WARNING TO STUDENTS

The rental program is designed to enable all students to have the main textbooks for their courses at the start of classes. The college has made a major financial investment towards this endeavor.

Students are required to ensure that the books are properly maintained and returned to the bookstore at the end of the semester undamaged and with all components attached (eg. CD, password, etc.). This ensures that the books are available for use by other students.

Accordingly, if books are not returned to the Bookstore timely, or are returned damaged, or with any component missing, you will be charged the full cost of the books.

Twelfth Edition

Social Psychology

Shelley E. Taylor
University of California, Los Angeles

Letitia Anne Peplau
University of California, Los Angeles

David O. Sears
University of California, Los Angeles

Prentice Hall, Upper Saddle River, New Jersey 07458

Library of Congress Cataloging-in-Publication Data

Taylor, Shelley E.
Social psychology / Shelley E. Taylor, Letitia Anne Peplau, David O. Sears.—12th ed.
p. cm.
Includes bibliographical references and index.
ISBN 0-13-193281-0
1. Social psychology. I. Peplau, Letitia Anne. II. Sears, David O. III. Title.
HM1033.T39 2005
302—dc22 2005002262

Editorial Director: Leah Jewell
Senior Editor: Jeff Marshall
Managing Editor: Stephanie Johnson
Editorial Assistant: Patricia Callahan
Director of Marketing: Heather Shelstad
Assit.Managing Editor: Maureen Richardson
Production Liaison: Fran Russello
Manufacturing Buyer: Ben Smith
Interior Design: Rose Design
Cover Design: Laura Gardner
Cover Illustration/Photo: Macduff Everton/CORBIS
Director, Image Resource Center: Melinda Reo
Manager, Rights and Permissions: Zina Arabia
Manager, Visual Research: Beth Brenzel
Manager, Cover Visual Research & Permissions: Karen Sanatar
Image Permission Coordinator: Cynthia Vincenti
Photo Researcher: Beaura Kathy Ringrose
Composition/Full-Service Project Management: Kelly Ricci/Techbooks/GTS

This book was set in 10.5/12.5 Galliard by Techbooks/GTS. It was printed and bound by Courier Companies, Inc. The cover was printed by The Lehigh Press, Inc.

Credits and acknowledgments borrowed from other sources and reproduced, with permission, in this textbook appear on page 554.

Pearson Education LTD. London
Pearson Education Singapore, Pte. Ltd
Pearson Education, Canada, Ltd
Pearson Education–Japan
Pearson Education Australia PTY, Limited
Pearson Education North Asia Ltd
Pearson Educación de Mexico, S.A. de C.V.
Pearson Education Malaysia, Pte. Ltd
Pearson Education, Upper Saddle River, New Jersey

10 9 8 7 6 5 4 3 2 1
ISBN 0-13-193281-0

Brief Contents

Contents

Part Three

Preface

Social psychology is more useful today than ever before. Whether we want to understand ourselves or the social world around us, social psychology offers valuable insights. Social psychologists study our sense of personal identity, our impressions of other people, our beliefs about world events, the pressure we feel to conform to social groups, and our search for love and meaningful social relationships. Social psychology also helps us to understand the stories behind today's news headlines on topics such as international terrorism, ethnic prejudice, sexual harassment, the impact of the Internet on social life, changing roles for women and men, or eyewitness identification in criminal trials. Not surprising, teachers, health professionals, lawyers, business leaders, and people in many different professions find social psychology valuable in their work. In the 12th edition of *Social Psychology,* we have tried to present the basic theories and findings of social psychology and show how its principles are relevant to our daily lives.

Today, we face the challenge of living in a society that becomes more diverse and multicultural each year. Television, air travel, and the Internet bring the citizens of the world closer together and make it essential that we take a broader perspective on social life. Social psychologists increasingly use sociocultural and global perspectives in their research, and we have included the best of this new work in our book. To give these issues the emphasis they deserve, we introduce a sociocultural perspective in Chapter 1. We also present new work on culture and ethnicity throughout the text.

This new edition of *Social Psychology* has been guided by certain basic principles and goals:

- We believe that social psychology, like any science, is cumulative. As researchers push toward exciting new frontiers, they build on the accumulated knowledge of the field. The latest findings are best understood as adding to this core body of knowledge. A primary goal in this text is to present the "basics" of the field—the classic theories and findings that form the shared heritage of our discipline.
- We have also been sensitive to important advances in social psychology. Over time, the core of the field has gradually shifted. This changing core is reflected in the 12th edition. For example, there is more emphasis on social cognition, the self, personal relationships, and evolutionary psychology. We have also expanded coverage of the role of emotion and the importance of automatic processes. Throughout the book, we have made every effort to include the most recent research and the most up-to-date theories in social psychology.
- Another goal has been to offer an integrated presentation of the field. As we discuss different topics, we try to keep the main theoretical ideas and traditions of social psychology firmly in view, so that readers can see the underlying conceptual continuities in the field. For example, we introduce social cognition and attribution theories early in the book and then show how these theories have been applied to such topics as the self, attitude change, stereotyping, aggression, and bias against women and minority groups.
- The application of research methods and theories to the understanding of social issues is a major theme in social psychology. Throughout the text, we highlight ways in which social psychology sheds light on everyday experiences and social problems. We conclude the book with two chapters that explore the most recent social psychological research on health and the law.
- The success of any text depends ultimately on its ability to communicate clearly to student readers and to spark interest in the field. Our goal has been to present materials simply, without oversimplifying. The text is comprehensive, but not encyclopedic. We have written a textbook for undergraduate students, not a handbook of social psychology for professionals. We have paid special attention to selecting examples that illustrate basic principles in a lively way and to sharing our own personal enthusiasm for the field.

SPECIAL FEATURES OF THE 12TH EDITION

In The News

Social psychology helps us to understand world events as they unfold around us. So students can comprehend the relevance of social psychological principles to current events, each chapter begins with a feature called *In The News* that highlights the social psychological questions raised by a current issue. For example, we begin the chapter on attitudes with a discussion about "stealth" advertising targeted to children. In the interpersonal attraction chapter, we examine the increasing popularity of Match.com, Friendster, and other Internet companies that help young singles find prospective dates. The chapter on groups considers factors that contributed to the failure of U.S. intelligence to provide accurate information about weapons of mass destruction in Iraq. The health chapter describes the alarming increase in obesity, which may soon overtake tobacco as a top killer. The law chapter describes the story of an innocent man, wrongly convicted of rape on the basis of mistaken eyewitness identification, who gained his freedom based on the results of DNA testing.

Cultural Perspectives

We have made every effort to include the newest multicultural and global perspectives in social psychology throughout the book. For example, in the chapter on personal relationships, we show that the disclosure of personal information contributes to marital satisfaction in our culture, where love is the basis for mate selection, but not in cultures where marriages are arranged by parents. In the chapter on groups, we present research showing that American boys tend to be competitive, Mexican boys tend to be cooperative, and Mexican American boys are in between the two. In the chapter on aggression, we analyze how a historical "culture of honor" may increase certain kinds of violence in the American South. Research comparing the behavior of people from individualist cultures and collectivist cultures is also incorporated throughout the book.

Research Highlights

To help students learn to think like social psychologists, we have included throughout the text detailed discussions of several key research studies, which describe the research process and the decisions researchers make. In addition, many chapters feature a *Research Highlights* Section that focuses on a topic at the forefront of contemporary social psychology, such as the planning fallacy, the measurement of implicit stereotypes, the dark side of intimate relationships, the accuracy of gender stereotypes, the promotion of safer sex behaviors, and the recovered memory debate.

ORGANIZATION

The book is organized to provide a systematic presentation of the material. A beginning chapter on theories and methods is followed by five major sections that progress from individual-level topics to dyads and groups, and then to the specific applications of social psychology.

Part One, on perceiving people and events, provides coverage of new research on social cognition. Here we explore how people think about and make sense of their social world. Chapter 2 presents research on person perception. Chapter 3 reviews basic principles of social cognition. Chapter 4 applies these basic principles to understanding how we view ourselves.

Part Two discusses attitudes and influence. Chapter 5 reviews research and theory on attitude formation and change. This review is followed by an analysis of prejudice and a chapter on processes of social influence that includes discussions of conformity and compliance.

Part Three examines social interaction and relationships. A chapter on interpersonal attraction is followed by a chapter on personal relationships that surveys current research in this growing area. We then broaden our focus to study group behavior and the pervasive influence of gender in social life. Part Four focuses on helping and hurting others, with chapters on prosocial behavior and aggression. Part Five, on social psychology in action, presents social psychological perspectives on health and the law.

We think this sequence will fit well with the teaching preferences of many instructors. However, each chapter is self-contained so the chapters can be covered in any order.

HIGHLIGHTS OF THE 12TH EDITION

In response to reviewer comments, we have shortened this edition to 15 chapters. We have added marginal definitions of key terms, so that concepts are fully explained when they first appear in the text. The many content changes throughout this edition reflect current trends in social psychology today. Some highlights of the new material include:

- Chapter 1 on theories and methods has been thoroughly updated. A new section has been added on the growing use of the Internet as a research tool.
- The social cognition section has been reorganized and now includes extensive coverage of

automatic inference and evaluation. The person perception chapter has streamlined sections on categorization, central traits, dual processing, and context effects. There is expanded coverage of goals in person perception and the impact of the perceiver on person perception. The social cognition chapter has greater coverage of the impact of emotion and mood on inference. There is also expanded coverage of automatic inference and of affective forecasting as well as new material on emotional suppression and thought.

- The self chapter gives less emphasis to the classic work of Schachter and Singer and provides expanded coverage of self-discrepancy theory, especially behavioral activation and inhibition. Work on terror management theory, which investigates how people cope with the fear of death, is increased, as is coverage of the self-enhancement debate. Emphasis is given to cultural influences on the self and self-enhancement. A new section titled "What Makes Us Happy" presents research on well-being.
- The attitudes chapter adds new coverage of persuasion directed at children and the ethical issues when youngsters are the target. There is greater coverage of implicit attitudes and of mood and persuasion. Attention is also given to research on prevention focus versus promotion focus in attitude change.
- The prejudice chapter has been substantially revised and updated. There is more extensive coverage of stereotype threat, implicit prejudice and stereotyping, aversive racism, and evolutionary theory. There is added coverage of prejudice-reduction techniques, especially the reduction of implicit prejudice. Attention is also given to a broader set of cultures, for instance, a new study of aboriginal peoples in Australia.
- The chapter on interpersonal attraction has been reorganized for greater clarity and coherence. It begins with a new section on the need to belong. This is followed by an analysis of loneliness and social rejection. Next, an integrated presentation of theory and research about attachment includes both children and adults. A section on mate selection includes both social role and evolutionary interpretations.
- The personal relationships chapter reflects the growing research emphasis on cognition in relationships. There is more extensive coverage of the investment model of commitment and of cultural effects on self-disclosure. Also featured are the strategies that individuals use to maintain commitment to a partner over time. Throughout, male–female differences are considered.
- The chapter on groups enriches classic concepts like "groupthink" with new examples, such as the decision making that led the United States to go to war with Iraq. The chapter also includes new coverage of women as leaders.
- The gender chapter presents the latest findings from meta-analyses of sex differences in social behavior, considers the health consequences of exaggerated masculinity and femininity, and introduces new research on ambivalent sexism. Research on the gender gap in wages is discussed along with studies of the division of labor in both heterosexual and same-sex couples.
- The aggression chapter has new coverage of terrorism as well as expanded information about violence in our schools. New research is presented on the possible impact of violent video games and music on children and adolescents. The materials on domestic violence have been updated and the section on aggression schemas has been reorganized for better flow.
- The health psychology chapter presents new evidence that a person's state of mind and social support influence health and illness. The chapter highlights the obesity epidemic, considering both its causes and consequences. The use of self-affirmation to increase receptivity to health behavior change is also discussed.
- A chapter on law, written by Jennifer Hunt and Eugene Borgida, has been substantially expanded. New topics include the influence of pretrial publicity on jurors, how jurors use character evidence, and the use of *amicus curiae* briefs to convey social psychological research to the courts. The chapter has been updated throughout with new research added to sections on eyewitness identification, false confessions, jury selection, and jury decision making. Links to concepts presented in earlier chapters are given greater prominence.

HELPING STUDENTS TO LEARN SOCIAL PSYCHOLOGY

To enhance the effectiveness of this text, we have kept the clarity and interest level high and have made a particular effort to avoid technical language. Our new design is modern and open, integrating visuals to facilitate easy reading and comprehension.

Each chapter opens with an outline of its main topics and concludes with a point-by-point summary of major concepts and findings. Key terms are highlighted in the text in bold type, and definitions are provided immediately in the margins of the page. There is also a complete glossary at the end of the book. Important findings and concepts are illustrated graphically in tables and charts.

ANCILLARY MATERIALS

A good textbook should become part of the classroom experience, supporting and augmenting the professor's vision for the class. *Social Psychology* offers a number of supplements that will enrich both the professor's presentation of social psychology and the students' understanding of it.

NEW* for 2005.** Prentice Hall is pleased to announce the American Psychological Society (APS) reader series, *Current Directions in Psychological Science.* For classes starting in 2005, you can package the *Current Directions in Social Psychology* reader for ***free with this text (ISBN 0-13-194070-8). This Reader contains selected articles from APS's journal *Current Directions in Psychological Science. Current Directions* was created for scientists to quickly and easily learn about new and significant research developments outside their major field of study. The journal's concise reviews span all of scientific psychology, and because of the journal's accessibility to audiences outside specialty areas, it is a natural fit for use in college courses. These Readers offer a rich resource that connects students and scholars directly to leading scientists working in psychology today.

The American Psychological Society is the only association dedicated solely to advancing psychology as a science-based discipline. APS members include the field's most respected researchers and educators representing the full range of topics within psychological science. The Society is widely recognized as a leading voice for the science of psychology in Washington, and is focused on increasing public understanding and use of the knowledge generated by psychological research.

Supplements for Instructors

- **Instructor's Resource Manual** (ISBN 0-13-193285-3), prepared by Lisa Finkelstein of Northern Illinois University, is a true "course planner." It includes expanded and updated lecture suggestions, classroom demonstrations and activities, handouts, video resources, and information on how to integrate Prentice Hall's *Classic and Contemporary Videos in Social Psychology* CD-ROM and the *Current Directions in Social Psychology* reader into your course (see a description of this CD-ROM under the *Supplements for Student* section below).
- **Test Item File** (ISBN 0-13-193283-7), prepared by Melissa Solomon of Bridgewater State College is a test bank revised to include more than 2,000 questions that offer instructors a wide selection of items. Conceptual, applied, and factual questions are available in multiple choice, short answer, true/false, and essay formats.
- **Prentice Hall Test Generator** (ISBN 0-13-193288-8), one of the best-selling test-generating software programs on the market, is available in Windows and Macintosh formats, both of which are included on one CD-ROM. The Test Generator includes a gradebook, online network testing, and many tools to help you edit and create tests quickly and easily.
- **Prentice Hall Color Transparencies for *Social Psychology*** (ISBN 0–13–060512–3) includes figures and tables from this text, as well as from other sources.
- **PowerPoints** provide an active format for presenting concepts from each chapter. The PowerPoint files can be downloaded from the Companion Website.
- **Prentice Hall Online Catalog Page** (www.prenhall.com/psychology) is password-protected for instructors' use only and allows online access to all Prentice Hall psychology supplements at any time. You'll find a multitude of resources (both text-specific and non-text-specific) for teaching social psychology—and many other psychology courses. From this site, you can download the files for the Instructor's Resource Manual, Test Item File, and PowerPoint presentation for *Social Psychology.*

Supplements for Students

- **Companion Website** (www.prenhall.com/taylor), prepared by Georgia Klamon-Miller, is a free online resource that allows students to take practice tests for each chapter, with immediate scoring and feedback. It also offers links to related Web sites, as well as interactive self-assessments that students can complete to learn more about themselves and their social styles.
- **Classic and Contemporary Videos in Social Psychology** (ISBN 0-13-048829-1) is a CD-ROM that contains a series of clips that can be used as lecture openers or discussion lead-ins. Some of the clips are from classic psychology

films, while others are from documentaries that are excellent illustrations of social psychological concepts. The Instructor's Manual includes notes that discuss the principles covered in each clip, providing discussion questions for students and listing relevant references.

- **Practice Tests,** prepared by Amy Dickie Bohmann of Texas Lutheran University, is a brief booklet that can be packaged free with the text to help students test themselves on key concepts before exams. Each chapter features practice multiple choice and short answer questions with explanations for correct answers.
- **Research Navigator** is a reliable, relevant, and resourceful program from Prentice Hall that helps students make the most out of your current research. Complete with extensive help on the research process and three exclusive databases full of relevant and reliable source material—including EBSCO's *ContentSelect* Academic Journal Database, the *New York Times* Search by Subject Archive, and the *Best of the Web* link library. *Research Navigator* is the one-stop research solution for your students.
- ***Insights into Social Psychology*** by Marianne Miserandino, Beaver College is a customizable reader that allows instructors to choose from 130 classic and contemporary readings across all of the key topics in social psychology. Unlike traditional readers, students pay only for the readings that the instructor chooses to include. The custom readings book can also be packaged with *Social Psychology* at a discount. Contact your local representative for a list of readings and details on how to order.
- ***Sociocultural Perspectives in Social Psychology,*** edited by Anne Peplau and Shelley Taylor (ISBN 0-13-241860-6) is a paperback book of readings that examines the influence of culture and ethnicity in social life. Nineteen articles were chosen to complement the major topics in social psychology and were screened by a panel of undergraduate students for their interest and readability. Pedagogical features of the book include an introduction to each article that highlights key issues and a set of questions about each article designed to stimulate thought or classroom discussion.

Acknowledgments

Special thanks go out to Heang Chov, Nikki Duong, Steve Gordon, Marilyn Hart, Cristina Nguyen, Margaret Samotyj, Larissa Schmersal, and Will Welch for their invaluable assistance in researching and preparing this manuscript. We are grateful to Prentice Hall for its continuing support, and especially to Jeff Marshall, Senior Acquisitions Editor; Stephanie Johnson, Sponsoring Editor; Patricia Callahan, Editorial Assistant; Dawn Stapleton, Assistant Editor; and Fran Rusello, our Production Editor. We also appreciate the useful feedback we have received from students who have used this book.

The text has benefited greatly from thoughtful reviews of this edition by Arnie Cann, University of North Carolina–Charlotte; Randy D. Fisher, University of Central Florida; Richard J. Harnish, Penn State University; Randy Kleinhesselink, Washington State University–Vancouver; Colin W. Leach, University of California–Santa Cruz; Edgar C. O'Neal, Tulane University.

We are also thankful to those who reviewed prior editions, including Kelly Anthony, Wesleyan University; Jeff Bryson, San Diego State University; Serena Chen, University of Michigan; Cynthia W. Esqueda, University of Nebraska–Lincoln; Katherine Gannon, Texas Tech University; Norine L. Jalbert, Western Connecticut State University; Joann M. Montepare, Emerson College; Warren Reich, Rutgers University–Newark; Salomon Rettig, Hunter College; and Ann Zak, College of St. Rose.

—Shelley Taylor, Anne Peplau, David O. Sears

About the Authors

Shelley E. Taylor is professor of psychology at the University of California, Los Angeles. Dr. Taylor received her BA in psychology from Connecticut College and her PhD in social psychology from Yale University. She taught at Harvard University until 1979, when she joined the faculty at UCLA. She has won a number of awards for her work, including the Donald Campbell Award for Distinguished Scientific Contribution to Social Psychology, the Outstanding Scientific Contribution Award in Health Psychology, the Distinguished Scientist Award from the American Psychological Association, and the William James Fellow Award from the American Psychological Society. She has served on the editorial boards of many journals. Her other books include *Social Cognition* (with Susan T. Fiske), *Health Psychology*, *Positive Illusions*, and *The Tending Instinct*. She has published numerous articles and book chapters in social cognition, health psychology, and social neuroscience.

Letitia Anne Peplau is professor of psychology at the University of California, Los Angeles. Dr. Peplau received her BA in psychology from Brown University and her PhD in social psychology from Harvard University. Since 1973, she has taught at UCLA, where she has served as chair of the social psychology program and co-director of the Center for the Study of Women. She was elected president of the International Society for the Study of Personal Relationships and received the Distinguished Scientific Achievement Award from the Society for the Scientific Study of Sexuality. Her other books include *Loneliness: A Sourcebook of Current Theory, Research, and Therapy* (edited with Daniel Perlman), *Close Relationships* (with Harold H. Kelley et al.), and *Gender, Culture, and Ethnicity* (edited with Rose Veniegas et al.). She has published numerous articles and book chapters on such topics as loneliness, friendship, gender roles in heterosexual dating and marriage, the relationships of lesbians and gay men, and the development of sexual orientation.

David O. Sears is professor of psychology and political science, former dean of social sciences, and current director of the Institute for Social Science Research at the University of California, Los Angeles. Dr. Sears received his BA in history from Stanford University and his PhD in psychology from Yale University. Since 1962, he has taught at University of California, Los Angeles. He has been elected a Fellow of the American Academy of Arts and Sciences, president of the Society for the Advancement of Socio-Economics, and president of the International Society of Political Psychology. His other books include *Public Opinion* (with Robert E. Lane), *The Politics of Violence: The New Urban Blacks and the Watts Riot* (with John B. McConahay), *Tax Revolt: Something for Nothing in California* (with Jack Citrin), *Political Cognition* (edited with Richard R. Lau), *Racialized Politics: The Debate About Racism in America* (edited with Jim Sidanius and Lawrence Bobo), and the *Oxford Handbook of Political Psychology* (edited with Leonie Huddy and Robert Jervis). He has published articles and book chapters on a wide variety of topics, including attitude change, mass communications, ghetto riots, political socialization, voting behavior, racism in politics, and the politics of multiculturalism.

Twelfth Edition

Social Psychology

In The News

Foul Play Among College Sports Fans

College basketball once offered a welcoming environment for fans and their children. But in recent years, student spectators have shown increasingly vulgar and boorish behavior. At basketball games student "cheering" sections have jeered at the name, appearance, imputed sexual orientation, and rumored personal problems of opposing players, their girlfriends, or even their parents (Brady, 2004). As Eric Hoover (2004) described it, "In sports arenas throughout the nation, boos have become passé, and fans are getting personal." Four-letter chants and use of the f-word are more common.

For college administrators, this mean-spirited behavior by students can be a public relations nightmare, tarnishing the image of their school and offending spectators (Snider, 2004). The situation is magnified when college games are broadcast on national television.

Some students say they use vulgarity because it's fun. Many students believe that it helps their home team by upsetting and intimidating the visiting players. Offensive chanting occurs most often in traditional college league rivalries, where emotions run strong among fans and motivation to intimidate the opposition is high. It may also be more common when the outcome of the game is likely to be close and victory is uncertain.

How are well-educated students transformed from polite individuals into a foul-mouthed group? Is profane jeering simply a result of a "mob mind," where normally decent individuals are swept up in the excitement of the crowd? It's not that simple. Not all students join in the jeering, and even the offensive chanters respect some limits. Racial slurs are rarely heard, for example. There are also differences across sports. Offensive taunts are most frequent among basketball audiences, less so for football and hockey crowds, and rare among gymnastics, tennis, and swimming spectators. Vulgar crowd displays are almost unknown at some colleges, but routine at others. Clearly student behavior is influenced by social rules that differ across situations.

When challenged by officials to stop this cruel and offensive behavior, some students insist on their rights to free speech. But many students do clean up their language if their home team coach takes to the microphone and urges good sportsmanship. Crowd misbehavior also decreases when there are pregame warnings that threaten obscene rooters with ejection from the arena. Colleges are grappling with this problem through campaigns to change social norms about acceptable behavior, both by promoting sportsmanship and by warnings that student seating sections can be disbanded. Administrators admit that they want a winning team and appreciate the benefits of a vocal and supportive home team audience. But the dividing line between enthusiastic loyalty and obnoxious insults needs clarification. Successful solutions must ultimately involve students themselves, by finding ways to change acceptable standards of behavior at college games.

Chapter 1

Theories and Methods in Social Psychology

Social psychologists use scientific methods to study how we perceive people and social events, how we influence others, and the nature of our social relationships. In reading this book, you will learn that some social psychologists study perceptions and attitudes: how people view themselves and each other, how they interpret people's behavior, and how their attitudes form and change. Other social psychologists focus on interactions among people, including friendship and altruism, prejudice and aggression, and conformity and power. Social psychologists also study how people act in groups and how groups affect their members. We can define **social psychology** as the scientific study of how people think about, influence, and relate to others. Social psychological principles help us understand a variety of important issues, including ways to promote healthier lifestyles, the influence of the media on public attitudes, and eyewitness testimony about crimes.

Focus of This Chapter

THE SOCIAL PSYCHOLOGICAL APPROACH

Of course, many scholarly fields study social behavior. What is unique about social psychology is its approach. The social psychological approach differs from disciplines that study large-scale societal processes and from those that focus on the individual. Let's compare these three approaches or levels of analysis using the specific example of violent crime in big cities.

The *societal level of analysis* is used by sociologists, economists, political scientists, and other social scientists. These scholars attempt to understand general patterns of social behavior, such as homicide rates, voting behavior, or consumer spending. According to this viewpoint, social behavior can be explained by such forces as economic hard times, class conflicts, clashes between competing ethnic groups, regional crop failures, governmental policies, or technological change. The goal of societal analysis is to identify links between broad social forces and general patterns of social behavior. To study violence in urban areas, social scientists might identify relationships between rates of violent crime and such factors as poverty, immigration, or the industrialization of a society.

Social Psychology

The scientific study of how people think about, influence, and relate to each other.

The *individual level of analysis* is typically used by clinical and personality psychologists, who explain behavior in terms of a person's unique life history and psychological characteristics. According to this viewpoint, personality traits and motives can explain why individuals behave as they do, and why two people may react quite differently to the same situation. Emphasis is given to individual differences in childhood experiences, in ability and motivation, and in personality or psychological adjustment. The individual approach explains violent crime in terms of the unique histories and characteristics of the criminal. For example, of all the bank tellers in Chicago, why does one individual go berserk and shoot five of his coworkers? To understand such behavior, the psychologist using the individual approach would consider the personality and background of the person: Was the bank teller depressed or suffering from paranoid delusions or using drugs? What kind of life had the bank teller led? For example, was he physically abused as a child?

Social psychologists adopt a different level of analysis: the *interpersonal level*. Social psychologists typically focus on a person's current social situation. That social situation includes the other people in the environment, their attitudes and behaviors, and their relationship to the individual. This emphasis on the power of the situation is based on the idea that people are malleable, flexible, and adaptable (Markus, 2004). The same teenage boy who is outgoing and talkative with his close friends may be shy and withdrawn with unfamiliar adults. The same teenage girl who got As in math in her supportive all-girl high school may struggle with math in her competitive, largely male college math classes. Change the social context, and the individual will change.

To understand violent crime, social psychologists might consider what kinds of interpersonal situations create feelings of anger that may increase violent behavior. One social psychological explanation is that frustrating situations make people angry and increase their tendency to act aggressively. This explanation is called the **frustration-aggression hypothesis**. It predicts that when people are blocked from achieving a desired goal, they feel frustrated and angry and are more likely to lash out. This effect of frustration is one explanation for violent crime.

Frustration-Aggression Hypothesis

Frustration creates feelings of aggression.

The frustration-aggression hypothesis can also explain how large-scale economic and societal factors create situations that lead to violence and crime. For instance, people who are poor and crowded into urban slums are frustrated: They cannot get good jobs, find affordable housing, provide a safe environment for their children, and so on. This frustration may produce anger, which can be the direct cause of violent crime. The frustration-aggression hypothesis focuses on the immediate social situation, the feelings and thoughts such situations produce in people of many different backgrounds, and the effects of those subjective reactions on behavior.

These demonstrators hold strong and opposite views about whether abortion should be legal. What individual, interpersonal, or societal factors might explain which viewpoint a person supports?

Chapter 1

Theories and Methods in Social Psychology

Social psychologists use scientific methods to study how we perceive people and social events, how we influence others, and the nature of our social relationships. In reading this book, you will learn that some social psychologists study perceptions and attitudes: how people view themselves and each other, how they interpret people's behavior, and how their attitudes form and change. Other social psychologists focus on interactions among people, including friendship and altruism, prejudice and aggression, and conformity and power. Social psychologists also study how people act in groups and how groups affect their members. We can define **social psychology** as the scientific study of how people think about, influence, and relate to others. Social psychological principles help us understand a variety of important issues, including ways to promote healthier lifestyles, the influence of the media on public attitudes, and eyewitness testimony about crimes.

Focus of This Chapter

THE SOCIAL PSYCHOLOGICAL APPROACH

Of course, many scholarly fields study social behavior. What is unique about social psychology is its approach. The social psychological approach differs from disciplines that study large-scale societal processes and from those that focus on the individual. Let's compare these three approaches or levels of analysis using the specific example of violent crime in big cities.

The *societal level of analysis* is used by sociologists, economists, political scientists, and other social scientists. These scholars attempt to understand general patterns of social behavior, such as homicide rates, voting behavior, or consumer spending. According to this viewpoint, social behavior can be explained by such forces as economic hard times, class conflicts, clashes between competing ethnic groups, regional crop failures, governmental policies, or technological change. The goal of societal analysis is to identify links between broad social forces and general patterns of social behavior. To study violence in urban areas, social scientists might identify relationships between rates of violent crime and such factors as poverty, immigration, or the industrialization of a society.

The *individual level of analysis* is typically used by clinical and personality psychologists, who explain behavior in terms of a person's unique life history and psychological characteristics. According to this viewpoint, personality traits and motives can explain why individuals behave as they do, and

Social Psychology

The scientific study of how people think about, influence, and relate to each other.

why two people may react quite differently to the same situation. Emphasis is given to individual differences in childhood experiences, in ability and motivation, and in personality or psychological adjustment. The individual approach explains violent crime in terms of the unique histories and characteristics of the criminal. For example, of all the bank tellers in Chicago, why does one individual go berserk and shoot five of his coworkers? To understand such behavior, the psychologist using the individual approach would consider the personality and background of the person: Was the bank teller depressed or suffering from paranoid delusions or using drugs? What kind of life had the bank teller led? For example, was he physically abused as a child?

Social psychologists adopt a different level of analysis: the *interpersonal level.* Social psychologists typically focus on a person's current social situation. That social situation includes the other people in the environment, their attitudes and behaviors, and their relationship to the individual. This emphasis on the power of the situation is based on the idea that people are malleable, flexible, and adaptable (Markus, 2004). The same teenage boy who is outgoing and talkative with his close friends may be shy and withdrawn with unfamiliar adults. The same teenage girl who got As in math in her supportive all-girl high school may struggle with math in her competitive, largely male college math classes. Change the social context, and the individual will change.

To understand violent crime, social psychologists might consider what kinds of interpersonal situations create feelings of anger that may increase violent behavior. One social psychological explanation is that frustrating situations make people angry and increase their tendency to act aggressively. This explanation is called the **frustration-aggression hypothesis**. It predicts that when people are blocked from achieving a desired goal, they feel frustrated and angry and are more likely to lash out. This effect of frustration is one explanation for violent crime.

Frustration-Aggression Hypothesis

Frustration creates feelings of aggression.

The frustration-aggression hypothesis can also explain how large-scale economic and societal factors create situations that lead to violence and crime. For instance, people who are poor and crowded into urban slums are frustrated: They cannot get good jobs, find affordable housing, provide a safe environment for their children, and so on. This frustration may produce anger, which can be the direct cause of violent crime. The frustration-aggression hypothesis focuses on the immediate social situation, the feelings and thoughts such situations produce in people of many different backgrounds, and the effects of those subjective reactions on behavior.

These demonstrators hold strong and opposite views about whether abortion should be legal. What individual, interpersonal, or societal factors might explain which viewpoint a person supports?

Each of these three approaches (societal, individual, and interpersonal) is worthwhile and indeed essential if we are to understand complex social behavior fully. A single question—What causes violent crime?—can be answered in many different ways. This book introduces you to the social psychological perspective on human behavior.

HISTORICAL ROOTS OF SOCIAL PSYCHOLOGY

In the early 1900s, three major theoretical perspectives were developed by pioneering psychologists, each of which has left a mark on contemporary social psychology.

Sigmund Freud, the founder of **psychoanalytic theory**, was fascinated by the rich mental life of the human animal. Freud proposed that behavior is motivated from within by powerful internal drives and impulses, such as sexuality and aggression. He also believed that adult behavior is shaped by unresolved psychological conflicts that can be traced to childhood experiences in the family. Psychoanalytic theorists seek to understand the inner forces, both conscious and unconscious, that energize and direct behavior.

Psychoanalytic Theory

Freud's theory emphasizing unconscious motivation.

A second major theory, **behaviorism**, offered a very different perspective on human experience. As developed by Ivan Pavlov, B. F. Skinner, and others, behaviorism focused on the observable behavior of humans and other animals. Behaviorists were not interested in subjective thoughts and feelings; they preferred to study what they could observe and measure directly, that is, overt behavior. Behaviorists examined ways in which the environment shapes the behavior of animals, and they proposed that current behavior is the result of past learning. They identified a series of principles to explain the specific processes through which this all-important learning occurs. Although much of their research was conducted with rats and pigeons, behaviorists believed that the same principles applied to humans.

Behaviorism

Analysis of learning that focuses on observed behavior.

The perspective of **Gestalt psychology** was developed by Wolfgang Kohler, Kurt Koffka, Kurt Lewin, and other European psychologists who immigrated to the United States in the 1930s. Their focus was on the way individuals perceive and understand objects, events, and people. In their view, people perceive situations or events not as made up of many discrete elements but rather as "dynamic wholes." Think about your best friend. When you last saw her, did you perceive her as a collection of arms, legs, fingers, and other features? Probably not. More likely, you perceived her as a total unit that integrates the relationships among her various body parts into the familiar "whole" or person you know and like. This emphasis on perceiving the environment as a whole that is more than the sum of its parts is known as "Gestalt psychology," from the German word for "shape" or "form."

Gestalt Psychology

Theory that people form coherent and meaningful perceptions based on the whole, not individual parts.

Each of these three important theories arose from the work of a few charismatic individuals who inspired fierce loyalty to their ideas and, often, an equally fierce rejection of other viewpoints. These pioneers modeled their theories on those of the physical sciences. Their goal was to explain and predict all human behavior, and they wanted theories as detailed, universal, and complete as those in physics or chemistry. Many of these theories were applied to the analysis of social behavior. The idea of developing general theories is important, but in the long run, the problems that are studied by social psychologists have proved to be too complex to be explained by any one general theory.

Even so, social psychological approaches to a wide variety of different problems have been guided by a few basic ideas that are easily traced back to the general theories of the past. In contemporary social psychology, the legacy of psychoanalytic theory can be seen most clearly in the analysis of motivation and emotion in social life. Social psychologists recognize that behavior is influenced by personal motives and by the emotional reactions individuals have to situations and other people. The legacy of behaviorism is our continuing concern with how learning shapes social behavior. Social psychologists are interested, for example, in how we learn to be helpful or to obey authority or to espouse conservative political views.

Finally, the legacy of Gestalt psychology is found in the emphasis on social cognition, the study of how we perceive and understand our social world. Basic Gestalt principles have been greatly expanded in recent years, as discussed in Chapter 2.

THEORIES IN SOCIAL PSYCHOLOGY

In the following sections, we introduce some of the major contemporary theories in social psychology. These sections are not intended to be comprehensive or detailed. Rather, we want to convey the essence and particularly the contrasts among these theories so that we can refer to them in later chapters. To permit a clear comparison of the theories, we apply each approach to the specific problem of understanding violent crime.

Consider this situation: At 3 A.M. one morning, a police officer sees a high school dropout, Larry, coming out of the rear door of a liquor store with a bag full of money. The store, like everything else in the neighborhood, has long been closed for the night. The officer yells at Larry to stop and put his hands up. Larry turns, pulls a pistol from his pocket, and shoots the officer, wounding him in the leg. Larry is later apprehended and ultimately sent to jail. We will refer to Larry as we describe major contemporary theories in social psychology.

Motivational Theories

One general approach focuses on the individual's own needs or motives. Both everyday experience and social psychological research provide many examples of the ways in which our needs influence our perceptions, attitudes, and behavior. For example, to enhance our self-esteem and satisfy a need to feel good about ourselves, we may blame others for our failures and take personal credit only for successes.

The Freudian, or psychoanalytic, view of human motivation emphasizes the importance of a few powerful inborn impulses or drives, especially those that are associated with sexuality and aggression. In contrast, social psychologists consider a much more diverse range of human needs and desires. Social psychologists also emphasize ways in which specific situations and social relationships can create and arouse needs and motives. For example, the experience of moving away from home to go to college often creates feelings of loneliness among young adults. Geographical moves disrupt established social networks and sources of companionship, and they arouse unmet needs for intimacy and a sense of belonging. The desire to create a group of friends at college may lead new students to join clubs, go to social events, and talk to strangers in the cafeteria. Unmet needs for companionship can also lead some students to seek distractions from this discomfort by throwing themselves into their studies or by abusing alcohol or drugs. The core idea is that situations can create or arouse needs that, in turn, lead people to engage in behaviors to reduce those needs.

To understand Larry's behavior in robbing the liquor store, a social psychologist who was using a motivational approach would try to uncover Larry's psychological needs. Was he motivated by a need for money, perhaps to buy food or to support a drug habit? Or was the robbery a way to gain status in Larry's peer group? Did Larry shoot the police officer out of fear or anger? A social psychological analysis might go further, to try to identify in detail ways that Larry's social environment fostered the particular needs and motives that led to the robbery and shooting. Social psychologists would also want to study other young men who have committed armed robberies, in order to try to arrive at generalizations about the links between motivation and criminal behavior.

Learning Theories

The central idea in learning theory is that a person's current behavior is determined by prior experience. In any given situation, a person learns certain behaviors that, over time, may become habits. When presented with a similar situation,

One of the most powerful mechanisms of learning is imitation. Like this boy, children often imitate a parent or other adults they admire and respect.

the person tends to behave in the same habitual way. For example, when a traffic light turns red, we typically stop, because that is how we have learned to respond in the past. As applied to social behavior by Albert Bandura (1977) and others, this approach has been called **social learning theory**.

Social Learning Theory

Learning is based on reinforcement and modeling.

There are three general mechanisms by which learning occurs. One is association, or classical conditioning. Pavlov's dogs learned to salivate at the sound of a bell because they were presented with food every time the bell was rung. After a while, they would salivate to the sound of the bell even in the absence of the meat because they associated the bell with meat. Humans sometimes learn emotions by association. After a particularly painful visit to the dentist, the mere mention of the word "dentist" or the sound of any kind of drill may arouse anxiety.

A second learning mechanism is **reinforcement**, a principle studied by B. F. Skinner and others. People learn to perform a particular behavior because it is followed by something that is pleasurable or that satisfies a need (or they learn to avoid behavior that is followed by unpleasant consequences). A child may learn to help other people because her parents praise her for sharing her toys and smile approvingly when she offers to help with chores. Or a high school student may learn not to contradict his history teacher in class because each time he does, the teacher frowns, looks angry, and snaps at him.

Reinforcement

Learning based on rewards.

A third mechanism is **observational learning**. People often learn social attitudes and behaviors simply by watching other people, known technically as "models." Children learn regional and ethnic speech patterns by listening to the speakers around them. Adolescents may acquire their political attitudes by listening to their parents' conversations during election campaigns. In observational learning, other people are an important source of information. Observational learning can occur without any external reinforcement. However, whether people actually perform a behavior that is learned through observation is influenced by the consequences the action has for them. For example, a little boy may learn a lot about baby dolls from watching his sisters but may be discouraged from playing with them himself because his traditional parents say, "Dolls aren't for boys." Imitation, or **modeling**, occurs when a person not only observes but actually copies the behavior of a model.

Observational Learning

Learning by watching others.

Modeling

Imitating or copying the behavior of another.

The learning approach seeks the causes of behavior in the past learning history of the individual. To return to the example of Larry shooting the police officer, we might find that in his previous encounters with the police, they had been rough, rude, antagonistic, suspicious, and unsympathetic. Perhaps Larry had been reinforced in the past for responding violently to situations involving conflict with authority. Or perhaps his father often acted in violent ways so that Larry learned to imitate a violent model. The learning theorist is especially concerned with past experiences and somewhat less concerned with the details of the current situation.

Cognitive Theories

The cognitive approach emphasizes that a person's behavior depends on the way he or she perceives the social situation. Kurt Lewin applied Gestalt ideas to social psychology, emphasizing the importance of the social environment as perceived by the individual. In Lewin's view, behavior is affected both by the individual's personal characteristics (such as ability, personality, and genetic dispositions) and by the social environment as he or she perceives it.

A core idea in the cognitive perspective is that people tend spontaneously to group and categorize objects. In a library, you see a row of books on a shelf as a unit, not as so many individual books. You probably perceive other people in the library in groups, perhaps as students and librarians, or as the line of people at the checkout desk, or as a couple in love. At home, you experience the pile of dirty dishes in the kitchen sink as an oppressive heap, not as individual dishes. We tend to group objects according to simple principles, such as similarity (dishes look more like each other than like the stove and refrigerator, so we group the dishes together), proximity (books stacked in a pile go together; the isolated books strewn all over the library table do not), or past experience (Santa Claus and Christmas trees go together, and so do doctors and stethoscopes, but Santa Claus and stethoscopes do not).

Second, people readily perceive some things as standing out ("figure") and some things as simply being in the background ("ground"). Typically colorful, moving, noisy, unique, nearby stimuli stand out as figure, whereas bland, drab, stationary, quiet, common, faraway stimuli constitute the background. Our attention is drawn to cheerleaders at a football game not because they are so numerous—there may be only a dozen in a crowd of 50,000 people—but because cheerleaders move a lot, yell, wave their arms, and wear colorful uniforms.

These two principles—that we spontaneously group or categorize the things we perceive and that we focus attention on the most prominent (figural) stimuli—are central to our perception of physical objects and of the social world. As social thinkers, we try to arrive at meaningful interpretations of how people feel, what they want, what kinds of people they are, and so forth. Research on social cognition focuses on how we put together information about people, social situations, and groups to make inferences about them (Fiske & Taylor, 1991). Social cognition researchers examine the flow of information from the environment to the person.

Cognitive approaches differ from learning approaches in two major ways. First, cognitive approaches focus on current perceptions rather than on past learning. Second, they emphasize the importance of the individual's perception or interpretation of a situation, not the objective "reality" of the situation as it might be viewed by a neutral observer. To return to Larry's run-in with the law, cognitive approaches would emphasize the importance of the way Larry interpreted his situation. How did Larry perceive his actions in taking the money? When the police officer shouted at Larry to stop, how did Larry interpret the event? He probably perceived the officer as someone whose job it is to arrest people. He may have seen the officer as threatening, biased, or perhaps even cruel. Ultimately, it was Larry's interpretation of the situation that led him to shoot the police officer.

Decision-Making Theories

Decision-Making Theories

Theory that people rationally calculate the costs and benefits of various actions.

Decision-making theories assume that individuals evaluate the costs and benefits of various actions and pick the best alternatives in a fairly logical, reasoned way. They choose the alternative that gives them the greatest rewards at the least cost. Decision making involves weighing the pros (benefits) and cons (costs) of possible alternatives and then adopting the best one. The relative strengths of the pros and cons determine the final decision. To return to Larry's situation, let's suppose that he has the choices of fleeing, surrendering, or shooting. He thinks that if he flees, he may be shot, which adds up to a considerable cost. If he surrenders, he will go to jail, another major cost. However, he may think that by shooting the police officer, he can get away—and with the money, too.

Expectancy-value theory extends the notion of costs and benefits by adding an assessment of the likelihood that each alternative will happen (Edwards, 1954). This theory holds that decisions are based on the combination of two factors: (1) the value of each possible outcome or alternative and (2) the probability, or "expectancy," that each outcome will actually result from the decision. Larry may try to flee even though he might get shot and killed, a major cost indeed. But he may estimate that the officer is not very likely to hit him with a bullet in the dark and in a backyard with many obstacles. So the probability of being shot is low. Going to jail is not as bad as being shot, but surrendering means almost certainly going to jail. The probability that surrender will lead to prison is very high.

Expectancy-Value Theory

Decisions are based on the value of outcomes and the probability each will occur.

Sometimes the decisions we make actually do follow the rational procedures suggested by decision-making theories. For example, in deciding which of two colleges to attend, a student might list the pros and cons associated with each, assess the importance of each factor listed, and come up with some kind of score that indicates which college is better. However, social psychologists also recognize that in real life, judgments and decisions do not always follow strict rationality. As discussed in Chapter 2, people often use shortcuts that enable them to make decisions, form judgments, or solve problems quickly and efficiently, but not always thoroughly and according to strictly rational standards. In addition, many judgments and decisions are swayed by motivational factors, such as emotional reactions or personal goals. The high school senior trying to decide between two colleges may come up with a formal "decision" based on the pros and cons of each school, but if the answer doesn't "feel right," that is, doesn't fit with his or her emotional leanings, the senior may ignore the score sheet in favor of emotional preferences. In short, rational decision-making models do not always apply to everyday decision making and problem solving. There are important limits on the degree to which people actually use rational principles in their daily lives.

Interdependence Theories

Interdependence theories shift the focus of analysis from the behavior of one individual to the behavior of two or more individuals who interact with each other. When people interact, they influence each other. For example, as a father helps his young son get dressed, he might show him how to button his shirt and be rewarded for his efforts by an appreciative hug. When two people have mutual influence on each other's thoughts, feelings, or behaviors, they are interdependent. In technical terms, **interdependence** means that the outcomes one person receives depend at least in part on the behavior of the other and vice versa. As any parent knows, children do not always appreciate attempts to help them get dressed. So, instead of hugging his father, the young boy in our example might have protested angrily that he could do it himself and run out of the room. The outcome of this parent-child interaction—whether or not father and son are in a pleasant mood and how quickly the boy gets dressed—depends on the actions of both partners.

Interdependence

Occurs when two or more people influence one anothers' feelings, thoughts, or behaviors.

A prominent example of an interdependence approach is **social exchange theory**. The principles of social exchange build on the work of both learning theorists and decision-making theorists. Social exchange theory analyzes the interaction between people in terms of the benefits and costs the individuals exchange with each other. Sometimes people make explicit exchanges. For example, you may agree to help your roommate learn Spanish in return for help with your advanced calculus course. Or in the heat of an argument, you and a friend may trade insults. But even when we are not aware of it, the process of interaction

Social Exchange Theory

Analyzes social interaction in terms of the outcomes (benefits minus costs) that the individuals exchange with each other.

creates benefits (information, smiles of approval, money, feelings of being loved, etc.) and costs (boredom, disapproval, feelings of being misunderstood, etc.) for the people involved.

Social exchange theory analyzes interpersonal interaction on the basis of the costs and benefits to each person of the possible ways he or she can interact. For example, the interactions between Larry and the police officer might turn hostile because of their conflicting interests. Larry would benefit from escaping, whereas the police officer would benefit from arresting him. In contrast, an exchange theory analysis of the interaction between a nurse and a patient might focus on the benefits to the patient from cooperating with the nurse (the patient gets the right care and is helped toward recovery) and the benefits to the nurse of being friendly (the patient cooperates and the nurse gets a reputation for doing a good job). In this case, the interests of both parties converge on sharing a cooperative and friendly interaction. Social exchange theory is particularly useful for analyzing bargaining situations in which two parties must come to an agreement despite their separate interests. It has also been elaborated by Harold Kelley and others to apply to personal relationships among friends and family. Social exchange theory is discussed in detail in Chapter 9.

Sociocultural Theories

In recent years, social psychologists have paid increasing attention to how people's diverse social backgrounds influence their thoughts, feelings, and behaviors (Fiske, Kitayama, Markus, & Nisbett, 1998). Consider the pace of life. In some cultures, punctuality is important and the general speed of life is relatively fast. In other cultures, people have more casual attitudes about time and a slower pace of daily life. Robert Levine has studied these cultural differences in the pace of life. In one study, Levine (1988) asked college students in the United States and Brazil when they would consider a friend late for a lunch appointment. Americans said a friend would be late after 19 minutes, but Brazilians gave the friend nearly twice as long, not considering a friend late until 34 minutes after the time of the appointment.

Edward Hall (1959) described unspoken cultural rules about the use of time as a "silent language" that we learn through experience in a culture. Lack of familiarity with cultural differences in time can create problems when people travel to other countries. For example, American Peace Corps volunteers reported having more trouble getting used to the relatively slow pace of life and lack of punctuality in other countries than they did in adjusting to unfamiliar foods or different standards of living (Spradley & Phillips, 1972).

Culture

Shared beliefs, values, traditions, and behavior patterns of a group.

Socialization

Process of acquiring the rules, standards, and values of a group.

Social Norms

Rules and expectations about how group members should behave.

In seeking to understand differences such as these, psychologists have come to recognize the importance of **culture**—the shared beliefs, values, traditions, and behavior patterns of particular groups. These groups can be nations, ethnic groups, religious communities, or even teenage gangs and college fraternities. Culture is taught by one generation to the next through a process known as **socialization**. Children learn about their culture not only from parents and friends, but also from storybooks and television programs. New fraternity and sorority members are expected to learn the traditions, songs, and secrets of their group from its senior members.

Social norms—rules and expectations about how group members should behave—are a building block of culture. Social rules govern a surprisingly broad range of behaviors, from how close we stand when talking with a friend to what we wear (or don't wear) at the beach. One reason for the growing problem of obesity among Americans may be norms about serving sizes at restaurants and fast food chains such as McDonald's and Haagen Dazs. A recent study found that, on average, portions served in the United States were 25 percent larger than those in France, although the cost of the food was comparable in the two countries (Rozin, et al., 2003). American consumers have come to expect to eat more than their French counterparts.

Some norms apply to everyone in a social group, regardless of his or her position or status. On a school campus, everyone is expected to obey traffic signs and to put litter in wastebaskets. But frequently the norms that apply depend on the individual's position, for instance, whether the person is a professor or a student. Professors are supposed to come to class on time, prepare lectures and lead class discussions, write and grade tests, serve on college committees, and so on. Different norms apply to students, who are expected to take notes in class, study for tests, write term papers, pay tuition, and so on.

The term **social role** refers to the set of norms that apply to people in a particular position, such as teachers or students. One perspective on social roles uses imagery borrowed from the theater. The individual acting in society is like an actor in a play. In the theater, the script sets the stage, defines the role that each actor will play, and dictates what actors say and do. Similarly, cultures present us with many preestablished social rules of behavior. For example, when children enter school, they learn many rules of classroom behavior, such as sitting quietly in their seats or raising a hand to speak. In marriage, traditional roles prescribe that the husband should be the breadwinner and the wife should be in charge of child care and housekeeping.

Social Role

Set of social norms about how a person in a particular social position should behave.

The sociocultural perspective is useful in understanding behavior within a particular social or cultural context. To return to the example of Larry robbing a liquor store and shooting a police officer, we might find that Larry belongs to a gang. Perhaps this group condones stealing money and accords higher status to gang members who carry a gun. His gang may have a shared history of violent encounters with the police, which led Larry to be suspicious and quick to fire his weapon. An analysis of the beliefs, traditions, norms, and other aspects of "gang culture" might help explain Larry's actions.

The sociocultural perspective also emphasizes comparisons of different cultures or social groups. Unless we attend specifically to cultural influences, we are likely to overlook their importance. We tend to assume that the behaviors of our own culture are "standard" or typical. One benefit of foreign travel is that it causes us to take a fresh look at aspects of our own behavior that we take for granted, such as our beliefs about punctuality and the use of time. Similarly, social psychologists are conducting cross-cultural studies as a way to learn how social behavior is affected by differences in cultural values, norms, and roles.

Larry's behavior reflects in part the larger U.S. culture in which he lives. As described in Chapter 13, the United States is one of the most violent societies on earth. American children watch countless acts of murder and mayhem on television and often engage in fierce competition at school and in sports. Further, life in many urban areas provides easy access to handguns and other weapons that can turn the expression of anger into a deadly act of violence. Larry's attitudes were shaped in part by exposure to cultural messages about violence, and his act of shooting the police officer was made possible by situational opportunities to obtain a gun and ammunition.

One goal of cross-cultural research on social behavior is to identify important ways in which cultures differ from each other. A particularly useful distinction contrasts cultures that emphasize **individualism** and those that emphasize **collectivism** (Triandis, 1995). The cultural values of U.S. and European societies emphasize the importance of personal independence and individualism. Western literature, from the *Iliad* to *The Adventures of Huckleberry Finn,* tells of self-reliant heroes who leave home to seek self-fulfillment (Triandis, 1990). In an individualist culture, a person's behavior is guided largely by individual goals rather than by the goals of collectives such as the family, the work group, or the tribe. If a conflict arises between an individual's personal goals and group goals, it is acceptable to put self-interest first. Further, a person's sense of self is based largely on individual attributes and accomplishments rather than on membership in social groups.

Individualism

Belief in the value of personal identity, uniqueness, and freedom.

Collectivism

Emphasis on loyalty to the family, adherence to group norms, and harmonious social relations.

In contrast, collectivist cultures emphasize loyalty to the family, adherence to group norms, and the preservation of harmony in social relations with members

Culture affects all facets of life from our favorite foods to our beliefs about masculinity and femininity. These traditional Moroccan women wear very conservative clothes in public to shield their bodies from view.

of one's own group. The cultural values of many African, Asian, and Latin American societies emphasize collectivism. This can be seen in Asian literature, which often celebrates a hero who performs his duty to his family or to the emperor, sometimes in the face of strong temptations to pursue more pleasurable pastimes. In a collectivist culture, group goals are expected to take priority over individual preferences, and the self is defined largely in terms of group membership. Collectivist cultures value a person who can fit in comfortably with the group. Thus, a Japanese folk saying warns, "The nail that stands out gets pounded down" (cited by Markus & Kitayama, 1991, p. 224). Individualist cultures applaud individuals who stand out from others; Americans note that "the squeaky wheel gets the grease."

Sometimes what appears to be the same concept has different meanings in individualist and collectivist cultures (Triandis, Bontempo, Villareal, Asai, & Lucca, 1988). In the United States, "self-reliance" typically implies freedom to do what one wants, freedom from the constraints of the group. In a collectivist culture, "self-reliance" is more likely to mean not being a burden on others, not making excessive demands on one's family or friends.

In large and complex societies such as the United States or Canada, individuals are often exposed to more than one cultural group. In the United States, collectivist tendencies are strongest in the Deep South; individualist tendencies are strongest in the Mountain West and Great Plains (Vandello & Cohen, 1999). Hispanic Americans tend to be more collectivist than non-Hispanics (Marin & Triandis, 1985). However, the longer Hispanic Americans are exposed to Anglo-American culture, the more individualist they tend to become. Collectivism also tends to be strong among Asian Americans (Triandis, 1990). Sometimes individuals who live in two cultural worlds have concerns about which cultural patterns to follow. One Chinese-born teenager who immigrated to the United States at age 12 described her feelings as follows:

> I don't know who I am. Am I the good Chinese daughter? Am I an American teenager? I always feel I am letting my parents down when I am with my friends because I act so American, but I also feel that I will never really be an American. I never feel really comfortable with myself anymore. (Cited in Olsen, 1988, p. 30)

The topic of identification with ethnic groups is explored further in Chapter 4. Throughout this book, we present research that seeks to understand cultural and ethnic diversity.

Evolutionary Social Psychology

The emerging field of **evolutionary social psychology** applies the principles of evolution and natural selection to the understanding of human behavior and social life (Buss & Kenrick, 1998). Evolutionary social psychology draws on ideas that were initially advanced by Charles Darwin and later elaborated by biologists to explain social behavior in insects, birds, and other animals. Whereas cultural approaches emphasize the amazing diversity of human behavior around the globe, evolutionary approaches emphasize the shared human qualities that are part of our heritage as a species.

Evolutionary Social Psychology

Analysis of human behavior in terms of evolution and natural selection.

In the distant past, some behavioral tendencies, such as the avoidance of snakes or a liking for foods rich in protein and sugar, increased the chances of survival among our ancestors. Individuals who showed these tendencies had more children who survived to reproduce, and so these patterns gradually became part of our human genetic inheritance. According to evolutionary social psychologists, similar evolutionary principles explain the origins of many social behaviors as well, including the tendency for infants to form strong emotional bonds with their parents, our preferences for particular mates, and our willingness to help others in need. In other words, many of the behavioral tendencies that we see in humans today are the end products of the history of natural selection in our species.

Several ideas are central to evolutionary social psychology (Brewer, 2004; Buss, 1996):

1. Many human tendencies and preferences are the result of natural selection. These are known as **evolved psychological mechanisms**. They can be seen as adaptive responses to specific problems that were encountered by our ancestors. Thus, a fear of snakes may have solved the problem of avoiding a dangerous hazard in the environment.
2. All human behavior reflects the joint influence of internal psychological dispositions (including evolved psychological mechanisms) and external situational demands. People are biological organisms that act in specific social contexts; both biological and social influences on behavior are important.
3. Some of the most important problems faced by our ancestors were social in nature. Humans are born and spend their lives in interdependent social groups. Consequently, many evolved psychological mechanisms have to do with relating to other people. These include a need for belonging and fear of ostracism by the group, an ability to cooperate with others, and a willingness to invest resources in one's children.

Evolved Psychological Mechanisms

Human tendencies and preferences resulting from natural selection.

What might an evolutionary perspective say about the case of Larry, who shot a police officer during the robbery of a liquor store? Evolutionary social psychologists would emphasize that aggression is a common human response to threat and presumably is a pattern that was adaptive thousands of years ago. They might further note that around the globe, violence is more common among men than among women, so it is not surprising that our young criminal is male. Evolutionary theorists might add that although there is a universal tendency to respond to a threat with aggression, the threshold or degree of threat required to trigger this response appears to vary depending on personal experience and cultural values.

The evolutionary theory of natural selection is very general in scope, comparable in some ways to the all-encompassing theories of psychoanalysis, behaviorism, and Gestalt theory. Within social psychology, researchers typically study more focused theories that are derived from this general evolutionary perspective. For instance, the theory of reciprocal altruism makes predictions about our greater willingness to help relatives than strangers in need. The theory of sexual selection predicts that men and women will prefer different qualities in prospective mates. We discuss these and other ideas from evolutionary social psychology in later chapters of this book.

Social Psychological Theories Today

Social psychologists often find that they cannot fully understand the topics they study by using any single general theory, such as social learning theory. Rather, it proves useful to combine and integrate ideas from different theoretical traditions. Instead of focusing primarily on overt behavior, thinking, or emotions, newer theorists seek to understand the interrelationships among behavior, thoughts, and feelings. For example, social learning theorists have come to appreciate the importance of subjective expectations for an understanding of human behavior. As you read about research on specific topics in social psychology, such as aggression or conformity, consider how current social psychological analyses try to encompass all facets of human experience, including behavior, cognition, and motivation.

Another trend is for social psychologists to develop theories that can account for a certain limited range of phenomena, such as helping a stranger in distress, forming a positive impression of another person, or conforming to peer pressure. These are called **middle-range theories** because they focus on a specific aspect of social behavior and do not try to encompass all of social life. The frustration-aggression hypothesis is one illustration of a middle-range theory. In this book, you will be introduced to many of these more focused theories. As you will see, these specific theories and models continue to reflect the influence of basic theoretical traditions.

Middle-Range Theories

Theories that account for a specific aspect of social behavior.

METHODS IN SOCIAL PSYCHOLOGY

An exciting feature of social psychology is that it explores topics relevant to our everyday experiences. Social psychologists study love and altruism as well as conflict and prejudice. Personal experience often leads psychologists to study particular topics and to generate initial hypotheses about social life. For example, social psychological research on prejudice was sparked by intense concerns about discrimination against African Americans, Jews, and other ethnic minorities in the United States. However, although social psychological research often begins with personal experiences and social concerns, it does not stop at armchair speculation. A hallmark of social psychology is its commitment to scientific methodology.

Social psychology is an empirical science. This means that social psychologists use systematic methods to gather information about social life and to test the usefulness of theories. Sometimes research confirms our commonsense views about social life, and sometimes it does not. Consider these statements and decide if each one is true or false.

- In choosing friends and lovers, a fundamental principle is that opposites attract.
- When people are anxious, they prefer to be with other people.
- TV ads that try to frighten people usually backfire and are less effective than ads that do not arouse fear.
- If you pay a man to give a speech that goes against his own beliefs, he will usually change his mind to agree with the speech. The more money you pay him, the greater will be the change in his personal attitudes.

You may not agree with all these statements, but it is fair to say that they all sound plausible. Yet research presented in later chapters in this book shows that all of these statements are oversimplifications and several are false.

When it comes to friends and lovers, research supports the old adage that "birds of a feather flock together." Similarity is a key ingredient in friendship and marriage.

Why do our informal observations of social life sometimes lead us to wrong conclusions? Often, our own experiences are simply not representative of those of most people or those that occur in most social situations. Sometimes we are biased and misinterpret what happens; we see things as we want them to be, not as they really are. Sometimes we see correctly but remember incorrectly. In contrast, scientific research collects data in ways that reduce bias. Psychologists strive to observe representative groups of people and to keep track of the "numbers." They do not rely on memory or general impressions. Psychologists have themselves noted some of the limitations and bias in the field. For example, some have suggested that most psychologists are politically liberal and that their liberal views may affect the topics studied and the policy recommendations drawn from psychological research (Redding, 2001). Psychology has also been criticized for relying too often on white middle-class college students as research subjects—a group that is hardly representative of society at large. What is unusual about scientific research, however, is the conscious effort to identify and overcome bias.

Social psychological research has four broad goals:

1. ***Description.*** A major goal is to provide careful and systematic descriptions of social behavior that permit social psychologists to make reliable generalizations about how people act in various social settings. Are men more aggressive than women? Are there typical reactions when a love affair ends? In thinking up solutions to problems, do people work better alone or in a group? A thorough knowledge of how people behave is essential.
2. ***Causal analysis.*** Much research in psychology seeks to establish relationships between cause and effect. Do expensive TV ad campaigns actually influence how people vote in elections? Does a college education cause students to become more liberal in their social attitudes? Fundamental to all scientific inquiry is the search to identify cause-and-effect relations.
3. ***Theory building.*** A third goal is to develop theories about social behavior that help social psychologists understand why people behave the way they do. As researchers learn more about general principles and the specifics of particular types of behavior, they gain a better understanding of social life. Theories help psychologists organize what they know about social behavior and suggest new predictions that can be tested in further research.
4. ***Application.*** Social psychological knowledge can help to solve everyday social problems. For example, the application of social psychology may help people learn to control their own aggressive impulses or develop more satisfying personal relationships. It may assist policymakers to find ways to encourage people to recycle aluminum cans and conserve water. Today, researchers are using social psychological principles to understand prejudice against people with AIDS and to help sexually active people to engage in safer sex practices.

The American population is becoming more and more ethnically diverse. This U.S. shopping mall advertises in Spanish, English, Chinese, and Korean. Yet ethnic minority groups are often underrepresented in psychological studies.

Specific examples of social psychological research are described throughout this book. These examples include both classic studies that have been influential in the history of social psychology and very recent studies on the forefront of contemporary research. You will also find a special feature called "Research Highlight," which profiles research on a particularly interesting or timely topic.

Selecting Research Participants

How do researchers decide which people to study? One obvious starting point is to study the people about whom they later want to generalize. If they want to generalize about women who work full time, they should study employed women. But clearly they will never be able to study all working women. So instead they study some smaller number of women, chosen in such a way that they are representative of the larger group. This is known as a representative sample.

The best way to ensure this general representativeness is to study a random sample of the larger population. In formal terms, a **random sample** means that each person in the larger population has an equal chance of being included in the study. If researchers selected a sample of telephone numbers from the phone directory at random (e.g., using a table of random numbers), they could be assured that theirs was a random sample of all listed phone numbers in the area covered by that telephone list. The laws of probability assure us that a large and truly random sample will almost always be representative of the population within a certain

Random Sample

Sample that represents the population of interest.

margin of error. It will include approximately the same proportion of women, ethnic minorities, married people, and older adults as the larger population.

Most of the time, social psychologists want their research results to apply to people in general, not only to college students in Boston or to first-grade children in Toronto or to people who use laundromats in Nashville. Yet it is difficult and expensive to study random samples of the general population, as you can readily imagine. So social psychologists try to make realistic compromises between practicality and the goal of collecting data that can be generalized beyond the few people studied.

A common compromise is to use college students as subjects. It has often been said that American social psychology is based on college sophomores, because they are a readily available population. About 75 percent of all published articles in social psychology use undergraduate subjects (Sherman, Buddie, Dragan, End, & Finney, 1999). How dissatisfied should we be with this reliance on college student samples?

The need for a representative sample depends on the question asked. In some basic theory-testing research, the representativeness of the sample may not be crucial. For example, the frustration-aggression hypothesis should apply equally to schoolchildren, commuters driving to work, shoppers at a suburban mall, or college students. On the other hand, college students are not appropriate for all research. Suppose researchers are hired to study how best to introduce computers into business offices where the employees have worked together for years, are almost all older women, and have no more than a high school education. It would be entirely unreasonable to study this question with a sample of unacquainted college students who had no experience with office work and used computers regularly. For a research question of this sort, studies of college students would be misleading.

In general, in comparison to the general population, college students are much younger, higher in social class, and better at test taking (Sears, 1986). Their attitudes may be less well developed and more open to change. As a result, using college students in studies in which any of these factors make a difference could be unwise. Although college students are convenient subjects, they are not always the most appropriate participants for social psychological research.

Psychological research has also been criticized for an overrepresentation of white males among research participants. Beginning in the 1970s, feminist psychologists documented a common tendency to use male subjects rather than females or samples that included both sexes. Further, research on particular topics such as aggression and achievement motivation was almost entirely based on male subjects. Critics questioned whether theories based on male subjects would be applicable to females. In recent years, heightened awareness of gender bias and increased numbers of women students and researchers have improved the gender balance of research samples (Gannon, Luchetta, Rhodes, Pardie, & Segrist, 1992).

Ethnic minority groups have also been seriously underrepresented in psychological studies, a pattern that continues to this day. For example, Sandra Graham (1992) analyzed trends in published research on African Americans in six major psychology journals from 1970 to 1989. She counted the proportion of journal articles in which African Americans were the focus of the study, or in which data from two or more racial groups were compared. Overall, only 3.6 percent of the articles she reviewed met one of these criteria, and the proportion of articles on African Americans actually declined from 5.2 percent in the early 1970s to 2.0 percent in the late 1980s. Noting that the U.S. population is becoming more ethnically diverse, Graham (1992) cautioned that "academic psychology cannot maintain its integrity by continuing to allow ethnic minorities to remain so marginalized in mainstream research" (p. 638).

As the population of Canada and the United States becomes more diverse, the challenge of studying all segments of society becomes both more difficult and more important. According to the U.S. Census Bureau (2001), slightly over 70 percent of Americans are non-Hispanic whites, 13 percent are African or Caribbean

Americans, 12 percent are Hispanics (of any race), 4 percent are Asian Americans and Pacific Islanders, and about 1 percent are American Indians or Alaskan Natives. However, demographers predict that the ethnic mix of the United States will change dramatically during this century, with the proportion of European Americans declining and the proportion of citizens from Asia, Latin America, and the Caribbean increasing (U.S. Census Bureau, 2004). In addition to having both English-speaking and French-speaking citizens, Canada is also experiencing increased immigration, most notably from Asia (Statistics Canada, 2004).

The face of American society is changing in other ways as well. The public visibility of lesbians and gay men has increased dramatically. Although no one knows for sure the sexual orientation distribution of the U.S. public, conservative estimates are that at least 7 to 10 million people are gay and lesbian, and an unknown number of others are bisexual. In addition, the number of older adults is increasing steadily. There is also growing awareness of the many people with physical disabilities. It is estimated that about 12 percent of Americans have a severe disabling condition that limits their daily activities, preventing them from going to school, keeping house, or having a job. These examples highlight the enormous social and cultural diversity of the American population, and the increasing difficulty of studying truly representative samples in scientific research.

Correlational Versus Experimental Designs

After an investigator has decided what research questions to ask, another difficult decision remains: How will the study be conducted? There are two basic research designs: correlational and experimental. In correlational studies, the researcher carefully observes and records the relationship between (or among) two or more factors. For example, a researcher might ask whether physical attractiveness is related to a student's popularity with other students. In a correlational design, the researcher does not influence the students' behavior in any way but merely records information about the attractiveness of each student and how much he or she is liked by other students.

In contrast, the hallmark of an experimental design is intervention: The researcher puts people in a controlled situation and assesses how they react (Aronson, Wilson, & Brewer, 1998). To study the link between physical attractiveness and popularity, a researcher using an experimental design might enlist the assistance of a paid confederate who is sometimes dressed to look very attractive and sometimes dressed to look very unappealing. The researcher might then bring student volunteers into the laboratory for a brief interaction with another student (really the paid confederate). After a short meeting, the degree to which the student likes the confederate is measured. In this experimental design, the researcher controls the student's exposure to an attractive versus an unattractive peer, the setting in which they interact, and the way in which liking for the peer is measured. The following sections look closely at both correlational and experimental research designs and highlight the advantages and disadvantages of each.

Correlational Research

Testing the association between two or more factors.

Correlational research consists of observing the relationship between two or more factors, known technically as *variables.* Correlational research asks if there is an association between the variables. More specifically, when variable A is high, is variable B also high (a positive correlation) or low (a negative correlation), or is B's value unrelated (no correlation)? Height and weight are positively correlated because tall people tend to weigh more than short people. In contrast, on a given day, the amount of clothing worn and the temperature tend to be negatively correlated: People usually wear less clothing on hot days. However, height and amount of clothing are probably uncorrelated; in general, tall people and short people probably wear about the same number of pieces of clothing.

A good example of correlational research comes from studies of whether or not watching violence on television is related to aggressive behavior. Correlational studies have examined the association between how much time a child spends watching violent programs on television and the amount of aggressive behavior in which the child engages. Are the children who watch the most violence on television also the most aggressive in their daily behavior? Huesmann (1982) found that elementary school children who watched violent programs the most were also described by their peers as the most aggressive. In this study, viewing violent programs on television was positively correlated with children's aggressive behavior.

There are several advantages to correlational designs. First, they enable researchers to study problems in which intervention is impossible. For example, scientists cannot randomly assign people to experience passionate love, earthquakes, or cancer; nor can we randomly assign people to live in big cities or to grow up in small families. Such factors are clearly beyond the control of even the most ingenious and dedicated researchers. Both ethical and practical considerations limit the opportunities that researchers have to intervene in the lives of others. In such situations, correlational designs offer the best possible method for understanding the connections among various facets of people's lives.

A second advantage of correlational research is efficiency. Correlational studies allow researchers to collect more information and test more relationships than they can in most experiments. When they use a correlational approach to study what causes some children to be more aggressive than others, researchers can collect information on a great many factors, including television viewing, family history, intelligence, personality, and relationships with other children. Moreover, researchers can measure aggressive behavior in a number of different ways: in terms of teachers' impressions, their own observations of children in school, a child's reputation for aggressiveness among other children, and parents' reports. They can then use statistical procedures to uncover associations among these many variables. The experimental method is relatively inefficient for collecting large amounts of data on many variables.

Reverse-Causality Problem

In correlational research, the direction of causality is uncertain: Does A cause B, or vice versa?

A major limitation of correlational research is that it does not provide clear-cut evidence of cause-and-effect relationships. In correlational studies, the cause-and-effect relationship can be ambiguous in two ways. The **reverse-causality problem** occurs whenever two variables are correlated with each other, yet each one can just as plausibly be the cause as the effect. In this case, we know that variables A and B are related, but we cannot tell whether A causes B or whether B causes A. Studies that show a correlation between watching television and levels of aggressive behavior illustrate this problem. Such results could indicate that TV violence causes aggression in children. But the opposite might also be true: Perhaps children who are very aggressive in their daily lives are especially interested in watching people fight and so spend more time watching violent TV programs. In other words, perhaps children's aggressive behavior is the cause of their TV viewing patterns. A correlation between two variables does not, by itself, indicate which variable is the cause and which is the effect.

Third-Variable Problem

If two variables are correlated with each one, is one the cause of the other? Or is some third variable the cause of both?

The other serious ambiguity in correlational research is the possibility that neither variable A nor variable B directly affects the other. Rather, some other unspecified factor may influence both of them. This is called the **third-variable problem**. For example, the correlation between TV violence and aggressive behavior may be created by a third factor. Perhaps disadvantaged families who live in cramped households and experience a good deal of frustration in their lives tend both to watch more TV and to be more aggressive. Among such families, TV viewing and aggressive behavior would be correlated, but the correlation might be due to a third variable—poverty and frustration—that caused both. The correlation between watching televised violence and aggressive behavior would be called spurious because it was artificially created by a third variable that was not considered. Television would have no causal role itself in producing aggressive behavior.

These two ambiguities are often, but not always, a problem in correlational studies. Sometimes psychologists can rule out the reverse-causality problem. For example, many studies have found a correlation between gender and aggressive behavior; such studies have found boys to be more aggressive than girls. In this case, we can be confident that aggressive behavior is not the cause of the child's sex. Here the direction of causality is clear: Something about being a boy versus being a girl affects a child's aggressiveness.

The third-variable problem is not always a fatal difficulty, because researchers can sometimes check to see whether the most plausible third variable is really responsible for the correlation they have observed. For example, in Huesmann's (1982) correlational study of TV viewing and aggression among school children, measures of frustration and anger in the child's family could be included. The researcher could then check to see whether the correlation of TV viewing with aggressive behavior was in fact due to home life. Does it hold both in angry, frustrated families and in happy, peaceful families? If so, the researcher could conclude that the third variable (home life) was not responsible for the original correlation.

Of course, this procedure does not completely eliminate the third-variable problem. Some other third variable (now actually a fourth) could exist that researchers had not measured, such as verbal skills. Perhaps children with poor verbal skills prefer watching TV shows with a great deal of physical activity rather than slower paced shows with more dialogue. Again, to test this possibility, the solution would be to measure this new third variable—verbal skill—and then see if the original correlation held up for both highly verbal children and those below average in verbal skills.

This process sounds as if it could go on and on. But at some point it ends because researchers can no longer think of any more plausible third variables—not because no more variables exist, but because, for the moment, researchers accept the correlation as reflecting a cause-and-effect relationship. Eventually someone may think of another possible variable to be examined.

Experiment

Research that randomly assigns people to conditions, varies treatment in each condition, and measures effect on responses.

In an **experiment**, the researcher creates two (or more) conditions that differ from each other in clearly specified ways. Individuals are randomly assigned to one of these different conditions and then their reactions are measured. For example, in experiments on media violence, one group of children might be shown a violent film and another group shown a nonviolent film. All the children might then be placed in a test situation in which their aggressive behavior can be measured. If those who were shown the violent film behave more aggressively, we can say that filmed violence is a cause of aggressive behavior in this setting.

A study of media violence by Hartmann (1969) illustrates this experimental approach. Teenage boys were randomly assigned to one of two conditions. Half the boys watched a 2-minute film that showed two boys shooting basketballs and then getting into an argument and finally a fistfight. A second group of boys watched another 2-minute film that depicted an active but cooperative basketball game. After seeing the film, each boy was asked to help out in what was described as a study of the effects of performance feedback on learning. The subject was supposed to be a "teacher" who would administer a shock to a "learner" every time that "learner" made a mistake in the learning task. The "teacher" could deliver as strong a shock as he wanted, within certain limits. (In reality, the shocks were fake, and the "learner" was a confederate of the experimenter.) The boys who had seen the violent film delivered stronger shocks than those who had seen the nonviolent one. In this situation, at least, observing filmed violence caused an increase in aggressive behavior.

Independent Variable

In an experiment, the factor that is systematically manipulated by the researcher.

Dependent Variable

In an experiment, the response to the independent variable being manipulated.

The great strength of the experimental method is that it avoids the ambiguities about causality that plague most correlational studies. Experimenters randomly assign people to different conditions to see if there is any difference in their responses. If the experiment has been done properly, any difference in responses between the two conditions must be due to the difference in the conditions. In more formal terms, the factor controlled by the researcher (the "cause") is called the **independent variable**, because it is determined by the researcher. In the Hartmann study, the independent variable was the type of film the boys watched. The outcome, or "effect," that is being studied is called the **dependent variable**, because its value is dependent on the independent variable. In the Hartmann (1969) study, the dependent variable was the amount of electric shock the subject administered to another person. Experiments provide clear evidence that differences in the dependent variable are caused by differences in the independent variable.

Table 1–1

Comparing Correlational and Experimental Research

	Correlational	Experimental
Independent variable	Varies naturally	Controlled by researcher
Random assignment	No	Yes
Unambiguous causality	Usually not	Yes
Exploratory	Often	Usually not
Theory testing	Often	Usually
Tests many relationships	Usually	Usually not

In experimental research, much attention is given to the creation of the independent and dependent variables. The psychologist usually starts with an abstract or conceptual definition of the variable in question. For example, the variable "observing violence" might be defined as watching acts that hurt or are intended to hurt another person. The researcher must then go from this fairly general conceptual definition to an **operational definition**. An operational definition is the specific procedure or operation that is used to manipulate or measure the variable in the experiment. For example, the experimenter might create two versions of a film: one violent and another nonviolent. If the experimenter is attempting to manipulate only the amount of violence in a film, then the two films should not differ in other ways; for example, they should run the same length of time, and they should both be either color or black and white. Control over the independent variable is crucial because it allows the experimenter to pinpoint the cause of any differences that emerge between the two groups of people.

Operational Definition

The specific procedure used to measure or manipulate a variable.

The second essential feature of an experiment is that subjects must be randomly assigned to conditions—by the flip of a coin, by the cutting of a deck of cards, or, more commonly, by the use of a table of random numbers. **Random assignment** of subjects to conditions is crucial because it means that differences between subjects in all conditions are due solely to chance. If subjects in each group differ in some systematic way beforehand, researchers cannot interpret any later differences in behavior as being due solely to the experimental conditions. The differences in behavior could be due to those preexisting factors and not to the independent variable. Table 1–1 compares correlational and experimental research designs.

Random Assignment

Guaranteeing that subjects are placed in experimental conditions on the basis of chance.

Field Versus Laboratory Settings

Another decision in designing research concerns where the study should be conducted: in a field setting or in a laboratory. Research done in the field examines behavior in its "natural habitat." Researchers might study factory workers' productivity right in the factory, or commuters' responses to an emergency on the subway train they normally ride to work, or college students' relationships with their roommates in a dormitory.

Laboratory research, in contrast, is done in an artificial situation, one that the research participant does not normally inhabit. Some laboratory research is conducted in a specially outfitted room in a psychology building at a college or research institute. The lab may have all kinds of special equipment, such as video monitors to show films to subjects, audio equipment to record conversations between subjects, one-way mirrors to permit observation of group interactions, physiological recording equipment, or computers. Or the laboratory may simply be a room or lecture hall where people can fill out questionnaires. The point is that the subject comes to a setting that is selected and controlled by the researcher. Both experimental and correlational research can be done in either the laboratory or the field, and each setting has advantages and disadvantages.

Social psychological research is not confined to the laboratory. As you will see in reading this book, studies have also been conducted at summer camps, in airport waiting rooms, on urban subways, and even at the beach.

The major advantage of laboratory research is the control it permits over the situation. Researchers can be quite certain about what is happening to each subject. If they are doing experimental work, they can randomly assign the participants to conditions, expose them to specific experiences, minimize the effects of extraneous factors, and go a long way toward eliminating unwanted variations in the procedures. Laboratory researchers also have great control over the dependent variable and can measure results more precisely than is often possible in the field. Therefore, the laboratory is the ideal place to study the exact effects of one variable on another. All these advantages fall under the heading of internal validity. **Internal validity** is high when researchers can be confident that the effects they observe in the dependent variable are actually caused by the independent variables they manipulated in the experiment (and are not caused by other uncontrolled factors).

Internal Validity

Extent to which cause-and-effect conclusions can be drawn.

In field settings, it is generally difficult to assign subjects to conditions randomly, to be certain that they are all experiencing the same thing, and to get precise measures of the dependent variable. In particular, it is difficult to design pure manipulations of the independent variable and to obtain pure measures of the dependent variable. The researcher must find or arrange circumstances that produce specific differences among the conditions.

In an ambitious field study of the effects of TV violence, Feshbach and Singer (1971) studied adolescent boys who lived in seven different boarding schools in California and New York. With the help of the school staff, the researchers were able to assign boys randomly to two different "TV diets." All boys watched selected prime-time TV shows for at least 6 hours a week for 6 weeks. In the violent TV condition, the boys watched shows with aggressive content, including Westerns and crime stories. In the nonviolent condition, boys watched situation comedies and other nonaggressive programs. Staff ratings of the boys' behavior constituted the measure of aggression. Contrary to what you might expect, the researchers found that the boys who were shown the violent programs were actually somewhat less aggressive than the boys who were shown the nonviolent programs. Watching TV violence seemed to reduce aggressive behavior. Why might this unexpected result have occurred?

The researchers discovered that most of the boys preferred the more violent programs. Therefore, those boys who were assigned to the nonviolent television condition may have been more frustrated than the other group because they were prevented from watching their favorite programs. Consequently, it is not clear whether the results are due to the content of the shows the boys watched or to differences in the level of frustration between boys in the violent and in the nonviolent TV conditions. This problem would not arise in a laboratory study, because the researchers would not have had to interfere with the boys' normal television-viewing practices.

Other advantages of the laboratory are convenience and cost. It is usually much easier and cheaper for researchers to set up a study in a room down the hall from their office than to go to the places where people live or work.

The most obvious advantage of field settings is that they are more realistic and therefore allow results to be generalized more readily to real-life situations. This is called **external validity** to reflect the fact that the results are more likely to be valid in situations outside (external to) the specific research situation itself (Campbell & Stanley, 1963). External validity is high when the results of a study can be generalized to other settings and populations. Consider the differences between two studies of TV violence described in this chapter: the Hartmann (1969) laboratory experiment and the Feshbach and Singer (1971) field experiment.

External Validity

Extent to which results of a study generalize to other populations and settings.

In Hartmann's (1969) laboratory study, the independent variable—filmed violence—was artificial. The researcher created a brief film that was especially prepared for the study. In Feshbach and Singer's (1971) field study, the independent variable was the violence actually shown on national prime-time television. In Hartmann's laboratory study, the dependent variable—aggressive behavior—was artificial: the amount of shock delivered in the teacher-learner situation that was constructed especially for the study. In the Feshbach and Singer field study, the dependent variable was naturalistic and consisted of observers' ratings of how much physical and verbal aggression the boys engaged in during their normal interactions with peers and teachers. Suppose we want to generalize from these two studies to the effects of prime-time television on teenage boys' aggression in their everyday lives. The field study deals with exactly the kinds of TV violence, everyday aggressive behavior, and real-life situations of interest. So it would be more appropriate to generalize from the field study. The field study, therefore, has greater external validity.

Another advantage of work in the field is that researchers are sometimes able to deal with extremely powerful variables and situations that could not be studied in the laboratory. Researchers can observe people in extreme situations, for example, when they are waiting for open-heart surgery in a hospital or huddled together under artillery bombardment. Sometimes ingenious researchers are able to take advantage of "natural experiments"—cases in which the independent variable is manipulated by nature rather than by the experimenter. For example, experimenters could not randomly assign homeowners to a destructive natural disaster in order to see if this experience changed their perceptions of personal control over their lives. But Parker, Brewer, and Spencer (1980) were able to approximate this design by studying a community that had suffered a devastating brushfire. Chance factors such as rapid changes in the wind direction determined which homes were destroyed and which were saved and so provided a rough equivalent of random assignment to conditions of disaster and nondisaster.

Because research in the field deals with everyday life, it tends to minimize suspicion by the subjects. Their responses are more spontaneous and less susceptible to the kinds of bias that suspicion can produce in the laboratory. Whenever people know they are participants in an experiment, there is always the possibility that they are not behaving naturally. For instance, they may try to please the experimenter or present themselves in a socially desirable manner, or they may distrust the experimenter and not believe the experimental manipulation. Any of these effects could produce bias in the results or obscure any actual cause-and-effect relationships. Table 1–2 compares characteristics of field and laboratory research.

Methods of Data Collection

The next step is to decide on a technique of data collection. Basically, researchers have three options: (1) They can ask research participants to report on their own behaviors, thoughts, or feelings; (2) they can observe participants directly; or (3) they can go to an archive and use data originally collected for other purposes.

Table 1–2

Comparing Laboratory and Field Research

	Laboratory	Field
Control over variables	High	Low
Random assignment	Almost always	Seldom
Convenience	Usually high	Usually low
Realism	Low	High
Impact of independent variables	Tends to be lower	Tends to be higher
Suspicion and bias	Tends to be higher	Tends to be lower
External validity	Low	High

Self-Report. Perhaps the most common technique of data collection in social psychology uses self-reports. People can be asked for their preference between two presidential candidates, their feelings toward their parents, or their attitudes about their personal appearance. Children can be asked to report on their perception of their classmates' aggressiveness or their own television-viewing behavior. One big advantage of self-report questionnaires or interviews is that they allow the investigator to measure subjective states such as perceptions, attitudes, or emotions. These can be inferred only indirectly from observational studies. For example, it would be difficult for observers to tell how lonely another person feels without getting that person's self-report. The principal disadvantage of self-report is that we must rely on people to give honest descriptions of their own internal feelings. People are often willing to give honest and full answers, especially when their privacy is carefully protected. But researchers also know that people sometimes disguise socially unacceptable feelings (such as racial prejudices) and that people are sometimes not fully aware of their own feelings.

Observational Research. Direct observation is a widely used research technique. For example, to study helping behavior, researchers have staged fake emergencies in public places to see how many people are willing to come to the aid of a stranger in distress. Marriage researchers have obtained permission to place microphones in homes and to record family interactions so that they can learn about the frequency of conflict, fighting, praising, and other types of interaction.

Archival Research. In **archival research**, the investigator uses data that were previously collected for another purpose. For example, in the 1940s, researchers wanted to examine whether whites' violence against blacks was associated with frustration based on economic difficulties. They used historical records to correlate cotton prices and lynching of blacks in the southern United States (Hovland & Sears, 1940). They found that the greatest number of lynching deaths occurred during the years with the lowest cotton prices. Perhaps the best known archival data come from the U.S. Census, which has been conducted every 10 years for 2 centuries. But many specialized databanks also exist with the records of polls, surveys, and large-scale studies.

Archival Research

Analysis of existing data collected for another purpose.

There are many advantages to using archival data. The most obvious is that this technique is inexpensive. The U.S. Census costs millions of dollars to collect, but the data can be used for next to nothing. Archival data also allow researchers to test hypotheses about changes in attitudes or behavior over time rather than be limited to one historical moment. We might want to know how many people say they would vote for a woman for president; the availability of archival data on that question over many years can provide a rich historical context for the findings. On the other hand, in almost all cases, archival data were originally collected with some research topic in mind other than the one researchers now wish to

Social psychologists are concerned about possible bias in their research. Here, a white woman interviews a Korean American teenager. How might the gender and ethnic background of these individuals affect their interactions and the information the participant is willing to reveal?

investigate. As a result, the questions are usually not exactly the ones the present researchers would ask, or they may be worded the wrong way for their purposes, or the participants in the study might not be exactly the group researchers would prefer. Nevertheless, data archives can often provide a useful source of data for social psychological research.

Internet Research. Recently, psychologists have started to conduct research using the Internet. The Internet offers several advantages to researchers (Gosling, Vazire, Srivastava, & John, 2004). First, the Internet makes it easier to recruit participants who are not college students and who come from diverse backgrounds, distant geographical regions, or specialized groups. Second, when participants complete a survey or research task online, their information is automatically recorded. This increases the efficiency of data collection. Third, Internet research is usually much less expensive than comparable research conducted using more traditional methods. Fourth, Internet chat rooms and bulletin boards provide a rich sample of human social behavior where people discuss current social issues or hobbies, share advice about medical problems, or swap technical tips about computer use. Online forums can be used to study many topics including communication, prejudice, and the spread of new ideas (Kraut et al., 2004).

At the same time, there are also important unresolved issues about using the Internet for research. There are concerns about possible bias in Internet samples. Without safeguards, some individuals might participate in a study more than once. Others might present a fake identity, or respond in a frivolous or malicious manner. Another problem concerns the data-collection setting. When participants are studied in laboratory settings, the researcher can control the environment. In contrast, when participants use a computer at home or work, it is impossible to monitor their behavior or to prevent undesirable distractions. Psychologists are aware of these concerns and are striving to find ways to minimize the problems associated with this valuable new research method (Gosling et al., 2004).

Bias in Research

All scientists are concerned about possible bias in their research, and social psychologists are no exception. Two kinds of bias are particularly troublesome in social psychology: the effects of the experimenter's behavior and bias associated with a subject's feelings about taking part in a study.

Experimenter Bias. Research participants are extremely susceptible to influence by the researcher. If the experimenter implies, consciously or otherwise, that he or she would like subjects to respond in a certain way, there is a tendency for participants to respond in that way. Subtle cues tend to be picked up by subjects and to influence their behavior. This problem is known as **experimenter bias**. For example, consider the studies of media violence in which subjects give electric shocks to another person after watching either a violent or a nonviolent movie. A well-intentioned but perhaps overly eager experimenter, expecting that subjects in the violent-movie condition might be the most aggressive, could subtly encourage these subjects to give more shocks by smiling, nodding, or making eye contact when they pushed the shock button. Similarly, the experimenter might frown or communicate disappointment to nonviolent-movie subjects who gave the shock because they violated the hypothesis.

Experimenter Bias

Unintentional acts by the researcher can bias results.

There are two solutions to the problem of experimenter bias. One is to keep the people who actually conduct the research (often research assistants) uninformed about the hypotheses or about the experimental condition a particular subject was assigned. For example, in research on TV violence, the experimenter could have one researcher show the movies and a second researcher administer the shock task, arranging it so that the second experimenter did not know which movie each subject had seen. The second experimenter is said to be "blind" to the condition the subject is in.

A second solution is to standardize the situation in every way possible. If everything is standardized and there are no differences between conditions other than those that are deliberate, there should be no bias. In the extreme case, subjects might arrive for an experiment and find a written instruction on the door telling them to enter and sit down at a computer. All instructions might be given by the computer, and the subjects might respond by typing in their answers to questions presented on the screen. Subjects might actually complete the experiment before they met the experimenter. In this way, every factor in the situation would be absolutely standardized, and experimenter bias would be eliminated.

In actual practice, the solution to the problem of bias is usually a combination of the two procedures we have described. As much as possible, the researcher is kept "blind" to the subjects' experimental conditions. Also as much as possible, instructions are standardized by the use of written materials, audio- and videotapes, and computers.

Subject Bias. Another source of bias stems from the subject's motives and goals when serving in the role of a research participant. **Demand characteristics** are "features introduced into a research setting by virtue of the fact that it is a research study and that the subjects know that they are part of it" (Aronson, Brewer, & Carlsmith, 1985, p. 454). The basic idea is that the mere fact of knowing that one is being studied may alter one's behavior. Subjects may try to "figure out" the true purpose of the experiment and alter their responses on the basis of their guesses about the study. They may try to give the "correct" or socially desirable response—to portray themselves as smart or politically liberal or religious or sexually responsible, depending on their interpretation of the situation. If subjects' responses are biased in these ways, researchers cannot draw accurate conclusions.

Demand Characteristics

Aspects of research that make people aware that they are being studied can bias their behavior.

Weber and Cook (1972) carefully analyzed the roles subjects adopt in laboratory experiments. They distinguished several different roles: "good subjects," who try to help the researchers by confirming the hypothesis; "negativistic subjects," who try to sabotage the experiment; "faithful subjects," who scrupulously follow the instructions and try to avoid acting on the basis of any suspicions about the nature of the study (either to help or to hurt the research); and "apprehensive subjects," who are anxious about their own performance. These biases are almost impossible to eliminate entirely, but they can be minimized in a variety of ways. The goal is to produce a situation in which subjects respond spontaneously without worrying about the correctness of their response or trying to figure out what the situation "demands." When possible, researchers may use unobtrusive

META-ANALYSIS IN SOCIAL PSYCHOLOGY

As the number of studies on a particular topic increases, researchers are confronted with a new problem: how to synthesize research findings to arrive at general conclusions. Consider work on sex differences in helping behavior. Eagly and Crowley (1986) identified no fewer than 172 separate studies that investigated male–female differences in helping behavior! How are researchers to handle this ever-increasing quantity of empirical research?

In recent years, statistical techniques called meta-analysis have been developed to help researchers review and synthesize empirical findings systematically (Miller & Cooper, 1991; Rosenthal, 1991). The first step is for the researcher to find as many studies as possible on the same topic. Then, meta-analysis uses statistical methods to pool information from all available studies. The goal is to arrive at an overall estimate of the size of the finding, for instance, the size of a particular sex difference. Researchers might find, for instance, that the average sex difference on a problem-solving test is less than a tenth of a standard deviation—quite a small effect that may not be of much practical importance.

In meta-analysis, statistics are also used to test for the consistency (homogeneity) of findings across studies. When results from different studies are found to be highly consistent, researchers can have much confidence in the findings. When results of studies differ, meta-analysis techniques direct researchers to look for other factors that may be important. For example, if 40 studies show that men are better at this type of problem solving and 40 studies show that women are better at this skill, scientists might suspect that some factor other than gender makes a difference. Perhaps men are better only when tested by a male experimenter, or only in group testing situations, or only if they come from middle-class backgrounds. Instead of merely commenting that the findings are inconsistent, the goal is to try to identify the reasons for the inconsistency. So additional analyses would be conducted that take these new factors into account.

As you read this textbook, you will find references to meta-analyses of numerous facets of social behavior.

measures so the subjects do not know that they are being studied. For instance, pedestrians who encounter a person who has fallen on a city street may never know that the person is actually a researcher conducting a study of helping behavior. Another approach is to guarantee participants that their responses will be anonymous; no one, including the researcher, will know how any individual responded.

Perhaps the most common approach is to try to keep subjects unaware of the goals and hypotheses of the study. For instance, a researcher interested in sex differences in initiating conversations with strangers might ask subjects to volunteer for a study of taste preferences. While the subjects are waiting for the alleged study to begin, their behavior in the waiting room might be observed, perhaps with the help of a confederate who behaves in a standardized way in the waiting room. In this situation, subjects would expect to participate in one type of study and might not suspect that the time they spend in the waiting room is of any interest to the researcher. All these techniques reduce the possibility that participants' reactions will be distorted or changed by their concerns about social desirability.

Replication. No single study, however beautifully crafted, is ever perfect. Each procedure has its own limitations. And researchers can virtually never test the entire population of interest to them, so there is always some margin of error in their ability to generalize their results. Because any single study is flawed, a hallmark of good research is **replication**. In its simplest form, replication means that researchers are able to reproduce the findings of others if they re-create their methods. This is a fundamental requirement for all science, that different researchers working in different settings can all produce the same effects. Of course, in social research, it is seldom possible to re-create precisely every aspect

Replication

Repeating a study more than once.

of a study because the subject population may be somewhat different, and the social and political climate may have changed over time. Consequently, when social scientists are able to replicate results, they have much greater confidence in their accuracy.

In addition to conducting exact replications, it is important to conduct conceptual replications. In a conceptual replication, different research procedures are used to explore the same conceptual relationship (Aronson, Brewer, & Carlsmith, 1985). For example, we have seen that research concerning the effects of TV violence on aggressive behavior has been conducted in both lab and field settings, has used both correlational and experimental designs, and has used diverse measures of aggressive behavior and a wide variety of violent films. To the extent that all these different techniques yield similar results, researchers become increasingly confident that they understand the phenomenon in question. The Research Highlight for this chapter discusses **meta-analysis**, a popular method for interpreting the results of many studies on the same topic.

Meta-Analysis

Quantitative approach to summarizing results of many studies.

The basic point is that researchers should be cautious about taking too seriously the results of a single study on a topic. Rather, they should ask whether a particular finding has been confirmed in other studies. And they should also ask how large and important the finding is in practical terms. For example, of all the possible variations in human aggression, how much can be attributed to TV violence? Are the sex differences we hear about so often really big enough to make a difference in everyday life? As you read magazines and newspapers or watch the news on TV, you will often hear about research on such diverse topics as the health dangers of cholesterol, the latest word on teen sex, the virtue of seatbelts, and the causes of child abuse. Use your knowledge of research methods and the importance of replication to be a sensible and cautious consumer of research reports.

RESEARCH ETHICS

Until the mid-20th century, few people worried about the ethics of research with human participants. After World War II, however, the discovery of Nazi atrocities, such as the dangerous and often fatal medical experiments carried out by doctors in concentration camps on unwilling prisoners, came to light. Concerns were also raised by the discovery of unethical medical experimentation in the United States, such as the notorious Tuskegee case: In 1932, the U.S. Public Health Service began a 40-year study in Tuskegee, Alabama, on 399 poor and semiliterate African American men who had syphilis, a progressive disease that can lead to brain damage and death. The goal was to trace the effects of syphilis on untreated males over many years. The men were told they were being treated, but in fact they were never given medication, even though penicillin became available in the 1940s and was highly effective against the disease. Even as late as 1972, treatment was still being withheld from the survivors while the study continued.

In the field of social psychology, ethical concerns have often focused on the use of deception by researchers. Consider some of the lab studies of the effects of TV violence on aggression. Is it ethical for a researcher to tell a subject to administer what he or she believes are painful electric shocks to another person when, in fact, the shock machine is fake and the other person is a confederate? Might the experiment cause the participant to feel guilty for hurting another person? If at the end of the study the researcher explains that the shock machine was fake, will the subjects feel foolish that they were duped by the experimenter?

Studies that use deception have raised a number of ethical issues. When are researchers justified in deceiving subjects about the research they are participating in? When (if ever) is it legitimate to do harmful things to subjects? Is it justifiable to expose subjects to risks if the potential scientific value of a study is great? These questions have led to efforts within many professional associations to define ethical behavior. The American Psychological Association (APA) first developed guidelines for the ethical conduct of psychological research in 1972 and revises these guidelines as new issues arise (APA, 1992). In addition, the U.S. government has also established procedures for the review of all the research it funds. The government requires each university and research institution that receives federal funds to establish a committee of researchers to review all proposed research that uses human subjects. This institutional review board is responsible for ensuring that all research is conducted according to a set of general principles laid down by the federal government. Three important ethical issues in psychological research are informed consent, debriefing, and minimal risk.

Informed Consent

Agreeing to participate in research after learning about the study, including possible risks and benefits.

Informed Consent. A subject must voluntarily agree to participate in research, without any coercion, and must understand what the participation involves. This is known as **informed consent**. The researcher has an obligation to tell potential subjects as much as possible about the study before asking them to participate. Subjects should be informed about the research procedures, any risks or benefits of the research, their right to refuse to participate, and their right to withdraw at any time during the research without penalty. Any exception to this general guideline must be approved by the institutional review board after careful examination of the planned research.

The requirement of informed consent sounds quite reasonable but sometimes creates problems for social psychologists. As we have just seen, it may be important not to tell subjects the true purpose of the study to avoid introducing bias into their responses. Even in the simplest research, subjects are rarely told the specific hypotheses that are being tested. Several of the studies we discussed in this chapter did not provide fully informed consent, and it is hard to see how they could have. Imagine what would happen if researchers first told subjects that the study concerned willingness to help strangers in distress and then tested to see if the subjects would help in an emergency. It is difficult to believe that this research would be valid.

Some people believe that deception of any kind in psychological research is unethical. They think it demeans the subjects and should never be used. A more moderate position that is endorsed by most research psychologists is that deception should not be used if possible or should be used only after a consideration of whether the benefits of the study outweigh any possible harmful effects. Participants need not be told everything that will happen, but they should know that they are in a study and should freely give their permission. In other words, only someone who has given informed consent or consent based on trust should be exposed to potentially distressing conditions.

Debriefing

Explaining the purpose and procedures of research to participants.

Debriefing. At the end of their participation in a study, subjects should always be debriefed. **Debriefing** means explaining in some detail the purposes and procedures of the research. Participants should be given an opportunity to ask questions and express their feelings. A friendly discussion between the researcher and the participant can help a subject to recover from any upset the research may have caused and to learn from their research experience. When research deals with very sensitive topics, it may be important for the researcher to suggest ways in which participants can learn more about the topic by reading or consulting with experts. Sometimes researchers offer to send participants written information about the results of the study once the research findings have been analyzed.

Minimal Risk

The risk to research participants is no greater than the risk of daily life.

Minimal Risk. A third ethical guideline for research is to minimize potential risks to the subjects. **Minimal risk** means that the possible risks of participating in the research are no greater than those ordinarily encountered in daily life. What kinds of risks can social psychological research pose?

One of the most important risks is the invasion of privacy. An individual's right to privacy must be respected and valued. Researchers who study especially sensitive topics, such as sex, drug or alcohol use, illegal behavior, or religious beliefs, must protect the subjects' right to withhold such information and to have their responses kept in strict confidence. On the other hand, public behavior and events on the public record do not have to be protected as carefully. Anyone can go to the local courthouse and look up information on births, marriages, and deaths. Threats to privacy, like all risks involved in social psychological research, can change over time as the society itself changes. For example, people are much more willing to discuss details of their sexual relationships now than they were a generation ago. Today there is widespread concern about keeping the results of AIDS testing confidential, because disclosure that a person has been infected can jeopardize his or her health insurance, employment, and standing in the community. The use of the Internet for research also poses new challenges (Kraut et al., 2004). Responsible researchers protect the privacy of subjects by guaranteeing confidentiality and often by having the person participate in the study anonymously.

The other main category of risk in social psychology research comes from stresses of various kinds. Subjects in some studies may become bored, anxious, or fearful. Some studies may threaten the individual's self-respect. As we see in Chapter 3, many studies in recent years have investigated the causal explanations that people have for their own successes and failures. Such studies frequently require that subjects be exposed to success or failure at an experimental task. A gratuitous failure experience in a psychology experiment is no fun. Being deceived is itself an unpleasant experience for some people. Smith and Richardson (1983) surveyed students who participated in psychology experiments at the University of Georgia. Twenty percent of students reported experiencing some harmful consequence, such as being deceived, feeling humiliated, experiencing physical discomfort, or being angered. Such reports were almost twice as common among students who had participated in deception experiments as among those who had not. Most students did not report harm, but a substantial minority did.

How much risk should a subject be exposed to? The first and most important principle is informed consent. If at all possible, subjects must be allowed to make that decision for themselves based on adequate information. This decision is similar to the decision people face when electing to undergo surgery: Ultimately, the decision must be in the hands of the patient, and it must be as informed a decision as possible.

It is not always possible to inform a subject fully about the exact nature of a study. In such cases, the researcher and the institutional review board must decide how much risk to allow. As stated previously, the risks faced in the research should be no more severe than those likely to be encountered in normal life. Being threatened with an injection may be frightening, but it is a usual occurrence. Being threatened with isolation for 10 hours is also frightening, but it is not a common occurrence; most people never face this threat. So researchers would be more hesitant to deceive a person about isolation than about a harmless injection.

Finally, another criterion many researchers and review boards use in evaluating risk is that the subjects should leave the study in essentially the same state of mind and body in which they entered. That is, participation in the research should have no substantial effects that carry over once the subject has finished the study. Whether a study is pleasant, interesting, and enjoyable; or mildly unpleasant, boring, or tedious, the subjects' state of mind, knowledge of themselves, and general attitudes should not be altered by the experiences. This guideline, if followed closely, ensures that participants will not be exposed to excessive risk.

At its best, social psychological research offers the joy of new discoveries about human experience. The thoughtful use of scientific methods can do much to advance our understanding of social life and social problems. But psychological research also carries with it the responsibility to treat research participants with sensitivity and high ethical standards and to repay their valuable assistance by sharing the research results with the public. The chapters that follow offer a guided tour of the major findings and theories in social psychology.

Summary

1. Social psychology is the scientific study of how people think about, influence, and relate to others. Social psychologists often emphasize the power of the immediate social situation to influence behavior.
2. Major theoretical approaches in social psychology include motivational theories, learning theories, cognitive theories, decision-making theories, and interdependence theories. These are not necessarily contradictory. Rather, each emphasizes one aspect of the causes of behavior without necessarily claiming that the others are unimportant or irrelevant.
3. A sociocultural perspective emphasizes how behavior is affected by cultural values, social norms, and social roles. Cultures differ in the relative emphasis they give to individualism and collectivism.
4. The emerging field of evolutionary social psychology applies the principles of evolution and natural selection to the understanding of human behavior and social life. Evolutionary approaches emphasize the shared human qualities and evolved psychological mechanisms that are part of our heritage as a species.
5. Many social psychologists are working to develop middle-range theories or models to explain specific aspects of human behavior, such as the frustration-aggression hypothesis.
6. We all know a great deal about social behavior from our daily observations and experiences. Systematic research is necessary to test which of our intuitions are right and which are wrong. Social psychological research has four goals: description, causal analysis, theory building, and application.
7. Research participants should represent the people about whom researchers seek to generalize. A random sample is ideal but costly; therefore, many researchers use convenience samples such as college students. Critics warn that an overreliance on white middle-class college students may bias research results and limit their generalizability.
8. Correlational research asks whether two or more variables are related without trying to manipulate either variable. Correlational research can deal with many variables at once and can investigate phenomena that cannot be manipulated in the laboratory, such as crime, divorce, or rape. Correlational research usually does not allow strong causal conclusions to be drawn.
9. In an experiment, subjects are randomly assigned to conditions that differ only in specific, deliberately varied ways (independent variable). If there is any difference in the resulting behavior (dependent variable), it is due to the independent variable controlled by the researcher. Experiments permit unambiguous causal statements.
10. Laboratory research provides more control and greater internal validity, but research in field settings is closer to the real world and often has greater external validity. The most common sources of data in social psychology are self-reports, systematic observations of behavior, and data archives. Use of the Internet for research is gaining in popularity.
11. Great care must be taken to avoid bias in research, including experimenter bias and demand characteristics of the research situation. Because any one study is inevitably limited, replication is an essential feature of good research. Meta-analysis helps researchers to synthesize the results of many topics on a single topic.
12. Social psychologists face many ethical issues in doing research. They must protect the welfare of subjects and respect their privacy. Current guidelines emphasize obtaining informed consent and exposing subjects to no more than minimal risk.

Key Terms

archival research **23**
behaviorism **5**
collectivism **11**
correlational research **17**
culture **10**
debriefing **28**
decision-making theories **8**
demand characteristics **25**
dependent variable **19**
evolutionary social psychology **13**

In The News

Man on a Leash or Woman Holding a Leash?

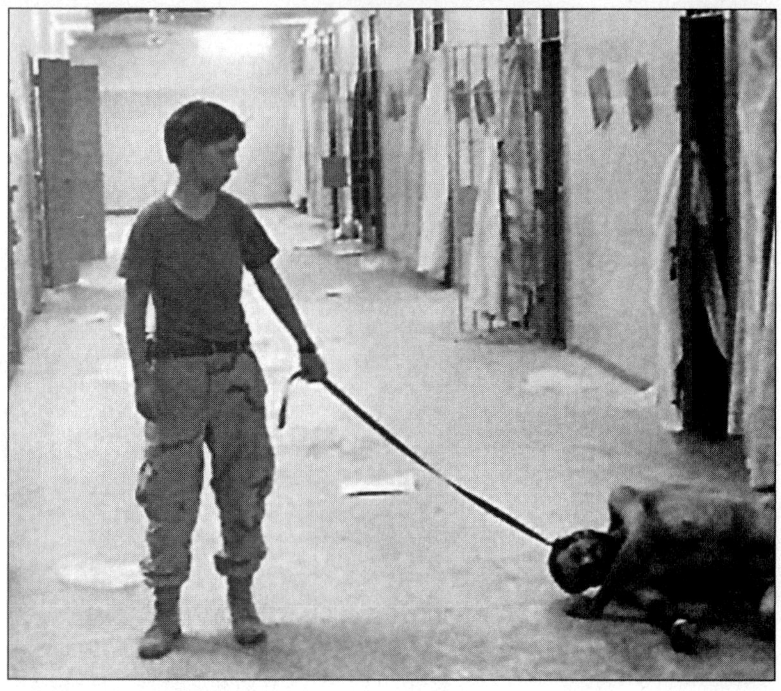

Photographs can be compelling, even disturbing, statements about people and the meaning of their activities. When this and similar photos were released to the press in spring of 2004, the reaction was horror throughout much of the world. But person perception is clearly in the eye of the beholder.

Those who perpetrated these actions regarded them very differently. They saw themselves as having done their jobs very successfully. They perceived their mission to be to "soften up" prisoners for interrogation by subjecting them to humiliating and debasing postures and activities, as with this man on a leash held by a woman. Their superiors apparently believed that the threat that family and friends might see the photographs and thereby think poorly of the prisoners would motivate those prisoners to give up information.

But outsiders looking at the photographs saw them as outrageous and inexcusably insulting, with actual smiling constituting additional evidence of an appalling lack of judgment.

Person perception depends critically on your perspective. If you are an interrogator, you see a man on a leash ready for questioning. If you are not, you see a young woman treating a prisoner in an unconscionable way and appearing to enjoy it.

Part One

Chapter 2

Person Perception: Forming Impressions of Others

Focus of This Chapter

Our impressions of others are among the most important judgments we form. We use whatever information is available to form impressions of others—to make judgments about their personalities or form hypotheses about the kinds of persons they are. In this chapter we deal with this process, which is called "person perception": how we form impressions of people, what kinds of information we use in arriving at those impressions, how accurate our impressions are, and what biases affect our impressions.

In thinking about how people form impressions of others, it is useful to keep in mind six quite simple and general principles:

1. People form impressions of others quickly on the basis of minimal information and go on to impute general traits to them.
2. People pay special attention to the most salient features of a person, rather than pay attention to everything. We notice the qualities that make a person distinctive or unusual.
3. Processing information about people involves perceiving some coherent meaning in their behavior. To a degree, we use the context of a person's behavior to infer its meaning, rather than interpret the behavior in isolation.
4. We organize our perceptions by categorizing or grouping stimuli. Rather than see each person as a separate individual, we tend to see people as members of groups—the people wearing white lab coats are doctors, even though each may have features that make him or her quite different from other doctors.
5. We use our enduring cognitive structures to make sense of people's behavior. On identifying a woman as a doctor, we use our information about doctors more generally to infer her attributes and the meaning of her behavior.
6. A perceiver's own needs and personal goals influence how he or she perceives others. For example, the impression you form of someone you will meet only once is different from the impression you form about your new roommate.

WHAT INFORMATION DO WE USE?

A glance at someone's picture or at an individual passing on the street gives us ideas about the kind of person he or she is. Even hearing a name tends to conjure up images of what its owner is like. When two people meet, if only for an instant, they form impressions of each other. With more contact, they form fuller and richer impressions that determine how they behave toward each other, how much they like each other, and whether they will associate often.

Roles

When we seek ways to organize information about people, knowing their social roles is important, perhaps more so than knowing their traits. There are many ways to be extroverted (e.g., such as being a comedian, a political leader, or a bully), but there are relatively fewer ways to fulfill a concrete role (such as being a politician). Consequently, roles are informative, rich, and well articulated, summarizing a lot of information across a wide range of situations. Roles are also more distinctive than are traits, leading to more associations. Knowing that someone is a cheerleader, for example, says a lot about exactly how he is outgoing and in what situations he is outgoing, whereas merely being told that he is an extrovert does not convey nearly as much information.

Moreover, role schemas are more useful than traits for recall. To see the advantage of role in memory, think of all the people in a particular seminar that you are taking. How easy is that? Now think of all the self-centered people you know. How easy is that? Chances are that social groupings lead to the generation of more names more quickly than do traits. People tend to think of others within a role context first, and only then according to personality traits.

Physical Cues

Our first impressions often draw on other people's appearance and behavior to infer qualities about them (Livingston, 2001). Such factors can lead us to form remarkably detailed impressions. The observation that a person is wearing conservative clothes, for example, may lead to the imputation of a variety of other characteristics, such as being conservative politically. We also use behavior to draw inferences about people. We observe a classmate helping an elderly person across the street and infer that she is kind. We even infer personality traits from a person's face (Fiedler & Schenck, 2001), imputing trait qualities to people on the basis of their physical features. For example, we expect baby-faced individuals to be warm, affectionate, honest, and weak (Andreoletti, Zebrowitz, & Lackman, 2001); and facially attractive individuals to be intelligent (Zebrowitz, Hall, Murphy, & Rhodes, 2002).

Salience

Figure-Ground Principle

Attention is drawn to stimuli that stand out against a background.

Salience

Attention is drawn to bright, noisy, colorful, unusual, and novel stimuli.

People direct their attention to those aspects of the perceptual field that stand out (the figure) rather than to the background or setting (the ground; Nelson & Klutas, 2000). This is termed the **figure-ground principle**. In the case of impression formation, the main implication is that salient cues will be used most heavily. If a student appears in a wheelchair the first day of class, everyone else in the room is likely to form an impression that is most heavily influenced by the fact of the person's physical disability. Clothing, hair style, and perhaps even age, race, and sex will all be secondary.

What determines the **salience** of one cue as opposed to another? A number of clearly specifiable objective conditions make cues stand out. Brightness, noisiness, motion, and novelty are the most powerful conditions, according to Gestalt principles of object perception (McArthur & Post, 1977). A man in a bright red sweater stands out in a crowded classroom, and the sweater is his most salient feature. The student who stands up shouting in the middle of a lecture and leaves the room draws our attention because she is noisy and moving when almost everything else in the classroom is quiet and stationary. Anything that makes a

Which person in this group is most salient? Does the white girl stand out? Salient people attract attention, we remember more about them, and we often interpret their behavior in stereotyped terms.

cue objectively unusual in its context makes it subjectively more salient and more likely to be noticed.

Salience has a number of consequences for person perception. First, salient behaviors draw more attention than do subtler, less obvious ones (Taylor & Fiske, 1978). Second, salience influences perceptions of causality in that more salient people are seen as having more influence over their social context (Taylor & Fiske, 1975). The student who sits in the front row of the classroom and asks an occasional question is more likely to be perceived as dominating the discussion than the student who sits in the back and contributes just as much.

Because salient stimuli draw the most attention, they also produce extreme evaluative judgments. These effects of salience have been described as "top of the head" by Taylor and Fiske (1978) because they seem to occur at the relatively superficial level of simply directing our attention. As might be expected, therefore, they seem to be strongest when the stimuli are sufficiently interesting and exciting to attract the perceiver's attention. The effects of salience occur even in important situations when people are motivated to make accurate impressions (Borgida & Howard-Pitney, 1983).

From Behaviors to Traits

From observable information, such as appearance, behavior, and even gestures, we quickly form personality trait inferences about what the person is like (Gawronski, 2003). Referring to traits is a more economical and general way of describing a person than is referring to behaviors. If someone asked you what your roommate is like and you had to recount each behavior you could remember, it would take you a long time, and the person to whom you were describing your roommate might not become much better informed by the process. Instead, you would use traits to summarize aspects of your roommate ("He is a good-natured, sloppy night person with a penchant for loud rock music."). This process appears to occur spontaneously, even automatically, as behavior is perceived (Uleman, Hon, Roman, & Moskowitz, 1996). These traits, in turn, can act as bases for predicting future behavior (Newman, 1996).

The fact that we move from behaviors to traits so quickly is compounded by the fact that traits imply each other. On observing a person patting a dog in a friendly manner, we may infer that she is kind, and from our inference of kindness, we may infer that she is friendly, warm, and helpful (Sedikides & Anderson, 1994). The implications that traits have for other traits is called **implicit personality theory**. From a very simple behavior, then, we can infer almost a whole personality.

Implicit Personality Theory

Beliefs about which personality traits go with other traits.

Table 2-1

Effect of "Warm" and "Cold" Descriptions on Ratings of Other Qualities

	Instructions[a]	
Quality	**Warm**	**Cold**
Self-centered	6.3	9.6
Unsociable	5.6	10.4
Unpopular	4.0	7.4
Formal	6.3	9.6
Irritable	9.4	12.0
Humorless	8.3	11.7
Ruthless	8.6	11.0

[a]The higher the rating, the more the person was perceived as having the quality.

Source: Adapted from H. H. Kelley (1950). *Journal of Personality, 18,* p. 434. Used with permission of Duke University Press.

Central Trait

A trait that is associated with many of a person's other characteristics.

Central Traits. Debate has raged over whether some traits are more central than others. For example, the pair of traits "warm–cold" appears to be associated with a great number of other characteristics, whereas the pair "polite–blunt" is associated with fewer. A trait that is highly associated with many of a person's other characteristics is called a **central trait** (Asch, 1946).

In a classic demonstration of the importance of traits, Kelley (1950) gave students in psychology courses personality trait descriptions of a guest lecturer before he spoke. Half the students received a description containing the word "warm," and the other half were told the speaker was "cold"; in all other respects, the lists were identical. The lecturer then came into the class and led a discussion for about 20 minutes, after which the students were asked to give their impressions of him. The results are shown in Table 2-1. There were great differences between the impressions formed by students who were told the lecturer

People form impressions of each other quickly. They use minimal information, such as sex, appearance, or a brief interaction to draw inferences about each other. What information do you think these students are using to form impressions of each other?

was warm and those formed by students who were told he was cold. In addition, those students who expected the speaker to be warm tended to interact with him more freely and to initiate more conversations with him. The different descriptions affected not only the students' impressions of the lecturer but also their behavior toward him.

The trait inferences that we make about other people fall out along two important dimensions. We tend to evaluate others in terms of both their task-related qualities or intellectual competence and their interpersonal or social qualities (Kim & Rosenberg, 1980).

Categorization

Social categories, such as gender, race, and social class, influence our perceptions as well. Perceivers do not respond to salient stimuli in isolation; they immediately and spontaneously perceive stimuli as part of some group or category. For example, we do not see that unshaven, dirty, disheveled man in the park with worn-out shoes and a couple of old shopping bags as just another human being; we immediately categorize him as a derelict.

What are the consequences of **categorization**? Determining that an individual is a member of a particular category may lead to social judgments about that person that are consistent with the category-based stereotype (Baron, Albright, & Malloy, 1995; Corneille & Judd, 1999; Jones, 1990). The observation that someone is an African American may call up a stereotype about African Americans in general (Devine, 1989).

Categorization

Perceiving people as members of groups or categories rather than as distinct individuals.

Categorizing a person also speeds information-processing time. For example, Brewer, Dull, and Lui (1981) presented participants with photos of people in three different categories—"grandmother," "young woman," and "senior citizen"—along with verbal labels clearly identifying their category. Then they presented the participants with additional information about each target person and measured how long the participants took to incorporate the information into their impressions. Information consistent with the prototype of the category ("kindly" for "grandmother") was processed faster than was information inconsistent with it (such as "aggressive" for "grandmother").

Once we regard a person as a member of a social category, the way in which we process information about that person may change (McConnell et al., 1994). When we form impressions about individuals in isolation, we tend to use a piecemeal approach, in which we examine individual pieces of information about the person and form it into an overall impression. However, if we place a person in a category, often our impression of the person is based on that category, and the person's individual characteristics are assimilated into the overall impressions we have of that category (Brewer, 1988; Fiske & Neuberg, 1990).

On the whole, perceivers seem to have a preference for category-based judgments over individuated judgments (Pendry & Macrae, 1994). This preference seems to exist because category-based evaluations are simpler and more efficient: They draw on our already-existing impressions about social groups. We are more likely to save our complex contextualized impressions of others for the people we know well (Welbourne, 2001): We regard the grouchy postal clerk as a grouch, but recognize that our grouchy roommate is only so just before a midterm.

The Continuum Model of Impression Formation

As the previous discussion implies, our impressions of other people can range from stereotypical, category-based impressions to much more individuated impressions based on information about particular behaviors. This distinction has been called **dual processing.** Under conditions when people are motivated to make impressions quickly or when people need to form their impressions rapidly, they will often use their schematic, stereotypic and category-based modes of inference to form their impressions of others. Under such conditions, a bus driver may be little more than a bus driver to us. Usually people attempt to make category-based inferences

Dual Processing

People can process information in a careful, systematic fashion or in a more rapid, efficient fashion.

Are these people acting in isolation or are they working together? We organize our perceptions by categorizing and grouping people, and in so doing we see them as a structured whole.

before they process individual information because it is easy to do and because the cues that suggest categories (such as sex or race) are often highly salient.

Under conditions that motivate us to learn about an individual, our impressions are constructed piecemeal from the available data. Motivated to be accurate, we attempt to understand another's goals. When efforts to use categories to understand another person fail, we also turn to individuated processing. When the bus driver is quoting Shakespeare and singing Puccini, we are motivated to learn a little more about him (Fiske & Neuberg, 1990).

The continuum model of impression formation integrates what we know about how people form their impressions of others. Sometimes we use heuristics to decide what kind of impression we should form of a person. A heuristic is a rule of thumb that reduces complex information to a simple cue. The informal guideline that any man who wears a gold chain is sleazy would be a heuristic. We use this rapid, heuristic-based processing, based on the categories of which a person is a member for a rapid determination of that person's traits (Ruscher, Hammer, & Hammer, 1996). When we need to be accurate, if the person does not fit our categories or if we have other reasons for wanting to know a person more thoroughly, we construct our impressions more carefully, in a systematic, piecemeal fashion (Verplanken, Jetten, & van Knippenberg, 1996).

Context Effects

Contrast

The tendency to perceive a communicator's position as further away from the individual's own position than it actually is.

Assimilation

Perceiving a communicator's position as closer to one's own position than it actually is.

Social judgment is also strongly dependent on the context in which it is made (Bless & Wänke, 2000). There are two major types of contextual effects on social judgments: contrast and assimilation. **Contrast** refers to a biasing effect on judgments away from the environmental context. Thus, for example, photographs of faces are rated as much less attractive when they are preceded by exposure to a very attractive face (Wänke, Bless, & Igou, 2001). **Assimilation** refers to the biasing of a judgment in the same direction as a contextual standard. For example, simultaneously presenting a highly attractive person and a less attractive one tends to produce more favorable ratings for the less attractive face than if the other attractive face is not present for comparison (Geiselman, Haight, & Kimata, 1984).

What determines whether contrast or assimilation effects occur? Assimilation of impressions to the context is more likely to occur when people are processing information about another person at a categorical or stereotypic level; it may be less likely to occur when the behavioral information about a target person is processed more thoroughly and systematically (Thompson, Roman, Moskowitz,

Chaiken, & Bargh, 1994), as when people are motivated to be accurate (Stapel, Koomen, & Zeelenberg, 1998).

Social context is itself informative with respect to impressions. Specifically, when people receive information about another person's traits and behaviors, they often focus on the pragmatic implications of the information; that is, they focus on why the information was conveyed (Wyer, Budesheim, Lambert, & Swan, 1994). For example, if your roommate tells you something negative about a mutual friend, it may somewhat modify your impression of that friend, but it will also cause you to question why your roommate made the remark. Thus, information about another does not always have the same impact. It depends on the context in which it is delivered and the purpose that is discerned for its delivery (Wyer et al., 1994).

For many behaviors, the importance of context information may not be appreciated. Context may be subtle, and so when the perceiver attempts to infer the characteristics of a target individual, he or she may not observe the role that the context or situation plays in the behavior. Inferring the role of context in producing behavior appears to be a secondary process that occurs after people have inferred the dispositions of another person (e.g., Trope & Liberman, 1993).

INTEGRATING IMPRESSIONS

How do we combine all of these separate inferences about a person into an overall impression?

Evaluation

The most important and powerful aspect of impressions is **evaluation**. Do we like or dislike a person? Put more formally, the evaluative dimension is the most important of a small number of basic dimensions that organize our unified impressions of other people (Osgood, Suci, & Tannenbaum, 1957).

Evaluation

The "goodness" or "badness" of another person, object, or concept.

Negativity Effect. During impression formation, we tend to pay special attention to negative or potentially threatening information (Ohman, Lundqrist, & Esteves, 2001). And when we come to form an overall impression of the person, that negative information is weighed more heavily (Coovert & Reeder, 1990; Taylor, 1991; Yzerbyt & Leyens, 1991). That is, a negative trait affects an impression more than a positive trait, everything else being equal (Vonk, 1993). This has been called the **negativity effect**. The main explanation for this fact is that negative traits are more unusual and therefore more distinctive. People may simply pay more attention to those negative qualities and give them more weight.

Negativity Effect

Impressions are influenced more by negative traits than by positive traits.

Positivity Bias. A general evaluative bias in person perception is to evaluate people positively, a phenomenon termed the **positivity bias** (Sears, 1983a). For example, in one study, students rated 97 percent of their professors in college favorably (i.e., above "average" on a rating scale), despite all the mixed experiences students have in their college classes (Sears, 1983a).

Positivity Bias

People perceive people positively more often than negatively.

How do we reconcile the positivity bias with the negativity bias? In fact, they work together. The reason we feel positively about most people is that most behavior is positive. People act in a generally good way toward each other, and situational norms dictate that people will behave appropriately in social situations. Moreover, when we have positive expectations about others, we tend to test those expectations and remember positive information better. Negative information, which initially attracts attention, often leads us to ignore or reject other people. And consequently we may limit both our contact with them and whatever additional information we might otherwise learn about them (Ybarra, Schaberg, & Keiper, 1999). People who are naturally optimistic seem to have a stronger attentional bias for positive stimuli relative to negative stimuli and thereby may exhibit the positivity bias more (Segerstrom, 2001).

Emotional Information. Perceivers also notice emotionally charged information and make great use of it in their judgments about others. That is, we infer what people are like from the emotions they express. In fact, emotional information is one of the most difficult sources of information to ignore when perceiving others (Edwards & Bryan, 1997).

Which particular emotion is being communicated by a target also influences processing. In one study, participants saw a videotape of a person who was in a neutral, happy, or angry mood. The happy mood elicited rapid, heuristic, stereotypic processing of the person's characteristics, whereas a neutral mood elicited more systematic processing of the information that was conveyed by the target. Angry displays led to a processing style between these extremes (Ottati, Terkildsen, & Hubbard, 1997). However, when perceivers are highly accountable for their inferences, the judgment process is more systematic, regardless of the emotional cues in the situation (Lerner, Goldberg, & Tetlock, 1998; Ottati et al., 1997).

The Averaging Principle

Averaging Principle

Idea that evaluative information about a person is averaged together to form an overall impression.

Most of our impressions are not purely positive or purely negative but a mixture of impressions that vary in valence and content. How do we combine separate pieces of information about a person to form a simple overall impression? Our impressions of others seem to follow a weighted **averaging principle** (Anderson, 1968). According to this model, people form an overall impression by averaging all traits but give more weight to those they believe are most important. For example, an administrator interviewing scientists as candidates for a laboratory job would probably weight "intelligence" more heavily than "attractiveness," but someone hiring an actor for a television commercial might reverse that priority. In summary, the best way to account for integrating our impressions of others is the weighted averaging principle (see Table 2–2).

Imputing Meaning

Perceivers try to arrive at a meaningful impression of a person, rather than to absorb each new piece of information separately. Their understanding of any new piece of information depends in part on the other information they have about the person. The meaning of "intelligent" in the context of knowing that a person is a "warm, caring therapist" will probably be quite positive. But the meaning of "intelligent" when the person is otherwise a "cold, ruthless foreign spy" will probably be more negative; it makes the person seem even more dangerous. Our perceptions of others' personal qualities may undergo a **shift of meaning** when they are placed in a new context (Asch, 1946; Zanna & Hamilton, 1977).

Shift of Meaning

The meaning of a trait changes when placed in a different context.

Imputing Consistency

People tend to form evaluatively consistent characterizations of others, even when they have only a few pieces of information. Because evaluation is the most

Table 2–2

Susan Evaluates Her Blind Date, John

Individual Traits	Susan's Evaluation
Witty	+10
Intelligent	+10
Courteous	+4
Very short	−5
Poorly dressed	−9
Overall impression	+10/5 = +2.00

important dimension in person perception, it is not surprising that we tend to categorize people as good or bad, not as both. We may then go on to perceive other traits as consistent with this basic evaluation. This tendency toward evaluative consistency is called the **halo effect**. If a person is likable, we assume that she is also attractive, intelligent, and generous. If she is bad, she is assumed to be sneaky, ugly, and inept.

Halo Effect

A liked person is assumed to have many other good qualities.

Resolving Inconsistencies. Sometimes the information we have about other people is internally inconsistent. For example, you may have an impression of your roommate as a kind and generous person—and then you may be told by a mutual acquaintance that your roommate is conceited and a snob. How is incongruent information incorporated into overall impressions?

Information that is incongruent with our impressions often gets remembered. You are not likely to soon forget your acquaintance's negative impression of your roommate. Why is this the case? Because in order to integrate this information into your overall impression, you had to do a lot of work. You had to think about why the incongruent information occurred, whether the acquaintance's report is trustworthy, and why your roommate might have behaved in this way on this particular occasion. As a result of the complicated process people go through to understand inconsistent information, it comes to play a more important role in their overall impression than does information consistent with the impression they hold (Hastie & Kumar, 1979; Trafimow & Finlay, 2001). Indeed, when we are kept from being able to do the cognitive work required to make inconsistent information more comprehensible, as by being kept too cognitively busy with other tasks, the bias for remembering inconsistent information is eliminated (Macrae, Bodenhausen, Schloerscheidt, & Milne, 1999).

Of course, it isn't always possible to make an impression of a person entirely evaluatively consistent. A man may be very nice to his friends but treat his dog quite badly. A woman may be very outgoing with her friends but become quiet when she is with strangers. When incongruent information is confined to a particular situation, the situational specificity helps people recall them (Trafimow, 1998). In addition, when traits are at least mildly congruent or evaluatively consistent with each other, they are easy to integrate (Hampson, 1998). When they are incongruent and difficult to reconcile with each other, people sometimes leave them unintegrated and recognize the incongruency (Casselden & Hampson, 1990).

Schemas

As already noted, much of the time we process information about others using the stereotypes or preconceptions we hold about the categories that define people (such as gender and occupation). Another word for these preconceptions or stereotypes is "schemas." A schema is an organized, structured set of cognitions, including some knowledge about the category, some relationships among the various cognitions about it, and some specific examples (Taylor & Crocker, 1981). Schemas help us process complex bodies of information by simplifying and organizing them. They can help us to remember and organize details, speed up processing time, fill in gaps in our knowledge, and interpret and evaluate new information. Several types of schemas figure importantly in person perception in forming impressions of others.

Person schemas are structures about people. They can focus on one particular person, for example, Abraham Lincoln. The schema might include such elements as his being deliberate, honest, serious about his duties, and concerned for oppressed people. Person schemas can also focus on particular types of people. For example, our schema of an "extrovert" might include such elements as "spirited," "outgoing," "enthusiastic," and "self-assured." The reasons we develop schemas for individuals is to help us gather information about those individuals and to guide our subsequent social interactions with them (Mayer, Rapp, & Williams, 1993). Figure 2–1 presents a diagrammable representation of a schema for a "cultured person."

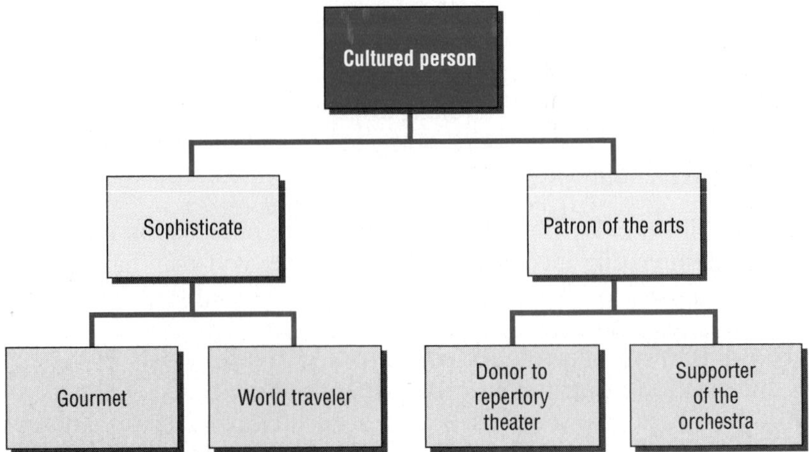

Figure 2–1 **A Schema for a "Cultured Person."**

Source: Adapted from Cantor and Mischel (1979).

People also have role schemas. These represent the organized, abstract concepts we have of people in a particular role, such as cowboy, professor, receptionist, or devoted lover. Sometimes these schemas are unrealistic. If our schema for "devoted lover" includes elements such as always understanding, always supportive, never angry, never childish, and always concerned first with the other person's happiness, we could be in trouble. Not many people will live up to that schema.

Stereotype

Beliefs about typical characteristics of members of a group or social category.

Other schemas focus on groups. The most familiar is the group **stereotype**, which attributes specific traits to a particular group of people. (Stereotypes are discussed in some detail in Chapter 6.) Other group schemas include schemas for group leader and group follower. Perceivers form inferences about others based on the particular group role they hold. For example, occupying the leadership role, even without having any attendant authority, or responsibility, may trigger a role schema that leads to the assumption of greater responsibility for group performance (Kerr & Stanfel, 1993).

Prototype

A schema for a particular type of person or situation.

Prototypes. In drawing inferences about another person, we often draw on the **prototype** of the schema. The prototype is an abstract ideal of the schema. In our category for football player, for example, we probably have an abstract idea of what the person's body type is, what he does in his free time, and perhaps even what fraternity he belongs to. When you categorize a new person as a football player, you may compare his attributes with those of the prototype for the schema.

Exemplars. When we learn the abstract attributes of categories, we also learn particular instances or examples of the category that we have actually encountered. In many cases, then, we categorize objects and people by seeing if they resemble the exemplars that we store in that category. For example, if you are evaluating a new partner as a possible long-term boyfriend or girlfriend usually you compare the person not only with your prototype for the ideal boyfriend or girlfriend but also with "old flames," particular past boyfriends or girlfriends who made your heart beat faster for a time (Fiske et al., 1987).

As can be seen, we rely on a complex mix of ways for recognizing and classifying people and their behavior. When we have very little information, we are most likely to fall back on prototypes for particular categories (e.g., what the typical police officer is like). When we have a little more information, we are likely to use both exemplars and prototypes to help us understand a person (e.g., what roommates are like in general and what your roommate last year was like) (Judd & Park, 1988; Linville, Fisher, & Salovey, 1989). For categories about which we have a great deal of information, we are likely to use our more well-developed and formal schemas (Sherman & Klein, 1994), although examples of specific behaviors may be drawn on as well (Budesheim & Bonnelle, 1998).

MOTIVATED PERSON PERCEPTION

We have discussed person perception as if it were a relatively rational process of taking in information about others and organizing it according to particular principles. Our goals and feelings about other people also influence the information that we gather about them.

Goals

One factor that influences how we gather information about others is the goals we have for interacting with them. Psychologists have studied goals and their impact on person perception by manipulating them experimentally, such as by telling participants either to form a coherent impression of a person (impression formation goal) or to remember the separate bits of information they might be exposed to (remembering goal). Generally speaking, under impression goal conditions, people form more organized impressions of others than when their goal is simply to remember the information (Matheson, Holmes, & Kristiansen, 1991).

Anticipating future interactions with somebody creates very different social goals from simply trying to learn about that person, and research shows that people remember more and organize the information differently when they expect to interact with someone in the future. For example, Devine, Sedikides, and Fuhrman (1989) asked participants to learn information about five people under various goal conditions. They either anticipated interacting with the target, were told to form an impression of the target, were told to compare themselves with the target, were asked to compare the target with a friend, or were simply asked to recall the target's attributes. As Table 2–3 shows, anticipating interactions with the target in the future produced the greatest recall of the target's behavior. Paradoxically, compared to all the other goal conditions, simply being instructed to remember the target's attributes produced the lowest recall.

The dual-processing distinction between rapid, heuristically based information processing and more systematic, piecemeal use of information is also relevant to motivated person perception. We note that social perceivers often use rapid, heuristically based processing when their inferences are not particularly important to them, but they are able to switch to the more systematic style of processing when inferences are important. For example, we may need to decide if a certain student should be our lab partner, if we should hire a friend to tutor us in chemistry, or if we should go out with the persistent person in math class. Circumstances like these tend to foster efforts to form accurate impressions.

The need to be accurate usually produces more extensive and less biased information gathering about a person (Boudreau, Baron, & Oliver, 1992). In one study (Neuberg, 1989), students were asked to interview a job candidate. Half were led to expect that the candidate would be unpleasant, and the other half were given no expectation about the interviewee. Cross-cutting this expectation, half the students were encouraged to form accurate impressions about the target; the others were not. Students who did not have a goal of accuracy formed impressions of the person that were relatively negative and thus consistent with

Table 2–3

The Impact of Goals on Recalling a Person's Attributes: Expecting to Interact Led to Greater Recall Than in Any Other Goal Condition

Recall	Anticipated Interaction	Form an Impression	Compare to Self	Compare to Friend	Remember
Target	4.38	4.00	3.31	3.38	3.00
Comparison	1.80	2.33	2.53	2.22	2.23

Source: Based on Devine, Sedikides, and Fuhrman (1989, p. 686).

the expectation they had been given. However, participants who had been encouraged to be accurate formed more positive impressions, actively undermining the expectation they had been given, through their more extensive and less biased efforts to gather information about the target. Thus, the goal to be accurate generally leads to more thorough and systematic processing of information about people than is true under conditions when accuracy is not a goal (Chen, Shechter, & Chaiken, 1996).

The type of impression one forms of another person also depends on the kind of interactions one anticipates having with that individual. Outcome dependency—that is, the situation in which achievement of an individual's own goals depends heavily on the behavior of another person—typically leads the individual to form a careful impression of the other (Vonk, 1999). Participants whose goals do not depend on the behavior of another person are more likely to form their impressions quickly and casually.

Another powerful goal is communication. What we say to others affects what we believe. Sedikides (1990) asked participants to form impressions of a target but then to communicate positive, negative, or neutral information about the target to a third individual. Communication goals completely determined the information that was provided to the third individual, so that they overrode the participant's own impressions. In fact, participants actually reformulated their own impressions in the direction of the positive, negative, or neutral impression they had been instructed to convey (Skowronski, Carlston, May, & Crawford, 1998).

When people communicate information about a target individual to a listener, they not only modify their own perceptions about the target but also systematically affect the impressions formed by the listener (Malle, Knobe, O'Laughlin, Pearce, & Nelson, 2000). Specifically, when we transmit information about another person, we typically omit information about mitigating circumstances that may have influenced the behavior and instead present the behavior as if it represented characteristics of the target individual. Our goal instead is to construct a simple, easily communicated story (Lassiter, Geers, & Apple, 2002). The result is that listeners may make more extreme positive or negative judgments of target individuals than the tellers do themselves (Baron, David, Brunsman, & Inman, 1997).

The influence of social goals on the kinds of impressions that people form of others is substantial. Moreover, many of these effects appear to occur without intention or awareness (Chartrand & Bargh, 1996). People who have a particular social goal when they interact with another person make inferences that are consistent with their goals about the other person, even when they do not intend to do so or are completely unaware that they are doing so (Uleman & Moskowitz, 1994).

The Perceiver's Cognitive and Emotional State

We have concentrated primarily on what information the perceiver extracts from a person to form an impression, but the perceiver also contributes to the person perception process in a variety of ways. Often when we form impressions of others, there is little else on our mind, and so we can focus our attention closely on the other person's behavior and infer what he or she is like. Many times, though, we are simultaneously pursuing other tasks—trying to present ourselves well, preparing for some future activity, thinking about something that happened the day before—and so our attention is not fully focused on the person about whom we are forming an impression.

When we are busy—namely, otherwise preoccupied—we are more likely to see other people's personal qualities as stable and enduring dispositions. As we listen to a professor give a boring lecture, we may assume that he is always dull and humorless, instead of realizing that his role may make him so, at least for the short term. This bias occurs because people often fail to consider external influences on another's behavior (Osbourne & Gilbert, 1992; see also Weary, Reich, & Tobin, 2001).

We all have different things that we notice in other people. One person may be especially focused on whether someone is attractive, whereas another person may focus on whether that person is smart. Indeed one of the reasons that the same person can provoke so many different impressions in others is that those others are each interested in or engaged by particular qualities of the person.

One factor that influences how we react to others is whether we see ourselves as similar to them. For the most part, seeing another person as potentially similar is a source of attraction, but when the other person shares a characteristic that we fear in ourselves, we may instead psychologically distance ourselves from the person or avoid her or him altogether (Schimel, Pyszczynski, Greenberg, O'Mahen, & Arndt, 2000).

Sometimes the qualities we use to evaluate others are salient in our minds for reasons having nothing to do with the person being evaluated. For example, if Ellen has just left her boyfriend, Todd, because he is controlling, she may evaluate all new dates in terms of how controlling they seem to be; this tendency to use an activated trait for evaluating others is remarkably resistant to correction (Staple, Koomen, & Zeelenberg, 1998). Compared to Todd, everyone else may come out looking less controlling (Moskowitz & Skurnik, 1999).

Do animals have personalities? Apparently, they do. The agreement among perceivers about the personal qualities of dogs is about as high as their agreement on judgments of humans (Gosling, Kwan, & John, 2003).

Not everyone moves from the observation of behavior to trait inferences immediately (Tormala & Petty, 2001). Some of us are entity theorists, who believe that traits are fixed; we make global trait judgments quickly and see them as strong determinants of behavior. Others of us are *incremental theorists,* who believe that traits are more malleable qualities. Entity theorists, not unexpectedly, make stronger inferences about the behavior of a target and seek more information about his or her character to support their theory about the person's behavior (Gervery, Chiu, Hong, & Dweck, 1999). Entity theorists are more inclined to see others in terms of their dispositions or traits. They pay particular attention to information consistent with their traits (Plaks, Stroessner, Dweck, & Sherman, 2001), and they notice negative behavior. They are also more likely to make a racial identification of racially ambiguous faces with the result that they may remember a person as a member of a particular racial group (Eberhardt, Dasgupta, & Banaszynski, 2003). In contrast, those with a more incremental orientation are more likely to notice and remember positive behavior (Ybarra & Stephan, 1999) and behavior that is inconsistent with trait impressions (Plaks et al., 2001). Entity theorists form their impressions of others quite quickly, at the time they interact with them, whereas incremental theorists are more likely to form their theories based on their memories of those individuals (Tong & Chiu, 2002).

When we use our own internal state as a basis for judging other people, we may bias our impressions. For example, when people are emotional, they are more likely to attend to emotional information and use that in their impressions (e.g., Halberstadt & Niedenthal, 1997). When we are aroused, we tend to perceive other people in a more extreme manner than we do when we are not aroused (Stangor, 1990). If you have just finished playing a brisk tennis game and you meet someone who strikes you as sleazy, your impression of the person as sleazy is likely to be more extreme than it would be if you have just come from reading a book.

The perceiver's impressions are also influenced by his or her own specific emotional state. Being in a bad mood might lead us to form a less positive impression of a person (e.g., Edwards, Weary, VonHippel, & Jacobson, 2000; Gasper & Clore, 2000; Strack & Neumann, 2000), and when we are in a good mood, we tend to see another person more positively. These biasing effects of mood are especially strong when the other person is behaving neutrally (Stangor, 1990; see also Isen, 1999, for a review).

Mood may influence not only the content of impressions we form of others but also the process we use in forming them. Specifically, a negative mood makes

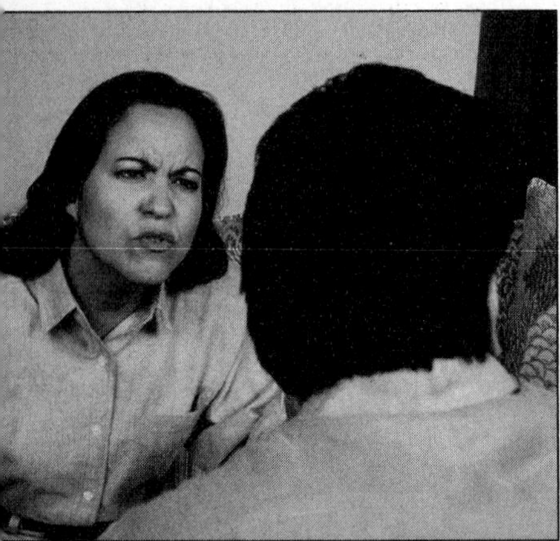

Causal attributions help us predict and control the environment. They determine our feelings and reactions to others, and help influence our future behavior. If you encountered these two people, you would want to know what was wrong.

people more likely to use piecemeal processing than categorical processing in impression formation, whereas people in a more positive mood use category information (Edwards & Weary, 1993) and are susceptible to making strong trait inferences about the causes of others' behavior (Forgas, 1998).

In summary, the process of putting together information about people often depends on motivational factors, including our particular goals and the affective state that we are in, or on a motivation to hold a particular belief about another person.

ATTRIBUTING THE CAUSES OF BEHAVIOR

Attribution Theory

The principles that determine how causal attributions are made and what effects they have.

One of the most important inferences we make about other people is why they behave as they do. What causes one individual to be shy at a party and another to be outgoing? What prompts the romantic breakup of two people who seemed so close? **Attribution theory** is the area of psychology concerned with when and how people ask "why" questions. Theorizing about causal attributions—that is, how and why people infer what causes what—began with Fritz Heider (1958). He argued that all human beings have two strong motives: the need to form a coherent understanding of the world and the need to control the environment. In order to achieve understanding and control, we need to be able to predict how people are going to behave. Otherwise, the world is random, surprising, and incoherent.

To keep our world predictable and controllable, we do not need to ask "why" questions all the time. Many of our causal attributions are virtually automatic, implicit in the impressions we form of other people and situations. However, sometimes a particular person or a surprising set of circumstances catches us up and makes us pay special attention to what is going on, in order to try to understand why events are unfolding as they are or why they occurred as they did (Olson & Janes, 2002). In particular, we are especially likely to make causal attributions when something unexpected or unpleasant happens, because unexpected or negative events create a need for greater predictability (Kanazawa, 1992; Wong & Weiner, 1981). Unexpected and negative events especially, then, elicit a search for causal attributions, because by making them, we restore a sense of predictability and control over the environment.

Jones and Davis's Correspondent Inference Theory

Dispositional Attribution

Perceiving a person's action as stemming from stable characteristics, such as personality.

Situational Attribution

Perceiving the cause of a person's action as due to situational forces.

Correspondent Inference Theory

Theory of attribution that details how people infer that a person's action is due to his or her enduring personal characteristics.

One of the most important tasks of causal attribution is to understand why people do what they do. People engage in a variety of actions, but only some of those reveal their personal qualities (Hilton, Smith, & Kim, 1995). For example, if your new roommate smiles and greets your mother graciously, this behavior is unlikely to be very revealing about her. Most college students know that this is the courteous way to greet someone's parents. What information about your roommate will tell you what she is really like? That is, in what circumstances do we infer that another's actions reflect real dispositions, such as traits, attitudes, and other internal states, and when do we assume that others are simply responding to the external situation? The terms we use to describe these very different kinds of attributions are **dispositional**, or internal, **attributions** to the person and **situational**, or external, **attributions** to the environment.

Jones and Davis (1965) developed **correspondent inference theory**, which details how we infer whether a behavior of a person is due to that person's personal characteristics or to situational influences. Essentially, we use the context in which a person's behavior occurs to infer whether that behavior is a result of the influence of the situation or of an underlying disposition, such as a trait. Actions perceived to be reflective of underlying dispositions lead to correspondent inferences; that is, they are judged to be meaningful and useful for illuminating a person's character.

A first important factor a social perceiver uses to infer the causes of another person's behavior is the social desirability of that behavior. Socially undesirable behavior leads people to infer an underlying disposition, whereas socially desirable behavior is not clearly revealing of personal characteristics. For example, if Kate is applying for a job at a summer camp and knows that having people skills is an important requirement, and if she behaves in an extroverted manner during the interview, it is difficult to know whether she is really socially skilled or simply appearing so to create a positive impression during the job interview. However, if Kate behaves in an introverted, rather shy and retiring manner, the interviewer could infer with some confidence that Kate is introverted. Otherwise, why would she behave in that way when the situation calls for different behavior?

Another important basis for inferring dispositions is knowing whether an individual's behavior is freely chosen or situationally constrained. Behavior that is freely chosen is more informative about a person's underlying characteristics than is behavior that is not chosen. For example, if you are a reporter for the student newspaper and are asked to write a story favoring the right to bear arms, readers would be unwise to infer that you hold a negative attitude toward gun control. However, if you were told you could write on either side of the issue and chose to write in favor of guns in the home, your readers could more confidently infer that your article reflected your true attitude (see Jones & Harris, 1967).

People consider the intended effects or consequences of another's behavior when inferring the causes of behavior. When a person's actions produce many outcomes, it is hard to know the person's actual motives, but when the behavior produces a distinctive consequence, a motive may more confidently be inferred. For example, if you give up a desirable high-paying summer job in Boston in favor of a lower paying, less attractive job in Oregon, your interest in being in Oregon over the summer would be evident to anyone observing your behavior. The distinctive features of people's choices are often used as a basis for inferring their underlying qualities through what is termed the "analysis of noncommon effects." For example, if you are choosing between two graduate school programs that are equally reputable, both at good universities that have offered you the same stipend, and you choose the program that has an internship, one might infer that the training received during an internship is important to you.

Another condition that can help a social perceiver determine whether an action is produced by a person's dispositional qualities is knowing whether the behavior is part of a social role. Behavior that is constrained by a role is not necessarily informative about a person's underlying beliefs or behaviors. If a firefighter helps to put out a fire, we do not infer that he is helpful; he is simply doing his job. But if a stranger from the street helps put out a fire, we more confidently infer his helpfulness.

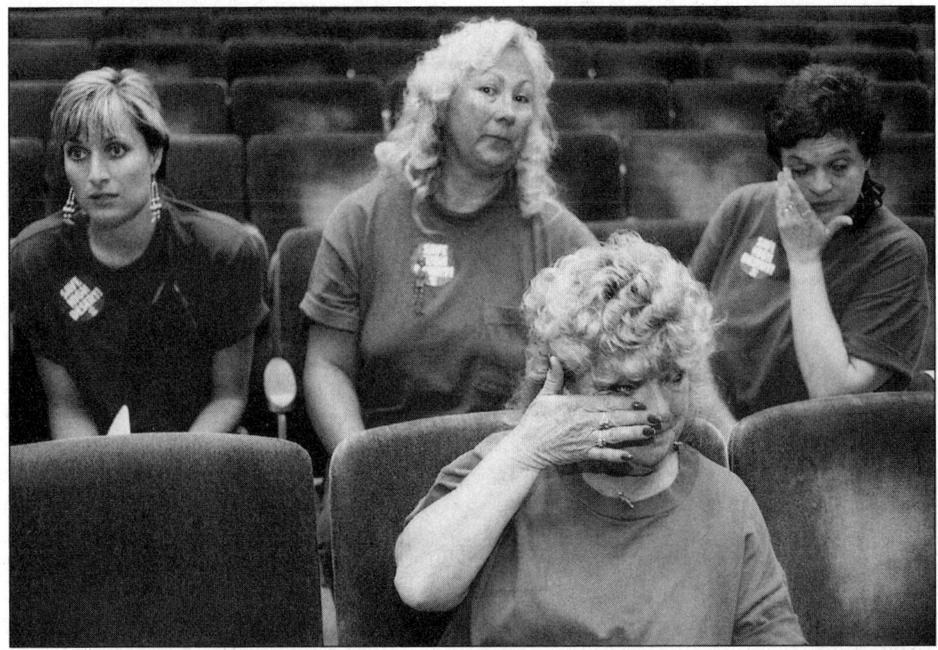

Unexpected or negative events that leave people uncertain are most likely to lead them to ask why the event occurred. Workers who are laid off may be in great need of an adequate casual explanation.

Finally, we interpret others' behavior on the basis of our preexisting expectations about their true dispositions (Jones & McGillis, 1976). For example, if you know that your roommate is politically liberal but you observe her nodding agreeably at her parents' conservative statements over dinner, you may nonetheless continue to believe that she is a strong supporter of liberal politics and make an external attribution for her nodding, namely, that she is trying to avoid an argument with her parents.

In summary, then, often we are in the position of wanting to know why a person committed a particular action. The goal of our attributional search is often to make a dispositional attribution, that is, to try to find a stable internal quality of the person that explains the action. To arrive at a dispositional attribution, we use cues about the person in the situation as well as our past knowledge about the person, and taken together, this knowledge helps us infer others' dispositional qualities through the observation of their behavior.

Kelley's Covariation Theory

Covariation

Judgments of how strongly two things are related.

Sometimes, during the search for causal attributions, we have the opportunity to gather additional evidence. Is the professor really as stern and humorless as she seems? If so, it will be a long semester. Harold Kelley's (1967) **covariation** model refers to the fact that people try to see if a particular effect and a particular cause go together across different situations. In order for something to be the cause of the behavior, it must be present when the behavior occurs and absent when it does not. Kelley suggests that we use three types of information to validate our tentative causal attributions: consistency, distinctiveness, and consensus.

Suppose your friend Mary tells you about a comedian she saw the night before. She says that he was the funniest comic she'd heard in years and that you should definitely go to see him. Before doing so, you may want to know if the comedian really is funny or if there is something unusual about Mary or about the situation that night, such as the mood she was in, the people she was with, or the drinks.

Discounting Principle

Tendency to de-emphasize the role of one particular cause to the extent that other plausible causes exist.

Kelley suggests that we ask at least three questions:

1. Is the behavior distinctive? That is, does Mary laugh at any comedian, or does she laugh really hard at this one?
2. Is there consensus? Do other people feel the same way? Did other people like this comedian as well?
3. Is the behavior consistent? Did Mary react this way only on this particular evening, or does she find him funny in other situations as well?

Consensus is one of the sources of information people use to make causal attributions. If everyone laughs at a comedian, we infer that he is funny, but if only a few people laugh, we infer that he is not funny.

For us to infer confidently that the comedian caused Mary's enthusiastic recommendation, three tests have to be passed: high distinctiveness, high consensus, and high consistency. Her reaction has to be distinctive to this comedian and not to others; other people have to like him, too; and she has to react similarly to him in other situations. To make an internal attribution—that is, for her laughter to be attributed to her, rather than to the comedian—we should see low distinctiveness, low consensus, and high consistency: Mary laughs at all comedians, no one else laughs at this comedian, and she laughs in a lot of situations. These predictions are illustrated in Table 2–4. The basic predictions of Kelley's theory and the use of consistency, consensus, and distinctiveness to draw causal attributions have been widely confirmed by research. However, it appears that we are at our best when we are assessing covariation along just one factor rather than several at a time (Fiedler, Walther, & Nickel, 1999). What this finding suggests is that we tend to simplify the attribution process.

Sometimes there are several possible causal explanations for behavior, and we need guidelines to determine which attribution is correct. Kelley (1972) discussed a second major principle used for making causal attributions, termed the **discounting principle**. We are less likely to attribute an effect to any particular cause if more than one potential cause is likely. If an insurance salesperson is nice to us and offers us coffee, we may not want to conclude that he or she is intrinsically

Table 2–4

Why Did Mary Laugh at the Comedian?

	Available Information			
Condition	**Distinctiveness**	**Consensus**	**Consistency**	**Most Common Attribution**
1	High—she didn't laugh at anyone else	High—everyone else laughed too	High—she always laughs at him	Stimulus object: The comedian (61%)
2	Low—she always laughs at comedians	Low—hardly anyone else laughed	High—she always laughs at him	Person: Mary (86%)
3	High—she didn't laugh at anyone else	Low—hardly anyone else laughed	Low—she has almost never laughed at him	Context: (72%)

Source: Adapted from McArthur (1972).

friendly. We may, instead, suspect that the salesperson wants our business. If a stranger brings us a glass of water and a cookie after an automobile accident while we are waiting for the police to come, we are likely to infer that she is being kind; she has no other reason for being nice to us. By and large, research findings do seem to follow the patterns described by the covariation and discounting principles (e.g., Morris & Larreck, 1995; Van Overwalle & Rooy, 2001).

Biases in the Attribution Process

We have described the process of making causal attributions as a fairly rational and logical one. We look at a person's behavior and reasonably infer the causes from the systematic knowledge we have of that individual and the circumstances in which the behavior occurred. But is the attribution process always this reasonable? Considerable research suggests that there are several prominent biases in the ways we make causal attributions.

Fundamental Attribution Error. As research on correspondent inference and the covariation principle suggests, generally speaking, we are likely to attribute others' behaviors to their general dispositions—that is, to their personality traits or attitudes—rather than to the situation they are in. This tendency is called the **fundamental attribution error** (Ross, 1977). When we ask the clerk in the college administration building for help and he seems impersonal and brusque, we assume that he is a cold, unfriendly person and ignore the fact that his whole day must be taken up with anonymous complaining students (Ross, 2001; Sabini, Siepmann, & Stein, 2001). Predictions of distant future behavior reflect the fundamental attribution error even more than do predictions about current behaviors (Nussbaum, Trope, & Liberman, 2003).

Fundamental Attribution Error

People overestimate how much a person's actions are due to dispositions, such as personality.

As an example of the fundamental attribution error, consider a study by Jones and Harris (1967) that looked at attributions about the attitudes of people who had written essays on a controversial topic, in this case, an essay about Cuba under the rule of Fidel Castro. Students were given copies of essays and were told that the essay writers had freely chosen to take either a pro-Castro position or an anti-Castro position; or they were told that the essay writers had been assigned the position and had no choice about which perspective to adopt in the essay. Even when the writers had been assigned the essay position, observers overestimated the role of internal dispositions (the writers' true position on Castro) and underestimated the strength of the external situation (i.e., the lack of choice about what position to take) to explain the position taken in the essay. Data from Jones and Harris's two very similar experiments are shown in Table 2–5.

Table 2–5

Attitude Attributed to Writer

Condition	Pro-Castro	Anti-Castro
Experiment 1		
Choice	59.6[a]	17.4
No choice	44.1	22.9
Experiment 2		
Choice	55.7	22.9
No choice	41.3	23.7

[a]A high score indicates a pro-Castro position attributed to the writer.

Source: Jones and Harris (1967, pp. 6, 10).

Research suggests that attributions of dispositional qualities to others on the basis of their behavior may be made spontaneously and without awareness, perhaps even automatically, when we observe or hear about these others' behavior (Gilbert & Mallone, 1995). Using information about the situational context to qualify dispositional inferences seems to be part of a second, less spontaneous, and more thoughtful process that involves correcting the initial disposition or inference (Gilbert, McNulty, Giuliano, & Bentson, 1992; Yzerbyt, Corneille, Dumont, & Hahn, 2001). Often, we do not get to this second stage of correction, unless the contextual information is very compelling or salient (Trope & Gaunt, 2000).

People also fail to reach the correction phase when they are cognitively "busy," that is, thinking about their future activities, trying to make a good impression, or engaging in other tasks that consume attention (e.g., Gilbert, Pelham, & Krull, 1988). When we are busy, we focus on the most salient or meaningful aspects of the situation and pay less attention to nonsalient contextual factors (Chun, Spiegel, & Kruglanski, 2002). As a result, we are especially likely to make dispositional attributions for others' behaviors. When we are not busy, however, we can take in at least some of the qualifying contextual information that may have produced another person's behavior and use it to correct our extreme dispositional inferences (Weary, Reich, & Tobin, 2001). Most of us are cognitively busy most of the time, however.

Nonetheless, there are reliable circumstances in which we make circumstantial attributions. We are more likely to make situational attributions for the behavior of people we know very well than for those we know less well. We are more likely to make situational inferences for people we expect to have contact with in the future and when situational information is especially salient. As we become more familiar with another person, we are more likely to take more information into account, such as their personal goals or how they see the world, and draw less on general abstract traits to build an impression of the person (Idson, & Mischel, 2001). And when we do not know a person's motive for behaving as he does, we may be more inclined to look to the situation for an explanation (Reeder, Vonk, Ronk, Ham, & Lawrence, 2004; Welbourne 2001).

The tendency to explain behavior in terms of enduring dispositions appears to be a common bias more so in the United States and much of Western Europe than in Asian countries. In Eastern countries, such as India (Miller, 1984), China (Morris & Peng, 1994), and Japan (Miyamoto & Kitayama, 2002), the role of context and situational factors as causes of behavior is more likely to be acknowledged. In these cultures, dispositional inferences may be confined to those circumstances where the context and situational factors suggest that indeed a person's beliefs reflect his underlying qualities (Church et al., 2003; Miyamoto & Kitayama, 2002). As noted earlier, Westerners may require extra time and attention to correct their dispositional inferences for plausible situational or contextual causes; but East Asians, in contrast, correct for the effect of situational information automatically (Knowles, Morris, Chiu, & Hong, 2001; Norenzayan, Choi, & Nisbett, 2002). Generally speaking, the causal theories of East Asians are more holistic and complex than those of Americans, and so the amount of information that East Asians consider before they make an attribution is greater than is true for Americans; this fact, as well, contributes to the more situational and contextual attributions that East Asians make for behavior (Choi, Dalal, Kim-Prieto, & Park, 2003).

The Actor-Observer Effect

One of the more interesting aspects of the fundamental attribution error is that it applies when we explain the behaviors of other people, but not when we explain our own behavior. This phenomenon is called the **actor-observer bias**. It refers to the fact that when we observe other people's behavior, we tend to attribute their behavior to their dispositional qualities, but when we explain our own behavior, we explain it in terms of situational forces (Jones & Nisbett, 1972).

Actor-Observer Bias

Observers overestimate the importance of an actor's dispositions for causing the actor's behavior; actors overestimate the importance of the situation in explaining their own behavior.

In one of the earliest demonstrations of this bias, Nisbett, Caputo, Legant, and Maracek (1973) asked male students to write a paragraph on what they liked most about the women they dated and why they had chosen their major. They were then asked to answer the same questions as if they were their own best friend. Responses were scored for the extent to which the behavior was attributed to the actor's disposition (e.g., "I need someone I can relax with") and the extent to which the behavior was attributed externally, to aspects of the girlfriend (e.g., "She's smart and fun."), or to the major ("Chemistry is a high-paying field."). The participants gave more situational reasons for their own behavior and more dispositional reasons for a friend's behavior.

Why do actors and observers give different explanations for the same events? One reason is that actors and observers have access to different information and may come to different conclusions (see Johnson & Boyd, 1995). Actors know more historical information about their own behavior in different situations than do observers. They know their behavior has varied across situations and may therefore be more likely to attribute it to a particular situation. In other words, they know they have behaved differently in different situations, whereas an observer has only the one situation to go on. Essentially actors pay more attention to events that others cannot observe, whereas observers draw on events that can be directly observed and that consequently seem to be the result of personal intention (Malle & Pearce, 2001).

Another explanation is that the difference may be due to different perspectives. The visual field of the observer is dominated by the actor, and the special salience of the actor may lead the observer to overattribute the actor's behavior to dispositions. The actor, however, is looking not at her own behavior, but at the situation—the place, the other people, and their expectations. The actor's own behavior is not as salient as it is to an observer; instead, the situation is more salient and therefore more causally potent (Taylor & Fiske, 1978).

In certain circumstances, the actor-observer effect is weakened. For example, when we feel empathy for a person whose behavior we are observing, we tend to explain the behavior the way that the other person does, namely, in terms of situational factors (Regan & Totten, 1975). We are more likely to attribute positive outcomes to dispositional factors and negative outcomes to situational factors, regardless of whether they are committed by actors or by observers (Taylor & Koivumaki, 1976). Empathy may be the exception, rather than the rule, however, as the next bias suggests.

False Consensus

People tend to imagine that everyone responds the way they do. We tend to see our own behavior as typical. This tendency to exaggerate how common our own behavior and opinions are is called the **false consensus effect**.

False Consensus Effect

Exaggerating how common one's own opinions or behaviors are.

In an early demonstration of this effect, students were asked if they would walk around their college campus for 30 minutes wearing a large sandwich board with the message "Eat at Joe's." Some students agreed; others refused. Both groups estimated that about two thirds of the other students on the campus would make exactly the same choice that they did. Clearly, both groups could not be right (Ross, Greene, & House, 1977). This false consensus effect has been found in a broad array of situations (Kulig, 2000).

Why does the false consensus effect occur? One possibility is that people seek out the company of others who are similar to them and who behave as they do (Krueger & Zeiger, 1993). Consequently, estimates of the beliefs and behaviors of others may simply reflect the biased sample of people one has available for social inference. Another possibility is that our own opinions are especially salient, and so our beliefs about consensus are increased because our own position is the only one we are thinking of (Marks & Miller, 1987). A third possibility is that in trying to predict how we might behave or think in a certain situation, we resolve ambiguous details in our mind in a way that favors a preferred course of action. We fail to realize that our own choices are a function not only of the objective situation but also of our construal of it (Gilovich, 1990). For example, the person who imagines that others will point and laugh if she appears in a sandwich board will probably refuse to wear one and assume that others, anticipating the same harassment, would do the same. A fourth possibility is that people need to see their own beliefs and behaviors as good, appropriate, and typical, and so they attribute them to others to maintain their own self-esteem. Research suggests that all these explanations may play some role in the false consensus effect (Fabrigar & Krosnick, 1995; Marks & Miller, 1987).

False Uniqueness Effect

Exaggerating how unique one's own positive abilities are.

On certain personal attributes, people show a **false uniqueness effect** (Marks, 1984; Snyder & Fromkin, 1980). For example, when people are asked to list their best abilities and estimate how others stand on these abilities, they usually underestimate their peers' standing. We need to feel distinctive and to feel that we are uniquely good at some of our abilities. Highly valued skills and abilities, then, show this false uniqueness effect, whereas attitudes and opinions are more likely to show a false consensus effect.

The Self-Serving Attributional Bias

After your football team has soundly beaten an opponent, how often do you hear a gratifying, "Gee, you're better than we are, aren't you?" Usually you hear that it was bad luck, the field conditions were poor, and they'll beat you next year. On the other hand, when you have just been badly beaten, the smug look and condescending "bad luck" from the opponent are particularly grating, because you know that they do not believe it was bad luck at all; they think they are better. The tendency to take credit for success and deny responsibility for failure is known as the **self-serving attributional bias** (Miller & Ross, 1975). Evidence for the self-serving attributional bias is extensive, although there are a couple of qualifications.

Self-Serving Attributional Bias

People see their positive behaviors as internally caused; their negative behaviors may be seen as caused by external circumstances.

Overall, there is more evidence that people take credit for success than that they deny responsibility for failure. People are sometimes willing to accept responsibility for failure, especially if they can attribute it to a factor over which they have personal control, such as effort. By so doing, they can preserve the belief that they will not fail in the future. Even though the self-serving attributional bias plays fast and loose with the facts, it may actually be quite adaptive. Attributing success to one's own efforts, particularly one's enduring characteristics, may make people more likely to attempt related tasks in the future (Taylor & Brown, 1988). For example, in one study, unemployed workers who attributed their firings to external factors made greater efforts to become reemployed and were actually more likely to find jobs than those who attributed their firings to their personal characteristics (Schaufeli, 1988).

Biases: Where Do They Come From?

Why are there such reliable biases in the attribution process? There are several reasons. Some biases represent cognitive shortcuts or heuristics, ways of cutting through masses of information quickly to reach a good explanation. The tendency to attend to salient stimuli and to attribute behavior to internal dispositions may simply make the process of forming causal attributions more rapid and efficient. Other attributional biases come from people's efforts to satisfy their own needs and motives. In addition to needing a coherent understanding of the world, we need to feel good as well. The self-serving and false consensus biases enhance self-esteem and the perception that we can control our lives. In short, our attributional biases come from a combination of cognitive and motivational needs.

ACCURACY OF JUDGMENTS

How accurately do people perceive others? Our impressions of others—our friends and family, for example—are rich and detailed, leading us to be confident that we know what they are like (Gill, Swann, & Silvera, 1998). But do we really? As we will see, this is a thorny question. On the one hand, people must be reasonably accurate in their judgments of others for society to function as smoothly as it does. On the other hand, having considered various evaluative and cognitive biases to which impression formation is subject, the research suggests that in many circumstances our impressions may be quite inaccurate.

People perceive external, visible attributes fairly accurately. A man in a blue uniform with a gun strapped to his side is a police officer. Person perception becomes more difficult, however, when we try to infer internal states, such as traits, feelings, emotions, or personalities.

Judging Personality

Considerable research has examined how accurate people are in judging others' personality traits, such as dominance or sociability. The results of this work suggest that accuracy is compromised by several factors. First, people's perceptions of others are sometimes determined more by their idiosyncratic preferences for particular personality dimensions than by objective attributes of the person being evaluated. For some people, knowing how intelligent a person is is important, whereas for another person, being trustworthy or not might be more important. Second, it is difficult to measure personality traits, and so it is difficult to establish the proper criteria for accuracy. A third problem has to do with how consistent people's personality traits are, especially for predicting their behavior. Often, personality traits predict behavior in only a limited set of circumstances. If a man cheats at pool but is scrupulously honest in dealing with his coworkers and subordinates, is he an honest or dishonest person?

Because of the difficulty in establishing criteria for accuracy, research has focused on when people agree about traits of others (Funder, 1987). Some traits have behavioral manifestations that are especially observable, and observable traits show high levels of agreement. For example, people show a lot of agreement in their ratings of whether someone is extroverted or intelligent (because these qualities are easy to observe), but less agreement on whether the person is honest or conscientious—traits that are more difficult to observe and confirm or disconfirm clearly (Park & Krauss, 1992; Reynolds & Gifford, 2001).

Accuracy has also been measured by whether a rater's judgments of another person match that person's own self-perception. For example, if you were asked to rate your roommate Suzie's friendliness, your rating would be compared with Suzie's self-rating to show how much you agree. Generally speaking, agreement between peer ratings and target ratings depends on how well the two people are acquainted (Kenny & Acitelli, 2001; Malloy & Albright, 1990). When you know a person better, you are more likely to see the person the way that person sees himself or herself. When you know a person less well, agreement may be high on publicly visible qualities, but not on qualities less open to observation (Fuhrman & Funder, 1995; Robins, Mendelsohn, Connell, & Kwan, 2004).

Accurate perception of another person's attributes can be improved when we have information about the situation in which the trait occurs. For example, if people learn that an individual has a particular goal in a situation, they are more likely to make a trait inference from observation of behavior. Thus, for example, if Linda wants to make the field hockey team and trips an opponent during practice, one may infer her ruthlessness with greater confidence than if she trips an opponent in the absence of a particular goal.

Perceivers agree more on the likability of specific target persons than they do on their traits or other attributes (Park, 1986). When one person talks about another's warmth and sense of humor and someone else talks about his kindness and good-naturedness, the only disagreement may be one of semantics. Perceptions of specific personality traits are another matter. People use more idiosyncratic trait definitions when they are making judgments about ambiguous traits than when they are making judgments about traits that have lots of observable referents. When people are forced to use the same trait definition for ambiguous traits, their agreement increases (Hayes & Dunning, 1997).

Somewhat surprisingly, even strangers are able to rate others in a manner consistent with those others' self-perceptions after relatively brief exposures to their behaviors. However, stranger-self agreements seem to occur primarily for behaviors that have many observable referents, such as extroversion, intelligence, and warmth (e.g., Borkenau & Liebler, 1993; Levesque & Kenny, 1993). Sharing a cultural background usually leads to more accurate inferences than if the perceiver and the perceived come from different cultures (Coleman, Beale, & Mills, 1993). Accuracy can be improved by inducing empathy because when we feel empathy for others, we seem to get inside their heads, see the world as they see it, and more accurately infer the content of their thoughts and feelings (Gesn & Ickes, 1999). The most consensus about a target's attributes is found when perceivers share information about targets who behave consistently across situations (Malloy, Agatstein, Yarlas, & Albright, 1997) or when perceivers are judging behavior in the same situation (Malloy, Albright, Diaz-Loving, Dong, & Lee, 2004). The lowest consensus occurs when perceivers do not communicate with each other and have different kinds of information about targets who behave differently in different situations.

People are more likely to agree on another person's characteristics if that person's behavior is not overly variable (Biesanz, West, & Graziano, 1998). People are also more likely to reach consensus about another person's attributes if their outcomes are dependent on their inferences (Bernieri, Zuckerman, Koestner, & Rosenthal, 1994; Paulus & Bruce, 1992). Participants in one study (Flink & Park, 1991) were told that they would observe eight of their peers being interviewed and then choose one of the interviewees to teach them a game (outcome dependency). The judges then rated each of the targets on a number of attributes. Outcome dependency greatly increased the consensus among the judges and reduced idiosyncratic judgments based on factors irrelevant to the judgment, such as liking. Outcome dependency also seemed to make judges more sensitive to the variability in a person's behavior across situations. That is, they noticed when a person was inconsistent and when he or she was not. Consequently, consensus in impressions improved (Wright & Dawson, 1988).

Unfortunately, though, when we attempt to predict future behavior, we fare rather badly. That is, for the most part we are overconfident about predicting the behavior of both other people and ourselves (Dunning, Griffin, Milojkovic, & Ross, 1990; Vallone, Griffin, Lin, & Ross, 1990). This inaccuracy seems to be due to two factors. First, when people express high confidence that certain things will happen to themselves or to others in the future, it is rarely warranted. As confidence increases, the gap between accuracy and confidence widens. For example, when California college students were asked to indicate how likely it was that their roommate would take his or her first job in California, many students expressed high confidence in this outcome. Many of them were wrong, because finding and accepting a first job depends on many factors in addition to the geographic locale in which you might want to live. Second, predictions that are statistically unlikely are very rarely accurate. Thus, for example, when asked how likely it was that most of their close college friends would be from outside their dorm, those students who said "highly likely" were usually wrong; people usually form friendships on the basis of propinquity, namely, who lives close by (Vallone et al., 1990).

The evidence suggests that we are not particularly accurate in perceiving other people, but perhaps we are accurate enough. The evidence suggests that people achieve **pragmatic accuracy**, namely, accuracy that enables them to achieve their relationship goals (Gill & Swann, 2004). For example, romantic partners are fairly accurate about each other on personal qualities that are relevant to the relationship, but may be somewhat less so on qualities that are less relevant to the relationship (Gill & Swann, 2004). Thus, pragmatic accuracy need not be terribly accurate, so long as it enables people to meet the goals they have with respect to their relationship partners (Gill & Swann, 2004).

Pragmatic Accuracy

Knowing enough about a person to achieve one's relationship goals.

Recognition of Emotions

Much of the work on the accuracy of person perception has focused on the recognition of emotions—on whether a person is happy or afraid, horrified or disgusted. In a typical study, a person is presented with a set of photographs of people portraying different emotions and asked to judge what those emotions are (see Figure 2–2). More recent research has made use of videotaped clips of emotional reactions. Research shows that there is near universal recognition of several facial expressions of emotion in both literate (Ekman, 1972; Izard, 1971) and preliterate (Ekman & Friesen, 1971; Ekman, Sorensen, & Friesen, 1969) cultures.

Why are we fairly accurate in our perception of emotional states? In 1871, Charles Darwin proposed, on the basis of his evolutionary theory, that facial expressions convey the same emotional states in all cultures. His argument was that universal expressions have evolved because they have great survival value: They allow people to communicate emotions and thereby control the behavior of others. Ekman and Friesen (1975) maintained that this universality is manifested in facial affect programs, biologically hardwired sets of cues that allow one person to know the emotion of another (Wehrle, Kaiser, Schmidt, & Schere, 2000). In fact, virtually all species of Old World monkeys and apes have been found to use facial gestures to signal dominance or submissiveness. Differing eyebrow positions seem to be crucial: Typically the brows are lowered on dominant or threatening individuals and raised on submissive or receptive individuals (Keating et al., 1981). As another example, Craig and Patrick (1985) induced

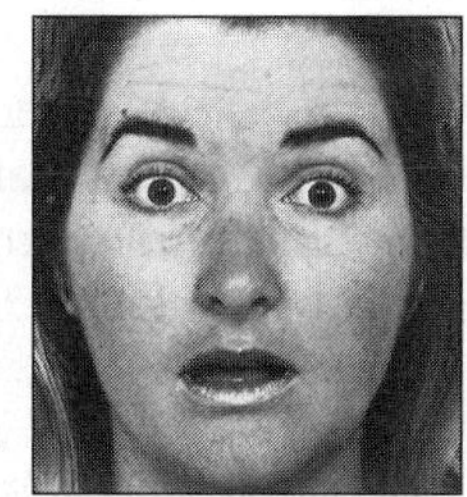
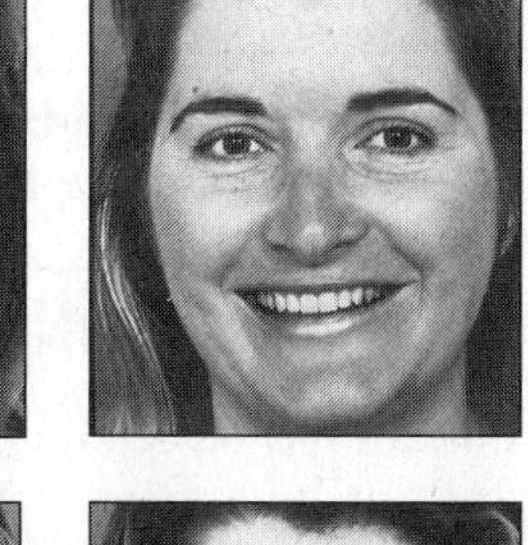
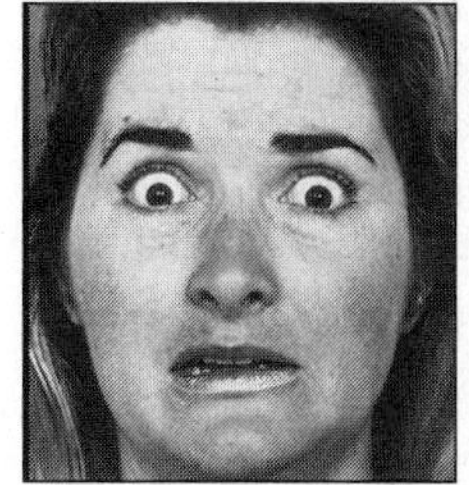
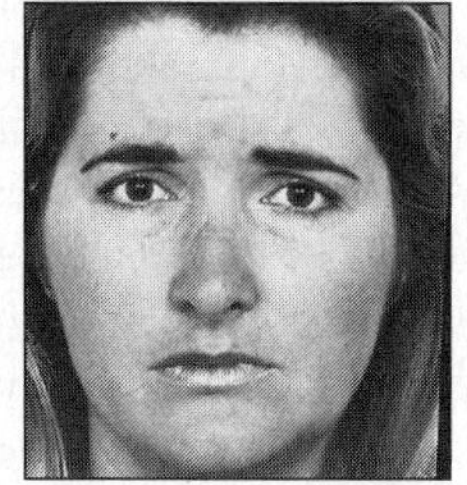
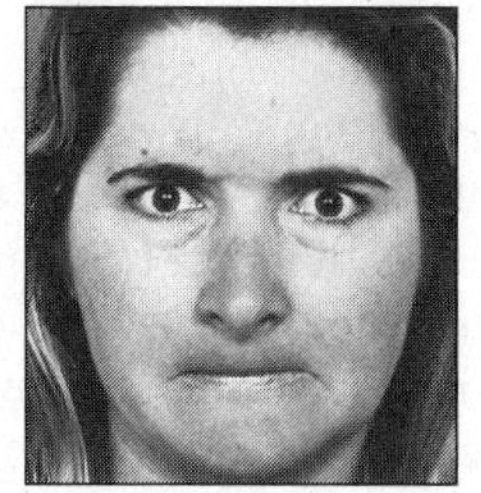

Figure 2–2 **Examples of Stimuli Used in the Study of Perceptions of Emotion.**

Each picture portrays a different emotion. Try to identify them before looking at the answers. (Top, left to right: neutral, surprise, happiness. Bottom, left to right: fear, sadness, anger)

pain by immersing participants' hands and wrists in icy water just at freezing temperature. They found consistent responses across cultures, including raising the cheeks and tightening the eyelids, raising the upper eyelids, parting the lips, and closing the eyes or blinking. The evolutionary argument is that there may be a link between the facial expressions used by subhuman primates to communicate with and control other species' members and those used by humans for the same purpose. If so, presumably the same link between emotion and facial expression would exist among humans across all (or most) cultures.

Of course, not all individual emotions can be discriminated well, but people can typically distinguish the major groups of emotions using facial cues. In an early study, Woodworth (1938) suggested that emotions can be arranged on a continuum; the relationship between any two emotions is distinguished by the distance between them on this continuum. The continuum of emotions is:

1. Happiness, joy
2. Surprise, amazement
3. Fear
4. Sadness
5. Anger
6. Disgust, contempt
7. Interest, attentiveness

People seem to be quite good at distinguishing emotions in categories that are 3, 4, or 5 points apart—they rarely confuse happiness with disgust or surprise with contempt (e.g., Rozin, Lowery, & Ebert, 1994). But it is almost impossible to discriminate emotions in the same category or only one group away. Happiness and surprise are frequently confused, as are anger and disgust, for example.

Two basic dimensions of emotional expression are pleasantness and arousal (Russell & Bullock, 1985), and people are reasonable judges of emotional states within the categories that these dimensions form. For example, positive emotions such as excitement and happiness are easily distinguished from negative ones such as fear, anger, and disgust. Among the positive emotions, arousing ones such as excitement can be distinguished from nonarousing ones such as contentment. Similarly, negative arousing emotions such as fear and anger can be distinguished from nonarousing ones such as sadness. On the whole, though, the pleasantness dimension is more easily discriminated than is the arousal dimension.

Despite the fact that there seems to be near universal recognition of certain emotions, there are also important differences among cultures. Not every emotion is communicated the same way in every culture, and there are emotions in some cultures that do not exist in others (Frank & Stennett, 2001; Markus & Kityama, 1994). Moreover, recent research shows that people are generally more accurate at judging emotions when those emotions are expressed by members of their own cultural group than when they are expressed by members of a different cultural group (Elfenbein & Ambady, 2003). This widely documented in-group advantage in recognizing emotions underscores the importance of continuing to attend to cultural differences in the expression and interpretation of emotion.

NONVERBAL COMMUNICATION

Much of our communication is verbal, but we communicate nonverbally as well. We mimic the behavior of our interaction partners, as we will see; we use nonverbal behavior to communicate dominance, sympathy, or liking. When another person communicates dominance nonverbally through posture or stance, we spontaneously become more submissive, and when a person communicates submission through their posture, we behave in a more dominant fashion (Tiedens & Fragale, 2003).

Often we are completely unaware of what we are communicating to others and, in turn, learning about them through these nonverbal cues. But, in fact, much communication occurs nonverbally, and the effects of nonverbal communication on impressions of others can be extremely potent. In a study by Amaby and Rosenthal (1993), students were presented with 30-second silent video clips of college professors' lectures, and they rated the professors on a variety of personal qualities. Students were able to make reliable ratings of the professors' qualities, ratings that showed a fair degree of consensus and were significant predictors of end-of-semester student evaluations of those teachers. The impact of even small amounts of nonverbal behavior can be substantial indeed (see also Borkenau, Mauer, Riemann, Spinath, & Angleitner, 2004).

Generally speaking, people communicate information about themselves through three main channels. The most obvious is verbal communication, the content of what a person says. The other channels are nonverbal and provide a set of much subtler cues. Nonverbal communication comes to us through a visible channel that includes such features as facial expression, gesture, posture, and appearance. It also comes to us through a paralinguistic channel, namely, the remainder of the speech signal when the content has been removed, such as the pitch, amplitude, rate, voice quality, and contour of speech.

The Visible Channel

Some of the main nonverbal cues of the visible channel are expressed through distance, gesture, and eye contact. This is called **body language**.

Body Language

Information transmitted about opinions by nonverbal bodily movements, such as posture.

Distance. In general, the more friendly and intimate a person feels toward another, the closer he or she will stand. Friends stand closer than strangers, people who want to seem friendly choose smaller distances, and people who are sexually attracted to each other stand close. Although most people do not think much about personal space, we are all aware that standing close is usually a sign of friendship or interest. It may be one of the most important and easiest ways of telling someone you have just met that you like him or her. The other person is immediately aware of your interest, and if not interested, he or she will probably move farther away to make that clear.

Gestures. Bodily gestures and posture carry information. Many bodily movements are generally accepted and convey specific information or directions—the gestures for "stop" and "come" are examples, as are gestures for "sit down," "yes,"

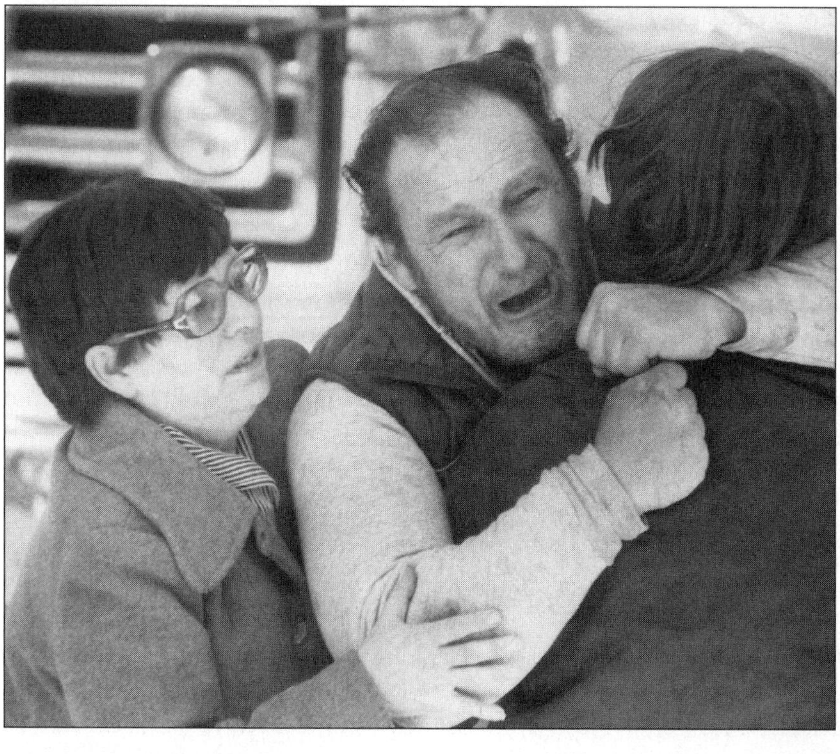

Because certain emotional expressions are universal, most people looking at this picture would assume that the man is deeply unhappy about something. In fact, he has just learned that his family was killed in a fire.

People from different cultures have different customs regarding touching and other nonverbal communication during casual conversation. These North American women, for example, are not comfortable touching, whereas the two men on a street in Spain stand close together and touch repeatedly during their conversation.

"no," "go away," and "good-bye." Various obscene gestures have well-known meanings. In a sense, all these gestures are a sign language.

Gestures have meaning mainly when observers and participants understand the context, and especially when they understand the culture. An open palm is not always an invitation: Sometimes, putting a hand up with palm out means "stop," not "go"; the reverse gesture, with the palm in and the fingers moving toward the body, means "come" or "enter." The meaning of gestures depends on context, on the person doing the action, on the culture, and on the recipient of the communication (Bavelas, Chovil, Coates, & Roe, 1995).

The importance of nonverbal communications and gestures in particular has now made its way into the popular culture. Media experts who "handle" political candidates often work as much on those candidates' gestures and other nonverbal communication as on the content of their presentation. During the 1988 campaign season, Roger Ailes, George Bush's media consultant, was quoted in *Newsweek* (Warner & Fineman, 1988, p. 19) as telling Bush during a rehearsal for one of the debates, "There you go with that f-ing hand again. *You look like a f-ing pansy!*" (cited in DePaulo, 1990).

Eye Contact. Eye contact is an especially interesting form of nonverbal communication, and its meaning varies greatly, depending on the context. At the minimum, eye contact indicates interest or lack of it. In movies, couples stare into each other's eyes to portray love, affection, or great concern. An otherwise casual conversation can become an expression of romantic interest if one of the speakers maintains eye contact. In other cases, a stare may be a challenge or a threat, as when two athletic opponents try to stare each other down (Ellsworth & Carlsmith, 1973). It is perhaps not surprising that eye contact can have seemingly contradictory meanings, for example, friendship or threat. In both cases, eye contact indicates greater involvement and higher emotional content. Whether the emotion is positive or negative depends on the context; the nonverbal cues themselves have no fixed meaning.

Conversely, avoiding or breaking the contact is usually a sign that the person is not interested. Indeed, when someone does not make eye contact during a conversation, we tend to interpret this as an indication that he or she is not really involved in the interaction. However, there are obvious exceptions to this general principle. Someone who is conveying bad news or saying something painful may avoid eye contact. Lack of eye contact can sometimes mean the person is shy or frightened as well.

Facial Expressions. Facial expressions can also be forms of communication, conveying warmth, sympathy, confusion, or anger, for example (Grahe & Bernieri 2002; Reynolds & Gifford, 2001). A smile from an acquaintance when you are undertaking an effortful task may be construed as supportive and increase self-regard, but the same smile when a competitor is undertaking the same task may instead be construed as support for the competitor and thus lower one's personal regard (Tamir, Robinson, Klor, Martin, & Whittker, 2004).

A particularly intriguing aspect of facial communication is mimicry. People (and chimpanzees) physically mimic the responses of others. Darwin noted that, in particular, people mimic distress when others are feeling it. It is possible that this mimicry is an expression of sympathy for the victim; the mimic may want the other person to know that distress about the painful experience is shared. Mimicry may also reflect an unconscious strategy that people spontaneously engage in to get along with the people with whom they interact (Cheng & Chartrand, 2003).

To test this idea, Bavelas, Black, Lemery, and Mullett (1986) had undergraduate women view a person accidentally drop a heavy TV monitor on an already injured finger, one with a heavily taped splint on it. In some cases, the victim, a (badly bruised) confederate, then looked directly at the observer; in other cases, no eye contact was made. Most of the observers in turn displayed an expression of pain, but it quickly faded in the absence of eye contact. Moreover, the observers were considerably more likely to smile when eye contact was made, probably in an effort to be reassuring. The facial expressions of the observers in the eye-contact condition were in fact rated as more "knowing" and "caring" than were those of the observers in the no-eye-contact condition, a finding suggesting that the former were successfully communicating feelings of empathy and sympathy. People are especially likely to mimic others if they are especially attentive to the people around them and the context in which their behavior occurs (van Baaren, Horgan, Chatrand, & Dijkmans, 2004).

Paralanguage. Variations in speech other than the actual verbal content, called **paralanguage**, carry a great deal of meaning, especially emotional meaning (Banse & Scherer, 1996). Voice pitch, loudness, rhythm, inflection, and hesitations convey information. Parents can often tell whether their baby is hungry, angry, or just mildly cranky by the sound of his or her cry. Dogs bark in different ways, and each type of bark means something different to someone familiar with the animal. And of course, the significance and meaning of adult speech depends in part on these paralinguistic factors.

Paralanguage

Information conveyed by speech other than words, such as pitch or loudness.

A simple statement such as "You want to move to Japan" can mean entirely different things depending on emphasis and inflection. Say it aloud as a flat statement with no emphasis, and it sounds like a mere statement of fact. Say it with an inflection (rising voice) at the end, and it questions the wisdom of going to Japan; you are expressing doubt that it is a good place to move to. Say it with added emphasis on the first word, and it turns into a question as to whether the person addressed is qualified; you are raising doubts about whether the person is capable of getting along in such a foreign country. The short phrase "I like you" may indicate almost anything from mild feelings to intense passion, depending on its paralinguistic characteristics.

Multiple Channels

Which of these three channels of communication—verbal, visible, or paralinguistic—provides the most information about a person's real emotions? Typically, and not surprisingly, people tend to form more accurate judgments about another person when they have access to all channels of communication (Chawla & Krauss, 1994). But generally, the verbal channel—that is, the information that people convey about themselves—seems to be much more influential for inferences about people (e.g., Berry, Pennebaker, Mueller, & Hiller, 1997).

The question of which channels communicate most powerfully becomes important, however, when the observer is receiving conflicting cues from different channels. How do you interpret your girlfriend's feelings when she says she loves you but moves away from you and won't look at you? The verbal and visible channels of her communication seem to conflict. We turn next to this issue.

THE PROBLEM OF DECEPTION

A particularly important area of conflict between verbal and nonverbal cues is judging when people are lying or otherwise trying to deceive observers. Police, judges, and jurors are constantly trying to learn the truth from people who try to mislead them. Closer to home, college students report telling about two lies a day during the course of normal social interactions (DePaulo, Kashy, Kirkendol, Wyer, & Epstein, 1996). Are people successful or unsuccessful liars, especially to people whose feelings they were attempting to spare?

Nonverbal Leakage

People sometimes betray the fact that they are lying through nonverbal cues even when they are successful in lying verbally. People attend more to what they are saying than to what they are doing with their bodies, which may lead to **nonverbal leakage** (Ekman & Friesen, 1974). That is, true emotions can "leak

Nonverbal Leakage

True feelings may be evident in nonverbal behavior.

out" even when a person tries to conceal them. For example, a student may say she is not nervous about taking a test but will bite her lower lip and blink more than usual, actions that often indicate nervousness.

Liars often betray themselves through paralinguistic expressions of anxiety, tension, and nervousness. It is sometimes possible to tell when someone is lying by noting the pitch of the voice. In general, the voice is higher when someone is lying than when he or she is telling the truth (Ekman, Friesen, & Scherer, 1976; Krauss, Geller, & Olson, 1976). The difference is often so small that an individual cannot tell simply by listening; however, electronic vocal analysis reveals lying with considerable accuracy. In addition, shorter answers, longer delays in responding, more speech errors, and more nervous, less serious answers are all characteristic of people who are perceived as liars or who are instructed to tell lies (Apple, Streeter, & Krauss, 1979; Kraut, 1978; Zuckerman, DePaulo, & Rosenthal, 1981). People also infer deception from "weird" nonverbal behavior. When an individual engages in odd nonverbal behavior, such as arm raising, head tilting, or staring that seems inappropriate to the perceiver, the perceiver is more likely to infer that the other's purpose is deceptive (Bond et al., 1992). The tendency to engage in nonverbal leakage may be fairly consistent across situations, because people who are perceived to be truthful by others tend to be seen this way across multiple situations (Frank & Eckman, 2004).

The concept of leakage implies that some nonverbal channels leak more than others because they are less controllable. The musculature of a smile, for example, is different when people are being truthful and when they are lying (Ekman, Friesen, & O'Sullivan, 1988). Several studies (e.g., Zuckerman et al., 1981) have found that the body is more likely than the face to reveal deception. Paralinguistic cues can also leak because, like the body, tone of voice is less controllable than is facial expression. Liars, for example, may be better able to modify—that is, suppress and exaggerate—facial expressions than tone of voice (Zuckerman, Larrance, Spiegel, & Klorman, 1981). Typically, successful deceivers make eye contact with their listeners and inhibit smiling while they are delivering deceptive messages.

Accuracy in Detecting Deception

Perceivers consistently perceive deceptive messages as somewhat less truthful than truthful messages (see DePaulo, 1990, for a review), but rarely by an impressive margin. Even friends aren't particularly good at detecting whether a friend is lying (Anderson, DePaulo, & Ansfield, 2002). When we are successful at detecting deception, we are better at detecting the fact of lying better than we can figure out the nature of the liar's true feelings. It is especially difficult to discriminate lying from ambivalence, because some of the same nonverbal cues characterize both states.

Lies are easiest to detect when they are apparently motivated by ingratiation, that is, when the sender has a motivation to lie, such as communicating false agreement with an attractive partner of the opposite sex (DePaulo, Rosenthal, Green, & Rosenkrantz, 1982). Deception is harder to detect when the motive is unknown. Moreover, detecting deception is undermined by many of the person-perception biases we have just discussed, such as the tendency to see people positively (O'Sullivan, 2003).

Does it help to be warned explicitly that a target person may be lying? One would think so, because perceivers then would attend more closely to "leaky" channels, such as the face and tone of voice. However, it seems not to help very much. In a study by Toris and DePaulo (1984), involving simulated job interviews, the "applicants" were told to be honest in some cases and dishonest in others, whereas the "interviewers" were told to expect the applicant to try to convey a false impression in some cases or were given no warning. Compared with interviewers who had not been warned to anticipate dishonest behavior, the warned interviewers perceived all applicants as more deceptive, and they were no more accurate than the unwarned interviewers in singling out the dishonest applicants from the honest ones. Moreover, they were less confident of their judgments than were their unwarned counterparts.

Paradoxically, people may be somewhat better at discerning deception when they are less involved. Highly involved participants tend to process people's messages carefully, and they therefore attend more to the verbal message, whereas less involved participants are more likely to pay attention to peripheral cues and attend more to nonverbal behavior (Forrest & Feldman, 2000). However, much of the time we may not be particularly motivated to notice whether a person is lying or not. In most social situations, deceptive self-presentations are likely to be taken at face value (DePaulo, 1990).

The Giveaways

When observers are able to discover deception, what cues do they use? Is the leakage hypothesis correct? Is the body less controllable than the face, and do people catch deception primarily through nonverbal bodily cues? Or is the voice—pitch, loudness, and speed—an even leakier channel than the body? Most of the research shows that all these cues help to expose a potentially deceptive communicator. However, they are really useful only when the observer also has access to the content of the person's speech.

Psychologists now know the specific behaviors that reliably distinguish lies from truth. Liars blink more, hesitate more, and make more errors when they are speaking, perhaps because it is arousing to lie. They tend to speak in higher pitched voices, and their pupils are more likely to be dilated. Liars are more likely to feel guilty or anxious, and this may explain why liars fidget more, speak more hesitatingly and less fluidly, and make more negative and distancing statements than do those who tell the truth (Vrij, Edward, & Bull, 2001). The voice tone of liars also often sounds negative. Interchannel discrepancies are more likely to occur. For example, someone attempting to convey an impression of warmth may smile and make eye contact but lean away, rather than lean forward, from the person with whom he is conversing (DePaulo, 1990). Linguistic cues may also give away the fact of lying. Compared to truth tellers, liars describe events in less cognitively complex terms, and they use fewer references to themselves and to other people. They also use more negative emotion words (Newman, Pennebaker, Berry, & Richards, 2003).

Paradoxically, one of the best sources of information regarding deception may be the sender's motivation to lie. When people are motivated to get away with their lies, they actually become more obvious to observers (e.g., DePaulo, Kirkendol, Tang, & O'Brien, 1988; DePaulo, LeMay, & Epstein, 1991). Motivated liars seem to work harder to control their nonverbal behavior, sometimes attempting to suppress it altogether in a rigid effort not to give anything away. In other cases, they may deliberately try to control all their verbal and nonverbal behaviors. Both strategies fail because observers can perceive this rigid or controlled behavior through the nonverbal channels and more successfully discern the effort to lie (DePaulo, 1990).

Nonverbal Behavior and Self-Presentation

Our discussion here implies that nonverbal behavior is either spontaneous and unself-conscious or a potential source of leakage about deception. However, nonverbal behavior is also subject to a certain amount of self-regulation (DePaulo, 1992). Whenever people are motivated to convey a particular impression in a social setting, they often do so, in part, by managing their nonverbal behaviors.

Think about the last time a friend shared a problem with you. If you listened patiently and sympathetically, as most of us do, at least initially, you were probably aware of saying the right things, such as "That's too bad" or "That's a terrible way to treat anybody." You may also have been aware of the appropriate nonverbal behaviors, such as making eye contact with your friend while he talked and nodding sympathetically. You knew, for example, not to smile, but to look serious, and not to open your mail and skim it while he was explaining his problem. Although not intending to deceive your friend in any way, your nonverbal behaviors were clearly monitored, at least to a degree, so that you conveyed the appropriate sentiments and reactions to your friend's disclosures.

Over a lifetime, we learn a great deal about the self-presentation of nonverbal behavior—indeed, so much so that it becomes almost automatic in adulthood. For example, by the time we are in college, we may not have to think much about the fact that we should stop fidgeting, make extended eye contact, and look sympathetic when another person is telling us a problem. Cultural norms regarding how one conveys emotions to others are orderly and follow what psychologists call "display rules" (Ekman, 1992a, 1992b). Display rules govern not only which emotion should be conveyed in a particular situation but also how the emotion should be conveyed.

Nonverbal behavior can also be used to further social goals. When he is talking with a woman he wishes to date, a man may smile a great deal, make extended eye contact, stand fairly close, and rest his hand against the wall behind his intended partner. Caught in a conversation with someone to whom he is not attracted, he stands farther away, glances from time to time around the room, maintains a more serious expression, and keeps his arms folded in front of him.

Gender

People vary in how effectively they use nonverbal communication. Girls and women tend to be more expressive, more involved in their interpersonal interactions, and more open in the expression of emotion (DePaulo, 1992). They tend to use more nonverbal behavior in interacting with others, such as touching, eye contact, expressive body movements, smiling, and gazing. Women are also more accurate interpreters of nonverbal cues than are men (Hall, 1978). There are also gender differences in the communication of different emotions. Women are better able to communicate happiness, whereas men are better able to communicate anger (Coats & Feldman, 1996).

It is easy to interpret gender differences in sex-role terms. Generally, women have been regarded as the experts in the social and emotional areas of life, and nonverbal behavior can clearly help in this regard. However, some studies suggest that these sex differences develop very early in life, as early as 3 months of age (Malatesta & Haviland, 1982). Consequently, it is difficult to disentangle the roles of nature and nurture in attempting to understand these significant sex differences (DePaulo, 1992).

In conclusion, it appears that when people are motivated to convey a particular impression of themselves in a social interaction, they attempt to do so, in part, by controlling their nonverbal behaviors. Although sometimes people exhibit such behaviors to deceive others, more commonly people use them to convey an accurate impression of themselves and their feelings in a particular situation. Moreover, people seem to be fairly successful at exercising this nonverbal control, as long as they are not trying to convey a false impression.

Summary

1. People often decide very quickly what other people are like and base their decisions on minimal information, such as appearance or gender. They infer enduring qualities in others from brief exposure to behavior in limited situations.
2. The qualities we infer about another are influenced by physical features, salience, the social categories to which the individual belongs, and our own motives and goals for forming the impression.
3. The evaluative dimension is the most important organizing principle behind first impressions. People tend to decide first how much they like or dislike another person and then ascribe characteristics to that person that fit this pleasant or unpleasant portrait.
4. Various perceptual biases distort our judgments of others, such as the halo effect (we tend to think that a person we like is good in every dimension), the positivity bias (we tend to like most people, even some who are not so likable), and the negativity effect (more emphasis is placed on negative than on positive information).

5. People tend to form highly consistent impressions of others, even with very little information.
6. When combining information into an integrated impression, we tend to use a weighted averaging approach, in which all information is considered but certain information is given more importance. When we are able to identify a person as a member of a particular social group, we are able to use our schemas or stereotypes to draw inferences about them.
7. Attribution theory is concerned with how people infer the causes of social events. Although causal attributions can be made by most people for most events, people are most likely to ask "why" questions when something unexpected, unusual, or unpleasant happens. Causal attributions help people predict and control the environment.
8. To infer the causes of behavior, people use a covariation principle, meaning that they look for an association between a particular effect and a particular cause across a number of different conditions. A second important principle is that people discount the role of one cause in producing a given effect if other plausible causes are also present.
9. There are several systematic biases in the attribution process. The fundamental attribution error and the actor-observer bias both suggest that people ascribe a greater causal role to more salient stimuli. People are also influenced by the need to provide causal explanations that protect their self-esteem. This need leads to the self-serving bias and the false consensus bias.
10. Our judgments of other people are not always accurate. In particular, we have a hard time judging people's emotions from their facial expressions. We can tell fairly easily if the emotion is a positive or a negative one, but we have difficulty telling which positive or negative emotion is being experienced. Nevertheless, there do seem to be some universal connections across cultures between certain emotions and certain facial expressions.
11. We use nonverbal cues, as well as verbal and visual ones, to infer the qualities of others. Nonverbal communication includes cues from both the visible channel (such as facial expressions, gestures, and posture) and the paralinguistic channel (cues in speech when the content has been removed, such as the pitch, rate, and delays of speech). Nonverbal cues not only help us form impressions but also enable us, in some circumstances, to detect deception.
12. Verbal communication is probably the single most important source of information about other people. However, visible and paralinguistic information makes an important additional contribution, particularly when the content helps us to interpret its meaning.
13. Deception leaks out in numerous nonverbal ways, such as nervous gestures or high-pitched and rapid speech. Observers can usually detect deception at levels slightly better than chance, but they need all three channels of communication to do so effectively.

Key Terms

actor-observer bias **51**
assimilation **38**
attribution theory **46**
averaging principle **40**
body language **57**
categorization **37**
central trait **36**
contrast **38**
correspondent inference theory **46**
covariation **48**
discounting principle **48**
dispositional attribution **46**
dual processing **37**
evaluation **39**
false consensus effect **51**
false uniqueness effect **52**
figure-ground principle **34**
fundamental attribution error **49**
halo effect **41**
implicit personality theory **35**
negativity effect **39**
nonverbal leakage **59**
paralanguage **59**
positivity bias **39**
pragmatic accuracy **55**
prototype **42**
salience **34**
self-serving attributional bias **52**
shift of meaning **40**
situational attribution **46**
stereotype **42**

In The News

Do Increasing Casualties Justify a Pullout or a Continued Presence?

On March 19, 2003, President George Bush declared war on Iraq and sent in troops to overthrow Saddam Hussein. On May 1, following a successful advance on and occupation of Baghdad, he announced the end of major combat. At that time, there had been 977 deaths among the coalition forces.

But keeping the peace in Iraq proved to be more costly than making war, and by July 20, 2004, an additional 1,020 coalition deaths had occurred. With increasing casualties, public pressure in the United States to end the war mounted.

In the long frustrating debate that followed, both sides used the casualties to make their cases. Those who advocated a pullout pointed to the waste of American lives in the face of little evidence that Iraq had been a threat to the United States. But those who advocated a continued presence in Iraq pointed to the causalities as evidence of the ongoing instability in Iraq, the lack of central leadership, and the need to monitor and control warring factions.

As will be seen in this chapter, there is nothing surprising or unexpected about the same evidence being used to support entirely contradictory positions. Social cognition is guided by prior expectations, and often, evidence can be interpreted to mean what a person wants it to mean.

Chapter 3

Social Cognition: Understanding the Social World

In this chapter, we take up the topic of **social cognition**, the study of how people form inferences from the social information in the environment. Research on social cognition explores how people make social judgments about other individuals or social groups, about social roles, and about their own experiences in social settings. Making social judgments is more difficult than we might imagine. Often, the information available to us is incomplete, ambiguous, or downright contradictory. How do we use all this information to arrive at a coherent judgment? This is the core question in research on social cognition.

You might assume that social cognition involves seeing the world accurately and forming unbiased, clear assessments of the social life that swirls around us. In fact, however, one of the earliest discoveries that social psychologists made is that social cognition is often marked by apparent errors and biases. Certainly there are logical and correct ways to put information together to make wise decisions, but people's social inferences often depart in quite predictable ways from logic and accuracy. As we'll see, though, these errors and biases are themselves informative about how we actually form inferences about the social environment. First, let's look at a social situation to see how it is marked by these departures from logic and accuracy, and then we'll see how they've shaped our current view of how we form social judgments.

Imagine that you have completed college and are interviewing at a company for your first job. You have met the personnel director and some prospective coworkers. You also have toured the facilities, seen where your office would be, and learned a great deal about the work the company does and your prospective responsibilities to the company. How do you decide if this is indeed the kind of company you want to work for and if you would like the work itself and the people you would work with?

Focus of This Chapter

SOCIAL INFERENCE

Any social inference is composed of several steps: gathering information, deciding what information to use, and integrating the information into a judgment. For example, as you are learning about your possible new employer, you are gathering information about the people, products, and general feel of the organization, and you are gathering information from people around you through the questions you ask and the types of facilities or people you request

Social Cognition

The study of how people form inferences and make judgments from social information.

to see. When you return home and mull over your visit, you must then decide what information, of the multitude of information you received, will be most relevant to your decision and then integrate that information into an overall impression or judgment concerning whether this company is the right one for you.

Gathering Information

When people gather information that is relevant to some inference they will ultimately form, they might plan to do so in an evenhanded and unbiased manner. However, research suggests that actual information gathering is often subject to several sources of bias.

Prior Expectations

Suppose you learn that a college acquaintance of yours, a tense, serious, humorless fellow, works for the company you are considering and finds it very much to his liking. If he likes the company so much, you might suspect that it is because he has found people there who are similar to him. Consequently, you might infer that everyone at the company must be stiff and uptight. Accordingly, as you learn about the company with this suspicion in mind, you might selectively gather information consistent with this prior expectation. You might note that prospective coworkers seem a little rigid or formal when you meet them and might conclude that indeed your classmate is typical of the people at this firm. But in doing so, you might fail to remember that most people are a little stiff or formal when they are meeting someone for the first time. Their formality might simply be due to the fact that you are a stranger to them, and they might actually turn out to be very friendly people. But with your prior expectations in mind, you might dismiss them as stiff and formal people without giving them a chance. This is how prior expectations can bias the process of gathering information.

Of course, prior expectations are very helpful in sifting through a lot of information that may otherwise be uninterpretable. They can provide structure and meaning for information that would otherwise be hard to interpret. However, sometimes prior expectations can cause us to draw inaccurate inferences. Four conditions are especially problematic (Nisbett & Ross, 1980). The first is faulty expectations. For example, your belief that the company is stiff and stodgy merely because it attracted one such individual to its ranks is likely to be incorrect. Therefore, letting this expectation guide your collection of information will probably lead you to incorrect answers. A second condition under which prior expectations can be problematic occurs when the social perceiver fails to recognize how prior expectations bias the collection of information. For example, you may be unaware that your impressions of your stodgy college classmate are actually guiding your judgments of your prospective coworkers. This lack of awareness means that later on you will be unable to correct the biasing effect of your prior impression. Your judgments concerning your prospective coworkers will stray on the stodgy and serious side without your realizing that your own biases contributed to this inference. Third, prior expectations can create problems when they overrule consideration of information altogether. If you decide on the basis of your college classmate's attributes not to interview at the company, you have made this error. And finally, if information is inconsistent with what you want to believe, you are likely to scrutinize it far more carefully, potentially rejecting it in favor of information that supports what you want to believe (Ditto, Scepansky, Munro, Apanovitch, & Lockhart, 1998).

Biases in the Information

Once the social perceiver has decided what information is relevant to an inference, the information must actually be collected. The individual must determine which bits of information from the available wealth of data should be examined. For example, obviously you cannot meet everybody at the company during your

What are these people doing? Helping an injured companion? Playing a game? Going through a survival exercise? Because much behavior is fundamentally ambiguous, social inference processes give social interaction structure and meaning.

job interview visit, and so the people you do meet will help give you an impression of the qualities of your prospective coworkers. But judgments made on the basis of limited information can be distorted when there are biases in the information. For example, if you are introduced to a particularly outgoing and friendly coworker, your impression of the attributes of the workers in the company may be falsely influenced toward the outgoing and friendly side.

Even when people are warned that information may be biased, they sometimes fail to understand the full implications of that bias. For example, in one study (Hamill, Wilson, & Nisbett, 1980), researchers told participants that they would be viewing a videotape of an interview with a prison guard. Some participants were told that this prison guard was typical of most prison guards, whereas others were told that he was very different from most prison guards. In the third condition, participants were not given information about how typical the guard was. Half the participants then saw a tape in which the prison guard appeared as a highly compassionate, concerned individual. The other half saw a tape that portrayed him as an inhumane, macho, cruel person. Participants were later asked a set of questions about the criminal justice system that included questions about what kinds of people become prison guards. The results showed that participants exposed to the interview of the humane guard were more favorable in their attitudes toward prison guards than were participants who saw the interview with the inhumane prison guard. Importantly, participants' inferences about prison guards were unaffected by whether they had been told that the prison guard was typical.

Small Sample

Inferences are also problematic when they are based on very little information. A small sample of information can actually produce a very biased picture (Schaller, 1992). For example, if you are introduced to only 2 of your prospective coworkers, who seem pleasant enough, but you will actually be working with 20 individuals, there is the possibility that these 2 are not typical of the larger group. The other 18 may not be quite as pleasant. Sometimes people forget that they are dealing with very little information, and they make confident inferences nonetheless (see Nisbett & Kunda, 1985).

Statistical Information

Information based on averages or totals.

Case History Information

Information about a specific person or event.

Statistical Versus Case History Information

Another distinction that is important in how people use information is that between **statistical information** and **case history information**. Statistical information provides data about a large number of individuals, whereas case history information usually tells a story about a few specific individuals. When people are exposed to both statistical information and a contradictory but colorful case history, the case history often has more influence on their judgment (Taylor & Thompson, 1982). This reaction occurs even when the statistical information is objectively more accurate. For example, one type of information you might want to gather during your job interview is about how quickly people advance in the company. Clearly, the most appropriate information to look at is the statistical information about promotion rates for all the employees and for those in your prospective division particularly. However, suppose you are told about Mark Comet, a particularly dynamic employee who managed to go from clerk to associate vice president in 3 short years. It is likely that the case history of Mark Comet's dramatic rise to fame and fortune within the company will bias your impression of how quickly people advance. It may lead you to ignore the more appropriate statistical information, which would suggest that people typically advance fairly slowly within the company.

Most of us know that we really should use broadly based statistical information in making our judgments. People draw on statistics all the time when they are trying to make a persuasive argument, and a person who has statistical information available can often be quite persuasive. If a case history does not lead us to a strong conclusion, we are more likely to rely on the statistical evidence. However, generally speaking, when more engaging anecdotal case history evidence is present, people often ignore relevant statistical evidence and are instead persuaded by case histories (Beckett & Park, 1995).

Impact of Negative Information

Suppose that during the course of gathering information about your prospective company, you learned one or two negative pieces of information. For example, one disgruntled employee, about to be let go for poor performance, may question why you would ever want to work at this place. Chances are, you would attach some significance to this observation, perhaps more than it was worth. This is a common finding in research on judgments and decisions.

Negative information attracts more attention than does positive information (Pratto & John, 1991). Consequently, negative information is weighted more heavily than are positive aspects when judgments are made (Coovert & Reeder, 1990). In studies of all kinds, ranging from forming impressions about other people to evaluating positive and negative information in order to reach a decision or judgment, negative information figures more prominently (Taylor, 1991).

Integrating Information

The next task in the inference process involves bringing information together and combining it into a social judgment. When people's integrative capabilities are compared with rational models, it appears that the human judgment process is rather haphazard and does not closely follow the principles of a rational model.

Consider the example of college admissions. When there are many applicants and only a few openings, criteria must be developed for deciding which people to admit and which to reject. Most college admissions departments have a formula for admitting students that dictates how heavily to weight SAT scores, high school grades, letters of recommendation, the personal essay, and other sources of information. With such clear standards available, one would assume that the college admissions decision makers do a good job of using this formula to determine who will be admitted and who will not. However, studies show that when there are clear standards for combining information into a judgment, computers typically outperform human decision makers (Dawes, Faust, & Meehl, 1989).

Why is this true? Human decision makers have great faith in their abilities to make decisions. When asked what procedures they use to make decisions, they

Decision making often involves collecting and integrating complex information. People typically think they are more consistent, use more information, and make more complex judgments than is actually the case.

typically report that they are more consistent, use more information, and make more complex judgments than they actually do. The reason that computers typically outperform human judges is that the computer consistently uses criteria established by people, weights information in a standard way, combines the information according to the formula, and reaches a judgment. Human decision makers, in contrast, may be swayed by pet theories or stereotypes that influence the information they select.

Imagine how this process might work after your job interview. A small group of individuals who met you during your visit is assigned the task of deciding whether to hire you. Each person has only a modest amount of information about you. One person points out that you seemed nervous under pressure, as evidenced by the fact that you dropped your roll on the floor during lunch. Another, however, argues that you could be a potential Mark Comet, given that you both have competitive tennis in your background. Another points out that your college transcript shows you have high grades in virtually every subject, suggesting great ability. The next person, however, complains that although you did well in everything, you have not shown any special talents. In short, then, each evaluator may have certain idiosyncratic ways of viewing the information derived from your brief visit that he or she considers relevant to the overall judgment of whether you should be hired. It is indeed unnerving to realize one's fate often depends on this type of decision-making process.

Judgments of Covariation

In addition to putting information together to form coherent impressions of people and events, we are also concerned about figuring out what goes with what in social life. Many of our beliefs involve statements about the relationship between things. For example, the adage "All work and no play makes Jack a dull boy" implies that working too hard and being dull are related and that playing and not being dull go together. Similarly, the statement "Blonds have more fun" implies a relationship between being blond and having fun and between not being blond and having less fun. Technically, such ideas about the associations between things are called judgments of **covariation**.

Covariation

Judgments of how strongly two things are related.

In making judgments about covariation, people are prone to certain errors. Specifically, they tend to see things as going together when they think they ought to go together or when they share features that make them seem similar. Thus, when a relationship between two variables is expected, a person is likely to overestimate how closely related those two things are or impose a relationship when none exists. This process is called **illusory correlation**.

Illusory Correlation

The mistaken belief that two things are related to each other because they seem to go together.

Illusory Correlation. Several factors can produce an illusory correlation (Klauer & Meiser, 2000). The first is associative meaning, in which two items are seen as belonging together because they "ought" to be, on the basis of prior expectations. Thus, members of minority groups are often seen as having attributes stereotypically associated with their group because of their membership, when, in fact, any given individual in the group may not exhibit the stereotypical behavior or may contradict it (Hamilton & Gifford, 1976). A second basis of illusory correlation is paired distinctiveness, in which two items are thought to go together because they share some unusual feature. For example, distinctive social groups, such as religious groups that dress differently, are especially likely to evoke distinctive, novel stereotypes (Mullen & Johnson, 1995), and social groups that do not appear to be any different from the people around them may be erroneously assumed to have less extreme attributes (Sanbonmatsu, Shavitt, & Gibson, 1994). Illusory correlations, then, can substitute for real correlations when people have expectations or theories about whether two factors go together.

Framing Effects

How decision alternatives are framed, that is, the terms in which they are cast, often strongly influences people's judgments. For example, if someone you admire tells you that a particular summer job will "be a great opportunity," you are likely to be disposed favorably toward the job even before you know what it is. In contrast, if someone tells you that "at least it's a job," you are likely to approach the position with some dread, feeling that at least it will pay the bills but it probably won't be very exciting.

Framing effects are well established in social cognition. One of the most common and influential ones is whether a decision is presented in terms of the gains it will create or the losses that might be incurred (Kahneman & Tversky, 1982). For example, research generally suggests that people become very cautious when alternatives are phrased in terms of their risks, but they are far more likely to take chances when the alternatives are framed in terms of gains (e.g., Roney, Higgins, & Shah, 1995). Consider the following example:

> Imagine the United States is preparing for the outbreak of an unusual Asian disease, which is expected to kill 600 people. Two alternative programs to combat the disease have been proposed. Assume that the exact scientific estimate of the consequences of the program is as follows: If Program A is adopted, 200 people will be saved. If Program B is adopted, there is a one-third probability that 600 people will be saved, and a two-thirds probability that no people would be saved. Which program would you favor?
>
> Now imagine the same situation with these two alternatives: If Program C is adopted, 400 people will die. If Program D is adopted, there is a one-third probability that no one will die, and a two-thirds probability that 600 people will die. (Based on Tversky & Kahneman, 1982)

Tversky and Kahneman (1982) presented these problems to college students. When the problem was framed in terms of lives saved, 72 percent of the participants chose Program A. However, when the program was phrased in terms of lives lost, 78 percent favored Program D, and only 22 percent favored Program C, which has the same outcome as Program A!

This result, that people are more risk-averse when decision alternatives are framed in terms of losses, has been found in many studies, and the implications are important. Such findings may affect how health warnings and information about other risks (e.g., the benefits of sunscreen use) should be presented and may illuminate systematic biases in the everyday decisions people make (Rothman & Salovey, 1997).

EMOTION AND INFERENCE

Many of the errors and biases we consider share an important feature. They represent evaluative beliefs. Often we form an emotional commitment to a particular theory or belief that overrides the information as we see it. We think we've done well on a job interview because we want the job so badly, for example. You might therefore assume that emotion is a process that derails cognition in the search for accuracy. In certain respects, you would be correct. However, emotion is also a vital part of decision making, and when people ignore their emotions they may make decisions that work against their interest. We pick our partners, our jobs, even our college on the basis of the emotional cues we get from the decision-making context. At one time, emotion was cast as the nemesis of cognition. The belief was that when people made decisions on the basis of their emotions, almost inevitably the result would be biased. But increasingly researchers are realizing that emotion and cognition are integrated and often work together (Gray, 2004). For example, emotions may provide useful information when people are trying to decide between two seemingly valid courses of action. Emotions can provide a warning when a risky decision seems attractive but is accompanied by a gnawing sense of dread (Gray, 2004). This is not to say that our emotions are always on target. Like cognitions, emotions can lead us astray, but the role that emotions play in all forms of social cognition is becoming more evident, as the next sections suggest.

Mood and Inference

Perhaps you have noticed that when you get a good grade on a test, you're nicer to your roommate, or that when you've had a nice time with your girlfriend or boyfriend, you're more likely to help someone who needs it. Or perhaps you've noticed that when you're feeling anxious, all of your activities seem more risky. These examples illustrate some of the effects that mood has on inference and behavior (Murphy & Zajonc, 1993).

How have psychologists uncovered the effects of mood on people's beliefs and behavior? Like Peter Pan teaching the Darling children how to fly, psychologists lead people to think happy thoughts by surprising them with an unexpected gift, inducing them to concentrate on happy experiences ("Think of Christmas, think of snow."), asking them to recall a time in the past when they were very happy or having them read a series of statements that suggest a progressively happier state of mind. Before very long, people exposed to these techniques report that they feel more cheerful, even euphoric. Alternatively, psychologists can make people unhappy by getting them to think about times in the past when they were sad or having them read a series of statements that produce a progressively negative mood. But negative moods are harder to induce than positive moods, and once in them, people are more likely to try to escape negative moods (e.g., Tykocinski, 2001).

What is the effect of mood on behavior? When we are in a good mood, we tend to be more sociable and more altruistic in our behavior. We spend more time with others and help others more, for example. What happens when we're in a bad mood? You might think that people in a bad mood would be more withdrawn and help other people less, and sometimes this is true. But often people who are in a bad mood want to escape that bad mood, and so instead of acting in a way that is consistent with their bad mood, they try to work themselves out of it by being sociable, by helping others, or by engaging in other positive actions.

But aren't these effects short lasting? After all, mood changes quickly (Forgas & Ciarrochi, 2002). Although mood may be short lasting, its effects can be long term. A bad mood, or even just the stress of the day, can lead people to make decisions with short-term benefits but with long-term adverse effects (Gray, 1999), and so the effects of mood on immediate judgments can have important effects.

Mood also influences memory. Perhaps you have had the experience of receiving a piece of good news and then finding yourself remembering other past experiences of being happy, feeling good, or feeling competent. In many circumstances, people remember material whose valence fits their current mood state

Mood-Congruent Memory

The tendency for people to remember material whose valence fits their current mood state.

(Fiedler, Nickel, Muehlfriedel, & Unkelbach, 2001). This effect is called **mood-congruent memory**. People tend to recall positive material when they're in a positive mood. Does mood-congruent memory work for negative moods as well? Sometimes people recall more negative material when they're in a negative mood. This seems to be especially true of people who are depressed (Lyubomirsky, Caldwell, & Nolen-Hoeksema, 1998). But remember that the effects of negative mood are more variable; sometimes people in a negative mood think of positive things, in part so they can work themselves out of the bad mood (Rusting & DeHart, 2000).

Mood also affects judgments. Cheerful people like just about everything better than do people who are not in a good mood: themselves, their health, their cars, other people, the future, and even politics (see Fiske & Taylor, 1991, for a review). Do unhappy people dislike everything? Again, the evidence is mixed. Sometimes unhappy people make negative judgments about others; other times they do not. Negative mood has a less reliable impact on judgments than does positive mood. Mood also influences the predictions people make about the future (DeSteno, Petty, Wegener, & Rucker, 2000). People who are depressed tend to be accurate in making pessimistic predictions but relatively off base in predicting positive events. The opposite is true of people who are more optimistic (Shrauger, Mariano, & Walter, 1998).

However, mood influences perceptions of risk as well. People in a negative mood make more pessimistic estimates about likely future events than people in a good mood. However, which negative mood a person is in matters as well. Whereas fearful people make risk-averse choices and express pessimism about risk, angry people express more optimistic risk estimates and make risk-seeking choices, rather like happy people. The reasons seem to be that anger and happiness share a sense of being in control and having confidence in one's assessments, whereas fearful people do not feel either certain or in control of events around them (Lerner & Keltner, 2001).

Mood influences not only our judgments, what we remember, and how we evaluate our world, but also how we make judgments. Happy people are expansive, inclusive, and impulsive in their decision making. They make decisions quickly, they work quickly at simple tasks, they make more unusual connections among the things they are thinking about, they have looser and less organized associations, they group more varied things together into the same category, and they think in a more stereotyped fashion (Isen, 1987; Park & Banaji, 2000). A negative mood seems to slow down the processing of information: People are more methodical and precise, they make decisions more slowly, they make more complex causal attributions, and they work more slowly (Ruder & Bless, 2003; Tiedens & Linton, 2001). But this style does not appear to pay off in terms of accuracy. In fact, a sad mood may actually impair accuracy because it promotes a more deliberate information-processing style (Ambady & Gray, 2002).

People who are chronically in a good or poor mood also make decisions differently. For example, extroverted people are especially influenced by positive information, whereas people who are high in neuroticism are more responsive to negative information (Zalenski & Larsen, 2002). People who are more extroverted, outgoing, or positive in their behavior also show trait-consistent mood effects, such that they are faster to link events to their personal qualities if they are in a positive mood state. Introverts, on the other hand, are faster to do so in a negative or neutral mood state (Tamir, Robinson, & Clore, 2002).

Our judgments and emotional reactions to situations are also heavily determined by our emotional expectations. According to the affective expectation model (AEM) (Wilson, Lisle, Kraft, & Wetzel, 1989), people's beliefs about how they will feel are as important in determining their reactions as are the experiences they actually have. For example, how much you think you will like a particular movie may affect how much you like it as much as the actual experience of the movie itself. Basically, people form affective expectations about how they will feel, and when asked afterward how they feel, they refer back to their expectations to see whether their actual experience matched them. What happens if an experience doesn't match your expectations? The answer depends on whether you notice the discrepancy. After you've seen a movie and it turns out not to be as good as what you expected, if you notice that fact, you may see the movie as worse than it was ("Not his best work."). But if you do not think about the fact that the experience was discrepant from your expectations, you may assimilate your experience to your previous expectation ("I knew it would be wonderful!") (Geers & Lassiter, 2002).

What, then, might be the effect of your mood on extracting and processing information from your job interview? If you were in a good mood at the time you visited the prospective workplace, you would probably pay disproportionate attention to all the positive features of the job and work environment. If you were in a bad mood, however, you might focus more on the apparent disadvantages of the position. Later, when you had to make a decision about the job, if you were in a good mood you might make the decision quite impulsively based on the positive features of the experience. On the other hand, if you were in a bad mood you might survey your impressions more methodically and even become quite bogged down in making the decision. In short, affective factors such as mood can influence judgments and decision making in important ways.

Automatic Evaluation

In recent years, social psychologists have provided compelling evidence that many social cognition processes occur virtually automatically and without awareness (Bargh, 1997; Greenwald & Banaji, 1995). Essentially, the years of practice we have had responding to positive and negative cues in the environment have made our emotional, our cognitive, and even our behavioral responses to many situations automatic (Aarts & Dijksterhuis, 2003). We respond to these evaluative cues without needing to attend to them or think about them (Rosner & Gazzaniga, 2004).

In a study that shows these automatic associations, John Bargh and his associates gave students word puzzles to solve very much like that shown in Figure 3–1. Students were told to circle any words that they saw in the puzzle. For some of the students, the words embedded in the figure related to aging and included such terms as "elderly," "slow," and "aged" (as is true in Figure 3–1). For others, the words were related to neutral topics ("corn" and "classroom"). Bargh and his associates reasoned that for those students who received the word puzzle with the aging-related clues, the stereotype of the elderly would be automatically primed in such a way that it would effect future thoughts and behaviors. The results bore out this hypothesis. When leaving the experiment, those participants who had been primed with the stereotype of the elderly walked more slowly than did the participants who had not been so primed (Bargh, Chen, & Burrows, 1996).

This automatic evaluation can occur very rapidly (Sohlberg & Birgegard, 2003). In one study, Fazio, Sanbonmatsu, Powell, and Kardes (1986) presented participants with a series of word-pair sequences and asked them to judge whether the target adjectives were negative or positive. The first word, a prime, appeared

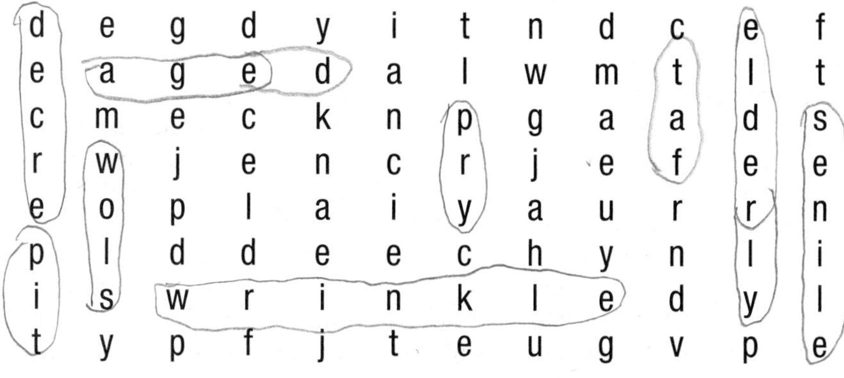

Figure 3–1 **Word Puzzle.**

See how many words you can find in this word puzzle. What do those words suggest? Puzzles like these have been used to prime concepts automatically, in this case a stereotype of the elderly.

Source: After Bargh, Chen, and Burroughs (1996).

for 200 milliseconds and the second, the target, appeared 100 milliseconds after the prime had disappeared. Despite the very rapid speed at which this task had to be accomplished, participants' rating of the target word as positive or negative was much faster when the prime and target had the same evaluative content (both were negative or both were positive) than when they were incongruent.

Such evidence clearly shows that evaluation is one of the most rapid and fundamental judgments that we make that guides our processing of subsequent information. Automatic evaluation seems to come from the fact that evaluatively tinged stimuli are easily and quickly noticed and prompt the behavioral tendencies of approach or avoidance (Chen & Bargh, 1999; Wentura, Rothermund, & Bak, 2000). In essence, these early and rapid judgments set the stage for the actions we will take.

Identifying a situation as good or bad arouses an action tendency to approach or avoid a situation or stimulus. In one study (Chen & Bargh, 1999) that showed this, participants responded to attitude statements either by pulling a lever toward them or by pushing it away from them. Consistent with the hypothesis, participants were faster to respond to negatively valenced words when they pushed the lever away from them (avoided it) than when they pulled it toward them (approached it) (see also Neumann & Strack, 2000).

Another example of this automatic evaluation-to-behavior link is the fact that people often nonconsciously mimic postures, mannerisms, and facial expressions of the people they interact with. If you doubt this, you can try an experiment. Smile at the person you are speaking to and see if your smile isn't reciprocated; then rest your hands on your hips and see if your partner doesn't mirror your behavior; then scratch your head and smooth your hair and see if your partner doesn't move his or her hand in that direction. This nonconscious mimicry is very common in social interaction, and it is a good example of the direct effect of the perception of other people's behaviors on our own behavior, usually without any awareness or intention on our part (Chartrand & Bargh, 1999).

How would you regard this scene if you were the girl's father? The boy's ex-girlfriend? The person who had arranged the first date between these two? The interpretations we make and the affect we experience are heavily determined by the motives we bring to social situations.

Goals can also influence behavior automatically (Bargh, Gollwitzer, Lee-Chai, Barndollar, & Trotschel, 2001). Some of these goals may be chronic concerns, whereas others may be primed by the situation. Goal-related cues can lead to virtually automatic reactions in some cases (Levesque & Pelletier, 2003). For example, a habit may be thought of, in part, as an association between a goal and an action so that if a goal is primed, the action will occur automatically. Perhaps you've had the experience of thinking about something you need to do at school and discovering that you are now driving in that direction, even though you were headed elsewhere. Or perhaps you made late dinner plans with friends and found yourself accidentally cooking dinner at your usual time. Habits do indeed seem to be a result of goal-dependent automatic behavior (Aarts & Dijksterhuis, 2000; Wood, Quinn, & Kashy, 2002). The fact that many of our emotions, thoughts, and actions occur as automatic responses to cues that are rapidly, effortlessly, and unconsciously processed is a very important insight from social cognition research. It helps to explain how human beings accomplish the vast amount of information processing that they seem to do so effortlessly. And it helps us understand why so often we are the creatures of our own habits.

Motivation and Inference

The particular content of one's motivation also influences inferences. How we process and put information together can be heavily influenced by the inferences we want to make. People often generate and evaluate information in a self-serving manner, constructing theories that are consistent with the belief that good things will happen to them and bad things will not (Dunning, Leuenberger, & Sherman, 1995; Kunda, 1987). For example, on learning that the divorce rate for first marriages is 50 percent, most people predict that they will not fall within that 50 percent group and will remain married to their spouse for life. They convince themselves that this is the case by highlighting their personal attributes that might be associated with a stable marriage and downplaying the significance of or actively refuting information that might suggest a vulnerability to divorce. Thus, for example, one might point to one's parents' enduring marriage, the close family life that existed in one's early childhood, and the fact that one's high school relationship lasted a full 4 years as evidence for a likely stable marriage. The fact that one's husband has already been divorced once, a factor that predicts a second divorce, might be interpreted not only as not leading to divorce in one's own case but as a protective factor ("He does not want this marriage to fail like the last one, so he's working especially hard to keep our relationship strong.").

When we are motivated to make a good decision or to reach a careful inference, do we do a better job or a worse job than if the inference matters less to us? Pelham and Neter (1995) undertook several studies to address this intriguing question. They manipulated motivation in several ways, including a financial incentive to be accurate, personal accountability for the decision made, and personal involvement in the decision. In the three separate studies, they found that higher levels of motivation increased the accuracy of judgments when those judgments were easy to make but decreased judgmental accuracy in the case of difficult judgments. Thus, a desire to be accurate does not necessarily translate into reality.

Another motivational factor that may influence the nature of social inference concerns one's assessment of one's knowledgeability or expertise in a particular area. If we consider ourselves to be experts on a topic, are we? And does that expertise actually translate into better judgments? For example, if you believe yourself to be very knowledgeable about cars, will that information translate into better or worse information gathering when you go to purchase one? Radecki and Jaccard (1995) found that people know less than they think and that their incorrect beliefs about their level of knowledge can actually hurt them. They found that people who perceived themselves to be knowledgeable gathered less information, with the result that they made poorer decisions. The Research Highlight captures another all-too-familiar example of motivated inference.

Suppressing Thoughts and Emotions

As the previous discussion has implied, we often try to regulate our emotions by engaging in a behavior that might restore a good mood, by reinterpreting the negative circumstances, or in some cases by simply trying to suppress emotion-laden thoughts. Perhaps you've tried to forget about an exam you took that you didn't think you did very well on, and despite your efforts, you kept thinking about the test. You are not alone. Suppressing one's thoughts is difficult, and many of these efforts not only fail but also may actually produce a rebound effect (Förster & Liberman, 2001; Wegner, 1994). Many people find themselves thinking about exactly what they're trying to forget.

Emotions guide the information we seek out and how we process it. What emotions do you think these women are experiencing as they are recalling the events pictured in the scrapbook?.

Theoretical accounts of this process suggest that when you are trying to suppress a thought, you are simultaneously trying to find things to distract yourself and also automatically monitoring the environment for cues you might have to suppress. This is why, despite your best efforts, you may find yourself thinking about exactly what you're trying to forget. For example, a stray remark about applying to graduate school by a friend might remind you about the test you just took (e.g., Liberman & Förster, 2000).

There are costs to this suppression (Richards & Gross, 2000). Trying to suppress an emotional response to an event involves a lot of effort, and as a result, not only do people find it hard to suppress these feelings, but also their physiological processes are affected and they are more aroused (Harris, 2001). Even the immune system may be influenced adversely when people are actively trying to avoid thinking about the difficult aspects of their lives (Petrie, Booth, & Pennebaker, 1998). Research suggests that suppression can become a chronic way of dealing with negative aspects of life.

What is the alternative to suppressing negative events? Many people try to reappraise negative experiences instead of suppressing them. Which strategy is

"I'LL GET IT DONE BY FRIDAY": THE PLANNING FALLACY IN ACTION

How many times have you convinced yourself that you could complete a paper long before it was due, only to find yourself writing furiously the night before you have to turn it in? How many times have you promised yourself you would keep up with the course readings, only to find that you are going through chapters for the first time as you're studying for the course midterm? These experiences are familiar to most—perhaps all—college students, and they are examples of a well-established phenomenon called the **planning fallacy** (Buehler, Griffin, & MacDonald, 1997).

Planning Fallacy

Consistently overestimating how quickly and easily one can achieve a goal.

The planning fallacy refers to the fact that people consistently overestimate how quickly and easily they will achieve a goal and underestimate the amount of time or effort that will be required to reach that goal. In a study that examined the planning fallacy (Buehler, Griffin, & Ross, 1994), college students were asked to list an academic project that had to be completed within the next week and to estimate when they intended to begin the project, when they expected to complete the project, and how many hours they expected to put into it. A week later, the students were asked if they had completed the project and when. Although all the students had estimated that they would complete the project comfortably in the time indicated, 1 week later more than half the projects remained uncompleted. Those that had been completed had typically taken, on average, nearly 5 days longer than had been estimated. So much for planning!

If our best-laid plans do not guide our behavior, what does? If you think back to when you typically complete a paper or project, you will realize that often the answer is "Right before it is due." Deadlines have a major impact on whether people complete projects and when they do so. Surprisingly, most of us are unaware of the effect of deadlines. When participants in the studies by Buehler and colleagues (1994) were asked about the factors that influenced when they completed their projects, most were oblivious of the role that deadlines had played. Yet well over two thirds of the participants finished their projects the day or night before they were due.

better? On the whole, reappraisers experience more positive emotions, get along better with other people, and have better well-being, whereas suppressors experience more negative emotions (despite their efforts to suppress them), get along more poorly with others, and have lower well-being (Gross & John, 2003).

Affective Forecasting

Imagine that the dean of your university has called you, personally congratulated you on the grades you have achieved, and told you that you will have a scholarship for the remainder of your academic career. How would you feel, and how long would you feel that way? Most people are good at inferring how they would feel—elated and thrilled, for example—but they are typically rather poor at estimating how long they will feel that way. This bias gets in the way of a common phenomenon called "affective forecasting."

Affective forecasting refers to the ways in which we use our emotions to make decisions about the future. Generally speaking, people believe that their emotional reactions to events will be more intense and last longer than is actually the case. In most cases, we do not respond emotionally to an event as strongly as we thought we would (Gilbert & Wilson, 2000). We see our affective responses as more durable than they actually turn out to be. This seems to occur in large part because we overestimate the impact of one event on our future thinking and emotions ("I'll be so happy if the Lakers win this year.") and fail to realize how much our future thoughts and feelings will be influenced by other intervening events (Buehler & McFarland, 2001; Gilbert & Ebert, 2002; Wilson, Wheatley, Meyers, Gilbert, & Axsom, 2000).

When people learn that their beliefs about how long their emotional reactions will persist are wrong, do they learn from experience? Do they come to realize that most emotional reactions are short lived? It depends, in part, on whether the events are positive or negative. Most of us persist in believing that positive events will make us happy for a long time, but we are somewhat relieved to find out that negative events will not distress us as long as we think they will. On the whole though, the degree to which people learn from their affective forecasting errors appears to be fairly minimal (Wilson, Myers, & Gilbert, 2001).

Inference: A Summing Up

Overall, how well does the social perceiver fare on tasks of social inference? The evidence we have considered suggests that when evaluated against appropriate standards, social inference suffers from some predictable errors and biases (Fiske & Taylor, 1991) as shown in Figure 3–2. This evaluation prompts at least two reactions. The first is concern over the disconcerting ways in which social perceivers let their prior expectations override and ignore relevant information. The second reaction is puzzlement. How do people manage in their social lives as well as they seem to if their social judgments are biased?

One answer to this question is that many of the rational models that psychologists expect people to use are very difficult to employ on a daily basis. Moreover, much of our social information is unreliable, biased, and incomplete, and it may not be presented to the average person in a way that is clear or usable. The conditions that maximize accuracy seldom occur in real life, and accordingly, in many situations, social perceivers could not apply a rational model even if they were so inclined.

Perhaps most significant is the fact that it is often more important for people to be efficient—that is, to process information quickly—than to be 100 percent accurate. Consider the sheer volume of information that an individual encounters in a particular day. Even an act as simple as crossing the street requires watching the lights and signs, the flow of the traffic, and the pedestrians on one's own side and the other side of the street. If people truly had to make all their inferences

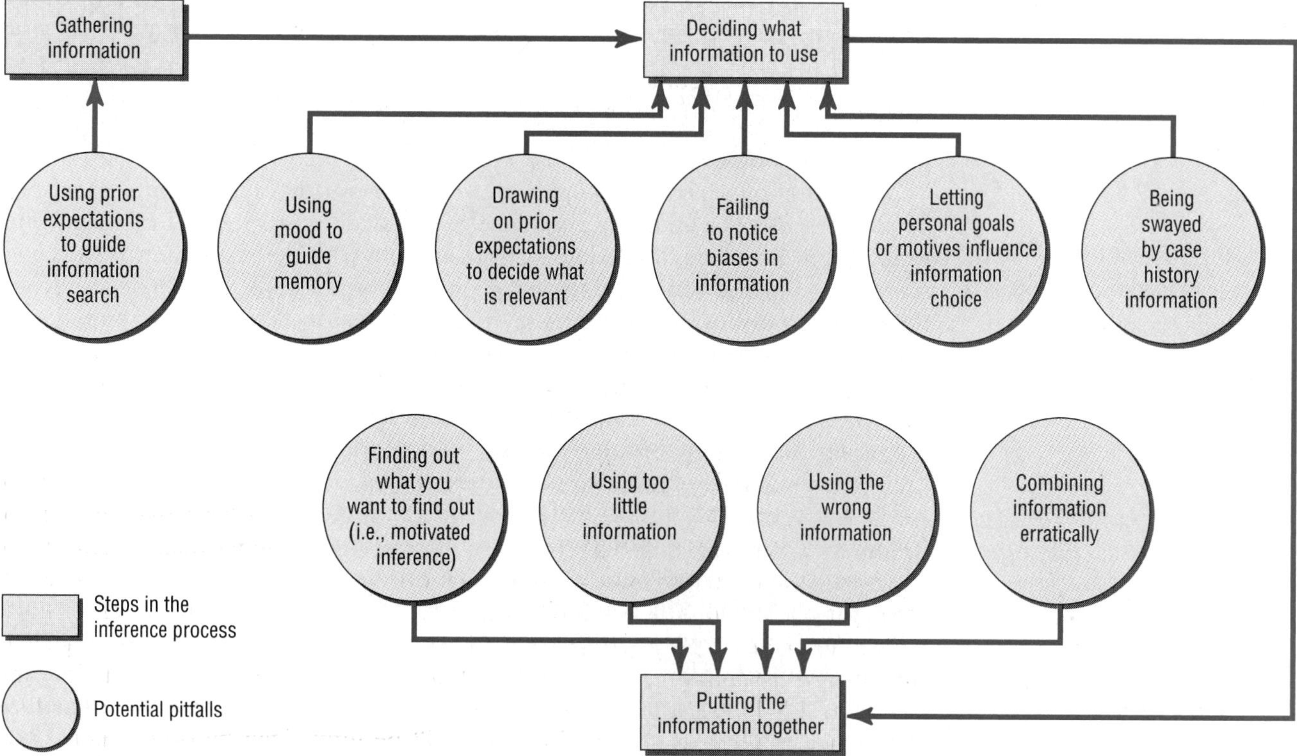

Figure 3–2 **Social Inference and Its Pitfalls.**

using rational models of inference, they might still be plotting a course to follow across the street when the light changed back to "Don't walk." In other words, careful, complex, and rational decisions require time, and given the busy, stressful nature of the real world, time is a very expensive commodity.

Consequently, people draw on their preexisting conceptions of people and situations and use inferential shortcuts to make social judgments quickly and efficiently. This is not to say that the errors we have just documented in the social inference process are inconsequential. Indeed, they can often have problematic consequences. Moreover, people are not very good at discriminating their poor and biased evaluations from their good ones, nor do they respond with the vigilance one might expect when they are warned that their inferences may be biased (Stapel, Martin, & Schwarz, 1998). Training people in appropriate reasoning strategies can therefore be essential, leading people to make better inferences (Bushman & Wells, 2001). Improving the inference process, then, is an important priority for social cognition researchers. But it must be done in the context of understanding the processes people typically use.

To understand how the social perceiver actually forms inferences requires an important observation. The act of bringing information together and solving a problem, as we have noted, can be a time-consuming task involving substantial processing capabilities. However, memory seems to have an almost limitless capacity. Think, for example, of the number of popular songs to which you know all the lyrics. The number may total in the hundreds or even thousands. This important difference is fundamental to how people actually make inferences. Rather than engaging in elaborate and often time-consuming problem solving for each individual task the environment presents, people often draw on the knowledge they have stored in memory to interpret the environment that confronts them, namely, their schemas. This process is accomplished quickly, efficiently, and often automatically, that is, without intention or awareness. It draws on the schemas we hold for people, situations, and events.

SCHEMAS

Schema

An organized system or structure of cognitions about a person, group, place, or things.

Scripts

A schema that describes the expected sequence of events in a well-known situation, such as going to a restaurant.

As we saw in Chapter 2, a **schema** is an organized, structured set of cognitions about some concept or stimulus. It includes knowledge about the concept or stimulus, relations among the various cognitions about it, and specific examples (Fiske & Taylor, 1991). Schemas can be about particular people, social roles, or the self; attitudes about particular objects; stereotypes about groups; or perceptions of common events.

Schemas about extremely common events are usually called **scripts** (Abelson, 1976). A script is a standard sequence of behavior over a period of time. One script might be called "ordering for a group in a Chinese restaurant." Everyone sits down, and the waiter brings the menus. Several people talk at once, giving their favorite dishes, while others say they never know what to have and would someone else just please decide. Then people go through the menu section by section, haggling over which soup to have, bargaining away their favorite beef dish (which no one else wants) for sweet and sour pork (which at least one ally does), and finally appointing the most self-confident and brash person to communicate the whole negotiated package to the waiter.

We could generate similar scripts for other ritualized series of events, such as having a baby, taking a shower, taking a final exam, or playing a basketball game. The essence of a script is in its boundedness in time, its causal flow (early events cause later ones), and its being a simple, coherent perceptual unit.

Schemas and scripts are important because people draw on them to interpret the environment. That is, each time we are confronted with a new situation, instead of trying to understand it afresh, we draw on our stored knowledge of similar past situations. In this way schemas help us to process information. They help us to recognize what aspects of a situation or stimulus are important. They add structure and organization to information. Schemas enable us to remember

People have scripts for common, organized sequences of behavior, such as ordering food in a restaurant or paying for a purchase in a store. These scripts help us anticipate what will happen next and to prepare our behavior accordingly.

information better, to organize details, and to process information relevant to the schema very quickly. Schemas can sometimes fill in gaps and knowledge as well as help us interpret and evaluate new information.

Exemplar

An example of a category that embodies the significant attributes or ideal of the category.

Organization of Schemas

An important feature of schemas is that they often have some hierarchical organization. They have some abstract and general elements and some more concrete, specific ones that are linked to each other. Suppose we had a schema of a party. We know that parties are usually held in the late afternoon or evening, usually in someone's home. They have guests and usually a host or hostess; they might have some food and some alcoholic drinks. Normally people interact by standing and talking to each other rather than by watching one common event (such as a singer). In short, we have in our minds a clear, well-developed, somewhat abstract picture of a party. It has a standard sequence—a number of elements with clear causal interrelationships.

At a more specific level, the schema might well have different categories of parties, all of which would be clearly distinct. For example, a wine-and-cheese party held at the opening of an art exhibition would be clearly different from the weekly Saturday night bashes at the country club, where all the local businesspeople and their spouses get together and drink too much, or from a formal diplomatic reception at a foreign embassy. At a still more specific level, our schema might include several specific parties we have attended, especially if those parties had some distinctive or memorable event, such as the hostess being thrown into the pool by her guests. All told, we might have a hierarchical schema of a party that would include a general, abstract concept covering all kinds of parties we have gone to.

Many schemas contain **exemplars**, which are the most common or best examples of a schema. For example, your schema of "bird" probably includes being small, feathered, and mottled brown in color, with a long tail and little clawed feet. But the exemplar or best example of the category may be a robin or a blue jay (Smith & Medin, 1981). Exemplars need not correspond to all the schema's typical features and may, in fact, be rather different from those typical features, like the robin and the blue jay.

Our discussion of schemas makes them sound very orderly. However, the associations contained within a schema often more closely resemble a tangled web than

An exemplar is a model example of a category. Michael Jordan is an exemplar of the category, "basketball star."

a hierarchy (Cantor & Kihlstrom, 1987). For example, a politician, a con man, and a clown are all examples of extroverts. Being socially skilled is associated with each of them, yet being self-confident is associated with being a politician, or a con man, but not necessarily with being a clown. Thus, the more specific attributes embedded in a schema (socially skilled and self-confident) may overlap with many or few of the upper level concepts (politician, clown, and con man) (Andersen & Klatsky, 1987). Social categories, then, are very flexible and complex, and not always neat, tidy, and hierarchical.

SCHEMATIC PROCESSING

Advantages

Schemas and Information Processing. Schemas are important because they help us process an enormous amount of information swiftly and economically. Indeed, schemas make processing more efficient in several different ways. They help us remember and interpret new information, draw inferences from it, and evaluate whether we agree with it. They help us fill in gaps in our knowledge by suggesting what is likely to be true. They help us to perceive and label information that is either consistent or inconsistent with the schema (Sherman, Lee, Bessenoff, & Frost, 1998). And they help us prepare for the future by structuring our expectations about what is likely to happen. These advantages of schematic processing have been demonstrated in a wide variety of studies.

Schemas Aid Recall. Memory often works best when we have a schematic representation of past events or people, because the schema will bring many details along with it (Hirt, 1990). For example, Cohen (1981) presented participants with a videotape of a woman and her husband sitting in their home. Half were told that the woman was a librarian; and half, that she was a waitress. Some of the features of the woman fit the schema of a librarian (as measured separately), such as wearing glasses, eating salad, drinking wine, and playing the piano. Others fit the schema of a waitress, such as having a bowling ball in the room, having no bookshelves in the room, and eating a chocolate birthday cake. Later the participants were asked to recall the details of the videotape. They remembered the schema-consistent details better, whether recall was assessed immediately or a week later (see also Corneille, Huart, Becquart, & Bredart, 2004).

But schema-inconsistent material is not always recalled poorly. Both schema-consistent material and schema-inconsistent material are remembered much better than items that are simply irrelevant to the schema (Brewer, Dull, & Lui, 1981; Hastie & Kumar, 1979), perhaps because it is difficult to learn material that is irrelevant to a schema.

Sometimes information that contradicts a schema is better recalled than information that is consistent with it, especially when a person has a very poorly developed or an extremely well-developed schema. People who are unfamiliar with a schema and attempt to learn it show an initial advantage in remembering schema-inconsistent information (Ruble & Stangor, 1986). Similarly, people who are highly familiar with a domain may more easily recognize inconsistencies. People with moderately well-formed schemas may be most attentive to consistent information (Higgins & Bargh, 1987). Consider, for example, the impressions that might be formed of Harry, a police officer who raises kittens and does needlepoint in his spare time. Those just meeting Harry and those who know him very well may be especially attentive to the schema-inconsistent behaviors, whereas those with a moderately well-developed conception of Harry may attend more to his schema-consistent behavior, such as his concern for abiding by the law or helping people in need.

Schemas Speed Up Processing. When people have a schema for a particular person or situation, it is easier for them to process information relevant to the schema. People who have watched a lot of soccer games, for example, simply see more and take in more information than do people who know relatively little about soccer.

But schemas do not always speed up processing. In some cases, having a well-developed schema slows things down by introducing a more complex mass of information that must be processed (Fiske & Taylor, 1991). For example, an experienced soccer fan may spend a lot of time commenting on a dubious foul call because he or she knows that players often fake injuries, that apparent fouls may represent inadvertent stumbles, and that soccer action looks very different from different angles. To a novice, however, the referee's foul call might be sufficient to process what is happening in the game.

Schemas Aid Automatic Inference. Schematic processing can occur almost automatically, without any conscious effort. For example, when meeting an especially friendly person, you may automatically attribute to him other characteristics associated with friendliness, such as kindness and warmth, and may be completely unaware that you have done so. These automatic effects are most likely to occur if the information in the environment strongly suggests a particular schema, or if the schema involves a person or life domain about which you have strong emotional concerns (Bargh, 1994).

Schemas Add Information. A schema can help us fill in missing information when there are gaps in our knowledge. If we read about a police officer but have no information about his or her clothing, we imagine him or her to be wearing a blue uniform. We assume a nurse will be warm and caring, and that a queen will be rather aloof and haughty. Missing information is filled in by schema-consistent details, even when we must invent them.

Exemplars of schemas are often used to fill in missing information (Sia, Lord, Blessum, Thomas, & Lepper, 1999). For example, if "blue jay" is your exemplar, or best example, of the category "birds," then on briefly glimpsing some new bird, you may assume that the bird has a crest because the blue jay has a crest. If the exemplar of your category for birds is "robin," however, you might be less likely to assume that the new bird has a crest.

Schemas Aid Interpretation. Because schemas tell you how information in a particular domain relates to other information relevant to that domain, they help you interpret ambiguous situations. For example, a pediatrician diagnosing a child as having mumps can make a whole series of other inferences with confidence: how the child got the disease, what symptoms should be present, what the course of the disease will be, and what treatment is best. For a person with no schema for mumps, none of this would be possible. Schemas allow confident inferences about matters that would otherwise not be clear (Read & Cesa, 1991). This effect seems to occur more for strong schemas than for weak ones, however (Fiske & Neuberg, 1990).

Schemas Provide Expectations. Schemas also contain expectations for what should happen. These expectations, in turn, can determine how pleasant or unpleasant we find a particular situation. When experience matches expectations, the result may be pleasant, whereas violations of expectations are often experienced as unpleasant. Suppose a black student who had worked to educate himself was nonetheless unable to find a job at his level of expertise. This experience might violate his expectations and would likely make him quite angry. A sense of deprivation relative to expectation has been cited as one of the causes of riots and other forms of social rebellion (Sears & McConahay, 1973).

Schemas Contain Affect. Affect consists of the feelings we have about the content of the schema. Consequently, use of a particular schema can produce an emotional response, called "schema-driven affect." For example, most of us have a fairly well-developed schema for "politician." It may include information about what the politician does in his or her job and what kinds of people are attracted to being a politician. The schema also includes any affective responses we have to the concept of politician. For example, some of us feel positively about politicians, thinking of them as helpful lawmakers; others may feel negatively about politicians, thinking of them as sly, self-serving, and power hungry. When information in the environment fits a particular schema, it triggers the affect attached to that schema (Fiske & Neuberg, 1990). The affect triggered by a schema is an efficient affective processing device: One can say, "I know that type and I know how I feel about him or her."

In some circumstances, bringing a schema to bear on an object or an event can actually change the feelings one has toward that object or event. A series of studies by Tesser (see Millar & Tesser, 1986; Tesser & Conlee, 1975) suggest that simply thinking about something with a schema in mind can intensify the affect one feels for that person or object. For example, if you feel that a professor belittled the comments you made in class, then the longer you think about it the more upset you are likely to become. In other circumstances, however, schemas may make affect more complex, not more extreme (Linville, 1982; Linville & Jones, 1980). For example, if a good friend of yours snaps at you one day, this behavior may produce a fairly complex evaluation. You have so much information about your friend and about yourself that coming up with an explanation for this behavior may be difficult.

Liabilities of Schemas

All these advantages of schematic processing have their accompanying disadvantages, and many of them are precisely the errors and biases discussed at the beginning of this chapter. The tendencies to be overly accepting of information that fits a schema or theory, to fill in gaps in thinking by adding elements that do not belong but are schema consistent, to apply schemas even when they do not fit very well, and to be unwilling to change schemas are all potential liabilities. We can easily be misled by oversimplifications. Schematic processing has the advantage of speed and efficiency and of making events comprehensible and predictable; it has the disadvantage of leading to wrong interpretations, inaccurate expectations, and inflexible modes of response. There are so many familiar examples of the dangers of this kind of stereotyping that it hardly seems necessary to belabor the point. (We discuss these issues in somewhat more detail in Chapter 6.)

MENTAL SHORTCUTS: USING COGNITIVE HEURISTICS

As we've seen, efficiency pressures often lead people to fall back on their prior schemas or scripts for events to manage the rapid and complex flow of information in the social world. Still, we need a way to get from the information we see around us to the schemas. That is, we need to know which of these complex structures in long-term memory are appropriate for understanding any given social situation. This complex task is solved in part through the use of **heuristics** (Tversky & Kahneman, 1974).

Heuristic

A shortcut for problem solving that reduces complex or ambiguous information to more simple judgmental operations.

The Representativeness Heuristic

Is John, the new guy in your math class, really the incurable romantic he seems to be, or is he a cad who moves on every woman he meets? The act of identifying people or events as examples of particular schemas is fundamental to all social inference and behavior. The question "What is it?" must be answered before any other cognitive task can be performed. A mental shortcut called the "representativeness heuristic" provides a rapid method for accomplishing this task.

Basically, the representativeness heuristic matches information in the environment against schemas to determine the likelihood that the match is appropriate.

Consider the following description: "Steve is very shy and withdrawn, invariably helpful, but with little interest in people or the world of reality. A meek and tidy soul, he has a need for order and structure and a passion for detail" (Tversky & Kahneman, 1974). Suppose you are now asked to guess Steve's occupation. Is he a farmer, a circus clown, a librarian, a con artist, or a pediatrician? With adequate information about the number and characteristics of the people in these different occupations, one could conceivably estimate the likelihood of a meek clown and a shy con artist. This task, however, is likely to take a long time, and good information on which to form these judgments would undoubtedly be lacking. In such cases, the representativeness heuristic provides a quick solution. One decides whether Steve is representative of (or similar to) the average person in each of the occupational categories and makes one's judgment about his occupation accordingly. Students given this task usually guessed that Steve was a librarian because the description of Steve is representative of attributes that are stereotypically associated with librarians (Tversky & Kahneman, 1974).

The representativeness heuristic, then, helps one to decide if a particular person or event is an example of a particular schema. However, this quite rapid method of identifying people and events is occasionally fallible because people sometimes fail to take into account other important qualifying information. For example, if Steve lives in a town with lots of farmers and only one librarian, the likelihood that he is a farmer and not a librarian is very high. The representativeness heuristic would not incorporate this qualifying information. As we noted earlier, people often ignore relevant statistical information that they ought to incorporate into their inferences. In these kinds of circumstances then, use of the representativeness heuristic would probably produce an incorrect answer.

The Conjunction Error. The representativeness heuristic can also lead us to combine information that does not belong together, simply because the information seems as if it ought to go together. In one study, students were told that a fellow student was gregarious and literary. When asked how likely it was that he was an engineering major, they responded that it was very unlikely. However, when asked how likely it was that he would start out as an engineering major but switch to journalism, participants gave this possibility a much higher rating (Slovic, Fischhoff, & Lichtenstein, 1977). Presumably, they could readily imagine how a gregarious, literary person would decide journalism, and not engineering, was for him, but they could not imagine how such a person would remain an engineer. But note that the likelihood that any given student is an engineering major is much higher than the likelihood that a student beginning as an engineering major will switch to journalism. Thus, although starting out in engineering and switching to journalism seems more likely because journalism fits our ideas of what gregarious and literary people do, it is far less probable than the likelihood of staying in engineering. This error is called the **conjunction error**. It is an error because people believe the combination of two events (majoring in engineering and switching to journalism) is more likely than either of the events alone (majoring in engineering or majoring in journalism), which is incorrect reasoning (Gavanski & Roskos-Ewoldsen, 1991; see also Bar-Hillel & Neter, 1993).

Conjunction Error

Error that occurs when people believe that several events that seem to go together will co-occur.

The Availability Heuristic

How often does a person break a leg when skiing? How many college students are psychology majors? These are questions about the frequency of events or the likelihood that a particular event will happen. A common way that people answer such questions is to use examples that come to mind. If you can think of many college students who are psychology majors among your friends and acquaintances, you may assume that there are many psychology majors on campus. Or if you can think of several people who broke their legs in skiing accidents, you may assume that the chances of breaking your leg while skiing are rather high. Using the ease of remembering examples or the amount of information you can quickly remember as a guide to making an inference is called using the availability heuristic (Tversky & Kahneman, 1974).

As is the case with the representativeness heuristic, little cognitive work need be performed to accomplish this task. If you have no trouble thinking of psychology majors among your acquaintances, you will probably assume that a great many people in college are psychology majors; whereas if you have trouble bringing to mind examples of psychology majors, you may conclude that relatively few individuals are psychology majors (Rothman & Hardin, 1997).

In many circumstances, use of the availability heuristic produces correct answers. After all, when examples of something can be easily brought to mind, it is usually because there are lots of them. Therefore, availability is often a good estimate of frequency. However, biasing factors can increase or decrease the availability of some kinds of phenomena or events without altering their actual overall frequency. For example, if you are a psychology major, many of your friends and acquaintances are likely to be psychology majors as well, and consequently you will have relatively little difficulty bringing examples of psychology majors to mind. Because of this bias, you are likely to overestimate the frequency of psychology majors. In contrast, another student who is a chemistry major and who spends most of her time with chemists or physicists would probably underestimate the number of psychology majors because she cannot bring to mind examples of many psychology majors.

The availability heuristic, then, enables you to answer questions concerning quantity and frequency on the basis of how quickly or easily you can retrieve examples from memory. The ease with which the process can be accomplished or the volume of information that can be retrieved quickly determines the answer (e.g., MacLeod & Campbell, 1992; Manis, Shedler, Jonides, & Nelson, 1993).

The Simulation Heuristic

Suppose you borrowed your father's car during a college vacation and smashed it up after a party you attended. How would you answer the question "What is Dad going to think when he finds out I've smashed up the car?" You may think through what you know about your father and his reaction to crises, run through this information in your mind, and generate several possibilities. The ease with which particular endings come to mind is used to judge what is likely to happen. Your father could refuse to pay your college tuition next term or he could ignore the whole thing, but in your mind, it is easiest to imagine that he will strongly suggest that you find a job so that you can help pay for the car. This inferential technique is known as the "simulation heuristic" (Kahneman & Tversky, 1982).

The simulation heuristic may be used for a wide variety of tasks, including prediction ("What will Dad say?"), causality ("Was I driving badly or was the other guy driving badly?"; Mandel & Lehman, 1996), and affective responses (Kahneman & Miller, 1986). On this latter point, consider the situation of a near miss:

> Mr. Crane and Mr. Tees were scheduled to leave the airport on different flights, at the same time. They traveled from town in the same limousine, were caught in a traffic jam, and arrived at the airport 30 minutes after the scheduled departure time of their flights.
>
> Mr. Crane is told his flight left on time. Mr. Tees is told that his flight was delayed, and left just 5 minutes ago.
>
> Who is more upset: Mr. Crane or Mr. Tees? (Kahneman & Tversky, 1982, p. 203)

Virtually everyone says, "Mr. Tees." Why? Presumably, one can imagine no way that Mr. Crane could have made his plane, whereas were it not for that one long light or the slow baggage handler or the illegally parked car or the error in the posted departure gate, Mr. Tees would have made it. Thus, the simulation heuristic and its ability to generate "if only" conditions can be used to understand the psychology of near misses and the frustration, regret, grief, or indignation they may produce (Seta, McElory, & Seta, 2001). The contrast between the exceptional circumstance and the normal situation intensifies the emotional reaction to the unusual situation.

Counterfactual Reasoning. Abnormal or exceptional events lead people to imagine alternatives that are normal and consequently dissimilar to the actual outcome (Kahneman & Miller, 1986). This process is called **counterfactual reasoning**. For example, after you have done badly on a test, you may hold the counterfactual thought, "If only I had studied, I would have passed the test." As this example suggests, people are most likely to generate counterfactual thoughts when they have experienced unexpected or negative outcomes (Markman & Tetlock, 2000). When such an outcome is preceded by abnormal or unusual events, people are especially likely to undo the event mentally through counterfactual reasoning. For example, if the reason you failed to study was that you had to take your roommate to the hospital, you might be more likely to think "if only" than if you simply ran out of time.

Counterfactual Reasoning

Imagined alternative versions of actual events ("What if?").

When they construct their "if only" thoughts, people typically focus on only certain kinds of events or actions. They do not introduce unlikely antecedent events, called "uphill changes." Thus, for example, in thinking through how you might have studied more, the idea that the day could have been extended by 10 additional hours is not likely to occur to you, because it is an impossibility. On the other hand, you might think, "If only I had studied earlier" or "If only I hadn't had to take my roommate to the hospital." These changes are termed "downhill changes" because they delete unlikely antecedent events (e.g., the fact that your roommate had to be taken to the emergency room). For example, role-playing jurors deciding how much compensation an individual was entitled to after he was injured during a store robbery believed that he was entitled to more compensation when the store was presented as one in which he had never shopped before than when it was described as a routine stop for him (Miller & McFarland, 1986).

Why do people engage in counterfactual reasoning? Are they simply trying to make themselves miserable? After all, when something unexpected or negative takes place, imagining how it could have been otherwise is hardly going to change the situation. Research suggests that counterfactual thoughts about what might have been may serve any of several motives (Sanna, Chang, & Meier, 2001). First, in some circumstances, counterfactual thoughts may help people feel better. For example, when people have been through a stressful event, they often imagine how much worse it could have been (Taylor, Wood, & Lichtman, 1983). An automobile accident victim may focus less on the damage done to her car than on the fact that she could have been killed if the car had hit her driver's-side door. Imagining how much worse things could have been makes one feel better about the unpleasant situation that exists.

Counterfactual thoughts may also serve a preparatory function for the future. If you realize that your car battery wouldn't have died if you hadn't left the inside light on, you probably won't do that again. When imagining how easily you could have avoided the problem produces negative affect, the motivation to change and improve—an emotional wake-up call—is increased (McMullen & Markman, 2000). And when there isn't anything we can do mentally to change the outcome or prepare for the future, we embrace a counterfactual explanation that puts us in the best light ("I could have really bombed the test. At least, I studied a little.") (Tetlock, 1998). Not surprisingly, this tendency to come up with self-enhancing counterfactual thoughts is particularly true of people with high self-esteem, especially when they are in a bad mood (Sanna, Turley-Ames, & Meier, 1999). People who think well of themselves may use counterfactual reasoning to repair a bad mood.

Mental Simulation. Simulating how events may happen provides a window on the future by helping people envision possibilities and develop plans for bringing those possibilities about (Taylor, Pham, Rivkin, & Armor, 1998). But people can focus on different aspects of the future. They may envision the future as filled with bountiful possibilities, what some call "wishful thinking" or "fantasy" (Oettingen, & Mayer, 2002). Or they might focus on the steps they need to take in order to achieve a future that is desired. Which type of mental simulation about the future helps people to achieve their goals?

If you are an avid reader of self-help books, you know that this advice-filled genre urges people to actively envision the state they hope to achieve in the future. Yet research suggests that this idea is badly misleading. In a study that tested this point, Pham and Taylor (1999) asked college students who were studying for an exam a few days away to envision either their satisfaction and celebration in achieving a good grade on the exam or to envision themselves studying so as to produce a good grade on the exam. That is, one group focused on the outcome to be achieved, whereas the other group focused on the process for achieving it. Those students who had focused on the process in fact improved their grade substantially over a control group that practiced neither mental simulation; but those students who focused on the outcome they wanted to achieve actually had lower scores on the exam than the control group (see also Armor & Taylor, 2003).

Clearly, if you want to use mental simulation to further your goals, it is best not to engage in wishful thinking and fantasy, but to focus your simulations clearly on what you will need to do to get there (Oettingen, Pak, & Schnetter, 2001; Taylor et al., 1998).

The Anchoring and Adjustment Heuristic

Imagine that someone asks you to guess how many people attended the UCLA-USC football game last night in the Los Angeles Coliseum. You have absolutely no idea, but you do know that last week's game in the Coliseum drew a crowd of 55,000. Assuming that the UCLA-USC contest drew a much bigger crowd, you might guess that 70,000 people attended. In this case, you have no information about the specific event in question, but you use information about a similar event as a reference point, or "anchor." You then adjust reference information to reach a conclusion (Tversky & Kahneman, 1974). In fact, when people are attempting to form judgments from ambiguous information, they will often reduce ambiguity by starting with the beginning reference point, or anchor, and then adjusting it. Social judgments are no exception, because information about social situations is often ambiguous; anchors can be helpful when one is trying to interpret the meaning of ambiguous information and behavior (Mussweiler, Strack, & Pfeiffer, 2000).

A common anchor used in social perception is the self. For example, suppose someone asks you whether Ellen, a classmate of yours, is smart. It may be easiest for you to answer this question by trying to decide whether or not Ellen is smarter than you. If she seems to be smarter than you are, you may decide that she is very smart. But if she seems to be not as quick as you are, you may decide that she is not very bright. Your judgment about Ellen's intelligence is based not on her absolute standing on an IQ test or some other objective information, but on whether she seems brighter or less bright than you (Markus, Smith, & Moreland, 1985). The anchoring heuristic, then, provides people with a departure point for a judgment task that might otherwise be ambiguous. In social judgment tasks, the self seems to be a common anchor. For a description of the various heuristic strategies, see Table 3–1. Heuristics help us get from the cues we perceive in the environment to our schemas. But which cues and schemas do we use?

WHICH SCHEMAS ARE USED?

Suppose you observe two people feverishly searching a room. How do you decide what they are doing? In other words, how do you select which schemas to apply to the situation? Sometimes appropriate schemas are suggested by the nature of the information itself. For example, if you know the two people in

Table 3–1

Some Heuristic Strategies for Making Judgments Under Uncertainty

Heuristic	Definition	Example
Representativeness	Representativeness is a judgment of how relevant A is to B; high relevance yields high estimates that A originates from B.	Deciding that George (A) must be an engineer because he looks and acts like your stereotype of engineers (B)
Availability	Availability is the estimate of how frequent or likely a given instance or occurrence is, based on how easily or quickly an association or examples come to mind.	Estimating the divorce rate on the basis of how quickly you can think of examples of divorced friends
Simulation	Simulation is the ease with which a hypothetical scenario can be constructed.	Getting angry because of a frustrating event on the basis of how easily you can imagine the situation occurring otherwise
Anchoring and adjustment	Anchoring and adjustment make up the process of estimating some value by starting with some initial value and then adjusting it to the new instance.	Judging how hard a friend studies by how hard you yourself study

question are roommates who keep gerbils and you see an empty cage, you may guess that they are trying to find their missing gerbils. In other circumstances, information in the environment may not immediately suggest what schemas to invoke. Are the two searchers looking for something that they have lost? Are they burglars? Are they undercover police officers conducting a drug bust? In this section, we consider the factors that influence which schemas people use to interpret information.

Natural Contours

The most obvious and probably also the most powerful determinant of which schema is used is the structure of the information itself. That is, schemas follow the natural contours of the information we receive. For example, if you are watching a football game, you will employ your schemas for football games, football players, and plays to interpret what is happening on the field. The information in the environment makes it obvious which schemas to use, and you would not invoke your schemas for cocktail parties, tennis games, or final examinations to interpret what is going on (cf. Gavanski & Hui, 1992).

But we do not take in all the environmental information when we form an inference. Rather, we absorb meaningful, structured chunks of it. For example, in a baseball game, we would notice the pitch, the batter's swing, and the outfielder catching the ball and recognize that the batter was out. The chunking process is imposed on the flow of behavior partly by the perceiver's own experiences and expectations. And the chunks partly reflect the real changes within the behavioral sequence (Newtson, 1976).

Salience

Environmental salience is another factor that influences which schemas people use to interpret information. Sometimes our interpretation of other people's behavior is influenced by what information about them is made salient by the environment. For example, if Linda is the only woman in a group that is otherwise composed of men, her gender will be particularly salient; therefore her behavior may be interpreted according to a gender schema for women (Taylor, Fiske, Close, Anderson, & Ruderman, 1977). For example, her request for help from a newcomer to the group might be interpreted as a sign of dependence, a trait sometimes stereotypically associated with women. However, if Linda is in a group composed of several men and several women, her behavior toward the newcomer might not be interpreted in gender-related terms. Instead, a schema for "newcomers" might be invoked, and her gesture might simply be interpreted as an effort to make the newcomer feel at home. Salience, then, can influence the processing of information in the environment by determining which schemas will be invoked to interpret information that may be subject to multiple interpretations.

Primacy

Often, which schema is used to analyze a person or a situation is determined very early by information present in the situation. For example, when introduced to someone with the words, "This is Susan, she's running for student body president," one is inclined to think of Susan and her subsequent behavior in terms of whether she would be a good student body president and to consider her behavior as determined at least in part by the fact that she is running for office. One reason **primacy** is so important is that when people have an organizing structure from the very outset, it influences the interpretation of information as that information is taken in. The effects of that influence are more powerful than if the schema is applied afterward (see Fiske & Taylor, 1991, for a review).

Primacy

Using an initial impression to interpret subsequent information.

Priming

When a schema has been used recently, it is likely to be used again to interpret new information (Bargh, 1994). Suppose you have just come from a classroom discussion in which the professor castigated the class for its lack of commitment to intellectual pursuits. Walking across campus, you meet Stan, who enthusiastically tells you that he has just been appointed to the cheering squad. How do you interpret his enthusiasm? In the context of the prior lecture, you may regard his behavior as shallow and unintellectual. In contrast, if you had just come from a discussion of the importance of being a well-rounded college student, you might interpret his behavior as a sign of extracurricular interests. This tendency for recently used schemas to be used in unrelated subsequent situations is called the **priming effect**, and it often occurs entirely without awareness (Stapel, Koomen, & Ruys, 2002).

Priming Effect

Recent thoughts influence the interpretation of subsequent information.

A study that demonstrates priming was conducted by Higgins, Rholes, and Jones (1977). Participants were first exposed to trait words designed to invoke either the positive schema of adventurousness (e.g., "brave") or the negative schema of recklessness (e.g., "foolish" or "careless"). In a second study, ostensibly

People perceive behavior in coherent, meaningful chunks of action, marked by breakpoints. For example, in a football game, a completed pass would form a natural unit, marked at the beginning by the throw and at the end of the successful reception.

unrelated to the first task, participants read about Donald, who shot rapids, drove in a demolition derby, and planned to learn skydiving. People who had previously been exposed to the positive schema of adventurousness evaluated Donald more positively than did people who had been primed with the negative schema of recklessness. This priming effect did not occur when the primed schemas were not applicable to the description of Donald (e.g., "neat" or "shy") (see Higgins & Bargh, 1987). Essentially, then, activating a schema puts it at the top of the mental heap, making it easily accessible for interpreting new information (Wyer & Srull, 1981).

Importance

Which schemas are used to interpret information from the environment and how many schemas are used can also be influenced by the importance of the information being processed. When the circumstances for making inferences are relatively trivial, people may make schematic inferences relatively quickly, with little thought. They may, for example, invoke a schema on the basis of which information is most salient. However, when the outcome of an inference is important, or when a person is accountable for the inference, that person may spend more time studying the situation and invoke more schemas, which yield more complex inferences (Chaiken, 1980; Tetlock & Boettger, 1989). For example, if asked your impression of a classmate, you may answer relatively quickly that he or she seems pleasant if your judgment of the person has no particular importance to you. However, if you were trying to decide whether to ask this classmate on a date, you would probably spend more time thinking through what you know about the person to decide whether he or she is fun to be with, attractive, pleasant, and attracted to you. Your inferences might consequently be more complex and based on more than one schema.

Individual Differences

Not everyone interprets the same information the same way. One reason is that different people have different schemas. For example, one person might describe other people primarily in terms of their sense of humor or warmth, whereas someone else might consider these characteristics relatively unimportant and instead might be concerned with another person's diligence and religiousness.

People also differ in their needs for structure, that is, the degree to which they need to create and use schemas to simplify previous experience (Neuberg, Judice, & West, 1997). Generally speaking, those with a high need for structure are more likely to rely on cognitive schemas than those who have a low need for structure (Bar-Tal, Kishon-Rabin, & Tabak, 1997).

A related construct, need for closure, is the desire to achieve a firm answer to a question and an aversion to ambiguity. Need for closure also leads people to make use of schemas as opposed to a more piecemeal consideration of available information (Chiu, Morris, Hong, & Menon, 2000; Kruglanski et al., 1997).

As we noted in the last chapter, Westerners and East Asians vary in how much attention they pay to contextual information. Whereas Westerners are more likely to make dispositional attributions for another's behavior and be relatively inattentive to important contextual information that might qualify the inference, East Asians are more likely to make situational attributions that explicitly take context into account. This pattern seems to characterize differences in social cognition between Westerners and East Asians generally. East Asians, more than people from the United States, explain events with reference to the context and qualify their inferences in terms of relevant situational information and relationships (Mauata & Nisbett, 2001). Essentially, East Asian cognition is more holistic than Western cognition. That is, attention is paid to the field as a whole, whereas among Westerners, cognition tends to be focused on a salient object (Ji, Peng, & Nisbett, 2000).

Goals

Which schemas are brought to bear on information in the environment is also based on the goals a social perceiver has in a particular situation (Hastie, Park, & Weber, 1984; Wyer & Srull, 1986). As we have seen, schemas are not simply passive reflections of the information in the environment. The person must actively organize the information into a more abstract, cognitive structure. One way in which this organizing cognitive activity is triggered is through an individual's goals (e.g., Trzebinski & Richards, 1986). When we have a particular goal in a situation, such as trying to remember what someone says or trying to form an impression of someone, we organize information in a way that fits our particular goals.

WHEN ARE SCHEMAS USED?

Schemas are important because they help people make sense of experience quickly. If we approached every situation as if for the first time, it would be impossible for us to function in our everyday lives. Schemas, then, represent our social learning, the social categories that we use to assign meaning to the people we meet and the situations we encounter.

But as we also noted earlier in the chapter, there are liabilities to schematic processing. Sometimes we make assumptions about people and situations on the basis of our schemas that turn out not to be true. If we could pay more attention to the information at hand instead of jumping to conclusions on the basis of our schemas, we could avoid certain mistakes. For example, categorizing another person as loud-mouthed, opinionated, arrogant, and conservative may not matter much in most circumstances, but if the person happens to be the father of the woman you are hoping to date, you might want to pay closer attention to his qualities and opinions.

Dual Processing of Information

Dual-Process Model

People can process information in a careful, systematic fashion or in a more rapid, efficient, heuristic fashion.

The distinction between the rapid, heuristically based use of schemas and the careful, systematic, piecemeal construction of inferences from evidence illustrates an important issue throughout social psychology: People have qualitatively different ways in which they can form inferences. This has been called the **dual-process model** of inference. According to this model, people may process information in a relatively effortless heuristic mode by using schemas, or in a more cognitively demanding, systematic mode, by drawing on more of the evidence in the specific situation. Under which conditions do we pay more attention to our schemas and somewhat less to the evidence at hand, and in what circumstances do we do the reverse?

Outcome Dependency. One condition that leads to less frequent use of schemas and more attention to the information is outcome dependency. When your outcomes depend on someone else's actions, you pay more attention to the other person (Berscheid, Graziano, Monson, & Dermer, 1976; Rush & Russell, 1988) and to schema-inconsistent information, apparently because it is potentially informative (Erber & Fiske, 1984). When people's outcomes are involved, they probe for more information about others (Darley, Fleming, Hilton, & Swann, 1988). For example, competitors remember more about members of a group with which they are in competition than do those not in competition with them (Judd & Park, 1988).

Accountability. Accountability or the need to be accurate is another condition that leads people to pay more attention to data and less attention to their schemas. When people have to justify their decisions to other people and accountability is therefore high, they tend to go beyond the schema to look more closely at the data (Pennington & Schlenker, 1999; Tetlock & Boettger, 1989). Asked if a particular nerdy person is smart, you may draw on your schema that tells you that nerds usually are smart. However, if it is up to you to decide whether to admit him to your debating team, you will probably want more information than your stereotype about nerds will provide. Consequently, you will pay closer attention to his actual behavior and will focus less on the ways in which he matches your schema for nerds (Lerner & Tetlock, 1999).

Time Pressure. Conversely, other facts favor schema use over careful consideration of the data. For example, when people are forming impressions or making decisions under time pressure, they tend to use their schemas more. In one study, male and female participants were asked to judge the suitability of male and female candidates for particular jobs. When the decisions were made under time pressure, male participants as well as female participants with conservative attitudes toward women tended to discriminate against the female job applicants. In the absence of time pressure, however, discrimination toward the female applicants was less strong. Under time pressure, then, the participants resorted to their stereotypes about men and women in jobs to make the judgments, whereas when they had time to consider the evidence and found that the female applicants were as well qualified as the male applicants, their degree of discrimination against the female candidates was considerably less (Bechtold, Naccarato, & Zanna, 1986).

We also fall back on our schemas when all the available information seems to fit the schema well and when we are not particularly motivated to examine the data more thoroughly. However, when we are told that a task is important or when some of the information is incongruent with the schema, we are more likely to engage in systematic processing of the data (Maheswaran & Chaiken, 1991).

To summarize, then, when there are pressures in the situation to be accurate, people tend to look at data more closely, sometimes rejecting easy, schematically based conclusions. They attend to more of the information and pay particular attention to schema-inconsistent information. Conditions that seem to favor this kind of data-driven processing are outcome dependency, accountability, and other situational cues that suggest a need to be accurate. In contrast, other circumstances favor more schematically based processing. In particular, any pressure to form a quick or coherent judgment that can be communicated easily to others may favor the use of schemas (Fiske & Taylor, 1991). As we see in Chapter 5, this distinction is also very important for understanding processes of attitude change.

SCHEMAS IN ACTION

The use of schemas for processing information is important not only because it helps people to form judgments and make decisions but also because it provides guidelines for interactions with others.

Confirmatory Hypothesis Testing

We learn about other people in many ways. We may hear about them before we meet them, or we may have hints about the kind of people they are on the basis of their initial behavior. Regardless of how we form an impression of another person, we may relatively quickly develop ideas about what the person is like. As we interact with the person, how do these ideas (or schemas) influence our behavior?

How does this process work? Suppose you learned that Susan, an attractive young woman in your psychology class, is with the cheering squad for the school; you quickly form an image of her as an outgoing, athletic, and enthusiastic person. In talking with her, you might ask her about the various sports she has played, the parties she has been to this year, what she thinks of the games she has attended, and so on. All this information tends to confirm your view of her as an extroverted, athletic, fun-loving person. However, after seeing her for several weeks, you might discover that she is actually rather shy and introverted, that she's not particularly athletic, and that she is not a cheerleader at all but rather coordinates uniform purchases and bus transportation to out-of-town games.

You might wonder how you came to be so deceived. Looking back on the situation, however, reveals that Susan may have done nothing at all to deceive you. Rather, you deceived yourself by selectively seeking information that supported your beliefs. Many college students have played some kind of sport in high school or attended at least a couple of parties. Because you asked Susan about these kinds of activities, that is the information she gave you, it augmented your image of her as an outgoing, athletic person (Swann, Giuliano, & Wegner, 1982). This process has been called **confirmatory hypothesis testing**, and it has been demonstrated in a broad range of circumstances.

Confirmatory Hypothesis Testing

Selectively extracting from others information that preferentially confirms a preexisting belief.

Snyder and Swann (1978) told college student participants that they would be interviewing another student. Half were told to find out if the other was an extrovert (i.e., outgoing and sociable), and half were told to find out if the other was an introvert (i.e., shy and retiring). All participants were then given a set of questions assessing introversion and extroversion, and they were told to pick out a set of questions to ask the other student. Students who were told to find out if the person was an extrovert preferentially selected extroversion questions (e.g., "What would you do if you wanted to liven things up at a party?"), and those who were told to find out if the person was an introvert picked introversion questions, which, in turn, made the target students appear especially extroverted or introverted, respectively, simply because they answered the questions they were asked (see also Davies, 1997; McDonald & Hirt, 1997).

Considerable research suggests that people behave toward others in ways that tend to confirm the beliefs they hold about those others (Garcia-Marques, Sherman, & Palma-Oliveira, 2001). Perceivers employ interaction strategies to elicit information from others that preferentially supports these schemas (Snyder & Gangestad, 1981).

Although a number of studies have found evidence for confirmatory hypothesis testing, there are conditions under which we are less likely to confirm a hypothesis selectively through leading questions. Holding an opposite hypothesis or having a need for valid information reduces the degree to which people selectively confirm hypotheses (Devine, Hirt, & Gehrke, 1990). For example, when people expect to have to work with a target in the future, they ask better questions and are less likely to engage in question-asking techniques that selectively confirm their expectations (Darley, Fleming, Hilton, & Swann, 1988). And when they have more than one hypothesis in mind, they will test for these alternative hypotheses as well (McDonald, 1990).

Self-Fulfilling Prophecy. Sometimes a prior schema we have about an individual will not only influence the kind of information we seek from the person and the subsequent inferences we draw, but will also affect the other person's actual behaviors and self-impressions. When a perceiver's false expectations about another person lead that person to adopt those expected attributes and behaviors, this is called a **self-fulfilling prophecy** (see Figure 3–3). For example, Snyder, Tanke, and Berscheid (1977) gave male college students a folder of information about a woman on campus that included a picture that represented the woman as either highly attractive or unattractive. In actuality, the photos were fake and were randomly assigned to women regardless of their true looks. Each student was then asked to phone the woman whose folder he had read and chat for 10 minutes. Tape recordings were made of the conversations. The men who believed they were talking to attractive women behaved more warmly on the phone than did the men who called supposedly unattractive women. Even more remarkable, the women who had been miscast as highly attractive were perceived by other students who judged the tapes to be more friendly, likable, and sociable in their interactions with the men than those who were miscast as unattractive. These kinds of self-fulfilling prophecies have been widely demonstrated.

Self-Fulfilling Prophecy

The tendency for people's expectations to create reality.

Self-Conceptions. The implication of the discussion thus far is that schemas are so powerful, they not only influence how information in the environment is

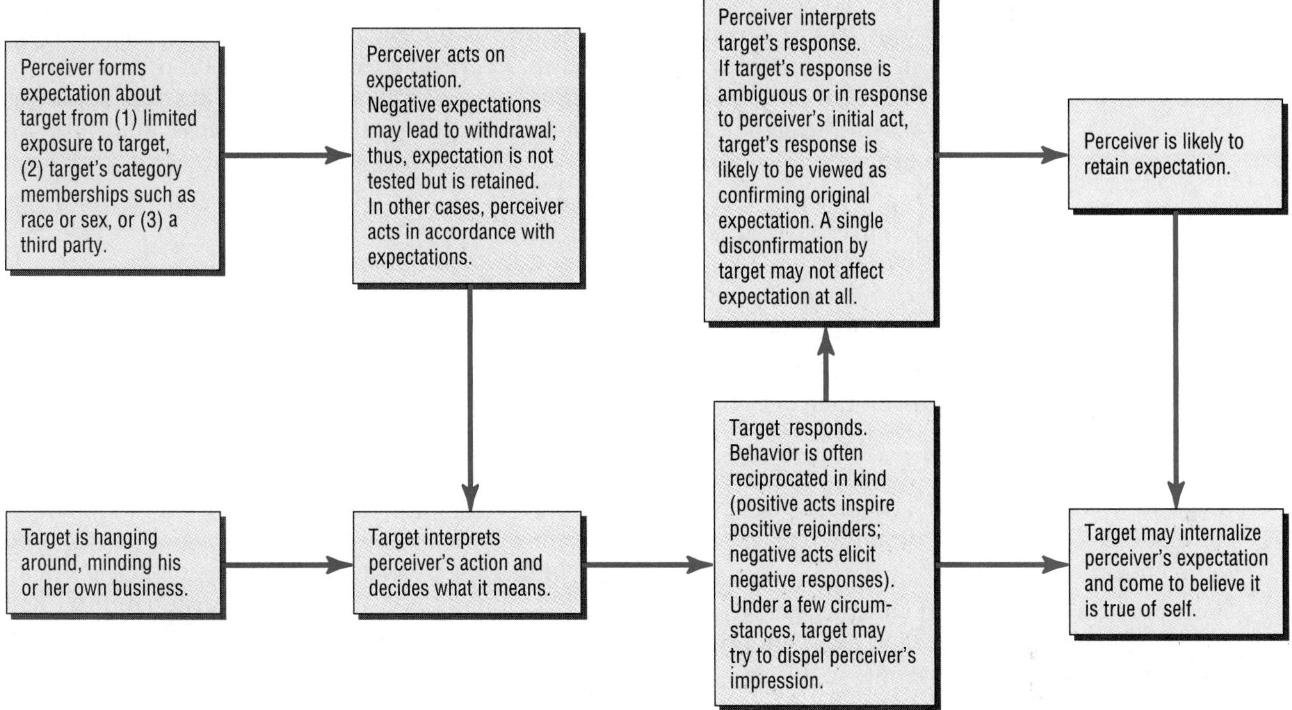

Figure 3–3 **The Development of a Self-Fulfilling Prophecy.**

Source: Adapted from Darley and Fazio (1980).

interpreted but also help push the environment to become consistent with the schema. Obviously, this is not always the case. For example, sometimes people hold beliefs about others that those others feel are untrue about themselves. Consequently, those others may be motivated to disconfirm what they feel is an incorrect belief (Smith, Neuberg, Judice, & Biesanz, 1997). For example, if a professor whose opinion you value saw you commit a foolish prank with some of your friends, you might be highly motivated to correct the professor's low opinion of you.

In these circumstances, whose viewpoint will triumph? The perceiver's misconceptions or the target's beliefs about himself or herself? Research by Swann and Ely (1984) attempted to address this question by considering the certainty of the perceiver's expectations and the target's self-conceptions. Perceivers first formed relatively certain or uncertain expectations about targets that were inconsistent with the target's self-conceptions. Thus, for example, some perceivers were led to believe that the target was extroverted (when the target perceived herself to be introverted), whereas other perceivers were led to believe the target was introverted (when the target considered herself extroverted). The perceivers then interacted with targets who possessed either relatively certain or uncertain self-conceptions about their introversion or extroversion. The results indicated that the target's self-concept was a stronger determinant of the perceiver's ultimate opinion of the target than was the perceiver's expectation. That is, after they had interacted together, the perceivers' impressions of the targets were more in line with the targets' self-concepts than with the perceivers' initial expectations. Only when targets were uncertain about their introversion or extroversion and perceivers were certain about their expectations did behavioral confirmation occur. That is, when perceivers were certain and targets were uncertain about their attributes, the perceivers' expectations tended to prevail. The general point, then, is that perceivers' expectations may have some effect on a target's behavior. But they do not lead targets to act in ways that are counter to their self-concepts (e.g., Snyder & Haugen, 1995).

Overall, then, schemas and schematic processing are important for several reasons. They help people organize their past experiences in ways that can be useful in new situations. They help in the processing of new information by determining what is relevant, by filling in gaps, by influencing what is recalled, and by making some inferences automatic. And they can act as effective guidelines for behavior in social interactions.

Summary

1. Social cognition is the branch of social psychology that examines how people form inferences based on social information in the environment.
2. Social perceivers are prone to certain errors and biases in their judgments. In particular, prior expectations and theories weigh heavily in the judgment process.
3. These predictable errors and biases appear to stem from the fact that people need to make judgments relatively quickly and efficiently to process the volume of information they encounter.
4. Cognitive structures called schemas help us organize information about the world. Schemas make information processing more efficient and speedy, aid recall, fill in missing information, and provide expectations. However, they sometimes lead to erroneous inferences or may lead us to reject good but inconsistent evidence.
5. Heuristics are shortcuts that help relate information in the environment to schemas. Heuristics reduce complex or ambiguous problems to more simple, judgmental operations.
6. The schemas that are most likely to be used to interpret information are those that match the natural contours of that information. In addition, which schemas a social perceiver uses is influenced by salience, social roles, goals, primacy, priming, the importance of the judgment context, and individual differences.
7. People sometimes attend more to the evidence than to their schemas, especially if they need to be very accurate, if they will be held accountable for their judgments, or if their future outcomes depend on their judgments.
8. Schemas not only help people form judgments and make decisions but also provide guidelines for interactions with others. In some cases, schemas may be so powerful that they bring about self-fulfilling prophecies.

Key Terms

case history information **67**
confirmatory hypothesis testing **92**
conjunction error **83**
counterfactual reasoning **85**
covariation **69**
dual-process model **90**
exemplar **79**
heuristic **82**
illusory correlation **70**
mood-congruent memory **72**
planning fallacy **76**
primacy **88**
priming effect **88**
schema **78**
scripts **78**
self-fulfilling prophecy **92**
social cognition **65**
statistical information **67**

In The News

Governor Girlie Man

In 2003, in an unprecedented recall election that led to the ouster of Governor Gray Davis, Arnold Schwarzenegger was elected governor of California. The former star of such films as *Terminator* and *Predator* now had to transcend his prior lives as bodybuilder, action hero, and actor to add "statesman" to his resume.

But prior selves are hard to overcome. Throughout his first year as governor, Schwarzenegger peppered his public persona with *Terminator* allusions in what the *Los Angeles Times* characterized as a "self-parodic testosterone swagger" (July 12, 2004).

In one well-publicized incident, the governor baited the Democrats as "girlie men" for holding up passage of the state budget. The Democratic majority leader responded by castigating the governor for insulting the manhood of the state's Democratic legislators. Not to be left out of the fray, a *Los Angeles Times* editorial speculated that "it takes one to know one," noting that the governor had largely failed to extract concessions from the lobbies with which he had negotiated over budget issues.

Almost ignored in these exchanges were the back-handed insults to women contained in these barbs, implying that being a "girl" is somehow contrary to political ability or decisiveness—this, in a state with two women senators.

What these exchanges illustrate perhaps better than any individual's or party's leadership (or lack thereof) is how threats to the self can be potent, upsetting, and in this case, even newsworthy.

Chapter 4

The Self: Learning About the Self

WHAT IS THE SELF?

The self is first and foremost the collection of beliefs that we hold about ourselves. What are our important characteristics? What are we good at? What do we do poorly? What kinds of situations do we prefer or avoid? One person may think of herself as a black woman who plans to become a sociology professor. Another might think of himself as not academically inclined but good at most sports. A third person may think of herself primarily in terms of a future goal, such as the desire to become the biggest real estate mogul in the Midwest. The set of beliefs we hold about who we are is called the **self-concept**.

Often we have a clear idea of who we are, whereas at other times we hold self-doubts and confusion and feel we are buffeted by external pressures and evaluations by others. This distinction refers to self-concept clarity and a sense of self that is clearly and confidently defined, providing a coherent sense of direction (Campbell, 1990; Kernis, Paradise, Whitaker, Wheatman, & Goldman, 2000).

Self-esteem is the evaluation we make of ourselves. That is, we are concerned not only with what we are like but also with how we value these qualities. Table 4–1 shows some of the items from a commonly used measure of self-esteem (Rosenberg, 1965). As you can see, the items measure the general value that people place on themselves—whether they are fundamentally good or bad people, talented or not, and so on.

People with high self-esteem have a clear sense of what their personal qualities are. They think well of themselves, set appropriate goals, use feedback in a self-enhancing manner, savor their positive experiences (Wood, Heimpel, & Michela, 2003), and cope successfully with difficult situations. For example, when people with high self-esteem receive feedback implying that they have been rejected by others, they are more likely than those with low self-esteem to respond by reminding themselves of their positive qualities or by persisting at an alternative goal (Sommer & Baumeister, 2002). And conveniently, people with high self-esteem remember their daily experiences more favorably—a memory bias that may itself strengthen high self-esteem (Christensen, Wood, & Barrett, 2003).

People with low self-esteem, on the other hand, have less clear self-conceptions, think poorly of themselves, often select unrealistic goals or shy away from goals altogether, tend to be pessimistic about the future, remember

Focus of This Chapter

Self-Concept

The collection of beliefs we hold about ourselves.

Self-Esteem

The value one places on oneself.

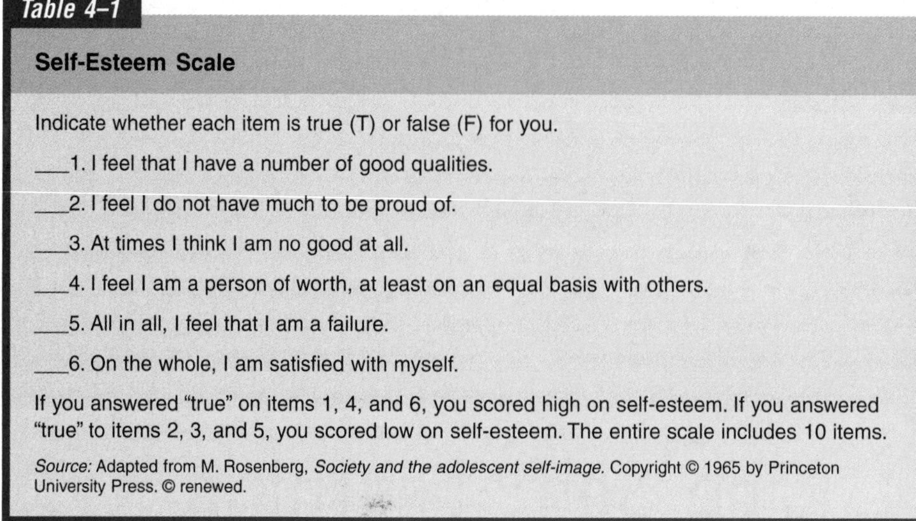
Table 4-1

Self-Esteem Scale

Indicate whether each item is true (T) or false (F) for you.

___1. I feel that I have a number of good qualities.

___2. I feel I do not have much to be proud of.

___3. At times I think I am no good at all.

___4. I feel I am a person of worth, at least on an equal basis with others.

___5. All in all, I feel that I am a failure.

___6. On the whole, I am satisfied with myself.

If you answered "true" on items 1, 4, and 6, you scored high on self-esteem. If you answered "true" to items 2, 3, and 5, you scored low on self-esteem. The entire scale includes 10 items.

Source: Adapted from M. Rosenberg, *Society and the adolescent self-image.* Copyright © 1965 by Princeton University Press. © renewed.

their past more negatively, wallow in their negative moods (Heimpel, Wood, Marshall, & Brown, 2002), have more adverse emotional and behavioral reactions to criticism or other kinds of personal negative feedback, are less able to generate positive feedback for themselves, are more concerned about their social impact on other people, and are more vulnerable to depression or rumination when they encounter setbacks or stress (Brown & Marshall, 2001; DiPaula & Campbell, 2002; Heatherton & Vohs, 2000; Josephs, Bosson, & Jacobs, 2003; Kernis et al., 2000; Leary, Tambor, Terdal, & Downs, 1995; Setterlund & Niedenthal, 1993; Sommer et al., 2002).

In addition to our overall sense of self-esteem, we hold specific evaluations of our abilities in particular areas. Joan may think well of herself generally but may know that she is not very diplomatic and not very talented artistically. David may generally think poorly of himself but know that he is organized and a good pianist. Two dimensions that are central to self-esteem are self-competence and self-liking, that is, evaluations of ourselves as capable and personal fondness for the self (Tafarodi, Marshall, & Milne, 2003). The importance and value we attach to these more specific self-views also influence global feelings of self-worth. That is, people are selective about the domains on which they base their self-worth. For one person, being attractive might be important; for another person, being smart might be more important (Crocker & Luhtanen, 2003).

For the most part, researchers have studied people's explicit self-esteem, that is, the concrete positive or negative evaluations they make of themselves. But more recent research suggests the importance of implicit self-esteem as well (Greenwald & Banaji, 1995; Greenwald & Farnham, 2000). Implicit self-esteem refers to the less conscious evaluations we make of ourselves. Studies of implicit self-esteem sometimes reveal things that studies of explicit self-esteem do not (Egloff & Schmukle, 2002; Woike, Mcleod, & Goggin, 2003). For example, implicit self-esteem seems to be more sensitive than explicit self-esteem to the specific situation a person is in (Bosson, Swann & Pennebaker, 2000; Dijksterhuis, 2004).

As we will see, one strong cultural difference is that Asians, especially the Japanese, are much less likely to answer explicit self-esteem scales in a self-enhancing manner. Instead, they report relatively modest self-esteem. However, in a test of implicit self-esteem (Kitayama & Karasawa, 1997), Japanese students were found to hold a preference for alphabetical letters contained in their own names over letters that were not in their names. They were also found to prefer numbers that corresponded to the month or the day of their birthdays over numbers that did not appear in their birthdays. These measures of implicit self-esteem, then, suggested a self-enhancing quality that the students did not acknowledge more directly (see also Koole, Dijksterhuis, & van Knippenberg, 2001).

How does a sense of self develop? One of the most influential theories of how the self develops was put forth by Erik Erikson (1963), who argued for a stage theory of ego development. He maintained that although identity formation is a lifelong task (Whitborne, Zuschlag, Elliot, & Waterman, 1992), it is of critical importance during adolescence and young adulthood. This time, when identity begins to come together, marks the transition between childhood and adulthood. Erikson (1963) believed that the goal of this process is "the ability to experience one's self as something that has continuity and sameness, and to act accordingly" (p. 38). Once the young adult has acquired a firm sense of identity, he or she has a basis for making job or career plans and for establishing intimate relationships.

Although Erikson was no doubt correct in his assessment of adolescence and young adulthood as pivotal times for developing a sense of self, it would be false to claim that the sense of self develops and is maintained only or primarily during this time. The sense of self begins in infancy with the recognition that one is a separate individual (Butterworth, 1992; Pervin, 1992a, 1992b). Very young children have fairly clear concepts of their personal qualities and what they do or don't do well. Moreover, many changes occur in middle and late adulthood that may influence the self-conceptions that people hold. Thus, although psychologists continue to believe that Erikson was essentially right when he argued that issues of identity are especially important in adolescence and young adulthood, it is also clearly the case that the development of a personal sense of self is a lifelong process that begins in childhood and never truly ends.

WHERE DOES SELF-KNOWLEDGE COME FROM?

Knowledge of the self comes from many sources. Some of it may seem to be spontaneous: a realization that something is true of one's self without any certainty of where that knowledge comes from. More commonly, however, we can identify the origins of our beliefs about ourselves in specific experiences.

Socialization

Much of our self-knowledge comes from **socialization**. During childhood we are treated in particular ways by parents, teachers, and friends, and we participate in religious, ethnic, or cultural activities that later come to be significant aspects of ourselves. From attending synagogue at an early age, taking Hebrew lessons, and eventually participating in a bar mitzvah, a Jewish boy may come to regard being

Socialization

How a person acquires the rules, standards, and values of his or her family, group, and culture.

Much self-knowledge comes from socialization. By participating in activities that are important to our families, we come to regard these activities as important to ourselves as well.

Jewish as an important part of his identity. A child whose parents take her to art exhibits and concerts every weekend may come to think of herself as a cultured person. Socialization forms the core of our early experience, and the regularity of those experiences may eventually come to be internalized as important aspects of the self-concept.

Reflected Appraisal

We also learn about ourselves through the reactions that other people have to us. C. H. Cooley (1902) developed the concept of the "looking-glass self," which maintains that people perceive themselves as others perceive and respond to them (Leary et al., 2003). Our perceptions of how other people react to us are called **reflected appraisals**.

Reflected Appraisals

Self-evaluation based on the perceptions and evaluations of others.

In a humorous example of the importance of reflected appraisal, Baldwin, Carrell, and Lopez (1990) recruited Catholic students for a study during which the students encountered a picture of the scowling face of either the pope or an unfamiliar other person and were later asked to evaluate some of their own personal qualities. Practicing Catholics who were exposed to the picture of the scowling pope evaluated themselves more harshly than did both the nonpracticing Catholics who were exposed to the same picture of the pope and the Catholics who were exposed to the picture of the unfamiliar other person. Apparently, the picture of the scowling pope was enough to shake the self-images of these students.

Feedback from Others

Sometimes people give us explicit feedback about our qualities. This process often begins in socialization, when our parents tell us not to be so shy, that we are good at playing the piano, that math is not our strong point, or that we are good readers. Generally speaking, there is a strong relationship between what parents think of their children's abilities and children's own self-conceptions about these same dimensions (Felson & Reed, 1986).

In later childhood and early adolescence, feedback from peers may be more important (Leary, Cottrell, & Phillips, 2001). All of us can remember being picked early or late when captains were choosing members for athletic teams, and we measured our popularity in terms of how quickly we were picked to be in someone's carpool for a field trip (see Leary, Haupt, Strausser, & Chokel, 1998). Adolescence brings with it additional sources of direct feedback, such as whether one is asked out on dates by many people or few, or whether the people that one asks out accept or decline. Also, students get direct feedback from teachers about their academic abilities in the form of comments and grades (Jussim, Soffin, Brown, Ley, & Kohlhepp, 1992).

Research has suggested that, on the whole, people prefer objective feedback (such as test scores) about their personal attributes (Festinger, 1954). Objective feedback is regarded as less biased and more fair than personal opinion. But the opinions of others also count. In particular, when those opinions are shared by a large number of people, we may come to believe that they are true.

Self-Perception

As we see in Chapter 3, people also infer their personal qualities from observing their own behavior. That is, in the process of observing ourselves, we see ourselves consistently preferring certain activities over others, certain foods over others, or certain people over others. From observing these regularities, we may gain self-knowledge.

Self-Perception Theory

Idea that people sometimes infer their attitudes from their overt behavior, rather than from their own internal state.

However, as Daryl Bem's (1967, 1972) **self-perception theory** also suggests, this source of self-knowledge may be useful primarily for aspects of the self that are not particularly central or important. For example, you do not need to observe yourself avoiding anchovies on your pizza to know that you do not like anchovies.

You do not need to observe yourself ordering flowers for your mother on Mother's Day to know that you love your mother. Many important aspects of the self have clear internal referents in the form of enduring beliefs, attitudes, and affective preferences. And so it is likely that self-perception as a source of self-knowledge applies primarily more to incidental than to important aspects of the self.

Labeling Arousal States

Sometimes we infer our internal states and personal qualities from our own physiological arousal. We respond to things that we perceive—a threatening dog, an attractive prospective partner—and recognize our emotions by considering our mental and physiological reactions. But many emotional reactions are biochemically similar. We can distinguish high arousal from low arousal, but often not specific emotions.

Stanley Schachter (1964) suggested that perceptions of our own emotions depend on (1) the degree of physiological arousal we have and (2) the cognitive label we apply, such as angry or happy. To arrive at a cognitive label, we review our own behavior and the situation. For example, if we feel physiologically aroused and are laughing at a comedy show on television, we might infer that we are happy. If we are snarling at someone for shoving us on a crowded street, we might infer that we are angry. Like Bem's theory of self-perception, this point of view emphasizes the ambiguity of internal states and proposes that self-perception depends at least somewhat on perceptions of overt behavior and of the external environment.

Usually our arousal states are not ambiguous. We usually know what is causing our emotional states. However, Schachter's theory of emotion (physiological arousal plus label) provides a cogent understanding of those circumstances in which our emotional states are ambiguous, and we must infer them from what goes on around us.

Environmental Distinctiveness

The environment provides us with other cues about our personal qualities. In particular, the self-concept is heavily influenced by factors that make us distinctive. For example, McGuire and his associates (McGuire & McGuire, 1982; McGuire & Padawer-Singer, 1976) asked students to "tell us about yourself" and found that students often mentioned aspects of themselves that make them distinctive. For example, a boy is more likely to mention his gender if he is the only boy in his family. If he has three sisters, none of them is as likely to mention the fact that she is a girl.

We also mention things about ourselves that make us distinctive in the particular situation. So, for example, an African American woman is more likely to mention that she is African American if there are relatively few African Americans in a group; she is more likely to mention the fact that she is a woman if she is in a group composed predominantly of men. When we are in a group of other people like ourselves, we tend to think of ourselves in terms of our personal identity, that is, the characteristics that distinguish us from those who are otherwise similar to us. Thus, a college student athlete in a room filled with other college students is likely to think of himself in terms of his athletic ability. However, when we are in a situation with several different groups—such as college students and their parents—we tend to think of ourselves in terms of our category membership (e.g., college student) (Turner, Oakes, Haslam, & McGarty, 1994). This tendency is especially true of people from cultures that foster a norm of relatedness to others, such as in Asian countries, as we see in the following section (Kanagawa, Cross, & Markus, 2001).

Comparative Self Assessments

Sometimes when we want to evaluate ourselves on a particular dimension or quality, information is not readily available. For example, if you want to know if you are a graceful dancer, there is no test you can take to find that out. You could conceivably consult an expert, but perhaps an expert isn't available. You could ask other people if you are a graceful dancer, but you might be shy about doing so. Consequently, sometimes we assess our personal qualities by comparing ourselves to other people. You know if you are a good dancer in part by observing those around you and noting whether you seem to be dancing more gracefully than those other people. This process is termed **social comparison**, which is discussed in more detail later in this chapter.

Social Comparison

The act of comparing one's abilities, opinions, or emotions with those of another person or persons.

Often we evaluate our current situation in terms of our past (Ross & Wilson, 2002). Our personal storehouse of memories, for example, lets us know how much progress we have made on particular skills or lets us assess our current qualities. Have we grown more or less tolerant with age? Are we more or less skilled at tennis than we were a year ago? These temporal comparisons are a common source of self-knowledge, particularly about how one has changed (Libby & Eibach, 2002; Wilson & Ross, 2000, 2001). A caveat, however, is that such comparisons are often biased, because it is easy to distort one's prior position on an attribute when trying to gauge progress. In effect, an individual says, "I was bad at it before; I've made a lot of progress" (Conway & Ross, 1984). As this example implies, these temporal comparisons, especially self-serving ones, can help people cope with threatening life experiences (McFarland & Alvaro, 2000).

Social Identity

Social Identity

The part of an individual's self-concept that derives from his or her membership in a social group.

Social identity is the "part of an individual's self-concept which derives from [his or her] membership in a social group (or groups) together with the value and emotional significance attached to that membership" (Tajfel, 1981, p. 248; see also Turner et al., 1994). These groups include your family and other personal relationships; your work; your religious, political, ethnic, or community group; and other groups that highlight or reinforce important aspects of the self (Deaux, Reid, Mizrahi, & Ethier, 1995). In childhood, the groups in which one participates often occur as a part of socialization. We are born into a particular family, a particular ethnic group, and sometimes a particular religious group. As we get older, the attributes we value in ourselves lead us to choose social groups that reflect and reinforce those values. Self-concept and social identity mutually determine and shape each other (see Bettencourt & Dorr, 1997; Luhtanen & Crocker, 1992).

Ethnic Identity

An individual's self-knowledge that concerns membership in a particular ethnic group.

Much of the research on social identity has focused specifically on **ethnic identity**. Ethnic identity is the part of an individual's self-knowledge that concerns his or her membership in a particular ethnic group. Developing a sense of self can raise particular issues for minority group members. During the adolescent and young adult years, when people are forming their sense of themselves, reconciling ethnic background with mainstream culture can be difficult for African Americans, Asian Americans, Native Americans, those from Hispanic backgrounds, and other ethnic minority members (Sellers, Rowley, Chavous, Shelton, & Smith, 1997; Spencer & Markstrom-Adams, 1990). This process becomes more difficult when it is coupled with change, such as occurs when a student changes schools or enters college (Ethier & Deaux, 1994).

As Table 4–2 suggests, some adolescents may identify with both mainstream culture and their ethnic group, creating what is called a "bicultural" or "integrated identity" (Phinney, 1990; Ryder, Alden, & Paulhus, 2000). Others may maintain a strong ethnic identity but have few ties to the majority culture, maintaining a separated identity. Individuals who give up their ethnic heritage in favor of mainstream culture are said to be assimilated. Finally, some adolescents and young adults develop only weak ties to both their ethnic culture and the mainstream culture and feel marginal, like outsiders in both cultures (LaFromboise, Coleman, & Gerton, 1993; Phinney, 1990, 1991; Rowley, Sellers, Chavous, & Smith, 1998).

Research shows that these distinctions are important because they predict the amount of contact that individuals will have with their ethnic group and with the larger society. For example, Dona (1991) found that Central American refugees in Canada who were assimilated spent less time with other Central Americans

Table 4–2

Four Identity Orientations Based on Degree of Identification with One's Ethnic Group and the Majority Group

	Identification with Ethnic Group	
Identification with Majority Group	**Strong**	**Weak**
Strong	Integrated Acculturated Bicultural	Assimilated
Weak	Separated Ethnically identified Ethnically embedded Dissociated	Marginal

Source: Phinney (1990).

than did those who were integrated or those who maintained a separated ethnic identification (see also Gurin, Hurtado, & Peng, 1994). In turn, those who were integrated had more contact with Canadian society than did individuals who maintained a separate identity (Dona, 1991).

An interesting aspect of ethnic identity and of social identities more generally is that they can lead to self-stereotyping. Self-stereotyping involves perceiving oneself as a member of a particular group and consequently behaving in line with this social identity (Turner, Hogg, Oakes, Reicher, & Wetherell, 1987). Sometimes this means that people assume the negative as well as the positive attributes of the group with which they identify. For example, a professor may think of herself as smart, but also as absent-minded. When negative aspects of a social identity are salient or threatened, people are especially likely to identify with the positive aspects of their social identity, that is, to self-stereotype only on positive dimensions (Biernat, Vescio, & Green, 1996).

In a review of research on ethnic identity, Phinney (1991) found that a strong ethnic identity is typically related to high self-esteem, but only when accompanied by a positive mainstream orientation (see also Sanchez & Fernandez, 1993). Among individuals who hold a strong ethnic identity without some adaptation to the mainstream culture, self-esteem can be more problematic. Similarly, other research suggests that individuals may be able to gain competence within two cultures without losing cultural identity and without having to choose one culture over the other. This notion of **bicultural competence** has been related to successful functioning in both one's culture of origin and the new culture (LaFromboise et al., 1993).

Bicultural Competence

Working knowledge and appreciation of two cultures.

What leads people to become highly identified with their ethnic or racial group? A study of African American college students found that those students whose parents were members of predominantly black organizations, who had taken black studies courses, and who had experienced racism or racial prejudice were more likely to include their African American background as a strong feature of their self-concept (Baldwin, Brown, & Rackley, 1990; Thompson, 1990, 1991). Thus, participation in ethnically related activities and being treated in particular ways because of one's ethnic or racial background foster a sense of ethnic identity.

Culture and the Self

Cross-cultural research suggests that concepts of the self vary greatly, depending on one's culture (Rhee, Uleman, Lee, & Roman, 1995; Triandis, McCusker, & Hui, 1990). In an investigation of this point, Markus and Kitayama (1991) explicitly contrasted American culture with Japanese culture to illustrate the substantial differences in self-conceptions that may exist between Western and Eastern cultures.

Independent Self

The sense of oneself as bounded, unitary, and separate from the social context.

In America, there is a strong emphasis on individuality and how one can best distinguish oneself from others by discovering and making use of one's unique talents. This **independent self** is "a bounded, unique, more or less integrated motivational and cognitive universe, a dynamic center of awareness, emotion, judgment, action, organized into a distinctive whole and set contrastively, both against other such wholes and against a social and natural background" (Geertz, 1974, p. 48). Not only do Westerners construe the self as an independently functioning unit, but also they actually define independence as a fundamental task of socialization. Westerners teach their children how to be independent (Kitayama, 1992).

Interdependent Self

The sense of self as flexible, variable, and connected to the social context.

The **interdependent self** of many Eastern, southern European, and Latin cultures consists of seeing oneself as part of an encompassing social relationship and realizing that one's behavior is determined and dependent on what one perceives to be the thoughts, feelings, and actions of others in the relationship (Markus & Kitayama, 1991). The self becomes meaningful and complete largely within the context of a social relationship, rather than through independent, autonomous action. Although the interdependent self is regarded as possessing a set of internal qualities, such as abilities or opinions, these attributes are thought to be situation specific and unstable, rather than defining characteristics of the self (Bochner, 1994; Cousins, 1989). Thus, the interdependent self is not a bounded whole but changes its structure with the nature of the social context (Kanagawa, Cross, & Markus, 2001). In interdependent cultures, so fundamental is the emphasis on blending in that those attributes that uniquely differentiate one person from another are not regarded as particularly representative of the self. So, for example, although people from the United States would regard great musical talent in a child as a distinctive quality of that particular child, the Japanese might not.

The Western viewpoint regards the self as composed of individual attributes, such as ambition, good humor, or extroversion (Trafimow, Triandis, & Goto, 1991). These attributes are considered to be distinctively one's own, even when they are shared with others. A student, for example, may regard herself as creative, but this judgment is unrelated to judgments she might make about her roommate's creativity. Even if she regards both herself and her roommate as creative, her creativity is independent of her roommate's, not shared. In contrast, the collectivist view of the interdependent self regards the individual not in terms of distinctive qualities, but in terms of those that are shared. Because people are regarded as fundamentally connected to each other, they are thought to have attributes in common rather than attributes that they uniquely possess (Bochner, 1994; Trafimow et al., 1991). Thus, two students might be creative interdependently and not independently. These different culture-based views of the self are illustrated in Figure 4–1.

Ethnic identity is an important part of self-knowledge that comes from membership in a particular ethnic group and participation in the group's valued activities.

Markus and Kitayama (1991, 1994) suggest that this conception of self as independent versus interdependent is a fundamentally important aspect of an individual's self-system. It influences how people think about their own personal characteristics, how people relate to others, what emotions are experienced in different situations, and what motivates people to engage in action. Moreover, this cultural conception of the self becomes rooted in the ideas, values, and social scripts of a culture, further shaping individual experience and the expression of the self (Han & Shavitt, 1994; Markus & Kitayama, 1994). Table 4–3 shows items from a scale that assesses independence and interdependence. Which are you?

Culture, Cognition, and Emotion. Different construals of the self have potentially important cognitive consequences. For example, those with an independent sense of self see themselves as distinctive. Although they may regard other people as like them, they do not regard themselves as similar to other people. In contrast, among those with interdependent selves, the self and others are considered part of a specific social context in which both are embedded. Thus, both self and others are construed as quite similar.

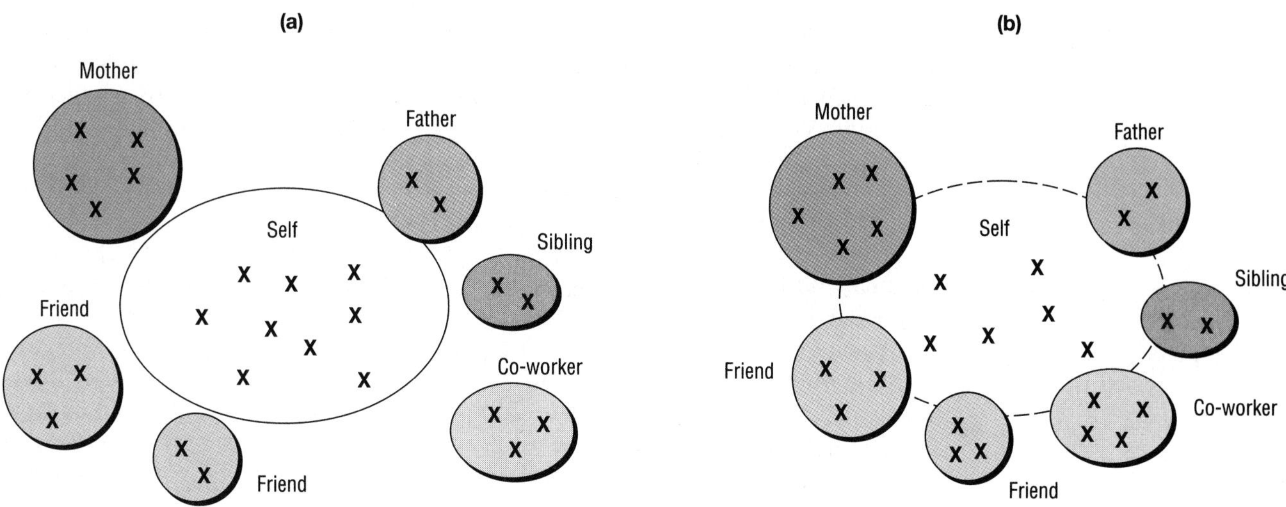

Figure 4–1 **Conceptual Representations of the Self.**
(a) Independent Construal; (b) Interdependent Construal.

Source: H. R. Markus and S. Kitayama (1991). Culture and the self: Implications for cognition, emotion, and motivation, *Psychological Review, 98,* 224–253. Copyright © 1991 by the American Psychological Association. Reprinted with permission.

The factors underlying personal motivation to achieve may be different as well. For example, Americans tend to strive for personal achievement, whereas the Japanese tend to strive for the achievement of group goals. Personal choice of tasks or activities enhances motivation for those in the United States, whereas it has a lesser effect on Asian students' intrinsic motivation (Iyengar & Lepper, 1999). For example, European Americans are more likely to select a task if they think they will do well on it or have done well on it in the past, whereas Asians' choice of task is not based on such expectations or prior performance (Oishi & Diener, 2003).

Individualistic (or agentic) motives versus interdependent (or communal) ones are even used to organize information about the social world in memory (Woike, Gershkovich, Piorkowski, & Polo, 1999). People with independent self-construals

Table 4–3

The Measurement of Independent and Interdependent Self-Constructs

Indicate the extent to which you agree or disagree with each of the items below based on the following scale:

1	2	3	4	5	6	7
Strongly disagree						Strongly agree

___1. I have respect for authority figures with whom I interact.

___2. I am comfortable with being singled out for praise or rewards.

___3. My happiness depends on the happiness of those around me.

___4. Speaking up in class is not a problem for me.

___5. I should take into consideration my parents' advice when making education and career plans.

___6. My personal identity independent of others is very important to me.

If you answered "agree" on items 1, 3, and 5, you scored high in interdependence, whereas if you answered "agree" on items 2, 4, and 6, you scored high in independence. Note that the entire scale is longer than the excerpt above.

Source: T. M. Singelis, *Personality and Social Psychology Bulletin, 20* (5), pp. 580–591, copyright © 1994 by Sage Publications, Inc. Reprinted by permission of Sage Publications, Inc.

are more likely to ignore the context in the inferences they draw about the social environment, whereas those with interdependent self-construals process social stimuli by paying attention to their relation to the context (Kuhnen, Hannover, & Schubert, 2001). For example, whereas North Americans often describe events in terms of the specific actors involved and their personal qualities, those with collectivist orientations are more likely to refer to the social groups to which those others belong (Menon, Morris, Chiu, & Hong, 1999).

People with independent versus interdependent selves may experience fundamentally different kinds of emotions. Those with an independent sense of self, as found in U.S. culture, frequently experience ego-focused emotions, such as the experience of pride ("I did well.") or frustration ("I was treated unfairly."). In contrast, cultures with interdependent conceptions of self tend to experience other-focused emotions (e.g., Mesquita, 2001). As an example, Markus and Kitayama (1991) use *amae*, the Japanese word for the sense of being lovingly cared for and dependent on another's indulgence. *Amae* is the formation and maintenance of a mutually reciprocal interdependent relationship with another person. There is no equivalent for *amae* in the English language. The differences between independent and interdependent self-conceptions are summarized in Table 4–4.

Similarly, self-esteem is likely to vary, depending on the sense of self that a person holds (Crocker, Luhtanen, Blaine, & Broadnax, 1994). Recall from Table 4–1 the kinds of items that assess self-esteem, such as "I feel I am a person of worth." Members of cultures with an independent sense of self are more likely to endorse these items than are members of cultures where the self is viewed interdependently (Markus & Kitayama, 1991; Yik, Bond, & Paulhus, 1998). More generally, the importance one attaches to self-esteem and its implications for life satisfaction vary between independent and interdependent countries. Evidence for this assertion was reported by Diener and Diener (1995). In a study of 31 countries, they found that the relation between self-esteem and life satisfaction was lower in interdependent or collectivist countries, whereas in independent countries, individuals with high self-esteem reported high life satisfaction as well (Diener & Diener, 1995; see also Crocker et al., 1994). In collectivist cultures, social norms (such as social approval) are better predictors of life satisfaction, whereas individual emotions are stronger predictors of life satisfaction in individualistic cultures (Suh, Diener, Oishi, & Triandis, 1998). So different are these patterns that some have questioned how psychologists should measure self-esteem,

Table 4–4

Summary of Key Differences Between an Independent and an Interdependent Perception of Self

Feature Compared	Independent	Interdependent
Definition	Separate from social context	Connected with social context
Structure	Bounded, unitary, stable	Flexible, variable
Important features	Internal, private (abilities, thoughts, feelings)	External, public (statuses, roles, relationships)
Tasks	Be unique Express self Realize internal attributes Promote own goals Be direct: say what's on your mind	Belong, fit in Occupy one's proper place Engage in appropriate action Promote others' goals Be indirect: read other's mind
Role of others	*Self-evaluation:* others important for social comparison, reflected appraisal	*Self-definition:* self defined by relationships with others in specific contexts
Basis of self-esteem[a]	Ability to express self; validate internal attributes	Ability to adjust, restrain self, maintain harmony with social context

[a]Esteeming the self may be primarily a Western phenomenon, and the concept of self-esteem should perhaps be replaced by "self-satisfaction," or by a term that reflects the realization that one is fulfilling the culturally mandated task.

Source: H. R. Markus and S. Kitayama. (1991). Culture and the self: Implications for cognition, emotion, and motivation. *Psychological Review, 98,* 224–253.

arguing that important components of self-esteem in interdependent cultures are missing from traditional Western definitions. Nonetheless, as our previous discussion of the bicultural self attests, people are capable of thinking of themselves in more than one culture simultaneously. How does biculturalism affect their self-perceptions? In an ingenious study, Ross, Xun, and Wilson (2002) gave several questionnaires to Chinese-born students, who were randomly assigned to participate in either Chinese or English; Canadian-born participants served as a control group and participated in English. Chinese-born participants who responded in Chinese endorsed more collective self-statements in their self-descriptions, scored lower on self-esteem, and expressed more agreement with Chinese cultural views than did their Chinese-born counterparts responding in English. The results suggest that these Chinese-born students had both East Asian and Western identities, with each being correspondingly activated by its associated language.

Despite differences between independent and interdependent cultures in willingness to endorse items on self-esteem scales, people in interdependent cultures who score high in self-esteem show many of the same effects as those from independent cultures who score high in self-esteem. For example, even in interdependent cultures, those who see themselves especially positively have higher levels of self-esteem (Yik et al., 1998). Members of interdependent cultures who have more independent self-construals appear similar to those from independent cultures, for example, and show self-protective responses to negative feedback. Moreover, as already noted, measures of implicit self-esteem suggest that even in interdependent cultures, there is some tendency to self-enhance indirectly, as by overvaluing the letters in one's name (Kitayama & Karasawa, 1997).

Relatedly, although Westerners are more likely to express the independent sense of self just described, there is much variability in the degree to which this is true. Members of some Western ethnic and religious groups think of themselves in interdependent or relational terms, despite living in a Western culture. Women are more likely than men to have an interdependent sense of self and to think of themselves in terms of their relationships with others rather than primarily as independent others (Cross, Bacon, & Morris, 2000; Cross & Vick, 2001). Thus, although there are cultural differences in self-construals, there is also considerable variability in whether members of a particular culture will think of themselves in independent or interdependent terms.

ASPECTS OF SELF-KNOWLEDGE

What form does our self-knowledge take? That is, how are the beliefs that we hold about ourselves represented cognitively?

Self-Schemas

In Chapter 2, we consider the concept of a schema. A schema is an organized, structured set of cognitions about some concept or stimulus. Just as people hold schemas about the nature of other people and events, they also hold schemas about themselves. **Self-schemas** describe the dimensions along which you think about yourself. You may, for example, be very concerned about maintaining and displaying your independence. You might refuse to take money from your parents for college, might do your own laundry, or might not ask your roommate for help with your math. Or you might consider yourself more dependent and think a lot about ensuring security for yourself by surrounding yourself with people you can depend on, like your brother, girlfriend, doctor, and minister. In either case, you have a strong self-schema concerning the independence–dependence dimension. On the other hand, you may not think of yourself very much in connection with that dimension, in which case you are not thinking schematically in those terms. You would be described as aschematic on the dimension of independence-dependence.

Self-Schemas

How one thinks about one's personal qualities in a particular life domain.

People are schematic on dimensions that are important to them, on which they think of themselves as extreme, and on which they are certain that the opposite

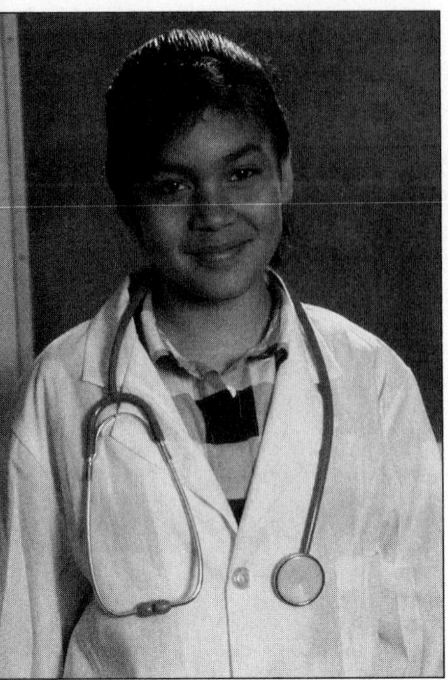

Possible selves are goals or roles to which people aspire that are currently not self-descriptive but may become so.

Possible Selves

Schemas that people hold concerning what they may or could become in the future.

is not true. If independence is important to you and you think of yourself as extremely independent and not at all dependent, this belief implies that you have accumulated considerable knowledge about yourself on that domain. For example, you are certain that you would never ask anyone for help setting up your stereo, even at the potential cost of damage to it or yourself. When you hold a schema for yourself on a particular dimension, it helps you to identify situations as relevant to that dimension. For example, if you think of yourself as independent, you are likely to see that the purchase of a new stereo system with complex instructions for installation requires independent behavior. Moreover, the recognition that situations are schema-relevant sets guidelines for your own behavior (Kendzierski & Whitaker, 1997). You are likely to recognize not only that the situation calls for independent behavior but also that you will be the one to play through the instructions and set up the stereo.

Not all self-schemas are positive. People also hold well-articulated, highly organized beliefs about themselves regarding negative qualities (Malle & Horowitz, 1995). For example, someone who thinks of himself as overweight will quickly notice that eating situations are relevant to him; he might plan what he will eat and may count the calories that he consumes. Being weight-schematic also means that he is likely to notice weight-relevant behaviors in others. Thus, for example, he may more quickly notice and infer that someone who has only cottage cheese and peaches for lunch is on a diet than would someone who is not so concerned with weight (Sedikides & Skowronski, 1993). Generally people are most likely to hold self-schemas about the personal attributes that make them distinctive (von Hipple, Hawkins, & Schooler, 2001).

People hold self-conceptions not only about their current qualities, but also about traits that may become self-descriptive at some time in the future (Markus & Nurius, 1986). These are called **possible selves**. Some of these involve goals or roles to which people aspire, such as the 5-year-old's desire to be a firefighter or the student's expectation of becoming a doctor. Most possible selves are positive. That is, people think of themselves in the future primarily in good terms (Markus & Nurius, 1986). However, some possible selves represent fears concerning what one might become in the future, such as the suspicion that one's enthusiastic consumption of alcohol on certain occasions could eventually lead to alcoholism. Contemplating feared selves can, not surprisingly, induce anxiety and guilt (Carver, Lawrence, & Scheier, 1999).

Possible selves function in much the same way as self-schemas. They help people to articulate their goals and develop behaviors that will enable them to fulfill those goals. In a study by Ruvolo and Markus (1992), participants were told to imagine themselves being successful at work, lucky at work, failing at work despite clear effort, or failing because of bad luck. Subsequently, participants worked on a task that measured persistence. Those participants who were asked to envision themselves as successful because of their own efforts worked longer on the task than did participants who envisioned themselves as failing or as succeeding due to luck, presumably because they had a vision of the successful possible self firmly in mind. Thus, possible selves provide focus and organization for the pursuit of goals. They help people gather appropriate self-knowledge and develop plans so they can rehearse the actions they need to undertake in pursuit of their goals (Markus & Ruvolo, 1989).

Self-schemas, including possible selves, then, have many important functions regarding self-knowledge and the self in action. Knowing our personal qualities enables us to identify quickly whether situations are relevant to us. Self-schemas help us to remember schema-relevant information. They help us to make inferences about the meaning of our past behavior and to make decisions and judgments that guide our future behavior.

Self-Discrepancies

Other aspects of the self that influence our thoughts and behavior concern discrepancies between how we actually are and how we ideally want to be or think we ought to be. Psychologist Tory Higgins (1987, 1989) suggests that these **self-discrepancies** produce strong emotions. When we perceive a discrepancy between our personal qualities and what we would ideally like to be **(ideal self)**, we experience disappointment, dissatisfaction, or sadness (what are called "dejection-related emotions"), as well as a reduction in self-esteem (Moretti & Higgins, 1990). Discrepancies between our actual self and what we think we ought to be **(ought self)** produce agitation-related emotions such as fear or anxiety (e.g., Boldero & Francis, 2000). Although the actual content of beliefs about the self shifts over time, the use of the ideal self and the ought self as standards and the psychological impact of discrepancies from those standards on well-being remain relatively stable (Strauman, 1996).

Self-Discrepancies

Discrepancies between how we perceive ourselves and how we would ideally like to be or believe others think we should be.

Ideal Self

The personal attributes one would like to have.

Ought Self

The personal attributes one believes one should possess.

To test these points, Higgins, Klein, and Strauman (1985) asked college students to fill out a questionnaire that assessed their self-perceptions, including how they would ideally like to be and how they felt they ought to be. The first time, the participants filled the questionnaire out for themselves. At a later time, they filled it out from the standpoint of their father, mother, and closest friend. They also rated the extent to which each of the personal attributes they rated was relevant or meaningful to them.

Discrepancies between the actual self and the ideal self did indeed produce dejection-related emotions (Higgins & Bargh, 1987) and loss of self-esteem (Higgins, Shah, & Friedman, 1997; Moretti & Higgins, 1990). For example, wanting to be editor of the school newspaper but failing to attain that position produced disappointment and sadness. Perceived discrepancies between one's actual self and a friend's or parent's ideal self produced anxiety. For example, perceiving that one was not going to be the successful entrepreneur of one's father's dream produced anxiety but not sadness. The more important the personal attribute was to the respondent, the greater the emotion experienced (see also Higgins, 1999).

Self-discrepancy theory postulates that concerns about the ideal or the ought self emerge from temperament and from early socialization. That is, we are predisposed, and may be taught as well, to think in terms of becoming our ideal self or meeting the standards of others. Generally speaking, people who are more concerned with becoming their ideal self recall having been raised by their parents in a warm and supportive way, whereas those who are more concerned about the opinions of others report a parenting style marked more by rejection (Manian, Strauman, & Denney, 1998). Cultural differences also affect whether the ideal or the ought self governs self-regulatory behavior. Specifically, people with an independent sense of self are more likely to be motivated by discrepancies between themselves and their ideal selves, whereas people raised with an interdependent self are more attentive to the concerns or demands of others (Lee, Acker, & Gardner, 2000). Overall, people experience a greater sense of well-being when there is a fit between the goals they are pursuing and their regulatory orientation (Bianco, Higgins, & Klem, 2003; Higgens, Idson, Freitas, Spiegel, & Molden, 2003).

SELF-REGULATION

How do we take all of this information we have about ourselves and employ it in our daily life? **Self-regulation** refers to the ways in which people control and direct their own actions. As we have seen, people have enormous quantities of information about themselves, including their personal characteristics and desires and their conceptions of themselves in the future. They formulate goals and pursue them, drawing on their social and self-regulatory skills. In this section, we deal explicitly with how conceptions of the self regulate thought, emotion, and action in social situations. Much of this self-regulation occurs virtually automatically without any awareness or conscious thought. We respond to the cues that are salient in the environment and that guide our behavior (e.g., Verplanken & Holland, 2002). But other times we consciously and actively intervene to control

Self-Regulation

The ways people control and direct their own actions.

our thoughts, reactions, and behaviors (Brandstatter & Frank, 2002). The ability of human beings to control, override, and interrupt their responses is a significant, important, and energy-consuming aspect of the self (Schmeichel, Vohs, & Baumesiter, 2003). To understand self-regulation, we begin with the working self-concept.

The Working Self-Concept

Working Self-Concept

Those aspects of the self-concept that are salient in a particular situation.

Which aspect of the self influences our thoughts and ongoing behavior depends in large part on what aspect of the self-concept is relevant to a particular situation. The aspect of the self-concept that is accessed for a particular situation is called the **working self-concept**. In a classroom situation, the academic self is likely to be the dominant determinant of our thoughts and feelings, whereas if we are reminded about a party on Friday, the social self may be accessed. The working self-concept is important because it draws on our overall self-concept but guides social behavior in specific situations and is, in turn, modified by what goes on in the situation (Ehrlinger & Dunning, 2003).

Earlier we noted the fact that self-esteem may be based on different attributes for different people. The athlete's self-esteem, for example, may be contingent on his performance during a game, whereas the gifted student's self-esteem may be contingent on her academic performance. These findings underscore an important point: In situations that call for attributes that are central to one's self-esteem, the self may be especially vulnerable (Crocker & Luhtanen, 2003). Crocker, Sommers, and Luhtanen (2002) studied students who applied to graduate school and then examined their self-esteem on days when they heard from graduate programs to which they had applied. Those participants who based their self-esteem heavily on academic competence showed greater increases in self-esteem on days they had been accepted and greater decreases in self-esteem on days when they had been rejected than students whose self-esteem was less based on their academic competence.

As this example suggests, the working self-concept can sometimes be at odds with the stable self-concept (Arndt, Schimel, Greenberg, & Pyszczynski, 2002). Think about a time when you had an argument with a friend and snapped at her. Afterward, you probably didn't feel good about yourself, and she probably didn't think much of you either. Yet you probably have a stable sense of yourself as a nice person who is easy to get along with. After that particular incident, you may not have thought well of yourself for at least several hours or perhaps even a few days (Nezlak & Plesko, 2001). Over time, however, your stable self-concept won out, and you again thought of yourself as pleasant and easy to get along with, even though occasionally you are not this way at all. As this example implies, changes in self-esteem may fluctuate with day-to-day activities as well (Nezlek & Plesko, 2001). These fluctuations in feelings about the self seem to depend most heavily on whether one feels competent, in control, and connected with others during daily activities (Reis, Sheldon, Gable, Roscoe, & Ryan, 2000).

Changes in the working self-concept produce changes in the permanent self-concept only when the working self-concept is stable over time. For example, while in college, you may not think of yourself as particularly authoritative. Yet, after graduating, if you get a job supervising several other people in a bank and you do this day in and day out for months or even years, you may come to think of yourself as authoritative, and that view may become an important part of your stable self-concept. It was not so before, but it became so because you are now consistently in a situation that requires an authoritative manner. The working self-concept, in this case, became part of the stable self-concept.

Self-Complexity

Self-Complexity

The number of dimensions that people use to think about themselves.

Another aspect of the self that is important for self-regulation involves **self-complexity**. Some people think of themselves in one or two predominant ways, whereas others think of themselves in terms of a variety of qualities. One college student may think of herself primarily as a student, focusing her attention and beliefs about herself on how well she does in her courses. Another may think of herself in more complex ways, as a student, a daughter, a girlfriend, a member of the track team, and a part-time employee (Linville, 1985; Woolfolk, Novalany, Gara, Allen, & Polino, 1995).

Linville (1985) suggests that people with simple self-conceptions are buoyed by success in their particular area of importance but are very vulnerable to failure. So, for example, the student who is focused primarily on her grades and who receives a bad grade may feel very upset and depressed because of it. People who are more complex, however, may be buoyed by success but have other aspects of themselves that buffer them in the case of failures or setbacks. The student who has an academic setback but has a complex self may temporarily turn her attention away from her schoolwork to prepare for a track meet and thus cope somewhat more successfully with the academic setback. Thus, self-complexity can act as a buffer against stressful life events and may help prevent people from becoming depressed or ill in response to setbacks (Showers & Ryff, 1996).

Considerable research has demonstrated the importance of self-complexity for buffering people against setbacks, with one caveat: Only positive complex self-representations achieve this function. Negative complex self-representations, by contrast, represent a risk factor for depression and predict poorer recovery from depression (Woolfolk et al., 1995). It stands to reason that thinking about oneself as inadequate or as likely to do poorly in a variety of domains is not going to buffer a person against failures or setbacks.

Self-Efficacy and Personal Control

Other aspects of the self that influence self-regulation include **self-efficacy** beliefs, the expectations that we hold about our abilities to accomplish certain tasks (Bandura, 1986). Whether we will undertake a particular activity or strive to meet a particular goal depends on whether we believe we will be efficacious in performing those actions. The smoker will not stop smoking unless she believes she can do it, no matter how badly she may want to stop. Faced with a challenging paper, the student who believes he has the ability to do a good job will be more likely to start it and persist at it than the student who has doubts about his ability to complete it successfully. Psychologists believe that early experiences with success and failure lead people to develop fairly stable conceptions of their self-efficacy in different life domains (Bandura, 1986).

Self-Efficacy

Specific expectations about our abilities to accomplish certain tasks.

It is important to realize that self-efficacy beliefs are highly specific, control-related perceptions of one's ability to perform a particular behavior. They are not general feelings of control. So, for example, if you want to know if someone will work hard to try out for the tennis team, you need to know his self-efficacy beliefs specifically related to making the tennis team, not his general feelings about himself as an effective person.

More generally, a sense of personal control enables people to plan, cope with setbacks, and generally engage in self-regulatory processes. In a study that illustrates this point, Pham, Taylor, and Seeman (2001) exposed college students who were either high or low in their sense of personal mastery to a manipulation that made salient the unpredictable aspects of college, the predictable aspects of college life, or the neutral features of the college environment. For example, the students in the unpredictable condition were reminded how sometimes it is impossible to get into a class of one's choice, whereas those in the predictable circumstances were reminded that exam times and paper dates are always posted at the beginning of the quarter. The students then listed their thoughts and feelings about college. Blood pressure and heart rate were also assessed. The students who had been exposed to the predictable college manipulation made more references to the future and more references to personal goals in their list of thoughts. They also had lower blood pressure and heart rates compared to those who had read about

Certain experiences, such as being filmed, put us in a state of self-awareness. Self-awareness causes people to compare and evaluate themselves according to available standards.

neutral features of the college environment or the unpredictable aspects of the college environment, suggesting that the manipulation emphasizing the predictable aspects of college reduced stress. The students who were chronically high in personal mastery were more optimistic and future oriented than were those low in personal mastery. A sense of personal control, whether generally true of one's life or true with respect to specific goals, plays an important self-regulatory role in helping people plan and make progress toward their futures.

Behavioral Activation and Inhibition

Self-regulation involves fundamental decisions about what people and activities to approach and which ones to avoid. Psychologists have argued that people have two quite independent motivational systems that control these tasks: an appetitive system, referred to as the "behavioral activation system" (BAS) and an aversive system, or "behavioral inhibition system" (BIS). When BAS is activated, people tend to approach people or activities in the environment; when BIS is activated, people are more likely to avoid people and activities.

One way to think about this distinction is as an individual difference. Some people are more BAS oriented and some people are more BIS oriented. For the most part, people who experience a lot of positive events and positive affect have a strong behavioral activation system, whereas people whose experience is dominated by negative affect have a stronger behavioral inhibition system. Daily experience influences the activation of these systems as well. If good things are happening to you, you are more likely to be in an activation state (BAS) than in an inhibited state (BIS) (Gable, Reis, & Elliot, 2000).

Earlier we discussed people's concerns with discrepancies from their ideal self versus their concerns with other's expectations for them. This distinction may map onto the difference between BAS (activation or goal promotion) and BIS (inhibition or prevention) (Shah & Higgins, 2001). Discrepancies from one's ideal facilitate efforts toward attaining the ideal (activation), whereas concerns that one may not meet the expectations of others represents a prevention (inhibition) orientation (Forster, Higgins, & Idson, 1998). Perhaps because it is fueled by anxiety, people motivated by a prevention focus are faster off the mark to meet prevention-related goals than people who are promotion oriented (Freitas, Lieberman, Salovey, & Higgins, 2002). This general orientation toward promotion or approach versus prevention or avoidance may reflect stable personality traits, with extroversion the exemplar of approach and neuroticism the exemplar of avoidance (Carver, Sutton, & Scheier, 2000).

Self-Awareness

Self-regulation is also influenced by our direction of attention, specifically, whether attention is directed inward toward the self or outward toward the environment (Duval & Wicklund, 1972). Usually our attention is focused outward toward the environment, but sometimes it is focused inward on ourselves. Certain experiences in the world automatically focus attention inward, such as catching sight of ourselves in the mirror, having our picture taken, or, more subtly, being evaluated by others, or even simply being a minority in a group situation. We begin to think of ourselves not as moving actors in the environment, but as objects of our own and others' attention. This state is called **self-awareness** (Duval & Wicklund, 1972; Wicklund & Frey, 1980).

Self-Awareness

Experiencing oneself as an object of one's own attention.

In general, self-awareness leads people to evaluate their behavior against a standard and to set an adjustment process in motion for meeting the standard. Suppose, for example, that you go out to an elegant restaurant and you are seated facing your date but also, to your irritation, you are looking directly into a mirror on the wall behind you. Try as you might, each time you look up, you catch sight of your own face. You notice your windblown hair, the awkward way you smile, and the unattractive way you chew. Feeling utterly foolish by the time the main course arrives, you flee to the bathroom to comb your hair, vowing that if you still look as bad when you return, you will change tables (Duval, Duval, & Mulilis, 1992; Sedikides, 1992).

Self-attention causes people to compare themselves to standards, such as those for physical appearance, intellectual performance, athletic prowess, or moral integrity (Macrae, Bodenhausen, & Milne, 1998). We attempt to conform to the standard, evaluate our behavior against that standard, decide that it either matches the standard or does not, and continue adjusting and comparing until we meet the standard or give up. This process is called "feedback," and the theory is called the **cybernetic theory of self-regulation** (Carver & Scheier, 1998). As the "mirror" example suggests, self-awareness is often experienced as aversive, and so people strive to find ways to reduce objective self-awareness, that is, to direct their attention away from themselves (Flory, Räikkönen, Matthews, & Owens, 2000). For example, at the end of a hard day people often need to keep themselves from focusing on personal issues and problems, and there are a variety of methods to do so. Television, for example, seems to effectively direct attention away from the self and consequently makes people less aware of how they are falling short of their standards (Moskalenko & Heine, 2003).

Cybernetic Theory of Self-Regulation

People compare their behavior to a standard, decide that it matches the standard or does not, and continue adjusting their behavior until a match is made or the goal is abandoned.

People also differ in the degrees to which they attend to public or private aspects of themselves. This distinction has been called "public" versus "private self-consciousness" (Fenigstein, Scheier, & Buss, 1975). People high in **public self-consciousness** are concerned with autonomy and issues of identity (Schlenker & Weigold, 1990). They worry about what other people think about them, the way they look, and how they appear to others. Those high in **private self-consciousness** try to analyze themselves, think about themselves a great deal, and are more attentive to their inner feelings. People high in private self-consciousness seem to have better articulated self-schemas, and they are more aware of their internal dispositions (Shrum & McCarty, 1992). When the public self is made especially salient, people tend to place more weight on their personal attitudes, but when their attention is diverted outward, they are more likely to place weight on social norms (Ybarra & Trafimow, 1998). Public and private forms of self-consciousness are not opposites. People can be high in both, low in both, or high in one or the other. Which are you? Or are you high in both? Answer the questions in Table 4–5 to find out.

Public Self-Consciousness

A tendency to be concerned with how one appears to others.

Private Self-Consciousness

A tendency to focus on the internal self.

Table 4–5

Self-Consciousness Scale

Indicate whether you generally agree (A) or disagree (D) with each of the following items.

___1. I'm always trying to figure myself out.

___2. I'm concerned about my style of doing things.

___3. Generally, I'm not very aware of myself.

___4. I reflect about myself a lot.

___5. I'm concerned about the way I present myself.

___6. I'm self-conscious about the way I look.

___7. I never scrutinize myself.

___8. I'm generally attentive to my inner feelings.

___9. I usually worry about making a good impression.

If you answered "agree" on items 1, 4, and 8 and "disagree" on items 3 and 7, you scored high on the private self-conciousness scale. If you answered "agree" to items 2, 5, 6, and 9, you scored high on the public self-conciousness scale. Note that the entire scale is considerably longer than the excerpt above.

Source: Adapted from Fenigstein, Scheier, and Buss (1975).

MOTIVATION AND THE SELF

This chapter has considered the working self-concept, self-efficacy expectations, and focus of attention among other determinants of how people regulate their activities in the environment. It is also important to know the motivations that drive self-regulation. Generally speaking, people seek an accurate, stable, and positive self-concept and will seek out situations or behave in ways that further those aspects of the self.

The Need for an Accurate Self-Concept

To make our future outcomes predictable and controllable, we need to have a fairly accurate assessment of our abilities. Psychologist Yaacov Trope (1975, 1983) has argued that in the absence of factors that might induce people to save face or strive to succeed, people tend to pick tasks that will be most informative about their abilities, tasks that he calls "diagnostic." For example, if you, a college student, want to know if you are a good dancer, you are unlikely to go to a children's dancing class or to a ballroom competition. You will do extremely well in the first setting and incredibly poorly in the second (unless you have been trained in competitive ballroom dancing). The situation most diagnostic for your dancing ability is a college dance or party.

Overall, Trope's work suggests that having an accurate sense of self is an important determinant in the selection of a task, especially when our knowledge of our ability is uncertain (Sorrentino & Roney, 1986). Accurate self-assessment enables us to anticipate and control our future performance (Trope & Bassok, 1982). Research suggests that we are most likely to seek accurate self-relevant information when we anticipate that the news will be good, but we also sometimes show a desire for self-assessment when we anticipate that the news may be bad (Brown, 1990).

The Need for a Consistent Self-Concept

Related to the need for accuracy is the need to have a consistent sense of self. We do not want to think of ourselves as changing dramatically from situation to situation; rather, we need to believe that we have certain intrinsic qualities that remain relatively stable over time (Swann, 1983). People seek out situations and interpret their behavior in ways that confirm their pre-existing self-conceptions, and they avoid or resist situations and feedback that are at odds with their existing self-conceptions. This process is termed **self-verification**. Imagine, for example, that a seminar has just ended and a classmate comes up to you and says, "Boy, you don't talk much in class, do you?" Perhaps you didn't talk in class that particular day, but you may think of yourself as someone who usually does. You may find that during the next class, you talk even more than you usually do in order to convince your classmate, as well as yourself, that your conception of yourself as an active class participant is a correct one.

Self-Verification

Seeking out and interpreting situations that confirm one's self-concept.

A series of studies by Swann and Read (1981b) suggests that this need to see ourselves as consistent is quite pervasive. In one study, college students were led to believe that other college students' evaluations of them would be either consistent or inconsistent with their own self-image. When given a chance to see those evaluations, the students spent more time perusing consistent than inconsistent feedback. This was true even when the consistent attributes were ones on which people perceived themselves negatively (see Swann & Schroeder, 1995).

When interacting with others, people also use behavioral strategies that confirm their self-conceptions. That is, they deliberately act in ways that confirm the existing self-image (McNulty & Swann, 1994), especially when they are certain of their self-views (Pelham & Swann, 1994). This tendency is especially strong when people believe that others have incorrect beliefs about them. The earlier example of volunteering more in class to counteract a classmate's false impression illustrates this point.

This need to see the self in a consistent manner extends to several other strategies of self-regulation. We selectively interact with others who see us as we see ourselves (Swann & Pelham, 1990; Swann, Stein-Seroussi, & Giesler, 1992). Generally speaking, we like the people who see us positively on the attributes that we are confident we hold (Katz & Beach, 2000). We choose signs and symbols in our clothing and appearance that say things about who we are (Swann, 1983). So, if you want people to think of you as an athlete, you are more likely to wear your athletic jersey than a T-shirt to class. We remember feedback that is consistent with our self-attributes better than we remember incongruent feedback (Story, 1998). People attempt to verify not only their own self-qualities but also the attributes they share with others. Many of the attributes we hold most dear concern our relationships with others and the personal qualities that we share with them, such as being a daughter or being a Democrat. People strive to maintain consistent beliefs on these qualities too, especially when their memberships in these groups are important to them (Chen, Chen, & Shaw, 2004).

The previous discussion implies that people spend much of their time seeking out situations and ways of behaving in accordance with their existing self-concept. In fact, this picture is probably not accurate. Most of the time, people are able to maintain their views of themselves without any active or conscious effort. Maintaining a consistent sense of self is part of the process of interacting with family, friends, and coworkers in familiar settings, performing familiar tasks. However, when people receive discrepant feedback from others, they may be especially motivated to focus active attention on the threat to a consistent self-conception and thus act to dispel the incorrect view (Madon et al., 2001). Self-verification can also influence whether people feel the need to self-enhance or not: When we are accepted for who we are by people who are important to us, our need to bolster self-esteem may decline (Schimel, Arndt, Pyszczynski, & Greenberg, 2001). The tendency to seek self-verifying feedback is influenced by self-esteem; people with high self-esteem tend to seek self-verifying feedback whether it is positive or negative. But people low in self-esteem, who are especially concerned with self-protection, tend to seek positive more than negative feedback, even when that positive feedback is non-self-verifying (Bernichon, Cook, & Brown, 2003).

Although the desire for a consistent self can be a potent motive for gaining self-verifying feedback, there may be cultural constraints on this process. Choi and Choi (2002) found that Koreans were more likely than Americans to express inconsistent beliefs about themselves across different contexts. Thus, although Americans saw themselves as moderately honest across several contexts, the Korean participants held less consistent beliefs that varied across situations, portraying themselves as very honest in some situations, and less so in others. Thus, the desire for a consistent self may partly reflect a cultural value. Consistent with these findings, East Asians may view themselves as more flexible across situations, whereas European Americans may view themselves as more consistent across situations (Suh, 2002).

People choose signs and symbols in their clothing and appearance to make statements about who they are. This process is called "self-verification."

Self-Improvement

In addition to the desire for an accurate sense of self, people are motivated by the desire to improve. The educational process, for example, assumes that people will strive to enhance their ability to master fundamental learning tasks. Many people aim to improve their performance in sports and other leisure activities rather than maintain a static level of ability. Once we are employed, we want to improve our job skills so we can maintain or enhance our standing in our work organization. Many self-regulatory activities serve this need to improve (Kasser & Ryan, 1996).

What kinds of information and situations do we seek when our goal is self-improvement? Earlier in this chapter, Markus's concept of possible selves, the visions that people have of themselves in the future, is discussed. Markus argues that by clearly articulating visions of ourselves in desired activities, we are able to set appropriate goals, make progress toward achieving those goals, and chart how well we are doing with respect to those goals. For example, the would-be college professor can chart and plan her personal progress better if she has a clear view of how she will perform in this future role. Thus, possible selves give explicit vision to the goals we set for ourselves in the future and help us to attain them.

Self-improvement may also be facilitated by social contact with other people. Specifically, comparing the self with someone who possesses a desired skill or attribute can enable a person to improve (Taylor & Lobel, 1989). This process is called "upward comparison." For example, a college football player may keep pictures of his favorite professional players on his wall to inspire him and remind him of the steps he needs to take to reach the same level of success. People who embody the attributes or skills we wish to attain can motivate us and can also be a source of specific information that is helpful for improvement.

Self-improvement is often motivated by criticism, whether explicitly from others or implicitly in one's performance. The perception that one has failed or not achieved as much as one hoped can be esteem reducing. Self-improvement processes are more pronounced, and negative emotional reactions are weaker when failure is particular to a highly specific task, rather than to a more global trait, such as intelligence. In this way, the specificity of the failure can be self-protective, inspiring improvement in the specific situation or skill (Kurman, 2003). By restricting need for self-improvement to a particular personal quality, overall self-esteem may be maintained. Self-improvement appears to be a particularly important motivation for East Asians (Heine et al., 2001).

Although social psychologists have not yet exhaustively explored the area of self-improvement—namely, the conditions under which we seek to improve ourselves, the attributes on which we wish to improve, and the sources of information and inspiration we turn to—they have begun to address the issue.

Self-Enhancement

Clearly, we need to have accurate information about our abilities and opinions. Without some degree of accuracy and consistency in our self-image, we would be vulnerable to a host of faulty judgments and decisions. We also need to set goals, acquire new skills and information, and generally improve on the abilities and skills that are important to us. Yet our self-regulatory activities are also heavily determined by the need to feel good about ourselves and to maintain self-esteem. These **self-enhancement** needs appear to be important, perhaps even preeminent, most of the time (Sedikides, 1993), and they become especially important following situations of threat, failure, or blows to self-esteem (Beauregard & Dunning, 1998; Krueger, 1998; Wills, 1981).

Self-Enhancement

The need to hold a positive view of oneself.

One way that people satisfy their self-enhancement needs is by holding self-perceptions that are falsely positive and somewhat exaggerated with respect to their actual abilities, talents, and social skills (Taylor & Brown, 1988). Taylor and Brown have called these **positive illusions**. There are at least three types of positive illusions: People see themselves more positively than is true; they believe they have more control over the events around them than is actually the case; and they are unrealistically optimistic about the future. For example, when students are asked to describe how accurately positive and negative personality adjectives describe themselves and others, most evaluate themselves more favorably than they evaluate others (e.g., Suls, Lemos, & Stewart, 2002). We remember positive information about ourselves, but negative information often slips conveniently from the mind (Sedikides & Green, 2000). We respond to threats by bolstering our self-perceptions in other life domains (Boney-McCoy, Gibbons, & Gerrard, 1999). If pressed, most of us would have more difficulty reconstructing circumstances when we have failed than circumstances when we have succeeded (Story, 1998). We believe we are more likely than others to engage in selfless, kind, and generous acts (Epley & Dunning, 2000). We often remember our performance as more positive than it actually was (Crary, 1966). We believe we are happier than most other people (Klar & Giladi, 1999). And perhaps most poignant of all, we see ourselves as less biased than we believe others to be (Pronin, Lin, & Ross, 2002).

Positive Illusions

Mild, falsely positive self-enhancing perceptions of one's personal qualities.

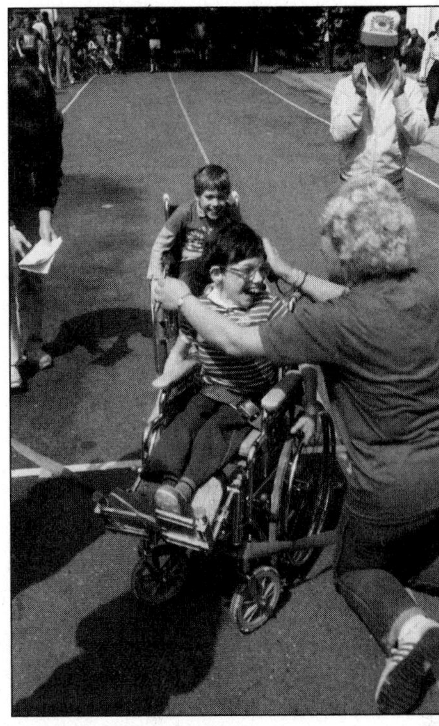

Sometimes just feeling good about ourselves (self-enhancement) is important.

As we see in Chapter 3, people are more likely to attribute positive than negative outcomes to themselves (Miller & Ross, 1975). We credit the volleyball win to our own spectacular plays, but we attribute the loss to "a bad day" or "poor team coordination." When we do acknowledge our negative qualities, we often regard them as less important or consequential than our positive qualities (e.g., Campbell, 1986; Haraciewicz, Sansone, & Manderlink, 1985). Although we may dimly recognize that we have no talent in some areas of our lives (such as athletics), we keep those negative self-perceptions from mind by avoiding thinking about them, avoiding situations that would bring them to the fore (Showers, 1992), or by remaining oblivious to just how bad we are (Kruger & Dunning, 1999). Alternatively, we may develop unique definitions of talents and shortcomings, so that we value more highly the things we do well than the things we do poorly (Greve & Wentura, 2003).

Are there conditions when people are more accurate or balanced in their self-appraisals? It appears that when people are about to receive feedback from others they are reasonably realistic, even pessimistic about the news they will get (Taylor & Shepperd, 1998). When people are in the process of deciding between alternative courses of action or setting goals, they are fairly accurate and honest with themselves. But once they move on to the task of implementing those goals, their positive illusions become more evident (Taylor & Gollwitzer, 1995). As these findings imply, viewing oneself in an unrealistically favorable light is more feasible about the future than about the present (Robinson & Ryff, 1999).

People who are low in self-esteem or moderately depressed may be more even-handed in their self-perceptions. They tend to recall both positive and negative information, their self-perceptions are more congruent with others' evaluations of them, and they are less likely to show the self-serving attributional bias of taking credit for good but not bad outcomes (Taylor & Brown, 1988). People are also more modest in their self-appraisals when they expect that others will have accurate information about their abilities, when their self-descriptions can be relatively easily verified, or when they expect to receive self-relevant feedback (Armor & Taylor, 1998; Shepperd, Ouellette, & Fernandez, 1996). In summary, people are much more likely to be self-aggrandizing when they won't get caught by their little white lies than when disconfirming evidence is likely to be forthcoming.

Why are most people so apparently self-enhancing in their self-perceptions; moreover, why do these self-enhancing perceptions exist if they do not conform to reality? Taylor and Brown (1988) argued that self-enhancing positive illusions are adaptive (Taylor, Lerner, Sherman, Sage, & McDowell, 2003). Unrealistic optimism about the future and a false sense of personal control may help us feel better about ourselves (Regan, Snyder, & Kassin, 1995) and persist longer in trying to achieve our goals. When we feel good about ourselves, we are happy, our social interactions go more smoothly, and we are more likely to help others. Feeling good about ourselves keeps us motivated and engaged in productive and creative work. Who, for example, would continue to work on a major project if he or she anticipated that it would be unsuccessful? Believing that we are talented and that our efforts will be successful keeps us going.

In short, then, our self-enhancing self-perceptions may foster many of the tasks that are regarded as evidence of a successful life adjustment: a sense of personal well-being, pleasant social interactions, and the ability to engage in creative, productive work (see Brown & Dutton, 1995). Positive self-regard is thought to foster good social relationships as well (Taylor et al., 2003); however, it appears that this relation has an upward limit. People who are noticeably self-enhancing can alienate their peers, as we will see shortly in our consideration of self-presentational skills (Bonanno, Field, Kovacevic, & Kaltman, 2002; Robins & Beer, 2001).

The need to feel good about oneself is often caricatured as blatant self-aggrandizement or self-deception. Yet feeling good about ourselves—not feeling threatened or undermined—is important in other aspects of personal and social life. When people are feeling less threatened, they are, perhaps paradoxically, more

IS SELF-ENHANCEMENT ASSOCIATED WITH A HEALTHY OR UNHEALTHY STRESS RESPONSE? A SOCIAL NEUROSCIENCE APPROACH

Self-enhancement, namely, seeing one's self more positively than may actually be true, has been a controversial topic within social psychology. Some psychologists have suggested that self-enhancement can foster mental and physical health (Taylor & Brown, 1988), but others have suggested that self-enhancement may be little more than defensive neuroticism that makes people overreact to stress and is therefore maladaptive for mental and physical health.

We all know the experience of stress. Our heart beats faster, blood pressure goes up, and we feel anxious. But what many of us may not know is that repeated exposure to experiences like these can actually compromise our health. Recently, social psychologists have tested the potential health impact of self-enhancement by examining whether self-enhancement is tied to stronger or to weaker biological responses to stress.

In one study (Taylor, Lerner, Sherman, Sage, & McDowell, 2003), college students completed measures of self-enhancement, which asked people to rate their personal qualities (such as intelligence or attractiveness) relative to their peers. Those who regarded themselves more favorably than their peers were judged to be self-enhancing. Participants also completed measures of mental health and psychological resources, such as optimism and social support. A few days later, they performed a series of challenging tasks in the laboratory. These included counting backwards as rapidly as possible by 7s from 2,085. While they were attempting to perform this task, they were harassed by an experimenter who told them to go faster and announced their mistakes. If you try to do this task under these kinds of harassing conditions, you will see how stressful it can be. While the stressful tasks were being performed, participants' heart rate and blood pressure were measured, and cortisol, a hormone that indicates stress, was collected through samples of saliva.

Were self-enhancing individuals more or less stressed out by these tasks compared to people who did not self-enhance? The result indicated that people who were higher in self-enhancement had lower heart rate and blood pressure responses to the stressful tasks, recovered normal heart rate and blood pressure more quickly after the tasks had ended, and had lower baseline cortisol levels. These patterns suggest that the self-enhancers had a healthier response to stress. Furthermore, the relation between self-enhancement and cortisol depended on psychological resources. That is, self-enhancing participants were more likely to be optimistic, have a sense of personal control, and have a supportive social network, and it was these resources that influenced their lower cortisol levels.

These findings are consistent with a growing body of research that ties positive mental states including self-enhancement to healthier physiological and neuroendocrine functioning (e.g., Taylor et al., 2000). As such, this study illustrates the value of a *social neuroscience* approach to social psychological issues. Social neuroscience integrates social behavior with its biological underpinnings, an approach that will be seen increasingly in social psychological research.

receptive to negative information about themselves. On a day when you get a good grade in one course, you may be more ready to hear a more qualified assessment in another course, for example. And when people are feeling good about themselves, they are less likely to be negative about other people (Ybarra, 1999).

Whether people are primarily motivated to be accurate or self-enhancing in their self-assessments has been a particular area of controversy, and the answer seems to depend, in part, on the circumstances in which feedback is sought. Specifically, self-enhancement is greater at the beginning of a project, when it has the power to motivate people to carry through their efforts toward their goals, than at the end of a project, when modest achievements and their discrepancies from hoped-for results might be dispiriting (Shepperd, Ouellette, & Fernandez,

1996). Self-enhancement is more evident when personal qualities are ambiguous than when they are concrete; people are more accurate if their self-assessments can potentially be disconfirmed (e.g., Dunning, Meyerowitz, & Holzberg, 1989). Self-enhancement is more in evidence when a course of action has been selected than when it is under debate; when people are debating the pros and cons of a particular course of action, their perceptions both of that undertaking and of their personal abilities to achieve it are more modest and in line with reality than is the case when they are preparing to implement it (Taylor & Gollwitzer, 1995). Thus, people are most likely to be self-enhancing at the general level when the chances that they will be proven wrong are negligible, but they become more accurate and modest in specific situations when exaggerated self-assessments may be subject to scrutiny or might lead them down risky paths (e.g., Sedikides, Herbst, Hardin, & Dardis, 2002).

The salience of these motives also appears to vary culturally. People from Western cultures, such as the United States, are more likely to self-enhance, whereas those from interdependent cultures, such as the Japanese, may be more concerned with self-improvement and therefore more likely to engage in self-criticism (Kitayama, Markus, Matsumoto, & Norasakkunkit, 1997).

Of the motives that guide self-regulation, self-enhancement has been the most studied; several specific theories that address important aspects of self-enhancement are presented in the following discussion.

Self-Affirmation. Psychologists believe that self-enhancement needs become especially important under conditions of threat. When people have received a blow to their self-worth brought about by a failure at some important task, they may try to emphasize or otherwise recruit positive features of themselves in order to compensate for the setback. For example, the attractive male student who fails an exam may seek out female classmates who will flatter his ego. Or the college student who is not making friends easily may proudly display high school sports trophies. **Self-affirmation** theory, developed by Claude Steele (1988), explicitly predicts that people will cope with specific threats to their self-worth by affirming unrelated aspects of themselves (Aronson, Blanton, & Cooper, 1995; Blanton, Cooper, Skurnik, & Aronson, 1997; Koole, Smeets, van Knippenberg, & Dijksterhuis, 1999).

Self-Affirmation

People cope with specific threats to their self-worth by reaffirming unrelated aspects of themselves.

In an experiment that tests some of these points, Brown and Smart (1991) gave students who were either high in self-esteem or low in self-esteem a success or a failure experience through an alleged test of their intellectual ability. Subsequently, the students were asked to rate themselves on a series of trait adjectives. Half the items referred to social traits and attributes and half referred to traits and attributes that were related to the task on which the students had received feedback—namely, achievement-related traits and attributes. Participants high in self-esteem who had failed on the intellectual task exaggerated the positivity of their social qualities; this result is consistent with the predictions of self-affirmation theory. However, participants low in self-esteem actually did the reverse. They generalized the failure experience: Both their self-ratings of intellectual attributes and their self-perceptions about social activities were low. Although the predictions of self-affirmation theory appear to be true generally, they may be more true of individuals who are high in self-esteem than of those low in self-esteem (Steele, 1988; Wicklund & Gollwitzer, 1982). For example, high self-esteem individuals are more likely to make spontaneous use of self-affirmation processes following a threat; that is, they are more likely to reaffirm their strengths and pay less attention to their weaknesses (Dodgson & Wood, 1998).

In addition to its specific arguments about the value of self-affirmation, the theory suggests an important aspect of self-enhancement more generally, namely, that some self-enhancement may be enough. An opportunity to reaffirm an important value or personal quality may undercut an otherwise potent threat to self (Cohen, Aronson, & Steele, 2000). That is, when it comes to self-esteem people are "satisfisers" rather than "maximizers": Once a certain level of self-esteem is reached, activities that might enhance it further are more likely to be avoided (Tesser, Crepaz, Collins, Cornell, & Beach, 2000). For example, focusing on one's good qualities may reduce the need to draw on additional experiences (such as success) that might otherwise be an opportunity for enhancing the self (Lockwood & Kunda, 1999). When people have the opportunity to self-affirm, they may also be less defensive and more accepting of potentially negative information (Sherman, Nelson, & Steele, 2000), because, paradoxically, the fact that they feel good about themselves allows them to think about potential threats to the self as well.

Terror Management Theory. Nonetheless, threat is an important stimulus to the need to enhance the self, and there is, perhaps, no greater threat than death itself. A theory that draws on this important insight is terror management theory. The theory maintains that people are vulnerable to fears about their own mortality and seek ways to manage and minimize the anxiety that this vulnerability causes (Greenberg, Pyszczynski, & Solomon, 1986). For example, when death is made salient, people actively suppress death-related thoughts (Greenberg, Arndt, Schimel, Pyszczynski, & Solomon, 2001).

According to the theory, the terror of mortality is kept under control by at least two factors: a cultural worldview that makes sense of an otherwise threatening world and personal self-esteem that confirms one is an object of value in a meaningful universe.

On the first point, the theory maintains that subscribing to and living up to culturally approved standards of behavior protect people from the anxiety that their vulnerability to death might otherwise create (e.g., Greenberg, et al., 1992; Greenberg, Porteus, Simon, Pyszczynski, & Solomon, 1995). The act of following a social or cultural norm is, in essence, soothing or reassuring. The reverse is also true: When fears of death are engaged, the threat of mortality leads people to want to affiliate with others (Wisman & Koole, 2003) and motivates allegiance to cultural beliefs (Arndt, Greenberg, Pyszczynski, & Solomon, 1997).

The theory also predicts that people are most likely to act on their beliefs when a mortality threat is made salient. For example, in one study, people were more likely to aggress against a person who challenged their worldview following a manipulation in which their mortality had been made salient; they were less likely to do so if no threat of mortality had been made (McGregor et al., 1998).

High self-esteem is also thought to help people manage the terror of mortality by allowing them to reaffirm their value and importance. Other self-enhancement theories stress the psychological benefits of enhancing the self. In contrast, from the standpoint of terror management theory, self-esteem is not so much an effort to enhance the self as an effort to protect it against the forces that threaten to destroy it.

Tesser's Self-Evaluation Maintenance Model. Abraham Tesser and his associates (see Tesser, 1988, for a review) have suggested another social mechanism whereby people facilitate and maintain their positive impressions of themselves, namely, how they deal with the performances of other people around them who might threaten or enhance their own sense of self. For example, John's best friend, Mark, recently won a prestigious prize for writing a short story. How will John react? Will he be overjoyed and eager to tell others about his friend's success? Or might he instead feel envious of Mark's success and unhappy to be reminded that he is a less talented writer? More generally, when does the successful performance of another individual enhance our self-evaluation, and when does it threaten our sense of self-worth? Tesser (1988) has developed a **self-evaluation maintenance theory** to answer this question.

Self-Evaluation Maintenance Theory

Reacting to the success of others with pride (basking in reflected glory) or discontent (suffering by comparison) and consequent efforts to restore a sense of self.

The performance of other people in our social environment can affect our self-evaluations, especially when we are psychologically close to them. In the model, perceived closeness can come from having a relationship with another person, such as a friend or relative. But closeness can also be based on shared characteristics, such as race, gender, religion, or physical proximity. In general, the behavior of people who are close has greater impact on us than the behavior of people who are psychologically distant.

In addition, Tesser focuses on situations in which the other person performs relatively better than we do. The performance of others is less important to our self-evaluation when it is mediocre or poor. According to Tesser, the critical situation arises when a person we are close to performs well. In such situations, what determines our reaction? Do we take pride in the other person's accomplishments or do we compare ourselves negatively to that person? A key factor is whether the performance is relevant to our self-definition. If John aspires to be an award-winning creative writer, his knowledge that a close friend has outperformed him is likely to threaten his self-evaluation and lead to feelings of envy and discomfort (Morf & Rhodewalt, 1993). On the other hand, if John has no particular concern about his writing ability and sees creative writing as irrelevant to his sense of self, he should take pleasure in the success of a close friend, because it poses no threat to his self-evaluation (cf. Brown, Nowick, Lord, & Richards, 1992).

However, there is an important qualification to these findings. When another person is construed as part of the self, such as one's best friend or partner, his or her successes become cause for celebration rather than cause for self-evaluation. The dynamics of Tesser's self-evaluation theory do not operate to nearly the same degree when the people whose performance we are appreciating are perceived as part of ourselves (Gardner, Gabriel, & Hochschild, 2002).

In more technical terms, the main ideas of the self-evaluation maintenance model can be summarized as follows:

1. *The comparison effect.* When another person outperforms us on a behavior that is relevant to our self definition, the better his or her performance and the closer our relationship, the greater is the threat to our self-evaluation. We feel envious, frustrated, or even angry.
2. *The reflection effect.* When another person outperforms us on a behavior that is irrelevant to our self-definition, the better his or her performance and the closer our relationship, the more we can gain in self-evaluation. A process of reflection leads us to feel positive and to take pride in the other person's success.

It is important to note the crucial role of the personal relevance of the behavior in question. The very same factors—closeness and high performance—can lead to opposite effects, depending on whether the behavior is relevant or irrelevant to our self-definition. Emotional arousal also appears to be critical to self-evaluation maintenance. That is, when another person outperforms us on a behavior important to our self-definition, we attempt to maintain high self-evaluation only if we actually experience strong emotions in response to the other person's success. If emotional arousal does not occur or if it is misattributed to some neutral source, the dynamics of self-evaluation maintenance take place to a far lesser degree (Tesser, Pilkington, & McIntosh, 1989; see also Tesser & Collins, 1988).

Culture and Self-Enhancement. The phenomenon of self-enhancement may represent an insight about the self that is culturally bounded. Japanese people are far more self-critical than are their Western counterparts, for example (Heine & Renshaw, 2002). The self-serving bias is another example. Recall from Chapter 2 that people tend to see themselves as the origin of actions that have good, not bad, consequences. Such attributions are thought to have self-enhancing qualities. We would expect to find that the self-serving bias is greatly lessened or even nonexistent in cultures such as that of Japan that have an interdependent sense of self. Indeed, some research suggests that this is the case. Takata (1987) found no self-enhancing bias among Japanese students, but the opposite: a bias in a self-effacing direction. When Japanese students outperformed another person, they tended to regard their success as situationally caused, whereas when they were outperformed by another, they were more likely to see that other person's qualities as responsible for her or his success. The more modest self-attributions and self-perceptions of the Japanese and others with an interdependent sense of self appear to be consistent findings (Heine, Takata, & Lehman, 2000; Oishi, Wyer, & Colcombe, 2000).

Nonetheless, one may ask the question, might people from interdependent cultures self-enhance on communal traits? That is, it may be that self-enhancement is not absent from Eastern cultures but merely assumes a different form, namely, enhancing the group and one's standing with respect to the group rather than to individual autonomous qualities. Kurman (2001) examined this possibility in collectivistic (i.e., Singapore, China) and individualistic (Israeli Jews) cultures and found that self-enhancement of traits reflecting personal agency was associated with an independent self-construal, but self-enhancement of communal traits was associated with an interdependent self-construal. These findings imply that self-enhancement may not be absent in some cultures and present in others, but may assume different forms depending on the values of the culture in which it is explored (see also Sedikides, Gaertner & Toguchi, 2003).

SOCIAL COMPARISON THEORY

Earlier we noted that comparisons with other people can be an important source of self-knowledge. When we want to know where we stand on a particular quality or ability and objective information is not available, we may compare ourselves with others. This strategy is the core of one of social psychology's most important theories—social comparison theory.

Social Comparison Theory

Idea that people are driven to evaluate themselves through comparisons with other people.

In 1954, Leon Festinger, a pioneer in modern social psychology, developed **social comparison theory**. Festinger believed that people are motivated to make accurate assessments of their level of ability and the correctness of their attitudes. To do this, they assess their own standing in comparison to that of others like themselves. As an illustration of the choice of similar others for comparison, Festinger suggested that beginning chess players prefer to compare themselves to other beginners rather than to master players. Festinger's theory of social comparison can be summarized in three statements:

1. People have a drive to evaluate their opinions and abilities accurately.
2. In the absence of direct physical standards, people evaluate themselves through comparisons with other people.
3. In general, people prefer to compare themselves to similar others.

Psychologists' current understanding of social comparison processes is considerably more complex than Festinger's (1954) original model (Goethals & Darley, 1987; Taylor & Lobel, 1989; Wood, 1989). The scope of social comparison theory has been broadened. It is now known that people make comparative judgments about not only their abilities and opinions but also their emotions, their personality, and their outcomes on such dimensions as salary and prestige. The process of social comparison affects many aspects of social life. For example, the belief that our current dating partner is more wonderful than anyone we have ever dated before or could be dating now has important implications for our satisfaction in and commitment to the relationship. The belief that our social or ethnic group is economically or socially disadvantaged compared to other groups in society can increase discontent and intergroup conflict (see Chapter 15). In fact, virtually any circumstance that makes the self salient can evoke social comparisons (Staple & Tesser, 2001).

The Goals of Social Comparison

Festinger's (1954) assertion that accuracy is the goal of social comparison has been challenged. It now appears that social comparisons can be made in the service of a variety of other personal goals and motives. These motives, not surprisingly, are the same ones that drive self-regulation more generally.

Accurate Self-Evaluation. As Festinger (1954) suggested, people sometimes desire truthful knowledge about themselves, even if the feedback is not favorable. For example, learning that you are the worst player on the volleyball team may spur you to greater effort or encourage you to change sports. On the whole, people feel more confident when the feedback is consistent with their standing on stable attributes, such as their ability or education and less confident when it is derived from their standing on an unstable attribute, such as practice (Arnkelsson & Smith, 2000).

Self-Enhancement. Rather than seeking truthful self-evaluation, people may seek comparisons that show them in a favorable light. In particular, when self-esteem has been threatened by unfortunate or frustrating circumstances people often prefer to compare themselves with someone worse off than themselves (Gibbons et al., 2002). A desire for self-enhancement can lead people to make **downward social comparisons** with others who are less fortunate, less successful, or less happy (Lockwood, 2002; Wills, 1981). For example, a student who is struggling to learn calculus may comfort himself with the observation that he's doing better than those students who are failing the course. Comparing oneself with a person who is worse off virtually guarantees that one will look better by comparison. Self-enhancement may also operate to mute the effects of an unfavorable social comparison. When one has compared oneself with another person and come off poorly, strategically emphasizing one's positive qualities may mute the effect of the social comparison (Mussweiler, Gabriel, & Bodenhausen, 2000), restoring self-esteem.

Downward Social Comparisons

Comparing one's traits or abilities with someone who is worse off than oneself.

Self-Improvement. As we noted earlier, people sometimes compare themselves to others who can serve as models of success. Contrary to what Festinger assumed, an aspiring chess player may compare her opening strategies to those of great masters to gain an assessment of her stage of learning, to learn from the insights of the masters, or to be inspired by their example (Buunk, Collins, Taylor, Van Yperen, & Dakof, 1990; Gibbons, Blanton, Gerrard, Buunk, & Eggleston, 2000; Taylor & Lobel, 1989; Wood, 1989). That is, a desire for self-improvement can lead to **upward social comparisons** with people who are more successful.

Upward Social Comparisons

Comparing one's traits or abilities with someone who is better off than oneself.

The danger, of course, is that comparisons with much better performers can be discouraging and lead to feelings of incompetence, jealousy, shame, or inadequacy (Patrick, Neighbors, & Knee, 2004). For example, after rating models from popular women's magazines, women who based their self-esteem heavily on their appearance had worse self-esteem (Patrick et al., 2004). Yet studies suggest that people can sometimes extract helpful information from upward social comparisons without suffering in self-esteem. In fact, even when comparing themselves with others who are performing well, they can maintain a view that they are better than most people on the attribute (Blanton, Buunk, Gibbons, & Kuyper, 1999). Whether upward comparisons are inspirational or discouraging also depends on the person's sense of whether the better performing person's standard is achievable (Lockwood & Kunda, 1997). Achievable standards are inspirational, whereas unachievable success is discouraging.

Sense of Communion. Much social comparison research has stressed how people compare themselves to others on objective characteristics that invite evaluation. Typically, such comparisons result in contrast effects, whereby one sees one's own attributes as different from or distinctive relative to others (Stapel & Koomen, 2001). But people often compare their feelings or reactions with those of others in situations that may yield a sense of bonding (Stapel & Kooman, 2001). For example, if you're on a plane that suddenly begins to rock and lurch rather wildly before settling down, you may well compare your reactions with those of nearby passengers. Your purpose in so doing might be less a desire to evaluate your own response of fear than to experience a sense of solidarity and comfort with others who are sharing the experience.

Consistent with this viewpoint, comparisons with people we believe are similar to us leads us to assimilation: For example, upward comparisons are inspiring if one perceives oneself as similar to the target but it may be deflating if one sees oneself as dissimilar (Mussweiler, 2001). Indeed, when people are making social comparisons for the purpose of bonding, they are less likely to make upward comparisons; rather, they make "horizontal" comparisons with people, which enhances a sense of solidarity (Locke, 2003).

In a study that illustrates the importance of bonding in social comparison, Locke and Nekich (2000) had undergraduate students record their spontaneous social comparisons for 1 week. They found that the students often compared their subjective responses in situations with the other people they were close to during these events. For example, in talking about their reactions to a test, the students would often make statements such as "we all thought it was a really tough test" (see also Mussweiler & Rüter, 2003).

Similarly, when a person reflects on the successes of others close to him or her, rather than feeling deflated, the others' successes may be cause for celebration. These comparisons increase a sense of connectedness and similarity to others, rather than a sense of difference (Gardner, Gabriel, & Hochschild, 2002). This tendency to include others in the self, to celebrate their successes and to share in their hardships, may be more true for women and for those with more relational self-construals than for men and those with independent self-construals. In summary, social comparison need not result only from a desire to understand, enhance, or improve one's individual attributes; it may also stem from a desire to bond with others.

The Comparison Process

Festinger focused on situations in which a person deliberately chooses to make a social comparison. Illustrations of such situations are easy to find. For example, after surviving a frightening earthquake, a person may actively seek to compare his reactions with those of others and spend hours talking with neighbors and friends about their experiences. At other times, however, social comparisons are not intentionally sought but forced on people by the situation (Wood, 1989). For example, when elementary school children play baseball, it is very clear who is good at the sport and who is not. Many children may not want to undergo this social comparison experience, but they find it an unavoidable part of their life at school (see McFarland & Buehler, 1995).

Unsolicited comparisons can have important effects on a person (Marsh, Kong, & Hau, 2000). This point was demonstrated in a classic experiment by Stanley Morse and Kenneth Gergen (1970). Participants in their study were undergraduate men who responded to an ad in the school newspaper offering two part-time jobs in "personality research." When each student arrived for his job interview, he was asked to fill out some questionnaires that included a measure of self-esteem. He was then exposed to another job applicant, who was brought into the same room to fill out the application materials. The experimental manipulation varied the appearance of the other job candidate (actually a confederate of the researchers).

Half the participants were confronted with "Mr. Dirty," a young man wearing ripped trousers, a smelly sweatshirt, and no socks. He seemed very disorganized and glanced around the room frequently while filling out the forms. In contrast, half the participants were randomly assigned to encounter "Mr. Clean," a well-groomed and confident young man who wore a dark suit and carried an attaché case. Later in the study, the participants' self-esteem was reassessed to see what impact the exposure had to Mr. Clean or Mr. Dirty. As predicted, participants who had an opportunity for downward comparison with Mr. Dirty increased their self-esteem; based on the comparison, they felt better about themselves. Participants who had an opportunity for upward comparison with Mr. Clean suffered a drop in self-esteem; based on the comparison, they felt less good about themselves. The results show that unsolicited opportunities for social comparison can have important effects on our self-evaluation.

Festinger (1954) emphasized that people prefer to compare themselves to similar others. But just what dimensions of similarity are most important? Consider the case of a college student enrolled in a large history class who wants to evaluate how well she is doing. She might decide to compare herself with all the other students in the class. She could do this by finding out where she ranks in the class on the basis of her grades. However, she might decide that this is not the best comparison because students taking the course differ widely in how many history courses they had in high school.

Instead, she might decide to compare herself only to other nonhistory majors who, like herself, have a limited background in the subject. In technical terms, this is a comparison based on **related-attributes similarity**. The basis of similarity is not her performance, but her background or preparation for the course, an attribute that should be related to performance (Goethals & Darley, 1987; Martin, Suls, & Wheeler, 2002).

Related-Attributes Similarity

Similarity to another person on attributes related to a target attribute, such as background or preparation.

Or the student might want information about the range of performance in this course and may be interested in comparing herself to the best and to the worst students in the group. People are especially likely to seek information about the best and the worst cases when the meaning of the underlying dimension is unclear to them. For example, if you are told you are moderately good at integrative orientation and you don't know what "integrative orientation" means, you will probably seek out information about the characteristics of those who are either very successful or very unsuccessful at this skill, because this information may clarify what the attribute is.

Social comparisons sometimes lead us to see ourselves either as similar to others (assimilation) or as quite different from those others (contrast effects). Several factors influence whether assimilation or contrast is more likely. When comparison information comes from another person, we tend to contrast that other with ourselves, whereas when we evaluate our own qualities, we are more likely to assimilate information about others into our own self-perceptions (Stapel & Koomen, 2000). Not surprisingly, when we compare ourselves with similar others we tend to assimilate the information the comparison yields to ourselves, whereas when we compare ourselves with someone who is highly dissimilar, we tend to contrast ourselves with the other person (Mussweiler, 2001).

Overall, social comparison processes can exert powerful effects on our lives and how we feel about ourselves. Social comparisons influence our self-evaluations, moods, and responses to others. They can boost our confidence and instill motivation and at other times lead us to feel quite incompetent and unsuccessful.

What Makes Us Happy?

We have looked at the ways in which people acquire information about themselves and at the ways they use to feel good about themselves, both conscious and unconscious. These issues lead logically to the question, what makes us happy? Subjective well-being is the evaluation of one's life in terms of satisfaction. What leads to a sense of subjective well-being? Many of us may immediately answer "money." In fact, wealthier people are a little happier than their poorer counterparts, but the difference is small (Diener, Suh, Lucas, & Smith, 1999). Rather, people adjust to whatever level of wealth they have. "Keeping up with the Joneses" implies that subjective well-being depends on being at least as well off as one's neighbors. However, the material aspects of one's immediate social environment do not have a particularly strong effect on subjective well-being. Overall, it is surprisingly easy for people to adjust to apparently advantaged or disadvantaged circumstance, whatever they may be. Lottery winners, for example, are no happier after 1 year than people roughly their age who did not win the lottery (Brickman & Bulman, 1977).

Well-being is more dependent on the experiences we have or create for ourselves than on the material possessions we have. Experiences may make people happier because experiences are open to positive reinterpretation, more than is the case with material possessions. Moreover, experiences may be a more meaningful part of identity than the things one acquires and thus contribute to more successful social relationships as well (van Boven & Gilovich, 2003).

The ability to pursue our goals is also related to well-being. When people are actively involved in the pursuit of their goals, their sense of well-being is high. In addition, the ability to withdraw from unattainable goals and switch to goals that are attainable can lead to effective self-regulation and a sense of well-being (Wrosch, Scheier, Miller, Schulz, & Carver, 2003). People report greater life satisfaction when there is agreement between their day-to-day strivings and their progress in meeting important life goals (e.g., Bianco, Higgins, & Klem, 2003). Happy people tend to base their life satisfaction on life domains that are going well for them, whereas unhappy people tend to dwell on the domains in which they are doing badly (Diener, Lucas, Oishi, & Suh, 2002). When people pursue goals that are consistent with their sense of self, they have greater subjective well-being. For example, when European Americans pursue independent goals (fun and enjoyment), it increases their subjective well-being. This is not the case with Asian Americans. In contrast, interdependent goal pursuits, such as pursuing a goal in order to please parents or friends, increase the well-being of Asian Americans but not European Americans (Oishi & Diener, 2001).

Social psychologists now believe that, although life circumstances can influence well-being, much of the subjective well-being comes from intrinsic personal qualities. For example, people from all cultures appear to have basic needs for autonomy (i.e., the ability to direct their own future), competence, and positive relationships with others. If these basic needs are thwarted, well-being is diminished (Chirkov, Ryan, Kim, & Kaplan, 2003; Kang, Shaver, Sue, Min, & Jing, 2003). Personality also matters. People who are extroverted, conscientious, and lower in neuroticism have a higher sense of well-being across a broad array of circumstances (e.g., Keyes et al., 2002; Schimmack, Radhakrishnan, Oishi, Dzokoto, & Ahadi, 2002). Basically, the happy person is blessed with an upbeat temperament, tends to look on the bright side of things, does not ruminate about bad events, has people he or she can confide in, and has adequate resources for making progress toward valued goals (Diener, Suh, Lucas, & Smith, 1999). Not surprisingly, having an approach motivation toward life influences well-being by maintaining positive emotions over time and by influencing the experiences that people draw on when they think about whether their lives are satisfying or not (Updegraff, Gable, & Taylor, 2004).

SELF-PRESENTATION

George is carefully preparing for an important job interview. He rehearses what he'll say about his work experience. He gets his hair trimmed and ponders which suit to wear and whether a vest would look too formal. He buys a new briefcase to carry his papers and makes a point of arriving early for his appointment. When he meets the interviewer, George remembers to give a strong handshake and smiles pleasantly. During the interview, George tries to look attentive and answer questions thoroughly. In short, he makes every effort to present himself as an energetic, competent person who would be successful in the position.

Human beings are undeniably social and depend critically on each other for bringing about individual and collective goals (Baumeister & Leary, 1995). So important is the experience of social inclusion, that is, the feeling that one belongs, that signs of social exclusion are among the most stressful conditions that people experience (Eisenberger, Lieberman, & Williams, 2003; Twenge, Cantanese, & Baumesister, 2003). A pervasive aspect of social interaction, therefore, is the desire to manage the impression we make on others (Nezlek & Leary,

2002). The term **self-presentation** refers to our efforts to control the impression we convey. The fundamental goal of self-presentation is to structure the interaction so that we obtain a desired outcome. In George's case, the goal is to obtain a job offer.

Self-Presentation

Deliberate efforts to act in ways that create a particular impression of the self.

Why is self-presentation important for understanding the self? There are several reasons. We often want people to view us positively—as an interesting, friendly, intelligent, and caring person. But sometimes we strive to convey other images instead (Kowalski & Leary, 1990). For example, the schoolyard bully might want to present himself as tough and intimidating. At other times, our goal may be to minimize a bad impression, for instance, by finding a plausible excuse for showing up late for an exam. Self-presentation helps us describe and understand the manifold and different presentations of ourselves that we may want to make to others. In addition, though, self-presentation influences self-knowledge. The ways in which we make ourselves known to others has an impact on our self-concept. When we perform behaviors publicly, they can have a greater impact on our self-concept than when we perform them privately (Tice, 1992). Through our own behavior and actions, we gain self-relevant knowledge.

Self-presentation is often a deliberate activity. In his job interview, George is quite conscious of his desire to present himself as hard working and talented. However, in familiar situations, self-presentational activities can become automatic (Baumeister, Hutton, & Tice, 1989). With his friends, George may habitually present himself as a fun-loving guy who doesn't take work too seriously. When self-presentation in a particular setting becomes routine, people are not as conscious about impression management and can focus their attention on other aspects of the situation.

An important aspect of self-presentation is knowing one's audience. For a fashion-conscious teenager, the trendy clothes and hairstyles that are popular among peers may be considered outlandish by older relatives. The ability to "take the role of the other," to anticipate how others will perceive and react to our actions, is essential for successful impression management. Thus, one of the challenges of social interaction is being able to change our behavior from situation to situation, depending on our self-presentational goals and on the nature of the audience.

Making a Good Impression

Perhaps the most common motive in self-presentation is to make a good impression (Schlenker, 1980). How do people accomplish this objective? Several tactics of successful impression management have been identified (Fiske & Taylor, 1991). One strategy is to conform to the norms of the social situation. For example, at a dinner party, a person might tell interesting stories and jokes. In contrast, at a funeral, expressions of sadness and sympathy for the family are more appropriate. Another strategy is to match the behavior of other people. For example, if your new acquaintance boasts about her tennis prowess, you might do well to boast about your own accomplishments. But if she behaves modestly and downplays her expertise, a similar degree of modesty might create the most positive impression.

A useful distinction can be made between two additional strategies for creating a positive impression: self-promotion and ingratiation. **Self-promotion** refers to conveying positive information about the self, either through one's actions or by saying positive things about the self. In contrast, **ingratiation** or flattery refers to saying positive things about the listener. Jones and Pittman (1982) have suggested that these two tactics reflect different goals: Whereas the self-promoter wants to be seen as competent, the flatterer wants to be liked. In some situations, such as a job interview, the person may try to accomplish both goals simultaneously, coming across as both likeable and talented.

Self-Promotion

Conveying positive information about oneself to others.

Ingratiation

Flattering or doing favors for a person to get that person to like you or to do things for you.

Self-promotion can be tricky. Telling about your accomplishments can enhance your self-presentation, but it can also backfire and create the impression that you are conceited or insecure (Cialdini & De Nicholas, 1989; Jones & Pittman, 1982). The reason is that observers often evaluate a person on more than one dimension at the same time. The blatant self-promoter may indeed convince others that he or she is competent but may also display conspicuous egotism.

An important factor in self-promotion is the context in which people talk about themselves. One study compared impressions of people who made positive statements about their intellectual ability under several different conditions (Holtgraves & Srull, 1989). People who mentioned their intellectual accomplishments were seen more favorably when these statements were made in response to specific questions. For instance, when a person was asked how he had done on his midterm, his answer that he had received a grade of 93 made a favorable impression. In contrast, people who went out of their way to say good things about their own ability without being asked and without others providing similar information were perceived as less likeable, less considerate, and more egotistical. The context of the conversation made a crucial difference in how observers interpreted self-promoting statements.

Another tactic of positive impression management is the careful use of modesty (Cialdini & De Nicholas, 1989). For example, the female basketball star whose brilliant plays have just saved her team from losing the championship might describe her performance as "pretty good" and emphasize that she couldn't have done it without the work of the entire team. By understating her accomplishments, she will probably be seen as both likeable and competent. The trick, of course, is to know when modesty will be effective. There are two rules of thumb. First, modesty boosts a person's public image only when the performance has actually been successful. Modesty about a poor performance does not enhance one's image. Second, modesty boosts one's public image only when the audience already knows the full extent of the person's success. The champion athlete can afford to be modest because her fame precedes her.

Self-presentation involves both verbal and nonverbal behavior. Chapter 3 describes ways in which nonverbal behavior contributes to self-presentation. In general, self-presentations are most convincing when verbal and nonverbal messages are the same. A person who says he's "very happy" in a glum and depressed tone of voice is not very credible.

We engage in impression management not only by the things we do but also by associating with people who are successful, powerful, or famous. Robert Cialdini and his coworkers have used the term "BIRGing" to refer to the tendency to "bask in the reflected glory" of others (Cialdini et al., 1976; Cialdini & De Nicholas, 1989). People enhance their individual self-presentation by highlighting their associations with successful others, even when these connections are quite trivial. If a person tells us he comes from the same hometown as the president, or that he once met Barbra Streisand, or that his friend won a million dollars in the lottery, he is trying to impress us by his indirect association with the rich and famous.

Ineffective Self-Presentation

Self-presentation is not always effective. Sometimes our actions do not show us in a positive light. For example, you may forget your mother's birthday or spill a bowl of soup in your lap at a restaurant. In such cases, the best you can do is minimize your losses.

Embarrassment is a common and unpleasant emotion experienced when there is a disruption in self-presentation (Parrott, Sabini, & Silver, 1988; Schlenker, 1980). This can involve minor lapses in impression management, for instance, when a waiter drops a tray of food or when you inadvertently call someone by the wrong name. Flaws in self-presentation can also involve more serious failures in performance, such as when a professional actor forgets his lines or a famous scientist is shown to have misinterpreted her data. The embarrassed person usually responds with efforts to resume the interrupted pattern of interaction. The person may apologize or give an excuse—and then attempt to pick up where he or she left off. Because embarrassing situations are uncomfortable for everyone present, others are motivated to help the embarrassed person save face.

One way to handle a less than stellar performance is to give excuses (Kernis & Grannemann, 1990; Snyder & Higgins, 1988). Consistent with attribution theory (Chapter 3), people often try to attribute their failures to external and uncontrollable causes. It is more gratifying to say you failed the test because it was unfair and all the other students also flunked (external and uncontrollable cause) than to admit that the test was easy and you were not able to master the material (low ability).

The importance of excuses is not limited to achievement settings. Failure to meet a social obligation, such as being late for an appointment, can also create impression management problems. You will probably make a better impression—and avoid arousing anger in the other person—if you blame your late arrival on a flat tire (external and uncontrollable cause) than if you say you forgot to set the alarm clock (carelessness) (Weiner, Amirkhan, Folkes, & Verette, 1987).

Self-Handicapping

A related but more desperate strategy for dealing with failure has been called **self-handicapping** (Baumeister & Scher, 1988; Berglas & Jones, 1978). People sometimes engage in actions that produce insurmountable obstacles to success so that when they experience the resulting inevitable failure, they can attribute it to the obstacle, not to their own lack of ability (see Figure 4–2). The student who stays up all night before the calculus exam can attribute his low grade to fatigue, not to his lack of ability to comprehend math; the golfer who rarely practices can attribute her afternoon in the woods and sand traps to lack of practice, not to lack of skill; the alcoholic can attribute the loss of his job to his drinking, not to poor performance. In Harold Kelley's (1967) attribution framework, the ability attribution is discounted because another plausible cause is present: the handicap.

Self-Handicapping

Engaging in actions that provide obstacles to success, so that failure can later be attributed to these obstacles.

People may also protect their images of their own competence by claiming to have handicaps that prevent success even when those handicaps do not exist. Snyder and Higgins (1988) and others have shown that in evaluative situations that threaten failure, people may claim such symptoms as learning disabilities, test anxiety, social anxiety, shyness, depression, or a history of traumatic incidents. Reporting such symptoms can also protect people from having to make ability attributions for their own failures: By announcing that you need new glasses after an embarrassing session on the tennis court, you can spare yourself both self-censure and the criticism of others. As you might expect, using

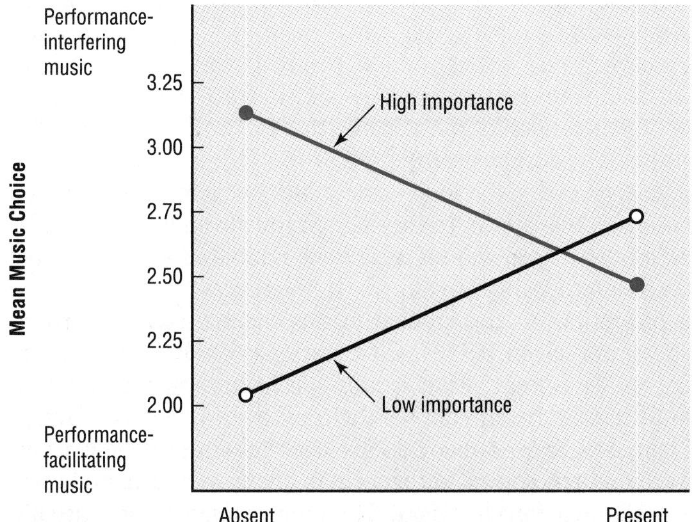

Figure 4–2 Subjects who expected to take an important test chose distracting music, apparently to have an advance explanation for their failure on the test. However, this effect occurred only when there was no preexisting distraction in the environment.

Source: Adapted from J. A. Shepperd and R. M. Arkin. Determinants of self-handicapping: Task importance and the effects of preexisting handicaps on self-generated handicaps. Personality and Social Psychology Bulletin, 15, 101–112. Copyright 1989, by Sage Publications, Inc. Reprinted by permission of Sage Publications, Inc.

such excuses tends to reduce a person's negative affect over the failure, at least as long as no one else knows the truth about the situation (Mehlman & Snyder, 1985). Other people are not always easily persuaded by a person's self-handicapping strategies, however (Rhodewalt, Sanbonmatsu, Tschanz, Feick, & Waller, 1995).

There are two versions of the self-handicapping strategy. One is behavioral self-handicapping by which people actively create genuine handicaps, such as fatigue, alcohol or drug abuse, lack of punctuality, and inattention (e.g., Sharp & Getz, 1996); men are more likely to practice this particular form of self-handicapping (Hirt, McCrea, & Kimble, 2000). The other is self-reported handicaps, by which people claim to be ill, anxious, shy, or the victims of traumatic incidents, when such states might excuse poor performance (Arkin & Baumgardner, 1985; Leary & Shepperd, 1986); it is a form of self-handicapping practiced by both genders. In both cases, as with self-serving attributional biases in general, the key motives are self-enhancement, or the need to boost one's ego, and self-protection, or the ego-defensive motive of avoiding a stable, uncontrollable, internal attribution for failure, such as an inherent lack of ability (McCrea & Hirt, 2001). Not surprisingly, self-handicapping behavior increases when people are self-focused in a situation with the potential to fail (Hirt, McCrea, & Kimball, 2000).

An unfortunate implication of this analysis is that self-presentational pressures may sometimes cause people to lie—to others and to themselves—about the true reasons for their actions. At times, the desire to impress others may conflict with a desire to be honest. Moreover, it is now clear that people who self-handicap to protect their self-esteem do themselves long-term damage. People who regularly engage in self-handicapping are more likely to use coping strategies of withdrawal and focus on negative outcomes. As a result, they have poor study habits, do poorly academically, and have poorer psychological adjustment (Zuckerman, Kieffer, & Knee, 1998). Self-handicapping may work in the short term, but it certainly is not a successful strategy for self-management in the long term.

A related strategy is "sandbagging," that is, feigning inability or generating false predictions of lack of success (Gibson, Sachau, Doll, & Shumate, 2002). For example, a sandbagging poker player may bet as if he or she has a weak hand in the early betting round so as to draw others in. Sandbagging has clear benefits: It can reduce performance pressure by setting other people's expectations at a low level and also provide a low baseline against which subsequent performance can be compared. Almost anything looks better than the sandbagger's estimate (Gibson & Sachau, 2000).

Staying up all night before an exam may help you learn overlooked material, but it can also be a self-handicapping strategy: When you fail, you can attribute your low grade to fatigue and not have to question your ability.

CULTURE AND THE SELF: A COMMENT

Early in this chapter, we noted some fundamental differences in self-conceptions, depending on cultural orientation. In particular, those from the United States and other Western cultures are often said to have an independent sense of self, whereas individuals from Eastern and Southern cultures are said to have a more interdependent sense of self. Because so much of the research that has explored the self has come from Western cultures, the coverage of the self in this chapter has disproportionately emphasized characteristics of the independent self. We have already noted several self-relevant phenomena that appear to vary significantly from independent to interdependent cultures. For example, self-enhancement is ubiquitous in Western cultures and uncommon in interdependent cultures. It seems reasonable to assume that many of the other processes we have studied in this chapter—self-affirmation (Steele, 1988), self-verification (Swann, 1983), self-consciousness (Fenigstein et al., 1975), self-control (Carver & Scheier, 1981), and self-handicapping (Jones & Berglas, 1978)—take a different form in cultures that construe the self in interdependent terms (Simon, Pantaleo, & Mummedy, 1995). Psychologists are only beginning to understand the self and the cultural differences in the ways in which the self is experienced. Although research on the self has assumed a clearer direction and focus over recent decades, it nonetheless leaves many important issues to be explored.

Summary

1. The self is the collection of beliefs we hold about ourselves. The content of these beliefs is called the "self-concept." The evaluation we make of them is called "self-esteem."
2. Self-knowledge comes from early socialization, reflected appraisals of others, direct feedback from others, self-perception, environmental distinctiveness, social comparison processes, social identity, and culture.
3. Cultural analyses suggest that Westerners construe the self as independent, unique, important, and freestanding, whereas collectivist cultures construe the self as interdependent as part of an encompassing social relationship. This distinction is thought to profoundly influence self-relevant phenomena.
4. Beliefs about ourselves may be represented as self-schemas (which serve for the self the same functions that schemas serve more generally) and possible selves (images of ourselves in the future that represent what we may become). Discrepancies between our self-concepts and our ideals or sense of what we ought to be produce strong emotions.
5. "Self-regulation" refers to how we control and direct our actions. It is influenced by the working self-concept, beliefs in our self-efficacy, our degree of self-complexity, and our focus of attention, called "self-awareness."
6. Several motivations drive self-regulation. People seek to have an accurate, consistent, and positive self-concept. They also seek information and situations that help them improve.
7. "Self-affirmation" refers to efforts to bolster our self-conceptions in one area after a threat to self-conceptions in another aspect of self. "Self-evaluation maintenance" refers to the processes we engage in when someone close to or distant from us outperforms us on a personally relevant or irrelevant task.
8. Often we compare our own attributes, opinions, and emotions with those of other people, a process called "social comparison." Typically, we prefer comparisons with someone similar, but sometimes we make upward comparisons to people who are better off than ourselves or downward comparisons with people who are doing more poorly than ourselves. Social comparison can aid in accurate or self-enhancing evaluations, and can also foster self-improvement.
9. Self-presentation concerns the efforts we make to control the impression we convey. As in theater, we construct our behavior in situations in order to make a desired impression, usually a positive one. Appropriate self-promotion and modesty are two strategies that often lead to positive impressions.
10. Poor impressions can be managed or controlled by making excuses or by self-handicapping, that is, engaging in actions or claiming to have problems that produce insurmountable obstacles to success.

Key Terms

In The News

Sweet Talking the Kids? How Persuasion May Not Be So Hidden

A recent issue briefing for health reporters issued by the Center for the Advancement of Health (2004) pointed to some disturbing facts regarding advertising efforts targeted to children. On average, children see 40,000 television advertisements each year. Most of these are directed specifically to them and sell candy, cereal, and fast food. Virtually all of the food marketed to children through advertisements is high in calories, salt, saturated fat, and/or refined sugars, and they are, for the most part, low in nutrients as well. These are not advertisements for broccoli or bananas!

Scientific studies consistently reveal that children prefer products they've seen on television and respond to the ads by asking their parents to get the products for them. Yet, children younger than 7 or 8 years old have not yet reached a stage in their critical thinking so that they can understand the persuasive intent of these commercials and argue against it. What is the long-term effect of watching children's programs coupled with a steady dose of ads that bombard children daily?

The Kaiser Foundation recently reported that one of the main contributors to childhood obesity, which has in recent years reached unprecedented levels, may well be children's exposure to the billions of dollars in food advertising that is directed to them. So called "stealth marketing," in which a persuasive message is slipped into a product or program, is also practiced by some of these companies. For example, McDonald's now offers a Barbie with french fries and a fast-food tray.

At present, one-third of elementary schools, half of middle schools, and the majority of high schools have a contract with a company that sells soft drinks on campus. Many hot-lunch programs are now sponsored or supplemented by established fast-food companies. Vending machines in elementary schools are common sources of high-fat, low-nutrition snacks, yet, as of 2004, only one state, Arkansas, has passed legislation banning vending machines in elementary schools.

Although this advertising may be especially problematic for young children who do not have the capacity to argue against persuasive messages, the barrage is no less evident with teens. Beer and liquor advertising (although not wine) is specifically targeted to adolescents, despite the fact that they are not of legal drinking age.

Policymakers are now holding debates about whether advertising targeted to children should be regulated. Of particular concern are the bulging waistlines produced by the "toxic environment of low-cost, high-fat food and less exercise" reports Harold Goldstein of the Californian Center for Public Health Advocacy (Center for Advancement of Health, 2004). What are the ethics of targeting these populations that are clearly much too young to actively resist persuasion?

Part Two

Chapter 5

Attitudes and Attitude Change

DEFINING ATTITUDES

Attitudes are evaluations of objects, issues, or persons. They are based on affective, behavioral, and cognitive information (the "ABCs" of attitudes). The **affective component** consists of the person's emotions and affect toward the stimulus, especially positive or negative evaluations. The **behavioral component** consists of how the person tends to act regarding the stimulus. The **cognitive component** consists of the thoughts the person has about that particular attitude object, including facts, knowledge, and beliefs. These three components of attitudes are not always highly related to each other, so it is important to consider all three aspects (Crites, Fabrigar, & Petty, 1994).

As an example, consider Evan's attitude toward safe sex, shown in Figure 5–1. The focus of the attitude is the attitude object, which in this case is condom use. The attitude would typically be measured by asking Evan direct questions concerning safe sex, such as, "Are you favorably or unfavorably inclined toward safe sex?" or "How important is the practice of safe sex to you?" or "Would you rate yourself as being for or against safe sex?" Surrounding the object are the various factors that are perceived as relevant to attitudes toward condoms. Some of these are impersonal factors, such as qualities of condoms. Other factors include people, such as Evan's parents, roommates, or friends, and their beliefs about safe sex and condom use. Others are personal states, such as Evan's feelings about condoms, and others are simply attributes of the object itself, such as its availability or cost. These clusters of cognitions and their links to the main attitude object constitute the cognitive component of an attitude.

The affective component consists of the positive or negative feelings associated with the attitude object. In Figure 5–1, positive and negative evaluations of the elements and central object are indicated by plus and minus signs, respectively. Evan's negative feelings about condoms may come from the awkwardness of purchasing them and later using them, and the concern that they may reduce sexual enjoyment. But there are also many positive links to condom use, such as the safety it provides, peer approval regarding the importance of safe sex, and the belief that one is doing the right thing.

Finally, there is a behavioral component. An attitude contains some tendency to behave in connection with the attitude object, in this case, whether or not Evan is willing to buy and use condoms.

Attitudes tend to be cognitively complex, but they are often evaluatively quite simple. As noted in Chapter 2, impressions of other people tend to quickly become evaluatively consistent, and the same is true of attitudes.

Focus of This Chapter

Attitudes

Enduring response dispositions with affective, behavioral, and cognitive components.

Affective Component

A person's feelings associated with an attitude.

Behavioral Component

A person's tendencies to act toward an attitude object.

Cognitive Component

A person's beliefs, knowledge, and facts about an attitude object.

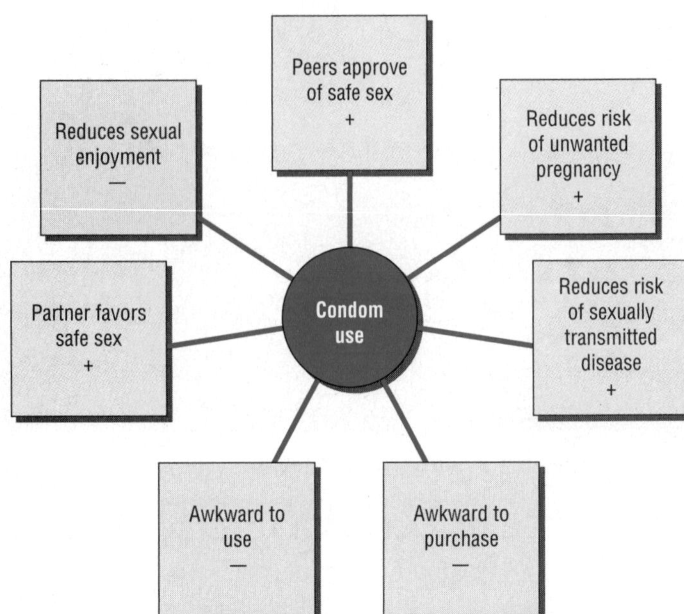

Figure 5–1 **Evan's Attitude Toward Condom Use.**
The core object is related to several other cognitions. The signs refer to the affective component of his overall attitude toward cognitions he associates with condom use. A positive sign (+) refers to a favorable affect; and a negative (−), to an unfavorable affect.

Despite some of his negative evaluations of condoms, Evan's attitude toward condom use is fundamentally positive.

When cognitive complexity is coupled with evaluative simplicity, one implication is the fact that whereas an individual may alter the cognitions that go into the makeup of an attitude relatively easily, overall evaluations toward attitude objects are often difficult to change. For example, Evan may learn that some of his peers don't think much of condom use, but that may not change his overall evaluation that the use of condoms for safe sex is a good thing.

A final important aspect of attitudes concerns their links to decision making and behavior. Attitudes make it possible to quickly access relevant information and related attitudes because they provide important links among pieces of information held in memory (Judd, Drake, Downing, & Krosnick, 1991). Consequently, attitudes enable people to make decisions very quickly because they provide information for making choices (Sanbonmatsu & Fazio, 1990).

The links to behavior are somewhat more tenuous. Sometimes behavior is controlled by attitudes and sometimes not. Evan may be in favor of condom use generally, but if there is a troop of 11-year-old Girl Scouts at the drugstore when he goes in to make his purchase, he may not actually purchase condoms, despite his generally positive attitude toward safe sex. Behavior can change attitudes, too. Suppose Evan's attitude toward safe sex was not positive, but more ambivalent. If he encountered a partner who insisted on safe sex, his attitudes might begin to shift in the direction of being more committed to safe sex. Relations between attitudes and behavior can go either way. Attitudes may control behavior, and behavior sometimes controls attitudes.

Many important attitudes are acquired in early childhood. We associate our country with the patriotic activities we experienced as children. In particular, we may imitate the attitudes of others who are strong, important people in our lives.

THEORIES OF ATTITUDES

Several theories are helpful for understanding how attitudes are formed and how they can be changed. The learning approach regards attitudes as habits, like anything else that is learned. Principles that apply to other forms of learning also determine the formation of attitudes. Motivational approaches based on the principle of cognitive consistency assert that we seek consistency among our attitudes and between attitudes and behavior. It emphasizes the acceptance of attitudes that fit into our overall cognitive structure. Expectancy-value approaches to attitudes maintain that we adopt attitudes that maximize our gains. Each side of an issue has costs and benefits; expectancy-value approaches maintain that an individual will adopt the side on which the net gains are greater. And finally, cognitive response theory considers the conditions that lead us to argue against or passively accept a persuasive communication designed to change our attitudes. These approaches are not necessarily contradictory or inconsistent with each other.

Learning Theory

Learning theory began at Yale University with the work of Carl Hovland and associates (Hovland, Janis, & Kelley, 1953). The assumption behind this approach is that attitudes are acquired in much the same way as other habits. People learn information and facts about different attitude objects, and they also learn the feelings and values associated with those facts. A child learns that a dog is an animal, that most dogs are friendly, and that most are good pets. Finally, the child learns to like dogs. As can be seen, the child acquires both the cognitions and the affects associated with the attitude object. Moreover, she or he learns them through the same processes and mechanisms that control other kinds of learning.

Learning Theory

Approach that assumes that a person's attitudes are based on principles of reinforcement, association, imitation, and punishment.

Thus, basic learning processes should apply to the formation of attitudes. We acquire information and feelings by the process of **association**. For example, if a history teacher shows you a picture of a mean-looking military man in a storm trooper's uniform and says the word "Nazi" in a hostile voice, you form an association between negative feelings and the word "Nazi."

Association

A link in memory between stimuli that are related.

Learning can also occur through **reinforcement** and **punishment**. If you take a class in psychology and get an A in it and enjoy it, the act of taking psychology classes is reinforced, and you are likely to take more such courses in the future. If you take a course and get an F, you are more likely to stay away from similar courses in the future.

Reinforcement

The process by which a person learns to exhibit a particular response by being rewarded when it is demonstrated.

Punishment

A response paired with a noxious stimulus reduces the likelihood that a response will occur again.

Attitudes can also be learned through **imitation**. People imitate others, especially when those others are strong, important people. Consequently, a major source of basic political and social attitudes in early life is the family. Children are likely to imitate the attitudes of their parents (Abramson, Baker, & Caspi, 2002). In adolescence, they are more likely to imitate attitudes of their peers on many matters.

Imitation

A form of learning involving thinking, feeling or behavior in a way that matches the thoughts, feeling, and behaviors.

The learning approach to attitudes views people as primarily passive agents in the process of attitude formation and change. They are exposed to stimuli; they learn through association, reinforcement, or imitation; and this learning process determines the person's attitude. The final attitude contains all the associations, values, and other bits of information the individual has accumulated. Learning theory accounts of attitude change and persuasion emphasize two main methods whereby attitudes may be acquired or changed: message learning and transfer of affect.

Message learning is regarded as crucial to attitude change. If a person learns a message, change is likely to follow. This obvious point is nonetheless quite controversial. Learning a persuasive message is actually much less important in attitude change than we might expect. Most studies show only modest relationships between memory of the content of a persuasive communication and attitude change (McGuire, 1985; Moser, 1992). Although it is vital that a listener know what position is being advocated, beyond this basic requirement, memory of the details of a message is not strongly related to its persuasiveness.

Message Learning

The idea that attitude change depends on the individual's learning the content of a communication.

Learning theory also suggests that people are persuaded when they transfer the affect from one object to another that is associated with it. To understand **transfer of affect**, imagine a television commercial for an automobile. To persuade you to adopt a positive attitude toward the car, the advertiser associates the car with many other positive objects, such as beautiful women, handsome men, lovely children, or cute dogs in the background. Presumably, you will associate all these attractive features with the car, and your positive feelings toward the car will increase. In other words, people simply transfer the affect they feel about one object (happy family life) to another (the car).

Transfer of Affect

Changing an attitude by transferring to it the affect associated with another object.

Research has supported this transfer-of-affect idea in a wide variety of contexts (e.g., Krosnick, Jussim, & Lynn, 1992), although it appears to work better for

We acquire attitudes in part by association. A car paired with a beautiful woman, for example, leads us to believe that the car is a good one and that owning it will bring social rewards.

material with which people are relatively unfamiliar and less well when people are already familiar with the attitude objects (Cacioppo, Marshall-Goodell, Tassinary, & Petty, 1992).

Cognitive Consistency

Cognitive Consistency

Tendency for people to seek consistency among their attitudes.

The second major theoretical framework for studying attitudes and persuasion is **cognitive consistency**. The cognitive consistency tradition depicts people as striving for coherence and meaning in their cognitions. Similarly, if their cognitions are already consistent and they are faced with a new cognition that might produce inconsistency, they strive to minimize that inconsistency. Several specific theories emphasize the importance of cognitive consistency.

Balance Theory

A theory addressing the need to maintain consistency among our feelings and beliefs about what goes together.

Balance Theory. The earliest consistency theory is **balance theory** (Heider, 1958). Balance theory considers the consistency among the affects and beliefs held by a person and are usually described in terms of a person, another person, and an attitude object. Thus, there are three relevant evaluations: (1) the first person's evaluation of the other person, (2) the first person's evaluation of the attitude object, and (3) the other person's evaluation of the attitude object. For example, consider Michelle's attitudes toward her teacher and toward legalized abortion. If we consider only simple positive-negative feelings, there are a limited number of combinations of these elements. These combinations are diagrammed in Figure 5–2, with the symbol P standing for Michelle (person), O for the teacher (other person), and X for legalized abortion (attitude object). The arrows indicate the targets of the feelings. A plus sign means a positive affect, and a minus sign means a negative one. The upper left triad shows that Michelle likes her teacher and that they both support legalized abortion.

Balanced relations between people fit; they go together; they make a sensible, coherent, meaningful picture. The main motive that drives people to achieve balance is their desire for harmonious, simple, coherent, and meaningful perceptions of social relationships. A balanced system is one in which you agree with a liked

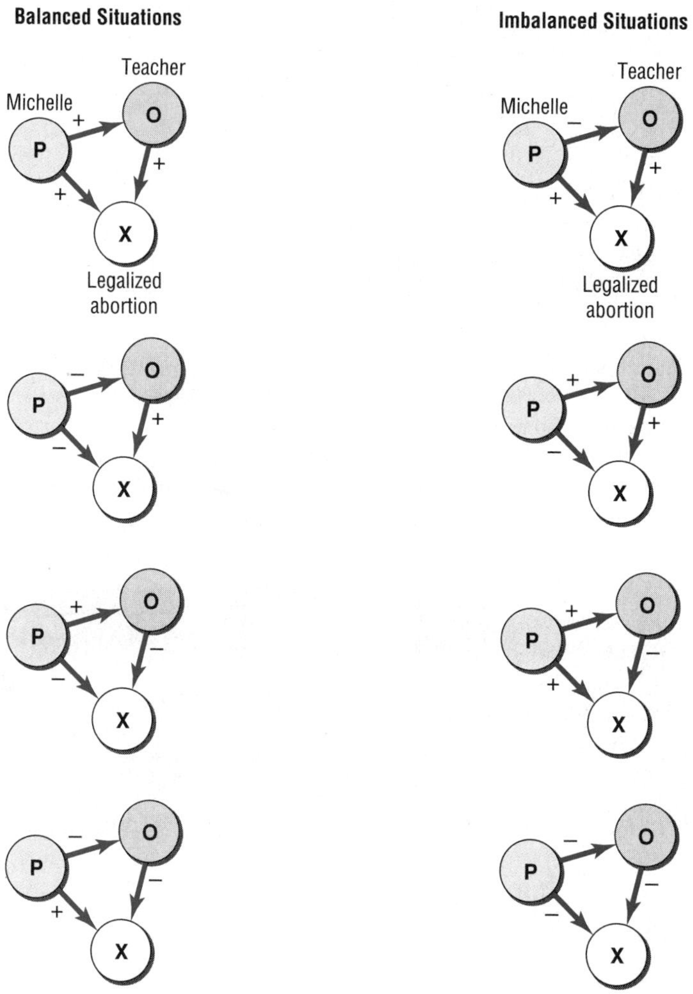

Balanced Situations

Imbalanced Situations

Figure 5–2 **The Balance Model.**

There are eight possible configurations of two people and one object. According to the model, the imbalanced structures tend to become balanced by a change in one or more elements.

person or disagree with a disliked person. Imbalance exists when you disagree with a liked person or agree with a disliked person.

On the left side of Figure 5–2 are the four balanced situations—situations in which the relations among the elements are consistent with each other. When Michelle likes her teacher and both support abortion, the system is balanced. When Michelle likes her teacher and both oppose abortion, balance also exists: Neither supports abortion, and they are united in opposition to it. Nor is there a conflict if Michelle and her teacher disagree about abortion, but Michelle dislikes the teacher. The imbalanced systems occur when Michelle and her teacher like each other but they disagree about abortion, or they dislike each other and agree about abortion. The inconsistency lies in the fact that we expect those we like to have attitudes similar to ours, and we expect those we dislike to have attitudes that are different from ours. In general, imbalance is present when the system has an odd number of negative relations.

Balance theory maintains that imbalanced configurations tend to change toward balanced ones. This assumption gives the model its importance. Imbalanced systems produce pressures toward attitude change and continue this pressure until they are balanced. That is, the systems on the right side of the figure eventually change into those on the left.

This attitude change can occur in many ways. Balance theory uses a least-effort principle to predict the direction of change. People tend to change as few affective relations as they can to produce a balanced system. Any of the relations may be altered to produce balance. For example, if Michelle supports abortion but her teacher does not and Michelle likes the teacher, balance could be produced in several ways. Michelle could decide that she really does dislike the teacher or that she actually opposes abortion. Alternatively, she might distort reality by misperceiving that the teacher really supports abortion. Which mechanism is chosen depends on the ease of using it and on the individual doing the changing. The important point is that various possibilities exist.

Research on balance theory has generally supported these predictions: People do adjust imbalanced systems toward balance, and in ways that minimize the number of changes that must be made (Abelson et al., 1968). People prefer balanced systems, and they remember balanced systems better (von Hecker, 1993). But balance pressures seem to be weaker when we dislike the other person than when we like him or her. We do not care very much whether we agree or disagree with someone we dislike; we simply end the relationship.

Cognitive Dissonance Theory

Cognitive Dissonance Theory

Inconsistency (dissonance) between two cognitive elements produces pressure to make these elements consonant.

Dissonance

Aversive arousal that results when a person simultaneously holds two beliefs that conflict with each other.

The most influential of the cognitive consistency theories is **cognitive dissonance theory**, proposed by Leon Festinger (1957). Like other cognitive consistency theories, cognitive dissonance theory assumes that there is a pressure to be consistent. Dissonance theory deals especially with inconsistencies between people's attitudes and their behavior.

Dissonance is defined as an aversive motivational state that results when some behavior we engage in is inconsistent with our attitudes. Dissonance appears to be most consistently aroused when the attitudes and behavior that are dissonant are important to the self (Aronson, 1968; Stone & Cooper, 2001).

Dissonance creates psychological tension and negative affect (Harmon-Jones, 2000), and consequently, people feel pressure to reduce or remove it. Reducing it means restoring consistency, or consonance. There are three ways of achieving this consonance. One way is to revoke or change our behavior in some way, although often this is not feasible. Sometimes individuals trivialize the dissonance so that they do not have to change their attitudes (Simon, Greenberg, & Brehm, 1995). Most often, however, people resolve dissonance between their attitudes and their behavior by changing their attitudes. Researchers have explored these implications of dissonance theory in several types of situations.

Dissonance Following a Decision. One action that almost always arouses dissonance is decision making. When we must decide between two or more alternatives, the final choice is virtually always inconsistent with at least some of our beliefs. After we make the decision, all the good aspects of the unchosen alternative and all the bad aspects of the chosen alternative are inconsistent with the decision.

We can reduce dissonance by improving our evaluation of the chosen alternative or by lowering our evaluation of the unchosen alternative. After making

Balanced relations occur when people achieve good form in their perceptions of each other. Mary likes Sara, Sara likes Elaine, and Elaine likes Mary. They go together, making a sensible, coherent, and meaningful picture.

decisions, we tend to increase our liking for what we chose and to decrease our liking for what we did not choose. In a study by Brehm (1956), female college students were shown eight products, such as a toaster, a stopwatch, and a radio, and were asked to indicate how much they would like to have each of them. They were then shown two of the products and asked to choose one. In the high-dissonance condition, Brehm gave the women a choice between a product they had ranked high and one they had ranked next best. In the low-dissonance condition, he gave the women a choice between a high-ranked product and one they ranked as far inferior. After they had made their decision, they were asked to rate all the objects again. On the second rating, there was a strong tendency for women in the high-dissonance condition to increase their evaluation of the item they had picked and to decrease their evaluation of the rejected item. In a no-dissonance control group, instead of choosing between two items and receiving their preference, the women were simply given one of the products they had rated favorably. When they rerated all the products, they showed no tendency to improve the evaluation of the object they owned. This condition demonstrates that the reevaluation in the high-dissonance condition was not simply due to pride of ownership; making the decision was the critical factor.

The tendency toward reevaluation is particularly strong when the two alternatives are initially rated as close in attractiveness. Brehm (1956) also tested this notion. When the women chose between two highly ranked products, they experienced more dissonance, and therefore, they reevaluated the products as more different from each other after having picked one than was true in the low-dissonance condition. The tendency to change evaluations of decision alternatives in favor of the decision actually made is especially great when people think about implementing their decision (Harmon-Jones & Harmon-Jones, 2002), suggesting that the impact on behavior may be direct.

Postdecisional dissonance can also be produced when we actually commit ourselves to a course of action. This point was dramatically illustrated in a classic study of a doomsday group that predicted the world was going to end on a particular day and believed that they would be saved by a ship from outer space. In the days and weeks after making their original prediction, group members sold many of their belongings and prepared for the end of the world. When the fateful day arrived and passed without the world being destroyed, they were initially greatly shaken. In a book describing this unusual group, *When Prophecy Fails* (Festinger, Riecken, & Schachter, 1956), the authors observed the group members' reactions to their own prophecy and, more important, to its ultimate failure. The group members' response was not to give up their beliefs and return to normal life. They could not have reduced dissonance by accepting that nothing had come of all the effort they had put into their plans. Instead, they decided that the day had been put off and that the end of the world was still coming soon. Moreover, they began to argue that their efforts had actually postponed the end of the world, and they became very active in trying to recruit new supporters to their cause. Presumably this activity helped reduce their dissonance by justifying their original behavior.

Part of the appeal of cognitive dissonance theory is that it often makes counterintuitive predictions. In this case, common sense might have suggested that the group would give up after its prediction had failed so miserably. But dissonance theory predicts that this disproof would lead them not to abandon the theory, but to argue it even more forcefully. And that is just what happened.

Counterattitudinal Behavior. Some people enter law school because they believe they can help the poor and needy and improve society. Yet, when they go into legal practice, most find themselves doing repetitious and uninteresting work that has more to do with business contracts and tax advantages than with helping others. Many of these once idealistic individuals eventually justify and even enjoy what they do. They may come to believe that nothing much can be done to help the poor after all.

When a person holds a belief and performs an act that is inconsistent with it, dissonance is produced. Dissonance theory argues that these attorneys began engaging in **attitude-discrepant behavior** when they first took a job, because that was the condition of the job. To get paid, they had to spend long hours doing relatively uninspiring work. But this requirement created dissonance: Their behavior was inconsistent with their attitudes. Because it is difficult to take back the action itself, the dissonance typically is relieved by a change in attitude. With time, these fledgling attorneys adjusted their attitudes to become more consistent with their behavior.

Attitude-Discrepant Behavior

Acts inconsistent with a person's attitudes.

Insufficient Justification. If you're asked to work on a political campaign and you put in long hours for a candidate about whom you have some misgivings, you should come to regard that candidate more positively. Why else would you be working so hard? However, if you're paid well for your efforts, you may not grow more positive in your attitude toward the candidate. When you ask yourself why you're putting in the long hours, the answer is easy: It's for the money.

The most interesting prediction of dissonance theory concerns the level of incentive that is required to produce attitude change. On the one hand, there has to be enough incentive to make a person commit a counterattitudinal act. But if there is too much pressure on the individual or too much incentive to perform the discrepant act, there is no inconsistency, and very little dissonance is produced. This principle is called **insufficient justification**: The less incentive one has for performing a counterattitudinal behavior, the more dissonance is experienced.

Insufficient Justification

When people perform a counterattitudinal behavior with inadequate reason, they may develop more positive attitudes toward that behavior.

Attitude change that is realized through this and similar methods is stronger, the more simple and clear-cut the attitude (Stalder & Baron, 1998). Therefore, it often involves significant attitudes that generalize to broad beliefs (Leippe & Eisenstadt, 1994). Thus, the phenomenon is by no means confined to inconsequential attitudes.

Threats. In principle, threats ought to work exactly the same way as incentives. That is, to get people to perform disliked tasks, you can pay them a lot or you can threaten them with punishment. For example, if you do not pay your income taxes or do your homework, you are penalized.

Greater threat should produce less dissonance and so less attitude change. In an experiment designed to test this idea, children were shown a group of toys and then were forbidden to play with a particularly desirable toy (Aronson & Carlsmith, 1963). They were threatened with either mild or severe punishment if they played with the forbidden toy. The children were then left alone in a room with the toys, and the amount of time they spent playing with the forbidden toy was assessed. After playing with the toys, they were asked how much they liked them, including the forbidden toy. Dissonance theory predicts that the children who were severely threatened would probably not play with the toy but would not devalue the toy either. After all, they know why they are not playing with it: They have been threatened with punishment. However, children who receive a mild threat do not have sufficient justification for avoiding the toy, and consequently, when asked to rerate the toys, they might reevaluate the toy, deciding that it isn't all that attractive anyway. This outcome is, in fact, what the experimenters found. The children reduced their evaluation of the forbidden toy more under mild threat than under severe threat.

Choice. Another major contributor to dissonance is the feeling of choice about the behavior. Attitude-discrepant behavior creates dissonance only when the behavior is freely chosen (or at least the person feels it is freely chosen). If you're working on a campaign for a political issue because your whole sorority is, and you don't feel you can get out of it, you shouldn't feel any dissonance over misgivings you might have about the issue.

Irrevocable Commitment. Another key to attitude change as a dissonance-reducing mechanism is the person's **commitment** to the decision or behavior. As long as we feel committed to a course of action, dissonance promotes attitude change (e.g., Jonas, Schulz-Hardt, Dieter, & Thelen, 2001). But when we feel that we can change our decision if it works out badly, or that we can do it half-heartedly, or that we may not have to go through with it at all, dissonance will not be present and no attitude change may occur.

Commitment

The perception that one's decision cannot be changed or revoked.

Foreseeable Consequences. For dissonance to occur, people need to believe that they could have foreseen the negative consequences of their decisions. If a classmate decides to walk to class on the left side of the street rather than on the right side, and as she walks along a brick suddenly falls off a roof and lands on her foot, this is a misfortune. But she is not likely to experience dissonance. On the other hand, if she knew that there was some chance that she might be injured, perhaps because there was high-rise construction on that side of the street, then dissonance would probably be aroused.

Responsibility for Consequences. The importance of perceived choice is that it brings with it perceived responsibility for all consequences, and whether or not it is "logical" to feel responsible for them, dissonance occurs. That is, when we choose something that works out badly, we feel responsible for the outcome, and dissonance is created, whether the consequences could reasonably have been foreseen or not. Indeed, some psychologists now argue that perceived personal responsibility for aversive consequences is so important in producing attitude change that it does not matter whether the behavior is counterattitudinal. Even acts that are consistent with our attitudes are likely to produce attitude change (strengthening our prior attitudes) if they produce negative outcomes and we feel responsible for the acts (Scher & Cooper, 1989).

Effort. The more effort one expends in executing acts that have aversive consequences, the more dissonance is likely to be aroused. If you volunteer for the U.S. Marine Corps and basic training is exhausting, painful, and stressful, dissonance will probably be created: You are likely to persuade yourself that you made the right choice and love the Marine Corps. The attitude change helps to justify the effort you have expended or even expect to expend (see Wicklund, Cooper, & Linder, 1967).

Self-Relevance. Dissonance is more likely to be experienced the more it undermines or questions self-relevant expectations. That is, when people perceive a discrepancy between their attitudes and their behavior, it may threaten assessments of their own competence or morality (Aronson, 1968). This important extension of dissonance theory maintains that dissonance should occur primarily under self-relevant conditions. A further prediction is that dissonance should be experienced primarily by people high rather than low in self-esteem. For people high in self-esteem, a threat to competence or morality will be more impactful than is true for people with low self-esteem. Generally speaking, this pattern has been found (Stone, 2003). A further implication is that anything that restores a strong sense of self, such as a self-affirmation, should reduce the need for dissonance-reduction processes, and indeed, this prediction is supported as well (Steele, 1988). Overall, these findings suggest that the experience of cognitive dissonance revolves around protection of a positive self, as well as the need to resolve logical inconsistencies among attitudes or between attitudes and behavior.

In summary, the main preconditions for cognitive dissonance, and for the attitude change that results from taking decisive action, are minimum incentives, perceived choice, irrevocable commitment, foreseeable consequences, personal responsibility for those consequences, and great effort.

Self-Perception Theory

Cognitive dissonance theory originally inspired research on the effects of behavior on attitude change, and for a number of years, it provided the only theoretical interpretation of these findings. Bem (1967) then offered another interpretation: **self-perception theory**. As we saw in Chapter 2, Bem argued that often we do not really know what our attitudes are and simply infer them from our behavior and the circumstances in which this behavior occurs. For example, if you choose to eat oranges from a basket of seven kinds of fruit and somebody asks you how you feel about oranges, you say to yourself, "I just chose oranges. Nobody forced me to. Therefore, I must really like oranges." Accordingly, you tell the person you like oranges.

Self-Perception Theory

The theory that people infer their attitudes from their behavior and perceptions of the external situation, rather than from their internal state.

It is easy to see how this theory might apply to attitude-discrepant behavior. A participant is paid 1 dollar to tell someone that a particular task was very enjoyable. When the participant is subsequently asked how enjoyable he himself thought the task was, he says to himself, "I said that the task was enjoyable and I was paid only 1 dollar. One dollar is not enough to make me lie, so I must really think that the task is enjoyable." On the other hand, if given 20 dollars, the participant might say to himself, "The reason I said it was enjoyable was just to get the 20 dollars; I didn't really believe it." Thus, self-perception theory and dissonance theory predict that the more people are paid to make a discrepant statement, the less they believe it.

Note that although cognitive dissonance theory and self-perception theory make the same prediction, they do so for entirely different reasons. The traditional view of attitudes reflected in dissonance theory is that they are strong, enduring predispositions. When people engage in counterattitudinal behavior, they suffer from unpleasant tensions that can be relieved only by their giving up these cherished attitudes. Bem's self-perception theory suggests that our expressions of attitudes are, instead, rather casual verbal statements. We observe the conditions under which our behavior occurred and then report on our attitudes.

Most psychologists now assume that aspects of both dissonance theory and self-perception theory are correct. When people have had few experiences with respect to the attitude or when the attitudes involve vague, uninvolving, minor, or novel issues, they may infer their attitudes from their self-perceptions of their behavior (Albarracin & Wyer, 2000), as self-perception theory predicts. When more controversial, engaging, and enduring issues are involved, dissonance theory is more likely to explain their attitudes and behavior.

Consistency: A Caveat. Generally speaking, the idea that consistency is an important aspect of attitudes is beginning to wane. One reason is that consistency seems to be an important concern in Western cultures—that is, of people in the United States and western Europe—but not as much a concern in southern European and Asian countries. For example, in their social interactions, Japanese people may express quite different attitudes depending on the situation they are in, because they believe it is appropriate to express agreement with others to ensure social harmony, rather than threaten social accord through disagreement.

But even Westerners are able to tolerate more inconsistency among their attitudes than consistency theories have described. Moreover, it is clear that people often hold attitudes about which they are ambivalent. Often these include attitudes such as abortion or the death penalty, about which a person may hold a strong opinion but nonetheless fully appreciate and be concerned about the issues on the other side. Or one may feel ambivalent about one's attitudes toward religion if they conflict with those of one's parents (Priester & Petty, 2001). Consistency, then, may be more of a value than a fundamental cognitive principle, whose importance may vary directly with the value placed on it.

Expectancy-Value Theory

People often respond to persuasive communications in terms of incentives, that is, the costs or benefits associated with particular attitude positions. According to

Table 5–1

Go to the Party or Study? An Expectancy-Value Analysis

	Value	×	Expectancy	=	Subjective Use
Choice 1—Go to Party					
Dance	+2	×	3	=	+6
Meet someone new	+3	×	1	=	+3
Drink beer	+1	×	3	=	+3
Get hangover	−3	×	2	=	−6
Do poorly on midterm	−3	×	3	=	−9
Total attitude					−3
Choice 2—Study					
Improve midterm grade	+3	×	3	=	+9
Be bored	−1	×	1	=	−1
No hangover	+2	×	3	=	+6
Total attitude					+14

Note: Value is on a +3 (very good) to −3 (very bad) scale; expectancy is on a 3 (certain to happen) to 0 (certain not to happen) scale; subjective use is the product of value and expectancy.

this theory, attitude formation and change is a process of weighing the pros and cons of various possible attitudes and then adopting the best alternative. This approach is best illustrated in **expectancy-value theory** (Edwards, 1954).

Expectancy-Value Theory

Maintains that decisions are based on the value of possible outcomes and the likelihood that each outcome will occur.

Expectancy-value theory assumes that people adopt a position based on their thoughtful assessment of its pros and cons, that is, on the values they place on its possible effects. They tend to adopt positions that will most likely lead to good effects and reject positions that will most likely lead to bad effects. Stated more formally, the theory assumes that in adopting attitudes, people try to maximize the subjective use of the various expected outcomes, which is the product of (1) the value of a particular outcome and (2) the expectancy that this position will produce that outcome.

Suppose you are trying to decide whether to go to your friend's party tonight. The expectancy-value analysis is presented in Table 5–1. You might think of the various possible outcomes of going to the party (dance, drink beer, not study for tomorrow's midterm, and meet someone new), the values of those outcomes (enjoy the dancing, drink beer, and meet someone new, but get a hangover and do poorly on the midterm), and the expectancy of those outcomes (certain to dance and to get a terrible grade, but unlikely to meet anyone new at a small party). Taking both expectancy and value into consideration, it's time to start studying: An inevitable terrible grade is not balanced by a little fun, dancing, and drinking.

In summary, expectancy-value theories look at the balance of incentives and predict that under conditions of conflicting goals, people will adopt the position that maximizes their gains. The approach treats people as calculating, active, and rational decision makers.

Dual-Processing Theories

In Chapter 2, we note that sometimes people engage in rapid, heuristically based inferential processing, whereas in other cases, they more systematically and deliberately process information relevant to their inferences. This same distinction—dual processing—applies to attitude change as well. Researchers working in the dual-processing tradition (Cacioppo & Petty, 1979; Chaiken, 1980) have found that people will process a persuasive message systematically when they have both the motivation and the ability to do so. At these times, we learn arguments, sift through them for the points that are relevant to us, and counterargue them if we disagree with them. At other times, however, we are seemingly lazy and not motivated to analyze the pros and cons of complex arguments.

Cognitive Response Theory

Maintains that attitude change following the receipt of a persuasive communication depends on the cognitive responses it evokes.

Cognitive Response Theory. One dual-processing approach to attitudes is **cognitive response theory**, which seeks to understand attitude change processes by understanding the thoughts that people generate in response to persuasive communications. The theory argues that people react to different aspects of a persuasive message with positive or negative thoughts (termed "cognitive responses"), which in turn influence whether the person will support the position (Romero, Agnew, & Insko, 1996).

Suppose you listen to a televised speech by a senator who advocates cutting government Medicare payments to the elderly and you say to yourself, "What about retired people on small pensions or people who can't support themselves, such as the disabled or the poor?" These negative cognitive responses mean that you are unlikely to adopt the senator's position. But if you say to yourself, "That's right. Taxes are too high, and those programs are probably paying for extravagant hospital costs for people who should pay their own medical bills anyway," you are likely to support the speaker's position. The key assumption of the cognitive response viewpoint is that people are active processors of information and generate cognitive responses to messages, rather than passive recipients of the messages they happen to be exposed to.

Counterarguing

Actively rebutting the arguments made by the communicator.

Cognitive response theory predicts that attitude change depends on how much and what kind of **counterarguing** a message triggers. If the message stimulates strong and effective counterarguing, resistance to change will follow. Conversely, persuasion can be produced by interference with the counterarguing process. If a person cannot think of any good counterarguments and is distracted from thinking about them while listening to a message, he or she is more likely to accept the communication.

Petty and Cacioppo (1986) drew a distinction between central routes to persuasion and peripheral routes to persuasion. Detailed information processing and reviewing and evaluation of arguments characterize the central route to persuasion. People are more likely to use the central route to persuasion when they are involved in the issue, are concerned about being accurate, or recognize that others are attempting to change their attitudes, among other factors (see Table 5–2) (Nienhuis, Manstead, & Spears, 2001). People draw on more superficial peripheral cues without thoughtful consideration of the important arguments when

Table 5–2

When Does Systematic Processing Take Place and When Is Heuristic Processing Used?

Category of Independent Variable	Conditions Promoting Systematic Processing	Conditions Promoting Heuristic Processing
Source	Number of independent sources	Likeability Physical attractiveness Expertise
Message	Repetition Rhetorical questions and arguments Written message High discrepancy	Length of message Number of arguments Video message
Target	Issue involvement Need for cognition Prior information	Response involvement
Situation	Forewarning Intent to persuade	Audience response Pleasant mood music Attractive models/actors

they pursue the peripheral route to persuasion. These include the attractiveness and prestige of the source or the pleasantness of the context (e.g., a beautiful woman or a handsome man smoking the advertised brand of cigarette). People are more likely to process a message peripherally when they are uninvolved in the issue, distracted by the source or pleasantness of the context, or overloaded with other things to do (e.g., Brannon & Brock, 2001).

These conditions, namely, whether a message is processed centrally or peripherally, affect elaboration likelihood, that is, the likelihood of whether an individual will generate thoughts to a persuasive communication. Generally speaking, one expects to see more cognitive elaboration when people are using the central route to persuasion than when they are drawing on peripheral cues. To test these predictions, researchers examine the cognitive responses that participants generate while they are being exposed to a persuasive communication. Generally speaking, predictions of cognitive response theory have held up well. There are important implications regarding whether a person elaborates on a persuasive message. For example, after people have elaborated on a message, it is easier to recall that message later on because one has generated more associations to it (Tormala, Petty, & Brinol, 2002). Thus, messages that are elaborated on may have a more enduring impact over time.

In a similar vein, Shelly Chaiken (1980, 1987) has distinguished **systematic processing**, which involves careful review and consideration of arguments, from **heuristic processing**, which involves using simple decision rules, such as the idea that longer arguments are stronger. Several investigations have shown that when people are motivated to peruse arguments carefully, they show more systematic processing, but that when motivation is low, heuristic processing tends to rule (Darke et al., 1998).

Systematic Processing

Careful evaluation of the arguments in a persuasive communication.

Heuristic Processing

Processing information rapidly and efficiently using shortcuts or rules of thumb to reduce complex problems to more manageable ones.

The dual-processing distinction between central and peripheral processing has become central to attitude change research. It is of particular importance because it bears directly on the question of how thoroughly and rationally we respond to persuasion attempts. Does the perceiver respond to the quality and price of a product or only to the "hype" that advertising specialists surround it with? Does the voter respond to real issues and real qualities of the candidates or only to superficial images presented on television? The answer is that we do both in different circumstances (Chaiken & Maheswaran, 1994).

This is not to suggest, however, that systematic processing always gives us the right answers and that peripheral or heuristic processing gives us wrong or simpleminded ones. Indeed, systematic processing can be heavily biased. Suppose, for example, the president is giving a speech on energy conservation, and your roommate remarks that the president is simply trying to support the interests of energy companies in his home state. You might process the president's message systematically, but with a negative lens, which might influence the conclusions you draw and how carefully you process the quality of the message and the arguments (Killeya & Johnson, 1998). At times, we bring defensive motivations, such as prior biases, to the processing of attitude messages. In these circumstances, our processing may be systematic, but it is highly likely to be biased through motives that guide the search for and elaboration of attitudinally relevant information and arguments (e.g., Darke et al., 1998; Lundgren & Prislin, 1998). The distinction between peripheral and systematic processing is covered in Table 5–2 and will be elucidated further in the sections on persuasion that follow.

Automatic Acquisition and Activation of Attitudes

Over the last decade it has become evident that many of the processes we have just discussed can occur automatically and preconsciously, rather than require the kind of rational effort suggested by several of the preceding models (Bargh & Ferguson, 2000). This viewpoint is, of course, implicit in cognitive response theory, because only sometimes do we actually process a message centrally, think about the arguments, evaluate them, and decide whether we are persuaded.

Much of the time we process messages by only vaguely attending to the quality of the arguments or even their source.

The notion that attitudes may be automatically activated takes this reasoning a step further and points out that attitude objects in the environment automatically and preconsciously activate our attitudes without any awareness on our part that this process has occurred. Thus, much of our behavior may be guided by our attitudes without our awareness or intention (Bargh, Chaiken, Govender, & Pratto, 1992; Smith, Fazio, & Cejka, 1996). This important observation means that we have a pervasive tendency to unconsciously classify most, perhaps all, incoming stimuli as either good or bad. One result is that almost immediately we develop a behavioral tendency to avoid negatively labeled stimuli and approach positive ones (Chen & Bargh, 1999). Thus, as we consider persuasion and the relation of attitudes to behavior in later sections, it is important to bear in mind that these processes do not require conscious or active engagement in a message for their impact on evaluation to occur.

One implication of this analysis is that attitudes can be subliminally primed through such techniques as advertising. Strahan, Spencer, and Zanna (2002), for example, found that thirsty people who were primed by a questionnaire to focus on their thirst were more susceptible to advertisements promoting sports beverages, compared to people who weren't thirsty or who were not primed to think about thirst. In other words, both the goal (needing to quench thirst) and the prime (thinking about thirst) needed to be present for the advertisements to be successful. So if we're not thirsty, the golden beer being poured into a glass may have no impact, but if we are thirsty, the ad that reminds us of our thirst may be more powerful.

The same dynamic is true of being subliminally exposed to the communicator of a message as well. After having been subliminally exposed to a communicator, participants in an experiment were more persuaded by a second message when that same source delivered it; participants who had not been subliminally exposed to the source previously did not find the source to be as persuasive (Weisbuch, Mackie, & Garcia-Marques, 2003).

The emphasis on unconscious aspects of attitudes extends to their existence themselves. Whereas early models of attitudes assumed that people know what their attitudes are, including their affect, cognitions, and behavioral tendencies toward an object, recent models of attitudes suggest that attitudes often exist outside of conscious awareness and control (Greenwald & Banaji, 1995). These implicit attitudes are nonetheless thought to shape the reactions that people have to attitude objects and to do so automatically.

An approach commonly used to assess implicit attitudes is the implicit attitudes test (IAT; Greenwald, 1998). The IAT measures implicit attitudes by assessing the automatic associations between an attitude object (such as dog) with evaluative works (pleasant or unpleasant words). If you were participating in a study of implicit attitudes that assessed your attitude toward dogs, you might be presented with pictures of dogs paired with positive (friendly) or negative (hostile) words. You might be asked to press the right key to indicate if you had seen a positive word and the left key to indicate that you had seen a negative word. If you like dogs, you should be quick to press the right key when the picture of a dog and a positive word are paired, because a positive response to dogs will occur automatically; you should be slower to press the left key when the dog picture is paired with a negative word, because you would have to override your automatic positive association to dogs. The opposite would, of course, be true of someone who did not like dogs (Greenwald, Nosek, & Banaji, 2003).

But how do implicit attitudes relate to explicit attitudes? Are they mirrors of the same thing, or are they fundamentally different? Research that has addressed this issue suggests that implicit and explicit attitudes are surprisingly independent (Karpinski & Hilton, 2001). Implicit attitudes may be more affected by what is going on in the immediate environment, whereas explicit attitudes may reflect more enduring evaluative associations. Thus, one could have an implicitly favorable attitude toward dogs as a result of a recent exposure to a particular affectionate dog, but one's attitude toward dogs in general might be more neutral.

PERSUASION

With this theoretical background in mind, we now turn directly to the important topic of persuasion. Persuasion is ubiquitous in our society. Advertisers attempt to convince us that their product is better than others. Politicians try to convince us that they deserve our vote. Citizens' groups attempt to influence our attitudes toward the environment, abortion, civil rights, and other heated topics of the day. When do people adhere to their original attitudes in the face of a persuasive communication, and when do they respond to a persuasive communication and change their attitudes? Figure 5–3 presents a model of the persuasion process, which will guide this discussion of the variables involved in successful persuasion.

The Communicator

The first thing we notice in a communication situation is the communicator, or the source. Some communicators are authoritative, such as a high school teacher or a scientist. Others may be humorous, such as the person wearing the elephant suit on television who urges us to buy a particular brand of peanuts. One of the most straightforward and reliable findings in persuasion research is that the more favorably people evaluate the communicator, the more they modify their attitudes in the direction of the communication. This finding follows directly from the transfer-of-affect idea in learning approaches to attitudes. Evaluations of communicators, whether positive or negative, transfer to the positions they advocate. Several aspects of a communicator influence whether the communicator is evaluated favorably.

Credibility. People are more persuaded by highly credible communicators than by those low in **credibility**. In an early study (Hovland & Weiss, 1952), participants heard communications on issues such as the advisability of selling antihistamines without a prescription. Each communication came from either a high-credibility source (*New England Journal of Medicine*) or a low-credibility source (a monthly mass-circulation pictorial magazine). Communications attributed to high-credibility sources produced more attitude change than those from low-credibility sources. The importance of high credibility in a source has been demonstrated many times and is no longer controversial. Subsequent research suggested, however, that there are two separate components of credibility, namely, expertise and trustworthiness.

Credibility

A communicator's credibility depends on expertise and trustworthiness.

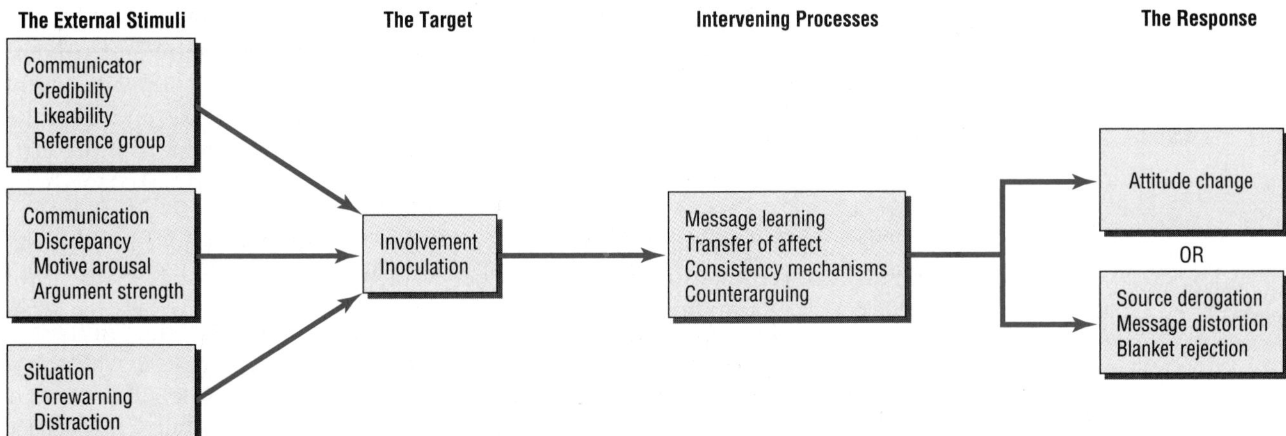

Figure 5–3 **Model of the Persuasion Process.**

Expertise. Expert sources are typically more persuasive than nonexpert sources. In a typical study of this point, participants were told they were participating in a study on aesthetics and were asked to evaluate nine stanzas from obscure modern poems. They then read someone else's evaluation of the stanzas they had not liked very much. The communicator argued that the poem was better than the participant had indicated. The crucial variable was the source of the communication: For some participants, it was represented as the poet T. S. Eliot, whereas for others, it was represented as a student at Mississippi State Teachers College. After reading the communication, the participants reevaluated the poems. There was more change in response to the high-credibility communicator, namely, T. S. Eliot, than to the low-credibility communicator (Aronson, Turner, & Carlsmith, 1963).

Trustworthiness. Regardless of expertise, it is important that a communicator be perceived as unbiased and trustworthy. One way that communicators can encourage this perception is to argue for positions that seem to be contrary to their self-interest. Consider a situation in which a district attorney and a criminal are each making statements about whether law enforcement agencies should be strengthened. Normally, a district attorney is seen as better informed and more prestigious than a criminal, and therefore as more persuasive. In a study by Walster, Aronson, Abrahams, and Rottman (1966), this was exactly the outcome—as long as the speaker was advocating less power for law enforcement agencies. But what if the criminal takes a position against his own self-interest and argues in favor of strengthened law enforcement? In this case, the criminal becomes quite persuasive. Communicators are seen as especially trustworthy when they have little to gain from the particular stance they adopt, but as somewhat less trustworthy when they have incentives for making statements or when they stand to gain personally from persuading others of their position.

Another factor that enhances perceptions of trustworthiness is multiple sources. When several people say the same thing, they are more persuasive than when a single person makes the same argument, presumably because several individuals are perceived to be less subject to a personal, idiosyncratic bias (Harkins & Petty, 1981). Yet multiple sources have this advantage only when their judgments are regarded as truly independent of each other (Ziegler, Diehl, & Ruther, 2002).

Liking. Because we try to make our cognitions consistent with our affect, it follows that we are likely to change our attitudes to agree with those of the people we like. In general, this has been shown to be true (e.g., Roskos-Ewoldsen & Fazio, 1992). Chaiken (1979), for example, showed that students who were rated by other students as physically attractive were also more persuasive communicators. Also, we tend to be influenced more by those who are similar to us than by those who are different from us (Brock, 1965). To test this point, Wood and Kallgren (1988) manipulated the likeability of a graduate student delivering a talk in the following way. He was described as having recently transferred to the participant's university, and then he either praised the faculty and student body in comparison to those at his old university or said that his previous school was better. Not surprisingly, he was liked better in the former case, and when he later gave a speech against environmental preservation, he produced more attitude change in his audience than when he had previously criticized his new school.

The source credibility effect cuts both ways. Not only is it the case that the messages of credible sources are more believable, but also it is the case that if we believe a set of arguments, we also believe they came from a credible source, even when that is not necessarily the case (Fragale & Heath, 2004).

Reference Groups

A group to which a person belongs or aspires that serves as a standard for the person's behavior and attitudes.

Reference Groups. We are also persuaded when a position is adopted by a group of people we like or identify with. Such groups are called **reference groups**. Diane Mackie (1987) told some participants that a majority (82 percent) of the students at their university supported the proposition that the United

Communicators who are perceived to be trustworthy and credible produce more attitude change in their audiences. Nelson Mandela embodies these qualities.

States should act to ensure a military balance in the Western Hemisphere. Others were told that 82 percent opposed the proposition. She then presented participants with speeches of equal strength on both sides; all participants received the same arguments. In four experiments, she found that the participants moved toward the side that their peers supported, whichever side that was.

Two reasons that reference groups are so effective in producing attitude change are liking and similarity (Holtz & Miller, 1985). If people admire a group, they want to be like the group's members. When the other members express a particular opinion, each member wants to hold a similar opinion. And consequently, people lean in the direction of changing their opinions to make them agree with those of their reference groups (Terry & Hogg, 1996).

Messages from in-groups are also more persuasive because they are processed differently from messages from out-groups. Mackie, Worth, and Asuncion (1990) found that communications from nonreference groups (out-groups) were processed at a very peripheral level and that participants were unpersuaded by either a strong or a weak message. Participants were, however, more persuaded by a strong message from the in-group than by a weak one, a finding that suggests more central processing of the reference group's message. This effect was especially true when the issue was relevant to an individual's reference group.

In short, who delivers a communication and the qualities of that communicator are clearly important in terms of how a message is evaluated. Attractive, likeable, credible, expert, trustworthy individuals are more persuasive than those who lack these attributes. Interestingly, however, it appears that communicator characteristics may be more important in audiovisual messages than in written messages. In audiovisual messages such as those on television, a great deal more information is available about the communicator, such as nonverbal information and appearance. In written communications, information about the communicator is less salient, and so message content tends to be relatively more important (Chaiken & Eagly, 1983).

Derogating the Source. Just as communicator characteristics can enhance the persuasiveness of a communication, they can also be used to discredit a communication. When faced with a communication that is inconsistent with our attitudes, we can reduce inconsistency by deciding that the source of the communication is unreliable or negative in some other way. This is called **source derogation**. Such an attack on the source of a communication is common in politics, informal

Source Derogation

Resisting persuasion by derogating the source of a communication.

debates, courtroom trials, and practically every kind of disagreement. The defense attorney in a trial tries to discredit the witness whose testimony is damaging to the defendant. The politician calls her opponent a liberal or a liar.

Attacking the source of the communication is an effective way to reduce the pressure produced by a discrepant communication. It has the additional benefit of making all future arguments from the opponent much less powerful. When an opponent has been discredited, anything he or she says carries less weight. Consequently, when a source that is vulnerable to being discredited delivers a message, people sometimes scrutinize the message more closely to guard against either their own or others' unfair reactions (Petty, Fleming, & White, 1999).

The Communicator as a Peripheral Cue. As we have seen, characteristics of a communicator, such as whether he or she is trustworthy, expert, or likeable, are important determinants of whether we accept a persuasive communication. People who dislike or do not trust a communicator often reject the message by attacking the source. But sometimes a communicator's conclusion is accepted simply because it comes from an expert or from an otherwise favorably evaluated source, regardless of the arguments put forth. How can the communicator have these different effects?

Elaboration-Likelihood Model

A theory of attitude change whose key variable is the amount of careful thought given to persuasive arguments (elaboration likelihood).

Peripheral Cues

Factors that are irrelevant to the content of the message, but that may influence attitude change.

The prediction from the **elaboration-likelihood model** is that communicator characteristics are often used as simple **peripheral cues** to persuasion when we cannot or are not motivated to process arguments carefully. When we engage in little cognitive effort, we know we can rely on a trusted communicator's viewpoint, so we can avoid thinking the argument through ourselves. If we cannot remember any of the arguments presented very well, we also tend to rely on the source to determine our attitude in response to the communication (Wood & Kallgren, 1988).

The Communication

In addition to the communicator, the communication itself, that is, its content, is clearly important. Counterattitudinal communications about attitudes that are important to people, for example, are very likely not to be persuasive because people already know what their attitudes are. But beyond this basic point, a number of variables in the communication itself have important effects on the degree to which people are persuaded by it.

Discrepancy

Distance between the communicator's and the target's position on an attitude issue.

Discrepancy. A major factor that influences the degree to which we are persuaded by a communication is how discrepant that communication is from our own position. Generally speaking, the greater the **discrepancy**, the greater the potential pressure to change (Hovland & Pritzker, 1957). But extremely discrepant statements cause us to doubt the credibility of the source rather than to change our attitudes (e.g., Eagly & Telaak, 1972; Freedman, 1964). These two points predict a U-shaped relationship between discrepancy and attitude change, namely, that relatively little attitude change will occur with low-discrepant and high-discrepant communications, and that maximum attitude change will occur with moderately discrepant communications.

It follows that greater credibility is likely to allow communicators to advocate more discrepant opinions successfully because such opinions will not be rejected easily. In contrast, a low-credibility source makes rejection relatively easy; therefore, the maximum amount of attitude change tends to occur at lower levels of discrepancy. These predictions were confirmed in a study by Bochner and Insko (1966). They had a Nobel Prize winner (high credibility) or a YMCA instructor (lower credibility) give messages regarding the number of hours of sleep the average person requires per night. As predicted, there was more change in opinion regarding the necessary amount of sleep at moderate levels of discrepancy than at higher levels. In addition, as expected, the optimal level of discrepancy was greater for the high-credibility source. The YMCA instructor produced the most attitude change when he advocated 3 hours of sleep, but the high-credibility source achieved the maximum attitude change when he argued that only 1 hour was necessary.

Discrepancy affects how a message is perceived. When a discrepant position is quite close to that of an audience, they perceive it as closer than it really is. This process is called "assimilation." Exaggerating the closeness of a discrepant position makes it easy to reduce the small discrepancy or may eliminate the need for change by making the two positions essentially identical. On the other hand, when the source's position is very discrepant from that of the audience, it is perceived to be farther away. This process is called **contrast**. When the position is perceived to be extreme, it may be perceived as so extreme as to be ridiculous, and the communicator is easily discredited (Hovland, Harvey, & Sherif, 1957).

Contrast

The tendency to perceive a communicator's position as being further away from one's own position than it actually is.

Strong Versus Weak Arguments. Sometimes the arguments in a communication are strong and compelling, and sometimes they are weak and specious. For example, the evidence for the role of unsafe sex practices in spreading AIDS is very compelling. The evidence that Elvis is still alive is very weak.

One would think that strong arguments always produce more attitude change than weak ones do, but that is not always the case. People respond more favorably to strong arguments in a persuasive communication primarily when they are motivated to pay close attention and are able to think carefully about the arguments. For example, when people are highly involved in a persuasive message, adding weak arguments to already strong ones actually dilutes the overall persuasiveness of a message (Friedrich, Fetherstonhaugh, Casey, & Gallagher, 1996). In many circumstances, however, people do not give a message very detailed or careful thought; in those circumstances, the sheer number of arguments may be a more important factor than how strong the arguments are (Wanke, Bless, & Biller, 1996). Thus, the strength of arguments is not necessarily a crucial factor in how persuasive they are (Petty & Cacioppo, 1986). The effects of strong arguments depend on whether people are involved in an attitude issue and process arguments systematically or heuristically.

Repetition. Does repetition increase the persuasiveness of a message? Consider your reaction to seeing the same athlete in the same television commercial downing the same brand of beer at the same bar week after week. Does the repetition reinforce your association of that brand with the athlete, or do you simply tire of the commercial and tune it out?

Much research by Zajonc (1968) shows that familiarity based on repetition increases liking. With persuasive communications, however, repetition appears to increase attitude change only up to a point (Cacioppo & Petty, 1979). Why? It is easy to imagine that repetition might have two separate effects: It may increase one's opportunity to consider the content of a persuasive communication and therefore enhance the processing of the message, but it may also increase the chances of tedium and therefore produce a negative reaction. For example, when the overly familiar beer commercial comes on, your reaction might be "Oh, not again!"

The implication of this argument is that repetition helps strong arguments because people process them more completely. But it may hurt weak arguments because it exposes their flaws or simply makes them tedious (Cacioppo & Petty, 1985).

How can tedium be dealt with? Presumably, the content can be varied. Consistent with this argument, repetition of commercials for a particular product seems to increase effectiveness if the commercials are varied somewhat, but not if the same commercial is used each time (Cacioppo & Petty, 1985).

Peripheral Cues and Message Characteristics. In some circumstances, peripheral cues are very important in determining attitude change. When we have little motivation to think about the arguments in a message (e.g., when the issue has little importance to us), or when we are unable to process the arguments well (e.g., when we are uninformed or distracted), peripheral cues become very important in determining attitude change.

The number of arguments in a message and the length of those arguments are two such peripheral cues (Cacioppo & Petty, 1985). Presenting more arguments in a message increases attitude change when the issue is not very relevant to the person: That person is swayed not by the issue but by the number of arguments. Presenting more arguments increases attitude change in response to strong and weak arguments alike, a finding indicating that little central processing is going on. Similarly, longer messages have a more persuasive impact than short messages, but only among those who are uninformed, because they presumably give the actual messages little thought. Among the better informed, strength of argument is a more important factor, presumably because people who are better informed are more motivated to pay attention to the nature of the arguments themselves (Wood, Kallgren, & Priesler, 1985).

A variety of factors, then, determine whether any given message will be persuasive. When people have the time and interest to pay attention to a message, strong arguments have a decided advantage. In the absence of strong arguments, peripheral cues, such as source characteristics or the sheer number of arguments, have more impact.

Matching the Persuasive Message to the Nature of the Attitude. A persuasive communication will be more so if it is matched to certain aspects of attitudes. For example, attitudes that are highly emotional may be more easily changed by persuasions that appeal to those emotions (DeSteno, Petty, Rucker, Wegener, & Braverman, 2004). If the thought of the death penalty enrages you, then a message that engages your anger should persuade you.

Attitudes are more strongly affected by messages that match the functional basis of the attitude. For example, if you support sports on campus because you think that it's a popular thing to do, a persuasive message that attacks this point (such as information suggesting that support for sports isn't so popular) would have a greater impact on your attitude than if your support of sports had to do with the physical health benefits of physical activity (Petty & Wegener, 1998).

In Chapter 4 on the self, we considered the fact that people differ as to whether they are motivated primarily by a prevention focus (behavioral avoidance system) or by a promotion focus (behavioral activation focus). That is, some peoples' goals involve approaching desired states, whereas others involve avoiding negative states. From this difference, it follows that messages may be more persuasive if they match the regulatory leanings of a participant (Cesario, Grant, & Higgins, 2004). Thus, for example, if someone is trying to persuade you to floss and you are prevention oriented, then arguments that stress how you can avoid painful dental procedures may appeal to you. In contrast, if you have a promotion orientation, then arguments that favor flossing might better be framed in terms of the goal of achieving good dental health (Mann, Sherman, & Updegraff, 2004). Generally speaking, this is what research has found. When a message feels right because it achieves regulatory fit, then the message arguments are more persuasive (Cesario et al., 2004).

Distorting the Message. Message factors may also be important in the rejection of a persuasive communication. Recall that cognitive consistency theories maintain that inconsistency between our own position and that advocated in a message may be resolved by distortion or misperception of the communication to reduce the discrepancy between it and our own position. For example, the U.S. Surgeon General writes an article recommending that sexually active young adults practice safe sex because they may be at risk for AIDS. Young adults who do not want to practice safe sex may read this message and erroneously decide that the Surgeon General says not to worry too much about AIDS because the evidence regarding heterosexual transmission is not yet conclusive. They can do this by misperceiving the article when reading it, by distorting the article in memory, or perhaps by reading only part of the article and reconstructing the rest of it mentally. However accomplished, the result is the same: The message becomes considerably less discrepant. Sadly, in the case of AIDS, the price of distorting a health warning can be high indeed.

Blanket Rejection. The most primitive (and perhaps most common) mode of inconsistency resolution is simply to reject the communication altogether. Rather than refute the arguments on logical grounds or weaken them by attacking their source, individuals simply reject the arguments. For example, a typical response by a smoker to a well-reasoned, logical attack on cigarette smoking is to say that the arguments are not good enough to make her stop. She does not answer them; she simply does not accept them. It often takes more than a good argument to convince people of something.

The Target

Target individuals—namely, the persons to be persuaded—vary in a number of respects that affect persuasion as well. Targets may be predisposed to agree with a message or to disagree with it. They may have personal motives that affect how willing they are to change in response to a persuasive message.

Aggression Arousal. In some persuasive messages, an effort is made to arouse feelings of aggression in the target. Aggression arousal should produce attitude change only when the communication urges an aggressive position. In a study by Weiss and Fine (1956), some participants underwent an annoying, frustrating experience that was designed to make them feel aggressive. Other participants had the opposite experience—a pleasant, satisfying one. Then both groups were exposed to a persuasive communication that either took a lenient attitude or a punitive stance toward juvenile delinquency. The experimenters found that participants who had been made to feel aggressive accepted the punitive communication because it would provide them with a way of expressing their aggression. The lenient message was less likely to satisfy the relatively nonaggressive needs of the participants who had had the pleasant experience. Personal frustrations, then, might make a person more vulnerable to persuasive communications that advocate military action, attacks on minorities, or harsh treatment of dissidents, but they probably would not increase susceptibility to such nonaggressive appeals as charity campaigns.

Fear Arousal. The case of fear is more complex. The learning theory approach suggests that fear-arousing messages will be accepted if the communication offers fear-reducing recommendations. But the empirical evidence suggests that the level of fear must also be considered. Increasing fear usually increases the effectiveness of a persuasive communication. When too much fear is aroused, the effects may be disruptive, causing people to be too frightened to act or leading them to ignore or reject the communication. At moderate levels, fear-arousing arguments can be more effective in producing attitude change than can arguments that cause little or no fear (Janis, 1967).

Whether persuasion is enhanced by fear appeals may depend on several additional factors. One is whether the message provides expectations of reassurance. If a message provides information about how to reduce fear, fear appeals can be effective. Another factor is whether the message topic is relevant to the fear. Although high fear sometimes erodes attention and makes it difficult for people to learn important information, to the extent that a persuasive communication is directly relevant to the source of the fear, it may be noticed more and processed somewhat more carefully (Sengupta & Johar, 2001). However, the very relevance of the message coupled with the presence of high fear or anxiety may lead people to use heuristic cues in a message that biases their systematic processing (Sengupta & Johar). In short, when people are fearful, they may try to process a fear-relevant message systematically but instead may seize on stray bits of information that bias their processing, precisely because they are fearful.

Persuasive communications designed to arouse fear usually are effective. However, if the message arouses too much fear, the effects may be disruptive and may lead people to ignore or reject the communication.

Many researchers now adopt an expectancy-value framework to understand the effect of fear on persuasion. This framework takes into account the nature of the feared event, the person's perceived vulnerability, and the perceived effectiveness of the recommended measures. This perspective (Leventhal, 1970) predicts that fear will increase attitude change when a person feels vulnerable to the feared event and when highly effective measures are recommended, but not when the person feels invulnerable or when there is little or no remedy (e.g., Das, Wit, & Stroebe, 2003). As we see in Chapter 14, the expectancy-value account of the relation between fear and attitude change is often used in health communications to encourage people to change their behaviors, such as using condoms, adopting a low-fat diet, or stopping smoking.

Ego Involvement

Ego Involvement

Subjected linking of an attitude to strong self-related needs.

Another factor related to the target and whether he or she will be persuaded by a communication relates to **ego involvement**. According to Sherif and Cantril (1947), attitudes that become highly entwined with the ego are highly resistant to change. Sherif and Cantril believed that ego involvement was more likely to occur when attitudes were linked to important reference groups, such as an individual's nation, religion, ethnicity, or social class. Later work has distinguished among several different kinds of ego involvement, however, with somewhat different dynamics. These include commitment, issue involvement, and response involvement.

Commitment. An important aspect of involvement is our commitment to our own initial attitude toward an issue. The strength of our commitment influences how vigorously we will resist a persuasive message.

Commitment may come from several sources. First, commitment increases when we engage in behavior on the basis of an attitude. A person who has just bought a new car, for example, is more committed to the belief that it is a fine car than he was before he bought it. Second, commitment is increased when we take a public stance on an attitude. For example, someone who has just told all her friends that she thinks drinking is evil and dirty is more committed to this attitude than if she had kept her thoughts to herself. A third source of commitment is direct experience with an attitude object. When one has had direct experience with an issue, attitudes are typically more strongly held. Fourth, freely choosing an attitude position produces a greater feeling of commitment than being forced or nudged into a position.

Commitment to an initial attitude position shifts the amount of discrepancy necessary to create maximum attitude change. The more an individual is committed to an initial attitude, the less deviation he or she will tolerate in a persuasive communication before rejecting it (Freedman, 1964; Rhine & Severance, 1970).

In general, then, commitment reduces the amount of attitude change produced by a discrepant, persuasive communication. If changing an attitude means giving up more, suffering more, or changing more of our other attitudes or behaviors, commitment to the initial attitude position increases and makes it more difficult to change.

Issue Involvement. A second type of ego involvement occurs when an issue has important consequences for the individual. This has been called "issue involvement" (or "personal relevance"), because we are involved in the issue rather than detached from it. Issue involvement is a key variable in the elaboration likelihood approach to attitude change (Petty & Cacioppo, 1986, 1990) because it motivates people to attend closely to the issue and to the relevant arguments. Consequently, when we are involved in an issue, strong arguments are more persuasive than weak ones (Petty & Cacioppo, 1990). For example, if you were told that your tuition might double next year, you would probably pay very close attention to the validity of the arguments for the increase. In contrast, if you heard that tuition was being increased at a college in Bulgaria, you might not scrutinize the arguments very carefully. An issue that is not personally relevant does not produce as much motivation to process the information. Under such conditions, people pay more attention to such peripheral cues as communicator expertise or to the length or number of the arguments.

Response Involvement. Even when we are not very committed to our prior attitude or the issue is not personally relevant, our attitudinal response may nonetheless be very important because it will receive public scrutiny and bring social approval or disapproval. This kind of involvement is called "response involvement" (Zimbardo, 1960). The response-involved person is concerned primarily with whether others will approve, whereas the issue-involved person is more concerned with the quality of arguments because the issue is what matters.

These contrasting effects of issue and response involvement were compared by Leippe and Elkin (1987). They manipulated issue involvement by telling participants that their university was considering instituting comprehensive examinations. Some students were told that the exams would be put into effect the next year, thereby affecting them, whereas others were told that the exams would not be put into effect until some years later. Response involvement was manipulated by telling some participants that they would discuss the issue with another student and a professor, whereas others were not told of any such discussions.

Only the participants who were both highly issue involved and weakly response involved—those who expected to be personally affected by the issue but did not have to worry about what image they would present to others—scrutinized the arguments closely, as reflected in greater attitude change in response to the stronger arguments. With high response involvement—that is, when participants were preoccupied with their self-presentation—the strength of arguments was virtually ignored. Likewise, when the issue had no personal relevance, strength of argument had no effect.

Personality and Persuasibility. In addition to ego involvement, there are individual personality characteristics that may affect persuasion and the kinds of messages that may persuade. These include authoritarianism/dogmatism and need for closure.

Authoritarianism/dogmatism refers to a general inclination to have a closed mind, to be intolerant, and to be deferential to authority, independent of specific ideological or political beliefs. Individuals who are low in dogmatism tend to be persuaded by strong, but not by weak, arguments. Highly dogmatic individuals, in contrast, are persuaded by strong arguments only when the source is non-expert. When the source is an expert one, highly dogmatic individuals respond to the authority of expertise and are equally persuaded by strong and weak arguments (DeBono & Klein, 1993). Dogmatism also influences the processes by which people respond to persuasive communications. For example, dogmatism is associated with more confident judgments as a result of generating more supportive and less contradictory evidence (Davies, 1998).

Another individual factor that influences persuasion is the need for closure. Need for closure is the desire to have a definite answer on a topic as opposed to remaining in a state of confusion or ambiguity. Participants who are high in need for closure are typically more resistant to persuasion than people low in need for closure because they don't like to change; those low in need for closure are more tolerant of the ambiguity that a persuasive communication creates and are more willing to change their attitudes. However, if a persuasive communication involves an issue on which people have relatively little information and they are distracted while listening to the persuasive communication, individuals with a high need for closure show more attitude change than those low in need for closure (Kruglanski, Webster, & Klem, 1993), presumably to escape the confusing state in which they find themselves.

Mood and Persuasion. A more transitory factor that can influence how a person processes a persuasive message is mood. Mood can act as information, and so people who feel negative when they are exposed to a message process that message more systematically than people who feel positively. Essentially, people interpret their negative mood as a signal that the situation might be problematic or threatening and therefore adapt a careful analytic strategy for processing the message.

Conversely, a positive mood signals that a situation is harmless, which may lead to a less effortful processing style. These effects occur primarily if the person feels that aspects of the situation are the cause of their affective state, but has a lesser effect on how persuasive messages are processed if the persuasive message is deemed irrelevant to the mood (Albarracin & Kumkale, 2003).

Affect may act as information in the persuasion process in other ways too. For example, a well-established effect in social psychology is the mere exposure effect, which finds that repeated exposure to any stimulus increases the positive affect (or reduces the negative affect) experienced about the stimulus. Thus, a sly implication of these findings, one on which advertisers commonly draw on, is that persuasion will increase the more one is exposed to a message. Generally speaking, research has supported this prediction (Harmon-Jones & Allen, 2001). Indeed, even if a message is subsequently shown to be based on faulty information, the impact of mere exposure may continue to endure (Sherman & Kim, 2002).

Mood acts not only as information in the persuasion process but also as a resource. Often, the persuasive messages we encounter have threatening consequences for the self. We may be urged to get a cancer-screening test or we may learn that our chosen major has few prospects for employment. On the one hand, this information is useful, but on the other hand it has the potential to undermine mood. How do people process positive and negative information based on their mood? The idea that mood is a resource suggests that positive mood may act as a buffer against the affective costs of negative information. That is, when people are in a good mood, it may enable them to focus on the knowledge that they can gain from negative information, despite the threat it poses to their mood. Thus, positive mood should facilitate processing negative self-relevant information, although at the potential cost of somewhat reducing positive mood. Generally speaking, research supports this idea. For example, in one study, college student subjects in a positive or neutral mood were exposed to information about the potential liabilities of consuming too much caffeine. Under positive mood, people for whom the message was relevant were more likely to process this negative information and to change their attitude (Raghunathan & Trope, 2002).

The Situation

So far, this chapter has considered the communicator, the message, and the target as factors that influence attitudes and responses to persuasive communications. However, a persuasive communication is usually delivered within a broader situational context, in which other things are happening that also affect the degree to which efforts to persuade succeed.

Forewarning. If you are highly committed to a position and are told that you are about to be exposed to a discrepant communication, you are more likely to be able to resist the persuasive nature of that communication (Chen, Reardon, Rea, & Moore, 1992; Freedman & Sears, 1965).

Why? Most likely, our defenses and counterarguments are exercised and therefore strengthened by being forewarned. When we hear that someone is going to try to change our attitude on an issue about which we care deeply, we may begin to counterargue the message, anticipating what the speaker is likely to say. The delay period between **forewarning** and exposure to a communication allows people to generate more counterarguments (Petty and Cacioppo, 1977). For example, a forewarned person can convince herself that the communicator is unreliable, prejudiced, or misinformed.

Forewarning

Informing people in advance that someone will try to change their attitudes.

When the listener is not very committed to a position, however, forewarning has the opposite effect; it actually facilitates attitude change. The warning seems to operate as a cue for the person to begin thinking about why the position to be advocated is a good one (Apsler & Sears, 1968).

Another kind of forewarning involves signaling the intent to persuade. We may not know the exact position a communicator is going to take, but we know that the communicator is going to try to persuade us of a position. When an issue is relevant and important to us and we are forewarned that someone intends to change our mind, we are likely to counterargue what we expect the arguments to be and thus show heightened resistance to attitude change.

Distraction. The ability to resist persuasion is weakened by anything that makes it harder to counterargue the discrepant communication. In particular, distracting the attention of listeners may enable a persuasive message to get through.

Mild amounts of **distraction** enhance persuasion (Petty & Brock, 1981), and cognitive response analysis suggests why. Distraction tends to foster persuasion when it interferes with an otherwise effective counterarguing process. Thus, distraction is more likely to lead to persuasion when the issue is a familiar one about which we

Distraction

The process of drawing attention away from a persuasive message.

Being forewarned about a person's intent to persuade usually makes people more skeptical about the message. Do you think the prospective customers will successfully resist the persuasive efforts of the salesman?

have established our arguments than when the issue is one about which we do not have ready arguments. If we do not have arguments against an issue, distraction does not keep us from counterarguing. Distraction appears to facilitate persuasion most when communications are very discrepant from our own attitude position and when we are very involved with the topic, presumably because these are the conditions that inspire the most vigorous counterarguing (Petty & Brock, 1981).

There are clear limits on the effects of distraction. Obviously, too much distraction prevents a persuasive message from being heard at all and reduces its effectiveness to zero. Advertisements in which the content of the message is very funny may have this paradoxical effect; the audience laughs so hard at the ads that they may forget what the product is.

Inoculation. In the aftermath of the Korean War, psychologists became interested in reports of the "brainwashing" of American prisoners of war (POWs) by the Chinese communists. A number of POWs had given public speeches that denounced the American government, and several said publicly that they wished to remain in China rather than return to the United States when the war was over. Psychologist William McGuire (1964) speculated that some soldiers might have been vulnerable to influence because their attitudes were assaulted on issues about which they were inexperienced and ignorant. Many soldiers, especially less educated ones, had never had to defend their beliefs about the United States against the sophisticated Marxist arguments used by the Chinese.

McGuire (1964) hypothesized that an important source of resistance to change comes from past experience with an issue. He likened the target faced with a persuasive communication to someone who is attacked by a virus or a disease. There are two ways people can strengthen their defenses against disease. They can strengthen their bodies generally by taking vitamins or by exercising (which supports bodily defenses), or they can strengthen their defenses against a particular disease by building up antibodies (as through inoculation). For example, when people are given a mild case of smallpox that they are able to fight off, their bodies produce antibodies that, in the future, provide an effective and strong defense against more powerful exposure. McGuire argued that these two defenses—support and inoculation—are also applicable to persuasion attempts.

A study by McGuire and Papageorgis (1961) used both support and inoculation methods to build up defenses. They used three groups of participants: One group received support for their position, one group had their position attacked weakly and refuted the attack, and the third group experienced neither approach. Afterward, all three groups were subjected to a strong attack on their initial position. The supportive method helped participants resist persuasion slightly, but the inoculation method helped a great deal. Participants who received this preparation changed their attitudes much less than did participants in the other two groups.

Supportive Defenses

Positive arguments for one's attitude position provided in advance of a persuasive attack help protect that attitude.

Inoculation Defense

People become more resistant to a persuasive communication when they are exposed to weak counterarguments first.

One implication is that **supportive defenses** work best when a person simply needs to be taught specific arguments, and the **inoculation defense** works better when people are stimulated to create their own defensive arguments (e.g., Bernard, Maio, & Olson, 2003). Consistent with this view, subsequent research has shown that supportive defenses are effective when subsequent attacks contain arguments similar to the content of the supporting arguments. But inoculation is effective even when an attack includes new arguments (McGuire, 1964).

Cognitive response theory provides a good explanation for inoculation effects. It suggests that when people refute a mild attack, they exercise their defenses. They prepare arguments that support their own position, construct counterarguments against the opposite position, derogate the source of the opposing view, and so on, thus providing themselves with a stronger and better defended position.

Culture and Persuasion

Is there a set of universal principles that make people more likely to be persuaded by an appeal, or are there cultural differences in what is persuasive?

Research suggests that a core dimension of cultural variability—individualism versus collectivism—may influence the kinds of messages that are most persuasive. In individualistic cultures, people value independence and often subordinate group interest to their personal goals. Therefore, persuasive messages that appeal to these values might be more persuasive. In contrast, in collectivist cultures, people value their relation to the various social groups to which they belong. Consequently, appeals to social relationships and social responsibility may be more common in persuasive messages in collectivist cultures.

To test these predictions, Han and Shavitt (1994) studied popular magazines in two countries: the United States, an individualist culture, and Korea, a collectivist culture. Two hundred product ads from each country were randomly selected from magazines and coded for appeals to individualism versus collectivism. Ads that were coded as reflecting an individualist orientation included appeals to individuality or independence, reflections of self-reliance or individual competition, emphasis on self-improvement or self-realization, and emphasis on the benefits of the product to the individual. In contrast, ads were rated as collectivist in orientation if they appealed to family integrity, focused on group well-being, expressed concerns for others or the support of society, focused on interdependent relationships with others, or focused on group goals. As expected, ads in the United States were significantly more likely to use individualistic appeals to induce people to buy products, whereas in Korea, collectivist appeals were more likely to be used.

In a second study, students in Korea and the United States were recruited for a study on persuasion and were presented with ads that were either collectivist or individualist in orientation. Individualist ads featured such headlines as "She's got a style all her own," "Alive with pleasure," "You . . . only better," "A leader among leaders," and "Treat yourself to a breath-freshening experience." Collectivist ads featured such headlines as "We have a way of bringing people closer together," "Celebrating a half century of partnership," "Sharing is beautiful," and "Share the breath-freshening experience." Students in the United States were more persuaded by ads that emphasized individualist benefits, whereas students in Korea tended to be more persuaded by ads that emphasized collectivist benefits.

Advertisers, then, seem to be on the right track. Not only do they develop ads that reflect the values of their particular culture, but their ads also tend to be more persuasive when they do.

ATTITUDE CHANGE OVER TIME

We have focused on immediate responses to communications. For example, under what conditions does a televised speech, radio ad, or conversation with a friend immediately produce attitude change? In many cases, however, we want to know how attitudes change over time. For example, in order to assess the likely impact of a commercial, an advertiser may want to know the effects of repeated exposure to a message and whether the effects will last after the ad ends.

Spontaneous Attitude Change

Thinking about an attitude object tends to make the attitude more extreme. According to Tesser (1978), we review and rehearse our beliefs, and consistency pressures move them toward more evaluatively consistent clusters. For example, if you spend more than the usual amount of time thinking about your best friend, you will probably like her better. You might remember additional qualities or enjoyable experiences you have shared. And you might reinterpret some of your less pleasant memories to excuse your friend's behavior. However, if you think about your enemy more often, you will probably dislike her even more. You might lengthen your list of offenses and find negative motives for her apparently good and generous acts.

Basically, Tesser's hypothesis is that thinking about an issue produces more polarized attitudes because thinking allows people to generate more consistent attitudes. All this cognitive activity requires that the individual have a preconceived structure, or schema, concerning the person or issue. Without some schematic understanding of the issue, it is difficult for a person to generate new beliefs or to know how to reinterpret old ones.

The implication is that thought polarizes attitudes only when people have a schema about the issue. To test this implication, Chaiken and Yates (1985) studied two groups of people: some who already had a highly consistent knowledge structure about an issue (capital punishment) and others who did not. Each person wrote an essay either about this issue or about a different, irrelevant issue (censorship). Only the highly consistent participants who wrote an essay on capital punishment developed more extreme attitudes on that topic. No significant polarization occurred in any of the other conditions. To polarize attitudes, then, people's thoughts must be relevant to the issue, the people must have sufficient cognitive resources, and there must be no alternative issues competing for attention (Liberman & Chaiken, 1991).

Persistence of Attitude Change

Another question concerns the persistence of attitude change over time following exposure to a persuasive communication. Generally, memory of the details of an argument decays rapidly at first and then less rapidly. However, the persistence of attitude change does not necessarily depend on retention of the details of arguments. Other events that occur after the communication are of much greater significance.

One important factor that aids persistence is whether the recipient is later reminded of important cues, such as the credibility of the source. Kelman and Hovland (1953) manipulated source credibility and found the usual difference on an immediate posttest: The high-credibility source produced more attitude change. Three weeks afterward, the credibility difference was gone. The low-credibility source's message was, by then, just as effective. This rebound in the persuasiveness of the low-credibility source's message is called the **sleeper effect**. The original credibility difference can be reinstated, however, when a person is reminded of the original source of the message.

Sleeper Effect

Delayed attitude changes that are not apparent immediately after exposure to a communication.

The reason for the sleeper effect is unknown. It may be that as time goes on, the credibility of the source becomes increasingly dissociated from the message; that is, the recipient remembers the message but forgets who said it. An alternative interpretation is the differential decay hypothesis (Pratkanis, Greenwald, Leippe, & Baumgardner, 1988), which assumes that the impact of a discounting cue (such as a low-credibility source) on persuasion dissipates more quickly than does the impact of the message itself. Regardless of the reason, sleeper effects are commonly found.

The sleeper effect applies to the intention to persuade as well. Recall that when a person is forewarned about another's intent to persuade, attitude change is less. However, over time it is easy to forget that the person intended to persuade, with the result that attitude change over time may actually increase (Watts & Holt, 1979).

ATTITUDES AND BEHAVIOR

Much of the interest in attitudes comes from the assumption that they affect behavior. Yet, in many instances, behavior does not follow from attitudes. The degree of influence of attitudes over behavior is one of the most important controversies in attitude research.

In a classic study, La Piere (1934), a white professor, toured the United States with a young Chinese student and his wife. They stopped at 66 hotels and motels and ate at 184 restaurants. Although at the time there was rather strong prejudice against Asians in the United States, all but 1 of the hotels and motels gave them space, and they were never refused service at a restaurant. Some time later, a letter was sent to the same establishments asking whether they would accept Chinese people as guests. Of the 128 that replied, 92 percent said they would not. That is, the Chinese couple experienced nearly perfect service in actuality, but nearly universal discrimination in the subsequent letters. La Piere, and many psychologists after him, interpreted these findings as reflecting a major inconsistency between behavior and attitudes (Wicker, 1969).

Yet this conclusion has been widely criticized as underestimating attitude-behavior consistency. Indeed, later studies have shown much higher degrees of consistency between attitudes and behavior (Kraus, 1995). There is, however, variation across situations in precisely how consistent the relation is. In recent years, much research has gone into determining the conditions that yield greater or lesser degrees of consistency between attitudes and behavior. It now appears that stable attitudes, important attitudes, easily accessed attitudes, attitudes formed through direct experience, attitudes about which people are certain, and attitudes that show a high degree of consistency between cognition and affect are most likely to predict behavior (Kraus, 1995). Some of these characteristics are discussed next.

Strength of the Attitude

One important condition for high attitude-behavior consistency is that the attitude be a strong and clear one. Strong attitudes are typically stable, have personal implications, and are held about personally important issues about which one feels extreme and certain. They are often formed through direct experience and become highly accessible as a result (Armitage & Conner, 2000; Bizer & Krosnick, 2001). When we see inconsistency between attitudes and behavior, it is often because the attitudes are weak or are held ambivalently.

Anything that contributes to a strong attitude also tends to increase attitude-behavior consistency. One contributing factor is the amount of information we have about the attitude object. For example, Kallgren and Wood (1986) found that environmental behaviors (agreeing to a home visit to hear about a recycling

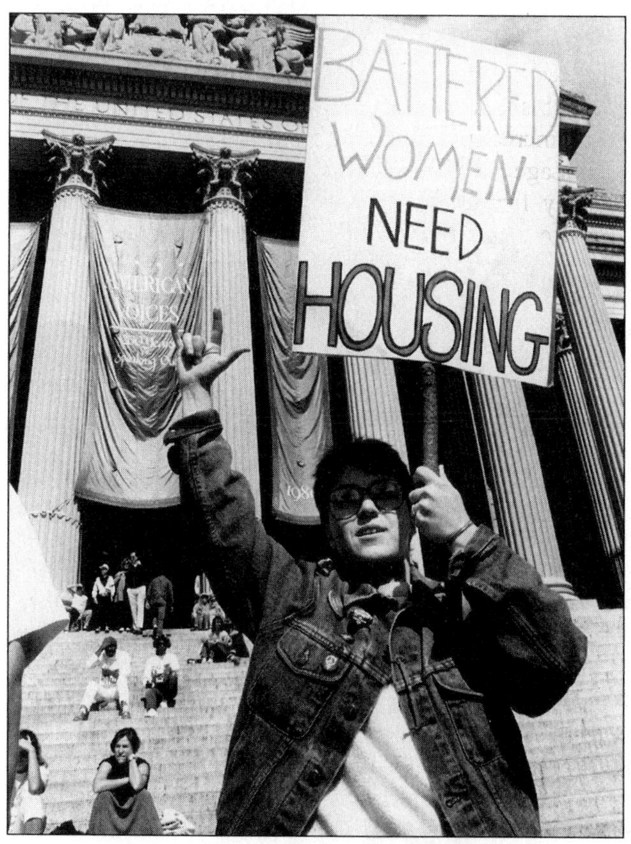

Sometimes attitudes influence people's behavior, but other times they may not. In this picture, the demonstrator is clearly acting on behalf of her attitudes. Yet although many of the bystanders no doubt hold similar attitudes, they are not participating in the protest for other reasons.

project or signing petitions to protect the environment) and attitudes about the environment were more consistent among students who knew the most about preservation of the environment.

Another factor that strengthens attitudes is rehearsing and practicing them. Attitude-behavior consistency is greater when people think about and express their attitudes, presumably because this helps to strengthen the attitude (Fazio, Chen, McDonel, & Sherman, 1982). Strong attitudes are often highly embedded attitudes; that is, they are tied to other beliefs that people hold. Embedded attitudes, therefore, should predict behavior well. Consistent with this point, Prislin and Oullette (1996) found that highly embedded attitudes about preservation of the environment were more strongly related to behavior than were less embedded attitudes.

Having direct personal experience with an issue encourages us to think and talk about it more than if the issue is remote to us. It follows that attitude-behavior consistency is greater when we have direct experience with the attitude object than when we only hear about it from someone else or read about it (Kraus, 1995). Regan and Fazio (1977) showed this effect with students at Cornell University during a severe housing shortage. Many first-year students had to spend the first few weeks of the fall semester in temporary housing—usually a cot in a dormitory lounge. Unlike students who were assigned immediately to permanent housing, they experienced the shortage personally. The researchers measured students' attitudes toward the crisis and their interest in possible behavioral actions, such as signing and distributing petitions or joining committees to study the crisis. Attitudes and behavior were closely related for the students with direct personal experience with the crisis. In contrast, behavior was not at all related to attitudes among students with only secondhand experience, such as those who only talked to friends or read about the crisis in the student paper.

Another source of attitude strength comes from having some vested or selfish interest in the issue. Sivacek and Crano (1982) found support for this idea by using the issue of the minimum drinking age. A ballot proposal in Michigan in 1978 would have raised the legal drinking age from 18 to 21. Presumably students under age 21 had more of a selfish interest in the issue than did older students. Indeed, attitudes toward the proposal were considerably more tightly correlated with behavior (volunteering to call voters) among those with a vested interest than among the disinterested.

A concept closely related to attitude strength is importance. Important attitudes are ones that reflect fundamental values, self-interest, or identification with individuals or groups that an individual values (i.e., reference groups or reference individuals) (Boninger, Krosnick, & Berent, 1995). Such attitudes are highly resistant to persuasion and also show a strong relationship to behavior (Zuwerink & Devine, 1996).

Stability of the Attitude

Stable attitudes that are easily remembered are more likely to predict behavior than attitudes that are less stable and not accessible in memory (Kraus, 1995). When people's attitudes are unstable, their current attitudes predict behavior more than the attitudes they held some months or years ago. You would not necessarily find a close relationship between a college student's evaluation of different careers and her career plans if her evaluations were measured when she was a first-year student and her plans were measured when she was a senior. Therefore, consistency between attitudes and behavior is at a maximum when they are measured at about the same time.

Longer time intervals diminish the attitude-behavior correlation because attitudes change. Also, people and situations change. For example, the fact that a 25-year-old woman says she does not want to have children will not necessarily reflect her behavior at age 30. The longer the interval between measuring the attitude and measuring the behavior, the more such unforeseen contingencies can arise.

Accessibility of the Attitude

Attitudes that are more accessible in memory influence behavior more strongly (Kraus, 1995). A primary factor that determines whether an attitude is accessible in memory is how frequently it is expressed. For example, suppose your school eliminates grade curving, and you believe that the change in the grading system is unfair. If you have frequent opportunities to express this attitude, it is likely to affect your behavior toward a particular professor with whom you are discussing a grade; if you have less opportunity to express your attitude about the grading policy, you might talk with the professor without being influenced by the grading policy (Fazio, 1986, 1989). Attitude accessibility also influences how people process persuasive messages. The more accessible the attitude, the more likely a person will be to elaborate on the persuasive message as opposed to processing it heuristically (Fabrigar, Priester Petty, & Wegener, 1998).

Attitudes also become more extreme when they are expressed more frequently (Downing, Judd, & Brauer, 1992). Thus, if you have multiple opportunities to express your attitude toward the grading policy, you may come to feel more strongly about it in the process. Easily accessible attitudes also come to be viewed as important (Roese & Olson, 1994). That is, the more opportunities you have to express an attitude, the more you come to regard that attitude as important to you (Blascovich et al., 1993).

Relevance of Attitudes to Behavior

Another obvious, but often ignored, point is that when attitudes are relevant to behavior, the two are more closely related. Attitudes vary quite a bit in their relevance to the act in question. La Piere's (1934) asking proprietors about their feelings toward Chinese people in general is plainly not as relevant as asking about their attitudes toward a particular couple. In general, behavior tends to be more consistent with attitudes that are specifically relevant to it than with very general attitudes that apply to a much larger class of potential behaviors.

Salience of the Attitude

In most situations, several different attitudes may be relevant to behavior. For example, cheating on college examinations might be determined by lax attitudes about honesty or by a strong desire to get into law school. A school superintendent's decision about whether to prevent a gay rights sympathizer from addressing a high school assembly might be dictated by her belief in free speech or by her personal attitudes toward homosexuality. The particular attitude that is salient is more likely to influence her behavior. Salience is particularly crucial when the attitude is not a very strong one. When an attitude is strongly held, presumably it does not have to be brought forcefully to the person's attention to be strongly related to behavior.

Affective Versus Cognitive Aspects of an Attitude

Some attitudes depend heavily on cognitions to back them up, that is, beliefs about the attitude object. Other attitudes are more affectively based, dependent on the positive or negative feelings or emotions that a person associates with an attitude object. Making the affective component of the attitude (i.e., the feelings the attitude issue prompts) more salient increases the influence of the affective component over behavior, whereas making the cognitive component (i.e., the beliefs one holds about the attitude object) more salient makes the cognitive component the stronger determinant of behavior (Millar & Tesser, 1986). However, when the cognitive and affective components of an attitude are consistent with each other, it does not matter which is made more salient: Both will be highly correlated with the behavior when either is made salient (Millar & Tesser, 1989; see also Posavac, Sanbonmatsu, & Fazio, 1997).

Whether an attitude is affectively or cognitively based also influences susceptibility to persuasion. Specifically, when an attitude is based heavily on affect, persuasive appeals to emotion are more successful, whereas when attitudes depend more on the cognitions that support them, cognitively based persuasive appeals are more successful in bringing about persuasion (Fabrigar & Petty, 1999).

Reasoning About One's Attitudes

If one were trying to decide whether to take a particular summer job or choose a particular major, an obvious strategy might be to evaluate each of the various aspects of the decision and analyze one's evidence for the pros and cons of each alternative. Despite the intuitive appeal of such a strategy, it actually reduces the relation between attitude and behavior. Wilson and Hodges (1992) found that introspecting about the reasons one likes or dislikes some attitude object has a disruptive effect on those attitudes and reduces the influence of those attitudes on subsequent decisions. In essence, analyzing the reasons that underlie one's attitudes actually causes the attitudes themselves to change temporarily (Wilson, Hodges, & LaFleur, 1995; Wilson & LaFleur, 1995), especially if those attitudes have little cognitive support, that is, beliefs that buttress the attitude (Maio & Olson, 1998).

The reason this happens may be that people generally don't think a lot about their attitudes, and so, when they are induced to do so, they focus on particular aspects of the attitudes, and thus, those aspects become more salient. In doing so, they may fail to discriminate important from unimportant information or to properly perceive the relevance of particular information; the result is a poorer quality decision (Tordesillas & Chaiken, 1999). Therefore, reasoning leads to increased inconsistency in the impact that attitudes have on other judgments and decisions.

Situational Pressures

Whenever people engage in overt behavior, they can be influenced both by their attitudes and by the situation. When situational pressures are strong, attitudes are not as strong determinants of behavior, especially weak attitudes, as when situational pressures are weak (Lavine, Huff, Wagner, & Sweeney, 1998). This effect is easy to see in the La Piere (1934) study. Well-dressed, respectable-looking people who are asking for rooms are hard to refuse, despite feelings of prejudice against their ethnic group. The external pressures are even stronger when the law requires that a room be given to anyone who wants one and can pay for it.

So strong is the effect of situational pressures on attitudes that people sometimes evolve completely different attitudes toward the same attitude object in different situations. As an example, Minard (1952) reported how white coal miners in the Pocahontas Coal Field of McDowell, West Virginia, treated black coworkers as equals in the mines, but as social inferiors when they encountered them in the outside world. Often, then, we form context-dependent attitudes toward a single social target that lead to discrepancies between our attitudes and our behavior, which may actually reflect multiple context-dependent attitudes (McConnell, Leibold, & Sherman, 1997).

The strongest influence on behavior is past behavior. People who have behaved in a certain way at one time usually do so again, and attitudes are only one input into this process. Accordingly, the sheer role of habit and knowledge of past behavior influence what a person will do in a given situation (Albarracin & Wyer, 2000).

Overall, then, sometimes attitudes are strongly related to behavior, and sometimes they are not. Some factors that are important are shown in Table 5–3.

The Reasoned Action Model

Perhaps the most influential effort to generate and test a general theory of attitude-behavior links is Fishbein and Ajzen's (1975; Ajzen & Fishbein, 1980) theory of reasoned action. This theory is an attempt to specify the factors that

Table 5–3

Conditions That Contribute to High Attitude-Behavior Consistency
Attitude is strong.
Unconflicted attitude
Consistent affective and cognitive components
Information about attitude object
Direct personal experience with attitude object
Attitude is stable over time.
Attitude is relevant to the behavior.
Attitude is salient.
No conflicting situational pressures are present.

determine attitude-behavior consistency. It begins with the assumption that we behave in accord with our conscious intentions, which are based, in turn, on our rational calculations about the potential effects of our behavior and about how other people will feel about it. The **reasoned action model** is diagrammed in Figure 5–4.

Reasoned Action Model

Predicts an individual's overt behavior from behavioral intentions.

The central point of the theory of reasoned action is that a person's behavior can be predicted from **behavioral intentions**. If a woman says that she intends to use birth control pills to avoid pregnancy, she is more likely to do so than is someone who does not intend to. Behavioral intentions can themselves be predicted from two main variables: the person's attitude toward the behavior (Does she think taking the Pill is a positive step for her?) and subjective social norms (her perception of what others think she should do: Does her partner want her to? What about her church? Her mother?). A person's attitude toward his or her own behavior is predicted by the expectancy-value framework: The desirability of each possible outcome is weighted by the likelihood of that outcome (e.g., avoiding pregnancy is extremely important to this woman, and the Pill is almost certain to prevent pregnancy; the Pill can have mildly unpleasant side effects, but not for everyone who takes it). Subjective **social norms** are predicted by the perceived expectations of significant others weighted by the motivation to conform to those expectations (e.g., her husband may strongly want her to take the Pill, and she wants to please him; her church strongly opposes it, but she thinks its views are outdated and no longer cares about them).

Behavioral Intentions

The conscious intention to carry out a specific act.

Social Norms

Expectations about how members of a social group should think or behave.

The reasoned action model appeals to many social psychologists both because it makes people seem reasonable and because it places attitudes in a central place in determining behavior. It also has the value of great simplicity: It explains a wide range of behaviors using a small number of variables. Consequently, the model has been widely used. A simple example is a study by Manstead, Proffitt, and Smart (1983), who examined whether pregnant women would breast-feed or bottle-feed their babies. In prenatal questionnaires, the researchers measured behavioral intentions (Did the woman intend to breast-feed?), attitudes toward

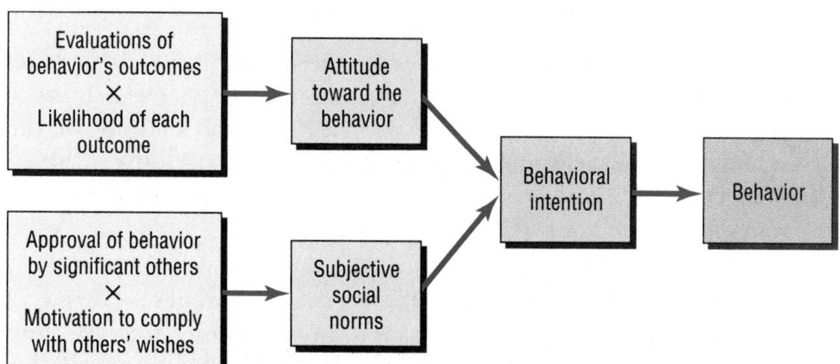

Figure 5–4 **The Reasoned Action Model of Factors that Determine a Person's Behavior.**

the behavior (Did she believe that breast-feeding establishes a closer mother-baby bond, and how important is that bond?), and subjective social norms (What did the woman's partner, mother, closest female friend, and doctor prefer, and how motivated was the woman to follow their wishes?). The researchers found that the reasoned action model was very successful in predicting later behavior. The correlation of these various attitudes with actual postbirth breast-feeding was .77, which is quite high. The model has also been used successfully to predict a variety of other behaviors. When intentions are stable, they predict behavior change; when intentions are weak or unstable, past behavior is the best predictor of current behavior (Conner & Abraham, 2001; Sheeran, Orbell, & Trafimow, 1999).

Of course, no theory is perfect. What are some of the difficulties with this one? It is sometimes difficult to obtain measures of behavioral intention that are truly independent of attitudes, on the one hand, and actual behavior, on the other. Sometimes a behavioral intention, as measured, is not very different from attitude toward the behavior.

Also, as everyone knows, good intentions are not always enough. Sometimes we do not have the ability or the resources to do something we intend to do. One may intend to stop smoking but doubt one's ability to do so. For example, Schifter and Ajzen (1985) found that female students' intentions to lose weight resulted in genuine weight loss only among those who believed they could control their weight and could successfully lose weight if they tried. Attitudes about the desirability of weight loss had little effect on the behavior of those who felt helpless about their ability to lose weight. Adding perceived control to the theory improves its ability to predict intentions and behavior; this is especially true when the behaviors present potential problems with respect to control (such as losing weight or stopping smoking). The revision of the model that includes perceived control over outcomes as an additional element is called the **theory of planned behavior**.

Theory of Planned Behavior

A theory of how people consider and weigh the implications that a behavior may have, as they form their intentions to act.

Summary

1. Attitudes have a cognitive (thought) component, an affective (feeling) component, and a behavioral component. Attitudes are usually cognitively complex but evaluatively simple.
2. The learning approach views attitudes as learned by association, reinforcement, and imitation. Cognitive consistency theories view people as attempting to maintain consistency among their attitudes and among the affective, cognitive, and behavioral components of a particular attitude. The expectancy-value approach views attitudes as cost-benefit calculations by the individual based on the pros and cons of the arguments.
3. Dissonance theory focuses on how behavior affects attitudes. Dissonance arises when decisions and behavioral acts are contrary to the individual's attitudes. Dissonance is typically resolved by changing attitudes. Postdecisional dissonance is greatest when people have free choice, remain committed to their decisions, and feel responsible for foreseeable consequences.
4. Dissonance resulting from attitude-discrepant behavior depends on barely sufficient incentives to commit the behavior, such as threats or promised rewards. The maximum dissonance occurs when incentives are low and clear personal responsibility for negative consequences of the behavior is high.
5. Alternative explanations for these dissonance effects have been generated by self-perception theory. When we have rather vague, undefined attitudes, behavioral acts may lead to new perceptions of our own attitudes, thus leading to attitude-behavior consistency through self-perception rather than through dissonance reduction.
6. Cognitive response theory and the elaboration likelihood model distinguish between systematic processing, which involves close scrutiny of the arguments, and heuristic processing, which involves the use of peripheral cues that are irrelevant to message content.
7. A useful model of the persuasion situation classifies possible influences on the target in terms of communicator (or source), communication, and situational and target variables.

8. Credible, trustworthy, and liked sources are the most potent communicators, as are reference groups with which the target identifies. Source characteristics are often processed as peripheral cues. To avoid changing attitudes, people sometimes derogate the source.
9. An important aspect of a communication is its discrepancy from the target's initial attitude. Attitude change tends to increase with more discrepancy up to a point; then it starts to fall off again. With high source credibility or low commitment, this falloff point occurs at higher levels of discrepancy.
10. Communications can arouse emotional needs such as anger or fear and tend to be accepted if the position that is advocated reduces the need it has aroused. Very high levels of fear seem to arouse defensive reactions, however, and reduce the likelihood of attitude change.
11. The degree of commitment to an attitude (position involvement) is a critical determinant of persuasion. With high commitment, there is less persuasion.
12. Strong arguments are more effective than weak ones when the target can be induced to think about them, such as when the issue is personally relevant (high issue involvement).
13. Repetition of a message is important if attitude change is to be maintained. However, too much repetition leads to boredom and lessens support.
14. A person can become inoculated against persuasion by being exposed to weak versions of the forthcoming persuasive arguments and learning to combat them.
15. Forewarning of the position to be advocated increases resistance to change when the listener is highly committed to a very discrepant position.
16. Distraction can facilitate persuasion by reducing the listener's defenses against highly discrepant messages.
17. Sometimes behavior arises from attitudes, and sometimes it does not. Attitude-behavior consistency is high when attitudes are strong, stable, salient, accessible, and clearly relevant to the behavior, and when there are few conflicting situational pressures.
18. The reasoned action model holds that behavior is controlled by behavioral intentions, which in turn are determined by attitudes toward the behavior and by subjective social norms.

Key Terms

affective component **133**
association **135**
attitude-discrepant behavior **140**
attitudes **133**
balance theory **136**
behavioral component **133**
behavioral intentions **165**
cognitive component **133**
cognitive consistency **136**
cognitive dissonance theory **138**
cognitive response theory **144**
commitment **141**
contrast **151**
counterarguing **144**
credibility **147**
discrepancy **150**
dissonance **138**
distraction **157**
ego involvement **154**
elaboration-likelihood model **150**
expectancy-value theory **143**
forewarning **157**
heuristic processing **145**
imitation **135**
inoculation defense **158**
insufficient justification **140**
learning theory **135**
message learning **135**
peripheral cues **150**
punishment **135**
reasoned action model **165**
reference groups **148**
reinforcement **135**
self-perception theory **142**
sleeper effect **160**
social norms **165**
source derogation **149**
supportive defenses **158**
systematic processing **145**
theory of planned behavior **166**
transfer of affect **135**

In The News

The Israelis and Palestinians

One of the longest running and most intractable intergroup conflicts in modern times pits the Israelis against the Palestinians. Jews have a long history of living amid the Arabs in the Holy Land, going back to the days of the Old Testament. About a century ago, the Zionist movement began to promote immigration of European Jews to Palestine as part of an establishment of a Jewish homeland, after centuries of slaughter and forcible expulsion from other nations. After the near-extermination of European Jews by the Nazi regime during World War II, the Zionists decided to establish their own nation. Their victory in the 1948 war over the armies of the surrounding Arab states resulted in the establishment of the State of Israel. Another war in 1967 expanded Israel's boundaries to include the Gaza Strip and the West Bank, both primarily inhabited by Palestinians. In the years since then, Israelis have increasingly settled in both areas, claiming a religious justification that goes back over 2 millennia, exacerbating tensions between the two peoples. A tentative peace agreement, the "Oslo Agreement," was reached in the early 1990s, and began to give the Palestinians some self-government and control over some lands in the West Bank and Gaza Strip. An effort in 2000 to make further progress toward a final settlement, brokered by President Bill Clinton, ended in failure when the two sides could not agree. It was followed by the resumption of the "intifada," the Palestinian rebellion against Israeli control; mass suicide bombings of Israelis by Palestinians; Israeli military occupation of the West Bank and the Gaza Strip; the beginnings of a massive wall built by Israel to separate it from the West Bank; proposals to return the Gaza Strip to Palestinian control; and thousands of deaths. Almost every aspect of this chapter on prejudice has some parallel in this tragic struggle, and the road to a happy solution seems to be a long one.

Chapter 6

Prejudice

Prejudice can be one of the most destructive aspects of human social behavior, often producing chilling acts of violence. More than 6 million European Jews were murdered by the Nazis in the 1940s under the guise of "purifying" the European racial stock. Today only a fraction of that number of Jews remain in Europe. In the United States, perhaps the most severe and tenacious prejudice has been against African Americans. When Africans were brought to America as slaves, they were treated as property. Even after emancipation, most lived under the Jim Crow system of formal segregation. Black men were often lynched without a trial if they "stepped out of line." In the 1950s and 1960s, the civil rights movement ended most forms of formal segregation and resulted in many other improvements in the lives of African Americans. However, poverty, substandard housing and schools, and crime have continued to plague the African American community.

African Americans are not the only minority group in the United States subjected to prejudice. In fact, virtually every ethnic and racial group has been the victim of prejudice at one time or another, as indicated by the derogatory ethnic labels applied to the Irish (micks), Germans (krauts), French (frogs), Italians (wops, dagos), Poles (polacks), Jews (kikes, hebes, hymies), blacks (niggers, coons, jigaboos, jungle bunnies), Hispanics (spics, greasers, wetbacks, beaners), and Asians (slants, slopes, Chinks, Japs, flips). Even white Anglo-Saxon Protestants are called WASPs on occasion, not usually fondly.

Prejudice is not limited to ethnic and racial groups. For example, gay men and lesbians have also historically been subject to such intense prejudice from the heterosexual majority that until recently most kept their sexual preferences secret to protect themselves. Overweight individuals are often targets of prejudice, and elderly people are often assumed to be less capable physically and mentally.

In the United States, the "peculiar institution" of slavery, and its successor, the Jim Crow system of legalized discrimination, were applied almost entirely to Americans of African descent. Achieving equality has been more difficult for them than for any other minority group. Racial prejudice has been a central reason. Most of the research on prejudice in the United States has focused on African Americans. Much of this

Focus of This Chapter

African Americans were the only peoples in the United States ever to be systematically bought and sold as property. Slave auctions, like livestock auctions, were routine parts of life in the South before the Civil War.

discussion therefore also focuses on African Americans, though other groups are discussed as well.

COMPONENTS OF GROUP ANTAGONISM

In-Group

The group to which an individual belongs.

Out-Group

Any group other than the in-group.

Stereotype

Beliefs about the typical characteristics of members of a group or social category.

Prejudice

Negative evaluations of a group, or of the members of a group without considering them as individuals.

Discrimination

People discriminate against a disliked group by refusing its members access to desired resources.

Group antagonism is exhibited when members of one group, called the **in-group**, display negative attitudes and behavior toward members of another group, called the **out-group**. Such group antagonisms have three interrelated but distinguishable elements. In theory, at least, **stereotypes** are cognitive: beliefs about the typical characteristics of group members. **Prejudice** is affective, referring to negative feelings toward a target group. And **discrimination** is behavioral, referring to behavior that disadvantages individuals simply because of their group membership.

Stereotypes

Stereotypes, the cognitive component of group antagonism, are beliefs about the personal attributes shared by people in a particular group or social category. Some stereotypes involve personality traits. Nineteenth-century stereotypes of Native Americans described them as dirty, cruel, and warlike savages. Twentieth-century stereotypes tend to depict them as silent, passive, drunken, and lazy (Trimble, 1988). In other cases, stereotypes involve attributions, such as those discussed in Chapter 2. For example, many whites attribute the lower educational and income levels among African Americans to a lower level of motivation (Kluegel, 1990). One of the most important ethnic and racial stereotypes in the United States today is displayed in Table 6–1.

Are stereotypes generally accurate? Many stereotypes do indeed have a "grain of truth." For example, crime and welfare rates are in fact relatively high for African Americans; Asian Americans tend to do relatively well academically; and alcoholism is an unusually common problem among Native Americans. But blanket stereotypes about groups, even when they contain a grain of truth, usually contain much inaccuracy because they are overgeneralizations about many quite different individuals. As a result, they can be destructive because they are applied to individual group members whom they may not fit at all. The stereotype of blacks as violent is quite widespread, as shown in Table 6–1. There is a grain of truth to that: It is true that the violent crime rate is higher among black men than among white men. But because there are many more whites than there are blacks, there are more white criminals than black criminals. And one effect of the stereotype is that black men often report experiencing fear and avoidance from whites in public places (Feagin,

Table 6–1

Racial Stereotypes about Violence

	Not Violence Prone	Neutral	Violence Prone	Net Evaluation
Whites	35	47	18	+18
Blacks	15	35	49	–34

Note: The General Social Survey interviews a representative sample of American adults. Each respondent is shown a 7-point scale with the endpoints labeled (not violence prone and violence prone) and asked to rate each of several groups on the scale. "Neutral" includes the midpoint (point 4) or "don't know" or "no answer." "Net evaluation" is the percentage positive minus the percentage negative.

Source: 1990 (*n* = 1,372). General Social Survey (Davis & Smith, 1996).

1991). More generally, stereotypes usually overemphasize certain attributes, especially very unfavorable or very favorable attributes. And they usually underestimate variability within a group (Fiske, 1998; Judd & Park, 1993).

Most research on the effects of stereotypes has emphasized how they bias and distort the stereotype holder's judgment, especially perceptions of individual group members. One typical experiment examined the effects of the racial stereotype of black criminality on behavior in a videogame. The participants were shown both black and white targets and were instructed to shoot armed targets and not to shoot unarmed targets. The stereotype-consistent decisions, to shoot an armed target if he was African American or not to shoot an unarmed target if he was white, were made more quickly than were the stereotype-inconsistent decisions (not to shoot an unarmed African American or to shoot an armed white target; Correll et al., 2002). In another experiment, adults were presented with vignettes describing a criminal suspect. The race of the suspect was varied, as was whether his behavior had been respectful or disrespectful. White participants who held stereotypes of blacks as violent had the most negative evaluations of the suspect, but only when the suspect was both black and disrespectful, not when he was respectful and/or white (Peffley & Hurwitz, 1998).

Recent research also has increasingly focused on the effect of stereotypes on their targets (see, e.g., Swim & Stangor, 1998). One particularly destructive effect is that a stereotype can be a self-fulfilling prophecy that produces stereotype-confirming behavior on the part of the out-group members. Members of the victimized group begin to live up to the stereotype and exhibit the very characteristics the stereotype says they have (Snyder & Swann, 1978). For example, older Americans who accept the standard stereotype that memory declines with age are themselves more likely to show memory declines than are those who reject the stereotype (Levy & Langer, 1994). Why? Stereotype holders behave toward an elderly person as if she can't remember anything. As a result, the older person begins to doubt her own memory, and that lost self-confidence can result in actual forgetfulness. In the end, the victim's self-perceptions and behavior come to reflect the stereotype. This sequence is mapped out in Figure 6–1.

People are usually well aware of the most common stereotypes about their own groups. Knowing that one is being judged stereotypically, that one might behave in ways that will confirm the negative stereotype, and that the stereotype might provide a plausible explanation for one's own poor performance—all this can be quite threatening. Indeed this has been called **stereotype threat**. Stereotype threat tends to occur when a negative stereotype is both relevant and salient. For example, a businesswoman in a contentious meeting with several male colleagues may, in frustration, find herself about ready to cry. She knows that crying would just confirm their stereotype of women as unable to deal with stressful situations and might damage her own standing within the organization. But she would not experience stereotype threat if she began to cry at a memorial service for a close friend because crying in mourning is not generally regarded negatively.

Stereotype Threat

Threat felt when stereotype is salient to targets of negative stereotypes.

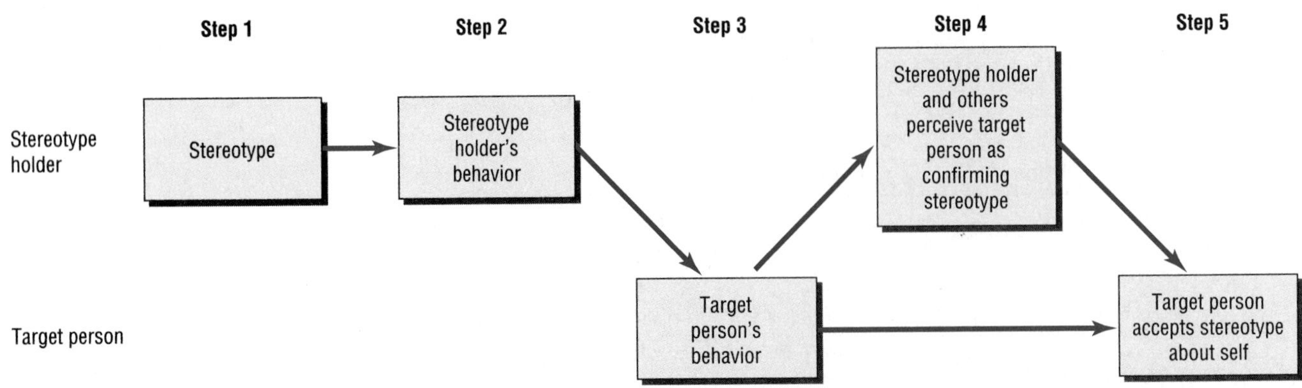

Figure 6–1 **Stereotypes as Self-Fulfilling Prophecies.**

This was nicely illustrated in a study carried out by Steele and Aronson (1995) using black and white students as participants. They gave the same test under two different conditions, in one case describing it as a genuine test of academic abilities, and in the other, as just a laboratory exercise. Negative stereotypes about the lesser academic ability of blacks would have been relevant only in the academic-ability condition. In fact, the black students showed evidence of stereotype threat only in that condition. For example, they were more likely to respond to word completion tests with racially relevant words, such as completing the word "—ce" by putting the letters "ra" in the blanks. They also were more likely to fill in the blanks with words related to self-doubt. And stereotype threat did in fact interfere with blacks' performance on the test only when it was described as a diagnostic of academic ability, the target of the stereotype.

Stereotype threats have also been shown to harm the performance of other groups. For example, women often are stereotyped as being less good at math than are men. In one study, high-achieving females performed significantly worse than did males on a standardized math test when the stereotype about their math ability was made salient (Spencer, Steele, & Quinn, 1999). Another study looked at the common stereotype of poor white athleticism. White students tended to practice less when expecting to take a test of their natural athletic ability, as if they were preparing to excuse poor performance on the basis of lack of practice (Stone, 2002). Stereotypes can also be positive and have positive effects through a similar process. When tested on a mathematics test, Asian American women performed better when their Asian identity was cued, but worse when their gender identity was cued, alternately confirming the stereotype of Asians as good at math or the stereotype of women as bad at it (Shih, Pittinsky, & Ambady, 1999).

Recent research has suggested that stereotype threat may have long-term negative consequences. Victims of it may come to devalue performance in the domain in question, a process that has been called "disidentification" (Major et al., 1998). Young blacks may come to view academic success as not very worthwhile, and women may devalue math performance as less important than other goals in life, such as artistic performance or having a family. Stereotype threat may have damaging physiological as well as psychological consequences. On average, African Americans have a higher incidence of hypertension (high blood pressure) than do white Americans. This may in part result from the stresses associated with stereotype threat. Blascovich and his colleagues (2001) varied stereotype threat while giving black and white students a written test. The blacks showed considerably higher blood pressure in the high stereotype threat condition than did the white participants, but they did not differ in the low stereotype threat condition.

Prejudice

Prejudice is the evaluation of a group or of a single individual based mainly on the person's group membership. It is based on the same evaluative or affective dimension discussed earlier regarding impressions (Chapter 2) and attitudes (Chapter 5). In addition, it is based on prejudgment, often reflecting an evaluation made before knowing much about the person's characteristics as an individual. Prejudice does not apply exclusively to attitudes about out-groups. **Ethnocentrism** refers to the belief that the in-group is superior to all out-groups, and can also influence evaluations of in-group members before they are known as individuals.

Ethnocentrism

The belief that the in-group is the center of the social world and superior to out-groups.

Overall, people do have a tendency to evaluate the attributes of out-groups less favorably than those of members of their own group. In one experiment, white and black students evaluated either a black or a white job applicant and made attributions explaining why the applicant had been fired or laid off from a previous job. Members of both groups gave more favorable evaluations and attributions to the applicant of their own race than to the applicant of the other race (Chatman & von Hippel, 2001). It is tempting to view any such gap as reflecting prejudice against the out-group. But by themselves these group differences do not demonstrate the role of prejudice. All we know is that whites differed from blacks. To more directly establish the role of prejudice, we would need to show that the most prejudiced students showed the least favorable judgments of the out-group job applicant.

The effects of prejudice against gay males have been directly demonstrated by a study in which people with the most negative attitudes toward gay men were the least willing to interact with someone with AIDS (Pryor, Reeder, & McManus, 1991). In another study, participants read two purportedly scientific studies. One concluded that homosexuality was associated with psychopathology; and the other, that it was not. Participants who were most prejudiced against homosexuals responded more favorably to the more derogatory report (Munro & Ditto, 1997).

The effects of prejudice, like those of stereotypes, are also destructive and wide ranging. An extreme example is that merely sitting next to a person from a stigmatized group seems to be enough to create harm. Male job applicants were more likely to be evaluated negatively if they were simply sitting next to an obese woman, even if they were thought not to know the woman or when positive information was presented about her (Hebl & Mannix, 2003).

Prejudice also influences preferences about public policy. Prejudice against blacks contributes to opposition to affirmative action and other government efforts to help blacks (Bobo & Kluegel, 1997). Prejudice against Latinos contributes to support for restrictive immigration policies and opposition to bilingual education (Sears, Citrin, van Laar, & Cheleden, 1999). Prejudice against gays produces support for restrictions on HIV-positive individuals, such as requiring them to carry identification, quarantining them, or tattooing them (Price & Hsu, 1992).

Are stereotypes and prejudice really different? At the beginning of this chapter, we stated that stereotypes are cognitive and prejudice is affective. That is a useful rule of thumb, but in fact both reflect a mixture of cognition and affect. For example, consider perceptions of people with AIDS. Those who are prejudiced against gay people are likely to store in memory both a group label (e.g., "gays") and its accompanying stereotypical traits (e.g., "immoral"), and they associate negative affect with the group label. We can distinguish the stereotypical traits from the prejudice, but in fact the two tend to go together (Dovidio, Brigham, Johnson, & Gaertner, 1996). As a result we do not attempt to make a sharp distinction between them in this chapter.

The distinction may be important in at least one respect, however. It is possible for unprejudiced people to be familiar with common cultural stereotypes even if they do not believe they are true (Devine & Elliot, 1995). However, most studies show that highly prejudiced people are the most likely to recognize conventional stereotypes (e.g., Gordijn, Koomen, & Stapel, 2001). It seems likely that the most widespread stereotypes are familiar to almost everyone, whether they agree with them or not. But subtler and less common stereotypes may be most familiar to people who themselves are highly prejudiced and who therefore are most preoccupied with the many supposed flaws of the out-group.

Discrimination

Discrimination is the behavioral component of group antagonism. It consists of negative behaviors toward individuals based on their group membership. For example, in 1942 the U.S. government sent 120,000 Japanese Americans to internment camps for the duration of World War II, generally without benefit of individual review or due process, and forced them to abandon most of their possessions. The use of quotas in college admissions to limit the number of Jewish students, as many private universities did before 1960, or of Asian American students, as is sometimes charged today, is another example of discrimination. The opponents of affirmative action to increase admission of minority members to schools and jobs often describe it as "reverse discrimination" because they say it favors a minority group at the expense of the majority.

When are people most likely to be judged as prejudiced and engaging in discrimination? Perceptions of *intent* to harm a target seem to increase perceptions of discrimination among both targets and outside observers, but only the targets care enough to take the *degree* of harm into account (Swim et al., 2003). Interestingly enough, people who have failed to discriminate in the past are more likely to be perceived as unprejudiced and therefore seem to feel freer to engage in discriminatory actions in the future. In one study, some participants were first given an opportunity to disagree with blatantly sexist statements, and others were not. Those given a chance to demonstrate their lack of prejudice were later more likely to favor a male for a stereotypically male job (Monin & Miller, 2001).

Blatant discrimination is obviously emotionally difficult for its victims. But even subtle acts of discrimination can be damaging. For example, several experiments have shown that exposure to sexist humor can increase tolerance of sex discrimination (Ford, 2000). The reason seems to be that humorous communication induces a noncritical mindset and therefore allows people to tolerate sexist acts more than if they scrutinized such acts more skeptically.

Attributional Ambiguity

Uncertainty about whether one's failures are due to discrimination or to one's own inadequate efforts.

Indeed discrimination can be particularly difficult when it is disguised as something else. Acts of discrimination often contain **attributional ambiguity**. A person turned down for promotion cannot necessarily tell whether it was because her performance was inadequate or because she was discriminated against. Crocker and Major (1989) hypothesized that the damaging effects of such negative evaluations can be lessened if the victim is able to attribute them to discrimination. In their study, a white evaluator gave negative feedback to African American students seated in an adjacent room. The students knew that the evaluator could see some of them and not others. Those who could be seen were more likely to

Early in World War II, Japanese Americans were taken from their homes and sent to isolated concentration camps far from their means of livelihood. They had not been accused of any wrongdoing. Here a group is being marched under army escort to an evacuation point for transport to the camps.

attribute the negative evaluation to discrimination, and their self-esteem suffered less from the negative feedback. Ironically, then, reducing blatant discrimination may actually increase the threat to self-esteem for members of minority groups because it increases attributional ambiguity (Crocker et al., 1998).

However, attributing negative events to discrimination is no panacea. The victim of discrimination may be perceived as a complainer, leading to still further devaluation of her performance (Kaiser & Miller, 2001). That produces an obvious dilemma for the victim of discrimination: Making an issue of it can help protect one's own self-esteem, but at the risk of being perceived as a troublemaker and bringing still further criticism to oneself. Similarly, explicitly addressing the negative effects of discrimination with special programs such as affirmative action may also have some negative side effects on perceptions of one's own abilities. Women who believed they had been selected to be leaders in a team problem-solving task because of their gender performed significantly worse on a subsequent problem-solving test than did women who believed they had been selected at random (Brown et al., 2000).

Discrimination and prejudice are not always perfectly consistent. This was illustrated in the classic study by La Piere (1934). As described in Chapter 5, almost all restaurant and hotel owners politely served the well-dressed Chinese couple who appeared on their doorsteps, even though in a separate letter they expressed strong prejudice against Asian customers in general. Obviously, eliminating discrimination as much as possible is a good thing, and many laws exist to prevent discrimination based on race, gender, and national origin. But it means that today this kind of inconsistency, in which attitudinally prejudiced people do not behaviorally discriminate, is quite common. Even quite prejudiced restaurant owners are generally not allowed to refuse service based on the customer's group membership.

Nevertheless, discrimination tends to be more consistent with prejudice when the situation is more ambiguous. In one study, participants were asked to evaluate applicants for admission to their university. When the applicants' credentials were consistently strong or consistently weak, prejudiced evaluators did not discriminate against black applicants. However, the most prejudiced participants did discriminate against blacks when the case was somewhat ambiguous because the applicant's credentials were mixed (Hodson, Dovidio, & Gaertner, 2002).

LEARNING PREJUDICE

There are a number of theories about the origins of group antagonism, most of which derive from the general theories introduced in Chapter 1 and applied to attitudes in Chapter 5. Perhaps the simplest, social learning theory, views it as being learned the same way people learn other attitudes and values.

Socialization

Children are not born with stereotypes and prejudice. They must learn them—from their family, their peers, the media, and the society around them. As indicated in Chapter 1, socialization refers to the process by which children learn the conventional social norms of their surroundings. Prejudice can be learned inside or outside the home. It can take place through any of the standard social learning mechanisms. For example, children may simply imitate the prejudices of adults and friends; they may be positively reinforced for using derogatory ethnic humor; or they may simply learn to associate particular minority groups with poverty, crime, dirtiness, and other negative characteristics.

It is easy to document the existence of social norms of ethnic and racial prejudice all over the world. For example, white North Americans have historically tended to be more prejudiced against those who originally came from Africa, Asia, and Latin America than against those who came from Western Europe. Russians have historically been more prejudiced against Jews, the English against Africans, the Chinese against Japanese, and the Japanese against Koreans.

In the United States, racial prejudice has historically been stronger in the South than it has in the North. For example, whites who live in the South are

Table 6–2

Percentage of White Adults Who Support Laws Against Racial Intermarriage

	Currently Residing In	
Grew Up In	**South**	**North**
South	36	26
North	20	15

Source: Adapted from Glaser and Gilens (1997, p. 81). Based on General Social Surveys from 1980 to 1993.

considerably more likely than those living in the North to think there should be laws against marriages between blacks and whites, as shown in Table 6–2. A similar cultural difference is that white Americans show more prejudice against heavy women than do blacks. In one study, white and black women were shown photographs of thin, average-weight, and heavy women (Hebl & Heatherton, 1998). White women tended to rate heavy women as less attractive, less happy, and less popular than thin women. However, black women actually rated heavy women as more popular and just as happy as thin women.

Conventional prejudices are often learned very early in life. By age 4 or 5, most urban white children living in the United States differentiate between blacks and whites, are aware of the prevailing norms about race, and display some signs of racial prejudice by the age of 5 at least in some form. Their recognition of less salient ethnic groups, such as Latinos or Asian Americans, tend to be delayed a few years, but by age 7, most also show signs of prejudice against them as well (Aboud, 1988). Children acquire prejudices about foreign peoples in the grade school years as well (Lambert & Klineberg, 1967).

Parents and peers are most responsible for passing on these social norms, but sometimes children do not discuss such matters very much with either their peers or their parents, especially when the target groups concerned are not very salient (Sears & Levy, 2003). Other vehicles for socialization are available. One study looked at ethnic slurs in children's literature (Mullen, 2004). The immigrant groups that attracted the most stereotypically simple slurs were the least commonly discussed, tended to be described in terms of physical appearance rather than of personal traits, had the least pleasant folk songs, and were even pictured with smaller heads!

The experiences children have during these early years are crucial because prejudices toward highly salient groups do not change much later in an individual's life (Sears & Levy, 2003). As can be seen in Table 6–2, whites brought up in the South are still more prejudiced than those brought up in the North, regardless of where they live as adults. That is not to say that later experience does not matter at all. As shown in the table, people who moved from the South to the North were less prejudiced than were people who lived their whole lives in the South. But the norms of one's early environment, as reflected in the region one is brought up in, the educational levels of one's parents, or the religion in which one is raised, have stronger effects on one's adult levels of prejudice than do such later experiences as adult occupation or adulthood region (Miller & Sears, 1986).

How does it happen that prejudices remain so constant through adulthood? Continuing reinforcement from like-minded people in one's own in-group helps maintain conformity to such social norms. In one experiment, participants were asked to estimate what percentage of African Americans possessed various stereotypical traits (Stangor, Sechrist, & Jost, 2001). Next they were given falsified feedback about the estimates made by members either of their in-group (fellow students at their own university) or of an out-group (students at a rival university) and reestimated those trait percentages. False feedback about others' attitudes influenced their reestimates significantly more when it came from the in-group than when it came from the out-group. The majority views of members of our own group play a powerful role both in reinforcing our stereotypes and in protecting them from change.

The Media

The media represent another potential source of social learning. Until the last several decades, racial minorities were largely "invisible" in the mass media, appearing relatively infrequently on television or in the printed media. Moreover media coverage of any given group is likely to reflect the broader society's current stereotypes about that group. For example, fewer than 1 percent of the cartoons in *The New Yorker* showed blacks even in the 1980s (Thibodeau, 1989). Those that did appear were usually relegated to stereotypical roles, such as cleaning ladies or sanitation workers. Although Latinos now make up 13 percent of the American population, they made up only 4 percent of the regular characters on prime-time television in 2003 (Hoffman & Noriega, 2004). And the few Latino characters that are shown tend to be depicted as illegal immigrants, drug runners, or gangbangers (Pachon & Valencia, 1999).

Gilens (1999) argues that the media are partly responsible for the increasingly negative view of "welfare" in the United States. He argues that Americans have increasingly viewed welfare as rewarding undeserving poor blacks, as reflected in the widespread stereotype that poor people are mostly unemployed blacks. But in fact, as of 1990, only 29 percent of those living below the poverty line were black, and half of them were employed. Where does this false stereotype come from? Gilens showed that the great majority of the pictures of poor people presented in the media are of nonworking blacks. They tend to ignore the very large number of white poor and working poor. What is the effect of this biased coverage? Among the strongest predictors of opposition to liberal welfare policies are the stereotypes that blacks and poor people are lazy.

Television coverage also tends to reinforce stereotypes that link racial minorities to violent crime. Violent crime is a staple of local television news. This coverage can exacerbate racial stereotyping, as shown in a clever experiment by Gilliam and Iyengar (2000). They showed adults a videotape of a 15-minute local newscast in a room furnished like a typical living room. One of the stories reported a murder, showing either a black male or a white male as the perpetrator. His race was varied by digitally changing the skin color of the same face. Showing a black perpetrator led white viewers to support more punitive responses to crime (such as "three strikes" laws). Watching a newscast about a black man committing a crime presumably activated stereotypes linking blacks and crime.

Sometimes the media do rise above simple stereotypical images. In the 1960s, for example, media coverage played an important role in mobilizing public support for the civil rights movement in the South. More recently, much of the public's information about AIDS has come from the media, and that has helped to reduce misinformation about the epidemic and increase tolerance toward its victims (Price & Hsu, 1992). Ironically, anti-gay prejudice in the general public actually interferes with reception of accurate media information about AIDS (Pryor, Reeder, & McManus, 1991). In other words, the mass media are products of their own society and tend to reflect its stereotypes and prejudices. However, even when the media present information that would dispel inaccurate stereotypes, the audience's prejudices may interfere with its reception.

MOTIVES FOR PREJUDICE

Other theories focus on how prejudice helps to satisfy the needs of individuals. As indicated in Chapter 1, they are motivational theories because they focus on the motives of individuals and on the incentives that induce individuals to adopt prejudiced attitudes.

Psychodynamic Approaches

Authoritarian Personality

A personality type characterized by exaggerated submission to authority; extreme conformity to conventional standards; hostility toward deviants; and ethnocentrism.

"Psychodynamic" theories analyze prejudice as an outgrowth of the particular dynamics of an individual's personality, indeed usually of a personality disorder. The best known describes the **authoritarian personality**, displaying exaggerated submission to authority, extreme levels of conformity to conventional standards of behavior, self-righteous hostility, and punitiveness toward deviants and members of minority groups (Adorno, Frenkel-Brunswik, Levinson, & Sanford, 1950). In keeping with this perspective's roots in psychoanalytic theory, authoritarian personalities were said to originate in abusive and rigid treatment during childhood. Adults with the most authoritarian personalities also showed high levels of ethnocentrism and prejudice. The theory, proposed soon after World War II, naturally focused particularly on anti-Semitism. It was quite a provocative point of view and stimulated a great deal of research. However, it ultimately became mired in methodological disputes (see Christie & Jahoda, 1954) and lay dormant for many years.

The authoritarian personality has resurfaced in recent years as "right-wing authoritarianism" (see Table 6–3), also strongly associated with prejudice toward racial and ethnic groups and with hostility toward homosexuals, AIDS victims, drug users, and the homeless (Altemeyer, 1988; Peterson, Doty, & Winter, 1993). It differs from the original concept in two ways. It is most common among political conservatives because right-wing authoritarians tend to support established authority rather than challenge it, as those on the political left do. Also its roots are described not as lying in psychopathology but as originating in social learning, especially from conservative parents and peers, and from direct personal experience. That is, right-wing authoritarians tend to have been raised in highly religious and socially narrow environments, with little direct experience with unconventional people and minorities. In a sense, this view is more hopeful: Authoritarianism is not ingrained in the human personality, reversible only through years of psychotherapy. Rather, it can be reduced through exposure to nonauthoritarians, to more diverse kinds of people and ideas, and to higher education (Peterson & Lane, 2001).

Displaced Aggression

The expression of aggression against a target other than the source of attack or frustration, usually a safer target.

Another psychodynamic theory treats prejudice as **displaced aggression** (see Chapter 13). People who are angry or frustrated normally try to express their aggression toward the source of their unhappiness. However, if the source of annoyance cannot be attacked because of fear of retaliation or simple unavailability, aggression may be displaced toward another target. For example, people who lose their jobs during an economic depression may feel angry and aggressive, but no obvious person is at fault. In these circumstances, people look for a scapegoat—someone whom they can blame for their difficulties and whom they can attack. One study showed that lynchings of African Americans in the Old South increased in bad economic times (Hovland & Sears, 1940). Poor whites could not aggress against the large economic forces that were the real source of their frustration, so they aggressed against a more convenient and safer target—local

Table 6–3

Items Used to Measure Right-Wing Authoritarianism

1. What our country really needs is a strong determined leader who will crush evil and take us back to our true path. (agree)
2. The facts on crime, sexual immorality, and the recent public disorders all show we have to crack down harder on deviant groups and troublemakers if we are going to save our moral standards and preserve law and order. (agree)
3. A "woman's place" should be wherever she wants to be. The days when women are submissive to their husbands and social conventions belong strictly to the past. (disagree)
4. We should treat protestors and radicals with open arms and open minds, since new ideas are the lifeblood of progressive change. (disagree)

Source: Duckitt (2001, p. 46).

African Americans. In this perspective, social norms again play a key role, with racial prejudice determining the targets of displaced aggression.

Intergroup Competition

A second motivational idea is that prejudice stems from intergroup competition. This idea begins with the assumption that society is composed of groups that differ in power, economic resources, social status, and other desirable attributes. Dominant groups are motivated to maintain their privileged positions, and subordinate groups are motivated to reduce that inequality. That competition produces intergroup conflict and therefore prejudice. There are several versions of such theories.

Realistic group conflict theory views prejudice as an inevitable consequence of competition among groups for resources or power (Le Vine & Campbell, 1972). For example, prejudice may stem from competition between blacks and Latinos for blue-collar jobs, or between whites and minorities for admission to selective colleges. A related but more psychologically realistic theory argues that intergroup hostility stems from the perception of deprivation relative to others, or **relative deprivation**, rather than from absolute levels of deprivation. For example, in a fast-growing economy, most people's economic situations may be improving. But those whose situations are improving more slowly may be resentful because they see others increasingly able to afford things they cannot, leading to antagonism against the more advantaged group. Relative deprivation was one factor in the riots in black ghettoes in the 1960s. Although blacks' lot was improving economically, they believed (quite accurately) that their situation remained much worse than that of whites, contributing to anti-white sentiment and violence (Sears & McConahay, 1973).

Realistic Group Conflict Theory

The theory that prejudice arises from real conflicts of interest between groups.

Relative Deprivation

Discontent due to the belief that oneself or one's group is faring more poorly than others, or more poorly than in the past.

Another such theory focuses on a **sense of group position** (Bobo, 1999). Privileged groups work actively to protect their privileged status and all the perks that come with it against challenges from subordinate groups. The dominant group's sense of group position involves four elements: (1) a belief in the superiority of the dominant group; (2) perceptions of members of the subordinate group as alien and different; (3) proprietary claims over superior resources such as access to the best neighborhoods, schools, and jobs; and (4) feelings of threat from subordinate groups coveting those superior resources. Evidence presented for this theory includes the greater opposition among whites than among blacks to government actions providing special help to blacks, and whites' stronger belief that affirmative action has primarily negative effects, even taking into account most other relevant differences between the races (Bobo, 2000).

Sense of Group Position

Members of a dominant group believe their advantaged position is deserved and that members of subordinate groups are threatening to take those privileges away.

Social dominance theory also assumes that groups in any society tend to be organized in hierarchies, with some groups at the top and others at the bottom. But it goes a step further to argue that societies with stable group hierarchies have more evolutionary success (Sidanius & Pratto, 1999). Its central predictor is support for a rigidly hierarchical society, indexed by levels of "social dominance orientation." Some items used to measure it are shown in Table 6–4. Individuals high in it may choose to enforce the existing hierarchy, perhaps by serving in law enforcement. Those who are low in it may try to promote more equality, perhaps by serving as left-wing political activists or as social workers. Social dominance orientation proves to have strong effects on racial and ethnic prejudices among members of the dominant group, indeed somewhat independent of the effects of right-wing authoritarianism (Duckitt, 2003). They may reflect somewhat different dynamics, authoritarianism being more closely associated with social conformity, and social dominance orientation, tough mindedness (Duckitt et al., 2002).

Social Dominance Theory

The theory that all societies are organized in group hierarchies, which are sustained through discrimination, legitimizing myths, and the efforts of individuals high in social dominance orientation.

How do dominant groups maintain their privileged positions, according to these theories? Physical force is generally not adequate by itself. It is too disruptive, costly, and inefficient. Instead these theories focus on two other mechanisms. One is interpersonal. Mary Jackman (1994) argues that when groups are in close daily contact with each other, the existing hierarchy is maintained not by coercion and violence, but by **benevolent paternalism**, a combination of

Benevolent Paternalism

Members of dominant groups control subordinate group members through affectionate and benevolent treatment, demanding deference in return.

Table 6–4

Items Used to Measure Social Dominance Orientation

Agree with these items:

Superior groups should dominate inferior groups.

Inferior groups should stay in their place.

It is probably a good thing that certain groups are at the top and other groups are at the bottom.

Disagree with these items:

Group equality should be our ideal.

It would be good if all groups could be equal.

No one group should dominate in society.

Source: Sidanius et al. (2000, pp. 234–235).

paternalism by the dominant group and deference by the subordinate group. Members of the two groups may even have close and affectionate relationships with each other, as long as the subordinates "stay in their place." One example is the traditional relationship between men and women. A man may both love his wife and insist that she stay in a subordinate role, doing the cooking and child care. Another is the warm relationship developed by some white women in the Old South with the black slaves who took care of their children—indeed such slaves might have been treated as "a member of the family." But of course they had to eat in the kitchen and were not free to quit their job or take a better one.

Legitimizing Myth

An ideology that justifies inequalities in the current social hierarchy.

A second mechanism is ideology. Dominant groups create **legitimizing myths** to justify maintaining the existing hierarchy. For example, stereotypes that women are nurturant and not capable of competing at the highest levels of business, politics, or war help to justify keeping women in the economically disadvantaged role of primary caregivers. Many whites attribute minorities' lesser education and income to a poor work ethic, loose morals, or inherent racial inferiority. Such attributions to internal, controllable traits are associated with greater racial prejudice (Kluegel, 1990). Similarly, heterosexuals who attribute homosexuality to a deliberately chosen lifestyle rather than to inherited dispositions are the most prejudiced against gay people (Whitley, 1990). Group hierarchy theories interpret these associations as reflecting the dominant group's use of stereotypes as a way to justify their superior position, though they may arise for other reasons as well.

Self-Interest

Attitudes or behaviors that are motivated by people's attempts to improve their own short-term material well-being.

Group competition theories lead to a useful distinction about whose interests are at stake. On the one hand, group members might be concerned about their own personal betterment—their sense of **self-interest**—or they might be concerned about their group's well-being—their sense of "group interest." An analogous contrast in relative deprivation theory is between "egoistic deprivation" (I am deprived relative to others) and "fraternal deprivation" (my group is deprived relative to other groups). For example, some whites might oppose affirmative action because it threatens their own children's access to elite colleges (self-interest) or because they see it as unfair to whites in general (group interest).

A number of studies have shown that self-interest has surprisingly little impact on levels of prejudice or other racial attitudes among whites (Sears & Funk, 1991). For example, opposition to affirmative action for African Americans does not usually stem from the fears of whites that it will deprive them personally of jobs, promotions, or educational opportunities. On the other hand, there are convincing examples of the power of perceived group interest. A survey of working women in the Boston area found that they earned significantly less than men in comparable jobs (Crosby, 1982). The women believed that women in general faced unfair situations in their work (fraternal deprivation) even though they reported relatively little dissatisfaction with their own personal work situations (egoistic deprivation). Fraternal deprivation has also been shown to be a stronger force than egoistic deprivation in producing prejudice in Europe against immigrant minority groups such as Algerians and Turks (Pettigrew & Meertens, 1995). It is generally easier to mobilize people on the basis of supposed group mistreatment than on the basis of their own individual mistreatment.

COGNITIVE BASES OF PREJUDICE

Chapters 2 and 3 extensively analyzed the cognitive processes involved in perceptions of other individuals. The central theme was that systematic cognitive biases naturally accompany the perception of other people because we need to simplify a complex world. Extending this idea to perceptions of groups, and of group members, has been an active area of research on prejudice in recent years. These seemingly harmless cognitive biases can produce stereotyping and prejudice even in the absence of the socialization of prejudice, personality disorders, or competition among groups for resources.

Categorization

Categorization

The process by which we perceive people as members of groups or categories rather than as distinct individuals.

Perceptual **categorization** into groups is the first step. Perceivers naturally categorize other people into groups. We immediately notice whether a stranger is a man or woman, black or white, child or adult, young or old and so immediately categorize the person into the appropriate group. This is a largely automatic, unconscious, and involuntary process. Even wanting to be fair and rational about treating someone as an individual may not be enough, because our perception is structured in group terms before we are even aware of it.

On what basis do we categorize others into groups? The perceptual salience of various cues is obviously important. Skin color often differentiates racial groups; body type, clothing, and voice can differentiate men and women; accent differentiates people from different countries, and so on. As indicated in Chapter 3, we pay the most attention to salient stimuli, so we tend to focus on these differences when we encounter members of other groups.

But perceptual salience only scratches the surface of the bases for group categorization. People differentiate others in terms of many categories, but in every society they tend to rely heavily on only a few. The social norms of each society focus particular attention on some cues and not on others, and these norms may have little or nothing to do with perceptual salience. For people in Northern Ireland, Bosnia, or Israel, religion is a defining characteristic. People are either Catholic or Protestant, Muslim or Christian or Jew, and anything else is important only within those groups. The ethnic distinction between Hutus and Tutsis was of deadly significance in the genocide involving these groups in Rwanda and Burundi in the mid-1990s.

Even the seemingly simple categorization of Americans on the basis of skin color into blacks and whites is controlled to a significant degree by arbitrary social norms. This was vividly illustrated by the famous "separate but equal" Supreme Court decision in 1896 in the case of *Plessy v. Ferguson*. It concluded that a Louisiana man had to be restricted to all-black railway cars. He had seven white great-grandparents and only one black great-grandparent, but state law at the time defined any individual as "colored" who had as much as "one drop" of African blood. The state law was arbitrary: It could have stated that a person is "colored" only if more than half of his or her great-grandparents claimed African descent, or if none of his or her ancestors were white. Instead this rule reflected the overriding stigma of having any African origins at all. Indeed, to this day, informal social norms in the United States tend to categorize people as "black" if they have any known African ancestry.

Categorization into social groups is important because it often is affectively loaded, unlike the classification of insects or trees. The category label usually has an evaluation associated with it. Different labels, even for the same category, can evoke very different evaluations. Consider the category of people of above-average weight. The category label "large people" might usually carry a fairly neutral evaluation, whereas the label "fat people" usually carries a strongly negative evaluation. Because category labels are so emotionally charged, they are often the focal points of intense controversy. Most people who have weight problems might prefer not to be categorized in terms of their appearance at all. Yet labels persist, and "large" triggers less negative affect than does "fat."

Category-Based Processing

Category-Based Processing

Cognitive processing in which perceivers attend to individuals mainly as members of a social category.

The categorization process has a number of important consequences. Information about individuals is simplified and processed more efficiently when they can be categorized into groups. In **category-based processing**, the perceiver categorizes the target person based on information he or she has stored in memory concerning social categories. The perceiver attends to the person's individual characteristics only to make sure they are consistent with the particular social category. This is another version of the "schematic processing" discussed in Chapter 3. The tedious alternative is to process information about the individual on a piecemeal basis, attribute by attribute, which is called "attribute-based processing" (Fiske & Neuberg, 1990). Category-based processing also tends to be more affective than cognitive, consisting more of emotional responses toward the group than of factual beliefs about it (Stangor, Sullivan, & Ford, 1991).

Once the person is categorized into a group, priming of group stereotypes usually occurs quickly, unconsciously, and involuntarily. For example, virtually all of us learn a standard set of stereotypes about children and the elderly, men and women, the French and Chinese, and other commonly encountered groups. These stereotypes tend to be activated automatically by the presence of a group member or anything else that makes us think about the group. They are evoked so quickly that we are scarcely aware of it, almost before we know it. For example, in one study participants were first shown either black or white faces, and then briefly shown a range of objects. They were able to identify a particular object as a gun more quickly when it followed a black face than when it followed a white face, presumably because of the strong stereotypic association between blacks and violent crime (Payne, 2001). In contrast, which face was first presented did not affect the identification of objects with no such stereotypic associations, such as insects or fruits (Judd, Blair, & Chapleau, 2004).

The categorization process is not necessarily blunt or simple; on the contrary, it can be quite sophisticated. For example, one study found that people with more Afrocentric features were judged as having personality traits more stereotypic of African Americans even if they were actually black or white (Blair et al., 2002). People who were unambiguously African American were evaluated more negatively when they had prototypical African American facial features. The stereotypes that are primed, and the accompanying evaluation, stemmed not just from crude group categorizations but involved responses to specific facial features (Livingstone & Brewer, 2002).

Priming a stereotype makes it salient and increases its influence over an individual's thinking. Even imagining stereotypes seems to increase their believability. In one study, subjects were asked to imagine a situation involving a stereotype about an occupational group (such as "aggressive lawyers"). They subsequently believed those stereotypes more than did subjects who were not asked to imagine them or who were asked to imagine a scene involving nonstereotyped behavior instead (Slusher & Anderson, 1987).

Accessibility

The speed with which stereotypes and prejudice come to mind and are applied.

At any given moment, our attitudes toward some categories have greater **accessibility** than others. When multiple categories are potentially relevant, we generally tend to use the category toward which we have the most accessible attitudes. A category may be more accessible because we have just been reminded of it. In one experiment, either students' university or their major was made salient. That affected which stereotypes were assigned to the student, even though all of

Even imagining aggressive lawyers makes stereotypes about them seem more valid.

the students fit into both categories (van Rijswijk & Ellemers, 2002). Or a category may be more accessible because we habitually use it more often. Highly prejudiced individuals are particularly likely to categorize others in terms of race or ethnicity (Brewer & Brown, 1998).

Stereotypes are particularly likely to be applied to a specific individual when the person is perceived as a typical member of the outgroup. This is called the **typicality effect**. Lord and his colleagues tested this hypothesis in an interesting study of male Princeton students' stereotypes of homosexuals. They presented each student with the description of a specific individual, "John B.," who was thinking of transferring to Princeton and who either fit the gay stereotype closely or did not. The students were then asked if they would be willing to show John B. around campus, introduce him to their friends, and host a weekend visit. The students' willingness to help John B. was more consistent with their general attitudes toward homosexuals (positive or negative) when he was described as fitting their stereotypes of gay men than when he did not (Lord, Lepper, & Mackie, 1984). However, this typicality effect depends on paying attention to the specific attributes of the target person, not just to the category. So, like the other examples of central or systematic processing given in the earlier chapter on attitudes, it may not occur when the perceiver is distracted or otherwise has a heavy cognitive load (Blessum et al., 1998).

Typicality Effect

Stereotypes get applied most forcefully to those out-group members who are most typical of the out-group.

Ambiguous or inadequate information about the individual member of the outgroup is especially likely to lead people to rely on stereotypes when interpreting their actions. When you have enough information about the individual action itself, you may be less likely to rely on the stereotype. Suppose you are given the somewhat ambiguous report that someone had "hit someone who annoyed him or her." Then you are told either that the hitter was a construction worker or a homemaker. In evaluating the person's aggressiveness, you might use your stereotypes and so rate the construction worker as more aggressive. But what if the report was clear about whether it was a highly aggressive act ("Decked a neighbor who had been taunting him or her") or a more customary, less aggressive act ("Spanked his or her son for trekking mud all over the carpet")? In that case, the stereotype is less likely to influence the perceived aggressiveness of the individual. When the circumstances of the behavior are clear, the stereotype is more likely to be ignored (Kunda & Sherman-Williams, 1993).

We are sometimes confronted with actions or individuals inconsistent with our stereotypes. But such inconsistent information often does not produce any change in our use of stereotypes. For one thing, we are still likely to apply our stereotypes even when we know that the individual has committed a single act inconsistent with it. If we have the stereotype of football players as not being very good students, we may still not expect Joe Fullback to be very bright even though we know that he got an A− on his social psychology midterm. But we are less likely to apply the stereotype if we know that he has engaged in stereotype-inconsistent behavior over some period of time. If his fraternity brother tells us that Joe got As in all but one of his courses last semester, we are more likely to treat him as an exception to the general stereotype (Beckett & Park, 1995; Krueger & Rothbart, 1988).

Subtyping

Breaking down large categories of people such as women into subcategories, such as homemakers, professional women, and grandmothers.

Subtyping is the process of making such finer distinctions within large group categories. For example, the large category "older people" may be subtyped into "elder statesmen," "senior citizens," and "Medicare recipients" (Brewer, Dull, & Lui, 1981). Similarly, the category "blacks" may be subtyped into "black athletes," "black businessmen," and "black mothers on welfare" (Devine & Baker, 1991). Subtyping is one particularly common way of preventing stereotype change because it helps to explain seemingly disconfirming evidence (Park et al., 2001). The tough Israeli soldiers we see on television violate the more customary stereotypes of Jews as artistic or sharp businessmen, but "Israeli soldiers" have become a distinctive subtype of the larger category "Jews."

Most of us believe we should judge others as individuals rather than as stereotypical members of a particular group. How then do we justify using stereotypes? One possibility is that we only need to *believe* we have considered information about the specific target individual; we do not *actually* have to have considered it. In a clever test of this hypothesis, Yzerbyt and colleagues (1994) gave participants information about either a library archivist or a comedian. Those in the experimental condition were then told they were going to receive additional information about the individual. However, this "extra information" was actually incomprehensible, because they heard a message from one person through one earphone and another message at the same time from another person through the other earphone. So they only had the illusion of receiving extra information about the specific individual. Those in the control condition did not receive even this incomprehensible "extra information." Those who thought they had received more information (even though that information was impossible to understand) were more likely to respond to all later questions about the target individual, were more confident in their ratings, and evaluated the targets more in line with the stereotypes of librarians and comedians. So even the illusion of having information about a specific individual seems to allow people to feel justified in judging the person according to stereotypes.

Advantages and Disadvantages

Category-based processing has both advantages and disadvantages in information processing. One advantage is that it reduces the amount of data we have to process. Reality is too complex for any person to represent precisely; we must simplify it if we are to process each experience and respond appropriately. By creating categories, we filter everyday experience and direct our attention to the most important aspects of that experience. To show this, one experiment had students perform two completely different tasks at the same time—form impressions of a target individual on the basis of visually presented trait words and at the same time listen to a tape-recorded passage about the basic geography and economy of Indonesia (Macrae, Milne, & Bodenhausen, 1994). Half of the students were then given a categorical group label (such as "doctor" or "skinhead") for the target individual to allow them to focus on relevant information and screen out irrelevant data. Those who were given the group label (and therefore able to use category traits) were indeed

Table 6–5

Mean Number of Words Located in Puzzle

	Word Type	
Prime	**Stereotypic**	**Nonstereotypic**
Child abuser	3.25	2.33
Soccer hooligan	3.25	2.08

Source: Adapted from C. N. Macrae, C. Stangor, and A. B. Milne (1994). Activating social stereotypes: A functional analysis. *Journal of Experimental Social Psychology, 30,* 378. Reproduced by permission of Academic Press.

better able to recall attributes consistent with the category. They were even better able to learn the irrelevant material on Indonesia. Categories allow the perceiver to process a great deal of information quickly and effortlessly, especially individual attributes of another person that are relevant to the category.

A second advantage of category-based processing is that it allows us to go beyond the information we are given and thereby enrich it. Thinking about a stereotype brings to the forefront the broad set of traits associated with it. To illustrate this, students at the University of Wales were asked to list their thoughts regarding either a "child abuser" or a "soccer hooligan" (Macrae, Stangor, & Milne, 1994). Then they were presented with various trait words in a complex puzzle. As Table 6–5 shows, thinking about the group made it easier to locate category-consistent words, but not category-inconsistent words. Activating the category increased the accessibility of the traits associated with each stereotype.

The most obvious disadvantage of category-based processing is that it leads to the formation of oversimplified stereotypes that serve only to feed prejudices. Stereotypes do not include the important individual characteristics of people in each category. One illustration of this point is a study in which people observed group discussions that included equal numbers of African American and white people (Taylor, Fiske, Eticoff, & Ruderman, 1978). The observers were more likely to confuse the contributions of people within a race than across races. They remembered that something was said by a black person or a white person, but not which specific person said it.

Second, stereotypes almost always overgeneralize, ascribing the same attributes to all members of a group, even those they do not fit. To be sure, the grain of truth argument holds that both group categorization and the accompanying stereotypes are based on real cues that are salient. However, it must be remembered that salience also depends not only on what our attention receives, but also on where we *direct* our attention. That direction depends to a large degree on the social norms we have learned, which may direct us to quite subtle cues. In the United States, because of the historic cleavage over race, our attention is likely to be directed to skin color. In Great Britain, cues relating to social class are of great importance. In multilingual nations such as Canada or Belgium, accent is important. Moreover, social norms also play a large role in forming the overgeneralizations underlying our stereotypes. Even if on average football players get relatively low grades, some are quite good students, and it is not fair to ignore their academic accomplishments.

A third disadvantage is that category-based processing can generate false memories. In one study, for example, exposure to either a list of stereotypically female roles or a list of stereotypically male roles later resulted in an increase in false recognition of roles and traits that were consistent with the stereotypes (Lenton, Blair, & Hastie, 2001). Participants were not even aware that they were biasing their memories. This bias also affects how people describe a target individual to others: Stereotype-consistent information is most easily communicated to others, even through multiple transmissions. In one study, participants were given a story about a man and a woman who exhibited some behaviors consistent with gender stereotypes, and some inconsistent with them. They transmitted the story through five successive storytellers. The parts of the story consistent with gender stereotypes were transmitted more accurately than those inconsistent with gender stereotypes (Kashima, 2000). The stereotypes were maintained best if the transmitters believed that their recipients shared the same stereotypes as they did (Lyons & Kashima, 2003). So even when one person is able to break through her stereotypes and perceive a target individual accurately, her accurate account may be distorted once again as it gets transmitted through others.

SOCIAL IDENTITY

The concept of social identity is a crucial element in the cognitive approach to prejudice. As shown in Figure 6–2, it is the part of the self-concept derived from membership in one or more social groups, along with the evaluation associated with it. In this chapter, however, our concern is not merely with our own groups, but with other groups with which our own group may be in conflict.

In-groups Versus Out-groups

Numerous studies show that the act of categorization can also quickly group people into "us" (an in-group) and "them" (an out-group). Perceiving people as members of in-groups and out-groups has three important consequences. One is the **in-group favoritism effect** (Tajfel, Billig, Bundy, & Flament, 1971). People generally evaluate in-group members more positively, make more favorable attributions for their behavior, reward them more, expect more favorable treatment from them, and find them more persuasive than out-group members (Brewer & Brown, 1998). In other words, once people feel they belong to a group, they tend to favor fellow group members at the expense of members of other groups.

In-Group Favoritism Effect

The tendency to give more favorable evaluations and greater rewards to members of one's in-group than to members of out-groups.

This in-group favoritism has been found in many contexts and in numerous ways. But does it simply reflect group members' efforts to maximize their own real interests, as the group competition theories would suggest? Apparently not; real interests need not be involved at all. The purely cognitive act of categorization, on whatever basis, seems to be sufficient to produce in-group favoritism even when there are no selfish gains to be made and when there have been no pleasurable interactions with the in-group or unpleasant interactions with the out-group.

Minimal Intergroup Situation

People are arbitrarily classified into groups and then allowed to allocate rewards to each other.

To show this, Tajfel's (1969) **minimal intergroup situation** randomly assigned students to two groups under some vague pretext, such as relative preferences for the painters Kandinsky and Klee. There was no actual interaction with fellow in-group members or with members of the other group. Then the students were asked to evaluate all individuals in the experiment and distribute some rewards to them. Merely being arbitrarily categorized into groups induced students to show

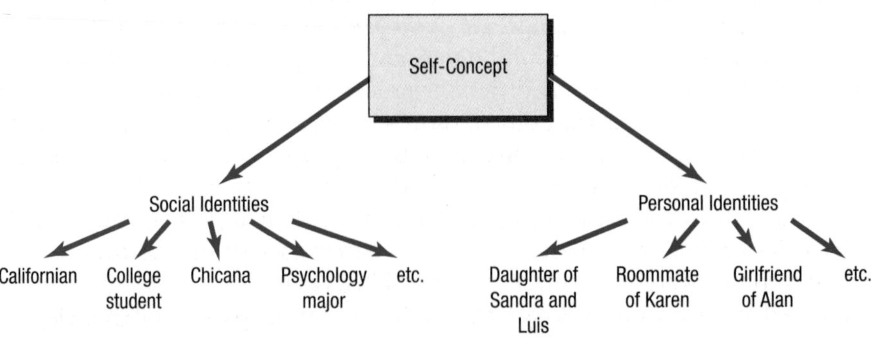

Figure 6–2 The self-concept is made up both of social identities that are based on group affiliations and personal identities that are based on our unique individual characteristics.

more favorable attitudes and behavior toward members of the in-group than toward members of the out-group. In-group favoritism in this minimal intergroup situation seems to be a remarkably robust phenomenon: Dozens of studies have found such effects (Brewer & Brown, 1998). This is not to say that people reward only in-group members. Rather they most commonly try to introduce some element of fairness by rewarding both in-group and out-group members. But there is usually a systematic bias toward greater rewards for the in-group.

Several important systematic biases follow from the general tendency toward in-group favoritism. People tend to make more sympathetic attributions for an in-group's successes and failures than for the out-group's outcomes. Like the self-serving attributional biases discussed in Chapter 2, these **group-serving biases** lead people to make internal attributions for an in-group's successes and external attributions for its failures, and just the opposite for the out-group. For example, a standard gender stereotype is that women are weak in math and science. Men tend to give external attributions when women succeed in those areas—to luck, an easy task, or a smart partner—and to give internal attributions for women's failures—to a lack of skill. In contrast, men typically attribute their own successes to skill and their failures to a difficult task (Islam & Hewstone, 1993a).

Group-Serving Biases

Members of an in-group make favorable attributions for the performance of in-group members and unfavorable attributions for performance by out-group members.

Second, in-group members tend to perceive other in-group members as more similar to themselves than to out-group members. This is the **assumed similarity effect**. In one study, fraternity members perceived themselves as more similar to each other than to commuter students who lived off campus, and vice versa (Holtz & Miller, 1985). Even when group members have been arbitrarily or randomly assigned to a group, they perceive members of their own groups as more similar to themselves than are members of other groups. Allen and Wilder (1979) randomly assigned students to groups (though ostensibly on the basis of artistic preference) and found that they assumed other in-group members were more similar to them than were out-group members, even on matters wholly unrelated to art.

Assumed Similarity Effect

Members of an in-group assume that other in-group members share their attitudes and values.

Third, although we tend to see out-group members as alien and different from us, we also tend to see them as quite homogeneous in terms of traits, personality, and even number of subtypes: "*They* are all alike, whereas *we* are all diverse individuals!" This is called the **out-group homogeneity effect**. For example, Brauer (2001) tested the stereotypes held by each of four different groups of participants (doctors, lawyers, hairdressers, and waiters) about the other groups. He asked them to give the location of the highest and lowest group member on each trait (e.g., "naive" for hairdresser or "helpful" for doctors). Ratings of the highest and lowest were more similar for the out-group than for the in-group in almost all cases, reflecting out-group homogeneity. Part of the reason is that we are more likely to see refining subtypes in the in-group than in other groups. In one case, business and engineering students were able to list more subtypes within their own group (such as "engineering students who seem to live in the computer center" or "business students who just want to make money") than in the other group (Park, Ryan, & Judd, 1992). In another case, Latino students were more likely than Anglo students to use such subtypes as Chicano, Cuban, and Puerto Rican (Huddy & Virtanen, 1995).

Out-Group Homogeneity Effect

Perception that members of the out-group are more similar to each other than members of the in-group are to each other.

In like fashion, we tend to perceive members of our in-group as being more complex individuals than members of the out-group. Their personalities are seen as more multidimensional and as having more variety and richness. For example, young people see the young as more complex than the elderly (and vice versa!), and sorority members see their sister members as more dissimilar from each other than they do members of other sororities (Linville & Jones, 1980; Park & Rothbart, 1982). As a result of seeing "them" as all alike, the in-group tends to perceive fewer subtypes in the out-group, and therefore to see the out-group more stereotypically (Judd, Ryan, & Park, 1991).

The out-group homogeneity effect is surely based partly on ignorance. We generally have more experience with our own group, so we are likely to know more about its members (Park & Rothbart, 1982). And greater familiarity with any group not surprisingly does lead us to perceive greater individuality among the members and greater variability of their attributes. But the out-group

Table 6–6

Differential Responses to In-groups and Out-groups

	In-group	Out-group
In-group favoritism	Positive evaluations	Negative evaluations
	Preferential treatment	Withhold resources
Assumed similarity	Similar to self	Different from self
Out-group homogeneity	All individuals are different	All individuals are similar
	Complex individuals	Simple individuals

homogeneity effect occurs even when the participants have approximately equal real experience with members of both groups. And even when the perceiver has no experience with either group, mere categorization into in-group and out-group has powerful effects. So less familiarity with the out-group does not fully explain the out-group homogeneity effect; mere categorization can produce the effect all by itself (Judd & Park, 1988; Linville, Salovey, & Fischer, 1986).

Social Identity Theory

These effects of categorizing people into in-groups and out-groups are summarized in Table 6–6. In-group favoritism is the most important of these effects because it has the most influence on how people are treated. Why does the mere act of categorizing individuals into an in-group and an out-group produce in-group favoritism effects? Evolutionary theory has become one popular way of explaining this tendency. It argues that the principle of inclusive fitness, an inbred tendency for people to try to reproduce their own genes, led to hunter-gatherer tribes' favoring relatives and engaging in intertribal hostilities. Both in-group favoritism and out-group antagonism could help protect limited resources and increase survival of one's own family (Fishbein, 1996). There may even be a physiological basis for in-group favoritism. Recent research has begun to find cardiovascular indicators of threat responses when people interact with stigmatized minorities, such as blacks, disadvantaged people, or people with facial birthmarks (Blascovitch et al., 2001). Similarly, whites who reported less prior contact with blacks exhibited more physiological threat (Mendes et al., 2002).

Social Identity Theory

The theory that an individual's self-concept derives partly from membership in an in-group.

At a more psychological level, Tajfel (1982) proposed **social identity theory**, incorporating three basic assumptions: (a) People categorize the social world into in-groups and out-groups; (b) people derive a sense of self-esteem from their social identity as members of an in-group; and (c) people's self-concepts partly depend on how they evaluate the in-group relative to other groups. We are likely to have high self-esteem if we belong to a superior in-group and to have lower self-esteem if the in-group is inferior. Social identity theory, then, is a mixture of cognitive and motivational theories: It is cognitive because the mere act of categorization in a group is sufficient to trigger these effects, and motivational because social identity fulfills self-esteem needs.

Social identity theory has several important implications that generally have been borne out in empirical tests. As discussed in Chapter 4, our sense of self is in part linked to our identification with social groups. When asked to answer the question "Who am I?" people typically refer to social groups. One person might explain that she is a woman, a Catholic, a Canadian, and a physician. Another person might say that he is a born-again Christian, a Texan, and a member of the Republican party. Groups provide individuals with a sense of meaning and identity.

Optimal Distinctiveness

A social identity in a group that is large enough to give the individual a sense of inclusion, but small enough to provide a sense of differentiation from others.

Marilynn Brewer's (1991) theory of **optimal distinctiveness** is even more specific. It suggests that people have two competing needs: for inclusion in larger collectives and for differentiation from other people. Brewer believes these needs are adaptive in an evolutionary sense; banding together in groups helped prehistoric people survive. So distinctive social identities can satisfy both needs, but they must be developed at the optimal level. Merely being a member of one's own family does not satisfy the need for inclusion in larger groups, and merely being a woman usually does not satisfy the need for distinctiveness.

The presumed role of self-esteem has proven to be the most troublesome aspect of social identity theory. The theory actually offers two separate hypotheses about the relationship between self-esteem and in-group favoritism. One is that in-group favoritism enhances social identity and thus raises self-esteem. Discriminating in favor of the in-group should imbue the identity with "positive distinctiveness," which should establish a positive social identity and enhance self-esteem (Hogg & Abrams, 1990). One simple example is the finding of Cialdini and colleagues (1976) that students were more likely to show their group pride by wearing school sweaters and scarves on the day after their college's football team was victorious than on a day after a defeat. The vast majority of studies support this hypothesis, showing that successful competition with out-groups does increase the self-esteem of in-group members, at least among people who are actively participating in their group (Aberson, Healy, & Romero, 2000; Rubin & Hewstone, 1998).

The second hypothesis is that individuals get high self-esteem from identifying with high-status groups (Brewer & Brown, 1998). If so, low or threatened personal self-esteem should produce stronger in-group favoritism, which in turn should increase self-esteem. However, there is little evidence to support this hypothesis. To be sure, people with low self-esteem tend to be the most prejudiced against out-groups, but, contrary to the hypothesis, they also are most negative about the in-group (Rubin & Hewstone, 1998). So if anything, the opposite holds: In-group identification may actually be stronger among people with high self-esteem.

These findings are clarified by distinguishing between a private self and a collective self (Crocker & Luhtanen, 1990; Tajfel & Turner, 1986). The private self is closely linked to our sense of personal identity and to our personal self-esteem. For example, if you receive a pay raise, you feel better about yourself. However, your collective self-esteem may depend more on how well your in-group does. If your college's football team wins, your collective self-esteem may improve, even though your personal self-esteem may not change. So threats to collective self-esteem, rather than to private self-esteem, may be responsible for prejudice

The victory of the American women's soccer team in the 2004 Olympics was an occasion for great pride and celebration of membership in an in-group.

against out-groups. This parallels the earlier finding that fraternal deprivation is more central to prejudice than is a sense of egoistic deprivation.

Comparison of Theories

We have now considered four main theories of prejudice: social learning, motivational, cognitive, and the mixture that is found in social identity theory. Each of these broad theoretical approaches points to different factors as causes of prejudice. There is some truth in all of them. Presumably cognitive processes increase stereotyping in all societies: The perceptual categorizations people routinely make may facilitate the formation of stereotypes and help to maintain prejudices. However, although distinguishing group categories may reflect a need to simplify life cognitively, they also are the result of specific social norms. Social learning plays the major role in defining which groups are targeted for prejudice in each culture, what the agreed-upon stereotypes are, and what is and is not acceptable behavior toward other groups. The cultural framework determines how much prejudice exists, when it can be expressed, and toward whom. The major disagreement among researchers is whether or not those cultural differences stem primarily from competition between groups for real resources or from other sources such as early socialization or personality differences.

THE CHANGING FACE OF PREJUDICE

Much has changed since the earliest sociopsychological studies of prejudice were conducted in the 1930s. Hitler has come and gone. The civil rights movement helped end the institution of racial segregation. The women's movement and activism on behalf of people with AIDS have filled the news and occasionally the streets as well. How have these developments changed social psychology's view of prejudice?

Declining Old-Fashioned Racism

In the years since World War II, racial and ethnic prejudice has generally declined in the United States. The traditional form of prejudice against African Americans has been called **old-fashioned racism** (McConahay, 1986). It had three components: a belief in innate white superiority, especially intellectually and morally; racial segregation in such areas as schools, public accommodations, and marriage; and discrimination against blacks in such areas as employment and higher education.

Old-Fashioned Racism

Beliefs in white racial superiority, segregation, and formal discrimination.

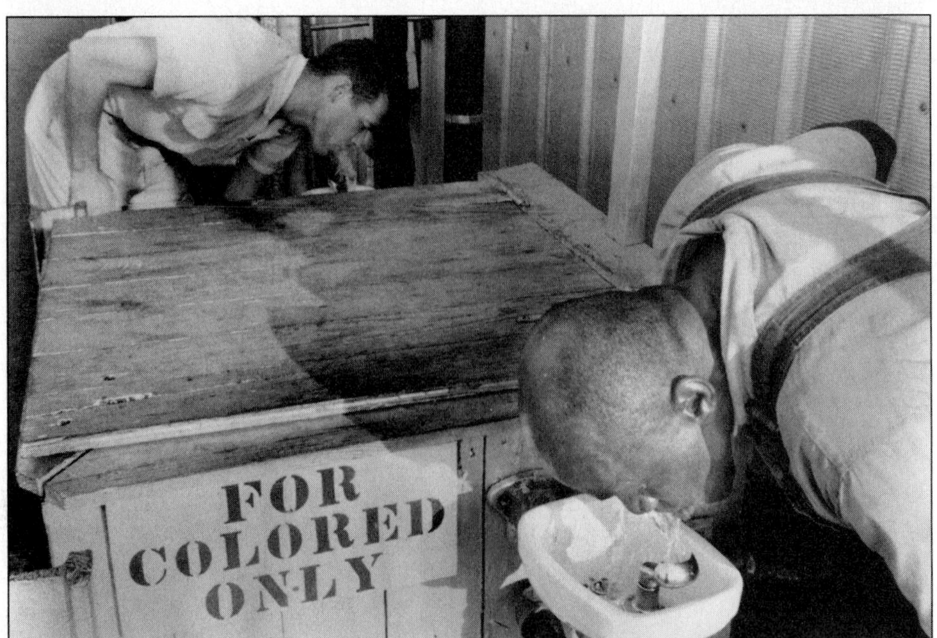

Until 1964, Southern states required African Americans and white people to drink from separate public drinking fountains.

Table 6–7

Changes over Time in Whites' Racial Attitudes

	Historical Era		
	Early (percent)	Late (percent)	Change (percent)
Reduced old-fashioned racism			
Oppose laws against intermarriage	38 (1963)	87 (1996)	+49
White and black students should go to same, not separate, schools	32 (1942)	96 (1995)	+64
Vote for well-qualified black person for president if nominated by own party	37 (1958)	92 (1996)	+55
Continued opposition to race-targeted policies			
Federal government should ensure that white and black children go to same schools	47 (1964)	38 (1994)	–9
Government should provide special aid to minorities	22 (1970)	22 (1988)	0

Note: The years involved in the comparison are shown in parentheses.

Source: Adapted from Schuman, Steeh, Bobo, and Krysan (1997).

Old-fashioned racism has declined quite sharply in recent decades, as shown in Table 6–7. The vast majority of whites in the United States now endorse the general principle of racial equality. This type of racism is likely to continue to decline in the future because its main supporters are whites born before World War II, especially white Southerners who never finished high school, and there are fewer and fewer such people (Schuman, Steeh, Bobo, & Krysan, 1997).

Other forms of prejudice have declined as well. The widespread anti-Semitism in Europe and the United States of the 19th and early 20th centuries has also declined (Quinley & Glock, 1979). The Israeli-Palestinian conflict has recently stimulated more anti-Semitic outbursts and hate crimes in Europe, however. Anti-gay prejudice seems to be declining as well: In 1982, 34 percent of American adults agreed that "homosexuality should be considered as an accepted lifestyle," whereas by 1999, 50 percent agreed (Sherrill & Yang, 2000). Dislike of gays has become a less important factor over time in determining opposition to equal rights for gays, such as protection against job discrimination or being allowed to serve in the armed forces (Brewer, 2003).

Less prejudice among adults has also resulted in less prejudice being passed on to children. As a result, younger generations have shown increasing support for equal racial opportunity and less prejudice toward newer immigrant groups such as Hispanics and Asians (Citrin et al., 2001; Schuman et al., 1997). In Western Europe, too, the younger generations show less prejudice toward immigrant minority groups (Pettigrew & Meertens, 1995).

Nevertheless, there is evidence of continuing resistance to full racial equality in the United States. A few whites do continue to support old-fashioned racism; in 1996, 13 percent said they favored laws against marriages between blacks and whites. Negative stereotypes of minorities persist, as shown earlier in Table 6–1. Whites give only weak support, at best, to government action to promote racial equality in the form of school integration, affirmative action, and other types of special aid for minorities, as shown in Table 6–7. And finally, African Americans, the targets of racial prejudice, are much less convinced than are whites that prejudice and discrimination are diminishing; in 2000, 63 percent of the blacks and 30 percent of the whites felt that blacks "are being discriminated against" (Parmelee, 2001, p. 24). In Australia, an in-depth study of Aborigines, the dark-skinned people who inhabited that continent before Europeans settled there, revealed that they continue to perceive much blatant and direct racism, despite much legislation protecting their equal rights (Mellor, 2003).

A lively set of controversies has arisen over the discrepancy between the erosion of old-fashioned racism and this apparent persisting evidence of prejudice. There are four discernibly different interpretations of this contrast.

Illusory Change

Some group competition theorists are skeptical that dominant groups like white Americans or Australians are really willing to accept major changes in their advantaged positions. Some argue that the apparent decline in racism may represent only illusory change. In their view, expressing racist ideas may have become socially unacceptable, but whites may retain the same old resistance to change behind their polite facade of opposition to segregation (Jackman & Muha, 1984; Sidanius & Pratto, 1999).

There is indeed evidence that whites express less prejudice to black interviewers than to white interviewers, presumably trying to avoid giving offense (McConahay, Hardee, & Batts, 1981; Schuman et al., 1997). However, this bias usually has little practical effect in research on prejudice, because almost all white respondents are normally interviewed by white interviewers. Moreover, there is evidence that old-fashioned racism is not greatly disguised in normal interviews. Krysan (1998) found just as much of it in face-to-face interviews with an interviewer as in private self-administered questionnaires collected by mail. Most social scientists today believe that the decline in old-fashioned racism is quite real. Few white Americans really want to go back to the formally segregated ways of the Old South. So most researchers have gone on to analyze what they believe to be a genuine contrast between vanishing old-fashioned racism and evidence of continuing white resistance to change in the racial status quo.

Symbolic Racism

Symbolic Racism

A contemporary form of antagonism toward a racial group based on prejudice and values rather than on self-interest.

A second view is that old-fashioned racism has been replaced by a more modern and more potent form of prejudice called **symbolic racism** (Kinder & Sears, 1981), sometimes described as "modern racism" (McConahay, 1986) or "racial resentment" (Kinder & Sanders, 1996). This reflects beliefs that racial discrimination is no longer a major obstacle to blacks and that blacks simply do not make enough of an effort to help themselves; it also reflects the resentment of blacks' demands for special treatment and the resentment of their gains in recent decades. These beliefs are thought to have roots in a combination of negative affects toward African Americans (such as anger, fear, or disgust) and the perception that blacks violate traditional American values (such as the value of hard work). They are thought to be acquired more through preadult socialization than because of intergroup competition, such as racial threats posed by blacks to whites. Some items used to measure symbolic racism are shown in Table 6–8.

There are critics of the concept of symbolic racism. "Principled objection" critics believe that racial prejudice no longer has much force in American society

Table 6–8

Items Used to Measure Symbolic Racism
It's really a matter of some people not trying hard enough; if blacks would only try harder, they could be as well off as whites. (agree)
How much discrimination against blacks do you feel there is in the United States today, limiting their chances to get ahead? (just a little, none at all)
Over the past few years, blacks have gotten more economically than they deserve. (agree)
How much of the racial tension that exists in the United States today do you think blacks are responsible for creating? (all of it, most)

Source: Henry and Sears (2002).

(e.g., Sniderman et al., 2000). Rather, they say, whites evaluate racial issues mainly on the basis of their nonracial values and ideologies. For example, whites oppose affirmative action not because they are racially prejudiced, but because they believe people should be appraised on the basis of their merits, because it violates the value of color-blind racial equality, and because they oppose government interference with either principle.

Research on symbolic racism makes several points. First, these several beliefs do go together in a quite popular belief system among many white Americans (Tarman & Sears, 2005). A few whites hold both old-fashioned racism and symbolic racism. Many more whites reject both of them. But the third important group both rejects old-fashioned racism and accepts symbolic racism, opposing racial segregation and discrimination but resenting African Americans' complaints about discrimination and mistreatment. Second, symbolic racism is a strong predictor of whites' opposition to black political leaders and to policies such as affirmative action, whereas old-fashioned racism is not (Sears et al., 1997). Third, contrary to the principled objection perspective, such opposition stems as much or more from symbolic racism than from political ideology or values, or ostensibly race-neutral justifications such as that affirmative action unfairly discriminates against groups not benefitting from it (Federico & Sidanius, 2002; Tarman & Sears, 2005). And fourth, symbolic racism is indeed rooted partly in anti-black affect, probably anger more often than sadness (DeSteno et al., 2004; Sears & Henry, 2003). The principled objection view is comforting if one wants to believe Americans have now largely put racial prejudice in the past. But it is inconsistent with most empirical evidence.

This idea of a new racism has been extended to a distinction between "blatant" and "subtle" prejudice against minorities in Great Britain, Holland, France, and Germany (Pettigrew & Meertens, 1995). Subtle prejudice is more common than blatant prejudice in all four countries and is a better predictor of anti-immigration sentiment. Similarly, old-fashioned sexism (endorsement of traditional gender roles and stereotypes about lesser female competence) is distinct from, but correlated with, "neosexism" (denial that women are still discriminated against, antagonism toward women's demands). Neosexism strongly contributes to opposition to affirmative action for women, whereas old-fashioned sexism does not (Swim, Aikin, Hall, & Hunter, 1995; Tougas, Brown, Beaton, & Joly, 1995).

Other kinds of modern prejudice prove to have roots in the same mixture of group antagonism and traditional values, especially individualism, as does symbolic racism."Anti-fat attitudes" (based on items such as "If I were an employer looking to hire, I might avoid hiring a fat person") are closely related both to symbolic racism and a belief in the Protestant work ethic (Crandall, 1994). Indeed in six different nations, "anti-fat" attitudes were most common among those who most believed their culture devalues fatness ("In our culture, being thin is an important part of being attractive") and that people are morally responsible for controlling their own lives (Crandall et al., 2001). Highlighting the role of beliefs in internal control, this model explained anti-fat attitudes better in the more individualist cultures of the United States, Australia, and Poland than in the more collectivist cultures of India, Turkey, and Venezuela. Finally, support for restrictive policies toward AIDS victims are predicted by negative evaluations of gay people and the belief that they violate fundamental religious and family values (Haddock, Zanna, & Esses, 1993; Price & Hsu, 1992).

Aversive Racism

A similar but somewhat distinct concept of a new racism is **aversive racism**. It too is thought to reflect both repudiation of formal racial inequality and negative feelings toward blacks, such as discomfort, uneasiness, and sometimes fear (Gaertner & Dovidio, 1986). How do whites resolve this conflict? The theory suggests it depends on the norms governing the particular situation in which interracial contact takes place. In situations with egalitarian norms, when whites know they are supposed to be treating everyone equally, they are likely to engage

Aversive Racism

Attitudes toward a racial group combining egalitarian social values and negative emotions, resulting in avoidance of that group.

Aversive racism leaves whites torn between their beliefs in equality and their negative affect toward blacks, and results in discomfort and avoidance.

in egalitarian action. Examples would be grading term papers or evaluating job applicants. But when the norms are more ambiguous, whites are more likely to be confronted with their distaste for blacks, which they feel ashamed of, leading them to avoid African Americans. Examples would be deciding to sit next to a white rather than a black student in a classroom, or avoiding eye contact with a pregnant black woman on a crowded subway car rather than offering her a seat.

A review of studies testing aversive racism theory found that egalitarian contexts, such as evaluations of highly qualified job applicants, employed individuals, or defendants in a trial, did tend to produce equal treatment, or sometimes even to slight biases in favor of African Americans (Aberson & Ettlin, 2004). However, ambiguous contexts led to white-favoring biases most of the time. Indeed, in interactions with African Americans, whites generally tended to sit farther away, use less friendly voice tones, make less eye contact, and terminate interactions more quickly than they did in interactions with whites (see Pettigrew, 1985).

Another feature of ambiguous contexts is that they provide plausible nonracist justifications for discriminating against blacks, which can help the aversive racist to maintain an unprejudiced self-image. In one study (Gaertner & Dovidio, 1977), participants were placed in a situation in which they witnessed an emergency. Two variables were manipulated. The victim was either black or white, and the participant was either in a group of three witnesses or was the only witness. When there were no other witnesses and refusal to help could be interpreted as due to racism, white participants actually helped black victims slightly more than they did the white victims. But when other witnesses were available, they helped the black victim only half as often as they helped the white victim, because they could safely avoid the black victim and justify the refusal by letting others take care of it. This aversive behavior in ambiguous situations allows aversive racists to protect their self-images as egalitarian, unprejudiced individuals because they avoid being confronted with their true prejudices.

Implicit Stereotypes

Automatic Processing

Mental processes that look like reasoning, but that occur unconsciously, without intention or awareness.

Up to now we have mainly been discussing stereotypes and prejudices that are measured by asking an individual how he or she feels about the group, assuming that everyone has a "true attitude" that they are aware of and can tell us about. However, Patricia Devine (1989) has developed a more complex model that applies a distinction from cognitive psychology, between **automatic processing**, that occurs outside of awareness in a quick, involuntary, unintentional, and effortless way, and **controlled processing**, the more familiar, conscious, deliberate, and voluntary thinking and expression we engage in every day. Her "dissociation" model opened up a new line of work on prejudice and stereotyping.

This approach has led to an innovative distinction between two kinds of measures of stereotypes and prejudice. Conventional self-report measures are described as reflecting "explicit" attitudes, presumably reflecting controlled processing. In contrast **implicit stereotypes** reflect well-learned sets of associations that can be automatically activated, and so are spontaneous, uncontrollable, and unintentional. They are not available to introspection, and in that sense people may not be aware of them or how they might influence perceptions of others (Greenwald & Banaji, 1995). As a result, they cannot be measured as readily with self-report measures, as indicated in the Research Highlights.

Controlled Processing

The more familiar, conscious, deliberate, and voluntary thinking and expression we engage in every day

Implicit Stereotypes

Reflect well-learned sets of associations that can be automatically activated, and so are spontaneous, uncontrollable, and unintentional.

Implicit stereotypes about many different groups have been measured: among them are blacks, women and men, elderly people, skinheads, soccer hooligans, child abusers, and college professors. For example, Rudman and Kilianski (2000) studied stereotypes about female and male authorities. Using the evaluative priming task, they primed stereotypes with pictures of women and men in either high or low authority roles. One picture depicted a female doctor, for example; and another, a female maid. Then either positive or negative stereotype words were presented (e.g., "competent" or "likable" or "dishonest" or "annoying"), and the participant pressed either the "good" or the "bad" key as quickly as possible. Implicit sexism was indicated by speedier responses (low reaction times) to the combination of a female authority picture with bad traits. By this measure both men and women had more negative attitudes toward female authorities than toward female nonauthorities or either kind of males.

There has been great enthusiasm among social psychologists about the development of these measures of implicit attitudes. They potentially can reveal components of attitudes that lie outside conscious awareness and control. This is a new and exciting theoretical approach and parallels the renewed attention to automatic, nonconscious cognition elsewhere in cognitive science (see Bargh & Chartrand, 1999). Nevertheless, these new measures are still in a formative stage and have not yet met all the standard criteria for good psychological measurement. For example, different measures of implicit attitudes often are not very consistent with each other. Rather, they seem to be quite sensitive to the particular technique used, such as whether the prime is a category label or an actual member of the group (Kawakami & Dovidio, 2001), or whether the participant is asked whether a word is good or bad or merely whether it is a real word or not (Wittenbrink, Judd, & Park, 2001a). Moreover, individuals' responses to any given measure have not yet been shown to be very consistent over time, unlike such explicit measures as of symbolic racism (e.g., Cunningham et al., 2001; Kinder & Sanders, 1996). On the other hand, proponents of implicit measures believe that they meet appropriate standards for psychometric techniques, with some statistical corrections for these difficulties (Banaji et al., 2005).

Are implicit measures of prejudice and stereotyping getting at the same thing as explicit self-reports, or something different? Some studies report strong relationships between the two, whereas others report relatively weak associations (see Banaji et al., 2005; Blair, 2002). One interpretation of the weak associations is that explicit and implicit measures tap into different psychological processes. There are some intriguing differences in the outcomes predicted by the two kinds of measures. Explicit measures of prejudice, such as symbolic racism, correlate strongly with conscious, deliberate, and thoughtful judgments, such as support for black leaders, ratings of a black defendant's guilt, or evaluations of a black interviewer. On the other hand, implicit measures seem to correlate more strongly with spontaneous, involuntary responses to blacks, such as physical proximity, blinking, avoidance of eye contact, or friendliness (Banaji et al., 2005; Dovidio et al., 2002).

It is important not to overdraw the distinction between explicit and implicit prejudice. Recent evidence indicates that implicit prejudice may not be as automatic and uncontrollable as initially thought, because in a variety of ways it proves to be sensitive to changes in context (Blair, 2002). For example, implicit

MEASURING IMPLICIT STEREOTYPES

A variety of techniques have been used to measure implicit stereotypes. They all begin with the basic idea that priming a particular group activates an unconscious network of associations between a target group and favorable or unfavorable stereotypes. If those associations have been strongly learned (such as "black–violent"), people will respond more quickly and accurately than if the association had not been strongly learned. So all of these techniques are intended to measure automatic associations in long-term memory.

Evaluative Priming Technique

A measure of implicit stereotypes based on the idea that the evaluation of a stereotype-consistent word is speedier after the presentation of a prime of the group.

Implicit Association Test

A measure of implicit stereotypes based on the idea that the response to stereotype-consistent pairs of words is speedier than that to stereotype-inconsistent pairs.

One is the **evaluative priming technique**. This involves three steps, as shown in Figure 6–3. First, the participant is briefly shown a prime, such as the face of a black person or of a white person. This is supposed to activate unconscious associations to stereotypes. Then a stereotypical word is briefly shown, such as "lazy" or "intelligent," and the participant is asked to indicate as rapidly as possible whether it is a positive or negative word. A person who is high in implicit racial stereotypes should respond quickly and accurately to the word "lazy" after being primed with a black person's face, or to the word "intelligent" after being primed with the white person's face. The person's response should be slower and less accurate to the word "lazy" after being primed with a white face or to the word "intelligent" after being primed with a black face (Cunningham, Preacher, & Banaji, 2001; Fazio et al., 1986).

A second is the **implicit association test** or IAT (see Figure 6–4; Greenwald, McGhee, & Schwartz, 1998). In this case, the participant is shown both the prime and a word at the same time, and then asked to make a response to the combination of the two. For example, a name might be shown that is usually associated with either elderly people or young people, along with a word that reflects a positive or negative stereotype of the elderly or of youth. Older names might include "Thelma," "Bertha," or "Edith," while younger names might include "Lisa," "Jackie," or "Michelle." Bad words might be "boring," "slow," or "stiff," whereas good words

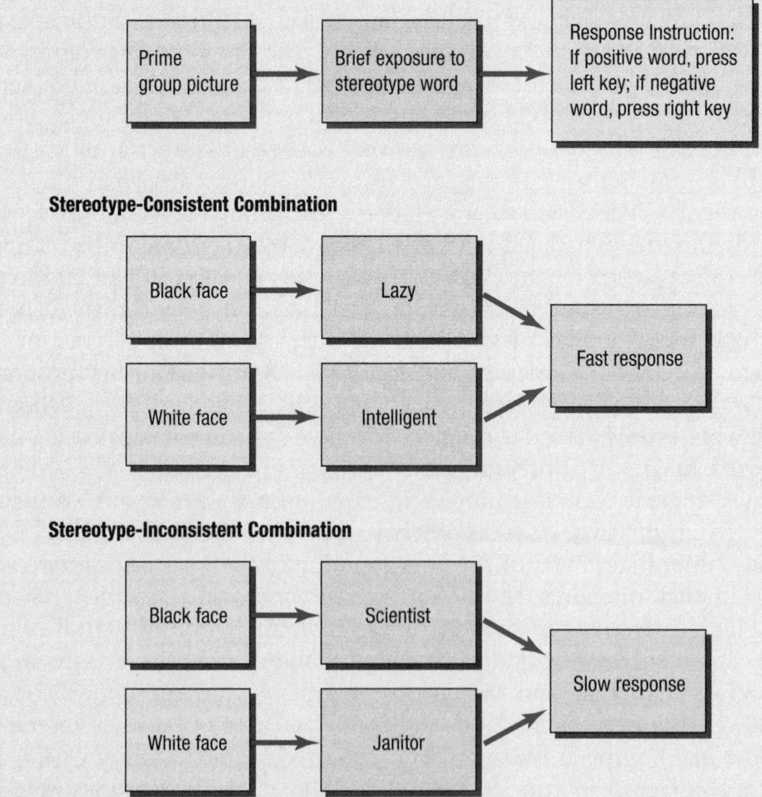

Figure 6–3 **Evaluative Priming Technique.**

Those high in implicit racism should show faster response times to stereotype-consistent than to stereotype-inconsistent combination.

might include "witty," "fast," or "cool." There would be two experimental conditions. Under one (the stereotype condition), the participant would be asked to quickly press one key on the keyboard if an elderly name plus a bad word (e.g., "Thelma" and "boring") is shown; and the other key, if a youthful name plus a good word (e.g., "Lisa" and "witty") is shown. A person with strong anti-elderly implicit stereotypes should show speedy reaction times to both combinations. Under the other (counterstereotypic condition) one key should be pressed if an elderly name is shown with a good word (e.g., "Bertha" and "fast"); and the other key, if a youthful name is shown with a bad word (e.g., "Michelle" and "stiff"). Because these combinations are not closely associated in long-term memory, people with strong stereotypes should show slow reaction times to either combination.

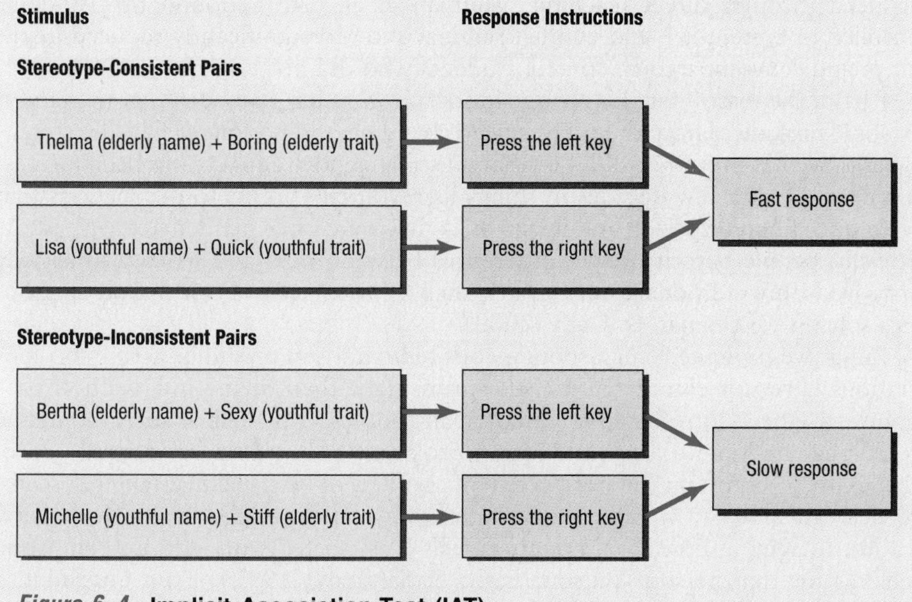

Figure 6–4 **Implicit Association Test (IAT).**

Those high in implicit ageism should respond more quickly to stereotype-consistent pairs than to stereotype-inconsistent pairs.

prejudice against blacks seems to be reduced when a black experimenter, rather than a white experimenter, administers the measures (Lowery, Hardin, & Sinclair, 2001). Exposure to pictures of admired blacks or disliked whites has significantly weakened automatic pro-white attitudes (Dasgupta & Greenwald, 2001), and prior exposure to a pleasant stereotypic situation (a family barbecue) has reduced implicit stereotyping, whereas exposure to a negative stereotypic incident (a gang incident) increased it (Wittenbrink, Judd, & Park, 2001b). Still, on balance, explicit and implicit attitudes do seem to reflect somewhat different systems of processing, one more automatic than the other.

REDUCING PREJUDICE

How can prejudice be reduced? An obvious first step would be to try to reduce intergroup competition by redistributing jobs, income, wealth, good housing, and medical care. Prejudice might decline if the needs of competing groups were better satisfied, but it probably could not be eliminated because some conflicts of interest between groups are inevitable. Efforts to help one group often come at the expense of the other and might increase antagonism. There will never be enough resources to satisfy everyone. So social psychologists have turned to other techniques.

Socialization

As indicated earlier, prejudice seems to be learned fairly early in life, and it tends to be stable over many years (Sears & Levy, 2003). Thus, another approach would be to change early socialization. Not so long ago, it was thought that socialization was liberalizing naturally, so prejudice would be reduced spontaneously. Indeed every new generation has shown less old-fashioned racism than its predecessors have. Much of the change is due to younger people growing up with less prejudice and older, more prejudiced whites dying off (Firebaugh & Davis, 1988). Also levels of formal education have been rising. The more education people have, the less prejudiced they are likely to be, especially if they have college degrees (Schuman et al., 1997). Why higher education has this effect is not known for certain. Part of the reason may be direct teaching. College students in the social sciences tend to give up their prejudices more than do students in engineering or the natural sciences. Even automatic prejudice can be reduced through direct teaching. Rudman et al. (2001) found that students enrolled in a prejudice and conflict seminar showed significantly reduced implicit prejudice, compared to control students who did not take the seminar.

Part of the reason for this change in socialization has also been that the targets of some prejudices have themselves been changing and no longer fit older stereotypes as well as they once did. For example, real gender equality has been increasing over the past few decades in things like women's access to occupations that were once limited to men and in activities that were once gender stereotyped. As a result, people perceive fewer differences between men and women in socially approved but traditionally male traits, such as "competitive" or "good at problem solving" (Diekman & Eagly, 2000).

But as we have seen, such spontaneous reductions in prejudice across the generations have not eliminated it. Not surprisingly, then, many intervention programs have been introduced for children and adolescents, such as social-cognitive retraining, multicultural, or mediation programs (Aboud & Levy, 2000). Also, the ability to entertain the perspective of another, or "perspective-taking," seems to decrease stereotypic biases and in-group favoritism (Galinsky & Moskowitz, 2000). Imagining how another person feels is associated with increased empathic feelings for that person (Batson, Early, & Salvarani, 1997). Even imagining a counterstereotypic individual, such as a strong woman, reduces implicit prejudice (Blair, Ma, & Lenton, 2001).

Sometimes the norms of tolerance that people learn as they are growing up contradict the conventional group stereotypes they have learned early in life. Devine has proposed, based on her two-process dissociation model described earlier, that people feel guilty when they become aware of the discrepancy between the automatically evoked stereotypes they learned early in life and the tolerance they have learned later on. Some people can then consciously inhibit the automatically evoked stereotypes by activating contrary personal beliefs, through deliberate, voluntary, controlled processing (Devine & Baker, 1991). In one study, low-prejudiced individuals were successfully able to inhibit prejudiced responses to anti-gay jokes after they received information that they had scored high on a questionnaire measuring subtle prejudice against gays (Monteith, 1993). In another study, extensive direct training in negating stereotypes proved effective (Kawakami et al., 2000). Such controlled suppression is most likely when people both have a clear intention to control their prejudice and are undistracted so that their maximum cognitive resources are available (Amodio et al., 2003; Blair & Banaji, 1996). However, such people probably cannot eliminate stereotyped responses altogether. Rather, they will slip on occasion and then react with some guilt and self-criticism. Devine calls this "prejudice with compunction."

But the direct effort to reduce prejudice can go too far and produce a backlash. Czopp and Monteith (2003) found that directly confronting people with racial bias tended to produce guilt and apologies, although confronting them with gender bias tended to elicit some amusement. Confrontation directly by a member of the group targeted with prejudice tended to elicit irritation and antagonism from more prejudiced participants.

Intergroup Contact

After World War II, the pervasiveness of racial segregation in the United States in housing, schools, jobs, and most other areas of life led many social scientists to conclude that sheer ignorance about African Americans and their lives helped to create erroneous and oversimplified racial stereotypes. Today blacks in particular remain quite segregated from whites in the United States. The level of residential segregation of whites and blacks declined slightly during the 1990s, but blacks continued overwhelmingly to live in predominantly black neighborhoods, and there has been relatively little shift toward mixed white and black neighborhoods (Fasenfest, Booza, & Metzger, 2004). Relatively few whites have close black friends or even acquaintances (Jackman & Crane, 1986).

If sheer ignorance, due to little interracial contact, produces erroneous stereotypes, more contact between the races should increase accurate perceptions and decrease prejudice. Some classic early studies of the effects of desegregation indeed found that contact reduced prejudice. At the beginning of World War II, the U.S. military avoided racially mixed units in order to minimize possible racial conflict. However, as casualties rose and the number of available white replacements dwindled, the army allowed African American volunteers to join previously all-white units. Surveys showed that most white soldiers initially opposed desegregation, but opposition was much reduced after it occurred (Stouffer, Suchman, DeVinney, Star, & Williams, 1949). Opposition declined most sharply among the white soldiers who were most in contact with the African American soldiers, as their unrealistic stereotypes decreased. And more recent studies often have shown that more intergroup contact is indeed associated with less prejudice. Several surveys in Europe have found that having more friends in minority groups is associated with less prejudice (Pettigrew, 1997). Similarly, having more contact with gay men and lesbians was associated with having reduced prejudice against them a year later (Herek & Capitanio, 1996).

One problem with contact as a general solution to stereotypes and prejudice is that the most prejudiced individuals often avoid contact and therefore are not exposed to its beneficial effects. A lack of positive previous experiences with members of an out-group can produce negative expectations about what future interactions might be like, and therefore "interracial anxiety" (Plant & Devine, 2003). That in turn can produce avoidance of interaction.

But what if interracial contact does occur anyway? Most experts have concluded that the specific type of interracial contact, rather than mere contact itself, is the crucial factor. Gordon Allport's classic (1954) **contact theory** identified four specific conditions that might help intergroup contact to reduce prejudice (see also Brewer & Brown, 1998; Pettigrew & Tropp, 2000):

Contact Theory

The theory that prejudice against a social group can be reduced by appropriate contact with individuals from that group.

Cooperative Interdependence

Relationship in which the outcomes of two people or groups depend on each other's actions.

- **Cooperative interdependence** with common goals is the key element in contact theory. This is composed of two elements: interacting together and sharing outcomes (Gaertner et al., 1999). Members of the two groups need to be working together with common goals that depend on each other's efforts for success rather than competing for scarce resources. The classic study demonstrating the destructive effects of competition on intergroup relations is the Robbers' Cave experiment conducted by Sherif and colleagues (1961). They initially encouraged competition between two groups of boys at a summer camp. However, the competition created so much hostility that it emerged even at noncompetitive events, such as watching a movie. The researchers later successfully reduced this hostility by encouraging the boys to work cooperatively to solve a common problem.
- Contact must also occur among individuals with equal status. If the traditional status imbalance is maintained, stereotypes cannot easily be broken down. Typically, interracial contact occurs when minorities are introduced into

entry-level jobs, as students or apprentices, or in the least desirable jobs; contact of this kind often simply perpetuates traditional stereotypes.

- The contact must have acquaintance potential (Cook, 1978). It should be of sufficient frequency, duration, and closeness to allow for the development of friendship. Brief, impersonal, or occasional contact is not as likely to help (Brewer & Brown, 1998). One study of contact with gays and lesbians found that multiple contacts, intimacy, and direct disclosure were required if prejudice against them was to be reduced (Herek & Capitianio, 1996).
- Finally, there needs to be some institutional support for the contact. Those in positions of authority need to endorse it unambiguously. If a fire chief makes snide public comments about the capabilities of female firefighters at the same time that the courts are ordering the fire department to accept women, sexism is likely to continue in local firehouses.

To try to reduce conflict in desegregated schools, social psychologists have developed educational materials consistent with the principles of contact theory. One is a "jigsaw technique" (Aronson & Gonzales, 1988). Children meet in a small multiracial group for about an hour a day to focus on one particular lesson. Each person is assigned one portion of the day's lesson and is responsible for teaching that material to the rest of the group. Because no one can complete the whole assignment without the information contributed by others, the students are interdependent. Furthermore, because each student assumes the role of expert, each has equal status. Ultimately, each student's level of learning is evaluated separately, but unless all cooperate in contributing their unique pieces of knowledge, none can succeed. As a result, the students are motivated to cooperate and learn from each other. This technique generally increases peer liking across ethnic and racial groups, increases the self-esteem of minority children, and improves academic performance (Johnson & Johnson, 2000).

How common are the optimal kinds of intergroup contact situations? In theory, being teammates on a professional football team or being fellow conspirators in a prison break (or a corporate takeover!) or having interracial teams solve homework problems in a statistics class should reduce prejudice. Merely having students of different groups in a lecture class probably would be less successful, as would having a Latino custodian in an office building. Helpful kinds of interracial contact occur more frequently today than they once did, especially in work situations. But in many other areas of life, different ethnic and racial groups often have relatively little contact with each other. As a result, intergroup contact is not a panacea.

Playing a game together is a good example of an interdependent activity for this multiethnic group of children.

Even when social settings are formally integrated, they may remain informally quite segregated.

Recategorization

Another major current approach focuses on the cognitive bases of stereotyping. Even when there is contact between the in-group and out-group members and out-group members prove not to fit the stereotype, the tendency toward category-based processing is strong and stereotypes are quite powerful. What strategies might be suggested by a more cognitive approach to overcoming stereotypes and reducing prejudice?

One strategy is to try to recategorize members of both the original in-group and out-group as members of a larger, more inclusive group. When football players from both teams join together to pray on the field after a hard-fought game, they are forming a common **superordinate group** of observant Christians that transcends their team subgroups. Producing superordinate categories depends on situational variables that reduce the salience of subgroup membership (Gaertner et al., 1989). For example, one experiment sought to create superordinate categories despite very visible differences between in-group and out-group members. The in-group was created by giving half the participants laboratory coats to wear, whereas the out-group continued to wear their normal clothes. The in-group did feel quite separate and expressed negative evaluations of the out-group. Half the participants in each group were then enlisted in a larger superordinate category by being given candy bars. The in-group subjects included in this superordinate group evaluated their out-group colleagues more positively (Dovidio, Gaertner, Isen, & Lowrance, 1995). They did so because it increased the perception that both in-groups and out-groups were part of a larger, more inclusive group (Dovidio et al., 1998b). The creation of superordinate groups may then help us discard the old stereotypes of the out-group.

Superordinate Group

Large and inclusive group categories, often created to defuse conflict among smaller groups.

Recategorization can also reduce prejudice by making cross-cutting categories more salient. If some members of our church play on the same intramural soccer team as members of another church, the social cleavage should be less severe and both should be less subject to in-group favoritism effects. This effect has been demonstrated with students from Bangladesh (Hewstone, Islam, & Judd, 1993). Some were Hindu and others were Muslim, a religious distinction that has divided that nation socially. The study was done at a university with many Indian as well as Bangladeshi students, so that religion and national identity formed two separate cross-cutting identities. The researchers found that the most extreme negative evaluations were of the double outgroup (e.g., a Hindu Indian who was evaluating Muslim Bangladeshis), whereas those who were in only one out-group were evaluated more moderately.

Many nations have been formed with the hope that they would unify previously warring groups in a more inclusive superordinate category (a "big tent"). Sometimes it works, as in the case of Catholics and Protestants in the United States. Sometimes it works at the expense of continuing tensions, as in the case of the Flemish-speaking and French-speaking Belgians. Sometimes it does not work at all, as in the case of the former Yugoslavia, and the nation ultimately breaks up into separate nations, each controlled by different ethnic and religious groups. Or separate land must be given to both groups, as in the case of the Palestinians and Israelis.

One tension that nation-building efforts create is between the desire for subgroup recognition and autonomy, on the one hand, and national integration and loyalty, on the other. In the United States this conflict is often played out in debates between advocates of a unified, color-blind society, and those of a more multicultural society in which many subgroups achieve recognition. The former see the advantage of superordinate categories, such as "Americans" or "Carolina students," and reduced emphasis on ethnic and racial subgroups or groups like sororities. The latter see the advantage of subgroups in providing social identities, self-esteem, and social support.

Some research shows the desirability of a superordinate identity, at least in terms of intergroup harmony. For example, Wolsko et al. (2000) found that exposure to multiculturalist messages increased stereotyping of out-groups, whereas exposure to color-blind messages decreased it. Similarly, in the United States, members of ethnic minority groups who identify with the superordinate culture tend to judge fairness more in terms of the procedures applied to all, not just in terms of how their own subgroup fares. But those who identify primarily with their own ethnic group are likely to be most concerned with how it fares in competition for resources (Huo, Smith, Tyler, & Lind, 1996).

Today, countries such as France, Germany, the Netherlands, England, Canada, and the United States are facing the problems posed by increasing ethnic diversity. Violent ethnic conflicts are in the headlines worldwide: in the former Soviet Union, the former Yugoslavia, throughout Africa, in Sri Lanka and India, and in Mideast nations such as Iraq. In the United States, large ethnic groups pose new challenges: Latinos have entered labor markets where they displace African Americans and other minorities; African American politicians have been elected to local governments, leading to charges of discrimination against other minorities; Korean family merchants have come under fire from other minorities in cities such as Los Angeles and New York; the academic success of many Asian American students has led to resentment from others; and urban schools struggle to accommodate newly arrived children from many different countries, many of whom speak only their native language.

Many modern nations have tried to accommodate an increasingly broad variety of groups. At the same time, many have embarked on a program to achieve equal rights for all groups. Such an effort is historically unprecedented. Through the many millennia of human history, such equality has been extremely unusual. It should not surprise us that prejudice has not been eradicated. However, the practical difficulties in reducing prejudice should not overshadow the equally practical, as well as important moral and legal, reasons for doing so. Indeed, reducing prejudice may be more important than ever. No one approach is going to solve the problem. Intergroup antagonism seems to be a fundamental aspect of the human condition. In the case of modern democratic nations, however, it is important to acknowledge the considerable measure of harmony and group tolerance that allows such Noah's arks of humanity to coexist and cooperate reasonably well.

Summary

1. Prejudice, stereotypes, and discrimination correspond to the affective, cognitive, and behavioral components of intergroup antagonism.
2. Stereotypes and prejudice strongly influence the individual's attitudes and behavior in a variety of areas.
3. Social learning is probably the strongest determinant of stereotypes and prejudices against minority groups. Prejudices frequently develop in childhood and adolescence and are difficult to change thereafter.

4. Psychodynamic theories see prejudice as stemming from the individual's particular personality dynamics.
5. Intergroup competition theories view prejudice as stemming from the realities of conflict over resources. They suggest that resistance to group equality is based partly on its costs to dominant groups and that group hierarchies are very difficult to change.
6. Cognitive approaches hold that stereotyping and prejudices arise from normal cognitive processes, especially categorization of individuals into in-groups and out-groups. Category-based processing tends to be automatic and often unconscious. Category labels are important in attaching affect to the category.
7. Social identity theory argues that intergroup antagonism can arise even without real conflicts of interests, because people's self-esteem is closely tied to their social identities and to the evaluation of their own in-groups as superior to out-groups.
8. Although old-fashioned racial prejudice has diminished in recent years, other forms have emerged to take its place, such as symbolic racism and aversive racism. These combine affect-based racial prejudices with other values, especially about self-reliance or equality.
9. An important new distinction is between explicit stereotypes, which are conscious and whose expression we can control, and implicit stereotypes, which are nonconscious, automatic, and uncontrollable.
10. Socialization of tolerance and especially education are effective in reducing prejudice, although they work slowly.
11. Intergroup contact is another important technique for reducing prejudice if it involves cooperative interdependence with common goals, equal status, close and sustained contact, and institutional support. Society is not always well organized to provide the kinds of intergroup contact that best break down prejudices.
12. Recategorization strategies can reduce prejudice. Conflicting groups can be included in a superordinate group, and other cross-cutting group loyalties can be made more salient.

Key Terms

accessibility **182**
assumed similarity effect **187**
attributional ambiguity **174**
authoritarian personality **178**
automatic processing **194**
aversive racism **193**
benevolent paternalism **179**
categorization **181**
category-based processing **182**
contact theory **199**
controlled processing **195**
cooperative interdependence **199**
discrimination **170**
displaced aggression **178**
ethnocentrism **173**
evaluative priming technique **196**
group-serving biases **187**
implicit association test **197**
implicit stereotypes **195**
in-group **170**
in-group favoritism effect **186**
legitimizing myth **180**
minimal intergroup situation **186**
old-fashioned racism **190**
optimal distinctiveness **188**
out-group **170**
out-group homogeneity effect **187**
prejudice **170**
realistic group conflict theory **179**
relative deprivation **179**
self-interest **180**
sense of group position **179**
social dominance theory **179**
social identity theory **188**
stereotype **170**
stereotype threat **171**
subtyping **184**
superordinate group **201**
symbolic racism **192**
typicality effect **183**

In The News

Where Have All the Susans Gone?

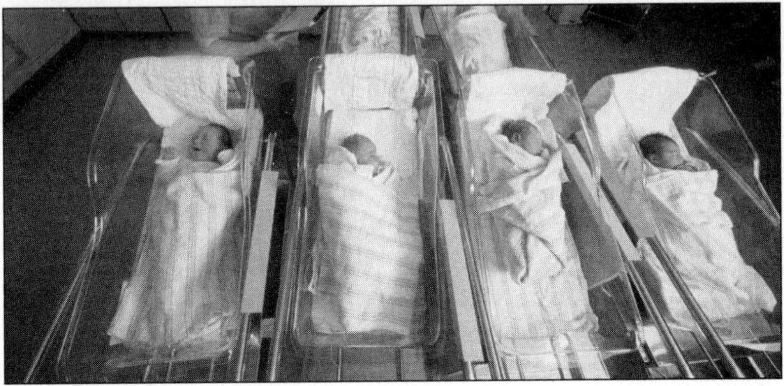

Not so long ago, Jacob was an uncommon name for boys in the United States—perhaps sounding old-fashioned to many prospective parents. But by 1990, the name Jacob had risen to 20th in the popularity rankings for newborn boys, and in 1999 Jacob moved into first place. Meanwhile, the name Christopher is slipping in popularity, and Ethan is moving up. In the 1980s, the name Madison began inching its way up the popularity ladder for girls. By 1990 it was ranked 206, and today it is the third most common girls' name in the United States. Although some names, like Sarah and Michael, are perennial favorites, other names wax and wane in popularity, like trends in fashion and hairstyles (Orenstein, 2003).

Many expectant parents fret for weeks about the best name for their new baby. In a culture that values individuality, some Americans place a premium on finding an innovative name. Few parents want their son to be one of three boys in preschool named Jake. So widespread is the search for the perfect baby name that the U.S. Social Security Administration now operates a Web site, "Popular Baby Names," ranking the 1,000 most common boys and girls names (www.ssa.gov/OACT/babynames/).

If so many parents are seeking original names, how do they wind up with the same choices? What social forces shape their decisions? A new book, *Cool Names for Babies* (Satran & Rosenkrantz, 2003), offers hints about the categories that parents may use. Some may emulate the famous, looking to movie stars (Keanu), rappers (Ludacris), or athletes (Venus). Currently, spiritual names (Pax and Eden) and color names (Indigo and Lavender) may be gaining popularity. Another emerging trend is planetary constellation names (Elara or Orion), which may one day replace the more earthbound place names (Madison, Dakota, or Paris) in vogue today.

Stanley Lieberson (2000) suggests that current trendy names are often a variation on earlier fads. For example, popular Biblical names for girls have shifted during the 20th century from Rachel in the early 1900s to Judith and Deborah at mid-century. Currently, Hannah, Abigail, and Sarah are moving up. Sometimes a sound becomes popular, such as names ending in "a" (Emma and Mia) or beginning with a hard "k" (Kylie and Caitlin). Another source of inspiration may be the desire to give a child a name that reflects parental aspirations for social mobility. Today, naming a child after an expensive brand such as Armani, Chanel, or Tiffany may not be so different from the parents of an earlier era who named their kids Ruby or Opal.

The irony is that in their quest for originality, parents often create a new social fad, only to discover that their child's name is all too common on the school playground. Overuse can spell the end of a name, at least for a while. As Peggy Ornstein (2003) suggested, "If you really want to ensure your baby girl will be unique among her peers, name her Barbara, Nancy, Karen or Susan . . . Those sound like the names of middle-aged women because—guess what?—they are."

Chapter 7

Social Influence

Social psychologists have long been interested in how an individual's behavior is influenced by other people and groups. Chapter 5 explored some aspects of social influence in its analysis of the processes of attitude change. In this chapter, we examine three important types of social influence: conformity, compliance, and obedience to authority.

Focus of This Chapter

CONFORMITY

Conformity is the tendency to change one's beliefs or behaviors to match the behavior of others (Cialdini & Goldstein, 2004). Most teenagers are presumably free to pick their own clothes and hairstyles. However, young people often prefer to dress like others in their social group, thus conforming to current fashion trends.

Conformity

Voluntarily performing an act because others also do it.

Americans are ambivalent about conformity. On the one hand, we know that sometimes a person has to "go along to get along." Conforming to group norms is often the price we pay for acceptance and social harmony. On the other hand, we value individualism and worry that people can easily be pressured to go against their personal beliefs "because everyone is doing it."

When is conformity a social good, and when is it harmful? The answer can be a matter of heated controversy, as a U.S. Supreme Court decision illustrates. In 1992, the high court ruled in a 5-to-4 decision that public schools may not include prayers or invoke the name of God during a school ceremony. Justice Anthony M. Kennedy explained that schoolchildren are a captive audience and are acutely sensitive to peer pressure. Consequently, he reasoned, a school-sponsored prayer poses a special "risk of compelling conformity" in religious beliefs: "What to most believers may seem nothing more than a reasonable request that the nonbeliever respect their religious practices, in a school context may appear to the nonbeliever or dissenter to be an attempt . . . to enforce a religious orthodoxy" (cited in Savage, 1992, p. A1). Kennedy concluded that the Court must protect children's freedom of conscience from subtle coercive pressures in school. Critics immediately denounced the decision as censoring the religious expression of the majority of schoolchildren.

Some of the earliest research in social psychology investigated conformity. The two classic studies discussed next are noteworthy.

A Guess in the Dark: The Sherif Studies

In pioneering research by Muzafer Sherif (1936), the task seemed simple: Individual male college students sat in a darkened room and watched a single point of light. Each man was told that the light would move and that his job was to estimate how far it moved. Most participants found it extremely difficult to estimate how far the light moved because it often appeared to move at varying speeds and in different directions. Actually, the study used a perceptual illusion known as the "autokinetic effect": A single point of light seen in the dark appears to move, even though it is really stationary. Given the ambiguity of this situation, the participants could not be sure of their own judgments, and their initial estimates varied enormously. Many people thought the light moved only 1 or 2 inches, whereas one person thought it moved as much as 800 feet! Apparently, this person thought he was in a gymnasium, although he was actually in a small room.

In a series of experiments, Sherif brought together groups of two or three individuals. The light was presented, and each person gave his estimate out loud. On the first trial, individuals usually gave quite different answers. But over time, as they made more judgments and listened to the responses of others in the same situation, the participants' answers became more and more similar. Lacking an objective yardstick to measure the distance, people gave weight to the judgments of others in the group. What Sherif had demonstrated was the emergence of a group norm or standard for judging the lights. Later, when participants were once again asked to make their judgments alone, their answers still fell within the approximate range established by the group. In everyday life, we might see the emergence of a social norm as teenage friends slowly evolve a group standard about appropriate dress, correct behavior at school, or the best place for pizza.

In a further variation, Sherif investigated whether he could systematically influence participants' conformity. In this experiment, participants made their judgments in a two-person group. However, only one person was a real subject; the second person was a confederate of the researcher. The confederate had been trained to make his estimates consistently lower or higher than those of the real subject. The judgment procedure was repeated for a number of trials. Under these conditions, the real participant soon began to give estimates that were more and more similar to those of the confederate. For instance, if the real subject began by estimating that the light moved between 10 and 14 inches and the confederate said it moved only 2 inches, on the next trial the subject tended to lower his estimate, and on the following trial he would lower it even more. By the end of the series, the participant's estimates were very similar to those of the confederate. Sherif had demonstrated that in an uncertain and ambiguous situation, people tend to conform to the norm established by a consistent peer. In everyday life, a student who transfers to a new school midyear may adopt the norms of dress and behavior already established by other students in the class.

As Plain as Day: The Asch Studies

Solomon Asch wondered if conformity occurs only in ambiguous situations, such as the Sherif study, in which people are quite uncertain about the correct answer. Would people conform if the stimulus situation were clear? Asch reasoned that when people face an unambiguous situation, they would trust their own perceptions and give their independent judgment, even when every other member of a group disagreed with them. Asch (1955) designed an experiment to test this hypothesis.

Five male college students arrived to take part in a study on perception. They sat around a table and were told they would be judging the lengths of lines. They were shown a card containing only one line (the "standard") and a second card on which three lines of varying lengths had been drawn. Their task was to choose the line on the second card that was most similar in length to the standard line on the first card. As shown in Figure 7–1, it was an easy task. One of the lines was exactly the same length as the standard, whereas the other two were quite different from it.

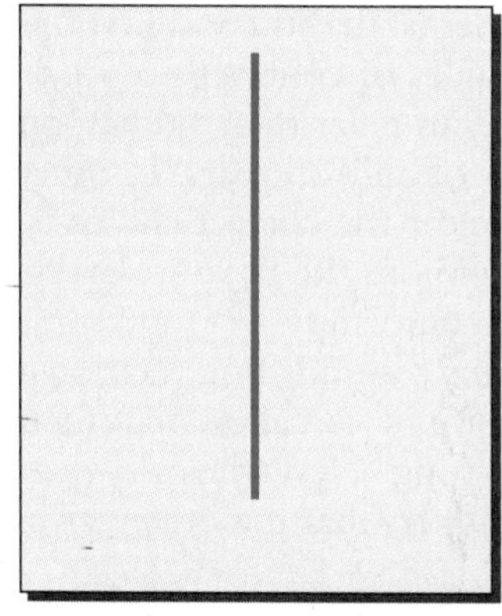

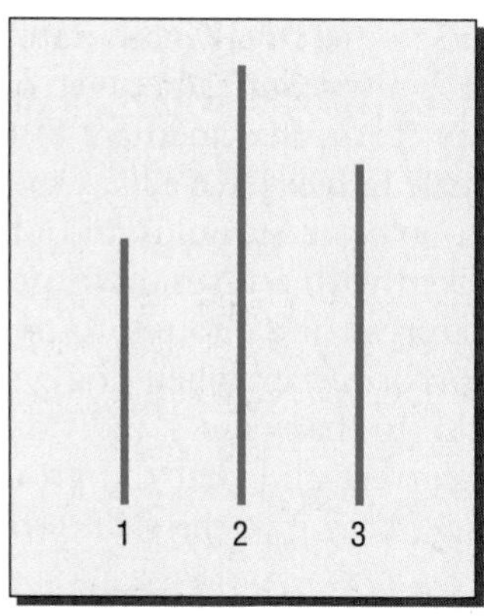

Figure 7–1 **A Stimulus Like the Ones Used in the Asch Conformity Study.**

In each trial, participants were shown two cards. One contained the "standard." The second contained three comparison lines, one of which was the same length as the standard. Subjects were asked which comparison line was the same as the standard.

When the lines were shown, the five participants answered aloud in the order in which they were seated. The first person gave his choice, and then each of the others responded in turn. Because the judgment was so easy, there were no disagreements. When all had responded, a second set of lines was shown, responses were given, and a third set of lines was presented.

At this point, the experiment seems dull and pointless. On the third trial, however, the first participant looked carefully at the lines as before and then gave what was obviously the wrong answer. In the example in Figure 7–1, he might have said line 1 rather than line 2. The next participant gave the same wrong answer, as did the third and fourth. When it was time for the fifth participant to respond, he was quite disturbed. It was clear to him that the others were giving wrong answers. He knew that line 2 was most similar to the standard. Yet everyone else said it was line 1.

In these circumstances, people sitting in the fifth position sometimes gave the wrong answer: They went along with the others even though they knew the answer was incorrect. In fact, among these college men with good eyesight and presumably sharp minds, the wrong answer was given about 35 percent of the time. Some participants never gave the wrong answer, and some did all the time, but overall they averaged about one wrong response in three. Of course, in this classic study, the situation was staged. The first four "subjects" were confederates of the experimenter and were responding according to a prearranged script. But the real subject did not know this, and he gave the wrong answer rather than disagree with the others.

It is important to keep the clarity of this judgment task in mind. There is a tendency to think that the conforming subjects were uncertain of the correct choice and therefore were swayed by the majority. This was not the case. The participants were quite sure of the correct choice and, in control groups with no group pressure, chose correctly 100 percent of the time. When participants conformed, they conformed even though they knew the correct answer.

Is the amount of conformity that Asch found in his studies of college students in the United States relatively high or relatively low? There is no easy answer to this question. Most participants (75 percent) conformed at least once during the study. On the other hand, most answers (two out of three) given by participants were correct despite group pressure. Conformity was clearly evident, but so, too, was considerable independence of judgment. Asch (1955) apparently expected to find very little conformity among college students and worried about his findings: "That we have found the tendency to conformity in our society so strong that reasonably intelligent and well-meaning young people are willing to call white black is a matter of concern" (p. 35). Asch might have been pleased to learn that a meta-analysis of 133 conformity studies (Bond & Smith, 1996) found a steady decline in general levels of conformity since his work in the 1950s.

Asch's pioneering work led to many other studies of conformity. Research has demonstrated similar conformity effects using a variety of judgment tasks, including evaluating opinion statements, statements of fact, and logical syllogisms.

Participants have agreed to extremely inaccurate statements: that there is no population problem in the United States because 6,000 miles of continent separate San Francisco from New York, that men are 8 to 9 inches taller than women on the average, and that male babies have a life expectancy of only 25 years! In other words, regardless of the type of stimulus and of how clear the correct choice is, when individuals are faced with a unanimous group opinion, the pressure exerted by the majority is often strong enough to produce conformity.

People sometimes conform even when doing so means contradicting their own perceptions of the world. In many cases, individuals continue to believe that their private judgments are correct and that the group is wrong. Nevertheless, when asked to respond publicly, they give the same wrong answers that the others give.

Culture and Conformity

Everyday experiences of conformity are shaped by the cultural context (Kim & Markus, 1999). Individualist cultures such as those of the United States and western Europe emphasize personal freedom and independence. Child rearing teaches self-reliance and assertion; children are given a good deal of independence, and creativity is encouraged. In this cultural context, the negative aspects of conformity tend to be emphasized. Group pressure to conform is seen as a threat to the uniqueness of the individual. Conformity may be seen as a loss of personal autonomy and control. In contrast, in collectivist cultures such as those in Africa, Asia, and Latin America, the meaning of conformity is quite different. Collectivist cultures emphasize the importance of ties to the social group. Parents are concerned with obedience, proper behavior, and respect for group traditions (Berry, Poortinga, Segall, & Dasen, 1992). In this cultural context, the positive aspects of conformity are emphasized. Conformity is viewed not as a response to social pressure but as a way to be connected to others and to fulfill one's moral obligations as a responsible person. Indeed, the Korean word for conformity means maturity and inner strength (Kim & Markus, 1999). From a collectivist perspective, a desire for independence is seen as immature and selfish. The willingness to adjust oneself to group norms is viewed as desirable and essential for group harmony.

Cross-cultural research has shown greater conformity to group norms in collectivist cultures than in individualist cultures (Bond & Smith, 1996). In an early study, Berry (1967) used an Asch-type line-judgment task to compare conformity in three cultural groups. Participants from Scotland and from the Eskimo people of Baffin Island represented individualist cultures that value self-reliance. Individuals from the Temne farming culture, an African group that strongly values tradition and conformity, represented a collectivist culture. All participants had normal vision. As predicted, clear cultural differences emerged. The Eskimo respondents showed the least conformity (mean of less than 3 out of 15 trials), followed by the Scots (mean of about 4). The greatest conformity was shown by the Temne respondents (mean of almost 9 out of 15). A meta-analysis of 133 cross-cultural conformity studies (Bond & Smith, 1996) has confirmed this pattern, finding significantly more conformity among people from collectivist societies than among those from individualist societies. The meta-analysis also showed that cultural values had more impact on conformity than did other factors such as group size or the ambiguity of the stimulus.

In a recent study, researchers investigated whether American and Japanese cultures provide different opportunities for individuals either to conform or to act independently (Morling, Kitayama, & Miyamoto, 2002). College students from the United States and Japan described personal experiences in which they adjusted themselves to a situation. For example, a Japanese student wrote, "When I am out shopping with my friend, and she says something is cute, even when I don't think it is, I agree with her." Other students wrote about times when they influenced or changed a situation in line with their own wishes. One American student wrote, "I talked my sister out of dating a guy who I knew was a jerk." Students in both countries had experienced both types of situations, but they differed in frequency. Japanese students remembered more adjustment situations than independence situations; Americans showed the opposite pattern of remembering more instances of independence than of fitting in.

Kim and Markus (1999) demonstrated the divergent cultural attitudes toward conformity and uniqueness between people from the United States and those from Asian cultures. In one study, participants evaluated sets of abstract figures. In each set, most figures appeared several times and one figure was unique. Compared to Asian and Asian American participants, European Americans showed a greater preference for the unique figures. In another study, students were offered a free pen in exchange for completing a brief questionnaire. As a measure of preference for uniqueness, students chose one pen from a set of pens in which most pens were of the same color and a minority were of a different color. Again, European Americans showed a strong preference for the unique pen. Finally, a content analysis of advertisements from Korean and American magazines highlighted this cultural difference. American ads emphasized freedom, choice, uniqueness, and rebelling against tradition. Korean ads emphasized tradition and harmony within group norms.

These studies indicate that there is consistency between the cultural values that people learn in growing up and see in the mass media, and the preferences and behavior they exhibit as adults. In interpreting these findings, it is essential to remember that conformity has different meanings in different cultures. To make this point, Kim and Markus (1999, p. 785) contrasted the experiences of an American ordering coffee in a café in San Francisco and a Korean ordering coffee in a café in Seoul. The American may take special pleasure in being able to order coffee exactly the way he or she wants it—a large decaffeinated cappuccino with nonfat milk. In the United States, "The best taste is one's individualized taste, and being sure of one's own particular taste contributes to being an appropriate person." In contrast, a Korean who ordered such a distinctive drink might feel strange, worry that he or she will be perceived oddly by other patrons, or fear that the waiter might be annoyed. "In Korea, the normal, regular, and traditional are usually the best tastes for the individual, and a particular taste that differs from the 'right' taste is typically taken as bad taste."

Why Do People Conform?

People conform for many reasons. Two of the most important reasons are to be right and to be liked (Martin & Hewstone, 2003). This idea is consistent with the analysis of attitude change presented in Chapter 5. There, we saw that people are more likely to be influenced by a persuasive communication from a person who is knowledgeable, trustworthy, and likeable. Similarly, people are more apt to conform to group behaviors when they think the group members are right and when they want to be liked by the group.

Informational Influence: The Desire to Be Right. One reason for conformity is that the behavior of other people often provides useful information. This is known as **informational influence**. An American tourist trying to figure out how to buy a ticket for the Paris subway may carefully observe the behavior of Parisians, noting where they go to purchase a ticket, how they make their way through the turnstile, and where they head to find the trains. By following the steps used by knowledgeable travelers, the tourist may succeed in mastering the basics of the subway system. The tendency to conform based on informational influence depends on two aspects of the situation: how well informed we believe the group is and how confident we are in our own independent judgment.

Informational Influence

Conforming because the behavior of others provides useful information.

The more we trust the group's information and value its opinions, the more likely we are to go along with the group. Our American tourist would be more likely to emulate the behavior of people who appear to be frequent subway users than to emulate other individuals who are carrying tourist paraphernalia and look equally perplexed. Anything that increases confidence in the correctness of the group is likely to increase conformity.

Balanced against confidence in the group is the individual's confidence in his or her own views. Early studies found that the more ambiguous or difficult the task, the more likely people are to conform to group judgments (Coleman, Blake, & Mouton, 1958), presumably because they are less certain of their own judgment. The Sherif task was more difficult than the Asch task and so produced more conformity. Other research has found that the less competent and knowledgeable we feel about a topic, the more likely we are to conform.

A useful distinction can be made between change in a person's public actions (overtly going along with the group) and change in a person's private beliefs (actually agreeing with the group). When conformity is based on informational influence—on the belief that group members are right—we usually change our minds as well as our behavior. Informational influence can thus be seen as a fairly rational process by which the behavior of others alters our beliefs or interpretation of a situation and consequently leads us to act in accord with the group (Griffin & Buehler, 1993).

Normative Influence

Conforming to be liked or accepted by others.

Normative Influence: The Desire to Be Liked. A second reason for conformity is the desire for social approval. This is known as **normative influence**. We often want others to accept us, like us, and treat us well. Simultaneously, we want to avoid being teased, ridiculed, or rejected (Janes & Olson, 2000). Normative influence occurs when we alter our behavior to conform to group norms or standards in order to gain social acceptance or maintain our standing in a group. For example, when we're with our health-conscious friends, we may exaggerate our interest in salads and fresh fish, even though we don't especially like them; when we're alone, we're more likely to follow our personal preferences, which may be for hamburgers or tacos. In such situations, conformity leads to an outward change in public behavior, but not necessarily to a change in private opinions.

Of course, if we change our behavior to conform to group norms, we may also have a tendency to change our beliefs as well. Cognitive dissonance theory, presented in Chapter 5, predicts such a change in attitudes. The idea is that people may engage in a process of "postconformity justification," by which they reconsider their initial views, try to understand the perspective of other group members, and construct a new interpretation of the situation that is consistent with their conforming behavior. Research provides evidence for precisely this sort of postconformity change in a person's beliefs (Buehler & Griffin, 1994).

It's common for teenagers to dress like their friends. Conformity is a way to fit into a group and feel accepted.

When Do People Conform?

We are more apt to conform in some situations than in others (Cialdini & Trost, 1998). The size of the group, the unanimity of group opinions, and our commitment to the group can all affect conformity. In addition, there are individual differences in the desire for individuation or uniqueness that can also influence whether we conform or dissent.

Group Size. Conformity usually increases as the size of the majority increases—at least up to a point. Imagine that you're in a room that feels uncomfortably chilly to you. If there is one other person in the room who complains that it's too hot, you may decide that the other person is mistaken or feverish. But if five other people all say the room feels hot to them, you may reconsider, wondering if something is wrong with you. Five people tend to be more trustworthy than one; it is harder to mistrust or discount a group than a single individual.

In some of his early experiments, Asch (1955) varied the size of the majority from 2 to 15. He found that 2 people produced more conformity pressure than 1, 3 a lot more than 2, and 4 about the same as 3. Surprisingly, increasing the size of the group past 4 did not substantially increase the amount of conformity in his line judgment task.

Group Unanimity. A person faced with a unanimous majority is under great pressure to conform. If, however, a group is not united, there is a striking decrease in the amount of conformity. When even one other person dissents, conformity drops to about one fourth the usual level. It does not seem to matter who the nonconforming person is. Regardless of whether this dissenter is a highly prestigious expert or someone of low prestige and uncertain expertise, conformity tends to drop to low levels (Asch, 1955; Morris & Miller, 1975). Furthermore, a sole dissenter can reduce conformity even if he or she gives wrong answers. If the correct answer is A, the majority says B, and another person says C, the real subject is less likely to conform than if everyone else agrees on one incorrect answer. Even slight disagreement within the group makes it easier for an individual to remain independent.

The dramatic decrease in conformity when unanimity is broken seems to be due to several of the factors we have already discussed. First, the amount of trust or confidence in the correctness of the majority decreases whenever there is disagreement, even if the dissenter is less knowledgeable or less reliable than those who make up the majority. The mere fact that someone else also disagrees with the group indicates that there is room for doubt, that the issue is not perfectly clear, and that the majority might be wrong. This situation reduces the individual's reliance on the majority opinion as a source of information and accordingly reduces conformity. Second, another group member's endorsement of the position that the individual favors serves to strengthen the individual's self-confidence about that judgment. Greater confidence reduces conformity. A third consideration involves reluctance to appear deviant. The lone dissenter stands out. When someone else also disagrees, neither person is quite as deviant as he or she would be alone.

One nonconformist can have an important effect as long as there are other people who inwardly disagree with the majority but are afraid to speak up. It may also explain why totalitarian governments allow no dissent. Even one small dissenting voice could encourage others to do likewise, and the regime might be endangered.

Commitment to the Group. Conformity is affected by the strength of the bonds between each individual and the group (Forsyth, 1999). **Commitment** refers to all the forces, positive and negative, that act to keep an individual in a relationship or group.

Positive forces that attract an individual to a group include liking other group members, believing that the group accomplishes important goals, feeling that group members work well together, and expecting to gain from belonging to the

Commitment

All the forces, positive and negative, that act to keep a person in a relationship or group.

Table 7–1

Blending In Versus Standing Out

Maslach and her colleagues used statements similar to those listed below to assess the strength of a person's desire for individuation. How strongly would you agree or disagree with each statement?

I would be willing to present a controversial point of view to a group of strangers.

When I'm in a group, I try not to call attention to myself.

I enjoy dressing in a distinctive way that calls attention to my appearance.

I am reluctant to speak out in class unless I am certain I'm correct.

group. Groups with high morale, in which members enjoy working together and believe they function well as a team, are more vulnerable to conformity pressures than are less cohesive groups.

Negative forces that keep an individual from leaving a group also increase commitment. These include such barriers as having few alternatives and having made large investments in the group that would be costly to give up. For example, some people stay in a work group only because they need the money, not because they like or respect their coworkers. In general, the more committed a person is to a group, the greater the pressures are for conformity to group standards.

The Desire for Individuation. People differ in their willingness to do things that publicly differentiate them from others. Some people are more comfortable blending in with a group and going along with group opinions; others prefer to stand out. Christina Maslach and her colleagues developed a paper-and-pencil test to measure people's willingness to engage in public behaviors that set them apart from others (Maslach, Stapp, & Santee, 1985; Whitney, Sagrestano, & Maslach, 1994). They called this phenomenon the **desire for individuation**.

Desire for Individuation

A person's willingness to do things that publicly differentiate him or her from others or make him or her stand out.

A person scores high on individuation by indicating a willingness to do things that would call attention to himself or herself. In contrast, a person scoring low on individuation would hesitate to take actions that would set him or her apart from the group. Questions similar to those used by Maslach are given in Table 7–1. Research indicates that high-individuation people are more likely to say that they have distinctive ways of dressing, use a distinctive nickname, and own unique possessions. In laboratory studies, high-individuation subjects were less likely to go along with the majority view and were more likely to engage in what the researchers called "creative dissent." High-individuation subjects have also been rated by observers as less socially compliant, more critical, and less polite. This research emphasizes the importance of individual differences in susceptibility to group influence.

Using Conformity to Change Unhealthy Behavior: The Case of Social Norms Marketing

For decades, high school and college administrators have sought ways to reduce student binge drinking, promote safer sex, discourage smoking, and foster sensible eating. Today, many schools are trying a new approach known as "social norms marketing." The basic idea is familiar. When a teenager asks for parental permission to stay out late or see an R-rated movie because "everyone is doing it," the appeal is based on information about social norms. When advertisers try to influence consumers by associating their product with appealing groups, for example, showing successful young professionals drinking a particular brand of liquor, they are also providing information about social norms. Can the power of social norms be harnessed for health education? Many schools seem to think so (Campo et al., 2003; Perkins, 2003).

In this approach, school officials use questionnaires and other methods to assess the frequency of alcohol consumption, condom use, smoking, and other

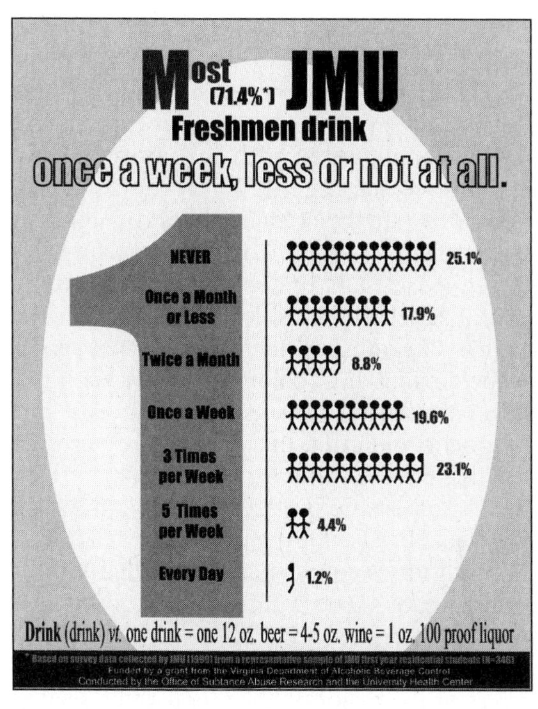

At many colleges, ad campaigns urge students to drink sensibly, exercise, and practice safer sex. These ads seek to persuade students that healthy living is, in fact, "normal" among the majority of their peers.

behaviors on their campus. Students often misperceive the actual frequency of these behaviors. By providing information showing that healthy behavior is, in fact, "normal," administrators hope to influence students' attitudes and behaviors. At the University of Arizona, an ad proclaimed, "Most U of A students (69%) have 4 or fewer drinks when they party." At James Madison University (JMU), a poster advertised that 9 out of 10 JMU men stop the first time their date says no to sexual activity. Some schools use humor. At Virginia Commonwealth University (VCU), a poster showing a gloved hand with two fingers extended asked, "Do you want to grow up to be a proctologist?" Then the poster asked, "Do you want to grow up to be a daily smoker?" The poster concluded, "Most VCU students say 'no way' to both!" At Hobart and William Smith Colleges, "campus factoids" are posted on the school's computer network and on their computer screen-saver program. These provide facts about the percentage of students who participate in volunteer service or who exercise or play sports regularly.

A growing number of colleges are adopting this approach. *The New York Times Magazine* named social norms marketing an "Idea of the Year" (Frauenfelder, 2001). Currently, however, the actual effectiveness of social norms marketing is a topic of debate (Campo et al., 2003). Advocates such as the National Social Norms Resource Center at Northern Illinois University argue than when used appropriately, the social norms approach can increase safer sex practices and decrease students' use of drugs and alcohol (Perkins, 2003). Skeptics, however, worry that these ad campaigns may not be helpful to all students. Information that most students are moderate drinkers might encourage heavy drinkers to cut down but could also encourage light drinkers to drink more. Others note that students may be influenced more strongly by the norms of their own small group of friends than by campus-wide standards.

Minority Influence: Innovation in Groups

Conformity to majority patterns is a basic aspect of social life. However, our emphasis on majority influence should not blind us to the importance of **minority influence**. Sometimes a forceful minority with a new idea or a unique perspective can effectively change the position of the majority (DeDreu & DeVries, 2001).

Minority Influence

Influence that members of a minority have over the majority in a group.

Early studies showing that dissent reduces conformity challenged the idea that majorities are "all-powerful." This challenge led researchers to investigate the possible influence of minorities. Pioneering work by the French psychologist Serge Moscovici (1985) has been especially important. In one experiment, researchers used an Asch-type conformity paradigm but with a majority of naive subjects and a minority of confederates (Moscovici, Lage, & Naffrechoux, 1969). Members of six-person groups were asked to rate the color of slides. In actuality, all slides were blue but varied in their luminance. In control groups of six naive participants, virtually all slides were described as blue. In the experimental group, however, two confederates consistently labeled the blue slides as "green." Participants had previously been told that all group members had normal vision, so these "green" responses could not be attributed to color blindness. With this minority pressure, about a third of the participants reported seeing at least one "green" slide, and 8 percent of all judgments indicated that slides were "green." Clearly, the minority view had a noticeable effect on the naive majority.

The "behavioral style" of a minority is important. To be effective, a minority must be consistent and forceful (Wood et al., 1994). This behavioral style is interpreted by the majority as a sign of the minority's confidence and certainty in its position. Further, a minority has a better chance of success if its behavioral style is logically consistent but not rigid, that is, when the minority has a well-defined position but a flexible style of presentation. Although members of a consistent minority may be liked less than members of the majority, they tend to be seen as more competent and honest (Bassili & Provencal, 1988). As a minority persists in its position over time, the majority may start to question the correctness of its views. Ultimately, some majority members may convert by changing their own position in the direction of the minority members. If enough members change their views, the minority may be transformed into a new majority (Clark, 2001).

Research has identified other factors that determine the influence of minorities (Mackie & Hunter, 1999). First, minorities are more influential when they are able to refute the majority viewpoint effectively, by logical arguments, for instance (Clark, 1990). Second, minorities are more likely to succeed when the issue is not of great personal relevance or importance to majority group members (Trost, Maass, & Kenrick, 1992). Third, the general social climate of the society can also make a difference. A minority will be more effective if it argues for a position in line with current social trends outside the group. For example, in an era of increasing sexual conservatism, a minority that argues for sexual permissiveness will be less effective than a minority that argues for sexual restraint.

Minorities are also more likely to succeed when they are similar to the majority group in most respects except for the particular behavior or attitude in question (Volpato, Maass, Mucchi-Faina, & Vitti, 1990). For example, a member of the Republican Party who tries to convince other Republicans to change their views on foreign aid would be a "single minority" (also called an "in-group

The first American women who demonstrated for the right to vote were a small minority. Over time, this resourceful and determined minority successfully changed public opinions, obtaining the right to vote for women in 1920.

minority") because of differing from the Republican majority only in beliefs about foreign aid. In contrast, a member of the Democratic Party who tries to get Republicans to change their policies on foreign aid would be a "double minority" (or "out-group minority") because of differing from the majority in two ways: political party and in views about foreign aid. Research suggests that the single-minority is usually more influential than a double minority.

A study by Maass and Clark (1984), for example, found that an ostensibly gay minority arguing for gay rights had less influence on heterosexuals than did a heterosexual minority arguing for gay rights, in part because the gay minority was seen as having more self-interest in the issue. Another study showed that conservative male subjects were more strongly influenced by a man who argued for a liberal position on abortion than by a woman who took the same liberal stance (Maass, Clark, & Haberkorn, 1982). When a minority group is perceived as having a personal stake in its position, its views can more easily be discounted as reflecting self-interest. In summary, minorities have more influence when their position is taken seriously and is seen as reflecting certainty and competence. Minorities are less influential when they can be discounted as bizarre, dogmatic, or self-serving.

A current controversy among social psychologists is whether the processes of majority influence (conformity) and minority influence (innovation) are fundamentally the same or different (Forgas & Williams, 2001). One view, known as the "dual-process hypothesis," is that minorities and majorities induce different cognitive processes among group members. Minority influence leads group members to think seriously about the issues involved and to engage in systematic processing of information. As a result, the influence of minorities is more likely to result in changed attitudes, to produce a "conversion" in people's opinions. In contrast, majority influence is seen as a less thoughtful process of conformity to group views. Majority influence may lead to changes in overt behavior but not necessarily to changes in private attitudes.

Proponents of this dual-processing perspective emphasize the value of minority influence. Although a dissenting minority can challenge the harmony of group interaction, disagreement may have important benefits. Charlene Nemeth and her associates have shown that minorities can cause other group members to think more carefully about an issue and to consider a wider variety of possible explanations or novel solutions (e.g., Nemeth & Kwan, 1987). In other words, the expression of minority viewpoints sometimes improves group functioning and can have a beneficial effect out of proportion to the minority's small numbers. This positive effect of minority viewpoints is most likely to occur on tasks that are enhanced by creative thinking and the introduction of multiple perspectives (Nemeth, Mosier, & Chiles, 1992). These demonstrations of the positive effects of a dissenting minority have provided a useful correction to the view that majorities are all-powerful. The influence of minorities can be very important indeed.

Yet many researchers are skeptical of the idea that the processes through which minorities influence groups are unique (David & Turner, 2001; Kruglanski & Mackie, 1990). For instance, there is evidence that majority endorsement of a position sometimes also leads to careful scrutiny of a message (Baker & Petty, 1994). Both majorities and minorities are capable of influencing groups in a variety of ways and can produce both private attitude change and public conformity.

COMPLIANCE

One of the basic ways people influence each other is to ask them to do something. Think of some of the direct requests you might make of your friends: to drive you to the airport, to lend you money, to refrain from smoking in your car, to tell you what they really think of your new haircut, or to join the volunteer group you're organizing. **Compliance** is defined as doing what we are asked to do, even though we might prefer not to. The distinguishing feature of compliance is that it involves responding to a request from another individual or group.

Compliance

Performing an act at another's request.

Imagine that as you approach the local supermarket, a young woman stops you and asks you to sign a petition urging the city to build a new shelter for homeless families. You reluctantly agree to sign the petition. Next the woman asks you to donate $5 to help the homeless. You give her a dollar and duck into the market. Why did you comply, at least partially, with her requests?

Sometimes we comply with requests seemingly for no reason at all. In one study, researchers approached people waiting to use a photocopying machine and asked to go to the head of the line because "I have to make copies" (Langer, Blank, & Chanowitz, 1978). This so-called explanation provided no logical justification for going out of turn. Yet many people went along with the request, apparently not paying much attention to the content of the explanation. Ellen Langer refers to this behavior as "mindlessness," because the response is made almost without thinking. Perhaps out of habit, we have learned that when someone asks for something, especially something trivial, and gives a reason (even a meaningless reason), we should go along. We spare ourselves the mental effort of thinking about the situation and simply comply with the request. Mindlessness may not explain most instances of compliance, but it is a fascinating aspect of human behavior.

Six Bases of Social Power

People can influence each other in a wide variety of ways. When David Kipnis (1984) asked managers in business organizations how they try to influence their coworkers to do things, they said:

"I simply order him to do what I ask."

"I act very humble while making my request."

"I explain the reasons for my request."

In contrast, when Kipnis asked dating couples how they influence their partners, they said:

"I get angry and demand he give in."

"I act so nice that she cannot refuse when I ask."

"We talk about why we don't agree." (p. 186)

A useful way to classify how people influence each other was developed by Bertram Raven and his colleagues (French & Raven, 1959; Raven, 1992). This model identifies six major bases of power, each reflecting a different type of resource a person might use to influence someone. These are summarized in Table 7–2. Let's consider each one.

Table 7–2

The Six Bases of Power

	Power Is Based On	Example of Parent Influencing a Child
Reward	Providing or promising a positive outcome	If you brush your teeth every night this week, I'll take you to the zoo on Saturday.
Coercion	Providing or threatening a negative outcome	If you don't brush your teeth, you can't watch TV.
Expertise	Having special knowledge or ability	The dentist told you to brush twice a day, and she knows best.
Information	The persuasive content of the message	If you don't brush your teeth, you'll get cavities that will hurt. The dentist will have to drill holes in your teeth to fill the cavities.
Referent	Identifying with or wanting to be like another person or group	Your big brother Stan always brushes every day.
Legitimate	The influencer's right to make a request	I'm your mother, and I'm telling you to brush your teeth—now!

Note: Our examples consider how a parent might use each power base to influence a child to brush her teeth.

Rewards. One basis for power is the ability to provide positive outcomes for another person—to help that person accomplish a desired goal or to offer a valued reward. Some rewards are highly personal, such as a smile of approval from a special friend. Other rewards, such as money, are impersonal. Sometimes people use reward power by making explicit bargains: A boss might offer to pay a worker a bonus for finishing a project over the weekend. At other times, the possibility of rewards is more subtle: An employee may hope that his hard work and attention to his boss's wishes will lead to a pay raise, even though no formal agreement has been discussed.

Coercion. Coercion can range from actual physical force to threats of punishment or subtle signs of disapproval. For example, after trying unsuccessfully to convince a young child to take a nap, a parent may simply place the resistant child in the crib, walk out of the room, and close the door. Or a supervisor may threaten disciplinary action if an employee continues to arrive late for work.

Expertise. Special knowledge, training, and skill are sources of power. We defer to experts and follow their advice because we believe that their knowledge will help us to achieve our personal goals. If a trusted physician advises us to take three little green pills daily for an infection, we are likely to comply whether or not we know precisely what the pills contain or understand how the medicine works. Likewise, a group of mountain climbers scaling the summit of a hazardous peak will follow the route suggested by their experienced guide.

Information. We often try to influence people by giving them information or logical arguments that we think will suggest the right course of action to them. A friend might influence you to go to a concert by informing you that your favorite music group is performing. In this case, the influencer is not an expert. Rather, it is the content of the message that produces the desired effect. Information is a pervasive factor in social influence. As noted earlier in this chapter, the need for information can motivate conformity. Chapter 5 investigated another type of informational influence: the use of persuasion.

Referent Power. A basis of influence with special relevance to personal relationships and groups is referent power (Orina, Wood, & Simpson, 2001). This power exists when we identify with or want to foster a relationship with another person or group. In such cases, we may voluntarily copy their behavior (conformity) or do what they ask (compliance) because we want to become similar to

A 3-year-old copies the gestures of his brother and friends. In Raven's model, social influence based on identification is called "referent power."

them or have a continuing relationship. In everyday life, we may not think of identification as a type of influence, but it can be very effective. A young child who looks up to an older brother, tries to imitate his mannerisms, and adopts his interests is one illustration. A young woman who smokes a particular brand of cigarettes because she identifies with the image of the beautiful, thin, independent woman promoting the product in ads is being influenced by referent power. Newlyweds who try to influence each other by appealing to the importance of their marriage are using referent power.

Legitimate Authority. Sometimes one person has the right or authority to ask another person to act a certain way. The high school teacher who orders a tardy student to do extra homework and the general who orders troops into battle are exercising **legitimate authority**. Similarly, in most families, parents believe they have the right to tell young children when to go to bed, and children usually feel obligated to comply. Children may try to renegotiate bedtime rules or ask to make an exception for a special occasion, but they usually accept their parents' authority to make rules.

Legitimate Authority

Social norms permit those in authority to make requests.

Social roles such as parent and child, police officer and citizen, or supervisor and employee dictate the legitimate rights and responsibilities of each person in the relationship. Even very young children seem to sense that the requests of doctors and dentists are meant to be obeyed. When people deviate from agreed-upon social rules, we believe we have the right to remind them of their obligations.

There are many ways to signal one's authority in a situation. The black robe of a judge, the white coat of a physician, and the blue uniform of a police officer are visible markers of status and authority. A field experiment at the Bronx Zoo illustrates the potential importance of uniforms to indicate that an individual has legitimate authority (Sedikides & Jackson, 1990). As visitors entered the Tropical Lagoon, they were approached by a person who told them not to touch the handrail of the bird exhibit. Visitors were significantly more likely to comply with this request when it came from someone dressed as a zookeeper than when it came from a person in casual clothes. Apparently the legitimate authority conveyed by the uniform increased the person's influence. Although the request not to touch the handrail was somewhat unusual (why put handrails there in the first place?), not one of the visitors questioned the reason for the request.

Power of Helplessness. A special case of legitimate authority is what Raven (1992) has called the "power of helplessness." Consider these requests: A small child asks his mother for help in taking off his snow boots; a polite foreign tourist asks a pedestrian for directions to the bus stop in broken English; a partially blind grocery shopper asks for help in reading the price marked on a can of soup. In each case, the person asking for help is in a powerless or helpless condition. In each case, others are likely to comply with the request, respecting a cultural **norm of social responsibility**. We expect people to help those who are less fortunate, and this social obligation makes it legitimate for those in need to ask for help. Raven (1992) cautions, however, that the legitimate power of helplessness can sometimes be costly for those who use it. People who constantly claim to be helpless may come to see themselves as incompetent. We will examine this issue further in Chapter 12 on helping behavior.

Norm of Social Responsibility

A norm dictating that we should help others who depend on us.

Raven has supplemented the six major bases of power with an analysis of other means of influence (Raven, 1992; Raven, Schwarzwald, & Koslowsky, 1998). For example, "environmental manipulation" occurs when the influencer changes the situation so that the target of influence must comply. An exasperated homeowner, tired of yelling at neighborhood children to stay off her property, may finally erect a sturdy fence to prevent their trespassing. By changing the physical environment, she has changed the children's behavior. Another approach is to invoke the power of third parties. In the heat of an argument, a child may say to his sister, "If you don't stop, I'm going to tell Daddy about what you did." The idea here is to change the sister's behavior by threatening to call on the greater power of a parent.

The bases of power can readily be applied to situations in everyday life, such as the efforts of teachers to influence their students. All teachers have the challenge of influencing students—getting students to pay attention, to complete assignments, to study, and to learn—but teachers differ dramatically in the influence strategies they use. A study of influence strategies used by teachers in American classrooms found that two forms of influence—expert power and referent power—were especially effective (Richmond & McCroskey, 1992). A teacher who uses expert power emphasizes his or her experience and knowledge, so that students comply with requests out of respect for the teacher's expertise. A teacher who uses expert power might say, "Trust me. I've done this a hundred times and it really works." A teacher who uses referent power seeks to build a positive relationship with students, so that students want to follow requests in order to please the teacher. The use of expert and referent power tends to set a positive tone in a classroom and can enhance students' motivation to learn.

In contrast, two other forms of influence—coercion and legitimate authority—appear to be less effective. A teacher who uses coercion might say, "Stop talking or I'll send you to the principal's office." A teacher who appeals to legitimate authority might say, "Do it because I told you to, and I'm your teacher." Both approaches can produce an immediate change in the behavior of students. They can get a student to stop talking or open a book. However, students in the United States tend to find these approaches oppressive. In the long run, coercion and appeals to authority may not motivate students to want to learn and may not foster an interest in course materials.

Mood and Compliance

If you want to ask a friend for a special favor, should you wait until he or she is in a particularly good mood? Will your own mood affect how you word your request for the favor? More generally, what part do emotions play in compliance? Australian psychologist Joseph Forgas (2001) designed a series of experiments to find out.

Forgas (1998) predicted that we are more willing to comply with a request when we are feeling happy than when we're feeling sad. Further, he predicted that mood would be especially important in how a person reacts to a rude versus polite request. In one study, students in a university library were first exposed to one of three mood-induction experiences. Some read a description of a humorous story (the positive-mood condition). Others read a sad story about death from cancer (the negative-mood condition). In a third, control condition, students read an information sheet about the library. After the student had read the materials, he or she was approached by an unfamiliar student (actually a confederate) who asked for a favor. In the polite condition, the confederate asked, "Excuse me, I need some paper to finish an assignment. Could I please get 10 sheets if you have any to spare?" In an intermediate politeness condition, the confederate asked, "Sorry, would you have 10 sheets of paper?" In the impolite condition, the confederate simply said, "Give me 10 sheets of paper."

A few minutes later, a second experimenter told the naive student that the earlier request for paper had actually been part of a psychology study and asked the student to evaluate the request and to indicate her or his degree of compliance. As predicted, mood had a significant effect on reactions to a request for a favor. Students in the positive-mood condition evaluated the request most favorably, those in the control condition were somewhat less favorable, and students in the negative-mood condition were the harshest of all in their assessments of the request. Compliance (the number of sheets of paper the student gave to the requestor) showed a similar pattern, being highest among happy students and lowest among sad students. Finally, as predicted, mood effects were larger when a request was rude than when it was polite: Happy people tended to ignore the way a request was worded, and sad people were significantly more responsive to the polite request than to the rude request.

In other research, Forgas (1999a, b) asked a complementary question: Does the mood of the person making a request affect how he or she formulates the request? As in the previous studies, mood was experimentally manipulated. In this case, students were asked to write about a specific event that occurred in their life that made them happy (positive-mood condition) or sad (negative-mood condition). They then were asked to think about three easy and three difficult requests. Easy requests included asking a stranger on the street for the time or asking a clerk for the price of a product in a supermarket. Difficult requests included asking a professor for an extension on an essay and asking a stranger on the street for money for a telephone call. For each situation, the participant was to write the "actual words you would use to make this request." These descriptions were then rated on such dimensions as politeness, friendliness, complexity, and elaboration. As you might imagine, students were more polite when making a difficult request than when making an easy request. You may be surprised to learn, however, that students in a sad mood consistently formulated their requests in a more polite way than did happy participants. Sad students also wrote more complex or elaborate request statements. Forgas suggested that being in a negative mood may bias people toward negative thoughts and so lead them to overestimate the dangers of giving offense, the result being more polite and elaborate requests. In contrast, those in a good mood may have more optimistic and confident thoughts, which would lead them to be more direct and less polite in asking for a favor.

Specific Compliance Techniques

One line of research has investigated the specific techniques people use to gain compliance. Robert Cialdini (2004) studied car salespeople, professional fundraisers, con artists, and others who earn a living by getting people to buy their products or go along with their schemes. He and other social psychologists have identified several important compliance techniques, which are summarized in Table 7–3.

The Foot-in-the-Door Technique. One way of increasing compliance is to induce a person to agree first to a small request. Once someone has agreed to the small action, he or she is more likely to agree to a larger request. This is the **foot-in-the-door technique**. It is used explicitly or implicitly in many advertising campaigns. Advertisers often concentrate on persuading consumers to do something minor that is connected with the product—to use a money-saving coupon at the supermarket or even to send back a card saying that they do not want the product. Advertisers apparently think that any act connected with the product increases the likelihood that the consumer will buy it in the future.

Foot-in-the-Door Technique

First persuade the person to comply with a small request, then make a larger request.

A classic study by Freedman and Fraser (1966) demonstrated this effect. Experimenters went from door to door and told women they were working for the Committee for Safe Driving. They said they wanted the women's support for this campaign and asked them to sign a petition that would be sent to the state's senators. The petition requested the senators to work for legislation to encourage

Table 7–3

Compliance Techniques

Technique	Description
Foot-in-the-door	First, make a small request. When the person complies, make another, larger request.
Door-in-the-face	First, make an unreasonably large request. Then immediately make a more modest request.
Low-ball	First, make a reasonable request. Then, reveal details that increase the costs involved.
That's-not-all	First, make a fairly large request. Then immediately offer a bonus or discount that makes the request more reasonable.
Pique	Make an unusual request that will disrupt the target's refusal script and capture his or her attention.

These members of the Hare Khrisna religion are using a common influence technique—offering a small present (free refreshments) in hopes that passersby will read their materials or make a financial donation. This strategy is based on the norm of reciprocity, the idea that when someone gives us something, we feel obligated to return the favor.

safe driving. Almost all the women agreed to sign. Several weeks later, different experimenters contacted the same women and also other women who had not been approached before. At this time, all the women were asked to put in their front yards a large, unattractive sign that read "Drive Carefully." The results were striking. Over 55 percent of the women who had previously endorsed the petition (a small request) also agreed to post the sign (a relatively large request). In contrast, under 17 percent of the other women agreed to post the sign. Getting the women to agree to the initial small request tripled the amount of compliance for the large request.

Several psychological processes explain the effectiveness of this technique (Burger, 1999). One explanation is based on self-perception theory, which was introduced in Chapter 4. The idea is that in some ways, the individual's self-image changes as a result of the initial act of compliance. In the safe driving experiment, for example, a woman may have thought of herself as the kind of person who does not take social action or, perhaps, who does not agree to things that are asked of her by someone at the door. Once she had agreed to the small request, which was actually difficult to refuse, she may have changed her perception of herself slightly. Once she had agreed to sign a petition, she may have come to think of herself as the kind of person who gets involved or who cares about safe driving. Then, when the second request was made, she was more likely to comply than she would have been otherwise.

The desire to view oneself as acting consistently may contribute to the foot-in-the-door effect: If I am the kind of person who cares about safe driving, then I should be willing to put a sign on my front lawn. Research shows that this technique is more effective among individuals who express a strong personal preference for consistency (Guadagno, Asher, Demaine, & Cialdini, 2001). Sample items used to assess preference for consistency are shown in Table 7–4.

Another explanation is that the initial small request may influence how the person interprets the request situation (Gorassini & Olson, 1995). Will Bob interpret Art's request for a donation to the cancer society as another annoying request for a handout or as an opportunity to show his compassion for the less fortunate? If Art uses the foot-in-the door technique, he may first hand Bob a booklet about children with cancer. This small request (accepting a booklet) and Art's comments about the suffering of children with cancer may define the issue and activate Bob's belief that people should care for the less fortunate. This belief then provides the context and interpretation for the larger request for money and may increase the likelihood that Bob will reach for his wallet to help.

Table 7–4

The Desire for Consistency
To assess individual differences in the preference for consistency versus inconsistency, Guadagno, Asher, Demaine, and Cialdini (2001) asked people to indicate their agreement or disagreement with statements similar to these:
I try to appear consistent to others.
I prefer my close friends to be predictable.
I admire people who are predictable and consistent.
It doesn't bother me if people think I'm inconsistent. (scored in reverse)

A third commitment explanation is that people who agree to a small request become involved and committed to the issue itself, to the behavior they perform, or perhaps simply to the idea of taking some kind of action. All of these processes may operate simultaneously to determine an individual response to a foot-in-the-door request.

Door-in-the-Face Technique

First ask for a large request, then make a smaller request.

The Door-in-the-Face Technique. Sometimes a technique opposite to the foot-in-the-door also works. Asking first for a very large request and then making a smaller request can increase compliance to the small request. This approach is sometimes called the **door-in-the-face technique**, because the first request is typically so outrageously large that people might be tempted to slam the door in the requester's face. In one study, people were asked to volunteer time for a good cause (Cialdini et al., 1975). Some were asked first to give a huge amount of time. When they refused, as almost all did, the researcher immediately said that then perhaps they might agree to a much smaller commitment of time. Other participants were asked to give only the smaller amount of time, whereas a third group was given a choice between the two. The results were striking. In the small-request-only condition, 17 percent of participants agreed. In the choice condition, 25 percent complied with the smaller request. However, when participants had first turned down a large request, 50 percent complied with the smaller request.

This effect is familiar to anyone who has ever bargained about the price of a used car or been involved in negotiations between a labor union and management. The tactic is to ask for the moon and then settle for less. The more you ask for at first, the more you expect to end up with eventually. The idea is that when you reduce your demands, the other person thinks you are compromising and the amount seems smaller. In a compliance situation, such as asking for money for charity, the same technique might apply. Five dollars doesn't seem like so much when the organization initially asked for a hundred dollars.

Clearly, both the foot-in-the-door and the reverse tactic work at times, but we do not yet know when each of them is most effective. Both seem to work best when the behavior involved is prosocial, that is, when the request is to give money or to help a worthwhile cause. One difference seems to be that the door-in-the-face technique works when the smaller request follows the larger request immediately and is obviously connected. The foot-in-the-door technique works even when the two requests are seemingly unconnected.

The Low-Ball Technique. Consider how likely you would be to agree to the following requests. In one case, a researcher calls you on the phone and asks you to participate in an experiment scheduled for 7:00 A.M. In a second case, a researcher calls and asks you to participate in a study. Only after you agree to participate does the researcher inform you that the study will be scheduled for 7:00 A.M.. When Robert Cialdini and his associates (1978) compared these two procedures, they found that the second approach was much more effective. When students were told from the outset that an experiment would be conducted early in the morning, only 25 percent agreed to participate and showed up on time. In contrast, when the time of the study was initially concealed, 55 percent of students agreed to the request, and almost all of them actually showed up for the early-morning appointment. Once having agreed to participate, few people backed out of their agreement when they were informed about the time of day.

This tactic, in which a person is asked to agree to something on the basis of incomplete information and is later told the full story, is called the **low-ball technique**. Essentially, the person is tricked into agreeing to a relatively attractive proposition, only to discover later that the terms are actually different from those expected. This technique appears to work because once an individual has made an initial public commitment to a course of action, he or she is reluctant to withdraw, even when the ground rules are changed (Burger & Cornelius, 2003). Although this technique can be effective, it is clearly deceptive. To protect consumers from unscrupulous salespersons, laws have been enacted to make low-balling illegal in several industries, such as automobile dealerships.

Low-Ball Technique

Obtain agreement with a modest request, then reveal hidden costs to the request.

The That's-Not-All Technique. Consider this situation: A salesperson describes a new microwave oven to a potential customer and quotes a price. Then, while the customer is mulling over the decision, the salesperson adds, "But that's not all. Today only, we're having a special deal. If you buy the microwave now, we'll give you a five-piece set of microwave dishes at no additional cost." In actuality, the dishes always come with the oven, but by presenting the dishes as a "special deal" or as something "just for you," the salesperson hopes to make the purchase even more attractive. The essence of this "that's-not-all" technique is to present a product at a high price, allow the customer to think about the price, and then improve the deal either by "adding" a product or by lowering the price.

In a series of experiments, Burger (1986) demonstrated the potential effectiveness of this **that's-not-all technique**. In one study, experimenters held a psychology-club bake sale on campus. At random, half the people who stopped at the table and asked about the cupcakes were told that they could buy a prepackaged set including one cupcake and two cookies for 75 cents. In this control condition, 40 percent of those who inquired actually purchased a cupcake. In the that's-not-all condition, people who inquired were first told that the cupcakes were 75 cents each. A moment later, they were told that actually, they would get not only the cupcake but also two cookies for the 75-cent price. In this that's-not-all condition, 73 percent of people bought a cupcake, a substantially higher proportion than in the control condition.

That's-Not-All Technique

Make a deal and then improve the offer.

Pique Technique

Making an unusual request to disrupt the target's refusal script.

The Pique Technique. Another compliance technique has been proposed based on the idea that people sometimes turn down requests without thinking much about them. In many cities today, pedestrians are often approached by panhandlers asking for money. Many pedestrians, weary from repeated requests, routinely avert their gaze and continue on their way, relying on what might be called a mindless refusal script. Without giving it much thought, they turn down the panhandler's request for assistance.

Michael Santos and his colleagues (1994) reasoned that to be successful in this situation, a panhandler must somehow disrupt the pedestrian's refusal script and capture his or her attention. A successful request should somehow pique the target's interest and consequently increase the chances of compliance with the request for a handout. To study this so-called **pique technique**, college women confederates posed as panhandlers and approached adult pedestrians in Santa Cruz, California. Sometimes the panhandler made a typical request: "Can you spare a quarter?" or "Can you spare any change?" In the pique condition, however, the panhandler made a novel request: "Can you spare 17 cents?" or "Can you spare 37 cents?" As the researchers predicted, pedestrians were significantly more likely to give money in response to an unusual request than to the typical request, and the total amount of money given in response to novel requests was higher. Apparently the unusual request piqued the interest of the targets and interfered with the

To be effective, a panhandler's request for money must pique the interest of passersby. How effective do you think this man will be?

WHAT A COINCIDENCE! HOW INCIDENTAL SIMILARITY AFFECTS COMPLIANCE

If your best friend asked you to read a term paper and give him feedback on it, you might agree readily without giving the request much thought. After all, friends are expected to help each other from time to time. But what if the same request came from a woman you just met? Recent research suggests that the stranger may be successful if she can get you to engage in mindless, unsystematic processing of her request—essentially, leading you to treat her like a friend. (You'll remember that we first introduced the idea of such mental shortcuts or cognitive heuristics in Chapter 3 and also discussed heuristic processing of information in Chapter 5.)

In a series of studies, Burger and his associates (2004) demonstrated that incidental similarity can substantially increase compliance. In one study, women participants met a person who was ostensibly another participant in the study. In reality, she was a confederate of the researchers. As an incidental part of the study, the participant learned the woman's birthdate. In a similarity condition, the two women had identical birthdays. In a control condition, they had different birthdates. Later, the woman asked the naive participant for a favor: "I wonder if you could read this eight-page essay for me and give me one page of written feedback on whether my arguments are persuasive and why?" Would the minor similarity manipulation make a difference in compliance? In fact, it did. In the control condition, only 34 percent of participants complied with the request, but in the similarity condition, 62 percent complied.

In subsequent studies, the researchers manipulated other types of incidental similarity, such as having the same first name or the same unusual type of fingerprint. Regardless of how similarity was created, it was associated with increased compliance. For example, participants donated twice as much money to charity when requested to do so by a person with their own first name as by a person whose name differed from theirs. The researchers explain these findings as resulting from relatively mindless, heuristic processing of the request (Burger et al., 2004, p. 41): "This research paints a picture of cognitively thrifty individuals relying on relatively effortless shortcuts." If, by coincidence, a person is like you in some minor way, you may invoke the "I say yes to people like this" heuristic and treat them as you would a friend. Although this type of mental shortcut can help us to process information efficiently, it can also make us vulnerable to shrewd salespeople who may play on trivial similarities to boost the effectiveness of their sales pitch. As one example, Burger and his associates noted that some automobile dealers may try to match customers to salespeople with similar attributes, such as age or a regional accent.

mindless refusal script of the pedestrians. The novel requests may also have increased liking or sympathy for the person making the unusual request. The Research Highlight for this chapter considers how similarity can be caused to gain compliance.

Resisting External Pressure

Although external pressure can increase compliance, there are limits to the effectiveness of these tactics. Savvy consumers who understand influence strategies are able to resist high-pressure sales clerks. Many people turn down panhandlers, regardless of the cleverness of their request. In wartime, heroic soldiers refuse to divulge secret information even when cruelly tortured, putting commitment to principle above personal safety. Influence attempts do not always produce the desired effects.

Reactance Theory

When our sense of freedom is threatened, we may restore it by refusing to comply.

Sometimes too much pressure may actually cause a person to do the opposite of what the influencer wants. Brehm (1966) called this phenomenon "reactance." The basic idea in **reactance theory** is that people attempt to maintain their personal freedom of action. When this freedom is threatened, they do whatever they can to reinstate it. If an individual perceives an influence attempt as a threat to freedom of action, the person protects this freedom by refusing to comply or by doing the opposite of what is requested.

A study of alcohol consumption illustrates this point. The researchers reasoned that a very strongly worded antidrinking message might be perceived as a threat to personal freedom and so be less effective than a milder antidrinking message (Bensley & Wu, 1991). This might be especially true for heavy drinkers who consume alcohol on a regular basis. To test this idea, the researchers compared the impact of two messages. A very strong message emphasized that there is "conclusive evidence" of the harm of drinking and that "any reasonable person must acknowledge these conclusions." A more moderate message said that there is "good evidence" of the harm of alcohol and that "you may wish to carefully consider" these findings. In a first study, students read one of the two messages and then indicated how much alcohol they intended to drink during the next few days. As predicted, students who read the strong message intended to drink more than students who read the moderate message. In a second study, college men who were fairly heavy alcohol drinkers actually consumed more beer after exposure to a strong antidrinking message than after exposure to a moderate message. It appears that, at least in the United States, when people are told they "must" do something, they tend to assert their independence by refusing to comply.

OBEDIENCE TO AUTHORITY

In this final section, we take a closer look at one of the six bases of power: obedience to legitimate authority. In some social situations, we perceive one person or group as having the legitimate authority to influence our behavior. The government has a right to ask citizens to pay taxes; parents have a right to ask their children to wash the dinner dishes; and medical personnel have the right to ask us to take off our clothes for a physical exam. In wartime, generals expect soldiers to obey orders, and they severely punish disobedience. In these cases, social norms permit those in authority to make requests and dictate that subordinates should obey them.

Obedience is based on the belief that authorities have the right to make requests. Research shows that people are more likely to defer to authorities such as an employer or a religious leader if they receive benefits from belonging to the group or organization (Tyler, 1997). Compliance with authorities is also increased when people believe they are treated fairly, trust the motives of the authorities, and identify with the group or organization (Huo, Smith, Tyler, & Lind, 1996).

Crimes of Obedience

In many cases, we agree with the policies of those in charge and obey orders willingly. But what happens when the demands of authorities conflict with our own beliefs and values? Do we follow our conscience and risk punishment, or do we go along with the request of the authority? Herbert Kelman and Lee Hamilton (1989) used the term "crimes of obedience" to describe immoral or illegal acts that are committed in response to orders from an authority. When soldiers obey orders to torture or kill unarmed civilians, they are engaging in crimes of obedience. Less extreme forms of criminal obedience are more commonplace. Examples include employees who carry out orders of corporate executives that violate the law and political leaders who ask their subordinates to engage in unethical campaign practices. Social psychologists have extensively investigated this sort of obedience.

For many people, the mass murder of European Jews by the Nazis is a tragic and compelling case study in obedience to authority. Before World War II, nearly 9 million Jews lived in Europe. The European Jewish community had a long tradition of culture, artistic and intellectual achievement, and religious devotion. When Adolf Hitler and the Nazi Party came to power in Germany in 1933, they contended that the Aryan race was superior to such "mongrel races" as the Jews and the Gypsies, and that Europe needed to be racially purified. Within a few years, the Nazi regime began to arrest and imprison Jews in Germany. By 1939, when Germany invaded Poland, hundreds of thousands of Jews were already in concentration camps. Soon thereafter, Nazi officials began secretly exchanging memos on "a final solution to the Jewish problem." Under the effective management of Adolf Eichmann, a dedicated career bureaucrat, Jews throughout Europe were systematically rounded up and shipped to concentration camps, where they were starved, gassed, or shot. By 1945, six million European Jews had died, along with many Gypsies, homosexuals, and political dissidents.

At the end of the war, Eichmann fled to Argentina. In 1961, he was captured by Israeli investigators and taken to Israel to stand trial for murder. His defense was that he was not personally responsible for the deaths of the Jews because he had simply been following orders. The court rejected this argument, found Eichmann responsible, and sentenced him to death. The Eichmann defense has come to stand for the claim that a person is justified in committing terrible actions because he or she is "just following orders."

The virtual annihilation of the European Jewish community could not have happened without the cooperation of thousands of ordinary citizens—bureaucrats, soldiers, janitors, doctors, railroad workers, and carpenters. Why did so many people comply with the Nazi regime? Did their compliance emerge from pathological characteristics of the German people? Or more frighteningly, did following orders arise out of the normal operation of everyday social processes, such as simple obedience to authority? Social psychologists have used scientific methods to seek answers to these questions.

The Milgram Experiments

In the 1960s, Stanley Milgram (1963, 1974) designed a series of laboratory experiments to understand the issues involved in obedience to authority. Because Milgram's work has become an enduring classic in social psychology (Blass, 2000), we describe it in some detail. Milgram began his research by placing newspaper ads asking for men to participate in a psychology study. The volunteers were scheduled in pairs and were told that the purpose of the study was to investigate the effects of punishment on learning. One of them was selected by chance as the "learner" and the other as the "teacher." The teacher's job was to read aloud pairs of words that the learner was supposed to memorize. Each time the learner made a mistake, the teacher was to administer a punishment.

The teacher sat in front of a large, impressive "shock machine" containing a long series of levers, each labeled with the amount of shock it would deliver. The range was from 15 to 450 volts. Above the numbers representing voltage were labels describing the severity of the shock such as "Slight," "Extreme Intensity Shock," and "Danger: Severe Shock."

The learner was put in a chair in another room. His arm was strapped down to the chair and electrodes were taped to his arm. He could not be seen by the teacher or anyone else; they communicated entirely by intercom. Before the testing began, the learner mentioned that he had a slightly weak heart. He was

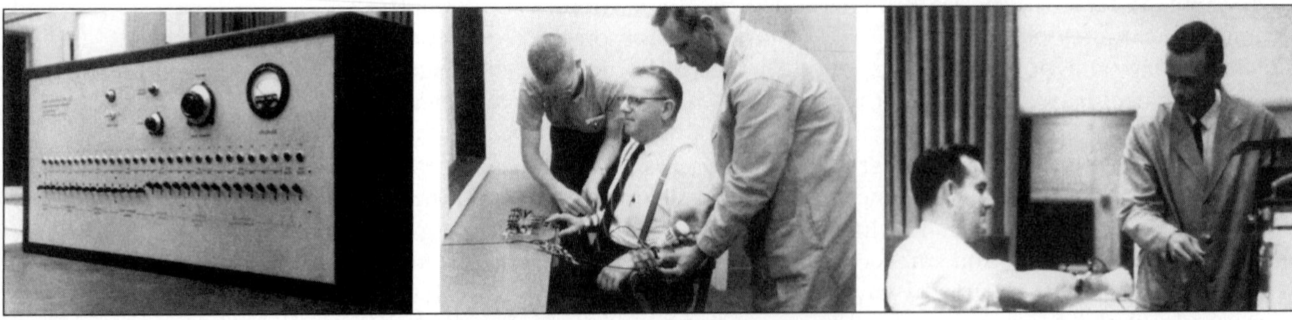

The Milgram study of obedience to legitimate authority. Left: the "shock machine." Middle: the "learner" being strapped to a chair. Right: the researcher giving instructions to the "teacher."

Table 7–5

Experiment 1 in Milgram's Obedience Studies

Shock Level	Percentage of Subjects Obeying the Experimenter's Orders
Slight to very strong shock (0–240 volts)	100%
Intense shock (255–300 volts)	88%
Extreme intensity shock (315–360 volts)	68%
Danger: Severe shock (375–420 volts)	65%
"XXX" (435–450 volts)	65%

Note: In a condition where the teacher and learner were in separate rooms, 65 percent of subjects went all the way to administer the strongest level of shocks.

Source: Data adapted from Milgram (1974, p. 35).

assured by the experimenter that the shocks were not dangerous. Then the experimenter gave the teacher a sample shock, to give him some idea of what the shocks he would be delivering felt like. It was actually fairly severe and hurt considerably, but the teacher was told it was a mild shock.

During the testing, the learner made a number of errors. Each time, the teacher told him he was wrong and delivered a shock. Whenever a shock was given, the learner grunted. As the level of shock increased, the learner's reactions became increasingly dramatic. He yelled, begged the teacher to stop shocking him, pounded the table, and kicked the wall. Toward the end, he simply stopped answering and made no response at all. Through all this, the experimenter urged the teacher to continue: "Please continue," "The experiment must go on," "It is necessary for you to continue." The subject was assured that the responsibility was the experimenter's, and not his.

In these circumstances, a large number of subjects dutifully delivered supposedly severe electric shocks. These results are summarized in Table 7–5. All 40 subjects delivered the 300-volt shock, and 65 percent continued to the final 450-volt level. They did this even though the person they were shocking screamed for mercy, had a heart condition, and was apparently experiencing great pain. In reality, of course, the "learner" was a confederate of the experimenter and did not receive any shocks. All responses, including errors, grunts, and groans, were carefully rehearsed and then tape-recorded to make them identical for all subjects. The "teacher," however, had no way of knowing that the situation was staged.

In a series of 18 studies, Milgram (1965, 1974) identified conditions that increase or decrease obedience. Figure 7–2 summarizes Milgram's findings. Situations that made individuals feel more responsible for their own actions or that emphasized the suffering of the victim reduced the amount of obedience. For example, bringing the victim closer to the subject substantially reduced obedience. Obedience was greatest when the victim was in another room and could not be heard or could be heard only through an intercom. Obedience decreased when the victim was in the same room, and it dropped still more when the subject had to touch the victim to administer the shock. Reminding subjects of their own personal responsibility for their actions also reduced the number of shocks they administered (Tilker, 1970).

Milgram found that the physical presence of the experimenter also made a difference. Obedience was greatest when the experimenter was in the same room with the subject and decreased if the experimenter communicated by phone from another room or simply left tape-recorded instructions. It was harder to disobey the authority figure if he was closely monitoring the subject's behavior. Finally, in other variations of the experiment, subjects administered shocks as part of a

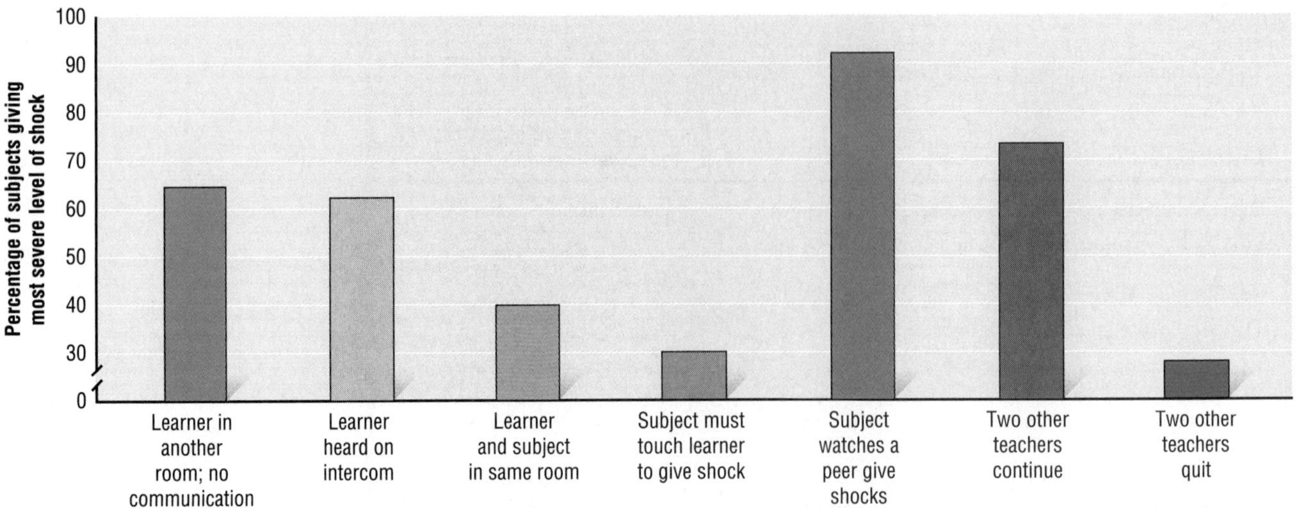

Figure 7–2 In the Milgram studies, variations in experimental conditions affected the percentage of participants who completed the entire sequence of shocks as the experimenter ordered. When the suffering of the learner was made more salient, obedience to authority decreased. The presence of peers who obeyed the experimenter increased the subject's level of obedience; defiant peers reduced obedience.

Source: Data from Milgram (1974).

group of teachers. (In reality, only one of the teachers was a naive subject.) When the real subject merely watched as peers administered shocks, 93 percent of subjects obeyed the experimenter fully. In contrast, when two defiant peers (actually confederates) stopped administering shocks early in the experiment, 90 percent of subjects also stopped. The behavior of peers proved a powerful force that could support—or defy—the authority of the experimenter.

Participants in the Milgram studies often experienced considerable stress. Some began to sweat; others broke out into nervous laughter or stuttered. They often pleaded with the experimenter to end the study. The participants were not callous about the situation; rather, they experienced great conflict. They felt enormous pressures from the situation and from the experimenter to continue. But they were also concerned about the welfare of the victim and about their personal responsibility for inflicting pain. As long as subjects could shift responsibility to the experimenter and minimize in their own minds the pain the victim was enduring, obedience was high. To the extent that they felt personally responsible and were aware of the victim's pain, they were less obedient.

No one anticipated the levels of obedience that Milgram observed. To demonstrate this point, Milgram (1974) described his procedures in detail to psychiatrists, college students, and middle-class adults. Virtually everyone predicted that subjects would quickly stop giving shocks once the learner protested. The psychiatrists predicted that most subjects would not go beyond 150 volts when the victim first demanded to be let go, and that only 1 person in 1,000 would administer the highest level of shock on the board. One contribution of this research was to show that even experts could not accurately predict what subjects would actually do in the powerful situation created in Milgram's laboratory.

Milgram interpreted his findings as showing that "normal" people can be led to perform destructive acts when exposed to strong situational pressure from a legitimate authority: "Men who are in everyday life responsible and decent were seduced by the trappings of authority . . . and by the uncritical acceptance of the experimenter's definition of the situation into performing harsh acts" (Milgram, 1965, p. 74). Miller (1986) called this the "normality thesis"—the idea that evil acts are not necessarily performed by abnormal or "crazy" people. Rather, average individuals who see themselves as mere agents in an organization, carrying out the orders of those in command, can behave in destructive ways. The Milgram studies are a compelling reminder of the power of social situations to influence human behavior (Cialdini & Goldstein, 2004).

Although the pressures to obey legitimate authorities are strong, individuals do not inevitably obey. In Chapter 12, we describe the actions of Christians who risked their lives to shelter Jews from Nazi persecution. What enabled these individuals to resist Nazi policies, and more generally, how can we account for principled resistance to authority? Several factors seem to make a difference. First, obedience is reduced when the suffering of the victims is highly salient. Second, obedience is reduced when an individual is made to feel personally responsible for his or her actions. Third, people are more likely to resist authority when others in the situation disobey. Fourth, encouraging individuals to question the motives, expertise, or judgment of authorities can also reduce obedience.

The Ethics of Obedience Research

Milgram's research sparked an unprecedented debate about the ethics of psychological research. Diana Baumrind (1964) severely criticized Milgram for exposing participants to psychological distress, embarrassment, and loss of dignity. She suggested that Milgram did not take seriously enough how subjects reacted to his study, and she questioned whether the debriefing following the experiment was able to restore the subjects' psychological well-being. She worried that in the long run, those who participated in Milgram's research may have suffered a loss of self-esteem and that the deception used in the study may have reduced participants' trust in authorities.

Milgram (1964) offered a strong defense of his research. He emphasized that the study was not ultimately harmful to the subjects. He explained the detailed and thoughtful nature of the explanations given to participants at the end of the experimental session. He also noted that a 1-year follow-up of participants found no evidence of long-term psychological harm. Indeed, most subjects expressed positive feelings about the research. Milgram also emphasized the value of his research. Neither he nor his colleagues had expected the high levels of obedience they found, and so important new information about human behavior was provided.

Psychological science has weathered the storm created by the Milgram controversy and has learned a good deal in the process (Miller, 1986). Today, psychologists are much more aware of the potential risks of psychological research. In addition, as we noted in Chapter 1, the U.S. government has established strict guidelines for the protection of human research participants. An important part of current procedures is that research projects must be evaluated in advance by a panel of experts, so that an individual researcher can no longer decide that a study is ethically sound. It is doubtful that the Milgram studies would gain approval today. Baumrind (1964), among others, would see this as a victory. Other psychologists would argue that the important information gained from the Milgram studies made them ethically justifiable. Do you think that the risks to Milgram's subjects were outweighed by the benefits gained from the research?

Summary

1. Conformity is the tendency to change one's beliefs or behaviors in ways that are consistent with group standards.
2. Classic studies by Sherif on the autokinetic effect and by Asch on line judgments showed that individuals will often conform to group norms in making both ambiguous and clear-cut perceptual judgments. People conform for two main reasons: to be right (informational influence) and to be liked (normative influence).
3. People are most likely to conform when the group is unanimous and when they feel strong commitment to the group. The size of the group also affects conformity. People who score high on a measure of the desire for individuation are less likely to conform than are low scorers. Conformity is significantly

affected by cultural values of individualism and collectivism.

4. A forceful minority can sometimes change the position of the majority in a group.
5. Compliance occurs when people do what they are asked to do, whether or not they want to do it.
6. We may comply with a request for many different reasons. Raven has identified six bases of power that can produce compliance: rewards, coercion, expertise, information, referent power, and legitimate authority. A special case of legitimate power is the "power of helplessness": A strong cultural norm of social responsibility dictates that we should help those who are less fortunate and less powerful than we are.
7. Researchers have identified several specific compliance strategies, including the foot-in-the-door, door-in-the-face, low-ball, that's-not-all, and pique techniques.
8. Obedience to authority is a particular kind of compliance; it occurs when we believe that the requester has a legitimate right to ask us to do something. In everyday life, obedience to legitimate authority is often adaptive and contributes to smooth social functioning. Sometimes, however, people obey orders that are harmful to others and that violate their own personal beliefs and values.
9. In one of the most famous research programs in social psychology, Stanley Milgram investigated obedience to authority. He found that a majority of "normal" adults would administer severe electric shocks to a helpless victim if ordered to do so by a researcher.
10. Obedience to legitimate authority is lessened when individuals are made aware of the suffering they cause, feel personally responsible for their actions, observe others who disobey the authority, and are encouraged to question the motives and judgment of the authority.

Key Terms

commitment **211**
compliance **215**
conformity **205**
desire for individuation **212**
door-in-the-face technique **222**
foot-in-the-door technique **220**
informational influence **209**
legitimate authority **218**
low-ball technique **223**
minority influence **213**
normative influence **210**
norm of social responsibility **218**
pique technique **223**
reactance theory **224**
that's-not-all technique **223**

In The News

The New Love Connection: Finding Romance Online

In today's fast-paced world, young singles are turning to technology to meet potential dates. It's estimated that 40 million Americans log on to dating Web sites each month. Although some people want a sexual encounter, many are hoping to find a serious love connection. Whatever their goal, users find the Internet an efficient way to meet new people.

Today, online dating companies compete to attract singles willing to pay fees in hopes of finding a partner. Trish McDermott, an executive at *Match.com,* extols the virtues of online dating: "Online you first see matches who meet some core criteria that you deem meaningful and important. You spend time getting to know this person, testing for good communication skills, a sense of humor, shared life goals and other areas of compatibility. Finally, if all seems right, you arrange to meet" (cited in Berney, 2004). *EHarmony* is headed by a psychologist. Their ads emphasize that users are matched on the basis of a free, "scientifically proven" personality test that assesses 29 dimensions of compatibility. *Friendster,* a site popular with younger daters, soared in popularity when it was founded in 2003. It provides opportunities for people to meet through a network of friends and friends of friends. Currently, the online dating world is expanding by catering to particular niche audiences, with Web sites geared toward college students, Jewish and Christian singles, gay men and lesbians, and individuals of every ethnic background.

Although many people like being able to exchange personal information before actually meeting someone, online dating does not offer a cure-all for the woes of conventional dates. Most people post one or more photos online and know that their looks will influence how much interest their personal ad generates. Further, experienced online daters can usually recount annoying stories of disappointing dates who fell far short of their inflated online self-descriptions, used outdated photos, and lied about their age, education, or even marital status.

Commentators have speculated about possible societal reasons for the increasing interest in online dating. Jennifer Egan (2003) notes that Americans are marrying at later ages and so are less likely to meet their spouses at high school or college. Young adults often devote long hours to work, leaving little time for chance encounters with other eligible singles. Although people do sometimes find partners at work, fear of sexual harassment lawsuits may cool passion among coworkers. Equally important, the generation of kids who grew up on the Internet is coming of age, and they find the Internet a comfortable way to make social connections. As New York City single Guillermo Fernandez explained, "You can search hundreds of people while sitting in your pajamas eating Krispy Kremes. You can even find out what the other person's hobbies are without having to ask" (cited in Lee, 2004).

The growing use of online dating services has slowly eroded the stigma that once identified online dating with lonely losers. As Michael McCarthy (2004) recently observed, "Online personals are not just for freaks and geeks anymore. Online dating is coming of age as lonely hearts surf the Net to find Web-savvy partners."

Part Three

Chapter 8

Interpersonal Attraction

From birth to death, relationships are at the core of human experience. Humans are social animals with a powerful need to relate to other people. Belonging to a group enables people to survive physically and psychologically (Fiske, 2004). In this chapter, we examine the basic human tendency to form relationships and the distress that people feel when they are lonely or rejected by others. We consider the special attachment bonds that individuals create throughout life. Next, we review general principles of interpersonal attraction that help explain why we like some people and keep our distance from others. We conclude with an analysis of romantic love.

Focus of This Chapter

THE NEED TO BELONG

The need to form social relationships is part of our human evolutionary heritage (Berscheid & Regan, 2005). Human infants must rely on others to feed and care for them during one of the longest periods of infant dependency in the animal world. From the first day of life, an infant's survival depends on other people. Human infants are born with an innate predisposition to look at faces. They are also equipped with the ability to form emotional bonds with their parents or other caregivers. Throughout life, people seek companions, friends, and lovers. It is not enough merely to be in the presence of others; rather, we want to have close ties to people who care about us. Indeed, some have proposed that the need to belong is a universal element of human nature, similar to hunger and thirst (Baumeister & Leary, 1995). Because social relations are so central to human life, it is not surprising that loneliness and social rejection are major sources of personal distress.

Loneliness

When our social relations lack some important feature, we experience the personal distress of **loneliness**. (Perlman & Peplau, 1998). This deficit may be quantitative: We may have no friends or fewer friends than we want. Or the deficit may be qualitative: We may feel that our relationships are superficial or less satisfying than we would like. Loneliness and aloneness are not the same. Loneliness goes on inside a person and cannot be detected simply by looking at someone. In contrast, aloneness is the objective state of being apart from other people.

Loneliness

Psychological discomfort we feel when our social relations are inadequate.

The pleasure of time spent alone is seen in this young woman's romp at the beach. There is no necessary link between solitude and loneliness.

There is no inevitable link between aloneness and loneliness: We can be happy alone or lonely in a crowd. Nonetheless, people are somewhat more likely to feel lonely when they are by themselves. In a carefully controlled study, Reed Larson and his colleagues (1982) asked teenagers to carry electronic pagers for a week. At random times from early morning to late evening, the researchers activated the pagers, sounding a beep that signaled participants to fill out a short questionnaire describing what they were doing and whether they were alone or with others. It also asked participants about their feelings. In general, teenagers felt lonelier when they were alone than when they were with others. This resulted primarily from being alone on Friday or Saturday night. Adolescents did not feel particularly lonely if they were alone during the week while studying or shopping. However, being alone on a weekend evening, when personal preference and social norms suggested they should be out with friends, often led to loneliness.

The Experience of Loneliness. Loneliness is quite common. In national surveys, roughly one American in four says he or she has felt very lonely or remote from other people in the past 2 weeks (Perlman & Peplau, 1998). Loneliness can range from fleeting twinges of discomfort to severe and persistent feelings of intense misery. Psychologists have developed paper-and-pencil tests, like the one shown in Table 8–1, to assess feelings of loneliness.

Sometimes loneliness is caused by a life change that takes us away from friends and intimate relationships. Situations that commonly cause loneliness include moving to a new town, going away to school, starting a new job, being separated from friends and loved ones, and ending an important relationship. Loneliness can also result when physical illness or a serious accident interferes with social relationships by confining a person to a hospital or reducing physical abilities. Most people eventually recover from situational loneliness and reestablish a satisfying social life, although doing so is obviously more difficult in some situations than in others.

Some people suffer from loneliness for many years, more or less independent of changes in their lives. They are experiencing chronic loneliness. Such an individual might describe himself or herself as a "lonely person," rather than as someone who is in a lonely period of life. Perhaps 10 percent of adults suffer from severe and persistent loneliness. Severe loneliness has been associated with a variety of personal problems, including depression, abuse of alcohol and drugs, and low grades in college. Loneliness is also associated with poorer health and, among

Table 8–1

Sample Questions from the Revised UCLA Loneliness Scale

INSTRUCTIONS: Indicate how often you have felt the way described in each statement using the following scale:

4 indicates "I have felt this way *often*."

3 indicates "I have felt this way *sometimes*."

2 indicates "I have felt this way *rarely*."

1 indicates "I have *never* felt this way."

	Never	Rarely	Sometimes	Often
I lack companionship.	1	2	3	4
There are people who really understand me.[a]	1	2	3	4
I am no longer close to anyone.	1	2	3	4
There is no one I can turn to.	1	2	3	4
I feel part of a group of friends.[a]	1	2	3	4
My social relationships are superficial.	1	2	3	4

[a]These items are scored in reverse so that high scores always indicate greater loneliness.

Source: Russell, Peplau, and Cutrona (1980).

older adults, with increased risk of hospitalization and death (Hawkley, Burleson, Berntson, & Cacioppo, 2003).

Two distinct types of loneliness have been identified (Weiss, 1973). **Emotional loneliness** results from the absence of an intimate attachment figure, such as might be provided for children by their parents or for adults by a spouse or an intimate friend. **Social loneliness** occurs when a person lacks the sense of social integration or community involvement that might be provided by a network of friends or coworkers. It is possible to experience one type of loneliness without the other. Young newlyweds who move from New Jersey to Alaska to seek adventure might not feel emotional loneliness: They have each other. However, they are likely to experience social loneliness until they make friends and develop a sense of belonging to their new community. A widow might feel intense emotional loneliness after the death of her husband but continue to have many social ties to relatives and friends at her church or synagogue (Green, Richardson, Lago, & Schatten-Jones, 2001).

Emotional Loneliness

Loneliness due to lack of an attachment figure.

Social Loneliness

Loneliness due to lack of friends and associates.

Who Is at Risk for Loneliness? No segment of society is immune from loneliness, but some people are at greater risk than others (Brehm, Miller, Perlman, & Campbell, 2002). Certain childhood experiences may predispose individuals to loneliness. For instance, children of divorced parents are at greater risk for loneliness as adults than are children from intact families. Loneliness is associated with greater shyness and with low self-esteem. The person who lacks self-confidence may be less willing to take risks in social situations and may subtly communicate a sense of worthlessness to others. Thus, she or he may set the stage for poor social relationships and for loneliness.

Not surprisingly, people who live with a partner are less likely than others to feel lonely (Pinquart, 2003). This benefit of living together is greater for those who are married than for those who live together without being married. It is interesting, however, that some married people do feel lonely. Married people may be lonely because their marriage is not personally satisfying or because they lack friends and associates outside the marriage.

Loneliness is more common among the poor than among the affluent. Good relationships are easier to maintain when people have the time and money for leisure activities. Loneliness is also related to age. Stereotypes depict old age as a time of great loneliness. However, research shows that loneliness is, in fact, highest among teenagers and young adults and lowest among older people (Perlman, 1990). In one large survey, 79 percent of people under age 18 said they were sometimes or often lonely, compared with only 53 percent of people ages 45 to 54, and 37 percent of those 55 years old and over (Parlee, 1979). Researchers have not yet determined the reason for this age pattern. Young people may be more willing than older adults to talk about their feelings and to acknowledge loneliness. It is also true, however, that young people face a great many social transitions, such as leaving home, living on their own, going to college, or taking a first full-time job—all of which can cause loneliness. As people get older, their social lives may become more stable. Age may also bring greater social skills and more realistic expectations about social relations.

During the journey from birth to death, few people escape the misery of loneliness. But rather than being a sign of weakness, loneliness reflects our human need for social relationships, a need that all people share. That's why the only real cure for loneliness is to establish relationships that meet our basic psychological need for connectedness.

Social Rejection

Across the globe, social exclusion is a widespread and effective form of punishment (Williams, 2001). Many adults use "time out" to punish children, requiring them to spend time alone. Rejection by peers is one of the most painful of childhood experiences and can lead to loneliness even in young children (Asher & Paquette, 2003). Adults also use social rejection to influence and change others' behavior, with varying levels of intensity. One way to get an intimate partner

Social rejection can be a very painful experience.

to do something or to stop doing something is to use the "silent treatment." A more extreme example is the practice of "silencing" that has been used at West Point and other military academies. A cadet who violates a serious rule may be sentenced to months of silencing—being forced to live and eat alone with all conversation prohibited, even to friends.

Ostracism

Experience of being ignored or rejected by others.

There is abundant evidence that **ostracism**, the experience of being ignored or rejected, deprives individuals of a sense of belonging. It is stressful and debilitating. In a recent study, computer users logged on to an experiment posted on an Internet Web site (Williams, Cheung, & Choi, 2001). Participants were asked to visualize themselves as they played a game with two other players that involved throwing and catching a flying disc on their computer screen. In fact, the other "players" were computer generated, and the naive participant was randomly assigned to one of several experimental conditions. With three players in the game, each person should, on average, receive the disc 33 percent of the time. Some participants had this experience of equal inclusion in the game. But other participants were randomly assigned to ostracism conditions. In a partial ostracism condition, players received the disc only 20 percent of the time. In a full ostracism condition, after initial learning trials, the real player was never thrown the disc. Results showed that participants in the ostracism conditions clearly experienced a sense exclusion from the group and showed a decrease in mood and self-esteem.

If ostracism reduces our sense of belonging, it may heighten our attention to information about the social environment that might help us to reconnect with other people. This would be similar to the impact of food deprivation: Hungry individuals think more about food than do individuals who are well fed. The hypothesis that social rejection would lead to greater monitoring of social information was tested in a study with college students (Gardner, Pickett, & Brewer, 2000). In this experiment, students participated in a computer chat room with four other people. In reality, the other "people" were computer-generated confederates. Some participants were randomly assigned to a social acceptance condition in which they received comments from others in the chat room that conveyed liking, agreement, and approval. In contrast, participants in the rejection condition were excluded from the online interaction. At the end of the chat room session, and without being told in advance, participants were unexpectedly asked to remember as many events from the interaction as they could. These events were later coded as social or nonsocial. As predicted, participants who had been rejected remembered significantly more social information than did participants who had been accepted.

A further possibility is that social rejection may lessen the internal controls that enable an individual to keep feelings of anger and aggressiveness in check. Some have suggested, for example, that school shootings, in which students attack and even murder other students and teachers, may be linked to prior experiences of ostracism and bullying. A recent series of experiments found support for this possibility (Twenge, Baumeister, Tice, & Stucke, 2001). Compared to college students who experienced social acceptance, rejected students responded more aggressively to a person who insulted them. Rejected students were not uniformly hostile toward everyone. Instead, they directed their aggression toward someone who criticized them and responded positively toward someone who praised them.

ATTACHMENT IN CHILDREN AND ADULTS

Infants become emotionally attached to the people with whom they interact most often and most lovingly. These usually include the mother and father, although they can be anyone with whom the infant has regular contact (Bowlby, 1988; Cassidy & Shaver, 1999). By **attachment** we mean that an infant responds positively to specific people, feels better when they are close, and seeks them out when frightened.

Attachment

Strong emotional bond to a significant other person.

There are four important features of children's attachment (Collins & Feeney, 2004). The first is *proximity maintenance.* The child seeks to stay close to the attachment figure, either physically or psychologically. The second is *separation distress.* The child experiences increased anxiety and distress during unwanted or prolonged separation from the attachment figure. Third, the attachment figure serves as a *safe haven.* In times of stress, when the child is frightened or confronted with an unfamiliar situation, the attachment figure is a source of comfort and security. Fourth, the attachment figure provides a *secure base,* a sense of safety and security that enables the child to explore the social and physical environment.

All children develop an attachment to their primary caretaker. However, the nature of this attachment bond can vary. Mary Ainsworth and her associates (1978) identified three major styles of attachment between infants and parents:

1. *Secure attachment* occurs when the parent is generally available and responsive to the child's needs. The secure child generally feels supported and secure.
2. *Avoidant attachment* occurs when the parent is generally cool, unresponsive, or even rejecting. Infants may initially "protest" this lack of attention but ultimately become "detached" from the caretaker. The avoidant child may suppress feelings of vulnerability and neediness and become prematurely self-reliant.
3. *Anxious/ambivalent attachment* occurs when the primary caretaker is anxious and does not respond consistently to the infant's needs. The caretaker may sometimes be available and responsive but at other times be unavailable or intrusive. This child may be vigilant for threats and feel anxious or angry.

We can think of a child's style of attachment as an answer to the question, "Can I count on my parent to respond to my needs?" The securely attached child has learned that the answer is yes; the avoidant child, that the answer is no; and the ambivalent child, that the answer is maybe.

Because of the crucial survival value of relationships for human infants, it is likely that the capacity to form attachment bonds is part of our human evolutionary heritage. Human infants are helpless creatures who need to be cared for, protected, fed, and kept warm. When children are old enough to move around, it is important that they not wander too far from their parents because they might put themselves in danger or get lost. Attachment was adaptive in human evolution because it ensured that children would get the attention they needed to survive.

During infancy, babies form strong attachments to their parents.

Work on infant attachment supports the idea that the tendency to form relationships is, at least in part, biologically based. As a species, humans are disposed to form emotional attachments to those with whom they interact regularly and to feel more comfortable and secure in the presence of these familiar people. The capacity for emotional attachment that first appears in infancy continues throughout life.

Adult Romantic Attachment

Social psychologists have found that the attachment theory perspective is useful in understanding the social relationships of adults. In an early analysis, Cindy Hazan and Phillip Shaver (1987) identified several ways that adult love relationships are similar to infant attachments. Both infants and adult lovers typically show intense fascination with the other, distress at separation, and efforts to maintain proximity and to spend time together. Like infant attachments, adult romantic bonds are believed to have a biological origin: "Romantic love is a biological process designed by evolution to facilitate attachment between adult sexual partners who, at the time love evolved, were likely to become parents of an infant who would need reliable care" (Hazan & Shaver, 1987, p. 423).

Adult romantic attachments are also similar in form to the three types of infant attachment. Several studies have found adults, like children, can be categorized as secure, avoidant, or anxious/ambivalent. The proportion of adults classified into each of the three attachment types is fairly similar across studies and is roughly comparable to the proportion of infants typically found in each group. For example, research using a large nationally representative sample of Americans found that a majority of adults (59 percent) were currently securely attached, roughly 25 percent were avoidant, and 11 percent were anxious/ambivalent (Mickelson, Kessler, & Shaver, 1997). Of course, there are also differences between the attachment of infants and that of adults. Adult attachments are typically reciprocal: Each partner not only receives care but also gives care in return. The relationship between infant and adult is not reciprocal in this sense. Another difference is that adult attachments are usually formed between peers. Finally, adult attachments often involve sexual attraction.

An important idea is that a child's earliest love relationships with parents may influence the way he or she approaches romantic involvements in adulthood (Reis et al., 2000). For example, a securely attached child may come to expect that people will be generally trustworthy, responsive, and caring. These beliefs are known as a person's **working model** of relationships. As an adult, this person may also show a secure style of attachment to romantic partners and form satisfying and long-lasting relationships. In contrast, an anxious/ambivalent child might become an adult who seeks love but fears rejection. An avoidant child might become an avoidant adult who fears intimacy and distrusts other people.

Working Model

Beliefs about whether other people are trustworthy, responsive, and caring.

Of course, attachment styles can change as a person has new life experiences. For example, a rewarding relationship during adolescence may enable a person who was insecurely attached as a child to develop a more trusting working model of relationships and to learn to form secure attachments with peers. Evidence for the continuity of attachment style over time comes from a longitudinal study that followed individuals from ages 1 to 21 (Waters, Merrick, Albersheim, & Treboux, 1995). When no major attachment-related event had occurred, such as the death of a parent, parental divorce, or physical abuse, most participants (72 percent) had the same attachment style as young adults that they did as infants. In contrast, when individuals had experienced a negative relationship event, only 44 percent showed the same pattern of attachment. A recent meta-analysis of more than 20 longitudinal studies found a moderate degree of stability in attachment patterns over time (Fraley, 2002).

There is growing evidence that attachment styles affect the quality of adult romantic relationships (Collins & Feeney, 2004). Summarizing results of studies using college students and other adult samples, Brennan and Shaver (1995) painted this portrait of the three groups:

> *Secure Adults.* These adults are comfortable with intimacy and see themselves as worthy of receiving care and affection from others. They describe

themselves as finding it relatively easy to get close to others and say they seldom worry about being abandoned. Secure adults tend to describe their most important love relationship as especially happy, friendly, and trusting. They tend to share their ideas and feelings with a partner. Secure adults are also more likely than others to describe their parents in positive terms—as caring, fair, and affectionate, and as having a good marriage.

Avoidant Adults. These adults report being somewhat uncomfortable getting close to others or trusting a romantic partner completely. In describing their most important love relationship, avoidant adults note emotional highs and lows, jealousy, and fear of intimacy. Avoidant adults tend to deny their attachment needs, view the ending of a romantic relationship as inconsequential, and focus more on work. They place great value on independence and self-reliance. They are less personally revealing to partners and (among college students) are more likely to engage in casual sexual encounters. Compared to secure adults, avoidant individuals tend to describe their parents as more demanding, critical, and uncaring.

Anxious/Ambivalent Adults. These adults seek intimacy but worry that others won't reciprocate their love. Anxious/ambivalent people describe their most important love relationship as involving obsession, desire for reciprocation, emotional highs and lows, and extreme sexual attraction and jealousy. They are more likely to fall in love at first sight and to feel unappreciated by romantic partners and coworkers. Compared to secure adults, anxious/ambivalent people tend to describe their parents as more intrusive and demanding, and their parents' marriage as unhappy.

Securely attached people tend to have more satisfying, committed, close, and well-adjusted relationships than do avoidant people. In one study, college students kept daily diaries of all their social interactions for an entire week (Tidwell, Reis, & Shaver, 1996). In general, secure individuals reported high levels of intimacy, enjoyment, and positive emotions in their contacts with other-sex people. Avoidant participants reported less intimacy and less enjoyment; they also reported feeling more tense, worried, and bored in their other-sex interactions.

Attachment style may also affect the way romantic partners behave toward each other. An illustrative study examined how dating couples react when the woman is confronted with a stressful situation (Simpson, Rholes, & Nelligan, 1992). Dating couples were brought into the laboratory, and a questionnaire measure of attachment style was obtained. Next, each woman was told that she would be "exposed to a situation and set of experimental procedures that arouse considerable anxiety and distress in most people. Due to the nature of these procedures, I cannot tell you any more at the moment" (p. 437). The woman was then shown a darkened, windowless room used for psychophysiological research, where the "procedures" were to take place. However, the researcher explained, the equipment was not ready yet, and so the woman was asked to wait for a few minutes with her boyfriend.

During the next 5 minutes, the interaction between the woman and her boyfriend was recorded. Analyses of these videotapes revealed that as their anxiety about the experiment increased, securely attached women turned to their partners as a source of comfort and reassurance. In contrast, avoidant women withdrew from their partners both emotionally and physically. In response to their girlfriends' growing anxiety, secure men tended to offer more support, and avoidant men offered less.

Other studies have investigated how attachment styles affect the social support and caregiving that dating and married partners provide to each other in times of need (e.g., Feeney & Collins, 2001; Feeney & Hohaus, 2001). In general, securely attached individuals tend to be more responsive to their partner's needs and provide more effective care than do avoidant or anxious individuals.

So far, we have seen that humans have powerful needs for social connection that sensitize us to the threat of social rejection and set the stage for loneliness. Our childhood relationships with caretakers provide our first experiences of attachment and can have enduring consequences for our orientation toward close relationships in adulthood. In the next section, we present research on factors that influence how we select our friends and romantic partners.

LIKING: THE BASES OF INTERPERSONAL ATTRACTION

Why do we like some people and not others? What determines whom we select as our friends? Perhaps the most general answer is that we like people who reward us and who help us to satisfy our needs. One important type of reward is social approval, and many studies have shown that we tend to like people who evaluate us positively. There also tends to be a reciprocity of attraction: We like people who like us (Brehm et al., 2002).

Social Exchange Theory

Analysis of relationships in terms of the rewards and costs people exchange with each other.

Another general principle comes from **social exchange theory**: We like people when we perceive our interactions with them to be profitable, that is, when the rewards we get from the relationship outweigh the costs. Thus, we may like Jonathan because he is smart, funny, and a good athlete, and because these good qualities outweigh his annoying tendency to be late. Social exchange theory also emphasizes that we make comparative judgments, assessing the profits we get from one person against the profits we get from another. This social exchange perspective is considered in more detail in Chapter 9.

With these general principles in mind, we now turn to research on more specific factors that influence interpersonal attraction. Four important determinants of liking are proximity, familiarity, similarity, and personal qualities of the other individual. As we discuss each of these important factors, we will also note occasional exceptions that differ from the general pattern.

Proximity: Liking Those Nearby

Probably the single best predictor of whether two people will be friends is how far apart they live. If one person lives in Vancouver and the other in New York, or even if they live on opposite sides of the same city, it is unlikely they will be friends. In fact, if two people live only 10 blocks apart, it is much less likely that they will be friends than if they live next door to each other. Proximity is a powerful force in interpersonal attraction.

In the 1950s, a team of social psychologists studied the proximity effect in a large apartment complex known as Westgate West (Festinger, Schachter, & Back, 1950).

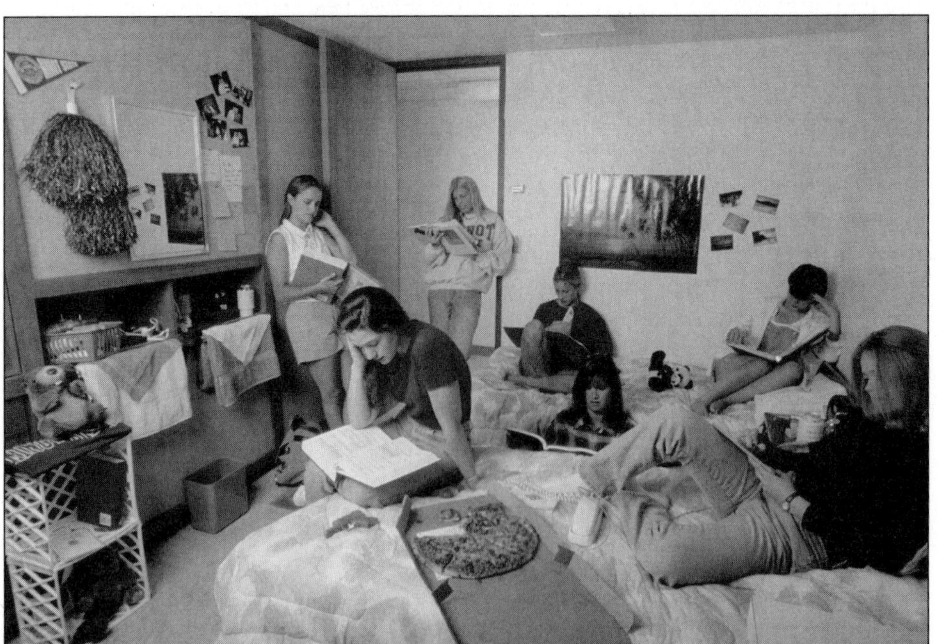

In a dormitory, it's usually easy to get to meet people who live nearby. Proximity is a powerful force in interpersonal attraction.

Westgate West had 17 separate 2-story buildings, each containing 10 apartments (5 on a floor). The apartments were almost identical. More important, residents did not choose where they lived; they were given apartments as the apartments became vacant. As a result, Westgate West came close to being a field experiment with residents randomly assigned to a condition.

All residents were asked, "Which three people in Westgate West do you see socially most often?" The results clearly showed that residents were most friendly with those who lived near them. People on the same floor mentioned their next-door neighbor more often than the neighbor two doors away, and the neighbor two doors away more often than the neighbor at the other end of the hall. Of next-door neighbors, 41 percent were chosen, whereas only 22 percent of those two doors away and 10 percent of those at the end of the hall were chosen. In addition, people who lived on different floors became friends much less often than those on the same floors even when the physical distance between them was roughly the same. The reason was probably that it takes more effort to go up or down stairs than to walk down a hall. Thus, people on different floors were in a sense further away psychologically than those on the same floor. The investigators referred to this as "functional distance," meaning that the probability that people would socialize was determined by the design of the apartment house as well as by actual distance. The closer people lived, as measured by either physical or functional distance, the more likely they were to be friends.

Other research has investigated how the physical design of college dormitories affects social interaction. College dormitories are generally built according to two different designs. One type has rooms located along a long corridor, with social areas and bathrooms shared by all corridor residents. A second type has suites of rooms consisting of several bedrooms located around a common living room, usually with the residents of these bedrooms sharing bathroom facilities. The amount of space available to each resident is approximately the same in both designs. Yet the two designs seem to have different effects on the residents. In one study, Baum and Davis (1980) obtained permission to assign first-year women students randomly to living conditions. To control the environment further, the researchers selected two identical long-corridor floors in the same building. One floor was left as a long corridor; the other floor was modified into smaller units with lounges. The researchers gave questionnaires to dorm residents at the beginning of the school year and at several times during the year. They also made systematic observations of social interaction in the dorm. The results of the experiment were clear. After living in the dorm for several weeks, students in the smaller residential units reported more success in making friends in the dorm and were observed to have more social interactions in lounges and corridors. Smaller residential units are more conducive than are larger units to friendship formation.

Further support for the importance of proximity comes from a study that asked people to describe "memorable interactions," that is, recent instances when they discussed something of personal importance with another person (Latané, Liu, Nowak, Bonevento, & Zheng, 1995). Participants were also asked to indicate the physical distance that separated them and the person involved in each memorable interaction. The results provided strong evidence for the impact of physical distance. Although 10 percent of the memorable interactions described were with people living more than 50 miles away, the great majority occurred with people living close at hand, either in the same residence or within a 1-mile distance. This finding was replicated in three diverse samples from the United States and China.

Explaining the Effects of Proximity. People who are physically close are more easily available than those who are distant. Obviously, we cannot like or be friends with someone we have never met. We choose our friends from people we know. The ready availability of people close by also affects the balance of rewards and costs of interacting, a point emphasized by social exchange theory. It takes little effort to chat with a neighbor or to ask her about bus service to the airport. Even if a neighbor's company is only moderately pleasant, we come by it "cheaply," and so we may find it profitable. In contrast, long-distance relationships require time, planning, and money. When good friends move apart, they often vow to keep in touch regularly. But many find that their contacts dwindle to an occasional birthday card or phone call.

A further explanation of the proximity effect is based on cognitive dissonance theory, introduced in Chapter 5. According to this theory, people strive to maintain harmony or consistency among their attitudes—to organize their likes and dislikes in a balanced, consistent way. It is psychologically distressing to live or work side by side with someone we dislike, and so we experience cognitive pressure to like those with whom we must associate. We are motivated to like those we are connected to and to seek proximity with those we like. For example, suppose you arrive at college to meet your assigned roommate and instantly dislike him or her. To try to reduce cognitive dissonance, you have two options. You can avoid the roommate as much as possible and try to move to another room. Or you can reevaluate the roommate, trying to see some good qualities in order to avoid conflicts and to make the best of the situation. The issue comes down to which is easier to change. Often it is nearly impossible to break off the relationship. Your dorm counselor may insist that you cannot change roommates until the term ends. Therefore, you experience pressure to increase your liking for your roommate.

Other studies have also shown that the mere anticipation of interaction increases liking. In one study, college students agreed to let the researchers organize their dating life for 5 weeks (Berscheid, Graziano, Monson, & Dermer, 1976). The participants were shown videotapes of various people, separated at random into those described as future dates and those described as people they would not date. The prospective dates were liked significantly more. In general, if we know we are going to interact with someone in the future, we tend to play up the person's positive qualities and to ignore or minimize the negative ones. A desire for cognitive consistency motivates us to like our neighbors, our roommates, and others in close proximity.

There are, of course, exceptions to the proximity-liking connection. Sometimes no amount of cognitive reevaluation will convince us that the rude secretary in our office is really nice or that our bratty kid sister is really a little angel. Proximity is most likely to foster attraction when the people involved have similar attitudes and goals. Indeed, when there are initial antagonisms or conflicts between people, increased proximity and contact may actually intensify negative feelings.

Familiarity: Liking Those We See Often

Mere Exposure Effect

Repeated exposure to a person increases our liking for the person.

People we live near or work with become familiar to us, and this familiarity can enhance interpersonal attraction. Indeed, simply being exposed frequently to a person can increase our liking for that person. This **mere exposure effect** was demonstrated by Robert Zajonc (1968, 2001). In one study, Zajonc showed college students pictures of faces. Some faces were shown as many as 25 times, others only once or twice. Afterward, subjects indicated how much they liked each face and how much they thought they would like the person pictured. The results are presented in Figure 8–1. The more often the subjects had seen a face, the more they said they liked it and thought they would like the person. The same result has been found for repeated exposure to actual people. Moreland and Beach (1992) enlisted the aid of four college women who served as confederates in a field experiment. A pretest showed that all the women were rated as equally attractive. In the main study, each woman attended a large lecture class in social psychology, posing as a student in the course. Each woman attended a different number of class sessions: 1 time, 5 times, 10 times, or 15 times during the term. At the end of the term, students in the class were asked to rate each woman, based on a photo shown as a slide. The more often students had seen a woman, the more they thought they would like her.

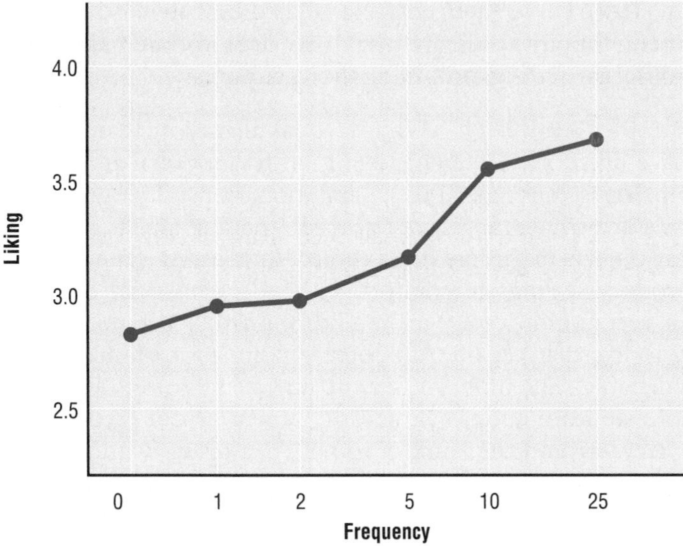

Figure 8–1 **The Association Between Frequency of Exposure and Liking.**

Subjects were shown photographs of different faces, and the number of times each face was shown was varied. The more often the subjects saw a particular face, the more they said they liked the person pictured.

Source: Data from Zajonc (1968).

Another ingenious demonstration of the familiarity effect involves people's reaction to their own faces. Faces are not perfectly symmetrical; the left eye may be a little higher than the right, the smile a little crooked, hair parted on the right instead of the left, and so on. Our friends see our face as it looks to an outside observer. But we see a different face—the mirror image of the one our friends see. For us, the right eye is higher, the part is on the left, and so on.

According to the mere exposure principle, our friends should prefer our face from the perspective they are used to, and we should prefer our mirror image. Research has supported this prediction (Mita, Dermer, & Knight, 1977). Researchers photographed college women and showed these pictures to the women and to their friends. Some pictures were true prints and others were made from reverse negatives (what we would see in the mirror). The women themselves preferred the mirror image (by 68 to 32 percent). Their friends, however,

Because the human face is not perfectly symmetrical, the way we see our own face in the mirror differs subtly from the way other people see us during interaction. The left photo shows a man as his friends view him. The right photo is a "reverse image" that shows the man as he appears to himself in the mirror. Research finds that people like best the face they have seen the most.

preferred the true prints (by 61 to 39 percent). Each liked best the face that she had seen the most often. Empirical research has also demonstrated the mere exposure effect using different settings and in different cultures.

Explaining the Effects of Familiarity. Why does familiarity increase liking? Several explanations have been offered, emphasizing both emotional and cognitive processes (Harmon-Jones & Allen, 2001). Evolutionary psychologists have speculated that humans may have an innate fear of the unfamiliar, because strangers and unfamiliar objects may represent a threat. In contrast, familiar people and things may produce feelings of comfort. Others suggest that repeated exposure improves our recognition of a person, and improved recognition is a helpful step in coming to like that person. As people become more familiar, they also become more predictable. The more we see the new neighbor in our apartment building, the more we learn about her, and the better we can predict how she will behave in the elevator and the laundry room. As a result, we feel more comfortable in her presence. Finally, we may assume that familiar people are similar to ourselves. The study described earlier, in which women attended a social psychology class from 1 to 15 times, addressed this issue (Moreland & Beach, 1992). Students rated women who attended class frequently as more similar to them in personality, background, and plans for the future.

Limits to Mere Exposure. As you might expect, there are limits to the mere exposure effect. Exposure is most effective in enhancing liking for a person or object that is initially perceived as pleasant or at least neutral, but not for one that is initially perceived as negative. To make this point, Zajonc (1968) used the example of repeatedly seeing a particular man in handcuffs. After a while, we become convinced he really is a criminal. Researchers tested this idea by showing subjects pictures of people presented positively (as scientists), neutrally (dressed in a sports shirt), or negatively (in a police lineup). Repeated exposure to positive and neutral pictures increased liking, but it had no effect in the case of negative pictures (Perlman & Oskamp, 1971). Another exception to the familiarity-liking connection occurs when two people have conflicting interests, needs, or personalities. As long as they see little of each other, the conflicts are minimized. They may not particularly like each other, but they have little reason to dislike each other. When contact is increased, however, the conflicts are aggravated. They come to dislike each other even more as a result of frequent contact. A third limitation is that a lot of repetition can cause boredom and satiation (Bornstein, Kale, & Cornell, 1990). There is probably an optimal level of exposure to maximize liking, depending on the people and the situation.

Similarity: Liking People Like Us

Another basic factor in interpersonal attraction is similarity. We tend to like people who are similar to us in attitudes, interests, values, background, and personality (AhYun, 2002). This similarity effect applies to friendship, dating, and marriage. There is much truth in the old adage that "birds of a feather flock together."

In a classic field study, Theodore Newcomb (1961) demonstrated that similarity leads to friendship. He rented a large house near the University of Michigan and offered male undergraduates free housing in return for taking part in his research. Before the students arrived, they filled out questionnaires about their attitudes and values. Newcomb controlled the assignment of rooms so that some roommates had very similar attitudes and other roommates had very different attitudes. By the end of the semester, roommates with similar preacquaintance attitudes generally liked each other and ended as friends; dissimilar roommates tended to dislike each other and did not become friends.

The similarity-liking connection has been the focus of much research. In a series of experiments, Donn Byrne (1971) carefully examined attitude similarity. To rule out other factors that might influence liking, such as appearance or personality, Byrne developed the so-called "phantom-other technique." In a typical study,

Shared interests are an important factor in interpersonal attraction and friendship.

participants fill out questionnaires about their own attitudes. They then read questionnaires allegedly filled out by a stranger. In actuality, there is no other person (hence, the term "phantom other"). Experimenters deliberately write answers to be very similar, moderately similar, or dissimilar to the subject's own answers. Subjects are then asked how much they think they would like the other person. The results of studies using this method have shown that attitude similarity strongly determines liking. The more similar the attitudes are, the greater is the anticipated liking. This effect has been demonstrated with very diverse groups, including children, college students, medical patients, job trainees, and alcoholics.

The importance of similarity extends well beyond attitudes. Similarity in ethnic background, religion, politics, social class, education, and age all influence attraction. For example, studies of elementary and high school students find that friends tend to be of the same race and gender. Friends are also similar in age, year in school, and academic achievement, as well as in patterns of aggressive behavior and social withdrawal (Kupersmidt, DeRosier, & Patterson, 1995). In college, randomly assigned roommates who have similar personalities tend to be more satisfied with their relationship and more likely to room together again the next year than are roommates with differing personalities (Carli, Ganley, & Pierce-Otay, 1991). A recent meta-analysis of 80 studies found consistent evidence for the similarity–attraction link, with a moderate effect size of .51 (AhYun, 2002).

In dating and marriage, the tendency to choose similar partners is called the **matching principle**. It is unusual for an ardent feminist to date a sex-role traditionalist, or for an orthodox Jew to date a fundamentalist Christian. Dating partners and spouses tend to be relatively matched not only in their values and attitudes but also in their physical appearance, social background, and personality. For example, one study of dating couples found that partners tended to resemble

Matching Principle

We tend to date and marry partners who are similar to us in attitudes, values, and background.

each other in age, intelligence, educational plans, religion, physical attractiveness, and even height (Hill & Peplau, 1998). They were also matched in their attitudes about sexual behavior and gender roles. Furthermore, couples who were most similar in background at the beginning of the study were most likely to be together 1 year and 15 years later.

Of course, to say that friends and spouses tend to be matched does not mean that they are necessarily identical in every way. When people of different races, religions, and social groups have a chance to interact and to discover shared values and interests, friendship and love often transcend differences in background.

Interethnic Relationships. Today, more Americans than ever are dating and marrying outside their own ethnic group (Fears & Deane, 2001). About 40 percent of young Americans say they have dated someone of another ethnic group, and 30 percent have had a "serious" relationship. Asian Americans of both sexes and African American men are most likely to have dated someone from another group. Interethnic marriage is also increasing (Saluter, 1996). Currently, there are about 2 million U.S. marriages in which one partner is Latino and the other is non-Latino white. This statistic represents roughly half of all interethnic marriages. Other common interethnic pairings are white/Asian (19 percent) and white/black (11 percent).

Relationships that cut across racial and ethnic lines are not new. However, attitudes toward such relationships have become increasingly accepting. For many years, laws banning interracial marriages were the norm in the United States. In 1967, the U.S. Supreme Court struck down the last of these state laws. In a recent national survey, 70 percent of white Americans approved of interracial marriage, as did 77 percent of Hispanics and 80 percent of blacks (Goodheart, 2004). Another survey asked a representative sample of Americans with a partner of a different ethnicity about their experiences (Fears & Deane, 2001). Most respondents said they had an excellent relationship. Although reporting that they had experienced some discrimination as a biracial couple, most said that their family was supportive of their relationship. Cynthia Vilanueva, an Anglo American married to a Latino American, explained that her husband's family initially had a problem with her ethnicity: "They thought I couldn't learn anything about his background . . . that I couldn't cook. I proved them wrong. Now I'm on a pedestal" (cited in Fears & Deane, 2001, p. A1). Although interethnic couples differ in their cultural background, they are typically similar in age and education. Like the majority of modern romantic couples, they are usually drawn together by shared interests and values.

Explaining the Effects of Similarity. Why is similarity so important for interpersonal attraction? Several mechanisms may be involved (e.g., Aron, 1988; Kalick & Hamilton, 1988). To understand each one, consider why a boyfriend and girlfriend might have similar beliefs about religion:

- ***Selective attraction.*** One possibility is that each person has strong religious views and uses them to screen potential dates. Only similar partners are acceptable; dissimilar others are rejected. This selection effect could occur very early in the initial choice of friends and dating partners, or later on as partners get to know each other better and decide whether to continue the relationship.
- ***Social influence.*** Another possibility is that partners are initially different in their attitudes but gradually persuade each other to change their views. As a result, they may become more similar over time. The mechanism here is one of social influence, in which partners' attitudes change in the direction of greater similarity.
- ***Environmental factors.*** A third possibility is that the relationship is strongly affected by shared environmental factors that lead people with similar attitudes to meet. For instance, students attending a religious college may all have fairly similar views about religion. In this case, their apparent "matching" is

actually an effect of a social environment that limits the pool of potential partners.

In everyday life, the causes of similarity and matching are complex, and several different mechanisms may work together to produce the often observed association of similarity and liking.

Limits to the Similarity Effect. Although similarity usually leads to liking, there are exceptions to this general pattern. Sometimes similarity is threatening. If someone similar to us has a heart attack or experiences some other unfortunate fate, we may worry that we are also vulnerable and so we may prefer to avoid that person (Novak & Lerner, 1968).

Another point is that differences among people are sometimes very rewarding. Few of us want to associate with clones, people who are identical to us in virtually every respect. The joys of friendship include stimulation and novelty—learning about new ideas and coming to appreciate the rich variety of human experiences. We are often more open to the rewards of difference when we feel that the other person likes and accepts us. A feeling of acceptance may be a prerequisite for disregarding differences.

A further advantage of having friends with different interests and skills is that it enables us to pool our shared knowledge in mutually beneficial ways. For example, in planning a group camping trip, it is convenient to have one person who knows about tents and equipment, someone else who can plan meals, and a third person who knows the area and can pick a good campsite. In a traditional marriage, where the wife is the "homemaking expert" and the husband is the "breadwinning expert," the spouses' roles are different but complementary. When we say that "opposites attract," we are often referring to complementary role relationships such as these, where people with different skills and knowledge contribute to a shared enterprise. However, most cases of complementarity require that partners have similar values and goals, such as a desire to spend a weekend camping in the wilderness or shared beliefs about how to organize married life.

In summary, research has shown that similarity, familiarity, and proximity are powerful forces in interpersonal attraction. We have also noted various exceptions to these patterns in order to give a complete account of the processes of interpersonal attraction. But these minor exceptions should not obscure the importance of the general principles involved.

These factors are not only causes of liking, but consequences as well. Proximity causes liking; however, once we like someone, we often take steps to ensure that we will be close to that person in the future. First-year roommates may be thrown together by chance. But if their proximity leads to friendship, they will probably try to live together the following year. Similarity can work in the same way. A longitudinal study followed married couples over 21 years (Gruber-Baldini, Shaie, & Willis, 1995). At the time of the initial testing, spouses were similar in age, education, and mental abilities such as verbal fluency, inductive reasoning, and attitudinal flexibility. Over time, spouses actually became more similar on several measures of mental abilities. As these results indicate, similarity can bring two people together in the first place, but as their relationship continues and they share ideas and experiences, they tend to become even more similar because of their association.

Desirable Personal Attributes: Warmth and Competence

Just what is it that makes us like one person more than another? There is no single answer to this question. Some people find red hair and freckles irresistible; others dislike them intensely. Some of us prize compassion in our friends; others value intelligence. Individuals vary in the attributes they find most attractive in other people. There are also large cultural differences in those personal qualities that are considered socially desirable. For example, in the United States, many people equate feminine beauty with being thin, but other societies consider plump women the most attractive. Researchers have sought to identify some of the general characteristics associated with liking in our U.S. society. Two qualities appear to be particularly important: personal warmth and competence. We feel affection for people who show interpersonal warmth, and we respect people we view as competent (Lydon, Jamieson, & Zanna, 1988; Rubin, 1973).

Warmth. What makes one person seem warm and friendly, whereas another comes across as cold and aloof? We don't yet have a complete answer to this question, but one important ingredient is having a positive outlook. People appear warm when they like things, praise them, and approve of them—in other words, when they have a positive attitude toward people and things. In contrast, people seem cold when they dislike things, disparage them, say they are awful, and are generally critical.

To test this idea, researchers had participants read or listen to interviews in which the interviewee was asked to evaluate a long list of items such as political leaders, cities, movies, and college courses (Folkes & Sears, 1977). Sometimes the interviewees expressed predominantly positive attitudes—they liked most of the politicians, cities, movies, and courses. In other cases, the interviewees expressed mainly negative attitudes. As predicted, participants liked the interviewees more if they were positive rather than negative in their attitudes. The researchers concluded that the explanation lay in the greater warmth communicated by the positive attitude. Other analyses showed that the liking effect was not due to any greater perceived intelligence, knowledge, or similarity of attitudes on the part of the positive interviewees. In addition to saying positive things, people can also communicate warmth by such nonverbal behaviors as smiling, watching attentively, and expressing emotions (Friedman, Riggio, & Casella, 1988).

Competence. In general, we like people who are socially skilled, intelligent, and competent. The particular type of competence that matters most depends on the nature of our relationship with the person: We are attracted to friends who are good conversationalists, to mechanics who are good at fixing cars, and to professors who are knowledgeable lecturers. Competent people are usually more rewarding to be with than inept people.

An illustration of the importance of competence comes from research on being a good conversationalist (Leary, Rogers, Canfield, & Coe, 1986). In a first study, college students gave descriptions of boring versus interesting speakers. Students reported being bored by speakers who talked too much about themselves or about trivial, banal topics. Students also reported being bored by people who were overly passive, tedious, and serious in their interactions. In a second study, students listened to taped conversations designed so that the target speaker was either boring or interesting. Students evaluated the boring speakers quite negatively. Boring speakers were liked less and rated as less friendly, less enthusiastic, less popular, and more impersonal. In contrast, being an interesting conversationalist enhanced a person's likeability.

An exception to the competence-leads-to-liking principle is the case of someone who is a little "too perfect" for comfort. In one study, participants listened to a tape recording of a male student who was trying out for a College Quiz Bowl team (Aronson, Willerman, & Floyd, 1966). In one condition, the candidate gave an outstanding performance and answered nearly every question correctly. In a second condition, the candidate gave a mediocre performance. As an added twist to the experiment, after the tryout was over, the candidate was sometimes heard to spill coffee on his suit.

The results showed the usual competence-leads-to-liking effect: The outstanding candidate was liked better than the mediocre one. However, the outstanding candidate was liked even better when he made a minor blunder than when his performance was flawless. Apparently, spilling coffee served to "humanize" the brainy student and so made him more likeable. In contrast, the blunder only detracted from the evaluations of the mediocre applicant. He was liked less when he spilled coffee than when he didn't.

Fatal Attractions. The personal qualities that initially attract us to someone can occasionally turn out to be fatal flaws in the relationship. A woman who is attracted to a man by his professional success and self-confidence may later find that he is a domineering workaholic. This point has been illustrated in research on so-called "fatal attractions" in college student romances and marriages (Felmlee, Flynn, & Bahr, 2004). In one study, the researcher asked students to think of their most recent romantic relationship that had ended and to list the qualities that had first attracted them to this previous partner (Felmlee, 1995). Common responses, in order of frequency, concerned the partner's physical appearance ("sexy" and "pretty eyes"), having fun with the partner ("a good sense of humor"), and the partner being caring, competent, and having similar interests. Later, students were asked to think, in retrospect, about the qualities they had found least attractive in the partner.

The important point of this research was that some of the attributes that initially attracted the partners eventually drove them apart. For example, one woman was drawn to her ex-boyfriend because of his "I don't care . . . I'll have fun anyway attitude." In retrospect, she reported that his greatest fault was being immature. In another case, a partner's initial "intense interest" was later faulted as a tendency to be jealous and possessive. Competence could also be a liability. One man had been attracted to his ex-girlfriend for her intelligence and confidence but later disliked her "ego." About 30 percent of the breakups students described involved a fatal attraction of some kind. Research has also found that fatal attractions are more common when an individual is drawn to a partner by a quality that is unique, extreme, or different from his or her own.

Physical Attractiveness

Although we are told not to judge a book by its cover, we can hardly avoid forming impressions of people based on their physical appearance (Berscheid & Reis, 1998; Langlois et al., 2000). A great many studies, both in North America and in other parts of the world, have investigated this topic, and they consistently show that beauty does indeed make a difference in social life.

Individuals with disabilities may have to overcome social stereotypes that portray them as unattractive and lonely.

Liking Good-Looking People. Other things being equal, we tend to like attractive people more than their less attractive peers. One reason is the stereotype that attractive people have other good qualities as well (Eagly, Ashmore, Makhijani, & Longo, 1991). Better looking adults are thought to be more socially skilled and friendly, but also more vain and sexually promiscuous. Attractive children tend to be evaluated as more popular than their peers. In fact, there is some evidence that attractive people are somewhat more comfortable in social settings and have more polished social skills than their less attractive peers (Feingold, 1992).

More surprising, attractive adults are also believed to possess qualities that seem irrelevant to physical beauty, such as mental health, dominance, and intelligence (Jackson, Hunter, & Hodge, 1995). For instance, students rated a lecture by a female instructor as more interesting and judged the woman to be a better teacher when she was made up to look attractive rather than plain. At times, we also treat good-looking people more favorably. More attractive adults are more likely to receive help, be accepted by others, or be recommended for a job. Cute children may receive more attention and be given more lenient punishments for misbehavior.

Physical attractiveness is often a factor in dating. In a classic study, Elaine Walster and her colleagues (1966) held a "computer dance" in which college students were randomly assigned to each other as dates for the evening. The researchers secretly made ratings of the physical attractiveness of each male and female participant. At the end of the evening, students were asked to rate how much they liked their assigned partner. People who were rated as more attractive were liked more.

People with physical disabilities are often the targets of stereotypes about physical attractiveness. In one study, college students associated the general category "woman" with such terms as "soft," "lovable," "married," and "intelligent," but they associated "disabled woman" with such terms as "ugly," "lifeless," "crippled," "lonely," and "someone to feel sorry for" (Asch & Fine, 1986). In another study, high school students rated a student with a hearing aid as more introverted, afraid, depressed, and insecure than a nondisabled student (Silverman & Klees, 1989).

Similarly, obese people are often viewed negatively, in part because they are seen as responsible for being overweight (Crandall & Biernat, 1990). The consequences of anti-fat attitudes can be quite harmful, ranging from jokes about fat people to wage discrimination in the workplace. Social attitudes are often especially harsh toward women who are overweight. In one study, college students evaluated an obese woman as less sexually attractive, skilled, and warm than an average-weight woman, but they did not differ in their perceptions of overweight and average-weight men (Regan, 1996). Another study found that heavier college women were less likely than were their slimmer peers to receive financial support from their own parents (Crandall, 1995). Anti-fat prejudice seems to be especially strong in individualistic cultures like the United States and weaker in collectivist cultures like Mexico (Crandall et al., 2001). Similarly, anti-fat attitudes are more negative among Anglo American women than among African American women (Hebl & Heatherton, 1998). A social climate that idealizes thinness in women can contribute to life-threatening eating disorders such as anorexia and bulimia in young women.

Who Is Attractive? To a considerable degree, culture influences standards of physical attractiveness. There are no universal norms about whether it is attractive or repulsive to pierce parts of one's body, to wear clothes that conceal or reveal the body, to dye one's hair or shave it off, to be pleasantly plump or stylishly thin. Fashion trends change and vary around the globe.

Nonetheless, there do seem to be a few features that are consistently associated with attractiveness (Berscheid & Reis, 1998). People tend to agree about who is and who is not physically attractive (Langlois et al., 2000). Agreement is high in ratings of both children's and adults' attractiveness. Furthermore, people who are attractive to others know that they are pretty or handsome (Marcus & Miller, 2003).

Researchers are beginning to understand what makes some faces more attractive than others (Fink & Penton-Voak, 2002). In general, we tend to view "average" faces as more attractive than faces that are atypical. We like faces that are symmetrical. In one study, college students rated the attractiveness of photos of the faces of identical twins. Although the twins looked quite similar, raters assessed the twin with the more symmetrical face as being more attractive (Mealey, Bridgstock, & Townsend, 1999). Beautiful faces seem to be more balanced and well proportioned.

Explaining the Effects of Good Looks. There seem to be several reasons for the association between physical attractiveness and liking. One reason may be that when meeting new people, we pay more attention to physically attractive individuals, especially women, than to their less good-looking peers (Maner et al., 2003). The stereotype that good-looking people have other good qualities as well may also enhance our liking for them. Evolutionary theory provides another explanation. Physical attractiveness may be an important clue to good health and reproductive fitness (Langlois et al., 2000). In other words, a pretty face may be a marker of "good genes." Another reason for liking attractive people is the "radiating effect of beauty." People may find it rewarding to be seen with a particularly attractive person because they think it will enhance their own public image. Michael Kernis and Ladd Wheeler (1981) hypothesized that this radiating effect of beauty occurs when a person is seen with an attractive friend, but not with an attractive stranger.

To test this idea, Kernis and Wheeler designed a laboratory experiment in which participants saw two people, a target person of average attractiveness and a same-sex person of either above-average or below-average looks. As a further variation, these people were sometimes presented as being friends and sometimes as strangers. As predicted, the friends' and strangers' conditions produced opposite results. When the two people were believed to be friends, a radiating effect occurred. The target person was rated as more attractive when seen with a very attractive friend, and as less attractive when seen with a very unattractive friend. However, when the two people were thought to be strangers, a contrast effect occurred. The average-looking target person was rated less favorably when paired with a very attractive stranger. Gender did not affect these patterns: The same results were found regardless of whether the people being evaluated were male or female. Other studies have also shown that both men and women are rated more favorably when they are accompanied by an attractive romantic partner or friend than when they have an unattractive companion (Geiselman, Haight, & Kimata, 1984).

Today, increasing numbers of people are getting acquainted through the Internet. The Research Highlight for this chapter considers whether the Internet facilitates the development of relationships or increases social isolation.

MATE SELECTION

When asked what they seek in a long-term partner or mate, people typically look beyond physical appearance to consider personal qualities that will contribute to compatibility over time. We want a mate who will be warm, kind, and trustworthy. We prize responsiveness and a sense of humor. Competence is also an asset (Fletcher & Simpson, 2000; Sprecher & Regan, 2002).

A recent analysis compared the mate preferences of college students across 6 decades, from the 1930s to the 1990s (Buss et al., 2001). Respondents ranked a wide variety of possible attributes ranging from good looks to dependability. In each time period, young adults gave greatest emphasis to having a mate who is dependable and emotionally mature and who has a pleasing disposition. Relatively little importance was given to having similar political, educational, or religious backgrounds. Several important differences were over time. In recent years, students gave increasing importance to mutual love and attraction. These qualities were ranked 4th by men and 5th by women in the 1930s but moved into first place for both sexes in the 1980s. The importance of education and intelligence also

DOES THE INTERNET BUILD SOCIAL CONNECTIONS OR INCREASE SOCIAL ISOLATION?

In the United States today, more than 50 percent of households are connected to the Internet. Although African Americans and Hispanics still lag behind other groups, their access to the Internet is increasing rapidly (Kraut & Kiesler, 2003). Growing numbers of people rely on e-mail not only for business but also to keep in touch with friends and relatives. Chat rooms are growing in popularity, and computer-based groups can connect people in distant corners of the world who share a similar interest. Just what impact does the Internet have on modern social life?

Critics worry that the Internet typically offers no more than superficial contact with strangers. They fear that the lure of computer games and impersonal news groups will siphon time away from face-to-face interaction or that people will use the Internet to hide from real relationships. Parents may worry that the Internet can expose their children to pornography and to sexual predators. The fact that young people often know more about computers than their parents do can add to concerns.

Psychological research suggests that the Internet is neither inherently good nor inherently bad (McKenna & Bargh, 2000). Rather, the impact of the Internet depends on how and why individuals use it. Although the Internet can pose hazards, psychological research suggests that most people use the Internet in ways that enhance their social relationships and personal well-being (Kraut et al., 2002).

In one survey, 94 percent of Internet users polled said that the Internet made it easier for them to communicate with family and friends, and 87 percent said they regularly used it for that purpose (D'Amico, 1998). A widowed grandfather in Pennsylvania can easily use e-mail to communicate with his grown children in California and New York, and family ties can be strengthened by the sharing of news and photos of children and pets online. Family researchers have suggested that men may find e-mail an especially appealing way to communicate with relatives, because messages can be written at any time of day, can be short without appearing to be rude, and can be constructed and reviewed at a leisurely pace (Bold, 2001). For older adults, who may have physical limitations or may be housebound, the Internet can be a valuable tool for maintaining contact with friends, obtaining information, and shopping.

A recent study investigated how seventh-graders from an affluent community used the Internet and what impact it had on their well-being (Gross, Juvonen, & Gable, 2002). Participants were asked to fill out

increased for both sexes, from 10th place in the 1930s to 5th place in the 1990s. Physical attractiveness never headed the list, but it increased in importance over time. For men, having a partner with good looks moved up from 14th place to 8th place; for women, the corresponding change was from 17th to 13th place.

Male–Female Differences

The extensive research on heterosexual mate selection also documents several consistent sex differences in the qualities people value in a mate. Although both sexes view a partner's physical attractiveness as an asset, men place greater value than do women on the physical attributes of a partner. For example, in a national survey of Americans, women were more willing than men to marry someone who was not good looking (Sprecher, Sullivan, & Hatfield, 1994). Second, age matters: Women prefer older partners and men prefer younger partners. Third, women place greater emphasis on a partner's economic resources than do men. In the national survey of Americans, men were more willing than were women to marry someone who was not likely to have a steady job, someone who earned less, and someone who had less education than they did. In contrast, women were more interested than men in marrying someone who had a steady job, earned more, and had more education. These sex differences have been found not only in the United States but also in a wide range of other cultures.

nightly logs describing their computer use and after-school activities. They also reported their feelings of loneliness, anxiety, and sense of well-being that day. Fully 90 percent of the students said they use the Internet occasionally or regularly, and 84 percent said they went online on a "typical day." Computer use represented a small portion of students' after-school activities, averaging 47 minutes. They spent much more time with friends, talking on the phone, doing homework, or watching TV; or in organized activities like clubs and lessons. These students were most likely to use instant messaging or e-mail, typically to communicate with friends, or to visit Web sites. Students' reports of loneliness, anxiety, and well-being were not associated with the amount of time they spent online. Rather, like the telephone, the Internet seemed to be another element in the students' communications repertoire.

The Internet provides a fascinating way to investigate factors that influence interpersonal attraction. Consider the case of physical attractiveness. If we meet a new person face to face, we are immediately struck by his or her appearance. In contrast, when people meet online, they can conceal their looks and other features that might decrease attraction, such as stuttering or being awkward in social situations. Further, the anonymity of the Internet may make it easier for people to disclose personal information. As a result, individuals may feel that they are better able to express important aspects of their real selves when interacting on the Internet. This possibility led Katelyn McKenna and her associates (2002) to predict that people may actually form initial friendships more rapidly online than in person.

To test this idea, college students were asked to engage in two 20-minute get-acquainted sessions with another student they had never met before. Some participants were randomly assigned to interact face to face with the same partner for both meetings. Some students had their first interaction online and their second meeting with the same partner face to face. At the end, the participants indicated how much they liked their partner. As predicted, participants who first met their partner online reported greater liking than did people who initially met face to face. In a third condition, participants were told that they would interact with two different partners, one online and a different person face to face. In reality, they interacted with the same person at both meetings. In this condition, the participants evaluated the same partner more favorably online than they did in person. In summary, first meeting someone online, without the influence of physical appearance, seems to foster interpersonal attraction.

Most research on mate preferences simply asks men and women to rate the importance they give to an array of qualities in a prospective partner, including attractiveness, and intelligence. In a more realistic approach, recent studies have attempted to simulate situations in which we do not have the perfect partner as an option. Instead, we have to make tradeoffs, perhaps deciding between a partner who is very attractive but interpersonally clumsy and a partner who is homely but charming. Results of studies requiring participants to choose among desirable qualities help to distinguish what people consider "necessities" versus "luxuries" in mate selection. Studies of college students have found male–female differences (Li, Bailey, Kenrick, & Linsenmeier, 2002). A prospective partner's physical attractiveness was considered a necessity by men but a luxury by women. In contrast, a partner's status and resources were a necessity for women selecting a male partner, but a luxury for men selecting a female partner. Both sexes considered kindness and intelligence to be necessities. Another study forced trade-offs among three main mate selection criteria: warmth/trustworthiness, attractiveness/vitality, and status/resources (Fletcher, Tither, O'Loughlin, Friesen, & Overall, 2004). Results again confirmed the expected sex difference. In selecting a long-term partner, women (compared to men) gave greater emphasis to warmth/trustworthiness and status/resources. In contrast, men (compared to women) gave greater importance to attractiveness/vitality.

Two contrasting explanations have been offered for these consistent sex differences. A sociocultural perspective emphasizes that men and women have traditionally had distinct social roles; men have been cast as the providers who determine the family's economic and social status, and women have been cast as homemakers who care for the home and children (Eagly & Wood, 1999). In addition, women have typically had poorer economic and educational opportunities than have men. Consequently, it is sensible for women to seek husbands who will be resourceful providers and for men to seek youthful wives who will devote themselves to the domestic arena.

Evolutionary psychologists offer a different interpretation (Buss & Kenrick, 1998). They propose that men and women have evolved different mating preferences to maximize their reproductive success. Because women "invest" heavily in the production of a child (9 months of pregnancy, a period of nursing, and care for a dependent infant), they seek partners who can provide valuable material resources. In modern society, this desire translates into a preference for men with a good education and a good job. Because men can impregnate many females and do not necessarily make a large investment in parenting, a key issue is the identification of characteristics that signal women's reproductive capacity: Men prefer women who are young and physically attractive because in our evolutionary history these were cues to women's health and fertility.

If a sociocultural explanation is correct, we may see shifts in men's and women's mate preferences as the educational opportunities and work experiences of the two sexes become more similar. In contrast, if the evolutionary explanation is correct, changing social roles for women and men should have relatively little impact on mate preferences. Currently, the evidence about changing preferences is mixed. For example, the study of college students across 6 decades described earlier found that the sexes were more similar in their mate preferences in the 1990s than they had been in the 1930s (Buss et al., 2001). Across time, men increased the importance they gave to having a wife with good financial prospects and decreased the importance they gave to a woman's domestic skills. Both sexes shifted toward greater emphasis on physical attractiveness. These changes appear consistent with the idea that changing gender roles in society can alter mate-selection criteria. Similarly, Eagly and Wood (1999) presented data showing that across 37 cultures, sex differences in mate preferences shifted as women gained greater economic equality and political power in society.

On the other hand, consistent with the evolutionary perspective, recent social changes have not fully erased sex differences in the value placed on age, attractiveness, and resources. Among college students surveyed in 1996, men ranked good health and good looks higher than did women; women ranked ambition and good financial prospects higher than did men. One possible conclusion is provided by David Buss and his associates (2001): "The stability of sex differences, in concert with the relative convergence between the sexes in mate preferences over the past half century, suggests the value of an interactionist approach that integrates 'evolutionary' factors with 'cultural' factors" (p. 502).

Loving and being loved in return are vital to human happiness.

ROMANTIC LOVE

Long a favored subject for poets and songwriters, love is now a popular topic for scientific research as well (Berscheid & Regan, 2005).

Cultural Variations: Arranged Marriages versus Love Matches

Although love may feel like the most intensely personal of experiences, culture shapes our experiences of love and romance. In the United States, most people find it hard to imagine marriage without love. The individualist orientation of American culture places a high premium on personal choice in matters of the

Table 8–2

Would You Marry Without Love?

How college students answered the question "If a man (woman) had all the other qualities you desired, would you marry this person if you were not in love with him (her)?" (Numbers are percentages.)

	1967		1976		1984	
	Men	**Women**	**Men**	**Women**	**Men**	**Women**
Yes	11.7	4.0	1.7	4.6	1.7	3.6
Undecided	23.7	71.7	12.1	15.4	12.7	11.5
No	64.6	24.3	86.2	80.0	85.6	84.9

Note: In all years, data are questionnaire responses from college men and women. The earliest data were collected by Kephart (1967); his question was worded identically to the question above except that he used "boy (girl)" instead of "man (woman)."

Source: Data from J. A. Simpson, B. Campbell, and E. Berscheid. *Personality and Social Psychology Bulletin,* (vol. 12, no. 3), pp. 364–368. Copyright 1986 by The Society for Personality and Social Psychology, Inc. Reprinted by permission of Sage Publications, Inc.

heart. In the 1960s, Kephart (1967) asked young adults about the love–marriage connection. The question he posed to more than 1,000 college students was whether they would marry a man (woman) if they weren't in love with that person. The results are shown in Table 8–2.

In 1967, most men said no, they wouldn't marry a woman they didn't love. However, most women said they were undecided; only one woman in four answered no. In the intervening years, both sexes—but especially women—became more romantic in their approach to marriage. In 1976 and again in 1984, researchers asked new generations of U.S. college students the same question (Simpson, Campbell, & Berscheid, 1986). By 1984, most men and women said they would not marry without love, and the difference between the sexes had disappeared.

In contrast, many traditional societies throughout the world reject individual choice and romance as a basis for marriage. In parts of India, for example, marriages are arranged by parents. Giri Raj Gupta (1992) explained that love is not viewed as an important basis for marriage. When parents select a bride, they emphasize her good character, obedience, domestic skills, religiousness, and appearance. In selecting a groom, the social and economic standing of the family and the young man's education and earning potential are paramount.

Teenagers who grow up in traditional societies often welcome their parents' help in selecting a mate. When David and Vera Mace (1960) explained U.S. marriage customs to girls in India, the girls expressed serious concerns about the hazards of free choice. One girl asked if a girl from the United States who is shy and does not call attention to herself might not get married. Another girl said it would be humiliating to have to attract a boy: "It makes getting married a sort of competition in which the girls are fighting each other for the boys. And it encourages a girl to pretend she's better than she really is" (pp. 144–145). Other girls praised their parents' judgment about a potential husband: "It's so important that the man I marry should be the right one. I could so easily make a mistake if I had to find him for myself" (p. 145). Proponents of arranged marriage emphasize that parents are better judges of character than are children, that passion is an unrealistic basis for marriage, and that well-matched partners from compatible families gradually learn to find love and satisfaction with each other.

Robert Levine and his colleagues (1995) studied attitudes about love and marriage among college students in 11 different countries. The researchers expected that people in Western individualistic cultures would differ significantly from people in underdeveloped collectivist cultures in their views about love. To test this prediction, they had students respond to the question about love as a prerequisite for marriage originally shown in Table 8–2. The researchers also rated the values of each culture on a continuum from individualist to collectivist.

As predicted, young adults from Western individualist cultures (in the United States, Australia, and England) gave much more importance to romantic love as a basis for establishing a marriage than did people from Eastern collectivist cultures (in India, Pakistan, Thailand, and the Philippines). The link between measures of individualism and the necessity of love for marriage was relatively high, with a correlation of .56. The economic standard of living in a culture was even more strongly related to beliefs about love, with a correlation of .76. People from wealthier nations had more romantic views of love than did people from poorer nations. The researchers noted that in Japan and Hong Kong, two traditional collectivist cultures that have recently achieved economic prosperity, the importance of love as a prerequisite for marriage was ranked between that of the developed Western nations and that of the underdeveloped Eastern nations. Finally, there is correlational evidence that beliefs about love are linked to the success of marriage. The rate of divorce was significantly higher in individualist cultures, such as in the United States, where people emphasize the importance of love in the decision to marry, than in collectivist cultures, which take a more practical approach to marriage.

Research on Romantic Love

Before turning to research findings on romantic love, consider this newspaper story of young love:

> On Monday, Cpl. Floyd Johnson, 23, and the then Ellen Skinner, 19, total strangers, boarded a train at San Francisco and sat down across the aisle from each other. Johnson didn't cross the aisle until Wednesday, but his bride said, "I'd already made up my mind to say yes if he asked me to marry him." "We did most of the talking with our eyes," Johnson explained. Thursday the couple got off the train in Omaha with plans to be married. Because they would need to have the consent of the bride's parents if they were married in Nebraska, they crossed the river to Council Bluffs, Iowa, where they were married Friday.

This account may remind you of such star-crossed lovers from literature as Romeo and Juliet. But have you personally ever experienced this rather magical love at first sight?

When university students were asked how closely their own most intense love experience corresponded to this romantic model, only 40 percent said that there was a strong resemblance (Averill & Boothroyd, 1977). Another 40 percent said that they had never experienced anything at all like this story. The rest thought their most intense love relationship bore only a partial similarity to this one. This range of answers highlights one of the dilemmas of the love researcher: how to capture the essential features of love and at the same time depict the diverse experiences of people in love. Some common ways people conceptualize love are presented in Table 8–3.

Undaunted by this challenge, researchers have begun to identify the various feelings, thoughts, and behaviors that are characteristically associated with romantic love. Most of the information we have about love comes from studies of young middle-class white adults in the United States and Canada.

Feelings of Love. One feature that often distinguishes romantic love from friendship is the experience of physical symptoms. According to popular songs, a lover's heart skips a beat now and then, and a lover loses sleep and has trouble concentrating. To investigate this matter, researchers asked 679 university students to rate the intensity of various feelings they had had during their current or most recent love experience (Kanin, Davidson, & Scheck, 1970).

The most common reactions were a strong feeling of well-being (reported by 79 percent of students) and great difficulty concentrating (reported by 37 percent of students). Other reactions included "floating on a cloud" (29 percent), "wanted to run, jump, and scream" (22 percent), feeling "nervous before dates" (22 percent), and feeling "giddy and carefree" (20 percent). Strong physical sensations

Table 8–3

Love Styles

When people say, "I love you," they can mean very different things. Researchers have identified six different ways that people commonly define love (Lee, 1988). These love styles are idealized types; each individual may define love in a way that combines more than one style. The statements quoted below are from a love questionnaire developed by Clyde and Susan Hendrick (1986).

Romantic love:	Love is an all-consuming emotional experience. Love at first sight is typical, and physical attraction is essential. A romantic lover might agree with the statement "My lover and I have the right physical 'chemistry' between us."
Possessive love:	The possessive lover is emotionally intense, jealous, and obsessed with the beloved. The possessive lover is highly dependent on the beloved and therefore fears rejection. He or she might agree that "when my lover doesn't pay attention to me, I feel sick all over."
Best-friend love:	Love is a comfortable intimacy that slowly grows out of companionship, mutual sharing, and self-disclosure. A best-friend lover is thoughtful, warm, and companionate. He or she might agree that "my most satisfying love relationships have developed from good friendships."
Pragmatic love:	This is the "love that goes shopping for a suitable mate, and all it asks is that the relationship work well, that the two partners be compatible and satisfy each other's basic needs" (Lee, 1973, p. 124). The practical lover seeks contentment rather than excitement. He or she might agree that "one consideration in choosing a partner is how he or she will reflect on my career."
Altruistic love:	This style of love is unconditionally caring, giving, and forgiving. Love means a duty to give to the loved one with no strings attached. An altruistic lover might agree that "I cannot be happy unless I place my lover's happiness before my own."
Game-playing love:	This person plays at love as others play tennis or chess: to enjoy the "love game" and to win it. No relationship lasts for long and usually ends when the partner becomes boring or too serious. A game player might agree that "I enjoy playing the 'game of love' with a number of different partners."

such as cold hands, butterflies in the stomach, or a tingling spine were reported by 20 percent; and insomnia was reported by 12 percent of students.

Researchers also found differences between the love experiences of women and men; women were more likely to report strong emotional reactions (Dion & Dion, 1973). Whether these results reflect actual sex differences in the experience of love or women's greater willingness to disclose such feelings is not known.

Thoughts of Love. In the 1970s, Zick Rubin conducted research in order to understand the typical thoughts of people in love. Rubin (1970, 1973) conceptualized love as an attitude toward another person, that is, as a distinctive cluster of thoughts about the loved person. Rubin identified three main themes in people's thoughts of love. One theme, which Rubin called "attachment," is a sense of needing the partner and an awareness of one's dependence on the other to provide valued rewards. A second theme concerns caring for the other person: the desire to promote the other person's welfare and to be responsive to his or her needs. The third theme emphasizes trust and self-disclosure. Rubin used these three themes to create a paper-and-pencil Love Scale that measures the strength of a person's thoughts of love about another. Sample items from Rubin's Love Scale are presented in Table 8–4.

Behaviors of Love. In assessing whether someone loves us, we usually depend not only on words, but also on actions. If someone professes love but forgets our

Table 8–4

Sample Items from Rubin's (1973) Love Scale

It would be hard for me to get along without _______.

I would do almost anything for _______.

I feel I can confide in _______ about virtually anything.

birthday, goes out with other people, criticizes our appearance, and never confides in us, we may doubt his or her sincerity. Swensen (1972) asked people of different ages what behaviors they thought were most closely associated with love for a romantic partner or spouse. The answers fell into seven categories or types of love behaviors:

- Saying "I love you" and other verbal statements of affection
- Physical expressions of love, such as hugging or kissing
- Verbal self-disclosure
- Communicating nonverbally such feelings as happiness and relaxation when the other is present
- Material signs of love, such as giving presents or doing tasks to help the other person
- Nonmaterial signs of love, such as showing interest in the person's activities, respecting his or her opinions, or giving encouragement
- Showing a willingness to tolerate the other and to make sacrifices to maintain the relationship

Swensen found that many of these romantic love behaviors were also seen as signs of love for parents, siblings, and same-sex friends.

King and Christensen (1983) identified specific events that indicate how far a heterosexual dating couple has progressed toward marriage. In most cases, the college couples in this research went through a predictable sequence of events that moved toward greater commitment. Events that usually occurred early in the development of a relationship included spending a whole day together and calling the partner by an affectionate name. At a later stage, partners started referring to each other as "boyfriend" and "girlfriend" and received invitations to do things together as a couple. A further development was to say "I love you" and to date each other exclusively. A common next step was to discuss living together or marriage and to take a vacation together. Events indicating greatest progress included living together or becoming engaged. Although couples varied in how far their relationship developed and in the speed with which they moved toward permanence, most couples followed a similar sequence of key events.

In summary, research has identified some of the feelings, thoughts, and behaviors that people in the United States commonly associate with love. However, studies also find that individuals differ in their specific love experiences. These findings suggest that there are distinct types of love. The next section contrasts passionate and companionate love.

Passionate Love and Companionate Love

Passionate Love

The emotionally charged type of love that sometimes occurs early in a romantic relationship.

Passionate love has been described as "a wildly emotional state: tender and sexual feelings, elation and pain, anxiety and relief, altruism and jealousy coexist in a confusion of feelings" (Berscheid & Walster, 1978, p. 177). Emotions play a central role in passionate love. People are swept off their feet by uncontrollable passions that draw them irresistibly toward the loved person. Elaine Hatfield and Susan Sprecher (1986) developed a Passionate Love Scale to assess the intensity of people's experiences with this type of love. Sample items from this measure are presented in Table 8–5. Hatfield believes that the capacity to experience passionate love is universal, although sociocultural factors may shape the way in which passionate love is expressed.

The physiological arousal that fuels passionate love can have many sources. Sexual desire, the fear of possible rejection, the excitement of getting to know someone, the frustration of outside interference from parents or a rival suitor, the anger of a lover's quarrel—all may contribute to the strong emotions experienced in passionate love. For example, Hatfield and her associates (1989) reasoned that anxiety may contribute to passionate love. In two studies, they showed that

Table 8–5

Sample Items from the Passionate Love Scale

I sense my body responding when _______ touches me.

I would feel deep despair if _______ left me.

I possess a powerful attraction for _______ .

_______ always seems to be on my mind.

Source: Hatfield and Sprecher (1986).

young adolescents who scored higher on measures of anxiety were more likely to report feelings of passionate love. Whatever its diverse sources, the experience of passionate love seems to have an uncontrollable quality that may provide a convenient justification for lovers to engage in behaviors they might otherwise consider unacceptable, such as an extramarital affair (Berscheid, 2002). The lovers' defense is that they "couldn't stop" themselves.

Another element of passionate love is preoccupation with the other person. The lover is obsessed with thoughts of the new love. There is a tendency to idealize the loved person, to see the person as wonderful and perfect in every way. Passionate love is often said to strike suddenly and fade quickly. This type of love is intense but fragile and often short-lived.

Companionate love has been defined as "the affection we feel for those with whom our lives are deeply intertwined" (Berscheid & Walster, 1978, p. 177). This is a more practical type of love that emphasizes trust, caring, and tolerance of the partner's flaws and idiosyncrasies. The emotional tone of companionate love is more moderate; warmth and affection are more common than are extreme passions. Companionate love develops slowly as two people build a satisfying relationship. Individuals differ sharply in their beliefs about whether passionate or companionate love is the better or truer form. However, many family researchers believe that companionate love provides the most enduring basis for long-term relationships.

Companionate Love

Affectionate type of love that emphasizes trust and caring.

The contrast between passionate and companionate love raises interesting questions about the experience of emotions in close relationships. For example, the early stages of a romantic relationship are often characterized by extreme emotions, whereas the later stages are marked by emotional tranquility and moderation. Why might this be? Ellen Berscheid (2002) suggested that over time, the novelty and surprise of the relationship wear off. Idealization of the partner confronts the reality of human imperfection. The couple develops routine ways of interacting, and life together becomes more settled.

However, Berscheid also suggested that as a relationship continues over time and interdependence grows, the potential for strong emotion actually increases. The greater our dependence on another person, the greater the possible influence of the partner in our lives. But paradoxically, because long-term couples learn to coordinate their activities smoothly, the actual frequency of strong emotions tends to be fairly low. The latent potential for strong emotion may emerge occasionally, however. When partners are separated because of travel or illness, they often have intense feelings of loneliness and desire.

A Triangular Theory of Love

In an effort to provide a comprehensive theory about love in different types of relationships, Robert Sternberg (1986) suggested that all love experiences have three components, which are shown as the points of a triangle in Figure 8–2.

The intimacy component includes feelings of closeness, connectedness, and bondedness in a relationship, as well as admiring and wanting to take care of the

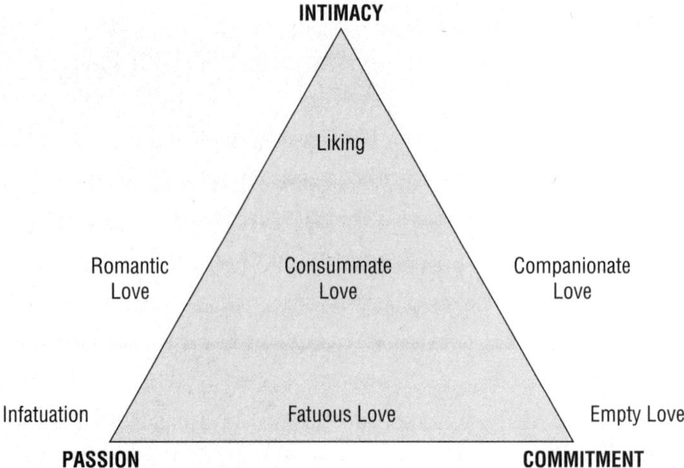

Figure 8–2 **A Triangular Theory of Love.**

According to Sternberg (1986), different types of love reflect different combinations of intimacy, passion, and commitment.

loved one. Self-disclosure and intimate communication are important. Sternberg believes that this component is essentially the same in love for a romantic partner, a child, or a best friend. Intimacy is a common core in each of these loving relationships.

The passion component comprises the drives that lead to intense emotions in love relationships. In a romantic relationship, physical attraction and sexuality may be prominent. However, other motives, such as needs to give or receive nurturance, needs for self-esteem, and needs for dominance, may also be involved.

In the short term, the commitment component is the decision that one loves someone else, and in the long term, it is a commitment to maintain that love. This is the most cognitive component of love.

An analysis of these three components led Sternberg to identify seven distinct kinds of love, depending on the presence or absence of each component:

1. Liking is the experience of intimacy without passion or commitment, as in a friendship.
2. Infatuated love is the experience of passion without intimacy or commitment, as in "puppy love."
3. Empty love is the experience of commitment without passion and intimacy, as in stagnant or "empty-shell" marriages.
4. Romantic love is the experience of passion and intimacy without commitment, as in a romantic affair.
5. Companionate love is the experience of intimacy and commitment without passion, as in a long-term marriage.
6. Fatuous love is the experience of passion and commitment without intimacy, as in love at first sight.
7. Consummate love is the ultimate experience of a love that combines all elements of intimacy, passion, and commitment that might be found in an adult love relationship or in some relations between parents and children.

Sternberg's theory is an interesting attempt to pull together many previous findings and concepts.

Jealousy

Jealousy

Emotion triggered when we perceive a threat by a rival to a valued friendship.

Jealousy occurs when a person perceives a real or potential attraction between the partner and a rival (DeSteno & Salovey, 1994). Jealousy is a reaction to a perceived threat to the continuity or quality of a valued relationship, such as a husband's discovery that his wife is secretly dating another man. Jealousy involves two types of threats: threats to the relationship from the possible loss of the partner and threats to the person's self-esteem from being rejected by the partner or losing to the rival. Feelings of anger, anxiety, and depression are common.

Several factors contribute to jealousy (White & Mullen, 1989). A person who is highly dependent on a relationship, who cares deeply about the relationship, and who has few alternatives is more susceptible to jealousy. For example, married people who believe they would have few alternatives if their current spouse left them are more vulnerable to jealousy. There is also evidence linking jealousy to insecurity. People who feel inadequate in a relationship or think that their behavior falls short of their own expectations are more likely to feel jealous (Attridge, Berscheid, & Sprecher, 1998).

As you might imagine, there are also cross-cultural differences in the situations that give rise to jealousy (White & Mullen, 1989). In the United States, for instance, a wife might feel jealous if her husband had a sexual affair with another woman. In contrast, in societies where cultural rules dictate that a man may have several wives, jealousy among the co-wives is unusual. Instead, co-wives typically have cordial relations unless the husband shows favoritism toward one wife or her children in ways that violate cultural dictates. Similarly, when cultures permit one woman to have multiple husbands, jealousy among the men is unusual.

There is currently a controversy about possible sex differences in the events that are most likely to trigger jealousy. David Buss (2000) and other evolutionary theorists have proposed that for men, uncertainty about the paternity of offspring is a prime concern. Hence, sexual infidelity should be most likely to evoke jealousy, because such acts might result in the man unknowingly supporting someone else's offspring. In contrast, women cannot be tricked into unknowingly bringing up another woman's offspring, so the mate's sexual unfaithfulness is of relatively less importance. Rather, women fear the loss of a mate's resources and help in bringing up their children. Consequently, a mate's emotional involvement with another woman should be particularly distressing. Evidence from self-report studies of college students has typically supported these predictions. In an illustrative set of studies, college students from the United States, Korea, and Japan were asked to react to several hypothetical situations in which their partner had either an emotional (but not sexual) relationship with another person or a sexual (but not emotional) relationship with another person (Buss et al., 1999). Consistent with the evolutionary predictions, in all three countries women reported that they would feel more distress about an emotional infidelity, and men anticipated greater distress from a sexual infidelity.

Other researchers have seriously questioned the empirical support for an evolutionary theory of jealousy. Recently, Christine Harris (2003) reviewed a wide range of evidence including self-reports about jealousy experiences, physiological measures such as heart rate and blood pressure used to assess distress reactions while participants imagined a mate's infidelity, and jealousy-inspired homicides. She found relatively little support for evolutionary predictions.

What seems clear is that both sexes experience considerable distress when they perceive a threat to a valued relationship. Both emotional and sexual infidelity can be powerful triggers of jealousy.

In this chapter, we have examined human needs for social connectedness and discussed why we like some people and not others. We also reviewed psychological studies of romantic love. The next chapter explores research about interaction processes in personal relationships.

Summary

1. Humans are social animals with a powerful need to relate to other people. Belonging to a group helps people to survive physically and psychologically.
2. Loneliness is the subjective discomfort we feel when our social relations are deficient in quantity or quality. Loneliness ranges from a temporary state resulting from a change in our social life to a chronic and enduring condition.
3. Emotional loneliness is caused by the lack of an attachment relationship; social loneliness is caused by the lack of social integration.

4. Social rejection, a distressing experience that threatens our need to belong, is often used as a form of punishment. Rejection can lower self-esteem, increase sensitivity to social experiences, and may increase the tendency to respond aggressively to provocation.
5. Infants form strong attachments to the significant adults in their lives. An attachment perspective is also useful in understanding adult romantic relationships. Three major attachment patterns are secure, avoidant, and anxious/ambivalent.
6. In general, we like people who reward us and who help to satisfy our needs.
7. Interpersonal attraction is increased by proximity and familiarity (the mere exposure effect).
8. We tend to like people who are similar to us in attitudes, values, interests, background, and personality. In dating and marriage, the tendency to select similar partners is called the "matching principle." The processes that lead to similarity among friends include selective attraction, social influence, and environmental factors.
9. Personal attributes that tend to increase attraction include warmth, competence, and physical attractiveness. Being seen with a physically attractive date or friend may have a "radiating effect," causing others to evaluate us more favorably.
10. Research on heterosexual mate selection finds a few consistent male–female differences: Men place greater emphasis on a partner's youth and beauty; women place greater emphasis on a partner's economic and social resources. Both cultural and evolutionary explanations of these patterns have been offered.
11. Most Americans consider love an essential prerequisite for marriage. Yet, in many traditional collectivist societies, marriages are arranged by parents or other adults.
12. Theorists have distinguished between passionate love (the exciting and emotionally charged experience some people have early in a love relationship) and companionate love (the deep affection, trust, and caring a person feels for a long-term partner).
13. Jealousy is a reaction to a perceived threat to a valued relationship by a rival.

Key Terms

attachment **237**
companionate love **259**
emotional loneliness **235**
jealousy **260**
loneliness **233**
matching principle **245**
mere exposure effect **242**
ostracism **236**
passionate love **258**
social exchange theory **240**
social loneliness **235**
working model **238**

In The News

The Pros and Cons of Same-Sex Marriage

Few social issues are more hotly debated than the legalization of same-sex marriage. Opponents of legalization warn that granting marital status to lesbians and gay men would threaten the institution of marriage and undermine the family. Opponents also suggest that it's unfair to heterosexuals to tamper with the time-honored formula that equates marriage with the union of a man and a woman. Supporters of same-sex marriage counter that it's unfair to deny citizens the many benefits associated with civil marriage, simply because of their sexual orientation. Supporters also note that marriage is already in trouble, as seen in our high divorce rate.

According to *Forbes Magazine* (Lagorce, 2004), one group that stands to reap windfall profits from legalizing same-sex marriage is the wedding industry. If even a fraction of the same-sex couples currently living together in the United States were to have formal weddings, they would likely spend many billions of dollars. This would include increased sales for wedding rings and clothing, for catering and flowers, for cakes and gifts, and for honeymoon vacations. Even without legal marriage, many businesses have already expanded their wedding registry services to include same-sex couples who are holding commitment ceremonies.

Several professional associations have issued statements about civil marriage for same-sex couples. In 2004, the American Anthropological Association opposed a constitutional amendment to limit marriage to heterosexual couples. The association explained, "The results of more than a century of anthropological research on households, kinship relationships, and families, across cultures and through time, provide no support whatsoever for the view that either civilization or viable social orders depend upon marriage as an exclusively heterosexual institution." The Council of the American Psychological Association also passed a resolution. The APA noted that there are currently thousands of federal, state, and local laws covering such issues as taxation, federal loans, social security benefits, medical insurance, and more that are based on marital status. The resolution concluded that it is "unfair and discriminatory to deny same-sex couples legal access to civil marriage and to all its attendant benefits, rights, and privileges."

The majority of Americans disapprove of same-sex marriage. In recent national polls, two thirds of Americans oppose legalizing same-sex marriage. About half of those polled say that they personally consider a same-sex relationship between consenting adults to be morally wrong and that allowing gays and lesbians to marry legally would undermine the traditional American family (Kaiser Foundation, 2001; Peplau & Beals, 2004). At the same time, growing numbers of Americans are concerned about treating same-sex couples fairly and would support legalizing same-sex civil unions as an alternative to marriage.

The outcome of the national debate over same-sex marriage is far from certain. What is clear, however, is the crucial importance that intimate relationships play in our lives. Both sides of this controversy, those who want to protect traditional marriage and those who want to extend civil marriage to lesbians and gay men, are motivated by a belief in the central value of family bonds.

Chapter 9

Personal Relationships

Social psychologists try to see beneath the great variation in human relationships to discover general principles that apply to many relationships. An essential feature of any relationship is that two people influence each other or, in more technical terms, that they are interdependent. The specific ways that people influence each other are diverse. A person can help us or hinder us, make us feel happy or sad, tell us the latest gossip or criticize our opinions, give us advice or tell us off. The progress from a casual interaction with a stranger to a close relationship that lasts many years involves increasing levels of interdependence between the two individuals.

Close relationships involve much interdependence (Berscheid, Snyder, & Omoto, 1989; Kelley et al., 2002). These can be relationships with a parent, a best friend, a teacher, a spouse, a coworker, or even an important rival or competitor. All close relationships share three basic characteristics. First, they involve frequent interaction that continues over a relatively long period of time. Second, close relationships include many different kinds of activities or events. In a friendship, for example, people discuss different topics and generally share a wide range of activities and interests. Third, in close relationships, the influence between people is strong. We may quickly forget a snide remark by a salesclerk but agonize for weeks about a comment made by our best friend.

In this chapter, we examine some of the most important features of social relationships. We begin with interdependence theory and then discuss the dynamics of self-disclosure and intimacy. We next analyze the nature of power and conflict in relationships. We consider factors that contribute to satisfaction and commitment in relationships. We conclude by examining ways people strive to maintain committed relationships.

Focus of This Chapter

INTERDEPENDENCE THEORY

The most influential perspective on social relationships is provided by various social exchange theories (Berscheid & Regan, 2005). In social psychology, researchers have most often emphasized **interdependence theory** (Berscheid & Reis, 1998; Kelley & Thibaut, 1978). This perspective analyzes the patterns of interaction between partners. One way to conceptualize these interactions is in terms of the outcomes—rewards and costs—that partners give and receive. We generally try to arrange our interactions to

Interdependence Theory

The most important social exchange perspective in social psychology.

maximize our rewards and minimize our costs. To receive rewards, however, we must also give them. As children, we learn a general rule or norm of reciprocity: We are expected to reward those who reward us. If people help us, we feel obligated to help them. If we invite someone to dinner, we expect that person to return the invitation in the future. Social interaction involves the exchange and coordination of outcomes between interdependent partners.

Rewards and Costs

A reward is anything a person gains from an interaction, such as feeling loved or receiving financial assistance. What is rewarding to one person may be of little value to someone else. A useful analysis of the rewards of social interaction was proposed by Foa and Foa (1974), who identified six basic types of rewards: love, money, status, information, goods, and services. These can be classified along two dimensions. The dimension of particularism concerns the extent to which the value of a reward depends on who provides it. The value of love or, more specifically, the value of such things as hugs and tender words depends very much on who provides them. Thus, love is a particularistic reward. In contrast, money is useful regardless of who it comes from; money is a nonparticularistic or universal reward. When we say that a relationship is very special to us, we often mean that it provides unique or particularistic rewards that we cannot get elsewhere. The second dimension, concreteness, captures the distinction between tangible rewards—things we can see, smell, and touch—and nonconcrete or symbolic rewards, such as advice and social approval.

Costs are the negative consequences that occur in an interaction or relationship. An interaction may be costly because it requires a great deal of time and energy, because it entails much conflict, or because other people disapprove of the relationship and criticize us for being involved in it. An interaction may also be costly if it deprives us of the opportunity to do other rewarding activities: If you spend the weekend partying with friends, you won't have time to study for an exam or visit your parents.

A study asked college students to describe the rewards and costs they experienced in a romantic dating relationship (Sedikides, Oliver, & Campbell, 1994). They listed such benefits as companionship, feeling loved, happiness, intimacy, self-understanding, and sexual gratification. The perceived costs of a romantic relationship included stress and worry about the relationship, the lack of freedom to socialize with or date other people, the time and effort required by the relationship, fights, and feelings of dependency on the partner. Although men and women generally identified similar rewards and costs, a few gender differences emerged. For example, women expressed greater concern about being dependent on a partner and about loss of identity; men expressed greater concern about monetary costs and about investments of time and energy.

Evaluating Outcomes

Interdependence theory assumes that people keep track of the rewards and costs of a particular interaction or relationship. We do not usually make lists of the good and bad aspects of a relationship; nonetheless, we are aware of the costs and rewards involved. In particular, we focus on the overall outcome we get in a relationship, that is, whether on balance the relationship is profitable for us (rewards outweigh costs) or whether we are experiencing an overall loss (costs outweigh rewards). When people say, "I'm really getting a lot out of this relationship" or "I don't think our relationship is worth it anymore," they are assessing their relationship outcomes.

People use several standards to evaluate relationship outcomes. Consider this example: At a party, you avoid talking to John, an obnoxious person you really dislike. Instead, you gravitate to Mike, a rather friendly person who tells good stories. You continue to chat with Mike until you notice that your best friend, Seth, has just arrived. At this point, you excuse yourself and go to talk to Seth.

The simplest standard for evaluating a relationship is whether it is profitable or costly. In this example, a conversation with John is seen as negative, and conversing with both Mike and Seth is rewarding.

In addition to determining whether a relationship is profitable, we make comparative judgments, assessing how one relationship compares to another. Two comparison standards are especially important (Thibaut & Kelley, 1959). The first standard is the **comparison level**. It reflects the quality of outcomes a person believes he or she deserves. Our comparison level reflects our past experiences in relationships. For example, you may compare your new boss to your past supervisors. Or you may consider whether a current dating relationship is as good as those you have had in the past. You may also compare a current relationship to those you have seen in your family, heard about from friends, watched in movies, or read about in popular psychology books. The comparison level is our personal belief about what constitutes an acceptable relationship.

Comparison Level

The outcomes (benefits and costs) we expect or believe we deserve.

The second major standard is the **comparison level for alternatives**. This involves assessing how one relationship compares to other relationships that are currently available to us. Is your current dating partner better or worse than the other people you could be going out with right now? Is your current boss better or worse than other people you might realistically work for at this point in your life? If your relationship is the best you think possible, you may stay in it, even if the actual benefits you receive are small. In contrast, even if a relationship is profitable in absolute terms, you may leave it if a better alternative becomes available.

Comparison Level for Alternatives

Our belief about the best alternate relationship currently available.

Coordinating Outcomes

An issue in all relationships is how to coordinate activities to maximize the benefits to both partners. Consider the coordination problems of two strangers who sit next to each other on a cross-country airplane trip. Carl arrives first, takes the only pillows and blanket, and claims the middle armrest for his use. A rather gregarious type, Carl hopes to spend the trip talking to the person who sits next to him. His seatmate, Kathy, on the other hand, has brought along work to do and plans to spend the trip reading. She's annoyed to find no pillow on her seat but manages to get one from the flight attendant. After a few pleasantries, Kathy makes it clear that she does not want to begin a long conversation, and Carl thumbs idly through a magazine. Some time later, Carl pulls down the window shade and tries to take a nap. His actions further annoy Kathy, who was hoping for a glimpse of the Grand Canyon. As Carl nods off, he begins to snore. In frustration, Kathy finally gets up to see if there is another vacant seat. In this example, a failure in coordination prompts one person to try to avoid any further interaction.

How easy or difficult it is for two people to coordinate their outcomes depends on how much they share common interests and goals. When partners like to do many of the same things and value the same activities, they have relatively few coordination problems (Surra & Longstreth, 1990). In such cases, they are said to have "correspondent outcomes" because their outcomes correspond: What is good for one is good for the other, and what is bad for one is bad for both (Thibaut & Kelley, 1959). In general, partners with similar backgrounds and attitudes tend to have fewer problems of coordination and so may find it easier to develop a mutually rewarding relationship. When partners have different preferences and values, they have "noncorrespondent outcomes" and, as a result, are more prone to conflicts of interest and coordination problems.

Of course, even well-matched partners experience conflicts of interest from time to time. When they occur, the partners must negotiate a settlement. Consider a young married couple deciding how to spend the income tax refund they have just received. The wife wants to buy a new sofa; the husband wants to buy a new TV. The couple has a limited amount of money available and cannot afford both the sofa and the TV; therefore, they must coordinate their use of the funds and resolve their conflicting interests. One common solution is to select a

When friends enjoy many of the same activities, they have an easy time coordinating their interaction. In technical terms, they have correspondent outcomes—what is rewarding for one is rewarding for the other.

less preferred alternative that is acceptable to both partners. The young couple might decide to spend the money on a trip—neither person's first choice, but an alternative that is attractive to both. Another possibility is to take turns, buying the sofa this year and the TV next year.

Settling conflicts of interest by negotiation is at best a time-consuming activity and at worst a source of arguments and bad feelings. Over time, partners often develop rules or social norms about coordinating their behavior. Neither spouse may like to take out the garbage or pay the bills, but they may agree that he will do one if she will do the other. Shared norms reduce the need for continual negotiation in order to arrive at coordinated behavior patterns.

Chapter 1 defined social roles as clusters of rules about how people should behave in a particular type of interaction or relationship. Roles provide solutions for some of the problems of coordination that people are likely to encounter. In many relationships, cultural rules prescribe certain coordinated patterns. At work, there are usually fairly clear understandings about what the employer and the employee are to do and how they are to interact. Lawyers and their assistants do not negotiate about who will draft legal briefs and who will type them, or about who will answer the phone and who will make court appearances.

When individuals act on the basis of preexisting cultural rules, they are engaging in the process of role taking (Turner, 1962). As we grow up, we learn many social roles that guide our interactions with other people. We can contrast this process of role taking, in which people adopt or conform to cultural roles, with the process of role making, in which people develop their own shared norms for social interaction. In many social settings, people improvise and create their own solutions to problems of interdependence. When two friends decide to share an apartment, for example, they need to negotiate who will do what, when, and how: Who will be in charge of paying bills? How will housekeeping be arranged? What are the rules about overnight guests? Many social interactions involve a mix of role taking and role making. When social guidelines are vague or in the process of change, individuals have greater freedom of action, but they also must put more effort into coordinating interaction successfully.

Fair Exchange

People are most content when they perceive their social relations to be fair. We don't like to feel exploited by others, nor do we usually like to take advantage of others. We use various rules for determining whether the benefits and costs in a relationship are being given and received fairly (Clark & Chrisman, 1994).

Consider the situation of two teenage boys trying to decide how to divide a pizza. They might decide to "share and share alike," using the "equality rule" that everyone should receive equal outcomes. People are more likely to use the equality principle when they are interacting with friends than when interacting with strangers (Austin, 1980). Children are more likely than are adults to use the equality principle, perhaps because it is the simplest rule.

A second principle for exchanging benefits in a relationship takes into account the needs of everyone involved. If the boys about to eat a pizza were to adopt this "relative needs" principle, one boy might get a larger piece of pizza if he were especially hungry, or if he hadn't had pizza in a long time. This principle of "to each according to need" is illustrated by parents who spend much more money on a child who needs dental braces than on another child who has perfect teeth. Parents gear their medical and dental expenditures to the needs of each child. Engaged and married couples view this principle as an ideal for their relationship, believing that "benefits should be given in response to needs, as needs arise, with no strings attached" (Clark, Graham, & Grote, 2002, p. 172).

A third fairness rule is **equity**, also known as distributive justice. The key idea is that a person's profits should be proportional to his or her contributions (Hatfield, Traupmann, Sprecher, Utne, & Hay, 1985). Here, the boy who contributed more to the cost of buying the pizza, or who exerted greater effort by making the pizza himself, is entitled to a larger portion. In this view, equity exists when two or more people receive the same ratio of outcomes to contributions. In more technical terms:

Learning to share with friends is an important step in understanding principles of fairness in social relationships.

Equity

Fairness exists when the ratio of profits to contributions is the same for everyone.

$$\frac{\text{Outcomes of person P}}{\text{Contributions of person P}} = \frac{\text{Outcomes of person O}}{\text{Contributions of person O}}$$

Equity theory has four basic assumptions:

1. In a relationship or group, individuals try to maximize their outcomes.
2. Dyads and groups can maximize their collective rewards by evolving rules or norms about how to divide rewards fairly among everyone concerned.
3. When individuals perceive that a relationship is inequitable, they feel distressed. The greater the inequity, the greater the distress experienced.
4. Individuals who perceive inequity in a relationship will take steps to restore equity.

Research has supported several predictions from equity theory (Hatfield et al., 1985). When relationships are not equitable, both partners feel distressed. It makes sense that the underbenefitted (exploited) person feels distress. But research shows that the overbenefitted person may also feel distress, perhaps because he or she feels guilty or uncomfortable about the imbalance.

There is also evidence that people try to restore equity when they perceive unfairness in a relationship (Hatfield et al., 1985). People can do this in two ways. One approach is to restore actual equity. For example, a roommate might agree that she hasn't been doing her share of the housework and will therefore do extra work to compensate. A second approach is to use cognitive strategies to alter the perception of the imbalance, thus restoring psychological equity. The roommate might distort reality and argue that she really has done a fair share of the work, thus avoiding the need to change her behavior. Whether people restore actual or psychological equity depends on the costs and benefits associated with each particular strategy. Finally, if it is not possible to restore equity in either of these ways, a person may try to end the relationship.

Satisfaction in dating and marriage is affected by perceptions of equity (Sprecher, 2001). Underbenefitted partners generally report lower satisfaction. A study of married and cohabiting couples found that individuals who reported less equity were less happy with their relationship, and the negative effects of inequity on satisfaction persisted 1 year later (Van Yperen & Buunk, 1990). A concern with fairness may be especially important at the beginning of a relationship. A longitudinal study found that equity is a factor in satisfaction early in dating relationships but not a few months later (Cate, Lloyd, & Long, 1988). Over time, individuals may develop trust in their partner's good intentions and may not monitor exchange patterns as closely.

However, when long-term relationships encounter stressful changes, such as the transition to parenthood, partners may again begin to assess fairness in their relationship. A recent study followed married couples from before the birth of their first child until a year after the birth (Grote & Clark, 2001). Those couples who experienced greater marital distress after the arrival of their baby were more likely to report an inequitable division of household work. The researchers suggested that feelings of unhappiness trigger a search for the sources of distress and lead partners to perceive inequities that might be overlooked in happier times.

There are also individual differences in the effects of equity on relationship satisfaction. Individuals who score high on a measure of general concern about fairness in relationships may be more negatively affected by inequity than are other people (Sprecher, 1992). Further, women with feminist or nontraditional attitudes about sex roles may be especially sensitive to equity concerns and so may experience greater dissatisfaction than other women or men if they believe their relationship is unfair (Van Yperen & Buunk, 1991).

Finally, research has generally found that in close relationships, equity is less important to happiness than the absolute level of rewards a person receives. Satisfaction is highest when people believe they are receiving many rewards, whether or not they perceive the distribution of rewards to be entirely fair (Surra, 1990). If you believe you are getting a lot from a relationship, you tend to be happy, even if you think you may be getting a bit less than you deserve. Furthermore, in our closest relationships, we may move beyond strict principles of equity and social exchange (Berscheid & Reis, 1998).

Beyond Exchange

Social exchange principles help us understand many different kinds of relationships. Most people recognize that exchange influences casual relationships, but they may resist the idea that exchange factors also govern our most intimate relationships. It is certainly unromantic to suggest, as sociologist Erving Goffman (1952) once did, that "a proposal of marriage in our society tends to be a way in which a man sums up his social attributes and suggests that hers are not so much better as to preclude a merger or a partnership in these matters" (p. 456).

Social psychologist Zick Rubin (1973), voiced a common concern about exchange theory:

> The notions that people are "commodities" and social relationships are "transactions" will surely make many readers squirm. Exchange theory postulates that human relationships are based first and foremost on self-interest. As such, it often seems to portray friendship as motivated only by what one person can get from another and to redefine love as a devious power game. . . . But although we might prefer to believe otherwise, we must face up to the fact that our attitudes toward other people are determined to a large extent by our assessments of the rewards they hold for us. (p. 82)

It may be helpful to remember that although exchange theory borrows terminology from economics, the rewards and costs involved are often personal and unique: An attractive smile and shared secrets are as much a part of exchange theory as are fancy cars and expensive gifts.

You may have noticed that exchange issues seem to be much more important in some of your relationships than they are in others. For example, you may be willing to trade work shifts with a coworker this week, but you clearly expect that she'll do the same for you next week. In contrast, you and your best friend may do many favors for each other and help each other in times of need without consciously keeping a mental record of what you give and receive.

To help understand these differences, Clark and Mills (1979) distinguished between two types of relationships: exchange relationships and communal relationships. In both types of relationships, exchange processes operate, but the rules governing the giving and receiving of benefits differ significantly. In exchange relationships, people give benefits with the expectation of receiving comparable benefits in return soon afterward. Exchange relationships occur most often with strangers or casual acquaintances and in business relations. In **exchange relationships**, people feel no special responsibility for the welfare of the other person. In contrast, in **communal relationships**, people do feel a personal responsibility for the needs of the other. Communal relationships usually occur between family members, friends, and romantic partners. In these relationships, people provide benefits to the partner in order to show concern and to respond to the other's needs, with no expectation of receiving similar benefits in the near future.

Exchange Relationships

When partners give benefits to each other, they expect to receive comparable benefits in return.

Communal Relationships

Partners provide benefits to show concern and respond to the other's needs.

Mills and Clark (1994, 2001) have conducted a program of research to identify differences between these two relationship orientations. Here are some of their findings:

- People pay more attention to the needs of a partner in a communal relationship than in an exchange relationship.
- People in a communal relationship prefer to talk about emotional topics, such as what makes them happy or sad; people in an exchange relationship prefer such unemotional topics as their favorite restaurant or their knowledge of gardening.
- A person is perceived as more altruistic if he or she offers to help a casual acquaintance (weak communal relationship in which assistance is not necessarily expected) than if he or she offers to help a close friend (strong communal relationship in which assistance is typically expected).
- A person is seen as more selfish if he or she does not offer to help a close friend than if he or she fails to assist an acquaintance.

In long-term relationships, patterns of reciprocity and rules of exchange become complex. In our most intimate relationships, we may develop a sense of unity or "we-ness" so that we perceive benefiting a loved one as a way of benefiting ourselves. Art and Elaine Aron (2000) have investigated the idea that in a close relationship, an individual comes to see the other person as part of himself or herself. To assess the inclusion of the other in the self, researchers showed participants the drawings depicted in Figure 9–1 and asked them to indicate which picture best described their relationship with a dating partner, parent, or other specific person (Aron, Aron, & Smollan, 1992). People had no difficulty using these drawings to characterize a relationship. The greater the overlap between self and other in a relationship, the more likely people were to report feelings of closeness and interconnected behaviors, such as spending time together. In another study, researchers found that the more committed young adults felt to their romantic partner, the more likely they were to use "we" and other plural pronouns rather than to use "I" in describing their relationship (Agnew, Van Lange, Rusbult, & Langston, 1998). The inclusion of the other as part of the self is one way close relationships can move beyond simple acts of social exchange.

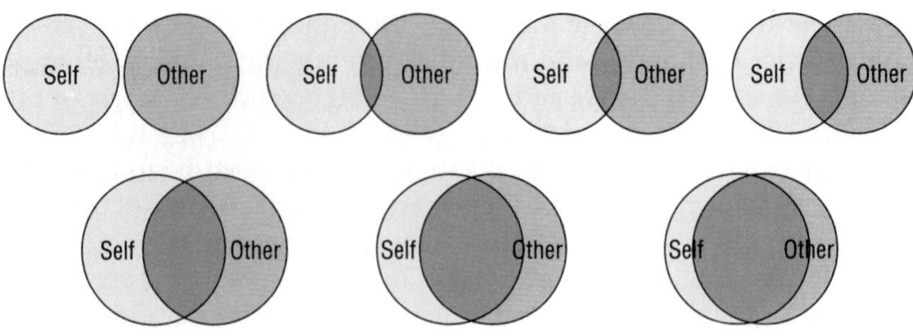

DIRECTIONS: Please circle the picture which best describes your relationship.

Figure 9–1 **The Inclusion of Other in the Self (IOS) Scale.**

Source: A. Aron, E. Aron, and D. Smollan (1992). Inclusion of other in the self scale and the structure of interpersonal closeness. *Journal of Personality and Social Psychology, 63*, p. 597. Copyright 1992 by the American Psychological Association. Adapted with permission.

SELF-DISCLOSURE

Self-Disclosure

Revealing intimate information or feelings about oneself with another person.

Conversation is an essential aspect of human interaction. When a friend reveals that his childhood fear of lawn sprinklers forced him to walk blocks out of his way to get to elementary school, we feel closer to him emotionally. When a coworker takes us aside to explain that her absence from work was not due to the flu as most people believed, but to a miscarriage, we sense a bond of trust and openness. **Self-disclosure** is a special type of conversation in which we share intimate information and feelings with another person (Canary, Cody, & Manusov, 2003; Dindia, 2002).

Sometimes we reveal facts about ourselves that might otherwise be unavailable to a listener—the kind of work we do, where we live, or how we voted in a recent election. This is known as "descriptive disclosure" because our revelations describe things about ourselves. A different type of self-disclosure occurs when we reveal our personal opinions and feelings—our affection for another person, our guilt about being overweight, or how much we hate our current job. This is called "evaluative disclosure" because emphasis is given to our personal assessment of people and situations.

We disclose information to another person for many reasons (Derlega & Grzelak, 1979; Omarzu, 2000). For example, we might tell someone a secret as a way to create greater intimacy in a relationship. Here are some of the main reasons for self-disclosure:

- ***Social approval.*** We reveal information about ourselves to increase social acceptance and liking by others.
- ***Relationship development.*** The sharing of personal information and confidences is an important way to begin a relationship and to move toward increasing levels of intimacy.
- ***Self-expression.*** Sometimes we talk about our feelings to "get them off our chest." After a hard day at work, we may eagerly tell a friend how angry we are at our boss and how unappreciated we feel. Being able to express our feelings can be a way to relieve distress.
- ***Self-clarification.*** In the process of sharing our feelings or experiences with others, we may gain greater understanding and self-awareness. Talking to a friend about a problem may help us to clarify our thoughts about the situation. Another person may reassure us that our reactions are "perfectly normal" or may suggest that we're "blowing things out of proportion." In either case, listeners provide useful information about social reality.
- ***Social control.*** We may reveal or conceal information about ourselves as a means of social control. For instance, we may deliberately refrain from talking about ourselves in order to protect our privacy. We may emphasize topics or ideas that we think will make a favorable impression on our listener. In extreme cases, people may deliberately lie to exploit others, as when an imposter claims to be a lawyer but actually has no legal training.

Self-Disclosure, Liking, and Reciprocity

Liking and self-disclosure tend to go hand in hand—a point demonstrated in a meta-analysis of many studies of self-disclosure (Collins & Miller, 1994). Liking is an important cause of self-disclosure. We reveal much more to people we like and trust than to those we dislike or barely know. Self-disclosure can also be a cause of liking. We tend to like people who reveal information about themselves to us, perhaps because we see them as warm, friendly, and trusting. Finally, the act of revealing personal information about ourselves to someone can enhance our liking for that person.

An important factor in the liking–disclosure link is reciprocity. Self-disclosure tends to be reciprocated (Dindia, 2002). If we share intimate information with another person, he or she is likely to respond with equally personal information. If we talk in superficialities, so will the other person. One explanation of this effect is the norm of reciprocity: If someone tells us something personal, we are expected to respond with a comparable revelation. In general, we like people most whose self-disclosure is reciprocal and gradual (Altman & Taylor, 1973).

There is much evidence that disclosure reciprocity is a key factor in liking. In an early study, Chaikin and Derlega (1974) used a procedure that enabled them to manipulate experimentally the intimacy level of self-disclosures in a pair. Their method was to videotape two actresses improvising a first-acquaintance encounter in a school cafeteria. Each actress improvised in two ways: at a high and a low level of self-disclosure. Then the experimenters presented the videotaped conversations to participants in each of the four combinations of self-disclosure: both women high in self-disclosure, both low, high-low, or low-high.

In the high-self-disclosure case, one woman immediately confided about her relationship with her boyfriend, who was her first sexual partner, and about her parents' reactions to her relationship. The other woman's high-intimacy disclosures concerned her mother's nervous breakdown and hospitalization, her fighting with her mother, and the possible divorce of her parents. In the low-self-disclosure cases, the women talked about the problems of commuting to school, the high schools they went to, and the courses they were taking. After watching one of the videotapes, the subjects indicated how much they liked each of the women. The main finding was that liking for both women was higher when they disclosed at the same level of intimacy than when they were at different levels. Breaking the reciprocity norm led to less liking, but for different reasons. The woman who disclosed

Self-disclosure is a special type of conversation in which we share intimate information and feelings with another person.

relatively little was perceived as cold, whereas the more intimate norm breaker was seen as maladjusted.

The link between self-disclosure and liking also depends on the meaning we attach to a person's revelations and to our own goals in the relationship (Miller, 1990). For example, if Suzanne wants to get closer to her roommate, Barbara, she may view Barbara's disclosure that her father has life-threatening cancer as a positive sign of growing trust in their relationship. Eager to help her friend, Suzanne may welcome Barbara's tearful revelation as an opportunity to show understanding and sympathy. In contrast, if the stranger sitting next to Suzanne in the lecture hall strikes up a conversation and begins to talk about her father's struggles with alcoholism, Suzanne may feel embarrassed, wonder about the person's judgment, and try to change the topic. The impact of self-disclosure on liking depends on the nature of the relationship between the individuals.

The Hazards of Self-Disclosure

Although self-disclosure can enhance liking and the development of a relationship, it also entails certain risks (Derlega, 1984). Revealing personal information makes us vulnerable. One college student hesitated for many months to tell her mother that she was a lesbian, fearing a rift in her close-knit family. When she did reveal her sexual orientation, her mother not only expressed shock and displeasure but also insisted that her daughter seek psychotherapy. Many lesbians and gay men would like to be open about their sexual orientation with relatives, friends, and coworkers but fear that disclosure may lead to hostility, rejection, or discrimination (Franke & Leary, 1991).

Some of the many possible risks individuals incur when they self-disclose include:

- ***Indifference.*** We may share information with another person in a bid to begin a relationship. Sometimes our disclosure is reciprocated by the other person and a relationship develops. At other times, however, we may find that the other person is indifferent to our disclosures and not at all interested in getting to know us.
- ***Rejection.*** Information we reveal about ourselves may lead to social rejection. For example, a college student may not tell her roommate that she has epilepsy, out of a concern that misinformation and fear will lead the roommate to reject her.
- ***Loss of control.*** There is some truth to the old adage that "knowledge is power." Sometimes, others use information we share with them to hurt us or to control our behavior. A teenage boy may tell a friend some little-known but potentially embarrassing information about his fear of women. In an angry moment, the friend may try to intimidate the young man by reminding him of this fear.
- ***Betrayal.*** When we reveal personal information to someone, we often assume, or even explicitly request, that the knowledge be treated confidentially. Unfortunately, such confidences are sometimes betrayed.

Not surprisingly, people are most likely to disclose personal information to trusted confidants such as a spouse, a close friend, a therapist, or a religious adviser or occasionally to someone they will never meet again, such as a stranger on a bus.

Because of the possible risks of self-disclosure, we sometimes conceal our deepest feelings, keep secrets from those we love, and protect parts of our lives from scrutiny (Finkenauer & Hazam, 2000). In short, there may be a tension between wanting to disclose and wanting to protect our privacy. Our goal is often to control the information others have about us—sharing what we want to when we want to.

Culture and Self-Disclosure

In the United States, the sharing of personal feelings is often considered the hallmark of a good friendship or marriage. This belief is consistent with a cultural emphasis on the importance of the individual and the expression of each person's

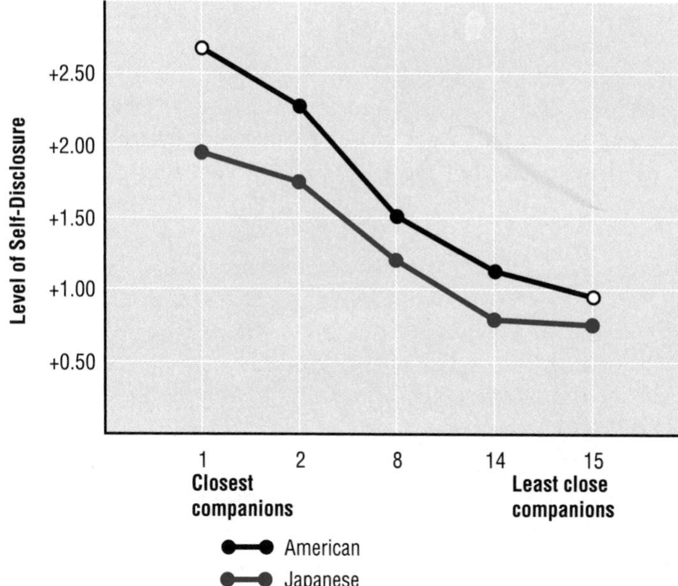

Figure 9–2 **A Comparison of Self-Disclosure to Closest and Least Close Companions by College Students in the United States and Japan.**

Everyone discloses more to close than to distant companions. But at each level of closeness, Japanese students report revealing less than do their American peers.

Source: Data from Barnlund (1989, p. 111).

unique feelings and experiences. However, other cultures have different norms and values about self-disclosure.

Consider, for example, differences between the individualist culture in the United States and the more collectively oriented culture of Japan (Barnlund, 1989). In general, social relations in Japan are more formal and restrained. The Japanese are generally less revealing than are their peers in the United States. When two Americans meet for the first time, it is common to ask whether the other person is married and has children, what type of work the person does, and where he or she went to school. This questioning is viewed as a routine way to get to know another person. In contrast, two Japanese people meeting for the first time would not ask such personal questions. In Japan, such inquiries would be considered forward and impertinent.

In a cross-cultural study of self-disclosure, Barnlund (1989) asked several hundred college students from Japan and the United States how much they had disclosed to friends and companions about various topics. Disclosure was rated on a 7-point scale, from no disclosure to disclosure in "great detail." As shown in Figure 9–2, everyone revealed more to close friends than to distant companions. Cultural differences also emerged: The Japanese revealed significantly less than did the Americans.

If culture influences the general amount and content of verbal disclosure, it may also affect the connections between personal revelations and satisfaction with a relationship. People in the United States might view low levels of self-disclosure within a marriage as a sign of marital problems, but couples from other cultures might not consider verbal disclosure indicative of the quality of a marriage. Evidence of such cultural differences comes from a study that compared the correlates of marital satisfaction among couples from the United States and couples from India, some of whom had arranged marriages and some of whom had chosen their spouse in a "love match" (Yelsma & Athappilly, 1988). For U.S. couples, higher satisfaction was associated with greater verbal disclosure; couples who talked more about personal matters were happier. The same was also true of Indian women and men in love-based marriages. But for Indian couples in arranged marriages, marital satisfaction was not related to patterns of verbal communication. In other words, the link between self-disclosure and marital satisfaction depends on cultural beliefs.

Gender and Self-Disclosure

In the United States, stereotypes depict men as "silent types" who keep their feelings to themselves and women as "talkers" who freely share confidences. As one wife complained about her husband, "He doesn't ever think there's anything

In same-sex friendships, women tend to disclose more personal information to women than men disclose to men.

to talk about. I'm the one who has to nag him to talk" (cited in L. Rubin, 1976, p. 124). How accurate is this stereotype about gender differences in regard to self-disclosure? A meta-analysis of 205 studies of self-disclosure found a small but statistically significant gender difference (Dindia & Allen, 1992). Women tend to reveal more than do men.

In same-sex friendships, women tend to disclose more to women than men disclose to men. Throughout adult life, women are more likely than are men to have an intimate same-sex confidant and to emphasize the sharing of personal information. In a study of college students, for example, women were more likely than were men to say that they enjoyed "just talking" to their best female friend and to indicate that talking helped form the basis of their relationship. In contrast, college men emphasized sharing activities with their best male friend (Caldwell & Peplau, 1982).

In cross-sex relationships, particularly heterosexual dating and marriage, gender differences in self-disclosure are more complex. The norm of reciprocity encourages male and female partners to disclose at comparable levels, some couples disclosing a great deal and others revealing relatively little personal information. In general, people disclose more to their romantic partner or spouse than to anyone else. Young people expect more self-disclosure in their intimate relationships than did earlier generations (Rands & Levinger, 1979). College dating couples usually disclose at quite high and equal levels (Rubin, Hill, Peplau, & Dunkel-Schetter, 1980). However, when exceptions to this equal-disclosure pattern occur in male–female couples, it is usually the man who discloses less.

The fact that men and women often disclose at equal levels does not mean that they necessarily reveal the same kinds of personal information. One study of college students found that in male–female relationships, women were more likely than men to reveal their weaknesses and to conceal their strengths; men showed the reverse pattern of disclosing their strengths and concealing their weaknesses (Hacker, 1981). Another study found that men disclosed more about "masculine" topics, such as when they had been aggressive or taken risks. Women disclosed more about "feminine" topics, such as when they felt childlike or were sensitive about their appearance (Derlega, Durham, Gockel, & Sholis, 1981).

In summary, research does not support the stereotype that all men are inexpressive all the time. There is a tendency for women to reveal more than men, but this effect is small and varies from situation to situation. In heterosexual dating and marriage, men and women often disclose at similar levels. Sex differences are most pronounced in same-sex relationships; women friends show a preference for talking, and men friends show a greater interest in shared activities.

How are we to explain these sex differences? There is much evidence that cultural norms affect patterns of self-disclosure. In the United States, emotional expression is generally acceptable for women. In contrast, men are taught to conceal tender emotions and personal concerns, especially from other men (Doyle, 1995). Men are encouraged to channel their emotional revelations exclusively to women, especially to a girlfriend or wife. In other cultures, however, norms about self-disclosure are quite different. As a result, individuals from non-Western cultures do not necessarily show the same patterns of self-disclosure and intimacy that are found in the United States.

Harry Reis and Ladd Wheeler (1991) compared the self-disclosure patterns of college students in the United States, Hong Kong, and Jordan. Cultural traditions in both Hong Kong and Jordan downplay cross-sex intimacy among unmarried students and encourage same-sex bonds, especially among men. Consequently, the researchers hypothesized that men in the United States would disclose relatively little to each other, and that men in Hong Kong and in Jordan would show higher levels of male–male disclosure. As predicted, the mean level of disclosure in male–male pairs was 6.6 in the United States, 8.2 in Hong Kong, and 8.4 in Jordan. These findings confirmed that U.S. culture suppresses intimacy among men, compared to the cultures of Hong Kong and Jordan.

INTIMACY

Like "love," "intimacy" is one of those common terms that can be difficult to define precisely. Self-disclosure is one component of intimacy, but the mere revelation of personal information is not sufficient to create the psychological experience of closeness. Rather, we experience a relationship as intimate when we feel understood, validated, and cared for by our partner (Reis, Clark, & Holmes, 2004; Reis & Shaver, 1988). Intimacy is created when we perceive another person as being responsive–paying attention to us and reacting in a supportive way. This model of intimacy is illustrated in Figure 9–3, which

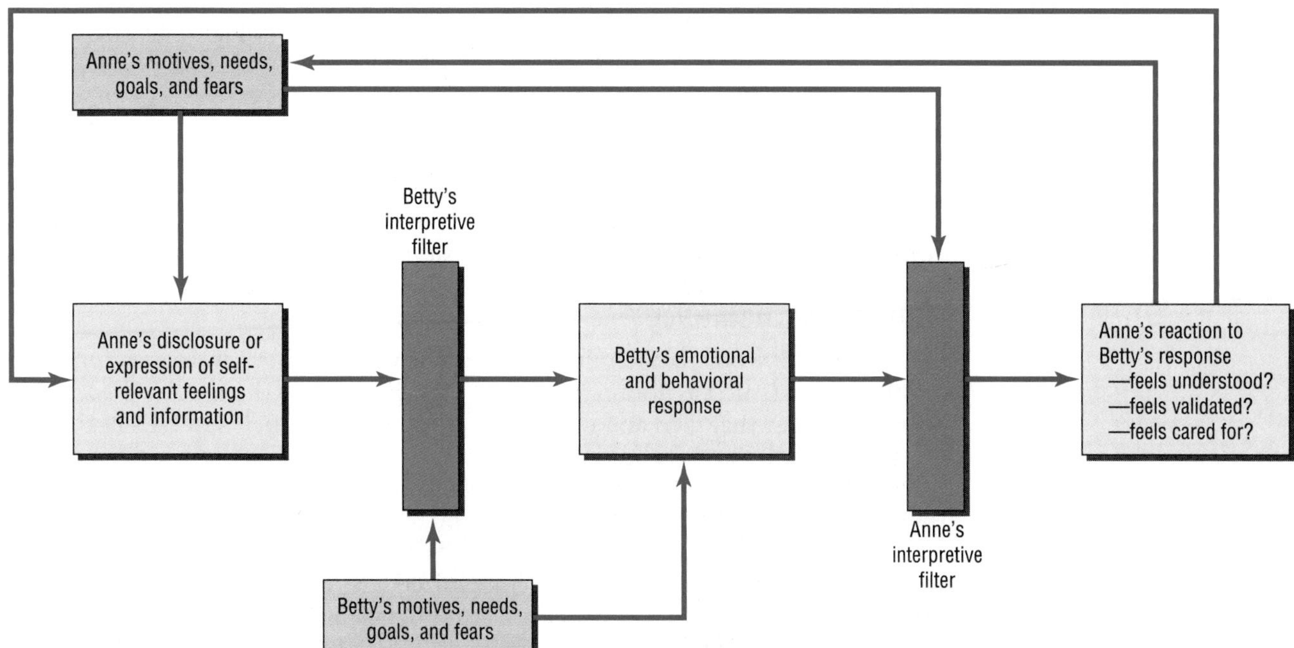

Figure 9–3 **Intimacy as an Interpersonal Process.**

Source: Data from H. T. Reis and P. Shaver (1988).

provides an example of an interaction between Anne and Betty. The model involves three major steps.

Step 1. The intimacy process begins when one individual reveals personal feelings or information to another. This sharing of information can be done verbally, through self-disclosure, or nonverbally, by "body language." In this example, Anne is upset about a problem she is having at work and decides to share her feelings with her friend, Betty. Anne's revelation is triggered by her private mental state—her motives, needs, goals, or fears.

Step 2. As the interaction continues, Betty responds to Anne's disclosure with sympathy and warmth. She moves her chair closer to Anne and asks relevant questions. Betty's behavior reflects her own motives (to be a good, supportive friend) and her personal interpretation of Anne's story (technically, her "interpretive filter"). Betty believes that her friend has been treated unfairly at work and tells her so.

Step 3. Anne appreciates Betty's concern. She interprets Betty's questions as a sign of interest and a desire to be helpful (this interpretation is shown as Anne's interpretive filter). As a result, Anne feels that Betty has understood her and has agreed with her views. She feels that Betty cares for her well-being.

Intimacy results from interactions of this sort, in which one person's actions evoke a response from another that makes the person feel understood, cared for, and validated. A growing body of empirical research demonstrates the importance of each of these ingredients in feelings of intimacy and satisfaction in close relationships (Berscheid & Reis, 1998). In several studies, college students have kept daily diaries in which they recorded their social interactions and described their feelings of closeness and intimacy toward the people they interacted with (Laurenceau, Barrett, & Pietromonaco, 1998; Reis, Sheldon, Gable, Roscoe, & Ryan, 2000). The more participants engaged in meaningful talk and the more they felt understood and appreciated, the more connected and intimate they felt to their social partners. In a recent study, partners in long-term heterosexual and homosexual relationships were interviewed about intimacy in their relationship (Mackey, Diemer, & O'Brien, 2000). Participants generally equated intimacy with being able to share their inner thoughts and feelings with their partner and with being accepted by their partner. As one participant explained, "I feel like I can be who I am . . . I don't have to pretend. . . . There are parts of myself that I don't particularly like . . . but it's OK to share with her. . . . She'll understand where it's coming from" (p. 214).

Self-disclosure by itself does not create intimacy. Rather, the discloser must feel that the listener accepts and understands the discloser's views. The listener's responsiveness and willingness to reciprocate disclosure both make a difference. In turn, intimate interactions promote feelings of trust and emotional closeness that are fundamental to the development of personal relationships.

Gender and Intimacy

Do men and women differ in their experiences of intimacy in relationships? Popular books such as John Gray's *Men Are from Mars, Women Are from Venus* (1992) suggest that men and women are worlds apart in their approaches to close relationships. What does research indicate? (See Reis, 1998, for a review.)

A first question is whether men and women tend to define intimacy differently. Based on studies in the United States, the answer appears to be "no." In one study, husbands and wives were asked, "What does intimacy mean to you?" (Waring et al., 1980). Both sexes emphasized expressing personal feelings and affection. In another study, participants gave detailed descriptions of two intimate and two distant-past experiences (Helgeson, Shaver, & Dyer, 1987). Both sexes listed disclosure of personal feelings, appreciation, warmth, and shared activities as central to intimacy. Using a very different methodology, Reis et al. (1985) had male and female raters evaluate the intimacy of videotaped conversations. Men and women did not differ in their evaluations of the conversations, a finding suggesting that they used similar standards to gauge the level of intimacy. Similarly, Burleson (2003) reviews research with different ethnic and cultural groups demonstrating that men, and women place relatively equal importance on emotional support in close relationships.

A second question is whether men and women differ in the degree of intimacy they actually experience in their interactions with friends and romantic partners. We have already seen that women tend to disclose somewhat more than do men and that this pattern is most evident in women's same-sex friendships. Interactions between female friends also tend to be more emotionally expressive than those of men (Aries, 1996).

The most comprehensive test of sex differences in intimacy is provided by Reis (1998). He compiled results of eight separate studies that used a daily-diary method. In these studies, participants rated the intimacy of each of their social interactions lasting 10 minutes or longer, using a 7-point scale from "superficial" to "meaningful." Across this set of studies, men's same-sex interactions were substantially less intimate than were women's same-sex interactions. By the standards of meta-analysis, the overall effect size ($d = .85$) was large. Indeed, this is one of the largest male–female differences reported to date. In contrast, no differences were found in the degree of intimacy men and women experienced in their interactions with other-sex friends and dating partners. The explanation for this pattern of intimacy is not entirely clear. A sociocultural explanation might suggest that women are expected to be the emotional leaders in relationships and so place a greater value on achieving intimacy and become more skilled in this domain. In contrast, men may be taught to inhibit self-disclosure and expressions of tender emotions, particularly in their relations with other men. (We discuss other male–female differences in social behavior in Chapter 11.)

THE BALANCE OF POWER

In any interaction, people often have different preferences and so try to influence each other in order to accomplish their own goals. The term **social power** refers to a person's ability to influence deliberately the behavior, thoughts, or feelings of another person (Huston, 2002). In some relationships, both individuals are equally influential. In other relationships, there is an imbalance of power; one person makes more of the decisions, controls more of the joint activities, wins more of the arguments, and is generally in a position of dominance.

Social Power

A person's ability to influence deliberately the behavior, thoughts, or feelings of another person.

Assessing the Balance of Power

Most research on the balance of power has investigated heterosexual couples. Today there is much variation among couples, ranging from relationships in which one partner (usually the man) makes virtually all the decisions to couples in which the partners share equally in power and decision making. Most heterosexual couples in the United States describe their romantic relationships as relatively equal in power. However, some couples report male dominance or, less frequently, female dominance.

In a survey of more than 3,000 married American couples, 64 percent said that the balance of power in their marriage was equal (Blumstein & Schwartz, 1983). Most of the remaining couples said the husband was more powerful, and less than 9 percent said the wife was dominant. Studies of dating couples have generally found similar patterns. For example, in a study of college students, 48 percent of women and 42 percent of men reported equal power in their current dating relationship (Felmlee, 1994). When the relationship was unequal, it was usually the man who had more say.

Partners can achieve equal power in different ways. Some couples strive to share all decisions completely: They shop together, discuss vacation plans, and so on. Other couples adopt a pattern in which each partner has "separate but equal"

Most American couples share in decision making about family matters.

areas of responsibility. Diane explained that she and her boyfriend, Alan, had equal power overall but that "in almost every situation, one of us is more influential. There are very few decisions that are fifty-fifty" (Peplau, 1984, p. 129). Diane picked their new apartment but Alan decided about moving the furniture. Diane said, "I make the aesthetic decisions and Alan makes the practical ones." Dividing areas of responsibility, sharing decisions totally, and some mixture of the two are all possible avenues to equal power.

In general, relationship satisfaction is equally high in male-dominant and egalitarian relationships. Consensus between a man and a woman may be more important for couple happiness than the particular pattern a couple follows. The exception occurs in female-dominant relationships. Such relationships are uncommon and tend to be less satisfying for both partners (Peplau, 1984). It is apparently easier to follow a traditional pattern of male dominance or a newer pattern of equality than to experience a female-dominant relationship.

Ethnicity and Power in American Marriages

Stereotypes often depict striking ethnic differences among married couples in the United States. Arlene Skolnick (1987) described ethnic stereotypes about marital power in these terms: "While the black family was seen as pathological because of its presumed female dominance, the Mexican American family was viewed as unhealthy because of its patriarchy. In contrast, the ideal middle-class Anglo family was seen as egalitarian and democratic" (p. 179). However, the results of several careful studies of the balance of power in Mexican American and African American marriages strongly refute these stereotypes.

Mexican American Marriages. Are Chicano families typically dominated by an all-powerful husband? To find out, Hawkes and Taylor (1975) interviewed Mexican American farm labor families in California. The interviewers were women who themselves lived in the migrant worker family camps and had been trained to assist in the research. Power was measured by responses to two different kinds of questions: questions about decision making and questions about who actually acts on the decisions. Decision-making questions assessed such topics as who decided how to spend the money, how many children the family should have, and how to raise the children. Action-taking questions asked about such issues as who paid the bills, who took steps to control how many children to have, and who disciplined the children. In the results, 62 percent of the families were classified as egalitarian, that is, as having marriages in which both the husband and the wife made decisions and carried them out. The remaining marriages were fairly evenly divided between ones in which the husband or the wife had more influence.

Other studies with both middle-class and working-class families have replicated the finding that a majority of Mexican American marriages are egalitarian (Peplau & Campbell, 1989). Staples and Mirande (1980) concluded that "virtually every systematic study of conjugal roles in the Chicano family has found egalitarianism to be the predominant pattern across socioeconomic groups, educational levels, urban-rural residence, and region of the country" (p. 894).

African American Marriages. Black families in the United States have often been depicted as matriarchal, or female-dominated. Some have used the term "matriarchy" to refer to the greater frequency of African American households headed by a single woman. The question posed here is a different one: In African American marriages, is the wife typically the dominant spouse? In an illustrative study, Dolores Mack (1971) recruited 80 couples, evenly divided among black working-class, black middle-class, white working-class, and white middle-class families. Mack used three separate measures of power. She assessed spouses' perceptions of the power balance in their marriage. She observed how couples behaved in power-relevant situations, such as coming to a joint decision about a matter on which they initially disagreed. She also observed couples in a bargaining situation. In general, couples tended to show fairly equal amounts of power in these situations. No racial differences were found on any of Mack's measures. Black wives were no more—or less—powerful than their white counterparts in any of the research activities. Other studies have also found that equal power is the most common pattern among black couples (DeJarnett & Raven, 1981; Peplau & Campbell, 1989).

In summary, research on Mexican American, African American, and Anglo marriages in the United States finds few overall differences in the frequency of egalitarian, male-dominant, and female-dominant relationships. There is considerable diversity within each ethnic group and much commonality across groups. Stereotypes that African American marriages are matriarchal and Chicano marriages are patriarchal are not supported by empirical research.

Tipping the Balance of Power

What determines whether a relationship is equal in power? Three important factors have been identified: social norms and attitudes relative resources, and the principle of least interest. These principles are likely to apply in a wide variety of relationships—not only in dating and marriage but also in relationships among friends, coworkers, and family members.

Social Norms and Attitudes. Patterns of influence in relationships are often dictated by social norms. In heterosexual dating and marriage, social convention has traditionally conferred greater authority on men. State laws once gave husbands legal control over all family property and permitted husbands, as the "head of the household," to decide where the family should live. More informally, women were taught to "look up to" the man they married and to defer to his wishes. Individuals who endorse traditional beliefs about sex roles consider it appropriate for a boyfriend and husband to be the leader and primary decision maker in heterosexual relationships.

Relative Resources. Norms and attitudes are not the only determinants of the balance of power. Social exchange theories propose that the relative resources of the two partners also affect their relative power. A resource is anything that "can be used to satisfy or frustrate needs or move persons further from or closer to their goals" (Huston, 2002, p. 206). When partners are imbalanced in their resources, the person who has more resources has more power. For example, when two students work together on a biology lab assignment, the person who is more knowledgeable or who owns a better microscope is likely to be more influential. In both heterosexual and same-sex romantic relationships, the situation becomes more complex. The partner who earns more money, has more education, or has a more prestigious job tends to have a power advantage, especially if the partner with greater resources is a man (Blumstein & Schwartz, 1983; Scanzoni & Scanzoni, 1981). In couples where the woman has a better job or earns more money than her partner, the result is more likely to be shared decision making. A study of marriages in which the wife earned at least 50 percent more than her husband illustrates this point. In these marriages, partners strove to minimize the wife's income and avoid linking her greater financial resources to decision making in their relationship (Tichenor, 1999).

The Principle of Least Interest. Another determinant of power is the relative dependency of the two partners on the relationship, based on their comparison level for alternatives. When both partners are equally attracted and committed, power tends to be equal. When one partner is more dependent on the relationship or cares more about continuing the relationship, the stage is set for an imbalance of power.

Principle of Least Interest

The partner who is less dependent on a relationship tends to have greater power.

Sociologist Willard Waller (1938) called this the **principle of least interest**: The less interested partner in a relationship has greater power. An implicit bargain is struck in which the more interested and dependent person defers to the other's wishes in order to ensure that the relationship will continue. An illustration of this principle is provided by Margaret, an unpopular young woman who had an affair with an older man:

> I accepted his structuring of our relationship. When he chose to deal in wit rather than in real information, I followed suit. When he acted casual about sex, so did I. I wanted something real from him. . . . Even when I knew this was impossible on my terms, I went ahead with it in his way. . . . I didn't back off, because I thought the potential was there, and a dateless summer had taught me that opportunities didn't come up all that often. (Cited in Goethals & Klos, 1970, p. 283)

Ultimately relationships based on lopsided dependencies usually prove unsatisfactory to both partners. Over time, these relationships tend either to change toward more equal involvement or to end.

CONFLICT

Even in the best of relationships, conflict seems to be inevitable (Holmes & Murray, 1996). In a recent study, adolescents kept daily records of their social interactions, including conflicts (Jensen-Campbell & Graziano, 2000). During 2 weeks, teenagers reported an average of one or two conflicts per day. Conflict was most frequent with siblings, then with parents, and was least frequent with friends. Although conflict can occur in relationships between coworkers and supervisors, family and neighbors, and friends and roommates, most research has investigated conflict in heterosexual dating and married couples.

Conflict is the process that occurs when the actions of one person interfere with the actions of another. The potential for conflict increases as two people become more interdependent. As interactions become more frequent and cover a more diverse range of activities and issues, there are more opportunities for disagreement.

Conflict is usually low during casual dating but increases significantly in serious dating relationships (Braiker & Kelley, 1979). Among married couples, conflict is fairly common. In one survey, nearly all the married people polled reported having "unpleasant disagreements" with their spouse at least occasionally (McGonagle, Kessler, & Schilling, 1992). On average, the married couples had one or two disagreements per month. Couples fight about almost anything, from politics and religion to work and money, from how to spend their time to how to divide household chores (Fincham, 2003). Life stressors and transitions, such

Conflict and arguments are common in close relationships. Parents can help children learn effective strategies for settling disputes.

as the birth of a child, the loss of a job, or a serious illness, increase the likelihood of conflict (Bradbury, Rogge, & Lawrence, 2001).

Conflict problems can be grouped into three general categories:

- ***Specific behaviors.*** Some conflicts focus on specific behaviors of a partner. A college student might be irritated because her roommate's loud stereo interferes with her studying for a test. Or a wife might be annoyed that her husband keeps forgetting to buy new tires for their station wagon.
- ***Norms and roles.*** Some conflicts focus on more general issues about the rights and responsibilities of partners in a relationship. Conflicts of this sort might concern a failure to live up to promises, a lack of reciprocity, or the neglect of some agreed-upon task. Thus, one roommate might complain that the other is not doing a fair share of the cleaning. Or a worker and a supervisor might disagree about the worker's job responsibilities.
- ***Personal dispositions.*** Some conflicts focus on a partner's motives and personality. People frequently go beyond specific behaviors to make attributions about the intentions and attitudes of a partner. One person might complain that the partner is lazy, lacks self-discipline, or doesn't really care about the relationship.

These three types of conflict reflect the fact that people are interdependent at three levels (Braiker & Kelley, 1979). At the behavioral level, partners have problems coordinating specific activities. At the normative level, they have problems negotiating rules and roles for their relationship. At the dispositional level, they may disagree about each other's personality and intentions. Conflicts can escalate as partners use specific problem behaviors to make more general attributions about each other's character. Dan may initially complain that his roommate left the sink full of dirty dishes. As the discussion continues, Dan may add that the roommate seldom lives up to their agreements about housekeeping. Dan may finally conclude that the roommate is hopelessly sloppy and self-centered.

Conflict can harm or help a relationship, depending on how it is resolved (Gottman, 1994; Holman & Jarvis, 2003). Because conflicts arouse strong emotions, they may not provide the best setting for constructive problem solving. The escalation of conflict is unlikely to benefit a relationship, especially if it leads to defensiveness, stubbornness, and withdrawal from interaction. At its worst, conflict leads to physical threats and actual violence. On the other hand, conflict can also provide an opportunity for couples to clarify disagreements and change their

THE DARK SIDE OF RELATIONSHIPS

We like to think of our close relationships as providing companionship, comfort, and support. Yet there can also be a darker side to relationships that involves rudeness, deceit, infidelity, and even physical abuse. Researchers use the term "interpersonal betrayal" to refer to actions taken toward a partner that violate three basic understandings about close relationships (Jones et al., 2001). First, we expect partners to "play by the rules" and to live up to both formal agreements such as wedding vows and informal expectations that have developed between partners (e.g., not to embarrass the partner in front of others). Second, we assume that we can trust a partner to fulfill his or her promises and to be faithful to the relationship. Third, we expect a partner to honor commitments that have been made to protect the future of the relationship. Sadly, partners often fail to live up to these expectations.

Lying

Research finds that lying is a fact of everyday life (Anderson, Ansfield, & DePaulo, 1999). On average, people tell at least one lie a day. Most college students have lied to a romantic partner at least once (Cole, 2001). Only a small percentage of adults say that they never lie. Some lies can be considered "altruistic," because they are designed to benefit another person. People sometimes bend the truth, telling a friend that his mediocre homemade dinner was "wonderful" or reassuring a friend that she made the right decision, even if we don't think so. In contrast, other lies are "self-serving," designed to help make a good impression, conceal wrongdoing, or avoid responsibility. Examples include falsely denying that we have spread gossip about a friend or that we have a contagious sexually transmitted disease. In general, people are less likely to lie to close friends and romantic partners than to acquaintances and strangers, and the lies told to intimates are more likely to be altruistic. Nonetheless, people often tell their most serious lies to a romantic partner, for instance, covering up a romantic infidelity that might jeopardize their primary relationship.

Infidelity

Romantic couples differ in their views about the kinds of relationships that each partner can have with other people. Although many married couples agree to be sexually faithful, other couples view extramarital liaisons as acceptable. Researchers define "infidelity" as a violation of a couple's norms regulating the acceptable level of emotional or physical intimacy with people outside the relationship (Drigotas & Barta, 2001). It is estimated that 20 to 24 percent of Americans will have sex with someone other than their spouse while they are married, with reports of extramarital sex higher among husbands than among wives.

Infidelity is more likely if a partner is less committed to a primary relationship, finds the primary relationship less satisfying, has invested less, and has attractive alternatives available (Drigotas, Safstrom, & Gentilia, 1999; Previti & Amato, 2004). A study of dating couples found that the way an infidelity is discovered makes a difference (Afifi, Falato, & Weiner, 2001). In general, discovering that a partner had been unfaithful diminished the deceived partner's satisfaction and trust. But the harm to the relationship was greatest if the infidelity was revealed by a third party or if the partner was caught in the act. Harm was least when the unfaithful partner voluntarily confessed. An unfaithful partner was most likely to be forgiven if he or she confessed rather than being found out.

Obsession and Stalking

Sometimes a former partner or a rejected suitor becomes obsessed with the person he or she desires (Regan, 2000). These individuals may engage in endless rumination about the person they "love" and may pursue him or her relentlessly. They may call repeatedly during the night, leave notes or flowers, hang out at the target's favorite restaurant or store, and generally become very intrusive. Stalking is an extreme form in which the person is followed, spied on, and sometimes threatened or even harmed (McCann, 2001). Most often, the stalker is a man and the victim is a woman, although men may also be stalked by women. It has been estimated that as many as 8 percent of women and 2 percent of men have been stalked at some time in their lives. In Chapter 13, we discuss violence that occurs in intimate relationships.

expectations about the relationship. Lovers' quarrels allow lovers to test their own and their partner's dependence on the relationship, to discover the depth of their feelings for each other, and to renew their efforts to create a satisfying relationship. The Research Highlight for this chapter goes beyond conflict to consider other negative features of relationships, including lying and infidelity.

SATISFACTION

What makes a relationship happy and satisfying? According to an interdependence perspective, we are satisfied if a relationship is profitable, that is, if the rewards we receive exceed the costs incurred (Rusbult, 1980, 1983). Many studies have demonstrated a positive correlation between receiving rewards and feeling satisfied in a relationship. The impact of costs on relationship quality has been less consistent. Recently researchers have suggested that the inconsistent impact of costs may stem from a confusion between costs and sacrifices (Clark & Grote, 1998; Van Lange et al., 1997). Costs are events we perceive as unpleasant, such as a partner criticizing our clothes or embarrassing us in public. Costs are always negative. In contrast, sacrifice involves doing something to promote the welfare of our partner or our relationship, such as giving up sleep to drive our partner to the airport or spending time with in-laws we dislike in order to please our partner. Sacrifice involves putting aside our own self-interest for the sake of the relationship, and it may not be experienced as costly.

According to interdependence theory, relationship satisfaction is also affected by our general comparison level. We are satisfied if a relationship compares favorably to our hopes and expectations. Downward social comparisons, a concept we introduced in Chapter 4, can also be important. One way to feel better about our own relationship is to tell ourselves that we are doing better than other, less successful couples (Buunk, Oldersma, & De Dreu, 2001). The occasional argument we have with our partner may seem minor when we consider another couple who seem to fight all the time.

Perceptions of fairness also affect satisfaction: Even if a relationship provides many benefits, we may not be fully satisfied if we believe that we are being treated unfairly. In business, partners are usually dissatisfied if they perceive the relationship to be inequitable. Similarly, in friendship and love, lopsided relationships, in which one person gives much more or gets much more than the other, are usually not as satisfying as are balanced relationships (Cate & Lloyd, 1992).

Other characteristics of relatively happy dating and married couples have also been identified. Happy couples tend to spend more time together in joint activities. For some couples, engaging in novel, exciting, and challenging activities may help to rekindle passion and increase relationship satisfaction (Aron, Norman, Aron, & Lewandowski, 2002). Adventurous couples might relish parasailing or kayaking; other couples might find mutual enjoyment in a rousing bridge tournament or visit to a new city together. Happy couples tend to use more humor and express less criticism and hostility toward each other.

Earlier, we saw that environmental factors such as unemployment can increase relationship conflict. Not surprisingly, research also shows that the situational context affects relationship satisfaction. As Ellen Berscheid (1999) observed, "Some fragile relationships survive forever because they never encounter a relationship-toxic environment and some very strong relationships dissolve . . . because fate . . . put their relationship in harm's way" (p. 265). Financial strain, the demands of work, the necessity of caring for ill relatives, and many other stressors external to the couple can detract from relationship quality (Cutrona et al., 2003; Neff & Karney, 2004).

COMMITMENT

People who are strongly committed to a relationship are likely to stay together "through thick and thin" and "for better or for worse." In technical terms, **commitment in a relationship** refers to all the forces, positive and negative, that

Commitment in a Relationship

All the forces (attractions and barriers) that keep a person in a relationship.

Some married couples succeed in creating committed relationships that withstand the test of time.

act to keep an individual in a relationship. Three major factors influence commitment to a relationship (Johnson, 1999; Surra & Gray, 2000).

First, commitment is affected by the positive forces of attraction to a particular partner and relationship. If we like another person, enjoy that person's company, and find that person easy to get along with, we will be positively motivated to continue the relationship. In other words, commitment is stronger when satisfaction is high (Rusbult & Van Lange, 1996). This component has been called "personal commitment" because it refers to an individual's desire to maintain or improve a relationship (Johnson, Caughlin, & Huston, 1999).

Second, commitment is influenced by our values and moral principles—the feeling that we ought to stay in the relationship. This "moral commitment" is based on our sense of obligation, religious duty, or social responsibility. For some people, a belief in the sanctity of marriage and a sense of having made a lifelong commitment to a spouse are strong deterrents to divorce.

Third, commitment is based on negative forces or barriers that make it costly for a person to leave a relationship. Factors that can restrain us from leaving a relationship include the lack of attractive alternatives and the investments we have already made in the relationship. A married person may fear the social, financial, and legal consequences of divorce and so feel trapped in an unhappy marriage. This situation, in which a person feels that he or she has to continue a relationship, has been called "constraint commitment." According to interdependence theory, two important types of constraints are the lack of attractive alternatives and investments we had already made in a relationship.

Availability of Alternatives. Our comparison level for alternatives affects our commitment. We may dislike our boss and regret having to interact daily but continue the relationship because we need the salary and can't find another job. We may date someone who falls below our comparison level because he or she is the only eligible person we know. When we are dependent on a relationship to provide things we value and cannot obtain elsewhere, we are unlikely to leave (Attridge, Creed, Berscheid, & Simpson, 1992). The lack of better alternatives increases commitment.

Investments. Commitment is also affected by the investments we have made in a relationship (Rusbult, 1980, 1983). Investments include time, energy, money, emotional involvement, shared experiences, and sacrifices for a partner. To invest a great deal in a relationship and then find it unrewarding can arouse cognitive dissonance, and so we may feel psychological pressures to see the relationship in a positive light and to downplay its drawbacks (Rubin, 1973).

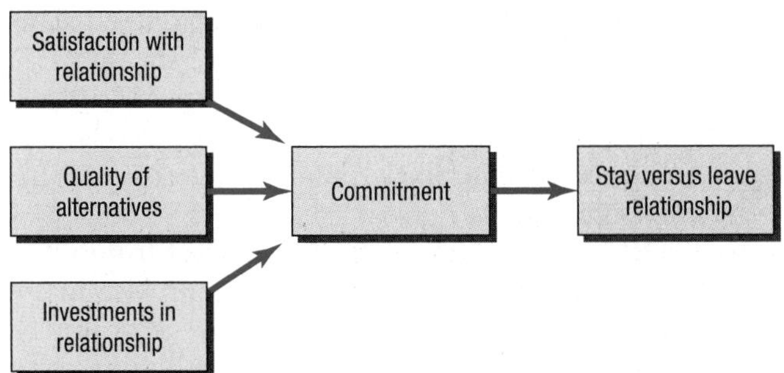

Figure 9–4 The Investment Model of Commitment and Relationship Stability.

The more we have put into a relationship, the more costly it would be for us to leave it.

Empirical research provides strong support for the interdependence model of commitment. A recent meta-analysis of 52 studies tested the model shown in Figure 9–4. As expected, satisfaction, alternatives, and investments were significant predictors of commitment which, in turn, predicted whether the relationship stayed together or ended (Le & Agnew, 2003).

Association Between Satisfaction and Commitment

In many relationships, there is a close association between satisfaction and commitment. As young lovers discover the special rewards of their developing relationship, they take steps to build commitment. They stop dating other people and forgo alternative activities to be with each other. As their affection blossoms into love, they take public action to demonstrate their feelings and to build a future together. Having a wedding ceremony, buying a home together, having children—these investments in the relationship are usually based on love and further serve to build commitment. If the couple encounters difficult times of conflict and disagreement, their investments may provide the motivation to work to improve the relationship and to rekindle their flagging affection.

Yet satisfaction and commitment are not invariably linked. Although some unhappy couples are able to improve their relationships and others terminate unrewarding relationships, some couples stay together despite low satisfaction (Previti & Amato, 2003). A U.S. national survey found that about 7 percent of married people were relatively unhappy in their marriage but expected to stay together nonetheless (Heaton & Albrecht, 1991). To understand the sources of commitment in unrewarding relationships, the researchers compared the experiences of those in unhappy marriages who expected to stay together and those who considered divorce a possibility. In general, the more highly committed couples had invested more in their relationship; they had been together for a longer time and had more children. The lack of alternatives to marriage also made a difference. For both sexes, the belief that life would be worse if they separated contributed to commitment. For women, the threat of economic loss from divorce was especially important. For men, the fear that their sex life would worsen was especially important. Moral commitment also made a difference. Individuals who believed that marriage is a lifetime commitment and that couples should stay together for the sake of the children were more likely to stay together despite marital dissatisfaction. Finally, people who believed they had greater personal control over their lives reported less commitment to an unhappy marriage. As these data suggest, people sometimes find themselves stuck in unsatisfying relationships.

Satisfaction and Commitment in the Relationships of Lesbians and Gay Men

Although heterosexual college students often expect gay and lesbian relationships to be less successful than heterosexual relationships (Testa, Kinder, & Ironson,

1987), this does not appear to be the case. Several studies have compared samples of gay, lesbian, and heterosexual couples, using standardized measures of love, satisfaction, and relationship adjustment (Kurdek, in press; Peplau & Beals, 2004). No significant differences have been found on any measures of relationship quality. Lesbians and gay men are no more likely than are heterosexuals to have happy—or miserable—relationships.

Researchers have begun to identify factors that enhance or detract from satisfaction in same-sex relationships (Peplau & Beals, 2004). Consistent with interdependence theory, satisfaction is high when a person perceives a relationship as providing many rewards and relatively few costs. Satisfaction is also higher when gay and lesbian partners believe that they share relatively equally in power and decision making (Kurdek, 1998).

It is estimated that roughly one in every two recent heterosexual marriages will end in divorce. Without official marriage records and census reports, it is not possible to offer similar estimates for the stability of the relationships of lesbians and gay men. Rather, researchers have investigated factors that affect commitment in gay and lesbian relationships (Beals, Impett, & Peplau, 2002; Kurdek, 2000). Factors identified by interdependence theory are useful in understanding same-sex couples. Commitment is high when partners perceive their relationships as providing many positive attractions, have made substantial investments in the relationship, and perceive few available alternatives.

Differences between homosexual and heterosexual couples are most likely to involve barriers to ending a relationship, rather than the positive attractions of the relationship. Heterosexual marriage creates barriers against divorce such as investment in joint property, concerns about children, or one partner's financial dependence on the other. These obstacles may encourage married couples to work toward improving a deteriorating relationship, rather than ending it. In contrast, gay and lesbian couples are less likely to experience comparable barriers. With a few exceptions, gay men and lesbians cannot marry legally. They are less likely than heterosexual married couples to pool their financial resources or own property jointly, and are less likely to have children in common. This absence of barriers reduces the chances that lesbians and gay men will be trapped in hopelessly miserable and deteriorating relationships. However, weaker barriers may also encourage partners to end relationships that might have improved if given more time and effort. In short, research finds many commonalities among close relationships, regardless of the sexual orientation of the people involved.

RELATIONSHIP MAINTENANCE

All relationships encounter problems and disappointments from time to time. How we respond to dissatisfaction is both a cause and a consequence of our satisfaction and commitment. There is growing evidence that happy, committed partners think about and treat each other differently from partners in dissatisfied relationships. In turn, how partners respond to today's disappointments and frustrations has important implications for their future happiness together and the ultimate longevity of their relationship. Researchers are beginning to uncover some of the many ways that partners' thoughts and behaviors can affect the quality of their relationship.

Positive Illusions about Relationships

We saw in Chapter 4 that people tend to hold positive illusions about themselves, reflecting a tendency toward self-enhancement. There is growing evidence that a similar process occurs in relationships. People, especially those in happy, committed relationships, tend to idealize their partner and to view their own relationship as superior to those of others (Murray & Holmes, 1997; Neff & Karney, 2002). Members of happy couples tend to emphasize their partner's virtues and downplay weaknesses. Although it may be hard to overlook specific annoying behaviors (e.g., he's late for our dates), these flaws are typically placed in the context of more global positive qualities (e.g., he's easygoing and warm-hearted). Viewing our romantic partner as favorably as possible can enhance our satisfaction and bolster our confidence that we have found the "right" partner and are in a good relationship.

One example comes from research on predictions about the chances that one's own romantic relationship will be successful. In the United States, roughly half of marriages end in divorce. Yet, when asked about their own marriage, most people are exceptionally optimistic. In three studies of ethnically diverse samples, most individuals said that the probability they would divorce was 0 percent (Fowers, Lyons, Montel, & Shaked, 2001). In contrast, these same individuals were much more accurate in estimating their chances of experiencing other negative events, such as becoming physically disabled or having a car accident. The researchers also gathered information from unmarried college students. Most students expected to marry and painted a rosy picture of their future relationship. Only 4 percent of single students thought that their future marriage would be below average in quality, and the majority thought it would be above average. Most students estimated a 0 percent likelihood that they would ever divorce, and only 12 percent thought the chances were greater than 50–50. The researchers noted that in contemporary society, marriage is both extremely important and fragile. Positive marital illusions may help to promote a sense that marriage is worth maintaining.

Other evidence of positive illusions comes from a longitudinal study of college students. In this research, students were asked to assess the quality of their current dating relationship and to predict the likelihood that they and their partner would be together 6 months and 1 year later (MacDonald & Ross, 1999). Participants' parents and roommates were also asked to make similar assessments. Students, roommates, and parents gave similar reports about the strengths in the relationship. However, consistent with the tendency for people to idealize their own relationship, students listed fewer challenges or obstacles facing the couple than did parents or roommates. In other words, students were primarily positive in their assessments; observers were more evenhanded and paid attention to problems as well as to strengths. Whose predictions about the longevity of the couple would be most accurate? Six months and 1 year later, parents' and roommates' predictions proved to be more accurate than students' own predictions.

Research has also investigated whether positive beliefs about relationships are found in diverse cultures (Endo, Heine, & Lehman, 2000). In two studies, Japanese, European Canadian, and Asian Canadian university students rated their own relationships with a best friend, a romantic partner, and the closest family member. They also evaluated the relationships of an "average" student from their university. Participants from all cultural groups rated their own relationships as significantly better than those of the average student on such dimensions as closeness, supportiveness, and enjoyment of being together. These findings suggest that the relationship enhancement bias is not limited to North Americans.

Sandra Murray (1999) suggests that "lasting satisfaction and relationship stability depend on individuals over-stating the case for commitment—interpreting and structuring the available evidence in ways that support the most positive possible view of their relationships" (p. 30). There is growing evidence that positive illusions about romantic relationships contribute to relationship satisfaction and longevity.

Misremembering the Past

Another way partners maintain confidence in their current relationship is to perceive steady progress toward greater love and intimacy. In essence, people may believe that even if their relationship isn't perfect, it's getting better all the time (Frye & Karney, 2004). This point was vividly illustrated in a study by Susan Sprecher (1999) of changes in the love of dating partners for each other over time. Sprecher followed a sample of dating couples for 4 years, obtaining information about the couples at 1-year intervals. At each testing, the partners filled out measures that assessed their love and satisfaction. Participants whose relationships endured remembered their love and satisfaction as increasing steadily from year to year. In fact, assessments of love and satisfaction taken throughout the 4 years did not corroborate the participants' memories. Instead, couples had relatively high love and satisfaction scores at all time points, and they did not show an overall pattern of increase over time.

Memory bias was also found in a 20-year longitudinal study of wives (Karney & Coombs, 2000). Women's actual satisfaction in their marriage declined over time. However, when asked to remember the early days of their marriage, wives reported a pattern of improvement over time: They believed their marriage was currently better than it had been in the past. If human memory was like a tape recorder, it would provide an accurate record of past events. In reality, human memory is more creative, constructing stories about the past that may take liberties with the facts in order to maintain current commitment. Indeed, the ability to perceive improvement may be a source of hope for the future.

Forgoing Tempting Alternative Partners

One of the potential threats to a relationship is created by the existence of attractive alternative partners (Rusbult et al., 1999). One purpose of commitment ceremonies and wearing wedding rings is to announce to tempting alternatives that a person is unavailable. People who are highly committed to a relationship may also use cognitive mechanisms to protect and maintain their relationship. For example, committed partners may actively devalue alternatives as a way of resisting temptation (Lydon, Fitzsimons, & Naidoo, 2003). Convincing ourselves that our current dating partner is more wonderful than all others makes it easier to sustain commitment (Rusbult, Van Lange, Wildschut, Yovetich, & Verette, 2000). There is also evidence that highly committed individuals pay less attention to potentially attractive alternative partners (Miller, 1997). Inattentiveness may help to preserve a desirable relationship.

Explaining a Partner's Behavior

When a partner does something that annoys or disappoints us, we are motivated to figure out the reasons for the action. In more technical terms, we make attributions about the causes of our partner's behavior. Research finds that, generally, happy and distressed couples tend to explain their partner's actions in different ways (Bradbury & Fincham, 1990; Karney & Bradbury, 2000). More often than not, happy couples tend to make "relationship-enhancing attributions";

Why is this husband bringing his wife flowers? Is it to show his love, or to conceal the fact that he just bought himself an expensive watch?

that is, they interpret a partner's behaviors in a positive light (Holzworth-Munroe & Jacobson, 1985). For example, a happily married wife might attribute her husband's recent lack of interest in sex to the stress he is under at work. She attributes a negative behavior to factors that are temporary and outside her husband's control. The same wife might attribute her husband's unexpectedly bringing her flowers to his desire to do something special to show his love. She attributes a positive event to factors that are intentional and enduring. In both cases, the wife's interpretation casts the husband's actions in a relationship-enhancing way.

In contrast, a wife in an unhappy marriage might make "distress-maintaining attributions" for her husband's actions. She might interpret his recent lack of interest in sex as a sign that he no longer loves her, thus attributing a negative behavior to an intentional and long-lasting cause. The same distressed wife might view her husband's gift of flowers as an attempt to justify spending money on himself—for a selfish and short-lived cause. Such attributions cast the husband in a negative light and serve to maintain the wife's discontent.

A comparison of relationship-enhancing and distress-maintaining attributions is provided in Table 9–1. In the terminology introduced in Chapter 3, happy couples tend to attribute negative partner behaviors to external, unstable, and unintentional causes. They give the partner the benefit of the doubt and attribute a problem to something that is outside the person's control, is temporary, and is unintended. Such attributions minimize the partner's responsibility for negative events and behaviors. Happy couples attribute positive partner behaviors to internal, stable, and intentional causes. A partner's kind act is seen as motivated by enduring, positive qualities of the partner. Such attributions give a partner credit for positive events and behaviors in the relationship. Distressed couples show an opposite pattern, attributing rewarding behaviors to unstable, external, and unintentional causes; and attributing negative behaviors to internal, stable, and intentional causes.

Happy and distressed couples also differ on the attributional dimension of globality. This dimension concerns whether the causes of the partner's behavior are seen as specific to a particular situation ("He hates washing dishes") or as something more global that affects many situations ("He refuses to do anything around the house"). A global attribution for a negative event might be "You're such a jerk," implying that many negative outcomes are caused by your personality. A more specific attribution for a negative event would be "There are times when you can be very annoying," implying that your personality occasionally affects a specific set of outcomes.

Taken together, these differences in attributions can lead partners in distressed relationships to view each other as relatively selfish and blameworthy, and partners

Table 9–1

A Comparison of Relationship-Enhancing and Distress-Maintaining Attributions

	Relationship-Enhancing Attributions	Distress-Maintaining Attributions
Positive Event		
My husband takes me out for an expensive dinner.	Internal, stable, global *He's always such a sweet and thoughtful person. He loves me.*	External, unstable, specific *He took me out because it's the end of the year, and he can write it off of his expense account.*
Negative Event		
My husband forgot my birthday.	External, unstable, specific *Something unexpected must have come up at work. This isn't like him.*	Internal, stable, global *He's always so thoughtless. He never remembers anything or cares about my feelings.*

in happy relationships to see each other as relatively caring and responsible. Research is beginning to show that attributions such as these can have important consequences in close relationships. For unhappy couples, issues of responsibility and blame are often salient. Interpreting a partner's behaviors as based on selfish and malevolent intentions can magnify feelings of distress and foster criticism of the partner and emotional withdrawal.

Over time, partners' attributions can influence their level of overall marital satisfaction (Fincham, Harold, & Gano-Phillips, 2000). In contrast, generous attributions that cast the partner's actions in the best light possible serve to preserve feelings of goodwill and may facilitate more productive problem solving.

Willingness to Sacrifice

Sometimes partners in a relationship encounter situations in which the best choice for each person is different. When a conflict of interest occurs, one partner may decide to sacrifice his or her immediate self-interest for the good of the partner or their relationship (Whitton, Stanley, & Markman, 2002). For example, a wife may decide to spend the holidays with her husband's family, even though she would personally prefer a romantic vacation for two.

The more committed partners are to a relationship, the more willing they usually are to sacrifice. For example, in a longitudinal study of dating and married couples, researchers investigated whether initial levels of commitment would predict subsequent willingness to sacrifice (Wieselquist, Rusbult, Foster, & Agnew, 1999). To measure willingness to sacrifice, the participants were asked to identify four "most important activities" in their life other than their relationship. Participants listed such things as their relationship with their family or friends, education, a career, religion, or leisure activities like soccer or reading. They were then asked to rate to what extent they would consider giving up this activity for the good of their relationship. Among both married and dating couples, greater commitment predicted greater willingness to put aside self-interest to promote the relationship.

The impact of sacrifice on a relationship may depend on the person's reasons for making the sacrifice. It is useful to distinguish between approach and avoidance reasons. Sometimes people sacrifice for a partner to show their love and concern. Examples include "I get a great deal of pleasure out of making my partner happy" or "I want my partner to appreciate me." Sacrifice for these and other approach motives can lead to positive feelings of happiness and satisfaction. In contrast, sometimes people give in to a partner in order to avoid conflict or for fear of jeopardizing the relationship itself. Examples include "I feel obligated to sacrifice for my partner" and "I have to sacrifice or my partner won't love me." Sacrifice for these and other avoidance motives can lead to lingering feelings of resentment and anger. In a recent study, college student dating couples kept daily records of sacrifices they made for their partner during a 2-week period. In addition, they also recorded their reasons for making the sacrifice and their emotions at the end of each day (Impett, Gable, & Peplau, 2004). On days when people sacrificed for approach reasons, they felt happier and more content with life. In contrast, when they sacrificed for avoidance reasons, they felt worse. Further, people who reported sacrificing for avoidance reasons were significantly more likely than other participants to break up during the following month.

Turning the Other Cheek: Accommodation and Foregiveness

From time to time, most of us act badly toward our friends and lovers—we say or do thoughtless and angry things (Rusbult et al., 1999). Consider a woman who returns home from a hard day at work. When her husband tries to start a conversation, she rebuffs him, saying in annoyance, "Just be quiet for a while." How will the husband react? He could respond to her hurtful comments with an angry remark of his own, such as "You're a real joy!" Or he could "turn the other cheek" and respond in a more conciliatory way, perhaps by giving his wife a little time to herself or acknowledging that she's probably had a rough day. By responding to a potentially destructive comment in a positive, constructive way, the husband can prevent the situation from escalating from a minor incident into a larger argument.

The technical terms "accommodation" refers to the willingness, when a partner engages in a potentially destructive behavior, to inhibit the impulse to reciprocate and instead to respond constructively (Rusbult et al., 1999). Research shows that being able to avoid trading insults and criticisms is an important factor in the quality of a close relationship. As one researcher noted, "It is less important to exchange positive behaviors than it is not to exchange negative behaviors" (Montgomery, 1988, p. 345). But it is not always easy for partners to put aside their own feelings of annoyance or anger and to respond constructively. Several factors increase the likelihood of a constructive response (Arriaga & Rusbult, 1998; Wieselquist et al., 1999). Partners who are strongly committed to a relationship and who are securely attached are less likely to retaliate. In addition, the way people interpret their partner's behavior makes a difference. People who are able to take their partner's perspective, who try to understand how their partner is thinking and feeling, are less likely to reciprocate negative acts. Individual differences in self-control, in the ability to inhibit self-interested impulses in favor of more constructive behaviors, can also make a difference (Finkel & Campbell, 2001).

Recently, social psychologists have turned their attention to the nature of forgiveness in personal relationships (e.g., Fincham, 2000). There are many ways in which a person may harm or transgress against a partner, such as embarrassing a partner at a party or having a secret extramarital affair. Consider a husband who finds that his wife has forgotten his birthday. The husband's disappointment or anger may lead to a sense of distance or estrangement in their relationship. He may contemplate hurtful acts in return. The husband's interpretation of the wife's actions and, in particular, her responsibility for the act is crucial. Did she intend to be hurtful or was this an inadvertent slip due to overwork at her job? Frank Fincham (2000) suggested that this unhappy interpersonal situation might be resolved in one of three ways, shown in Figure 9–5. First, new information might lead to a reinterpretation of the situation. If the husband discovers that his wife failed to mention his birthday at breakfast because she had planned a surprise dinner party to celebrate that evening, the harm would be nullified or removed. Second, the husband might take no action or might seek to distract himself from the situation. Over time, his hurt feelings would be likely to dissipate, although they might be reactivated by later events. Third, the husband might deliberately decide to forgive his wife's thoughtlessness. His forgiveness might be made easier by his wife acknowledging her harmful act and apologizing for it.

Research is beginning to illuminate the process of forgiveness in close relationships (Finkel et al., 2002; Katchadourian et al., 2004; McCullough, 2001). Individuals in generally happy and committed relationships are more likely to forgive than those in less satisfactory relationships. People who feel empathy for an offending partner are more likely to show forgiveness and to engage in efforts at conciliation rather than retaliation. Further, there is preliminary evidence that acts

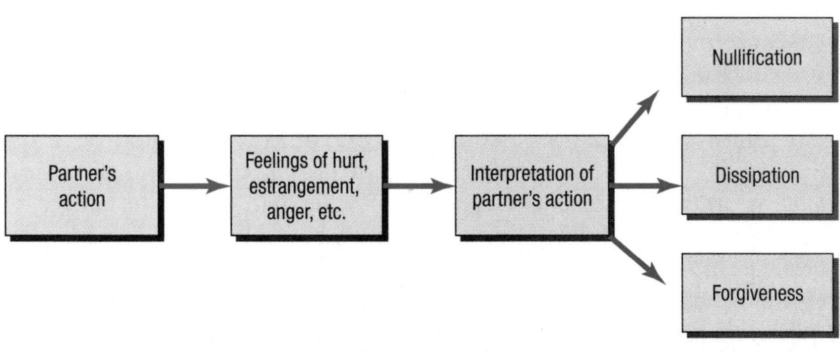

Figure 9–5 **A Model of Forgiveness in a Close Relationship.**

of forgiveness help to restore feelings of closeness between partners. Compared to harboring grudges, forgiving interpersonal offenses may reduce stress and enhance physical health as well (Witvliet, Ludwig, & Vander Laan, 2001).

RESPONSES TO DISSATISFACTION: VOICE, LOYALTY, NEGLECT, AND EXIT

Caryl Rusbult and her colleagues have investigated the diverse ways people react when they are dissatisfied with a relationship (Drigotas, Whitney, & Rusbult, 1995; Rusbult, 1987). Rusbult's model is quite general and has been applied to job dissatisfaction as well as to dissatisfaction with romantic relationships. Rusbult has identified four common reactions to dissatisfaction, which she calls "voice," "loyalty," "neglect," and "exit."

Voice occurs when a person actively discusses the problems; tries to compromise; seeks help; tries to change the self, the partner, or the situation; or more generally works to improve the relationship. Fundamentally, voice is an effort to rescue a relationship in trouble. In a job situation, a worker might give voice to his or her dissatisfaction by discussing problems with a supervisor, suggesting solutions, consulting with a union official, or blowing the whistle on corporate wrongdoing. In a romantic relationship, voice might take the form of trying to talk with the partner, suggesting improvements in the relationship, or offering to enter counseling. Voice is most often used when the person has previously been satisfied with the relationship and has invested fairly heavily in it. In romantic relationships, this response is somewhat more likely from women than it is from men.

Loyalty means passively but optimistically waiting for things to improve. Loyalty is a conservative response that attempts to maintain the status quo. In a job situation, a worker might publicly support the organization and perform his or her job well while hoping that conditions will change. In a personal relationship, a dissatisfied but loyal partner would respond by waiting, hoping, or praying that things will improve with time. This reaction is most likely when the person views the relationship problems as relatively minor, has poor alternatives, has invested a good deal in the relationship, or is not seriously dissatisfied overall.

Neglect refers to passively allowing a relationship to deteriorate. In a job situation, this might mean letting conditions at work worsen through lack of effort or frequent lateness or absences or using company time for personal business. In a personal relationship, neglect might be displayed by spending less time with the partner, ignoring the partner, refusing to discuss problems, treating the partner badly, or "just letting things fall apart." This response is most common when the person has not been satisfied in the past and has made low investments in the relationship.

Exit refers to actively ending a relationship. In a work situation, exit occurs when a person searches for a different job, transfers, or quits. In a romantic relationship, exit might take the form of moving out of a joint residence, physically abusing the partner, or ending the relationship by leaving or getting a divorce. People are most likely to leave a personal relationship when they believe they have little to lose, as when the relationship is unhappy, the person has invested relatively little, or the person has reasonable alternatives.

Rusbult has shown that satisfaction and commitment influence the type of problem solving used in personal relationships. For example, in one study, college students were more likely to use relationship-promoting responses of voice and loyalty when they had been satisfied with the relationship before problems arose, when they had made substantial investments in the relationship, and when they had poor alternatives (Rusbult, Zembrodt, & Gunn, 1982). In contrast, students were more likely to use exit strategies when their preproblem satisfaction was relatively low, their investments were low, and they had good alternatives.

From the perspective of continuing the relationship, loyalty and voice are constructive, relationship-promoting responses; neglect and exit are destructive to the relationship. Of course, for the individuals involved, ending a relationship or quitting a job may sometimes become the best course of action.

Summary

1. When two people interact, they influence each other. Interdependence refers to mutual influence between two or more people.
2. According to social exchange theories, people are concerned with the outcomes (rewards minus costs) they receive in a relationship. Interdependence theory is the most important social exchange perspective in social psychology.
3. People use several standards to evaluate their relationship outcomes, including a general comparison level and a comparison level for alternatives. When two people are interdependent, they try to coordinate their activities to maximize their joint profits.
4. In a relationship, coordination problems arise because one person's outcomes depend on the partner's actions and vice versa. Coordination is easier when partners have correspondent outcomes (similar interests) than when they have noncorrespondent outcomes (dissimilar interests). Social norms and roles provide solutions to coordination problems.
5. People care whether their relationships are fair. Three major rules of fairness are equality, relative needs, and equity. Equity exists when each person's outcomes are proportional to his or her contributions to the relationship. According to equity theory, when individuals perceive inequity in a relationship, they feel distress and take steps to restore actual equity or psychological equity.
6. Close relationships often move beyond simple exchange. Clark and Mills distinguished between exchange relationships and communal relationships. In exchange relationships, people give benefits with the expectation of receiving comparable benefits in return. In communal relationships, people provide benefits to respond to others' needs without expecting similar benefits in return.
7. Self-disclosure is the sharing of personal feelings and information with another individual. There is a norm of reciprocity for self-disclosure; therefore, partners tend to disclose at similar levels.
8. Patterns of self-disclosure reflect cultural norms. In the United States, disclosure tends to be lower in male–male friendships than it is in female–female friendships or in male–female relationships.
9. We experience intimacy in a relationship when we feel understood, validated, and cared for by our partner.
10. Social power refers to a person's ability to deliberately influence the behavior, thoughts, or feelings of another person. The balance of power describes whether partners have equal power or whether one person is dominant. In general, most African American, Mexican American, and Anglo couples describe their marriages as fairly equal in power. Three determinants of the balance of power are social norms, the relative resources of the partners, and the principle of least interest.
11. Conflict occurs when the actions of one person interfere with the actions of another. Conflicts can be about specific behaviors, norms and roles, or personal dispositions.
12. Satisfaction refers to an individual's subjective evaluation of the quality of a relationship.
13. Commitment refers to all the forces, positive and negative, that keep a person in a relationship. It is useful to distinguish among personal commitment, moral commitment, and constraint commitment.
14. Maintaining a close relationship over time depends, in part, on how we respond to the problems and disappointments that arise. Research has highlighted the importance of such cognitive processes as creating positive illusions about a relationship, remembering the past in ways that suggest the relationship is improving, and devaluing tempting alternatives. It also makes a difference whether partners interpret each other's behaviors in relationship-enhancing or distress-maintaining ways.
15. Relationships are strengthened when partners show patterns of accommodation and forgiveness.
16. Rusbult identified four common reactions to dissatisfaction in relationships: voice, loyalty, neglect, and exit.

Key Terms

commitment in a relationship **285**
communal relationships **271**
comparison level **267**
comparison level for alternatives **267**
equity **269**
exchange relationships **271**
interdependence theory **265**
principle of least interest **282**
self-disclosure **272**
social power **279**

In The News

Groupthink and U.S. Intelligence Failures about Iraq

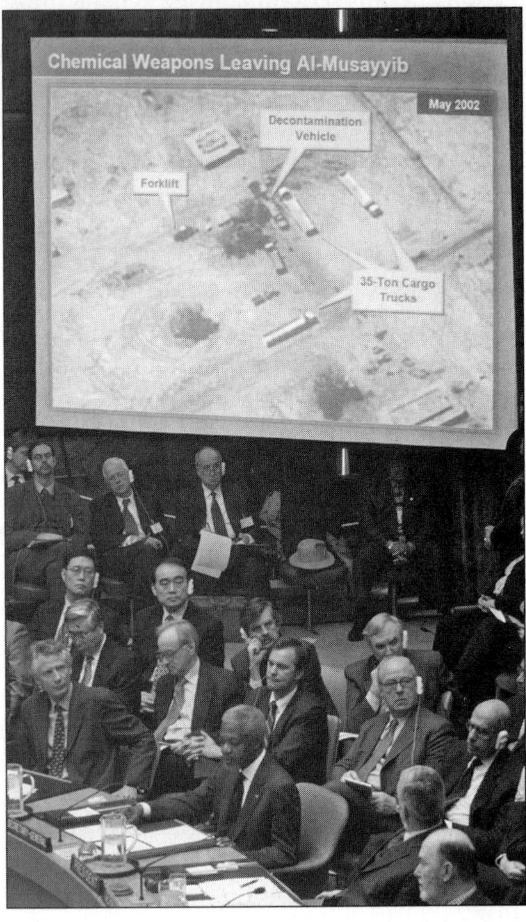

In the wake of the September 11 terrorist attacks on the United States and questions about the intelligence information that led President Bush to attack Iraq, the U.S. Senate Intelligence Committee launched an investigation. In a 511-page report released in July 2004, the committee documented major and repeated failures at the Central Intelligence Agency (CIA) and other U.S. intelligence agencies. The report noted the CIA's failure to provide an accurate assessment of Iraq's weapons of mass destruction before the American invasion. False conclusions were drawn about Iraq's capabilities based on flawed information. Rather than send American spies to Iraq, the CIA depended on reports from paid informants and Iraqi defectors. Warnings about the unreliability of these uncorroborated sources were ignored. Conflicting evidence was dismissed. Sources that denied the existence of stockpiles of weapons of mass destruction in Iraq were viewed as not knowledgeable or as lying. As summarized by the *Los Angeles Times* (2004, p. A15), "Intelligence agencies suffered from a collective presumption that Iraq had an active and growing program to develop weapons of mass destruction. This bias led analysts . . . to interpret ambiguous evidence as conclusive and to ignore evidence that pointed to a lack of such a weapons program."

How could America's premier intelligence agency function so poorly? The Senate report suggested that part of the answer was to be found in the process of "groupthink," a concept developed in the 1970s by social psychologist Irving Janis. Groupthink occurs when members of a decision-making group fail to obtain systematic information about an issue and do not evaluate all options critically. In assessing Iraq's weapons of mass destruction, intelligence community staff showed several aspects of groupthink. They gathered information selectively and gave undue weight to unreliable information. They examined few alternatives. They felt pressure to conform within the group and to withhold criticism of group decisions. They developed a collective rationalization for their views. The report explained that groupthink bias developed as members of key intelligence groups attempted to conform to the consensus of the group.

Later in this chapter, we delve more deeply into the concept of groupthink and consider steps that can be taken to avoid such faulty decision making in groups.

Chapter 10

Behavior in Groups

This chapter focuses on social groups. We begin by considering how the mere presence of other people affects behavior. Next, we discuss some of the basic processes of interaction in groups, including group performance, group decision making, and competition versus cooperation. We conclude the chapter by investigating leadership in groups.

Focus of This Chapter

BEHAVIOR IN THE PRESENCE OF OTHERS

Jessica is an outstanding high school runner who hopes to try out for the Olympics. She trains very hard and notices that she runs better with a training partner than by herself. Her best performances have been during actual track meets when she ran against tough competition. Jake is taking his first class in acting. At home in the privacy of his bedroom, he delivers his lines with accuracy and self-confidence. But in front of his classmates, he stumbles over his part. As these examples suggest, the presence of other people sometimes enhances and sometimes impairs an individual's performance (Williams, Harkins, & Karau, 2003).

Social Facilitation

Sometimes people perform better in the presence of others than when they are alone. This reaction is called **social facilitation**. Social psychologists have long been fascinated by this occurrence. Indeed, a study of social facilitation was conducted by Norman Triplett in 1898. Triplett observed that cyclists seemed to ride faster when they raced against other cyclists than when they were alone. To test this observation, he devised an experiment to see whether children would work harder pulling in a fishing line in a group or when they were alone. As predicted, the children worked harder in the presence of others.

Social Facilitation

Performing better when others are present than when alone.

Many studies have demonstrated this effect. In the 1920s, Floyd Allport (1920, 1924) had participants work on such tasks as crossing out all the vowels in a newspaper column, doing easy multiplication problems, or writing refutations of a logical argument. Even though the participants always worked individually on the task, they were more productive when there were five other people in the room than when they were alone. Social facilitation has been found to occur when the others who are present are actually performing the same task (when they are "co-actors") and when they are

All eyes are on golf pro Tiger Woods as he hits his tee shot during a tournament.

merely observers. Social facilitation is not limited to humans. It has also been demonstrated in rats, cockroaches, and parakeets. For instance, individual ants dig three times more sand when they are in groups than when they are alone (Chen, 1937).

On the other hand, the presence of others sometimes inhibits individual performance, as suggested by the example of Jake, who could recite his lines flawlessly when he was alone but stumbled over his words in public. This reaction is called the **social inhibition** of performance. In Allport's early studies, people in a group setting wrote more refutations of a logical argument, but the quality of the work was lower than when they worked alone. Another early study found that the presence of a spectator reduced individual performance on a memory task (Pessin, 1933). Why does the presence of others sometimes improve performance and at other times diminish the quality of performance?

An answer was offered by Robert Zajonc (1965). He suggested that being in the presence of others increases an individual's drive or motivation, as shown in Figure 10–1. Whether increased arousal facilitates or interferes with performance depends on the task. When a task requires a response that is well learned or innate, called a "dominant response," increased motivation is helpful. The presence of others facilitates performance on relatively simple tasks, such as crossing out vowels or doing easy arithmetic. Similarly, for a highly trained athlete, the presence of others is likely to improve performance. But when a task requires behavior that is complex or poorly learned, the increased arousal from having others present impairs performance. Examples would be solving difficult arithmetic problems, memorizing new material, or writing complex logical deductions. For Jake, struggling to remember his lines in a play, an audience may simply increase stage fright and inhibit a good performance. If Jake were more experienced and had performed the part every night for months, the presence of an audience might improve his performance. In summary, when a dominant or well-learned response is involved, heightened motivation improves performance, particularly on simple rather than complex tasks.

Social Inhibition

Performing more poorly when others are present than when alone.

An interesting demonstration of this effect comes from an observational study of the behavior of people playing pool in a college student union building (Michaels, Bloommel, Brocato, Linkous, & Rowe, 1982). The researchers identified pairs of players who were either above or below average in their level of play and secretly recorded their scores. Then teams of four confederates approached the players and watched them closely during several more rounds of play. Zajonc's theory predicts that good players will benefit from an audience, but poor players will not. The results provided clear support for this prediction. When good players were being watched by four others, their accuracy rose from 71 to 80 percent. When poor players were being watched, their accuracy dropped from 36 to 25 percent. The Research Highlight for this chapter investigates a related question: Does the presence of a supportive audience enhance performance?

Why does the presence of others motivate us? A first explanation is the one offered by Zajonc, that there is a fairly simple, innate tendency to become aroused by the mere presence of others. A second view is that others motivate us

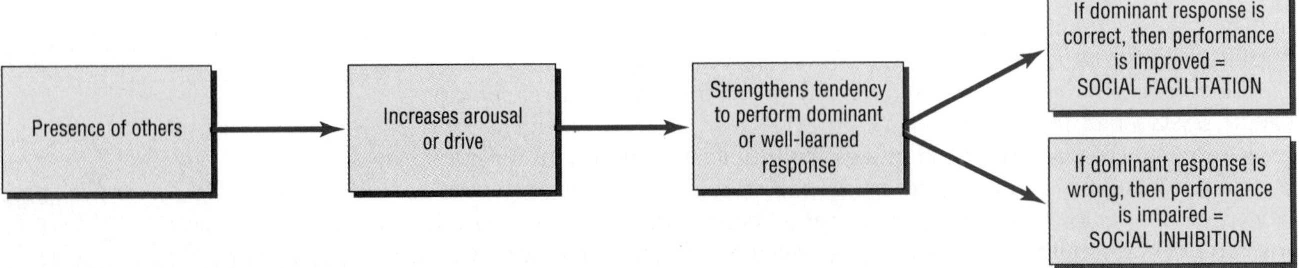

Figure 10–1 **Processes Leading to Social Facilitation versus Social Inhibition.**

DOES A SUPPORTIVE AUDIENCE IMPROVE PERFORMANCE?

In an upset victory in 1998, the French national soccer team won the soccer World Cup by beating the favored Brazilian team. Did it help the French team to play the championship game in France? Research shows that in competitive sports, teams tend to do better when playing at home than on the road. This "home field advantage" has been documented both in the United States and in Europe, and for a variety of team sports (Schlenker, Phillips, Boniecki, & Schlenker, 1995). For example, a study of professional basketball, baseball, and football teams found that teams won a greater percentage of home games than of games played elsewhere (Hirt & Kimble, 1981). The home field advantage was most striking for basketball: Professional teams won about 65 percent of home games but only 35 percent of away games.

Many reasons have been suggested for this home field advantage (Schlenker et al., 1995). The fatigue of travel and greater familiarity with the home field may contribute. In some cases, officiating bias by referees may favor the home team in close calls. Territorial dominance may also play a part: Home teams may do better because they are on their own turf. However, the most important advantage appears to be the presence of a supportive audience. Teams usually have more fans on hand for home games than they do for away games. Therefore, a team playing at home can usually expect approval and support from the spectators (Sanna & Shotland, 1990). In contrast, visitors may feel wary and inhibited and may expect the audience to be unsupportive or even hostile.

Studies of the home field advantage in sports have often relied on correlational analyses of archival records about team performance. In addition, researchers have conducted experimental investigations of the impact of a supportive audience on performance (Butler & Baumeister, 1998). In these studies, the emphasis has shifted from sports teams to individual performance. If you were going to give an important speech or play a difficult concerto at a piano recital, would you want your friends and relatives to be in the room, or would you prefer to perform for an anonymous audience? Would a supportive audience make a difference in your performance?

Research suggests that a supportive audience may not necessarily enhance individual performance (Butler & Baumeister, 1998). In one experiment, college students performed better on a stressful mental arithmetic task when observed by a stranger than when observed by a close same-sex friend. In a second experiment, students performed better on a difficult computer video game when they were observed by a disinterested stranger than when observed by a supportive stranger who would receive a cash prize if the participant performed successfully. A third experiment demonstrated that a supportive audience was detrimental if the standard for success was high, but not if the criterion was easy. In all studies, participants with a supportive observer engaged in what the researchers called "futile caution." They worked more slowly but not more accurately on the task than did participants with a nonsupportive audience. As a result, their overall performance suffered. Nonetheless, participants in all three experiments preferred having a supportive audience and felt better in front of them. If the results of this first set of studies are replicated, it appears that individuals planning a stressful performance may face a difficult choice between feeling better (with a supportive audience) or doing better (with a neutral or unfamiliar audience).

because we are concerned about how they will evaluate us and we want to make a positive impression. This reaction is known as **evaluation apprehension**. On simple tasks, an awareness that we are being judged can spur us to greater effort. On complex tasks, however, the pressure of being evaluated may be harmful to performance.

Evaluation Apprehension

Concern about making a good impression on others.

A third view is that the presence of others is distracting. On easy tasks that do not require our full attention, we may compensate for the distraction by concentrating and trying harder; thus, we may actually perform better. However, the distraction created by other people is harmful to performance on complex tasks.

Distraction-Conflict Model

Individual performance can be impaired if we focus on the audience rather than on the task.

An extension of this idea is the **distraction-conflict model** (Baron, 1986), which suggests that the presence of others creates a conflict between two basic tendencies: (1) to pay attention to the audience and (2) to pay attention to the task. This conflict can increase arousal, which then either helps or hinders task performance, depending on whether the task calls for a dominant response. Further, conflict can also create cognitive overload if the effort required to pay attention simultaneously to a difficult task and to other people exceeds the individual's mental capacities.

More recently, a fourth biopsychological explanation was offered by Jim Blascovich and his colleagues (1999). They proposed that the presence of others can evoke one of two distinctive physiological response patterns: challenge or threat. When the individual has sufficient resources to meet the demands of the task, a challenge response occurs. Physiologically, this pattern is similar to the changes that occur during aerobic exercise and is associated with efficient cardiovascular functioning. In contrast, when the individual's resources are insufficient to meet the demands of the task, a threat response occurs, as though the body is mobilizing to cope with danger. In research using sophisticated cardiovascular measures, participants worked on an unlearned or well-learned task either alone or in the presence of others. As predicted, the participants who performed the unlearned (difficult) task in front of an audience showed the physiological pattern of threat and performed worse than did the participants with no audience. The participants who performed the well-learned (easy) task in front of an audience showed the physiological pattern of challenge and performed as well as those working alone. The various explanations of social facilitation are not necessarily contradictory: It is possible that all these processes affect human performance, depending on the situation.

Before we leave the topic of social facilitation versus inhibition, it is important to emphasize a special feature of these situations. The quality of the individual's performance—how fast the person runs or how many problems the person solves—can be evaluated both by the individual and by observers. This possibility of judgment is an important factor in explaining why social facilitation occurs. What would happen if the contributions of each member of a group could not be evaluated individually? For example, if four people stop to help a motorist push his stalled car to the side of the road, there is no way to judge the efforts of any one person. In this case, how does the presence of others influence individual performance? This question brings us to the next topic, social loafing.

Social Loafing

Social Loafing

Working less hard as part of a group than alone.

When an individual's contribution to a collective activity cannot be evaluated, individuals often work less hard than they would alone. This effect, known as **social loafing**, is illustrated in Figure 10–2. Social loafing was first studied in the late 1880s by a French agricultural engineer named Max Ringelmann (see Kravitz & Martin, 1986). As part of a study of work efficiency, Ringelmann asked male student volunteers to pull as hard as they could on a rope. Using a strain gauge, he measured their effort in kilograms of pressure. Sometimes the participants worked alone and sometimes in groups of 7 or 14 people. Common sense and

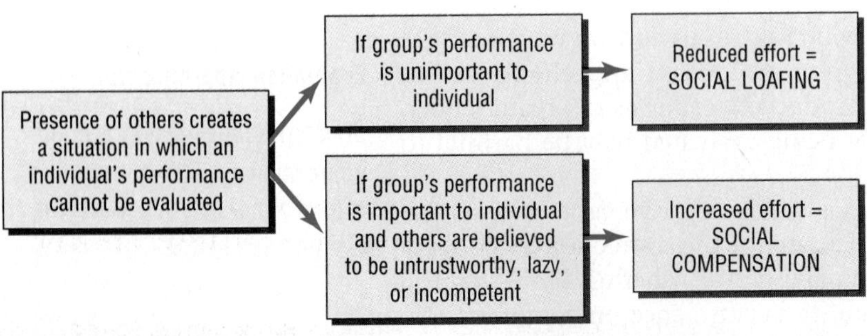

Figure 10–2 **Processes Leading to Social Loafing versus Social Compensation.**

research on social facilitation might predict that the men would work harder when they were part of a team than when they were alone. Just the opposite happened. When pulling alone, individuals averaged about 85 kilograms per person. In groups of 7, the total group force was only 65 kilograms per person, and in the largest group, each individual's contribution fell to 61 kilograms.

More than 100 studies have demonstrated the social loafing effect (Williams, Harkins, & Karau, 2003). In one study, undergraduate men were asked to make as much noise as they could by cheering or by clapping (Latané, Williams, & Harkins, 1979). Each person performed alone, in pairs, in groups of four, and in groups of six. The results, presented in Figure 10–3, clearly show that the noise produced by each individual decreased as the size of the group increased. This is the same pattern Ringelmann found. Other studies show that social loafing can occur on a wide range of tasks including swimming, navigating mazes, identifying radar signals, writing songs, and evaluating job candidates.

Why does social loafing occur? Steven Karau and Kipling Williams (1993) proposed an integrative framework for understanding social loafing that is an elaboration of the expectancy-value approach introduced in Chapter 1. According to their *collective effort model,* how hard an individual works on a group task depends on two main factors: (a) the person's belief about how important or necessary his or her own contribution is to group success and (b) how much the person values the potential outcome of group success. Working in a group leads to a relaxation of effort when individuals believe that their own work will be "lost in the crowd"—that no one will know how well they performed and that they cannot be held responsible for their individual actions. Not surprisingly, the tendency toward social loafing increases as the size of the group increases. The antidote to social loafing is to make each individual's contribution identifiable. If people believe that their contribution can be evaluated by others, social loafing can be eliminated. This effect of identifiability may explain why social loafing is greatest when people work with strangers, is reduced when people work with acquaintances, and disappears when people work with close friends or in a highly valued group.

The possible consequences of group performance also make a difference. Providing rewards for high group productivity can reduce social loafing. In one study, some students were told they could leave an experiment early if their group generated many solutions to a problem; other students were given the same problem-solving task but were not offered the incentive of leaving early (Shepperd & Wright, 1989). In this case, the anticipation of a reward for high effort counteracted the social loafing effect. Social loafing is also less likely to occur on tasks that are meaningful, complex, or interesting. When the task is difficult or challenging, individuals are less likely to slack off.

In an interesting twist on social loafing, researchers have found that people sometimes work extra hard in order to compensate for unmotivated or inept

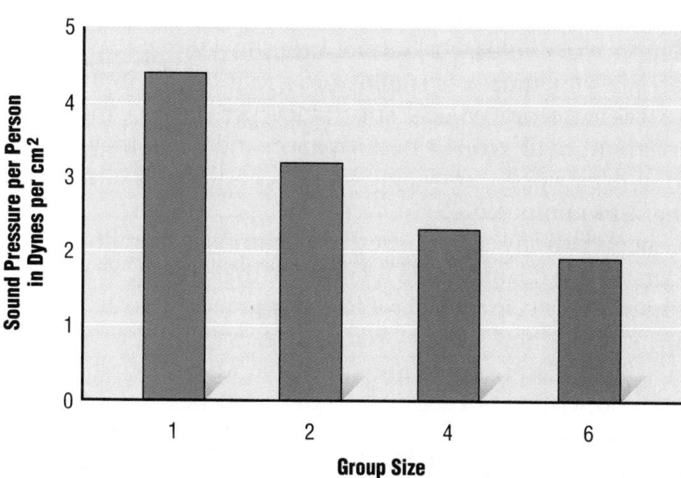

Figure 10–3 **Comparison of the Average Intensity of Noise One Individual Produced When Cheering Alone or in a Group.**

Source: Data from Latané, Williams, and Harkins (1979, pp. 822–832).

coworkers. Consider the situation of Alex, a highly motivated college student, eager to earn top grades so he can get into law school. When the teacher divides Alex's history class into study groups and assigns each team a topic for a jointly graded oral presentation, Alex has a dilemma. He wants to get an A on the project, but he's sure that his teammates won't work as hard as he usually does. Should he go along with the group and risk getting a C, or should he compensate for their low effort by doing most of the work himself? What would you do in this situation? Research on social loafing might suggest that Alex, like his coworkers, will slack off in the study group. Yet common sense and psychological research suggest that sometimes an individual will expend great effort to compensate for others in the group. This effect is known as **social compensation**. Williams and Karau (1991) believed that two conditions are necessary for an individual to show social compensation: (a) The person must believe that coworkers are performing inadequately, and (b) the person must consider the quality of the group product important. For Alex, lack of trust that his teammates will work hard creates concern about the shared grade they will receive for their report.

Social Compensation

Working especially hard to make up for lazy or incompetent teammates.

Williams and Karau (1991) conducted three experiments to test their ideas. In a first study, they assessed the link between personal effort and trusting one's coworkers. They found that students who scored high on a measure of interpersonal trust—and so might expect coworkers to carry their own weight—showed the usual pattern of social loafing in a group. In contrast, students who scored low in trust—who might expect others to loaf—showed a compensatory pattern of working harder in the group. In a second study, the researchers directly manipulated the subject's expectations about a coworker's effort. Sometimes the coworker (actually a confederate) said that he was going to work hard on the experiment, and sometimes he said he didn't think he would work very hard. As predicted, subjects with a hardworking teammate performed less well than did subjects with a low-effort teammate. A third study focused on the personal importance of the task. Some subjects were told that the task was important and related to intelligence; others were told that the task was relatively trivial. The researchers also varied whether subjects believed that their partner was high or low in ability and predicted that the social compensation effect would be seen only when the subject believed that the task was important and that the partner was low in ability. In other conditions, a pattern of social loafing (lower effort) was anticipated. The results provided strong support for these predictions.

A recent study found that when people lack information about the motivation or ability of a teammate, they may rely on stereotypes instead (Plaks & Higgins, 2000). In one experiment, participants were assigned to work individually on a portion of the Graduate Record math exam. They were told that they had been paired with either a male or a female teammate and that they would receive a joint team score based on their combined scores. Given the stereotype that men are better than women at math, the researchers predicted that participants paired with a female teammate would work harder (social compensation effect) than those with a teammate of unknown gender or with a male teammate (social loafing effect). This prediction was confirmed. Several other experiments provided further evidence that people sometimes use stereotypes about the attributes of an unknown teammate to calibrate how much effort they personally expend. In short, when people care about their group's performance, and when they believe that their coworkers are untrustworthy, unwilling to work hard, or unable to perform well, they work hard to compensate.

Finally, research has begun to investigate the cross-cultural generality of the social loafing effect (Karau & Williams, 1993). Several studies using the sound production task (making noise by clapping) have found evidence of social loafing in India, Thailand, Japan, and China. These studies suggest that the tendency toward social loafing may be widespread. At the same time, there is evidence for cultural differences in social loafing. In particular, the tendency toward social loafing may be greater among people from the United States than among people from Asian cultures (Karau & Williams, 1993). A study conducted in the United

States and China illustrated this point (Gabrenya, Wang, & Latané, 1985). In this study, researchers created a sound-tracking test, which was described to participants as a measure of their auditory ability. The researchers predicted that U.S. students, from an individualist culture, would show the typical social loafing pattern on this task when working in a group. In contrast, they predicted that Chinese students would show an opposite pattern. Because China has a more group-oriented culture, in which individuals are taught to work toward group goals and put the welfare of the group ahead of individual interests, Chinese students were expected to perform better in groups than alone. As predicted, significant differences were found in the behavior of ninth-grade students in Florida and in Taiwan. In groups, U.S. students performed only 88 percent as well as they did when alone. In contrast, Chinese students in groups performed at 108 percent of their individual level. A puzzling and unexpected finding was that these cultural differences in social loafing were found only for boys; girls performed equally well when working alone or in a group. These findings provide some preliminary support for the existence of cultural differences in tendencies toward social loafing, at least on some types of tasks and for males. But more research is needed to reach definite conclusions about the impact of culture on social loafing.

In this section, we have seen that the presence of others sometimes leads to social facilitation and sometimes causes social loafing. Working in the presence of others can spur us to greater effort or lull us into complacency about our individual efforts. Which effect occurs depends on whether the group context increases our concerns about social evaluation (because others are judging our performance) or reduces social evaluation concerns (because our individual effort is hidden by working in a group). It also depends on the complexity of the task and how much we care about the outcome.

Social Impact Theory

The discussion so far has concerned the question of when the presence of others has positive or negative effects on individual performance. **Social impact theory** addresses the issue of how strong an influence (either positive or negative) these others have. As developed by Latané (1981), this theory suggests that the total impact of other people on an individual depends on three characteristics of the observers (source of influence): their number, their strength, and their immediacy. Figure 10–4 illustrates schematically a situation in which a group of people (sources) are influencing a single individual (target).

Social Impact Theory

The influence of observers depends on their number, strength (importance), and immediacy.

As the number of observers increases, so does their impact. To return to the earlier example of the fledgling actor, Jake, who is learning lines for a play, the impact of the audience should increase with the number of people present. Jake should experience more stage fright when performing in front of 50 people than in front of 5 people.

Another factor is the strength of the social forces, that is, the importance or power of the observers. Strength is determined by such factors as the status and age of the observers and their relationship to the individual. Jake might feel significantly worse about performing in front of his teacher or a casting director than in front of his friends.

The third factor is the immediacy of the audience, that is, its closeness to the individual in space or time. Jake's reactions should be stronger if he has a live audience than if he is being watched on a video monitor located in another room (Borden, 1980) or if his performance is being taped for future viewing. Latané, (1981) suggested that social impact can be compared to light falling on a surface: The total amount of light depends on the number of light bulbs, the wattage of the bulbs, and their closeness to the surface. Latané believes that social impact theory can help explain why the presence of others sometimes leads to social facilitation and sometimes causes social loafing. In facilitation situations, the person is the sole target of the influence of an audience or of coworkers, as shown in Figure 10–4. The

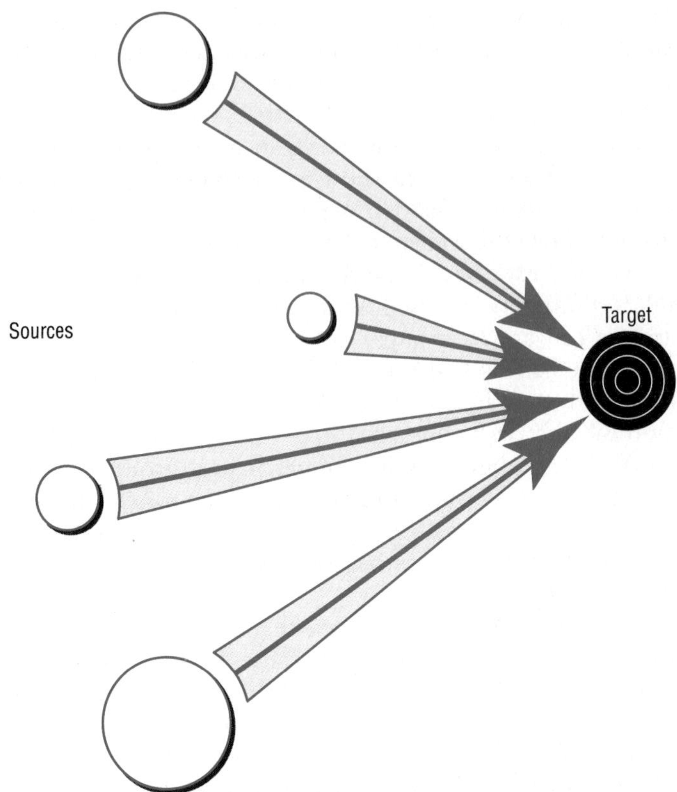

Figure 10–4 The impact of an audience on a target depends on the number of people present (the number of circles or "sources"), the immediacy of the people (the nearness of the circles to the target), and the strength or importance of the people (the size of the circles).

Source: Latané (1981, p. 344). Copyright 1981 by the American Psychological Association. Adapted by permission.

social impact of the others is directed entirely at the single individual; as the number of people present increases, their social impact on the individual also increases. In contrast, social loafing situations occur when several people work together on a task assigned by an outsider. This situation is depicted in Figure 10–5: Each individual is only one of several targets of forces coming from outside the group. Consequently, the social impact of the outsider is divided among group members. As the size of the group increases, the pressure felt by each individual decreases. Put in a broader context, social impact theory illustrates a major goal of social

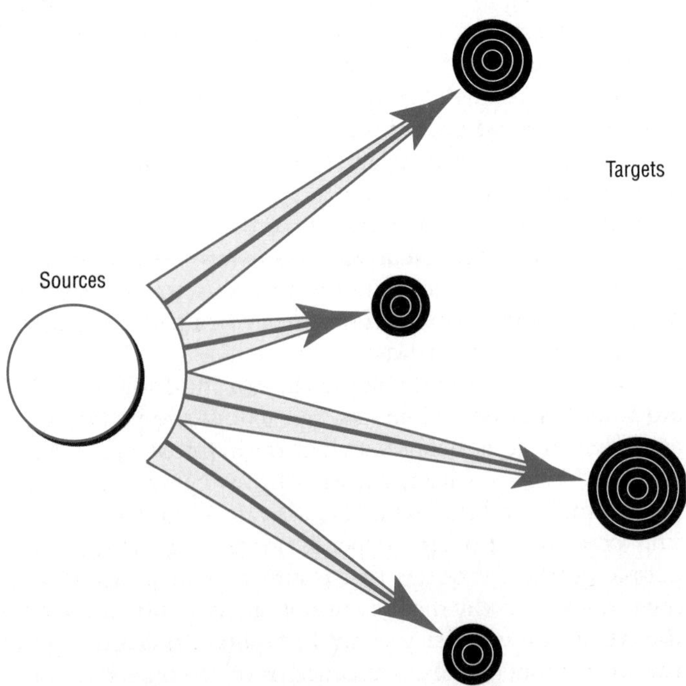

Figure 10–5 When each individual is only one of several targets of social influence, the impact of the audience (sources) on the target is lessened.

Source: Latané (1981, p. 349). Copyright 1981 by the American Psychological Association. Adapted by permission.

psychology: to create theories that can explain diverse social phenomena with a single set of unified principles (Nowak, Szamrej, & Latané, 1990).

Deindividuation

Sometimes people seem to lose themselves in a crowd and act differently from how they would if they were alone (Reicher, 2003). During spring break, college students in many parts of the country flock to resort towns for vacation. News accounts sometimes describe large gatherings of young people cruising the streets. Occasionally the crowd's behavior gets out of control. In one town, students antagonize homeowners with late-night partying and acts of public nudity. In another city, a police crackdown on underage drinking leads students to riot, breaking windows and vandalizing cars.

How can we explain such crowd behavior? The 19th-century French sociologist Gustave Le Bon suggested that in a mob, the emotions of one person spread through the group. When one person does something, even if it would ordinarily be unacceptable to most of the others, everyone else tends to do it also. Le Bon (1896) called this reaction "social contagion": Mob behavior is infectious, like a cold spreading among students in a classroom. Le Bon explained social contagion in terms of a breakdown of normal control mechanisms. Our actions are usually controlled by our values, our ethics, and the social rules we have learned while growing up. In crowd situations, however, we sometimes lose a sense of responsibility for our own actions. Our own control system is weakened, and so aggressive and sexual impulses are free to be expressed. The result can be violent, immoral acts. Social psychologists have studied this phenomenon, which they call **deindividuation** (Postmes & Spears, 1998). A naturalistic demonstration of the deindividuation effect involved children who were trick-or-treating on Halloween (Diener, Fraser, Beaman, & Kelem, 1976). The researchers stationed themselves in homes in the neighborhood. When children arrived at the door, some were asked their names by the adults in the homes, and others were not. Then the children were all given an opportunity to steal extra candy when the adult was not present. Those children who had been asked their names were less likely to steal, even though the chances of being caught were virtually zero in all cases.

Deindividuation

The anonymity of a group can lead people to do things they would not do alone.

Another experiment demonstrated deindividuation in a laboratory setting (Zimbardo, 1970). Groups of four young women were recruited to take part in a study supposedly involving empathic responses to strangers. In one condition, the participants were greeted by name, wore name tags, and were easily identifiable. In another condition, the subjects wore oversized white lab coats and hoods, were never called by name, and were difficult to identify. All the groups were given an opportunity to deliver electric shocks to a person not in the group. (In fact, the shocks were fake and the "victim" was a confederate.) The subjects who were not identifiable gave almost twice as many shocks as the others.

As you may have noticed, in both these studies, people wore a "disguise" of some kind—a Halloween costume or a white lab coat and hood. Johnson and Downing (1979) pointed out that in many studies of deindividuation, participants wore disguises or masks that had negative implications: Most Halloween masks are of monsters or ghosts, and the white hoods that were used in some lab studies were reminiscent of Ku Klux Klan outfits. What would happen if the costumes people wore had neutral or positive implications?

To test this hypothesis, Johnson and Downing (1979) had people wear either Ku Klux Klan outfits or nurses' outfits, consisting of white hats and coats. Those wearing outfits were compared to others wearing normal clothing. It was found that the Ku Klux Klan outfit had only a slight effect on the level of shock subjects gave (thus, this study did not replicate Zimbardo's [1970] results). Perhaps more important, wearing the nurses' uniforms actually reduced the number of shocks people gave. Although anonymity sometimes produces increased aggression, these results indicate that people are influenced by the social context, in this case, by the type of uniform they wore. If the uniform implies positive, prosocial behavior, the wearer may behave accordingly.

Halloween costumes often mask personal identity. This and other forms of anonymity increase the tendency toward deindividuation.

Researchers agree that deindividuation increases when individuals are anonymous and as the size of the group gets larger. There is controversy, however, about the psychological mechanisms involved. Some social psychologists emphasize that deindividuation creates a special psychological state in which individuals become less aware of their own personal values and behaviors and instead focus on the group and the situation (Diener, 1980). In contrast, others emphasize that deindividuation conditions heighten an individual's identification with the group and so increase conformity to the norms of that specific group (Postmes, Spears, Sakhel, & de Groot, 2001). This conformity can set the stage for antisocial acts, if the group favors such actions. From this perspective, college students who are partying on spring vacation may violate general norms of proper behavior or break city laws, but they are actually going along with the emerging "let's have a good time" norms of the student vacationer group. It is important to note that the behavioral consequences of deindividuation depend on the norms of the situation, which can be either antisocial or prosocial.

Crowding

Finally, another important consequence of being in the presence of others can be the experience of crowding. Rush-hour commuters crammed into a bus are likely to feel crowded. So, too, are holiday shoppers swarming down the escalators of a department store and competing for the attention of an overworked salesclerk. **Crowding** refers to the psychological state of discomfort and stress associated with wanting more space than is available. Feeling crowded can occur regardless of the amount of space we actually have. We are more likely to feel crowded when we are physically cramped, but we sometimes feel crowded even when we have plenty of space around us. There are times when three is a crowd, no matter how much space is available. If you like to swim at deserted beaches, the presence of a few other people may make you feel that the beach is overcrowded, whereas you might not feel crowded at a party even if there are many other people in a fairly small room.

Crowding

The subjective feeling of having too little space.

Researchers who study crowding find it essential to distinguish between subjective feelings of being crowded and objective measures of population density. **Social density** is the objective number of people in a given space and might be measured by the number of people per square foot. In contrast, crowding is the subjective experience of feeling cramped and not having enough space. High social density may or may not be unpleasant, but crowding is always unpleasant

Social Density

Objective number of people in a given space.

and negative, by definition. When we say we feel "crowded," we are usually complaining.

When do people experience the presence of others as crowding? Several theories of crowding have been proposed (reviewed by McAndrew, 1993). Most emphasize cognitive processes, that is, the way people perceive, interpret, and react to their social environment.

Sensory Overload. Stanley Milgram (1970) proposed that whenever people are exposed to too much stimulation, they experience sensory overload. Social density can produce overstimulation and feelings of being crowded (Baum & Paulus, 1987). Individual differences in reactions to social density may reflect differences in preferred levels of stimulation. Some people may like high levels of stimulation: They like the radio blaring all the time, prefer to study in busy rooms, and watch television while carrying on a conversation or reading a magazine. Others like low levels of stimulation. When they work, it has to be quiet; if they watch television, they do not want any distraction. For high-stimulation people, high social density may be the right level of stimulation and may so be perceived as pleasant and exciting. In contrast, for low-stimulation people, high social density may be disruptive and may be perceived as crowding.

Loss of Control. High social density can make people feel they have lost control over their actions (Baron & Rodin, 1978). The idea is that when there are many people in a confined space, each individual is less able to control the situation, to move around freely, or to avoid undesired contact. The result is feeling crowded. This loss of control can have several negative features. In the United States, people often want to feel in control of their lives, so being unable to control the environment may, in itself, be negative. Further, high social density may prevent people from maintaining a desired degree of privacy. High density may also lead to problems in the coordination of activities. When three people share a small dormitory room, they may literally bump into each other and have trouble studying or sleeping without interruption. Under high-density conditions, people are more likely to interfere with each other's activities, and thus to feel frustration and anger.

Attributions. A third explanation for crowding emphasizes causal attributions, a concept first discussed in Chapter 2. In this view, the subjective experience of crowding requires two elements: a physiological state of arousal and a cognitive label that attributes the arousal to the presence of too many people (Worchel & Teddie, 1976). In general, if people can be distracted from focusing on the others present in a situation, they will feel less crowded (Webb, Worchel, Riechers, & Wayne, 1986). For example, when research subjects in high-density conditions were exposed to arousing (humorous, sexual, or violent) television shows, they experienced significantly less crowding than did people who watched a nonarousing program under the same conditions. Indeed, people in cramped quarters rated the humorous movie as funnier and the violent movie as more violent and tended to enjoy the movies more.

Culture. There are also cultural differences in the experience of crowding (Evans, Lepore, & Allen, 2000). In general, people from Asian, Latin, and other collectivist cultures prefer closer interpersonal distances for conversation and are less likely to experience high-density living arrangements as crowded. In contrast, people from North America, northern Europe, and other individualist cultures prefer greater distances in their social interactions and are more likely to experience high-density housing as crowded. Do these cultural differences buffer collectivists from the adverse health effects of high-density conditions? A study of Anglo Americans, African Americans, Mexican Americans, and Vietnamese Americans investigated this question (Evans et al., 2000). As expected, Mexican and Vietnamese Americans tended to perceive their homes as less crowded than did Anglo and African Americans. However, regardless of cultural background, individuals living in households with more people per room were more likely to experience psychological distress. There is no evidence that some cultural groups are better able to tolerate high-density living spaces.

BASIC FEATURES OF GROUPS

This chapter discusses ways in which the mere presence of others affects an individual's behavior. At this point, the focus turns to the dynamics of interaction in small groups (Moreland & Levine, 2003). We spend time in many different kinds of social units, not all of which qualify as groups. Table 10–1 provides some common examples, including being part of an audience or crowd. In everyday language, we may speak of all collectivities as "groups." But social scientists use the term "group" in a narrower, more technical way. In a **group**, people are interdependent and have at least the potential for mutual interaction. In most groups, members have regular face-to-face contact. This definition of a group is an extension of the basic definition of an interpersonal relationship that was given in Chapter 9. The essential feature of a group is that its members are interdependent, that is, that they influence one another in some way.

Group

People who are interdependent and have mutual influence on each other.

Based on this definition, a social category such as all professional basketball players does not constitute a group, because all the people in this category do not know one another, have face-to-face contact, or influence one another directly. However, the members of the Los Angeles Lakers basketball team are a group because they interact regularly and their actions affect one another. Similarly, all the children who watch *Sesame Street* on television are part of a common audience, but they are not a group. However, all the children in Ms. Asawa's second-grade class are a group.

The increasing use of the Internet has led to the creation of many new types of online groups. These include newsgroups, forums for the discussion of current topics and hobbies, support groups for individuals with common problems, fantasy sports leagues, and interactive games. These "virtual groups" mix features of a traditional small group, such as the potential for interaction, and features of an audience, such as anonymity and physical distance. Participants can generally be differentiated into "regulars," who interact frequently; "newbies," who have just joined a group; and "lurkers," who may simply read what others post without revealing their presence. Social psychologists are beginning to study these computer-based social groupings (McKenna & Bargh, 2000).

Table 10–1

Types of Social Groupings

There are a variety of social groupings or categories, not all of which meet the criteria for being a "group."

- *Social categories:* We often group people together on the basis of a shared attribute. Examples are teenage boys, unemployed heads of household, Canadians, Sunday-school teachers, and truck drivers. All members of a social category have some common characteristic, although they are not likely to know each other or to interact.
- *Audience:* All the people watching the 6 o'clock news on Channel 4 are part of the same audience, even though they are not necessarily aware of each other and do not interact.
- *Crowd:* When people are in physical proximity to a common situation or stimulus, we call them a "crowd." Examples are fans gathered outside a rock star's dressing room, people waiting outside for a bank to open, or people gathering to watch a street brawl.
- *Team:* A set of people who interact regularly for some particular purpose or activity, such as a work group, sports team, or bridge club, make up a team.
- *Family:* Although there are many types, families usually consist of a set of people who are related by birth or legal arrangements and who may share a common residence.
- *Formal organization:* Larger aggregates of people often work together in some clearly structured way to accomplish a joint goal. Examples are a school system, the American Cancer Society, or the National Rifle Association.

In climbing a dangerous stretch of the mountain, the lives of these individuals are interlinked. Interdependence is a basic feature of groups.

Group Structure

When people are together in a group, they do not remain entirely undifferentiated. They develop patterns of behavior, divide tasks, and adopt different roles. For example, Merei (1949) observed that after only three or four meetings, groups of young children established many informal rules: They decided where each child would sit in the room, who could play with each toy, and what sequence of activities should be followed when the group got together. These patterns are referred to as the "social structure" of the group (Levine & Moreland, 1998). Three important elements of social structure are social norms, social roles, and social status.

Social Norms

Rules and standards for appropriate behavior.

Social norms are shared rules and expectations about how members of a group should behave (Forsyth, 1998). A study by Simon, Eder, and Evans (1992) traced the development of norms about romantic love among groups of teenage girls in sixth through eighth grades in a midwestern community. The researchers conducted in-depth interviews and observations at school over a 3-year period. One norm that emerged in these friendship groups was that romantic relationships should be important, but not everything in life. Group members who deviated from this rule were criticized. Girls who made boys their central concern were teased and called "boy crazy." Girls who showed too little interest in boys risked being labeled as deviant, for instance, as "queer" or lesbian.

In sixth grade, relatively little dating actually occurred and it was common for several girls to express interest in the same boy, much as female friends might like the same rock musician or movie star. During seventh grade, however, as group members began to pursue boys more actively, the norms changed. A new rule of exclusivity gradually developed, dictating that a girl should not have romantic feelings for a boy who was already attached. Now it was considered inappropriate for a girl to express romantic feelings for a boy who was "going out with" someone else, or who was being pursued by another girl in the group. Through the creation of these and other norms, the groups set guidelines for appropriate attitudes and behavior. A girl who failed to follow group norms was often pressured to conform through criticism expressed in jokes and gossip. Thus, norms determine whether an individual's specific actions and beliefs are approved or disapproved by the social group.

A recent illustration of norm formation comes from a study of students enrolled in a "distance-learning" course taught entirely on the Internet (Graham, 2003). The instructor assigned students to work in teams and then observed the emergence of team rules over time. Team members quickly developed a variety of norms, including rules that team members should do an equal share of the work; volunteer rather than wait to be asked to do tasks; check email twice a day in the morning and evening; provide a phone number in case of a team emergency; inform the group if they planned to be out of town; and so on.

Among friends, social norms are typically informal and are created through face-to-face interaction. In other settings, however, the basic structure of a group is predetermined. The new recruit joining the army and the woman joining a sorority are both confronted with a preexisting social structure. For example, in a student government organization, there may be such positions as President, Vice President, Treasurer, Secretary, and chairs of the major committees. Associated with each position is a particular set of rules and understandings about what the person in that position is expected to do, what the responsibilities are, and so on.

Social Role

Set of norms about how a person in a particular social position should behave.

The cluster of norms that apply to people in a particular position, such as the senior law partner or the administrative assistant, constitutes their **social role**. Roles define the division of labor in the group. In some organizations, roles are explicit and may even be described in a formal organizational chart, in written job descriptions, or in a legal contract. Many of our daily activities are structured by the social roles that we occupy in school, at work, and in our families and communities.

Social Status

A person's rank or privilege in a group.

Another important feature of group structure concerns differences in the **social status** of group members. The positions in most social systems differ in prestige and authority. In a formal organization such as a software company, the owner has the highest status, the largest salary, and the most authority to make decisions for the company; the secretary probably has the lowest status, the lowest salary, and the least influence in directing company policies and group activities. Even in groups whose members are supposedly equal in status, such as groups of friends or members of a jury, some individuals may emerge as more influential than others.

Expectation States Theory

A person's status in a group is affected by such diffuse status characteristics as age, gender, ethnicity, and wealth.

Expectation states theory, developed by Joseph Berger and his colleagues (1986), analyzes the creation of status differences in groups. According to this perspective, group members want to achieve certain goals and are willing to confer high status on members who can help the group succeed. When group members first meet, they try to assess each person's ability to contribute to the achievement of group goals, and these assessments, in turn, form the basis for each person's status in the group.

Consider, for example, how the 12 members of a newly formed jury might select someone as group leader (Forsyth, 1999). Imagine that the group includes these three individuals:

- Susan Able, a 40-year-old white college professor who has written several books on management
- John Black, a 35-year-old African American business executive with many years of leadership experience
- Fred White, a 58-year-old white physician who has an active general practice

In deciding on the person to head the jury, the jurors might consider specific task-relevant information, such as Mr. Black's leadership experience in industry or Professor Able's experience in leading classroom discussions. However, the jurors might also use what Berger calls "diffuse status characteristics"—that is, general attributes of the person, such as age, sex, ethnicity, or wealth—that people tend to associate (sometimes wrongly) with ability. For instance, the jurors might discount Professor Able's task-relevant qualifications because she is a woman, and women are generally given less status and authority than are men in U.S. society. Jurors might also give special weight to Dr. White's high-prestige job as a physician and to his seniority in age, even though these attributes may have little relevance to his abilities to head the jury. Research indicates that a person's status in a group is affected both by task-relevant characteristics and by potentially irrelevant diffuse status characteristics, such as age, ethnic background, and occupational prestige. Both gender and race can serve as diffuse status characteristics in groups, sometimes working to the disadvantage of women and members of ethnic minority groups (Forsyth, 1999).

Cohesiveness

In some groups, the bonds among members are strong and enduring, morale is high, and there is a general sense of community. In other groups, members are loosely linked, lack a sense of "groupness," and tend to drift apart over time. **Cohesiveness** refers to the forces, both positive and negative, that cause members to remain in a group. Cohesiveness is a characteristic of a group as a whole, based on the combined commitment of each individual to the group.

Cohesiveness

Forces, both positive and negative, that cause members to remain in a group.

Many factors affect the cohesiveness of a group (Brown, 2000). When group members like each other and are connected by bonds of friendship, cohesiveness is high (Paxton & Moody, 2003). Indeed, researchers have often measured cohesiveness by assessing the amount of liking among group members. A second source of cohesiveness is the extent to which a group interacts effectively and harmoniously with minimal conflict. We would undoubtedly prefer to be on a team that works efficiently than to be on one that wastes our time and misuses our skills. Our sense of identification with the group may also be important (van Vugt & Hart, 2004). More generally, anything that increases group satisfaction and morale tends to enhance cohesiveness.

Third, people's motivation to remain in a group is also influenced by the instrumental goals of the group. We participate in many groups as a means to an end—as a way to earn a salary, to play a sport we enjoy, or to work for a worthy cause. Our attraction to a group depends on the match between our goals and those of the group, and on how successfully the group accomplishes its objectives. Finally, group cohesiveness is also affected by forces that discourage members from leaving, even if they are dissatisfied. Sometimes people stay in groups because the costs of leaving are high or because they have no available alternatives. You may despise your coworkers but stay at the job because there are no other job openings in town. You may dislike your teachers but stay in their classes because you have no choice in the matter.

High levels of cohesiveness are usually beneficial to group functioning. When group members enjoy working together and endorse group goals, both morale and motivation tend to be high (Mullen & Cooper, 1994). Further, members of highly cohesive groups are more likely than are members of less cohesive groups to be influenced by the group and to conform to group norms (McGrath, 1984). Thus, cohesiveness can sometimes enhance productivity and sometimes hamper it. If the norms of the group are to work hard, to put in long hours, and to do your best, cohesiveness will increase productivity. In contrast, if group standards are to slack off and spend more time talking than completing tasks, high cohesiveness will decrease productivity.

GROUP PERFORMANCE

Are two heads better than one? Are groups usually more successful in completing a task than individuals alone would be? Social psychologists have studied these questions in depth. To understand when a group is better than an individual, consider the variety of tasks that groups can perform.

Types of Group Activities

An "additive task" is one in which group productivity is the sum of the effort of each group member. When several friends work together to push a pickup truck with a dead battery out of a busy intersection, the group effort is the sum of each person's efforts. A crucial factor in additive tasks is whether group members are able to coordinate their efforts effectively. In the truck example, it would be important for everyone to push at the same time and in the same direction. The

Amish neighbors work together to raise the side of a new barn. In an additive task, the success of the group depends on the combined efforts of all individuals.

rope-pulling task used by Ringelmann was also an additive task: The total effort exerted was the sum of the effort of each individual. Although social loafing may diminish each individual's contribution to an additive task, the total contribution does usually exceed what any one person could do alone. (Try pushing a stalled truck by yourself if you doubt this generalization.) On additive tasks, group productivity is generally superior to the efforts of any one person, and larger groups tend to be more productive than smaller groups.

In a "conjunctive task," all group members must succeed for the group to succeed. For a terrorist team to slip successfully onto an airplane, it is essential that every member remain undetected. A false move by any one person could endanger the whole mission. Similarly, workers on an automobile assembly line can work only as fast as the slowest person on the line. For conjunctive tasks, group productivity is only as good as the least competent group member, the "weakest link." Successful coordination among group members is also essential for conjunctive tasks.

In a "disjunctive task," only one person needs to solve a problem for the entire group to succeed. If a research group is trying to solve a complex mathematical equation, any one person with the right answer can ensure the group's effectiveness. Group performance on this type of task depends on the skill of the most competent member. Another example is the phenomenon of transactive memory in groups (Wittenbaum, Vaughan, & Stasser, 1998). Group members develop shared beliefs and assumptions about who will remember and be able to retrieve specific types of information based on each person's interests, skills, and previous behavior. If staff members in the psychology department are planning their annual holiday party, they may depend on specific group members to remember crucial details. Grace, who is a food enthusiast, may be counted on to remember where the refreshments were ordered last year and how much they cost. Cary, who works in the main office, may be assumed to remember where the lights and decorations were stored.

An even more complex situation occurs when a group has a task that can be subdivided among group members. In a medical operating room, the success of a delicate heart transplant depends on the skill of a team of professionals—not only the surgeon who performs the surgery but also the anesthesiologist who administers drugs and monitors vital signs, technicians who keep equipment working properly, surgical nurses, and so on. A mistake by any member of the operating team could put the patient at great risk. On complex tasks such as these, group productivity depends not only on the effort and skill of the best or worst player but also on the group's ability to coordinate individual activities, often under time pressure.

Brainstorming

If an advertising executive must develop catchy slogans for a campaign to encourage drivers to use seat belts, should she ask her staff members to work on the problem individually, or should she bring them together as a group to work jointly on the task? In the 1950s, advertising executive Alex Osborn (1957) proposed that groups are better than individuals at generating creative new ideas and solutions. The particular technique that he advocated is called **brainstorming**, and it is still used today in advertising and industry. A brainstorming group is given a specific problem to discuss, such as writing slogans to advertise a new brand of toothpaste. Members are instructed to think of as many different suggestions as they can in a short time. The rules of brainstorming, as outlined by Osborn, include the following:

Brainstorming

Group members work together to generate many new ideas or solutions to a problem.

1. Criticism is ruled out. Negative evaluations of ideas must be withheld until later.
2. Freewheeling suggestions are welcomed. The wilder the idea, the better. It is easier to tame down an idea than to perk it up.
3. Quantity is wanted. The greater the number of ideas, the greater the likelihood of winners.
4. Combinations and improvements are sought. In addition to contributing ideas of your own, you should suggest how the ideas of others can be turned into better ideas or how two or more ideas can be joined.

In an early study on brainstorming, participants were assigned at random to five-person groups or to an individual condition (Taylor, Berry, & Block, 1958). The people in both conditions were then given five problems and 12 minutes to work on each one. One problem was stated as follows: "Each year a great many American tourists visit Europe, but now suppose that our country wished to get many more European tourists to visit the United States during their vacations. What steps can you suggest that would get more European tourists to come to this country?" The participants were asked to offer as many solutions as possible and to be as creative as they could. There were obviously no "correct" solutions.

Subjects in the alone condition were divided at random into five-person aggregates or "nominal" groups. That is, although each person worked alone, for purposes of analysis he or she was considered part of a unit. The researchers compared 5 hours of work done by a five-person interacting group with 5 hours done by five individuals working alone. Quantity consisted of the number of different ideas produced by the real groups and the aggregates. If two people in an aggregate produced the same idea, it was counted only once. The results were clear. Five individuals working alone produced almost twice as many solutions and unique ideas as five people working together. Subsequent research has replicated this finding: In general, individuals produce more ideas—and often better ideas—when working alone than when working in brainstorming groups (Paulus, Larey, & Dzindolet, 2001).

Why isn't brainstorming more effective? There are several possible explanations (Brown & Paulus, 1996). The norm that only one person should speak at a time in a group means that a person who thinks of a new idea cannot immediately share the idea but must wait to speak. During this waiting time, the person may "rehearse" the idea but can't simultaneously be thinking up additional new ideas. Further, a person who is trying to think of creative slogans or ideas may find it distracting to have to listen to other people, rather than be able to give full attention to pursuing his or her own ideas.

In addition, even though members are asked to listen to all ideas uncritically, group members may experience evaluation apprehension, worrying that others won't like their suggestions. This concern about making a good impression may inhibit their creative thinking. One study found that working in a brainstorming group was especially harmful to the performance of individuals who are high in social anxiety and uncomfortable in group interactions (Camacho & Paulus, 1995). In addition, most members of a brainstorming group tend to perform at relatively similar levels, generating about the same number of ideas. Paulus and Dzindolet (1993) referred to this as "social matching." The presence of group members who perform at low levels may actually decrease the general performance level of other members of the group by setting a low norm for group productivity. Finally, research suggests that members of brainstorming groups may not pay much attention to the ideas of other group members and so may miss out on the possible cognitive stimulation that others' ideas could provide (Dugosh, Paulus, Roland, & Yang, 2000).

In summary, brainstorming is not typically a more effective technique than having individuals work alone. Yet many people continue to believe that group brainstorming increases productivity (Paulus et al., 2001). Why does this illusion of group productivity persist? First, people may evaluate group productivity inaccurately. After a brainstorming session, group members may be impressed by all the different ideas generated by the discussion. Individuals may recognize that the group produced more solutions than one person would have but may forget that the correct comparison is to the productivity of many individuals simultaneously working alone. In other words, people readily agree that "two heads are better than one" but don't ask the relevant question of whether two heads together are better than two heads alone. In addition, individuals may take credit for more than their actual share of contributions to the group product. A further reason for the popularity of group discussions is that many people enjoy being in groups and may prefer group discussions to working alone. Group discussions contribute to morale and motivation, even though the process takes more time.

Because of the popularity of brainstorming, researchers have begun looking for ways to improve the benefits of group brainstorming (Brown & Paulus, 2002). Promising possibilities include the creation of heterogeneous groups of individuals with diverse knowledge, alternating periods of group brainstorming with time alone generating ideas, and exchanging ideas by computer rather than in face-to-face group interaction.

GROUP DECISION MAKING

After weeks of hearing testimony, the jurors meet to discuss a controversial case and reach a verdict. A woman has stabbed her husband to death. The prosecutor argued that this was a vicious act of premeditated murder, worthy of the death sentence. The defense attorney argued that the woman had been the victim of years of physical beatings and psychological abuse and that the stabbing was actually an act of self-defense. How will the jury arrive at a joint decision?

Decision Rules

Rules about how a group should reach a decision.

Psychologists have identified a set of **decision rules** that groups use in arriving at decisions (Miller, 1989). In the United States, many states require that a guilty verdict in a murder case be unanimous; the dissent of even one juror will result in a hung jury and a possible retrial. When a unanimity rule is in effect, the group must pay careful attention to the views of dissenting minorities. In contrast, when the president of a company considers relocating her business to a new city, she may discuss the move with staff members but will ultimately make an individual decision. The rule here is that the boss decides.

Research has sought to identify factors that affect the decision rules used by groups. The type of decision is a defining factor. For example, in situations where a group is discussing a matter of opinion—whether the new yearbook cover should be green or blue—there is no objectively correct opinion. In such cases, when the topic is familiar, the alternatives are limited, and there is no correct

The foreperson of this jury reads the group's verdict to the defendant and others in the courtroom.

answer, a majority-wins rule often prevails. In a majority-wins decision, the group ultimately decides to go along with the position that has the most supporters, even if the majority wins by the slimmest of margins. When groups are discussing matters of fact rather than of opinion, when one solution is correct and another is wrong, groups tend to adopt a truth-wins rule (Laughlin & Adamopoulos, 1980). As a result of the presentation of information and arguments, group members are persuaded by the truth of a particular position, even if it was initially held by only a minority of the group members. Research on these and other decision rules suggests that by knowing the initial opinions of group members and the type of issue being discussed, we can often predict the group's decision in advance. Group decision rules have consequences for the functioning of the group (Miller, 1989). Strict rules, such as the requirement that a group reach a unanimous decision, usually require more discussion than less stringent rules. Unanimous decisions are harder to reach, often involve compromises, and sometimes result in a failure to reach a decision. However, when groups are able to reach a unanimous decision, they tend to be more satisfied with the outcome than when a minority of members disagree with a group decision.

Unfortunately, groups do not necessarily make wise decisions. Social psychological research indicates that groups are vulnerable to special social forces that can bias decision making. Three important issues in group decision making are the biased use of information, group polarization, and groupthink.

Biased Use of Information in Groups

When a group meets to discuss an issue, members often have different information about the topic and different points of view. Indeed, one reason that groups may make wiser decisions than individuals is precisely that they can pool their collective information to arrive at a more thoughtful group decision.

Consider how a psychology department might decide among three candidates for a new assistant professorship. All faculty members would hear the candidates give a lecture and would read the candidates' résumés and letters of recommendation. Each faculty member would interview each candidate individually, asking many questions about the candidate's background, experience, and interests. When the faculty meet to make a final decision, they would all have some shared common knowledge about the candidates, and they would each have unique unshared information about the candidates. For instance, one faculty member might learn that a particular candidate had just won a teaching award, another might learn that the candidate had worked two jobs to pay for graduate school, and a third might learn that the candidate was fluent in Chinese and planned to conduct cross-cultural research. To arrive at the best decision among the three candidates, faculty members should spend considerable time describing the unique or unshared information they learned about the candidates. Do groups really engage in this systematic sharing of information?

To answer this question, social psychologists have asked a variety of participants to take part in decision-making studies. In one study, three-person groups of college students decided which of two professors would be nominated for a teaching award (Winquist & Larson, 1998). In another study, three-person teams of physicians were given hypothetical medical cases to diagnose (Larson et al., 1998). In both studies, all group members were given some shared and some unshared information. All the information might be vitally important to making a wise decision. The group discussions were coded for how much discussion time was spent on shared versus unshared information.

Common Knowledge Effect

Group members spend more time discussing shared than unshared information.

The results of these and other studies are clear: Group members spend considerably more time discussing shared than unshared information (Wittenbaum & Park, 2001). This is the so-called **common knowledge effect**. By devoting so much of their discussion time to common information, groups fail to take advantage of unshared information that may be particularly revealing or important. Why does this bias occur? It appears that group interactions are easier and more comfortable when mutual information is discussed and everyone can participate. Group members who communicate common information are evaluated as more competent and knowledgeable by others in the group than by individuals who bring up unique information. Several suggestions have been offered to increase the use of unshared, novel information. For example, leaders can take the initiative to introduce unshared information and encourage group members to do so. Further, because unshared information tends to be mentioned later in group discussions, it may be important to have longer group meetings that permit adequate time for a full discussion of all information.

Another tendency that can influence group decision making is the confirmation bias, a concept introduced in Chapter 2. People often seek out and prefer information that supports their initial beliefs. In group decision making, therefore, individuals may use group discussions to confirm rather than challenge their own initial decision (Schulz-Hardt, Frey, Luthgens, & Moscovici, 2000). In other words, group members may use the group discussion to justify their own initial decision, not to learn new information that might conflict with their initial preference and require them to change their opinion (Kelly & Karau, 1999).

In summary, although groups have the potential to make better decisions than individuals, they do not always take advantage of this possibility.

Group Polarization

Do groups tend to make riskier or more conservative decisions than individuals? In 1968, James Stoner reported that the decisions groups make are often riskier than the individual views held by the members before discussion. This finding, called the **risky shift**, sparked considerable interest, in part because it seemed to contradict the popular belief that groups are relatively conservative and stodgy about decision making. In a typical risky-shift study, subjects read about several complex situations. In each situation, choices ranging from very high risk to very low risk were available. Consider this problem:

Risky Shift

Group discussion can lead individuals to make riskier decisions than they would make alone.

> Carol is a successful teacher at a community college. She makes a comfortable salary and enjoys her work. But Carol has always wanted to be her own boss and run a restaurant. A year ago, Carol began looking into the possibility of opening a small restaurant. She has found a young chef who would be interested in working with her, has identified a prime location for a new restaurant, and has

talked to loan officers at her bank. To run the restaurant, Carol would need to quit her job and use all of her personal savings. If the restaurant is successful, Carol will realize her lifelong ambition and make a good income. On the other hand, Carol knows that many new businesses are not successful. If the restaurant fails, she will have spent a great deal of time and money and give up her secure teaching job. Imagine that you are advising Carol. Check the lowest probability that you would consider acceptable for Carol to open the restaurant.

Carol should open the restaurant if the chances of success are at least:

___ 1 in 10 (Open the restaurant even if success is unlikely.)
___ 2 in 10
___ 3 in 10
___ 4 in 10
___ 5 in 10
___ 6 in 10
___ 7 in 10
___ 8 in 10
___ 9 in 10
___10 in 10 (Open the restaurant only if success is certain.)

How do you think other students would answer this question?

In the original study by Stoner (1968), research participants read each situation and made their own decision individually. Then subjects were brought into a group and asked to discuss each problem and to reach a unanimous group decision. Under these conditions, there was a strong tendency for the group decision to involve greater risk than the average of the decisions made by the individuals.

Many studies conducted in the United States, Canada, and Europe have replicated this basic finding of a group shift toward greater risk, but some researchers have found exceptions. Some groups actually make more conservative decisions. Today, research has shown that when the initial opinions of group members tend toward risk, group discussion results in a shift toward greater risk. In contrast, when the initial opinions are conservative, group discussion results in a shift toward more extreme conservatism. The basic finding is that group discussion leads to more extreme decisions, a phenomenon called **group polarization** (Levine & Moreland, 1998). Several explanations for group polarization have been offered.

Group Polarization

Groups often make more extreme decisions than do individuals alone.

The persuasive-arguments perspective emphasizes that people gain new information as a result of listening to pro and con arguments in the group's discussion (Burnstein & Vinokur, 1977). The more numerous and persuasive the arguments in favor of a position, the more likely group members are to adopt that position. However, if most members initially support one position and largely discuss reasons for their initial opinion, people will hear more reasons in favor of their own opinion than against it. In addition, group discussion may encourage members to think about various arguments and to commit themselves more actively to a particular position. The information presented during the discussion may thus convince people of the correctness of their original views and so may lead to more extreme opinions. Further, as part of the group discussion, individuals may repeatedly express their own ideas, and this process of restatement may actually increase the shift toward more extreme views (Brauer, Judd, & Gliner, 1995).

A second explanation of group polarization emphasizes social comparison and self-presentational processes (Goethals & Darley, 1987). The idea is that group members are concerned with how their own opinions compare with those of others in the group. During discussion, individuals may learn that others have similar attitudes and indeed that some people have even stronger (more extreme) views than they do. A desire to be seen positively, as confident or bold, may lead individuals to shift toward positions that are more extreme than those of the other group members. This shift is essentially a form of one-upmanship, by which individuals try to be "better" than average. Research provides support for both persuasive arguments and social comparison processes and suggests that they occur simultaneously (Isenberg, 1986).

A third possibility is that social identity processes are at work (Abrams, Wetherell, Cochrane, Hogg, & Turner, 1990; Mackie, 1986). The idea is that discussion causes individuals to focus on their group membership and to identify with the group. This identification, in turn, leads individuals to feel pressure to shift their own views to conform with the perceived norm of their group. However, rather than perceive the "true" average opinion of the group (as assessed by prediscussion scores), members perceive the group norm as more stereotyped or extreme. Consequently, they conform to what they believe is the group's position by shifting their own attitudes toward a greater extreme. Whatever its possible causes, group polarization is an important facet of group decision making.

Do group discussions always result in polarization? The answer is no. When members of a group are more or less evenly split on an issue, discussion often leads to a compromise between the opposing views of group members (Burnstein & Vinokur, 1977). This process has been called "depolarization."

Groupthink

Groupthink

Poor group decision making based on inadequate considerations of alternatives.

Sometimes a seemingly reasonable and intelligent group makes a decision that in retrospect was obviously a disaster. Irving Janis (1982) proposed that this phenomenon may result from a process he called **groupthink**. As outlined in Figure 10–6, groupthink is characterized by a group that feels invulnerable and is excessively optimistic. The group reaches a decision without allowing members to express their doubts. Members shield themselves from any outside information that might undermine this decision. Finally, the group believes its decision is

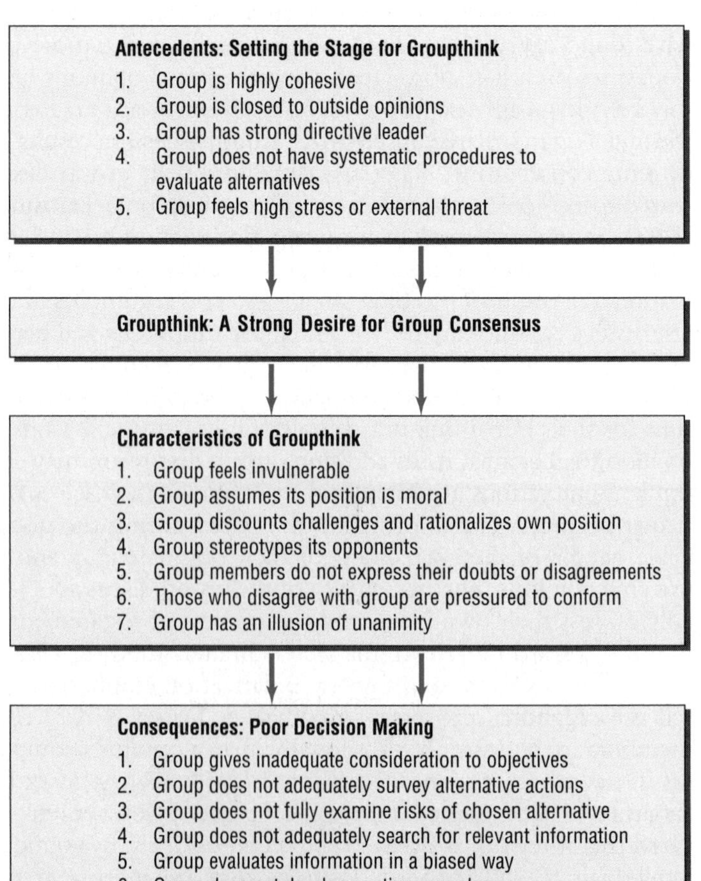

Figure 10–6 **Janis's Theory of Groupthink.**
Irving Janis (1982) analyzed the antecedents, characteristics, and consequences of groupthink.

unanimous, even when considerable unexpressed dissent exists. Because disagreements both inside and outside the group are prevented, the decisions are sometimes disastrous.

Janis claimed that groupthink contributed to several important episodes in U.S. foreign policy. He cited the lack of preparation for the Japanese attack on Pearl Harbor in 1941, the failed invasion of the Bay of Pigs in Cuba in the 1960s, the escalation of the Vietnam War, and President Nixon's attempted Watergate cover-up in the early 1970s. In each case, a small group of powerful politicians, generally led by the president, made a decision in isolation from dissenting voices or from information that would have changed the eventual decision. Other researchers have applied the groupthink model to other types of disasters, such as the explosion of the space shuttle Challenger.

On January 28, 1986, Challenger was launched from the Kennedy Space Center. Seventy-two seconds later, the spacecraft exploded, killing everyone on board as a horrified nation watched the tragedy on television. Expert engineers had warned against the launch, arguing that the air temperature was too cold for safety. But top decision makers disregarded this advice. According to one analysis, many elements of groupthink were present in the decisions leading up to the launch (Moorhead, Ference, & Neck, 1991). For example, the people who made the decision to launch the shuttle had worked together for years, had a strong sense of camaraderie, and were led by two top managers who strongly supported the launch even in the face of opposition. The decision makers dismissed the warnings of expert engineers, and they pressured the manufacturer of the shuttle to recommend the launch. At the time, the decision makers seemed confident in the correctness of their position. The fact that the National Air and Space Administration had had a series of 55 successful missions added to a sense of invulnerability. Ultimately, failure to heed the warnings of experts led to the fateful launch.

Janis (1982) identified several possible causes or antecedents of groupthink. He suggested that groupthink occurs most often in highly cohesive groups that are able to seal themselves off from outside opinions and have very strong, dynamic leaders. These leaders propose a particular solution to a problem and argue strongly for it. Group members do not disagree or consider alternative actions. Members may fear being rejected and do not want to lower group morale by voicing concerns. According to Janis, skeptical members may go along with the group or even convince themselves that their own doubts are trivial and not worth expressing. Janis offered various suggestions for combating groupthink and enhancing the effectiveness of group decision making:

1. The leader should encourage each group member to air objections and doubts about proposed decisions. For this suggestion to be effective, the leader must be willing to accept criticism of his or her ideas.
2. The leader should initially remain impartial in discussions, stating preferences and expectations only after group members have expressed their own views.
3. The group should divide into subcommittees to discuss issues independently and then come together to hammer out differences.
4. Outside experts should be invited to participate occasionally in group discussions and should be encouraged to challenge the views of the group members.
5. At each meeting, at least one person should be assigned to play devil's advocate to challenge group ideas.

These suggestions are designed to force the group to consider many alternatives, to avoid an illusion of consensus, and to consider all relevant information.

Despite the intuitive appeal of the concept of groupthink, empirical support for Janis's (1982) ideas is limited (Esser, 1998; Paulus, 1998). Several studies have supported parts of groupthink theory. For example, Philip Tetlock and his colleagues (1992) conducted a sophisticated analysis of the records of 12 different political decisions, such as President Jimmy Carter's unsuccessful attempt to rescue U.S. hostages in Iran. Tetlock concluded that it was possible to distinguish reliably between groups whose decisions reflected groupthink and groups whose decision making showed good judgment and "vigilance." These results provide support for the existence of the groupthink process. However, these researchers had mixed success in testing factors that Janis proposed as causes of groupthink. Their results confirmed the important role of the leader in determining the quality of decision making but found no support for Janis's supposition that groupthink is caused by high group cohesiveness.

What are we to conclude about groupthink? Clearly, as noted in the CIA story at the beginning of this chapter, the idea remains popular to this day. Groupthink seems to offer valuable insights into specific historical incidents. However, supporters of the groupthink concept now agree that the processes that cause groupthink are more complex than what Janis believed. Many cohesive groups with strong leaders make excellent decisions. Indeed, the groups involved in the disasters studied by Janis often made reasonable decisions on other occasions. Furthermore, as politicians and generals can readily attest, thoughtful decision making is no guarantee of ultimate success. Sometimes groups engage in careful decision making, take reasonable action, and then, through bad luck or unforeseeable circumstances, fail miserably. Nevertheless, Janis's analysis of groupthink and the research it has sparked provide a useful reminder of some of the potential pitfalls of group decision making.

GROUP INTERACTION: COMPETITION VERSUS COOPERATION

Sometimes people in groups interact cooperatively: They help each other, share information, and work together for mutual benefit. At other times, group members compete: They put their own individual goals first and strive to outperform the rest. Social psychologists have long been interested in understanding these human tendencies. In a series of classic studies, researchers developed ingenious ways to study competition and cooperation systematically in the laboratory.

Classic Laboratory Studies

Much of the research on competition and cooperation has used laboratory games that simulate key features of everyday interaction (Bornstein, 2003). This section discusses research using two of the most popular games: the trucking game and the prisoner's dilemma. A common finding from these studies is that participants—usually middle-class, white college students in the United States—tend to compete, even when cooperation would be a more rewarding strategy.

The Trucking Game. In a pioneering experiment on competition, Deutsch and Krauss (1960) used a simple two-person game called the "trucking game." Participants were asked to imagine that they were running a trucking company (either the Acme Company or the Bolt Company) and had to get a truck from one point to another as quickly as possible. The two trucks were not in competition; they had different starting points and different destinations. There was, however, one hitch: The faster route for both converged at one point to a one-lane road, and the two trucks had to go in opposite directions. This scenario is shown in Figure 10–7. The only way both could use the road would be for one of them to wait until the other had passed through. If either truck entered the road, the other could not use it; if they both entered the road, neither of them could move until one had backed up. In addition, each player had a gate across the direct route that could be raised by pressing a button. If the gate was raised, it prevented the road from being used.

Each truck was provided with an alternative route that did not conflict with the other's but was much longer. In fact, the game was set up so that taking the alternative route was guaranteed to lose points, whereas taking the direct route would gain points for both sides, even if they alternated at the one-lane section of the road. The players were told that their goal was to earn as many points as

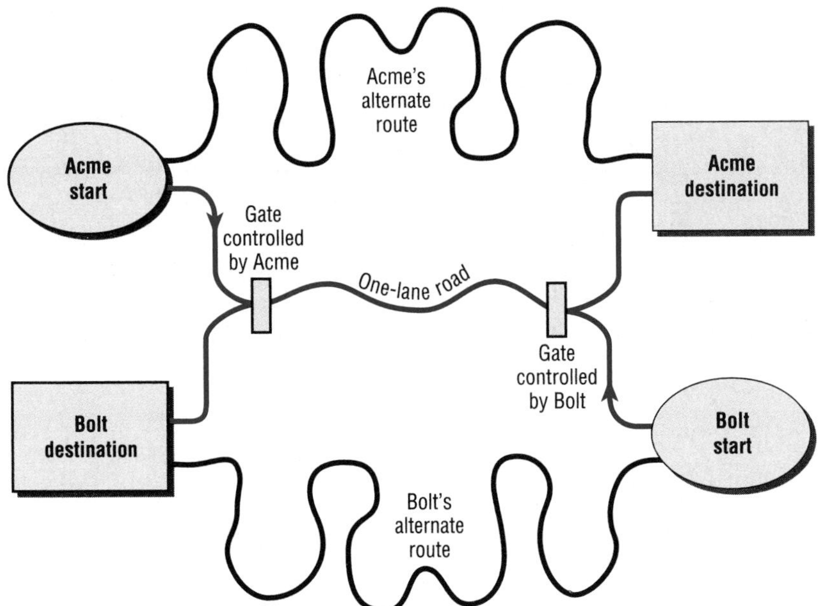

Figure 10–7 **Road Map of the Trucking Game.**

The players must get their truck to its destination as quickly as possible. Although they can do this efficiently only by cooperating and sharing the one-lane road, they often compete.

Source: Data from Deutsch and Krauss (1960, p. 183).

possible for themselves. Nothing was said about earning more points than the other player. Once the instructions were fully explained, each participant played the trucking game with the same partner for a series of trials.

The results of this study were striking. It was clear to the participants that the optimal strategy was to cooperate by alternating in using the one-lane road. In this way, they could both use the direct route, and one would be delayed only a few seconds while the other was getting through. Nevertheless, there was little cooperation between the players. Instead of allowing each other to use the one-lane road, they fought for its use, they raised their gates, and both players ended up losing points.

In a typical trial, both sides would try to use the road and would meet in the middle, head on. They would stubbornly stay there for a while, each refusing to retreat. The players might laugh nervously or make nasty comments. Finally, one of them would back up, erect the barrier, and use the alternate route. On the next trial, they would do the same thing, and so it went. An occasional cooperative trial might occur, but most trials were competitive.

The Prisoner's Dilemma. The tendency to compete is not triggered by the unique characteristics of the trucking game. It also occurs in many other games, such as the **prisoner's dilemma,** so called because it is based on a problem faced by two suspects at a police station. The district attorney thinks the suspects have committed a major crime together but has no proof against either one. The prisoners are put into separate rooms, and each is told that he has two alternatives: to confess or not to confess. If neither suspect confesses, neither can be convicted of a major crime. But the district attorney tells them they can still be convicted of minor crimes so that both will receive minor punishments. Of course, if they both confess, they will both definitely be convicted of the major crime. But the district attorney tells each suspect that he will ask for leniency if the suspect confesses. So if one of them confesses and the other does not, the confessor will be freed for helping the state, and the other suspect will get the maximum penalty. The situation is shown in Figure 10–8.

Prisoner's Dilemma

A game used by researchers to study cooperation and competition.

Obviously, there is a conflict. If one suspect thinks his partner is going to confess, it is best for him to confess also; on the other hand, the best joint outcome is for neither to confess and then for both to take the minor sentences. Thus, if the suspects trust each other, they should not confess. However, if one suspect is convinced that the other will not confess, he or she would do even better to confess and in that way be freed. We do not know what real prisoners would do in

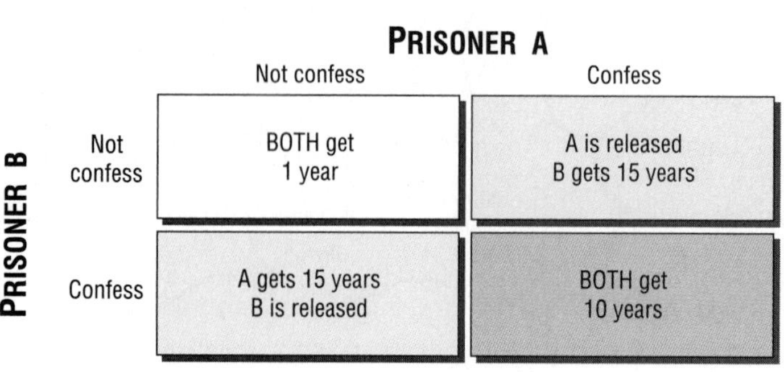

Figure 10–8 **Example of the Prisoner's Dilemma Game.**

Two prisoners have the choice of confessing or not confessing. If they trust and support each other by not confessing, each receives a light sentence; if they both confess, they receive relatively heavy sentences; and if one confesses and the other does not, the former is released and the latter gets a very heavy sentence. The dilemma is that one who has complete trust in the other would do best by being untrustworthy and confessing.

these circumstances. In research on the problem, much of the drama is removed, but the situation is basically similar. Instead of playing for their freedom, subjects play for points or money. They play in pairs but usually are not allowed to talk to each other. Each player has a choice of two strategies, and each player's reward or "payoff" depends on the actions of both the player and the partner.

The exact pattern of payoffs varies; a typical one is shown in Figure 10–9 for two players, Pete and Joe. If both choose option X, each gets 10 points. If Pete chooses X and Joe chooses Y, Pete loses 15 points and Joe wins 15. If both choose Y, they both lose 5 points. In other words, they can cooperate (choose X) and both win 10 points, or they can compete (one or both choosing Y) and try to win even more (15 points) but risk losing. The players are told that the goal is to score as many points as they can. It is clear to virtually all of them that the way to have the highest score is for both to select X (the cooperative choice) on every trial in a series of trials. However, as in the trucking game, there is a strong tendency to compete. In a typical game, only about a third of the choices are cooperative. Moreover, as the game progresses (and the players have usually won only a few points), the number of cooperative choices usually goes down. The players choose the competitive strategy more and more often, even though they know they can win more by cooperating. This effect has been demonstrated not only when one individual plays against another but also when one group plays

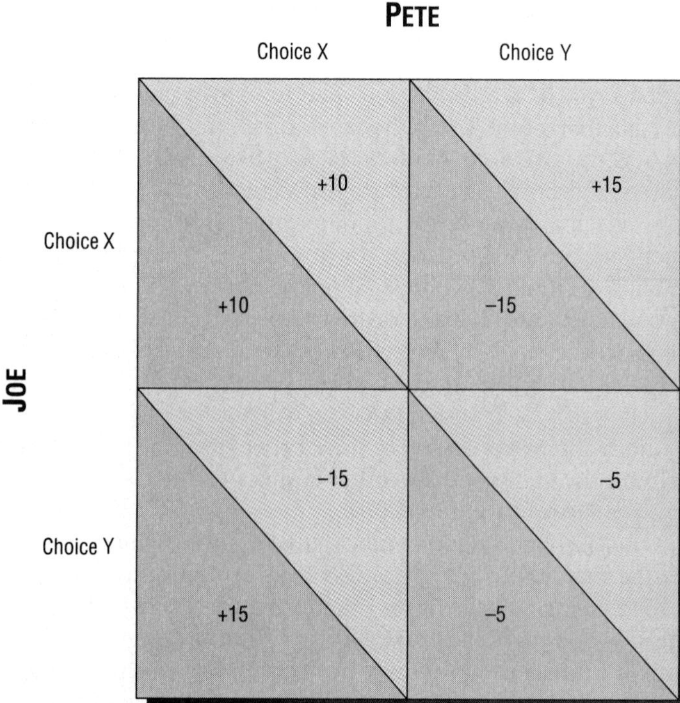

Figure 10–9 **Typical Prisoner's Dilemma Game Matrix or Reward Structure.**

Pete's payoff is shown in blue; Joe's payoff is shown in gray. Choice X is cooperative because it allows both players to win. Choice Y is competitive because only the player who chooses it has a chance of winning and both players may lose. With this reward structure, there is a great deal of competition.

against another. Indeed, the typical finding is that groups are more competitive than are individuals (Schopler et al., 2001).

Determinants of Competition versus Cooperation

Many factors determine whether people interact cooperatively or competitively including the reward structure of the situation, individual differences in competitiveness, communication patterns, and the effects of reciprocity.

Reward Structure. The nature of the social interdependence among group members determines the reward structure of the situation. A competitive reward structure exists when one person's gain is another's loss. If you win a pot in poker, the other players must lose. In an Olympic swimming match, only one person can win the gold medal. If a college course is graded on a curve, only a few students can get As. In these situations, the outcomes of group members are linked in a negative way: An individual does best when others do poorly. This is a situation of "competitive interdependence." In such situations, a person who wants the available rewards will do best to compete.

Situations in which there is a cooperative reward structure and the outcomes of group members are linked in a positive way are situations of "cooperative interdependence." For a soccer team to win games, teammates must work together. The better each player does, the more likely it is that the entire team will be victorious. In families and friendship groups, there are usually norms of cooperation. It has been found, for instance, that children are generally more cooperative and less competitive with friends and siblings than they are with strangers (Knight & Chao, 1991). In a cooperative reward situation, an individual who desires rewards will do best to cooperate.

An "individualistic reward structure" exists when the outcomes of individuals are independent of each other. Here, individuals are socially independent rather than interdependent. What happens to one person has no impact on the others. If a teacher gives an A to everyone who gets 90 percent correct on a test, it is possible for all students to get an A, or for none to get an A. Each person's grade is independent of how other classmates perform. In this type of situation, there is no extrinsic reason to compete. Often, however, the reward structure in a situation is mixed or unclear. People have choices about whether to cooperate or to compete. This is the case in the trucking game and the prisoner's dilemma game. As we saw, experimental game studies show that when there is a mixed reward

Team sports foster fierce intergroup competition when one side can win only at the expense of the other team.

structure, many middle-class U.S. college students adopt a competitive strategy that actually prevents them from maximizing their rewards.

Personal Values. There also appear to be individual differences in people's personal values about competition. Individuals tend to have one of three value orientations or strategies for interacting with other people (McClintock & Liebrand, 1988):

- Cooperators are concerned with maximizing the joint rewards received by both the self and the partner.
- Competitors are oriented toward maximizing their own gains relative to those of the partner. They want to do better than the partner.
- Individualists are oriented toward maximizing their own gains, with no concern for the gains or losses of the partner.

When people are faced with a situation such as the trucking game or prisoner's dilemma, their value orientation has a strong impact on their initial behavior. Cooperators usually initiate cooperative interactions; competitors begin in a more competitive mode. Over time, however, people will change their own behavior if the partner does not reciprocate. Confronted with a highly competitive partner, even the most dedicated cooperator may begin to behave competitively.

Communication. In general, more communication leads to more cooperation (Orbell, van de Kragt, & Dawes, 1988). For example, in the trucking-game study, three different communication conditions were included. Some participants were required to communicate, some were given the opportunity to talk if they wanted to, and others were not allowed to communicate. Cooperation was greatest when communication was required and was least when communication was impossible.

Similar results have been found in the prisoner's dilemma game. Wichman (1970) showed that competition was greatest when no communication was possible, somewhat less when partners could talk but not see each other, and least when partners could see and talk to each other. When there was no communication, about 40 percent of responses were cooperative; when verbal communication was permitted, cooperation increased to more than 70 percent of trials. Communication enables partners to urge each other to cooperate, to discuss their plans, to make promises, to convince each other that they are trustworthy, and to learn about each other.

Reciprocity. We have seen throughout this book that there is a general norm of reciprocity: People often feel obligated to return both favors and insults. There is some evidence that in the course of interaction, initial competition provokes more competition, and initial cooperation sometimes (but not always) encourages further cooperation. One strategy that seems especially successful in fostering cooperation is reciprocal concessions. The parties take turns giving up a little. This is the traditional compromise solution to most conflicts: Each side starts with an extreme position and then retreats gradually until a common meeting ground is found.

If one party makes a small concession and then waits for the other to do the same, there is usually greater cooperation eventually (Esser & Komorita, 1975). A crucial element of this strategy is timing. A person who gives in too much at once may appear weak and the other will not reciprocate. The concessions must be gradual and sequential. An effective technique is to make reciprocal concessions only slightly larger than those made by the other person. This approach reinforces the other's cooperation and results in even larger concessions and quick agreement. Obviously, it does not work unless both sides are willing to cooperate to some extent. If one is totally competitive, only the one who tries cooperating will be exploited and will end up in a weaker position than before.

Psychologists have learned a good deal about competition and cooperation from laboratory studies using games such as the prisoner's dilemma. There are many important applications of this research to everyday social situations. For example, teachers sometimes use cooperative learning groups to reduce competition and prejudice in the classroom. In a cooperative learning group, children work together to master course materials. Students know that they will do best if all members of their group do well. One benefit of cooperative learning groups is that they can foster liking among children from different social backgrounds and can therefore reduce prejudice. However, research shows that cooperative groups can have other benefits as well (Deutsch, 1993; Johnson & Johnson, 1992). Cooperative learning can lead to greater achievement than would occur in competitive or individualist settings. Cooperative groups can also provide individuals with a greater sense of social support from their peers, can enhance self-esteem, and can foster greater psychological well-being. These benefits are most likely to occur when individuals are fully aware that the reward structure is cooperative, and when each individual is accountable to the group for his or her performance. In addition, cooperative groups are most likely to work successfully when group members interact frequently face to face and when individuals are trained in the social skills necessary for working together effectively.

Culture and Competition

Cross-cultural studies suggest that the United States is one of the most competitive societies on the planet. This point is strikingly illustrated in research comparing white children from the United States with children from Mexico (Kagan, 1977). In one study, 8-year-old children played a game of marbles with same-sex children from their own culture (Madsen, 1971). The children had the option of cooperating or competing, but the game was set up so that they could get marbles only by cooperating. The Mexican children cooperated on roughly 7 of 10 trials. In contrast, children from the United States cooperated on fewer than 1 trial in 10. Another study compared Mexican children, Mexican American children, and Anglo children (Kagan & Madsen, 1971). Among 7- to 9-year-olds, Mexican children cooperated 63 percent of the time, Mexican Americans 29 percent of the time, and Anglos only 10 percent of the time.

How can we explain these clear-cut group differences? Spencer Kagan (1984) systematically examined possible explanations. In general, people living in cities are more competitive than those who live in rural areas, and people from higher economic classes are more competitive than those from poorer backgrounds. But neither of these factors explains the Mexican American versus Anglo differences. When researchers compare children from similar residential and economic backgrounds, the cultural differences remain. Further, these differences in competitiveness are not due to differences in family size or patterns of parental discipline.

It appears that the cross-cultural patterns reflect broad cultural values about cooperation and competition that are taught not only at home but also in schools, through the media, and through sports and games (Kagan, 1984). The more exposure Mexican American children have to U.S. culture, the more competitive they become. We noted earlier that Mexican American children show a pattern of competitiveness between that of Anglos and that of Mexicans. Other research suggests that Mexican American children whose parents were born in the United States are more competitive than are children whose parents were born in Mexico (Knight & Kagan, 1977). Similarly, Mexican American children who speak only Spanish (and so, presumably, are less influenced by Anglo culture) are less competitive than are bilingual children (cited in Kagan, 1984). Taken together, these findings suggest that as the influence of U.S. culture and values increases, children tend to become more competitive.

Social Dilemmas

A perplexing aspect of social life is the **social dilemma**—a situation in which a desirable choice for the individual results in undesirable consequences for the

Social Dilemma

A situation that pits short-term self-interest against the long-term welfare of the group.

With rainfall at a historic low and a summer drought predicted, this homeowner collects rainwater in a barrel to use to water his garden. Conservationists ask individuals to make small personal sacrifices that will benefit the community as a whole.

group. Consider an example used by Glance and Huberman (1994): Imagine that you and a group of friends are dining at a fine restaurant with an unspoken agreement to divide the check evenly. What do you order? Do you choose the modest chicken entree or the pricey lamb chops? The house wine or the aged Cabernet Sauvignon? If you are extravagant, you could enjoy a superlative dinner at a bargain price. But if everyone in the party reasons as you do, the group will end up with a hefty bill to pay. And why should others settle for pasta primavera when someone is having grilled pheasant at their expense? What would you do in this situation? Would you order a modest dinner, doing your part to keep the expenses low for the group? Or would you order something expensive, hoping to get a "free ride" at the expense of the group—a choice known as the "free rider effect"?

Today, as we are becoming more aware of the dangers of pollution and the wanton use of natural resources, an understanding of social dilemmas is especially timely. In the Southwest, for example, many communities have suffered severe droughts for years, and water conservation is essential. Individuals who live in drought-stricken areas face many personal decisions, for example, forgoing the pleasure of a long shower today so that there will be more water for all in the future.

In technical terms, a social dilemma is a situation in which the most rewarding short-term choice for an individual will ultimately lead to negative outcomes for all concerned. As Brewer and Kramer (1986) wrote, "Social dilemmas exist whenever the cumulative result of reasonable individual choices is collective disaster" (p. 543). Social dilemmas pit the short-term interests of the individual against the long-term interests of the group (which includes the individual).

Social dilemma research is currently an active field in social psychology (Foddy, Smithson, Schneider, & Hogg, 1999). This research extends earlier studies of the trucking game and the prisoner's dilemma to more complicated situations. Much of this research has been done in the laboratory, in game-playing situations that replicate essential features of real-life social dilemmas (Parks & Sanna, 1999). Because individuals who are confronted with social dilemmas sometimes act selfishly and sometimes cooperate for the good of the collective, researchers have investigated factors that can tip the balance in one direction or the other. Not surprisingly, some of the same factors identified in the earlier discussions of competition and cooperation are also relevant to social dilemmas.

First, the reward structure in the situation makes a difference. For example, an effective way to encourage people to use less water is to change the billing system so that customers are charged higher rates if they use more of this valued resource (Messick & Brewer, 1983). Similarly, we can encourage people to insulate their homes (and use less energy) by offering tax incentives for energy-saving home improvements. Second, reminding people of social norms of cooperation can make a difference. Research shows that people are less likely to litter if they have been reminded that most people disapprove of littering, in other words, that there is a social norm against littering (Reno, Cialdini, & Kallgren, 1993). Another way to reduce future littering is to clean up the environment, because a litter-free environment shows that other people are following the social norm against littering. A mountain hiker will be less likely to toss trash along the trail if the path is free of litter, if others are seen putting empty food wrappers in their backpacks, or if others pick up a stray piece of trash on the ground. In addition, individuals are more likely to follow government policies, such as rules about water rationing during a drought, when they believe that the people creating the rules are acting in a way that is fair to all concerned (Tyler & Degoey, 1995).

Other factors are also important in solving social dilemmas (Kerr & Park, 2001). A person's value orientation—whether cooperative, competitive, or individualist—can make a difference in how he or she approaches a social dilemma. The size of the group also matters. In a large group, the effect of one person's selfish behavior is diluted. In the example of the diners splitting the bill, one person's expensive meal would matter less if divided among 12 people than if divided among only 4. The relationship among individuals also matters. We are more likely to forgo our short-term self-interest if we know and care about individuals in the group, and if we expect to interact with them again in the future. A diner who goes out regularly for dinner with the same friends is unlikely to splurge at the expense of the group.

Communication among the individuals involved can increase cooperation. Discussion provides an opportunity for individuals to make public commitments to cooperate. If the diners discussed the cost of dinner before making their individual choices, they might mutually agree to order frugally. Communication may also enhance feelings of identification with the group. Fostering a sense of group identity can increase the tendency to show restraint and to use resources wisely, especially in small groups.

LEADERSHIP

Some form of leadership exists in all groups. The central attribute of leadership is social influence (Burn, 2004; Chemers, 2001). The leader is the person who has the most impact on group behavior and beliefs. He or she is the one who initiates action, gives orders, makes decisions, settles disputes among group members, offers encouragement, serves as a model, and is in the forefront of group activity.

Groups differ in whether they have formal or informal leaders. Large organizations such as businesses or schools have formal organization charts indicating the official chain of command and giving guidelines about patterns of decision making and supervision. Even in smaller groups, such as clubs and fraternities, there may be elected officers with specified responsibilities. At the other extreme, some groups have no formal leaders at all. Friendship groups illustrate a pattern of informal leadership. One person may be more articulate and persuasive than others in group discussions and so may have more influence on decisions.

Paths to Leadership

Individuals can become group leaders in many ways. Some leaders are appointed. An army lieutenant is appointed by people higher up in the military organization to run his or her unit. Because of this position, the lieutenant can give orders to everyone else in the company, but none of them can give the lieutenant orders. In other situations, such as clubs or student government, a leader is elected.

Not all leaders are appointed or elected. In some cases, a group member gradually emerges as a leader over time. When people interact repeatedly, as in a group of friends or classmates, some individuals typically emerge as informal leaders. These leaders do not have official titles, yet most group members would generally agree that a particular person or set of people is the leader. Outside observers can also spot emergent leaders by monitoring such indicators as who talks the most in group discussions and whose opinions are most likely to prevail in group decision making. Many studies have found a strong tendency for the person who talks the most to be perceived as the leader both by other members of the group and by outside observers (Mullen, 1991). Specific leadership activities also make a difference. For instance, a study asked groups of grade-school children to decide which of eight pictures was most suitable for displaying in children's hospital rooms (French & Stright, 1991). Those children who frequently asked others their opinions, who kept the group focused on the task, and who made records of group decisions were perceived as leaders by group members, by teachers, and by other observers.

Another path to leadership arises when an individual turns a personal tragedy into a social cause (Huffington, 2001). When her daughter was killed by a drunk driver, Candy Lightner took action. She formed Mothers Against Drunk Driving, an organization that has successfully crusaded for designated-driver programs, stricter drunk-driving laws, and ad campaigns against irresponsible drinking. When Kathy Fackler's son was maimed on a ride at Disneyland, she began a campaign to improve amusement park safety that has resulted in tougher state laws and ride inspection programs. These unlikely leaders emerged when tragedy spurred them to take public action.

Task Leadership

Directing and organizing a group to accomplish a task or a goal.

Social Leadership

Maintaining the social and emotional well-being of group members.

In general, leaders must perform two types of activities. **Task leadership** concerns accomplishing the goals of the group—getting the work of the group done successfully. The task leader gives suggestions, offers opinions, and provides information to the group. He or she controls, shapes, directs, and organizes the group in carrying out a specific task. In contrast, **social leadership** focuses on the emotional and interpersonal aspects of group interaction. The social leader concentrates on keeping the group running smoothly and harmoniously, is concerned about people's feelings, uses humor to relieve tension, and tries to encourage group cohesiveness.

Both task and social leadership are important to successful group functioning. The qualities necessary for the two types of leadership are somewhat different. A task leader must be efficient, directive, and knowledgeable about the particular task at hand. A social leader must be friendly, agreeable, conciliatory, concerned with feelings, and socially oriented. In some groups, one person is the task leader and a different person is the social leader. There is some evidence, for instance, that in informal discussion groups, men are more likely to emerge as task leaders and women as social leaders (Eagly & Karau, 1991). Often, however, a single person serves both functions. A study of Girl Scouts in fourth to sixth grade illustrated this point (Edwards, 1994). Girls who were viewed as leaders by their peers and by adults were described as having more new ideas and as being more organized than other girls in the troop. These young leaders were also rated as more friendly than their peers.

Cross-cultural research confirms the importance of these two types of leadership activities (Hui, 1990). In Japan, Jyuji Misumi (1995) studied leadership in education, government, and industry. He found that four types of leaders can be distinguished: those who are high on task orientation and low on social orientation; those who are high on social orientation and low on task orientation; those who are high on both; and those who are low on both. In general, "hybrid" leaders who emphasized both group productivity and group morale were more effective than other types of leaders in a variety of settings, ranging from teaching school to running a successful engineering project.

Who Becomes a Leader?

What makes a person a leader? Two contrasting views have emerged: One emphasizes the unique personal characteristics of the leader, and the other emphasizes the situational forces acting on the group (Chemers, 1997). The great-person theory of leadership suggests that some people, because of personality or other unique characteristics, are destined to lead. To test this hypothesis, many empirical studies have compared the characteristics of leaders and followers (Burn, 2004). A few qualities have been found that consistently separate leaders from followers.

First, leaders tend to excel in those abilities that help the group to accomplish its goals. Depending on the situation, leadership might be linked to intellectual ability, political expertise, physical strength, or skills that are relevant to the activities and goals of the group (Riggio, Murphy, & Pirozzolo, 2001). The star quarterback on a football team often becomes a task leader of the team.

Second, leaders tend to have interpersonal skills that contribute to successful group interaction. In general, it is an asset to be cooperative, organized, articulate, and interpersonally sensitive. Leaders tend to be sociable, empathic, and emotionally stable (Hogan, Curphy, & Hogan, 1994). The ability to perceive group needs and to respond to them is important. Such characteristics enhance a person's functioning as a social leader. A third factor is motivation. Leaders usually desire recognition and prominence (e.g., Whitney, Sagrestano, & Maslach, 1992). Leaders are more ambitious, achievement oriented, and willing to assume responsibility. It is important to note, however, that although these qualities enhance a person's leadership potential, they do not guarantee an actual position of leadership. Finally, leaders tend to be confident in their own abilities and are optimistic about the success of group efforts (Chemers, Watson, & May, 2000).

Another approach to leadership emphasizes situational factors. During World War II, U.S. Navy admiral William ("Bull") Halsey was quoted as saying, "There are no great men. There are only great challenges which ordinary men are forced by circumstance to meet" (Boal & Bryson, 1988, p. 11). Times of crisis that threaten the goals of a group can set the stage for the emergence of a new leader (Pillai, 1996). Today, most researchers believe that becoming a leader depends in large part on the match between the characteristics of the person and the needs of the situation confronting the group. It should be obvious that different situations require different qualities in a leader. Being a star pitcher may be a real asset in becoming captain of the intramural softball team, but it would not contribute much to heading the debate team.

Styles of Leadership

Leaders vary enormously in their style and effectiveness. Fred Fiedler (1978, 1993) has investigated ways in which a leader's style and the nature of the situation interact to determine the leader's effectiveness. Fiedler called his analysis a **contingency model of leadership effectiveness**. The model identifies two styles of leadership, corresponding roughly to the distinction that we made earlier between task and social leadership. Those leaders who give higher priority to completing a group task successfully and who deemphasize relations among group members are called "task-oriented leaders." The coach who says that "winning is the only thing" and ignores the feelings of team members is an example. In Fiedler's model, those leaders who reverse these priorities by putting group relations first and task accomplishment second are called "relationship-oriented leaders." This sort of coach would say that it doesn't matter whether you win or lose, as long as you enjoy playing with your teammates.

Contingency Model of Leadership Effectiveness

Task and social leaders differ in their effectiveness, depending on the situation.

Fiedler also classified group situations along a continuum. At one extreme are high-control situations in which a leader has high legitimate power and is well liked and respected by the group. In addition, the group's task is structured and clear-cut. An example would be a popular scout leader showing a group of children how to set up a tent. At the other extreme are low-control situations in which the leader has little legitimate authority, has poor relations with group members, and is confronted with a task that may require creative or complex solutions. An example would be an inexperienced and unpopular student teacher who is asked to lead a group discussion with high school seniors about ways to improve school spirit. A main goal of Fiedler's research has been to determine which types of leaders are most effective in which situations. His results, replicated in a number of different studies, are shown in Table 10–2. Task-oriented leaders are more effective in increasing group productivity in both extremely high-control and extremely low-control situations. In other words, both the scout leader and the student teacher would be advised to focus on the task at hand. Relationship-oriented leaders are most effective when the leader has moderate control: when the leader gets along well with group members but has a complex task, or when the leader is disliked but the task is clear.

One conclusion to be drawn from Fiedler's model is that the effectiveness of either type of leader changes when there is a change in control. For example, a study of army infantry squads found that a squad leader's situational control increased from moderate to high as he gained experience and on-the-job training (Bons & Fiedler, 1976). In accord with Fiedler's theory, task-oriented squad leaders were at first less effective than relationship-oriented leaders. However, as

Table 10–2

Effects of Leader's Style and Situational Control on Performance Quality

	Leader's Situational Control		
	Low	**Moderate**	**High**
Task-oriented leader	Good	Poor	Good
Relationship-oriented leader	Poor	Good	Poor

Note: Fiedler's model predicts that task-oriented and relationship-oriented leaders will be most effective in encouraging good group performance under different conditions. Task-oriented leaders are most effective when their situational control is either low or high. In contrast, relationship-oriented leaders are most effective when situational control is moderate.

the leaders gained more situational control, the task-oriented leaders became more effective and the relationship-oriented leaders decreased in effectiveness. The key point is that no one style of leadership is effective in all situations. Ultimately the most effective leader may be the person who can adapt his or her leadership style to the situation.

The models of leadership that we have considered so far have paid little attention to the role of followers in determining who becomes a leader. The transactional approach to leadership serves to fill this gap (Hollander, 1993). The central point of this approach is that the influence between the leader and the followers works both ways. The perceptions and attitudes of followers partly determine who becomes the leader. Leaders, in turn, usually pay close attention to the views of followers and may modify their leadership behavior in response to the actions of their followers. In small groups, the willingness of group members to accept the leader's influence depends on the processes of social exchange, discussed in Chapter 9. Leaders who fail to provide rewards or to move the group toward its goal, who are perceived as unfair, and who are unresponsive to group needs will be disliked and may jeopardize their leadership position. For example, elected officials who ignore the wishes of their constituents may not win reelection.

Some leaders go beyond meeting the present needs of their followers and, instead, inspire hope in new possibilities. The Reverend Dr. Martin Luther King, Jr., motivated many people in the United States to dream of and work for a changed society of racial justice and harmony. Similarly, in his bid for the U.S. presidency, Robert Kennedy said, "Some men see things as they are and say, why? I dream things that never were and say, why not?" (*The New York Times,* 1968, p. 53). Leaders who provide a vision of a better future and inspire followers to take on new challenges are called "charismatic" or "transformational leaders." Such leaders can be found not only in politics but also in business, the military, and religion, and they range across the liberal–conservative spectrum (Zaccaro, 2001).

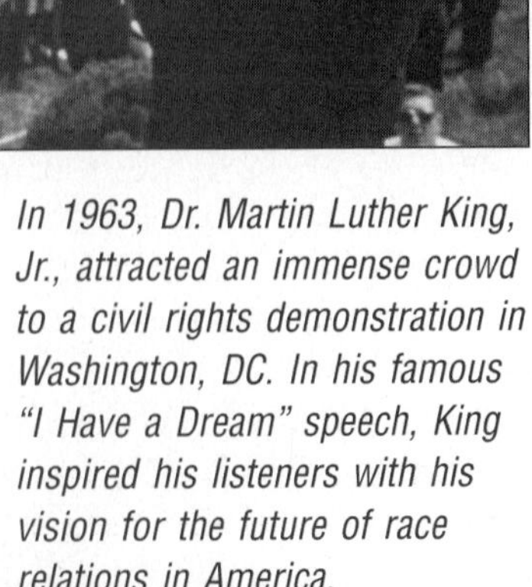

In 1963, Dr. Martin Luther King, Jr., attracted an immense crowd to a civil rights demonstration in Washington, DC. In his famous "I Have a Dream" speech, King inspired his listeners with his vision for the future of race relations in America.

Transformational leaders have several important characteristics (Avolio, 2004). They create trust and a sense of purpose. They treat followers as individuals, not merely as members of a group, and promote the self-development of subordinates. They show their followers how to think about problems in new and creative ways. They serve as important role models. They appeal to the hopes and desires of their followers. Transformational leaders are often seen by their followers or subordinates as outstanding and unusually effective leaders. For example, a study of sailors in the U.S. Navy found that subordinates reported working harder and feeling greater satisfaction when their superior officer had a transformational style (Yammarino & Bass, 1990).

Gender and Leadership

Do men and women typically differ in their styles of leadership? Traditional gender roles pose a dilemma for women leaders. Male leaders are often viewed positively for being assertive, directive, and self-promoting. But when women leaders adopt a similar task-oriented style, they may be viewed negatively, as unfeminine and lacking in warmth (Ayman & Frame, 2004; Eagly, Makhijani, & Klonsky, 1992). "Women can be disliked and regarded as untrustworthy in leadership roles, especially when they exert authority over men, display very high levels of competence, or use a dominant style of communication" (Eagly, Johannesen-Schmidt, & van Engen, 2003, p. 573). Women can avoid these negative evaluations by conveying warmth, smiling, and showing an interest in helping others to reach their goals (Carli, 2001). Not surprisingly, women leaders are less likely than men to adopt directive, task-oriented styles of leadership. Men and women do not differ, however, in their use of more interpersonally focused and democratic approaches to leadership.

Recent work on transformational leadership has raised a fascinating question. Are women more likely than men to adopt a transformational leadership style that involves gaining the trust of subordinates, serving as a role model, and mentoring and empowering followers? A recent meta-analysis of 45 studies identified two small but consistent sex differences (Eagly, Johannesen-Schmidt, & van Engen, 2003). First, women scored higher on measures of transformational leadership. Second, women scored higher on the use of rewards, such as noticing and praising subordinates for their good work. These two approaches to leadership may permit women to be competent leaders who get the job done but are still liked by their subordinates.

Summary

1. Working individually in the presence of others sometimes improves performance (social facilitation) and sometimes impairs performance (social inhibition). Which effect occurs depends on the complexity of the task. Explanations include the effects of increased arousal, evaluation apprehension, and distraction/conflict.
2. Working collectively on a task so that a particular individual's own efforts cannot be evaluated may result in social loafing, a decrease in effort and performance. However, if a person cares about the group's performance and believes that his or her coworkers are unwilling or unable to perform well, the individual may work especially hard, an effect known as "social compensation."
3. Social impact theory proposes that the influence of an audience on an individual depends on the number of observers, the strength (importance) of the audience, and the immediacy of the audience.
4. People in groups sometimes behave in much more unusual or antisocial ways than would individuals alone, a phenomenon known as "deindividuation." Deindividuation occurs because anonymity reduces the individual's feelings of personal responsibility.
5. Sometimes the presence of other people results in the psychological state of discomfort and stress known as "crowding."
6. In a group, people are interdependent: What happens to one person affects the outcomes of other group members. Social norms are rules and expectations about how people should behave; social roles define the rights and responsibilities of individuals in particular positions in the group.
7. "Cohesiveness" refers to the positive forces that cause members to want to stay in a group and also to the negative forces that discourage members from leaving a group.
8. Whether individuals or groups are better at solving problems depends on the type of task to be performed. Brainstorming is a popular method for generating creative ideas in a group setting, but it may not be as efficient as having several individuals work alone.
9. Decision-making groups can adopt a variety of decision rules, such as majority-wins or truth-wins rules.
10. Groups tend to make more extreme decisions than individuals would alone. This group polarization effect sometimes leads to riskier decisions and sometimes to more conservative decisions. Explanations of group polarization emphasize the importance of persuasive arguments, social comparison processes, and social identity.
11. Decision-making groups with a directive leader may be vulnerable to groupthink. This is a decision-making process that discourages criticism and can lead to poor decisions.

12. Much research has used laboratory games such as the trucking game and the prisoner's dilemma to study competition and cooperation. People in the United States often compete, even when they would obtain greater external rewards from cooperation. Factors that affect competition include the reward structure of the situation, personal values, communication, and reciprocity. There are important cultural differences in the tendency to be competitive.
13. A social dilemma exists when the most rewarding short-term choice for an individual will ultimately lead to negative outcomes for the group.
14. Group leaders are those who have the most impact on group behavior and beliefs. A task leader focuses on accomplishing group goals successfully. A social leader strives to maintain harmony and high morale. People who become leaders tend to be socially skilled, to excel in abilities that help the group achieve its goals, and to be ambitious. According to Fiedler's contingency model, the success of a leader depends on the match between the leader's style (task oriented versus relationship oriented) and the nature of the situation.

Key Terms

brainstorming **313**
cohesiveness **311**
common knowledge effect **316**
contingency model of leadership effectiveness **329**
crowding **306**
decision rules **314**
deindividuation **305**
distraction-conflict model **300**
evaluation apprehension **299**
expectation states theory **310**
group **308**
group polarization **317**
groupthink **318**
prisoner's dilemma **321**
risky shift **316**
social compensation **302**
social density **306**
social dilemma **325**
social facilitation **297**
social inhibition **298**
social impact Theory **303**
social leadership **328**
social loafing **300**
social norms **309**
social role **310**
social status **310**
task leadership **328**

Women in the Military

Of the 255,000 U.S. soldiers stationed in Afghanistan and Iraq in 2004, 1 in 10 was a woman. Although women are banned by law from land combat, they perform a variety of jobs as helicopter pilots, convoy drivers, and clerks (Scarborough, 2004). And women soldiers share in many of the risks of warfare, including ambush attacks and suicide bombings.

In a recent interview, Carol Burke, author of a book about women in the military, tackled the objections that some raise about including women in one of society's most masculine institutions (Callahan, 2004). For example, in addressing the issue of physical strength, Burke noted that some women are tall and muscular. "A strong athletic, six-foot-tall woman will outperform a slim, five-foot-tall man who lacks substantially developed muscle mass." In addition, she emphasized that physical strength and size are not always essential for modern warfare. "In some areas of combat, the smaller size and greater agility of women would be an advantage. Inside a tank or a submarine, for example, a small quick female soldier might be more effective than a thickly-muscled linebacker-sized man."

In fact, throughout history, courageous women have risked their lives in times of war (WREI, 2004). During the American Revolution, Margaret Corbin took over her fallen husband's cannon in the Battle of Fort Washington and was the first woman awarded a disability pension by Congress for wounds she incurred during combat. During the Civil War, women disguised as men served on both sides of the conflict, and women also served as spies and nurses. Dr. Mary Walker received the Congressional Medal of Honor for her service as a surgeon in the field of combat. In 1901, the U.S. government established the Army Nurse Corps. The first African-American women to serve in the U.S. military were recruited during World War I by the Navy to serve as "yeomanettes," working in offices in Washington, DC. In more recent times, military women have served and died in the line of duty in World War II, Vietnam, and the Persian Gulf.

Today, as the percentage of women in the military is increasing, restrictions on women's roles continue. For example, women are not permitted to serve in direct ground combat or in submarine warfare. Nonetheless, there is growing recognition of the importance of women soldiers to American's volunteer military. As Army Major Rhonda Cornum noted, "The qualities that are most important in all military jobs—things like integrity, moral courage, and determination—have nothing to do with gender" (cited in Curphey, 2003, p. 3).

and cooking utensils are for girls and that toy trucks and guns are for boys (Powlishta et al., 2001). Most 4-year-olds believe that doctor, police officer, and construction worker are male jobs and that secretary, teacher, and librarian are female jobs. The process of gender typing continues in adulthood. Married couples often distinguish between "men's work," such as mowing the lawn, taking out the garbage, and barbecuing, and "women's work," such as housecleaning or child care. Although a few occupations, such as psychologist, journalist, and comedian, are seen by adults as gender-neutral, most jobs are perceived as gender-typed (Beggs & Doolittle, 1993). You should have no trouble guessing how most people categorize the following jobs: receptionist, brain surgeon, elementary school teacher, auto mechanic, nurse, and stock broker.

The distinction between male and female is a universal organizing principle in social life. As children, boys and girls are expected to learn different skills and to develop different personalities. As adults, men and women typically assume distinctive gender-linked roles as husband or wife, mother or father. Cultures vary in exactly what is defined as masculine or feminine and in the degree to which they accentuate gender differences or similarities, but the use of gender to structure social life has been basic (Helgeson, 2005).

In the sections that follow, we investigate the importance of gender in everyday life. We begin with stereotypes about males and females and then consider how gender influences a person's self-concept. We review theoretical perspectives on gender and present the latest research that compares the social behavior of women and men. We conclude with a discussion of changing roles for women and men.

A word about terminology is useful at this point. Some psychologists believe we should distinguish between the terms "sex" and "gender." At present, however, no consensus has been reached about how to define these two terms (Haig, 2004). For simplicity, we will use these terms interchangeably.

GENDER STEREOTYPES

Consider a seemingly simple question: How does a person's sex influence our perception and evaluation of the person and his or her behavior? The emphasis here is on gender as a characteristic of the target of impression formation. Research shows that our beliefs about what typical men and women are like can color our perception of individuals and bias our evaluations of their performance.

How do you think men and women differ? Do you believe that one sex tends to be more aggressive or more nurturant than the other? How do the sexes typically compare on such qualities as being courageous, neat, logical, gentle, squeamish, dominant, or gullible? Beliefs about the personal attributes of females and males are **gender stereotypes** (Deaux & Kite, 1993). As discussed in Chapter 2, every stereotype, whether based on gender, race, ethnicity, or other groupings, is an image of the typical member of a particular social category. Depictions of the sexes in the mass media illustrate the nature of gender stereotypes in U.S. society.

Gender Stereotypes

Beliefs about the typical attributes of males and females.

Media Images of the Sexes

Television, movies, popular music, and other mass media convey messages about the nature of masculinity and femininity (Matlin, 2004). You probably know these stereotypes quite well, although you may not have thought about them very much.

In TV commercials, for example, we can see anxious housewives desperately trying to avoid tell-tale spots on the family's clothes or pondering the best food for a finicky cat. Young women appear to be obsessed with staying thin or compete for a man's attention by wearing the right perfume or jeans. Off camera, the voices of male experts solemnly offer advice. On screen, men in impressive offices extol the virtues of electronic equipment. During weekend sports events, ads for alcoholic beverages show groups of men engaged in rugged outdoor activities.

Systematic research has found that the most common commercial depicts a male expert instructing a female consumer about a product. In a study of TV ads

Chapter 11

Gender

You glance casually at the driver of the sports car stopped at a traffic light. Noticing a gray sweatshirt and a prominent chin, you assume the person is a man. But something about the face makes you look again. You quickly study the person's physique. The smooth cheeks give no hint of stubble. The shoulders are a bit broad for a woman, but perhaps she's a swimmer. The arm resting on the car door conceals the person's chest, but reveals slender, delicate fingers. Neither rings nor earrings are visible. Then the light changes and the car drives off, leaving you puzzled about the driver's sex.

When we encounter new people, we inevitably try to identify them as male or female. The reason is that gender is one of the most basic categories in social life. The process of categorizing people and things as masculine or feminine is called **gender typing** (or "sex typing"). This process usually occurs automatically, without our giving it much thought (Glick & Fiske, 1999). Most of the time, cues about gender are readily available from physical characteristics such as facial hair or breasts and from style of dress. People usually display their gender as a prominent part of their self-presentation.

Parents typically dress their children in ways that readily communicate the child's sex. An observational study that was conducted in suburban shopping malls found that 90 percent of infants were dressed in clothes that were gender-typed in color or style. Although 75 percent of the girls wore or carried something pink, none of the boys did. In contrast, 79 percent of the boys wore or carried something blue, and only 8 percent of girls did (Shakin, Shakin, & Sternglanz, 1985). Halloween costumes can mask the wearer's identity. But in a recent analysis, more than 90 percent of children's were clearly gender-typed (Nelson, 2000). Girls' costumes clustered in a narrow range depicting such traditional feminine roles as princess, beauty queen, bride, or ballet dancer. Girls were also more likely than boys to have costumes representing animals or food; a butterfly, a puppy, and a lollipop are examples. Boys' costumes were more varied and emphasized warriors, police, cowboys, villains, monsters, and such symbols of death as Dracula, an executioner, or the Grim Reaper. Situations in which we cannot identify a person's gender are rare. They call attention to the gender categorization process and typically lead us to seek information about whether the person is male or female.

The tendency to divide the world into masculine and feminine categories is not limited to person perception; many objects and activities are also defined as masculine and feminine. At an early age, children learn that dolls

Focus of This Chapter

Gender Typing

Labeling things, activities, and people as "masculine" or "feminine".

We are exposed to thousands of ads on billboards, in magazines, and on television that reinforce images of women as sex objects.

conducted in the 1970s, 70 percent of men were shown as experts, whereas 86 percent of women were product users (McArthur & Resko, 1975). Female authorities and male consumers were the exception. This general pattern has been replicated in studies conducted on five continents since the mid-1970s (Furnham & Mak, 1999; Ganahl, Prinsen, & Netzley, 2003).

Although gender stereotypes in the media are often blatant, more subtle gender patterns can also be found. Dane Archer and his colleagues (1983) analyzed thousands of photographs from newspapers and magazines in the United States. The researchers discovered that photos of men tended to emphasize their faces, but photos of women gave greater emphasis to their bodies. In the typical photo of a man, almost two thirds of the picture was devoted to the face; in the typical photo of a woman, less than half was devoted to the face. Archer and his coworkers found the same tendency in 11 different countries, from Hong Kong to Kenya. Archer created the term **face-ism** for this tendency to emphasize men's faces and women's bodies.

Face-ism

Tendency to emphasize men's faces and women's bodies.

Subsequent research has provided additional support for this tendency. Ads in such magazines as *Glamour, Ebony,* and *Esquire* were four times more likely to display women's buttocks, legs, stomach, shoulders, or back than to show men's (Plous & Neptune, 1997). On TV talk shows, there tend to be more close-up (face) camera shots of male guests and more entire body shots of female guests (Akert, Chen, & Panter, 1992). An analysis of television beer commercials also documented this tendency: The camera shots in these ads were significantly more likely to focus on women's bodies than on men's bodies (Hall & Crum, 1994). By emphasizing men's faces and women's bodies, the media may subtly reinforce stereotypes of men as thinkers and women as sex objects.

These studies and other analyses of newspaper articles, award-winning children's books, elementary school and college textbooks, modern art, and other diverse elements of culture have found several general themes in the portrayal of the sexes (Matlin, 2004):

- Whereas men are shown in a wide variety of social roles and activities, women are more often restricted to domestic and family roles.
- Men are commonly portrayed as experts and leaders; women, as subordinates.
- Men are usually depicted as more active, assertive, and influential than women.
- Although females constitute slightly more than half the population, they are underrepresented in the media.

In recent years, there have been efforts to change media images so they portray men and women in less rigidly gender-typed ways. On TV, for example, we are beginning to see women in the business world and men in the kitchen. In animated cartoons, female characters are showing somewhat more independence, assertiveness, and competence than they did 20 years ago, although both sexes are still depicted in stereotyped ways (Thompson & Zerbinos, 1995, 1997). As in the past, cartoons continue to feature male characters more prominently, and males do significantly more of the talking and important action in the story.

Do these media portraits of the sexes actually have an effect on people's daily lives? As we have seen elsewhere in this book, it is surprisingly difficult to show the extent to which the mass media influence people's behavior (Durkin, 1987). Several studies have found that children who watch more television tend to have more stereotyped views about men and women, and also about the types of jobs that are best suited to each sex. The amount of television children watch correlates with their attitudes about the gender typing of household chores (Signorielli & Lears, 1992). Further, children who watch more television believe more strongly that only girls should wash dishes and help with cooking and that only boys should mow the lawn and take out the garbage. However, in correlational studies such as these, the direction of causality is not clear. Does TV encourage traditional attitudes in viewers? Or do sex-role traditionalists watch more television because they find media portrayals of women and men consistent with their preexisting personal beliefs?

Experimental studies provide stronger evidence about the potential impact of the media. Experiments demonstrate that television can affect viewers' beliefs about gender. In a field experiment, Kimball (1986) studied a Canadian community before and after television became available. After the introduction of television, children's beliefs became more sex-typed and more similar to those of children in other communities with access to television.

Cultural and Personal Stereotypes

Cultural Stereotypes

Societal images of members of a social group.

Personal Stereotypes

An individual's own beliefs about the typical attributes of members of a social group.

A useful distinction can be made between cultural and personal stereotypes. **Cultural stereotypes** are beliefs about the sexes that are communicated by the mass media, religion, art, and literature. As individuals, we are familiar with cultural stereotypes, but we may or may not agree with them. We may know, for instance, that the culture portrays women as less competent than men, but we may reject this idea as untrue. **Personal stereotypes** are our own unique beliefs about the attributes of groups of people such as women and men.

The content of stereotypes has often been described in terms of general personality traits that characterize each sex. Most of us have beliefs about the global features that distinguish males and females. To get some idea of your own views, read the traits listed in Table 11–1, and decide whether you personally think each trait is more characteristic of men or of women, or equally true of both sexes. You will probably find this a fairly easy task.

Research shows that men are commonly rated higher than women on traits associated with competence and instrumentality, such as leadership, objectivity, and independence (Deaux & LaFrance, 1998). In contrast, women are usually rated higher on traits associated with warmth and expressiveness, such as gentleness and awareness of the feelings of others. Since the mid-1970s, there have been many changes in the roles of women in the United States, including a dramatic increase in the proportion of women employed outside the home. However, despite these changes, stereotypes about the personal attributes of men and women have remained remarkably stable over time (Spence & Buckner, 2000).

Cross-cultural research finds that core elements of gender stereotypes are quite similar in many countries. John Williams and Deborah Best (1990a) studied gender stereotypes among college students in 25 countries around the globe, including Nigeria, Spain, New Zealand, India, Japan, Canada, and Brazil. Respondents in

Table 11–1

Common Gender Stereotypes

Typical Woman	Typical Man
Gentle	Aggressive
Cries easily	Unemotional
Enjoys art and literature	Likes math and science
Does not use harsh language	Worldly
Tactful	Ambitious
Religious	Objective
Interested in own appearance	Dominant
Aware of feelings of others	Competitive
Strong need for security	Self-confident
Talkative	Logical
Neat in habits	Acts as leader
Dependent	Independent

every single country identified being adventurous, independent, dominant, and strong as masculine qualities and being sentimental, submissive, and superstitious as feminine qualities.

At the same time, there are variations in gender stereotypes about people from different racial, ethnic, and cultural backgrounds. This point is illustrated by a study of an ethnically diverse sample of students from the University of Houston (Niemann, Jennings, Rozelle, Baxter, & Sullivan, 1994). Students were asked to list the first 10 adjectives that came to mind when they thought of members of a particular group, such as Anglo males or Mexican American females. Each participant described eight groups that varied in gender and ethnicity. The results, shown in Table 11–2, give the most common adjectives used to describe members of each group. Some stereotypes were based on gender regardless of ethnicity. Women from all groups were stereotyped as pleasant and friendly. Other stereotypes were based on ethnicity without regard to gender. For example, African Americans were described as athletic and Asian Americans as intelligent. In addition, there were also male–female differences within ethnic groups. For example, Anglo and Mexican American women but not men were described as attractive. Asian American and Mexican American men but not women were described as hard workers. The results of this study of Texas college students may not be representative of stereotypes in the general population. Nor do these results tell us how people stereotype members of their own ethnic group versus members of other ethnic groups. What these results do illustrate, however, is the interplay between gender and ethnicity in the creation of stereotypes.

Gender Subtypes

In addition to thinking about the general traits that distinguish males from females, there is a second way that people think about gender. We often construct images of different categories or subtypes of males and females (Deaux & LaFrance, 1998; Schneider, 2004). This process of subtyping was introduced in Chapter 6. Instead of thinking about females in general, we may think of more specific categories of women, such as mothers, beauty queens, tomboys, feminists, sluts, or career women. Thus, one person might believe that mothers are nurturant and self-sacrificing; that beauty queens are gorgeous but empty-headed; or that tomboys are youthful, athletic, and adventurous.

Table 11–2

Stereotypes of Women and Men from Different Ethnic Groups

Women	Men
African American	**African American**
Speak loudly	Athletic
Dark skin	Antagonistic
Antagonistic	Dark skin
Athletic	Muscular appearance
Pleasant and friendly	Criminal activities
Anglo American	**Anglo American**
Attractive	Intelligent
Intelligent	Egotistical
Egotistical	Upper class
Pleasant and friendly	Pleasant and friendly
Blond or light hair	Racist
Asian American	**Asian American**
Intelligent	Intelligent
Speak softly	Short
Pleasant and friendly	Achievement oriented
Short	Speak softly
Attractive	Hard worker
Mexican American	**Mexican American**
Black, brown, or dark hair	Lower class
Attractive	Hard workers
Pleasant and friendly	Antagonistic
Dark skin	Dark skin
Lower class	No college education

Note: The table presents some of the most common terms (or synonyms) used by college students to describe members of each group.

Source: Adapted from Niemann, Jennings, Rozelle, Baxter, and Sullivan (1994, p. 20).

Similarly, instead of having a single, uniform image of males, our stereotypes may distinguish such types as fathers, businessmen, hardhats, sissies, jocks, chauvinists, or nerds. A recent analysis of *Sports Illustrated, GQ,* and other men's magazines identified nine main types of men who were shown in ads (Rohlinger, 2002). These included the hero, who is a celebrity in sports, business, or politics; the outdoorsman who conquers nature or animals; the family man who is depicted with children or other family members; the urban man who enjoys fashion and is shown in restaurants, bars, theaters, or other social settings; and the erotic man whose body, rather than the setting, is emphasized.

As these examples suggest, stereotypes often represent specific types of males and females who embody distinctive clusters of traits. An important point is that these subtypes sometimes incorporate attributes typically associated with the other sex: A sissy is a boy who avoids sports, seeks the company of girls, and shows tender emotions. A career woman may be recognized by her focus on work and her assertive and competitive personality.

Activating Stereotypes

What determines whether we relate to a person largely on the basis of stereotypes or as a unique individual? The analysis of category-based processing of information presented in Chapter 6 is relevant to answering this question. Three factors are particularly important in activating the use of gender stereotypes: the amount of information available about the person, the salience of the person's group membership, and the balance of power.

Amount of Information. The less information available about a person, the more likely we are to perceive and react to him or her on the basis of stereotypes. For example, when people know nothing about a baby except its gender, they sometimes react to the child in stereotyped ways. In one study, adults watched a videotape of a baby (Condry & Condry, 1976). Although everyone watched the same videotape, half were told they were watching a boy and half were told they were watching a girl. People who thought the child was a boy rated the child as significantly more active and forceful than did people who thought the child was a girl. The child's ambiguous response to a jack-in-the-box toy that popped up unexpectedly was rated as showing more "fear" when the child was a girl and more "anger" when the child was a boy. In another study, children (ages 5, 9, and 15), college students, and mothers watched videotapes of infants labeled as male or female (Vogel, Lake, Evans, & Karraker, 1991). Both the children and the college students rated the "female" infants as smaller, nicer, softer, and more beautiful than the "male" infants. The mothers' evaluations of the infants were not affected by gender labels, perhaps because their personal experience with babies made it less important to rely on gender stereotypes.

When we have more information about the unique attributes of a particular person, we rely less on stereotypes. For instance, you may believe that most males are highly assertive and so assume when you meet a new man that he too will be assertive. However, you may also have learned from experience that your friend Leon is shy and unassuming. The effect of gender stereotypes can usually be reduced or eliminated when we have relevant information about a specific person.

Salience of Group Membership. A second factor that can activate the use of stereotypes is the salience of the person's group membership, in this case, gender. By "salient," we mean that the person's gender stands out and is a prominent characteristic. For example, a woman's gender is more salient if we can see her in person than if we read an article she has written. Another factor affecting gender salience is the proportion of women to men in a group. A person's gender is more salient when he or she is in a numerical minority, such as being the only woman in an all-male work group. "Token integration" often creates groups with only one minority person. Token or solo status calls attention to the person's distinctive social category and makes solos especially vulnerable to stereotyping. For example, when Shannon Faulkner entered the Citadel, an all-male military college in South Carolina, she was the only woman student. Many students and administrators objected to Faulkner's presence. Eventually, Faulkner left the Citadel, citing as reasons the isolation of being the only woman and the stress of her long legal battle to gain admission.

An experiment by Shelley Taylor (1981) illustrates how solo status can contribute to gender stereotyping. Students evaluated the members of a six-person tape-recorded discussion group. Some groups had a solo man or a solo woman; others were evenly divided between men and women. After listening to the tape recording, subjects rated the group members. In actuality, the solo's contribution to the discussion was identical to that of one of the members of the gender-balanced group. But Taylor found that the solos were perceived as talking more and making a stronger impression than members of the more gender-balanced groups. In addition, solos tended to be perceived as playing gender-stereotyped roles. Solo women were seen as "motherly, nurturant types, bitches, or the group secretary." Solo men were perceived as "father figures, leaders, or macho types." Group composition accentuated the solo's gender and fostered stereotyped perceptions of the solo's behavior.

Another study found that college women and men have different reactions to the prospect of being the lone person of their gender in a group (Cohen & Swim, 1995). College students who anticipated being the only man or the only woman in a group expected to be treated in a stereotyped way by other group members. For women, this was a negative prospect; the possibility of being stereotyped was associated with expecting to feel less comfortable in the all-male group and preferring to switch to a different group. This effect was especially strong for women with lower self-confidence about the task involved. In contrast, for men, the prospect of being stereotyped was positive; it correlated with expecting to take a leadership role in the all-female group. Men's self-confidence about the task was unrelated to their expectations about being a solo member of a group.

Power and Stereotyping. Susan Fiske (1993) proposed that the balance of power affects the tendency to stereotype. In a work situation, for example, the boss has considerably more power and control than do the employees. In such a situation, the relatively powerless employees will attend carefully to the more powerful boss, who has control over their jobs. Paying attention enables the subordinates to predict what the powerful person is likely to do, and it leads to the formation of more complex and usually less stereotypical impressions of the powerful person. In contrast, the powerful person pays less attention. The powerful don't need to pay careful attention, may not have the time or ability to watch many subordinates closely, and may not want to be bothered. As a result, the powerful are more likely to form stereotyped impressions of their subordinates. Support for Fiske's theory comes from several laboratory experiments designed to simulate work situations.

If you saw this woman at a shopping mall, you might assume that she is a suburban homemaker or school teacher. In reality, Ruth Bader Ginsburg is a distinguished lawyer and justice of the Supreme Court of the United States.

Fiske suggested that this analysis is relevant to understanding gender stereotypes because women are often in positions of low power relative to men. She illustrated this point with the case of Lois Robinson, a woman who worked as a welder in a Florida shipyard. The shipyard was almost exclusively a male domain; Robinson was often the only woman on her shift. Robinson and the other women workers were greatly outnumbered and resented by the men. Male workers teased, touched, and humiliated the women. Sexual pranks were common, and the men often called women by stereotyped terms such as "babe," "sugar," "momma," or more sexually explicit terms. The women's relatively powerless position at the shipyard permitted men to engage in stereotyping and sexual harassment with impunity. When Robinson voiced her concerns, male managers dismissed her complaints. Eventually Robinson filed a lawsuit for sexual harassment.

The Dangers of Stereotypes

It is quite natural to simplify complex life experiences by categorizing and generalizing. Personal stereotypes, like other social schemas, are one way we try to make sense of life. However, as we discussed in Chapter 6 on Prejudice, stereotypes have a number of problems.

Some stereotypes, such as the belief that men are more intelligent than women, are inaccurate and have been refuted by scientific research. Other stereotypes are essentially accurate: The generalization that men are on average taller and stronger than women is correct (Deaux & LaFrance, 1998). The Research Highlight for this chapter assesses the accuracy of common gender stereotypes. Inevitably, however, stereotypes oversimplify, ignoring cases of tall women and weak men. Unfortunately people don't always question the accuracy of their stereotypes. If we encounter someone who does not fit a stereotype, we may simply decide the person is "the exception that proves the rule." We do not necessarily reexamine

HOW ACCURATE ARE GENDER STEREOTYPES?

Some stereotypes concern groups of people we have never met and may know little about. Few of us have personal friends who are spies, serial killers, British royalty, tax collectors, sky divers, or strippers, yet we probably have stereotypes for each of these groups. In contrast, all of us have close relationships with women and men who are our relatives, friends, neighbors, or coworkers. Consequently the gender stereotypes we learn from the media may be tempered by our personal experiences with a wide variety of male and female individuals.

Just how accurate are gender stereotypes? To try to find out, Judith Hall and Jason Carter (1999) identified 77 behaviors and traits that had been tested empirically for sex differences, using the meta-analysis technique which we described in Chapter 1. These included nonverbal behaviors such as frequency of smiling and touching, as well as the ability to read others' emotions from their nonverbal cues. Measures of math, verbal, and spatial ability were also included. Personality traits (e.g., neuroticism, anxiety, conscientiousness, and achievement motivation), group behavior, and attitudes completed the set. The researchers used as their standard for the "true" sex difference the size of the difference for each attribute found in a meta-analysis. In some cases, these sex differences were quite large and in others very small. To assess gender stereotypes, the researchers had five samples of college students indicate how large or small they believed the sex difference was on each of the 77 behaviors and traits. Finally, the accuracy of stereotypes was determined by a comparison of the stereotype rating of each trait to the difference found in the meta-analysis of actual behavior. In other words, accuracy was based on students' ability to estimate not only which sex scored higher on a particular measure but also the magnitude of the male–female difference.

In general, stereotype accuracy was high across the full range of behaviors and traits examined. Correlations between students' ratings and the actual gender effects were typically about .70. These results do not mean that all gender stereotypes are accurate. But they do indicate that in some important areas of life, our general impressions of men and women as groups contain a kernel of truth.

Hall and Carter (1999) also found wide individual differences in gender stereotype accuracy: Some participants were very accurate and others were not. In general, men and women were equally accurate. To investigate correlates of stereotype accuracy, the participants also completed a variety of interpersonal sensitivity. Participants who were the most accurate were more attuned to information in the social environment, as reflected in their ability to identify another person's intended message through nonverbal cues alone. Accurate participants were also more cognitively flexible and reported liking intellectual stimulation and novel situations. Finally, accurate participants were less likely to believe that men and women generally behave extremely differently. These findings suggest that some people are more open than others to questioning their own stereotypes and may scrutinize more closely the behavior of the people they observe.

our stereotype. Further, stereotypes are often used to justify prejudice and discrimination against members of certain groups (Cejka & Eagly, 1999). Historically, false beliefs that women are not as smart as men and that women lack ambition were used to deny women an education and to keep them at home.

A second problem is that stereotypes exaggerate differences among groups and minimize differences within groups. Gender stereotypes can portray men as all alike, when in fact there are enormous individual differences among men. The same is true of differences among women. Gender stereotypes can also make it seem that men and women are utterly different, when in fact the similarities are usually much greater than the differences. For example, although men tend to be faster runners than women, there is enormous variation among men and women in running speed: Individuals of both sexes range from highly trained sprinters and long-distance runners to slow-paced couch potatoes who haven't run in years. Average differences between males and females in running speed, although real, are much smaller than within-group variation.

A third problem is that we sometimes act in ways that turn stereotypes into "self-fulfilling prophecies." For example, if you expect a woman to be pleasant and unassertive, you may act toward her in ways that lead her to act just as you believe she will. This point was cleverly demonstrated in a study by Berna Skrypnek and Mark Snyder (1982). A male college student was led to believe that his partner for an experiment was either a stereotypical man (independent, assertive, ambitious, and masculine) or a stereotypical woman (shy, gullible, soft-spoken, and feminine). In reality, the partner was always a woman, a naive subject who had been randomly assigned the label of "man" or "woman." The two partners communicated from separate rooms by a system of lights, so that the partner's true sex was never revealed. The woman was told nothing about her partner, how she had been described to him, or the goals of the study. In this way, the researchers systematically manipulated the gender expectations of the male subject.

In the first phase of the study, the partners negotiated how to divide work on 12 hypothetical tasks. Some tasks were stereotypically masculine (fixing a light switch or baiting a fish hook), some were stereotypically feminine (icing a birthday cake or ironing a shirt), and some were neutral (coding test results or washing windows). The rules set by the experimenter gave the man greater initiative in the bargaining process. As predicted, the man's expectations about his partner shaped his own actions significantly. If he thought his partner was a stereotypical woman, the male subject was more likely to select masculine tasks for himself and to refuse to switch tasks than if he thought his partner was a man. As a result, the female subject was assigned more of the feminine tasks when she was arbitrarily labeled a "female" than when she was believed to be a "male."

In the second phase, the researchers investigated whether this initial behavior pattern would continue over time. Accordingly, they changed the rules of the interaction so that the woman now had greater control over the bargaining. Nonetheless, a woman who had been labeled as "female" continued to select more feminine tasks than did a woman labeled as a "male." The woman actually came to initiate behaviors consistent with the gender to which she had been randomly assigned!

This study provides a powerful demonstration that in social interactions, one person's beliefs and stereotypes about another can channel the interaction so that the other person engages in stereotype-confirming behavior. Our actions are shaped not only by our own interests and preferences but also by the expectations of those with whom we interact. When others expect us to act in gender-typed ways and communicate these expectations through their behaviors, we sometimes put aside personal preferences and instead act out the other's expectations.

Evaluating Performance

Do we typically give women and men equal credit for equal work? Or do gender stereotypes distort judgments of performance? One of the first demonstrations of gender bias in evaluation was provided by Philip Goldberg in 1968. He investigated whether women were biased in evaluations of other women. Goldberg selected six professional journal articles from such fields as law, elementary education, and art history. The articles were edited to about 1,500 words each and combined into test booklets. The experimental manipulation concerned the gender of the authors. The same article bore a male name (e.g., John T. McKay) in one booklet and a female name (e.g., Joan T. McKay) in another. Each booklet contained three articles by "men" and three by "women." College women read the six articles and rated each on persuasiveness, style, and competence.

The same article was judged more favorably when it had a male author than when it had a female author. Goldberg's results appeared to show that women are indeed prejudiced against women. Before leaping to a hasty conclusion, however, it is important to know that Goldberg's findings sparked a flurry of research. The

Gender bias can color our evaluations of the performance of individuals who work in nontraditional jobs. This applies not only to women in "masculine" fields but also to men who work as elementary school teachers, nurses, or in other traditionally "feminine" jobs.

results of more than a hundred subsequent studies suggest that evaluation bias is considerably more complex than was first imagined (Graves, 1999; Hyde, 2004). Evaluation bias can cut both ways, sometimes favoring men and occasionally favoring women. The challenge today is to understand when and how gender bias occurs. Many factors are important.

First, the gender typing of the task or job can make a difference. Men may have an advantage in traditionally masculine jobs and women may have an advantage in feminine jobs (Heilman et al., 2004). In one study, professional personnel consultants rated applicants' résumés for traditionally masculine jobs such as automobile salesperson, feminine jobs such as office receptionist, and gender-neutral jobs such as motel desk clerk (Cash, Gillen, & Burns, 1977). For masculine jobs, men were perceived as better qualified, were expected to be more successful, and were given stronger recommendations. For feminine jobs, women were rated more favorably. For gender-neutral jobs, men and women were given similar ratings.

Another study investigated how employers react to male and female job applicants (Levinson, 1975). College students working on the research team responded by phone to actual job ads that had appeared in the local newspaper. Some of the jobs were traditionally masculine (bus driver, management trainee, and security guard) and some were feminine (receptionist, housekeeper, and dental assistant). None required advanced training. A male and female applicant with equivalent qualifications called about each job. How would the employers respond to the male and female applicants?

Gender bias was said to occur when the "sex-appropriate" caller was encouraged to apply but the "sex-inappropriate" caller was not. In one case, for example, a female caller for a restaurant management training program was told that she was disqualified because she had only 2 years of college and no prior management experience. However, a male with the identical background was scheduled for an interview. In all, 28 percent of the women asking about "masculine" jobs were discouraged, as were 44 percent of the men asking about "feminine" jobs. This result suggests considerable gender bias linked to the gender typing of occupations. In this case, the bias was actually stronger against men than it was against women.

A second factor that influences evaluation bias is the amount of relevant information available about the person. Gender bias in evaluations is least likely to occur when extensive information is provided about the individual's ability. One study gave detailed information about a male or female manager, including copies of letters, memos, and other materials allegedly written by the person (Frank & Drucker, 1977). Subjects used this material as a basis for evaluating the manager's sensitivity, organizing and decision-making abilities, and communication effectiveness. The experimental variable was the gender of the writer: "John Griffin" or "Joan Griffin." Given all this information about the specific individuals, John and Joan were rated identically. No evaluation bias occurred.

In a more recent study, psychology faculty volunteered to evaluate the dossier of a male or female candidate who was allegedly being considered either for initial hiring as an assistant professor or for tenure (Steinpreis, Anders, & Ritzke, 1999). Each participant read only one folder. By random assignment, half read about Karen Miller and half read about Brian Miller. In fact, the dossiers were identical except for the names. Gender bias favoring the male was found in the hiring decision but not in the tenure decision. Both male and female faculty members thought Brian Miller was a better hiring prospect and rated his research, teaching, and service qualifications more highly. In contrast, faculty evaluating the more experienced candidate for tenure rated Karen and Brian identically. The researchers suggested that bias occurred in the hiring decision because the younger candidate had less experience and the record was more ambiguous. In contrast, more information was available for the older tenure candidate and the record itself was quite strong.

Finally, it is important to add that the size of the sex bias in evaluations can be very small. In laboratory studies using college student evaluators, it is rare for Joan McKay to be seen as totally incompetent and John McKay to be rated as a stellar performer. When gender effects are found, they usually reflect small mean differences in ratings, perhaps a difference of 1 point on a 10-point rating scale (Swim et al., 1989).

There is ample evidence that sex bias does exist in actual job settings, although it is difficult to gauge the pervasiveness of this tendency. In one national survey, for example, male managers generally perceived women workers as lower than men in skill, motivation, and work habits (Rosen & Jerdee, 1978). Women were believed to be less employable and promotable and to have less ability to make decisions and to cope with stress. There is also evidence that women managers and leaders are sometimes evaluated less favorably than are their male counterparts (Rudman & Glick, 1999). Women managers tend to receive more negative ratings when they adopt a task-oriented and directive (or "masculine") leadership style, when they work in a traditionally masculine job (such as business executive), and when they are evaluated by men.

Consider the experience of Ann Hopkins, one of a handful of women accountants employed by the large firm of Price Waterhouse (Fiske, Bersoff, Borgida, Deux, & Heilman, 1991). In 1982, Hopkins had established herself as an outstanding worker; she had brought in $25 million worth of business, was praised by her clients, and had more billable hours than any of her 87 male peers. Yet, when candidates were considered for partnership in the firm, Hopkins was turned down. Critics said she was too "macho," had poor interpersonal skills, and needed a "course at charm school." Instead of changing her clothes and hairstyle, Hopkins filed a lawsuit against Price Waterhouse, alleging sex bias in promotion procedures. In 1990, after a lengthy trial, the U.S. Supreme Court ruled in her favor, noting that "gender-based stereotyping played a role" in the promotion decision.

During the trial, expert testimony was presented by social psychologist Susan Fiske, who reviewed the extensive research literature on sex stereotyping. Fiske argued that Hopkins was vulnerable to stereotyping because she was a token woman in a predominantly male environment and because she was a woman in a traditionally masculine field. Rather than basing the promotion decision on her actual performance, the firm had stereotyped Hopkins as a "lady partner candidate." Further, unsubstantiated rumors about her social skills were weighed equally with the opinions of people who knew her work well and the objective facts of her performance record. Behaviors that her supporters saw as determined go-getting were interpreted by her critics as abrasive and difficult. In short, gender stereotyping biased the evaluation of her job performance.

Another way that gender bias can occur is in the **attributions** people make to explain success or failure. There is some evidence that men's success is more likely to be seen as the result of ability, especially on masculine tasks (Swim & Sanna, 1996). In contrast, women's success is more often attributed to high effort rather than to ability. We usually evaluate a successful performance more favorably if we attribute it to skill, not to effort. Differences in attributions for men's and women's performance may create a subtle bias that diminishes the recognition of women's ability.

Attributions

Explanations for the causes of behavior.

Attributional bias is not limited to work settings. Consider two schoolchildren who both do well in math. When Lisa shows her mother the A in math on her report card, her mother proudly credits Lisa with "really working hard" in that course. In contrast, when Tom shows his A to his mother, she proudly credits Tom with being "a little math genius." The girl's success is attributed to high effort; and the boy's success, to high ability.

A study of junior high school students and their parents indicates that gender-based attributional differences such as these are common (Yee & Eccles, 1988). The researchers investigated how parents perceived their child's math performance. In general, parents were fairly accurate in their assessment of the level of their children's math achievement. However, parents gave significantly different explanations for the performance of sons and daughters. For example, mothers credited a son's success more than a daughter's to talent; mothers attributed a daughter's success more than a son's to effort. In this way, well-meaning parents may unintentionally discourage their talented daughters from pursuing the study of math by subtly communicating that the girl is hardworking rather than gifted. A similar pattern was recently found in the evaluations parents in Finland gave for their first-grade child's performance in both math and reading (Raty, Vanska, Kasanen, & Karkkainen, 2002).

In summary, a person's gender can influence the way we evaluate that person and the way we explain his or her performance. Evaluation bias sometimes favors men, especially in "masculine" situations. However, women may have an advantage in "feminine" situations. When substantial information is available about a person, gender bias in evaluation often disappears. Having seen how our perceptions of other people are affected by whether they are female or male, we turn our attention now to the question of how gender influences our self-perception.

GENDER AND THE SELF

Gender is a basic element in our self-concept. Knowing that "I am a woman" or "I am a man" is a core part of our personal identity. People often perceive themselves as having interests and personalities that are congruent with their gender.

Gender Identity

A cognitive perspective is valuable in understanding how children learn about gender (Martin & Ruble, 2004). Knowledge that we are male or female, our sense of **gender identity**, is acquired early in life. By about age 2, children are aware of their own gender and can tell us whether they are a girl or a boy. By age 4 or 5, children can correctly label other people by gender. However, children's understanding of gender differs from that of adults. Research by Lawrence Kohlberg (1966) and other developmental psychologists has documented the surprising fact that young children think they can change gender if they want to (Martin, Ruble, & Szkrybalo, 2002).

Gender Identity

Self-knowledge that one is male or female.

In one study, Kohlberg showed children a picture of a girl and asked whether she could be a boy if she wanted to, or if she played boys' games, or if she wore a boy's haircut and clothes. Most of the 4-year-olds said that she could become a boy. By age 6 or 7, however, children insisted that such a gender transformation would be impossible. Kohlberg believed that this shift in children's conception of

Claire Ashton as she appeared after sex-change surgery (left) and how she looked as the former Tom Ashton.

gender is part of a more general pattern of cognitive development. The same 4-year-old who says she could change gender might also say the family cat could become a dog by cutting off its whiskers.

Young children do not see the physical world as constant (a girl remains a girl, and a cat remains a cat). As children grow older, a combination of experience and maturation enables them to reach a more advanced stage of mental development in which they understand that sex and other physical properties remain the same despite changes in external appearance. An important developmental milestone occurs when children understand that gender is fixed and unchanging: once a boy, always a boy, and once a girl, always a girl.

In recent years, there has been growing awareness of individuals whose gender identity does not fit neatly into the categories of "male" or "female" (Fausto-Sterling, 2000). **Transsexuals** are a case in point. Such individuals are biologically members of one sex but at a young age develop the belief that they are really members of the other sex. In the most common case, a person is to all outward appearances a male, but his psychological reality is that he is a woman trapped in a male body.

Transsexual

Person whose psychological gender identity differs from their biological sex.

In 1996, David Buechner was a successful classical pianist and winner of a dozen international piano competitions (Jacobs, 1998). A child prodigy who had attended Juilliard, Buechner dazzled audiences with his solo performances with the New York Philharmonic and other world-famous orchestras. Friends described David as a "guy's guy," a Yankees baseball fan who enjoyed a good cigar. But behind the facade, David was deeply troubled. From a very early age, Buechner knew something was wrong. After years of anguish and unsuccessful therapy, he explained, "I came to accept the fact that I was just born with the body of a man and a head wired like a woman" (cited in Jacobs, 1998, p. 50). Finally deciding to risk his career for a chance at personal happiness, Buechner began the process of living life as a woman. In 1998, Sara Buechner returned to the concert stage, trading a tuxedo for a white silk gown and matching shoes.

No one knows what causes transsexualism (Cole, Denny, Eyler, & Samons, 2000). Most often, transsexuals show no signs of biological abnormality.

Genetically, hormonally, and physiologically, they are "normal" members of their sex. Yet, at a very early age, they develop a self-concept that is at odds with their physical characteristics. This puzzling phenomenon is profoundly disturbing to the individuals involved. Efforts to help transsexuals through psychotherapy have had very little success; it is not easy to change a deeply rooted sense of gender identity. As a result, some have advocated sex-change surgery as one way to reconcile this mind-body discrepancy by altering the body to fit the person's mental identity.

Today, a small but visible minority of individuals is challenging the traditional view that gender is a simple male-versus-female dichotomy. Often describing their experiences as "transgendered," such individuals include not only transsexuals but also heterosexual cross-dressers, people who view themselves as both male and female, and others who seek to bend the rigid gender rules of their society (Cole et al., 2000). In addition, many individuals who do not identify as transgendered nonetheless enjoy role-playing games that enable them to be a character of the other sex. It is apparently fairly common for players of online games such as "EverQuest" and "Ultima Online" to assume a cross-gender identity (Pham, 2001). It has been estimated that about half the female characters in "EverQuest" are played by men. The anonymity of the Internet lets people bend gender rules more freely than they would in everyday life.

Early Analyses of Psychological Masculinity, Femininity, and Androgyny

Individuals differ markedly in the degree to which they perceive themselves as having all the different masculine or feminine characteristics that make up conventional gender stereotypes. In terms of their gender self-concept, highly "masculine" individuals believe that they possess many attributes, interests, preferences, and skills that society typically associates with maleness. Highly "feminine" individuals believe that they possess many attributes, interests, preferences, and skills associated with femaleness (Lippa, 2002).

Early tests to measure psychological masculinity and femininity used a forced-choice format. A typical test might ask whether a person preferred showers (masculine) or tub baths (feminine), whether the person would rather work as a building contractor (masculine) or a librarian (feminine), or whether the person was active (masculine) or passive (feminine). An important feature of these tests was that they viewed masculinity and femininity as mutually exclusive polar opposites. People received a single score on the test: High scores indicated masculinity (many masculine choices) and low scores indicated femininity (few masculine choices).

In the 1970s, researchers challenged this one-dimensional view of psychological masculinity and femininity (Spence, 1991). Sandra Bem (1974, 1985) proposed that some people see themselves as having both masculine and feminine characteristics. Such a person might enjoy both carpentry and cooking and might be very assertive (a masculine trait) at work and very nurturant (a feminine trait) at home. Bem called these people "psychologically androgynous," borrowing from the Greek terms for male (*andro*) and female (*gyne*). Bem emphasized that the androgynous person is not a moderate who falls halfway between extreme masculinity and femininity. Rather, the androgynous person views himself or herself as combining strong masculine and strong feminine attributes. This two-dimensional model is shown in Figure 11–1.

To investigate **androgyny**, Bem (1974) constructed a new test with separate dimensions for masculinity and for femininity, making it possible for a person to score high on both. In the Bem Sex-Role Inventory, people rate their personal qualities using 60 adjectives: 20 masculine ("assertive," "independent"), 20 feminine ("affectionate," "understanding"), and 20 gender-neutral ("sincere," "friendly"). These masculine and feminine adjectives were selected from common gender stereotypes and included attributes like those listed in Table 11–1. When Bem administered her test to samples of college students, she found some traditionally gender-typed individuals, both masculine men (who scored high on

Androgyny

Combining high levels of both masculine and feminine attributes.

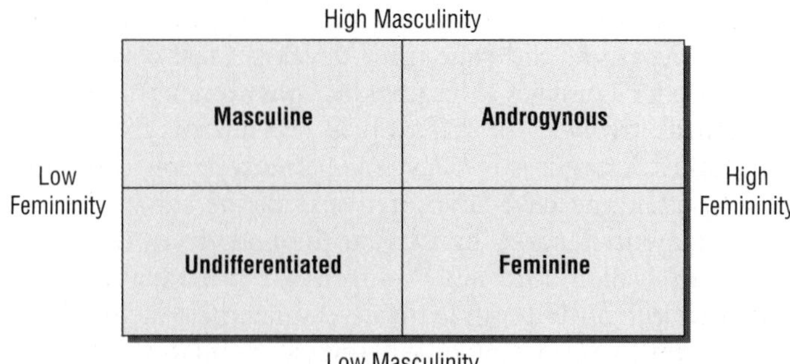

Figure 11–1 **A Two-dimensional Model of Psychological Masculinity and Femininity.**

M and low on F) and feminine women (who scored high on F and low on M). More interesting, however, was the fact that some people rated themselves high on both masculine and feminine characteristics, showing the androgynous pattern Bem had predicted.

The exact percentages of gender-typed and androgynous people vary from study to study. Typical are results from a study of California college students (Bernard, 1980). Roughly 40 percent of students perceived themselves as traditionally gender-typed, and 25 percent were androgynous. An "undifferentiated" subgroup included 29 percent of men and 21 percent of women who scored low on both masculine and feminine traits. Finally, a few people showed a pattern of reverse gender typing, specifically, feminine men (5 percent) and masculine women (12 percent). The important point is that although traditional gender typing is the most common pattern, a sizable minority of people perceive themselves as combining both masculine and feminine qualities.

Research on androgyny raised important questions about how psychological masculinity and femininity affect well-being. One long-standing view had been that to ensure mental health, boys and men should be masculine in their interests and attributes, whereas girls and women should be feminine. This "congruence model" (Whitley, 1983) proposed that adjustment is enhanced when there is an "appropriate" match between gender and self-concept. In contrast, the newer "androgyny model" of well-being argues that it is better for people to combine both masculine and feminine traits. In particular, it is proposed that androgynous individuals surpass traditionally sex-typed individuals in having greater behavioral flexibility and higher self-esteem.

Behavioral Flexibility. Bem hypothesized that masculine people will perform well in situations that call for task competence or assertiveness; feminine people will do well in situations that require nurturance or emotional expressivity; and androgynous people will do well in both types of situations. Some empirical support for this prediction has been found (e.g., Jose & McCarthy, 1988), although results are not entirely consistent.

Some research has focused on situations in which psychological masculinity should enhance performance. In one study, Bem (1975) found that masculine and androgynous individuals did better than feminine individuals on a test of ability to resist group pressure for conformity. In a study of Israeli soldiers, both masculine and androgynous individuals viewed themselves as more likely to succeed in the army and received more positive evaluations from other soldiers than did feminine individuals (Dimitrovsky, Singer, & Yinon, 1989). Other studies demonstrate situations in which femininity and androgyny are advantageous. In one study, feminine and androgynous individuals did better on tasks that required nurturance, including playing with a baby and talking to a transfer student who was having problems adjusting to a new college (Bem, Martyna, & Watson, 1976).

Self-esteem. Feeling good about oneself is a key ingredient in mental health. The congruence model predicts that self-esteem and psychological adjustment are highest for masculine men and feminine women—people with "appropriate" gender self-concepts. In contrast, the androgyny model asserts that androgynous individuals who perceive themselves as having both positive masculine and positive feminine attributes will have higher self-esteem than gender-typed individuals.

A large number of studies have investigated this topic, and they lead to an unexpected conclusion. Research provides no support for the congruence model and only weak support for the androgyny model. Instead, the biggest factor that influences self-esteem is how a person scores on the dimension of psychological masculinity. Both masculine and androgynous individuals usually have higher self-esteem. This finding holds for both adolescents and adults and has been found among Hispanic Americans, African Americans, and Asian Americans as well as among Anglos (Stein, Newcomb, & Bentler, 1992). The added benefit for androgynous people of being feminine as well as masculine is statistically significant, but very small in size.

Researchers are uncertain why masculinity appears to be central to self-esteem. One possibility is that in an individualist culture such as that of the United States, self-esteem is closely linked to traits traditionally labeled as masculine, such as independence, assertiveness, and competence. Another possibility is that self-esteem tests are biased and do not adequately assess elements of self-esteem that are associated with femininity; in other words, the pattern of results may be due to a methodological weakness in the tests being used (Whitley, 1988).

The concept of psychological androgyny and the research that it fostered seriously challenged the congruence model idea that "appropriate" gender typing is essential to mental health. Masculine men and feminine women do not seem to be better adjusted mentally than androgynous individuals. Over time, however, the newer androgyny analysis of masculinity and femininity has also been questioned.

Social critics observe that discussions of masculinity and femininity often reflect personal values. Those with traditional views about the sexes sometimes reject the concept of androgyny and seek to preserve clear-cut distinctions between masculinity and femininity. In contrast, some feminists view psychological androgyny as a new ideal for self-development. Other feminists, however, reject androgyny as an ideal because it preserves the notion that there are distinct masculine and feminine qualities even though it gives permission to people to have both types of attributes. Instead, some argue that we should move toward "sex-role transcendence" (Garnets & Pleck, 1979), in which personal attributes and preferences would no longer be associated with gender.

Current Views about Psychological Masculinity and Femininity

Gender researchers have also raised questions about the early psychological analyses of androgyny (Helgeson, 2005) . One concern is that the measures used to assess components of masculinity and femininity were very limited in scope. Measures of "femininity" focused fairly narrowly on self-perceptions of emotional expressiveness and nurturance. Measures of "masculinity" assessed self-perceptions of instrumentality or assertiveness (Spence, 1991). In actuality, most people view masculinity and femininity much more broadly. One common element is physical appearance. Masculinity is associated with such physical features as being tall, muscular, and strong. Femininity is associated with such attributes as being petite and soft. Men's and women's distinctive sexual characteristics and reproductive capacities are also seen as part of masculinity and femininity. Further elements in many people's views of masculinity and femininity are distinctive family roles as mother/homemaker and father/provider (Myers & Gonda, 1982). There is mounting evidence that these different components of masculinity and femininity are not part of a single, consistent dimension (Helgeson, 2005; Spence & Buckner, 2000). One woman might, for instance, think of herself as masculine in personality (assertive, self-confident, and independent), feminine in appearance (short and voluptuous), and androgynous in social roles (both a mother and a firefighter). Standard masculinity/femininity instruments do not capture this complexity.

Today we know that psychological masculinity and femininity are complex and multifaceted. To avoid confusion, many researchers have suggested that self-ratings of personal attributes such as active, self-confident, and decisive should be called measures of "agency" or "instrumentality" rather than of masculinity. Self-ratings of traits such as emotional, kind, and helpful to others should be called measures of "communion" or "expressivity" (Helgeson, 2002; Spence & Buckner, 2000).

A useful distinction has also been made between socially desirable and undesirable aspects of instrumentality and expressiveness. The traits typically used to assess instrumentality and expressivity measure qualities such as self-confidence and nurturance that are positively valued in society. In contrast, negative agency (also called "unmitigated agency") has been conceptualized as a tendency to focus on the self to the exclusion of others and to go beyond assertion to hostility toward others. Characteristic attributes include being arrogant, egotistical, dictatorial, and hostile. Negative communion (also called "unmitigated communion") has been conceptualized as the tendency to become overly involved with others and to neglect the self. This tendency might be reflected in putting the needs of others above one's own, worrying about others, and getting overly involved in others' problems.

In a program of research, Vicki Helgeson (2002) demonstrated that these exaggerated versions of instrumentality and expressivity can be harmful to health. In general, desirable aspects of communion or expressivity are unrelated to mental and physical health. But extreme or negative communion is associated with health problems. For example, individuals high on negative communion tend to report greater levels of anxiety and depression. They may have lower self-esteem. They adjust more poorly than do others to such illnesses as severe arthritis, diabetes, and breast cancer. Their overall level of well-being tends to be lower. Helgeson suggested several reasons for this association. Individuals who are excessively involved in the lives of others may experience more stress and interpersonal conflict in their efforts to nurture and control others. They may also tend to take on the problems of other people as though they were their own problems. In short, they may experience a greater burden of caring for others and simultaneously neglect their own health and welfare.

Exaggerated agency has also been associated with health problems (Helgeson, 2002). Individuals high on negative agency tend to be egoistic, cynical, and hostile. These characteristics have been associated with heart disease and also with poor adjustment to cancer and other serious illnesses. Among teens and younger adults, unmitigated agency has been linked to greater use of drugs and alcohol, and also to getting into trouble at school and with the police. A desire to remain in control may discourage these individuals from seeking help when they need it.

THEORETICAL PERSPECTIVES ON GENDER

Debates about sex differences raged long before the existence of social psychology. For centuries, personal experience and intuition were the bases for such discussions. Today, scientific theories and research are providing a more balanced and comprehensive understanding of gender differences and similarities.

Early discussions often asked whether gender differences are caused by "nature or nurture," by biology or learning. We now know that such simple dichotomies are misleading. A full explanation of gender differences must consider the biological capacities of the sexes, the social environment in which males and females live, and the interactions between biology and culture. It has also become clear that there is no single, general explanation for all differences between males and females. Rather, the causes of gender differences in math ability may be quite distinct from the causes of gender differences in helping behavior or in physical violence. Four broad perspectives on the origins of gender patterns emphasize the influence of biology, socialization, social roles, and social situations.

Biology

Gender differences are affected by diverse biological factors. Physical differences in height and muscular development, in the ability to bear children and to breast-feed, are obvious. The impact of sex hormones, both on the unborn fetus and on adults, is a lively topic of investigation, as are possible sex differences in the brain (Hines, 2004). Evolutionary psychologists propose that genetic evolution also contributes to gender differences in human behavior (Kenrick, Trost, & Sundie, 2004). Biologically oriented scholars believe that cross-cultural consistencies in certain gender patterns, such as men's greater tendency toward physical violence and social dominance, suggest a biological underpinning to sex differences in these behaviors.

Social psychologists do not deny biological contributions to human behavior. It is fair to say, however, that many social psychologists emphasize the ways that social forces and the nature of group living can modify basic biological dispositions (Caporael & Brewer, 1995; Wood & Eagly, 2002). Research on human aggression provides one illustration. The United States is one of the most violent countries in the world, and as we document later in this chapter, U.S. men commit the vast majority of violent crime. In other social settings, however, violence is rare and sex differences in aggression do not exist. Consider the remote South Pacific island of Vanatinai (Lepowsky, 1994). Among the 2,000 people living on this island toward the end of the 20th century, there were strong social norms of equality between the sexes. Aggression was socially disapproved of and extremely rare. Since 1943, only one murder by a Vanatinai person had been reported—a man who killed his wife in a jealous rage. An anthropologist who studied this culture for nearly a decade could find no instances of physical fights among children or adult men. Only five cases of violent behavior had been reported, all linked to sexual jealousy. In four of these cases, the aggressors were women; two attacked their husbands and two attacked other women. Physical attacks on women by men, all too common in the United States, were virtually unknown among the Vanatinai. Whatever biological sex differences in aggressive tendencies exist among these islanders are severely curbed by strong social norms that prohibit violence and by the relatively equal status of women in the society.

A contrasting example comes from research on mixed-sex teen gangs in Chihuahua, Mexico (Cummings, 1994). To gain entrance to a gang, a teenage girl must have a one-on-one fistfight with another girl. Once in a gang, girls often have rock-throwing brawls with girls from other gangs, and they rush to the aid of males in their gang if the males are outnumbered in a fight. In this tough youth culture, aggression is prized by both sexes, and women are apparently capable of considerable physical violence.

Finally, even basic biological functions, such as reproduction, are strongly influenced by social factors. Women are physically capable of having a dozen or more babies during a lifetime, but the implications of this biological ability can vary dramatically. In the past, women usually had many children and spent most of their adult life in the role of mother. Today, because of contemporary social attitudes and contraceptive methods, the typical woman in the United States has only two or three children. Consequently, mothering activities occupy a much smaller part of women's lives. In addition, before advances in medical technology, childbirth was hazardous and many women died at a relatively young age. As a result, men tended to live longer than women did. Today, women's biological capacity remains the same, but childbirth is safer. Now, women tend to live longer and typically outlive men by several years. In short, the impact of biological sex differences can vary markedly depending on the social environment (Deaux & LaFrance, 1998).

Socialization

The socialization perspective emphasizes the many ways in which people learn about gender and acquire "sex-appropriate" behavior beginning in childhood (Eckes & Trautner, 2000). An important idea is that society has different expectations and

Children's toys teach lessons about what males and females can and should do in society. Adults tend to give trucks and mechanical toys to boys but not to girls.

standards for the behavior of males and females. As children grow up, they learn these gender lessons through the processes of reinforcement and modeling described in Chapter 1. Imagine a father whose young daughter enters the living room dressed in Mommy's earrings, silk robe, and high heels and climbs on Daddy's knee. The father is likely to smile at his daughter, give her a big hug, and compliment her on being such a pretty little girl. Now imagine a 4-year-old boy doing exactly the same thing. Although a modern daddy might not punish his son, it is likely he would communicate firmly that feminine clothes are not appropriate for boys. There is considerable evidence that both mothers and fathers encourage sex-typed activities in their children.

Another major influence on children is peers—friends, classmates, and siblings. One of the most striking features of childhood is the tendency for children to segregate themselves into all-boy and all-girl groups and, often, to avoid persons of the other sex (Maccoby, 2002). On a preschool playground, Jake and Danny are on the big swing together. When Laura excitedly asks if she can join them on the swing, the boys emphatically shout, "No!" Jake adds, "We don't want you on here. We only want boys on here" (Rubin, 1980, p. 102). This pattern of same-sex play first appears in preschool and continues through early adolescence.

One reason why American children may prefer same-sex groups is that children develop sex-typed interests in toys and games. Many girls like to play with dolls and makeup kits, and many boys favor sports or video games. Another reason is that boys and girls tend to develop distinctive styles of interaction that make same-sex playmates more enjoyable (Maccoby, 1990a). In the United States, boys usually enjoy a rough-and-tumble style of play that emphasizes physical contact, competition, and dominance. Girls, in contrast, engage in less physical contact, try to minimize conflict, and so may find the boys' play style aversive. Eleanor Maccoby (1990b) explained that "on wheeled vehicles boys (3 to 5) play ramming games while girls ride around and try not to bump into each other" (p. 5). Consequently the preferred play styles of boys and girls are not compatible. In this case, initially small sex differences in activity level or rough-and-tumble play lead children to segregate themselves by sex. This segregating, in turn, leads to the creation of same-sex "cultures" with different play activities and norms about interacting. Recent research demonstrated that the more preschoolers played with same-sex peers, the more gender-typed their behavior became (Martin & Fabes, 2001).

Family and friends are not the only agents of socialization. As we saw earlier, television and other popular media also present many stereotypes of the sexes. Even children's toys convey cultural messages, which differ from one country to another (Watanabe, 1992). In the United States, one of the most popular fashion dolls is Barbie, a sexy blond who has a boyfriend, enjoys shopping, and goes to parties dressed in black vinyl. In contrast, Japan's best-selling fashion doll since the mid-1970s has been Licca, a demure, wide-eyed, rather flat-chested girl who suggests the innocence of a schoolgirl. In each country, manufacturers are selling not only a toy but also an idealized image of femininity, which emphasizes cuteness in Japan and sexiness in the United States. In the United States, a controversy arose when the makers of Barbie introduced a new talking Barbie whose repertoire included "Math class is tough." Critics argued that this message might discourage girls from taking math classes and perpetuate the cultural belief that boys are better suited to math. Ultimately, the manufacturer agreed to remove the statement about math.

According to the socialization perspective, the many different social experiences of boys and girls lead to relatively enduring sex differences in attitudes, interests, skills, and personalities that continue into adulthood.

Social Roles

A third perspective emphasizes that people's behavior is strongly influenced by their social roles (Eagly, Wood, & Diekman, 2000). The lives of adults are structured by their various roles as family members, workers, and community members. A key idea is that many important social roles are defined differently for the two sexes. Within the family, people usually have quite different expectations for mothers and fathers, for husbands and wives, and for sons and daughters. In the world of work, occupational roles are often sex-typed: Nursing, clerical work, and elementary education are traditionally female areas; medicine, construction, and college teaching are traditionally male areas. In business organizations, women's work roles are often lower in social status, prestige, and power than are those of men: He's the boss and she's the assistant.

Traditional social roles affect the behavior of women and men in several ways. They perpetuate a division of labor by gender, with women as homemakers and child-care providers and men as breadwinners. Roles influence the skills and interests people develop in childhood and later refine as adults. Little girls often play with cooking sets and baby dolls in preparation for adult roles as wives and mothers. In addition, the effects of gender-linked roles may spill over into new situations. We may learn from our family, our religious training or our work experiences that men have higher status and are more authoritative than, women. When we meet a new person, we may use his or her sex as a cue, assuming, for example, that a man is a confident leader and that a woman is a supportive follower (Eagly, 1987). As we saw earlier in this chapter, such expectations may become self-fulfilling prophecies.

According to social role theory, differences in the behavior of women and men occur because the two sexes occupy different social roles in their daily lives. People usually conform to the norms associated with specific roles and behave in socially appropriate ways. Thus, a husband who wants to be a good provider for his family may display ambition and dedication to his career. A wife who wants to be a good mother may read books on child care and devote much of her time to her children. Differing roles lead men and women to have different interests, develop different areas of expertise, and spend their days in different activities.

In contrast, when men and women occupy the same roles, their attitudes and behavior are often remarkably similar. This point is illustrated in a study of single fathers who, because of widowhood or divorce, had full-time responsibility for children under age 13 (Risman, 1987). Put in the role of caregiver, these fathers were very similar to mothers in their nurturance and parenting skills, but they differed markedly from married fathers who did little child care.

Cross-cultural research provides further evidence of the ways that social roles can influence behavior (Peplau, DeBro, Veniegas, & Taylor, 1999). Among the Luo people of Kenya, boys and girls are typically assigned to different sorts of household tasks, boys doing the heavy work and girls doing child care (Ember, 1973). When there is no older girl in the family to take care of the "female" tasks, however, a boy is assigned to this work. Boys who are assigned to female work tend to become less aggressive, less dominant, and more dependent than other boys. These boys are, of course, no different from other boys biologically. Rather, the fact that they are assigned to traditionally feminine role activities affects their personality and behavior.

Another illustration of the influence of social roles comes from a study of women and men who held the same blue-collar jobs in the steel industry (Deaux & Ullman, 1983). Very few sex differences were found: Men and women were similar in their self-evaluations, aspirations, and likes and dislikes about their work. Studies of managers in organizations also show great similarity in the managerial styles of women and men in similar job positions (Eagly & Johnson, 1990). It may be that similar sorts of people, regardless of their sex, tend to choose particular occupational roles. It is also likely, however, that the role itself shapes the person who occupies it.

Social Situations'

Another major influence on behavior is the current social context (Yoder & Kahn, 2003). A man may talk about football and cars with his male buddies, peppering his speech with four-letter words, but he may clean up his act and change the topic of conversation with a new girlfriend. The basic assumption in situational models is that "men and women are relatively equal in their potentialities for most social behaviors and [their] behaviors may differ widely as a function of personal choice, the behavior of others, and the situational context" (Deaux & Major, 1987, p. 371). Research is beginning to uncover important situational factors that contribute to sex differences in behavior.

For example, when we want other people to like us, we often try to conform to their expectations about how males and females should behave, regardless of our personal beliefs. In one experiment, college women participated in a simulated job interview (von Baeyer, Sherk, & Zanna, 1981). By random assignment, half the women were informed that the male interviewer was a traditional person who believed that the ideal woman should be gentle, sensitive, attractive, and passive and should be assigned to easier jobs such as making coffee. Other women were informed that the interviewer preferred nontraditional women who were independent and assertive and could assume equal job responsibilities with men. Not surprisingly, the women's knowledge about the interviewer influenced how they prepared for the interview. Women expecting a traditional interviewer "dressed up" by wearing more makeup and jewelry than did women expecting to meet a nontraditional interviewer. Women with traditional interviewers also talked less during the interview and tended to make more stereotypical, gender-linked statements about themselves. The desire to be liked and accepted by others can lead us to act in more or less gender-typed ways, depending on the situation.

Situational pressures can affect men as well as women (Morier & Seroy, 1994). In one study, college men were led to believe that they would interact with a woman who was either highly desirable (attractive, outgoing, unattached, and interested in meeting men) or less desirable (unconcerned about her appearance, not physically fit, and not interested in meeting men). In addition, half the men were led to believe that this woman had traditional beliefs about gender roles; half believed she had nontraditional views. What type of impression would the men try to make on this new woman? When the woman was desirable, the men tended to match their self-presentation to the woman's attitudes: They described themselves as more traditional to a traditional woman and less traditional to a nontraditional woman. When the woman was not seen as desirable, there was no difference in men's self-presentation to a traditional versus a nontraditional woman. In other words, men tended to conform to the gender-role attitudes of someone they wanted to impress.

In summary, the causes of sex differences are complex, and several broad theoretical perspectives on gender are useful. College students apparently agree that sex differences are multiply determined. In one study (Martin & Parker, 1995), researchers asked students how likely it is that sex differences are due to each of three factors: the way males and females are socialized (how they are treated by parents and others), biological factors (hormones, chromosomes, etc.), and different opportunities. Students reported that each of these factors is important; they rated socialization slightly ahead of biology and opportunities. In the next section, we present research that compares the sexes on several types of social behavior.

COMPARING THE SOCIAL BEHAVIOR OF WOMEN AND MEN

In recent years, a great deal of research has compared the abilities and behavior of males and females, especially those of children and college students in the United States. Sex differences in several social behaviors are examined here, including aggression, conformity, nonverbal communication, sexuality, and personal entitlement. Before we begin the discussion, however, it is necessary to review some basic ideas about meta-analysis, a statistical method first discussed in Chapter 1.

Meta-Analyses of Sex Differences

As the number of studies of sex differences has increased, it has become more difficult for investigators to summarize research findings to arrive at general conclusions.

Traditionally reviews of research literature have relied heavily on the judgment of the reviewers to select a balanced sample of studies and to eliminate methodologically flawed research. A persistent problem for reviewers has been inconsistency across studies. What can we conclude if 20 studies find that boys are better at some activity, 10 studies find that girls are better at the same activity, and 10 studies find no differences? Often researchers have used a "vote-counting" approach to resolve these discrepancies, assuming that a sex difference "exists" if it occurs in the majority of studies.

In an effort to develop more systematic ways to review and synthesize empirical findings, researchers have begun to use a technique called **meta-analysis** (Hyde & Frost, 1993). This approach uses statistical methods to pool information from many studies in order to arrive at an overall estimate of the size of sex differences. We might find, for instance, that the average sex difference on a particular measure is less than 1/10 of a standard deviation—quite a small effect. Meta-analyses also encourage reviewers to consider very carefully how they select a sample of studies to review. It has been suggested, for instance, that reviewers should include not only published studies but also unpublished doctoral dissertations. The reasoning here is that studies finding no sex differences may be less likely to be accepted for publication: thus, the published research is biased toward overestimating sex differences. In the following sections, we present some of the findings of recent analyses of sex differences.

Meta-Analysis

Quantitative approach to summarizing results of many studies.

Aggression

Around the world, males tend to be more aggressive than females in both childhood and adulthood. Boys are more likely than are girls to fight, taunt and insult others, and fantasize about aggressive themes (Perry, Perry, & Weiss, 1989). In adulthood, men are the warriors who defend their tribe or nation. Men are also the sex most likely to use physical force to achieve their goals, a fact reflected in statistics on rape, spouse abuse, and violent crime. According to statistics from the U.S. Federal Bureau of Investigation, 90 percent of those who are arrested for murder are men. See Table 11–3 for other statistics. One of the most consistent findings about mental health problems is that so-called externalizing problems, including aggression and other types of antisocial behavior, occur predominantly among men (Rosenfield, Vertefuille, & Mcalpine, 2000). Whether we consider socially approved aggression in wartime, illegal violence, or children's play, males

Table 11–3

FBI Statistics Comparing Percentage of Arrests for Various Crimes by Men and Women

	Percentage of Crimes Committed by	
Type of Offense	**Men**	**Women**
Murder and non-negligent manslaughter	89	11
Robbery	90	10
Aggravated assault	80	20
All violent crime	83	17
Weapons (carrying, possession)	92	8
Vandalism	83	17

Note: For 2002, a total of 447,048 arrests were made in the United States for violent crimes.

Source: Data from the Uniform Crime Reports for the United States 2002, Federal Bureau of Investigation (2004).

Competitive sports provide a socially approved context for male aggression. But theorists disagree about whether aggressive sports provide a wholesome outlet for innate male aggressive drives or teach men to become even more aggressive.

take the lead in aggressive behavior. Men are also more likely than women to endorse a social dominance orientation, tending to agree, for example, that "inferior groups should stay in their place" or that "sometimes war is necessary to put other countries in their place" (Sidanius & Pratto, 1999).

Several meta-analyses have reviewed more than a hundred studies of aggression (Eagly & Steffen, 1986; Hyde, 1986; Knight, Fabes, & Higgins, 1996). In general, males are more aggressive than females in both verbal and physical aggression, although the gender gap is wider for physical aggression. Sex differences are found to be larger in naturalistic settings (e.g., hitting and kicking on a playground) than in more controlled laboratory settings (e.g., hitting a plastic doll in a research room). Another meta-analysis investigated aggression that occurs in response to an action or provocation by another person (Bettencourt & Miller, 1996). The results showed that when a clear provocation occurred and aggression might be seen as justified, sex differences were greatly reduced. In contrast, in studies in which there was no obvious provocation, men were significantly more aggressive than were women.

Another factor that affects sex differences in aggression in the United States is that our society is more tolerant of aggression in males than in females. In childhood, boys are much more likely to be given toy guns and swords and to be taught about fighting and self-defense. A study investigated children's expectations about the consequences of various aggressive acts, such as hitting a child who takes a ball (Perry, Perry, & Weiss, 1989). Compared to boys, girls anticipated more parental disapproval for aggression and thought that they would feel greater guilt. There is also evidence that females are more concerned about the harm their aggression might cause the victim and about the danger of retaliation (Bettencourt & Miller, 1996). As a result, females may feel more guilt, anxiety, and fear about aggressive acts and so inhibit their aggressive impulses (Eagly & Steffen, 1986).

Conformity

Stereotypes portray women as more yielding, gullible, and conforming than men. According to Eagly (1987), traditional social roles dictate that men be less easily influenced than women. Social psychological studies have typically investigated conformity and compliance in laboratory settings where an individual interacts with strangers.

Careful reviews of the empirical research on social influence lead to two conclusions. First, when meta-analysis is used to pool findings from a large number of studies, there is a small but statistically significant tendency for women to be more easily influenced than men (Eagly, 1987). Second and equally important, results are often very inconsistent from study to study. Alice Eagly (1978, 1983) found 62 studies of sex differences in persuasion, that is, the extent to which a person is influenced by hearing arguments in favor of or against an issue. Only 16 percent of these studies found that women were significantly more easily persuaded; the vast majority found no differences. Similarly, Eagly found 61 studies of responses to group pressures for conformity, as in the Asch experiment described in Chapter 7. Here again, only 34 percent of the studies found that women conformed significantly more; in most cases, the sexes did not differ significantly. Whether sex differences occur appears to depend on specific details of the testing situation, such as the nature of the social influence task or the testing materials.

One interesting hypothesis is that sex differences in influenceability may have more to do with the gender typing of the task than with a general disposition for women to conform. People are generally more likely to conform if they lack information about a topic or consider it unimportant. Thus, women are more likely to conform on tasks traditionally viewed as masculine, and men are more likely to conform when confronted with feminine tasks. This point was demonstrated by Sistrunk and McDavid (1971). They asked college women and men to answer a questionnaire about matters of fact and opinion, some concerning traditionally masculine topics such as sports cars, politics, and mathematics; and others concerning traditionally feminine areas such as cosmetics, sewing, and cooking. To introduce conformity pressure, the questionnaire indicated next to each question how a majority of college students had supposedly responded. The results clearly showed the effect of gender typing. Men conformed more than women did on feminine items; women conformed more than men did on masculine items. Overall, there were no significant differences between the level of conformity of men and that of women. Although this interpretation seems quite plausible, more research is needed to establish its general applicability (Eagly, 1987).

If empirical studies find that sex differences in influenceability are somewhat elusive and small in magnitude, why does the stereotype persist that women are much more yielding than men are? The answer may be found in the roles that men and women typically play in society (Eagly & Wood, 1985). In real life, an important determinant of social influence is a person's prestige or power relative to others in a group. In a business, for example, subordinates are expected to go along with the boss; a nurse usually follows a physician's order. Because men typically have higher occupational status than do women, it is more common to observe a woman yielding to a man than vice versa.

Although this behavior pattern is actually based on job status, people may mistakenly infer that women have a general tendency to conform. To test this idea, Eagly and Wood (1982) had students read a description of a man influencing a female coworker or a woman influencing a male coworker. Participants then answered questions about the people described. When they had no information about the job titles of these persons, students assumed that the women held lower status jobs and that women were more likely to comply behaviorally with men than vice versa. When explicit job titles were provided, students believed that compliance would be based on status rather than on gender. Such results support the idea that stereotypes about women's greater influenceability are based in part on the perception that men often have more prestigious and powerful positions in society.

Nonverbal Communication

Stereotypes about female intuition suggest that women are better than men at decoding or "reading" nonverbal behavior. Thus, it might be speculated that mothers are more expert than fathers at telling whether a crying baby is hungry, wet, or suffering from gas pains. Similarly the stereotype suggests that women are

Can you tell what emotion this women is feeling? The ability to "read" a person's emotions from his or her nonverbal communication is a useful social skill.

better able to sense whether another person is feeling depressed or embarrassed or tired. Are women actually better than men at decoding another person's emotions from facial cues, body language, or tone of voice? Psychologists have studied the accuracy of this gender stereotype.

In a typical study, participants watch a videotape of a person expressing a series of emotions. After viewing each segment of the film, subjects indicate which of several emotions (such as happiness, disgust, or fear) they think is being expressed. In other studies, subjects listen to recordings of voices that have been content-filtered—altered so that the words are garbled and only the tone is distinct. More than a hundred studies of decoding accuracy have been conducted, and they consistently find that women perform better than men do. The female advantage is greatest for reading facial expressions, next greatest for body cues, and smallest for decoding voice tone. Women also tend to be better at recognizing faces. This gender difference has been found not only in adults but also in children and teenagers (McClure, 2000). The same gender difference appears in studies in the United States and in other cultures. Although the size of the sex difference in decoding nonverbal cues varies from study to study, research has consistently documented women's greater accuracy (Hall, 1998).

Researchers are much less certain about the reasons for this sex difference, although several possible explanations have been proposed (Hall, Carter, & Hogan, 2000). One possibility is that females have a genetically "programmed" sensitivity to nonverbal cues because of their role in caring for preverbal infants. Another suggestion is that women are expected to be experts in emotional matters, and so in growing up are trained to be more skillful in nonverbal communication. A third explanation is that women may be more relationship oriented than are men, and so more highly motivated to understand what others are feeling (Klein & Hodges, 2001). A final explanation suggests that the relationship among the individuals may make a difference. According to a subordination hypothesis, people in positions of lesser power (who tend to be women) pay more attention to the feelings of those in charge. Consistent with this interpretation is research showing that regardless of sex, subordinates are more accurate judges of the feelings of leaders than leaders are of the feelings of subordinates (Snodgrass, 1992). In some situations, leaders and other powerful individuals may be motivated to convey their feelings effectively to subordinates, thus making it relatively easy for subordinates to read their feelings. In contrast, subordinates may want to conceal their feelings toward a boss or leader (Hall, Halberstadt, & O'Brien, 1997; Snodgrass, Hecht, & Ploutz-Snyder, 1998). Currently all of these explanations must be considered speculative.

Sexuality

Gender differences in human sexuality have been widely documented (e.g., Baumeister & Tice, 2001; Peplau, 2003). A consistent finding is that women tend to have a more relational or partner-centered orientation to sexuality; men tend to have a more recreational or body-centered orientation. For example, compared to women, men have significantly more tolerant attitudes toward casual sex for both men and women. Men report greater acceptance of premarital intercourse, including casual sex early in a dating relationship. Men also report greater acceptance of extramarital intercourse. A meta-analysis (Oliver & Hyde, 1993) found that the size of this male–female difference in attitudes decreased from the 1960s to the present but continues to be relatively large. There are also cultural differences in sexual attitudes. Researchers have compared the sexual attitudes of adults in 24 countries (Widmer et al., 1998). Table 11–4 shows the percentage of people who thought that three types of sexual behavior were "always wrong." Note that the United States is one of the more conservative countries studied.

When young heterosexual adults are asked to define sexual desire, women tend to "romanticize" the experience and men to "sexualize" it (Regan & Berscheid, 1996, p. 116). For example, one young woman explained that "sexual desire is the longing to be emotionally intimate and to express love for another person." A young man equated sexual desire with "wanting someone . . . in a physical manner. No strings attached. Just for uninhibited sexual intercourse."

Men and women also differ in their reasons for having sex. Among married and dating heterosexuals, women emphasize the desire to gain intimacy from a sexual encounter; they viewed the goal of sex as expressing affection to another person in a committed relationship (Hatfield et al., 1989). In contrast, men emphasize sexual variety and physical gratification as the goal of sex. When it comes to engaging in casual sex, young men and women give many of the same reasons, including sexual desire, experimentation, and the attractiveness of the partner. Nonetheless, men are more likely to mention enhancing their status with male peers, and women more often say that sex might increase the probability of a long-term commitment with the sex partner (Regan & Dreyer, 1999). Research on sexual fantasies finds a similar pattern (Ellis & Symons, 1990). Women tend to fantasize about a familiar partner and to include affection and commitment. Men's fantasies are more likely to involve anonymous partners or strangers and to focus on specific sex acts. In summary, women are more likely than men to associate sexuality with an intimate relationship.

Is there a male–female difference in the strength of a person's sex drive? Psychologist Roy Baumeister and his associates (2001) reviewed relevant research and concluded that on average, the male sex drive is stronger than the female sex drive. They defined sex drive as sexual motivation or desire to have sex. Individuals can differ in both the frequency and the intensity of their sexual desire. Baumeister and associates found that men think and fantasize about sex more often than women do. Men report more frequent feelings of sexual arousal and are much more likely than women to masturbate. Among married couples, men generally report wanting sex more frequently than they have it with their wife; women report being content with the frequency of sex. In many heterosexual

Table 11–4

Percentage of Respondents Indicating That Each Type of Behavior Is "Always Wrong"

	Sex Before Marriage	Extramarital Sex	Homosexual Sex
Canada	12	68	39
Japan	19	58	65
Sweden	4	68	56
United States	29	71	70

Source: Data are from Widmer et al. (1998).

relationships, the frequency of sex reflects a compromise between the desires of the man and those of the woman. Consequently, same-sex relationships, in which partners have more similar preferences, may provide a window on gender and sexual desire. Research in the United States has found that gay male couples generally have more frequent sex than do lesbian couples (Peplau, Fingerhut, & Beals, 2004). These and many other findings led Baumeister and his associates to conclude that men do have a stronger sex drive.

Research on sexuality has identified some of the largest and most consistent male–female differences in human behavior. Of course, there are also substantial individual differences among men and among women (Bailey et al., 2000). Many explanations have been offered for gender differences in sexuality, some researchers point to our evolutionary heritage and the biology of reproduction, others emphasize childhood socialization, and others focus on adult social roles.

Personal Entitlement

What would you consider a good starting salary for your first full-time job after college? Beth Ann Martin (1989) asked this question of college seniors majoring in business. First, she provided students with detailed information about the salaries that previous graduates had earned in recent years. The sex of the previous graduates was not mentioned. Then Martin asked students what they personally expected to earn at their first job after graduation. On average, men expected to earn about 10 percent more than women expected to earn. In another study, Faye Crosby (1982) carefully matched a sample of full-time male and female workers on occupational prestige, seniority, and other job-related dimensions. In her sample, women workers were consistently paid less than men. Surprisingly, however, the women were not unhappy with their own pay or treatment on the job. Although these women workers recognized that other women often experience pay discrimination, they did not believe that they personally were being paid unfairly. Crosby termed this view the "paradox of the contented female worker."

Personal Entitlement

What a person believes he or she deserves from a job or relationship.

These and other findings suggest that women and men may differ in their sense of **personal entitlement**—what they believe they deserve from their jobs or relationships (Major, 1993). In general, men may expect to receive more benefits than women do for identical contributions. For example, when male and female research subjects work individually on a task and are then asked to determine fair payment for their work, women pay themselves less than men do (Desmarais & Curtis, 1997). In another study, researchers promised to pay college students a fixed amount of money to work on a task in their laboratory (Major, McFarlin, & Gagnon, 1984). Although both sexes were told they would receive identical pay, the women worked longer, did more work, and worked more accurately and efficiently than did the men. Apparently the women believed they had to do more work to merit the money they received.

Brenda Major (1989) proposed that sex differences in personal entitlement on the job stem from societal inequalities. In the United States, men and women tend to work in different types of jobs, and the types of work usually performed by women (e.g., being a secretary, a child-care worker, or an elementary school teacher) tend to pay less than work usually done by men. As a result, men and women may use different standards to evaluate their own performance, including a tendency to compare one's own rewards to those of others of the same sex. Consequently, women and men differ in their sense of personal entitlement. Major (1989) speculated that this pattern serves to maintain the status quo: "Because women do not feel as entitled to high pay for their work as men do, objectively underpaid women may not perceive their job situation as unjust" (p. 108).

Researchers have begun to test several specific hypotheses about sex differences in personal entitlement (Hogue & Yoder, 2003; Major et al., 1984). A social comparison explanation suggests that when people evaluate their outcomes (the pay or other rewards that they receive), they tend to make same-sex comparisons. Therefore, women may compare themselves to other underpaid women, and men may compare themselves to other more highly compensated men. Although this may be true in some work settings, especially where jobs are segregated by sex, it does not appear to be true among high-level professionals such as women lawyers (e.g., Mueller & Wallace, 1996). Second, a performance evaluation explanation is that women and men tend to make different evaluations of what they put into a job, that is, the quality of their work. In particular, women may devalue their personal efforts (Pelham & Hetts, 2001). Third, for some people, work satisfaction may be determined by factors other than pay, such as relations with coworkers, recognition for one's work, personal autonomy, or job stress. At present, we do not have a complete explanation for the paradox of the contented female worker.

Sex Differences in Perspective

From our review of research on gender comparisons, a few general points are worth remembering. First, average differences between the sexes in behaviors such as reading emotions from nonverbal cues do not mean that all males are socially insensitive and all females are nonverbal experts. There is much individual variation; some males excel and some females do poorly in these skills. Second, demonstrating differences between the sexes does not necessarily mean that an individual's skills and behaviors are unchangeable. Both men and women can learn to be more (or less) conforming, attuned to nonverbal cues, or aggressive.

In discussions of gender issues, a frequently asked question is this: Aside from the biological facts of life, just how different are males and females? Psychological research offers no simple answer. At the level of basic abilities and motivations, gender differences are typically small or nonexistent (Hyde, 2004). Men and women appear to be remarkably similar in many of their basic human talents. Yet consistent sex differences do exist (for whatever complex reasons) in several social behaviors, including aggression, conformity, the decoding of nonverbal messages, and sexuality.

Finally, it is important to acknowledge that the daily lives of men and women are often very different indeed. Men and women tend to engage in different roles and consequently use their talents in different ways. Women are more likely to change baby diapers and men are more likely to change flat tires than vice versa. The final section of this chapter takes a closer look at the changing social roles for women and men.

CHANGING ROLES FOR WOMEN AND MEN

Newspapers today are filled with stories about the changing roles of men and women. Whether people welcome these changes as "progress toward equality" or lament the collapse of "traditional values," few would deny that the lives of men and women are not what they used to be. Traditional gender roles were organized around two basic principles. One idea was that men and women should perform distinctive activities, that there should be a division of labor according to gender. The second idea was that men should be the dominant sex, both at home and in society at large. Researchers have charted changes in public beliefs about appropriate roles for women and men.

Changing Attitudes about Gender Roles

There is much evidence that strong beliefs favoring traditional roles for women and men are breaking down in the United States and other technological societies. Studies that assess public attitudes toward gender roles have documented these changes. For example, in 1936, only 18 percent of people in the United States approved of a married woman working for pay if her husband could support her. By 1976, a two-thirds majority of men and women approved of wives working outside the home (Boer, 1977). Similarly an annual national survey of first-year college students has found decreasing agreement with the statement "The activities of married women are best confined to home and family." In 1970, 48 percent of students agreed with this statement, but by 2000 agreement dropped to only 22 percent of college men and 10 percent of college women (Bryant, 2003). These shifts away from traditional views of gender roles appear to be continuing.

In the early 1970s, Janet Spence and Robert Helmreich (1972) developed a standardized paper-and-pencil test to measure attitudes about women's rights and roles in society. The Attitudes toward Women Scale (AWS) became the instrument most widely used to assess gender attitudes (also known as "sex-role attitudes"). The AWS asks respondents to indicate how strongly they agree or disagree with such statements as:

- Swearing and obscenity are more repulsive in the speech of a woman than a man.
- The intellectual leadership of a community should be largely in the hands of men.
- Women should worry less about their rights and more about becoming good wives and mothers.

Since the early 1970s, the AWS has been administered to more than 70 samples of American college students. Average scores on the AWS can range from 0 (strongly disagree) to 3 (strongly agree), with higher scores indicating more egalitarian beliefs. An analysis of this research (Twenge, 1997) found a steady trend toward more egalitarian attitudes, which is presented in Figure 11–2. Cross-cultural research indicates that traditional attitudes about gender roles are strongest in rural and nonindustrialized societies. Both in our society and around the world, men tend to have more traditional attitudes than women do (Williams & Best, 1990).

Hostile Sexism

Negative attitudes toward women who challenge men's power, try to act like men, or reject traditional gender roles.

Benevolent Sexism

Positive attitudes and willingness to help women who are seen as virtuous and who embrace traditional women's roles.

A new approach to understanding attitudes about gender has recently been presented by Peter Glick and Susan Fiske (2001). They observed that beliefs about gender often include both positive and negative components. Stereotypes depict women as less powerful and competent than men. But women are also seen as nicer and more nurturant than men. Glick and Fiske distinguished between two types of attitudes toward women. **Hostile sexism** reflects the view that women should be subservient to men and should "know their place." It can lead to animosity toward women who are seen as threatening men's power and authority. In contrast, **benevolent sexism** emphasizes women's niceness and purity. As a result, men should protect and honor women who embody these

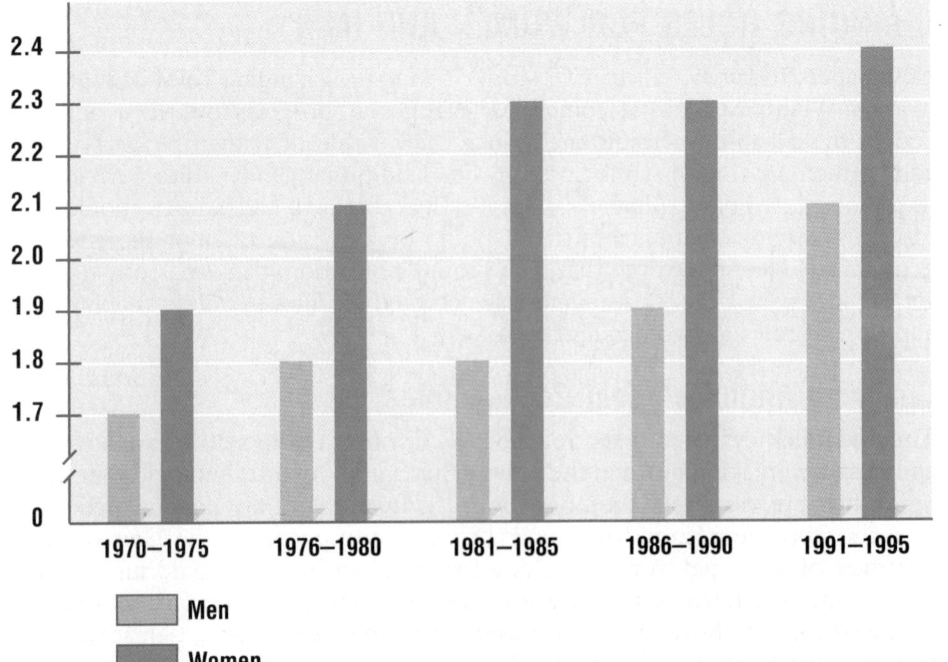

Figure 11–2 **Mean Scores for College Men and Women on the Attitudes Toward Women Scale from 1970 to 1995.**

Note: Mean scores can range from 0 (strongly disagree) to 3 (strongly agree). Higher scores indicate more egalitarian attitudes. At each time period, differences between scores of men and women are statistically significant.

Source: Data from Twenge (1997, p. 42).

Table 11–5

Items Used to Measure Ambivalent Sexism toward Women
Hostile sexism
Women are too easily offended.
Most women fail to appreciate fully all that men do for them.
Many women get a kick out of teasing men by seeming sexually available and then refusing male advances.
Benevolent sexism
In a disaster, women ought to be rescued before men.
Women, compared to men, tend to have a superior moral sensibility.
Men are incomplete without a woman.
Source: Glick and Fiske (2001, p. 124).

qualities and embrace traditional women's roles. Some of the items used to measure these two types of attitudes are presented in Table 11–5.

Glick and Fiske use the term **ambivalent sexism** to refer to this mix of positive and negative attitudes. These two types of attitudes are consistent with two distinctive images of women found in religion and mythology (Matlin, 2004). On the one hand, some women are virtuous, saintly, and devoted to family, an image reflected in the Christian depiction of the Virgin Mary as a symbol of caring and self-sacrifice. In contrast, other women as seen in negative terms, with examples ranging from seductive temptresses to career-oriented feminists trying to usurp men's power and positions in society.

Ambivalent Sexism

A mixture of benevolent attitudes toward women (protecting women) and hostile attitudes (resenting women's efforts to achieve equal power).

Recently, Glick and colleagues (2004) provided evidence that attitudes toward men are also ambivalent in nature. Negative attitudes portray men as arrogant and abusive of power, as incompetent in domestic life, and as sexual predators. Positive attitudes cast men as protectors and providers who need and value women's nurturance and care. Glick and colleagues emphasize that these ambivalent attitudes reward women who adhere to traditional feminine roles by providing male protection and adoration. In contrast, they criticize women who attempt to break out of traditional roles and who endorse more egalitarian relations between the sexes. In the view of these researchers, although benevolent sexism may seem to put women on a pedestal, this favored position comes at the price of reinforcing male dominance and preserving traditional differences between the sexes.

Men's Work and Women's Work: On the Job and at Home

In recent years, there have been major changes in the work performed by women and men. As one example, women in the United States are now relatively equal participants in higher education. In 1979, for the first time in history, more women than men entered college. Since then, the percentage of male students has continued to decline, slipping to 44 percent in 2000. Men are currently the new minority on college campuses. This gender gap in college attendance is most pronounced among African Americans (37 percent men) but is also true of Latino and white Americans (Fonda, 2000). The gender gap in going to college cuts across the economic spectrum, occurring among students from poor and affluent families alike.

Women are also training for many high-status professions such as law and medicine that were once dominated by men (Matlin, 2004). In 1965, women obtained only 11 percent of doctorate degrees and 3 percent of professional degrees in the United States. Today, women earn more than 40 percent of these advanced degrees. In the field of psychology, women now receive over 70 percent of doctoral degrees (APA Research Office, 2004)

Working for Pay. Perhaps the most dramatic change in the last century has been women's increased participation in paid work. Today, most adult women are in the paid work force and the typical American woman will hold a job for at least 30 years during her lifetime (Barnett & Hyde, 2001). In 1940, only 15 percent of married women worked for pay. Now, the majority of married women have paying jobs, including many mothers with preschool children (Matlin, 2004). Currently, the modal American family is a dual-earner family in which both partners have jobs.

Yet women are far from equal partners in the world of work. Women continue to be concentrated in lower status "female" jobs such as elementary school teacher, nurse, and secretary. Partly because of this sex segregation of jobs, the average U.S. woman worker earns only about 75 cents for every dollar earned by a man, with African American, Asian American, and Hispanic women faring worse than white women (Lips, 2003). Many factors contribute to this gender gap in wages: A greater percentage of women are in lower paying, traditionally female jobs and have less seniority. When factors such as these are taken into account, the gender difference in earnings decreases but does not disappear. Even in occupations traditionally dominated by women, men tend to earn more. According to 2000 U.S. Census Bureau statistics, 98 percent of kindergarten and preschool teachers were women, but the few men in the field earned $5,000 more per year than the women (Associated Press, 2004). Similarly, 91 percent of registered nurses were women, but the men in the field made $3,000 more per year.

Homemaking and Child Care. Are men today doing more domestic activities formerly considered "for women only"? Everyday examples of such changes are easy to find. It is increasingly common to see a man shopping for groceries or taking a toddler to the park. Research shows that American men are spending more time with their children now than in the past (Coltrane, 2000a). However, men's participation in housework and child care—"family work," as some call it—is still relatively small compared to that of women. Women who live with men typically do the majority of housework and, if they have children, the majority of child care. Despite minor variations, the same pattern is found across American ethnic groups (Coltrane, 2000b) and throughout the industrialized world (e.g., Batalova & Cohen, 2002). Consequently, marriage has opposite effects on the housework performed by men and women. Married men do less housework than do single and cohabiting men. In contrast, married women do substantially more housework than single and cohabiting women.

To celebrate Mother's Day, this father and son decorate a cake while mom watches in the background.

A surprising finding is that the total amount of time husbands spend on housework and child care is not strongly related to how many hours their wives work outside the home. Women perform most homemaking and child-care activities, whether they have a full-time paid job or not. A major change is that employed wives are finding ways to spend less time on family work, for example, by buying take-out food rather than cooking at home and, if they can afford it, by hiring others to help with housework. In general, men tend to participate more in child care and housework if they have nontraditional sex-role attitudes, are needed to do child care because of the mother's work schedule, and have incomes similar to those of their wives (Deutsch & Saxon, 1998; Presser, 1994). Nonetheless, in the majority of two-parent households, homemaking and child care continue to be largely "women's work."

Juggling Multiple Roles. What is the psychological impact for women of juggling responsibilities at work and at home? The demands of multiple roles can undoubtedly be difficult and stressful. Working mothers often complain about lack of time and lack of sleep. Despite these and other very real problems, many women enjoy having many roles. One woman explained, "It keeps life interesting. I think it makes you feel so much more whole to be able to do all these things" (Crosby, 1991, p. 88).

Research documents the potential psychological benefits for both women and men of having multiple roles as spouse, parent, and wage earner (Barnett & Hyde, 2001; Helgeson, 2005). Apparently the stresses of juggling jobs and family can be outweighed by the benefits, which include variety and social contact as well as money. For example, the emotional support a person receives in one role may help to allay the stresses of another role. As one woman explained, "Sometimes I have a really rough day at work and then I come home and these two little kids run to the door. . . . Then, I forget the day at work and put all that bad stuff in its pocket. If I didn't have these kids, if I weren't juggling, I'd probably sit there and think about the rotten day for five hours" (Crosby, 1991, p. 148).

Same-Sex Couples. A different perspective on the division of labor at home is provided by research on the intimate relationships of lesbians and gay men (Peplau & Beals, 2004). Most lesbians and gay men are in dual-earner relationships, so that neither partner is the exclusive breadwinner and each partner has some degree of economic independence. How do same-sex couples divide housekeeping responsibilities? To find out, Larry Kurdek (1993) compared the division of housework among gay and lesbian couples who lived together and heterosexual married couples. Among heterosexual couples, housework was allocated on the basis of gender: Wives did the bulk of the work, including cooking, cleaning, and grocery shopping. In contrast, gay and lesbian couples divided housework in much more balanced ways, so that neither partner did the majority of the work. Gay men tended to divide up the chores so that each partner had separate areas of specialization based on personal preference and ability. Lesbians were more likely to share tasks, either by doing the work together or by taking turns. In general, research finds that contemporary lesbians and gay men reject traditional husband–wife roles as a model for their relationships and strive to create more egalitarian patterns. A recent study comparing lesbian and gay couples who obtained civil union licenses in Vermont to heterosexual married coules also found much greater equality in housework among same-sex couples (Solomon, Rothblum, & Balsam, 2004).

Male Dominance

The second basic idea in traditional gender roles is that men should be the leaders both at home and in society at large. Changes are clearly occurring in both arenas. In the public sector, laws denying women the vote, forbidding women to own property, and in general defining women as second-class citizens are largely a thing of the past in modern technological societies. In the United States, for example, women serve as governors, members of Congress, and justices on the U.S. Supreme Court. Nonetheless, the numbers of women in the power circles of society are still small. Women make up only a tiny percentage of the members of the U.S. Senate and House of Representatives. The CEOs of major corporations are overwhelmingly men. For an example closer to home, consider the college or university you attend. Chances are that there are many women administrative assistants and some women professors, but that the chairperson of most departments, most of the deans and top-level administrators, and the president are men. Women are still very far from being equal partners at work and in public affairs (Deaux & LaFrance, 1998).

In personal relationships, the extent of male dominance is harder to assess. At the level of personal dispositions, men and women do not differ in their interest in power or their power motivation (Winter, 1988). However, social convention has traditionally conferred greater authority on men in dating and marriage. Until the 1970s, for example, state laws in the United States gave husbands legal control over all family property and permitted husbands, as the "head of the household," to decide where the family should live. As we saw in Chapter 9, many married couples today describe their relationships as equal in power, as do a majority of dating couples. However, when relationships are not equal, it is most often the man who has greater influence.

Even young couples who strongly endorse egalitarian norms sometimes find it hard to achieve these ideals. Individuals who reject the abstract principle of male dominance may nonetheless continue to follow social scripts that encourage male leadership. A study of dating illustrates this idea (Rose & Frieze, 1989). Researchers asked college students to list separately the actions that a young man and a young woman would do as each prepared for a first date, met the date, and spent time together. The typical dating script is presented in Table 11–6. Note that it is assumed that the man will take the leadership role on the date: ask the woman out, decide where to go, pay for the date, initiate physical contact, and be the one to ask for a second date. In other words, contemporary dating rules continue to cast the man as the person "in charge."

Two follow-up studies have demonstrated the generality of this dating script. In one study, college students described their most recent actual first date rather than a typical date (Rose & Frieze, 1993). In a more recent study, students described a date with someone they already knew from work or some other group context (Laner & Ventrone, 1998). In both cases, nearly identical scripts were reported. Laner and Ventrone speculated that "if these gender-stereotypic behaviors produce successful first dates, it is highly likely that their basis—woman

Table 11–6

Script for a Typical First Date

The Woman's Role	The Man's Role
Tell friends and family	Ask for a date* Decide what to do*
Groom and dress	Groom and dress
Be nervous	Be nervous
Worry about or change appearance	Worry about or change appearance
Wait for date	Prepare car, apartment Check money*
Welcome date to home	Go to date's house
Introduce parents or roommates	Meet parents or roommates
Leave	Leave Open car door for date*
Confirm plans	Confirm plans
Get to know date	Get to know date
Compliment date	Compliment date
Joke, laugh, and talk	Joke, laugh, and talk
Try to impress date	Try to impress date
Go to movies, show, or party	Go to movies, show, or party
Eat	Eat Pay* Initiate physical contact* Take date home
Tell date she had a good time	Tell date he had a good time Ask for another date* Tell date he will be in touch*
Kiss goodnight	Kiss goodnight
	Go home

**Note:* The man's script has more elements than the woman's. The man typically takes the leadership role, indicated by asterisks next to specific activities.

Source: Data from Rose and Frieze (1989, June), *Gender and Society* (Vol. 3, No. 2). Copyright 1989 by Sociologists for Women in Society. Reprinted by permission of Sage Publication.

as subordinate . . . and facilitator of men's plans; man as dominant, as planner and economic provider . . . will carry forward into future dates" (p. 469).

In addition, cultural standards for dating and marriage continue to create situations in which women have fewer personal resources than do their romantic partners. To the extent that women marry men who are older, have more education, earn more money, and have more prestigious jobs, women may be at a relative power disadvantage in heterosexual relationships. Young adults often have somewhat ambivalent attitudes toward power in dating and marriage. On the one hand, they endorse abstract democratic principles of shared decision making in male–female relationships. On the other hand, they follow traditional patterns of male–female interaction that can have the unintended consequence of giving men greater control.

In contemporary society, multiple definitions of gender roles coexist. The options available to people today, both at work and in personal relationships, are much less limited by gender than in the past.

Summary

1. Gender is one of the most basic categories in social life. The process of labeling people, things, and activities as "masculine" or "feminine" is called gender typing.
2. Gender stereotypes are beliefs about the typical personal attributes of males and females. Cultural stereotypes are societal-level images of the sexes found in the media, art, and literature. Personal stereotypes are the beliefs held by an individual about the typical attributes of men and women. The tendency to emphasize men's faces and women's bodies in the media is known as "face-ism."
3. Stereotypes are most likely to influence perceptions of other people when there is little information available, when a person's gender is especially salient, and when the person is relatively low in power. One problem with gender stereotypes is that they can bias evaluation of the performance of individual men and women at work or at school.
4. Gender identity, the knowledge that we are female or male, is acquired early in childhood. An important developmental milestone occurs when children come to understand that gender is constant and unchanging. Transsexuals have a severe gender identity conflict: They believe their true psychological gender is different from their biological sex.
5. Beliefs about masculinity and femininity are important elements of our self-concept. Androgynous people rate themselves high in both masculine (instrumental) and feminine (expressive) qualities. Research refutes the congruence model assertion that psychological well-being is greatest among traditionally masculine men and feminine women.
6. Some researchers believe that gender-neutral terms such as "instrumentality" ("agency") and "expressivity" ("communion") should replace the concepts of "psychological masculinity" and "femininity." There is evidence that undesirable aspects of instrumentality (a focus on the self to the exclusion of others) and expressiveness (a tendency to become overly involved with others and to neglect the self) can be harmful to one's health.
7. There are four major theoretical perspectives on the causes of sex differences. A biological approach emphasizes the impact of physical differences, sex hormones, and evolution. A socialization approach emphasizes ways in which we acquire relatively stable gender-typed characteristics through modeling and reinforcement that begin in childhood. A social roles perspective emphasizes that people tend to conform to the expectations of gender-linked social roles, such as husband or nurse. A final approach emphasizes that people's behavior varies from situation to situation, depending on such factors as the sex composition of the group, the nature of the task or activity, and the social expectations of others.
8. Much research has compared the social behavior of women and men. A technique called "meta-analysis" provides a quantitative way to integrate results from many different studies. Research finds that on average males are more aggressive and that in some situations men may be less vulnerable to social influence. Females tend to be better at decoding nonverbal communication. In general, women tend to have a more relational or partner-centered orientation to sexuality; men tend to have a more recreational or body-centered orientation. Males and females appear to differ in their sense of personal entitlement.
9. Attitudes about men's and women's roles (gender-role attitudes) have become less traditional over

time. Nonetheless, men continue to hold more traditional attitudes than women do.

10. In daily life, women and men often use their basic talents and motivation in distinctive, gender-linked ways. Traditional gender roles prescribe a division of labor by sex and confer greater power on men. Despite social change, both of these traditional patterns continue. In general, however, people today are less constrained by gender roles than they were in the past.

Key Terms

ambivalent sexism **365**
androgyny **349**
attributions **347**
benevolent sexism **364**
cultural stereotypes **338**
face-ism **337**
gender identity **347**
gender stereotypes **336**
gender typing **335**
hostile sexism **364**
meta-analysis **357**
personal entitlement **362**
personal stereotypes **338**
transsexual **348**

In The News

Helping Strangers in Distress

Derrick Harris, a professional truck driver, was headed toward Knoxville, Tennessee, to make a delivery when he noticed a roadside fire. "When I first saw the flames," Harris recounted, "I thought it was a brush fire. Then I noticed the fire was moving, and I realized it was a person. It seemed like something from TV or the movies, like it was a stunt man on fire." Instantly, Harris pulled off the highway. Grabbing a blanket and a cooler of water from his truck, he raced to the victim. He used the blanket to extinguish the fire and then soaked it with water to comfort the seriously injured man. Next, Harris went back to his truck to get a fire extinguisher to put out a fire that had started in nearby trees. He used his cell phone to call for help and waited with the burn victim until the police and paramedics arrived. The story didn't end there, however. Comments from the victim and the presence nearby of a kerosene container aroused Harris' suspicion that the fire was not accidental. Based on information from Harris, the police searched the surrounding woods and soon found a suspect who later admitted to setting the man on fire. When questioned by reporters, Harris was modest about his act of bravery. "It's a case of being in the right place at the right time," he said. His courage did not go unnoticed, however. Harris was awarded the 2003 Goodyear Highway Hero award (*Road & Travel Magazine,* 2004).

In another case of bravery, Andrew Johnson, 28, was driving to his home in Pittsburgh (Hirschl, 2004). Johnson drove past what he thought was a woman in a red shawl standing with a man and a child. Something in the scene caused Johnson to look back. "I had a feeling that what I saw didn't look right," he said. So he turned his truck around, fearing that the woman might be injured. As Johnson got out of his car and approached the group, the man began to attack the woman with a meat cleaver. Johnson yelled at him to stop. The man dropped the cleaver, and Johnson, a former high school wrestler, tackled the man and put him in a headlock. When the police arrived, they had to use mace to subdue the violent attacker. The woman was hospitalized but lived because of the quick action of a stranger. Regrettably, these and other acts of courage and selfless altruism seem to get less media attention than do stories of crime and brutality.

Part Four

Chapter 12

Helping Behavior

In this chapter, we consider several types of helping. Selfless acts of altruism toward strangers are important. So, too, are the countless acts of caregiving that occur among friends and family members and the volunteer organizations that offer aid to millions of people each year.

Focus of This Chapter

DEFINING ALTRUISM AND PROSOCIAL BEHAVIOR

To begin, we should be clear about the meaning of two key concepts: altruism and prosocial behavior. **Altruism** is performing an act voluntarily to help someone else when there is no expectation of a reward in any form, except perhaps a feeling of having done a good deed (Schroeder, Penner, Dovidio, & Piliavin, 1995). By this definition, whether an act is altruistic depends on the intentions of the helper. The stranger who risks his or her own life to pull a victim from a burning building and then vanishes anonymously into the night without any chance of receiving a reward or public recognition has performed an altruistic act.

Prosocial behavior is a much broader category (Batson, 1998). It includes any act that helps or is designed to help others, regardless of the helper's motives. Many prosocial acts are not altruistic. For example, if you volunteer to work for a charity to impress your friends or to build up your résumé for future job opportunities, you are not acting altruistically in the pure sense of the term. Prosocial behavior ranges over a continuum from the most selfless acts of altruism to helpful acts that are motivated entirely by self-interest.

Our everyday experiences provide many examples of prosocial behavior. In a study of young adults, McGuire (1994) asked college students to describe instances in which they had provided help and received help. These young adults had no trouble identifying 72 different types of helping, including casual help (e.g., giving someone directions, picking up dropped papers), substantial help (e.g., lending someone money, helping someone to pack or move), emotional help (e.g., listening to someone talk through a problem), and emergency help (e.g., taking someone to the hospital emergency room, pushing a car out of a ditch or snow).

Prosocial behavior is affected by the type of relationship between people. Whether because of liking, social obligation, self-interest, or empathy, we are more helpful to those we know and care about than to those we don't

Altruism

Helping another person with no expectation of receiving a reward.

Prosocial Behavior

Behavior that helps others, regardless of the helper's motive.

know. Although help offered to strangers is less common than help offered to friends, it is by no means a rare occurrence. Many studies have documented people's willingness to help a stranger in need. In a midwestern U.S. city, more than half of women shoppers were willing to give money for bus fare to a university student who explained that his wallet had "disappeared" (Berkowitz, 1972). In New York City, most pedestrians responded positively to requests for help from a passerby: 85 percent gave the time of day, 85 percent gave directions, and 73 percent gave change for a quarter (Latané & Darley, 1970). In another study on the streets of New York City, 50 percent of people who found a wallet that had been "lost" (intentionally by researchers) mailed it back to its owner (Hornstein, Fisch, & Holmes, 1968). Prosocial behavior even occurs on city subways. When a passenger (actually a researcher) fell down with an apparent knee injury, 83 percent of those in the subway offered assistance (Latané & Darley).

We begin this chapter with a discussion of theoretical perspectives on helping and then consider three important types of helping behavior: bystander intervention or helping a stranger in distress; volunteering time, services, or money to advance a social cause we care about; and caregiving in our relations with family and friends.

THEORETICAL PERSPECTIVES ON HELPING

Our understanding of prosocial behavior benefits from several broad theoretical perspectives that were presented in Chapter 1. First, an evolutionary approach suggests that a predisposition to help is part of our genetic, evolutionary heritage. Second, a sociocultural perspective emphasizes the importance of social norms that dictate when we should help people in need. Third, a learning approach proposes that people learn to be helpful, following basic principles of reinforcement and modeling. Fourth, a decision-making perspective focuses on the processes that influence judgments about when help is needed; it also emphasizes the weighing of costs and benefits in the decision to give help. Finally, attribution theory highlights the idea that our willingness to help depends on the "merits" of the case and, in particular, whether the person deserves assistance.

Throughout life, family and friends help each other in many ways, both small and large. Here a woman helps an elderly relative carry groceries.

An Evolutionary Perspective

Scientists have long observed prosocial behavior among animal species. Charles Darwin (1871) noted that rabbits make noise with their hind feet to warn other rabbits of predators. Some varieties of baboons have a characteristic pattern of responding to threats. The dominant males take the most exposed positions to protect the group and may even rush at an intruder. As the group moves away from the threat, the males risk their own safety by remaining behind to protect the rest of the group. Dolphins show a fascinating pattern of rescuing injured peers. Because dolphins are mammals, they must breathe air to survive. If an injured dolphin sinks below the surface, it will die. Several observers have reported that dolphins aid injured companions. In one case, a dolphin was stunned by an explosion in the water (Siebenaler & Caldwell, 1956). Two other dolphins came to its aid by holding the animal afloat until it recovered and was able to care for itself. Among many animals, parents sacrifice themselves when their young are threatened. An impressive example is the female nighthawk, which responds to a potential attack on her young by flying from the nest as if she had a broken wing, fluttering around at a low level, and finally landing on the ground right in front of the intruder but away from the nest (Armstrong, 1965).

This description of animals helping and sacrificing for each other runs counter to the dog-eat-dog, survival-of-the-fittest image that some people have of the animal kingdom. The existence of seemingly altruistic behavior among animals has posed a problem for evolutionary theorists: If the most helpful members of a species sacrifice themselves for others, they will be less likely to survive and pass along their genes to the next generation by having offspring. How, then, does a biological predisposition to act altruistically persist among animals and people?

Evolutionary psychology, a theoretical perspective introduced in Chapter 1, has tried to resolve this paradox (Bell, 2001; McAndrew, 2002). Briefly, any genetically determined trait that has a high survival value (that helps the individual survive) tends to be passed on to the next generation. The tendency to help others may have high survival value for the individual's genes, but not necessarily for the individual. Imagine a bird that has fathered six chicks. Half the genes in each chick come from the father. Together, the six chicks have three times as many of the father's genes as he does himself. If the father sacrifices himself to save the chicks, his particular gene pool has already been replicated. Similar analyses can be done for other relatives that have varying percentages of the individual's genes. Helping close relatives contributes to the survival of an individual's genes in future generations and so can be understood by the basic principles of evolutionary biology.

Sociobiologist Robert Trivers (1971) emphasized the likely biological basis of mutual or reciprocal altruism. In his view, the potential costs to the individual of giving aid to others are offset by the possibility of receiving help from others. However, such a system of mutual help giving is threatened by potential "cheaters" who accept help but offer none in return. To minimize cheating, natural selection may have favored a disposition to feel guilt and a tendency to enforce mutual helping through social means such as punishing those who do not follow group rules.

The evolutionary approach leads to several specific predictions. For example, animals should be most helpful to those that are genetically most closely linked to themselves. They should be more helpful to immediate family than to distant relatives or strangers (Burnstein, Crandall, & Kitayama, 1994). The theory also predicts that parents will behave more altruistically to healthy offspring than to unhealthy ones that are less likely to survive. Studies of human beings support these predictions, although evolution is not the only possible interpretation for such findings (Dovidio et al., 1991; Webster, 2003).

A further prediction is that mothers will usually be more helpful to their offspring than will fathers. The reasoning here is that in many species, males have the biological potential to sire a great many offspring and so can perpetuate their genes without investing much in any one infant. The female can produce only a relatively small number of offspring and so must help each offspring to thrive to ensure the survival of her own genes.

The idea that helping others is a genetically determined part of "human nature" is controversial (Batson, 1998). Just how well the theory applies to people is still an open question. Nonetheless, the theory raises the intriguing possibility that self-preservation is not always the overwhelming motive that we sometimes think it is. Biological dispositions toward selfishness and aggression may coexist with biological dispositions toward helpfulness and caregiving (Bell, 2001; Kottler, 2000).

A Sociocultural Perspective

Critics of evolutionary perspectives argue that social factors are much more important than biology is in determining prosocial behavior among people. Donald Campbell (1975) suggested that genetic evolution may help explain a few basic prosocial behaviors such as parents' caring for their young, but that it does not apply to more extreme instances of helping a stranger in distress.

Nor does evolution seem to offer an explanation of acts of generosity to strangers. Consider the case of Osceola McCarty. As a young black girl growing up in Mississippi, Osceola quit school in the sixth grade to go to work as a washerwoman. Over the years, Ms. McCarty never married or had children. Living frugally, she put her meager pay—mostly dollars and change—into the bank. At the age of 87, she donated her entire life savings of $150,000 to the University of Southern Mississippi for scholarships for needy black students. Explained Ms. McCarty, "I wanted to share my wealth with the children. . . . I never minded work . . . but maybe I can make it so the children don't have to work like I did"

Working as a washerwoman, Oseola McCarty saved $150,000 over the years. At age 87, she gave her life savings to the University of Southern Mississippi.

(cited in Bragg, 1995, p. 1). Such stories are better explained by what Campbell calls "social evolution"—the historical development of human culture. In this view, human societies have gradually and selectively evolved skills and beliefs that promote the welfare of the group. Because prosocial behavior generally benefits society, it has become part of the social rules or norms.

Cultural Similarities: Basic Norms of Responsibility, Reciprocity, and Justice. Three basic social norms are common in human societies. First, a **norm of social responsibility** prescribes that we should help others who depend on us. Parents are expected to care for their children, and social agencies may intervene if parents fail to live up to this obligation. Teachers are supposed to help their students; coaches, to look after team members; and coworkers, to assist each other. The religious and moral codes of many societies emphasize the duty to help others. Sometimes this obligation is even written into the law. For example, the state of Minnesota enacted a statute requiring that "any person at the scene of an emergency who knows that another person is exposed to or suffered grave physical harm shall, to the extent that he can do so without danger or peril to himself or others, give reasonable assistance to the exposed person."

Norm of Social Responsibility

Social rule that we should help those who depend on us.

Norm of Reciprocity

Social rule that we are obligated to help those who help us.

Second, a **norm of reciprocity** says that we should help those who help us. Several studies have shown that people are more likely to help someone from whom they have already received aid. In an illustrative study, pairs of college students worked individually on a judgment task (Regan, 1968).

After a while, the participants were given a short break. In one condition, one of the participants (actually a confederate of the experimenter) did a favor for the other participant. During the break, the confederate left the building and returned carrying two bottles of cola. He handed one to the subject, saying, "I asked him [the experimenter] if I could get myself a cola and he said it was okay, so I brought one for you, too." All subjects took the cola. In a second condition, the researcher gave the participants drinks. In a third condition, no drinks were provided. Participants then went back to work on the task. After a while, there was a second break. At this point, the confederate asked the experimenter (loud enough for the subject to hear) whether he could send a note to the subject. The experimenter said that he could as long as it did not concern the experiment. The confederate then wrote the following note:

> Would you do me a favor? I'm selling raffle tickets for my high school back home to build a new gym. The tickets cost 25 cents each and the prize is a new Corvette. The thing is, if I sell the most tickets I get 50 bucks and I could use it. If you'd buy any, would you just write the number on this note and give it back to me right away so I can make out the tickets? Any would help, the more the better. Thanks. (Regan, 1968, p. 19)

The measure of helping was how many tickets the subject agreed to buy. The results are shown in Figure 12–1. When the confederate gave the subject a drink and then asked him to do a favor, there was considerably more helping than when the experimenter gave the subject a drink or when no drink was given. This and other research show that the reciprocity norm is quite strong, not only in the United States but also in many other cultures (Gergen, Ellsworth, Maslach, & Seipel, 1975).

Norm of Social Justice

Social rules about fairness.

Third, human groups also develop a **norm of social justice**, rules about fairness and the just distribution of resources. As we discuss in Chapter 9, one common fairness principle is equity. According to this principle, two people who make equal contributions to a task should receive equal rewards. If one receives more than the other, the two will feel pressure to try to restore equity by redistributing the rewards. The shortchanged or underbenefitted person obviously feels distressed. The more interesting finding is that even the person who receives more than a fair share (the overbenefitted person) may give some to the person who received too little. A third person, observing the unfair situation, might also be tempted to give to the one who suffered. Everyday acts of "helping the less

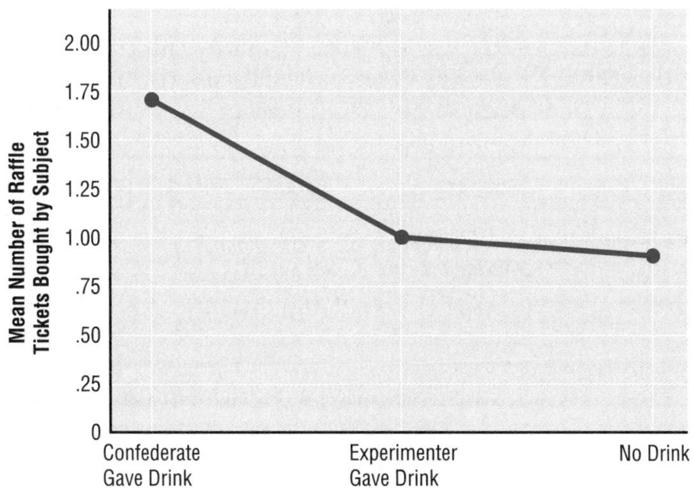

Figure 12–1 In this study, subjects who had been given a cola by another subject (actually a confederate) were more likely to help him by purchasing raffle tickets. Subjects who were given a cola by the experimenter or who received no cola purchased fewer tickets. In everyday life, favors are often reciprocated.

Source: Data from Regan (1968).

fortunate," such as donating to a charity, seem to be motivated by a desire to create a more equitable situation.

Numerous studies (e.g., Walster, Walster, & Berscheid, 1978) have demonstrated that overbenefitted people act to restore equity when they can. In several experiments, research subjects played a game in which one person, through no fault of her own, lost a lot of money or trading stamps whereas the partner won a good deal (Berscheid & Walster, 1967). At the end of the game, the winner (the real subject) was given an opportunity to give some of her winnings to the partner who lost. There was a strong tendency to give some of the money to the loser, even though the winner had won legitimately. In contrast, in a condition in which both partners had equal winnings, there was little tendency for the subject to give any winnings to the other player.

In another study, one member of a team was given more money than his partner was given. This overbenefitted person tended to give some of the money to the partner in order to make their rewards more equitable (Schmitt & Marwell, 1972). In addition, the overrewarded partner often chose to play a different game when assured that it would result in a more equal division of the rewards. In other words, not only did he give away some of his own money to produce an equitable division, but also he changed the situation to avoid producing more inequity in the future.

These three norms—social responsibility, reciprocity, and social justice—provide a cultural basis for prosocial behavior. Through the process of socialization, individuals learn these rules and come to behave in accord with these guidelines for prosocial behavior. Research showing that people are more likely to help relatives and friends than to help strangers can be explained in terms of social norms: We feel greater responsibility for those we are close to, and we assume that they will help us if a need arises (Dovidio et al., 1991).

Cultural Variation: When Are We Responsible to Help? All societies have norms relevant to helping, but the specifics of whom we are expected to help and when vary from culture to culture. Research by Joan Miller (1994) demonstrates this point. She systematically compared the beliefs about social responsibility of Hindus in India and of people in the United States. Hindu culture emphasizes the interconnectedness of people and the obligations of the individual to the social group. In contrast, U.S. culture values individualism and self-reliance. As a result, Miller believed that people in the United States tend to view the decision to help others as a matter of personal choice, whereas Hindus view the same decision to help in terms of duty and moral obligation.

In an illustrative study, 180 American and 180 Hindu subjects evaluated stories about a person in need (Miller, Bersoff, & Harwood, 1990). Sometimes the person's problem was relatively minor (needing an aspirin for a headache), and sometimes the problem was extreme (needing a ride to the hospital because of

Table 12–1

Percentage of Subjects Saying the Person Has an Obligation to Help

	Hindus			Americans		
	Parent	Friend	Stranger	Parent	Friend	Stranger
Extreme need	99	99	100	100	98	96
Moderate need	98	100	99	95	78	55
Minor need	96	97	88	61	59	41

Source: Data from Miller, Bersoff, and Harwood (1990, p. 38).

severe bleeding). The stories also varied the relationship of the helper and the person in need (strangers, friends, or a parent and a young child). The results are presented in Table 12–1. Both cross-cultural similarities and cross-cultural differences were found. When the person's need was life-threatening, both Hindus and Americans believed there was an obligation to help, even if the person in need was a stranger. In contrast, when the need was minor, Hindus were much more likely than were Americans to view assistance as a moral obligation. For example, 88 percent of Hindus believed that a person was obligated to help a stranger with a minor problem, compared to only 41 percent of Americans. It appears that Hindus have a broader definition of social responsibility that often extends beyond family and friends to include strangers in need. In contrast, Americans tend to have a more narrow view of social responsibility and so are likely to interpret more helping situations as optional matters of personal choice.

Further insights into the differences between individualist cultures and collectivist cultures are provided by a study that compared the United States and Brazil (Bontempo, Lobel, & Triandis, 1990). In this research, college students in Illinois and Rio de Janeiro were asked questions about helpful behaviors, such as lending money to someone or spending time caring for a seriously ill person. Students in both cultures acknowledged social obligations to help in such cases. However, whereas the Brazilians said they would actually enjoy doing what was expected of them, the Americans reported little enthusiasm for performing these required prosocial acts.

A Learning Perspective

A third perspective emphasizes the importance of learning to be helpful (Batson, 1998). As children grow up, they are taught to share and to help. You can probably remember times when you were praised for being helpful or chided for forgetting to help when you should have. We learn social norms about helping and may also develop habits of helpfulness. Two general learning principles discussed in Chapter 1 are again important here. People learn to help through reinforcement—the effects of rewards and punishments for helping. People also learn through modeling—by observing others who help.

Reinforcement. Studies clearly show that children tend to help and share more when they are rewarded for their prosocial behavior. One study found that 4-year-olds were more likely to share marbles with another child when they were rewarded with bubble gum for their generosity (Fischer, 1963). In everyday life, parents and teachers are more likely to reward helpfulness with praise than with bubble gum. Research suggests that some forms of praise may be more effective than others.

In one study, 8- and 9-year-old children played a game to win chips that could be traded for toys (Mills & Grusec, 1989). In an initial phase of the study, the researcher urged the children to share their chips with poor children who didn't have any toys. With prompting, all children gave away some of their chips.

Children were then given one of two types of praise for their helpfulness. In a dispositional praise condition, the experimenter emphasized the child's personality by saying, "I guess you're the kind of person who likes to help others whenever you can. Yes, you're a very nice and helpful person." In a general praise condition, the researcher emphasized the child's actions rather than personality, saying, "It was good that you gave some of your chips to the poor children. Yes, that was a nice and helpful thing to do." The children were then left alone to play the game again and were told that they could share "with the poor children if you want to, but you really don't have to." The children who had received the dispositional praise, emphasizing that they were helpful people, were significantly more likely to share than were the children who had received the general praise or no praise at all. Dispositional praise appears to be more effective than global praise, presumably because it encourages children to see themselves as the kind of people who will continue to help in the future.

When adults assist children, they provide an important model of helpfulness.

Observational Learning. Watching prosocial models can also be important, as shown by research on children's television programs. For example, one study exposed first-graders to different episodes from the then-popular children's TV show about a dog named Lassie (Sprafkin, Liebert, & Poulos, 1975). Half the children watched an episode that focused on Lassie's efforts to keep her puppy from being given away. At the story's climax, the puppy falls into a mine shaft. Unable to rescue the puppy herself, Lassie brings her owner, Jeff, and his grandfather to the scene. Jeff risks his life by hanging over the edge of the shaft to save the puppy. In the neutral condition, children watched an episode of Lassie that dramatized Jeff's attempt to avoid taking violin lessons. It contained no examples of people helping a dog, although Lassie was featured in a positive light. Children watched the Lassie episode individually and then were given an opportunity to help some puppies, but only at the cost of forgoing personal benefits. Children who had watched the prosocial TV show were significantly more helpful than were children who had watched the neutral show.

Other research has examined the combined effects of both modeling and reinforcement. In one study, a helpful adult model was used to get boys to behave altruistically by giving some of the tokens they had won at bowling to an orphan named Bobby (Rushton & Teachman, 1978). Then the model either rewarded the child for his generosity ("Good for you; that's really nice of you") or punished him ("That's kind of silly for you to give to Bobby"). There was also a no-reinforcement condition in which the adult said nothing. As Figure 12–2 shows, children who were rewarded gave more to Bobby on later trials than did children who were punished. Two weeks later, when children again played the same game

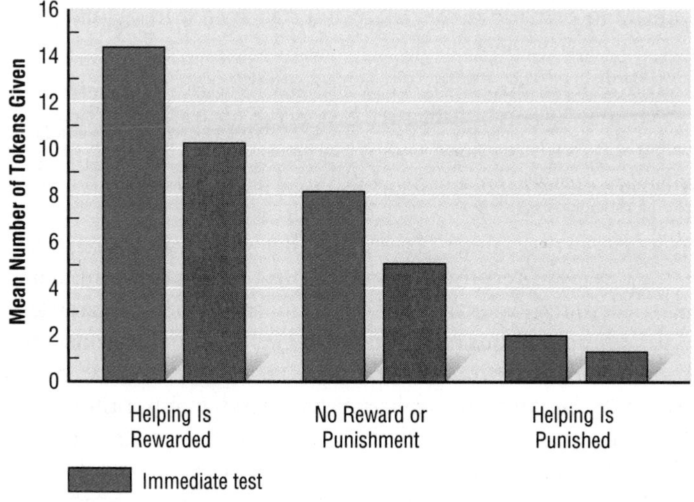

Figure 12–2 Rewards and punishments have clear effects on children's willingness to help. In this study, children were praised, criticized, or given no reinforcement for donating tokens to an orphan named Bobby. Children were then given other opportunities to help Bobby, both immediately and then 2 weeks later. Children who were rewarded gave the most tokens; children who were punished gave the fewest.

Source: Data from Rushton and Teachman (1978, p. 324).

and were reminded about Bobby, the effects of the earlier reward or punishment still influenced how much they gave to Bobby.

Adults can also be affected by observing helpful models, as a study of blood donors clearly showed. In this clever experiment, women college students first talked to a friendly woman (actually a confederate of the researchers) as part of a study of social interaction (Rushton & Campbell, 1977). The researchers arranged things so that as the two women left the interaction study, they passed a table set up in the corridor, staffed by people asking for blood donors. Half the time, the confederate immediately volunteered, modeling prosocial behavior. In the no-model condition, the confederate stepped aside to talk to someone else and did not volunteer to give blood. The effects of the model's behavior were striking. A helpful model led 67 percent of subjects to pledge to donate blood, compared to only 25 percent of subjects who saw no model. More impressive were data on whether the women actually followed through on their pledges to give blood. None of the women in the no-model condition actually gave blood, but 33 percent of those who saw the altruistic model did. Similar evidence of modeling effects has been found in a variety of situations, such as donating money to a Salvation Army kettle at Christmas or helping a stranded motorist fix a flat tire (Bryan & Test, 1967).

Taken together, these and other studies provide convincing evidence of the power of reinforcement and modeling to shape prosocial behavior. Over time, people develop habits of helping and learn rules about who they should help and when. For young children, prosocial behavior may depend largely on external rewards and social approval. As we grow older, however, helping can become an internalized value, independent of external incentives. It can be enough to know that you've lived up to your own standards and to feel the warm glow of having done a good deed.

A Decision-Making Perspective

When a mother rushes to pull her toddler from the path of an oncoming car, she seldom has time to think about her actions in advance. In many situations, however, helpful actions may result from more complex processes of decision making. Before trying to rescue a cat from a tree, passersby may discuss whether the cat will come down without aid and how best to effect a rescue. From a decision-making perspective, helping occurs when an individual decides to offer assistance and then takes action (Latané & Darley, 1970). Possible steps in the decision to help are shown in Figure 12–3. A person must first notice that something is happening and decide if help is required. If help is needed, the person considers the extent of his or her own personal responsibility to act. Third, the person evaluates the rewards and costs of helping or not helping. Finally, the person must decide what type of help is needed and just how to provide it. Let's consider each step in detail.

Perceiving a Need. It's 2 A.M., and a piercing scream fills the night air. You wake up with a start. A woman shouts, "Stop it! Leave me alone!" You hear an angry male voice, but you can't quite make out what he's saying. What is going on? Is it merely a noisy lovers' quarrel or a serious physical attack? Is this an emergency requiring outside intervention?

The crucial first step in any prosocial act is noticing that something is happening and deciding that help is required. Sometimes a need is clear: A child has gashed her head playing soccer and urgently needs medical attention. In many situations, however, such as hearing screams in the night, it can be difficult to decide. Uncertainty is a major reason people sometimes fail to offer assistance. One study found that when students heard an unmistakable emergency—a maintenance man falling off a ladder and crying out in agony—all of them went to the man's aid. In another condition, where students heard an ambiguous emergency—the sounds of an identical fall but without verbal cues that the victim was injured—help was offered only about 30 percent of the time (Clark & Word, 1972).

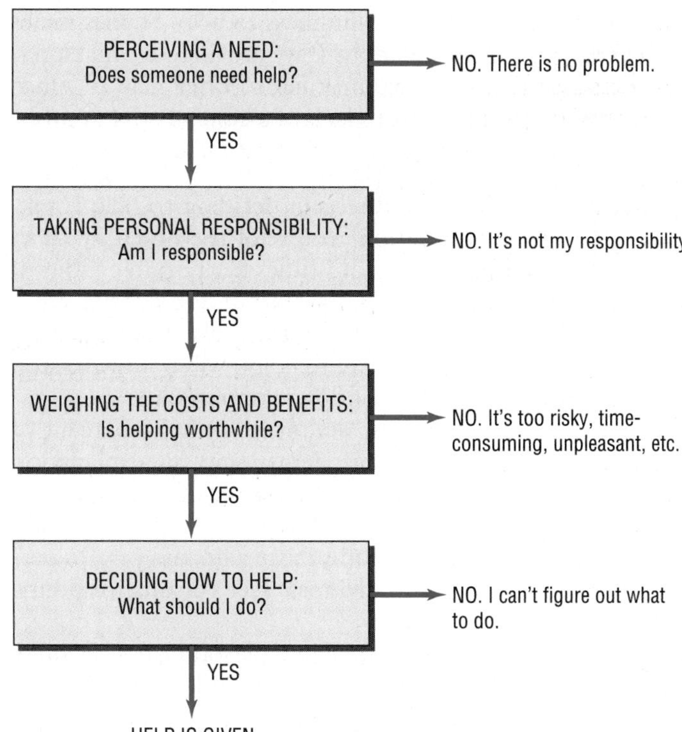

Figure 12–3 The decision-making perspective identifies four crucial steps in the process leading us to help a person in distress. At each point, different decisions may lead us not to offer assistance.

What cues do people use to decide if an emergency exists? Research by Shotland and Huston (1979) identified five important characteristics that lead us to perceive an event as an emergency:

1. Something happens suddenly and unexpectedly.
2. There is a clear threat of harm to a victim.
3. The harm to the victim is likely to increase over time unless someone intervenes.
4. The victim is helpless and needs outside assistance.
5. Some sort of effective intervention is possible.

Most people consider the following events to be emergencies: a heart attack, a rape in progress, and a car accident with the driver motionless on the ground. People are less certain that an emergency exists if there is a power blackout, if a friend says he is miserable and depressed, or if there is a disabled car on the side of a road.

Our interpretation or definition of a situation is a vital factor in whether we offer aid. Shotland and Straw (1976) found that people responded quite differently to an identical fight scene, depending on whether they perceived it as a lovers' quarrel or a fight between strangers. In this study, students came to the psychology department individually in the evening to fill out an attitude questionnaire. While working alone on the task, the student heard a loud fight break out in the corridor (actually staged by drama students). A woman screamed and pleaded with a man to "get away from me." In a "marriage" condition, where the woman yelled, "I don't know why I ever married you," only 19 percent of the students intervened. But in a "stranger" condition, where the woman yelled, "I don't know you," 65 percent of the subjects intervened either directly or by calling the police. Even though the fights were identical in all respects, the subjects perceived the situation as more serious and the woman as more eager for help in the "stranger" condition.

In a real-life fight in which the relationship between the participants is unclear, onlookers may assume it to be a lovers' quarrel and decide not to intrude. Although this reaction is unfortunate, it means that the lack of help is due to a misunderstanding of the situation, not to an unwillingness to help. Similar issues may arise in our relationships with friends and family. If we are unaware that a relative is undergoing tests for possible cancer, we may fail to offer help or emotional support, not from lack of concern but from lack of awareness that a problem exists.

Taking Personal Responsibility. The second step in deciding to help is taking personal responsibility. Consider this situation. You're at the beach, lying in the sun. A woman spreads her blanket near yours and tunes her portable radio to a local rock station. After a few minutes, she goes for a swim, leaving her radio on the blanket. A bit later a man comes along, notices the radio, snatches it up quickly, and walks off. What do you do? Chances are that you will not try to stop the thief, reminding yourself, perhaps, that it's not your responsibility.

In an experiment that re-created the scene just described, only 20 percent of people intervened by going up to the thief and demanding an explanation (Moriarity, 1975). In a second condition, however, the owner of the radio first approached the person next to her on the beach and asked if he or she would "watch my things" while she went swimming. Among those who said yes, 95 percent later intervened to stop the thief. When individuals feel personal responsibility, they are significantly more likely to help.

Another demonstration of the importance of taking personal responsibility comes from a clever field study (Maruyama, Fraser, & Miller, 1982). On Halloween, groups of children who came to a certain house while trick-or-treating were asked to donate candies for hospitalized children. There were three experimental conditions, designed to manipulate the children's perceptions of responsibility. In one condition, the woman who greeted the children made each one personally responsible for donating candies by putting the child's name on a bag for the candies. In another condition, she made one child responsible for the entire group. In the third condition, no one was given responsibility. The variations in responsibility had clear effects on the number of candies donated by the children, as shown in Figure 12–4. When each child was individually responsible, the average donation was five candies; when one child was responsible for the group, average donations dropped to three; when no one was responsible, an average of only two candies per child was given. The more personal responsibility a child was given, the more generously the child donated to help hospitalized children. One reason that we are more helpful to family members than to strangers is our greater sense of personal responsibility for the welfare of our relatives.

Another factor that influences perceived responsibility is competence. We feel a greater sense of obligation to intervene if we have the skills to help effectively. In one study, participants witnessed a person (actually a researcher) pass out from an electrical shock caused by malfunctioning equipment (Clark & Word, 1974).

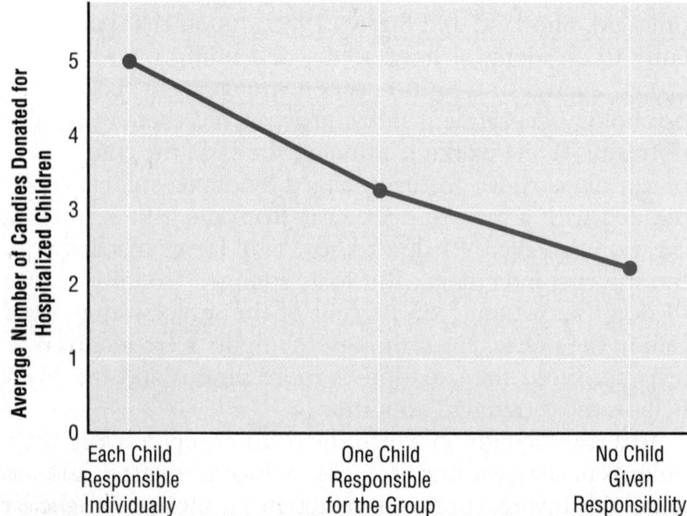

Figure 12–4 Increased personal responsibility increases helping. In this study, researchers varied the instructions given to Halloween trick-or-treaters about their responsibility for giving candy to needy children.

Source: Data from Maruyama, Fraser, and Miller (1982).

We are more likely to intervene in an emergency if we know how to help effectively. By taking a course in cardiopulmonary resuscitation (CPR), these people will have the knowledge to help heart attack victims.

Of the participants who had formal training or experience in working with electrical equipment, 90 percent intervened to help; among those with no electrical skills, only 58 percent intervened.

Weighing the Costs and Benefits. The decision-making perspective suggests that people consider the potential gains and losses that will result from a particular action, including helping someone (Dovidio, Piliavin, Gaertner, Schroeder, & Clark, 1991). A person will act prosocially if the perceived profits (rewards minus costs) of helping outweigh the profits of not helping.

Sometimes it is relatively easy to help. At other times, helping involves considerable costs in time, energy, and possible complications. Telling a passerby the time of day requires little effort; pulling off the freeway to help a stranded motorist would be more time-consuming. In both situations, the cost depends in part on whether you perceive any inconvenience or possible threat to your own safety. Does the person needing help look respectable, or is there some chance you will be robbed? The greater the perceived costs, the less likely you are to help. The benefits of giving help also affect our decision making. The greater the good you believe you can do, the more likely you are to help. The more the person deserves to be helped and the more help you are able to give, the better you may feel about offering assistance.

It is also important to consider the consequences of not giving assistance, including possible costs. Not helping a person in need may lead you to feel guilty. Other people may see that you have not been helpful and think badly of you. You may have a general moral value that says you should help when you can, so that not helping means you have failed to live up to your own ethical standards. Thoughts such as these influence whether you offer help.

Several researchers have tested this model of helping and have found supportive results (see review by Dovidio et al., 1991). Cost-benefit considerations do influence helping, at least in some situations. On the other hand, some altruistic acts occur quickly and perhaps even impulsively. The person who instantly jumps into an icy lake to save a drowning child is unlikely to have weighed carefully the expected profits of the action. Rather, such acts may be motivated by basic emotions and values having to do with human life and personal courage.

Deciding How to Help and Taking Action. A final step is deciding what type of assistance is needed and then taking action. Should you intervene directly in the fight outside your door or act indirectly by calling the police? Should you try to help the unconscious accident victim or call the paramedics? In emergencies, decisions are often made under great stress, urgency, and sometimes even personal danger. Well-intentioned helpers are not always able to give assistance or may even mistakenly do the wrong thing.

A decision-making analysis highlights the many reasons why people fail to give needed assistance. They may not notice that a problem exists or may perceive the problem as trivial. They may recognize a need but not feel personally responsible for helping. They may believe the costs of helping are too great. They may want to help but be unable to do so. Or they may hesitate, caught in a state of indecision.

Attribution Theory: Helping Those Who Deserve Help

Whether or not a person receives help depends in part on the "merits" of the case. For example, people in a supermarket were more likely to give someone money to buy milk than to buy cookie dough (Bickman & Kamzan, 1973), presumably because milk is more essential for health than cookies. Passengers on a New York City subway were more likely to help a man who fell to the ground if he appeared to be sick rather than drunk (Piliavin, Rodin, & Piliavin, 1969). In both cases, beliefs about the legitimacy or appropriateness of the problem made a difference.

Potential helpers also make inferences about the causes of the person's need, following the principles of attribution theory outlined in Chapter 2. A teacher might spend more time helping a student who missed classes because of a death in the family than helping a student who took a vacation to a ski resort. Several studies indicate that the key causal factor is personal control: We are more likely to help someone if we believe the cause of the problem is outside the person's control. For instance, in one study (Meyer & Mulherin, 1980), college students said they would be more willing to lend rent money to an acquaintance if the need arose due to illness (an uncontrollable cause) rather than if it was due to laziness (a controllable cause). In another study, students said they would be more likely to lend their lecture notes to a classmate who needed them because of something uncontrollable, such as the professor's being a poor lecturer, than because of something controllable, such as the classmate's not trying to take good notes (Weiner, 1980). If a person is responsible for his or her predicament, we are less likely to help.

Attributions also affect our emotional reaction to the person in need. Darren George (1992) studied actual incidents of help giving among college friends. He found that students felt more sympathy and less anger toward a friend who had an academic problem that was outside his or her control than toward a friend who was personally responsible for his or her academic difficulties.

In summary, we feel sympathy and concern for those who suffer through no fault of their own; we feel anger and contempt toward those who are responsible for their own problems. Attributing another person's need for help to a controllable cause may give rise to anger, avoidance, or neglect; in contrast, attributing the person's plight to uncontrollable causes may elicit sympathy and lead us to help the person (Schmidt & Weiner, 1988). Table 12–2 summarizes the impact of attributions on helping.

THE HELPER: WHO IS MOST LIKELY TO HELP?

Why are some people more likely than others to help? Researchers have investigated both relatively fleeting moods and emotions that influence our behavior and more enduring personality characteristics.

Mood and Helping

There is considerable evidence that people are more willing to help when they are in a good mood, for example, after they have found coins in a pay telephone (Isen & Simmonds, 1978), or when they have been given a free cookie at the college

Table 12–2

An Attribution Theory Analysis of Helping

Perceived Cause of the Person's Need	Emotional Reaction to the Person in Need	Willingness to Help
Uncontrollable		
Something outside the person's control Example: No jobs are available.	Sympathy, pity	High—The person is perceived as deserving help.
Controllable		
Something the person could control Example: A person is out of work because she is lazy and doesn't want to work.	Anger, irritation	Low—The person is perceived as not deserving help.

library (Isen & Levin, 1972), or have listened to soothing music (Fried & Berkowitz, 1979), than when these mood-enhancing events have not occurred. People in a large shopping mall were more likely to help a stranger by picking up a dropped pen or providing change for a dollar when in the presence of pleasant odors such as baking cookies and roasting coffee (Baron, 1997). Salespeople who rated themselves as being in a positive mood were evaluated by their supervisors as more helpful toward their coworkers and clients (George, 1991). Apparently, a warm glow of positive feeling increases the willingness to act prosocially.

Although the link between positive moods and helping is well established, the specific reasons for this pattern are topics for investigation (Carlson, Charlin, & Miller, 1988). For example, a mood-maintenance hypothesis suggests that we offer help to prolong our positive emotional state; "doing good" may enable us to continue to feel good. Another possibility is that being in a good mood leads us to have more positive thoughts. Therefore, when you see a young mother struggling to carry her baby and a stroller up an escalator, you might think "She could probably use a helping hand," rather than "How stupid! Why didn't she take the elevator?"

Finally, there are important limitations to the "feel-good" effect. The effects of positive moods can be short-lived—only 20 minutes in one study (Isen, Clark, & Schwartz, 1976). Second, a good mood may actually decrease helpfulness when giving assistance would detract from the person's good mood. People in a good mood apparently want to maintain their positive feelings.

The effects of bad moods on helping are more complicated, and research results have not been entirely consistent (Carlson & Miller, 1987). If a bad mood causes us to focus on ourselves and our own needs, it may lessen the likelihood of our helping another person. A depressed teenager may be too wrapped up in his own concerns to extend a helping hand to someone else. On the other hand, if we think helping someone else might make us feel better and so relieve our bad mood, we may be more likely to offer assistance (Cialdini et al., 1987). Robert Cialdini and his colleagues have proposed a **negative-state relief model** to explain why negative moods may increase helping (Cialdini, Darby, & Vincent, 1973; Schaller & Cialdini, 1988). In this view, people in a bad mood are motivated to try to relieve their own discomfort. If an opportunity to help arises and you perceive it as a way to improve your mood, you are more likely to offer help. Of course, helping another person is only one of many possible ways to make yourself feel better—talking to a friend or listening to your favorite music might work just as well. Negative moods do not always lead to helping.

Negative-State Relief Model

Asserts that people help to alleviate their own bad mood or personal distress.

Does providing assistance actually make helpers feel better? Research suggests that it can (Williamson & Clark, 1992). In one study, college students who were able to provide help reported feeling more cheerful and less nervous than did students who were not given an opportunity to help (Williamson & Clark, 1989). Helpful students also reported feeling better about themselves (e.g., more generous and considerate, and less selfish and unreliable). In short, helping can improve the helper's mood and self-evaluation.

Motives for Helping: Empathy and Personal Distress

As noted earlier, true altruism is defined by the person's intentions: We act altruistically only when we help with no expectation of receiving personal benefit. This definition has led researchers to study the motives that lead people to help (Batson, Van Lange, Ahmad, & Lishner, 2003).

A useful distinction can be made between helping based on personal distress and helping based on empathy. To understand this distinction, picture for a moment the sight of people in serious trouble: the mangled bodies of victims in a train crash, a starving child in ragged clothes, or an anguished father whose child has disappeared. Witnessing people in need often evokes powerful emotions.

Personal Distress

Negative emotions felt in response to the plight of another person.

Empathy

Feelings of sympathy and caring for others.

Personal distress means our own emotional reactions to the plight of others—our feelings of shock, horror, alarm, concern, or helplessness. Personal distress occurs when people who witness an event are preoccupied with their own emotional reactions. In contrast, **empathy** means feelings of sympathy and caring for others, in particular, sharing vicariously or indirectly in the suffering of others. Empathy occurs when the observer focuses on the needs and emotions of the victim. Personal distress leads us to feel anxious and apprehensive; empathy leads us to feel sympathetic and compassionate. Research suggests that the distinctive emotions generated by personal distress and empathy may actually be accompanied by distinctive physiological reactions, including heart rate patterns and facial expressions (e.g., Eisenberg & Fabes, 1990). Table 12–3 compares personal distress and empathy.

In general, personal distress motivates us to reduce our own discomfort. We might do this by helping a person in need, a possibility suggested by the negative-state relief model of helping. We might also feel better, however, if we escape from the situation or ignore the suffering around us. There is no necessary connection between personal distress and offering assistance. Further, helping motivated by a desire to reduce our own discomfort is egoistic and not altruistic. In contrast, empathic concern usually motivates us to help the person in need. Because the goal of empathic concern is to enhance the welfare of someone else, it provides an altruistic motive for helping.

Many studies conducted both in North America and in other cultures have shown that empathy increases prosocial behavior (Batson, 1998; Hoffman, 2000). Research has also identified some of the factors that tend to encourage empathy (Miller, Kozu, & Davis, 2001). We are more likely to feel empathy for someone we view as similar to us. We are also more likely to feel empathy for a person whose plight results from uncontrollable or unpredictable factors such as illness or an accident rather than laziness or poor judgment. Finally, empathy can be increased by a focus on the feelings of the person in need, rather than on the objective facts of the situation. For example, in one study, college students learned of the plight of Carol, a student who had broken both legs in a car accident and was seriously behind in her schoolwork (Toi & Batson, 1982). After listening to a tape-recorded interview with Carol, each participant was asked if she

Table 12–3

Comparing Empathy and Personal Distress

	Emotions	Motivation
Empathy	Compassion, sympathy	To reduce own distress
Personal distress	Anxiety, upset, disturbed	To reduce other's distress

would be willing to help Carol. The experimenter manipulated empathy by varying the instructions given to the subjects. In a high-empathy condition, the subjects were told, "Try to take the perspective of the person interviewed, imagining how she feels about what has happened and how it has affected her life." In a low-empathy condition, the subjects were told, "Try to be as objective as possible, paying careful attention to all the information presented. . . . Try not to concern yourself with how the person interviewed feels about what happened."

As expected, the people in the high-empathy condition experienced significantly greater empathy, as reflected in self-ratings of feeling sympathetic, compassionate, and "moved" by Carol's story. Also as predicted, people in the high-empathy condition were significantly more likely to volunteer to help Carol than those in the low-empathy condition, even when it would have been easy to avoid helping. Help was offered by 71 percent of the subjects in the high-empathy condition compared to only 33 percent in the low-empathy condition. Taking the perspective of someone in distress can increase empathy and result in greater helpfulness.

A controversy currently exists, however, about how to interpret studies showing this empathy-helping link. One view is that instructions emphasizing empathy increase altruistic motivation to help (Batson, 1998). But contrasting explanations are also possible. It has been suggested, for example, that when experimenters give instructions designed to enhance empathy, they may actually increase not only the subject's concern for the victim but also the subject's own personal feelings of sadness, depression, or distress (e.g., Maner et at., 2002). According to this interpretation, helping based on empathy is not entirely altruistic because the helper's goal is to improve his or her own mood.

As this continuing controversy suggests, it is often difficult to sort out the motives that lead one person to help another. Our behavior often has multiple causes. However, these theoretical debates should not diminish our admiration for individuals who risk their own safety in courageous acts of helping. The earthquake victims who are rescued from a collapsed building care little about the motives of the volunteers who take them to safety and consider the rescuers heroes regardless of whether their help was motivated by empathy or personal distress.

Personality Characteristics

Efforts to identify a single personality profile of the "helpful person" have not been very successful. Rather, it appears that particular personality traits and abilities dispose people to help in specific types of situations (Knight, Johnson, Carlo, & Eisenberg, 1994). For instance, one study found that adults with a high need for approval were more likely to donate money to charity than were individuals low in need for social approval, but only when other people were watching them (Satow, 1975). Presumably, people high in a need for approval are motivated by a desire to win praise from others and so act more prosocially only when their good deeds are likely to be noticed.

The Research Highlight for this chapter presents research on whether political liberals differ from political conservatives in their willingness to assist those in need. The three case studies described illustrate the complex ways in which personality affects helping by considering the experiences of Good Samaritans, blood donors, and the rescuers of Jews in Nazi Europe.

Good Samaritans. What personal qualities lead a person to intervene in a potentially dangerous emergency? Consider this true story: As a young man drove by a dance hall, he noticed a man assaulting a young woman. This is how he described the event and his intervention:

> I went over there and I grabbed the dude and shoved him over and I said lay off the chick. So me and him started going at it. I told him to get out of here, man, look at her, man, the girl's mouth's all bleeding, she got her teeth knocked out, she got a handful of hair pulled out. Everybody was just standing around. (Quoted in Huston, Ruggiero, Conner, & Geis, 1981, p. 17)

BLEEDING-HEART LIBERALS AND HEARTLESS CONSERVATIVES

In the United States, popular opinion often depicts Democrats and political liberals as "bleeding hearts" who are eager to spend government money to help the unfortunate. In contrast, Republicans and political conservatives are stereotyped as heartless tightwads who are unwilling to support programs to help those in need. Research drawing on attribution theory has begun to investigate these stereotypes.

A recent experiment assessed people's willingness to recommend financial assistance for needy individuals who were responsible or not responsible for their plight (Farwell & Weiner, 2000). Participants were asked to imagine that they were on the board of directors of a charitable organization. They read descriptions of individuals who suffered from various problems for reasons that contrasted high versus low personal control or responsibility. For instance, in an unemployment vignette, the person lost a job because of poor work habits or because the employer went out of business. In an obesity vignette, the person was obese because of poor diet and lack of exercise or because of a thyroid disorder. After reading each vignette, the participants indicated how much assistance they personally would recommend for the potential recipient. In addition, the participants indicated their own political views on a liberal to conservative continuum. Consistent with attribution theory, needy individuals who had no control over their plight were awarded substantially more money than those who had caused their own problems. Conservative and liberal participants did not differ in how much they allocated to those deserving individuals who had not created their problems. However, liberals allocated significantly more than did conservatives to those who had caused their own difficulties. In this way, liberals lived up to the stereotype of being more generous toward the needy.

To assess stereotypes of liberals and conservatives, participants in this study were also asked to indicate how much money they thought a politically conservative classmate and a politically liberal classmate would allocate in each case. Consistent with the bleeding-heart stereotype, both liberals and conservatives thought that liberals would be more generous than conservatives, especially toward those who had caused their own plight. Compared to what liberal participants had actually allocated, everyone tended to overestimate the generosity of liberals. This effect was strongest among conservative participants, who viewed liberals as particularly generous toward those who suffered as a result of their own actions. At the same time, everyone tended to underestimate the generosity of conservatives.

Another study of political views and helping studied reactions to victims of a natural disaster. In 1993, the American Midwest was ravaged by severe floods. Would public compassion and willingness to support government assistance for individuals and communities devastated by floods be influenced by political ideology? A representative survey of more than 1,000 adults investigated this question (Skitka, 1999). In general, people were more supportive of using federal funds to provide such immediate humanitarian aid as food and shelter and less supportive of using public money to assist in rebuilding or relocating homes and towns. Several differences were found between political liberals and political conservatives. Conservatives were less willing than were liberals to offer all types of aid. Further, conservatives tended to hold individuals and communities more responsible than did liberals for avoiding potential disaster by building flood barriers or buying flood insurance. A further difference emerged in reactions to victims who had taken precautions and to victims who had not taken precautions. Conservatives tended to limit their aid to those who had taken precautions (and so might be seen as more deserving); liberals were more likely to provide humanitarian aid to everyone, even to those who had done nothing to prevent the problem.

Before the police arrived, the men exchanged more blows, one of which broke the intervener's jaw. What motivated this man and motivates other Good Samaritans to endanger their own welfare to help a stranger?

To find out, Huston et al. (1981) conducted in-depth interviews of 32 people who had intervened in dangerous crime episodes such as bank holdups, armed robberies, and street muggings. The responses of these Good Samaritans were compared with those of a group of noninterveners who were matched for age, sex, education, and ethnic background. Given the dangerous situations involved, it is perhaps not surprising that the Good Samaritans were significantly taller, heavier, and better trained to cope with emergencies than were the noninterveners. All but one of the interveners were men, the exception being a woman who rescued her 83-year-old neighbor from a knife-wielding attacker. The Good Samaritans were more likely than were the noninterveners to describe themselves as strong, aggressive, and principled. Also, they had more lifesaving, medical, or police training. Often these interveners were not motivated primarily by humanitarian concern for the victim but acted from a sense of their own competence and responsibility, based on their training and physical strength.

The personal qualities that lead someone to stop a crime or mugging may be quite different from those that lead someone to donate money to charity or to help a stranger who collapses from a heart attack. Whether a potential helper intervenes depends on the match between the person's abilities, values, and motives and the requirements of the particular situation.

Blood Donors. Further insights into personality and helpfulness come from studies of individuals who regularly donate their services. Many people have never given blood or have done so only rarely. But a helpful minority donate blood frequently, perhaps every 2 or 3 months. How can we explain their persistent helpfulness? Research by Jane Piliavin and Peter Callero (1991) offers some answers.

Piliavin and Callero (1991) found that blood donors often knew a family member or friend who had donated blood and served as a positive model. This modeling enabled donors to overcome the reluctance many people have to give blood for the first time. Over time, committed blood donors gradually develop an internal motivation to give blood: They donate because they think they should, not because they have been asked to give blood. In addition, committed donors overcome or "neutralize" the fear of giving blood. Repeat blood donors come to view giving blood as a meaningful activity that enhances their self-concept. So, for

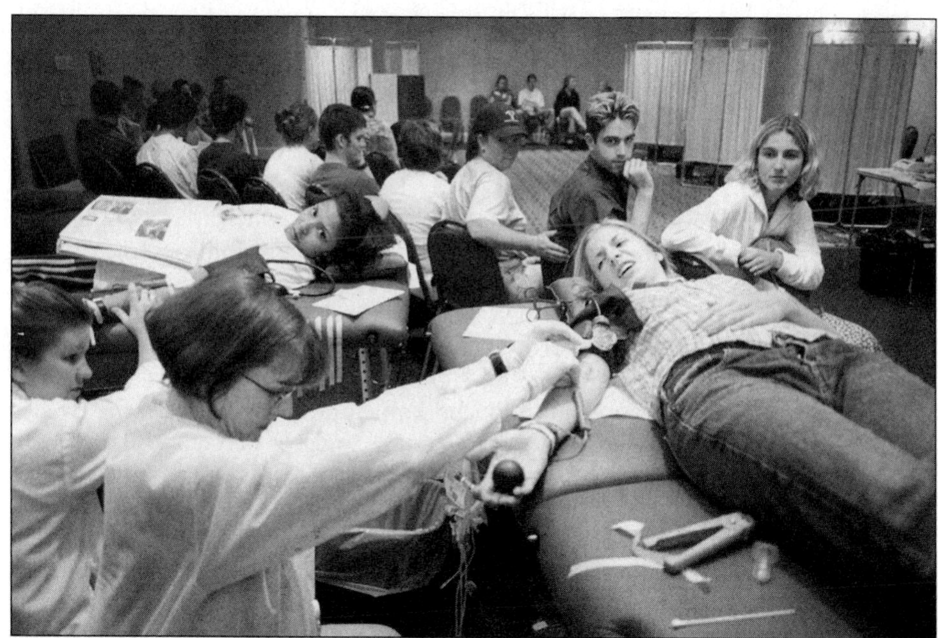

Some people become regular blood donors. For them, giving blood may become an expression of their personal identity.

example, repeat donors are more likely than others to agree that "blood donation is an important part of who I am" and that "for me, being a blood donor means more than just donating blood." In other words, the act of giving blood becomes a personal statement about the kind of people repeat donors are—a part of their personal identity. More generally, the development of an identity as a person who engages in a particular type of prosocial work, whether as a blood donor, a volunteer for the American Cancer Society, or a Big Brother, may be an important factor in maintaining helpfulness over time (Grube & Piliavin, 2000).

Rescuers of Jews in Nazi Europe. During World War II, Hitler's government and others systematically killed millions of Jews—a tragedy now known as the Holocaust. For many, the Holocaust symbolizes the worst aspects of human nature, not only in the brutal acts of murder and genocide committed by the Nazis but also in the complacency and inaction of the international community. Yet the Holocaust also provides examples of great altruism in the stories of individuals who risked their lives to shelter Jews from death.

In the summer of 1942, 12-year-old Samuel Oliner and his family were forced to live in the squalid, walled-in Bobowa ghetto in Poland. One day, Samuel's entire family was rounded up and shoved into trucks. Samuel's stepmother, hoping that the boy might escape from certain death, urged him to run and hide. Once outside the ghetto, he made his way to the home of a nearby peasant woman named Balwina, a casual acquaintance of his father. Despite grave danger to herself and her family, Balwina sheltered the Jewish boy, taught him ways to pass for Christian, and later arranged for him to work as a hired hand on a farm some miles away. Samuel's family was murdered, but the boy survived because of the brave and altruistic actions of a Christian woman he barely knew.

Samuel Oliner ultimately moved to the United States, became a professor of sociology, and undertook a detailed study of "rescuers" who had saved the lives of Jews in Nazi Europe. The research team conducted in-depth interviews with 406 rescuers from various European countries and a matched sample of 126 nonrescuers who were similar in sex, education, and geographic area during the war (Oliner & Oliner, 1988). The experiences of these rescuers illustrate several general concepts discussed in this chapter. Many rescuers emphasized the importance of social norms they had learned from their family, community, or religious group, such as the responsibility to help those in need and the religious injunction to "love thy neighbor." Others were motivated by empathy and compassion. In describing how she cared for a ragged and starving Jewish man who had escaped from a concentration camp, one woman said, "How could one not have helped such a man? . . . He was shivering, poor soul, and I was shivering too, with emotion. I am very sensitive and emotional" (Oliner & Oliner, 1988, p. 189). The capacity to respond to the suffering of others and the belief in moral principles of justice and responsibility enabled rescuers to overcome fear and to put aside serious risks to their own safety.

Gender and Helping

Is one sex more helpful than the other? The answer depends on the type of assistance required (see meta-analysis in Eagly & Crowley, 1986). Consistent with the traditional male role as protector, men are more likely to engage in helping that is defined as heroic—rescuing a drowning person or intervening to save a someone being attacked. Each year since 1904, the Carnegie Hero Fund Commission has recognized citizens who voluntarily and knowingly risk their own life to save another. Of the 8,706 recipients of this award, only 9 percent were women (Becker & Eagly, 2004). Men's greater physical prowess and upper-body strength coupled with sports training may contribute to this sex difference. In more mundane settings, men are also more likely than are women to help a stranger in distress, perhaps by stopping to assist a motorist stranded by the road. Men are especially likely to help when the victim or requester is female, and when there is an audience.

In other ways, however, women and men are equally likely to show extraordinary courage in helping other people. Becker and Eagly (2004) recently reviewed data on various selfless acts by men and women. During the Nazi era in Europe, brave non-Jews sometimes risked their own lives to save Jews from the Nazi Holocaust. In some cases, married couples worked together to rescue Jews. But what about individuals acting alone? In such cases, 63 percent of the rescuers were women. Women are also well represented in other helpful activities. Consider the case of individuals who donate a kidney to save the life of another person. Based on national data, 57 percent of kidney donors were women. A third example is provided by Peace Corps volunteers, individuals who face hardships overseas to serve communities in need of assistance. In the 1960s, more men than women served as volunteers but during the past 20 years, the gender balance has shifted. Currently, close to 60 percent of Peace Corps workers are women.

Another important form of helping involves caregiving. In general, women's social roles tend to emphasize nurturant forms of prosocial behavior, such as caring for children, comforting a friend, or taking an elderly relative to a clinic. Research has found that women are more likely than are men to do personal favors for friends and to provide advice about personal problems (Eagly & Crowley, 1986). Studies have also investigated social support, providing assistance, advice, and emotional encouragement to friends and relations. In general, women are more likely than are men to provide social support to others (Shumaker & Hill, 1991). Finally, women are more likely than men to be the primary caregivers for the family, taking major responsibility for the care of children and also of aging parents (Crawford & Unger, 2000). In other words, although there are many exceptions to this general pattern, men and women tend to specialize in different types of helpful behavior.

BYSTANDER INTERVENTION: HELPING STRANGERS IN NEED

Having reviewed the major theoretical perspectives on helping, we now take a closer look at three different forms of helping. We begin with **bystander intervention**, the technical term for helping a stranger in distress. The "In the News" stories about courageous strangers helping victims in need at the beginning of this chapter illustrate this concept.

Bystander Intervention

Technical term for helping a stranger in distress.

Psychological research into bystander intervention was sparked, not by acts of heroism, but by a highly publicized murder. In 1964, a young woman named Kitty Genovese came home from work late one night. As she neared the front of her apartment building in Kew Gardens, New York, she was viciously attacked and repeatedly stabbed. During a half-hour struggle with the attacker, Kitty repeatedly screamed that she was being stabbed and begged for help. Thirty-eight people living in adjacent houses and apartments later said they had heard her screams. But no one came to her aid or even called the police. The police were not called until 20 minutes after she died; they arrived 2 minutes later. Even then, none of her neighbors came out into the street until an ambulance arrived to take her body away. Why didn't anyone help Kitty Genovese? At the time, many commentators saw the event as a sign of growing apathy and callousness about human suffering. However, social psychologists responded to the tragedy by using scientific methods to study why bystanders sometimes fail to help strangers in distress and also why bystanders sometimes risk their own lives to save strangers in great need. Much of the early research on helping behavior was inspired by the death of Kitty Genovese. This research has documented the importance of several features of the situation, including the presence of other people, the nature of the physical environment, and the pressures of limited time.

The Presence of Others

One of the shocking aspects of the Kitty Genovese murder was that so many people heard the young woman's screams and yet did not even call the police. Many social commentators interpreted this lack of reaction as a sign of widespread moral decay and alienation in society. A very different hypothesis was offered by social psychologists Bibb Latané and John Darley (1970). They proposed that the very presence of so many onlookers may have caused the lack of helping. Those who witnessed the murder may have assumed that others had already called the police and so may have felt little personal responsibility to intervene. Latané and Darley called this the **bystander effect**.

Bystander Effect

The presence of other people makes it less likely that anyone will help a stranger in distress.

To test the idea that the number of witnesses affects helping, Latané and Darley (1970) designed a series of experiments, both in the laboratory and in naturalistic settings. In one experiment, college students taking part in a study overheard an "emergency" next door. They were much more likely to respond if they were alone than if they thought others also knew about the situation. The more people present, the less likely it was that any one individual would actually offer help, and the longer the average delay before help was given.

Many studies have replicated this finding in different settings. For example, Latané and Darley (1970) conducted a field study in the Nu-Way Beverage Center in Suffern, New York. The researchers staged a series of robberies with the help of the salesclerk and two pretend criminals. The robberies were staged when either one or two customers were in the store. When the salesclerk went to the back of the store to check on something, two husky young men entered muttering "They'll never miss this" and walked off with a case of beer. As expected, people who witnessed the crime alone were significantly more likely to report the theft to the clerk than people who were in the store with another customer.

Why does the presence of others inhibit helpfulness? A decision-making analysis suggests several explanations. One is the **diffusion of responsibility** created by the presence of other people. If only one person witnesses a victim in distress, he or she is totally responsible for responding to the situation and will bear all the guilt or blame for nonintervention. But if several people are present, help is possible from several sources. The obligation to help and the potential costs of failing to help are shared. Further, if a person knows that others are present but cannot actually talk to them or see their behavior, as in the Kitty Genovese case, the person may assume that others have already done something to help, such as calling the police.

Diffusion of Responsibility

The presence of other people makes each individual feel less personally responsible.

Experiments support this idea, that it is not simply the number of people present that is crucial, but the lessened feelings of personal responsibility that result from being in a group (Ross, 1971). Research also shows that a group leader—

We are more likely to help in an emergency if we are alone than if others are present. This is called the bystander effect. Here, a single witness to a bike accident rushes to help the injured rider.

presumably the person most responsible for group activities—is much more likely than are other group members to help a victim in distress (Baumeister, Chesner, Senders, & Tice, 1988). It appears that group leaders are less susceptible to the diffusion of responsibility than are other group members.

A second explanation for the bystander effect concerns ambiguity in the interpretation of the situation. Potential helpers are sometimes uncertain if a particular situation is actually an emergency. The behavior of other bystanders can influence how we define a situation and react to it. If others ignore a situation or act as if nothing is happening, we, too, may assume that no emergency exists. The impact of bystanders on interpreting a situation was demonstrated by Latané and Darley (1970). In this experiment, college men sat filling out a questionnaire. After a few minutes, smoke began to enter the room through an air vent. Soon the smoke was so thick that it was difficult to see and to breathe normally. When the subjects were alone, they usually walked around the room to investigate the smoke, and 75 percent reported the smoke to the researcher within 4 minutes. In a condition where the real subject was in a room with two confederates who deliberately ignored the smoke, only 10 percent of the subjects reported the noxious smoke.

A third factor in the bystander effect is **evaluation apprehension**. If we know that other people are watching our behavior, we may get "stage fright." We may worry that we will do something wrong or that others will evaluate our reaction negatively. Subjects in the smoke-filled room may have feared they would look foolish or cowardly by showing concern about the smoke when others were apparently so calm. The desire to avoid the cost of social disapproval can inhibit action. Of course, there are also situations in which evaluation apprehension makes us more likely to help. If we see someone fall down a flight of stairs or have a heart attack, the socially appropriate response is to offer assistance. In such situations, the knowledge that others are watching may actually increase our tendency to help (Schwartz & Gottlieb, 1980).

Evaluation Apprehension

Concern about how others are evaluating us.

Environmental Conditions

The physical setting influences helpfulness. Are you more likely to stop to help a stranded motorist on a pleasant, sunny day or on a cold, rainy one? On a dark street or a well-lighted one? On a country lane or in a big city? Much research has documented the impact on helping of environmental conditions such as weather and city size.

The effects of weather were investigated in two field studies by Cunningham (1979). In one study, pedestrians were approached outdoors and asked to help the researcher by completing a questionnaire. People were significantly more likely to help when the day was sunny and when the temperature was comfortable (relatively warm in winter and relatively cool in summer). In a second study, conducted in a climate-controlled restaurant, Cunningham found that customers left more generous tips when the sun was shining. Other research suggests that people are more likely to help a stranded motorist in sunny rather than in rainy weather (Ahmed, 1979) and during the day rather than at night (Skolnick, 1977). In short, weather makes a difference in helping.

A common stereotype is that city dwellers are unfriendly and unhelpful, whereas small-town residents are cooperative and helpful. Research finds that when it comes to helping strangers in distress, city size is important (Levine, Martinez, Brase, & Sorenson, 1994). Strangers are more likely to be assisted in small towns than in large cities. There is apparently something about being in a small town that encourages helping and, conversely, something about the urban context that reduces the tendency to help. Incidentally, studies show that the size of the hometown in which a person grew up is not related to helping; what matters is the current environmental setting in which the need for help occurs.

Amato (1983) investigated helping in 55 Australian communities, ranging from small villages to major cities. To ensure a diverse sample of prosocial behaviors,

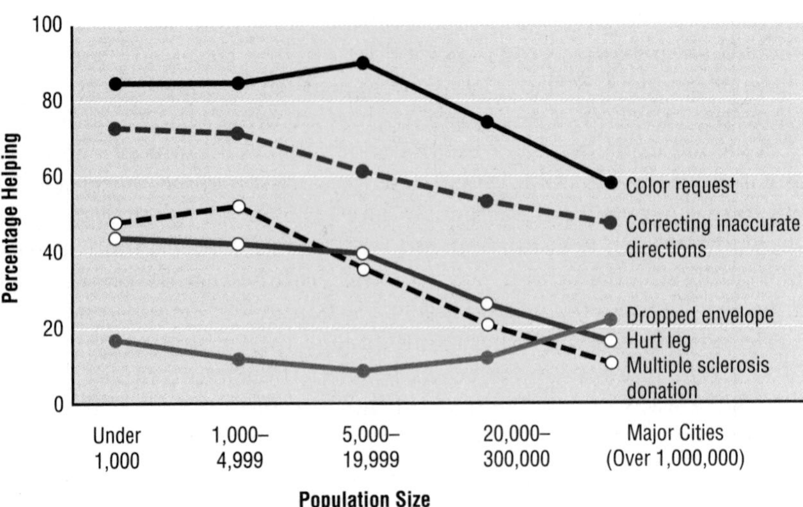

Figure 12–5 Research shows that strangers are more likely to receive help in small towns than in large cities. This figure shows the percentage of times that a stranger received five different kinds of help in cities of various sizes.

Source: P. R. Amato. Helping behavior in urban and rural environments. *Journal of Personality and Social Psychology, 45,* p. 579. Copyright 1983 by the American Psychological Association. Adapted with permission.

five different types of helping were studied: a student asking pedestrians to write down their favorite color as part of a school project, a pedestrian inadvertently dropping an envelope on the sidewalk, a request to donate money to the Multiple Sclerosis Society, a salesclerk giving obviously wrong directions to someone, and a man with a bandaged leg falling to the ground and crying out in pain. The results of this study are presented in Figure 12–5. On four of the five helping measures, the percentage of people who helped was significantly greater in small towns than in larger cities. The one exception to this pattern was the lost envelope, which generally did not elicit helping in this study.

In a more recent study, Levine (2003) tested rates of helpfulness in cities throughout the United States and in more than two dozen other countries. Several different measures of helping were used; researchers posed as a person who accidentally dropped a pen, a person with a leg brace who dropped papers on the street, and a blind person attempting to cross a busy intersection. Helping was more common in cities with low population density (fewer people per square mile) and with lower rates of violent crime. Topping the list of helpful cities were Rio de Janeiro, Brazil, and San Jose in Costa Rica. In general, people in Spanish- and Portuguese-speaking cities were the most helpful. Least likely to offer aid were people in Kuala Lumpur, Malaysia, and New York City.

In summary, research strongly suggests that helping behavior is related to city size. What should be kept in mind, of course, is that these studies dealt only with help offered to strangers. There is little evidence that city dwellers are any less helpful than small-town people when it comes to aiding friends and relatives. Many explanations for the less helpful behaviors of city dwellers toward strangers have been offered. These include the anonymity of urban life; the fear of crime in big cities; the overload experienced by city dwellers, who are constantly bombarded by stimuli, including other people; and possible feelings of helplessness from dealing with unresponsive urban bureaucracies. Researchers don't yet know which explanation is most important.

Time Pressures

Sometimes people feel that they are too hurried to help. A clear demonstration of this effect comes from an experiment by Darley and Batson (1973). As part of this study, individual male students were asked to walk to another building, where they were to give a short talk. Some were told to take their time, that the talk would not begin for several minutes. Others were told to hurry because they were already late and the researcher was waiting. As the subject went from one building to the other building, he encountered a shabbily dressed man slumped in a doorway, coughing and groaning. The question of interest was whether the subject would offer assistance.

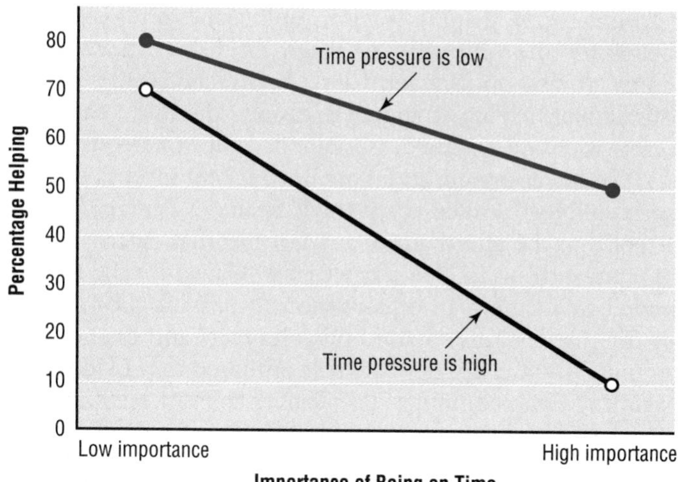

Figure 12–6 Time pressures can create conflicts: Should we help a stranger in distress or keep an important appointment? In this study, researchers varied both time pressure and the importance of being on time. This figure shows the percentage of subjects in each condition who offered to help a person in distress. Students in a hurry were less likely to help, especially when it was important to the experimenter that they be on time.

Source: Data from Batson et al. (1978, p. 99).

A further twist to the study was that all participants were students studying religion. For some, the assigned topic for the talk was the Bible story of the Good Samaritan, about a person who comes to the aid of a man who lies injured on the roadside, the victim of robbers. Other students were to talk about a topic not relevant to helping, namely, the sorts of jobs theology students might pursue after graduation. The results of the study showed that time pressure had a strong impact on helping. In a postexperiment interview, all students recalled seeing the victim. However, only 10 percent of those in a hurry helped, compared to 63 percent of those who were not in a hurry.

Surprisingly, the speech topic made no difference. Students expecting to talk about the Good Samaritan were no more likely to offer assistance than those preparing to talk about jobs. The researchers suggested that time pressure caused some students to overlook the needs of the victim. Another factor may have been a conflict about whom to help—the experimenter or the victim.

The possibility that conflict rather than callousness was at work is supported by a second study using a somewhat similar design (Batson et al., 1978). When the students, all males, arrived for this study, they were sent individually to another building to interact with a computer. Some were told to hurry, and others were not. In addition, some were led to believe that their participation was of vital importance to the researcher, whereas others were told that their data were not essential. As the student walked to the new building, he encountered a male undergraduate slumped on the stairs, coughing and groaning.

Would the subject help this victim? The results presented in Figure 12–6 show that students in a hurry were less likely to help (40 percent) than were those with no time pressures (65 percent). However, this was primarily true of subjects who thought their research participation was essential. When subjects thought the researcher was not counting on them, those in a hurry were nearly as likely to help (70 percent) as those not in a hurry (80 percent). These results are consistent with the cost-benefit model discussed earlier. Apparently, subjects weighed the costs and benefits to both experimenter and victim before arriving at a final course of action.

VOLUNTEERISM: MAKING A COMMITMENT TO HELP

Every Tuesday, Emily goes to a local hospital to assist nurses in the children's unit care for "crack babies," who are suffering painful withdrawal symptoms from drugs used by their mothers during pregnancy. Anthony spent last summer working with a church group to renovate rundown homes in his community. As a trained volunteer at the zoo, Alicia spends one day each week showing schoolchildren the wonders of animal life. What these and millions of other people have in common is that they volunteer their services to charitable causes. There are thousands of volunteer groups today, helping to clean up beaches after oil spills, to provide food and shelter for the homeless, to teach English to new immigrants, to support museums, and so on (Snyder, Clary, & Stukas, 2000).

Unlike the spontaneous acts of helping strangers in distress discussed earlier in this chapter, volunteer activities are planned, sustained, and time-consuming (Snyder & Omoto, 2001). Volunteer organizations are not a recent invention. One of the first volunteer agencies in North America was the Bureau des Pauvres (Office for the Poor), formed in 1688 in the aftermath of a major fire that destroyed the homes and belongings of many citizens in New France (now Canada). The townspeople of Quebec responded by forming an organization to provide food, clothing, housing, and money for the destitute. Staffed by volunteers and financed by donations from the community, the Bureau des Pauvres continued to provide relief to the poor, the elderly, and the disabled until 1700 (Pancer & Pratt, 1999).

Diverse Motives for Volunteering

What motivates these helpful volunteers? There is no single answer. Research has identified at least six functions that volunteerism may serve for individuals (Clary et al., 1998; Snyder, Clary, & Stukas, 2000). These are summarized in Table 12–4. Many volunteers emphasize such personal values as compassion for others, a desire to help the less fortunate, or a concern for a particular group or community. When asked why they do volunteer work related to AIDS, volunteers often mentioned their "humanitarian obligation to help others" and their concern "to help members of the gay community" (Snyder & Omoto, 1992). A second function of volunteering can be to gain greater understanding—to learn about a particular social cause, to explore personal strengths, to develop new skills, and to learn to work with a variety of people. Some AIDS volunteers indicated a desire to learn how people cope with AIDS. A third motive for volunteering can be social, reflecting a desire to be with friends, to engage in an activity that significant others value, or to gain social approval. A fourth motive may concern career development. Volunteering can help individuals to explore career options, to make potential work contacts, and to add a socially valued activity to their resume. Volunteering can also serve a fifth, self-protective function. Volunteer activities may help a person to escape from personal troubles, to feel less lonely, or to reduce feelings of guilt about being more fortunate than others. A final function concerns self-enhancement. Volunteering may help a person to feel needed or important, may enhance self-esteem, or may foster personal growth. AIDS volunteers emphasized that they were able "to gain experience dealing with emotionally difficult topics" and "to feel better about myself" (Snyder & Omoto, 1992). Religion can also be a factor in volunteering. Religiously committed individuals, those who rate religion as very important in their lives or belong to

Table 12–4

Volunteering Can Serve Many Functions

Values	Volunteering enables a person to express such personal values as compassion and concern for the less fortunate.
Understanding	Volunteering enables a person to gain new knowledge, skills, and experiences.
Social	Volunteering is a way to engage in an activity that others value, to gain social approval, and to strengthen social relationships.
Career	Volunteering provides opportunities to advance job or career goals.
Self-protection	Volunteering helps volunteers set aside their own problems and avoid feeling guilt for their own good fortune.
Self-enhancement	Volunteering provides opportunities for personal growth and enhanced self-esteem.

These volunteers at the Lunch Box, a soup kitchen in Poughkeepsie, New York, are preparing Thanksgiving meals to be delivered to homebound individuals in need. Each year, millions of people volunteer their time and services to help others in need.

religious organizations, are more likely to volunteer to help those in need and report donating a larger percentage of their incomes to charity (Hansen, Vandenberg, & Patterson, 1995; Putnam, 2000).

As people move through the life course, their motives for volunteering may change (Omoto, Snyder, & Martino, 2000). Among adolescents and younger adults, social reasons may be particularly important. Among older adults, the value of community service may become more important, along with a desire to feel productive and needed.

The diverse motives for volunteering help to explain why some individuals continue to volunteer for a long time and others do not. Research finds that volunteers are most likely to continue their involvement when the benefits they obtain from volunteering match their motives (Clary et al., 1998). For example, a high school student who wants to become a doctor might do volunteer work at a hospital to gain useful experience. Her commitment to this activity will be greater if she feels that her time is well spent, that she is learning how to interact skillfully with patients and is meeting medical personnel who encourage her career goals. In contrast, someone who moves to a new city and volunteers at the local hospital in hopes of meeting people and making friends may drop out if these social goals aren't met.

A longitudinal study of AIDS volunteers examined factors associated with continued commitment (Omoto & Snyder, 1995). People's initial reasons for volunteering affected how long they continued to serve. Those individuals who gave relatively self-focused reasons for helping, such as self-enhancement or understanding, were more likely to have continued 2 years later. The researchers believed that these somewhat "selfish" desires to feel good about oneself and to learn about AIDS may have helped to sustain commitment over time. In contrast, other-focused motives may provide the impetus to volunteer initially but may not sustain volunteers once the personal costs of volunteering become clear. Indeed, individuals who volunteer to help persons with a socially stigmatized disease such as AIDS may be exposed to special costs. In addition to the time that volunteering requires, those who quit being AIDS volunteers were more likely to say that they felt embarrassed to do work related to AIDS. Experiences of stigmatization led some AIDS volunteers to experience burnout and hastened their decision to quit (Omoto & Snyder, 2002).

In summary, the reasons for volunteering are complex and often combine both altruism and self-interest. Wanting to help other people and expressing deeply held values are important reasons to volunteer. So, too, is the opportunity to gain new skills, to meet new people, and to feel good about ourselves.

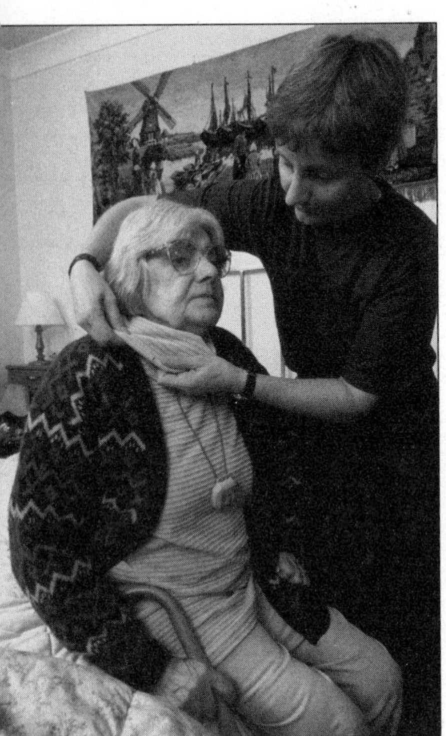

Family members often help and care for each other. Here, a woman helps her aged mother to get dressed.

CAREGIVING: HELPING FAMILY AND FRIENDS

We have seen that people can be remarkably helpful to strangers in need, intervening to offer aid when they witness a crisis and volunteering their time to service organizations. Nonetheless, most of the help that we give and receive occurs in the context of our close relationships with family, friends, and coworkers. When young adults were asked to describe recent times when they had helped another person, most of their help had been given to friends and relatives (Amato, 1990). Only 10 percent of the helping episodes concerned a total stranger. Assistance rendered to strangers was usually casual and spontaneous—giving someone directions, helping a person pick up dropped packages, or offering a seat to someone on a bus. In contrast, much of the help offered to friends and family was planned, such as helping a friend move into a new apartment or visiting a sick relative.

Even young children show the capacity to be helpful to those they know. One study observed children ages 3 to 5 at play in a preschool (Strayer, Wareing, & Rushton, 1979). On average, each child engaged in 15 helpful acts per hour, ranging from giving a toy to another child to comforting an upset friend or helping a teacher. Research also finds that children who share with, help, and comfort others are more popular with their peers (Eisenberg & Fabes, 1998).

The caregiving that occurs among friends and relatives is influenced by gender. In earlier times, the necessity of breast-feeding and other biological factors undoubtedly shaped women's nurturing role toward infants. Currently, social roles continue to cast women as the nurturers and caregivers (Crawford & Unger, 2000; Gerstel & Gallagher, 2001). In modern societies, women continue to be the main caregivers. Taylor (2002) estimated that overall, about 79 percent of caregiving is provided by mothers, daughters, and wives. In marriage, wives are typically defined as responsible for the emotional well-being of the couple. Women are also in charge of what has been called "kin work," the maintenance of ties with relatives through visits, letters, phone calls, presents, and social gatherings (di Leonardo, 2001).

Later in life, middle-aged women may find themselves caring not only for their children but also for their aging parents. In a U.S. national survey, daughters were three times more likely than sons to be the primary caregiver for an aging adult (Stephens & Franks, 1999). Care for aging family members may include running errands, helping with meals or bathing, or taking an older relative into one's home. In some cases, grandmothers are involved in caring for their grandchildren. It is common for wives to nurse husbands through the physical decline of old age, not only because husbands tend on average to be older but also because men's average life expectancy is shorter. Women are also more likely than men to maintain close same-sex friendships throughout life and often exchange help and support with their friends. Many women have mixed reactions to these caregiving activities. At its best, taking care of a loved one can be a source of pleasure, pride, and satisfaction, and may contribute to the health of the caregiver (Brown, Nesse, Vionokur, & Smith, 2003). But caregiving can also be a stressful burden (Stephens & Franks, 1999).

Of course, this description of women's major role as caregiver is not meant to diminish the many ways that men may also care for their families, not only through financial support but also by giving direct care and assistance to children, partners, and aging relatives (Kramer & Thompson, 2002). Nonetheless, there continues to be a general pattern of much greater caregiving by women.

SEEKING AND RECEIVING HELP

We have focused on the act of giving help to others. It is also important to understand why people are sometimes reluctant to seek the help they need and why reactions to being helped are sometimes negative. Sometimes we eagerly seek help. The novice swimmer floundering in the surf may call out for aid. At other times, however, we resist asking for help. Even though perilously close to bankruptcy, a young man may resist turning to his parents for help. To understand help-seeking, we need to consider not only the possible benefits of asking for aid but also the psychological barriers that may inhibit help-seeking (Vogel & Wester, 2003). Reactions to receiving help are also varied. A soldier may come to like and respect a particularly helpful platoon buddy. In contrast, when aunt Jenna offers to help her 5-year-old nephew get dressed, the boy may indignantly insist he would rather do it himself. An unemployed worker may be hesitant to seek welfare and, once receiving benefits, may react toward social workers with veiled hostility rather than warmth. Our feelings about seeking and receiving assistance can be quite varied. Several social psychological theories help to explain these mixed reactions.

Attribution Theory: Threats to Self-Esteem

According to attribution theory, people are motivated to understand why they need help and why others are offering to help them. If people can attribute their need to external or uncontrollable forces rather than to personal inadequacies, they will be able to maintain positive self-esteem. Several studies have found that people are more likely to seek help when they believe their problem is caused by a difficult situation than when they think the cause is a personal deficiency (Fisher, Nadler, & Whitcher-Alagna, 1982).

Attributions about the motives of those providing help are also important (Ames, Flyn, & Weber, 2004). If we perceive that people are helping us because they genuinely care about us and our welfare, we may get an ego boost. On the other hand, if accepting aid implies that we are incompetent, unsuccessful, or dependent, it may threaten our self-esteem (Fisher et al., 1982). This possibility was demonstrated by Graham and Barker (1990) in a study of attributions for help giving in the classroom. Children ages 5 to 12 were shown videos of classroom interactions between an elementary school teacher and a group of students who were working on math problems. In the film, the teacher circulated around the room. She stopped to gaze at one boy's paper and then moved on without comment. Later, she looked at the work of another boy and leaned down to offer him unsolicited advice: "Let me give you a hint. Don't forget to carry your tens." Later, the subjects rated the ability of the two boys. At all age levels, the children perceived the student who was offered help as lower in ability than the student who did not receive help. Apparently, a teacher's well-intentioned efforts to help may be perceived by the recipient and by observers as a sign of the recipient's incompetence. Threats to self-esteem may deter people from seeking help, even when it is badly needed.

The Norm of Reciprocity and the Costs of Indebtedness

Providing help involves an exchange of resources. As we saw earlier, there is a cultural norm of reciprocity, prescribing that we should help those who have helped us. As a result, help is often most appreciated when it can be reciprocated so that an equitable balance is maintained in the relationship. People are likely to ask for help when they think they will be able to repay the aid in some form (Fisher et al., 1982). People are more likely to appreciate a benefactor if they are able to give something in return for the aid they receive. In our personal relationships with friends and relatives, mutual assistance is typical. Friends offer each other advice, exchange gifts, and volunteer to help each other on a continuing basis. Knowing that we've helped a friend in the past and will have a chance to reciprocate help in the future reduces the costs of asking for help (Wills, 1992).

In contrast, when the exchange of help in a relationship is largely one-way, it leads to indebtedness and can create an imbalance of power in the relationship (Nadler, 1991). For example, young adults who receive financial support from their parents may appreciate the assistance but may also feel that accepting help gives their parents greater rights to influence their lives. In short, lopsided help giving can threaten equity in a relationship and create power imbalances.

Reactance Theory: Loss of Freedom

Reactance Theory

Idea that people react negatively when their freedom is threatened.

Reactance theory also offers insights into the experience of receiving help. According to this theory (Brehm, 1966), people want to maximize their personal freedom of choice. If we perceive that our freedom is threatened, we often react negatively, with annoyance and hostility. This unpleasant psychological state is called "reactance." The prospect of losing freedom may also lead us to reassert our independence. For example, when foreign aid recipients criticize U.S. policies, they may be symbolically proving their independence and thereby reducing feelings of psychological reactance. Similarly, when children adamantly refuse the help offered by their parents, they may be reacting to a perceived threat to their personal autonomy. Research on older adults who receive help from family members with such daily activities as getting dressed, preparing meals, or running errands (Newsom, 1999) often have negative reactions to the assistance they receive. In one study, older adults receiving aid from a spouse frequently reported feeling dependent, weak, or incapable (Newsom, Adams, Rahim, Mowry, & Rogers, 1998). They sometimes felt indebted and wished they could give more in return. Concerns about losing self-respect were also mentioned.

New Ways to Obtain Help: Computers and Self-Help Groups

We have seen that the experience of receiving help is not always positive. There are times when accepting aid can limit our freedom, diminish our power, and lower our self-esteem. An understanding of these processes helps to explain why people sometimes react negatively or ambivalently to help givers, and why people may prefer not to ask for help even when they badly need it. Social psychological factors also explain the popularity of two contemporary sources of help: computers and self-help groups.

Computers offer a unique opportunity to receive help from a machine rather than from a human being. Computer software programs have been developed to teach a variety of subjects, from spelling to chess. These teaching programs offer users help and advice and eliminate the embarrassment of acknowledging errors or problems to another person. The appeal of computer assistance was dramatically illustrated in a study by Karabenick and Knapp (1988). College students performed a complex and difficult task on a computer. Half were told they could receive help from a research assistant, and half were told that they could get help from the computer. The results were clear-cut. In the personal-help condition, the students were reluctant to request assistance; only 36 percent of the subjects asked the research assistant for help. In contrast, in the computer-help condition, 86 percent of the students requested help at least once, and most asked for help more than once. By providing private assistance with no expectation of reciprocity, computers can reduce the psychological costs of receiving help. In addition to specific educational software programs, the Internet is increasingly becoming a source of information and advice for many people. As one example, computers are now widely used for patient education: It is estimated that there are more than 100,000 Web sites devoted to specific diseases (Kalichman, Benotsch, Austin, Luke, & Chauncey, 2003)

In self-help groups, people with a common problem work together to help one another (Medvene, 1992). Examples include groups for pregnant teenagers, victims of child abuse, widowed men and women, and for older returning college students. It is estimated that more than 7 million people in the United States are currently in self-help groups. Self-help groups minimize the costs of receiving help because they are run by the people in need, offer opportunities for reciprocal helping, and foster the knowledge that others have the same problem. The Internet has also made it possible for people to form online support groups for people with similar concerns who may live many miles apart.

Gender and Seeking Help

Stereotypes often depict men as reluctant to seek help or advice. The image of a male driver, hopelessly lost in a new city but unwilling to ask for directions, is typical. Research suggests that there may be some basis for this impression (Addis & Mahalik, 2003). Men are less likely than women to seek professional help from physicians or psychotherapists. Although men are more likely than women to have problems with drug and alcohol abuse, they are less likely than women to seek help for these problems. One interpretation of these findings is that male socialization emphasizes toughness and self-reliance, characteristics that may be seen by men as inconsistent with asking for help. Male athletes, for example, are admired for playing despite pain and injuries, and all men are discouraged from admitting weakness. As Addis and Mahlik (2003) explained, men may be less likely to seek help if their peers emphasize self-reliance and toughness, if they fear social ridicule or rejection for showing weakness, if they are concerned about being seen as abnormal, or if they fear that help-seeking will compromise their independence. Although concerns about the psychological costs of seeking assistance clearly affect both men and women, cultural messages about gender may put stronger pressures on men.

Our analysis of the experience of receiving aid is continued in Chapter 14, where research about the health benefits of receiving social support is presented.

In reading this chapter, you have learned a good deal about helping behavior. You now understand many factors that inhibit people from helping, such as the diffusion of responsibility that comes from being with others. You also know that we can teach people to become more helpful, for instance, by showing children helpful models on TV or by giving adults training in lifesaving techniques such as cardiopulmonary resuscitation (CPR) that make it possible for them to help people in need.

Research shows that people who learn about factors that can discourage helping are more likely to overcome these obstacles. In one study, college students either heard a lecture or saw a film about prosocial behavior and how the bystander effect can inhibit helping (Beaman, Barnes, Klentz, & McQuirk, 1978). Two weeks later, in a seemingly unrelated context, students encountered a person in need of help, a student sprawled on the floor in a hallway. Some students were alone when they encountered the victim; others were with an unresponsive confederate who ignored the victim. In all conditions, the students who had learned about prosocial behavior were significantly more likely to intervene. What effect has learning about prosocial behavior had on you? Will knowledge increase your willingness to help people in distress?

Summary

1. Altruism is helping someone with no expectation of reward or personal benefit. Prosocial behavior includes any act that helps or is designed to help, regardless of the helper's motives.
2. Evolutionary theorists believe that a tendency to help is part of our human evolutionary heritage. In contrast, a sociocultural perspective emphasizes that societies create rules about helping that include social norms of responsibility, reciprocity, and justice.
3. A learning perspective emphasizes that people learn prosocial behaviors and norms by reinforcement and modeling.
4. A decision-making perspective emphasizes the complex cognitive processes that lead to prosocial behavior. The potential helper must perceive that help is needed, take personal responsibility, weigh the costs and benefits, and decide how to intervene.
5. According to attribution theory, people are more helpful to those who seem to suffer through no fault of their own and so deserve to receive help.
6. Characteristics of the helper are important. People are more likely to help when they are in a good mood and feel empathy for the victim. According to the negative-state relief model, people help others in order to improve their own mood or reduce personal distress. Efforts to identify a single personality profile of the "helpful person" have not been very successful.
7. "Bystander intervention" is the technical term for helping a stranger in distress. Research shows that situational factors affect this type of helping. People are less likely to intervene when others are present. There are several explanations for this bystander effect, including a diffusion of responsibility, the influence of other people on how an individual

interprets the situation, and evaluation apprehension. Other situational factors that influence helping are weather, city size, and time pressures.

8. Each year, millions of people volunteer their time and services to charitable causes. Researchers have identified six functions served by volunteering; these concern expression of personal values, gains understanding, the strengthening of social relationships, a career advancement, self-protection, and self-enhancement.
9. Most of the help people give and receive occurs with family, friends, and coworkers. In the family, traditional gender roles often cast women as the primary caregivers. Caregiving can be a source of both satisfaction and stress.
10. Although there are benefits to seeking and receiving help, people are sometimes reluctant to ask for or accept aid. Receiving help can lower our self-esteem, make us feel indebted to others, and threaten our sense of freedom.
11. Knowledge about factors that inhibit helping can enable people to overcome these barriers and act in more prosocial ways.

Key Terms

altruism **373**
bystander intervention **391**
bystander effect **392**
diffusion of responsibility **392**
empathy **386**
evaluation apprehension **393**
norm of social responsibility **376**
norm of reciprocity **376**
norm of social justice **376**
negative-state relief model **385**
prosocial behavior **373**
personal distress **386**
reactance theory **400**

In The News

Terrorism in Spain

On March 11, 2004, as morning commuter trains were winding their way from the suburbs into Madrid, Spain, 10 bombs exploded simultaneously, killing 190 people and wounding 1,900 others. Was this an act of aggression? One would be hard pressed to interpret it otherwise; but consider the context in which the bombings occurred.

Brought about by a faction of Al Qaeda, the bombs were said to be in retaliation against aggression in Iraq, an offense to which Spain had contributed troops. The next week, the Spanish elections occurred, and the sitting government was voted out; a socialist government was voted in, which pledged to withdraw the troops from the Iraqi offensive immediately.

As this news story suggests, violence often begets violence, but the interpretations made—whether this was an initial act of aggression or a retaliatory action in a spiral of aggressive behavior—strongly influences whether the action will be viewed as a first strike or as just a punishment for prior wrongdoings.

Chapter 13

Aggression

When we think of aggression and violence, most of us probably think first of crimes committed by one individual against another. In the United States, more than 16,000 murders occur each year, more than 95,000 rapes, and more than 11 million acts of violence overall—in reported crimes alone (U.S. Department of Justice, 2002). Unreported crimes increase these numbers. For example, the actual number of rapes each year is estimated at more than 683,000. Worldwide, the total number of deaths each year from war, murder, and suicide combined is 1.6 million, including an estimated 520,000 homicides and at least 310,000 casualties from war (Stolberg, 2002).

The United States has the dubious distinction of having the highest murder rate in the world. What accounts for these statistics? Several explanations have been offered. Compared to other countries, the United States has a more uneven distribution of economic resources. When there are many poor people in a country or substantial economic differences among groups within a country, the murder rate is higher. Another explanation is that the United States has a low level of social integration; that is, there are many different ethnic and language groups. Social instability is compounded by one of the highest divorce rates in the world. Such instability and lack of integration breed violence. A third explanation has to do with the age distribution of the population. Any country with a high percentage of population in the 15- to 29-year-old age group, like the United States, will have a higher murder rate.

Exposure to officially sanctioned violence increases the murder rate. If the government of a country engages in "legitimate" violence, such as using the death penalty or engaging in war, the murder rate is higher. Both conditions hold in the United States. Finally, the availability of firearms in the United States should not be ignored as a potential explanation. Because the U.S. Constitution protects the right to bear arms, relatively more people in the United States have guns available to them than do people in any other nation in the world, and sometimes they use them for murdering.

Most violence is committed by the people closest to us—those in our own families, our spouses, and our lovers. Only 44.4 percent of violent crimes are committed by strangers (U.S. Department of Justice, 2002). Each year about 1.6 million American husbands engage in severe violence (hitting with fists or using a gun or knife) against their wives. Similarly, parents commit a startling number of violent acts against their own children.

Focus of This Chapter

One in every 36 college women has experienced forced or unwanted sexual intercourse, which is the legal standard for rape (U.S. Department of Justice, 2000).

Of course, the United States has no corner on violence. Mass genocide, ethnic cleansing, and war may be found throughout the world, and patterns of intimate violence, though lower than those in the United States, are found in many countries as well. What are the origins of this ubiquitous behavior?

ORIGINS OF AGGRESSION

Scientists have long debated the origins of aggression. Freud (1930) assumed that we have an instinct to aggress. From his theory of the death instinct (*thanatos*), he argued that aggression may be turned inward self-destructively or directed outward, toward others. Although Freud recognized that aggression can be controlled, he maintained that it could never be eliminated, because aggression is natural to the human being.

Although most scientists no longer accept the idea that aggression derives from a death instinct, most concur that aggression springs from inherited tendencies that human beings share with many other species (Potegal & Knutson, 1994). Evolutionary biologists have developed the field of sociobiology, drawing on biological bases of behavior. Sociobiologists argue that many aspects of social behavior, including aggression, can be understood in terms of evolution (Buss, 1996; Buss & Kenrick, 1998). Because aggression aids males in obtaining desirable mates and aids females in protecting their young, principles of natural selection should operate over time to favor certain forms of aggression.

Although many social psychologists accept the sociobiological viewpoint (e.g., Buss, 1996; Buss & Kenrick, 1998), others believe that the perspective may shed only limited light on human aggression. Human aggression is more complex and takes different forms from animal aggression, and it often occurs in quite different social contexts that are governed by different social norms. Consequently, although the sociobiological perspective may provide an understanding of the underpinnings of human aggression, it is not, in itself, a sufficient theory to explain aggressive behavior in human beings.

This is not to say, however, that biology plays only a modest role in human aggression (Geen, 1998). Physical aggression is influenced by the male sex hormone testosterone (Dabbs, 1998), and it may also be influenced by other biochemical factors, including the neurotransmitter serotonin. Violence-prone individuals also have different patterns of brain activation (Harmon-Jones & Sigelman, 2001). There appears to be a genetic component in human aggression (Miles & Carey, 1997) and in criminality (DiLala & Gottesman, 1991; Stolberg, 1993), because certain types of aggressive, antisocial behavior clearly run in families (Miles & Carey, 1997). Aggression tends to be quite stable over the life span; relatively unaggressive people tend to stay that way, and highly aggressive individuals remain so into adulthood (Huesmann & Moise, 2000).

Despite the clear significance of the genetic and biochemical underpinnings of aggression, it is also clear that social factors greatly influence the expression of aggression in human beings, to which we now turn.

DEFINITION OF AGGRESSION

Although it might seem that everybody understands what aggression is, there is considerable disagreement about the precise definition (Geen, 1998). The simplest definition of "aggression," and the one favored by those with a learning theory or behaviorist approach, is that it is any behavior that hurts others.

But this definition ignores the intention of the person who does the act, and this factor is critical. If we ignored intent, some actions that are intended to hurt others would not be labeled aggressive because they turned out to be harmless. Suppose an enraged man fires a gun at a business rival, only to discover that the gun is not loaded. The act is harmless, yet we would still want to consider the act aggressive, because the man intended to kill someone.

Thus, we need to distinguish hurtful behavior from hurtful intentions. **Aggression** is defined here as any action that is intended to hurt others. Often it is difficult to know someone's intention, but we will accept this limitation because we can define aggression meaningfully only by including intent.

A second distinction needs to be drawn between **antisocial aggression** and **prosocial aggression**. Normally we think of aggression as bad; but some aggressive acts are good. Many aggressive acts are actually dictated by social norms and are therefore described as prosocial: Acts of law enforcement, appropriate parental discipline, and obeying the orders of commanders in wartime are regarded as necessary. For example, we applaud the police officer who shoots a terrorist who has killed innocent victims and is holding others hostage. Unprovoked criminal acts that hurt others violate social norms and thus are antisocial acts.

Some aggressive acts that fall between prosocial and antisocial might be labeled **sanctioned aggression**. This kind of aggression includes acts that are not required by social norms but that are well within their bounds; they do not violate accepted moral standards. For example, a coach who disciplines a disobedient player by benching him or her is usually thought to be well within his rights. And so is a woman who strikes back at a rapist.

A third useful distinction is between aggressive behavior and aggressive feelings such as **anger**. Our overt behavior does not always reflect our internal feelings. Someone may be quite angry inside but make no overt effort to hurt another person. In considering both the factors that increase anger and the restraints that may prevent it from being translated into aggressive action (Potegal & Knutson, 1994), we must examine two separate questions: What produces aggressive feelings, and what produces aggressive behavior?

The attributions that we make for frustration greatly influence the likelihood of aggression. In this picture, the umpire and the coach have clearly come to different interpretations of the meaning of a frustrating situation and they are nearly ready to come to blows over it.

Aggression

Any action intended to hurt another person.

Antisocial Aggression

Aggressive acts that violate commonly accepted social norms.

Prosocial Aggression

Aggressive acts that support commonly accepted social norms.

Sanctioned Aggression

Aggression that is permissible according to the norms of the individual's social group.

Anger

Aggressive feelings.

Frustration

The blocking or thwarting of goal-directed behavior.

SOURCES OF ANGER

We all experience anger, and virtually everyone at one time or another would like to hurt someone else. Indeed, most people report they feel at least mildly or moderately angry anywhere from several times a week to several times a day (Averill, 1983). What causes anger? Two main factors are discussed here: attacks by others and frustration. As will be seen, the victim's perceptions of the aggressor's motives play a major role in generating anger.

Attack

One of the most common sources of anger is an attack or intrusion by another person. Imagine that you are waiting at a red light, and the driver of the car behind you blows the horn just as the light turns green. Or suppose that you are reading a newspaper and someone unexpectedly pours a glass of water down your neck. In these cases, someone has done something unpleasant to you. Depending on how you react, you will perceive it as an annoyance or as an attack.

People often respond to attack with retaliation, in an "eye for an eye" fashion. This response can produce an escalation of aggression. Gang warfare often starts out with a few insults and ends up in murder. Similarly, domestic violence often breeds more domestic violence. Cases of family violence sometimes involve not one aggressor and one victim, but a pattern of mutual violence between a married couple or between parents and children (Straus, Gelles, & Steinmetz, 1980). Attack provokes retaliation, and the violence escalates.

Frustration

A second major source of anger is **frustration** (Geen, 1998). Frustration results from interfering with or blocking the attainment of a goal. When someone wants to go somewhere, perform some act, or obtain something and is prevented from doing so, that person becomes frustrated. Frustration, in turn, may beget aggression, in part because aggression alleviates the negative emotions (Bushman, Baumeister, & Phillips, 2001).

The behavioral effects of frustration were demonstrated in a classic study by Barker, Dembo, and Lewin (1941). Children were shown a room filled with attractive toys but were not allowed to enter it. They stood outside looking at the toys, wanting to play with them but unable to reach them. After the children had waited for some time, they were allowed to play with the toys. Other children were given the toys without first being prevented from playing with them. The children who had been frustrated smashed the toys on the floor, threw them against the wall, and generally behaved very destructively. The children who had not been frustrated were much quieter and less destructive.

Family life is a major source of frustration. Families argue about housekeeping, sex, money, in-laws, and children, for example. Economic problems produce especially high levels of frustration within families. There is more family conflict and more domestic violence in working-class than in middle-class families, and more in families with unemployed breadwinners and in families with especially large numbers of children (Straus et al., 1980). Of course, many working-class families with large numbers of children and marginal economic security are loving and relatively conflict free. On the average, however, stress leads to greater frustration, and ultimately to more violent incidents.

This effect of frustration is seen in broader perspective in society at large. Economic depressions produce frustration that affects almost everyone. The consequence is that various forms of aggression become more common. For example, before World War II, the economy in the southern United States was heavily dependent on cotton. Hovland and Sears (1940) found that lower cotton prices were associated with more lynchings of African Americans in the South during the years 1882 to 1930. A drop in the price of cotton signified a depressed period economically, which produced frustration and heightened aggressive behavior in the form of lynchings (see also Catalano, Novaco, & McConnell, 1997).

Job-related problems are also among the greatest sources of frustration and anger. In one study of employed women, problems such as conflicts between supervisors' and coworkers' expectations, job dissatisfaction, and perceived underutilization of skills were among the strongest predictors of general hostility levels (Houston & Kelly, 1989).

The well-established relation between hot temperatures and violence may also reflect frustration. Even in the writings of ancient Rome, hot temperatures were noted to increase aggressive behavior (Anderson, Bushman, & Groom, 1997; Rotton & Cohn, 2000). Hot temperatures increase hostile emotions and hostile thoughts toward others (Anderson, 2001). In addition, the irritation and discomfort that accompany hot temperatures may be misattributed to interpersonal tension, which may produce aggression (Anderson, Deuser, & DeNeve, 1995). (As we will see shortly, attributions are central to the occurrence of aggression.) Only at extremely hot temperatures do violence rates actually decrease (Rotton, & Cohn, 2000). Perhaps it just gets too hot!

Some researchers have suspected that frustration has contributed to the recent violence seen on high school and junior high school campuses around the country. A number of the boys who have perpetrated these crimes have been objects of teasing or bullying or otherwise believed themselves to have been mistreated or made fun of by their peers. The anger and frustration generated by these experiences, coupled with easy access to weapons, have erupted into dramatic acts of violence that have shocked the country.

The original frustration/aggression theory suggested that aggression always stems from frustration, and frustration always produces aggression (Dollard et al., 1939). It appears now that neither "always" in these assumptions is correct. Although frustration usually arouses anger, there are circumstances in which it does not; also, increased anger may not always lead to more aggressive behavior. And as we see in this chapter, factors other than frustration can also produce aggressive behavior.

Expectation of Retaliation

Another factor that may escalate the cycle of aggression is the motivation to retaliate. Experimental research shows that men who have been angered and who expect to be able to retaliate are more likely to remember negative information, including negative information unrelated to the initial cause of their anger. In short, people who expect to be able to retaliate may stay angrier longer about a wider variety of things. In contrast, when there is no expectation of retaliation, angered versus nonangered men experienced no differences in recall of negative information (Taylor, 1992). To the extent that anger and the expectation of retaliation keep negative thoughts in consciousness, the likelihood that aggression may beget further aggression is increased.

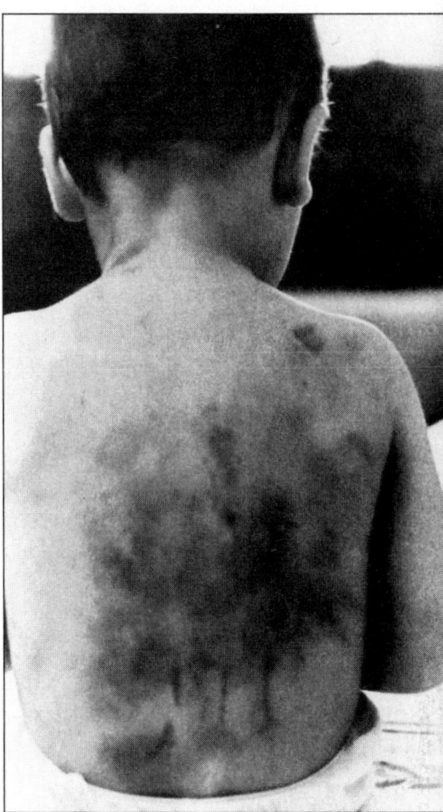

Much violence occurs in families, especially families encountering economic problems. Wives and children especially are victims.

Competition

Although most research on aggression has examined its emotional antecedents, such as anger and frustration, Deutsch (1993) suggested that "affectless aggression"—that is, aggression that is independent of emotional state—may be inadvertently fostered by situations that breed competition. In particular, he suggested that competitive circumstances are often the precursors to destructive patterns of anger, arguments, and aggression, and that when situations are cooperatively structured, aggression is less likely. In a study testing this theory (Anderson & Morrow, 1995), the participants were first induced to think of an ambiguous aggressive situation in competitive terms. Subsequently, when they played the video game "Mario Brothers," those induced to think about the situation competitively, unnecessarily killed more video-game characters than did participants who were induced to think about the ambiguous situation in cooperative terms. Deutsch's argument is an important one because it shows how aggression may be cued by the situation.

Situational cues to aggression may be especially important in eliciting aggression in people who are predisposed to it. For example, men who are characteristically high in aggression—that is, high in trait aggression—appear to have more well-developed cognitive associative networks for aggression than low trait-aggressive individuals. The result is that aggression may be more easily primed by cues in the environment suggestive of aggression (Bushman, 1996).

AGGRESSIVE BEHAVIOR

What is the relationship between anger and aggression? Attack and frustration tend to make people angry (Green, 1998). However, angry people do not always behave aggressively.

Learning to Be Aggressive

A main mechanism that determines human aggressive behavior is past learning (Miles & Carey, 1997). A newborn infant expresses aggressive feelings quite impulsively. Whenever it is the least bit frustrated, whenever it is denied anything it wants, it cries in outrage, flails its arms, and strikes out at anything within range. By the time the individual is an adult, however, these angry impulses and aggressive reactions are under control most of the time. This development is primarily due to learning. We learn habits of behaving aggressively in some situations and suppressing anger in others, of aggressing against some kinds of people (such as siblings) and not others (such as police officers), and of responding to some kinds of frustration and not to others. These habits are crucial to our control of our own aggressive behavior.

Imitation

A form of learning involving thinking, feeling, or behaving in a way that matches the thoughts, feelings, and behaviors of another person.

Imitation. One important mechanism that shapes a child's behavior is **imitation**. All people—children in particular—have a strong tendency to imitate others. A child watches people eat with a fork and tries to do the same. This imitation extends to virtually every kind of behavior, including aggression. A child observes other people being aggressive or controlling their aggression and copies them. Thus, the child's own aggressive behavior is shaped and determined by what he or she observes others doing.

A classic experiment by Albert Bandura and his coworkers (Bandura, Ross, & Ross, 1961) illustrated imitative learning of aggressive behaviors. Children watched an adult play with Tinkertoys and a Bobo doll (a 5-foot-tall inflated plastic doll). In one condition, the adult began by assembling the Tinkertoys for about a minute and then turned his attention to the doll. He approached the doll, punched it, sat on it, hit it with a mallet, tossed it in the air, and kicked it about the room, while shouting such things as "Sock him in the nose," "Hit him down," and "Pow." He continued in this way for 9 minutes, with the child watching. In the other condition, the adult worked quietly with the Tinkertoys and ignored the doll. Some time later, each child was frustrated mildly and then left alone for 20 minutes with a number of toys, including a 3-foot-tall Bobo doll. The children's behavior was rated as shown in Figure 13–1. They tended to imitate many of the actions of the adult. They punched, kicked, and hammered the doll and uttered aggressive comments similar to those expressed by the aggressive adult. The children who had witnessed the adult working quietly on the Tinkertoys played less aggressively.

The key theoretical notion in these experiments is that children learn specific aggressive responses by observing others perform them. Such vicarious learning is likely to increase when the adult's behavior is reinforced and when the situation promotes identification with the adult model. As predicted, in the Bandura experiments, more imitative aggression occurred when (a) the model was rewarded, (b) the model was of the same sex as the child, and (c) the model had had a previous nurturant relationship with the child, such as being a friend or a teacher of the child (Bandura, Ross, & Ross, 1963).

Would the children in this situation, who learned to attack a certain type of doll, also attack the same kind of doll in a different situation—and perhaps a different kind of doll as well? Just how far this imitative learning would extend—Would they also punch their siblings?—is not clear; it is clear, however, that with repeated exposure to aggression, these children might be more likely to react aggressively than was true previously.

Children do not imitate indiscriminately; they imitate some people more than others. The more important, powerful, successful, and liked the other people are, the more the children will imitate them. Also, the people they see most often are the ones they imitate most. Parents usually fit all these criteria, and they are the primary models for a child during the early years.

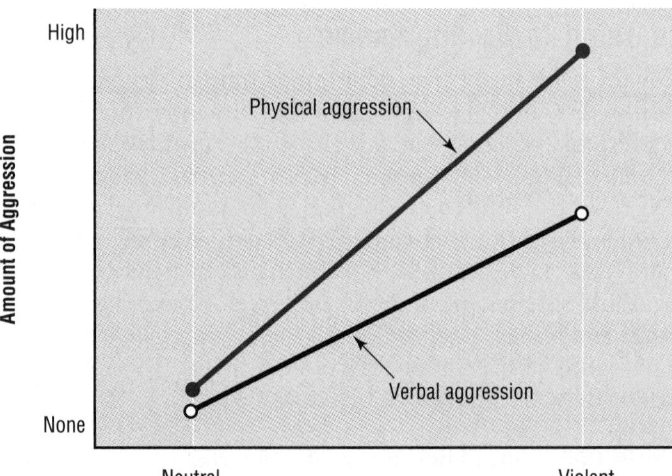

Figure 13–1 **Aggression by Children Witnessing Violent or Neutral Model.**

Note: The entry is the mean amount of physical or verbal aggression children administered to the Bobo dress doll after watching the type of model indicated.

Source: Data from Bandura, Ross, and Ross (1961).

Reinforcement. A second mechanism by which aggression is learned is **reinforcement**. When a particular behavior is rewarded, we are more likely to repeat that behavior in the future; when it is punished, we are less likely to repeat it. For example, a boy comes home in tears after being knocked down by another boy at school. His father chastises him for not hitting the boy back. The next time the boy is attacked, he does fight back, and even though he comes home with a bloody nose, his father praises him. This is one way that children learn the use of retaliatory aggression. In one study, the participants were verbally reinforced ("That's good," "You're doing fine") for shocking a confederate (Geen & Pigg, 1970). Other participants in a control group shocked the confederate but were not verbally reinforced. The reinforced participants gave considerably more intense shocks than did the nonreinforced participants. Aggressive acts are, to a major extent, learned responses, and reinforcement is a major facilitator of aggression.

Reinforcement

The process of learning a response by being rewarded when it is demonstrated.

Because parents are both the major source of reinforcement and the chief object of imitation, a child's future aggressive behavior depends greatly on how the parents treat the child and on how the parents themselves behave. This joint dependence on parents for reinforcement and imitation produces an interesting consequence. Punishing a child for acting aggressively might be considered an effective method of teaching the child not to be aggressive, but it often produces the opposite effect. A child who is punished for fighting does tend to be less aggressive—at home. Home is where the risk of punishment is greatest and therefore where the threat of punishment has the strongest inhibiting effect. Unfortunately, the situation is usually quite different when this child is out of the home. A child who is punished severely for being aggressive at home tends to be more aggressive outside the home (Sears, Whiting, Nowlis, & Sears, 1953).

The explanation for this effect is that the child imitates the parents' aggressive behavior. When he is in a situation in which he has the upper hand, he acts the way his parents do toward him. They are aggressive and so is he. The punishment teaches him not to be aggressive at home, but it also teaches him that aggression is acceptable if he can get away with it. Regardless of what parents hope, children will continue to do what their parents do, as well as what they say.

Attributions

In most cases, for an attack or frustration to produce anger and aggressive behavior, it must be perceived as intended to harm. Our reactions to another person's apparently aggressive behavior often depend more on the motives or intentions behind another person's actions—especially when they are potentially provocative—than on the nature of these actions (Reeder, Kumar, Hesson-McInnis, & Trafimow, 2002). Anger is the most likely reaction when an attack or frustration is perceived as intended by the other person, that is, as being under that person's internal control (Betancourt & Blair, 1992; Weiner, 1982). However, if a victim attributes the attack or frustration to mitigating circumstances—that is, to conditions beyond the frustrator's control—the incident is not as likely to create as much anger. For example, we would expect more anger among unemployed workers if they were fired by a boss who said she did not like them than if they were laid off because an economic recession forced the entire plant to shut down. Indeed, a survey of occasions on which people felt angry showed that anger was most likely in response to an act perceived as voluntary and unjustified (59 percent of the episodes), but very unlikely in responses to an unavoidable accident or event (2 percent of the time; Averill, 1983).

The importance of attributions in generating anger was shown clearly in an experiment by Greenwell and Dengerink (1973). Male college students were placed in a competitive task with a fictitious opponent. Each was allowed to shock the other. They received information, supposedly from the opponent, indicating either (a) that he was intentionally raising the level of his shock settings over trials or (b) that he was deliberately maintaining those shocks at a constant, moderate level. For half the participants within each of these groups, the strength of the shocks received actually did increase; for the others, it remained constant. When the participant was later given a chance to shock his opponent, the opponent's intentions were more important in determining the participants' own shock settings than was the strength of the actual shocks received from this person.

The timing of information about intention or mitigating reasons is also important. If people already understand the mitigating reasons before they are frustrated, they are less likely to get angry and become aggressive. Explaining all the good reasons afterward, while the person is already steaming, is not as likely to reduce the anger (Johnson & Rule, 1986). If the attack or other provocation to anger is very great, however, even prior information about mitigating circumstances or the other person's intentions may have little effect (Zillmann, 1988). Family violence often occurs because intense arguing escalates without any consideration of the reasons for the other person's actions. In these cases, mitigating information may come too late or may be ineffective in the heat of passion. People sometimes really do kill "in the heat of anger," no matter what information they are given.

Apologizing can undercut aggressive behavior. Generally speaking, we judge others less harshly if they apologize for behavior that might otherwise instigate aggression. A study conducted in Japan, in which undergraduates were harmed by another student but then received an apology (or not), revealed that the victims were more likely to refrain from aggression when the perpetrator had apologized. However, when the harm was severe, the effects of the apology were reduced (Ohbuchi, Kameda, & Agarie, 1989).

Attributions and Chronic Aggression

Aggression remains quite stable over time (Olweus, 1979). Children who are aggressive when they begin school tend to remain so throughout their early years of schooling. Aggression in children is important because it predicts such serious outcomes as low academic achievement, dropping out of school in adolescence, juvenile delinquency, and even criminality and psychopathology (Hudley & Graham, 1992).

Attributions play a role in chronic aggressive behavior just as in aggressive incidents. Chronically aggressive children have an attributional bias to perceive others as acting against them with hostile intent, particularly in ambiguous situations (Dodge, 1986; Dodge & Coie, 1987). For example, if a child who is prone to aggression is asked to imagine that a ball thrown by a peer hit him in the head, and no other information is given, that child is more likely to believe that the peer hit him on purpose than is a child not prone to chronic aggression. Aggression-prone children are inclined to attribute hostile intent to others, but this does not mean that they aggress indiscriminately against others. Rather, their aggressive behavior appears to be influenced not only by their own attributional tendencies, but also by the perpetrator of the behavior. In a classroom, for example, two boys may commonly go head-to-head, not only because each is habitually inclined to explain other's aggressive behavior in terms of intention, but also because they have evolved a relationship of this sort with each other (Hubbard, Dodge, Cillessen, Coie, & Schwartz, 2001).

Biased attributions of intention, in turn, evoke retaliatory behavior. Because aggressive children often make inappropriate attributions of intention, they feel justified when they retaliate aggressively. For example, Graham, Hudley, and Williams (1992) found that aggressive minority youths made more attributions of biased intent, reported feeling more anger, and were more likely to endorse aggressive retaliatory behavior than were nonaggressive minority youngsters. Moreover, this pattern of causal attribution occurred in the absence of anger or an instigating incident, a finding suggesting that the attributions are stable and cause subsequent aggression.

Social norms dictate that aggression may be tolerated in certain situations. War and sports are two of those circumstances.

Graham and her colleagues (1992) reasoned that if biased attributions instigate this kind of aggression, then changing attributions would be a good way to intervene with chronically aggressive children. They developed a 12-session intervention designed to train aggressive African American boys to infer nonhostile intent following an ambiguous peer provocation. The intervention taught these students to understand the meaning of intention, to discriminate between intentional and unintentional provocation, and to make attributions to nonhostile intent following ambiguous negative social outcomes. For example, they might be asked to consider how easy it is for a ball thrown by a peer to hit someone in the head accidentally.

Following the 12-session program, the researchers found marked reductions in these children's perceptions of hostile intention and less endorsement of aggressive behavior. Moreover, the boys' classroom teachers regarded them as significantly less aggressive than they had before the intervention. What is important about this finding is that the teachers were not even aware that the boys had been through the intervention. Even more convincing, when children were actually put in the position of experiencing frustration at the hands of a peer, those who had gone through the program were less likely to attribute hostile intention to the experience and to aggress against the peer than were chronically aggressive children who had not gone through the program. The study suggests, then, that changing attributions for unintentional negative outcomes can reduce what would otherwise be seen as justifiable retaliatory aggression (Hudley & Graham, 1992).

Schemas for Aggression

Reinforcement, imitation, and assumptions about others' motives all combine to produce schemas for aggression. As we saw in Chapters 2 and 3, schemas are organized, structured sets of beliefs about some life domain. In the case of aggression, people develop organized interconnected beliefs about the appropriateness of aggression, the circumstances in which it may or should occur, and the way it should be expressed, as, for example, through a temper tantrum versus punching or hitting another person. Through these observational and learning processes, children may come to develop schemas for aggression that, when combined with biological processes (such as physiological arousal), can lead to a high likelihood that they will engage in aggressive behavior.

The likelihood that aggression schemas will develop and lead to aggressive behavior increases with certain environmental risk factors, such as family violence or chronic exposure to neighborhood violence. Another factor that may contribute to the development and maintenance of these schemas for aggression is media portrayals of violence, an issue to which we will turn shortly (Huesmann, Moise, & Podolski, 1997). Once schemas for aggression are in place, aggressive behavior can be self-sustaining, maintained by the stability of the aggression schemas the individual has developed (Huesmann, 1997, 1998; Huesmann & Guerra, 1997).

Schemas for aggression may interact with some of the other factors that facilitate aggression to increase the likelihood of aggressive behavior. For example, one study (Zelli, Dodge, Lochman, & Laird, 1999) found that children who had well-developed schemas for aggression and who also had biased attributions about the meaning of others' behavior were especially likely to be aggressive. Schemas for aggression may vary by culture (Bond, 2004). Some cultures, for example, may have social norms dictating that aggression is a necessary response to a threat to one's honor, whereas other cultures may have quite different schemas for aggression.

Culture and Aggression

Historically, the southern United States has led the rest of the nation in homicide rates. Researchers (Cohen & Nisbett, 1994; Nisbett, 1993) have suggested that greater violence in the South has its roots in the herding economy that developed in the early southern settlements. Throughout the world, in areas where an economy depends on herding sheep, goats, or cattle, herders have gained reputations as people who are willing to use force to protect their property and livelihood, because herds are difficult to patrol and can easily be rustled away.

In such a system where self-protection is important, a "culture of honor" may develop, in which people feel a need to defend their reputations to establish that their property cannot be easily taken. If crossed or trifled with, an individual must let an adversary know in swift and certain terms that such behavior will not be tolerated. This culture of honor is prevalent in the South, according to Nisbett (1993), and in many places, the legal system has developed to enforce this culture of honor. For example, in colonial Louisiana, a wife and her adulterous lover were legally turned over to the husband for punishment, and he had the legal right to kill both of them. Compared to laws in the North, current laws in the South are more liberal with respect to defense of self and home, use of guns, and use of violence for coercion and punishment, such as spousal abuse, corporal punishment, and capital punishment (Cohen, 1996).

Table 13–1

Questions about Violence Used for Self-Protection

	Percentage Agreeing	Percentage Saying They Agree a Great Deal
A man has a right to kill another man in a case of self-defense.		
Non-South	88	57
South	92	70
A man has the right to kill a person to defend his family.		
Non-South	92	67
South	97	80
A man has the right to kill a person to defend his house.		
Non-South	52	18
South	69	56

Source: Data from Blumenthal, Kahn, Andrews, and Head (1972).

The greater violence that marks the South is not an indiscriminate form of violence. Rather, argument-related killings drive the southern homicide rate higher, as opposed to killings related to crimes such as robbery. According to the culture of honor, violence is appropriate only when it is used to protect oneself, to protect one's family, or to respond to affronts (Fischer, 1989). In fact, an analysis of data from surveys shows that southern white men do not endorse violence unconditionally but do endorse violence when it is used for self-protection or to defend their honor (see Table 13–1; Cohen & Nisbett, 1994).

Richard Nisbett and his associates have conducted experimental investigations of the culture of honor. In one study, male college student participants who had grown up in the North or the South were insulted by a confederate, who bumped into the participant and called him an "asshole." Northerners were relatively unaffected by the insult; Southerners were more likely to think their masculine reputation was threatened, were more upset by the incident, showed more physiological reactivity to the insult, and were more likely to engage in aggressive and dominant behavior subsequently (Cohen, Nisbett, Bowdle, & Schwarz, 1996). These findings show how the culture of honor is manifested personally in the ways in which people handle day-to-day insults.

Why have violence and tolerance of it persisted in the South long after the demise of the herding economy that initially gave rise to it? One possible reason is that Southerners are especially likely to endorse violence for the socialization of children. Typically, children in the South, especially boys, are trained to stand up for themselves and to use physical aggression to do so if needed (Cohen & Nisbett, 1994). Spanking is seen as a legitimate punishment for childhood misbehavior. Thus, children come to recognize through social learning and social norms that violence settles certain kinds of conflict. Another factor that may perpetuate the higher incidence of violence in the South is gun ownership. National surveys show that Southerners are more likely than are individuals in other regions of the United States to own guns, and rates of violence are higher in areas that have more firearms (Podell & Archer, 1994). Finally, the higher incidence of violence in the South may come from the fact that the culture of honor is esteemed and valued and is perpetuated in the conventional family, community, and religious institutions of the South; whereas in the North, these very same institutions may mitigate against violence (Cohen, 1998).

A General Model of Aggressive Behavior

As we saw earlier, the experience of anger and frustration is often a prelude to violence. Craig Anderson and his colleagues have proposed a general affective

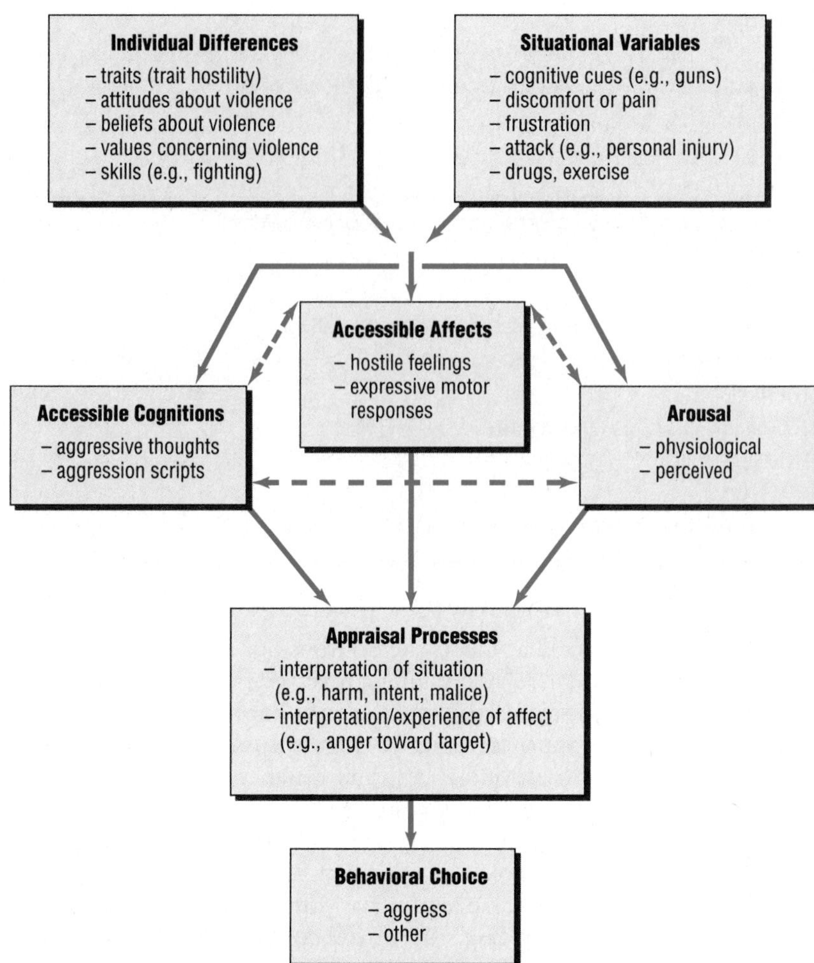

Figure 13–2 **General Affective Aggression Model.**

Source: Lindsay and Anderson (2000).

aggression model, arguing that factors that increase aggression do so by increasing aggressive affect, thoughts, and arousal (Anderson & Bushman, 2002). According to this viewpoint, such factors as media violence, exposure to weapons, the experience of pain, and other environmental cues or feelings may prompt aggressive behavior in part by increasing the accessibility of aggressive thoughts in memory (Anderson & Bushman, 2002). As can be seen in Figure 13–2, the general affective aggression model integrates what is known about the origins of aggression. These origins include individual differences, such as attitudes and personality traits that favor aggressive behavior, cultural factors, such as those just described, and situational factors, such as heat, frustration, or the availability of weapons. These origins, in turn, are argued to make aggressive cognitions, affect, and arousal salient, such that they act as input into the appraisal (or attribution) process during which an individual interprets whether behavior directed against him or her was intended to harm; this interpretation, in turn, leads to the decision whether to aggress against the other person. Aggression will be most likely when cues in the situation combine with aggressive predispositions in an individual.

Instrumental Aggression

Not all aggression is fueled by angry thoughts. Instrumental aggression occurs when a person uses aggression to attain some practical goal by hurting others, even when he or she is not angry. Boxers are paid to injure their opponents and may scarcely know them. Paid killers and paid assassins kill for money, not because of anger. Slave-trading Europeans committed many acts of violence against 17th- and 18th- century Africans not out of anger, but for commercial motives.

Realistic Group Conflict

The theory that antagonism between groups arises from real conflicts of interest.

One particularly important form of instrumental aggression stems from what Le Vine and Campbell (1972) called **realistic group conflict**. Sometimes two groups must compete for the same scarce resources. The two groups may aggress against each other as a way of trying to get those resources; they may or may not be angry at each other. For example, national leaders often take their countries to war with their neighbors not out of anger, but because they want to acquire territory, raw materials, or a better defensive position. In all these cases, aggressive behavior is committed simply as a way to attain other valued goods, and not necessarily because of angry feelings (Schwartz & Struch, 1989). We discussed this form of aggression in more detail in Chapter 6.

Contagious Violence and Deindividuation

One form of imitative aggression that is an important factor in crime and in crowd behavior is contagious violence. The French sociologist Tarde (1903) introduced this idea when he noted that news of a spectacular crime in one community produced imitative crimes. Mob behavior is another example of contagious violence. As was noted in Chapter 10, in crowds, people commit behaviors that they would be much less likely to commit if alone. Zimbardo (1970) described this phenomenon as "deindividuation" and suggested a number of factors that produce it: anonymity, diffused responsibility, the size of the group, the nature of the group's activity, a novel unstructured situation, arousal due to noise, and fatigue. For example, the most extreme violence in warfare is carried out in societies that use such deindividuating devices as masks, face and body paint, and special garments (Watson, 1973). Similarly, early-20th-century white lynch mobs in the United States engaged in more atrocities against black victims when the crowds were especially large and when the perpetrators were anonymous, as by wearing hoods (Mullen, 1986).

The companion process to deindividuation is **dehumanization**. When people are motivated to aggress against an individual, for whatever reason, they may dehumanize the victim by attributing different beliefs and values to the target of their aggression. One study of Israeli adults (Struch & Schwartz, 1989) examined aggression against ultraorthodox Jewish groups. Aggression was measured as opposition to the institutions that served the needs of these groups, support for acts that would be harmful to them, and opposition to personal interaction with them. Aggression was more likely when the respondents perceived an intergroup conflict of interests, that is, when they and the ultraorthodox groups were working at cross-purposes. But aggression was also associated with the perception of the Orthodox Jews as "inhuman" and the degree to which dissimilar values were attributed to them.

Dehumanization

Taking away the personhood or human qualities of another person.

REDUCTION OF AGGRESSIVE BEHAVIOR

Aggressive behavior is a major problem for human societies. Individual crimes and large-scale social violence are harmful both to individual well-being and to the general social fabric. All societies expend much energy to control this tendency toward violence; it is vital to understand how to reduce aggressiveness. However, every solution proves to have its own risks and unintended consequences. Let us look systematically at the possible techniques for reducing aggressive behavior.

Punishment and Retaliation

It seems obvious that the fear of punishment or retaliation will reduce aggressive behavior. We expect people to consider future consequences and to avoid behaving aggressively if punishment seems likely. Consistent with these findings, younger children are more likely than are older children to be victims of domestic violence because they are weaker and less likely to retaliate (Straus et al., 1981).

The threat of punishment or retaliation, however, is not a simple way of reducing aggression. As suggested earlier, children who are frequently punished for being aggressive tend to become more aggressive themselves (Sears, Maccoby, &

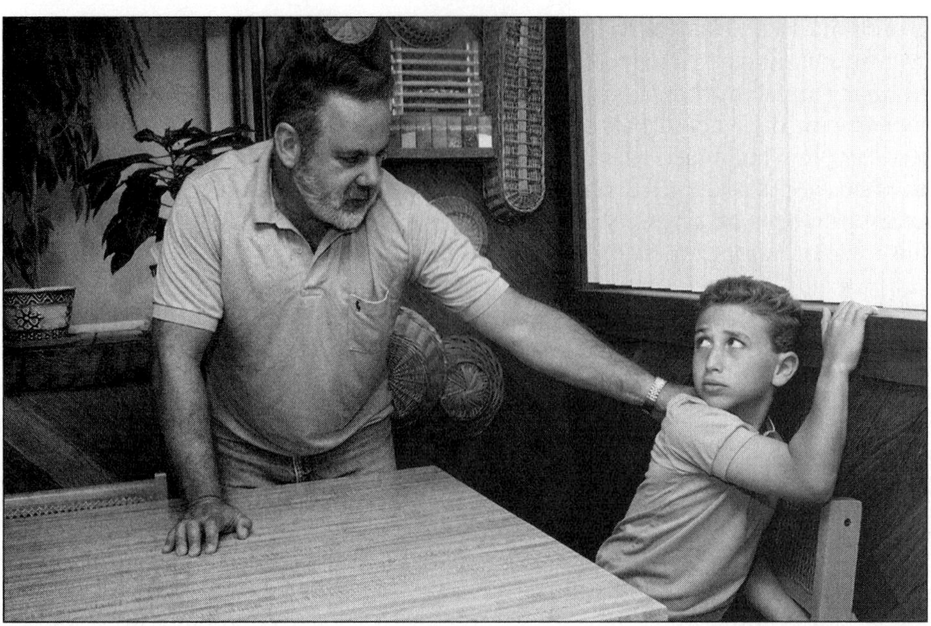

Children who are frequently punished often turn out to be aggressive as adults.

Levin, 1957). When they reach adulthood, they are also especially likely to abuse their spouses. Perhaps they model themselves on an aggressive parent. Perhaps frequent punishment, like any attack, generates anger. In any case, punishment of children's aggressiveness does not result in a reduction of their aggressive behavior.

A second problem is that fear of punishment or retaliation seems to spark counteraggression. People who are attacked have a tendency to retaliate against their attackers, even when retaliation is sure to provoke more attacks (Dengerink, Schnedler, & Covey, 1978). Many lives have been lost on battlefields because national leaders believed that "national honor" demanded counteraggression, even though it almost guaranteed further retaliation and bloodshed.

Even if punishment or threat of retaliation were usually temporarily effective in suppressing direct aggression, it is too expensive to be a widespread solution to the problem. There are too many people in too many places for all to be monitored constantly. As it is, many people who commit serious crimes, such as murder, are never caught and punished. It is impossible to depend on external controls to minimize violence, and people would not want to live in a society with such repressive control of individual behavior.

Reducing Frustration and Attack

Frustration and attack are major sources of anger; therefore, a more effective technique for reducing aggression might be to reduce the potential for them to occur. All societies, to one degree or another, try to ensure some minimal access to the necessities of life, such as food, clothing, shelter, and family. A major reason is to prevent large-scale violent disruptions of daily life by especially frustrated groups. Large-scale hostile political demonstrations resulting from collective frustration are usually met by government attempts to relieve that frustration. Sometimes government response is somewhat successful, as in the New Deal's response to the Great Depression of the 1930s; sometimes it is not, as in France in 1789 and in Russia in 1917.

Some societies, particularly those organized around socialist philosophies, make a particular effort to minimize the frustration of their citizens. Capitalist societies, on the other hand, tend to accept some frustration as part of the price of freedom. The evidence is that socialist societies generally provide more economic equality, sometimes at the expense of overall productivity, individual freedom, and other benefits.

Similarly, most societies make some provision for collective police protection so that people are not continually subject to attack from bandits or other violent persons. This protection helps to reduce the chances for widespread violence in two ways: People are protected, and they are not themselves goaded into retaliation. In the 19th century, life on the frontier in the United States was often lived without benefit of such tight community control over violence. The result was that people were quite vulnerable to attack and sometimes responded with retaliatory vigilantism.

Even nations conscientiously dedicated to the public's well-being cannot eliminate all individual frustration, attack, and instrumental aggression. Not all of us will have as much money as we want when we want it. That is the nature of life. Consequently, while forward-looking societies are wise to try to minimize as much large-scale frustration as they can, they can never completely eliminate it or probably even come close. Other techniques for reducing aggression are necessary.

Learned Inhibitions. One technique of reducing aggression is for people to learn to control their own aggressive behavior. Just as people learn when aggression is desirable or permissible, so, too, must they learn when aggressive behavior should be suppressed. Many factors affect the inhibition of aggression. Generalized learned inhibitions—and the cues that bring those inhibitions into play—are discussed here, along with the factors that cause those inhibitions to be overridden (Geen, 1998).

Distraction. As we mature and gain experience in a variety of situations, we learn strategies for coping with our emotions, including anger. We learn, for example, that if we ruminate on the causes of our anger and think about it continuously, anger tends to increase. However, if we learn to distract ourselves and to think about other things, would anger decrease? Several studies have compared whether ruminating about the source of one's anger or distracting oneself from it is more effective in controlling anger. The results suggest that rumination fairly consistently increases anger; distraction is less likely to feed aggressive behavior, but it is not always successful (Bushman, 2002; Rusting & Nolen-Hoeksema, 1998). Anger is a difficult emotion to dispel.

Aggressive Anxiety. Feeling anxious about the prospect of committing an aggressive act also acts as a deterrent to aggression. People may feel varying degrees of anxiety, depending on the inhibitions they have learned about aggression in general and aggressive acts in particular. Not everyone has equal amounts of **aggression anxiety**, of course. Women have more than men do. Children reared in middle-income homes tend to have more than do children raised in lower income homes. Parents who use reasoning and withdrawal of affection as disciplinary techniques produce children with more aggression anxiety than do parents who use high degrees of physical punishment (Feshbach, 1970). Presumably, reasoning produces more strongly internalized inhibitions about aggression, which are more effective than a fear of punishment by others.

Aggression Anxiety

Anxiety about expressing overt aggression.

We also learn anxiety about expressing aggression in specific situations. All through our lives, we are learning and relearning "the ropes," the norms of our social environments. Students learn not to swear at their professors, and professors learn not to throw things at their students. It is legal to kill animals for sport or food, but not to kill another person or someone's pet. We all possess a great many finely graded distinctions about what is and what is not permissible aggression. These learned inhibitions represent the most potent controls of human violent behavior we have.

Pain Cues. These learned inhibitions are triggered by cues that tell us what kind of a situation we are in—one that calls for expression of aggression or one that calls for inhibition of it. One particularly important set of cues concerns a potential victim's reactions. If a victim shows signs of pain, how will the aggressor react? Will the aggressor have empathy for the victim's suffering and end the attack? Or will the aggressor feel he or she is successfully hurting the victim, as intended, and redouble his or her aggressive efforts?

To test these possibilities, Baron (1971a, 1971b, 1974) conducted a number of studies, varying whether or not an aggressor received cues about the pain experienced by his victim. First, he led participants to believe they were delivering electric shocks to a fellow student during the course of an experiment on learning. He then transmitted the supposed physiological reactions of the shock victim to the participant in the form of a "pain meter." Such pain cues reduced further aggression. Even when the victim was quite dissimilar from the participant and therefore might be difficult to empathize with, pain cues proved to reduce aggression. Indeed, pain cues reduced aggressive behavior in all conditions except when the aggressor was extremely angry; then, the victim's pain cues promoted more aggression. In general, then, signs of a victim's suffering seem to inhibit further aggression, except in cases of extreme anger, when they are perceived as signs of successful hurting.

For such reasons, dehumanization is thought to increase aggression against victims who are far away from or anonymous to their attackers. For example, it may be easier to bomb an enemy from great heights than to attack on the ground at closer, more personal range. When the victim is distant or anonymous, it is easier to be aggressive because the pain cues are absent. Conversely, making the victim more human, so that the attacker empathizes with the person's suffering, tends to reduce aggression.

Disinhibition

A loosening of control over anger after it has been released under socially approved conditions.

Alcohol and Drugs. Inhibitions can be released as well as implemented, as all of us know. Such **disinhibition** can then result in outbursts of anger and aggression. It is sometimes said, "The conscience is soluble in alcohol." Learned inhibitions against expressing aggression may be ignored when one is drinking. Intoxicated offenders commit as many as 60 percent of the murders in the United States, as well as a high proportion of other violent crimes such as rape (including date rape), robbery, assault, domestic violence, and child abuse (Lisak & Roth, 1988; Steele & Southwick, 1985). Interestingly, some research suggests that inexperienced drinkers are more likely to react to intoxication with aggression than are individuals with more drinking experience (Laplace, Chermack, & Taylor, 1994).

Anecdotes and statistics do not isolate the particular effects of alcohol in these complex situations, however. Nor do they prove that alcohol reduces inhibitions against aggression. Belligerent men may be attracted to bars and to arguments, alcohol may stimulate sexual desire, and so on. To test more specifically the effects of alcohol on aggressive behavior, Taylor and Gammon (1975) gave participants either a high dose of alcohol (about three or four stiff drinks for the average participant) or a low dose (about one drink). First, the participants were put in a game situation, rigged so that the participant always won, and were given the opportunity to deliver what they believed was electric shock to their opponent. The participant delivered significantly more shock when he had drunk more alcohol. This is a typical finding: Most studies show that consumption of alcohol generally does increase aggression (Hull & Bond, 1986).

Why does alcohol consumption tend to produce more violence? When sober people are provoked to aggression, they respond to such inhibiting cues as the instigator's intent and potential retaliation, whereas intoxicated participants are less attentive to the potential consequences of their behavior (Zeichner & Pihl, 1979). In a shock study, intoxicated participants who expected their opponent to behave aggressively plunged ahead with retaliatory aggression even when the opponent actually gave the lowest level of shock possible. These participants seemed to be oblivious to the low level of shock actually given by the opponent. Nonintoxicated participants noted the discrepancy between their expectation and the opponent's actual behavior and reduced their own aggressive behavior (Leonard, 1989). In short, alcohol seems to produce a loss of inhibitory control, in part because of a loss of perceptiveness about oneself and others.

Alcohol may also heighten attention and reactions to conditions that typically instigate aggression (Taylor & Sears, 1988). In particular, alcohol tends to

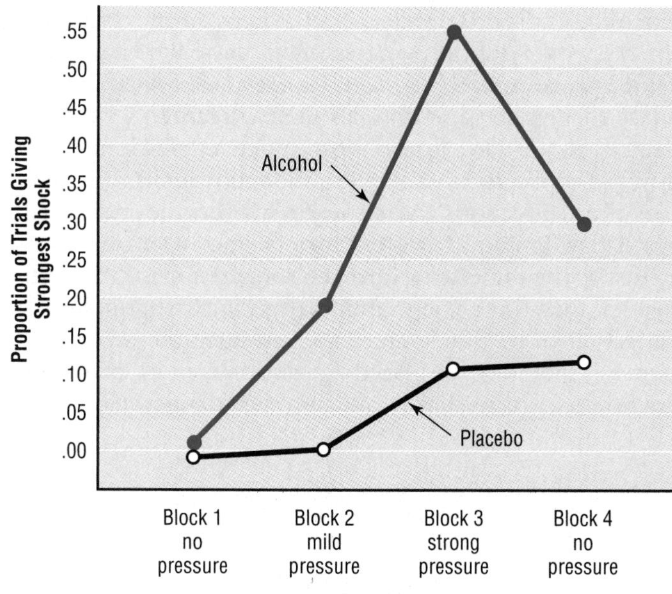

Figure 13–3 The amount of shock administered by participants to a nonaggressive component as influenced by whether they had consumed alcohol and had experienced social pressure to give shock.

Source: Data from Taylor and Sears (1988, p. 241).

increase a person's aggressive responses to such provocations as threat, frustration, and malicious intent. In a shock experiment, intoxicated participants initiated more attacks than did nonintoxicated participants, but only when the opponent was threatening. They did not differ when competing against a nonaggressive opponent (Taylor, Schmutte, Leonard, & Cranston, 1979).

Alcohol also makes people more responsive to social pressure to aggress. Taylor and Sears (1988) repeated their shock experiment using only an opponent who behaved nonaggressively. The participant was not threatened or attacked at all. The study varied how strongly two peer observers attempted to persuade the participant to deliver shock to the opponent; on some trials they tried hard, and on others, they tried a little or not at all. As can be seen in Figure 13–3, alcohol (relative to a placebo ginger ale drink with only the taste of alcohol) increased aggression in response to peer pressure even though the victim was totally innocent and harmless. So alcohol seems both to disinhibit the tendency to aggress generally and to heighten people's response to social pressures to aggress.

What about drugs? Do they reduce or increase aggression? A careful review of the extensive clinical and field research on marijuana use concludes that marijuana does not precipitate violence in the majority of those people who use it chronically or periodically. In fact, marijuana has been shown in experimental studies to reduce aggression (see Taylor, Gammon, & Capasso, 1976). It is possible that some people have such weak inhibitions against aggression that marijuana would trigger their aggressiveness, but the research evidence on this point is too skimpy to allow a firm conclusion. In contrast to marijuana, other drugs—such as PCP ("angel dust"), methamphetamines, and crack cocaine—seem to trigger violent behavior.

Displaced Aggression

What happens to aggressive feelings when, for one reason or another, they cannot be directed at the cause of the anger? We are often frustrated or annoyed by someone but unable to retaliate against that person. The person may be too powerful or not available, or we may be too anxious and inhibited to retaliate. In such situations, we may express aggression in some other way, as in **displaced aggression**—that is, expressing aggression against a substitute target. The child frustrated by her parents may deliberately pour her milk on the dog, or a man whose firm will not promote him may become increasingly angry at ethnic minorities. The individual expresses anger toward a safer target than the actual source of the frustration. The more negative the frustrating experience, the greater displaced aggression is likely to

Displaced Aggression

Expressing aggression against a target other than the original source of attack, usually a safer target.

be (Marcus-Newhall, Pedersen, Carlson, & Miller, 2000). Even small insults, such as a minor provocation, can provoke displaced aggression in those who have previously been the recipients of a provocation (Pederson, Gonxales, & Miller, 2000).

When people do displace their aggression onto an alternate target, what determines who will be selected as the target, and how much aggression will be expressed? The basic principle of displacement is that the more similar a target is to the original source of the frustration, the stronger will be the individual's aggressive impulses toward that target. However, anxiety operates in much the same way as does anger. Just as the impulse to hurt the source of frustration generalizes to other people, so does the anxiety about attacking the source. The more similar a potential target is to this source, the stronger the anxiety felt toward him or her. In general, therefore, displaced aggression is most likely to be directed toward targets who are perceived as weaker and less dangerous.

Catharsis

Catharsis

Idea that by expressing aggression, a person reduces the aggressive drive.

Can pent-up angry feelings be reduced by aggression? When anger is released, the chance of further aggression may be reduced. Freud called this process **catharsis**. In simple language, catharsis involves "letting off steam" or "getting it out of your system." If someone annoys you by honking a car horn at you, you may feel angry. If, at the next traffic light, you find yourself behind that car and honk at it, your level of anger is likely to decrease.

Catharsis can be successful in reducing aggression when an angry person expresses that anger directly against his or her frustrator. In one experiment, a confederate insulted the participants, criticized them for being slow on an experimental task, and expressed doubts about their intellectual abilities. Some of the participants were then given the opportunity to aggress against the confederate, whereas others were not. The results showed that delivering blasts of noise at the confederate reduced a subsequent tendency to aggress (Konecni & Ebbesen, 1976). That is, delivering loud noise to the confederate was cathartic for the participants.

Sometimes frustration leads to displaced aggression, that is, aggressing against a substitute target. This child may have a grievance against her parents or a more powerful sibling, but she is spanking her doll because it can't retaliate.

However, catharsis also has risks and may, in some circumstances, actually increase aggression (Bushman, Baumeister, & Stack, 1999). We all control our anger fairly well most of the time. Once it is released, however, we may relax our inhibitions about expressing hostility in the future. Geen and Quanty (1977) cited the reaction of a man who killed four people: "He said . . . he had a funny feeling in his stomach, but after the first [killing] . . . it was easy" (p. 29). Another risk is that within any given sequence of behavior, aggression seems to escalate rather than to decline. For catharsis to reduce aggression rather than escalate it, the sequence of behavior needs to be interrupted: There must be a break in the action, a change in the victim, or a change in how the aggression is expressed (Goldstein, Davis, & Herman, 1975).

The catharsis hypothesis also dictates that subsequent aggression can be reduced by expressions of aggression other than by direct physical acts against a frustrator, such as displaced aggression, vicarious aggression (that is, aggression against your tormentor actually committed by someone else), or verbal aggression. Although, some studies have found that cathartic effects come from indirect aggression, many more studies have not shown this result.

Social psychologists are now skeptical that expressing anger produces cathartic reduction in aggressive behavior. It does seem to reduce the expression of aggression when the person is angry and is able to express aggression in a fairly direct manner against the person whom he or she perceives as triggering the anger. But studies now suggest that catharsis actually increases rather than decreases aggression (e.g., Bushman, 2002).

Workplace Aggression

On December 26, 2000, Michael McDermott, a 42-year-old employee of the Wakefield, Massachusetts, Edgewater Technology firm shot seven of his coworkers, all of whom died. Five of the victims worked in the accounting department.

According to sources, McDermott was upset because the accounting department was garnishing a portion of his wages, at the request of the Internal Revenue Service.

Incidents like these have gained so much attention in the media that it might seem that the workplace, as a major source of frustration, leads reliably to aggression. In fact, the overwhelming majority of workplace aggressive incidents are committed by members of the public, not by employees, who seldom kill or assault their colleagues. This is not to say that frustration and consequent aggression in the workplace is nonexistent. Usually, though, workplace aggression involves less dramatic behaviors such as shouting or spreading rumors. Perhaps people realize that their chance of losing their jobs is high if their physical aggression is uncontrolled.

Factors that influence workplace aggression are those that influence aggression more generally. In terms of individual factors, both alcohol consumption and a hostile attributional bias can increase the likelihood of an employee becoming aggressive. But organizational factors are important as well. Perceiving that one's work situation is unjust or that one's supervisor is overcontrolling appear to be important workplace factors that increase the likelihood that aggressive incidents may occur. But it may be reassuring to know that despite the publicity these incidents have attracted, the workplace does not appear to be as dangerous an environment as one might assume (LeBlanc and Barling, 2004).

Violence in Schools

For teens the "workplace" is school, and there can be no doubt that school is becoming a more dangerous place to be. As the recent rash of school shootings underscores, teens are caught up in violence, and this problem is receiving increasing attention. In 2001, students between the ages of 12 and 18 were the victims of 161,000 violent crimes on campus (U.S. Department of Justice, 2002). In the 1999 to 2000 school year, 9 percent of elementary and secondary school teachers were threatened, and 4 percent were actually attacked (National Center for Education Statistics, 2002). About one out of every eight students reports that he or she has carried some kind of weapon to school. More than 772, 500 young people are involved in the more than 24,500 active gangs in 3,330 jurisdictions across the United States (Egley & Major, 2004).

Which teens kill? A teen's odds of committing murder are greatly increased if he comes from a criminally violent family, has a history of being abused, belongs to a gang, and abuses drugs or alcohol. In addition, having access to weapons, a history of skipping school and other school-related problems, or a neurological disorder, including epilepsy, mental retardation, or hyperactivity, increases the likelihood of school violence (Sleek, 1998).

School shootings have aroused particular concern among parents, school administrators, and psychologists, in large part because this type of violence seems so unpredictable. The profile of the school shooter varies somewhat from the profile of youngsters most likely to commit murder. Most of the perpetrators have been young white males, often as young as 14 or 15. Most have a history of social problems, although not necessarily ones relating to aggression. In some cases, a pattern of being bullied or taunted or feeling like an outsider has been implicated. Situational factors influence the likelihood of a school shooting as well. For example, the majority of these incidents have occurred in rural or suburban communities, rather than in urban ones, perhaps because students who are unusual or deviant in some way are better able to blend in the urban than in a rural setting (Newman, 2004).

There are as yet no foolproof solutions to the eruption of school violence that we have seen in recent years. However, a technique originally developed by Aronson and Gonzales (1988) to reduce prejudice may be applicable. In this technique, called the "jigsaw classroom," groups of late elementary and middle school students are divided into small groups to work on some lessons together. These groups are formed in such a way as to cut across the natural cliques that evolve along academic, racial, ethnic, and popularity lines. Although the jigsaw method can lead to some initial resentment, over time it appears to give way to greater acceptance, potentially breaking down the destructive clique structure that seems to be one of the roots of school violence. Other intervention efforts have worked toward building stronger ties between the school and the surrounding community and have shown modest success in reducing school violence (Howard, Flora, & Griffin, 1999). Attending to the problem of media violence may be important as well.

Reducing Aggressive Behavior: A Comment

The factors that contribute to aggression demand continued research investigation because of the importance of this issue to society. Government agencies indicate that hate crimes due to religion, race, ethnicity, and sexual orientation ("gay bashing") have received insufficient research attention (Costanzo & Oskamp, 1994). Increasing violence in the schools has terrified administrators, faculty, and students, impeding the realization of educational goals and sometimes turning schools into armed camps (Buckley, 1993). Displacement of aggression onto others, catharsis, the role of alcohol and drugs, and other, yet-to-be-identified influences on the likelihood of violence have not been thoroughly studied (Baron & Richardson, 1994).

Unfortunately, it has become increasingly difficult for scientists to study the causes of aggression (Stone, 1993). Research on potential genetic contributions to violence has been attacked by African American groups on the grounds that such work may be disproportionately targeted on blacks. The animal rights movement has made it difficult to use animals to study the determinants of aggressive behavior. Thus, the future of at least certain kinds of research on aggression is very much an issue (Stone, 1993).

MEDIA VIOLENCE

It is widely assumed that media violence stimulates people to behave aggressively. In 1983, the chief of the California state prisons adopted a policy of not showing "any movie that glorifies sick violence" after he discovered that the movie *The Texas Chainsaw Massacre* had been shown at the men's prison in Chino. As we have seen, however, aggression is a complex behavior. Does watching violent films have an effect on aggressive behavior?

The Surgeon General's Report

Both the public and the politicians are concerned about media violence. The U.S. Congress first held public hearings on TV violence in 1952. Later, the U.S. Surgeon General commissioned a report on the topic, which was published in 1972 by the Surgeon General's Scientific Advisory Committee. After reviewing the available research, the report concluded, rather cautiously:

> [There is] a preliminary and tentative indication of a causal relation between viewing violence on television and aggressive behavior; an indication that any such causal relation operates only on some children (who are predisposed to be aggressive); and an indication that it operates only in some environmental contexts. (Surgeon General's Scientific Advisory Committee, 1972, p. 11)

This report immediately came under harsh attack, partly because some of the members of the committee that prepared it had worked for the television networks. It was believed, therefore, that they could not be disinterested scientific observers (Cater & Strickland, 1975). Most critics argued that the commission had underestimated the effects of media violence.

Ten years later, the National Institute of Mental Health asked a panel of behavioral scientists to evaluate the effects of televised violence. This time, the reviewing committee concluded that "The consensus among most of the research community is that violence on television does lead to aggressive behavior by children and teenagers who watch the programs. . . . A causal link between televised violence and aggressive behavior now seems obvious" (National Institute of Mental Health, 1982, p. 6). A similar report was issued in seven volumes by the Canadian Royal Commission. These reports were supported by many researchers in the field (e.g., Friedrich-Cofer & Huston, 1986; Huesmann, 1982).

There are many theories of how and why media violence affects behavior. For example, learning theory would emphasize that observing aggressive models teaches viewers to behave violently through imitation. A related idea is that children learn entire scripts about aggression from the media. Then events in their later lives prime those memories and generate aggressive behavior (Berkowitz, 1984; Huesmann, 1988). For example, one common media script is that the bad guy provokes the good guy, who retaliates. The child who has learned this script from television might, in later life, be too quick to retaliate because of minor insults (see also Viemero & Paajanen, 1992). Individuals who have a predisposition to be aggressive may be especially affected by such exposure to media violence (Bushman, 1995).

Much violence in the media is rewarded rather than punished, as in the case of the retaliating good guy. Viewing such rewarded violence sends the message that learned inhibitions against aggression should be set aside, so that the individual can act more aggressively. Only the catharsis theory proposes that watching media violence is likely to reduce aggression among viewers, and as we've seen, support for this theory has been meager. What does research actually find about the effects of media violence? We next review three types of research: laboratory experiments, correlational surveys, and **field experiments**.

Field Experiments

A study in which variables are systematically manipulated and measured in a real-life, nonlaboratory setting

Laboratory Experiments

In some of the earliest research on this issue, Leonard Berkowitz (1974) conducted a series of laboratory experiments, typically showing a brief film with violent physical aggression to college students who had been angered and to some who had not been angered. One of the films often used was a 7-minute clip from *The Champion*, a boxing film starring Kirk Douglas. After viewing the film, the participants were given the opportunity to administer shock to a confederate in a shock-learning situation. People who viewed the violent film administered more shocks to the confederate.

Most of these studies were tests of the theory that the cue properties of the situation stimulate learned aggressive responses (Berkowitz, 1974). In this case, anything that associated the participant with the film aggressor, or the confederate with the film victim, would tend to increase aggression. In many respects, this theory was supported (see Berkowitz, 1984, for a review). For example, the participants displayed more aggression when told to identify with the winner of the boxing match than when they were told to identify with a referee; the confederate received more intense shocks when described as a boxer than when described as a speech major; and a confederate named "Kirk" received more shocks than did one named "Bob" after seeing the actor Kirk Douglas play the boxer who was beaten up in the film. When the film presented justified aggression, by presenting the loser of the boxing match in an unfavorable light, more aggression was displayed. Some studies found that the participants had to be frustrated or angered for the violent film to increase their level of aggression (though other studies did not find that prior angering had any effect; see Freedman, 1986).

Whether one explains the media effect as resulting from imitation, priming, activation, or disinhibition, the result is the same: In these laboratory experiments, observing aggression usually increased aggressive behavior.

More recent studies have helped identify how exposure to violence may increase aggressive behavior. For example, Bushman (1998) had participants view

Do the media cause aggression and violence? Research suggests that media portrayals of aggression and violence may have a modest role in increasing aggressive behavior in some people in some circumstances.

either a violent or a nonviolent video and afterward, in an ostensibly unrelated task, asked them to make free associations with words that could have an aggressive or nonaggressive connotation. The participants who had seen the violent video listed more aggressive associations. In a second study, Bushman asked participants exposed to the violent or nonviolent video to engage in a subsequent task of identifying whether particular strings of letters were English words. Half the words were aggressive and half were nonaggressive. The participants who had seen the violent video had faster reaction time to aggressive words. These findings suggest that violent media prime aggression-related material in memory, and that once activated, such links may set the stage for aggressive behavior.

What Do Laboratory Experiments on Media Violence Tell Us? As clear as the implications of these findings may be, it is a leap from such laboratory studies to the real-life situations to which researchers seek to generalize. Are these laboratory findings likely to hold up in real life? The laboratory experiments must be judged, therefore, in terms of their **external validity**, as discussed in Chapter 1.

External Validity

The extent to which results of a study are generalizable to other people and settings.

Certainly there are reasons to question whether the laboratory setting would generalize to the real world. Laboratory exposure to provoking conditions is brief and controlled. It provides little opportunity for retaliation or distraction, for example. Researchers have completed an analysis of these laboratory experiments and compared them with aggression in real-world studies. Overall, the conditions that provoke violence and the characteristics of the people who commit violent acts under those conditions seem to be remarkably similar when laboratory and real-world situations are compared (Anderson & Bushman, 1997). For example, in both laboratory and real-world situations, people are more likely to aggress when they have been provoked, have consumed alcohol, have been exposed to media violence, or have been allowed to aggress anonymously. And consistently, in both laboratory and real-world situations, men commit aggressive acts more than do women, trait aggressiveness is associated with aggressive behavior, and other personality traits associated with aggression similarly hold up across both kinds of settings. The clear implication is that these laboratory investigations of aggression indeed reflect many of the conditions that normally give rise to it in everyday life.

Correlational Surveys

Correlational Research

Measuring two variables and determining whether they are associated.

Other studies have examined aggression using **correlational research**. For example, are the children who watch the most violent television the ones who are the most aggressive? Does viewing violence in childhood produce more aggression in adulthood? The longitudinal study, a particularly important type of correlational survey, would attempt to answer this question by measuring children's television viewing during a specific time period and then assessing their aggressive behavior some years later. Several such studies have been done (Eron, Huesmann, Lefkowitz, & Walder, 1972; Huesmann, Eron, Lefkowitz, & Walder, 1984; Milavsky, Kessler, Stipp, & Rubens, 1982). Overall the correlations between early viewing of violence and later aggressive behavior are modest, but positive (Freedman, 1984; Friedrich-Cofer & Huston, 1986). These correlations can be stable over as long as 22 years. In one study, for example, viewing of TV violence at age 8 predicted a variety of aggressive behaviors at age 30. Moreover, the more frequently youngsters watched TV at age 8, the more serious were the crimes for which those individuals were convicted by age 30 (Eron, 1987).

If children who view violence the most are the most aggressive, the effects of their heavier viewing should accumulate over the years; therefore, the correlation between viewing violence and behaving aggressively should increase with age. Yet, in longitudinal studies, this has generally not been the case: The correlation between viewing violence and behaving aggressively has been about the same at each age level (Freedman, 1984). It is possible to argue that consistently positive, even if very weak, correlations reflect socially significant effects (Eron, 1987; Rosenthal, 1986). But the fact is that the relationship is not a very strong one. It is especially weak for girls and is somewhat stronger and more consistent for boys (Huesmann et al., 1984; Viemero & Paajanen, 1992).

Even if we take these relatively weak correlations as reflecting a real relationship, they lend themselves to other causal interpretations. Both of the standard problems with correlational designs pose dangers here. The "reverse causality" problem is that being aggressive may lead to watching violence rather than vice versa (Friedrich-Cofer & Huston, 1986). In fact current research suggests that both effects are true: Aggressive children may watch more television, but viewing television increases rates of aggression (Johnson, Cohen, Smailes, Kasen, & Brook, 2002). The "third-variable" problem also emerges. The viewing of violent programs is highly correlated with the amount of total television viewing, and when television watching has been taken into account, the effect of violent viewing often disappears (Friedrich-Cofer & Huston, 1986). Thus, viewing unusual amounts of television in general, rather than viewing violence in particular, may be more characteristic of children who are especially aggressive (Bushman, 1995). Also, other personality characteristics not considered in these studies may produce both aggressive behavior and a special interest in watching violent images (Freedman, 1986). So the correlational studies are equivocal concerning the causal role of media violence in producing aggressive behavior in real life. However, in laboratory experiments the direction of causality is clear; exposure to violent media causes aggression. And, the correlational data show that this relation holds up in the real world. Thus, taken together, the two types of evidence make a strong case for the role of violent media in influencing aggressive behavior (Anderson & Bushman, 2002; Johnson et al., 2002).

Overall, the results of violent versus nonviolent TV field investigations are not dramatic. Observed violence in movies or television seems to have fairly weak effects on aggressive behavior in real-life situations. As noted, the effect of media violence on behavior may occur primarily among boys or men predisposed to aggression.

As the preceding comment suggests, it must be obvious that the majority of research conducted on and demonstrating effects of media portrayal of violence on aggressive behavior have been done on boys and men. Part of the reason for this gender bias stems from the fact that boys and men are substantially more likely to commit acts of physical aggression than women are. In fact, cues that inspire aggression in men (such as viewing violence) actually inspire concern over aggression in women (Mussweiler & Förster, 2000). These findings may reflect the different experiences that men and women typically have with aggression.

Does Violence Sell?

The most common complaint in public surveys about television is the amount of violence depicted on the screen. Despite societal opposition, advertisers continue to sponsor violent programs. Is their investment well placed? If an advertisement is to be effective, people need to be able to remember the brand advertised and the message of the advertisement. Recent analyses of television programs indicate that TV violence in fact impairs memory both for brands and for the content of advertisements. This effect occurs in both men and women, in children and adults, and in people who like or do not like violence. Violence quite simply is distracting and engrossing in ways that detract from the effectiveness of the advertisements that sponsor it. "If the television program bleeds, memory for the advertisement recedes!" (Bushman & Phillips, 2001).

Violence in Music and Video Games

Most of the research on media violence has focused on television, but violence is increasing in other media as well, including rock music and video games. Do these media also have the potential to increase violence? Might they also increase aggressive thoughts and the possibility of aggressive behavior? Studies by Anderson and colleagues (Anderson, Carnagey, & Eubanks, 2003) examined the

DO VIDEO GAMES INCREASE AGGRESSION?

In recent years, psychologists, parents, and legislators have become concerned about the possible effects of aggressive video games on aggressive behavior. When Eric Harris and Dylan Klebold launched an assault on Columbine High School in Littletown, Colorado, observers pointed out that they had enjoyed playing a bloody, violent video game called "Doom." In fact, for a class project, Harris and Klebold had made a videotape similar to their version of "Doom," raising the possibility that the game had had some effect on their behavior.

But anecdotal evidence is not proof. To see whether video games actually increase aggression, two psychologists, Brad Bushman and Craig Anderson (2002), conducted an experimental study. They induced participants to play either a violent or a nonviolent videogame. They then asked the participants to describe the motives and actions of the main character in a subsequent ambiguous story. People who had played the violent video game described the main character as behaving more aggressively, thinking more aggressive thoughts, and feeling more angry than people who had played a nonviolent videogame, suggesting that exposure to the video game can lead to hostile expectations about others.

Evidence like this suggests that this more recent form of violence exposure merits attention (Anderson & Bushman, 2001). As has been found in other studies of media aggression, the effect of violent video games on aggression appears to be stronger for men than for women (Bartholow & Anderson, 2002). As video games become increasingly lifelike and the violence that occurs in the game looks more like the violence of real life, concerns over their impact, especially on boys and men prone to aggression, are likely to grow.

effects of songs with violent lyrics on aggressive thoughts and feelings in college student participants. The results of five studies suggest that those students who heard violent songs felt more hostile than those who heard a similar but nonviolent song and that aggressive thoughts increased in response to the violent songs. Whether exposure to music with violent lyrics may actually increase aggressive behavior is not yet known. More, however, is known about exposure to video games, as the Research Highlight suggests.

Conclusions and Comments

The effect of media violence has become one of the most passionate and most political research topics in social psychology. It seems fair to conclude that media violence is not a sufficient condition to produce aggressive behavior, nor is it a necessary one. Aggressive behavior is multiply determined, and media violence in and of itself is unlikely to provoke such behavior. However, it is clear that media violence can contribute to some aggressive acts in some individuals (Bushman & Anderson, 2001). Moreover, as evidence has accumulated from different types of studies across the years, the connection between media violence and aggression has only grown clearer (Bushman & Anderson, 2001). In addition, the relation between media violence and aggressive behavior, though weak, nonetheless shows considerable cross-cultural generalizability. In a number of countries—Israel, Australia, Finland, Poland, South Africa, the Netherlands, and the United States—aggressive children watch more media violence, and exposure to more media violence enhances aggressive behavior (Huesmann, 1986; Huesmann & Miller, 1994; Huesmann, Moise, & Podolski, 1997).

The primary professional organization of psychologists, the American Psychological Association, concurs with this judgment regarding the adverse effects of violence in the media on violent behavior, and for this reason the organization is currently actively involved in efforts to reduce violence in the media (Sleek, 1994). In particular, it has focused on spurring the mass media not only to reduce the amount of violence shown on television and in movies but also to generate more antiviolence presentations.

Table 13–2

Typology of Films Used in Research on Sexual Violence

	Sexual	Nonsexual
Violent	Some R-rated films *(Blue Velvet, Straw Dogs)*	Horror films *(Friday the 13th, The Texas Chainsaw Massacre)*
	Some X-rated films *(Story of 0)*	War films *(Rambo)*
Nonviolent	Teen sex comedies *(Spring Break)*	Situation comedies *(Rainman, On Golden Pond)*
	Nonviolent R-rated films *(Body Heat)*	Family films *(101 Dalmatians, E.T.)*
	Most X-rated films *(Emmanuelle)*	

Source: Data from Miller, Bersoff, and Harwood (1990, p. 38).

Sexual Violence and the Media

What is the role of sexually explicit films, books, and magazines in promoting sexual violence? Many argue that pornography degrades women and encourages sexual coercion and violence, at least in some vulnerable individuals (Malamuth, 1993). In a survey assessing public reaction to various forms of sexual, violent, and sexually violent media, a substantial majority of respondents supported censoring sexually violent media (71 to 77 percent), whereas only about half supported censoring non-sexually violent media, and only a third supported censoring nonviolent, sexually explicit movies (Fisher, Cook, & Shirkey, 1994; Fisher & Grenier, 1994). However, does the portrayal of explicit sexual violence actually increase its occurrence?

Much research on this question has been done in recent years. Most of it has been guided by the theories just discussed, hypothesizing that violent sex in the media increases sexual violence through imitation, association of sexual pleasure with violence, and disinhibition. Most of these studies have used either full-length feature films or short "stag" films. They have typically manipulated exposure to erotic and violent material independently. Table 13–2 shows some examples of feature films that represent each possible combination of these two dimensions.

Violent Erotica. A basic question is whether there is something special about the mixture of violence and sexual themes that triggers unusual levels of aggression against women. We have seen that violent films produce more aggression in laboratory experiments than do nonviolent films. However, what are the effects of witnessing uniquely sexual violence?

To answer this question, Donnerstein (1983) presented some participants with a violent-erotic stag film. The film depicts a young woman who apparently wishes to study with two men. They have been drinking, and she is forced to sit between them and drink. They then tie her up, strip her clothes off, slap her, and rape her. Other participants were presented with a violent but nonerotic film in which the woman is tied up and slapped without any nudity or sexual activity. Male participants who were angered by a female (a confederate in the experiment) before watching a violent-erotic film gave more intense shocks to the confederate than in any other condition (see also Scott, 1994; Weisz & Earls, 1995).

A second important finding is that the female film victim's emotional reaction to being sexually coerced is crucial in determining the viewer's later aggression. In a study by Donnerstein and Berkowitz (1981), participants were either angered or not by a female confederate, against whom they could later retaliate. Then they were shown the film, in which a female victim is raped by two men. However, the ending was varied: In one, the victim is smiling and not resisting and even becomes a willing participant. In the other, she seems to find the experience humiliating and disgusting. As shown in Figure 13–4, the male viewers delivered more intense shocks to the female confederate when angered, consistent with earlier research. When they were not angry, they administered more intense shocks only when the film depicted the woman as enjoying the experience.

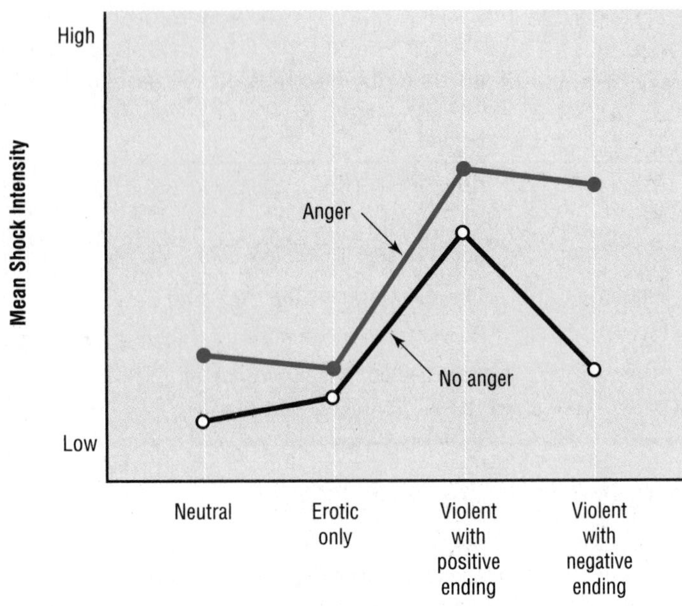

Figure 13–4 **Shock Intensity as a Function of Prior Angering and Type of Erotic Film.**

Note: Erotic film had little or no aggression; the positive ending depicted coercive sex with a woman who was a willing participant; and the negative ending, with a woman who was not.

Source: Data from Donnerstein and Berkowitz (1981, p. 150).

Desensitization

Becoming insensitive through overexposure to material that normally evokes strong emotions.

Exposure to violent erotica may also contribute to the **desensitization** of men to violence against women. It may lead to demeaning or callous attitudes toward women and therefore make violent or coercive sexual behavior more acceptable. Numerous studies have indeed shown that viewing violent sexuality produces more accepting attitudes toward violence against women and contributes to the acceptance of the myth that women often enjoy being forced to perform various sexual acts or even being raped (Donnerstein & Linz, 1994; Mullin & Linz, 1995; see also Scott, 1994; Weisz & Earls, 1995).

An example of desensitization comes from a study by Check and Malamuth (1981). They compared the effects of viewing the films *Swept Away* and *The Getaway,* which show women as victims of both erotic and nonerotic aggression, with the effects of viewing more neutral films. This study was particularly useful because the films were viewed at a movie theater, and the viewers' attitudes were measured in regular class sessions, so they were not aware of being participants in an experiment. The more aggressive films increased males', but not females', acceptance of violence against women. Subsequent studies found that repeated exposure over a period of days or weeks to stag films depicting sexual violence against women produced desensitization in terms of (a) reducing perceptions that the material was violent and degrading to women, (b) reducing support for sexual equality, and (c) lessening sympathy for victims of rape (e.g., Linz, Donnerstein, & Penrod, 1984; Zillmann & Bryant, 1974; see Malamuth & Briere, 1986, for a review).

Demand Characteristics

Aspects of a study that make subjects aware of a study's purpose that bias their behavior.

As in laboratory experiments on media violence, however, these studies raise problems of external validity. One problem is that most of these studies presented single, brief stag films depicting little other than a wide variety of sexual activities, rather than the full-length films to which most men are usually exposed. A second problem is that such studies may create experimental **demand characteristics** because the purpose of the experiment may seem obvious. That is, the danger is that the participants will then try to do the expected thing, to try to react "normally," and thus will inadvertently comply with the researcher's hypothesis. Watching a brief clip of women being sexually abused in a film and then being asked to shock another woman or express attitudes about sexual violence may be so obviously connected to each other that they yield a biased test of the hypothesis. One solution is to collect the dependent variable under different auspices and in a wholly different context from the films, thus disguising the connection between the two. This is called a "separated posttest." For example, after the film exposure, Linz and colleagues (1988) had another researcher phone the participants at home to ask them to participate in a study in the law school evaluating a trial. When they arrived, the participants were asked to be jurors in a rape case. Prior exposure to the films had no effect on evaluations of the rape victim (see also Malamuth & Ceniti, 1986).

What are the policy implications of these findings? Whether to control the portrayal of sexual violence in the mass media is a difficult question. Because the existing research leaves so many questions unresolved (Fisher & Grenier, 1994), it is probably premature to advocate more stringent legal restrictions. Labeling media products as dangerous, akin to labeling food or cigarettes, is not a viable scheme because it is difficult to establish what is harmful to viewers. Labels indicating what is contained in films (which then leave it up to viewers to determine whether they want to expose themselves to violent incidents) or warnings that alert parents to what children will see based on descriptions of a film's content may be the more practical solutions—and, indeed, are already in effect. Educational interventions that inform young men and women of one another's attitudes regarding sex and violence and that help them communicate more effectively with each other may be an alternative way to mitigate the effects of exposure to sexual violence (Linz, Wilson, & Donnerstein, 1992).

Nonviolent Erotica. The use of force is not a common theme in most men's sexual fantasies or in the erotic materials they most often see. For most men, fantasies about consensual sex or voyeuristic fantasies are more common (Arndt, Foehl, & Good, 1985). *Playboy,* which has the largest circulation of erotic men's magazines, rarely displays violence. Similarly, many popular R-rated movies display at least some female nudity and nonexplicit sexual acts, and many depict violence against women as well as against men, but relatively few portray sexual violence against women. Indeed, the written stories most sexually arousing to men are those that are sexually explicit and nonaggressive (Malamuth, Check, & Briere, 1986). Nevertheless, it is possible that even nonviolent erotica induces sexual coercion and aggression. Such erotica may promote the dehumanization of women by treating them as sexual objects, as subordinate to men, as existing solely for male sexual satisfaction, as promiscuous and insatiable, and even as desiring coercive sex. Consequently such erotica may encourage men to pursue women sexually, even when those women do not want sexual attention.

In general, nonviolent erotica seems not to increase aggression beyond the levels in no-film or neutral-film control groups (Smith & Hand, 1987). Exposure to nonviolent erotica may increase violent behavior under one set of limited conditions: when viewers are angry to start with, when the erotic materials are extremely explicit hard-core pornography, and when the predominant affect experienced by the viewer is negative (disgust or distaste).

INTIMATE VIOLENCE

The previous sections discuss the psychological dimensions of aggressive behavior and the effect of the media portrayal of violent acts on aggressive behavior. This section discusses several specific forms of aggressive behavior that share their intimate nature. These are domestic violence, rape, and sexual harassment.

Domestic Violence

Domestic violence is violence committed by one family member or cohabiting individual against another. The most common forms of domestic violence are parents abusing children and husbands abusing wives, although there are also cases of wives abusing their spouses and of children abusing their parents. The health care costs of partner rape, physical assault, and stalking exceed $5.8 billion each year, nearly $4.1 billion of which goes to direct medical and mental health care services (Centers for Disease Control, 2003).

Domestic Violence

Acts of violence committed by one family member against another family member.

In families where wives are beaten by their husbands, children are also at risk. A recent study of battered women revealed that almost 25 percent of their children reported to have been physically involved in a battering incident, and over half verbally intervened while in the same room (Edleson, Mbilinyi, Beeman, & Hagemeister, 2003). Witnessing violence is a risk factor for long-term physical and mental health problems (Felitti et al., 1998). Abused children experience many risks: They show signs of chronic stress, including difficulties in school and problems with concentration. Perhaps worst of all, they are more likely than those who come from nonabusive families to grow up to be abusers themselves.

Many children are not only physically abused but also sexually abused by fathers, stepfathers, boyfriends, and other male relatives. Sexually abused girls face special problems. Evidence suggests that girls who are sexually abused also have biological alterations in their development, including abnormal hormonal and neuroendocrine changes, as well as early puberty (Corneil, 1995; Jones, 1994; Trickett & Putnam, 1993).

Somewhat surprisingly, men and women are about equally likely to physically aggress against each other in partner relationships (Archer, 2000). In fact, in couple-abuse situations, women may be slightly more physically aggressive than men. However, women are far more likely to be injured by their partners than men are. And accordingly, the problems involved in partner abuse have fallen more heavily on women than on men.

Partner abuse is a major social problem. In the United States, almost 3 million women are physically abused by their husband or boyfriend each year (Commonweath Fund, 1999), and approximately one third of all women in the United States are physically assaulted by a man they know intimately some time during their adult lives (Family Violence Prevention Fund, 2001). Every month, more than 50,000 women in the United States seek restraining or protection orders against their partners. At least 25 percent of the women who are victims of domestic violence in the United States are beaten while they are pregnant. Unhappily, the response to this major crime remains inconsistent. Police are more likely to file a formal report if an individual is victimized by a stranger than if she is victimized by her partner.

What are the determinants of this source of violence? Studies of violent husbands suggest several contributing factors. Witnessing parental violence as a child, being sexually aggressive toward one's wife, and behaving aggressively toward one's children are all risk factors that distinguish husbands who beat their wives from husbands who do not (Koss, Heise, & Russo, 1994). A man's need to control or dominate women and an inability to empathize with others may make him more likely to resort to violence (Koss et al., 1994). There are also situational factors that trigger violence, such as jealously or a work-related frustration that spills over into the home environment (Puente & Cohen, 2003).

Cultural factors are also implicated. Domestic violence may be more likely in cultures that value honor, especially those that regard female fidelity as an important aspect of her partner's honor; if a woman's act of infidelity prompts her partner to retaliate against her, his aggressive act will not be evaluated as negatively in cultures that value this aspect of honor as it would be in cultures in which female fidelity is not an important part of a man's honor (Vondello & Cohen, 2003).

The psychological impact of domestic violence can be severe. Women who are assaulted by their partners, especially over a long period of time, experience shock, denial, withdrawal, confusion, psychological numbing, and fear. Often there are dramatic changes in self-esteem and chronic anxiety, which ultimately turn into physical symptoms, including fatigue, difficulty sleeping, eating disorders, nightmares, intense startle reactions, and other physical complaints (Koss et al., 1994). Some women are eventually killed.

The legacy of domestic violence extends beyond the immediate violent situation. More than half of abused women themselves beat their children, and the 3 million children who witness acts of domestic violence each year are six times more likely to attempt suicide and 50 percent more likely to abuse drugs and alcohol (Bray, 1994).

Why do women remain in violent relationships? The combination of economic dependence on men and society's willingness to turn a blind eye to this form of violence has given many women few options for escape (Browne, 1993; Rusbult & Martz, 1995).

Rape

The following letter appeared recently in the college newspaper of a prominent university:

> I am writing this letter to a well-respected young man [at my college] who belongs to a prestigious fraternity. You are good-looking, outgoing, and have many friends. I met you for the first and last time at a party last April, and it is a night I will never forget.
>
> I met you early on in the evening. . . . We were standing with a group of people when you introduced yourself and flashed me that winning smile. I was hooked. You asked me to dance and I quickly obliged. You were a great dancer and we were having a terrific time together.
>
> I had a couple of drinks, but you didn't seem to think that I was very relaxed. I believed you, so I took the drinks you kept offering me.
>
> Well, it worked. The punch did relax me for a while, and during that time, you catered to my every whim. . . . Even when I started feeling sick, you were there for me. . . . I asked you to please walk me home. . . .
>
> You, however, didn't think that walking home was such a good idea in my condition and you told me just to lie down until I felt better. . . . You were such a nice guy.
>
> [Then] the nice guy disappeared. You used force to hold me down, words to terrify and stun me, and your plan worked. Premeditated rape. You blamed me, though. You told me it was my fault because I was pretty and you couldn't help yourself.
>
> For you, it was a night of fun, something you can look back at and laugh, while I still look back, and I'm not laughing. You put me through hell. You didn't just rape me, you robbed me, you stole my life from me. Through the feelings of guilt, shame, and fear that you instilled in me, you isolated me from my world. . . . I don't have enough evidence to take you to court and [the college] won't kick you out of school because the party wasn't a university-condoned event. So don't worry, my hands are still tied. The system is stacked in your favor. Congratulations. You win! (Anonymous)

Rape

Forced sexual activity without one partner's consent.

Rape is one of the most common major crimes in the United States. What is rape? **Rape** is forced sexual activity without the partner's consent. Rape is believed to be largely a crime of aggression and power, involving a man's need for control and domination (Brownmiller, 1975; Donat & D'Emilio, 1992). Approximately 20 percent of women in the United States have been raped at least once in their lives (Family Violence Prevention Fund, 2001). Perhaps most startling is the fact that 44 percent of rape victims are younger than 18 at the time of the attack, and about 15 percent are under 12 (NCVS, 2002). Yet only 36 percent of these assaults were reported, possibly because in most cases the victim knew the rapist, as Figure 13–5 reveals (U.S. Department of Justice, 2001).

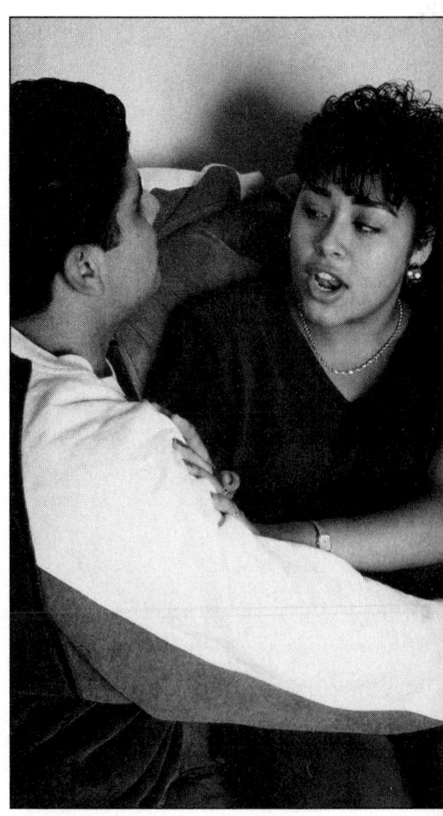

Date rape or acquaintance rape is on the rise. It appears to occur, in part, because men interpret ambiguous cues as sexual invitation, when women mean only to be friendly.

These statistics have shocked the American public, largely because they conflict so strongly with the stereotypes and myths that have traditionally been held about rape. The stereotypical conception of rape involves a woman walking down a dark street at night and being assaulted by a mentally deranged or socially deviant stranger. Yet more than 80 percent of rape victims know the rapist, and in over half the cases, the rapist is a relative or spouse, boyfriend, or ex-boyfriend. Statistics on date rape are also startlingly high. Depending on the particular survey, between 28 and 50 percent of college women report that they have been forced into sexual activity against their will (e.g., Koss & Oros, 1982; McCaul et al., 1990). Much rape also occurs within marriage, especially in already violent marital relationships (Frieze, 1983). Until recently, rape within families was

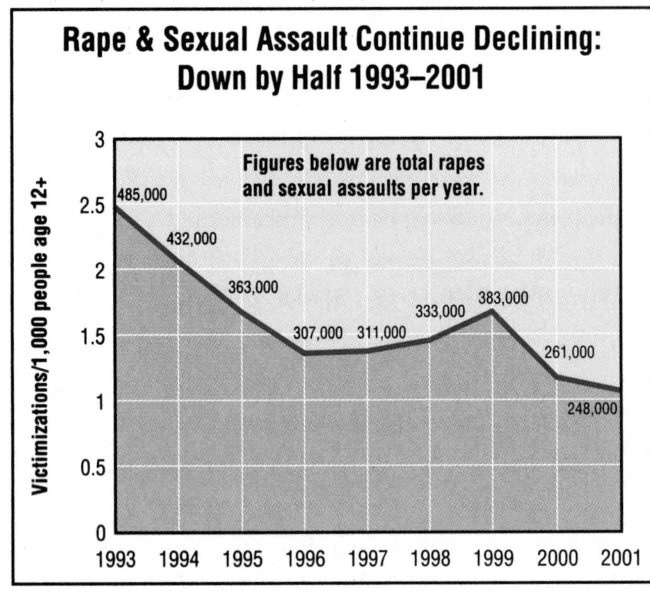

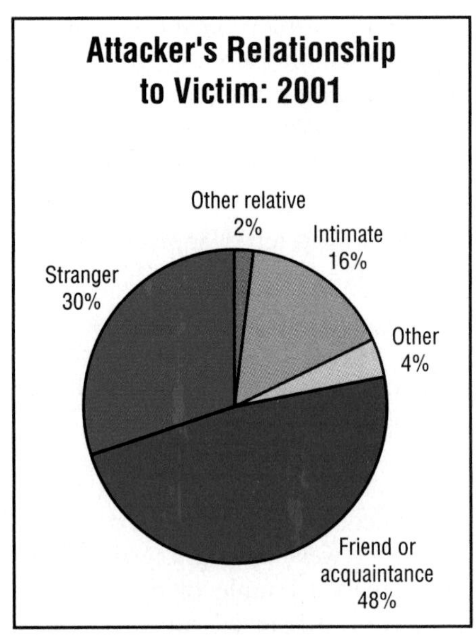

Figure 13–5 **Total Rapes/Sexual Assaults Per Year and the Relationship of the Attacker to the Victim.**

Source: Rape, Abuse, & Incest National Network (2001).

virtually ignored (Sorensen & White, 1992). Some states still do not consider marital rape a form of rape. Even in states where marital violence and rape are discouraged, conviction rates for partner violence are minuscule. Other seemingly potent deterrents, such as mandatory arrest and protection orders issued against an abusive spouse, appear to have little deterrent effect (Koss, 2000).

Myths about Rape. Rape myths abound and include such ideas as "Only bad girls get raped," "Any healthy woman can resist a rape if she wants to," "Women ask for it," and "Women cry 'rape' when they've been jilted" (Burt, 1980). The fact that at least 30 percent of all rapes involve children clearly contradicts these myths. As the patterns of rape (such as who gets raped by whom) become better known, **date rape**—that is, forced sexual activity between two people who are at least mildly acquainted and dating—is also coming to be recognized as a serious problem.

Date Rape

Forced sexual activity that occurs in the context of acquaintanceship or dating.

Among the most prevalent rape myths is the idea that only disturbed men rape. The reality is that many men make a distinction between forcing sexual activity on a woman and rape. Psychologist Neal Malamuth (1981) found that when male college students were asked if they would force a woman to have sex against her will if they could get away with it, about half said they would. But when asked if they would rape a woman if they knew they could get away with it, only about 15 percent of the men said they would. The men did not seem to realize that there is no difference between rape and forcing a woman to have sex against her will. Thus, it seems apparent that many men who have raped women are, on some level, unaware of that fact. Even men who have been convicted of rape typically argue away the seriousness of the crime by maintaining that their behavior was out of their own control or that the woman did something to ask for it (Scully & Marolla, 1984). Men may interpret signs of friendliness in a woman as an interest in sexual activity and may thus be inclined to force sexual activity despite the woman's protests.

The different perceptions of men and women of the circumstances surrounding rape were well illustrated in a study by Muehlenhard (1988). She gave male and female undergraduates 11 scenarios describing dates in which who initiated the date, who paid the expenses of the date, and what was done on the date were varied. Each respondent was then asked to indicate the degree to which the woman was interested in sex and how justified the man would be in having sex with her against her wishes. Muehlenhard found that ratings of willingness to have sex and justifications for use of force were highest when the woman initiated the date, when the couple went to the man's apartment, and when the man paid the dating expenses. Men perceived the woman in the scenario as significantly more interested in sex than women did, a finding suggesting that men may overestimate women's interest in sex. Men also rated force as more justifiable than women did, a finding suggesting that they may regard some circumstances as appropriate for forcing a partner to have sex (see also Goodchilds, Zellman, Johnson, & Giarusso, 1988; Jenkins & Dambrot, 1987).

How do rape myths contribute to the circumstances surrounding the high rate of rape in this country? They may contribute to the incidence of rape in at least three ways (Anderson, Cooper, & Okamura, 1997). First, rape myths are more commonly held by men than by women and may thus contribute directly to an inclination to rape. Second, men who hold rape myths are more likely to tolerate violence in general, to hold conservative gender-role stereotypes, to exhibit hostility toward women, and to regard sexual activity in adversarial "contest" terms, all of which may promote rape (Burt, 1980; Lonsway & Fitzgerald, 1995). Third, rape myths create a cultural climate of acceptance that may be more tolerant of rape than would otherwise be the case (Lonsway & Fitzgerald, 1995). As just noted, studies consistently find that women have more favorable attitudes toward rape survivors than do men, a finding that holds up cross-culturally (Lee, 1991; Levett & Kuhn, 1991). There also appear to be fairly consistent sex differences in the degree of fault attributed to the rapist. For example, a study in India found that female students recommended longer imprisonment for a rapist, attributed less fault to the woman who had been raped, and perceived a greater likelihood of rape overall than men (Kanekar, Shaherwalla, Franco, Kunju, & Pinto, 1991; see also Schult & Schneider, 1991).

Who Rapes? Originally rapists were thought to be characterized by a distinctive type of psychopathology. However, it is now clear that convicted rapists are heterogeneous and that sexual aggression is determined by many factors (Prentky & Knight, 1991). A study of college men who admitted having aggressed against women either sexually or nonsexually found that hostile childhood experiences were characteristic of both the sexual and the nonsexual aggressors (Malamuth, Sockloskie, Koss, & Tanaka, 1991; see also Barbaree & Marshall, 1991). Attitudes condoning coercive sex were correlated with delivering shock to a woman in a shock-learning experiment (Malamuth & Ceniti, 1986) and with unsympathetic responses to a rape victim (Linz, Donnerstein, & Penrod, 1988). Rapists also endorse rape myths more than do ordinary male citizens (Malamuth & Briere, 1986). Anger toward women and the need for dominance over them are strong characteristics of convicted rapists and of college men who have engaged in sexual aggression (Lisak & Roth, 1988). Narcissists seem more predisposed to sexually coercive behavior as well, perhaps because their self-serving interpretation of the world gives them little empathy for others and an inflated sense of entitlement (Bushman, Bonacci, van Dijk, & Baumeister, 2003).

Sexual attraction seems to prime aggression—that is, lead to aggressive thoughts—in at least some men (Mussweiler & Förster, 2000; Zurbriggen, 2000). Men who report that they have sexually aggressed against women in the past and who anticipate that they may do so in the future are more likely to hold authoritarian beliefs and conservative beliefs about appropriate sex roles for men and women (Walker, Rowe, & Quinsey, 1993), and they are more likely to be self-centered and insensitive to others' needs (Dean & Malamuth, 1997). They are characterized by a hostile masculinity and an interest in impersonal sex (Malamuth, Linz, Heavey, Barnes, & Acker, 1995). Some of these personality characteristics are evident long before these men exhibit any sexual aggression toward women, and therefore, they might well be considered modifiable risk factors for the tendency to aggress sexually against women.

Peer influence may also be a powerful factor in producing sexual aggression. Ageton (1983) and Alder (1985) found that in two separate samples of adolescent boys and adult males, the strongest predictors of sexual aggression were, in the case of adolescents, involvement with delinquent peers, and in the case of adults, having sexually aggressive friends. These findings underscore the fact that rape shares more with other crimes of aggression than it does with other forms of sexual activity.

Adjustment to Rape. There is no other crime for which the victim is so routinely blamed as rape (White & Sorensen, 1992). Myths die hard and are even accepted by many women. Unfortunately, rape survivors often also blame themselves for a rape. Is it maladaptive to blame oneself for a rape if one is the victim? Studies of rape victims (Frazier, 2003; Meyer & Taylor, 1986) and studies of perceptions of rape victims by rape counselors (Thornton et al., 1988) have found that self-blame is associated with poor adjustment to rape.

In fact, adjustment to rape can be difficult (Koss, 1993). Being raped has negative and often long-lasting physical and psychological consequences. Between one third and one half of rape victims sustain physical trauma, including beatings, sexually transmitted diseases, and pregnancies (Koss, 1993). More than a year after a rape, victims experience rape-related fear and anxiety (Kilpatrick, Resnick, & Veronen, 1981), sexual dissatisfaction (Feldman-Summers, Gordon, & Meagher, 1989), depression (Atkeson, Calhoun, Resnick, & Ellis, 1982), and family-related problems (Ellis, Atkeson, & Calhoun, 1981), compared with age-matched women who have not been raped. Symptoms of posttraumatic stress disorder comparable to those of combat survivors in war have been documented in rape survivors (Koss, 1993). Achieving a sense of control over one's personal recovery helps to reduce distress (Frazier, 2003).

Unfortunately, the legal system often perpetuates the misunderstandings and ambiguities surrounding rape. Studies of police officers suggest that they often hold some myths and stereotypes about rape and rape victims that may interfere with their effective handling of rape cases or may preclude sensitive interactions with rape victims (Krahe, 1991). The Supreme Judicial Courts' Gender Bias Study Committee issued a report in 1989 (Zeprun, 1990) indicating several sources of bias in rape trials. Jurors apparently expect more corroborating evidence in sexual assault cases than in cases involving other serious felonies. There is more of a tendency to call into question a victim's character and stability in sexual assault cases, whereas such evidence is unusual in comparable felony cases, such as nonsexual assault. Consequently, victims are often discouraged from reporting rape and may justifiably anticipate that the criminal justice system will put them, rather than the rapist, on trial. General political ideology also affects the perception of rape. Conservatives are more likely than are liberals to hold rape victims responsible for their situation (Lambert & Raichle, 2000).

It is evident that the factors fostering violence against women are complex. They cannot be fully understood from an examination of the individual psychology of men who sexually aggress against women. As the research on rape myths indicates, social and cultural institutions provide the context within which sexual aggression occurs (Goodman, Koss, Fitzgerald, Russo, & Keita, 1993). Researchers (Koss, 1993; Koss et al., 1994) and political figures (Biden, 1993) suggest that only programs that extract rape from its current social and cultural context may help to decrease its frequency. Specifically, more programs to help survivors, more education about rape, and more progress toward equal rights for women may reduce the cultural myths that surround rape, with a result that the incidence of rape may decline.

Sexual Harassment

Unwelcome sexual advances, requests for sexual favors, and other conduct of a sexual nature that create an intimidating or offensive environment.

Sexual Harassment

Sexual harassment is an umbrella term for many aggressive behaviors (Frazier, Cochran, & Olson, 1995). It includes unwelcome sexual advances, requests for sexual activity, and other verbal and physical conduct of a sexual nature that creates an intimidating, hostile, or offensive work environment, or it becomes a condition for new or ongoing employment. Sexual harassment may take the blatant form of repeated requests for sexual favors, or it may be more subtle, such as patting a man or woman on the behind, telling lewd stories, or placing pornography around the workplace.

Sexual harassment appears to be a widespread problem in the workplace. Within the public sector, the number of sexual harassment charges filed with the Equal Employment Opportunity Commission (EEOC) and with state and local fair employment practices agencies around the country totaled 15,836 in 2000, up from 10,532 in 1992 (Newman, Jackson, & Baker, 2003). Studies of college students find that 50 percent of women and 20 percent of men report some experience of harassment at school from faculty, other students, or staff (McKinney & Maroules, 1991). Large-scale survey studies of working women suggest that approximately one out of every two women is harassed at some point during her academic or working life. Sexual harassment can occur in any work situation and to anyone, but it is most common when women enter traditionally all-male environments. Typically, it is directed by a male supervisor toward a single woman under 35. Sexual harassment appears to be fueled in part by the politics of power (Sheets & Braver, 1999).

Anita Hill's accusations of sexual harassment against Supreme Court nominee Clarence Thomas brought the issue into the public eye and onto psychologists' research agenda.

Recently social psychologists have begun to study the dynamics of sexual harassment (Borgida & Fiske, 1995). Clearly, most people do not sexually harass their coworkers, and not all work situations promote sexual harassment. The person and the situation both seem to be important. That is, particular social or work situations, such as those involving unequal power, contribute to sexual harassment but cannot fully account for its occurrence. Characteristics of particular men who are prone to sexual harassment are also important but cannot fully account for harassment. Men predisposed to harass are likely to do so only to the extent that the environment implicitly condones such activity (Burgess & Borgida, 1997; Fiske & Glick, 1995; Pryor, Giedd, & Williams, 1995).

Research investigations reveal that men who are highly likely to sexually harass a coworker are individuals who associate sex with social dominance or power (Pryor et al., 1995). Psychologists have discovered some intriguing aspects of this power-sex association. Often men who sexually harass are not aware that their actions are inappropriate or that they constitute a misuse of power (Fitzgerald, 1993a, 1993b). One reason may be that, for many men, the link between power and sex is automatic and unconscious. In an intriguing experiment by Bargh, Raymond, Pryor, and Strack (1995), men were exposed to material that was either power related or neutral; later, they were asked to evaluate a woman with whom they were participating in the experimental study. The attraction ratings of the female confederate by men predisposed to aggress sexually were significantly higher when they had previously been exposed to the power-related materials than when they had been exposed to neutral materials. Other research has uncovered similar findings (Bargh & Raymond, 1995). This research may help to explain why some men accused of sexual harassment seem bewildered by the charges. Their behavior may develop without their awareness.

The psychological impact of sexual harassment can be substantial. Harassment is degrading, frightening, and sometimes physically violent. Often it extends over a considerable period of time, even years, and it can result in profound job-related, psychological, and health-related consequences (Fitzgerald, 1993a, 1993b). Costs of sexual harassment include job loss, decreased morale and absenteeism, lower job satisfaction, and damaged interpersonal relationships at work and at home. A state of California study (Coles, 1986) found that 50 percent of women who filed a sexual harassment complaint with the state of California were fired, and another 25 percent resigned because of the stress of the complaint process or the harassment itself. Knowledge or anticipation of these kinds of psychological, occupational, and legal implications of sexual harassment charges, in turn, may act as an impediment to women reporting the events they have experienced (Fitzgerald, Swan, & Fischer, 1995). Moreover, the ongoing effects and aftermath of sexual harassment can include long-lasting psychological and health problems. Symptoms that can result from sexual harassment include anxiety, depression, headaches, sleep disturbances, gastrointestinal disorders, weight problems, nausea, and sexual dysfunction (Fitzgerald, 1993a, 1993b).

Until recently, there has been little organizational or legal effort to control sexual harassment. If sexual harassment complaints are to have any impact, it is clear that organizations must provide a safe environment within which victims of harassment can register their grievances. At present, at least some of the mechanisms for reporting sexual harassment appear to discourage, rather than encourage, its reporting (Fitzgerald et al., 1995). There have been a number of legislative and legal initiatives to try to define sexual harassment and to specify the consequences should it occur. Clearly, though, much work must center on educating both women and men about the nature of sexual harassment. Moreover, it is important to realize that sexual harassment grows out of women's inferior status in the world of work; to the extent that women's work status improves, sexual harassment is likely to decline (Fitzgerald, 1993a, 1993b).

Summary

1. Aggression is defined as any action that is intended to hurt another person. It has both biological and social origins.
2. Aggressive acts can be antisocial, prosocial, or sanctioned, depending on whether they violate or conform with social norms.
3. Aggressive feelings, or anger, need to be distinguished from aggressive behavior.
4. The major determinants of anger seem to be attack and frustration, particularly if attributed to an intent to injure.
5. Major determinants of aggressive behavior are angry feelings and the learning of aggressive responses. Learning can take place through imitation or reinforcement of aggressive responses.
6. Social norms are crucial in determining what aggressive habits are learned.
7. Fear of punishment or retaliation can reduce aggressive behavior. However, these controls may sometimes foster covert aggression or may actually increase aggression over the longer run.
8. Learned inhibitions of aggression are the most important controls over it. However, such inhibitions can also result in the displacement of aggression to other, innocent parties.
9. Observed aggression generally increases aggression in laboratory studies, especially when the model is rewarded or when the observed victim is similar to the target of the participant's own aggression.
10. Viewing televised or movie violence has equivocal effects on aggressive behavior in real-life settings. Nonetheless, mounting evidence leads to the conclusion that media violence contributes to violent crime in society, although many other factors are also implicated.
11. Intimate violence, including child abuse, spousal abuse, rape, and sexual harassment, is now the most common form of aggression. Because of the prevailing stereotypes, myths, and misperceptions, men and women often regard sexual coercion in different ways, and many men condone it under a range of circumstances.
12. The main determinants of sexual violence and sexual harassment seem to lie in nonegalitarian and coercive attitudes toward women, peer group norms, abuse of substances such as alcohol, and situational norms that tacitly encourage aggression against women. Written and filmed erotica may play a relatively minor role as well.

Key Terms

aggression **407**
aggression anxiety **419**
anger **407**
antisocial aggression **407**
catharsis **422**
correlational research **426**
date rape **434**
dehumanization **417**

demand characteristics 430
desensitization 430
disinhibition 420
displaced aggression 421
domestic violence 431
external validity 426
field experiments 425
frustration 407
imitation 409
prosocial aggression 407
rape 433
realistic group conflict 416
reinforcement 411
sanctioned aggression 407
sexual harassment 436

In The News

Obesity Gaining on Tobacco as Top Killer

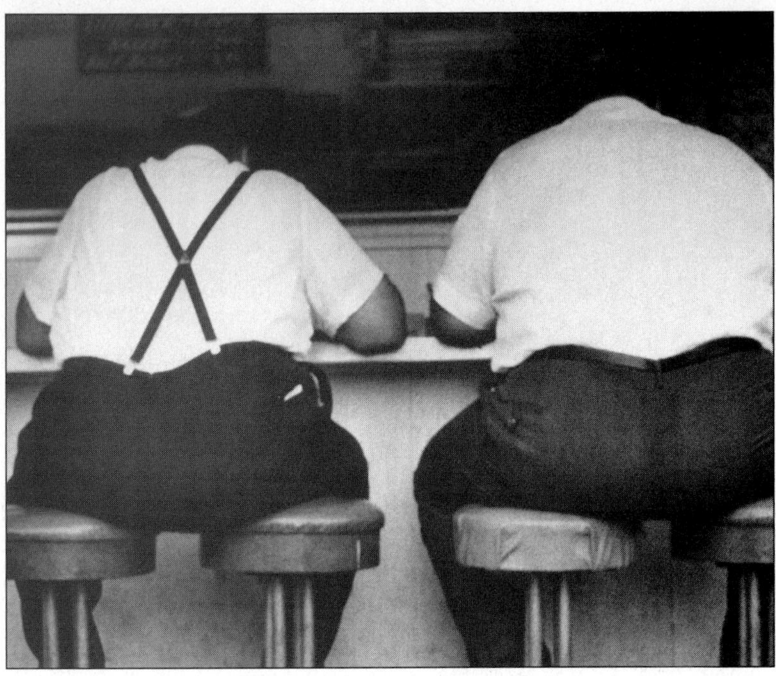

"Obesity Gaining on Tobacco as Top Killer," a recent headline read in the *Los Angeles Times* (March 10, 2004). For decades, smoking has been branded as our most lethal health-related habit because of its clear relation to heart disease, lung cancer, and other chronic disorders. But poor diet, physical inactivity, and the obesity that often accompanies them is rapidly closing in on tobacco as the leading cause of preventable deaths in the United States and other developed countries. It is currently estimated that about 400,000 deaths a year can be attributed to obesity, a figure that represents a 33 percent increase over the last decade.

These obesity-linked diseases and deaths will far outstrip any health strides we can make through changes in medical technology, immunizations, and the like. A study released by the RAND Corporation (RAND, 2004) estimates that by the year 2020, 20 percent of health care dollars will be spent on people over 50 with obesity-related disabilities.

Although experts have seen this problem coming, the very rapid increase in obesity rates and, in particular, the dramatic increase in the number of obese children, have caught many off-guard. As a result, obesity-related disorders such as high blood pressure, type 2 diabetes, cirrhosis of the liver, and nerve damage associated with diabetes are appearing earlier in life.

Over half of the U.S. population is now overweight or obese. The exact causes are not entirely clear, but inactivity, larger portion sizes, and a high content of sugar and fat in the diet are very likely contributors. Quite simply, we eat more calories than we burn off.

How can we overcome these alarming trends and what role can social psychologists play? Helping to enhance public awareness of factors that can reverse these trends such as increasing exercise, consuming smaller portions, and avoiding high-fat, high-sugar foods will go some distance. But much of the problem lies in our increasingly enticing environments, especially in schools where soft drinks and high-fat snacks are readily available. Overall, a combination of information, intervention, and restructuring of the environment may be needed to address this growing health problem.

Part Five

Chapter 14

Social Psychology and Health

The concept of health has been revolutionized in the last few decades. We used to think about our health in physical terms. We were either sick or healthy, and we knew which state we were in on the basis of the cues we got from our bodies; however, as the following anecdotes suggest, health is a heavily psychological issue as well as a physical one.

- Bob, a 22-year-old member of the tennis team, has been told to stop smoking because it is lowering his energy during matches. He wants to stop, but so far, he has been unable to do so.
- Lisa broke up with her boyfriend last week, and she faces a major test in her chemistry course next week. She has just come down with the flu.
- Ellen recently went to see a physician about her headaches. The doctor was cold and aloof and seemed to dismiss her complaints as trivial. She has decided not to follow her doctor's advice, but instead will take a relaxation-training course to see if it can help her.

The realization that health is a psychological as well as a physical issue has given rise to an exciting new field: health psychology.

The psychological study of health considers four main areas: (a) promoting and maintaining health, (b) preventing and treating illness, (c) identifying the causes and correlates of health and of illness and other dysfunctions, and (d) improving the health care system and the formation of health policy (Matarazzo, 1980; Taylor, 2003).

An important lesson of health psychology is that health is a **biopsychosocial process**. A person's state of health is a complex interaction of biological factors, such as a genetic predisposition to a particular disease or exposure to a flu virus; psychological factors, such as the experience of stress; and social factors, such as the amount of social support one receives from friends and family. Once we recognize that psychological and social factors as well as biological ones are involved in health and illness, it is clear that good health is something that people achieve by actively engaging in a healthy lifestyle, rather than something to be taken for granted. Moreover, promoting health and preventing illness before it occurs can save money and misery (Kaplan, 2000).

Focus of This Chapter

Biopsychosocial Process

A person's state of health is determined by biological, psychological, and social factors.

HEALTH BEHAVIORS

At one time, major health problems involved infectious diseases such as influenza, pneumonia, and tuberculosis. Now these problems are less threatening. Currently, the major health problems faced by citizens of industrialized nations are "preventable" disorders such as heart disease, cancer, and diabetes. These problems are called preventable because they result, at least in part, from health behaviors that people can control. For example, annual cancer deaths in the United States could be reduced by 25 to 30 percent if people stopped smoking (American Cancer Society, 1989). Deaths due to heart disease would decline substantially if people lowered the cholesterol in their diet, stopped smoking, and reacted more effectively to stress (American Heart Association, 1984). Deaths due to vehicular accidents could be reduced by 50 percent if drunk driving were eliminated (National Highway Traffic Safety Administration, 2003). An examination of the nation's health goals (see Table 14–1), developed by the U.S. Department of Health and Human Services, clearly shows that the majority of these goals are related to lifestyle factors.

What Is a Health Behavior?

Health Behaviors

Actions to enhance or maintain good health.

Health behaviors are actions undertaken by people who are healthy to enhance or maintain their good health. These behaviors include consuming healthful foods; getting regular exercise; avoiding the use of health-threatening substances such as tobacco, alcohol, and drugs; getting sufficient sleep; using seat belts; using sunscreen; using condoms; controlling weight; and making use of

Table 14–1

Fifteen Specific Ways to Improve Health

The U.S. Department of Health and Human Services has developed a set of goals to improve the health of the U.S. populace. These goals serve as targets for intervention by local health services. Note how many of them involve lifestyle changes and behavior modification.

A. Preventive health services

1. Teaching people how to control high blood pressure
2. Implementing effective family-planning programs
3. Establishing programs to improve health care for pregnant women and infants
4. Establishing effective immunization programs for children and at-risk adults
5. Educating adolescents and adults regarding the control of sexually transmitted diseases

B. Health protection

6. Managing toxic chemicals and wastes
7. Developing and implementing effective occupational safety and health standards
8. Developing procedures to reduce accidents (especially vehicular accidents and injuries)
9. Fluoridating water and improving preventive dental health
10. Monitoring and controlling the spread of infectious diseases

C. Health promotion

11. Reducing smoking
12. Reducing the misuse of alcohol and drugs
13. Developing programs for effective nutrition
14. Improving physical fitness and increasing exercise
15. Developing effective techniques for the control of stress and violent behavior

Source: Data from Harris (1989), Matarazzo (1983), and Department of Health and Human Services (2000).

Poor health habits, such as smoking, are the major causes of disease and death in this country. Unfortunately, these behaviors often begin early in life, before people realize the damage their actions will produce.

health-screening programs, such as opportunities to be screened for such high-prevalence disorders as breast cancer and coronary heart disease (see Taylor, 2003, for a review).

The importance of basic health habits was illustrated in a classic study conducted by Belloc and Breslow (1972). These scientists began by defining seven important health habits: sleeping 7 to 8 hours a night, not smoking, eating breakfast each day, having no more than one or two alcoholic drinks each day, getting regular exercise, not eating between meals, and being no more than 10 percent overweight. They then interviewed 6,000 residents of Alameda County, California, and asked them to indicate which of these behaviors they regularly practiced. The residents were also asked to indicate how many illnesses they had had, how much energy they had, and how disabled they had been (e.g., how many days of work they had missed) over the past 6 to 12 months. The more health behaviors people practiced, the fewer illnesses of all kinds they reported having, and the more energy they said they had. Other studies have found similar effects, as illustrated in Figure 14–1.

Unfortunately, few people follow all these good health behaviors. Although most of us practice some, such as not smoking or keeping our weight down, most of us violate at least a few others, such as not getting enough sleep or not exercising as much as we should. Some of the worst offenders are college students. Why? Most of the country's major health problems strike older people and are uncommon among college students. Therefore, these diseases often seem remote to students. It may seem almost impossible that the health habits developed in adolescence and young adulthood could possibly influence health so many years away. Yet this is clearly the case.

Health Attitudes and Health Behaviors

Since good health behaviors are essential to good health, it is important to understand the attitudes that lead people to practice good health behaviors or to continue to practice faulty ones. The practice of health behaviors centers on five sets

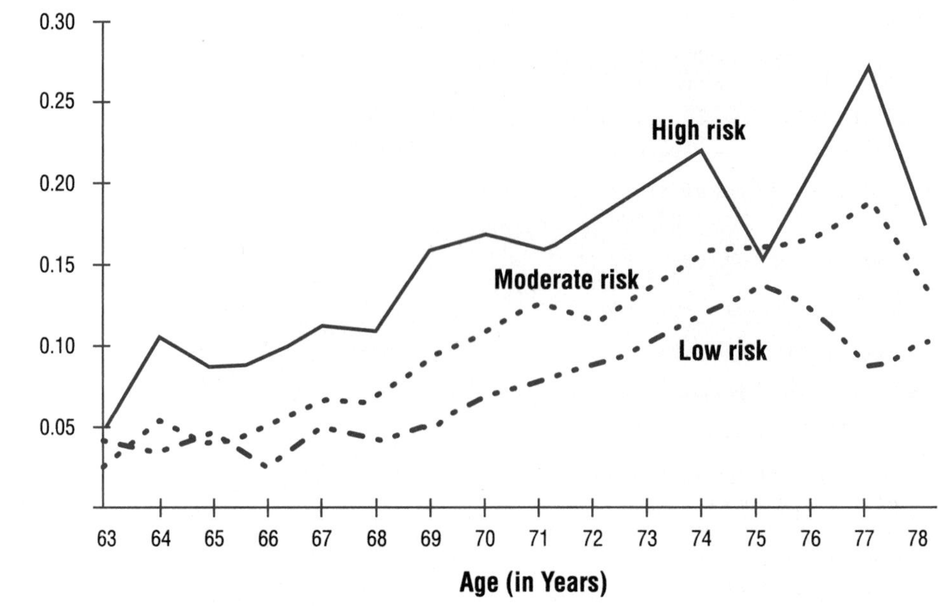

Figure 14–1 **Living Longer, Living Better.**

A study of University of Pennsylvania graduates, classes 1939 and 1940, indicates that those who practice healthy habits stay free of disabilities longer. Class members were divided into low-, moderate-, and high-risk groups based on their weight, exercise, and use of tobacco while they were still in college. Beginning at age 67, these people were then rated on a disability index based on eight basic tasks: dressing and grooming, arising, eating, walking, bathing and other hygiene, reaching, gripping, and executing basic chores. A score of 0.01 indicates some difficulty in performing one of the tasks. A score of 0.10 means some difficulty in performing all eight tasks. The maximum score of 0.30 indicates inability to perform all eight tasks.

Source: A. S. Vita, R. B. Terry, H. B. Hubert, and J. F. Fries (1988). Aging, health risks, and cumulative disability. *New England Journal of Medicine, 338,* 1035–1041. Copyright © 1998, Massachusetts Medical Society. All rights reserved. Adapted with permission.

of beliefs (Bandura, 1986; Hochbaum, 1958; Rogers, 1984; Rosenstock, 1966; Weinstein, 1993):

1. General health values, including interest in health and concern about health
2. The perception that the threat to health posed by a disorder or disease is severe
3. A belief in personal vulnerability to a disorder or disease
4. A belief that one can perform the response necessary to reduce the threat (self-efficacy)
5. A belief that the response will be effective in overcoming the threat (response efficacy)

To understand these points, consider the experience of one student in a health psychology class a few years ago. Bob was the only person in the class who smoked, and he was the object of some pressure from the professor and the students to quit. Although he acknowledged that smoking is linked to both lung cancer and heart disease, he believed the links to be fairly weak. Moreover, because he was in good health and played a number of sports, he felt relatively invulnerable to these diseases. However, over Thanksgiving vacation, Bob went home to a large family gathering and discovered to his shock that his favorite uncle, a chain smoker all his adult life, had lung cancer and was not expected to live more than a few months. Suddenly his general health became a more salient value for Bob. Bob's feelings of vulnerability to lung cancer changed dramatically because now a member of his own family had been affected. He came to realize in graphic fashion how severe the outcome of smoking can be. Bob's perceptions of the need to stop smoking changed as well. He concluded that stopping might be sufficient to ward off the threat of disease (response efficacy). Moreover, he developed a belief in his own self-efficacy, that he would be able to stop. When Bob returned from Thanksgiving vacation, he had stopped smoking altogether. These relations are diagrammed in Figure 14–2.

Health Beliefs

Beliefs that influence willingness to adopt a health behavior, such as personal susceptibility.

Generally, these **health beliefs** predict health behaviors quite well, including smoking reduction and cessation (Kaufert, Rabkin, Syrotuik, Boyko, & Shane, 1986), exercise (Wurtele & Maddux, 1987), skin cancer prevention activities (such as sunscreen use) (Leary & Jones, 1993), brushing and flossing teeth regularly (Tedesco, Keffer, & Fleck-Kandath, 1991), breast self-examination (Champion & Huster, 1995), AIDS-preventive sexual behavior (Aspinwall, Kemeny, Taylor, Schneider, & Dudley, 1991), condom use (Goldman & Harlow,

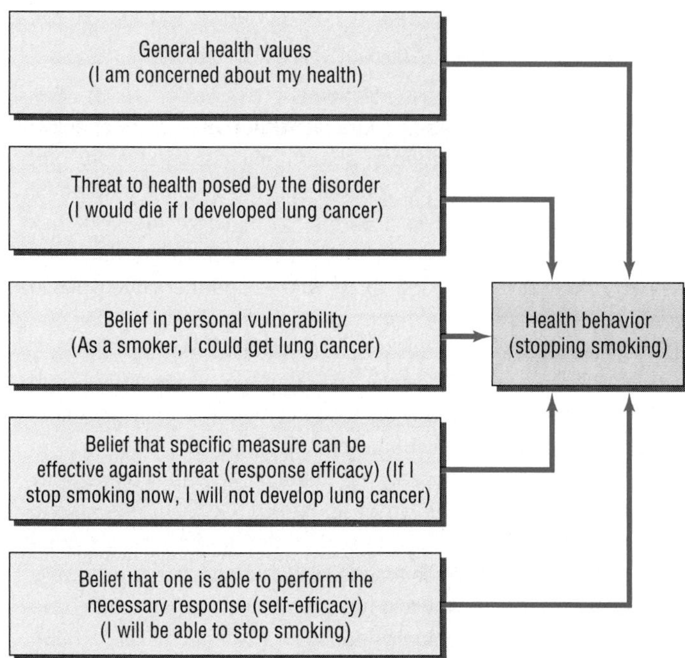

Figure 14–2 **The Relation of Health Attitudes to Health Behavior.**

1993), and dieting to control obesity (Uzark, Becker, Dielman, & Rocchini, 1987; see Taylor, 2003, for a review).

Another attitudinal component that predicts health behavior has been added by Fishbein and Ajzen (1980), whose reasoned action model was considered in Chapter 6. The theory of reasoned action maintains that a behavior is a direct result of a behavioral intention. Take the specific case of dieting to reduce cholesterol. Suppose that your father believes that cholesterol is a threat to his health and that the possible outcome (a potential heart attack) is serious. Suppose he also believes that he can change his diet in a healthier direction and believes that if he were to do so, he would reduce his risk. He still may not be inclined to undertake the behavior. Knowing whether he *intends* to change his diet, then, improves the ability to predict whether he will actually go on the diet. Knowing an individual's behavioral intentions can enable us to predict whether he or she will, for example, practice AIDS-preventive behavior (Fisher, Fisher, & Rye, 1995), use oral contraceptives (Doll & Orth, 1993), practice breast self-examination (Lierman, Young, Kasprzyk, & Benoliel, 1990), use sunscreen (Hillhouse, Stair, & Adler, 1996), use preventive screening programs (Sheeran, Conner, & Norman, 2001), and get exercise (Gatch & Kendzierski, 1990), among other health behaviors.

Beliefs about one's sense of self-efficacy or self-control are also important in the practice of health behavior (Bandura, 1986) and predict behaviors as diverse as condom use among college students (Wulfert & Wan, 1993), exercise (McAuley, 1993), diet change (Schwarzer & Renner, 2000), and quitting smoking (Borland, Owen, Hill, & Schofield, 1991). A woman attempting to diet might inadvertently undermine her diet by thinking, "I'll never be able to do this" or "I've tried to diet many times before and have always been unsuccessful." In contrast, if she reaffirms the fact that her diet is under her personal control and that she has the ability to modify it, she will be more successful.

Through understanding the determinants of health behaviors, it may be easier to see why so few people actually practice good overall health behaviors. The smoker may decide that it is too difficult to stop (low self-efficacy). The nonexerciser may believe that exercise alone will not reduce the risk of a particular disease (low-response efficacy). The obese individual may not perceive that being overweight is actually a threat to his health (low perception of threat). For a health behavior to occur, all these beliefs must fall into place, and a person may have numerous beliefs or rationalizations for not undertaking a particular health behavior.

SAFE SEX

In a recent television program, a man and a woman are fondling each other, removing each other's clothes, and making steady progress toward the man's bed. As they approach it, she whispers, "Have you had a blood test?" He responds, "Last month. Negative. You?" She responds, "Negative, too. Do you have protection?" His response: "I'm covered." They fall to the bed and . . . (fade out).

This is Hollywood's idea of a safe-sex encounter. But where did the magic condom come from? Did he put it on in the taxi on the way back to his apartment? Did he put it on in the kitchen while he was pouring them each a glass of wine?

Hollywood's safe-sex encounters may be seamless, but in real life, safe sex is not. A first important step is getting people to recognize that practicing safe sex is important. Engaging in unprotected sexual activity puts people at risk for contracting acquired immune deficiency syndrome (AIDS) and other sexually transmitted diseases. In the United States, AIDS has spread into the sexually active young adult population and is spreading fastest among African Americans and Hispanics. Yet the level of knowledge about sexuality in general and AIDS specifically is inadequate, especially among less acculturated Hispanics (Catania et al., 1993; Marin & Marin, 1990) and poor inner-city women (Hobfoll, Jackson, Lavin, Britton, & Shepherd, 1993).

Inducing young people to take steps to practice safe sex is a problem (Caron, Davis, Halteman, & Stickle, 1993). Sex researchers advocate asking prospective partners about their sexual history, yet many young adults indicate that they would lie to a partner to minimize their HIV risk history (Cochran & Mays, 1990). Moreover, young adults who ask partners questions in the hopes of reducing their HIV risk are actually less likely to use condoms (Mays & Cochran, 1993). One study found that many adolescents who reported risky sexual behaviors, such as promiscuity, were unlikely to use condoms consistently (Biglan et al., 1990). Condom use among intravenous drug users and safe-sex practices among Hispanic women are especially low and have remained unchanged or have actually declined (Catania et al., 1993). Adolescents and young adults typically regard condom use as "not cool" (Collins & Aspinwall, 1989). The very factors that the Hollywood encounter overlooked—namely, the interpersonal awkwardness and logistics of actually using condoms—act as barriers to their use.

Clearly, then, safe sex requires more than a couple of hurried questions and a claim of protection. Interventions to increase the practice of safe sex need to address knowledge about sex and sexually transmitted diseases such as AIDS, attitudes toward sexual protection, cultural differences that may bear on these attitudes, and intervention techniques that directly address how condoms are perceived by the young adult population.

In addition, other factors undermine even the best intentions to practice health behaviors. For example, among adolescents, many risky behaviors are not planned; they happen as a result of circumstances which lead to smoking, drinking, unprotected sex, and other risky behaviors (Gibbons, Gerrard, Blanton, & Russell, 1998). Other adverse health behaviors can result from a negative mood, as may contribute to some eating disorders (Heatherton, Striepe, & Wittenberg, 1998). Alcohol makes it more difficult for people to exert self-control and can increase the likelihood of smoking or unprotected sex in young adults (MacDonald, Zanna, & Fong, 1996). Some health behaviors are driven by the expectation of positive or negative consequences, and these factors are also not fully incorporated into attitude models. For example, people lie out in the sun so they will have an attractive tan, without considering the risks of skin cancer or other damage from the sun. An example of the difficulties associated with the practice of one health habit, safe sex, appears in the Research Highlight.

Finally, attitude models assume that people have and use extensive cognitive capabilities to make health behavior decisions. But as we see in Chapter 5, quite often, we make inferences or decisions rapidly, using highly salient or heuristic processes rather than the systematic piecemeal decision making the attitude models

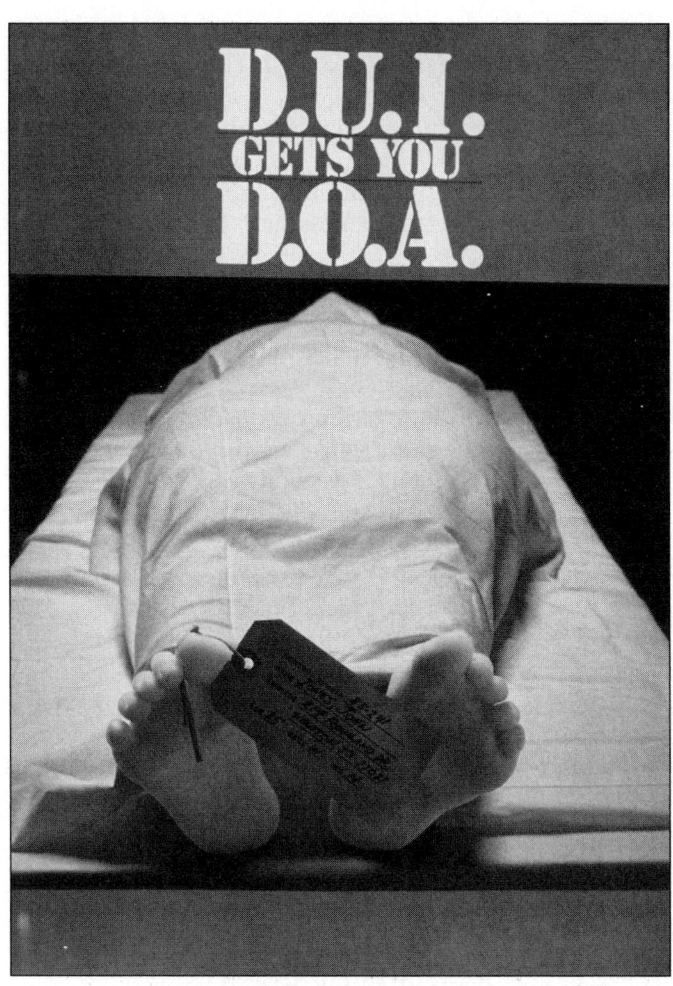

Mass-media messages designed to change health behaviors can be effective in inducing the motivation to change, but by themselves, they may bring about little behavior change.

propose. In general, when a health issue is perceived to be personally relevant, it is more likely to be processed systematically through central attitude-change routes; but when an issue is perceived to be less self-relevant, people are more likely to use heuristically based judgment strategies (Rothman & Schwarz, 1998).

The finding that health beliefs are important determinants of preventive health behaviors must also be qualified by the fact that much of this research is conducted on relatively affluent middle-class individuals with access to health care. When we look at poverty-level families and low-income black and Hispanic families, we find instead that the cost of preventive health care, such as whether a mammogram is free (Stein, Fox, & Murata, 1991), and access to health care are far more important determinants of health behavior than are health beliefs. For example, many lower income families have no regular source of health care and consequently either do not seek help or use hospital emergency facilities (Lewin-Epstein, 1991). These facts are especially problematic because low-income African Americans and Hispanics typically have poorer health than more affluent whites (Mutchler & Burr, 1991). This appears to be true because minority-group members and people with lower income, less education, and poorer occupational status are more likely to experience a wide range of highly stressful, undesirable life events (McCleod & Kessler, 1990). Far from waning, these social class and ethnic differences are actually growing.

Changing Health Attitudes

Research on health attitudes is useful because it not only helps us predict who will practice a particular health behavior but also explains the conditions under which people might change their health behaviors. In theory, persuasive messages that increase feelings of vulnerability while simultaneously increasing feelings of self-efficacy and response efficacy might induce people to modify their behaviors in a healthy direction. How can people get this information?

One of the goals of preventive health education is to reach as many people as possible, such as through the mass media. We have all been exposed to televised or radio messages urging us to increase the fiber in our diet, reduce our cholesterol, or stop smoking. How successful are these messages? Evaluation of these efforts suggests some success (Atkin, 1979; Lau, Kane, Berry, Ware, & Roy, 1980), especially in changing public opinion over time about particular risks and health behaviors.

Social psychologists have undertaken several types of interventions to induce people to change their health habits. One approach draws on self-affirmation discussed in Chapter 4. The idea guiding this intervention is that when people have an opportunity to affirm important values, their self-image becomes more positive, and therefore, paradoxically, these good feelings about the self enable them to confront personally relevant, potentially threatening information. Sherman, Nelson, and Steele (2000) tested this idea by having college women complete a self-affirmation task (or not) by writing about either their most important (or their least important value); they then read an article that linked caffeine consumption to breast cancer. Women for whom the information was relevant (i.e., women who consumed a lot of caffeine) rejected the information more often than did women for whom the issue was less relevant. But when women for whom the information was relevant had completed a self-affirmation task first, their response to the information was more positive, and they reported that they would be more likely to reduce their coffee consumption. In a second study, sexually active college students, who completed a self-affirmation task prior to being exposed to a threatening message on AIDS, saw themselves as being at greater risk for HIV infection and purchased condoms more often if they had not first completed a self-affirmation task. Thus, health messages can threaten an individual's self-image, but self-affirmation can increase receptivity to potentially threatening health information and lead to positive health behaviors.

Culture and Health Behaviors

Many of the interventions designed to change people's negative health behaviors are targeted to the individual. For example, although they may reach large audiences, media messages are designed to help each individual smoker reduce his or her level of smoking. Such an approach may have some degree of success in a culture that stresses independence. But health habits are also embedded in the dynamics of social relationships (Tucker & Mueller, 2000), and so the family unit has been increasingly adopted as the context for changing poor health habits and encouraging good ones.

An approach that focuses more on the social network and the individual's social environment may be especially successful in collectively oriented cultures. This social network approach seems to be especially valuable in appealing to Hispanic Americans. In many Hispanic cultures, anticipated social support or its absence is a better predictor of health habits than are health attitudes. The importance of the social network among Hispanics can have good or bad consequences. Among Hispanic smokers, for example, beliefs about how others respond to one's smoking are important in understanding whether a person will stop smoking or not (Marin, Marin, Otero-Sabogal, Sabogal, & Perez-Stable, 1989). Unfortunately, the fear of losing the social support of significant others, especially family members, may lead Hispanics to withhold their HIV-positive serostatus or their gay or bisexual orientation, both of which may prevent them from seeking HIV-related social support (Mason, Marks, Simoni, Ruiz, & Richardson, 1995).

Fortunately, appeals to social support can be used to design interventions to reduce adverse health behaviors. For example, to combat smoking, messages stressing that smoking cessation provides children with a good example, improves the health of one's family, eliminates bad breath, and saves money all appeal to the social interconnectedness of the Hispanic community much more than the individualist orientation we typically see in antismoking messages that emphasize personal health risks (Marin, Marin, Perez-Stable, Otero-Sabogal, & Sabogal, 1990). Thus, the traditional Hispanic values of familism (value placed on family) and simpatia (respect for polite and harmonious interpersonal relations) can become both benefits and liabilities by promoting or undermining health (Szapocznik, 1995).

Increasingly, researchers are recognizing that social support is important for changing health habits among non-Hispanics as well. Researchers find, for example, that weight loss and reductions in smoking are more successfully brought about in a work group situation than through individual intervention (Brownell, Stunkard, & McKeon, 1985). Physicians find that patients are more likely to adhere to their advice when spouses and even children are involved in understanding the treatment regimen (Wallston, Alagna, DeVellis, & DeVellis, 1983). People are more likely to practice certain health behaviors, such as safe sex, if they feel they have support from their family and friends (Catania et al., 1991).

We have learned an important lesson from collectivist cultures, then, about how to appeal to people to change negative health practices. Understanding how the social environment influences these habits, embedding interventions in the social context, enlisting the cooperation of people who are important in the target individual's life, and appealing to a person's social responsibilities all help to promote successful health behavior change.

STRESS AND ILLNESS

Good health habits alone are not sufficient to ward off the threat of illness, although they help substantially. Stressful life experiences and the ways people cope with those stressful events also have an impact on health and illness (Taylor, 2003).

Most of us have more experience with stress than we care to remember. **Stress** is discovering that your alarm clock did not go off the morning of a major test or finding out that your car won't start when you need to drive to a job interview. The experience is both physiological and psychological. Your body moves into a state of heightened arousal, your mouth goes dry, your heart beats faster, your hands may shake a little, and you may perspire more heavily. You have trouble concentrating on anything but the stressful event, which you replay in your mind over and over again (Holman & Silver, 1998).

Stress

Appraising environmental events as harmful, threatening, or challenging and responding to that appraisal with physiological, emotional, cognitive, and behavioral changes.

Most of us think of these experiences as unnerving but temporary, not producing any lasting damage. However, researchers now believe that over time, stress can wear down the body, making it more vulnerable to illness. Repeated exposure to stressful events and repeated subjection to the physiological changes that accompany stress (e.g., increases in blood pressure, blood sugar level, and respiration) exert wear-and-tear on physiological systems. This damage, in turn, may lay the groundwork for a variety of health problems, including heart disease, hypertension, and even cancer (e.g., Friedman & Rosenman, 1974; Jemmott & Locke, 1984; Selye, 1956, 1976).

What, precisely, is stress? Stress is a negative emotional experience accompanied by predictable physiological, biochemical, and behavioral changes that are designed to reduce or adapt to the stressor either by manipulating the situation to alter the stressor or by accommodating its effects (Baum, 1990). Most of us think of stress as particular events, such as being stuck in traffic, getting a poor grade on a test, being late for an appointment, or losing a notebook. Yet, despite some commonalities in the experience of stress, not everyone perceives the same events as stressful. For example, one person may experience a job interview as threatening, whereas another may welcome it as a challenge. The fact that stress is, to some degree, in the eye of the beholder makes it clearly a psychological process. That is, events are stressful when they are regarded as stressful, and not otherwise (Lazarus & Folkman, 1984).

What Makes Events Stressful

Some types of events are more likely than are others to be appraised as stressful. Any event that requires a person to adjust, make changes, or expend resources has the potential to be stressful. For example, although the December holidays are usually viewed as a positive event, they may also be highly stressful, because they can involve last-minute shopping, extensive travel, social occasions with relatives, excessive consumption of alcohol and rich food, and little sleep.

Unpleasant or negative events cause people more psychological distress and produce more physical symptoms than do more positive stressful events (e.g., Sarason, Johnson, & Siegel, 1978). For example, a $20 parking ticket typically causes a person more distress than does spending $20 to go to a noisy, crowded rock concert, even though the latter experience may actually be more physiologically challenging.

Uncontrollable or unpredictable events are more stressful than controllable or predictable ones (Bandura, Cioffi, Taylor, & Brouillard, 1988; McFarlane, Norman, Streiner, Roy, & Scott, 1980; Suls & Mullen, 1981). An uncontrollable event that is unpredictable does not allow the person experiencing the stress to develop ways to cope with the problem. For example, the sound of static on your own radio may be less distressing than static on a neighbor's radio, because you can always turn off your own radio, whereas you may not have the same degree of control over your neighbor's radio.

Ambiguous events are often perceived as more stressful than clear-cut events. For example, if you have been attracted to another student in a class, and one day this person treats you coldly, you may ruminate over the reason. Did you do something to offend this person? Is he or she simply having a bad day? Clear stressors enable people to find solutions and do not leave them stuck at the problem-solving stage (Billings & Moos, 1984).

Unresolvable events are more stressful than those that can be resolved. Although this point may seem obvious, researchers have tended to ignore the fact that people are conscious, active agents who try to overcome their problems. Often they are successful. Thus, the relationship between stressful experiences and adverse psychological responses, such as stress, physiological changes, and even illness, may be accounted for largely by stressful events that an individual has been unable to resolve (Holman & Silver, 1998; Thoits, 1994).

How Stress Can Cause Illness

The experience of stress is a problem for people not only because it produces emotional distress and physiological strain, but also because over time it may lay the groundwork for illness (Taylor, 2003). Moreover, the effects of stress are long-lasting, often continuing long after the stressor is over. Studies of environmental stress have found that when people are exposed to a stressful event such as noise or a crime-ridden neighborhood, they show fewer prosocial responses (such as helping others) and sometimes experience difficulty in performing cognitive tasks that they would otherwise be able to do (Cohen, Glass, & Phillip, 1978; Glass & Singer, 1972; Taylor, Repetti, & Seeman, 1997). How have the effects of stress on behavior and health been studied?

Stressful Life Event

An event (usually negative) that requires change.

Major Stressful Life Events. The earliest research to demonstrate the relation of stress to health examined the role of major **stressful life events** in the onset of illness. Newspapers and magazines often highlight colorful cases in which individuals who have experienced a major stressful event suddenly develop a serious illness or even die:

> A dramatic example is the death of the 27-year-old army captain who had commanded the ceremonial troops at the funeral of President Kennedy. He died 10 days after the president, of a "cardiac irregularity and acute congestion," according to the newspaper report of medical findings. (Engel, 1971, p. 774)

Much of the research designed to show the importance of major life events in the onset of illness have used questionnaires that list a variety of potentially stressful

Table 14–2

Measuring Stress

Some researchers ask people to indicate how much stress they've been under by recording what recent events have caused changes in their lives and whether they viewed them as having a positive or negative impact on their lives. The following items represent an excerpt from the Life Experiences Survey and are commonly used to measure stressors encountered by students.

For each item checked below, please indicate the extent to which you viewed the item as having either a positive or a negative impact on your life at the time the events occurred. That is, indicate the type and extent of impact that the event had. A rating of −3 would indicate an extremely negative impact. A rating of 0 suggests no impact, either positive or negative. A rating of 13 would indicate an extremely positive impact.

Rating scale:	−3	−2	−1	0	+1	+2	+3
	Extremely Negative	Moderately Negative	Somewhat Negative	No Impact	Slightly Positive	Moderately Positive	Extremely Positive

	0 to 6 Months	7 Months to 1 Year	Rating						
1. Beginning a new school experience at a higher academic level (college, graduate school, professional school, etc.)	—	—	−3	−2	−1	0	+1	+2	+3
2. Changing to a new school at same academic level (undergraduate, graduate, etc.)	—	—	−3	−2	−1	0	+1	+2	+3
3. Academic probation	—	—	−3	−2	−1	0	+1	+2	+3
4. Being dismissed from dormitory or other residence	—	—	−3	−2	−1	0	+1	+2	+3
5. Failing an important exam	—	—	−3	−2	−1	0	+1	+2	+3
6. Changing a major	—	—	−3	−2	−1	0	+1	+2	+3
7. Failing a course	—	—	−3	−2	−1	0	+1	+2	+3
8. Dropping a course	—	—	−3	−2	−1	0	+1	+2	+3
9. Joining a fraternity or sorority	—	—	−3	−2	−1	0	+1	+2	+3
10. Financial problems concerning school (in danger of not having sufficient money to continue)	—	—	−3	−2	−1	0	+1	+2	+3

To score: Add all scores that have a negative sign. This is your negative score. Separately add all scores that have a positive sign. This is your positive score. For a total score, add absolute scores (i.e., disregarding sign) for positive and negative events together.

Source: I. G. Sarason, J. H. Johnson, and J. M. Siegel (1978). Assessing the impact of life changes: Development of the Life Experiences Survey. *Journal of Consulting and Clinical Psychology, 46*, 932–946. By permission of the authors.

events that require people to make changes in their lives, such as getting married or having one's spouse die. To obtain a score, one checks the events that have occurred within the past year. Each of the events has a point value, reflecting the amount of change that a person must make to accommodate to the event. Thus, for example, if a person's spouse dies, virtually every aspect of life is disrupted, and so this event is assigned a very high number of life-change units. On the other hand, getting a parking ticket might be annoying, but it is unlikely to produce much change in a person's life. Although everyone will have experienced at least a few stressful events during the year, some will have experienced many, and it is this group that is most vulnerable to illness.

Table 14–2 shows the student section of the Life Experiences Survey by Sarason, Johnson, and Siegel, (1978); which is used as a college student supplement to life-event inventories like those noted previously. As you can see, the scoring system enables people to rate whether the impact of a life experience is predominantly positive or predominantly negative, which provides precision for relating stressful life events to subsequent health or mental health problems.

Daily Hassles. More recently, psychologists have begun to suspect that the more minor stressful events or the daily hassles of life may also have a cumulative and negative impact on health. Such hassles include being stuck in a traffic jam, doing household chores, or having difficulty making a small decision. Interpersonal conflicts are by far the most distressing daily hassles (Bolger, DeLongis, Kessler, & Schilling, 1989). Although the research is not yet conclusive, it is possible that the cumulative effect of the small irritations of daily life as well as major, less common stressful events predict illness and psychological stress (Kanner, Coyne, Schaeffer, & Lazarus, 1981; Kohn, Lafreniere, & Gurevich, 1991).

Chronic Stress. Increasingly, researchers are recognizing the importance of chronic stress in health. Living in a noisy, crowded, crime-filled environment not only is stressful day to day but also, over time, can have cumulative adverse effects on health. The well-known relationship between social class and mortality has been explained with reference to chronic stress (Taylor et al., 1997). That is, the higher one's income and level of education, the longer one will live, and the lower one's education and income, the more vulnerable one is to accidents, homicide, adverse health-related habits such as drug and alcohol consumption, and diseases such as heart disease and cancer. The environments in which we live, then, and the resources we bring to them substantially influence our vulnerability to disease and even our life expectancy (Adler, Marmot, & McEwen, 1999).

More specifically, researchers have increasingly turned their attention to the effects of long-term stressors on people's health. It is difficult to do these studies well, because long-term stress leads to a variety of life changes that may themselves increase the likelihood of illness, such as poor health habits and depression. Nonetheless, research is increasingly suggesting an important role for chronic stress in disease. For example, Cohen and his associates (1998) found that although severe acute stressful events that had lasted less than a month were not associated with an increased likelihood of developing colds, severe chronic events that had lasted a month or longer were associated with a substantial increase in risk.

COPING WITH STRESSFUL EVENTS

Coping

Managing internal or environmental demands that are appraised as taxing or exceeding one's resources.

Once we experience an event as stressful, we usually begin to make efforts to cope with that event. **Coping** is the process of attempting to manage demands that are viewed as taxing or exceeding our resources (Lazarus & Folkman, 1984; Lazarus & Launier, 1978).

Coping with a stressful event is a dynamic process (Aspinwall & Taylor, 1997). It begins with the appraisals people make of the situations with which they must cope (Major, Richards, Cooper, Cozzarelli, & Zubeck, 1998; Tomaka, Blascovich, Kibler, & Ernst, 1997). These appraisals are central to subsequent efforts to manage the stressful situation. Appraising a potentially stressful event as a challenge can lead to confident coping, little sense of threat, and positive emotions, whereas assessing a potential stressor as threatening can lower confidence in one's coping abilities and increase negative emotions (Skinner & Brewer, 2002). For example, the impending breakup of a romantic relationship can produce a variety of responses, including efforts at reconciliation or attempts to find activities that will distract us from emotions such as sadness or indignation.

Generally researchers distinguish between two types of coping efforts: problem-solving efforts and efforts at emotional regulation (Lazarus & Folkman, 1984; Leventhal & Nerenz, 1982; Pearlin & Schooler, 1978). Problem-solving efforts are attempts to do something constructive to change the stressful circumstances. Emotion-focused coping involves efforts to regulate or work through one's emotional reactions to the stressful event (Stanton, Kirk, Cameron, & Danoff-Burg, 2000). These two types of coping can occur simultaneously. For example, when romantic partners break up, both people may try to cope by cheering themselves up and by taking steps to meet new people. Generally speaking, the ability to be flexible in the use of one's coping strategies is associated with more successful coping (Cheng, 2001).

Psychologists also study more specific coping strategies (see Taylor, 2003, for a review) including active coping methods, such as seeking information, planning, or attempting to get help from others, and emotion-focused coping methods, which include positive reinterpretation, acceptance, or turning to religion. Active coping is used more often and is more adaptive in situations that are changeable (Park, Armeli, & Tennen, 2004), whereas emotion-focused coping may be more appropriate in situations that cannot be changed (e.g., Vitaliano, DeWolfe, Maiuro, Russo, & Katon, 1990). Psychologists also study avoidant coping methods, which involve disengaging behaviorally or mentally from a stressful event, as through substance abuse or distancing. These "coping" strategies are maladaptive for health and mental health. Table 14–3 presents examples of some coping strategies used by men with AIDS.

In Chapter 4, on the self, we made the important distinction between individualist or independent cultural orientation and collectivist or interdependent cultural

Table 14–3

Strategies for Coping with AIDS

AIDS has killed many thousands of people, and thousands more live, sometimes for years, with the knowledge that they have the disease. Such a threat requires and elicits many forms of coping, some of which are illustrated in the following excerpts from interviews with gay men living with AIDS.

Social Support or Seeking Information

A key point in my program is that I have a really good support network of people who are willing to take the time, who will go the extra mile for me. I have spent years cultivating these friendships.

Direct Action

My first concern was that, as promiscuous as I have been, I could not accept giving this to anyone. So I have been changing my lifestyle completely, putting everything else on the back burner.

Distraction, Escape, or Avoidance

It was important to me to focus on something besides AIDS, and my job is the most logical thing. I'm very good at what I do. I have a supervisory position, so I deal with other people's problems, which is good for me, because I take their job problems and solve them and I forget about mine. I think that's a real constructive distraction for me.

Emotional Regularity and Ventilation

Sometimes I will allow myself to have darker feelings, and then I grab myself by the bootstraps and say, okay, that is fine, you are allowed to have these feelings but they are not going to run your life.

Personal Growth

When something like this happens to you, you can either melt and disappear or you can come out stronger than you did before. I literally feel like I can cope with anything. Nothing scares me, nothing. If I was on a 747 and they said we were going down, I would probably reach for a magazine.

Positive Thinking and Restructuring

I have been spending a lot of time lately on having a more positive attitude. I force myself to become aware every time I say something negative during the day, and I go, "Oops," and I change it and I rephrase it. So I say, "Wonderful," about 42,000 times a day. Sometimes I don't mean it, but I am convincing myself that I do.

The last chapter has not been written. The fat lady has not sung. I'm still here.

Source: Reed (1989).

orientation. Not surprisingly, cultural orientation is associated with different types of coping strategies. A study of pregnant women in Japan and the United States (Morling, Kitayama, & Miyamoto, 2003) assessed whether women coped with the stresses of pregnancy by exerting personal influence, practicing acceptance, or obtaining social assurance. For women in the United States, acceptance predicted better pregnancy outcomes (less distress over time, better prenatal care, and less weight gain), whereas for Japanese women, social assurance predicted a better outcome (a positive maternal relationship). Surprisingly, personal influence was not associated with pregnancy outcomes in either culture. This is a surprising finding because personal influence or confluence is usually an adaptive, successful coping strategy. It may be that the time-limited nature of pregnancy is not conducive to this form of active coping.

What Is Successful Coping?

What constitutes successful coping? Coping efforts are generally considered more successful if they reduce physiological arousal and its indicators, such as heart rate, pulse, and skin conductivity. A second criterion of successful coping is whether and how quickly people can return to their previous life activities. Many stressful events disrupt ongoing daily life activities, interfering with work or leisure. To the extent that coping efforts enable a person to resume such activities, coping may be judged to be successful. Finally, and most commonly, researchers judge coping according to its effectiveness in reducing psychological distress, such as anxiety and depression (Lazarus & Folkman, 1984).

Successful coping depends on a variety of coping resources. Internal resources consist of coping styles and personality attributes. External resources include money, time, social support, and other life events that may be occurring at the same time. All these factors interact with each other to determine coping processes (Taylor, 2003). A model of the coping process is presented in Figure 14–3. The next section considers a few of these coping resources in detail.

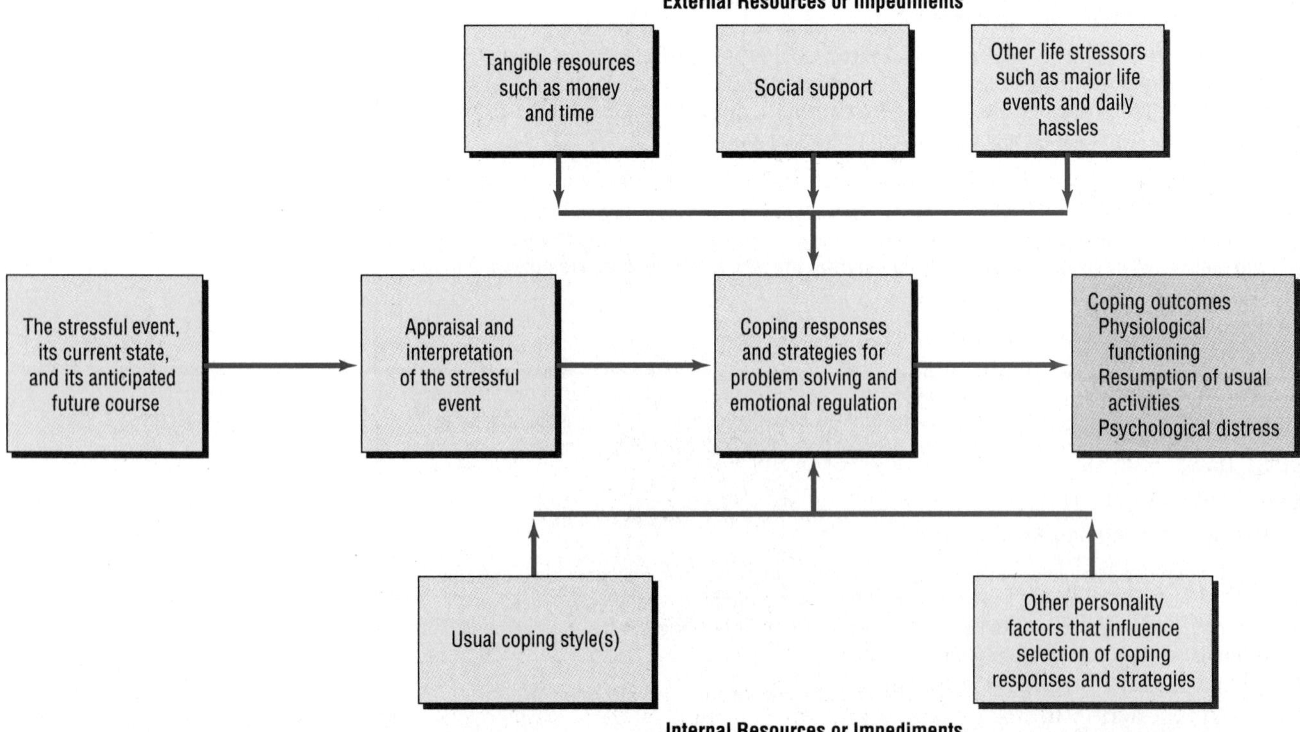

Figure 14–3 **The Coping Process.**

Coping Style

Coping style is one internal coping resource. It consists of a general tendency for a person to deal with a stressful event in a particular way.

Avoidance versus Confrontation. Some people meet stressful events head-on and tackle problems directly, whereas other people avoid stressful events by minimizing their significance or withdrawing from them through alcohol, drugs, or television.

People who cope by minimizing or avoiding stress appear to cope effectively with short-term threats. However, if the threat is repeated or persists over time, avoidance may not be a successful strategy. For example, the avoider may cope well with a trip to the dentist because he puts the event out of his mind until just before it happens. However, the avoider may cope poorly with constant job stress because this event cannot easily be put out of mind; the stress recurs daily despite efforts to avoid it. Avoiders may be unable to deal with the possibility of future threat and may not make enough effort to anticipate and manage future problems (Suls & Fletcher, 1985; Taylor & Clark, 1986). They may also pay a price in the form of physiological activation and poor health (Smith, Ruiz, & Uchino, 2000).

In contrast, individuals who cope with threatening events through confrontation may deal effectively with long-term threats. In the short run, however, they may be more anxious as they deal with the stressor directly (e.g., Miller & Mangan, 1983). The vigilant coper may fret over a visit to the dentist and may have internal distress. However, she may make constructive efforts to reduce her stress on the job and thereby ameliorate the situation. Generally speaking, active coping is more effective than avoidant coping, which actually seems to make stressful situations worse (e.g., Felton, Revenson, & Hinrichsen, 1984; Holahan & Moos, 1987).

Hostility. Some coping styles used to deal with stress have an adverse effect on health. A pattern of hostile responses to stressful circumstances seems to be associated with the development of coronary artery disease. A particular type of hostility is especially implicated, namely, cynical hostility, characterized by suspiciousness, resentment, frequent anger, antagonism, and distrust of others (Smith & Frohm, 1985; Williams & Barefoot, 1988). Individuals who have these negative beliefs about others are often highly verbally aggressive and exhibit controlling and subtly antagonistic behavior toward others (e.g., Smith, Limon, Gallo, & Ngu, 1996; see Table 14–4).

Interpersonal hostility may contribute to the development of coronary heart disease in several ways (Helmers et al., 1995). First, people who show this hostile response are more likely to have high levels of cardiovascular responses to stressful events, such as increased blood pressure and rapid heart rate. Such people may also take longer to recover from stressful episodes physiologically. Third, people who exhibit this pattern seem to derive fewer benefits from social support (Lepore, 1995). Consequently, they may be unable to extract the health benefits of social support that would otherwise be available.

The discovery that cynical hostility is a risk factor for coronary heart disease (at least in men) is an important breakthrough in research on coronary heart disease, which remains the chief cause of death in the United States and most other developed nations. This type of hostility is seen by early childhood (Woodall & Matthews, 1993), so it may be possible to intervene early in life.

Internal Coping Resources. Psychologists have identified several personality resources that people may bring to bear on a stressful event to improve psychological adjustment (see Taylor, 2003, for a review). **Dispositional optimism** is a general belief that good outcomes will occur in life. Such optimism may enable people to appraise stressful events more positively and to mobilize their resources to take direct action in response to a stressor (Chang, 1998; Scheier, Carver, & Bridges, 1994). Optimists may also show fewer adverse immune changes in response to stress than those who are less optimistic (Segerstrom, Taylor,

Dispositional Optimism

A generalized belief that positive outcomes will occur in one's life.

Table 14–4

Hostility and Cardiovascular Disease

Research has implicated hostility as a psychological culprit in the development of cardiovascular disease. Many studies employ the Cook Medley Hostility Scale (Cook & Medley, 1954) as a measure of hostility. Some of the items are presented below. "True" responses indicate high hostility.

1. No one cares much about what happens to me.
2. I have often met people who were supposed to be experts who were no better than I.
3. Some of my family have habits that bother and annoy me very much.
4. I have often had to take orders from someone who did not know as much as I did.
5. It makes me feel like a failure when I hear of the success of someone I know well.
6. People often disappoint me.
7. It is safer to trust nobody.
8. I have often felt that strangers were looking at me critically.
9. I tend to be on my guard with people who are somewhat more friendly than I had expected.
10. My way of doing things is apt to be misunderstood by others.

Source: W. W. Cook and D. M. Medley (1954). Proposed hostility and pharisaic-virtue scales for the *MMPI. Journal of Applied Psychology, 38,* 414–418.

Kemeny, & Fahey, 1998), as well as lower blood pressure (Räikkönen, Matthews, Flory, Owens, & Gump, 1999). Optimism may buffer people against illness itself (Schulz, O'Brien, Bookwala, & Fleissner, 1995).

Conscientious, socially dependable children are more likely to live longer into adulthood (Friedman et al., 1993, 1995a), whereas people with impulsive, undercontrolled personalities are more likely to die young (Friedman et al., 1995b). Specifically, conscientious individuals are less likely to have accidents and to use unhealthful substances such as alcohol, tobacco, and drugs. Conscientious people may also take a more active, self-conscious approach to their health than those who lack these personal qualities.

Hardiness

A set of attitudes that makes people stress-resistant.

Hardiness is a set of attitudes that makes people stress-resistant (Kobasa, 1979). These attitudes include a sense of commitment, a positive response to challenge, and an internal sense of control. These beliefs are believed to buffer hardy people from the negative effects of coping with stress or change (e.g., Soderstrom, Dolbier, Leiferman, & Steinhardt, 2000). People with a sense of personal control typically cope more successfully with stressful events, even stressful events that are largely uncontrollable (e.g., Helgeson, 1992; Thompson & Spacapan, 1991).

Pennebaker and his colleagues (e.g., Pennebaker & Beall, 1986; Pennebaker, Colder, & Sharp, 1990) have suggested that catharsis, the process of disclosing emotional traumas, may have psychological benefits (see also Lepore, 1997). In studies, where people are instructed to write or talk about the traumatic events that they have gone through, beneficial long-term changes in psychological adjustment and immune functioning and fewer visits to health services have been found (e.g., King & Miner, 2000; Lepore, Ragan, & Jones, 2000). Religion also provides many people with strength and solace in dealing with stressful events (Blaine & Crocker, 1995; McIntosh, Silver, & Wortman, 1993).

On the other side, personality problems such as neuroticism lead people to appraise events as more stressful, to become more distressed by problems, and to react more strongly to them (Gunthert, Armeli, & Cohen, 1999; Suls, Green, & Hillis, 1998). In addition, neurotics report more physical symptoms, although, in some cases, they are not actually more ill (e.g., Feldman, Cohen, Doyle, Skoner, & Gwaltney, 1999). Neurotics also seem to experience more social conflict and react more strongly to it, a finding suggesting that they create gaps in social support that might otherwise have been available to help them combat the effects of stressful events. In the next section, we consider how valuable a resource social support can be.

Social Support

In Chapters 9 and 10, we see how important social relationships are in satisfying people's social needs. Recent work by health psychologists indicates that socially supportive relationships may also mute the effects of stress, help people cope with stress, and enhance health (see Sarason, Sarason, & Gurung, 1997; Taylor, 2003, for reviews).

Social support may be provided in any of several ways. First, emotional concern expressed through liking, love, or empathy can be supportive. For example, if you are going through an awkward breakup with a romantic partner, expressions of caring from friends can be very welcome. Second, instrumental aid, such as the provision of goods or services during stressful times, can be an act of social support. For example, if you are having difficulty getting to your classes on time because your car is unreliable, a friend's offer to fix your car or to drive you to class would be supportive. Third, providing information about a stressful situation can be helpful. For example, if you feel poorly prepared for an exam and someone who took the course last year gives you information about the types of questions on the midterm and final, this information may be useful in helping you study. Finally, information may be supportive when it is relevant to self-appraisal, that is, self-evaluation. For example, if you are uncertain whether you have made the right decision in breaking up with your boyfriend or girlfriend, information from your friends telling you that you did the right thing for the right reasons can be very comforting. Social support can come from a spouse or partner, family members, friends, social and community contacts, fellow club members, people from churches or synagogues, and coworkers or supervisors on the job (Buunk, Doosje, Jans, & Hopstaken, 1993).

Social Support

Information from others that one is cared for and valued.

Some impressive evidence for the importance of social support in combating the threat of illness comes from a survey of adults in Alameda County, California (Berkman & Syme, 1979). Almost 7,000 people were interviewed regarding their personal, social, and community ties and their death rate was tracked over 9 years. The results showed that people who had few social and community ties were more likely to die during this period than were people who had more such ties.

Social support effectively reduces psychological distress during stressful times (Broman, 1993; see Taylor, 2003, for a review). For example, it helps students

Social support can help keep people well and help them to recover quickly from illness.

cope with the stressors of college life (Lepore, 1995). Social support also appears to lower the likelihood of illness and to speed recovery from illness (House, Landis, & Umberson, 1988), ranging from the common cold (Cohen, Doyle, Skoner, Rabin, & Gwaltney, 1997) to heart disease (Bruhn, 1965). Social support from marriage reduces the likelihood that a person will engage in a risky lifestyle and increases the practice of good health behaviors, which are, in turn, associated with better health (Wickrama, Conger, & Lorenz, 1995). Social support has also been tied to better immune functioning (Kiecolt-Glaser & Glaser, 1995), to reduced physiological responses to stress (Turner-Cobb, Sephton, Koopman, Blake-Mortimer, & Spiegel, 2000), and to more effective functioning in response to a variety of chronic diseases (see Taylor & Aspinwall, 1990, for a review). Social support influences health habits and health behaviors.

An obvious but important point is that social relationships can aid psychological adjustment, the practice of good health behaviors, and recovery from illness only when they are supportive (Ross, Lutz, & Lakey, 1999). Conflictual interpersonal interactions, such as may be found among fighting or divorcing couples, can have an adverse effect on adjustment (e.g., Holahan, Moos, Holahan, & Brennan, 1997; Major, Zubek, Cooper, Cozzarelli, & Richards, 1997) and on health (e.g., Kiecolt-Glaser & Newton, 2001).

Social support may be most effective when it is "invisible." When we are aware that other people are going out of their way to help us, we experience emotional costs, which mute the effectiveness of the social support we receive. But when social support occurs quietly, almost automatically, as a result of the relationships we have, it can reduce stress and promote health (e.g., Bolger, Zuckerman, & Kessler, 2000).

Stress Management

Some individuals have difficulty coping with stressful events on their own. Stress management programs have been developed to help people deal with these events more effectively. Such programs train people in techniques that can be used to cope with a wide variety of stressful events, or they may focus on coping with a particular stressful event (Taylor, 2003).

As an example, consider the stress of college. College is a trying experience for many students. For some, it is the first time they are away from home, and they must cope with the problems of living in a dormitory, surrounded by strangers. They may have to share a room with a person of very different background and habits. High noise levels, communal bathrooms, institutional food, and difficult academic schedules may all be very trying. In addition, fledgling college students may discover that academic life is more rigorous than what they had expected. An academic star in high school may discover that there is more competition in college. Receiving the first C, D, or F can be a deflating and anxiety-arousing experience.

Some colleges and universities have instituted programs to help students cope with these stressful events by learning stress management techniques. Commonly, in the first phase of such programs, students learn what stress is and how it creates wear-and-tear on one's system. Students learn that stress is in the eye of the beholder, and that college life is not inherently stressful but can become stressful depending on how a student perceives it. Through these messages, students begin to see that if they acquire appropriate stress management techniques, they may come to experience stressful events as less so. In sharing their experiences of stress, many students find reassurance in the fact that other students have had similar experiences.

In the next phase, students are trained to observe their own behavior closely and to record the circumstances they find most stressful. They also typically record their physiological, emotional, and behavioral reactions to stressful events. They may write down any efforts they make to cope with the stressful events, such as sleeping, eating, watching television, or using drugs or alcohol.

Once they learn to chart their stressful responses, students are encouraged to examine what triggers those reactions. For example, one student may feel overwhelmed by academic life only when she must deal with speaking out in class, whereas another student may experience stress primarily when he thinks about having to use the computer in a particularly demanding course. By pinpointing the circumstances that initiate their feelings of stress, students can more clearly identify their own particular trouble spots.

Students are next trained to recognize the negative self-talk they engage in when facing stressful events. For example, the student who fears speaking out in class may come to recognize how her self-statements contribute to the stress she feels ("I hate asking questions" and "I always get tongue-tied"). Such negative self-talk undermines feelings of self-efficacy and will become a target for modification later in the intervention.

Typically, students next set specific goals for reducing the stress of college life. One student's goal may be to learn to speak in class without experiencing overwhelming anxiety. For another, the goal may be to consult a particular professor about a problem. Once the goals have been set, the student identifies some behaviors that can help her or him meet those goals. For example, the student who fears speaking out in class may decide that she will begin to raise her hand whenever she knows the answer to factual questions that require only a one- or two-word response. By beginning with relatively little speaking in class, she can train herself to give longer answers and ultimately to speak more effectively.

Once the student has set some realistic goals and identified some target behaviors, he or she will learn how to engage in positive self-talk. For example, the student desiring to overcome a fear of oral presentations might remind herself of the occasions when she has spoken successfully in public. Once she has achieved some success in speaking publicly, the same student might encourage herself by highlighting the positive aspects of the experience (e.g., holding the attention of the audience or making some good points). As she becomes more effective, she might try to create opportunities to speak publicly and reward herself each time she does so by engaging in some desirable activity such as going to a movie.

Typically students also learn some ways of modifying the physiological reactions associated with stress. Usually these methods involve relaxation-training techniques and may include deep breathing, muscle relaxation, guided imagery, or meditation (English & Baker, 1983). Such methods can help reduce heart rate, muscle tension, and blood pressure. If a student finds a task overwhelming, he or she might take a 5- or 10-minute break, breathe deeply and relax completely, and then return to the task freer of previous tensions (Scheufele, 2000; Speca, Carlson, Goodey, & Angen, 2000).

College life is filled with many stressful events, and stress management techniques can help in controlling adverse reactions to them.

Most stress management programs include a wide array of techniques that an individual can use to combat stress. Some will work better for some students, and others will work better for other students.

SYMPTOMS, ILLNESS, AND TREATMENT

Deciding that one is ill is both a social and a psychological process.

The Recognition and Interpretation of Symptoms

To label yourself ill, you must first notice your symptoms, which is, in part, a psychological process that depends on focus of attention. People whose attention is chronically focused on themselves, who are socially isolated or live alone, or who have relatively inactive lives are more likely to notice symptoms in themselves. Conversely, people who are externally focused on their environment and activities, who have active social lives and work outside the home, or who live with others are less likely to notice symptoms (Pennebaker, 1983; Petrie & Weinman, 1997).

Situational factors influence whether a person directs his or her attention inward or outward. Boring situations make people more attentive to their internal states, whereas interesting situations distract them. Joggers, for example, are more likely to experience fatigue and to be aware of their running-related symptoms if they are running on a monotonous course than if they are running on one that is interesting (Pennebaker & Lightner, 1980; see also Fillingim & Fine, 1986).

People's expectations guide the interpretation of information, and so it is with symptom information (Leventhal, Nerenz, & Strauss, 1980). For example, women who believe that menstruation produces psychological distress and physical symptoms are more likely to report experiencing them. In fact, women who expected to have symptoms and distress exaggerated the degree to which they had experienced them, when their retrospective reports of distress and symptoms were compared with actual diary reports they had kept during their menstrual cycles (McFarland, Ross, & DeCourville, 1989).

Culture can be an important source of expectations about the meaning of symptoms. Many cultures subscribe to particular accounts of what causes symptoms, and these interpretations affect how people label their illness and what treatment they seek (Klonoff & Landrine, 1992; Landrine & Klonoff, 1994).

Mood influences the experience of symptoms. People who are in a poor mood report more aches and pains and greater discomfort than do happy individuals (Salovey & Birnbaum, 1989). Similarly, satisfaction with important areas of one's life, including work and home, is typically associated with low levels of symptoms; conversely, work overload and/or the responsibility for supporting many other people increases symptoms and compromises physical health (Barnett, Davidson, & Marshall, 1991; Shumaker & Hill, 1991). Women experience more symptoms (and actually have more physical illnesses) than men do (Kaplan, Anderson, & Wingard, 1991).

Experience also shapes reactions to symptoms (Jemmott, Croyle, & Ditto, 1988). For example, if you have a long history of sore throats, you are more likely to ignore any particular one than if it is an unusual symptom for you.

As seen in Chapter 3, cognitive theories or schemas about events often strongly affect how those events are perceived and interpreted. Research suggests that such beliefs can be important in symptom interpretation and the management of illness as well. People form organized, cognitive pictures of their symptoms that influence their illness-related activities (e.g., Bishop, 1990). In essence, these are illness schemas. They include such factors as the name of the illness and its symptoms (i.e., its identity), cause, duration, and consequences.

People have at least three models of illness (Nerenz & Leventhal, 1983). Acute illness is short in duration with no long-term consequences and is believed to be caused by specific viral or bacterial agents. An example is the flu. Chronic illness is caused by many factors, including poor health habits, is long in duration, and often has severe consequences. Cancer is an example. Cyclic illness is marked by alternating periods of symptoms and no symptoms. Recurrent episodes of herpes is an example.

Sometimes patients adopt inappropriate models for their illnesses (Weinman, Petrie, Moss-Morris, & Horne, 1996). For example, patients suffering from hypertension (high blood pressure) may believe the disease is acute when, in fact, it is chronic. Consequently, they may think that if they feel well, their blood pressure must be under control, and therefore they no longer need to take their medication (Meyer, Leventhal, & Gutmann, 1985). In fact, hypertension is called the silent killer precisely because patients often experience no symptoms and conclude erroneously that they no longer need treatment. It is important for practitioners and others involved in health care to explore patients' schemas of their illnesses to see if they are using an appropriate illness model in understanding their disorder and its treatment (Blascovich et al., 1992; Lacroix, Martin, Avendano, & Goldstein, 1991).

Social interaction also affects how people interpret symptoms. Sometimes when we are ill, we consult our friends or family to find out if they have had similar symptoms or to get their opinions on what the symptoms might mean. Often people exchange this information before seeking treatment. Warned that a minor sore throat is the first symptom of a serious flu, you might take better care of yourself than if you learned that others were experiencing a similar symptom and attributing it to air pollution. Finally, pain is an important determinant of whether people recognize symptoms and interpret them as serious.

In this section, we stress the psychological factors that influence when people experience and notice symptoms and interpret them as signs of illness. It is important to realize, though, that the experience of symptoms and the decision whether to seek treatment are heavily influenced by quality of life. For example, women get sick more than men do, a factor that has been attributed to less paid work; lower wages; more hours spent on household labor, child care, and helping others; and fewer hours of leisure and sleep. In general, men hold more highly rewarding social roles than women typically do; however, when gender differences in social roles are equal, men have poorer health than do women (Bird & Fremont, 1991). Thus, if gender roles were more equal, particularly in the stress they induce, women would experience health at least equivalent to that of men, and perhaps better.

Similarly, the vulnerability of African Americans to hypertension and stroke has been interpreted as arising at least in part from a combination of highly stressful living conditions, low income, and racial prejudice (Harburg et al., 1973; Williams & Collins, 1995). Thus, an emphasis on psychological factors must not obscure the very important influence of social roles and socioeconomic factors on the experience of symptoms and illness rates.

Patient-Practioner Interaction

Sometimes symptoms lead us to the medical practitioner's door. Interacting with a physician or a nurse regarding medical treatment is a complex social process involving interpersonal communication, person perception, social judgments, and social influence. One of the earliest judgments that most patients make is whether they think the practitioner is technically competent. However, most people know little about medicine and standards of practice, so they evaluate medical care using the only information they have: whether they like the practitioner and whether he or she is warm and friendly or cool and uncommunicative. When people are asked what is important to them in their medical care, they rate the manner in which the care is delivered at least as high as the technical quality of that care (Felitti, Firman, & Sanson-Fisher, 1986; Scarpaci, 1988).

One of the problems that arises in interactions with practitioners, even when patients and practitioners have some basic confidence in each other, is faulty communication. Practitioners often use jargon and technical language that patients

Communication between patient and practitioner can be improved by training physicians in effective communication techniques.

do not understand, and they may inadvertently depersonalize the patient by referring to the patient's symptoms rather than to the patient as a person (Chafetz, 1970; Kaufman, 1970):

> Recently, when I was being given emergency treatment for an eye laceration, the resident surgeon abruptly terminated his conversation with me as soon as I lay down on the operating table. Although I had had no sedative or anesthesia, he acted as if I were no longer conscious, directing all his questions to a friend of mine—questions such as, "What's his name?" "What occupation is he in?" "Is he a real doctor?" etc. As I lay there, these two men were speaking about me as if I were not there at all. The moment I got off the table and was no longer a cut to be stitched, the surgeon resumed his conversation with me, and existence was conferred upon me once again. (Zimbardo, 1970, p. 298)

Patients, too, contribute to faulty communication by failing to pay attention to what they are being told, and by responding to the wrong cues in the situation and reading too much into a physician's comment (DiMatteo & DiNicola, 1982; Golden & Johnston, 1970; Greer, 1974). For example, a patient may be so distressed by swollen glands that he fails to listen to a physician's instructions for taking penicillin at regular intervals.

The treatment setting contributes to the undermining of effective communication. Most people now receive their health care through a prepaid financing and delivery system, called a "health maintenance organization" (HMO; Spragins, 1996), that is associated with some dissatisfaction with health care. For example, a physician may have a backlog of patients in the waiting room and is accordingly under pressure to see each patient for as little time as possible.

Faulty communication between patient and practitioner is a problem for several reasons. First, it may undermine the use of health services in the future. Patients whose emotional needs are not met in their interactions with a physician are less likely to return to that physician (Ware, Davies-Avery, & Stewart, 1978). Even more important, patients may not adopt the behaviors and treatments recommended by the practitioner.

Adherence to Medical Treatment. Depending on the disorder and recommendation, noncompliance with treatment recommendations ranges from a low of 15 percent for such remedies as tablets or ointments to a staggering high of 93 percent for lifestyle advice such as to stop smoking or to lose weight (Haynes, McKibbon, & Kanani, 1996; Kaplan & Simon, 1990).

Failure to follow medical advice can be traced to several factors (see Taylor, 2003, for a review). First, patients who are dissatisfied with the quality of their care may choose not to follow advice. Second, to follow through on a treatment, a patient must understand it, and often understanding is not achieved. Adherence is high when a patient receives a clear, jargon-free explanation of the origin, diagnosis, and treatment recommendations associated with the disorder (Hauenstein, Schiller, & Hurley, 1987). Adherence also increases when the instructions are written down, when the patient has repeated the instructions, when any unclear sections are clarified, and when the instructions are repeated more than once (DiNicola & DiMatteo, 1984). Unfortunately, these seemingly simple steps are often not followed.

The nature of the treatment also influences the patient's behavior. For example, treatments that seem "medical," like taking a prescribed pill, have higher adherence rates than those that don't, like using an over-the-counter ointment. Complex combinations of several medications are less likely to be taken as directed than a single medication (Blumenthal & Emery, 1988; Siegel, Grady, Browner, & Hulley, 1988). Patients are less likely to follow treatments that must be continued over several months than they are to follow treatments that continue for only a few days; over time, adherence falls off. Treatments that interfere with everyday activities produce lower rates of adherence than those that can be implemented relatively easily (Kirscht & Rosenstock, 1979). For example, a patient who has been advised to rest in the middle of a busy working day might find it nearly impossible to do so (Turk & Meichenbaum, 1989).

Another reason the recommendations of physicians to alter lifestyle behaviors often show low rates of compliance is that these aspects of life are difficult to modify (Turk & Meichenbaum, 1991). As noted earlier in the chapter, such behaviors as overeating, smoking, or drinking to excess may have become habitual and may be tied to certain cues and stimuli in the social environment. These cues alone can maintain a behavior, even when the motivation to change the behavior is there.

Improving Patient–Practioner Communication. How can we improve patient–practitioner communication? Training practitioners to communicate effectively is a good way to begin. For example, in medical school, physicians could be trained to provide information to patients that is comprehensible and jargon-free without being simpleminded. Training programs also stress the importance of communicating information clearly and asking the patient to repeat the information to be certain that the patient has understood it. Methods of communicating warmth and friendliness to a patient through such simple nonverbal behaviors as smiling, leaning forward, and shaking hands can also improve the communication process (DiMatteo, Hays, & Prince, 1986).

Training physicians in the effective use of the social influence techniques identified in Chapter 8 can also improve the communication process and ultimately increase adherence to treatment. Physicians are high-status people and have a high degree of authority by virtue of their medical expertise. This type of power is called "legitimate power." Doctors can also draw on their "referent power" by becoming significant individuals in their patients' lives. If the patient feels that the physician's approval and acceptance are rewarding, then the practitioner has an additional mode of influence. When the practitioner is able to use both referent power and legitimate power, adherence is increased (Brown & Raven, 1994; Rodin & Janis, 1979).

Psychological Control and Adjustment to Treatment

As has already been noted, feelings of control over one's health and treatment regimen appear to be important in good health behaviors and adherence to treatment. So important is **psychological control** that many psychologists have used it to design interventions with medical patients (see Taylor, 2003, for a review).

Psychological Control

Belief that one can exert personal control over events.

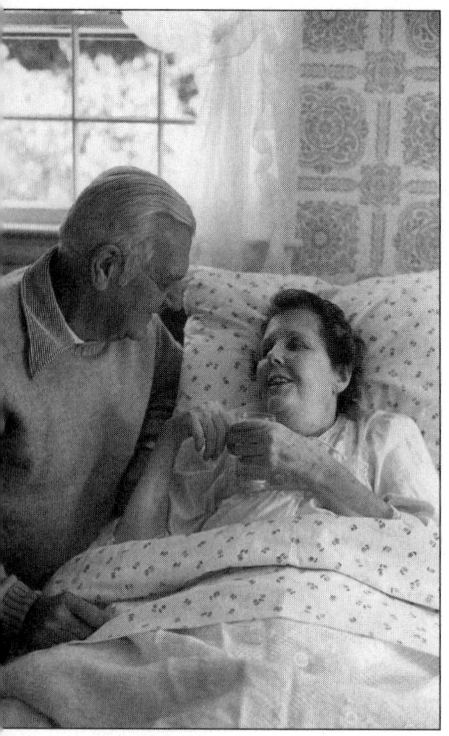

A chronic illness affects not only the patient's life, but the lives of family and other friends as well.

The idea is that if patients are given a sense of control during an unpleasant medical procedure, it will enable them to adjust to that procedure more successfully than if they do not have such feelings of control. A substantial amount of research now indicates that when medical patients anticipating uncomfortable procedures are informed about steps they can take either to control the unpleasantness of the procedure or to control their own reactions to it, they show fewer signs of distress and adjust more successfully to the procedures (Terry & Hynes, 1998; Thompson & Spacapan, 1991).

So beneficial has preparation been found to be for patients that many hospitals play videotapes for patients to prepare them for coming procedures. In one study by Mahler and Kulik (1998), patients awaiting coronary artery bypass graft (CABG) were exposed to one of three preparatory videotapes or to no preparation. One videotape conveyed information via a health care expert; the second featured the health care expert and also included clips of interviews with patients who reported on their progress; and the third presented information from a health care expert plus interviews with patients who reported their recovery consisting of "ups and downs." Overall, patients who saw the videotapes—any videotape—felt significantly better prepared for the recovery period, reported higher self-efficacy during the recovery period, were more compliant with recommended dietary and exercise changes during their recovery, and were released sooner from the hospital than were patients who did not receive videotaped preparation (see also Doering et al., 2000).

SOCIAL PSYCHOLOGICAL PERSPECTIVES ON CHRONIC ILLNESS

At any given time, 50 percent of the population has some chronic condition that requires medical management—major conditions such as cancer or heart disease, as well as more minor ones such as a partial hearing loss or recurrent episodes of herpes. Perhaps a more startling statistic is that most of us will eventually develop at least one chronic disability or disease that may alter our daily lives for many years and ultimately be the cause of our death. Chronic illnesses now account for the major health problems in the United States, conditions that people often live for many years. Because chronic diseases are long term, they often have a major impact on the social and psychological lives of those who have them (Taylor, 2003).

Illness Cognitions

Researchers have noted that most people suffering from chronic illness develop theories about where their illnesses came from (Weinman et al., 1996). Such theories about the origins of chronic illness include stress, physical injury, disease-causing bacteria, and God's will. Of perhaps greater interest is where patients ultimately place the blame for their illness. Do they blame themselves, another person, the environment, or a quirk of fate?

Self-blame for illness is widespread (e.g., Davis, Lehman, Silver, Wortman, & Ellard, 1996). Patients frequently perceive themselves as having brought on their own illnesses by engaging in bad health practices such as smoking or even simply by exposing themselves to stress. What are the consequences of self-blame? Some researchers have suggested that self-blaming patients may adjust poorly to their illness because they focus on things they could have done or should have done to prevent it (see Krantz & Deckel, 1983), but not all studies find these effects. Self-blame may be maladaptive for some disorders, but not for others.

It does appear, however, that individuals who blame other people for their disorders often adjust more poorly (Bulman & Wortman, 1977; Taylor et al., 1984). Perhaps poorly adjusted people single out others to blame for their illness, or it may be that by blaming other people, these patients adjust less well to their illness because of the unresolved anger and hostility they experience toward those who they believe are responsible for their illness (see Downey, Silver, & Wortman, 1990).

Researchers have also examined whether patients who believe they can control their illnesses are better adjusted than those who do not see their illnesses as being under personal control. For example, cancer patients may believe that they can prevent a recurrence of the disease through good habits or even sheer force of will (Taylor, Helgeson, Reed, & Skokan, 1991). Self-generated feelings of psychological control appear to be adaptive for chronically ill patients (Thompson, Nanni, & Levine, 1994), although it is not altogether clear whether it is control per se or the expectation of a positive outcome that affects psychological adjustment (Carver et al., 2000).

Chronic Disease and Patients' Changing Lives

A chronic disease such as cancer or diabetes can affect all aspects of a patient's life (Taylor, 2002). Work may be threatened or terminated by the need for extensive treatments or by the debilitating side effects of the disorder. The patient's psychological state is almost certainly affected. The diagnosis of a chronic illness can produce extreme fear and anxiety or depression, as the patient realizes that his or her activities may be permanently curtailed by the disorder (Holahan, Moos, Holahan, & Brennan, 1995; Taylor & Aspinwall, 1990). In addition, many patients need to learn a complex variety of self-care activities to aid in the management of their disorder (e.g., Glasgow, Toobert, Hampson, & Wilson, 1995).

Because of physical changes that can accompany chronic illness, loss of income due to job restriction, or the need for help from others, such as family and friends, may result. A patient's spouse may suddenly have to take on additional responsibilities that once fell to the partner who is now ill. Young children sometimes must assume more responsibilities than would normally be expected for their age group. Often, then, it is not only the patient who experiences psychosocial difficulties but also the spouse, children, and others who must adjust to these changes (Taylor, 2003).

Thus far, we have focused primarily on the problems and stressors created by chronic disease. This focus obscures an important point, namely, that chronic disease can confer positive as well as negative outcomes (Taylor, 1983). In one study (Collins, Taylor, & Skokan, 1990), over 90 percent of cancer patients reported at least some beneficial changes in their lives as a result of the cancer. They reported feeling stronger, more self-assured, and more compassionate toward the unfortunate. Similar results have been reported for patients with heart attacks, AIDS, and physical disabilities (McFarland & Alvaro, 2000). What seems evident, then, is that sometimes people are able to derive value and benefits from a chronic illness experience while simultaneously accommodating their lives to the adverse changes posed by disease.

Summary

1. Health psychology examines the role of psychological factors in the promotion and maintenance of health; the prevention and treatment of illness; the identification of the causes and correlates of health, illness, or dysfunction; and the improvement of the health care system and health policy formation.
2. The major health problems in the United States involve lifestyle disorders, including cancer, diabetes, heart disease, drug and alcohol abuse, and vehicular accidents. Lifestyle disorders are preventable and can be influenced by psychological interventions.
3. Attitude change techniques have been applied to understanding the practice of good health behaviors. Whether a person practices a health behavior depends on general health values, the perceived threat of the particular health hazard, the perceived severity of that hazard, the perceived effectiveness of the particular health practice, and a sense of self-efficacy that one can undertake the recommended health practice. Overall, however,

attitudinal approaches to the modification of health behaviors have had fairly modest effects.

4. Stress is a major health issue because it causes psychological distress and can have an adverse effect on health. Stress, however, is not intrinsic to situations but is the consequence of a person's appraisal processes. Negative, uncontrollable, ambiguous, and unresolvable events are most likely to be perceived as stressful.
5. Coping consists of problem-solving efforts and efforts at emotional regulation that attempt to reduce the stress of stressful events. Coping resources and liabilities include coping style, social support, time, money, and the presence of other stressful events in one's life. Stress management programs help people to make more effective use of their coping resources when dealing with stressful events.
6. Social support can be an effective resource in times of stress. It reduces psychological distress and the likelihood of illness.
7. The recognition and interpretation of symptoms are influenced by social psychological factors. When attention is directed outward, people are less likely to notice symptoms than when attention is directed inward. The interpretation of symptoms is influenced by prior expectations, experiences, and illness schemas. Communications with others influence whether people will seek treatment for symptoms.
8. Adherence to treatment is often very low, in part because of communication difficulties between patient and practitioner. Practitioners often provide jargon-filled and simplistic explanations, whereas patients are often guilty of not learning or following through on treatment recommendations. Interventions that draw on principles of social influence can help improve this situation.
9. Interventions that use the principle of psychological control with patients who are awaiting unpleasant medical procedures have been very successful in helping patients adjust to these procedures.
10. Adjustment to chronic illness depends in part on the cognitions people have about their illness, such as what was its cause and whether they feel they can control it.
11. Communication problems often occur between chronically ill patients and their family members. Friends and family members may not understand or may be unable to meet the communication needs of chronically ill patients who have to work through the impact that the illness is having on their lives.
12. Chronic illness can provide meaning and value to patients even as it also produces adverse changes and poses problems of adjustment.

Key Terms

biopsychosocial process **441**
coping **452**
dispositional optimism **455**
hardiness **456**
health behaviors **442**
health beliefs **444**
psychological control **463**
social support **457**
stress **449**
stressful life event **450**

In The News

DNA Test Frees Man Falsely Convicted of Sexual Assault and Attempted Murder

On July 29, 1985, 23-year-old Steven Avery helped his father pour cement for a barn. Later he went shopping with his wife and five children, buying some paint at a Shopko in Green Bay, Wisconsin.

At about 4:00 p.m. that day, a 36-year-old woman was jogging near Lake Michigan, about 20 miles away from where Avery was shopping. While jogging, the woman encountered an unknown man who forced her into a nearby wooded area. The man beat and raped her. When the woman reported the crime to the Manitowoc County Sheriff's Department, she felt confident about her ability to identify her attacker, saying "It's as if I have a photograph in my mind." The victim gave a description of her attacker that resembled Avery, who had previously been convicted for burglary.

Based on the woman's description, the Sheriff's Department arrested Avery. Despite Avery's claims of innocence, the woman picked his picture out of a photo lineup and later identified him in an in-person lineup. Avery was indicted and brought to trial.

At trial, defense attorneys presented 16 witnesses to support Avery's alibi. These witnesses included family members, friends, a cement contractor, and Shopko sales clerks. They also presented a sales receipt indicating that Avery purchased his paint just after 5 p.m., thereby placing him miles away from the crime scene near the time of the attack. However, the jury was more persuaded by the rape victim's in-court identification of Avery. On December 14, 1985, Steven Avery was convicted of sexual assault and attempted murder. In 1986, he was sentenced to 32 years in prison.

Over the next two decades, Avery maintained his innocence. In 2002, the Wisconsin Innocence Project, a group that represents individuals who allege that they have been wrongly convicted, obtained a court order to have powerful new DNA tests conducted on pubic hairs collected from the crime scene. Those tests indicated that, despite the victim's repeated identifications of Steven Avery, he was not the man who raped her. Comparisons with DNA databases indicated that the perpetrator was a man named Gregory Allen, who had been convicted of sexually assaulting other women.

Based on the new DNA evidence, Avery was released from prison on September 11, 2003. He had served 18 years in prison for a crime he did not commit. During that time Avery lost his job, his wife divorced him, and two of his children ceased to have contact with him (Kertscher, 2003; Kertscher & Garza, 2003; Wisconsin Innocence Project, 2003).

Steven Avery's story raises a number of important questions. How reliable are eyewitness identifications? The victim was inches away from Allen during the rape, yet she misidentified Avery as her assailant. Does the construction of police lineups and photospreads affect eyewitness identification? The victim selected Avery from police photos as well as a lineup; were there safeguards that the police could have used to protect him from misidentification? Finally, how do juries make decisions about guilt or innocence? Jury members seemed to give more weight to the victim's testimony than to the testimony of Avery's 16 alibi witnesses; why was this the case?

Chapter 15

Social Psychology and Law

WHAT IS SOCIAL PSYCHOLOGY AND LAW?

As you have seen throughout this book, social psychologists study a wide range of topics related to social thought and behavior. Therefore it is not surprising that social psychological research has been conducted on a number of legally relevant topics. This chapter considers such issues as eyewitness identification and testimony, false confessions, lie detection, jury decision making, expert testimony, attitudes toward the death penalty, and discrimination in the legal system. In addition, there has been a great deal of social psychological research on legally relevant aspects of rape, sexual harassment, and domestic violence. Because these topics were covered in depth in Chapter 13, we will not discuss them further here.

The legal system provides a unique opportunity for social psychologists to test basic theories in "real-world" situations. As you have seen, a great deal of social psychological research is conducted in laboratory settings. Studying the legal system helps psychologists see how behavior occurs in complex, personally relevant, and emotionally laden contexts. Some social psychologists also study legal issues because they are concerned with social justice. By conducting scientifically rigorous research into legal topics such as misconceptions about rape or mistaken eyewitness identification, social psychologists may be able to help ensure that justice is served.

Focus of This Chapter

EYEWITNESS IDENTIFICATION AND TESTIMONY

Mistaken eyewitness identification, such as the real-life story of Steven Avery that begins this chapter, may not be a rare event. Some scholars believe that eyewitness error is the leading cause of wrongful conviction, resulting in the incarceration of thousands of innocent individuals (Scheck, Neufeld, & Dwyer, 2000). A considerable amount of research has demonstrated that eyewitness identifications frequently are inaccurate (Wells & Olson, 2003). In one study, two research confederates posing as customers visited 63 convenience stores (Brigham, Maass, Snyder, & Spaulding, 1982). To make sure that the clerks noticed them, the confederates behaved in an unusual manner. For example, one confederate paid for a pack of cigarettes entirely with pennies, then asked the clerk for directions to a faraway location. Two hours later, a pair of men dressed in suits came into the store, identified themselves as law interns, and asked the clerks to identify each of the confederates from a group of six photographs. The clerks correctly identified the confederates only 34 percent of the time. In other words, only 2 hours after interacting with unusual individuals, the clerks misidentified them more than 65 percent of the time!

Why are eyewitness identifications sometimes so unreliable? Social psychologists distinguish between two groups of factors that influence eyewitness identification: **estimator variables** and **system variables** (Wells, 1978). Estimator variables are factors related to the eyewitness or the situation in which an event was witnessed. The distance from which the witness saw the event, the amount of fear the witness experienced, and the race of the witness and the perpetrator are all examples of estimator variables. In contrast, system variables are factors that are under the direct control of the criminal justice or legal system. Biases in police lineups and suggestive questioning by police or attorneys are examples of system variables.

Estimator Variables

Factors affecting eyewitness identification that are related to the witness or to the situation in which the event was witnessed.

System Variables

Factors affecting eyewitness identification that are under the direct control of the criminal justice or legal systems.

Acquisition

The process of perceiving and interpreting information.

Storage

The process of keeping information in memory.

Retrieval

The process of recalling information that is stored in memory.

Before discussing individual system and estimator variables, it is useful to think about three psychological processes that are involved in eyewitness identifications: the acquisition, storage, and retrieval of information. **Acquisition** is the process of perceiving and interpreting information. In order to provide reliable testimony, a witness must notice important aspects of the event, such as the physical characteristics of the perpetrator and the exact sequence of his or her behaviors. The witness also must interpret these events accurately. Imagine that a witness sees a man with his hands on the neck of another person who is lying on the street. It makes a great difference whether that witness interprets the behavior as strangling the individual or checking whether the individual has a pulse! **Storage** is the process of keeping acquired information in memory. Legal cases often progress slowly, so a great deal of time may pass between a witnessed event, police questioning, and courtroom testimony. It therefore is crucial that witnesses maintain the information they have acquired. Finally, **retrieval** is the process of recalling information that they have stored in memory. Witnesses may have to retrieve the information they know at several time points, including police questioning, lineup identification, and courtroom testimony. Keep these three processes in mind as you read about research on estimator and system variables and try to figure out which process is influenced by each variable.

Estimator Variables

Viewing Opportunity. In order for a witness to acquire complete, accurate information about an event, the witness needs to be able to see and/or hear it clearly. A person who witnesses an event that happens 20 yards away on a clear day will be able to provide better information than will a person who witnesses an event that occurs 100 yards away on a rainy night. It therefore is not surprising that the U.S. Supreme Court has held that a witness's opportunity to view an event and his or her degree of attention to the event are factors that should be considered when evaluating eyewitness testimony (*Neil v. Biggers,* 1972). A meta-analysis of over 100 studies on eyewitness identification and facial recognition confirms this insight. Witnesses are more likely to identify faces correctly when they are able to look at them longer and when they are able to devote a greater degree of attention to the faces during the acquisition phase (Shapiro & Penrod, 1986). Unfortunately, witnesses often fail to recognize the effects of poor viewing conditions. Lindsay, Wells, and Rumpel (1981) found that individuals who witnessed an event under poor viewing conditions were just as likely to make identifications as were individuals who witnessed an event under better viewing conditions.

Stress and Arousal. Individuals who witness crimes often experience stress or other negative emotions. Witnesses may be angry that a crime is taking place, worried about a person who is being victimized, or fearful that they may be harmed themselves. These negative emotions affect eyewitnesses' memories. Individuals who witness a negative emotional event tend to have accurate memories of the event itself, but less accurate or complete memories of what happened before and after the event (Christianson, 1992). For example, a person who witnesses a violent mugging is likely to have accurate memories of the actual assault, but less accurate memories of what the mugger did after the attack.

Weapon Focus. Imagine that you are depositing money in your bank account when the person behind you pulls out a gun. That person points the gun at you and threatens to use it if he is not immediately given all of the teller's money. Chances are, you will keep your eyes glued to the gun while the teller is getting the money. As a result, you may end up remembering more about the gun than about the actual bank robber. This phenomenon, known as the **weapon focus effect**, has been demonstrated in several studies (Steblay, 1992). The weapon focus effect may occur because witnesses who are trying to evaluate their level of danger find it useful to keep their eyes on any weapons. In addition, the novelty of weapons may draw people's attention (Pickel, 1999; Shaw & Skolnick, 1999).

Weapon Focus Effect

A phenomenon in which eyewitnesses remember more information about the weapon used to commit a crime than about the criminal who was holding the weapon.

Notably, the weapon focus effect occurs whether or not a witness is in physical danger. In a study by Kramer, Buckhout, and Eugenio (1990), participants watched a slide presentation in which a person walked through a room carrying either a bloody meat cleaver or a magazine. Even in this nonarousing situation, the participants in the meat cleaver condition remembered fewer details about the walker than did the participants in the magazine condition. The weapon focus effect is more likely to occur in contexts where weapons are unexpected or surprising (Pickel, 1999); for example, witnesses are more likely to focus on weapons in a church, where they are unexpected, than at a shooting range, where they are expected.

Own-Race Bias. Witnesses tend to be more accurate in identifying individuals who are members of their own race rather than another race (Meissner & Brigham, 2001). This **own-race bias** is an example of the out-group homogeneity effect first discussed in Chapter 6. People are able to distinguish among members of their own racial group, but often have the experience that people in other racial groups "all look alike." This effect tends to be stronger in white individuals than in black individuals (Anthony, Copper, & Mullen, 1992). However, research suggests that cross-racial contact diminishes the own-race bias (Chance & Goldstein,

Own-Race Bias

A phenomenon in which eyewitnesses tend to be more accurate when identifying members of their own race than when identifying members of another race.

The weapon focus effect occurs when eyewitnesses remember more information about the weapon used in a crime than about the person who committed the crime.

1996). The finding may help explain why black individuals are more accurate in identifying white individuals than white individuals are in identifying black individuals. Black individuals tend to have more exposure to white individuals than the reverse; as a result, black individuals may develop a greater ability to distinguish between white people.

Retention Interval. The amount of time that passes between witnessing an event and making an identification or providing testimony is known as the *retention interval.* It may not surprise you to learn that the accuracy of eyewitness identifications decreases with time. The longer the interval between witnessing an event and making an identification, the less accurate the identification tends to be (Wells, 2002). One reason that accuracy decreases over time is forgetting. As time passes, people forget details that could help them make accurate identifications. Accuracy drops dramatically soon after an event, then diminishes much more slowly afterward (Wells, 2002). For example, imagine you have seen a robbery. You will be able to remember the most information right after the event. After 24 hours, the amount of information you will be able to remember will drop dramatically. However, the decline in your memory will soon level off. A year later, the passage of 24 hours will not make much difference in the amount of information you can recall. Another reason why accuracy decreases with time is that people may be more likely to be exposed to things that can influence their memory. For example, witnesses may "contaminate" each other's memories by talking to each other. If one witness says that she remembers a detail, such as hair color, other witnesses often claim to "remember" that detail, too (Shaw, Garven, & Wood, 1997).

System Variables

Suggestive Questioning. As discussed earlier, system variables are factors affecting eyewitness accuracy that are directly under the control of the criminal justice or legal system. Of particular importance are the questioning techniques used by criminal investigators. A substantial body of research has demonstrated that the way witnesses are questioned influences not only the responses they provide but also their long-term memories of the event (Roebers & Schneider, 2000; Wells, 2002).

Some questions are suggestive even though they are not deliberately misleading. For example, seemingly minor changes in the wording of a question can influence the way people respond to it. In a classic study, participants watched a video of a car accident (Loftus & Palmer, 1974). They then were asked to estimate the speed of the cars at the time of the accident. The critical variable was the word used to describe the accident. Specifically, participants estimated the speed at which the cars "contacted," "hit," "bumped," "collided," or "smashed." As seen in Table 15–1,

Table 15–1

Speed Estimates Made by Participants in Loftus and Palmer's (1974) Study

Question: "About how fast were the cars going when they . . . "	Estimated Miles Per Hour
"Contacted"	31.8
"Hit"	34.0
"Bumped"	38.1
"Collided"	39.3
"Smashed"	40.8

participants who were asked about the speed at which the cars "contacted" gave estimates that were 9 miles per hour lower than did participants who were asked about the speed at which the cars "smashed." Thus, the witnesses' interpretation of what they saw was influenced by the way the event was described.

Some questions are deliberately misleading. For instance, people may ask witnesses questions that contain misleading postevent information—information about nonexistent details or events that did not actually happen. In another study by Loftus (1975), participants watched a video of a car accident. Afterward, the participants were asked one of two questions: "How fast was the white sports car going while traveling along the country road?" or "How fast was the white sports car going *when it passed the barn* while traveling along the country road?" In reality, there was no barn in the video. However, 17 percent of the participants who were asked the second question later reported that they had seen a barn, compared with only 3 percent of participants who were asked the first question. Thus, questions that include postevent information can make us believe that we remember something that did not actually exist—even something as big as a barn.

There are three major explanations about how postevent information affects memory. The first is the **overwriting hypothesis**. This hypothesis posits that postevent information actually replaces the information that witnesses encoded about an event, changing existing memories permanently (Loftus, 1979). The overwriting hypothesis suggests that memory is similar to something written on a chalkboard; it can be erased and replaced with something else. An alternative explanation is the forgetting hypothesis. According to this hypothesis, over time, people simply forget details of a witnessed event. When they are asked questions about material they have forgotten, they use other available information, including postevent information, to answer those questions. Thus, according to the forgetting hypothesis, postevent information does not change existing memories; it just fills in the gaps left by forgetting (McCloskey & Zaragosa, 1985). A third explanation, source monitoring theory, suggests that people retain memories of both the original event and postevent information. The problem is that witnesses frequently have difficulty with **source monitoring**, a process in which people determine where they acquired various pieces of information. As a result, witnesses may mistakenly conclude that pieces of postevent information came from their observations of the original event (Johnson, Hashtroudi, & Lindsay, 1993).

Overwriting Hypothesis

The hypothesis that information received by witnesses after seeing an event permanently replaces their original memories of the event.

Source Monitoring

The process of identifying the source of a piece of information stored in memory.

Source monitoring theory suggests that eyewitnesses can distinguish their original memories from postevent information if they are helped to identify the sources of their knowledge. There is evidence that this prediction is valid, at least for adult witnesses. In a study by Lindsay and Johnson (1989), participants examined a picture of an office that had many objects (e.g., a pencil holder) in it. They then read a misleading description of the office that included objects that were not actually in the picture. Finally, the participants were asked to identify which objects they actually had seen. The study found that participants who were asked yes–no questions (e.g., "Did you see a coffee cup?") made a large number of mistakes; they claimed that they had seen objects that were described only in writing. In contrast, participants who were asked source monitoring questions (e.g., "Did you see a coffee cup in the picture or did you read about it in the text?") had much greater accuracy in identifying where they learned about the object.

People's ability to report both original and postevent information when specifically asked indicates that the overwriting hypothesis is not the best explanation for errors in eyewitness testimony. Although memory change and forgetting undoubtedly affect eyewitness testimony in certain circumstances, source monitoring theory currently provides the best explanation for eyewitness suggestibility effects. The Research Highlight for this chapter examines another issue related to memory and eyewitness testimony, the controversial topic of "recovered memories" of childhood sexual abuse.

THE RECOVERED MEMORY DEBATE

Is it possible to experience an extremely traumatic event and not be able to remember it for years or even decades? Since the mid-1980s, a number of individuals have made this claim. They have asserted that, as adults, they "recovered" memories of childhood sexual abuse that they previously had repressed. These **recovered memories** have included vivid recollections of horrific experiences such as being gang raped, being forced to consume excrement, and being forced to watch adults ritually sacrifice human fetuses (Ofshe & Watters, 1994). The reliability of these recovered memories has important legal implications. There have been several cases in which adults who have recovered memories of childhood abuse have attempted to sue their alleged abusers as well as cases in which prosecutors have attempted to obtain criminal convictions on the basis of recovered memories (Loftus, 1994; Partlett & Nurcombe, 1998).

Recovered Memory

A memory that is forgotten for a period of time and then remembered.

Recovered memories of childhood sexual abuse are extremely controversial among psychologists. In fact, a group of well-known psychologists chosen by the American Psychological Association to summarize scientific knowledge about recovered memories was unable to reach a consensus on most issues (American Psychological Association Working Group on Investigation of Memories of Childhood Abuse, 1998). The biggest debate involves the accuracy of recovered memories.

Many clinical psychologists and other therapists believe that people are able to completely repress painful memories and then later remember them accurately (Alpert, Brown, & Courtois, 1998; Gleaves, Smith, Butler, & Spiegel, 2004). However, scientific research on eyewitness testimony has shown that people's recollections of events can be influenced by a number of factors, including suggestive questioning. Many of the adults who have recovered memories of childhood abuse have done so during therapy sessions that relied on highly suggestive questioning techniques (e.g., "You seem like you've been abused. Why don't you tell me about that?"), guided imagery (i.e., instructions to visualize specific events), hypnosis, or age regression. As a result, many other psychologists have questioned the accuracy of recovered memories (Kihlstrom, 2004; Ornstein, Ceci, & Loftus, 1998). They have expressed concern that suggestive questioning techniques may cause people to "remember"

Lineup Biases. Police investigators often ask witnesses to identify a suspect as the perpetrator of a crime. Witnesses usually make their identifications from either a group of police photographs known as a photospread or a live presentation of one or more possible suspects.

Showup

A lineup in which a single suspect is presented to an eyewitness.

In-person identification procedures include showups and lineups. A **showup** is a procedure in which a witness is asked to decide whether a single suspect is the perpetrator. For example, a police officer who catches someone running away from a crime scene may bring him to a witness and ask, "Is this the man who mugged you?" In contrast, lineups occur when a witness is shown several individuals in order to identify a perpetrator. It has long been thought that showups are more suggestive than lineups, because presenting a single individual to a witness strongly implies that the featured person is the actual criminal. A recent meta-analysis (Steblay, Dysart, Fulero, & Lindsay, 2003), however, found that the rate of correct eyewitness identifications is similar between showups and lineups. Moreover, when the perpetrator is absent (i.e., not present in the showup or lineup), witnesses may actually be *less* likely to make a false identification in a showup than in a lineup.

Simultaneous Lineup

A lineup in which several potential suspects are shown at one time.

The ways that lineups are constructed and administered can have substantial effects on the accuracy of eyewitness identifications. **Simultaneous lineups** occur when several potential suspects are shown at one time and the witness is asked to select the perpetrator. Identifications from simultaneous lineups can be problematic because they encourage relative rather than absolute judgments, that is, decisions about which person looks most like the perpetrator rather than decisions about whether the perpetrator actually is present in the lineup (Wells, 1984).

experiences of abuse that never actually happened.

Researchers have used a variety of approaches to investigate the accuracy of recovered memories. For ethical reasons, these studies typically examine distressing emotional experiences other than sexual abuse. An illustrative study was conducted by Porter, Yuille, and Lehman (1999) using college student participants. At the beginning of the study, the researchers sent questionnaires to the participants' parents asking whether their children had experienced six highly emotional events, such as being bitten or attacked by a dog. Using the parents' responses, the researchers chose one real and one nonreal experience for each participant.

The students then participated in a series of three interviews. In the first interview, each participant was asked whether he or she had experienced the real and the nonreal events. Almost all of the participants immediately remembered the real, but not the false, events. The interviewer then told the participants four fictitious details about one nonreal event that supposedly had been provided by their parents. The interviewer encouraged the participants to remember additional details about the event, telling them, "Most people are able to retrieve lost memories if they try hard enough." The interviewer also led the students through guided imagery exercises in which they tried to visualize the nonreal event.

During the next 2 weeks, the students participated in 2 more interviews that were similar to the first one. They also completed daily writing exercises in which they tried to remember details about the event. At the end of the 2 weeks, 26 percent of the participants had "recovered" a complete memory of the nonreal event; they were convinced that the event had happened and were able to describe details about the event other than the four details provided by the interviewer. An additional 30 percent "recovered" partial memories of the false event; they were able to describe some details about the event but were not completely sure that it had happened.

Although the exact nature of repressed and recovered memories still is unclear, research provides experimental evidence that people who are exposed to suggestive questioning techniques can develop memories of nonexistent, highly emotional childhood events. In the coming years, additional research will help resolve the scientific debate about recovered memories and will inform legal policies related to childhood sexual abuse.

Although this process can lead to correct judgments if the perpetrator is present, it can be highly problematic when the perpetrator is not in the lineup (Steblay, Dysart, Fulero, & Lindsay, 2001). The **sequential lineup** was developed to address this problem. In sequential lineups, potential perpetrators are shown one at a time, and witnesses must decide whether one person is the perpetrator before seeing the next person. This type of lineup results in more careful attention to each person and reduces the use of relative judgments. Eyewitnesses exposed to sequential lineups make fewer false identifications than do eyewitnesses exposed to simultaneous lineups (Steblay et al., 2001).

Sequential Lineup

A lineup in which potential suspects are shown one at a time.

In addition to lineup composition, the instructions given to eyewitnesses during lineups can influence identification accuracy. Some lineup instructions can be highly suggestive. For example, if a police officer asks a witness, "Which person is the one who hurt you?", she may imply that the real perpetrator is present in the lineup, making it more likely that the witness will make an identification (Steblay, 1997). As a result, identifications from lineups are more accurate when witnesses are told explicitly that the actual perpetrator may or may not be present in the lineup.

In Chapter 1, you learned about demand characteristics in research. As a reminder, demand characteristics occur when an experimenter gives subtle cues to research participants that lead them to confirm his or her hypothesis. There are many similarities between police lineups and research experiments (Wells & Luus, 1990). Police lineups involve a hypothesis—the belief that a particular suspect was the perpetrator of the crime. This hypothesis is tested by gathering data. Specifically, police officers accept or reject their hypothesis about the

As seen in the movie, The Usual Suspects, *police investigators often ask eyewitnesses to identify criminals from a lineup of several people. In a simultaneous lineup, these individuals are presented to the witness at the same time.*

perpetrator of a crime based on whether or not witnesses identify that individual in a lineup. These similarities between police lineups and experiments have led social psychologists to investigate whether demand characteristics also exist in eyewitness identification procedures (Garrioch & Brimacombe, 2001; Phillips, McAuliff, Kovera, & Cutler, 1999). In a study by Garrioch and Brimacombe (2001), participants administered a photographic lineup (photospread) to eyewitnesses. The participants were told that a particular picture was the "correct" choice, but, in actuality, the perpetrator was not included in the set of pictures. The study found that the eyewitnesses expressed more confidence about their choice when they selected the picture that the administrator believed was correct. This finding suggests that the administrators communicated subtle cues that those witnesses had selected the right picture. As a result, many social psychologists now recommend double-blind identification procedures, where neither the investigator nor the witness knows which individual in a lineup or photospread is the actual suspect.

Assessing Eyewitness Accuracy. Given the number of factors that can affect the accuracy of eyewitness identifications and testimony, how can we determine whether a particular witness is providing correct information? One possibility involves considering the eyewitness's confidence in his or her identification or testimony. The Supreme Court has held that the confidence of an eyewitness should influence the amount of weight given to his or her testimony (*Neil v. Biggers,* 1972). Likewise, several studies suggest that police officers, attorneys, and jurors are more likely to trust a witness who claims to be very confident about her identification than one who expresses less confidence (Brewer & Burke, 2002; Potter & Brewer, 1999). However, the relationship between eyewitness confidence and accuracy tends to be quite small, particularly when witnessing conditions are poor (Bothwell, Deffenbacher, & Brigham, 1987; Sporer, Penrod, Read, & Cutler, 1995). In other words, witnesses' confidence about their identifications or testimony often bears little relation to the accuracy of their claims.

Recently, researchers have been investigating other methods of assessing the accuracy of eyewitnesses. One promising method involves measuring the length of time it takes witnesses to make an identification. Witnesses who identify a suspect quickly are more likely to be accurate than are witnesses who take longer to make an identification (Dunning & Perreta, 2002; Smith, Lindsay, & Pryke, 2000). In one series of studies, witnesses who identified a perpetrator in 10 or fewer seconds were accurate 87.1 percent of the time, whereas witnesses who took longer than 10 seconds were accurate only 46.3 percent of the time (Dunning & Perretta, 2002). These studies suggest that correct eyewitness identifications may be associated with the use of automatic rather than controlled processes (which you learned about in Chapter 3).

Another approach involves having witnesses separately identify different features of the suspect. For example, a suspect might identify a perpetrator's face from one set of photographs, select his body from a second set of photographs, and finally identify his voice from a set of audio recordings. Pryke, Lindsay, Dysart, and Dupuis (2004) found that witnesses who consistently identified the same individual from different types of feature lineups were more accurate than were witnesses who selected different individuals for different features.

How Influential Is Research on Eyewitnesses? Social psychological research on eyewitness identification and testimony is being noticed and used by important policymakers. In the fall of 1999, the U.S. Department of Justice released guidelines for police to use when dealing with eyewitnesses. The task force that created the guidelines included six social and cognitive psychologists who conduct research on eyewitness identification and testimony (Wells, Malpass, Lindsay, Fisher, Turtle, & Fulero, 2000). As a result, the guidelines were based in part on the social psychological research reviewed in this section. For example, the guidelines recommend that police officers use open-ended questions (e.g., "Tell me what you saw") rather than leading questions. They also recommend that police officers explicitly tell eyewitnesses that the perpetrator may or may not be present in the lineup. By influencing national guidelines for police procedures, social psychological research may play an important role in improving the quality of eyewitness identification and testimony. An important goal now is to determine how frequently police officers are actually using procedures recommended by social scientists. Preliminary research suggests variability in the use of different procedures; for example, in a recent survey, 40 percent of police officers reported that they used sequential lineups, and 52 percent indicated that they explicitly told witnesses that they did not have to select a suspect from the lineup (Wogalter, Malpass, & McQuiston, 2004).

CRIMINAL DEFENDANTS

In addition to eyewitnesses, social psychologists also study the experiences of criminal defendants. In this section, we discuss research about two critical issues related to criminal defendants: false confessions and lie detection.

False Confessions

When police officers question criminal suspects, they generally try to get those suspects to confess, that is, to admit that they are guilty of committing a crime. Although it may seem odd to think that someone would confess to a crime that he or she did not commit, false confessions do occur. Kassin and Wrightsman (1985) identified three different types of false confessions. Sometimes people make **voluntary false confessions**; for example, a father may falsely confess to a crime in order to keep his child from going to jail. False confessions also may be coerced. **Coerced-compliant false confessions** occur when people are pressured to admit guilt, but privately continue to believe in their own innocence. In the case *Brown v. Mississippi* (1936), the U.S. Supreme Court overturned the murder convictions of three men who falsely confessed to murder to stop the police from whipping them with steel-studded leather belts. In contrast, **coerced-internalized false confessions** occur when people actually come to believe that they committed crimes they did not commit. A highly publicized case of coerced internalized false confession involved a man named Paul Ingram. He was arrested after his adult daughters "recovered" memories of sexual and satanic ritual abuse. Ingram initially claimed to be innocent. However, after numerous questioning sessions in which he was hypnotized and asked leading questions, Ingram began to believe that he in fact had abused his daughters.

Voluntary False Confession

When a person willingly confesses to a crime he or she did not commit.

Coerced-Compliant False Confession

When a person is pressured to confess to a crime but continues to believe that he or she is innocent.

Coerced-Internalized False Confession

When an innocent person is pressured to confess to a crime, then comes to believe that he or she actually committed the crime.

Even though no physical evidence of the abuse was ever found, Ingram pleaded guilty to several counts of third-degree rape (Ofshe & Watters, 1994).

The cases mentioned in the last paragraph involve false confessions that were elicited by physical torture and hypnosis. Social psychological research suggests that false confessions may occur even in less extreme circumstances. For example, a large proportion of students will falsely confess to deleting data from a computer by hitting a forbidden key when the behavior seems plausible and when a witness claims that she saw them do it (Kassin & Kiechel, 1996). False confessions seem to be especially likely among teenagers and individuals who are highly suggestible (Redlich & Goodman, 2003).

Minimization

An interrogation technique in which the investigator downplays the significance of a crime to make a confession seem less serious.

Certain questioning techniques also may increase the rate of false confessions. One technique, **minimization**, occurs when interrogators downplay the significance of a crime to make a confession seem less serious (Kassin & McNall, 1991). For example, a police officer using minimization might say, "Hey, I understand that mistakes happen. Why don't you just tell me what happened?" Another technique involves offering suspects a "deal"—that is, an explicit offer of leniency in exchange for a confession. A recent study by Russano, Meissner, Narchet, and Kassin (in press) demonstrates that the combination of minimization techniques and deals can substantially increase the likelihood of false confessions. In the study, participants were asked to complete a series of "individual problems" and "team problems." The team problems were supposed to be answered in conjunction with a confederate who ostensibly was another participant in the experiment. The experimenter warned participants that they should not discuss their answers on the individual problems because that would constitute cheating.

In one condition, once the experimenter left the room, the confederate asked the participant for the answer to one of the individual problems. Most participants gave the confederate their answer, thereby making them guilty of cheating. In another condition, the confederate did not ask the participant for an answer. Participants in this condition therefore were innocent of cheating.

The experimenter came back, collected the questionnaires from the participant and the confederate, and then left the room again. After a few minutes, he returned and told them that there was a problem with their answers and he would need to talk to each of them individually. When the experimenter spoke with the participant, he said that both students in the session had produced a highly unusual answer to one of the individual problems, suggesting that they had discussed their answers. The experimenter accused the participant of cheating and asked him or her to sign a confession that would be given to the professor in charge of the study. Depending on the condition, the experimenter's interrogation included minimization techniques (e.g., "I'm sure you didn't realize what a big deal it was;" Russano et al., in press, p. 9) or offers of a deal (e.g., avoiding a confrontation with the presumably angry professor).

Overall, 72 percent of the guilty participants and 20 percent of the innocent participants confessed to sharing answers with the confederate. However, the rates of both true and false confessions differed dramatically based on whether minimization techniques and "deals" were used in the interrogation. As seen in Table 15–2, guilty participants who were interrogated without minimization or a deal confessed 46 percent of the time, whereas guilty participants interrogated with both techniques confessed 87 percent of the time. Innocent participants who were interrogated without minimization or a deal very rarely confessed—only 6 percent of the time. In contrast, innocent participants interrogated with both techniques confessed nearly half of the time (43 percent). Thus, both minimization techniques and offers of leniency increase the likelihood that an individual will confess to committing a wrongful act. Unfortunately, these techniques seem to have a disproportionate influence on innocent individuals. As seen in Table 15–2, the ratio of true:false confessions was greater than 7:1 when basic interrogation techniques were used. That ratio dropped to 2:1 when minimization techniques were used and deals were offered. Thus, although these techniques are effective in increasing the rate of true confessions, they have the problem of

Table 15–2

Rates of True and False Confessions in Russano, Meissner, Narchet, and Kassin's (in press) Study

	True Confessions	False Confessions	Ratio of True: False Confessions
Interrogation only	46%	6%	7.67:1
Interrogation + deal	72%	14%	5.14:1
Interrogation + minimization	81%	18%	4.50:1
Interrogation + deal + minimization	87%	43%	2.02:1

greatly increasing the number of false confessions. As a result, the use of these techniques by police officers may be problematic, potentially leading to substantial numbers of false confessions by innocent suspects.

What are the potential consequences of false confessions in legal contexts? Once a suspect has made a confession, he or she is likely to be charged with the crime and indicted. Research has shown that a confession is one of the most powerful pieces of evidence that can be presented in court. Kassin and Neumann (1997) presented mock jurors with a simulated murder trial. There was very little direct evidence tying the defendant to the crime. In one condition, jurors heard that the defendant had confessed to the crime but then retracted his confession; 62 percent of those jurors voted to convict the man. In contrast, in another condition, jurors heard that an eyewitness had identified the defendant in a lineup; only 27 percent of those jurors voted to convict the defendant. This pattern suggests that false confessions can lead to the wrongful conviction of innocent individuals.

Lie Detection

What happens when a suspect does not confess to a crime and there is not enough physical evidence to conclusively link him or her to the act? How can the police determine whether the suspect is lying about his or her involvement in the crime? Conversely, how can people who are falsely accused of criminal behavior clear their names?

In Chapter 2, you learned that people who are lying often give off nonverbal cues, such as blinking or tilting their heads. However, even with this nonverbal leakage, observers usually are unable to detect lies at much above the level of chance (DePaulo, 1994; Frank & Ekman, 1997). Despite their training and experience in crime investigation, law enforcement professionals may not be much better (DePaulo & Pfeifer, 1986; Vrij, 2000). For example, Mann, Vrij, and Bull (2004) recently conducted a study in which British police officers watched video segments from police interrogations of actual criminal suspects. Some suspects were telling the truth and other suspects were lying. The officers correctly recognized truth-telling 66 percent of the time and lies 64 percent of the time, with somewhat higher levels of accuracy among officers with more experience at interviewing criminal suspects. In another study (Ekman & O'Sullivan, 1991), a variety of law enforcement professionals—including members of the U.S. Secret Service, Central Intelligence Agency, Federal Bureau of Investigation, National Security Agency, and California police department—watched videotapes of 10 individuals who told the truth or lied about their reactions to a film. Only the Secret Service members were able to detect lying at levels above chance (50 percent)—and even they were accurate only 64 percent of the time. Notably, in both studies, there was no correlation between participants' confidence in their judgments and their lie-detection ability. In other words, investigators who were confident that they could tell whether someone was telling the truth or lying were just as likely to be wrong as were investigators who were less certain about their judgments. This pattern is similar to research about the correlation between eyewitness confidence and accuracy discussed in an earlier section.

Why aren't trained criminal investigators better at detecting liars? The primary reason is probably that, as you learned in Chapter 2, lie detection is difficult for most people. Despite their experience, police officers, attorneys, and judges often have mistaken beliefs about the physical cues that may indicate deception. For example, police officers often believe that looking away during an interview indicates that a suspect is lying, but this has not been found in social psychological research (Strömwall & Granhag, 2003). Another reason why criminal investigators have difficulty detecting lies may be that they expect deception from suspects and therefore overestimate the likelihood that any given individual is telling a lie. Meissner and Kassin (2002) found that, due to this expectation of deceit, police officers have lower standards for deciding that someone is lying than do other individuals.

Law enforcement professionals' difficulty with lie detection is problematic when one considers the high stakes involved in criminal investigations. If police officers cannot reliably tell whether suspects are telling the truth or lying, how can we be sure that innocent suspects are not being arrested and that guilty individuals are not being released? One technique that commonly is used to help police officers involves polygraph, or "lie detector," tests. During these tests, suspects answer questions while hooked up to a machine that records various physiological responses. In the most common version of the polygraph test, the **control question test**, the suspect is asked questions about his or her involvement in the crime (e.g., "Did you embezzle $40,000 from your employer?"), as well as control questions about unrelated wrongdoings (e.g., "Have you ever told a lie?"). According to the logic of the test, an innocent person should become more aroused when answering control questions about previous wrongdoings (which he or she presumably did commit) than when answering questions about the crime (which he or she did not commit; Iacono & Patrick, 1999). In contrast, a guilty individual should become more aroused when answering questions about the crime.

Control Question Test

A method of polygraph testing in which a person's physiological responses to questions about a crime are compared with his or her physiological responses to questions about personal wrongdoings.

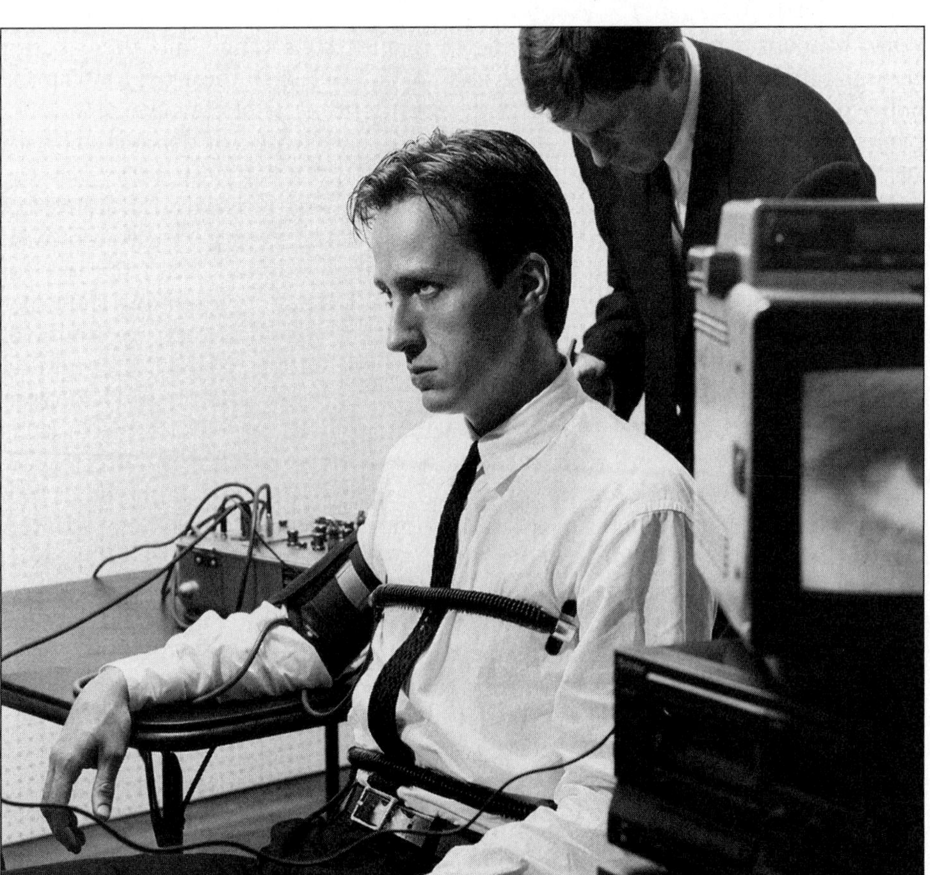

In this photo, an examiner administers a polygraph test to a criminal suspect. The accuracy of polygraph tests is hotly debated.

The accuracy of polygraph tests is debated. Advocates of the test, who are often professional criminal investigators, claim that polygraph testing is accurate approximately 90 percent of the time (Honts, Raskin, & Kircher, 2002). However, most research published in peer-reviewed scientific journals suggests that the accuracy rate is much lower, about 70 percent for the control question test (Fiedler, Schimd, & Stahl, 2002; Iacono & Lykken, 2002). In addition, research has shown that guilty individuals who are given a small amount of information about the logic of polygraph testing can "beat" the test and appear innocent by increasing their physiological responses to the control questions about previous misdeeds (Honts, Raskin, & Kircher, 1994). Hence, even with polygraph testing, police officers may not be able to determine consistently and accurately whether suspects are telling the truth.

JURY SELECTION AND DECISION MAKING

The U.S. Bill of Rights gives citizens the right to be tried before an impartial jury of their peers. Given the importance of trial by jury in our legal system, it is not surprising that social psychologists have conducted a considerable amount of research on jury decision making. In this section, we discuss some of the insights into jury selection and decision making that have emerged from this research.

Jury Selection

At the beginning of each trial, a process known as ***voir dire*** is conducted to select jurors. During *voir dire,* judges or attorneys question potential jurors about opinions or biases that could impair their ability to render a fair verdict. If there is reason to believe that a juror would not be able to decide a case fairly, that juror is dismissed from further participation in the trial. In addition, attorneys can use a limited number of **peremptory challenges** to dismiss jurors without having to state a reason. Peremptory challenges can be used to eliminate jurors for a number of reasons, including occupation and perceived personality traits; however, they cannot be used to dismiss jurors on the basis of race or gender (*Batson v. Kentucky,* 1986; *J.E.B. v. Alabama,* 1994).

Voir Dire

Jury selection that takes place at the beginning of every trial.

Peremptory Challenge

A process during *voir dire* in which attorneys can dismiss a limited number of potential jurors without stating a reason.

The rationale behind peremptory challenges is that attorneys will be able to eliminate jurors who will react unfavorably to their side of the case. An important question, then, is whether jurors' characteristics are related to their judgments about trial evidence. Overall, relationships between juror characteristics and trial judgments tend to be small, although they can be more pronounced in certain types of cases (Greene et al., 2002; Strier, 1999). For example, women are somewhat more likely to find defendants guilty in cases involving sex crimes against women or children (Bottoms, Davis, & Epstein, 2004; Kovera, Levy, Borgida, & Penrod, 1994). In cases with ambiguous evidence, jurors may render more favorable verdicts to defendants who are from the same race or socioeconomic status (SES) group (Devine, Clayton, Dunford, Seying, & Pryce, 2001). In addition, certain personality characteristics can influence juror verdicts. For example, more authoritarian jurors are more likely than less authoritarian jurors to convict defendants (Narby, Cutler, & Moran, 1993). Finally, jurors' attitudes about specific issues, such as mental health, can influence their verdicts in related cases (Greene et al., 2002; Strier, 1999).

To date, there has not been strong evidence that attorneys are able to use peremptory challenges based on juror characteristics to select more effective juries (Johnson & Haney 1994; Olczak, Kaplan, & Penrod, 1991). Attorneys frequently base peremptory challenges on their implicit personality theories, that is, intuitive beliefs about how different "types" of people tend to act. Not surprisingly, these intuitive beliefs are often idiosyncratic and not strongly related to juror performance (Wrightsman, Greene, Nietzel, & Fortune, 2002). Attorneys also tend to dismiss the prospective jurors who appear to be least favorable to their position. Because both sides are allowed to do this, the composition of the final jury remains fairly close to the overall composition of the jury pool (Johnson & Haney, 1994).

However, research on the relationship between juror characteristics and trial judgments has led to the development of a process known as scientific jury selection (Strier, 1999). In scientific jury selection, trial consultants (who are often psychologists) use social science methods, such as surveys, focus groups, and mock trials, to determine the relationship between various juror characteristics and reactions to a particular case. This information is gathered prior to *voir dire,* and the results are provided to the attorneys so they can use the data when selecting jurors. There have been relatively few systematic studies of scientific jury selection, and its effectiveness remains a controversial issue. To date, the evidence suggests that scientific jury selection has a small, but potentially important, influence on jury verdicts, particularly when cases are ambiguous and selections are based on case-specific attitudes (Strier, 1999; Wrightsman et al., 2002). It is important to realize, though, that the most important predictor of case verdicts is the evidence presented at trial, not the characteristics of the jurors who evaluate it.

Death Penalty Attitudes and Death Qualification. Cases involving the death penalty raise particularly important issues for jury selection. In capital cases, *voir dire* often is used to eliminate potential jurors who do not support the death penalty. Proponents of this **death qualification** process claim that jurors who do not support the death penalty may vote to acquit a guilty defendant to keep that individual from receiving the death penalty. However, opponents of death qualification assert that excluding people who oppose the death penalty results in a biased jury. For example, women and ethnic minorities are significantly more likely to hold attitudes that would exclude them from jury duty in a capital trial (Fitzgerald & Ellsworth, 1984). In addition, individuals who support the death penalty tend to be more prosecution oriented, punitive, and concerned about crime control than are individuals who do not support the death penalty (Fitzgerald & Ellsworth, 1984; Haney, Hurtado, & Vega, 1994); they also are more likely to be prejudiced against racial minorities (Young, 2004). Translating those attitudes into behavior, individuals who support the death penalty are more likely to convict defendants than are individuals who oppose the death penalty (Allen, Mabry, & McKelton, 1998; Nietzel, McCarthy, & Kern, 1999). Finally, eliminating potential jurors who oppose the death penalty can affect the quality of the deliberation process. Cowan, Thompson, and Ellsworth (1984) compared deliberations by juries with a mixture of pro- and anti-death-penalty jurors with deliberations by death-qualified juries. The mixed

Death Qualification

When individuals who do not support the death penalty are excluded from serving on a jury in a capital case.

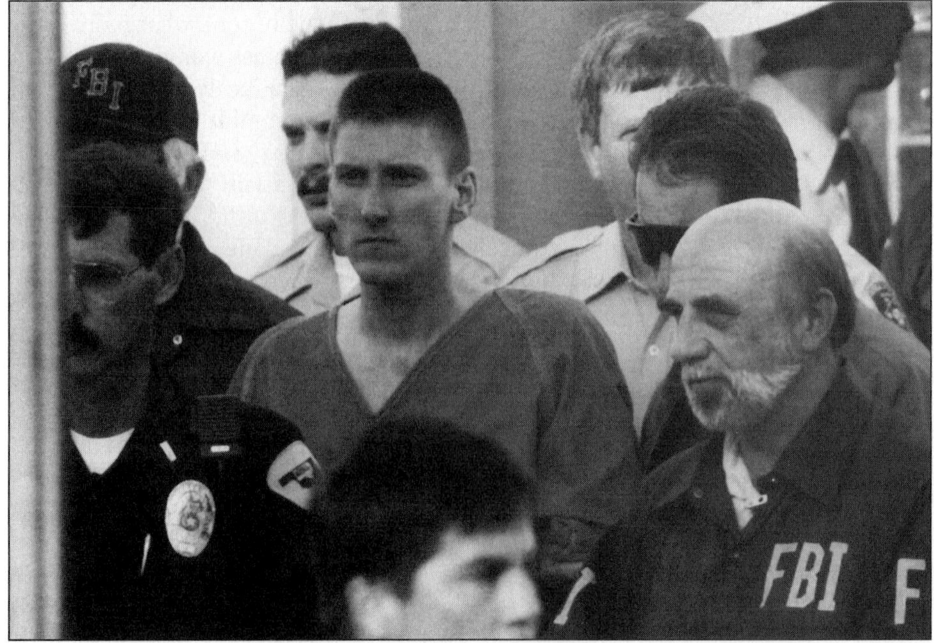

Timothy McVeigh was convicted of causing the blast that killed 168 people in the bombing of the Murrah Federal Building in Oklahoma City in 1995. McVeigh was sentenced to death and executed in 2001. Cases involving the death penalty raise important issues for jury selection.

juries were more critical of the prosecution's case, remembered more of the case facts, and found the case more difficult to decide. Thus, using jury selection to dismiss jurors who oppose the death penalty is likely to result in a less critical, more conviction-prone jury that may not be representative of the community from which it is drawn.

The Story Model of Juror Decision Making

Once jurors are selected, they must listen to the evidence against a defendant, decide whether he or she is guilty and, in some cases, recommend an appropriate punishment. To accomplish these tasks, jurors frequently must make sense of a great deal of complicated evidence and contradictory testimony. How do jurors integrate all of that information into a single verdict? Pennington and Hastie (1988, 1992; Hastie & Pennington, 2000) proposed the **story model** as a way to explain juror decision making. According to the story model, jurors use the evidence presented in trials to create stories about the events in question. For example, jurors may create a story about a robbery at a local convenience store that includes information about an alleged robber's motive and goals (e.g., whether he needed money for child support) and his actions toward the clerk (e.g., whether he pointed a gun at her). The story also may include situational characteristics (e.g., whether other people were present) and the outcome of the encounter (e.g., stolen money). By representing trial evidence in terms of characters who are involved in story-like plots that lead to specific outcomes, jurors can make sense of the overwhelming amount of information they are given.

Story Model

A model of juror decision making which asserts that jurors use the evidence presented at trial to form stories about the events in question.

Because trials usually involve contradictory accounts by the prosecution and the defense, jurors may generate a set of alternative stories. They then must choose between these competing accounts by considering factors such as which story provides the best explanation of the evidence, which story is the most plausible and internally consistent, and which story best matches the potential verdicts for the trial. Once jurors have identified the best story, they select the verdict that is the best possible match to that story. For example, Huntley and Constanzo (2003) investigated jurors' stories related to several sexual harassment trials. They found that the extent to which jurors' stories reflected the evidence presented by the plaintiff (alleged victim) versus the evidence presented by the defendant (alleged harasser) strongly predicted their verdicts. Specifically, jurors whose stories were similar to the alleged victim's determined that sexual harassment had occurred, whereas jurors whose stories were similar to the defendant's determined that it had not.

Factors That Affect Juror Decision Making

According to the story model, jurors construct their stories by actively interpreting and evaluating the information they receive during a trial. As a result, it is important to understand how the different pieces of information that jurors encounter influence their judgments about a defendant. In this section, we will review several factors that can affect juror decision making, including pretrial publicity, specific types of evidence, defendant characteristics such as race and attractiveness, and understanding of judicial instructions.

Pretrial Publicity. Turn on your television and watch the news. Chances are, you will soon hear about the latest high profile criminal investigation or trial. You might hear updates about child sexual abuse charges against Michael Jackson, sexual assault allegations against Kobe Bryant, or testimony in the trials of Martha Stewart or Scott Peterson. If you do, your experiences would not be unusual; content analyses indicate that TV news and newspaper articles frequently include prejudicial information about criminal suspects (Dixon & Linz, 2002; Imrich, Mullin, & Linz, 1995).

The U.S. Constitution guarantees defendants the right to a fair trial by an impartial jury. Some people claim that the large amount of **pretrial publicity** that

Pretrial Publicity

Media coverage about criminal investigations or preparations for particular trials.

Martha Stewart was convicted of obstructing justice and misleading investigators about her stock trades. There was extensive media coverage about these allegations prior to and during Stewart's trial. This kind of pretrial publicity may jeopardize defendants' right to a fair trial.

surrounds high-profile cases violates that right by biasing potential jurors against a defendant before the case begins. Pretrial publicity may also expose jurors to evidence that would not be admissible in court. For example, a judge might rule that evidence about weapons found in a suspect's house cannot be presented as evidence because the search was illegal. However, jurors still might know about those weapons—and consider them when deciding the defendant's guilt—because they read about them in a newspaper article or saw them on the news.

A number of social psychological studies have demonstrated that exposure to negative pretrial publicity about a criminal suspect increases the likelihood that jurors will convict that individual (Steblay, Besirevic, Fulero, & Jimenez-Lorente, 1999). For example, individuals who were exposed to more pretrial publicity about Timothy McVeigh were more likely to believe that he participated in the bombing of the Federal Building in Oklahoma City (Studebaker et al., 2002). Pretrial publicity also affects judgments about civil cases, such as lawsuits. Because there are two parties—the plaintiff and defendant—in civil cases, the effects of pretrial publicity are more complex. Research has shown that negative pretrial publicity about a defendant (e.g., learning that a company accused of dumping dangerous chemicals has been accused of other environmental violations in the past) *increases* the perceived liability of the defendant—that is, makes it seem more guilty. In contrast, negative pretrial publicity about the plaintiff (e.g., learning that the person suing the company has been accused of fraud in the past) tends to *decrease* liability judgments—that is, makes the defendant appear less guilty (Bornstein, Whisenhunt, Nemeth, & Dunaway, 2002).

Pretrial publicity appears to influence jurors' judgments by creating initial assumptions of guilt and affecting attributions made about a defendant (Otto, Penrod, & Dexter, 1994). Jurors who have been exposed to negative pretrial publicity may be quick to assume that the defendant is a typical criminal who probably committed the crime in question. In addition, pretrial publicity can affect jurors' standards for evidence, leading them to desire more or less evidence in order to find a defendant guilty (Kovera, 2002). Notably, the effects of pretrial publicity may increase over time (Steblay et al., 1999). As a result, pretrial publicity may be a considerable problem in actual criminal and civil trials where several months frequently elapse between initial publicity about an arrest and the ultimate verdict made at trial.

Inadmissible Evidence

Sometimes during trials, jurors are exposed to information that they are not supposed to have. For example, a witness might say, "The defendant's girlfriend told me that he stole $10,000 from his boss." This statement would not be admissible because it is hearsay. As a result, the judge would instruct jurors to disregard the witness's testimony. Instructions to disregard evidence are based on the assumption that people can decide not to be influenced by something they have heard or seen. However, research has shown that jurors' verdicts frequently are influenced by inadmissible evidence even when they are explicitly instructed to ignore that information (Kassin & Sommers, 1997; Pickel, 1995). As a result, exposing jurors to inadmissible evidence may jeopardize defendants' right to a fair trial.

There are several reasons why jurors may consider evidence that they have been instructed to ignore. Jurors who are motivated to make the right decision may be reluctant to disregard any information that may be useful—even if they are not supposed to consider it (Kassin & Sommers, 1997). Also, as you learned in Chapter 3, people often have difficulty suppressing unwanted thoughts; thus, even if jurors try to inhibit thoughts about inadmissible evidence, they may not be able to do it successfully (Lieberman & Arndt, 2000). However, the effects of inadmissible evidence on individual jurors may be reduced by jury deliberation. In a study by London and Nunez (2000), participants read a criminal trial related to child sexual abuse. During the trial, the judge instructed jurors to disregard a photograph seized during an illegal search or a statement made by the alleged victim's mother. These pieces of evidence had a strong influence on participants' verdicts prior to, but not following, deliberation. Thus, the process of jury deliberation may make jurors aware that they are being influenced by inadmissible evidence, leading them to correct their initial judgments.

Character Evidence. Earlier in this chapter, you learned about two types of evidence that jurors find highly persuasive: eyewitness testimony and confession evidence (Kassin & Neumann, 1997). Another important type of evidence is **character evidence**, that is, evidence about a defendant's traits and propensities. In certain circumstances, the defense can introduce witnesses to describe positive characteristics of a defendant that would make it unlikely that he committed a particular crime. For example, a witness might testify that the defendant is kind and gentle, suggesting that he would be unlikely to have committed a brutal assault. Although one might expect this kind of testimony to help the defendant, research shows that positive character evidence has little effect on jurors' guilt judgments or likelihood of conviction (Hunt & Budesheim, 2004).

Character Evidence

Evidence presented in court about a defendant's traits and/or propensities.

Paradoxically, the use of character evidence may actually *increase* the likelihood that a defendant will be convicted. This ironic outcome occurs because the prosecution is allowed to cross-examine character witnesses to try to show that they are not good judges of the defendant's character. During cross-examination, prosecutors might ask a witness whether she knows about previous behaviors by the defendant that contradict her testimony. For example, a prosecutor might say, "You said the defendant is kind and gentle. Are you aware that he was expelled from high school after injuring another student in a fistfight?" Although jurors are only supposed to use this information to evaluate the credibility of the character witness, it may influence their impressions of the defendant as well. Research shows that a defendant is more likely to be convicted when jurors hear positive character testimony that is cross-examined with negative information than when they hear no character evidence at all (Hunt & Budesheim, 2004). Thus, despite its intuitive appeal, introducing character evidence can be a risky move for a defendant.

Defendant Characteristics. The U.S. legal system is based on the idea that every person is equal before the law. The only thing that should affect jurors' decisions about defendants is the evidence presented against them. No matter who the defendants are, they should be convicted if there is strong evidence of their guilt and acquitted if there is weak evidence of their guilt. Unfortunately, a considerable amount of research, both experimental and archival, indicates that a number of factors other than evidence also influence juror decision making. Consistent with research about physical attractiveness discussed in Chapter 8, a meta-analysis of 80 juror decision-making studies found that physically attractive defendants are less likely than physically unattractive defendants to be found guilty for certain crimes, like rape and robbery and physically attractive defendants also receive more lenient sentences (Mazzella & Feingold, 1994). A similar effect was found for SES; high-SES defendants are less likely to be found guilty and, when convicted, receive lighter sentences than do low-SES defendants.

One of the most commonly studied defendant characteristics is race. Several archival studies of legal outcomes have shown that black defendants receive disproportionately harsh sentences compared to white defendants. Baldus, Woodworth, and Pulaski (1990) analyzed death penalty sentences in the state of Georgia. These researchers examined hundreds of capital cases, coding information about more than 200 variables that might affect the outcomes of the trials. Even when all of these factors were controlled, black defendants were more likely than white defendants to be sentenced to death. This bias was especially pronounced in cases involving white victims.

Many laboratory studies also have investigated racial bias in guilt and sentencing judgments made by mock jurors. These studies have generated somewhat inconsistent results, with some studies showing discrimination against black defendants, other studies showing discrimination only in certain circumstances, and still other studies showing no discrimination at all (Mazzella & Feingold, 1994; Sommers & Ellsworth, 2001). For example, Pfeifer and Ogloff (1991) found that participants who had been given jury instructions about the presumption of innocence and the need to set aside personal prejudices made similar judgments about black and white defendants; however, participants who had not been given such instructions were more likely to find the black defendant guilty.

Sommers and Ellsworth (2000, 2001) recently proposed that the inconsistent findings in these studies can be explained by aversive racism theory (Gaertner & Dovidio, 1986). As you learned in Chapter 6, aversive racism theory asserts that in the contemporary U.S. culture most people believe in equality but still have some negative beliefs and feelings about black individuals. Because of their belief in equality, most people attempt to suppress prejudiced thoughts and act in a nonbiased manner. However, when they are unaware of the influence of race or when their behavior can be justified by factors other than race, these individuals still engage in discrimination. Aversive racism theory makes the counterintuitive prediction that jurors will be more likely to discriminate against black defendants in trials where the race of the defendant is *not* salient. When a trial has racial overtones, jurors' beliefs about equality should be activated, so they should be more likely to monitor themselves for signs of bias. On the other hand, when the race of the defendant is not salient, jurors should be less likely to monitor their behavior. As a result, they may make judgments that are biased against black defendants, then use nonracial explanations to justify those decisions.

To test this explanation, Sommers and Ellsworth (2000) manipulated the salience of race in an assault trial. Half of the participants read about a black or white defendant who slapped his girlfriend in public, saying "You know better than to talk that way about a man in front of his friends." The other half of the participants received materials that were identical, except that the defendant said "You know better than to talk that way about a *black* [*white*] man in front of his friends." In the first condition, where race was not salient, white participants were significantly more likely to think that the black defendant was guilty. In contrast, in the second condition, where race was salient, there were no differences between white participants' judgments about the black and white defendant. Notably, black participants made more lenient judgments about the black defendant in both conditions, apparently because they saw both situations as racially charged. Sommers and Ellsworth's research therefore suggests that racial discrimination is likely to occur in many criminal and civil trials; however, jurors are not likely to be consciously aware that they are making biased judgments. As a result, trial outcomes may be more fair when jurors are reminded of their egalitarian beliefs prior to making judgments about the defendant's guilt or innocence.

Comprehension of Judicial Instructions. Before juries deliberate, judges give them instructions about issues such as what evidence they are allowed to consider and what verdicts they may reach. However, a considerable number of studies involving both actual trials and jury simulations indicate that jurors have difficulty understanding and applying such instructions (Ellsworth & Reifman, 2000; Lieberman & Sales, 1997). For example, one study found that jurors called for jury duty in Michigan understood less than 50 percent of the instructions they were given (Reifman, Gusick, & Ellsworth, 1992). Likewise, in death penalty cases, juries are asked to consider aggravating circumstances (i.e., factors that make the crime more serious), as well as mitigating circumstances (i.e., factors that make the crime less serious). However, jurors in capital cases do not seem to understand the concept of mitigation or the conditions under which mitigating or aggravating circumstances should lead to sentences other than the death penalty (Haney & Lynch, 1994; Wiener et al. 1998). The finding that many jurors may not understand the factors that they are supposed to consider when making death penalty judgments suggests that sentencing decisions in some capital cases may be inappropriate.

Because of the importance of this issue, several methods of helping jurors understand judicial instructions have been proposed (Ellsworth & Reifman, 2000; Lieberman & Sales, 1997). One method involves rewriting instructions to be more "user friendly," for example, by using everyday words rather than legal terminology. Another potential solution involves giving jurors a written copy of judicial instructions; that way, jurors can refer back to them when they have questions about what they are supposed to do (Heuer & Penrod, 1989). The evidence to date suggests that, although misunderstandings still occur, these reforms help improve jurors' comprehension of judicial instructions.

Jury Deliberation

Much of the research discussed in this section has investigated how individual jurors understand and evaluate trial information. However, in actual cases, a

Judges give jury members instructions about the laws that are relevant for deciding a verdict. However, research indicates that jurors frequently do not understand judicial instructions.

group of jurors must work together to reach a verdict. Although almost all of the factors that affect the decisions of individual jurors have similar effects on juries (Devine et al., 2001), it is important to consider how the small group processes you read about in Chapter 10 can influence jury deliberations.

Jury verdicts tend to be powerfully influenced by the initial verdict preferences of individual jurors (Kalven & Zeisel, 1966; Sandys & Dillehay, 1995). When two-thirds to three-fourths of the jurors initially support a particular verdict, the jury as a whole almost always returns that verdict (Devine et al., 2001). This finding reflects the importance of normative social influence; people often conform to the viewpoint of the majority, even if they do not privately agree. Juries appear, however, to have a **leniency bias** in which lower standards are used for deciding to acquit a defendant than for deciding to convict a defendant (MacCoun & Kerr, 1988). For example, a smaller majority is needed to sway a jury toward acquittal than toward conviction (Devine et al., 2001). In addition, as you may have seen in movies like *Twelve Angry Men,* there are some cases in which jurors in the minority persuade the rest of the jury to change positions. Consistent with research on group processes, minority jurors are more persuasive when they use informational social influence, that is, refute the majority opinion with well-reasoned arguments.

Leniency Bias

A bias in which juries have lower standards for acquitting a defendant than for convicting a defendant.

Juries tend to rely on two approaches for determining verdicts (Hastie, Penrod, & Pennington, 1983). **Evidence-driven juries** discuss the strength of the evidence presented at trial before assessing jurors' verdict preferences. In contrast, **verdict-driven juries** begin deliberations by assessing verdict preferences, then try to reach a consensus among individuals with different opinions. Some juries combine these two approaches, alternating discussions between evidence and verdict preferences. Research suggests that evidence-driven juries discuss the trial more thoroughly and therefore make better judgments about the case.

Evidence-Driven Jury

A jury that begins deliberation by discussing the strength of the evidence.

Verdict-Driven Jury

A jury that approaches deliberation by assessing verdict preferences.

A considerable number of studies have investigated two particular issues related to jury decision making. The first issue is jury size. The number of individuals required to be in a jury ranges from 6 or fewer to 12. In 1973, the U.S. Supreme Court held that there are no important differences between 6- and 12-person juries (*Colgrove v. Battin,* 1973). However, research shows that, compared to 6-person juries, 12-person juries spend more time deliberating and have better memory for trial evidence (Saks & Marti, 1997). Also, because there are more individuals in the jury, there is a greater chance that minority or dissenting opinions will be heard and considered. Finally, 12-person juries tend to be more

In criminal and civil trials, jury members must work together to reach a verdict. Normative and informational social influence both can affect jury deliberations.

representative of the demographic characteristics of the overall jury pool. Therefore, contrary to the Supreme Court's view, the quality and fairness of verdicts may be better in larger juries.

The second issue is the decision rule required for a jury to return a verdict. Sometimes juries must deliberate to a unanimous verdict, whereas in other cases they can return a verdict that is supported by a majority of the jurors. Juries who must reach a unanimous decision discuss evidence more thoroughly, are more likely to consider minority opinions, and take longer to reach a verdict compared to juries that require only a majority consensus (Hastie et al., 1983). Moreover, jurors, particularly those with dissenting opinions, tend to be more satisfied with their experiences in juries that require unanimous versus majority decisions. As a result, the decision rule used by juries affects the quality of their deliberations and judgments, as well as the subjective experiences of individual jurors.

SOCIAL PSYCHOLOGISTS' CONTRIBUTIONS TO THE LEGAL SYSTEM

As you have seen in this chapter, social psychologists have learned a great deal about factors that affect important legal behaviors, such as confessions, eyewitness testimony, and jury decision making. At this point, you may be asking yourself whether this research has made any impact on the legal system. In fact, social psychologists have communicated their findings to the legal system in a number of different ways. Earlier in this chapter, you learned that social psychologists collaborated with the U.S. Department of Justice to develop national guidelines for police to use when interacting with eyewitnesses (Wells et al., 2000). In this section, we discuss two other ways that social psychologists contribute to the legal system: through expert testimony and *amicus curiae* briefs.

Expert Testimony

One of the most common ways for social psychologists to share their knowledge is through **expert testimony**. Social psychologists frequently are asked to testify about research findings in order to give judges and jurors a framework for understanding and evaluating the evidence in a particular case (Monahan & Walker, 1998). The use of expert psychological testimony in trials appears to be growing steadily, but it has proved controversial. Two major issues are involved in expert testimony: the quality of the testimony and its effects on jurors.

Expert Testimony

Testimony by a qualified expert witness about research findings that are relevant to a particular case.

The quality of expert testimony is important because the courts do not want jurors to consider evidence that is unreliable or inconclusive. Thus, psychologists may testify only about research that meets the legal standards for admissibility. Until recently, most U.S. courts required that research be "generally accepted" by the relevant scientific community in order to be admissible (*Frye v. United States,* 1923). However, in 1993, the U.S. Supreme Court changed the legal standard for the admissibility of expert scientific evidence, including psychological science, in all federal courts as well as in some state courts (*Daubert v. Merrell Dow Pharmaceuticals, Inc.,* 1993; Walker & Monahan, 1996).

Today, judges must consider several indicators of scientific reliability:

- Has the research been subjected to peer review? That is, have other scientists evaluated it?
- Is the theory underlying research falsifiable? That is, can a hypothesis be disproven?
- Does the research have any known or potential error rate? That is, how likely is a conclusion to be false?
- Is the research generally accepted by the scientific community?

These newer standards have led psychologists to carefully evaluate the quality of research on topics such as eyewitness identification, repressed memories, gender stereotyping, polygraph testing, battered woman syndrome, rape trauma

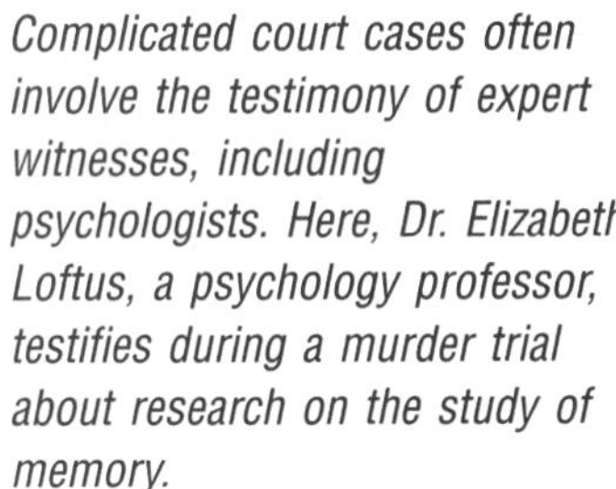

Complicated court cases often involve the testimony of expert witnesses, including psychologists. Here, Dr. Elizabeth Loftus, a psychology professor, testifies during a murder trial about research on the study of memory.

syndrome, children as witnesses, and predictions of dangerousness (e.g., Hunt, Borgida, Kelly, & Burgess, 2002; Kovera & Borgida, 1997). However, a problem with these standards is the reliance on judges as the "gatekeepers" or evaluators of scientific evidence. Many judges lack the necessary scientific background and may have difficulty weighing the scientific issues involved in admissibility decisions (Gatowski et al., 2001; Kovera & McAuliff, 2000). Notably, judges who know more about topics such as eyewitness testimony are more likely to allow a psychological expert to testify at trial (Wise & Safer, 2004).

In addition to assessing the quality of psychological evidence, judges also must determine whether expert testimony will help jurors to reach a trial decision without unduly biasing them toward a particular verdict. One question related to the helpfulness of expert testimony is whether jurors can use aggregate research findings to help them understand a particular case. In a study by Brekke and Borgida (1988), mock jurors listened to an audiotape of a rape trial. During the trial, a psychologist testified about some common misconceptions about rape and rape victim behavior. In one condition, the psychologist presented scientific information without tying it to the case; in another condition, she used a hypothetical example of a rape victim to show the connections between the research and the current case. Results indicated that the jurors were more likely to vote for conviction and recommend a harsh sentence for the defendant when the expert witness connected the research to the case rather than presented a generalized overview. The expert witness was most influential when she testified before the other witnesses, giving the jurors a framework within which to evaluate their testimony. Thus, expert testimony that draws links between research and a particular case has a larger influence on jurors than does expert testimony that simply presents a set of research findings. Other research has shown similar effects for expert testimony on battered woman's syndrome (Schuller, Wells, Rzepa, & Klippenstine, 2004), child sexual abuse (Kovera, Gresham, Borgida, Gray, & Regan, 1997), and eyewitness identification (Geiselman et al., 2002). However, jurors tend to discount expert testimony when an expert is highly paid or when he or she frequently testifies in court (Cooper & Neuhaus, 2000). The pattern suggests that experts who appear to be "hired guns" are not perceived as credible by jurors.

***Amicus Curiae* Brief**

A "friend of the court" document that summarizes research findings that are relevant to a particular case.

Amicus Curiae Briefs

Another common way for social psychologists to share their knowledge with the legal system involves ***amicus curiae*** or "friend of the court" briefs. *Amicus* briefs summarize relevant bodies of psychological science to provide judges with a scientific context for deciding a particular case. *Amicus* briefs, written by teams of expert psychologists and attorneys, have been filed by the American Psychological Association (APA) in almost 150 cases decided by appellate courts, including the U.S. Supreme Court (see http://www.apa.org/psyclaw/amicus.html for a complete list of cases). These 150 cases have involved some of the most significant and controversial public policy issues of our time, including affirmative action, abortion, employment discrimination, child sexual abuse, same-sex couples, and the death penalty.

For example, in *Price Waterhouse v. Hopkins* (1989), an *amicus* brief submitted by the APA summarized social psychological research on gender stereotyping and gender prejudice to assist the U.S. Supreme Court in deciding a case about employment discrimination (the case is discussed in Chapter 11). The brief included several studies about stereotyping, prejudice, and discrimination that are discussed in Chapters 3 and 6 of this textbook. Likewise, the APA recently filed an *amicus* brief with the U.S. Court of Appeals in the case, *Comfort et al. v. Lynn School Committee et al.* (2004), a case involving racial desegregation in a public school district. In question was a proposal by the Lynn, Massachusetts, school system to alleviate segregation and racial tension by creating conditions that would encourage sustained contact between white and minority students. The APA brief summarized social psychological research on intergroup contact theory, stereotyping, and social categorization (discussed in Chapters 3 and 6) suggesting that this kind of plan would decrease levels of harmful racial prejudice and discriminatory behavior. By developing *amicus* briefs for cases like *Price Waterhouse v. Hopkins* and *Comfort v. Lynn School Committee,* social psychologists can provide the courts with scientific evidence that can lead to more just outcomes for important legal cases.

Summary

1. Social psychologists study many topics related to the law. These issues include eyewitness identification and testimony, false confessions, lie detection, jury decision making, expert testimony, attitudes toward the death penalty, and discrimination in the legal system.
2. The reliability of eyewitness reports can be affected by estimator variables, which are factors related to the witness or the viewing situation. Eyewitnesses give more reliable information when they are not experiencing excessive stress, when weapons are not present, and when they are identifying members of their own race.
3. System variables, that is, factors under the control of the justice system, also can affect eyewitness reports. Witnesses who are exposed to misleading postevent information may claim to have seen things that did not actually happen. According to source monitoring theory, witnesses may have difficulty distinguishing whether a particular piece of information came from the event they witnessed or from an interviewer's questions.
4. The format of lineups is another system variable that makes a difference in eyewitness accuracy. Eyewitnesses make more accurate identifications when suspects are presented sequentially rather than simultaneously. Suggestive lineup instructions can decrease the accuracy of identification. Recent research suggests that eyewitnesses may be most accurate when they identify a suspect in less than 10 seconds.
5. People sometimes confess to crimes that they did not commit; occasionally, they may even start to believe that they actually committed the crimes. False confessions are more likely when interrogators minimize the severity of the crime and offer leniency in exchange for a confession.
6. Law enforcement professionals may not be able to detect deception at much better than chance levels. Polygraph ("lie detector") tests seem to have relatively low accuracy rates, and individuals may be able to manipulate their physiological responses in order to appear innocent.
7. Characteristics of jurors such as personality traits, social attitudes, and demographic variables are at best modest predictors of juror verdicts. Despite this fact, some attorneys attempt to use scientific jury selection to identify jurors who will be more favorable to their case.

8. In capital cases, efforts are often made to eliminate potential jurors who do not support the death penalty. Research suggests that this process of death qualification may result in a less critical, less representative, and more conviction-prone jury.
9. The story model of juror decision making proposes that jurors actively use the evidence presented at trial to create stories about the events in question. Jurors then determine which of these competing accounts most consistently fits the evidence and best matches the verdicts for the trial.
10. A number of factors can influence juror decision making. Negative pretrial publicity can increase the likelihood that a criminal defendant will be convicted as well as influence judgments in civil trials. Jurors frequently are influenced by inadmissible evidence, even after instructed by a judge to ignore it. Likewise, jurors may use information they learn from the cross-examination of character evidence to negatively evaluate the defendant.
11. Jurors are less likely to convict physically attractive defendants, as well as defendants who are high in socioeconomic status. In many cases, jurors are more likely to convict black defendants than white defendants. A defendant's race is most likely to influence juror decision making when his or her race is not salient; when race is emphasized, jurors may monitor themselves closely to avoid racial bias.
12. The final verdict reached by a jury frequently reflects the initial verdict preference of the majority of jurors; however, in some cases, jurors' judgments are changed through deliberation about the evidence. Compared to 6-person juries, 12-person juries deliberate more and consider a wider range of perspectives. In addition, juries required to reach a unanimous decision tend to discuss evidence longer and more thoroughly.
13. Social psychologists have contributed their knowledge to the legal system through expert testimony and *amicus curiae* ("friend of the court") briefs. At trial, psychologists may testify about research that meets standards for scientific reliability in order to provide a "framework" for considering the case. Expert testimony is more influential when it draws connections between research and the case at hand rather than simply presenting research findings. *Amicus curiae* briefs are documents written by psychologists and attorneys that summarize relevant scientific literature for the courts.

Key Terms

acquisition **470**
amicus curiae brief **490**
character evidence **485**
coerced-compliant false confession **477**
coerced-internalized false confession **477**
control question test **480**
death qualification **482**
estimator variables **470**
evidence-driven jury **488**
expert testimony **489**
leniency bias **488**
minimization **478**
overwriting hypothesis **473**
own-race bias **471**
peremptory challenge **481**
pretrial publicity **483**
recovered memory **474**
retrieval **470**
sequential lineup **475**
showup **475**
simultaneous lineup **475**
source monitoring **473**
storage **470**
story model **483**
system variables **470**
verdict-driven jury **488**
voir dire **481**
voluntary false confession **477**
weapon focus effect **471**

Glossary

Accessibility The speed with which stereotypes and prejudice come to mind and are applied.

Acquisition The process of perceiving and interpreting information.

Actor-observer bias The tendency for observers to overestimate the importance of the actor's dispositions, and for the actor to overestimate the importance of the situation in explaining the actor's behavior.

Additive principle In impression formation, the idea that pieces of information about a person or attitude are processed in terms of their evaluative implications and are then added together to form an overall impression. Sometimes contrasted with the averaging principle.

Affective component That part of an attitude consisting of a person's feelings associated with beliefs about an attitude object; consists mainly of the evaluation of the object (like–dislike, pro–con).

Agenda setting The process in which the mass media focus public attention on certain issues and thus determine which issues the public is concerned about.

Aggression Any action intended to hurt another person.

Aggression anxiety Anxiety about expressing overt aggression, usually with respect to a particular target.

Altruism An act performed voluntarily to help another person when there is no expectation of receiving a reward in any form. See also "prosocial behavior."

Ambivalence As applied to attitudes, ambivalence occurs when a person believes arguments on both sides of an issue. This person may express inconsistent opinions over time, depending on which arguments come to mind.

Ambivalent sexism A mixture of benevolent attitudes toward women (protecting women) and hostile attitudes (resenting women's efforts to achieve equal power). See also "benevolent sexism" and "hostile sexism."

***Amicus curiae* brief** A "friend of the court" document developed to help the court decide a particular case. Social psychologists use *amicus* briefs to summarize research findings that are relevant to a case.

Androgyny People who believe they possess both traditionally feminine and traditionally masculine characteristics are said to be androgynous. An androgynous person's self-concept includes both masculine, or instrumental, qualities (e.g., being independent and strong) and feminine, or expressive, qualities (e.g., being nurturant and gentle).

Anger Aggressive feelings.

Antisocial aggression Aggressive acts, such as murder, that violate commonly accepted social norms.

Archival research The analysis of data already collected for another purpose, such as census data or legal records of births, deaths, and marriages.

Assimilation In the study of attitude change, the tendency to perceive a communicator's position as closer or more similar to the individual's own position than it actually is.

Association A link in memory between different stimuli that occur together in time and place. Through pairing, reactions to one stimulus become associated with the other. This is one of the basic processes by which learning occurs.

Assumed-similarity effect In intergroup relations, the tendency for members of an in-group to assume that other in-group members share their attitudes and values.

Attachment The emotional bonds that form between people in a close relationship. During infancy, attachment is seen when a child responds positively to one special person, wants to be with that person, seeks the person out when frightened, and so on.

Attack advertising Political commercials that attack the opponent rather than advocate the strength of the favored candidate.

Attitude Enduring response disposition with an affective component, a behavioral component, and a cognitive component. We develop and hold attitudes toward persons, objects, and ideas.

Attitude-discrepant behavior Acts inconsistent with a person's attitudes. When an individual behaves in a way inconsistent with a belief, cognitive dissonance is produced, and there is a tendency for the attitude to change. See "cognitive dissonance theory."

Attribution The process by which people use information to make inferences about the causes of behaviors or attitudes.

Attributional ambiguity Being uncertain as to the cause of some circumstance or event; as applied to potential discrimination, it creates a dilemma for people who are often subject to discrimination, because they do not know whether their failures are due to discrimination or to their own inadequate efforts.

Attribution theory The principles that determine how attributions are made and what effects these causal attributions have.

Authoritarian personality A personality type characterized by exaggerated submission to authority; extreme conformity to conventional standards; self-righteous hostility, especially toward deviants; and ethnocentrism.

Automatic processing Mental processes that look like reasoning, but that occur unconsciously, without intention or awareness.

Averaging principle In impression formation, the idea that pieces of information about a person or attitude are processed in terms of their evaluative implications and are then averaged together, to form an overall attitude. Sometimes contrasted with the additive principle.

Aversive racism Attitudes toward members of a racial group that combine both egalitarian social values and negative emotions, resulting in avoidance of that racial group.

Balance theory Heider proposed that we strive to maintain consistency among our sentiment and unit relations. We are motivated to like people we are connected to by physical proximity or other links, to like people we agree with, and to dislike those we disagree with.

Behavioral component That part of an attitude consisting of a person's tendencies to act toward the attitude object. A child's attitude toward a pet cat may include tendencies to feed and cuddle the animal.

Behavioral intention The conscious intention to carry out a specific act.

Behavioral self-blame Blaming one's own actions for a victimization that has befallen oneself.

Behaviorism The influential analysis of learning associated with J. B. Watson, Ivan Pavlov, and B. F. Skinner. It investigates only overt behavior, not subjective states such as thoughts or feelings. Behaviorism identifies association and reinforcement as the key determinants of learning.

Benevolent paternalism Members of a dominant group control subordinate group members through affectionate benevolent treatment and demand deference in return.

Benevolent sexism Positive attitudes and willingness to help women who are seen as virtuous and who embrace traditional women's roles.

Bicultural competence The development and possession of awareness and information about two cultures; knowledge, appreciation, and internalization of the basic beliefs of both cultures.

Biopsychosocial process The view that a person's state of health is jointly determined by biological factors (such as exposure to a virus), psychological factors (such as stress), and social factors (such as degree of social support).

Body language Information transmitted about attitudes, emotions, and so on by nonverbal bodily movements and features, such as posture, stance, or touch.

Brainstorming A technique for coming up with new and creative solutions to problems. Members of a group discuss a problem and generate as many different solutions as they can, withholding criticism until all possibilities have been presented.

Bystander effect An effect that, when other people are present, makes it less likely that any one person will offer help to a stranger in distress. The diffusion of responsibility created by the presence of other people is one explanation for the bystander effect.

Case history information Information about a particular person or event. This kind of information often has a more persuasive impact on people's judgments than objectively better but less vivid statistical information.

Categorization The process by which we perceive people or other stimuli in groups or categories rather than perceiving each person as a distinct individual.

Category-based processing Cognitive processing in which perceivers attend to individuals mainly in terms of which group or social category they are in.

Catharsis Sigmund Freud's idea that by expressing aggression, a person reduces his or her aggressive drive.

Central traits A trait is central to the extent that it is associated with many of the stimulus person's other characteristics. Traits such as being warm or cold are considered central because they are important in determining overall impressions.

Character evidence Evidence presented in court about a defendant's traits and/or propensities. In certain circumstances, character evidence may be introduced by the defense to suggest that the defendant is not the kind of person who would commit this type of crime.

Coerced-compliant false confession A confession by a person who is pressured to confess to a crime but who continues privately to believe that he or she is innocent.

Coerced-internalized false confession A confession by an innocent person who is pressured to confess to a crime and then comes privately to believe that he or she actually committed the crime.

Cognitive component That part of an attitude consisting of the person's beliefs, knowledge, and facts about the attitude object.

Cognitive consistency Tendency for people to seek consistency among their attitudes; regarded as a major determinant of attitude formation and change.

Cognitive dissonance theory Theory developed by Festinger according to which inconsistency (dissonance) between two cognitive elements produces pressure to make these elements consonant. The theory has been applied to a wide range of phenomena, including decision making, attitude-discrepant behavior, and interpersonal attraction.

Cognitive response theory The theory that attitude change following the receipt of communication depends on the cognitive responses it evokes. If the change produces negative thoughts, it will be rejected; if it evokes positive thoughts, it will be accepted. Counterarguing is a crucial mechanism for resisting persuasion, according to this theory.

Cohesiveness In group dynamics, the forces, both positive and negative, that cause members to remain in a group. Cohesiveness is a characteristic of a group as a whole, and results from the degree of commitment of each individual to the group.

Collectivism The belief that the group's well-being is more important than that of the individual. Collectivist cultures emphasize loyalty to the family, adherence to group norms, and the preservation of harmony in social relations with members of one's own group.

Commitment The perception that one's decision cannot be exchanged or revoked.

Commitment to a relationship All the forces that act to keep a person in a relationship or group. Positive forces include interpersonal attraction and satisfaction with a relationship; negative forces include such barriers to ending a relationship as the lack of alternatives or having made large investments in the relationship.

Commitment to an attitude The perception that one's decision cannot be changed or revoked; a key determinant of cognitive dissonance.

Common knowledge effect Group members spend more time discussing shared than unshared information.

Communal relationships In these relationships, each partner provides benefits to the other in order to show concern and to respond to the other's needs, with no expectation of receiving similar benefits in the near future. See also "exchange relationships."

Companionate love A somewhat practical type of love that emphasizes trust, caring, and tolerance of the partner's flaws. Companionate love may develop slowly in a relationship as partners become more interdependent. Sometimes contrasted with "passionate love."

Comparison level A standard we use to evaluate the quality of our social relationships. Our comparison level is the level of outcomes (benefits and costs) we expect or believe we deserve based on our experience in relationships.

Comparison level for alternatives A standard we use to evaluate the quality of our social relationships. Our comparison level for alternatives is our evaluation of one particular relationship against other relationships that are currently available to us.

Compliance Performance of an act at another's request.

Confirmatory hypothesis testing Selectively extracting from others information that preferentially confirms a hypothesis, instead of gathering information evenhandedly that both favors and opposes the hypothesis.

Conformity Voluntary performance of an act because others also do it. Conformity often results from a person's desire to be right (informational influence) and/or desire to be liked (normative influence).

Conjunction error An error that occurs when people believe more in the likelihood that several events will happen at the same time (because the events seem to go together) than in the likelihood that any one of the events will happen by itself.

Contact theory The theory that prejudice against a social group can be reduced by appropriate kinds of contact with individual members of that group.

Contingency model of leadership effectiveness Fiedler's model distinguishing between task-oriented and relationship-oriented leaders. When the group situation is either highly favorable or highly unfavorable to control by the leader, task-oriented leaders are more effective. In intermediate situations, where the leader has moderate control, relationship-oriented leaders are more successful.

Contrast In the study of attitude change, the tendency to perceive a communicator's position as being further away from the individual's own position than it actually is.

Controlled processing The more familiar, conscious, deliberate, and voluntary thinking and expression we engage in everyday.

Control question test A method of polygraph testing in which a person's physiological responses to questions about a crime are compared with his or her physiological responses to questions about personal wrongdoings. An innocent person is expected to be more aroused when answering questions about personal wrongdoings, whereas a guilty person is expected to be more aroused when answering questions about the crime.

Cooperative interdependence Relationship in which the outcomes of two people or groups depend on each other, so that the rewards one gets increase the rewards the other gets. When members of a team work together to win, the success of one teammate benefits all members of the team.

Coping The process of managing internal or environmental demands that are appraised as taxing or exceeding one's resources. Coping may involve active problem-solving efforts and/or efforts at emotional control.

Correlational research Passively measuring two variables and determining whether they are associated. Studies relating smoking to lung cancer are correlational: They measure the amount of smoking each person has done and whether the person gets lung cancer, in order to determine if the two factors are related. The major problem with correlational designs is the difficulty in determining whether a correlation reflects cause and effect.

Correspondent inference theory A theory of attribution and person perception that details the conditions under which people assume that an individual's action is due to his or her enduring personal characteristics.

Counterarguing In attitude change, one mechanism for resisting influence by discrepant communications: The individual considers and actively rebuts the arguments made by the communicator.

Counterfactual reasoning Imagined alternative versions of actual events; people's "What if?" or "If only . . . " thoughts about past or present outcomes or circumstances.

Covariation Judgments of covariation involve determining how strongly two things are related, such as the time of day and the frequency of crime, or the ingestion of caffeine and alertness. When social perceivers expect two things to go together, they tend to overestimate the actual degree of covariation.

Credibility In attitude change, a communicator's credibility depends on his or her perceived expertise about the topic and how much he or she is trusted by the individual receiving the communication.

Crowding The subjective experience of feeling cramped or not having enough space.

Cultural stereotype Societal images of members of a social group such as those found in art, literature, religious teachings, and the mass media. For example, TV commercials may portray women as worried consumers and men as knowledgeable experts. See also "personal stereotype."

Culture The shared beliefs, values, traditions, and behavior patterns of a particular group.

Cybernetic theory of self-regulation The process by which people compare their behavior to a standard, decide whether it matches the standard, and continue adjusting and comparing until the standard is met or abandoned. Self-awareness is argued to be a precondition for this type of self-regulation.

Date rape (or acquaintance rape) Forced sexual activity that occurs between two people who are at least mildly acquainted and who may be dating.

Death qualification In selecting jury members for a capital case, jurors who express reservations about conviction are "death-qualified" and excluded from serving on the jury.

Debriefing An essential feature of ethical research, in which after the subjects' participation is over, the purposes and procedures of the research study are explained to the subjects, their questions are answered, and the scientific value of the research is discussed.

Decision-making theories According to decision-making theories, people calculate the costs and benefits of various actions and select the best alternative in a fairly logical way.

Decision rule A rule about how a group can reach a decision, such as majority-wins, two-thirds majority, or unanimity.

Dehumanization The process of taking away the personhood or human qualities of another person or group through one's actions or the ways one thinks about the person or group. Dehumanizing another person is thought to facilitate aggression against that person.

Deindividuation The process by which being part of a group leads people to do things they normally would not do if they were alone. Anonymity is the key factor in deindividuation. The behavioral consequences of deindividuation depend on the norms of the situation, which can be either antisocial or prosocial.

Demand characteristics Aspects of a study that make subjects more aware of their participation in research and thus bias their behavior. For example, subjects may try to avoid negative evaluations from the experimenter or may try to cooperate with the experimenter to verify the hypothesis.

Dependent variable In an experiment, the responses to the independent variable being manipulated or measured.

Desensitization Reaction to an overexposure to material that normally evokes strong emotions, such as violence or sexuality; the individual becomes insensitive to it.

Desire for individuation This refers to individual differences in a person's willingness to do things that publicly differentiate him or her from others or make him or her stand out.

Diffusion of responsibility A process by which the presence of other people makes each individual feel less responsible for causing events or solving problems. It may decrease the likelihood that a person will take action, for instance, to help a stranger in distress.

Discounting principle In making attributions, the tendency to reduce reliance on one particular cause to the extent that other plausible causes exist. If, for example, a judge gives the death penalty to a criminal, we might conclude that she is generally a tough judge, but we would be less likely to do so if we discover that the law requires the death penalty for this particular crime.

Discrepancy In the study of attitude change, the distance between the communicator's and the target's position on the issue discussed in the communication. For example, a communicator may argue that tuition should be doubled; that position will be highly discrepant to a student who believes it should not change, but only moderately discrepant to a student who thinks a modest increase is reasonable.

Discrimination The behavioral component of group antagonism. People discriminate against a disliked group by refusing its members access to desired jobs, educational opportunities, and so on.

Disinhibition As applied to aggression, a loosening of control over anger after it has been released under socially approved conditions; a person who has committed a socially approved aggressive act has fewer inhibitions about aggressing under other conditions.

Displaced aggression The expression of aggression against a target other than the source of attack or frustration, usually a safer target.

Dispositional attribution Perceiving the cause of a person's action as stemming from his or her disposition, such as personality, ability, or attitudes.

Dispositional optimism A generalized expectation, held by some people and not others, that positive outcomes will occur in one's life.

Dissonance The state of aversive arousal that results when a person simultaneously holds two beliefs that conflict with or contradict each other. See also "cognitive dissonance theory."

Distraction In attitude change, a stimulus that draws attention away from a persuasive message. Distraction can increase attitude change by making it harder for people to defend a position against the arguments in the message.

Distraction-conflict model An explanation of social facilitation effects. The presence of others creates a conflict between two basic tendencies: (a) to pay attention to the audience and (b) to pay attention to the task. This conflict creates arousal, which may inhibit task performance.

Domestic violence Acts of violence committed by one family member against another family member or by one of several cohabiting individuals against another of them.

Door-in-the-face technique A technique for gaining compliance with a request by first asking for a much larger request. After the larger request is refused, the person is more likely to agree to the second, smaller request.

Downward social comparison Comparison of one's traits or abilities with those of someone who is perceived as worse off than oneself.

Dual-processing model A model hypothesizing that people can process information in a careful, systematic fashion or in a more rapid, efficient, heuristic fashion. Aspects of the person or situation predict which mode of processing a person will use.

Ego involvement In attitude change, the subjective linking of an attitude to strong ego needs, thereby making the attitude more emotionally laden and more resistant to change.

Elaboration-likelihood model A theory of persuasion and attitude change in which the key variable is the amount of careful thought given to the arguments (elaboration likelihood): With more careful processing, attitude change depends more on the real strength of the arguments and less on peripheral cues.

Emotional loneliness Loneliness due to lack of an attachment figure.

Empathy Feelings of sympathy and caring for others, in particular, sharing vicariously or indirectly in the suffering of other people. Strong feelings of empathy can motivate a person to help someone in need.

Equity The principle that two people who make equal contributions to a task should receive equal rewards.

Estimator variables Factors affecting eyewitness identification that are related to the witness or to the situation in which the event was witnessed. The witness's arousal level and the viewing conditions at the time of the event are examples of estimator variables.

Ethnic identity The part of an individual's self-knowledge that concerns his or her membership in a particular ethnic group, together with the value and emotional significance attached to that membership.

Ethnocentrism The belief that the in-group is the center of the social world and superior to out-groups.

Evaluation The most important basic dimension underlying impression formation and attitudes; the "goodness" or "badness" of another person, object, or concept. See also "affective component."

Evaluation apprehension A person's concern about how others evaluate him or her; often a concern about making a good impression in public.

Evaluative priming technique A way to measure implicit stereotypes, based on the idea that the evaluation of a stereotype-consistent word (such as "gentle") is speedier after the presentation of a prime of the group (such as a picture of a woman).

Evidence-driven jury A jury that begins deliberation by discussing the strength of the evidence rather than by taking a preliminary vote about the verdict.

Evolutionary social psychology An emerging specialty in social psychology that uses the principles of evolution and natural selection to understand human behavior and social life.

Evolved psychological mechanism Term used to describe human tendencies and preferences that are the result of natural selection. These tendencies are responses adapted to specific problems encountered by our distant ancestors.

Exchange relationships Relationships in which people give benefits with the expectation of receiving comparable benefits in return soon afterward. See also "communal relationships."

Exemplar An example of a category that embodies the significant attributes of the category or the ideal of that category. For example, a robin is an exemplar of the category "bird."

Expectancy-value theory This theory states that decisions are based on the combination of two factors: (a) the value of the various possible outcomes of the decision and (b) the likelihood or probability that each outcome will actually occur.

Expectation states theory According to this theory, a person's status in a group may be affected by such diffuse state characteristics as age, ethnicity, and wealth.

Experiment Type of research in which the researcher randomly assigns people to two or more conditions, varies in a controlled manner the treatment each condition is given, and then measures the effects on the subjects' responses. Although experiments are often difficult to arrange, they have the advantage of yielding clear information about cause and effect. Any differences between groups in the outcome of the experiment must be due to the variables that were experimentally manipulated.

Experimenter bias A bias introduced into the results of a study, usually in the direction of falsely confirming the hypothesis, through unintentional actions of the researcher.

External validity The extent to which the results of a study are generalizable to other populations and settings.

Face-ism The tendency to emphasize men's faces and women's bodies, for instance, in advertisements and news photos.

False consensus effect Bias in perceptions of others so that one exaggerates how common one's own opinions or behaviors are.

False uniqueness effect Bias in perceptions of others that one exaggerates how uniquely positive one's own abilities are.

Field experiment A study in which variables are systematically manipulated and measured in a real-life, nonlaboratory setting.

Figure-ground principle In social perception, the basic principle that attention is drawn to stimuli that stand out against a background. Figural stimuli are those that stand out; the background is called the "ground." This principle has generated much of the research on salience in social perception.

Foot-in-the-door technique A technique for gaining compliance with a request by first persuading the person to comply with a small request. After agreeing to a small request, the person is more likely to comply with a larger request.

Forewarning In attitude change, informing recipients of the position to be taken in a persuasive communication, or of the communicator's intension to persuade them, prior to the receipt of the communication.

Frustration The blocking or thwarting of goal-directed behavior. For example, a child is frustrated when a parent refuses to let him color the bathroom wallpaper with crayons or smear ice cream on the dining room table.

Frustration-aggression hypothesis In its most absolute form, this hypothesis asserts that frustration always creates feelings of aggression, and that aggression is always caused by frustration.

Fundamental attribution error The tendency for observers to overestimate the causal importance of a person's dispositions and to underestimate the importance of the situation when they explain the person's actions.

Gender identity The self-knowledge that one is male or female. Gender identity is acquired early in life.

Gender self-concept The degree to which a person perceives that he or she possesses traditionally masculine or feminine characteristics. See also "androgyny."

Gender stereotype Beliefs about the typical personal attributes of males and females. According to traditional gender stereotypes, women have expressive or communal qualities, such as being nurturing and gentle, and men have instrumental qualities, such as being independent, assertive, and competent. See also "androgyny."

Gender typing The process of labeling things, activities, and people as "masculine" or "feminine." For example, many people consider dolls, ruffles, and housecleaning to be feminine.

Gestalt psychology A theory, developed by Wolfgang Kohler, Kurt Koffka, Kurt Lewin, and others, that focuses on the way individuals perceive and understand objects, events, and people. The theory emphasizes the idea that people form coherent and meaningful perceptions based on the entire perceptual field, so that the whole is different from the sum of its parts.

Group A social aggregate in which members are interdependent (have mutual influence on each other) and have at least the potential for mutual interaction.

Group polarization Groups often make more extreme decisions than do individuals alone. Polarization sometimes leads to a risky shift, and sometimes to a cautious shift, depending on the initial views of group members.

Group-serving biases Tendency for members of an in-group to hold favorable attributions for the performance of members of the in-group (internal attributions for success, external for failure) and unfavorable attributions for performance by members of the out-group.

Groupthink According to Janis, the impairment in decision making and sound judgment that can occur in groups. Group members ignore contradictory information, ostracize dissenters, and unify around their decision.

Halo effect The effect in which a liked person is assumed to have good qualities of many kinds, whether or not the observer has any information about those qualities.

Hardiness A personality variable consisting of a sense of commitment, a positive response to challenge, and an internal sense of control that seems to help people cope effectively with stress.

Health behavior An action undertaken by a person who is healthy to enhance or maintain good health.

Health belief An attitude about a particular health practice that influences willingness to adopt that practice; may include beliefs about personal susceptibility, the efficacy of the health practice, or the severity of the health risk.

Heuristic A shortcut for problem solving that reduces complex or ambiguous information to more simple judgmental operations.

Heuristic processing A way of processing information rapidly and efficiently that draws on cues, shortcuts, or rules of thumb to reduce complex problems to more manageable, simple ones.

Hostile sexism Negative attitudes toward women who challenge men's power, try to act like men, or reject traditional gender roles.

Ideal self The personal attributes one would like to have.

Illusory correlation The belief that two things are related to each other because expectations dictate that they ought to go together, when in fact those things bear little or no relationship to each other.

Imitation See "modeling."

Implicit association test A technique for measuring implicit stereotypes. Based on the idea that the response to stereotype-consistent pairs of words (e.g., Matilda and doddering) is speedier than to stereotype-inconsistent pairs (e.g., Hortense and sexy).

Implicit attitudes Attitude or stereotype or prejudice that reflects automatically activated evaluations.

Implicit personality theory The ordinary person's theory about which personality traits go with other traits, such as "weak" going with "cowardly" and "calm" going with "decisive."

Implicit stereotypes Stereotypes that are expressed outside the person's awareness and are not under the person's control.

Independent self The sense of oneself as bounded, unitary, and separate from the social context.

Independent variable The variable in a study that is interpreted as the cause of changes in the dependent variable. The independent variable may be systematically manipulated by the researcher in an experiment or passively measured in a correlational study.

Individualism Belief in the value of personal identity, uniqueness, and freedom. In an individualist culture, personal goals come before group goals, and a person's sense of self is based largely on personal accomplishments rather than on group membership.

Informational influence One reason for conformity is the desire to be correct in our behavior or interpretation of an ambiguous situation. Informational influence occurs when we conform because the behavior of others provides useful information. See also "normative influence."

Informed consent Consent given after research subjects are informed about the study, about the procedures that will be used, and about the costs and benefits of the research.

Ingratiation Flattering or doing favors for a person to get that person to like you or to do things for you.

In-group The group to which an individual belongs; membership in it forms part of his or her social identity. See also "out-group."

In-group favoritism effect The tendency to give more favorable evaluations and greater rewards to members of one's in-group than to members of out-groups.

Inoculation defense In attitude change, McGuire's notion that people become more resistant to the effects of persuasive communications when they have been exposed to weak counterarguments.

Insufficient justification One type of experiment that tests predictions from cognitive dissonance theory; subjects perform a counterattitudinal behavior with inadequate reason or incentive for doing so and consequently come to develop more positive attitudes toward that behavior.

Interdependence The condition in which two or more people have some degree of mutual influence on each other's feelings, thoughts, or behaviors.

Interdependence theory The theory that because members of a couple or group are interdependent (i.e., the outcomes one person experiences depend on what others do and vice versa), individuals must coordinate their behavior to maximize their joint benefits. Interdependence theory is the most important social exchange perspective in social psychology.

Interdependent self The sense of self as flexible, variable, and connected to the social context.

Internal validity The extent to which cause-and-effect conclusions can be validly drawn from the research.

Jealousy Emotion triggered when a person perceives a real or potential attraction between his or her partner and a rival. Jealousy is a reaction to a perceived threat by a rival to the continuity or quality of a valued relationship. Feelings of anger, anxiety, and depression commonly result.

Learning theory The central idea in learning theory is that a person's behavior is determined by prior learning. Current behavior is shaped by past experience. In any given situation, a person learns certain behaviors that, over time, may become habits. When presented with the same situation, the person tends to behave in the same habitual way.

Legitimate authority In many situations, social norms permit those in authority to make requests. Illustrations of legitimate authority include the government's right to ask citizens to pay taxes, parents' right to ask their children to wash the dinner dishes, and an employer's right to assign duties to an employee.

Legitimizing myth An ideology that justifies the current social hierarchy, for example, the belief that success stems from hard work and great talent.

Leniency bias A bias in which juries have lower standards for acquitting a defendant than for convicting a defendant.

Loneliness The psychological discomfort we feel when our social relations lack some essential feature. This deficit may be quantitative (too few relationships) or qualitative (unsatisfying relationships).

Low-ball technique A technique for gaining compliance in which the influencer obtains a commitment from the person before revealing hidden costs of the request.

Matching principle In dating and marriage, people tend to have partners who are similar to themselves in attitudes, values, ethnic background, religion, social class, education, and many other personal characteristics.

Mere exposure effect The effect by which simply being exposed frequently to a person or object tends to increase our liking for that person or object. Repeated exposure most often enhances liking when our initial reaction to the person is neutral or positive, when no conflict of interest exists, and when the exposure is not so great that it causes satiation.

Message learning The idea that attitude change depends on the individual's learning the content of the communication.

Meta-analysis A quantitative approach to summarizing and synthesizing the results of many empirical studies on a topic, such as sex differences in aggression. Statistics are used to estimate the overall size of the "effect," or sex difference, and also to test for the consistency (homogeneity) of a finding across studies.

Middle-range theories Theories that attempt to account for major categories of behavior but do not attempt to cover all human behavior in general. A middle-range theory might try to explain attitude change, attribution, or aggression, but not all three at once.

Minimal intergroup situation The basic research situation used to test social identity theory: People are arbitrarily classified into groups (e.g., the red and the blue teams) and then allowed to allocate rewards to each other.

Minimal risk A risk for the participants in a research project that is no greater than the risk encountered in daily life.

Minimization In legal contexts, an interrogation technique in which the investigator downplays the significance of a crime to make a confession seem less serious.

Minority influence Influence that members of a minority have over the majority in a group.

Mirror image The image held by members of two conflicting nations, so that each group believes that its own nation is peace-loving and that the other nation is hostile and threatening.

Modeling People often learn behaviors and social attitudes simply by observing the attitudes and behaviors of other people, known technically as "models." Modeling occurs when a person not only observes but actually copies the behavior of a model. Observational learning can occur without any external reinforcement. However, whether or not a person actually performs or models a behavior learned through observation is influenced by the consequences the action has for the person. Modeling is also known as "imitation" or "observational learning."

Mood-congruent memory The tendency for people to remember material whose valence fits their current mood state. For example, a person in a good mood is more likely to remember positive material.

Negative-state relief model According to this model of helping, people help in order to alleviate their own bad mood or personal distress at a victim's suffering.

Negativity effect Tendency for impressions to be influenced more by negative traits than by positive traits. Hence, positive impressions are more vulnerable to change than negative impressions.

Nonverbal leakage The communication of true emotions through nonverbal channels even when the person's verbal communications attempt to conceal the emotions.

Normative influence One reason for conformity is the desire to be liked. Normative influence occurs when we conform to group norms or standards in order to gain social acceptance or avoid social rejection. See also "informational influence."

Norm of reciprocity The social norm that we should reward those who reward us. For example, if someone helps us, we feel obligated to help them in return.

Norm of social justice A norm about fairness and the just distribution of resources. Norms of social justice, such as equity, may encourage prosocial behavior.

Norm of social responsibility A social norm dictating that we should help others who depend on us. This may contribute to prosocial behavior.

Observational learning Learning by watching what others do and doing the same; this learning also applies to forming attitudes by modeling those of others such as parents or teachers.

Old-fashioned racism Old-fashioned beliefs in white racial superiority, segregation, and formal discrimination.

Operational definition The specific procedure or operation that is used to measure or manipulate a variable in a research study.

Optimal distinctiveness A social identity in a group that is large enough to give the individual a sense of inclusion, but small enough to provide a sense of differentiation from others.

Ostracism Experience of being ignored or rejected by others

Ought self The personal attributes one believes one should possess, based on one's obligations and responsibilities or the expectations of others.

Out-group Any group other than the in-group.

Out-group homogeneity effect Perception that members of the out-group are more similar to each other than members of the in-group are to each other.

Overwriting hypothesis The hypothesis that information received by witnesses after seeing an event permanently replaces their original memories of the event.

Own-race bias A phenomenon in which eyewitnesses tend to be more accurate when identifying members of their own race than when identifying members of another race.

Paralanguage Information conveyed by variations in speech other than actual words and syntax, such as pitch, loudness, and hesitations.

Passionate love The emotionally charged type of love that sometimes characterizes the early stages of romantic relationships. Contrasted with "companionate love."

Peremptory challenge A process during *voir dire* in which attorneys can dismiss a limited number of potential jurors without stating a reason. Peremptory challenges cannot be used to eliminate jurors of a particular race or gender. See also *"voir dire."*

Peripheral cues Aspects of the communication situation that are irrelevant to the content of the message (e.g., pleasant music, long or beautifully written messages), but that may influence attitude change when the individual is not engaged in systematic processing.

Personal distress An individual's reactions to the suffering of others, including horror, shock, helplessness, or concern. Because personal distress focuses on the self, it can motivate people to ignore or avoid the suffering of others, rather than to offer assistance.

Personal entitlement What a person believes that he or she deserves from a job or relationship.

Personal stereotypes An individual's own beliefs about the attributes of members of a particular group. Personal stereotypes may be similar to or different from cultural stereotypes.

Pique technique A technique for gaining compliance by making an unusual request that will disrupt the target's refusal script and capture his or her attention.

Planning fallacy Consistently overestimating how quickly and easily one can achieve a goal and underestimating the amount of time, money, or effort required to reach that goal.

Positive illusions Mildly but falsely positive self-enhancing perceptions of one's personal qualities.

Positivity bias A general tendency to express positive evaluations of people more often than negative evaluations. Also called the "leniency effect" or "person positivity bias."

Possible selves Schemas that people hold concerning what they may become in the future.

Pragmatic accuracy Accuracy that enables people to achieve their relationship goals.

Prejudice The affective component of group antagonisms; disliking a group or the members of a group.

Pretrial publicity Media coverage about criminal investigations or preparations for a particular trial. Pretrial publicity may bias potential jurors against a defendant.

Primacy The tendency to use an initial impression to organize and interpret subsequent information.

Priming effect The tendency for recent thoughts about material to influence the interpretation of subsequent information.

Principle of least interest According to social exchange theory, the balance of power in a relationship is affected by the relative dependency of the two partners. The principle of least interest states that the partner who is less interested (less dependent) tends to have greater power.

Prisoner's dilemma A laboratory game widely used in studies of competition and cooperation. It poses the fundamental dilemma of whether to compete (with the hope of gaining large rewards at the expense of the other person) or to cooperate (with the hope of receiving lesser personal rewards but greater joint rewards).

Private self-consciousness A chronic tendency to focus on the private self. Privately self-conscious people try to analyze themselves, think about themselves a great deal, and be attentive to their inner feelings.

Prosocial aggression Aggressive acts that support commonly accepted social norms, such as a soldier shooting an enemy sniper during combat.

Prosocial behavior Behavior that helps or is intended to help others, regardless of the helper's motives. See also "altruism."

Prototype A schema defined by the specific features of a particular type of person, social role, or situation, such as snob, librarian, or birthday party.

Psychoanalytic theory Freud's theory of human personality and behavior. It emphasizes instincts, unconscious motivation, and the psychological defenses used for protection against one's own irrational drives.

Psychological control The belief that one can exert personal control over events, whether that control actually exists or is ever exercised.

Public self-consciousness A chronic tendency to be concerned with how one appears to others. Publicly self-conscious people are concerned about what others think of them, how they look, and how they appear to others. Contrasts with private self-consciousness.

Punishment An aversive stimulus that reduces the likelihood that the preceding response will occur again.

Random assignment Placement of subjects in experimental conditions in a manner that guarantees that assignment is made entirely by chance, such as by using a random numbers table. This is an essential characteristic of an experiment.

Random sample A group of people participating in a study who are selected from the broad population by a random process, and who therefore are representative of that broad population.

Rape Forced sexual activity without one partner's consent.

Rational choice theory A principal rival to political psychological theories, rational choice theory views people as motivated by self-interest and acting rationally within the limits of their information. This theory is derived from neoclassical economics.

Reactance theory Brehm's concept that people attempt to maintain their freedom of action. When this freedom is threatened, people do whatever they can to restore it, for instance, by refusing to comply with a request.

Realistic group conflict theory The theory that antagonism between groups arises from real conflicts of interest and the frustrations those conflicts produce.

Reasoned action model A model predicting an individual's overt behavior from conscious behavioral intentions, which, in turn, are based on calculations about the effects of his or her behavior and others' evaluations of it.

Recovered memory A memory that is forgotten for a period of time and then remembered. The accuracy of recovered memories is a topic of considerable debate.

Reference group A group to which a person belongs or that a person uses as a basis of comparison. The group serves as a standard for the person's own behavior and attitudes. The group's norms can act as a persuasive force leading to attitude change, or they can prevent change by supporting the individual's position when it is attacked.

Reflected appraisal Self-evaluation based on the perceptions and evaluations of others.

Reinforcement The process by which a person or animal learns to exhibit a particular response by being rewarded when it is demonstrated.

Related-attributes similarity Similarity to another person not in a target attribute, but in attributes related to that target attribute, such as background or preparation.

Relative deprivation Feelings of personal or social discontent that arise from the belief that some persons or groups are faring more poorly than others, or more poorly than they have in the past.

Replication Because any single study is flawed, a hallmark of good research is replication. In its simplest form, replication means that researchers are able to reproduce the findings of others if they re-create the methods. It is also important to conduct conceptual replications, in which different research procedures are used to explore the same conceptual relationship.

Retrieval The process of recalling information that is stored in memory.

Reverse-causality problem The problem that arises in correlational research when the presumed cause might in fact be the actual effect. Children who watch a great deal of television do less well in school than do children who watch little television. However, is their television viewing causing their poor grades? Or does their poor school performance cause them to escape from schoolwork by watching TV?

Risky shift After taking part in a group discussion of an issue, people are sometimes willing to support riskier decisions than they were before the group discussion. This is part of a more general process of group polarization, which can lead to either riskier or more cautious decisions, depending on the initial views of group members.

Salience The quality that makes a particular stimulus stand out and be noticed. Bright, noisy, colorful, unusual, and novel stimuli are usually the most salient.

Sanctioned aggression Aggression that is permissible (though not necessarily encouraged) according to the norms of the individual's social group.

Schema An organized system or structure of cognitions about a stimulus, such as a person, a personality type, a group, a role, or an event.

Script A schema that describes the expected sequence of events in a well-known situation. For example, the script for going to a restaurant includes being seated, looking over the menu, ordering, eating, and paying the server.

Self-affirmation People cope with specific threats to their self-worth by reaffirming unrelated aspects of themselves.

Self-awareness The state of experiencing oneself as an object of one's own attention.

Self-complexity The number of dimensions that people use to think about themselves. Some people think about themselves in many ways, whereas other people think of themselves primarily in one or two ways.

Self-concept The collection of beliefs we hold about ourselves.

Self-disclosure The sharing of intimate information or feelings about oneself with another person. Self-disclosure can be descriptive (revelations that describe things about oneself) or evaluative (the emphasis one gives to one's personal assessment of people and situations).

Self-discrepancy A discrepancy between how we perceive ourselves to be and how we would ideally like to be or believe others think we should be.

Self-efficacy Specific expectations that we hold about our abilities to accomplish certain tasks.

Self-enhancement The need to hold a positive view of oneself and to protect oneself from negative feedback.

Self-esteem The value one places on oneself.

Self-evaluation maintenance theory Tesser's analysis of when people react to the success of others with pride (basking in reflected glory) or discontent (suffering by comparison). A key factor is whether the performance of the other is relevant to one's self-concept.

Self-fulfilling prophecy The tendency for people's expectations to influence their attitudes and behavior. Prejudice can serve as a self-fulfilling prophecy by influencing how the prejudiced person acts toward the target, which may, in turn, influence the target to act in a way that confirms the first person's prejudices.

Self-handicapping Engaging in actions that produce insurmountable obstacles to success, so that the inevitable failure can later be attributed to the obstacle rather than to one's own lack of ability.

Self-interest The idea that attitudes or behavior is motivated by what is best for the individual's short-term material well-being.

Self-perception theory The theory that people infer their attitudes from their overt behavior and from their perceptions of the external situation, rather than from their own internal state.

Self-presentation Deliberate efforts to act in ways that create a particular impression of the self, often a favorable impression.

Self-promotion Conveying positive information about oneself to others through one's actions or by saying positive things about oneself.

Self-regulation The ways people control and direct their own actions.

Self-schema A cognitive structure that represents how one thinks about oneself in a particular domain and how one organizes one's experience in that domain.

Self-serving attributional bias The tendency for people to see their positive behaviors as internally caused and their negative behaviors (such as failures) as caused by external circumstances.

Self-verification The process of seeking out and interpreting situations that confirm one's self-concept and avoiding or resisting situations and feedback that differ from one's self-concept.

Sense of group position The sense of members of a dominant group that they are superior, that their advantaged position is deserved, and that members of subordinate groups are threatening to take those privileges away.

Sequential lineup A police lineup in which potential perpetrators are shown one at a time. The witness must decide whether each person is the perpetrator before seeing the next person.

Sexual harassment Unwelcome sexual advances, requests for sexual favors, and other verbal or physical conduct of a sexual nature that are connected to employment or create an intimidating, hostile, or offensive environment at work or school.

Shift of meaning The tendency of the connotations of a trait to change when placed in a different context. This is the explanation for context effects by cognitive theories of impression formation.

Showup A police lineup in which a single suspect is presented to an eyewitness, who must determine whether that individual is the perpetrator.

Simultaneous lineup A lineup in which several potential suspects are shown at one time and the witness is asked to select the perpetrator.

Situational attribution Perceiving the cause of a person's action as lying in situational forces acting on the person, such as social influence or economic incentives.

Sleeper effect Delayed attitude changes that are not apparent immediately after exposure to the communication.

Social cognition The study of how people form inferences and make judgments based on social information.

Social comparison The act of evaluating one's abilities, opinions, or emotions with those of another person or persons.

Social comparison theory Festinger proposed that people are driven to evaluate themselves. In the absence of objective nonsocial criteria, people evaluate themselves by comparison with other people. In an uncertain or ambiguous situation, people may want to affiliate with others in order to make social comparisons.

Social compensation A response that occurs when an individual expends great effort in a collective setting in order to compensate for others in the group who he or she believes are performing inadequately.

Social density The objective number of people in a given space, such as the number of people sharing a dormitory room or the number of people per square mile in a major city.

Social dilemma A situation in which the short-term choice that is most rewarding for an individual will ultimately lead to negative outcomes for all concerned. Social dilemmas pit the short-term interests of the individual against the long-term interests of the group (including the individual).

Social dominance theory The theory that all societies are organized in group hierarchies, which are sustained through discrimination, legitimizing myths, and the efforts of individuals with a high social dominance orientation.

Social exchange theory A theory that analyzes the interaction between people in terms of the outcomes (rewards minus costs) that the individuals exchange with each other.

Social facilitation The tendency for people (and other kinds of animals) to perform better on simple, well-learned tasks when others are present than when they are alone.

Social identity In the study of the self, that part of an individual's self-concept that derives from his or her membership in a social group or groups, together with the value and emotional significance attached to that membership.

Social impact theory A theory, according to Latané, in which the influence (either positive or negative) of an audience on a target individual depends on three factors: the number of observers, the strength of the audience (e.g., their importance), and the immediacy of the audience in time or space.

Social inhibition The impairment or inhibition of an individual's performance brought about by the presence of others.

Socialization The process by which a person acquires the rules, standards, and values of his or her family, group, and culture.

Social loneliness Loneliness due to lack of friends and associates.

Social leadership Activities designed to promote group harmony and cohesiveness. The social leader focuses on the social and emotional aspects of interaction in order to keep a group running smoothly and happily. Sometimes contrasted with "task leadership."

Social learning theory A modern offshoot of behaviorism that places primary emphasis on how people learn social behaviors from one another, especially through social reinforcement and modeling.

Social loafing Individuals sometimes work less hard as members of a group than they would if they worked alone. Individuals may feel that their own efforts will be less recognizable in a group, a belief that may lead to a diffusion of responsibility and diminished effort by individuals.

Social norms Rules and expectations about how members of a social group should think or behave. These standards determine whether an individual's specific actions, attitudes, or beliefs are approved or disapproved by the individual's social group. Also called "group norms."

Social power One person's ability to influence deliberately the behavior, thoughts, or feelings of another person.

Social psychology The scientific study of how people think about, influence, and relate to others.

Social role A set of social norms (rules and understandings) about how a person in a particular social position (such as mother or professor) is expected to behave. Roles define the rights and responsibilities of members of couples, groups, and other social units.

Social status A person's rank or privilege in a group, based on such characteristics as age, gender, or position in a business.

Social support An interpersonal exchange characterized by emotional concern, instrumental aid, the provision of information to another, or help in self-appraisal. Social support is believed to buffer people against the adverse effects of stress and may promote physical health as well.

Sociotropic voting Voting choices motivated by perceptions of what is good for the nation rather than by perceptions of what is good for the self.

Source derogation In persuasive communication situations, reducing inconsistency by derogating the source of a discrepant communication rather than by changing one's attitudes.

Source monitoring The process of identifying the source of a piece of information stored in memory. According to source-monitoring theory, eyewitnesses sometimes include postevent information in their descriptions of an event because they do not correctly identify the source of that information.

Statistical information Information based on averages or totals.

Stereotype Beliefs about the typical characteristics of members of a group or social category. In the study of prejudice, stereotypes are the cognitive component of group antagonism.

Stereotype threat The threat that targets of stereotypes feel in situations in which the stereotype is salient. This threat can harm their performance in ways that are consistent with the stereotype.

Storage The process of keeping information in memory.

Story model A model of juror decision making that asserts that jurors use the evidence presented at trial to form stories about the events in question. Jurors evaluate alternative stories about the events, then select the verdict option that matches the strongest story.

Stress A process of appraising environmental events as harmful, threatening, or challenging and of responding to that appraisal with physiological, emotional, cognitive, and behavioral changes. Stress occurs when people perceive that their personal resources may not be sufficient to meet the demands of the environment.

Stressful life event An event in a person's life that requires him or her to make changes; negative, ambiguous, and uncontrollable events are most likely to be perceived as stressful. Stressful life events are believed to contribute to the risk of illness.

Subtyping Breaking down large categories of people such as women or the elderly into subcategories, such as homemakers, professional women, and grandmothers.

Superordinate group Large and inclusive group categories, often created to defuse conflict between smaller groups.

Supportive defense In attitude change, positive arguments for an individual's own position, provided in advance of a persuasive attack to help protect that attitude.

Symbolic racism Antagonism toward a racial group based on prejudice and values rather than on self-interest.

Systematic processing Careful scrutiny of the arguments in a persuasive communication, which gives argument strength more weight, induces counterarguing, and makes attitude change more enduring; minimizes the role of peripheral cues.

System variables Factors affecting eyewitness identification that are under the direct control of the criminal justice or legal systems. Lineup construction and questioning techniques are examples of system variables.

Task leadership Activities designed to accomplish the goals of a group and to get the work of the group done successfully. The task leader directs and organizes the group in carrying out a specific task. Sometimes contrasted with "social leadership."

That's-not-all technique A technique for gaining compliance in which the influencer first offers one deal and then, while the person is considering this possibility, improves the offer.

Theory of planned behavior A theory of the relation between attitudes and behavior based on how people consider and weigh the implications that a particular behavior may have as they form their intentions with respect to actions.

Third-variable problem A problem with interpreting correlational research. When two variables are correlated with each other, is one the cause of the other? Or is some third variable the cause of both?

Transfer of affect Changing attitude A by transferring to it the affect one already has toward object B.

Transsexual Person whose psychological gender identity differs from their biological sex, for example, someone who is anatomically a male but believes that he is really a female trapped in a male body.

Typicality effect The tendency to behave toward an out-group member who is seen as most typical of that group in ways more consistent with one's stereotypes about the out-group.

Upward social comparison The comparison of one's traits or abilities with those of someone who is better off than oneself.

Verdict-driven jury A jury that approaches deliberations by assessing verdict preferences, then tries to reach a consensus among jurors with different opinions.

Voir dire Jury selection that takes place at the beginning of every trial. Jurors who exhibit biases or are unable to be open-minded about the case are dismissed by the judge. It is assumed that eliminating such individuals from jury service improves the quality of jury deliberations and verdicts.

Voluntary false confession When a person willingly confesses to a crime that he or she did not commit.

Weapon focus effect A phenomenon in which eyewitnesses remember more information about the weapon used to commit a crime than about the criminal who was holding the weapon.

Working model In attachment theory, a person's beliefs about whether other people are trustworthy, responsive, and caring.

Working self-concept Those aspects of the self-concept that are salient in a particular situational context.

References

Aarts, H., & Dijksterhuis, A. (2000). Habits as knowledge structures: Automaticity in goal–directed behavior. *Journal of Personality and Social Psychology, 78,* 53–63.

Aarts, H., & Dijksterhuis, A. (2003). The silence of the library: Environment, situational norm, and social behavior. *Journal of Personality and Social Psychology, 84,* 18–28.

Abelson, R. P. (1976). Script processing in attitude formation and decision making. In J. S. Carroll, & J. W. Payne (Eds.), *Cognition and social behavior* (pp.33–46). Hillsdale, NJ: Erlbaum.

Abelson, R. P., Aronson, E., McGuire, W. J., Newcomb, T. M., Rosenberg, M. J., & Tannenbaum, P. H. (Eds.). (1968). *Theories of cognitive consistency: A sourcebook.* Chicago: Rand McNally.

Aberson, C. L., & Ettlin, T. E. (2004). The aversive racism paradigm and responses favoring African Americans: Meta-analytic evidence of two types of favoritism. *Social Justice Research, 17,* 25–45.

Aberson, C. L., Healy, M., & Romero, V. (2000). Ingroup bias and self-esteem: A meta-analysis. *Personality and Social Psychology Review, 4,* 157–173.

Aboud, F. E., & Levy, S. R. (2000). Interventions to reduce prejudice and discrimination. In S. Oskamp (Ed.), *Reducing prejudice and discrimination* (pp. 269–293). Mahwah, NJ: Erlbaum.

Aboud, R. (1988). *Children and prejudice.* New York: Basil Blackwell.

Abrahamson, A. C., Baker, L. A., & Caspi, A. (2002). Rebellious teens? Genetic and environmental influences on the social attitudes of adolescents. *Journal of Personality and Social Psychology, 83,* 1392–1408.

Abrams, D., Wetherell, M., Cochrane, S., Hogg, M. A., & Turner, J. C. (1990). Knowing what to think by knowing who you are: Self-categorization and the nature of norm formation, conformity, and group polarization. *British Journal of Social Psychology, 29,* 97–119.

Addis, M. E., & Mahalik, J. R. (2003). Men, masculinity, and the contexts of help seeking. *American Psychologist, 58,* 5–14.

Adler, N. E., Marmot, M., McEwen, B. S., & Stewart, J. (1999). *Socioeconomic status and health in industrial nations: Social, psychological, and biological pathways.* New York: Annals of the New York Academy of Sciences.

Adorno, T. W., Frenkel-Brunswik, E., Levinson, D. J., & Sanford, R. N. (1950). *Authoritarian personality.* New York: Harper & Row.

Afifi, W. A., Falato, W. L., & Weiner, J. L. (2001). Identity concerns following a severe relational transgression: The role of discovery method for the relational outcomes of infidelity. *Journal of Social and Personal Relationships, 18,* 291–308.

Ageton, S. S. (1983). *Sexual assault among adolescents.* Lexington, MA: Lexington Books.

Agnew, C. R., Van Lange, P. A. M., Rusbult, C. E., & Langston, C. A. (1998). Cognitive interdependence: Commitment and the mental representation of close relationships. *Journal of Personality and Social Psychology, 74,* 939–954.

Ahmed, S. M. S. (1979). Helping behavior as predicted by diffusion of responsibility, exchange theory, and traditional sex norms. *Journal of Social Psychology, 109,* 153–154.

AhYun, K. (2002). Similarity and attraction. In M. Allen, R. W. Preiss, B. M. Gayle, & N. A. Burrell (Eds.), *Interpersonal communication research* (pp. 145–167). Mahwah, NJ: Erlbaum.

Ainsworth, M. D., Blehar, M. C., Waters, E., & Wall, S. (1978). *Patterns of attachment.* Hillsdale, NJ: Erlbaum.

Ajzen, I., & Fishbein, M. (1980). *Understanding attitudes and predicting social behavior.* Upper Saddle River, NJ: Prentice Hall.

Akert, R. M., Chen, J., & Panter, A. T. (1992). *Facial prominence and stereotypes: The incidence and meaning of faceism in print and television media.* Unpublished manuscript, Wellesley College, Wellesley, MA.

Albarracín, D., & Kumkale, G. T. (2003). Affect as information in persuasion: A model of affect identification and discounting. *Journal of Personality and Social Psychology, 84,* 453–469.

Albarracín, D., & Wyer, R. S. (2000). The cognitive impact of past behavior: Influences on beliefs, attitudes, and future behavioral decisions. *Journal of Personality and Social Psychology, 79,* 5–22.

Alder, C. (1985). An exploration of self-reported sexually aggressive behavior. *Crime and Delinquency, 31,* 306–331.

Allen, M., Mabry, E., & McKelton, D. (1998). Impact of juror attitudes about the death penalty on juror evaluations of guilt and punishment: A meta-analysis. *Law and Human Behavior, 22,* 715–731.

Allen, V. L., & Wilder, D. A. (1979). Group categorization and attribution of belief similarity. *Small Group Behavior, 10,* 73–80.

Allport, F. H. (1920). The influence of the group upon association and thought. *Journal of Experimental Psychology, 3,* 159–182.

Allport, F. H. (1924). *Social psychology.* Boston: Riverside Editions, Houghton Mifflin.

Allport, G. W. (1954). *Nature of prejudice.* Garden City, NY: Doubleday.

Alpert, J. L., Brown, L. S., & Courtois, C. A. (1998). Symptomatic clients and memories of childhood abuse: What the trauma and child sexual abuse literature tells us. *Psychology, Public Policy, and Law, 4,* 941–995.

Altemeyer, B. (1988). *Enemies of freedom: Understanding right-wing authoritarianism.* San Francisco: Jossey-Bass.

Altman, I., & Taylor, D. A. (1973). *Social penetration: The development of interpersonal relationships.* New York: Holt, Rinehart and Winston.

Amaby, N., & Rosenthal, R. (1993). Half a minute: Predicting teacher evaluations from thin slices of nonverbal behavior and physical attractiveness. *Journal of Personality and Social Psychology, 64,* 431–441.

Amato, P. R. (1983). Helping behavior in urban and rural environments: Field studies based on a taxonomic organization of helping episodes. *Journal of Personality and Social Psychology, 45,* 571–586.

Amato, P. R. (1990). Personality and social network involvement as predictors of helping behavior in everyday life. *Social Psychology Quarterly, 53,* 31–43.

Ambady, N., & Gray, H. M. (2002). On being sad and mistaken: Mood effects on the accuracy of thin-slice judgments. *Journal of Personality and Social Psychology, 83,* 947–961.

Ambady, N., & Rosenthal, R. (1992). Thin slices of expressive behavior as predictors of interpersonal consequences: A meta-analysis. *Psychological Bulletin, 111,* 256–274.

American Cancer Society. (1989). *Cancer facts and figures—1989.* Atlanta, GA.

American Heart Association. (1984). *Heartfacts, 1984.* Dallas, TX: Author.

American Psychological Association. (1992). Ethical principles of psychologists and code of conduct. *American Psychologist, 47,* 1597–1611.

American Psychological Association Research Office. (2004). *Demographic shifts in psychology.* Retrieved August 16, 2004, from http://research.apa.org/demoshifts.html

American Psychological Association Working Group on Investigation of Memories of Childhood Abuse. (1998). Final conclusions of the American Psychological Association working group on investigation of memories of childhood abuse. *Psychology, Public Policy, and Law, 4,* 933–940.

Ames, D. R., Flynn, F. J., & Weber, E. U. (2004). It's the thought that counts: On perceiving how helpers decide to lend a hand. *Personality and Social Psychology Bulletin, 30,* 461–474.

Amodio, D. M., Harmon-Jones, E., & Devine, P. G. (2003). Individual differences in the activation and control of affective race bias as assessed by startle eyeblink response and self-report. *Journal of Personality and Social Psychology, 84,* 738–753.

Andersen, S. M., & Klatsky, R. L. (1987). Traits and social stereotypes: Levels of categorization in person perception. *Journal of Personality and Social Psychology, 70,* 740–756.

Anderson, C. A. (2001). Heat and violence. *Current Directions in Psychological Science, 10,* 33–38.

Anderson, C. A., & Bushman, B. J. (1997). External validity of "trivial" experiments: The case of laboratory aggression. *Review of General Psychology, 1,* 19–41.

Anderson, C. A., & Bushman, B. J. (2002). Human aggression. *Annual Reviews of Psychology, 53,* 27–57.

Anderson, C. A., Bushman, B. J., & Groom, R. W. (1997). Hot years and serious and deadly assault: Empirical tests of the heat hypothesis. *Journal of Personality and Social Psychology, 73,* 1213–1223.

Anderson, C. A., Carnagey, N. L., & Eubanks, J. (2003). Exposure to violent media: The effects of songs with violent lyrics on aggressive thoughts and feelings. *Journal of Personality and Social Psychology, 84,* 960–971.

Anderson, C. A., Deuser, W. E., & DeNeve, K. M. (1995). Hot temperatures, hostile affect, hostile cognition, and arousal: Tests of a general model of affective aggression. *Personality and Social Psychology Bulletin, 21,* 434–448.

Anderson, C. A., & Morrow, M. (1995). Competitive aggression without interaction: Effects of competitive versus cooperative instructions on aggressive behavior in video games. *Personality and Social Psychology Bulletin, 21,* 1020–1030.

Anderson, D. E., Ansfield, M. E., & DePaulo, B. M. (1999). Love's best habit: Deception in the context of relationships. In P. Philippot, R. S. Feldman, & E. J. Coats (Eds.), *The social context of nonverbal behavior* (pp. 372–409). Cambridge, UK: Cambridge University Press.

Anderson, D. E., DePaulo, B. M., & Ansfield, M. E. (2002). The development of deception detection skill: A longitudinal study of same-sex friends. *Personality and Social Psychology Bulletin, 28,* 536–545.

Anderson, K. B., Cooper, H., & Okamura, L. (1997). Individual differences and attitudes toward rape: A meta-analytic review. *Personality and Social Psychology Bulletin, 23,* 295–315.

Anderson, N. H. (1968). Likableness ratings of 555 personality-trait words. *Journal of Social Psychology, 9,* 272–279.

Andreoletti, C., Zebrowitz, L. A., & Lachman, M. E. (2001). Physical appearance and control beliefs in young, middle-aged, and older adults. *Personality and Social Psychology Bulletin, 27,* 969–981.

Anthony, T., Copper, C., & Mullen, B. (1992). Cross-racial facial identification: A social cognitive integration. *Personality and Social Psychology Bulletin, 18,* 296–301.

Apple, W., Streeter, L. A., & Krauss, R. M. (1979). Effects of pitch and speech rate on personal attributions. *Journal of Personality and Social Psychology, 37,* 715–727.

Apsler, R., & Sears, D. O. (1968). Warning, personal involvement, and attitude change. *Journal of Personality and Social Psychology, 9,* 162–166.

Archer, J. (2000). Sex differences in aggression between heterosexual partners: A meta-analytic review. *Psychological Bulletin, 126,* 651–680.

Archer, D., Iritani, B., Kimes, D. D., & Barrios, M. (1983). Face-ism: Five studies of sex differences in facial prominence. *Journal of Personality and Social Psychology, 45,* 725–735.

Aries, E. (1996). *Men and women in interaction.* New York: Oxford University Press.

Arkin, R. M., & Baumgardner, A. H. (1985). Claiming mood as a self-handicap: The influence of spoiled and unspoiled public identities. *Personality and Social Psychology Bulletin, 11,* 349–357.

Armitage, C. J., & Conner, M. (2000). Attitudinal ambivalence: A test of three key hypotheses. *Personality and Social Psychology Bulletin, 26,* 1421–1432.

Armor, D. A., & Taylor, S. E. (1998). Situated optimism: Specific outcome expectancies and self-regulation. In M. P. Zanna (Ed.), *Advances in experimental social psychology* (Vol. 30, pp. 309–379). New York: Academic Press.

Armor, D. A., & Taylor, S. E. (2003). The effects of mindset on behavior: Self-regulation in deliberative and implemental frames of mind. *Personality and Social Psychology Bulletin, 29,* 86–95.

Armstrong, E. A. (1965). *Bird display and behavior: An introduction to the study of bird psychology* (2nd ed.). New York: Dover.

Arndt, J., Greenberg, J., Pyszczynski, T., & Solomon, S. (1997). Subliminal exposure to death-related stimuli increases defense of the cultural worldview. *Psychological Science, 8,* 379–385.

Arndt, J., Schimel, J., Greenberg, J., & Pyszczynski, T. (2002). The intrinsic self and defensiveness: Evidence that activating the intrinsic self reduces self-handicapping and conformity. *Personality and Social Psychology Bulletin, 28,* 671–683.

Arndt, W. B., Foehl, J. C., & Good, E. F. (1985). Specific sexual fantasy themes: A multidimensional study. *Journal of Personality and Social Psychology, 28,* 472–480.

Arnkelsson, G. B., & Smith, W. P. (2000). The impact of stable and unstable attributes on ability assessment in social comparison. *Personality and Social Psychology Bulletin, 26,* 936–947.

Aron, A. (1988). The matching hypothesis reconsidered again: Comment of Kalick and Hamilton. *Journal of Personality and Social Psychology, 54,* 441–446.

Aron, A., & Aron, E. N. (2000). Self-expansion motivation and including other in the self. In W. Ickes & S. Duck (Eds.), *Social psychology of personal relationships* (pp. 109–128). Chichester, England: Wiley.

Aron, A., Aron, E. N., & Smollan, D. (1992). Inclusion of other in the self scale and the structure of interpersonal closeness. *Journal of Personality and Social Psychology, 63,* 596–612.

Aron, A., Norman, C. C., Aron, E. N., & Lewandowski, G. (2002). Shared participation in self-expanding activities: Positive effects on experienced marital quality. In P. Noller & J. A. Feeney (Eds.), *Understanding marriage* (pp. 177–194). New York: Cambridge University Press.

Aronson, E. (1968). Dissonance theory: Progress and problems. In R. P. Abelson, E. Aronson, W. J. McGuire, T. M. Newcomb, M. J. Rosenberg, & P. H. Tannenbaum (Eds.). *Theories of cognitive consistency: A sourcebook* (pp. 5–27). Chicago: Rand-McNally & Company.

Aronson, E., Brewer, M., & Carlsmith, J. M. (1985). Experimentation in social psychology. In G. Lindzey & E. Aronson (Eds.), *Handbook of social psychology* (3rd ed., Vol. 1, pp. 441–486). New York: Random House.

Aronson, E., & Carlsmith, J. M. (1963). The effect of the severity of threat on the devaluation of forbidden behavior. *Journal of Abnormal and Social Psychology, 66,* 584–588.

Aronson, E., & Gonzales, A. (1988). Desegregation, jigsaw, and the Mexican-American experience. In P. A. Katz & D. A. Taylor (Eds.), *Eliminating racism: Profiles in controversy* (pp. 301–314). New York: Plenum Press.

Aronson, E., Turner, J. A., & Carlsmith, J. M. (1963). Communicator credibility and communication discrepancy as determinants of opinion change. *Journal of Abnormal and Social Psychology, 67,* 31–36.

Aronson, E., Willerman, B., & Floyd, J. (1966). The effect of a pratfall on increasing interpersonal attractiveness. *Psychonomic Science, 4,* 227–228.

Aronson, E., Wilson, T. D., & Brewer, M. B. (1998). Experimentation in social psychology. In D. T. Gilbert, S. T. Fiske, & G. Lindzey (Eds.), *Handbook of social psychology* (Vol. 1, pp. 99–142). New York: McGraw-Hill.

Aronson, J., Blanton, H., & Cooper, J. (1995). From dissonance to disidentification: Selectivity in the self-affirmation process. *Journal of Personality and Social Psychology, 68,* 986–996.

Arriaga, X. B., & Rusbult, C. E. (1998). Standing in my partner's shoes: Partner perspective taking and reactions to accommodative dilemmas. *Personality and Social Psychology Bulletin, 24,* 927–948.

Asch, S. E. (1946). Forming impressions of personality. *Journal of Abnormal and Social Psychology, 41,* 258–290.

Asch, S. E. (1955). Opinions and social pressure. *Scientific American, 19,* 31–35.

Asher, S. R., & Paquette, J. A. (2003). Loneliness and peer relations in childhood. *Current Directions in Psychological Science, 12,* 75–78.

Aspinwall, L. G., Kemeny, M. E., Taylor, S. E., Schneider, S. G., & Dudley, J. P. (1991). Psychosocial predictors of gay men's AIDS risk-reduction behavior. *Health Psychology, 10,* 432–444.

Aspinwall, L. G., & Taylor, S. E. (1997). A stitch in time: Self-regulation and proactive coping. *Psychological Bulletin, 121,* 417–436.

Associated Press. (2004). Census report: *It pays to be a man.* Retrieved June 5, 2004, from the CNN Web site: http://www.cnn.com/2004/US/06/04/gender.income.ap/index.html

Atkeson, B. M., Calhoun, K. S., Resick, P. A., & Ellis, E. M. (1982). Victims of rape: Repeated assessment of depressive symptoms. *Journal of Consulting and Clinical Psychology, 50,* 96–102.

Atkin, C. K. (1979). Research evidence on mass mediated health communication campaigns. In D. Nimmo (Ed.), *Communication yearbook 3* (pp. 655–669). New Brunswick, NJ: Transaction Books.

Atkins, D. C., Baucom, D. H., & Jacobson, N. S. (2001). Understanding infidelity: Correlates of a national random sample. *Journal of Family Psychology, 15,* 735–749.

Attridge, M., Berscheid, E., & Sprecher, S. (1998). Dependency and insecurity in romantic relationships: Development and validation of two companion scales. *Personal Relationships, 5,* 31–58.

Attridge, M., Creed, M., Berscheid, E., & Simpson, J. A. (1992). *Predicting the stability of romantic relationships from individual versus couple data.* Manuscript submitted for publication.

Austin, W. (1980). Friendship and fairness: Effects of type of relationship and task performance on choice distribution rules. *Personality and Social Psychology Bulletin, 6,* 402–408.

Averill, J. R. (1983). Studies on anger and aggression: Implications for theories of emotion. *American Psychologist, 38,* 1145–1160.

Averill, J. R., & Boothroyd, P. (1977). On falling in love in conformance with the romantic ideal. *Motivation and Emotion, 1,* 235–247.

Avolio, B. J. (2004). In G. R. Goethals, G. J. Sorensen, & J. M. Burns (Eds.), *Encyclopedia of leadership* (Vol. 4, pp. 1558–1566). Thousand Oaks, CA: Sage.

Avolio, B. J., & Yammarino, F. J. (2003). *Transformational and charismatic leadership.* New York: Elsevier.

Ayman, R., & Frame, M. C. (2004). Gender stereotypes. In G. R. Goethals, G. J. Sorenson, & J. M. Burns (Eds.), *Encyclopedia of leadership* (Vol. 2, pp. 549–559). Thousand Oaks, CA: Sage.

Bailey, J. M., Kirk, K. M., Zhu, G., Dunne, M. P., & Martin, N. G. (2000). Do individual differences in sociosexuality represent genetic or environmentally contingent strategies? *Journal of Personality and Social Psychology, 78,* 537–545.

Baker, S. M., & Petty, R. E. (1994). Majority and minority influence: Source-position imbalance as a determinant of message scrutiny. *Journal of Personality and Social Psychology, 67,* 5–19.

Baldus, D. C., Woodworth, G., & Pulaski, C. A. (1990). *Equal justice and the death penalty: A legal and empirical analysis.* Boston: Northeastern University Press.

Baldwin, J. J., Brown, R., & Rackley, R. (1990). Some socio-behavioral correlates of African self-consciousness in African-American college students. Incorporating an African world view into psychology: I [Special Issue]. *Journal of Black Psychology, 17,* 1–17.

Baldwin, M. W., Carrell, S. E., & Lopez, D. F. (1990). Priming relationship schemas: My advisor and the Pope are watching me from the back of my mind. *Journal of Experimental Social Psychology, 26,* 435–454.

Banaji, M. R., Nosek, B. A., & Greenwald, A. G. (2005). No place for nostalgia in science: A response to Arkes and Tetlock. *Psychological Inquiry.*

Bandura, A. (1977). *Social learning theory.* Upper Saddle River, NJ: Prentice Hall.

Bandura, A. (1986). *Social foundations of thought and action: A social cognitive theory.* Upper Saddle River, NJ: Prentice Hall.

Bandura, A., Cioffi, D., Taylor, C. B., & Brouillard, M. E. (1988). Perceived self-efficacy in coping with cognitive stressors and opioid activation. *Journal of personality and Social Psychology, 55,* 479–488.

Bandura, A., Ross, D., & Ross, S. A. (1963). Vicarious reinforcement and imitative learning. *Journal of Abnormal and Social Psychology, 67,* 601–607.

Bandura, A., Ross, R., & Ross, A. R. (1961). Transmission of aggression through imitation of aggressive models. *Journal of Abnormal and Social Psychology, 63,* 575–582.

Banse, R., & Scherer, K. R. (1996). Acoustic profiles in vocal emotion expression. *Journal of Personality and Social Psychology, 70,* 614–636.

Barbaree, H. E., & Marshall, W. L. (1991). The role of male sexual arousal in rape: Six models. *Journal of Consulting and Clinical Psychology, 59,* 621–630.

Bargh, J. A. (1994). The four horsemen of automaticity: Awareness, intention, efficiency, and control in social cognition. In R. S. Wyer, Jr. & D. K. Srull (Eds.), *Handbook of Social Cognition* (2nd ed., pp. 1–40). Hillsdale, NJ: Erlbaum.

Bargh, J. A. (1997). The automaticity of everyday life. In R. S. Wyer, Jr. (Ed.), *Automaticity of everyday life: Advances in social cognition* (Vol. 10, pp. 1–61). Mahwah, NJ: Erlbaum.

Bargh, J. A., Chaiken, S., Govender, R., & Pratto, F. (1992). The generality of the automatic attitude activation effect. *Journal of Personality and Social Psychology, 62,* 893–912.

Bargh, J. A., & Chartrand, T. L. (1999). The unbearable automaticity of being. *American Psychologist, 54,* 462–479.

Bargh, J. A., Chen, M., & Burrows, L. (1996). Automaticity of social behavior: Direct effects of trait construct and stereotype priming on action. *Journal of Personality and Social Psychology, 71,* 230–244.

Bargh, J. A., & Ferguson, M. J. (2000). Beyond behaviorism: On the automaticity of higher mental processes. *Psychological Bulletin, 126,* 925–945.

Bargh, J. A., Gollwitzer, P. M., Lee-Chai, A. Y., Barndollar, K., & Troetschel, R. (2001). The automated will: Nonconscious activation and pursuit of behavioral goals. *Journal of Personality and Social Psychology, 81,* 1014–1027.

Bargh, J. A., & Raymond, P. (1995). The naive use of power: Nonconscious sources of sexual harassment. *Journal of Social Issues, 51,* 85–96.

Bargh, J. A., Raymond, P., Pryor, J. B., & Strack, F. (1995). Attractiveness of the underling: An automatic power → sex association and its consequences for sexual harassment and aggression. *Journal of Personality and Social Psychology, 68,* 768–781.

Bar-Hillel, M., & Neter, E. (1993). How alike is it versus how likely is it: A disjunction fallacy in probability judgments. *Journal of Personality and Social Psychology, 65,* 1119–1132.

Barker, R., Dembo, T., & Lewin, K. (1941). Frustration and aggression: An experiment with young children, *University of Iowa Studies in Child Welfare, 18,* 1–314.

Barnett, R. C., Davidson, H., & Marshall, N. L. (1991). Physical symptoms and the interplay of work and family roles. *Health Psychology, 10,* 94–101.

Barnett, R. C., & Hyde, J. S. (2001). Women, men, work, and family: An expansionist theory. *American Psychologist, 56,* 781–796.

Barnlund, D. C. (1989). *Communicative styles of Japanese and Americans.* Belmont, CA: Wadsworth Publishing.

Baron, R. A. (1971a). Aggression as a function of magnitude of victim's pain cues, level of prior anger arousal, and aggressor–victim similarity. *Journal of Personality and Social Psychology, 18,* 48–54.

Baron, R. A. (1971b). Magnitude of victim's pain cues and level of prior anger arousal as determinants of adult aggressive behavior. *Journal of Personality and Social Psychology, 17,* 236–243.

Baron, R. A. (1974). Aggression as a function of victim's pain cues, level of prior anger arousal, and exposure to an aggressive model. *Journal of Personality and Social Psychology, 29,* 117–124.

Baron, R. A. (1997). The sweet smell of . . . helping: Effects of pleasant ambient fragrance on prosocial behavior in shopping malls. *Personality and Social Psychology Bulletin, 23,* 498–503.

Baron, R. A., & Richardson, D. R. (1994). *Human aggression (2nd ed.) Perspectives in social psychology.* New York: Plenum Press.

Baron, R. M., Albright, L., & Malloy, T. E. (1995). Effects of behavioral and social class information on social judgment. *Personality and Social Psychology Bulletin, 21,* 308–315.

Baron, R. M., & Rodin, J. (1978). Perceived control and crowding stress: Processes mediating the impact of spatial and social density. In A. Baum & Y. Epstein (Eds.), *Human response to crowding.* Hillsdale, NJ: Erlbaum.

Baron, R. S. (1986). Distraction-conflict theory: Progress and problems. In L. Berkowitz (Ed.), *Advances in experimental social psychology* (Vol. 19, pp. 1–40). New York: Academic Press.

Baron, R. S., David, J., Brunsman, B., & Inman, M. (1997). Why listeners hear less than they are told: Cognitive load and the teller–listener extremity effect. *Journal of Personality and Social Psychology, 72,* 826–838.

Bar-Tal, Y., Kishon-Rabin, L., & Tabak, N. (1997). The effect of need and ability to achieve cognitive structuring on cognitive structuring. *Journal of Personality and Social Psychology, 73,* 1158–1176.

Bartholow, B. D., & Anderson, C. A. (2002). Effects of violent video games on aggressive behavior: Potential sex differences. *Journal of Experimental Social Psychology, 38,* 283–290.

Bassili, J. N., & Provencal, A. (1988). Perceiving minorities: A factor-analytic approach. *Personality and Social Psychology Bulletin, 14,* 5–15.

Batalova, J. A., & Cohen, P. N. (2002). Premarital cohabitation and housework: Couples in cross-national perspective. *Journal of Marriage and Family, 64,* 743–755.

Batson v. Kentucky, 476 US 79, 90 L.Ed.2d 69, 106 S.Ct 1712 (1986).

Batson, C. D. (1998). Altruism and prosocial behavior. In D. T. Gilbert, S. T. Fiske, & G. Lindzey (Eds.), *Handbook of social psychology* (Vol. 2, pp. 282–316). Boston: McGraw-Hill.

Batson, C. D., Cochran, P. J., Biederman, M. F., Blosser, J. L., Ryan, M. J., & Vogt, B. (1978). Failure to help when in a hurry: Callousness or conflict? *Personality and Social Psychology Bulletin, 4,* 97–101.

Batson, C. D., Early, S., & Salvarani, G. (1997). Perspective-taking: Imagining how another feels versus imagining how you would feel. *Personality and Social Psychology Bulletin, 23,* 751–758.

Batson, C. D., Van Lange, P. A. M., Ahmad, N., & Lishner, D. A. (2003). Altruism and helping behavior. In M. A. Hogg & J. Cooper (Eds.), *Sage handbook of social psychology* (pp. 279–295). Thousand Oaks, CA: Sage.

Baum, A. (1990). Stress, intrusive imagery, and chronic distress. *Health Psychology, 9,* 653–675.

Baum, A., & Davis, G. E. (1980). Reducing the stress of high-density living: An architectural intervention. *Journal of Personality and Social Psychology, 38,* 471–481.

Baum, A., & Paulus, P. (1987). Crowding. In D. Stokols & I. Altman (Eds.), *Handbook of environmental psychology.* New York: Wiley. pp. 533–570.

Baumeister, R. F., Catanese, K. R., & Vohs, K. D. (2001). Is there a gender difference in strength of sex drive? *Personality and Social Psychology Review, 5,* 242–273.

Baumeister, R. F., Chesner, S. P., Senders, P. S., & Tice, D. M. (1988). Who's in charge here: Group leaders do lend help in emergencies. *Personality and Social Psychology Bulletin, 14,* 17–22.

Baumeister, R. F., Hutton, D. G., & Tice, D. M. (1989). Cognitive processes during deliberate self-presentation: How self-presenters alter and misinterpret the behavior of their interaction partners. *Journal of Experimental Social Psychology, 25,* 59–78.

Baumeister, R. F., & Leary, M. R. (1995). The need to belong: Desire for interpersonal attachments as a fundamental human motivation. *Psychological Bulletin, 117,* 497–529.

Baumeister, R. F., & Scher, S. J. (1988). Self-defeating behavior patterns among normal individuals: Review and analysis of common self-destructive tendencies. *Psychological Bulletin, 104,* 3–22.

Baumeister, R. F., & Tice, D. M. (2001). *The social dimension of sex.* Boston: Allyn & Bacon.

Baumrind, D. (1964). Some thoughts on the ethics of research: After reading Milgram's "Behavioral study of obedience." *American Psychologist, 19,* 421–423.

Bavelas, J. B., Black, A., Lemery, C. R., & Mullett, J. (1986). "I show how you feel." Motor mimicry as a communicative act. *Journal of Personality and Social Psychology, 50,* 322–329.

Bavelas, J. B., Chovil, N., Coates, L., & Roe, L. (1995). Gestures specialized for dialogue. *Personality and Social Psychology Bulletin, 21,* 394–405.

Beals, K., Impett, E., & Peplau, L. A. (2002). Lesbians in love: Why some relationships endure and others end. *Journal of Lesbian Studies, 6*(1), 53–64.

Beaman, A. L., Barnes, P. J., Klentz, B., & McQuirk, B. (1978). Increasing helping rates through information dissemination: Teaching pays. *Personality and Social Psychology Bulletin, 4,* 406–411.

Beauregard, K. S., & Dunning, D. (1998). Turning up the contrast: Self-enhancement motives prompt egocentric contrast effects in social judgments. *Journal of Personality and Social Psychology, 74,* 606–621.

Bechtold, A., Naccarato, M. E., & Zanna, M. P. (1986). *Need for structure and the prejudice–discrimination link.* Paper presented at the annual meeting of the Canadian Psychological Association, Toronto, Ontario.

Becker, S. W., & Eagly, A. H. (2004). The heroism of women and men. *American Psychologist, 59,* 163–178.

Beckett, N. E., & Park, B. (1995). Use of category versus individuating information: Making base rates salient. *Personality and Social Psychology Bulletin, 21,* 21–31.

Beggs, J. M., & Doolittle, D. C. (1993). Perceptions now and then of occupational sex typing: A replication of Shinar's 1975 study. *Journal of Applied Social Psychology, 23,* 1435–1453.

Bell, D. C. (2001). Evolution of parental caregiving. *Personality and Social Psychology Review, 5,* 216–229.

Belloc, N. B., & Breslow, L. (1972). Relationship of physical health status and health practices. *Preventive Medicine, 3,* 409–421.

Bem, D. J. (1967). Self-perception: An alternative interpretation of cognitive dissonance phenomena. *Psychological Review, 74,* 183–200.

Bem, D. J. (1972). Self-perception theory. In L. Berkowitz (Ed.), *Advances in experimental social psychology* (Vol. 6, pp. 1–62). New York: Academic Press.

Bem, S. L. (1967). Verbal self-control: The establishment of effective self-instruction. *Journal of Experimental Psychology, 74,* 485–491.

Bem, S. L. (1974). The measurement of psychological androgyny. *Journal of Consulting and Clinical Psychology, 42,* 155–162.

Bem, S. L. (1975). Sex role adaptability: One consequence of psychological androgyny. *Journal of Personality and Social Psychology, 31,* 634–643.

Bem, S. L. (1985). Androgyny and gender schema theory: A conceptual and empirical integration. In T. B. Sonderegger (Ed.), *Nebraska Symposium on Motivation: Psychology and gender* (pp. 179–226). Lincoln: University of Nebraska Press.

Bem, S. L., Martyna, W., & Watson, C. (1976). Sex typing and androgyny: Further explorations of the expressive domain. *Journal of Personality and Social Psychology, 43,* 1016–1023.

Bensley, L. S., & Wu, R. (1991). The role of psychological reactance in drinking following alcohol prevention messages. *Journal of Applied Social Psychology, 21,* 1111–1124.

Berger, J., Webster, M., Ridgeway, C., & Rosenholtz, S. J. (1986). Status cues, expectations, and behavior. In E. J. Lawler (Ed.), *Advances in group processes* (Vol. 3, pp. 1–22). Greenwich, CT: JAI Press.

Berglas, S., & Jones, E. E. (1978). Drug choice as a self-handicapping strategy in response to noncontingent success. *Journal of Personality and Social Psychology, 36,* 405–417.

Berkman, L. F., & Syme, S. L. (1979). Social networks, host resistance, and mortality: A nine-year follow-up study of Alameda County residents. *American Journal of Epidemiology, 109,* 186–204.

Berkowitz, L. (1972). Social norms, feelings, and other factors affecting helping and altruism. In L. Berkowitz (Ed.), *Advances in experimental social psychology* (Vol. 6). New York: Academic Press.

Berkowitz, L. (1974). Some determinants of impulsive aggression: Role of mediated associations with reinforcements for aggression. *Psychological Review, 81,* 165–176.

Berkowitz, L. (1984). Some effects of thoughts on anti- and prosocial influences of media events: A cognitive-neoassociation analysis. *Psychological Bulletin, 95,* 410–427.

Bernard, L. C. (1980). Multivariate analysis of new sex role formulations and personality. *Journal of Personality and Social Psychology, 38,* 323–336.

Bernard, M. M., Maio, G. R., & Olson, J. M. (2003). The vulnerability of values to attack: Inoculation of values and value-relevant attitudes. *Personality and Social Psychology Bulletin, 29,* 63–75.

Berney, K. (2004). Love at first byte. Retrieved September 1, 2004 from the Discovery Channel Health Web site: http://health.discovery.com/centers/loverelationships/articles/onlinedating.html

Bernichon, T., Cook, K. E., & Brown, J. (2003). Seeking self-evaluative feedback: The interactive role of global self-esteem and specific self-views. *Journal of Personality and Social Psychology, 84,* 194–204.

Bernieri, F. J., Zuckerman, M., Koestner, R., & Rosenthal, R. (1994). Measuring person perception accuracy: Another look at self–other agreement. *Personality and Social Psychology Bulletin, 20,* 367–378.

Berry, D. S., Pennebaker, J. W., Mueller, J. S., & Hiller, W. S. (1997). Linguistic bases of social perception. *Personality and Social Psychology Bulletin, 23,* 526–537.

Berry, J. W. (1967). Independence and conformity in subsistence-level societies. *Journal of Personality and Social Psychology, 7,* 415–418.

Berry, J. W., Poortinga, Y. H., Segall, M. H., & Dasen, P. R. (1992). *Cross-cultural psychology: Research and applications.* New York: Cambridge University Press.

Berscheid, E. (1999). The greening of relationship science. *American Psychologist, 54,* 260–266.

Berscheid, E. (2002). Emotion. In H. H. Kelley et al. (Eds.), *Close relationships* (pp. 110–168). Clinton Corners, NY: Percheron Press.

Berscheid, E., Graziano, W., Monson, T., & Dermer, M. (1976). Outcome dependency: Attention, attribution, and attraction. *Journal of Personality and Social Psychology, 34,* 978–989.

Berscheid, E., & Regan, P. (2005). *The psychology of interpersonal relationships.* Upper Saddle River, NJ: Prentice Hall.

Berscheid, E., & Reis, H. T. (1998). Attraction and close relationships. In D. T. Gilbert, S. T. Fiske, & G. Lindzey (Eds.), *Handbook of social psychology* (4th ed., Vol. 2, pp. 193–281). Boston: McGraw-Hill.

Berscheid, E., Snyder, M., & Omoto, A. M. (1989). Issues in studying close relationships: Conceptualizing and measuring closeness. In C. Hendrick (Ed.), *Close relationships* (pp. 63–91). Newbury Park, CA: Sage.

Berscheid, E., & Walster, E. (1967). When does a harm-doer compensate a victim? *Journal of Personality and Social Psychology, 6,* 435–441.

Berscheid, E., & Walster, E. (1978). *Interpersonal attraction* (2nd ed.). Reading, MA: Addison-Wesley.

Betancourt, H., & Blair, I. (1992). A cognition (attribution)–emotion model of violence in conflict situations. *Personality and Social Psychology Bulletin, 18,* 343–350.

Bettencourt, B. A., & Dorr, N. (1997). Collective self-esteem as a mediator of the relationship between allocentrism and subjective well-being. *Personality and Social Psychology Bulletin, 23,* 955–964.

Bettencourt, B. A., & Miller, N. (1996). Gender differences in aggression as a function of provocation: A meta-analysis. *Psychological Bulletin, 119,* 422–447.

Bianco, A. T., Higgins, E. T., & Klem, A. (2003). How "fun/importance" fit affects performance: Relating implicit theories to instructions. *Personality and Social Psychology Bulletin, 29,* 1091–1103.

Bickman, L., & Kamzan, M. (1973). The effect of race and need on helping. *Journal of Social Psychology, 89,* 37–77.

Biden, J. R. (1993). Violence against women: The congressional response. *American Psychologist, 48,* 1059–1061.

Biernat, M., Vescio, T. K., & Green, M. L. (1996). Selective self-stereotyping. *Journal of Personality and Social Psychology, 71,* 1194–1209.

Biesanz, J. C., West, S. G., & Graziano, W. G. (1998). Moderators of self–other agreement: Reconsidering temporal stability in personality. *Journal of Personality and Social Psychology, 75,* 467–477.

Biglan, A., Metzler, C. W., Wirt, R., Ary, D., Noell, J., Ochs, L., et al. (1990). Social and behavioral factors associated with high-risk sexual behavior among adolescents. *Journal of Behavioral Medicine, 13,* 245–261.

Billings, A. G., & Moos, R. H. (1984). Coping, stress, and social resources among adults with unipolar depression. *Journal of Personality and Social Psychology, 46,* 877–891.

Bird, C. E., & Fremont, A. M. (1991). Gender, time use, and health. *Journal of Health and Social Behavior, 32,* 114–129.

Bishop, G. D. (1990). Understanding the understanding of illness: Lay disease representations. In J. A. Skelton & R. T. Croyle (Eds.), *Mental representation in health and illness* (pp. 32–59). New York: Springer-Verlag.

Bizer, G. Y., & Krosnick, J. A. (2001). Exploring the structure of strength-related attitude features: The relation between attitude importance and attitude accessibility. *Journal of Personality and Social Psychology, 81,* 566–586.

Blaine, B., & Crocker, J. (1995). Religiousness, race, and psychological well-being: Exploring social psychological mediators. *Personality and Social Psychology Bulletin, 21,* 1031–1041.

Blair, I. V. (2002). The malleability of automatic stereotypes and prejudice. *Personality and Social Psychology Review, 6,* 242–261.

Blair, I. V., & Banaji, M. R. (1996). Automatic and controlled processes in stereotype priming. *Journal of Personality and Social Psychology, 70,* 1142–1163.

Blair, I. V., Judd, C. M., Sadler, M. S., & Jenkins, C. (2002). The role of Afrocentric features in person perception: Judging by features and categories. *Journal of Personality and Social Psychology, 83,* 5–25.

Blair, I. V., Ma, J. E., & Lenton, A. P. (2001). Imagining stereotypes away: The moderation of implicit stereotypes through mental imagery. *Journal of Personality and Social Psychology, 81,* 828–841.

Blanton, H., Buunk, B. P., Gibbons, F. X., & Kuyper, H. (1999). When better-than-others compare upward: Choice of comparison and comparative evaluation as independent predictors of academic performance. *Journal of Personality and Social Psychology, 76,* 420–430.

Blanton, H., Cooper, J., Skurnik, I., & Aronson, J. (1997). When bad things happen to good feedback: Exacerbating the need for self-justification with self-affirmations. *Personality and Social Psychology Bulletin, 23,* 684–692.

Blascovich, J., Brennan, K., Tomaka, J., Kelsey, R. M., Hughes, P., Coad, M. L., et al. (1992). Affect intensity and cardiac arousal. *Journal of Personality and Social Psychology, 63,* 164–174.

Blascovich, J., Ernst, J. M., Tomaka, J., Kelsey, R. M., Salomon, K. L., & Fazio, R. H. (1993). Attitude accessibility as a moderator of autonomic reactivity during decision making. *Journal of Personality and Social Psychology, 64,* 165–176.

Blascovich, J., Mendes, W. B., Hunter, S. B., Lickel, B., & Kowai-Bell, N. (2001). Perceiver threat in social interactions with stigmatized others. *Journal of Personality and Social Psychology, 81,* 828–841.

Blascovich, J., Mendes, W. B., Hunter, S. B., & Salomon, K. (1999). Social "facilitation" as challenge and threat. *Journal of Personality and Social Psychology, 77,* 68–77.

Blascovich, J., Spencer, S. J., Quinn, D., & Steele, C. (2001). African Americans and high blood pressure: The role of stereotype threat. *Psychological Science, 12,* 225–229.

Blass, T. (Ed.). (2000). *Obedience to authority: Current perspectives on the Milgram paradigm.* Mahwah, NJ: Erlbaum.

Bless, H., & Wänke, M. (2000). Can the same information be typical and atypical? How perceived typicality moderates assimilation and contrast in evaluative judgments. *Personality and Social Psychology Bulletin, 26,* 306–314.

Blessum, K. A., Lord, C. G., & Sia, T. L. (1998). Cognitive load and positive mood reduce typicality effects in attitude–behavior consistency. *Personality and Social Psychology Bulletin, 24,* 496–504.

Blumenthal, J. A., & Emery, C. F. (1988). Rehabilitation of patients following myocardial infarction. *Journal of Consulting and Clinical Psychology, 56,* 374–381.

Blumstein, P., & Schwartz, P. (1983). *American couples: Money, work, sex.* New York: Pocket Books.

Boal, K. B., & Bryson, J. M. (1988). Charismatic leadership: A phenomenological and structural approach. In J. G. Hunt, B. R. Baliga, H. P. Dachler, & C. A. Schriesheim (Eds.), *Emerging leadership vistas* (pp. 11–28). Lexington, MA: Lexington Books.

Bobo, L. (1999). Prejudice as group position: Micro-foundations of a sociological approach to racism and race relations. *Journal of Social Issues, 55,* 445–472.

Bobo, L. (2000). Race and beliefs about affirmative action: Assessing the effects of interests, group threat, ideology and racism. In D. O.

Sears, J. Sidanius, & L. Bobo (Eds.), *Racialized politics: The debate about racism in America* (pp. 137–164). Chicago: University of Chicago Press.

Bobo, L., & Kluegel, J. R. (1997). Status, ideology, and dimensions of whites' racial beliefs and attitudes: Progress and stagnation. In S. A. Tuch and J. K. Martin (Eds.), *Racial attitudes in the 1990s: Continuity and change.* Westport, CT: Praeger.

Bochner, S. (1994). Cross-cultural differences in the self concept: A test of Hofstede's individualism/collectivism distinction. *Journal of Cross-Cultural Psychology, 25,* 273–283.

Bochner, S., & Insko, C. A. (1966). Communicator discrepancy, source credibility, and opinion change. *Journal of Personality and Social Psychology, 4,* 614–621.

Boer, C. de. (1977). The polls: Women at work. *Public Opinion Quarterly, 41,* 268–277.

Bold, M. (2001). Impact of computer-mediated communication on families. *National Council on Family Relations Report, 46,*(1), F16–F17.

Boldero, J., & Francis, J. (2000). The relation between self-discrepancies and emotion: The moderating roles of self-guide importance, location relevance, and social self-domain centrality. *Journal of Personality and Social Psychology, 78,* 38–52.

Bolger, N., DeLongis, A., Kessler, R. C., & Schilling, E. A. (1989). Effects of daily stress on negative mood. *Journal of Personality and Social Psychology, 57,* 808–818.

Bolger, N., Zuckerman, A., & Kessler, R. C. (2000). Invisible support and adjustment to stress. *Journal of Personality and Social Psychology, 79,* 953–961.

Bonanno, G. A., Field, N. P., Kovacevic, A., & Kaltman, S. (2002). Self-enhancement as a buffer against extreme adversity: Civil war in Bosnia and traumatic loss in the United States. *Personality and Social Psychology Bulletin, 28,* 184–196.

Bond, C. F., Jr., Omar, A., Pitre, U., Lashley, B. R., Skaggs, L. M., & Kirk, C. T. (1992). Fishy-looking liars: Deception judgment from expectancy violation. *Journal of Personality and Social Psychology, 63,* 969–977.

Bond, M. H. (2004). Culture and aggression—from context to coercion. *Personality and Social Psychology Review, 8,* 62–78.

Bond, R., & Smith, P. B. (1996). Culture and conformity: A meta-analysis of studies using Asch's (1952b, 1956) line judgment task. *Psychological Bulletin, 119,* 111–137.

Boney-McCoy, S., Gibbons, F. X., & Gerrard, M. (1999). Self-esteem, compensatory self-enhancement, and the consideration of health risk. *Personality and Social Psychology Bulletin, 25,* 954–965.

Boninger, D. S., Krosnick, J. A., & Berent, M. K. (1995). Origins of attitude importance: Self-interest, social identification, and value relevance. *Journal of Personality and Social Psychology, 68,* 61–80.

Bons, P. M., & Fiedler, F. E. (1976). Changes in organizational leadership and the behavior of relationship-and task-motivated leaders. *Administrative Science Quarterly, 21,* 433–472.

Bontempo, R., Lobel, S., &Triandis, H. (1990). Compliance and value internalization in Brazil and the U.S. *Journal of Cross-Cultural Psychology, 21,* 201–213.

Borden, R. J. (1980). Audience influence. In P. B. Paulus (Ed.), *Psychology of group influence* (pp. 99–132). Hillsdale, NJ: Erlbaum.

Borgida, E., & Fiske, S. T. (Eds.) (1995). Gender stereotyping, sexual harassment, and the law. *Journal of Social Issues, 51(1).*

Borgida, E., & Howard-Pitney, B. (1983). Personal involvement and the robustness of perceptual salience effects. *Journal of Personality and Social Psychology, 45,* 560–570.

Borkenau, P., & Liebler, A. (1993). Convergence of stranger ratings of personality and intelligence with self-ratings, partner ratings, and measured intelligence. *Journal of Personality and Social Psychology, 65,* 546–553.

Borkenau, P., Mauer, N., Riemann, R., Spinath, F. M., & Angleitner, A. (2004). Thin slices of behavior as cues of personality and intelligence. *Journal of Personality and Social Psychology, 86,* 599–614.

Borland, R., Owen, N., Hill, D., & Schofield, P. (1991). Predicting attempts and sustained cessation of smoking after the introduction of workplace smoking bans. *Health Psychology, 10,* 336–342.

Bornstein, B. H., Whisenhunt, B. L., Nemeth, R. J., & Dunaway, D. L. (2002). Pretrial publicity and civil cases: A two-way street? *Law and Human Behavior, 26,* 3–18.

Bornstein, G. (2003). Intergroup conflict: Individual, group, and collective interests. *Personality and Social Psychology Review, 7,* 129–145.

Bornstein, R. F., Kale, A. R., & Cornell, K. R. (1990). Boredom as a limiting condition on the mere exposure effect. *Journal of Personality and Social Psychology, 58,* 791–800.

Bosson, J., Swann, W. B., Jr., & Pennebaker, J. (2000). Stalking the perfect measure of implicit self-esteem: The blind men and the elephant revisited? *Journal of Personality and Social Psychology, 79,* 631–643.

Bothwell, R. K., Deffenbacher, K. A., & Brigham, J. C. (1987). Correlation of eyewitness accuracy and confidence: Optimality hypothesis revisited. *Journal of Applied Psychology, 72,* 691–695.

Bottoms, B. L., Davis, S. L., & Epstein, M. A. (2004). Effects of victim and defendant race on jurors' decisions in child sexual abuse cases. *Journal of Applied Social Psychology, 34,* 1–33.

Boudreau, L. A., Baron, R. M., & Oliver, P. V. (1992). Effects of expected communication target expertise and timing of set on trait use in person description. *Personality and Social Psychology Bulletin, 18,* 447–451.

Bowlby, J. (1988). *A secure base: Parent–child attachment and healthy human development.* New York: Basic Books.

Bradbury, T. N., & Fincham, F. D. (1990). Attributions in marriage: Review and critique. *Psychological Bulletin, 107,* 3–33.

Bradbury, T. N., Rogge, R., & Lawrence, E. (2001). Reconsidering the role of conflict in marriage. In A. Booth, A. C. Crouter, & M. Clements (Eds.), *Couples in conflict* (pp. 59–81). Mahwah, NJ: Erlbaum.

Brady, E. (2004, February 6). How free should speech be at campus games? *USA Today,* p. A1.

Bragg, R. (1995, August 13). All she has, $150,000, is going to a university. *The New York Times,* pp. 1, 22.

Braiker, H. B., & Kelley, H. H. (1979). Conflict in the development of close relationships. In R. L. Burgess & T. L. Huston (Eds.), Social *exchange in developing relationships* (pp. 135–168). New York: Academic Press.

Brandstatter, V., & Frank, E. (2002). Effects of deliberative and implemental mindsets on persistence in goal-directed behavior. *Personality and Social Psychology Bulletin, 28,* 1366–1378.

Brannon, L. A., & Brock, T. C. (2001). Scarcity claims elicit extreme responding to persuasive messages: Role of cognitive elaboration. *Personality and Social Psychology Bulletin, 27,* 365–375.

Brauer, M. (2001). Intergroup perception in the social context: The effects of social status and group membership on perceived outgroup homogeneity and ethnocentrism. *Journal of Experimental Social Psychology, 37,* 15–31.

Brauer, M., Judd, C. M., & Gliner, M. D. (1995). The effects of repeated expressions on attitude polarization during group discussions. *Journal of Personality and Social Psychology, 68,* 1014–1029.

Bray, J. H. (1994). Does one plus one make two or one? Comment on Fine and Kurdek. *Journal of Family Psychology, 8,* 380–383.

Brehm, J. W. (1956). Post-decision changes in desirability of alternatives. *Journal of Abnormal and Social Psychology, 52,* 384–389.

Brehm, J. W. (1966). *A theory of psychological reactance.* New York: Academic Press.

Brehm, S. S., Miller, R. S., Perlman, D., & Campbell, S. M. (2002). *Intimate relationships.* Boston: McGraw Hill.

Brekke, N., & Borgida, E. (1988). Expert psychological testimony in rape trials: A social–cognitive analysis. *Journal of Personality and Social Psychology, 55,* 372–386.

Brennan, K. A., & Shaver, P. R. (1995). Dimensions of adult attachment, affect regulation, and romantic relationship functioning. *Personality and Social Psychology Bulletin, 21,* 267–283.

Brewer, M. B. (1988). A dual process model of impression formation. In T. K. Skrull & R. S. Wyer, Jr. (Eds.), *Advances in social cognition* (Vol. 1, pp. 1–36). Hillsdale, NJ: Erlbaum.

Brewer, M. B. (1991). The social self: On being the same and different at the same time. *Personality and Social Psychology Bulletin, 17,* 475–482.

Brewer, M. B. (2004). Taking the social origins of human nature seriously: Toward a more imperalist social psychology. *Personality and Social Psychology Review, 8,* 107–113.

Brewer, M. B., & Brown, R. J. (1998). Intergroup relations. In D. T. Gilbert, S. T. Fiske, & G. Lindzey (Eds.), *Handbook of social psychology* (4th ed., pp. 554–594). New York: McGraw-Hill.

Brewer, M. B., Dull, V., & Lui, L. (1981). Perceptions of the elderly: Stereotypes as prototypes. *Journal of Personality and Social Psychology, 41,* 656–670.

Brewer, M. B., & Kramer, R. M. (1986). Choice behavior in social dilemmas: Effects of social identity, group size, and decision framing. *Journal of Personality and Social Psychology, 50,* 543–549.

Brewer, N., & Burke, A. (2002). Effects of testimonial inconsistencies and eyewitness confidence on mock-juror judgments. *Law and Human Behavior, 26,* 353–364.

Brewer, P. R. (2003). The shifting foundations of public opinion about gay rights. *Journal of Politics, 65,* 1208–1220.

Brickman, P., & Janoff-Bulman, R. (1977). Pleasure and pain in social comparison. In R. L. Miller & J. M. Suls (Eds.), *Social comparison processes: Theoretical and empirical perspectives* (pp. 149–186). Washington, DC: Hemisphere.

Brigham, J. C., Mass, A., Snyder, L. D., & Spaulding, K. (1982). Accuracy of eyewitness identifications in a field setting. *Journal of Personality and Social Psychology, 42,* 673–681.

Brock, T. C. (1965). Communication-recipient similarity and decision change. *Journal of Personality and Social Psychology, 1,* 650–654.

Broman, C. L. (1993). Social relationships and health-related behavior. *Journal of Behavioral Medicine, 16,* 335–350.

Brown v. Mississippi, 297 U.S. 278 (1936).

Brown, J. D. (1990). Evaluating one's abilities: Shortcuts and stumbling blocks on the road to self-knowledge. *Journal of Experimental Social Psychology, 26,* 149–167.

Brown, J. D., & Dutton, K. A. (1995). Truth and consequences: The costs and benefits of accurate self-knowledge. *Personality and Social Psychology Bulletin, 21,* 1288–1296.

Brown, J. D., & Marshall, M. A. (2001). Self-esteem and emotion: Some thoughts about feelings. *Personality and Social Psychology Bulletin, 27,* 575–584.

Brown, J. D., Nowick, N. J., Lord, K. A., & Richards, J. M. (1992). When Gulliver travels: Social context, psychological closeness, and self-appraisals. *Journal of Personality and Social Psychology, 62,* 717–727.

Brown, J. D., & Smart, A. S. (1991). The self and social conduct: Linking self-representations to prosocial behavior. *Journal of Personality and Social Psychology, 60,* 368–375.

Brown, J. H., & Raven, B. H. (1994). Power and compliance in doctor/patient relationships. *Journal of Health Psychology, 6,* 3–22.

Brown, R. (2000). *Group processes* (2nd ed.). Malden, MA: Blackwell.

Brown, R. P., Charnsangavej, T., Keough, K. A., Newman, M. L., & Rentfrow, P. J. (2000). Putting the "affirm" into affirmative action: Preferential selection and academic performance. *Journal of Personality and Social Psychology, 79,* 736–747.

Brown, S. L., Nesse, R. M., Vinokur, A. D., & Smith, D. M. (2003). Providing social support may be more beneficial than receiving it: Results from a prospective study of mortality. *Psychological Science, 14,* 320–327.

Brown, V., & Paulus, P. B. (1996). A simple dynamic model of social factors in group brainstorming. *Small Group Research, 27,* 91–114.

Brown, V. R., & Paulus, P. B. (2002). Making group brainstorming more effective: Recommendations from an associative memory perspective. *Current Directions in Psychological Science, 11,* 208–212.

Browne, A. (1993). Violence against women by male partners: Prevalence, outcomes, and policy implications. *American Psychologist, 48,* 1077–1087.

Brownell K. D., Stunkard, A. J., & McKeon, P. M. (1985). Weight reduction at the worksite: A promise partially fulfilled. *American Journal of Psychiatry,* 142, 47–51.

Brownmiller, S. (1975). *Against our will.* New York: Simon & Schuster.

Bruhn, J. G. (1965). An epidemiological study of myocardial infarction in an Italian-American community. *Journal of Chronic Diseases, 18,* 326–338.

Bryan, J. H., & Test, N. A. (1967). Models and helping: Naturalistic studies in aiding behavior. *Journal of Personality and Social Psychology, 6,* 400–407.

Bryant, A. N. (2003). Changes in attitudes toward women's roles: Predicting gender-role traditionalism among college students. *Sex Roles, 48,* 131–142.

Buckley, J. (1993, November 8). The tragedy in room 108. *U.S. News and World Report,* pp.41–43, 46.

Budesheim, T. L., & Bonnelle, K. (1998). The use of abstract trait knowledge and behavioral exemplars in causal explanations of behavior. *Personality and Social Psychology Bulletin, 24,* 575–584.

Buehler, R., Griffin, D., & MacDonald, H. (1997). The role of motivated reasoning in optimistic time predictions. *Personality and Social Psychology Bulletin, 23,* 238–247.

Buehler, R., Griffin, D., & Ross, M. (1994). Exploring the "Planning Fallacy": Why people underestimate their task completion times. *Journal of Personality and Social Psychology, 67,* 366–381.

Buehler, R., & McFarland, C. (2001). Intensity bias in affective forecasting: The role of temporal focus. *Personality and Social Psychology Bulletin, 27,* 1480–1493.

Bulman, R. J., & Wortman, C. B. (1977). Attributions of blame and coping in the "real world": Severe accident victims react to their lot. *Journal of Personality and Social Psychology, 35,* 351–363.

Burger, J. M. (1986). Increasing compliance by improving the deal: The that's-not-all technique. *Journal of Personality and Social Psychology, 51,* 277–283.

Burger, J. M. (1999). The foot-in-the-door compliance procedure: A multiple-process analysis and review. *Personality and Social Psychology Review, 3*(4), 303–325.

Burger, J. M., & Cornelius, T. (2003). Raising the price of agreement: Public commitment and the low-ball compliance procedure. *Journal of Applied Social Psychology, 33,* 923–934.

Burger, J. M., Messian, N., Patel, S., del Prado, A., & Anderson, C. (2004). What a coincidence! The effects of incidental similarity on compliance. *Personality and Social Psychology Bulletin, 30,* 35–43.

Burgess, D., & Borgida, E. (1997). Refining sex-role spillover theory: The role of gender subtypes and harasser attributions. *Social Cognition, 15,* 291–311.

Burleson, B. R. (2003). The experience and effects of emotional support. *Personal Relationships, 10,* 1–23.

Burn, S. M. (2004). *Groups: Theory and practice.* Belmont, CA: Wadsworth.

Burnstein, E., Crandall, C., & Kitayama, S. (1994). Some neo-Darwinian decision rules for altruism: Weighing cues for inclusive fitness as a function of the biological importance of the decision. *Journal of Personality and Social Psychology, 67,* 773–789.

Burnstein, E., & Vinokur, A. (1977). Persuasive argumentation and social comparison as determinants of attitude polarization. *Journal of Experimental Social Psychology, 13,* 315–332.

Burt, M. R. (1980). Cultural myths and support for rape. *Journal of Personality and Social Psychology, 38,* 217–230.

Bushman, B. J. (1995). Moderating role of trait aggressiveness in the effects of violent media on aggression. *Journal of Personality and Social Psychology, 69,* 950–960.

Bushman, B. J. (1996). Individual differences in the extent and development of aggressive cognitive–associative networks. *Personality and Social Psychology Bulletin, 8,* 811–819.

Bushman, B. J. (1998). Effects of television violence on memory for commercial messages. *Journal of Experimental Psychology: Applied, 4,* 291–307.

Bushman, B. J. (2002). Does venting anger feed or extinguish the flame? Catharsis, rumination, distraction, anger and aggressive responding. *Personality and Social Psychology Bulletin, 28,* 724–731.

Bushman, B. J., & Anderson, C. A. (2001). Media violence and the American public: Scientific facts versus media misinformation. *American Psychologist, 56,* 477–489.

Bushman, B. J., & Anderson, C. A. (2002). Violent video games and hostile expectations: A test of the general aggression model. *Personality and Social Psychology Bulletin, 28,* 1679–1686.

Bushman, B. J., Baumeister, R. F., & Phillips, C. M. (2001). Do people aggress to improve their mood? Catharsis beliefs, affect regulation opportunity, and aggressive responding. *Journal of Personality and Social Psychology, 81,* 17–32.

Bushman, B. J., Baumeister, R. F., & Stack, A. D. (1999). Catharsis, aggression, and persuasive influence: Self-fulfilling or self-defeating prophecies? *Journal of Personality and Social Psychology, 76,* 367–376.

Bushman, B. J., Bonacci, A. M., van Dijk, M., & Baumeister, R. F. (2003). Narcissism, sexual refusal, and aggression: Testing a narcissistic reactance model of sexual coercion. *Journal of Personality and Social Psychology, 84,* 1027–1040.

Bushman, B. J., & Phillips, C. M. (2001). If the television program bleeds, memory for the advertisement recedes. *Current Directions in Psychological Science, 10,* 43–47.

Bushman, B. J., & Wells, G. L. (2001). Narrative impressions of literature: The availability bias and the corrective properties of meta-analytic approaches. *Personality and Social Psychology Bulletin, 27,* 1123–1130.

Buss, D. M. (1996). The evolutionary psychology of human social strategies. In E. T. Higgens & A. W. Kruglanski (Eds.), *Social psychology: Handbook of basic principles* (pp. 3–38). New York: Guilford.

Buss, D. M. (2000). *The dangerous passion.* New York: Free Press.

Buss, D. M., & Kenrick, D. T. (1998). Evolutionary social psychology. In D. T. Gilbert, S. T. Fiske, & G. Lindzey (Eds.), *Handbook of social psychology* (4th ed., Vol. 2, pp. 982–1026). Boston: McGraw-Hill.

Buss, D. M., Shackelford, T. K., Kirkpatrick, L. A., Choe, J. C., Lim, H. K., Hasegawa, M., et al. (1999). Jealousy and the nature of beliefs about infidelity: Tests of competing hypotheses about sex differences in the United States, Korea and Japan. *Personal Relationships, 6,* 125–150.

Buss, D. M., Shackelford, T. K., Kirkpatrick, L. A., & Larsen, R. J. (2001). A half century of mate preferences: The cultural evolution of values. *Journal of Marriage and Family, 63,* 491–503.

Butler, J. L., & Baumeister, R. F. (1998). The trouble with friendly faces: Skilled performance with a supportive audience. *Journal of Personality and Social Psychology, 75,* 1213–1230.

Butterworth, G. (1992). Self-perception as a foundation for self-knowledge. *Psychological Inquiry, 3,* 134–136.

Buunk, B. P., Collins, R. L., Taylor, S. E., Van Yperen, N. W., & Dakof, G. A. (1990). The affective consequences of social comparison: Either direction has its ups and downs. *Journal of Personality and Social Psychology, 59,* 1238–1249.

Buunk, B. P., Doosje, B. J., Jans, L. G. J. M., & Hopstaken, L. E. M. (1993). Perceived reciprocity, social support, and stress at work: The role of exchange and communal orientation. *Journal of Personality and Social Psychology, 65,* 801–811.

Buunk, B. P., Oldersma, F. L., & de Dreu, C. K. W. (2001). Enhancing satisfaction through downward comparison. *Journal of Experimental Social Psychology, 37,* 452–467.

Byrne, D. (1971). *The attraction paradigm.* New York: Academic Press.

Cacioppo, J. T., Hawkley, L. C., & Berntson, G. G. (2003). The anatomy of loneliness. *Current Directions in Psychological Science, 12,* 71–74.

Cacioppo, J. T., Marshall-Goodell, B. S., Tassinary, L. G., & Petty, R. E. (1992). Rudimentary determinants of attitudes: Classical conditioning is more effective when prior knowledge is low than high. *Journal of Experimental Social Psychology, 28,* 207–233.

Cacioppo, J. T., & Petty, R. E. (1979). Effects of message repetition and position on cognitive response, recall and persuasion. *Journal of Personality and Social Psychology, 27,* 97–109.

Cacioppo, J. T., & Petty, R. E. (1985). Central and peripheral routes to persuasion: The role of message repetition. In L. F. Alwitt & A. A. Mitchell (Eds.), *Psychological processes and advertising effects: Theory, research, and applications* (pp. 91–111). Hillsdale, NJ: Erlbaum.

Caldwell, M. A., & Peplau, L. A. (1982). Sex differences in same-sex friendship. *Sex Roles,* 8, 721–732.

Callahan, N. (2004, June 9). Drafting women. Retrieved August 20, 2004, from http://www.nathancallahan.com/burke.html

Camacho, L. M., & Paulus, P. B. (1995). The role of social anxiousness in group brainstorming. *Journal of Personality and Social Psychology, 68,* 1071–1080.

Campbell, D. T. (1975). On the conflicts between biological and social evolution and between psychology and moral tradition. *American Psychologist, 30,* 1103–1126.

Campbell, D. T., & Stanley, J. C. (1963). *Experimental and quasi-experimental designs for research.* Chicago: Rand-McNally.

Campbell, J. D. (1986). Similarity and uniqueness: The effects of attribute type, relevance, and individual differences in self-esteem and depression. *Journal of Personality and Social Psychology, 50,* 281–294.

Campbell, J. D. (1990). Self-esteem and clarity of the self-concept. *Journal of Personality and Social Psychology, 59,* 538–549.

Campo, S., Brossard, D., Frazer, M. S., Marchell, T., Lewis, D., & Talbot, J. (2003). Are social norms campaigns really magic bullets? Assessing the effects on students' misperceptions on drinking behavior. *Health Communication, 15*(4), 481–497.

Canary, D. J., Cody, M. J., & Manusov, V. L. (2003). *Interpersonal communication.* Boston: St. Martin's.

Cantor, N., & Kihlstrom, J. F. (1987). *Personality and social intelligence.* Englewood Cliffs, NJ: Prentice Hall.

Cantor, N., & Kihlstrom, J. F. (Eds.). (1981). *Personality, cognition, and social interaction.* Hillsdale, NJ: Erlbaum.

Caporael, L. R., & Brewer, M. B. (1995). Hierarchical evolutionary theory: There is an alternative, and it's not creationism. *Psychological Inquiry, 6,* 31–80.

Carli, L. L. (2001). Gender and social influence. *Journal of Social Issues, 57,* 725–741.

Carli, L. L., Ganley, R., & Pierce-Otay, A. (1991). Similarity and satisfaction in roommate relationships. *Personality and Social Psychology Bulletin, 17,* 419–426.

Carlson, M., Charlin, V., & Miller, N. (1988). Positive mood and helping behavior: A test of six hypotheses. *Journal of Personality and Social Psychology, 55,* 211–229.

Carlson, M., & Miller, N. (1987). Explanation of the relation between negative mood and helping. *Psychological Bulletin, 102,* 91–108.

Caron, S. L., Davis, C. M., Halteman, W. A., & Stickle, M. (1993). Predictors of condom-related behaviors among first-year college students. *Journal of Sex Research, 30,* 252–259.

Carver, C. S., Harris, S. D., Lehman, J. M., Durel, L. A., Antoni, M. H., Spencer, S. M., et al. (2000). How important is the perception of personal control? Studies of early stage breast cancer patients. *Personality and Social Psychology Bulletin, 26,* 139–149.

Carver, C. S., Lawrence, J. W., & Scheier, M. F. (1999). Self-discrepancies and affect: Incorporating the role of feared selves. *Personality and Social Psychology Bulletin, 25,* 783–792.

Carver, C. S., & Scheier, M. F. (1981). The self-attentioninduced feedback loop and social facilitation. *Journal of Experimental Social Psychology, 17,* 545–568.

Carver, C. S., & Scheier, M. F. (1998). *On the self-regulation of behavior.* New York: Cambridge University Press.

Carver, C. S., Sutton, S. K., & Scheier, M. F. (2000). Action, emotion, and personality: Emerging conceptual integration. *Personality and Social Psychology Bulletin, 26,* 741–751.

Cash, T. F., Gillen, B., & Burns, D. S. (1977). Sexism and "beautyism" in personnel consultant decision making. *Journal of Applied Psychology, 62,* 301–310.

Casselden, P. A., & Hampson, S. E. (1990). Forming impressions from incongruent traits. *Journal of Personality and Social Psychology, 59,* 353–372.

Cassidy, J., & Shaver, P. R. (Eds.). (1999). *Handbook of attachment.* New York: Guilford.

Catalano, R., Novaco, R., & McConnell, W. (1997). A model of the net effect of job loss on violence. *Journal of Personality and Social Psychology, 72,* 1440–1447.

Catania, J., Coates, T., Stall, R., Bye, L., Kegeles, S., Capell, F., et al. (1991). Changes in condom use among homosexual men in San Francisco. *Health Psychology, 10,* 190–199.

Catania, J. A., Coates, T. J., Peterson, J., Dolcini, M. M., Kegeles, S., Siegel, D., et al. (1993). Changes in condom use among black, hispanic and white heterosexuals in San Francisco: The AMEN Cohort Survey. *Journal of Sex Research, 30,* 121–128.

Cate, R. M., & Lloyd, S. A. (1992). *Courtship.* Newbury Park, CA: Sage.

Cate, R. M., Lloyd, S. A., & Long, E. (1988). The role of rewards and fairness in developing premarital relationships. *Journal of Marriage and the Family, 50,* 443–452.

Cater, D., & Strickland, S. P. (1975). *TV violence and the child: The evolution and fate of the Surgeon General's report.* New York: Russell Sage Foundation.

Cejka, M. A., & Eagly, A. H. (1999). Gender-stereotypic images of occupations correspond to the sex segregation of employment. *Personality and Social Psychology Bulletin, 25,* 413–423.

Center for the Advancement of Health. (2004, April). Sweet-talking the kids: Not-so-hidden persuasion. *Facts of Life, 9,* 1.

Centers for Disease Control. (2003). *National Center for Injury Prevention and Control, Intimate Partner Violence: Fact Sheet.* http://www.cdc.gov/ncipc/factsheets/ipvfacts.htm

Cesario, J., Grant, H., & Higgins, E. T. (2004). Regulatory fit and persuasion: Transfer from "feeling right." *Journal of Personality and Social Psychology, 86,* 388–404.

Chafetz, M. E. (1970). The alcoholic symptom and its therapeutic relevance. *Quarterly Journal of Studies on Alcohol, 31,* 444–445.

Chaiken, S. (1979). Communicator physical attractiveness and persuasion. *Journal of Personality and Social Psychology, 37,* 1387–1397.

Chaiken, S. (1980). Heuristic versus systematic information processing and the use of source versus message cues in persuasion. *Journal of Personality and Social Psychology, 39,* 752–766.

Chaiken, S. (1987). The heuristic model of persuasion. In M. P. Zanna, J. M. Olson, & C. P. Herman (Eds.), *Social influence: The Ontario Symposium* (Vol. 5, pp. 3–39). Hillsdale, NJ: Erlbaum.

Chaiken, S., & Eagly, A. H. (1983). Communication modality as a determinant of persuasion: The role of communicator salience. *Journal of Personality and Social Psychology, 45,* 241–256.

Chaiken, S., & Maheswaran, D. (1994). Heuristic processing can bias systematic processing: Effects of source credibility, argument ambiguity, and task importance on attitude judgment. *Journal of Personality and Social Psychology, 66,* 460–475.

Chaiken, S., & Trope, Y. (Eds.). (1999). *Dual-process theories in social psychology.* New York: Guilford Press.

Chaiken, S., & Yates, S. (1985). Affective–cognitive consistency and thought-induced attitude polarization. *Journal of Personality and Social Psychology, 49,* 1470–1481.

Chaikin, A. L., & Derlega, V. J. (1974). Liking for the norm-breaker in self-disclosure. *Journal of Personality, 42,* 117–129.

Champion, V., & Huster, G. (1995). Effect of interventions on stage of mammography adoption. *Journal of Behavioral Medicine, 18,* 169–187.

Chance, J. E., & Goldstein, A. G. (1996). The other-race effect and eyewitness identification. In S. L. Sporer, R. S. Malpass, & G. Koenken (Eds.), *Psychological issues in eyewitness identification* (pp. 153–176). Mahwah, NJ: Erlbaum.

Chang, E. C. (1998). Does dispositional optimism moderate the relation between perceived stress and psychological well-being? A preliminary investigation. *Personality and Individual Differences, 25,* 233–240.

Chartrand, T. L., & Bargh, J. A. (1996). Automatic activation of impression formation and memorization goals: Nonconscious goal priming reproduces effects of explicit task instructions. *Journal of Personality and Social Psychology, 71,* 464–478.

Chartrand, T. L., & Bargh, J. A. (1999). The chameleon effect: The perception–behavior link and social interaction. *Journal of Personality and Social Psychology, 76,* 893–910.

Chatman, C. M., & von Hippel, W. (2001). Attributional mediation of in-group bias. *Journal of Experimental Social Psychology, 37,* 267–272.

Chawla, P., & Krauss, R. M. (1994). Gesture and speech in spontaneous and rehearsed narratives. *Journal of Experimental Social Psychology, 30,* 580–601.

Check, J. V. P., & Malamuth, N. M. (1983). Sex role stereotyping and reactions to depictions of stranger versus acquaintance rape. *Journal of Personality and Social Psychology, 45,* 344–356.

Chemers, M. M. (1997). *An integrative theory of leadership.* Mahwah, NJ: Erlbaum.

Chemers, M. M. (2001). Leadership effectiveness: An integrative review. In M. A. Hogg & R. S. Tindale (Eds.), *Blackwell handbook of social psychology: Group processes* (pp. 376–399). Malden, MA: Blackwell.

Chemers, M. M., Watson, C. B., & May, S. T. (2000). Dispositional affect and leadership effectiveness: A comparison of self-esteem, optimism, and efficacy. *Personality and Social Psychology Bulletin, 26,* 267–277.

Chen, H. C., Reardon, R., Rea, C., & Moore, D. J. (1992). Forewarning of content and involvement: Consequences for persuasion and resistance to persuasion. *Journal of Experimental Social Psychology, 28,* 523–541.

Chen, M., & Bargh, J. A. (1999a). Consequences of automatic evaluation: Immediate behavioral predispositions to approach or avoid the stimulus. *Personality and Social Psychology Bulletin, 25,* 215–224.

Chen, M., & Bargh, J. A. (1999b). Nonconscious behavioral confirmation processes: The self-fulfilling consequences of automatic stereotype activation. *Journal of Experimental Social Psychology, 33,* 541–560.

Chen, S., Chen, K. Y., & Shaw, L. (2004). Self-verification motives at the collective level of self-definition. *Journal of Personality and Social Psychology, 86,* 77–94.

Chen, S., Shechter, D., & Chaiken, S. (1996). Getting at the truth or getting along: Accuracy and impression motivated heuristic and systematic processing. *Journal of Personality and Social Psychology, 71,* 262–275.

Chen, S. C. (1937). Social modification of the activity of ants in nest-building. *Physiological Zoology, 10,* 420–436.

Cheng, C. (2001). Assessing coping flexibility in real-life and laboratory settings: A multimethod approach. *Journal of Personality and Social Psychology, 80,* 814–833.

Cheng, C. M., & Chartrand, T. L. (2003). Self-monitoring without awareness: Using mimicry as a nonconscious affiliation strategy. *Journal of Personality and Social Psychology, 85,* 1170–1179.

Chirkov, V., Ryan, R. M., Kim, Y., & Kaplan, U. (2003). Differentiating autonomy from individualism and independence: A self-determination theory perspective on internalization of cultural orientations and well-being. *Journal of Personality and Social Psychology, 84,* 97–110.

Chiu, C-y., Morris, M. W., Hong, Y-y., & Menon, T. (2000). Motivated cultural cognition: The impact of implicit cultural theories on dispositional attribution varies as a function of need for closure. *Journal of Personality and Social Psychology, 78,* 247–259.

Choi, I., & Choi, Y. (2002). Culture and self-concept flexibility. *Personality and Social Psychology Bulletin, 28,* 1508–1517.

Choi, I., Dalal, R., Kim-Prieto, C., & Park, H. (2003). Culture and judgment of causal relevance. *Journal of Personality and Social Psychology, 84,* 46–59.

Christensen, T. C., Wood, J. V., & Barrett, L. F. (2003). Remembering everyday experience through the prism of self-esteem. *Personality and Social Psychology Bulletin, 29,* 51–62.

Christianson, S. (1992). Emotional stress and eyewitness memory: A critical review. *Psychological Bulletin, 112,* 284–309.

Christie, R., & Jahoda, M. (Eds.). (1954). *Studies in the scope and method of "the authoritarian personality."* Glencoe, IL: Free Press.

Chun, W. Y., Spiegel, S., & Kruglanski, A. W. (2002). Assimilative behavior identification can also be resource dependent: The unimodel perspective on personal-attribution phases. *Journal of Personality and Social Psychology, 83,* 542–555.

Church, A. T., Ortiz, F. A., Katigbak, M. S., Avdeyeva, T. V., Emerson, A. M., de Jesús Vargas Flores, J., et al. (2003). Measuring individual and cultural differences in implicit trait theories. *Journal of Personality and Social Psychology, 85,* 332–347.

Cialdini, R. B. (2004). *Influence: Science and practice.* Boston: Allyn & Bacon.

Cialdini, R. B., Borden, R. J., Thorne, A., Walker, M. R., Feeman, S., & Sloan, L. R. (1976). Basking in reflected glory: Three (football)

field studies. *Journal of Personality and Social Psychology, 34,* 366–375.

Cialdini, R. B., Cacioppo, J. T., Bassett, R., & Miller, J. A. (1978). Low-ball procedure for producing compliance: Commitment then cost. *Journal of Personality and Social Psychology, 36,* 463–476.

Cialdini, R. B., Darby, B. L., & Vincent, J. E. (1973). Transgression and altruism: A case for hedonism. *Journal of Experimental Social Psychology, 9,* 502–516.

Cialdini, R. B., & De Nicholas, M. E. (1989). Self-presentation by association. *Journal of Personality and Social Psychology, 57,* 626–631.

Cialdini, R. B., & Goldstein, N. J. (2004). Social influence: Compliance and conformity. *Annual Review of Psychology, 55,* 591–621.

Cialdini, R. B., Schaller, M., Houlihan, D., Arps, K., Fultz, J., & Beaman, A. (1987). Empathy-based helping: Is it selflessly or selfishly motivated? *Journal of Personality and Social Psychology, 52,* 749–758.

Cialdini, R. B., & Trost, M. R. (1998). Social influence: Social norms, conformity, and compliance. In D. T. Gilbert, S. T. Fiske, & G. Lindzey (Eds.), *Handbook of social psychology* (Vol. 2, pp. 151–192). Boston: McGraw-Hill.

Cialdini, R. B., Vincent, J. E., Lewis, S. K., Catalan, J., Wheeler, D., & Darby, B. L. (1975). Reciprocal concessions procedure for inducing compliance: The door-in-the-face technique. *Journal of Personality and Social Psychology, 31,* 206–215.

Citrin, J., Sears, D. O., Muste, C., & Wong, C. (2001). Multiculturalism in American public opinion. *British Journal of Political Science, 31,* 247–275.

Clark, M. S., & Chrisman, K. (1994). Resource allocation in intimate relationships. In M. J. Lerner & G. Mikula (Eds.), *Entitlement and the affectional bond: Justice in close relationships* (pp. 65–88). New York: Plenum Press.

Clark, M. S., Graham, S., & Grote, N. (2002). Bases for giving benefits in marrage: What is ideal? What is realistic? What really happens? In P. Noller & J. A. Feeney (Eds.), *Understanding marriage* (pp. 150–176). New York: Cambridge University Press.

Clark, M. S., & Grote, N. K. (1998). Why aren't indices of relationship costs always negatively related to indices of relationship quality? *Personality and Social Psychology Review, 2*(1), 2–17.

Clark, M. S., & Mills, J. (1979). Interpersonal attraction in exchange and communal relationships. *Journal of Personality and Social Psychology, 37,* 12–24.

Clark, R. D. (1990). Minority influence: The role of argument refutation of the majority position and social support for the minority position. *European Journal of Social Psychology, 20,* 489–497.

Clark, R. D. (2001). Effects of majority defection and multiple minority sources on minority influence. *Group dynamics, 5*(1), 57–62.

Clark, R. D., & Word, L. E. (1972). Why don't bystanders help? Because of ambiguity? *Journal of Personality and Social Psychology, 24,* 392–400.

Clark, R. D., & Word, L. E. (1974). Where is the apathetic bystander? Situational characteristics of the emergency. *Journal of Personality and Social Psychology, 29,* 279–287.

Clary, E. G., Snyder, M., Ridge, R. D., Copeland, J., Stukas, A. A., Haugen, J., et al. (1998). Understanding and assessing the motivations of volunteers: A functional approach. *Journal of Personality and Social Psychology, 74,* 1516–1530.

Coats, E. J., & Feldman, R. S. (1996). Gender differences in nonverbal correlates of social status. *Personality and Social Psychology Bulletin, 22,* 1014–1022.

Cochran, S. D., & Mays, V. M. (1990). Sex, lies, and HIV. *New England Journal of Medicine,* 322, 774–775.

Cohen, C. E. (1981). Goals and schemas in person perception: Making sense out of the stream of behavior. In N. Cantor & J. Kihlstrom (Eds.), *Personality, cognition, and social behavior* (pp. 45–68). Hillsdale, NJ: Erlbaum.

Cohen, D. (1996). Law, social policy, and violence: The impact of regional cultures. *Journal of Personality and Social Psychology, 70,* 961–978.

Cohen, D. (1998). Culture, social organization, and patterns of violence. *Journal of Personality and Social Psychology, 75,* 408–419.

Cohen, D., & Nisbett, R. E. (1994). Self-protection and the culture of honor: Explaining southern violence. The self and the collective [Special Issue] *Personality and Social Psychology Bulletin, 20,* 551–567.

Cohen, D., Nisbett, R. E., Bowdle, B. F., & Schwarz, N. (1996). Insult, aggression, and the southern culture of honor: An "experimental ethnography." *Journal of Personality and Social Psychology, 70,* 945–960.

Cohen, G. L., Aronson, J., & Steele, C. M. (2000). When beliefs yield to evidence: Reducing biased evaluation by affirming the self. *Personality and Social Psychology Bulletin, 26,* 1151–1164.

Cohen, L. L., & Swim, J. K. (1995). The differential impact of gender ratios on women and men: Tokenism, self-confidence, and expectations. *Personality and Social Psychology Bulletin, 21,* 876–884.

Cohen, S., Doyle, W. J., Skoner, D. P., Rabin, B. S., & Gwaltney, J. M., Jr. (1997). Social ties and susceptibility to the common cold. *Journal of the American Medical Association, 277,* 1940–1944.

Cohen, S., Frank, E., Doyle, W. J., Skoner, D. P., Rabin, B. S., & Gwaltney, J. M., Jr. (1998). Types of stressors that increase susceptibility to the common cold in healthy adults. *Health Psychology, 17,* 214–223.

Cohen, S., Glass, D. C., & Phillip, S. (1978). Environment and health. In H. E. Freeman, S. Levine, & L. G. Reeder (Eds.), *Handbook of medical sociology* (pp. 134–149). Upper Saddle River, NJ: Prentice Hall.

Cole, S. S., Denny, D., Eyler, A. E., & Samons, S. L. (2000). Issues of transgender. In L. T. Szuchman & F. Muscarella (Eds.), *Psychological perspectives on human sexuality* (pp. 149–195). New York: Wiley.

Cole, T. (2001). Lying to the one you love: The use of deception in romantic relationships. *Journal of Social and Personal Relationships, 18,* 107–129.

Coleman, J. F., Blake, R. R., & Mouton, J. S. (1958). Task difficulty and conformity pressures. *Journal of Abnormal and Social Psychology, 57,* 120–122.

Coleman, L. M., Beale, R., & Mills, C. (1993). Identifying targets of communication styles: An exploratory study. *Personality and Social Psychology Bulletin, 19,* 213–219.

Coles, F. S. (1986). Forced to quit: Sexual harassment complaints and agency response. *Sex Roles, 14,* 81–95.

Colgrove v. Battin, 413 U. S. 149 (1973).

Collins, B. E., & Aspinwall, L. G. (May, 1989). Impression management in negotiations for safer sex. *Negotiating safer sex: personal and interpersonal issues.* Symposium conducted at the Second Iowa Conference on Personal Relationships, Iowa City, IA.

Collins, N. L., & Feeney, B. C. (2004). An attachment theory perspective on closeness and intimacy. In D. J. Mashek & A. Aron (Eds.), *Handbook of closeness and intimacy* (pp. 163–188). Mahwah, NJ: Erlbaum.

Collins, N. L., & Miller, L. C. (1994). Self-disclosure and liking: A meta-analytic review. *Psychological Bulletin, 116,* 457–475.

Collins, R. L., Taylor, S. E., & Skokan, L. A. (1990). A better world or a shattered vision? Changes in perspectives following victimization. *Social Cognition, 8,* 263–285.

Coltrane, S. (2000a). *Gender and families.* New York: Altamira Press.

Coltrane, S. (2000b). Research on household labor. *Journal of Marriage and Family, 62,* 1208–1233.

Comfort et al. v. Lynn School System et al., 283 F. Supp. 2d 328 (D. Mass. 2003), Appeal No. 03-2415 (1st Cir. 2004).

Commonwealth Fund. (1999). *Health Concerns Across a Woman's Lifespan: 1998 Survey of Women's Health.* Retrieved on 7/1/04, from http://www.wellstone.org/stream_document.aspx?rID=2145 & catID=1770&itemID=2143&typeID=8.

Condry, J., & Condry, S. (1976). Sex differences: A study in the eye of the beholder. *Child Development, 47,* 812–819.

Conner, M., & Abraham, C. (2001). Conscientiousness and the theory of planned behavior: Toward a more complete model of the antecedents of intentions and behavior. *Personality and Social Psychology Bulletin, 27,* 1547–1561.

Conway, M., & Ross, M. (1984). Getting what you want by revising what you had. *Journal of Personality and Social Psychology, 47,* 738–748.

Cook, S. W. (1978). Interpersonal and attitudinal outcomes in cooperating interracial groups. *Journal of Research and Development in Education, 12,* 97–113.

Cooley, C. H. (1902). *Human nature and the social order.* New York: Scribners.

Cooper, J., & Neuhaus, I. M. (2000). The "hired gun" effect: Assessing the effect of pay, frequency of testifying, and credentials on the perception of expert testimony. *Law and Human Behavior, 24,* 149–171.

Coovert, M. D., & Reeder, G. D. (1990). Negativity effects in impression formation: The role of unit formation and schematic expectations. *Journal of Experimental Social Psychology, 26,* 49–62.

Corneil, W. (1995). Traumatic stress and organizational strain in the fire service. In L. R. Murphy & J. J. Hurrell (Eds.), *Job stress interventions* (pp. 185–198). Washington, DC: American Psychological Association.

Corneille, O., Huart, J., Becquart, E., & Bredart, S. (2004). When memory shifts toward more typical category exemplars: Accentuation effects in the recollection of ethnically ambiguous faces. *Journal of Personality and Social Psychology, 86,* 236–250.

Corneille, O., & Judd, C. M. (1999). Accentuation and sensitization effects in the categorization of multi-faceted stimuli. *Journal of Personality and Social Psychology, 77,* 927–941.

Correll, J., Park, B., Judd, C. M., & Wittenbrink, B. (2002). The police officer's dilemma: Using ethnicity to disambiguate potentially threatening individuals. *Journal of Personality and Social Psychology, 83,* 1314–1329.

Costanzo, M., and Oskamp, S. (1994). Violence and the law. *Claremont symposium on applied social psychology* (Vol. 7, pp. 246–272). Thousand Oaks, CA: Sage Publications.

Cousins, S. D. (1989). Culture and self-perception in Japan and the United States. *Journal of Personality and Social Psychology, 56,* 124–131.

Cowan, C. L., Thompson, W. C., & Ellsworth, P. C. (1984). The effects of death qualification on jurors' predisposition to convict and on the quality of deliberation. *Law and Human Behavior, 8,* 53–79.

Craig, K. D., & Patrick, C. J. (1985). Facial expression during induced pain. *Journal of Personality and Social Psychology, 48,* 1080–1091.

Crandall, C. S. (1994). Prejudice against fat people: Ideology and self-interest. *Journal of Personality and Social Psychology, 66,* 882–894.

Crandall, C. S. (1995). Do parents discriminate against their heavy-weight daughters? *Personality and Social Psychology Bulletin, 21,* 724–735.

Crandall, C. S., & Biernat, M. (1990). The ideology of anti-fat attitudes. *Journal of Applied Social Psychology, 20,* 227–243.

Crandall, C. S., D'Anello, S., Sakalli, N., Lazarus, E., Wieczorkowska, G., & Feather, N. T. (2001). An attribution-value model of prejudice: Anti-fat attitudes in six nations. *Personality and Social Psychology Bulletin, 27,* 30–37.

Crary, W. G. (1966). Reactions in incongruent self-experiences. *Journal of Consulting Psychology, 30,* 246–252.

Crawford, M., & Unger, R. (2000). *Women and gender* (3rd ed.). Boston: McGraw Hill.

Crites, S. L., Jr., Fabrigar, L. R., & Petty, R. E. (1994). Measuring the affective and cognitive properties of attitudes: Conceptual and methodological issues. *Personality and Social Psychology Bulletin, 20,* 619–634.

Crocker, J., & Luhtanen, R. (1990). Collective self-esteem and ingroup bias. *Journal of Personality and Social Psychology, 58,* 60–67.

Crocker, J., Luhtanen, R., Blaine, B., & Broadnax, S. (1994). Collective self-esteem and psychological well-being among White, Black, and Asian college students. *Personality and Social Psychology Bulletin, 20,* 503–513.

Crocker, J., & Luhtanen, R. K. (2003). Level of self-esteem and contingencies of self-worth: Unique effects on academic, social, and financial problems in college students. *Personality and Social Psychology Bulletin, 29,* 701–712.

Crocker, J., & Major, B. (1989). Social stigma and self-esteem: The self-protective properties of stigma. *Psychological Review, 96,* 608–630.

Crocker, J., Major, B., & Steele, C. (1998). Social stigma. In D. T. Gilbert, S. T. Fiske, & G. Lindzey (Eds.), *The handbook of social psychology* (4th ed., pp. 504–553). New York: McGraw-Hill.

Crocker, J., Sommers, S. R., & Luhtanen, R. K. (2002). Hopes dashed and dreams fulfilled: Contingencies of self-worth and graduate school admissions. *Personality and Social Psychology Bulletin, 28,* 1275–1286.

Crosby, F. J. (1982). *Relative deprivation and working women.* New York: Oxford University Press.

Crosby, F. J. (1991). *Juggling.* New York: Free Press.

Cross, S. E., Bacon, P. L., & Morris, M. L. (2000). The relational-interdependent self-construal and relationships. *Journal of Personality and Social Psychology, 78,* 791–808.

Cross, S. E., & Vick, N. V. (2001). The interdependent self-construal and social support: The case of persistence in engineering. *Personality and Social Psychology Bulletin, 27,* 820–832.

Cummings, L. L. (1994). Fighting by the rules: Women street-fighting in Chihuahua, Mexico. *Sex Roles, 30,* 189–198.

Cunningham, M. R. (1979). Weather, mood, and helping behavior: Quasi-experiments with the sunshine Samaritan. *Journal of Personality and Social Psychology, 37,* 1947–1956.

Cunningham, W. A., Preacher, K. J., & Banaji, M. R. (2001). Implicit attitude measures: Consistency, stability, and convergent validity. *Psychological Science, 12,* 163–170.

Curphey, S. (2003, March 22). 1 in 7 U.S. military personnel in Iraq is female. Retrieved August 16, 2004, from http://www.womensnews.org/article.cfm/dyn/aid/1265/context/cover

Cutrona, C. E., Russell, D. W., Abraham, W. T., Garner, K. A., Melby, J. N., Bryant, C., et al. (2003). Neighborhood context and financial strain as predictors of marital interaction and marital quality in African American couples. *Personal Relationships, 10,* 389–409.

Czopp, A. M. & Monteith, M. J. (2003). Confronting prejudice (literally): Reactions to confrontations and racial and gender bias. *Personality and Social Psychology Bulletin, 29,* 532–544.

Dabbs, J. M. (1998). Testosterone and the concept of dominance. *Behavioral and Brain Sciences, 21,* 370–371.

D'Amico, M. L. (1998, December 7). Internet has become a necessity, U.S. poll shows. Retrieved May 4, 1999, from the CNN Web site: http://cnn.com/tech/computing/9812/07/neednet.idg/index.htm

Darke, P. R., Chaiken, S., Bohner, G., Einwiller, S., Erb, H.-P., & Hazlewood, J. D. (1998). Accuracy motivation, consensus information, and the law of large numbers: Effects on attitude judgment in the absence of argumentation. *Personality and Social Psychology Bulletin, 24,* 1205–1215.

Darley, J. M., & Batson, C. D. (1973). "From Jerusalem to Jericho": A study of situational and dispositional variables in helping behavior. *Journal of Personality and Social Psychology, 27,* 100–108.

Darley, J. M., & Fazio, R. H. (1980). Expectancy confirmation processes arising in the social interaction sequence. *American Psychologist, 35,* 867–881.

Darley, J. M., Fleming, J. H., Hilton, J. L., & Swann, W. B., Jr. (1988). Dispelling negative expectancies: The impact of interaction goals and target characteristics on the expectancy confirmation process. *Journal of Experimental Social Psychology, 24,* 19–36.

Darwin, C. (1871). *The descent of man.* London: Murray.

Das, E. H. H. J., de Wit, J. B. F., & Stroebe, W. (2003). Fear appeals motivate acceptance of action recommendations: Evidence for a positive bias in the processing of persuasive messages. *Personality and Social Psychology Bulletin, 29,* 650–664.

Dasgupta, N., & Greenwald, A. G. (2001). On the malleability of automatic attitudes: Combating automatic prejudice with images of admired and disliked individuals. *Journal of Personality and Social Psychology, 81,* 800–814.

Daubert v. Merrell Dow Pharmaceuticals, Inc. 113 S. Ct. 2786 (1993).

David, B., & Turner, J. C. (2001). Self-categorization principles underlying majority and minority influence. In J. P. Forgas & K. D. Williams (Eds.), *Social influence: Direct and indirect processes* (pp. 293–313). Philadelphia: Psychology Press.

Davies, M. F. (1998). Dogmatism and belief formation: Output interference in the processing of supporting and contradictory cognitions. *Journal of Personality and Social Psychology, 75,* 456–466.

Davies, M. F. (1997). Positive test strategies and confirmatory retrieval processes in the evaluation of personality feedback. *Journal of Personality and Social Psychology, 739,* 574–583.

Davis, C. G., Lehman, D. R., Silver, R. C., Wortman, C. B., & Ellard, J. H. (1996). Self-blame following a traumatic event: The role of perceived avoidability. *Personality and Social Psychology Bulletin, 22,* 557–567.

Dawes, R., Faust, D., & Meehl, P. E. (1989). Clinical versus actuarial judgment. *Science, 243,* 1668–1674.

Dean, K. E., & Malamuth, M. N. (1997). Characteristics of men who aggress sexually and of men who imagine aggressing: Risk and moderating variables. *Journal of Personality and Social Psychology, 72,* 449–455.

Deaux, K., & Kite, M. (1993). Gender stereotypes. In F. L. Denmark & M. A. Paludi (Eds.), *Psychology of women: A handbook of issues and theories* (pp. 107–139). Westport, CT: Greenwood Press.

Deaux, K., & LaFrance, M. (1998). Gender. In D. T. Gilbert, S. T. Fiske, & G. Lindzey (Eds.), *Handbook of social psychology* (Vol. 2, pp. 788–827). Boston: McGraw-Hill.

Deaux, K., & Major, B. (1987). Putting gender into context: An interactive model of gender-related behavior. *Psychological Review, 94,* 369–389.

Deaux, K., Reid, A., Mizrahi, K., & Ethier, K. A. (1995). Parameters of social identity. *Journal of Personality and Social Psychology, 68,* 280–291.

Deaux, K., & Ullman, J. C. (1983). *Women of steel.* New York: Praeger.

DeBono, K. G., & Klein, C. (1993). Source expertise and persuasion: The moderating role of recipient dogmatism. *Personality and Social Psychology Bulletin, 19,* 167–173.

De Dreu, C., & De Vries, N. (Eds). (2001). *Group consensus and minority influence.* Oxford, England: Blackwell.

DeJarnett, S., & Raven, B. (1981). The balance, bases, and modes of interpersonal power in black couples. *Journal of Black Psychology, 7,* 367–374.

Dengerink, H. A., Schnedler, R. W., & Covey, M. K. (1978). Role of avoidance in aggressive responses to attack and no attack. *Journal of Personality and Social Psychology, 36,* 1044–1053.

Department of Health and Human Services. (1981). *Alcohol and health.* Rockville, MD: National Institute of Alcohol Abuse and Alcoholism.

Department of Health and Human Services. (2000). Fifteen specific ways to improve health: Information and tips for safety and wellness. Retrieved on 7/1/04, from http://www.hhs.gov/safety/index.html

DePaulo, B. M. (1992). Nonverbal behavior and self-presentation. *Psychological Bulletin, 111,* 203–243.

DePaulo, B. M. (1994). Spotting lies: Can humans learn to do better? *Current Directions in Psychological Science, 3,* 83–86.

DePaulo, B. M., Kashy, D. A., Kirkendol, S. E., Wyer, M. M., & Epstein, J. A. (1996). Lying in everyday life. *Journal of Personality and Social Psychology, 70,* 979–995.

DePaulo, B. M., Kirkendol, S. E., Tang, J., & O'Brien, T. P. (1988). The motivational impairment effect in the communication of deception: Replications and extensions. *Journal of Nonverbal Behavior, 12,* 177–202.

DePaulo, B. M., LeMay, C. S., & Epstein, J. (1991). Effects of importance on success and expectations for success on effectiveness of deceiving. *Personality and Social Psychology Bulletin, 1,* 14–24.

DePaulo, B. M., & Pfeifer, R. L. (1986). On-the-job experience and skill at detecting deception. *Journal of Applied Social Psychology, 16,* 249–267.

DePaulo, B. M., Rosenthal, R., Green, C. R., & Rosenkrantz, J. (1982). Diagnosing deceptive and mixed messages from verbal and nonverbal cues. *Journal of Personality and Social Psychology, 18,* 433–446.

Derlega, V. J. (1984). Self-disclosure and intimate relationships. In *Communication, intimacy, and close relationships* (pp. 1–10). New York: Academic Press.

Derlega, V. J., Durham, B., Gockel, B., & Sholis, D. (1981). Sex differences in self-disclosure: Effects of topic content, friendship, and partner's sex. *Sex Roles, 7,* 433–447.

Derlega, V. J., & Grzelak, A. L. (1979). Appropriate self-disclosure. In G. J. Chelune (Ed.), *Self-disclosure* (pp. 151–176). San Francisco: Jossey-Bass.

Desmarais, S., &Curtis, J. (1997). Gender and perceived pay entitlement: Testing for effects of experience with income. *Journal of Personality and Social Psychology, 72,* 141–150.

DeSten, D., Dasgupta, N., Bartlett, M. Y., & Cajdric, A. (2004). Prejudice from thin air: The effect of emotion on automatic intergroup attitudes. *Psychological Science, 15,* 319–324.

DeSteno, D., Petty, R. E., Rucker, D. D., Wegener, D. T., & Braverman, J. (2004). Discrete emotions and persuasion: The role of emotion-induced expectancies. *Journal of Personality and Social Psychology, 86,* 43–56.

DeSteno, D., Petty, R. E., Wegener, D. T., & Rucker D. D. (2000). Beyond valence in the perception of likelihood: The role of emotion specificity. *Journal of Personality and Social Psychology, 78,* 397–416.

DeSteno, D. A., & Salovey, P. (1994). Jealousy in close relationships: Multiple perspectives on the green-eyed monster. In A. L. Weber & J. H. Harvey (Eds.), *Perspectives on close relationships,* (pp. 217–242). Boston: Allyn & Bacon.

Deutsch, F. M., & Saxon, S. E. (1998). Traditional ideologies, nontraditional lives. *Sex Roles, 38,* 331–362.

Deutsch, M. (1993). Educating for a peaceful world. *American Psychologist, 48,* 510–517.

Deutsch, M., & Krauss, R. M. (1960). The effect of threat on interpersonal bargaining. *Journal of Abnormal and Social Psychology, 61,* 181–189.

Devine, D. J., Clayton, L. D., Dunford, B. B., Seying, R., & Pryce, J. (2001). Jury decision making: 45 years of empirical research on deliberating groups. *Psychology, Public Policy, and Law, 7,* 622–727.

Devine, P. G. (1989). Stereotypes and prejudice: Their automatic and controlled components. *Journal of Personality and Social Psychology, 56,* 5–18.

Devine, P. G., & Baker, S. M. (1991). Measurement of racial stereotype subtyping. *Personality and Social Psychology Bulletin, 17,* 44–50.

Devine, P. G., & Elliot, A. J. (1995). Are racial stereotypes really fading? The Princeton trilogy revisited. *Personality and Social Psychology Bulletin, 21,* 1139–1150.

Devine, P. G., Hirt, E. R., & Gehrke, E. M. (1990). Diagnostic and confirmation strategies in trait hypothesis testing. *Journal of Personality and Social Psychology, 58,* 952–963.

Devine, P. G., Sedikides, C., & Fuhrman, R. W. (1989). Goals in social information processing: The case of anticipated information. *Journal of Personality and Social Psychology, 56,* 680–690.

Diekman, A. B., & Eagly, A. H. (2000). Stereotypes as dynamic constructs: Women and men of the past, present, and future. *Personality and Social Psychology Bulletin, 26,* 1171–1188.

Diener, E. (1980). Deindividuation: The absence of self-awareness and self-regulation in group members. In P. B. Paulus (Ed.), *Psychology of group influence* (pp. 209–242). Hillsdale, NJ: Erlbaum.

Diener, E., & Diener, M. (1995). Cross-cultural correlates of life satisfaction and self-esteem. *Journal of Personality and Social Psychology, 68,* 653–663.

Diener, E., Fraser, S. C., Beaman, A. L., & Kelem, Z. R. T. (1976). Effects of deindividuation variables on stealing among Halloween trick-or-treaters. *Journal of Personality and Social Psychology, 33,* 178–183.

Diener, E., Lucas, R. E., Oishi, S., & Suh, E. M. (2002). Looking up and looking down: Weighting good and bad information in life satisfaction judgments. *Personality and Social Psychology Bulletin, 28,* 437–445.

Diener, E., Suh, E. M., Lucas, R. E., & Smith, H. L. (1999). Subjective well-being: Three decades of progress. *Psychological Bulletin, 125,* 276–302.

Dijksterhuis, A. (2004). I like myself but I don't know why: Enhancing implicit self-esteem by subliminal evaluative conditioning. *Journal of Personality and Social Psychology, 86,* 345–355.

DiLala, L. F., & Gottesman, I. I. (1991). Biological and genetic contributions to violence–wisdom's untold tale. *Psychological Bulletin, 109,* 125–129.

di Leonardo, M. (2001). The female world of cards and holidays: Women, families, and the work of kinship. In S. J. Ferguson (Ed.), *Shifting the center: Understanding contemporary families* (pp. 574–585). Mountain View, CA: Mayfield.

DiMatteo, M. R., & DiNicola, D. D. (1982). *Achieving patient compliance.* New York: Pergamon Press.

DiMatteo, M. R., Hays, R. D., & Prince, L. M. (1986). Relationship of physicians' nonverbal communication skill to patient satisfaction, appointment noncompliance, and physician workload. *Health Psychology, 5,* 581–594.

Dimitrovsky, L., Singer, J., & Yinon, Y. (1989). Masculine and feminine traits: Their relation to suitedness for and success in training for traditionally masculine and feminine army functions. *Journal of Personality and Social Psychology, 57,* 839–847.

Dindia, K. (2002). Self-disclosure research: Knowledge through meta-analysis. In M. Allen, R W. Preeiss, B. M. Gayle & N. A. Burrell (Eds.), *Interpersonal communications research* (pp. 169–185). Mahwah, NJ: Erlbaum.

Dindia, K., & Allen, M. (1992). Sex differences in self-disclosure: A meta-analysis. *Psychological Bulletin, 112,* 106–124.

DiNicola, D. D., & DiMatteo, M. R. (1984). Practitioners, patients, and compliance with medical regimens: A social psychological perspective. In A. Baum, S. E. Taylor, & J. E. Singer (Eds.), *Handbook of Psychology and Health, Vol. 4: Social psychological aspects of health* (pp. 55–84). Hillsdale, NJ: Erlbaum.

Dion, K. K., & Dion, K. L. (1996). Toward understanding love. *Personal Relationships, 3,* 1–3.

Dion, K. L., & Dion, K. K. (1973). Correlates of romantic love. *Journal of Consulting and Clinical Psychology, 41,* 51–56.

Di Paula, A., & Campbell, J. D. (2002). Self-esteem and persistence in the face of failure. *Journal of Personality and Social Psychology, 83,* 711–724.

Ditto, P. H., Scepansky, J. A., Munro, J. D., Apanovitch, A. M., & Lockhart, L. K. (1998). Motivated sensitivity to preference-inconsistent information. *Journal of Personality and Social Psychology, 75,* 53–69.

Dixon, T. L., & Linz, D. (2002). Television news, prejudicial pretrial publicity, and the depiction of race. *Journal of Broadcasting and Electronic Media, 46,* 112–136.

Dodge, K. (1986). A social information processing model of social competence in children. In M. Perlmutter (Ed.), *The Minnesota symposium on child psychology. Vol. 18: Cognitive perspectives on children's social and behavioral development* (pp. 77–126). Hillsdale, NJ: Erlbaum.

Dodge, K. A., & Coie, J. D. (1987). Social-information-processing factors in reactive and proactive aggression in children's peer groups. [Special Issue] *Journal of Personality and Social Psychology 53,* 1146–1158.

Dodgson, P. G., & Wood, J. V. (1998). Self-esteem and the cognitive accessibility of strengths and weaknesses after failure. *Journal of Personality and Social Psychology, 75,* 178–197.

Doering, S., Katzlberger, F., Rumpold, G., Roessler, S., Hofstoetter, B., Schatz, D. S., et al. (2000). Videotape preparation of patients before hip replacement surgery reduces stress. *Psychosomatic Medicine, 62,* 365–373.

Doll, J., & Orth, B. (1993). The Fishbein and Ajzen theory of reasoned action applied to contraceptive behavior: Model variants and meaningfulness. *Journal of Applied Social Psychology, 23,* 395–415.

Dollard, J., Doob, L., Miller, N. E., Mowrer, O. H., & Sears, R. R. (1939). *Frustration and aggression.* New Haven, CT: Yale University Press.

Dona, G. (1991). Acculturation and ethnic identity of Central American refugees in Canada. *Hispanic Journal of Behavioral Sciences, 13,* 230–231.

Donat, P. L., & D'Emilio, J. (1992). A feminist redefinition of rape and sexual assault: Historical foundations and change. *Journal of Social Issues, 48,* 9–22.

Donnerstein, E. (1983). Erotica and human aggression. In R. Green & E. Donnerstein (Eds.), *Aggression: Theoretical and empirical reviews,* (pp. 127–154). New York: Academic Press.

Donnerstein, E., & Berkowitz, L. (1981). Victim reactions in aggressive erotic films as a factor in violence against women. *Journal of Personality and Social Psychology, 41,* 710–724.

Donnerstein, E., & Linz, D. (1994). Sexual violence in the mass media. In M. Costanzo & S. Oskamp (Eds.). *Violence and the law. Claremont symposium on applied social psychology* (Vol. 7, pp. 9–36). Thousand Oaks, CA: Sage Publications.

Dovidio, J. F., Brigham, J. C., Johnson, B. T., & Gaertner, S. L. (1996). Stereotyping, prejudice, and discrimination: Another look. In C. N. Macrae, C. Stangor, & M. Hewstone (Eds.), *Stereotypes and stereotyping* (pp. 276–319). New York: The Guilford Press.

Dovidio, J. F., Gaertner, S. L., Isen, A. M., & Lowrance, R. (1995). Group representations and intergroup bias: Positive affect, similarity, and group size. *Personality and Social Psychology Bulletin, 21,* 856–865.

Dovidio, J. F., Gaertner, S. L., & Validzic, A. (1998). Intergroup bias: Status, differentiation, and a common in-group identity. *Journal of Personality and Social Psychology, 75,* 109–120.

Dovidio, J. F., Kawakami, K., & Gaertner, S. L. (2002). Implicit and explicit prejudice and interracial interaction. *Journal of Personality and Social Psychology, 82,* 62–68.

Dovidio, J. F., Kawakami, K., Johnson, C., Johnson, B., & Howard, A. (1997). On the nature of prejudice: Automatic and controlled processes. *Journal of Experimental Social Psychology, 33,* 510–540.

Dovidio, J. F., Piliavin, J. A., Gaertner, S. L., Schroeder, D. A., & Clark, R. D., III. (1991). The arousal: Cost-reward model and the process of intervention: A review of the evidence. In M. S. Clark (Ed.), *Prosocial behavior* (pp. 86–117). Newbury Park, CA: Sage.

Downey, G., Silver, R. C., & Wortman, C. B. (1990). Reconsidering the attribution-adjustment relation following a major negative event: Coping with the loss of a child. *Journal of Personality and Social Psychology, 59,* 925–940.

Downing, J. W., Judd, C. W., & Brauer, M. (1992). Effects of repeated expressions on attitude extremity. *Journal of Personality and Social Psychology, 63,* 17–29.

Doyle, J. A. (1995). *Male experience* (3rd ed.). Dubuque, IA: Brown & Benchmark.

Dresser, N. (1994, May 9). Even smiling can have a serious side. *Los Angles Times,* pp. 1, 5.

Drigotas, S. M., & Barta, W. (2001). The cheating heart: Scientific explorations of infidelity. *Current Directions in Psychological Science, 10,* 177–188.

Drigotas, S. M., Safstrom, C. A., & Gentilia, T. (1999). An investment model prediction of dating infidelity. *Journal of Personality and Social Psychology, 77,* 509–524.

Drigotas, S. M., Safstrom, C. A., & Rusbult, C. E. (1995). On the peculiarities of loyalty: A diary study of responses to dissatisfaction in everyday life. *Personality and Social Psychology Bulletin, 21,* 596–609.

Drigotas, S. M., Whitney, G. A., & Rusbult, C. E. (1995). On the peculiarities of loyalty: A diary study of responses to dissatisfaction in everyday life. *Personality and Social Psychology Bulletin, 21,* 596–609.

Duckitt, J. (2003). Prejudice and intergroup hostility. In D. O. Sears, L. Huddy, & R. Jervis (Eds.), *The Oxford handbook of political psychology* (pp. 559–600). New York: Oxford University Press.

Duckitt, J., Wagner, C., du Plessis, I., & Birum, I. (2002). The psychological bases of ideology and prejudice: Testing a dual process model. *Journal of Personality and Social Psychology, 83,* 75–93.

Dugosh, K. L., Paulus, P. B., Roland, E. J., & Yang, H-C. (2000). Cognitive stimulation in brainstorming. *Journal of Personality and Social Psychology, 79,* 722–735.

Dunning, D., Griffin, D. W., Milojkovic, J. D., & Ross, L. (1990). The overconfidence effect in social prediction. *Journal of Personality and Social Psychology, 58,* 568–581.

Dunning, D., Leuenberger, A., & Sherman, D. A. (1995). A new look at motivated inference: Are self-serving theories of success a product of motivational forces? *Journal of Personality and Social Psychology, 69,* 58–68.

Dunning, D., Meyerowitz, J. A., & Holzberg, A. D. (1989). Ambiguity and self-evaluation: The role of idiosyncratic trait definitions in self-serving assessments of ability. *Journal of Personality and Social Psychology, 57,* 1082–1090.

Dunning, D., & Perretta, S. (2002). Automaticity and eyewitness accuracy: A 10–12 second rule for distinguishing accurate from inaccurate positive identifications. *Journal of Applied Psychology, 87,* 951–962.

Durkin, K. (1987). Sex roles and the mass media. In D. J. Hargreaves & A. M. Colley (Eds.), *The psychology of sex roles* (pp. 201–214). New York: Hemisphere.

Duval, S., & Wicklund, R. A. (1972). *A theory of objective self awareness.* New York: Academic Press.

Duval, S. T., Duval, V. H., & Mulilis, J. P. (1992). Effects of self-focus, discrepancy between self and standard, and outcome expectancy favorability on the tendency to match self to standard or to withdraw. *Journal of Personality and Social Psychology, 62,* 340–348.

Eagly, A. H. (1978). Sex differences in influenceability. *Psychological Bulletin, 85,* 86–116.

Eagly, A. H. (1983). Gender and social influence: A social psychological analysis. *American Psychologist, 38,* 971–981.

Eagly, A. H. (1987). *Sex differences in social behavior: A social-role interpretation.* Hillsdale, NJ: Erlbaum.

Eagly, A. H., Ashmore, R. D., Makhijani, M. G., & Longo, L. C. (1991). What is beautiful is good, but. . . . A meta-analytic review of research on the physical attractiveness stereotype. *Psychological Bulletin, 110,* 109–128.

Eagly, A. H., & Crowley, M. (1986). Gender and helping behavior: A meta-analytic review of the social psychological literature. *Psychological Bulletin, 100,* 283–308.

Eagly, A. H., Johannesen-Schmidt, M. C., & van Engen, M. L. (2003). Transformational, transactional, and laissez-faire leadership. *Pschological Bulletin, 129,* 569–591.

Eagly, A. H., & Johnson, B. T. (1990). Gender and leadership style: A meta-analysis. *Psychological Bulletin, 108,* 233–256.

Eagly, A. H., & Karau, S. J. (1991). Gender and the emergence of leaders: A meta-analysis. *Journal of Personality and Social Psychology, 60,* 685–710.

Eagly, A. H., Makhijani, M. G., & Klonsky, B. G. (1992). Gender and the evaluation of leaders: A meta-analysis. *Psychological Bulletin, 111,* 3–22.

Eagly, A. H., & Steffen, V. J. (1986). Gender and aggressive behavior: A meta-analytic review of the social psychological literature. *Psychological Bulletin, 100,* 309–330.

Eagly, A. H., & Telaak, K.(1972). Width of the latitude of acceptance as a determinant of attitude change. *Journal of Personality and Social Psychology, 23,* 388–397.

Eagly, A. H., & Wood, W. (1982). Inferred sex differences in status as a determinant of gender stereotypes about social influence. *Journal of Personality and Social Psychology, 43,* 915–928.

Eagly, A. H., & Wood, W. (1985). Gender and influenceability: Stereotype versus behavior. In V. E. O'Leary, R. K. Unger, & B. S. Wallston (Eds.), *Women, gender, and social psychology* (pp. 225–256). Hillsdale, NJ: Erlbaum.

Eagly, A. H., & Wood W. (1999). The origins of sex differences in human behavior: Evolved dispositions versus social roles. *American Psychologist, 54,* 408–423.

Eagly, A. H., Wood, W., & Diekman, A. B. (2000). Social role theory of sex differences and similarities: A current appraisal. In T. Eckes & H. M. Trautner (Eds.), *Developmental social psychology of gender* (pp. 123–173). Mahwah, NJ: Erlbaum.

Eberhardt, J. L., Dasgupta, N., & Banaszynski, T. L. (2003). Believing is seeing: The effects of racial labels and implicit beliefs on face perception. *Personality and Social Psychology Bulletin, 29,* 360–370.

Eckes, T., & Trautner, H. M. (Eds.) (2000). *The developmental social psychology of gender.* Mahwah, NJ: Erlbaum.

Edleson, J. L., Mbilinyi, L. F., Beeman, S. K., & Hagemeister, A. K. (2003). How children are involved in adult domestic violence: Results from a four city telephone survey. *Journal of Interpersonal Violence, 18,* 18–32.

Edwards, C. A. (1994). Leadership in groups of school-age girls. *Developmental Psychology, 30,* 920–927.

Edwards, J. A., & Weary, G. (1993). Depression and the information-formation continuum: Piecemeal processing despite the availability of category information. *Journal of Personality and Social Psychology, 64,* 636–645.

Edwards, J. A., Weary, G., von Hippel, W., & Jacobson, J. A. (2000). The effects of depression on impression formation: The role of trait and category diagnosticity. *Personality and Social Psychology Bulletin, 26,* 462–473.

Edwards, K. & Bryan, T. S. (1997). Judgmental biases produced by instructions to disregard: The (paradoxical) case of emotional information. *Personality and Social Psychology Bulletin, 23,* 849–864.

Edwards, W. (1954). The theory of decision-making. *Psychological Bulletin, 51,* 380–417.

Egan, J. (2003, November 23). Love in the time of no time. *The New York Times Magazine.* Retrieved November 24, 2003 from www.nytimes.com/2003/11/23/magazine/23ONLINE.html

Egley, A., & Major, A. K., Jr. (2004). *Highlights of the 2002 National Youth Gang Survey.* Office of Juvenile Justice and Delinquency Prevention, U.S. Department of Justice Washington, D.C. Government Printing Office.

Egloff, B., & Schmukle, S. C. (2002). Predictive validity of an Implicit Association Test for assessing anxiety. *Journal of Personality and Social Psychology, 83,* 1441–1455.

Ehrlinger, J., & Dunning D. (2003). How chronic self-views influence (and potentially mislead) estimates of performance. *Journal of Personality and Social Psychology, 84,* 5–17.

Eisenberg, N., & Fabes, R. A. (1990). Empathy: Conceptualization, measurement, and relation to prosocial behavior. *Motivation and Emotion, 14,* 131–149.

Eisenberg, N., & Fabes, R. A. (1998). Prosocial development. In N. Eisenberg (Ed.), *Handbook of child psychology* (Vol 3, 5th ed., pp. 701–778). New York: Wiley.

Eisenberger, N. I., Lieberman, M. D., & Williams, K. D. (2003). Does rejection hurt? An fMRI study of social exclusion. *Science, 302,* 290–292.

Ekman, P. (1972). Universals and cultural differences in facial expressions of emotion. In J. K. Cole (Ed.), *Nebraska symposium on motivation, 1971* (pp. 207–283). Lincoln: University of Nebraska Press.

Ekman, P. (1992a). Are there basic emotions? *Psychological Review, 99,* 550–553.

Ekman, P. (1992b). Facial expressions of emotions: New findings, new questions. *Psychological Science, 3,* 34–38.

Ekman, P., & Friesen, W. V. (1971). Constants across cultures in the face and emotion. *Journal of Personality and Social Psychology, 17,* 124–129.

Ekman, P., & Friesen, W. V. (1974). Detecting deception from the body or face. *Journal of Personality and Social Psychology, 29,* 288–298.

Ekman, P., & Friesen, W. V. (1975). *Unmasking the face.* Upper Saddle River, NJ: Prentice Hall

Ekman, P., Friesen, W. V., & O'Sullivan, M. (1988). Smiles when lying. *Journal of Personality and Social Psychology, 54,* 414–420.

Ekman, P., Friesen, W. V., & Scherer, K. (1976). Body movements and voice pitch in deception interaction. *Semiotica, 16,* 23–27.

Ekman, P., & O'Sullivan, M. (1991). Who can catch a liar? *American Psychologist, 46,* 913–920.

Ekman, P., Sorensen, E. R., & Friesen, W. V. (1969). Pancultural elements in facial displays of emotion. *Science, 164,* 86–88.

Elfenbein, H. A., & Ambady, N. (2003). Universals and cultural differences in recognizing emotions. *American Psychological Society, 12,* 159–163.

Ellis, B. J., & Symons, D. (1990). Sex differences in sexual fantasy. *Journal of Sex Research, 27,* 527–555.

Ellis, E. M., Atkeson, B. M., & Calhoun, K. S. (1981). An assessment of a long-term reaction to rape. *Journal of Abnormal Psychology, 90,* 263–266.

Ellsworth, P. C., & Carlsmith, J. M. (1973). Eye contact and gaze aversion in an aggressive encounter. *Journal of Personality and Social Psychology, 28,* 280–292.

Ellsworth, P. C., & Reifman, A. (2000). Juror comprehension and public policy: Perceived problems and proposed solutions. *Psychology, Public Policy, and Law, 6,* 788–821.

Ember, C. R. (1973). Feminine task assignment and the social behavior of boys. *Ethos, 1,* 424–439.

Endo, Y., Heine, S. J., & Lehman, D. R. (2000). Culture and positive illusions in close relationships. *Personality and Social Psychology Bulletin, 26,* 1571–1586.

Engel, G. L. (1971). Sudden and rapid death during psychological stress: Folklore or folk wisdom? *Annals of Internal Medicine, 74,* 771–782.

English, E. H., & Baker, T. B. (1983). Relaxation training and cardiovascular response to experimental stressors. *Health Psychology, 2,* 239–259.

Epley, N., & Dunning D. (2000). Feeling "holier than thou": Are self-serving assessments produced by errors in self- or social prediction? *Journal of Personality and Social Psychology, 79,* 861–875.

Erber, R., & Fiske, S. T. (1984). Outcome dependency and attention to inconsistent information. *Journal of Personality and Social Psychology, 47,* 709–726.

Erikson, E. H. (1963). *Childhood and society.* New York: Norton.

Eron, L. D. (1987). The development of aggressive behavior from the perspective of a developing behaviorism. *American Psychologist, 42,* 435–442.

Eron, L. D., Huesmann, L. R., Lefkowitz, M. M., & Walder, L. O. (1972). Does television violence cause aggression? *American Psychologist, 27,* 253–263.

Esser, J. K. (1998). Alive and well after 25 years: A review of groupthink research. *Organizational Behavior and Human Decision Processes, 73*(2/3), 116–141.

Esser, J. K., & Komorita, S. S. (1975). Reciprocity and concession making in bargaining. *Journal of Personality and Social Psychology, 31,* 864–872.

Ethier, K. A., & Deaux, K. (1994). Negotiating social identity when contexts change: Maintaining identification and responding to threat. *Journal of Personality and Social Psychology, 67,* 243–251.

Evans, G. W., Lepore, S. J., & Allen, K. M. (2000). Cross-cultural differences in tolerance for crowding: Fact or fiction? *Journal of Personality and Social Psychology, 79,* 204–210.

Fabrigar, L. R., & Krosnick, J. A. (1995). Attitude importance and the false consensus effect. *Personality and Social Psychology Bulletin, 21,* 468–479.

Fabrigar, L. R., & Petty, R. E. (1999). The role of the affective and cognitive bases of attitudes in susceptibility to affectively and cognitively based persuasion. *Personality and Social Psychology Bulletin, 25,* 363–381.

Fabrigar, L. R., Priester, J. R., Petty, R. E., & Wegener, D. T. (1998). The impact of attitude accessibility on elaboration of persuasive messages. *Personality and Social Psychology Bulletin, 24,* 339–352.

Family Violence Prevention Fund. (2001). Domestic violence is a serious, widespread social problem in America: The facts. Retrieved November 23, 2004, from http://endabuse.org/ resources/facts/

Farwell, L. & Weiner, B. (2000). Bleeding hearts and the heartless: Popular perceptions of liberal and conservative ideologies. *Personality and Social Psychology Bulletin, 26,* 845–852.

Fasenfest, D., Booza, J., & Metzger, K. (2004). Living together: A new look at racial and ethnic integration in metropolitan neighborhoods, 1990–2000. *Living cities census series.* Washington, DC: The Brookings Institution.

Fausto-Sterling, A. (2000). *Sexing the body: Gender politics and the construction of sexuality.* New York: Basic Books.

Fazio, R. H. (1986). How do attitudes guide behavior? In R. M. Sorrentino & E. T. Higgins (Eds.), *The handbook of motivation and cognition: Foundations of social behavior* (pp. 204–243). New York: Guilford Press.

Fazio, R. H. (1989). On the power and functionality of attitudes: The role of attitude accessibility. In A. R. Pratkanis, S. J. Breckler, & A. G. Greenwald (Eds.), *Attitude structure and function* (pp. 153–179). Hillsdale, NJ: Erlbaum.

Fazio, R. H., Chen, J., McDonel, E. C., & Sherman, S. J. (1982). Attitude accessibility, attitude–behavior consistency, and the strength of the object-evaluation association. *Journal of Experimental Social Psychology, 18,* 339–357.

Fazio, R. H., Sanbonmatus, D. M., Powell, M. C., & Kardes, F. R. (1986). On the automatic activation of attitudes. *Journal of Personality and Social Psychology, 50,* 229–238.

Feagin, J. R. (1991). The continuing significance of race: Antiblack discrimination in public places. *American Sociological Review, 56,* 101–116.

Fears, D., & Deane, C. (2001, July 5). Biracial couples report tolerance: Survey finds most are accepted by families. The *Washington Post Online.* http://washingtonpost.com/ac2/wp-dyn/A19824-2001Jul4?Language=printer

Federal Bureau of Investigation (2004). Arrests by Sex, 2002 (Table 42). Retrieved August 22, 2004, from http://www.fbi.gov/ ucr/cius-02/html/web/arrested/04-table42.html

Federico, C. M., & Sidanius, J. (2002). Racism, ideology, and affirmative action revisited: The antecedents and consequences of "principled objections" to affirmative action. *Journal of Personality and Social Psychology, 82,* 488–502.

Feeney, B. C., & Collins, N. L. (2001). Predictors of caregiving in adult intimate relationships. An attachment theoretical perspective. *Journal of Personality and Social Psychology, 80,* 972–994.

Feeney, J. A., & Hohaus, L. (2001). Attachment and spousal caregiving. *Personal Relationships, 8,* 21–39.

Feingold, A. (1992). Good-looking people are not what we think. *Psychological Bulletin, 111,* 304–341.

Feldman, P. J., Cohen, S., Doyle, W. J., Skoner, D. P., & Gwaltney, J. M., Jr. (1999). The impact of personality on the reporting of unfounded symptoms and illness. *Journal of Personality and Social Psychology, 77,* 370–378.

Feldman-Summers, S., Gordon, P., & Meagher, J. (1977). The impact of rape on sexual satisfaction. *Journal of Abnormal Psychology, 88,* 101–105.

Felitti, G., Firman, D., & Sanson-Fisher, R. (1986). Patient satisfaction with primary-care consultations. *Journal of Behavioral Medicine, 9,* 389–399.

Felitti, V. J., Anda, R. F., Nordenberg, D., Williamson, D. F., Spitz, A. M., Edwards, V., et al. (1998). Relationship of childhood abuse and household dysfunction to many of the leading causes of death in adults: The Adverse Childhood Experiences (ACE) study. *American Journal of Preventive Medicine, 14,* 245–258.

Felmlee, D. H. (1994). Who's on top? Power in romantic relationships. *Sex Roles, 31,* 275–295.

Felmlee, D. H. (1995). Fatal attractions: Affection and disaffection in intimate relationships. *Journal of Social and Personal Relationships, 12,* 295–311.

Felmlee, D. H., Flyn, H. K., & Bahr, P. R. (2004, August). *Too much of a good thing: Fatal attractions in adult intimate relationships.* Paper presented at the biannual conference of the International Association for Relationship Research, Madison, Wisconsin.

Felson, R. B., & Reed, M. D. (1986). Reference groups and self-appraisals of academic ability and performance. *Social Psychology Quarterly, 49,* 103–109.

Felton, B. J., Revenson, T. A., & Hinrichsen, G. A. (1984). Stress and coping in the explanation of psychological adjustment among chronically ill adults. *Social Science and Medicine, 18,* 889–898.

Fenigstein, A., Scheier, M. F., & Buss, A. H. (1975). Public and private self-consciousness: Assessment and theory. *Journal of Consulting and Clinical Psychology, 43,* 522–527.

Feshbach, S. (1970). Aggression. In P. H. Mussen (Ed.), *Carmichael's Manual of Child Psychology.* (Vol. 2, pp. 159–259). New York: Wiley.

Feshbach, S., & Singer, R. D. (1971). *Television and aggression.* San Francisco: Jossey-Bass.

Festinger, L. (1954). A theory of social comparison processes. *Human Relations, 7,* 117–140.

Festinger, L. (1957). *A theory of cognitive dissonance.* Evanston, IL: Row, Peterson.

Festinger, L., Riecken, H. W., & Schachter, S. (1956). *When prophecy fails.* Minneapolis: University of Minnesota Press.

Festinger, L., Schachter, S., & Back, K. (1950). *Social pressures in informal groups: A study of human factors in housing.* Stanford, CA: Stanford University Press.

Fiedler, F. E. (1978). Recent developments in research on the contingency model. In L. Berkowitz (Ed.), *Group processes* (pp. 209–225). New York: Academic Press.

Fiedler, F. E. (1993). The leadership situation and the black box in contingency theories. In M. M. Chemers & R. Ayman (Eds.), *Leadership theory and research* (pp. 2–28). New York: Academic Press.

Fiedler, K., Nickel, S., Muehlfriedel, T., & Unkelbach, C. (2001). Is mood congruency an effect of genuine memory or response bias? *Journal of Experimental Social Psychology, 37,* 201–214.

Fiedler, K., & Schenck, W. (2001). Spontaneous inferences from pictorially presented behaviors. *Personality and Social Psychology Bulletin, 27,* 1533–1546.

Fiedler, K., Schmid, J., & Stahl, T. (2002). What is the current truth about polygraph lie detection? *Basic and Applied Social Psychology, 24,* 313–324.

Fiedler, K., Walther, E., & Nickel, S. (1999). The auto-verification of social hypotheses: Stereotyping through differential aggregation: Computer simulations and some new evidence. *European Review of Social Psychology, 10,* 1–40.

Fillingim, R. B., & Fine, M. A. (1986). The effects of internal versus external information processing on symptom perception in an exercise setting. *Health Psychology, 5,* 115–123.

Fincham, F. D. (2000). The kiss of the porcupines: From attributing responsibility to forgiving. *Personal Relationships, 7,* 1–23.

Fincham, F. D. (2003). Marital conflict: Correlates, structure, and context. *Current Directions in Psychological Science, 12,* 23–27.

Fincham, F. D., Harold, G. T., & Gano-Phillips, S. (2000). The longitudinal association between attributions and marital satisfaction: Direction of effects and role of efficacy expectations. *Journal of Family Psychology, 14,* 267–285.

Fine, M., & Asch, A., (Eds.). (1988) *Women with disabilities* (p. 15). Philadelphia: Temple University Press.

Fink, B., & Penton-Voak, I. (2002). Evolutionary psychology of facial attractiveness. *Current Directions in Psychological Science, 11,* 154–158.

Finkel, E. J., & Campbell, W. K. (2001). Self-control and accommodation in close relationships: An interdependence analysis. *Journal of Personality and Social Psychology, 81,* 263–277.

Finkel, E. J., Rusbult, C. E., Kumashiro, M., & Hannon, P. A. (2002). Dealing with betrayal in close relationships: Does commitment promote forgiveness? *Journal of Personality and Social Psychology, 82,* 956–974.

Finkenauer, C., & Hazam, H. (2000). Disclosure and secrecy in marriage: Do both contribute to marital satisfaction? *Journal of Social and Personal Relationships, 17,* 245–263.

Firebaugh, G., & Davis, K. E. (1988). Trends in antiblack prejudice, 1972–1984: Region and cohort effects. *American Journal of Sociology, 94,* 251–272.

Fischer, D. (1989). *Albion's seed: Four British folkways in America.* New York: Oxford University Press.

Fischer, W. F. (1963). Sharing in pre-school children as a function of amount and type of reinforcement. *Genetic Psychology Monographs, 68,* 215–245.

Fishbein, H. D. (1996). *Peer prejudice and discrimination: Evolutionary, cultural, and developmental dynamics.* Boulder, CO: Westview Press.

Fishbein, M., & Ajzen, I. (1975). *Belief, attitude, intention, and behavior: An introduction to theory and research.* Reading, MA: Addison-Wesley.

Fishbein, M., & Ajzen, I. (1980). *Understanding attitudes and predicting social behavior.* Upper Saddle River, NJ: Prentice Hall.

Fisher, J. D., Nadler, A., & Whitcher-Alagna, S. (1982). Recipient reactions to aid. *Psychological Bulletin, 91,* 33–54.

Fisher, R. D., Cook, I. J., & Shirkey, E. C. (1994). Correlates of support for censorship of sexual, sexually violent, and violent materials. *The Journal of Sex Research, 31,* 229–240.

Fisher, W. A., Fisher, J. D., & Rye, B. J. (1995). Understanding and promoting AIDS preventive behavior: Insights from the theory of reasoned action. *Health Psychology, 14,* 255–264.

Fisher, W. A., & Grenier, G. (1994). Violent pornography, antiwoman thoughts, and antiwoman acts: In search of reliable effects. *Journal of Sex Research, 31,* 23–38.

Fiske, A. P., Kitayama, S., Markus, H. R., & Nisbett, R. E. (1998). The cultural matrix of social psychology. In D. T. Gilbert, S. T. Fiske, & G. Lindzey (Eds.), *Handbook of social psychology* (Vol. 2, pp. 915–981). Boston: McGraw-Hill.

Fiske, S. T. (1993). Social cognition and perception. In M. R. Rosenzweig & L. W. Porter (Eds.), *Annual review of psychology* (Vol. 44, pp. 2–23). Palo Alto, CA: Annual Reviews.

Fiske, S. T. (1998). Stereotyping, prejudice, and discrimination. In D. T. Gilbert, S. T. Fiske, & G. Lindzey (Eds.), *Handbook of social psychology* (Vol. 2, pp. 357–411). New York: Oxford University Press.

Fiske, S. T. (2004). *Social beings.* New York: Wiley.

Fiske, S. T., Bersoff, D. N., Borgida, E., Deaux, K., & Heilman, M. E. (1991). Social science research on trial: Use of sex stereotyping research in Price Waterhouse v. Hopkins. *American Psychologist, 46,* 1049–1060.

Fiske, S. T., & Glick, P. (1995). Ambivalence and stereotypes cause sexual harassment: A theory with implications for organizational change. Gender, Stereotyping, Sexual Harassment, and the Law. *Journal of Social Issues, 51,* 97–115.

Fiske, S. T., & Neuberg, S. L. (1990). A continuum of impression formation, from category-based to individuating processes: Influences of information and motivation of attention and interpretation. In M. P. Zanna (Ed.), *Advances in experimental social psychology* (Vol. 23, pp. 1–73). New York: Academic Press.

Fiske, S. T., Neuberg, S. L., Beattie, A. E., & Milberg, S. J. (1987). Category-based and attribute-based reactions to others: Some informational conditions of stereotyping and the individuating processes. *Journal of Experimental Social Psychology, 23,* 399–427.

Fiske, S. T., & Taylor, S. E. (1991). *Social cognition* (2nd ed.). New York: McGraw-Hill.

Fitzgerald, L. F. (1993a). The last open secret: The sexual harassment of women in the workplace and academia [Edited transcript of a Science and Public Policy Seminar]. Washington, DC: Federation of Behavioral, Psychological, and Cognitive Sciences.

Fitzgerald, L. F. (1993b). Sexual harassment: Violence against women in the workplace. *American Psychologist, 48,* 1070–1076.

Fitzgerald, L. F., Swann, S., & Fischer, K. (1995). Why didn't she just report him? The psychological and legal implications of women's responses to sexual harassment. *Journal of Social Issues, 51,* 117–138.

Fitzgerald, R., & Ellsworth, P. C. (1984). Due process vs. crime control: Death qualification and jury attitudes. *Law and Human Behavior, 8,* 31–51.

Fletcher, G. J. O., & Simpson, J. A. (2000). Ideal standards in close relationships: Their structure and functions. *Current Directions in Psychological Science, 9,* 102–105.

Fletcher, G. J. O., Tither, J. M., O'Loughlin, C., Friesen, M., & Overall, N. (2004). Warm and homely or cold and beautiful? Sex differences in trading off traits in mate selection. *Personality and Social Psychology Bulletin, 30,* 659–672.

Flink, C., & Park, B. (1991). Increasing consensus in trait judgments through outcome dependency. *Journal of Experimental Social Psychology, 27,* 453–467.

Flory, J. D., Raikkonen, K., Matthews, K. A., & Owens, J. F. (2000). Self-focused attention and mood during everyday social interactions. *Personality and Social Psychology Bulletin, 26,* 875–883.

Foa, U. G., & Foa, E. B. (1974). *Societal structures of the mind.* Springfield, IL: Charles C Thomas.

Foddy, M., Smithson, M., Schneider, S., & Hogg, M. (Eds.). (1999). *Resolving social dilemmas: Dynamic, structural, and intergroup aspects.* Philadelphia: Psychology Press.

Fogel, J., Albert, S. M., Schnabel, F., Ditkoff, B. A., & Neugut, A. I. (2002). Internet use and social support in women with breast cancer. *Health Psychology, 21,* 398–404.

Folkes, V. S., & Sears, D. O. (1977). Does everybody like a liker? *Journal of Experimental Psychology, 13,* 505–519.

Fonda, D. (2000, December 11). The male minority. *Time,* pp. 58–60.

Ford, T. E. (2000). Effects of sexist humor on tolerance of sexist events. *Personality and Social Psychology Bulletin, 26,* 1094–1107.

Forgas, J. P. (1998a). Asking nicely? The effects of mood on responding to more or less polite requests. *Personality and Social Psychology Bulletin, 24,* 173–185.

Forgas, J. P. (1998b). On being happy but mistaken: Mood effects on the fundamental attribution error. *Journal of Personality and Social Psychology, 75,* 318–331.

Forgas, J. P. (1999a). On feeling good and being rude: Affective influences on language use and request formulations. *Journal of Personality and Social Psychology, 76,* 928–939.

Forgas, J. P. (1999b). Feeling and speaking: Mood effects on verbal communication strategies. *Personality and Social Psychology Bulletin, 25,* 850–863.

Forgas, J. P. (2001). On being moody but influential: The role of affect in social influence strategies. In J. P. Forgas & K. D. Williams (Eds.), *Social influence: Direct and indirect processes* (pp. 147–166). Philadelphia: Psychology Press.

Forgas, J. P., & Ciarrochi, J. V. (2002). On managing moods: Evidence for the role of homeostatic cognitive strategies in affect regulation. *Personality and Social Psychology Bulletin, 28,* 336–345.

Forgas, J. P., & Williams, K. D. (2001). *Social influence: Direct and indirect processes.* Philadelphia: Psychology Press.

Forrest, J., & Feldman, R. S. (2000). Detecting deception and judges' involvement: Lower task involvement leads to better lie detection. *Personality and Social Psychology Bulletin, 26,* 118–125.

Förster, J., Higgins, T. E., & Idson, L. C. (1998). Approach and avoidance strength during goal attainment: Regulatory focus and the "goal looms larger" effect. *Journal of Personality and Social Psychology, 75,* 1115–1131.

Förster, J., & Liberman, N. (2001). The role of attribution of motivation in producing postsuppressional rebound. *Journal of Personality and Social Psychology, 81,* 377–390.

Forsyth, D. R. (1998). *Group dynamics* (3rd ed.). Pacific Grove, CA: Brooks/Cole.

Fowers, B. J., Lyons, E., Montel, K. H., & Shaked, N. (2001). Positive illusions about marriage among married and single individuals. *Journal of Family Psychology, 15,* 95–109.

Fragale, A. R., & Heath, C. (2004). Evolving informational credentials: The (mis)attribution of believable facts to credible sources. *Personality and Social Psychology Bulletin, 30,* 225–236.

Fraley, R. C. (2002). Attachment stability from infancy to adulthood: Meta-analysis and dynamic modeling of developmental mechanisms. *Personality and Social Psychology Review, 6,* 123–151.

Frank, F. D., & Drucker, J. (1977). The influence of evaluatee's sex on evaluation of a response on a managerial selection instrument. *Sex Roles, 3,* 59–64.

Frank, M. G., & Ekman, P. (1997). The ability to detect deceit generalizes across different types of high-stake lies. *Journal of Personality and Social Psychology, 72,* 1429–1439.

Frank, M. G., & Ekman, P. (2004). Appearing truthful generalizes across different deception situations. *Journal of Personality and Social Psychology, 86,* 486–495.

Frank, M. G., & Stennett, J. (2001). The forced-choice paradigm and the perception of facial expressions of emotion. *Journal of Personality and Social Psychology, 80,* 75–85.

Franke, R., & Leary, M. R. (1991). Disclosure of sexual orientation by lesbians and gay men: A comparison of private and public processes. *Journal of Social and Clinical Psychology, 10,* 262–269.

Frauenfelder, M. (2001, December 9). Social-norms marketing. *New York Times Magazine,* p. 100.

Frazier, P. A. (2003). Perceived control and distress following a sexual assault: A longitudinal test of a new model. *Journal of Personality and Social Psychology, 84,* 1257–1269.

Frazier, P. A., Cochran, C. C., & Olson, A. M. (1995). Social science research on lay definitions of sexual harassment. *Journal of Social Issues, 51,* 21–38.

Freedman, J. L. (1964). Involvement, discrepancy, and change. *Journal of Abnormal and Social Psychology, 69,* 290–295.

Freedman, J. L. (1984). Effect of television violence on aggressiveness. *Psychological Bulletin, 96,* 227–246.

Freedman, J. L. (1986). Television violence and aggression: A rejoinder. *Psychological Bulletin, 100,* 372–378.

Freedman, J. L., & Fraser, S. C. (1966). Compliance without pressure: The foot-in-the-door technique. *Journal of Personality and Social Psychology, 4,* 195–202.

Freedman, J. L., & Sears, D. O. (1965). Warning, distraction, and resistance to influence. *Journal of Personality and Social Psychology, 1,* 262–266.

Freitas, A. L., Liberman, N., Salovey, P., & Higgins, E. T. (2002). When to begin? Regulatory focus and initiating goal pursuit. *Personality and Social Psychology Bulletin, 28,* 121–130.

French, D. C., & Stright, A. L. (1991). Emergent leadership in children's small groups. *Small Group Research, 22,* 187–199.

French, J., & Raven, B. (1959). The bases of social power. In D. Cartwright (Ed.), *Studies in social power* (pp. 150–167). Ann Arbor, MI: Institute for Social Research.

Freud, S. (1930). *Civilization and its discontents.* London: Hogarth Press.

Fried, R., & Berkowitz, L. (1979). Music hath charms . . . and can influence helplessness. *Journal of Applied Social Psychology, 9,* 199–208.

Friedman, H. S., Riggio, R. E., & Casella, D. F. (1988). Nonverbal skill, personal charisma, and initial attraction. *Personality and Social Psychology Bulletin, 14,* 203–211.

Friedman, H. S., Tucker, J. S., Schwartz, J. E., Martin, L. R., Tomlinson-Keasey, C., Wingard, D. L., et al. (1995). Childhood conscientiousness and longevity: Health behaviors and cause of death. *Journal of Personality and Social Psychology, 68,* 696–703.

Friedman, H. S., Tucker, J. S., Schwartz, J. E., Tomlinson-Keasey, C., Martin, L. R., Wingard, D. L., et al. (1995). Psychosocial and behavioral predictors of longevity: The aging and death of the "Termites." *American Psychologist, 50,* 69–78.

Friedman, H. S., Tucker, J. S., Tomlinson-Keasey, C., Schwartz, J. E., Wingard, D. L., & Criqui, M. H. (1993). Does childhood personality predict longevity? *Journal of Personality and Social Psychology, 65,* 176–185.

Friedman, M., & Rosenman, R. H. (1974). *Type A behaviour and your heart.* New York: Knopf.

Friedrich, J., Fetherstonhaugh, D., Casey, S., & Gallagher, D. (1996). Argument interpretation and attitude change: Suppression effects in the integration of one-sided arguments that vary in persuasiveness. *Personality and Social Psychology Bulletin, 22,* 179–191.

Friedrich-Cofer, L., & Huston, A. C. (1986).Television violence and aggression: The debate continues. *Psychological Bulletin, 100,* 364–371.

Frieze, I. H. (1983). Investigating the causes and consequences of marital rape. *Signs, 8,* 532–553.

Frye v. United States, 293 F. 1013 (D.C. Cir. 1923).

Frye, N. E., & Karney, B. R. (2004). Revision in memories of relationship development: Do biases persist over time? *Personal Relationships, 11,* 79–97.

Fuhrman, R. W., & Funder, D. C. (1995). Convergence between self and peer in response-time processing of trait-relevant information. *Journal of Personality and Social Psychology, 69,* 961–974.

Funder, D. C. (1987). Errors and mistakes: Evaluating the accuracy of social judgment. *Psychological Bulletin, 101,* 75–90.

Furnham, A., & Mak, T. (1999). Sex-role stereotyping in television commercials: A review and comparison of fourteen studies done on five continents over 25 years. *Sex Roles, 41,* 413–437.

Gable, S. L., Reis, H. T., & Elliot, A. J. (2000). Behavioral activation and inhibition in everyday life. *Journal of Personality and Social Psychology, 78,* 1135–1149.

Gabrenya, W. K., Wang, Y., & Latané, B. (1985). Social loafing on an optimizing task: Cross-cultural differences among Chinese and Americans. *Journal of Cross-Cultural Psychology, 16,* 223–242.

Gaertner, S. L., & Dovidio, J. F. (1977). The subtlety of white racism, arousal, and helping behavior. *Journal of Personality and Social Psychology, 35,* 691–707.

Gaertner, S. L., & Dovidio, J. F. (1986). Prejudice, discrimination, and racism: Problems, progress, and promise. In J. F. Dovidio & S. L. Gaertner (Eds.), *Prejudice, discrimination, and racism* (pp. 315–332). Orlando, FL: Academic Press.

Gaertner, S. L., Dovidio, J. F., Rust, M. C., Nier, J. A., Banker, B. S., Ward, C. M., et al. (1999). Reducing intergroup bias: Elements of intergroup cooperation. *Journal of Personality and Social Psychology, 76,* 388–402.

Gaertner, S. L., Mann, J., Murrell, A., & Dovidio, J. F. (1989). Reducing intergroup bias: The benefits of recategorization. *Journal of Personality and Social Psychology, 57,* 239–249.

Galinsky, A. D., & Moskowitz, G. B. (2000). Perspective-taking: Decreasing stereotype expression, stereotype accessibility, and in-group favoritism. *Journal of Personality and Social Psychology, 78,* 708–724.

Ganahl, D. J., Prinsen, T. J., & Netzley, S. B. (2003). A contextual analysis of prime time commercials: A contextual framework of gender representation. *Sex Roles, 49,* 545–551.

Gannon, L., Luchetta, T., Rhodes, K., Pardie, L., & Segrist, D. (1992). Sex bias in psychological research. Progress or complacency? *American Psychologist, 47,* 389–396.

Garcia-Marques, L., Sherman, S. J., & Palma-Oliveira, J. M. (2001). Hypothesis testing and the perception of diagnosticity. *Journal of Experimental Social Psychology, 37,* 183–200.

Gardner, W. L., Gabriel, S., & Hochschild, L. (2002). When you and I are "we," you are not threatening: The role of self-expansion in social comparison. *Journal of Personality and Social Psychology, 82,* 239–251.

Gardner, W. L., Pickett, C. L., & Brewer, M. B. (2000). Social exclusion and selective memory: How the need to belong influences memory for social events. *Personality and Social Psychology Bulletin, 26,* 486–496.

Garnets, L., & Pleck, J. (1979). Sex role identity, androgyny, and sex role transcendence: A sex role strain analysis. *Psychology of Women Quarterly, 3,* 270–283.

Garrioch, L., & Brimacombe, C. A. E. (2001). Lineup administrators' expectations: Their impact on eyewitness confidence. *Law and Human Behavior, 25,* 299–314.

Gasper, K., & Clore, G. L. (2000). Do you have to pay attention to your feelings in order to be influenced by them? *Personality and Social Psychology Bulletin, 26,* 698–711.

Gatch, C. L., & Kendzierski, D. (1990). Predicting exercise intentions: The theory of planned behavior. *Research Quarterly for Exercise and Sport, 61,* 100–102.

Gatowski, S. I., Dobbin, S. A., Richardson, J. T., Ginsburg, G. P., Merlino, M. L., & Dahir, V. (2001). Asking the gatekeepers: A national survey of judges on judging expert evidence in a post-Daubert, world. *Law and Human Behavior, 25,* 433–458.

Gavanski, I., & Hui, C. (1992). Natural sample spaces and uncertain belief. *Journal of Personality and Social Psychology, 63,* 766–780.

Gavanski, I., & Roskos-Ewoldsen, D. R. (1991). Representativeness and conjoint probability. *Journal of Personality and Social Psychology, 61,* 181–194.

Gawronski, B. (2003). Implicational schemata and the correspondence bias: On the diagnostic value of situationally constrained behavior. *Journal of Personality and Social Psychology, 84,* 1154–1171.

Geen, R. G. (1998). Aggression and antisocial behavior. In D. T. Gilbert, S. T. Fiske, & G. Lindzey (Eds.), *Handbook of social psychology* (4th ed., Vol. 2, pp. 317–356). New York: McGraw-Hill.

Geen, R. G., & Pigg, R. (1970). Acquisition of an aggressive response and its generalization to verbal behavior. *Journal of Personality and Social Psychology, 15,* 165–170.

Geen, R. G., & Quanty, M. B. (1977). The catharsis of aggression: An evaluation of a hypothesis. In L. Berkowitz (Ed.), *Advances in experimental social psychology* (Vol. 10, pp. 1–37). New York: Academic Press.

Geers, A. L., & Lassiter, G. D. (2002). Effects of affective expectations on affective experience: The moderating role of optimism-pessimism. *Personality and Social Psychology Bulletin, 28,* 1026–1039.

Geertz, C. (1974). From the native's point of view: On the nature of anthropological understanding. In K. Basso & H. Selby (Eds.), *Meaning in anthropology* (pp. 221–237). Albuquerque: University of New Mexico Press.

Geiselman, R. E., Haight, N. A., & Kimata, L. G. (1984). Context effects on the perceived physical attractiveness of faces. *Journal of Personality and Social Psychology, 20,* 409–424.

Geiselman, R. E., Putnam, C., Korte, R., Shahriary, M., Jachimowicz, G., & Irzhevsky, V. (2002). Eyewitness expert testimony and juror decisions. *American College of Forensic Psychology, 20,* 21–36.

George, D. M. (1992). *An attribution-empathy-efficacy model of helping behavior.* Unpublished doctoral dissertation, University of California, Los Angeles.

George, J. M. (1991). State or trait: Effects of positive mood on prosocial behaviors at work. *Journal of Applied Psychology, 76,* 299–307.

Gergen, K. J., Ellsworth, P., Maslach, C., & Seipel, M. (1975). Obligation, donor resources, and reactions to aid in three cultures. *Journal of Personality and Social Psychology, 31,* 390–400.

Gerstel, N., & Gallagher, S. K. (2001). Men's caregiving: Gender and the contingent character of care. *Gender and Society, 15,* 197–217.

Gervey, B. M., Chiu, C., Hong, Y., & Dweck, C. S. (1999). Differential use of person information in decisions about guilt versus innocence: The role of implicit theories. *Personality and Social Psychology Bulletin, 25,* 17–27.

Gesn, P. R., & Ickes, W. (1999). The development of meaning contexts for empathic accuracy: Channel and sequence effects. *Journal of Personality and Social Psychology, 77,* 746–761.

Gibbons, F. X., Blanton, H., Gerrard, M., Buunk, B., & Eggleston, T. (2000). Does social comparison make a difference? Optimism as a moderator of the relation between comparison level and academic performance. *Personality and Social Psychology Bulletin, 26,* 637–648.

Gibbons, F. X., Gerrard, M., Blanton, H., & Russell, D. W. (1998). Reasoned action and social reaction: Willingness and intention as independent predictors of health risk. *Journal of Personality & Social Psychology, 74,* 1164–1180.

Gibbons, F. X., Lane, D. J., Gerrard, M., Bergan-Reis, M., Lautrup, C. L., Pexa, N. A., & et al. (2002). Comparison-level preferences after performance: Is downward comparison theory still useful? *Journal of Personality and Social Psychology, 83,* 865–880.

Gibson, B., & Sachau, D. (2000). Sandbagging as a self-presentational strategy: Claiming to be less than you are. *Personality and Social Psychology Bulletin, 26,* 56–70.

Gibson, B., Sachau, D., Doll, B., & Shumate, R. (2002). Sandbagging in competition: Responding to the pressure of being favorite. *Personality and Social Psychology Bulletin, 28,* 1119–1130.

Gilbert, D. T., & Ebert, J. E. J. (2002). Decisions and revisions: The affective forecasting of changeable outcomes. *Journal of Personality and Social Psychology, 82,* 503–514.

Gilbert, D. T., & Mallone, P. S. (1995). The correspondence bias. *Psychological Bulletin, 117,* 21–38.

Gilbert, D. T., McNulty, S. E., Giuliano, T. A., & Bentson, J. E. (1992). Blurry words and fuzzy deals: The attribution of obscure behavior. *Journal of Personality and Social Psychology, 62,* 18–25.

Gilbert, D. T., Pelham, B. W., & Krull, D. S. (1988). On cognitive busyness: When person perceivers meet persons perceived. *Journal of Personality and Social Psychology, 54,* 733–739.

Gilbert, D. T., & Wilson, T. D. (2000). Miswanting: Some problems in the forecasting of future affective states. In J. P. Forgas (Ed.), *Thinking and feeling: The role of affect in social cognition* (pp. 178–197). Cambridge: Cambridge University Press.

Gilens, M. (1999). *Why Americans hate welfare: Race, media, and the politics of antipoverty policy.* Chicago: University of Chicago Press.

Gill, M. J., & Swann, W. B., Jr. (2004). On what it means to know someone: A matter of pragmatics. *Journal of Personality and Social Psychology, 86,* 405–418.

Gill, M. J., Swann, W. B., Jr., & Silvera, D. H. (1998). On the genesis of confidence. *Journal of Personality and Social Psychology, 75,* 1101–1114.

Gilliam, F. D., Jr., & Iyengar, S. (2000). Prime suspects: The influence of local television news on the viewing public. *American Journal of Political Science, 44,* 560–573.

Gilovich, T. (1990). Differential construal and the false consensus effect. *Journal of Experimental Social Psychology, 59,* 623–634.

Glance, N. S., & Huberman, B. A. (1994). The dynamics of social dilemmas. *Scientific American, 270,* 76–81.

Glasgow, R. E., Toobert, D. J., Hampson, S. E., & Wilson, W. (1995). Behavioral research on diabetes at the Oregon Research Institute. *Annals of Behavioral Medicine, 17,* 32–40.

Glass, D. C., & Singer, J. E. (1972). *Urban stress: Experiments on noise and social stressors.* New York: Academic Press.

Gleaves, D. H., Smith, S. M., Butler, L. D., & Spiegel, D. (2004). False and recovered memories in the laboratory and clinic: A review of experimental and clinical evidence. *Clinical Psychology: Science and Practice, 11,* 3–28.

Glick, P., & Fiske, S. T. (2001). An ambivalent alliance: Hostile and benevolent sexism as complementary justifications for gender inequality. *American Psychologist, 56,* 109–118.

Glick, P., & Fiske, S. T. (1999). Gender, power dynamics, and social interaction. In M. M. Ferree, J. Lorber, & B. B. Hess (Eds.), *Revisioning gender* (pp. 365–397). London: Sage Publications.

Glick, P., Lameiras, M., Fiske, S. T., Eckes, T., Masser, B., Volpato, C., et al. (2004). Bad but bold: Ambivalent attitudes toward men predict gender inequality in 16 nations. *Journal of Personality and Social Psychology, 86,* 713–728.

Goethals, G., & Klos, D. S. (Eds.). (1970). *Experiencing youth: First-person accounts.* Boston: Little, Brown.

Goethals, G. R., & Darley, J. M. (1987). Social comparison theory: Self-evaluation and group life. In B. Mullen & G. R. Goethals (Eds.), *Theories of group behavior* (pp. 21–48). New York: Springer-Verlag.

Goffman, E. (1952). On cooling the mark out: Some aspects of adaptation to failure. *Psychiatry, 15,* 451–463.

Goldberg, P. (1968). Are women prejudiced against women? *TransAction, 5,* 28–30.

Golden, J. S., & Johnston, G. D. (1970). Problems of distortion in doctor-patient communications. *Psychiatry in Medicine, 1,* 127–149.

Goldman, J. A., & Harlow, L. L. (1993). Self-perception variables that mediate AIDS-preventive behavior in college students. *Health Psychology, 6,* 489–498.

Goldstein, J. H., Davis, R. W., & Herman, D. (1975). Escalation of aggression: Experimental studies. *Journal of Personality and Social Psychology, 31,* 162–170.

Goodchilds, J., Zellman, G., Johnson, P., & Giarusso, R. (1988). Adolescents and the perceptions of sexual interactions outcomes. In A. Burgess (Ed.), *Sexual Assault* (Vol. 2). New York: Garland.

Goodheart, A. (2004, May-June). Change of heart. *AARP The Magazine,* 43–45.

Goodman, L. A., Koss, M. P., Fitzgerald, L. F., Russo, N. F., & Keita, G. P. (1993). Male violence against women: Current research and future directions. *American Psychologist, 48,* 1054–1058.

Gorassini, D. R., & Olson, J. M. (1995). Does self-perception change explain the foot-in-the-door effect? *Journal of Personality and Social Psychology, 69,* 91–105.

Gordijn, E. H., Koomen, W., & Stapel, D. A. (2001). Level of prejudice in relation to knowledge of cultural stereotypes. *Journal of Experimental Social Psychology, 37,* 150–157.

Gosling, S. D., Vazire, S., Srivastava, S., & John, O. P. (2004). Should we trust web-based studies? *American Psychologist, 59,* 93–104.

Gottman, J. M. (1994). *What predicts divorce?* Hillsdale, NJ: Erlbaum.

Governor girlie man. (2004, July 20). *The Los Angeles Times,* p. B12.

Graham, C. R. (2003). A model of norm development for computer-mediated teamwork. *Small Group Research, 34,* 322–352.

Graham, S. (1992). "Most of the subjects were white and middle class": Trends in published research on African Americans in selected APA journals, 1970–1989. *American Psychologist, 47,* 629–639.

Graham, S., & Barker, G. P. (1990). The down side of help: An attributional-developmental analysis of helping behavior as a low-ability cue. *Journal of Educational Psychology, 82,* 7–14.

Graham, S., Hudley, C., & Williams, E. (1992). Attributional and emotional determinants of aggression among African-American and Latino young adolescents. *Developmental Psychology, 28,* 731–740.

Grahe, J. E., & Bernieri, F. J. (2002). Self-awareness of judgment policies of rapport. *Personality and Social Psychology Bulletin, 28,* 1407–1418.

Graves, L. M. (1999). Gender bias in interviewers' evaluations of applicants. In G. N. Powell (Ed.), *Handbook of gender and work* (pp. 145–164). Thousand Oaks, CA: Sage.

Gray, J. (1992). *Men are from Mars, women are from Venus.* New York: HarperCollins.

Gray, J. R. (1999). A bias toward short-term thinking in threat-related negative emotional states. *Personality and Social Psychology Bulletin, 25,* 65–75.

Gray, J. R. (2004). Integration of emotion and cognitive control. *Current Directions in Psychological Science, 13,* 46–49.

Green, L. R., Richardson, D. S., Lago, T., & Schatten-Jones, E. C. (2001). Network correlates of social and emotional loneliness in young and older adults. *Personality and Social Psychology Bulletin, 27,* 281–288.

Greenberg, J., Arndt, J., Schimel, J., Pyszczynski, T., & Solomon, S. (2001). Clarifying the function of mortality salience-induced worldview defense: Renewed suppression or reduced accessibility of death-related thoughts? *Journal of Experimental Social Psychology, 37,* 70–76.

Greenberg, J., Porteus, J., Simon, L., Pyszczynski, T., & Solomon, S. (1995). Evidence of a terror management function of cultural icons: The effects of mortality salience on the inappropriate use of cherished cultural symbols. *Personality and Social Psychology Bulletin, 21,* 1221–1228.

Greenberg, J., Pyszczynski, T., & Solomon, S. (1986). The causes and consequences of a need for self-esteem: A terror management theory. In R. F. Baumeister (Ed.), *Public self and private self* (pp. 189–212). New York: Springer-Verlag.

Greenberg, J., Solomon, S., Pyszczynski, T., Rosenblatt, A., Burling, J., Lyon, D., et al. (1992). Why do people need self-esteem? Converging evidence that self-esteem serves an anxiety-buffering function. *Journal of Personality and Social Psychology, 63,* 913–922.

Greene, E., Chopra, S., Kovera, M. B., Penrod, S. D., Rose, V. G., Schuller, R., et al. (2002). Jurors and juries: A review of the field. In J. Ogloff (Ed.), *Psychology and law in the 21st century* (pp. 225–284). New York: Kluwer.

Greenwald, A. G., & Banaji, M. R. (1995). Implicit social cognition: Attitudes, self-esteem, and stereotypes. *Psychological Review, 102,* 4–27.

Greenwald, A. G., & Farnham, S. D. (2000). Using the Implicit Association Test to measure self-esteem and self-concept. *Journal of Personality and Social Psychology, 79,* 1022–1038.

Greenwald, A. G., McGhee, D. E., & Schwartz, J. L. K. (1998). Measuring individual differences in implicit cognition: The Implicit Association Test. *Journal of Personality and Social Psychology, 74,* 1464–1480.

Greenwald, A. G., Nosek, B. A., & Banaji, M. R. (2003). Understanding and using the Implicit Association Test: I. An improved scoring algorithm. *Journal of Personality and Social Psychology, 85,* 197–216.

Greenwell, J., & Dengerink, H. A. (1973). The role of perceived versus actual attack in human physical aggression. *Journal of Personality and Social Psychology,* 26, 66–71.

Greer, S. (1974). Psychological aspects: Delay in treatment of breast cancer. *Proceedings of the Royal Society of Medicine, 64,* 470–473.

Greve, W., & Wentura, D. (2003). Immunizing the self: Self-concept stabilization through reality-adaptive self-definitions. *Personality and Social Psychology Bulletin, 29,* 39–50.

Griffin, D., & Buehler, R. (1993). Role of construal processes in conformity and dissent. *Journal of Personality and Social Psychology, 65,* 657–669.

Gross, E. F., Juvonen, J., & Gable, S. L. (2002). Internet use and well-being in adolescence. *Journal of Social Issues, 58*(1), 75–90.

Gross, J. J., & John, O. P. (2003). Individual differences in two emotion regulation processes: Implications for affect, relationships, and well-being. *Journal of Personality and Social Psychology, 85,* 348–362.

Grote, N. K., & Clark, M. S. (2001). Perceiving unfairness in the family: Cause or consequence of marital distress? *Journal of Personality and Social Psychology, 80,* 281–293.

Grube, J. A., & Piliavin, J. A. (2000). Role identity, organizational experiences, and volunteer performance. *Personality and Social Psychology Bulletin, 26,* 1108–1119.

Gruber-Baldini, A. L., Schaie, K. W., & Willis, S. L. (1995). Similarity in married couples: A longitudinal study of mental abilities and rigidity-flexibility. *Journal of Personality and Social Psychology, 69,* 191–203.

Guadagno, R. E., Asher, T., Demaine, L. J., & Cialdini, R. B. (2001). When saying yes leads to saying no: Preference for consistency and the reverse foot-in-the door effect. *Personality and Social Psychology Bulletin, 27,* 859–867.

Gunthert, C. B., Cohen, L. H., & Armeli, S. (1999). The role of neuroticism in daily stress and coping. *Journal of Personality and Social Psychology, 77,* 1087–1100.

Gupta, G. R. (1992). Love, arranged marriage, and the Indian social structure. In J. J. Macionis & N. V. Benodraitis (Eds.), *Seeing ourselves: Classic, contemporary and cross-cultural readings in sociology,* pp. 262–270. Upper Saddle River NJ: Prentice Hall.

Gurin, P., Hurtado, A., & Peng, T. (1994). Group contacts and ethnicity in the social identities of Mexicanos and Chicanos. The self and the collective [Special Issue] *Personality and Social Psychology Bulletin. 20,* 521–532.

Hacker, H. M. (1981). Blabbermouths and clams: Sex differences in self-disclosure in same-sex and cross-sex friendship dyads. *Psychology of Women Quarterly, 5,* 385–401.

Haddock, G., Zanna, M. P., & Esses, V. M. (1993). Assessing the structure of prejudicial attitudes: The case of attitudes toward homosexuals. *Journal of Personality and Social Psychology, 65,* 1105–1118.

Haig, D. (2004). The inexorable rise of gender and the decline of sex: Social change in academic titles, 1945–2001. *Archives of Sexual Behavior, 33,* 87–96.

Halberstadt, J. B., & Niedenthal, P. M. (1997). Emotional state and the use of stimulus dimensions in judgment. *Journal of Personality and Social Psychology, 72,* 1017–1033.

Hall, C. C. I., & Crum, M. J. (1994). Women and "body-isms" in television beer commercials. *Sex Roles, 31,* 329–337.

Hall, E. T. (1959). *The silent language.* Garden City, NY: Doubleday.

Hall, J. A. (1978). Gender effects in decoding nonverbal cues. *Psychological Bulletin, 85,* 845–857.

Hall, J. A. (1998). How big are nonverbal sex differences? The case of smiling and sensitivity to nonverbal cues. In D. J. Canary & K. Dindia (Eds.), *Sex differences and similarities in communication* (pp. 155–178). Mahwah, NJ: Erlbaum.

Hall, J. A., & Carter, J. D. (1999). Gender-stereotype accuracy as an individual difference. *Journal of Personality and Social Psychology, 77,* 350–359.

Hall, J. A., Carter, J. D., & Horgan, T. G. (2000). Gender differences in nonverbal communication of emotion. In A. H. Fischer (Ed.), *Gender and emotion: Social psychological perspectives* (pp. 97–117). New York: Cambridge University Press.

Hall, J. A., Halberstadt, A. G., & O'Brien, C. E. (1997). "Subordination" and nonverbal sensitivity. *Sex Roles, 37,* 295–317.

Hamill, R., Wilson, T. D., & Nisbett, R. E. (1980). Insensitivity to sample bias: Generalizing from atypical cases. *Journal of Personality and Social Psychology, 39,* 578–589.

Hamilton, D. L., & Gifford, R. K. (1976). Illusory correlation in interpersonal perception: A cognitive basis of stereotypic judgments. *Journal of Experimental Social Psychology, 12,* 393–407.

Hampson, S. E. (1998). When is an inconsistency not an inconsistency? Trait reconciliation in personality description and impression formation. *Journal of Personality and Social Psychology, 74,* 102–117.

Han, S., & Shavitt, S. (1994). Persuasion and culture: Advertising appeals in individualistic and collectivistic societies. *Journal of Experimental Social Psychology, 30,* 326–350.

Haney, C., Hurtado, A., & Vega, L. (1994). "Modern" death qualification: New data on its biasing effects. *Law and Human Behavior, 18,* 619–633.

Haney, C., & Lynch, M. (1994). Comprehending life and death matters: A preliminary study of California's capital penalty instructions. *Law and Human Behavior, 18,* 411–436.

Hansen, D. E., Vandenberg, B., & Patterson, M. L. (1995). The effects of religious orientation on spontaneous and nonspontaneous helping behaviors. *Personality and Individual Differences, 19,* 101–104.

Haraciewicz, J. M., Sansone, C., & Manderlink, G. (1985). Competence, achievement orientation, and intrinsic motivation: A process analysis. *Journal of Personality and Social Psychology, 48,* 493–508.

Harburg, E., Erfurt, J. C., Hauenstein, L. S., Chape, C., Schull, W. J., & Schork, M. A. (1973). Socio-ecological stress, suppressed hostility, skin color, and black-white male blood pressure: Detroit. *Psychosomatic Medicine, 35,* 276–296.

Harkins, S. G., & Petty, R. (1981). The effects of source magnification of cognitive effort on attitudes: An information-processing view. *Journal of Personality and Social Psychology, 40,* 401–413.

Harmon-Jones, E. (2000). Cognitive dissonance and experienced negative affect: Evidence that dissonance increases experienced negative affect even in the absence of aversive consequences. *Personality and Social Psychology Bulletin, 26,* 1490–1501.

Harmon-Jones, E., & Allen, J. J. B. (2001). The role of affect in the mere exposure effect. *Personality and Social Psychology Bulletin, 27,* 889–898.

Harmon-Jones, E., & Harmon-Jones, C. (2002). Testing the action-based model of cognitive dissonance: The effect of action orientation on postdecisional attitudes. *Personality and Social Psychology Bulletin, 28,* 711–723.

Harmon-Jones, E., & Sigelman, J. (2001). State anger and prefrontal brain activity: Evidence that insult-related relative left-prefrontal activation is associated with experienced anger and aggression. *Journal of Personality and Social Psychology, 80,* 797–803.

Harris, C. R. (2001). Cardiovascular responses of embarrassment and effects of emotional suppression in a social setting. *Journal of Personality and Social Psychology, 81,* 886–897.

Harris, C. R. (2003). A review of sex differences in sexual jealousy, including self-report data, psychophysiological responses, interpersonal violence, and morbid jealousy. *Personality and Social Psychology Review, 7,* 102–128.

Harris, P. R. (1980). *Promoting health-preventing disease: Objectives for the nation.* Washington, DC: U.S. Government Printing Office.

Hartmann, D. P. (1969). Influence of symbolically modeled instrumental aggression and pain cues on aggressive behavior. *Journal of Personality and Social Psychology, 11,* 280–288.

Hastie, R., & Kumar, P. A. (1979). Person memory: Personality traits as organizing principles in memory for behavior. *Journal of Personality and Social Psychology, 37,* 25–38.

Hastie, R., Park, B., & Weber, R. (1984). Social memory. In R. S. Wyer & T. K. Srull (Eds.), *Handbook of social cognition* (Vol. 1, pp. 151–212). Hillsdale, NJ: Erlbaum.

Hastie, R., & Pennington, N. (2000). Explanation-based decision-making. In T. Connolly & H. R. Arkes (Eds.), *Judgment and decision making: An interdisciplinary reader* (2nd ed., pp. 212–228). New York: Cambridge University Press.

Hastie, R., Penrod, S. D., & Pennington, N. (1983). *Inside the jury.* Cambridge, MA: Harvard University Press.

Hatfield, E., Brinton, C., & Cornelius, J. (1989). Passionate love and anxiety in young adolescents. *Motivation and Emotion, 13,* 271–289.

Hatfield, E., & Sprecher, S. (1986). Measuring passionate love in intimate relationships. *Journal of Adolescence, 9,* 383–410.

Hatfield, E., Sprecher, S., Pillemer, J. T., Greenberger, D., & Wexler, P. (1989). Gender differences in what is desired in sexual relationships. *Journal of Psychology and Human Sexuality, 1*(2), 39–52.

Hatfield, E., Traupmann, J., Sprecher, S., Utne, M., & Hay, J. (1985). Equity and intimate relations: Recent research. In W. Ickes (Ed.), *Compatible and incompatible relationships* (pp. 91–118). New York: Springer-Verlag.

Hauenstein, D. J., Schiller, M. R., & Hurley, R. S. (1987). Motivational techniques of dietitians counseling individuals with Type II diabetes. *Journal of the American Diabetic Association, 87,* 37–42.

Hawkes, G. R., & Taylor, M. (1975). Power structure in Mexican and Mexican-American farm labor families. *Journal of Marriage and Family, 37,* 807–811.

Hawkley, L. C., Burleson, M. H., Berntson, G. G., & Cacioppo, J. T. (2003). Loneliness in everyday life: Cardiovascular activity, psychosocial context, and health behaviors. *Journal of Personality and Social Psychology, 85,* 105–120.

Hayes, A. F., & Dunning, D. (1997). Construal processes and trait ambiguity: Implications for self-peer agreement in personality judgment. *Journal of Personality and Social Psychology, 72,* 664–677.

Haynes, R. B., McKibbon, K., & Kanani, R. (1996). Systematic review of randomized trials of interventions to assist patients to follow prescriptions for medications. *Lancet, 348,* 383–386.

Hazan, C., & Shaver, P. (1987). Romantic love conceptualized as an attachment process. *Journal of Personality and Social Psychology, 52,* 511–524.

Heatherton, T., Striepe, M. I., & Wittenberg, L. (1998). Emotional distress and disinhibited eating: The role of self. *Personality and Social Psychology Bulletin, 24,* 301–313.

Heatherton, T. F., & Vohs, K. D. (2000). Interpersonal evaluations following threats to self: Role of self-esteem. *Journal of Personality and Social Psychology, 78,* 725–736.

Heaton, T. B., & Albrecht, S. L. (1991). Stable unhappy marriages. *Journal of Marriage and Family, 53,* 747–758.

Hebl, M. R., & Heatherton, T. F. (1998). The stigma of obesity in women: The difference is black and white. *Personality and Social Psychology Bulletin, 24,* 417–426.

Hebl, M. R., & Mannix, L. M. (2003). The weight of obesity in evaluating others: A mere proximity effect. *Personality and Social Psychology Bulletin, 29,* 28–38.

Heider, F. (1958). *Psychology of interpersonal relations.* New York: Wiley.

Heilman, M. E., Wallen, A. S., Fuchs, D., & Tamkins, M. M. (2004). Penalties for success: Reactions to women who succeed at male gender-typed tasks. *Journal of Applied Psychology, 89,* 416–427.

Heimpel, S. A., Wood, J. V., Marshall, M. A., & Brown, J. D. (2002). Do people with low self-esteem really want to feel better? Self-esteem differences in motivation to repair negative moods. *Journal of Personality and Social Psychology, 82,* 128–147.

Heine, S. J., Kitayama, S., Lehman, D. R., Takata, T., Ide, E., Leung, C., et al. (2001). Divergent consequences of success and failure in Japan and North America: An investigation of self-improving motivations and malleable selves. *Journal of Personality and Social Psychology, 81,* 599–615.

Heine, S. J., & Renshaw, K. (2002). Interjudge agreement, self-enhancement, and liking: Cross-cultural divergences. *Personality and Social Psychology Bulletin, 28,* 578–587.

Heine, S. J., Takata, T., & Lehman, D. R. (2000). Beyond self-presentation: Evidence for self-criticism among Japanese. *Personality and Social Psychology Bulletin, 26,* 71–78.

Helgeson, V. S. (1992). Moderators of the relation between perceived control and adjustment to chronic illness. *Journal of Personality and Social Psychology, 63,* 656–666.

Helgeson, V. S. (2002). Gender-related traits and health. In J. Suls & K. Wallston (Eds.), *Social psychological foundations of health.* Oxford, England: Blackwell.

Helgeson, V. S. (2005). *Psychology of gender* (2nd ed.). Upper Saddle River, NJ: Prentice Hall.

Helgeson, V. S., Shaver, P., & Dyer, M. (1987). Prototypes of intimacy and distance in same-sex and opposite-sex relationships. *Journal of Social and Personal Relationships, 4,* 195–233.

Helmers, K. F., Krantz , D. S., Merz , C. N. B., Klein, J., Kop, W. J., Gottdiener, J. S., et al. (1995). Defensive hostility: Relationship to multiple markers of cardiac ischemia in patients with coronary disease. *Health Psychology, 14,* 202–209.

Hendrick, C., & Hendrick, S. S. (1986). A theory and method of love. *Journal of Personality and Social Psychology, 50,* 392–402.

Herek, G. M., & Capitanio, J. P. (1996). "Some of my best friends": Intergroup contact, concealable stigma, and heterosexuals' attitudes toward gay men and lesbians. *Personality and Social Psychology Bulletin, 22,* 412–424.

Heuer, L., & Penrod, S. D. (1989). Instructing jurors: A field experiment with written and preliminary instructions. *Law and Human Behavior, 13,* 409–430.

Hewstone, M., Islam, M. R., & Judd, C. M. (1993). Models of crossed categorization and intergroup relations. *Journal of Personality and Social Psychology, 64,* 779–793.

Higgins, E. T. (1987). Self-discrepancy: A theory relating self and affect. *Psychological Review, 94,* 319–340.

Higgins, E. T. (1989). Self-discrepancy theory: What patterns of self-beliefs cause people to suffer? In L. Berkowitz (Ed.), *Advances in experimental social psychology* (Vol. 22, pp. 93–136). San Diego, CA: Academic Press.

Higgins, E. T. (1999). Self-discrepancy: A theory relating self and affect. In R. F. Baumeister (Ed.), *Self in social psychology. Key readings in social psychology* (pp. 150–181). Philadelphia: Psychology Press.

Higgins, E. T., & Bargh, J. A. (1987). Social cognition and social perception. *Annual Review of Psychology, 38,* 369–425.

Higgins, E. T., Idson, L. C., Freitas, A. L., Spiegel, S., & Molden, D. C. (2003). Transfer of value from fit. *Journal of Personality and Social Psychology, 84,* 1140–1153.

Higgins, E. T., Klein, R., & Strauman, T. (1985). Self-concept discrepancy theory: A psychological model for distinguishing among different aspects of depression and anxiety. *Social Cognition, 3,* 51–76.

Higgins, E. T., Rholes, W. S., & Jones, C. R. (1977). Category accessibility and impression formation. *Journal of Experimental Social Psychology, 13,* 141–154.

Higgins, E. T., Shah, J., & Friedman, R. (1997). Emotional responses to goal attainment: Strength of regulatory focus as moderator. *Journal of Personality and Social Psychology, 72,* 515–525.

Hill, C. T., & Peplau, L. A. (1998). Premarital predictors of relationship outcomes: A 15-year followup of the Boston Couples Study. In T. N. Bradbury (Ed.), *The developmental course of marital dysfunction* (pp. 237–278). New York: Cambridge University Press.

Hillhouse, J. J., Stair, A., & Adler, C. M. (1996). Predictors of sunbathing and sunscreen use in college undergraduates. *Journal of Behavioral Medicine, 19,* 543–561.

Hilton, D. J., Smith, R. H., & Kim, S. K. (1995). Processes of casual explanation and dispositional attribution. *Journal of Personality and Social Psychology, 68,* 377–387.

Hines, M. (2004). *Brain gender.* New York: Oxford University Press.

Hirschl, B. P. (2004, May 30). Carnegie hero fund commission celebrates centennial. *Tribune-Review.* Retrieved July 3, 2004 from http://www.pittsburghliv.com/x/tribune-review/news/s_195618.html

Hirt, E., & Kimble, C. E. (1981, May). *The home-field advantage in sports: Differences and, correlates.* Paper presented at the annual meeting of the Midwestern Psychological Association, Detroit, MI.

Hirt, E. R. (1990). Do I see only what I expect? Evidence for an expectancy-guided retrieval model. *Journal of Personality and Social Psychology, 58,* 937–951.

Hirt, E. R., McCrea, S. M., & Kimble, C. E. (2000). Public self-focus and sex differences in behavioral self-handicapping: Does increasing self-threat still make it "just a man's game?" *Personality and Social Psychology Bulletin, 26,* 1131–1141.

Hobfoll, S. E., Jackson, A. P., Lavin, J., Britton, P. J., & Shepherd, J. B. (1993). Safer sex knowledge, behavior, and attitudes of inner-city women. *Health Psychology, 12,* 481–488.

Hochbaum, G. M. (1958). *Public participation in medical screening programs: A sociopsychological study* (PHS Publication No. 572). Washington, DC: U.S. Government Printing Office.

Hodson, G., Dovidio, J. F., & Gaertner, S. L. (2002). Processes in racial discrimination: Differential weighting of conflicting information. *Personality and Social Psychology Bulletin, 28,* 460–471.

Hoffman, A. R., & Noriega, C. A (2004). *Looking for Latino regulars on prime-time television: The Fall 2003 season.* Los Angeles: UCLA Chicano Studies Research Center.

Hoffman, M. L. (2000). *Empathy and moral development: Implications for caring and justice.* New York: Cambridge University Press.

Hogan, R., Curphy, G. J., & Hogan, J. (1994). What we know about leadership: Effectiveness and personality. *American Psychologist, 49,* 493–504.

Hogg, M. A., & Abrams, D. (1990). *Social identifications: A social psychology of intergroup relations and group processes.* New York: Routledge.

Hogue, M., & Yoder, J. D. (2003). The role of status in producing depressed entitlement in women's and men's pay allocations. *Psychology of Women Quarterly, 27,* 330–337.

Holahan, C. J., & Moos, R. H. (1987). Personal and contextual determinants of coping strategies. *Journal of Personality and Social Psychology, 52,* 946–955.

Holahan, C. J., Moos, R. H., Holahan, C. K., & Brennan, P. L. (1995). Social support, coping, and depressive symptoms in a late-middle-aged sample of patients reporting cardiac illness. *Health Psychology, 14,* 152–163.

Holahan, C. J., Moos, R. H., Holahan, C. K., & Brennan, P. L. (1997). Social context, coping strategies, and depressive symptoms: An expanded model with cardiac patients. *Journal of Personality and Social Psychology, 72,* 918–928.

Hollander, E. P. (1993). Legitimacy, power, and influence: A perspective on relational features of leadership. In M. M. Chemers & R. Ayman (Eds.), *Leadership theory and research* (pp. 29–47). New York: Academic Press.

Holman, E. A., & Silver, R. C. (1998). Getting "stuck" in the past: Temporal orientation and coping with trauma. *Journal of Personality and Social Psychology, 74,* 1146–1163.

Holman, T. B., & Jarvis, M. O. (2003). Hostile, volatile, avoiding, and validating couple-conflict types: An investigation of Gottman's couple-conflict types. *Personal Relationships, 10,* 267–282.

Holmes, J. G., & Murray, S. L. (1996). Conflict in close relationships. In E. T. Higgins & A. W. Kruglanski (Eds.), *Social psychology: Handbook of basic principles* (pp. 622–654). New York: Guilford.

Holtgraves, T., & Srull, T. K. (1989). The effects of positive self-descriptions on impressions: General principles and individual differences. *Personality and Social Psychology Bulletin, 15,* 452–462.

Holtz, R., and Miller, N. (1985). Assumed similarity and opinion certainty. *Journal of Personality and Social Psychology, 48,* 890–898.

Holzworth-Munroe, A., & Jacobson, N. S. (1985). Causal attributions of married couples: When do they search for causes? What do they conclude when they do?. *Journal of Personality and Social Psychology, 48,* 1398–1412.

Honts, C. R., Raskin, D. C., & Kircher, J. C. (1994). Mental and physical countermeasures reduce the accuracy of polygraph tests. *Journal of Applied Psychology, 79,* 252–259.

Honts, C. R., Raskin, D. C., & Kircher, J. C. (2002). The scientific status of research on polygraph techniques: The case for polygraph testing. In D. L. Faigman, D. H. Kaye, M. J. Saks, & J. Sanders (Eds.), *Modern scientific evidence: The law and science of expert testimony* (2nd ed., Vol. 2, pp. 446–483). St. Paul MN: West Publishing.

Hoover, E. (2004, April 9). Crying foul over fans' boorish behavior. *Chronicle of Higher Education, 50*(31), p. A1.

Hornstein, H. A., Fisch, E., & Holmes, M. (1968). Influence of a model's feeling about his behavior and his relevance as a comparison other than observers' helping behavior. *Journal of Personality and Social Psychology, 10,* 222–226.

House, J. S., Landis, K. R., & Umberson, D. (1988). Social relationships and health. *Science, 241,* 540–545.

Houston, B. K., & Kelly, K. E. (1989). Hostility in employed women: Relation to work and marital experiences, social support, stress, and anger expression. *Personality and Social Psychology Bulletin, 15,* 175–182.

Hovland, C. I., Harvey, O. J., & Sherif, M. (1957). Assimilation and contrast effects in reactions to communication and attitude change. *Journal of Abnormal and Social Psychology, 55,* 257–261.

Hovland, C. I., Janis, I. L., & Kelley, H. H. (1953). *Communication and persuasion.* New Haven, CT: Yale University Press.

Hovland, C. I., & Pritzker, H. A. (1957). Extent of opinion change as a function of amount of change advocated. *Journal of Abnormal and Social Psychology, 54,* 257–261.

Hovland, C. I., & Sears, R. R. (1940). Minor studies of aggression: VI. Correlation of lynchings with economic indices. *Journal of Psychology, 9,* 301–310.

Hovland, C. I., & Weiss, W. (1952). The influence of source credibility on communication effectiveness. *Public Opinion Quarterly, 15,* 635–650.

Howard, K. A., Flora, J., & Griffin, M. (1999). Violence-prevention programs in schools: State of the science and implications for future research. *Applied and Preventive Psychology, 8,* 197–215.

Hubbard, J. A., Dodge, K. A., Cillessen, A. H. N., Coie, J. D., & Schwartz, D. (2001). The dyadic nature of social information processing in boys' reactive and proactive aggression. *Journal of Personality and Social Psychology, 80,* 268–280.

Huddy, L., & Virtanen, S. (1995). Subgroup differentiation and subgroup bias among Latinos as a function of familiarity and positive distinctiveness. *Journal of Personality and Social Psychology, 68,* 97–107.

Hudley, S., & Graham, C. (1992). An attributional approach to aggression in African-American children. In D. Schunk & J. Meece (Eds.), *Student perceptions in the classroom* (pp. 75–94). Hillsdale, NJ: Erlbaum.

Huesmann, L. R. (1982). Televised violence and aggressive behavior. In D. Pearl, L. Bouthiler, & J. Lazar (Eds.), *Television and behavior: Ten years of scientific progress and implications for the eighties. Vol. II: Technical reviews* (pp. 126–137). Rockville, MD: National Institute of Mental Health.

Huesmann, L. R. (1986). Psychological processes promoting the relation between exposure to media violence and aggressive behavior by the viewer. *Journal of Social Issues, 42,* 125–139.

Huesmann, L. R. (1988). An information processing model for the development of aggression. *Aggressive Behavior, 14,* 13–24.

Huesmann, L. R. (1997). Observational learning of violent behavior: Social and biosocial processes. In A. Raine, P. A. Brennan, D. P. Farrington, & S. A. Mednick (Eds.), *Biosocial bases of violence. NATO ASI series: Series A: Life sciences* (Vol. 292, pp. 69–88). New York: Plenum Press.

Huesmann, L. R. (1998). The role of social information processing and cognitive schema in the acquisition and maintenance of habitual aggressive behavior. In R. G. Geen & E. Donnerstein (Eds.), *Human aggression: Theories, research, and implications for social policy* (pp. 73–109). New York: Academic Press.

Huesmann, L. R., Eron, L. D., Lefkowitz, M. M., & Walder, L. O. (1984). Stability of aggression over time and generations. *Developmental Psychology, 20,* 1120–1134.

Huesmann, L. R., & Guerra, N. G. (1997). Children's normative beliefs about aggression and aggressive behavior. *Journal of Personality and Social Psychology,* 72, 408–419.

Huesmann, L. R., & Miller, L. S. (1994). Long-term effects of repeated exposure to media violence in childhood. In L. R. Huesmann (Ed.), *Aggressive behavior: Current perspectives* (pp. 153–183). New York: Plenum Press.

Huesmann, L. R., & Moise, J. F. (2000). The stability and continuity of aggression from early childhood to young adulthood. In D. J. Flannery & C. R. Huff (Eds.), *Youth violence: Prevention, intervention, and social policy* (pp. 73–95). Washington, DC: American Psychiatric Press.

Huesmann, L. R., Moise, J. F., & Podolski, C. L. (1997). The effects of media violence on the development of antisocial behavior. In D. M. Stoff, J. Breiling, & J. D. Maser (Eds.), *Handbook of antisocial behavior* (pp. 181–193). New York: Wiley.

Huffington, A. (2001, July 20). Private pain can foster public gain. *Los Angeles Times,* p. B15.

Hui, C. H. (1990). Work attitudes, leadership styles, and managerial behaviors in different cultures. In R. W. Brislin (Ed.), *Applied cross-cultural psychology* (pp. 186–208). Newbury Park, CA: Sage.

Hull, J. G., & Bond, C. F. (1986). Social and behavioral consequences of alcohol consumption and expectancy: A meta-analysis. *Psychological Bulletin, 99,* 347–360.

Hunt, J. S., Borgida, E., Kelly, K. M., & Burgess, D. (2002). Gender stereotyping. In D. L. Faigman, D. H. Kaye, M. J. Saks, & J. Sanders (Eds.), *Modern scientific evidence: The law and science of expert testimony* (2nd ed., Vol. 2, pp. 384–426). St. Paul, MN: West Publishing.

Hunt, J. S., & Budesheim, T. L. (2004). How jurors use and misuse character evidence. *Journal of Applied Psychology, 89,* 347–361.

Huntley, J. E., & Costanzo, M. (2003). Sexual harassment stories: Testing a story-mediated model of juror decision-making in civil litigation. *Law and Human Behavior, 27,* 29–51.

Huo, Y. J., Smith, H. J., Tyler, T. R., & Lind, E. A. (1996). Superordinate identification, subgroup identification, and justice concerns. *Psychological Science, 7,* 40–45.

Huston, T. L. (2002). Power. In H. H. Kelley et al., *Close relationships* (pp. 169–219). Clinton Corners, NY: Percheron.

Huston, T. L., Ruggiero, M., Conner, R., & Geis, G. (1981). Bystander intervention into crime: A study based on naturally-occurring episodes. *Social Psychology Quarterly, 44,* 14–23.

Hyde, J. S. (1986). Gender differences in aggression. In J. S. Hyde & M. C. Linn (Eds.), *Psychology of gender: Advances through meta-analysis* (pp. 51–66). Baltimore: Johns Hopkins University Press.

Hyde, J. S. (2004). *Half the human experience: The psychology of women.* Boston: Houghton Mifflin.

Hyde, J. S., & Frost, L. A. (1993). Meta-analysis in the psychology of women. In F. L. Denmark & M. A. Paludi (Eds.), *Psychology of women: A handbook of issues and theories* (pp. 67–104). Westport, CT: Greenwood Press.

Iacono, W. G., & Lykken, D. T. (2002). The scientific status of research on polygraph techniques: The case against polygraph testing. In D. L. Faigman, D. H. Kaye, M. J. Saks, & J. Sanders (Eds.), *Modern scientific evidence: The law and science of expert testimony* (2nd ed., Vol. 2, pp. 483–538). St. Paul, MN: West Publishing.

Iacono, W. G., & Patrick, C. J. (1999). Polygraph ("lie detector") testing: The state of the art. In A. K. Hess & I. B. Weiner (Eds.), *Handbook of forensic psychology* (2nd ed., pp. 440–473). New York: Wiley.

Idson, L. C., & Mischel, W. (2001). The personality of familiar and significant people: The lay perceiver as a social-cognitive theorist. *Journal of Personality and Social Psychology, 80,* 585–596.

Impett, E. A., Beals, K. P., & Peplau, L. A. (2002). Testing the investment model of relationship commitment and stability in a longitudinal study of married couples. *Current Psychology, 20,* 312–326.

Impett, E. A., Gable, S. L., & Peplau, L. A. (2004). Giving up and giving in: The costs and benefits of daily sacrifice in intimate relationships. *Journal of Personality and Social Psychology,* accepted for publication.

Imrich, D. J., Mullin, C., & Linz, D. (1995). Measuring the extent of prejudicial pretrial publicity in major American newspapers: A content analysis. *Journal of Communication, 45,* 94–117.

Isen, A. M. (1987). Positive affect, cognitive processes, and social behavior. *Advances in experimental social psychology* (Vol. 20, pp. 203–253). New York: Academic Press.

Isen, A. M (1999). Positive affect. In T. Dagleish & M. Powers (Eds.), *Handbook of cognition and emotion* (pp 521–539). Sussex, England: Wiley.

Isen, A. M., Clark, M., & Schwartz, M. F. (1976). Duration of the effect of good mood on helping: Footprints on the sands of time. *Journal of Personality and Social Psychology, 34,* 385–393.

Isen, A. M., & Levin, P. F. (1972). Effects of feeling good on helping: Cookies and kindness. *Journal of Personality and Social Psychology, 21,* 384–388.

Isen, A. M., & Simmonds, S. F. (1978). The effect of feeling good on a helping task that is incompatible with good mood. *Social Psychology Quarterly, 41,* 346–349.

Isenberg, D. J. (1986). Group polarization: A critical review and meta-analysis. *Journal of Personality and Social Psychology, 50,* 1141–1151.

Islam, M. R., & Hewstone, M. (1993). Dimensions of contact as predictors of intergroup anxiety, perceived out-group variability, and out-group attitude: An integrative model. *Personality and Social Psychology Bulletin, 19,* 700–710.

Iyengar, S. S., & Lepper, M. R. (1999). Rethinking the value of choice: A cultural perspective on intrinsic motivation. *Journal of Personality and Social Psychology, 76,* 349–366.

Izard, C. E. (1971). *The face of emotion.* New York: Appleton-Century-Crofts.

J.E.B. v. Alabama, 128 L.Ed.2d 89 (1994).

Jackman, M. R. (1994). *The velvet glove: Paternalism and conflict in gender, class, and race relations.* Berkeley: University of California Press.

Jackman, M. R., & Crane, M. (1986). "Some of my best friends are black...": Interracial friendship and whites' racial attitudes. *Public Opinion Quarterly, 50,* 459–486.

Jackman, M. R., & Muha, M. J. (1984). Education and intergroup attitudes: Moral enlightenment, superficial democratic commitment, or ideological refinement? *American Sociological Review, 49,* 751–769.

Jackson, L. A., Hunter, J. E., & Hodge, C. N. (1995). Physical attractiveness and intellectual competence: A meta-analytic review. *Social Psychology Quarterly, 58,* 108–122.

Jacobs, A. (1998, September 13). His debut as a woman. *The New York Times Magazine,* pp. 48–51.

Janes, L. M., & Olson, J. M. (2000). Jeer pressure: The behavioral effects of observing ridicule of others. *Personality and Social Psychology Bulletin, 26,* 474–485.

Janis, I. L. (1967). Effects of fear arousal on attitude change: Recent developments in theory and experimental research. In L. Berkowitz (Ed.), *Advances in experimental social psychology* (Vol. 3, pp. 166–224). New York: Academic Press.

Janis, I. L. (1982). *Groupthink: Psychological studies of policy decisions and fiascoes* (2nd ed.). Boston: Houghton Mifflin.

Jemmott, J. B., Croyle, R. T., & Ditto, P. H. (1988). Commonsense epidemiology: Self-based judgments from laypersons and physicians. *Health Psychology, 7,* 55–73.

Jemmott, J. B., & Locke, S. E. (1984). Psychosocial factors, immunologic mediation, and human susceptibility to infectious diseases: How much do we know? *Psychological Bulletin, 95,* 78–104.

Jenkins, M. J., & Dambrot, F. H. (1987). The attribution of date rape: Observer's attitudes and sexual experiences and the dating situation. *Journal of Applied Social Psychology, 17,* 875–895.

Jensen-Campbell, L. A., & Graziano, W. G. (2000). Beyond the school yard: Relationships as moderators of daily interpersonal conflicts. *Personality and Social Psychology Bulletin, 26,* 923–935.

Ji, J-l., Peng, K., & Nisbett, N. E. (2000). Culture, control, and perception of relationships in the environment. *Journal of Personality and Social Psychology, 78,* 943–955.

Johnson, C., & Haney, C. (1994). Felony voir dire: An exploratory study of its content and effect. *Law and Human Behavior, 18,* 487–506.

Johnson, D. W., & Johnson, R. T. (1992). Positive interdependence: Key to effective cooperation. In R. Hertz-Lazarowitz & N. Miller (Eds.), *Interaction in cooperative groups* (pp. 174–199). New York: Cambridge University Press.

Johnson, D. W., & Johnson, R. T. (2000). The three Cs of reducing prejudice and discrimination. In S. Oskamp (Ed.), *Reducing prejudice and discrimination.* (pp. 239–268). Mahwah, NJ: Erlbaum.

Johnson, J. G., Cohen, P., Smailes, E. M., Kasen, S., & Brook, J. S. (2002). Television viewing and aggressive behavior during adolescence and adulthood. *Science, 295,* 2468–2471.

Johnson, J. T., & Boyd, K. R. (1995). Dispositional traits versus the content of experience: Actor/observer differences in judgments of the "authentic self." *Personality and Social Psychology Bulletin, 21,* 375–383.

Johnson, M. K., Hashtroudi, S., & Lindsay, D. S. (1993). Source monitoring. *Psychological Bulletin, 114,* 3–28.

Johnson, M. P. (1999). Personal, moral, and structural commitment to relationships. In J. M. Adams & W. H. Jones (Eds.), *Handbook of interpersonal commitment and relationship stability* (pp. 73–87). New York: Kluwer Academic/Plenum.

Johnson, M. P., Caughlin, J. P., & Huston, T. L. (1999). The tripartite nature of marital commitment: Personal, moral, and structural reasons to stay married. *Journal of Marriage and Family, 61,* 160–177.

Johnson, R. D., & Downing, L. L. (1979). Deindividuation and valence of cues: Effects of prosocial and antisocial behavior. *Journal of Personality and Social Psychology, 37,* 1532–1538.

Johnson, T. E., & Rule, B. G. (1986). Mitigating circumstance information, censure, and aggression. *Journal of Personality and Social Psychology, 50,* 537–542.

Jonas, E., Schulz-Hardt, S., Dieter, F., & Thelen, N. (2001). Confirmation bias in sequential information search after preliminary decisions: An expansion of dissonance theoretical research on selective exposure to information. *Journal of Personality and Social Psychology, 80,* 557–571.

Jones, A. (1994, September/October). Where do we go from here? *Ms. Magazine, 5,* 38–43.

Jones, E. E. (1990). *Interpersonal perception.* New York: W. H. Freeman.

Jones, E. E., & Berglas, S. (1978). Control of attributions about the self through self-handicapping strategies: The appeal of alcohol and the role of underachievement. *Personality and Social Psychology Bulletin, 4,* 200–206.

Jones, E. E., & Davis, K. E. (1965). From acts to dispositions: The attribution process in person perception. In L. Berkowitz (Ed.), *Advances in experimental social psychology,* (Vol. 2, pp. 220–266). New York: Academic Press.

Jones, E. E., & Harris, V. A. (1967). The attribution of attitudes. *Journal of Experimental Social Psychology, 3,* 1–24.

Jones, E. E., & McGillis, D. (1976). Correspondence inferences and the attribution cube: A comparative reappraisal. In J. H. Harvey, W. J. Ickes, & R. F. Kidd (Eds.), *New directions in attribution research* (Vol. 1, pp. 389–420). Hillsdale, NJ: Erlbaum.

Jones, E. E., & Nisbett, R. E. (1972). The actor and observer: Divergent perceptions of causes of behavior. In E. E. Jones, D. E. Kanouse, H. H. Kelley, R. E. Nisbett, S. Valins, & B. Weiner (Eds.), *Attribution: Perceiving the causes of behavior* (pp. 79–94). Morristown, NJ: General Learning Press.

Jones, E. E., & Pittman, T. (1982). Toward a general theory of strategic self-presentation. In J. Suls (Ed.), *Psychological perspectives on the self* (Vol. 1, pp.231–262). Hillsdale, NJ: Erlbaum.

Jones, W. H., Moore, D. S., Schratter, A., & Negel, L. A. (2001). Interpersonal transgressions and betrayals. In R. M. Kowalski (Ed.), *Behaving badly* (pp. 233–256). Washington, DC: American Psychological Association.

Jose, P. E., & McCarthy, W. J. (1988). Perceived agentic and communal behavior in mixed-sex interactions. *Personality and Social Psychology Bulletin, 14,* 57–67.

Josephs, R. A., Bosson, J. K., & Jacobs, C. G. (2003). Self-esteem maintenance processes: Why low self-esteem may be resistant to change. *Personality and Social Psychology Bulletin, 29,* 920–933.

Judd, C. M., Blair, I. V., & Chapleau, K. M. (2004). Automatic stereotypes vs. automatic prejudice: Sorting out the possibilities in the Payne (2001) weapon paradigm. *Journal of Experimental Social Psychology, 40,* 75–81.

Judd, C. M., Drake, R. A., Downing, J. W., & Krosnick, J. A. (1991). Some dynamic properties of attitude structures: Context-induced response facilitation and polarization. *Journal of Personality and Social Psychology, 60,* 193–202.

Judd, C. M., & Park, B. (1988a). Definition and assessment of accuracy in social stereotypes. *Psychological Review, 100,* 109–128.

Judd, C. M., & Park, B. (1988b). Out-group homogeneity: Judgments of variability at the individual and group levels. *Journal of Personality and Social Psychology, 54,* 778–788.

Judd, C. M., & Park, B. (1993). Definition and assessment of accuracy in social stereotypes. *Psychological Review, 100,* 109–128.

Judd, C. M., Ryan, C. S., & Park, B. (1991). Accuracy in the judgment of in-group and out-group variability. *Journal of Personality and Social Psychology, 61,* 366–379.

Jussim, L., Soffin, S., Brown, R., Ley, J., & Kohlhepp, K. (1992). Understanding reactions to performance feedback by integrating ideas from symbolic interactionism and cognitive evaluation theory. *Journal of Personality and Social Psychology, 62,* 402–421.

Kagan, S. (1977). Social motives and behaviors of Mexican-American and Anglo-American children. In J. L. Martinez (Ed.), *Chicano psychology* (pp. 45–86). New York: Academic Press.

Kagan, S. (1984). Interpreting Chicano cooperativeness: Methodological and theoretical considerations. In J. L. Martinez & R. H. Mendoza (Eds.), *Chicano psychology* (2nd ed., pp. 289–333). New York: Academic Press.

Kagan, S., & Madsen, M. C. (1971). Cooperation and competition of Mexican, Mexican-American, and Anglo-American children of two ages under four instructional sets. *Developmental Psychology, 5,* 32–39.

Kahneman, D., & Miller, D. T. (1986). Norm theory: Comparing reality to its alternatives. *Psychological Review, 93,* 136–153.

Kahneman, D., & Tversky, A. (1982). The psychology of preferences. *Scientific American, 246,* 160–173.

Kaiser Foundation. (2001, November). *Inside-out: A report on the experiences of lesbians, gays and bisexuals in America and the public's view on issues and policies related to sexual orientation.* Menlo Park, CA: Author.

Kaiser, C. R., & Miller, C. T. (2001). Stop complaining! The social costs of making attributions to discrimination. *Personality and Social Psychology Bulletin, 27,* 254–263.

Kalichman, S. C., Benotsch, L., Austin, J., Luke, W., & Chauncey, C. (2003). Health-related Internet use, coping, social support, and health indicators in people living with HIV/AIDS. *Health Psychology, 22,* 111–116.

Kalick, S. M., & Hamilton, T. E. (1988). Closer look at a matching simulation: Reply to Aron. *Journal of Personality and Social Psychology, 54,* 447–451.

Kallgren, C. A., & Wood, W. (1986). Access to attitude-relevant information in memory as a determinant of attitude-behavior consistency. *Journal of Experimental Social Psychology, 22,* 328–338.

Kalven, H., Jr., & Zeisel, H. (1966). *The American jury.* Boston: Little, Brown.

Kanagawa, C., Cross, S. E., & Markus, H. R. (2001). "Who am I?" The cultural psychology of the conceptual self. *Personality and Social Psychology Bulletin, 27,* 90–103.

Kanazawa, S. (1992). Outcome or expectancy? Antecedent of spontaneous causal attribution. *Personality and Social Psychology Bulletin, 18,* 659–668.

Kanekar, S., Shaherwalla, A., Franco, B., Kunju, T., & Pinto, A. J. (1991). The acquaintance predicament of a rape victim. *Journal of Applied Social Psychology, 21,* 1524–1544.

Kang, S. M., Shaver, P. R., Sue, S., Min, K. H., & Jing, H. (2003). Culture-specific patterns in the prediction of life satisfaction: Roles of emotion, relationship quality, and self-esteem. *Personality and Social Psychology Bulletin, 29,* 1596–1608.

Kanin, E. J., Davidson, K. R., & Scheck, S. R. (1970). A research note on male-female differentials in the experience of heterosexual love. *Journal of Sex Research, 6,* 64–72.

Kanner, A. D., Coyne, J. C., Schaeffer, C., & Lazarus, R. S. (1981). Comparison of two modes of stress measurement: Daily hassles and uplifts versus major life events. *Journal of Behavioral Medicine, 4,* 1–25.

Kaplan, R. M. (2000). Two pathways to prevention. *American Psychologist, 55,* 382–396.

Kaplan, R. M., Anderson, J. P., & Wingard, D. L. (1991). Gender differences in health-related quality of life. Gender and health [Special Issue]. *Health Psychology, 10,* 86–93.

Kaplan, R. M., & Simon, H. J. (1990). Compliance in medical care: Reconsideration of self-predictions. *Annals of Behavioral Medicine, 12,* 66–71.

Karabenick, S. A., & Knapp, J. R. (1988). Effects of computer privacy on help-seeking. *Journal of Applied Social Psychology, 18,* 461–472.

Karau, S. J., & Williams, K. D. (1993). Social loafing: A meta-analytic review and theoretical integration. *Journal of Personality and Social Psychology, 65,* 681–706.

Karau, S. J., & Williams, K. D. (2001). Understanding individual motivation in groups: The collective effort model. In M. E. Turner (Ed.), *Groups at work: Theory and research* (pp. 113–141). Mahwah, NJ: Erlbaum.

Karney, B. R., & Bradbury, T. N. (2000). Attributions in marriage: State or trait? A growth curve analysis. *Journal of Personality and Social Psychology, 78,* 295–309.

Karney, B. R., & Coombs, R. H. (2000). Memory bias in long-term close relationships: Consistency or improvement? *Personality and Social Psychology Bulletin, 26,* 959–970.

Karpinski, A., & Hilton, J. L. (2001). Attitudes and the Implicit Association Test. *Journal of Personality and Social Psychology, 81,* 774–788.

Kashima, Y. (2000). Maintaining cultural stereotypes in the serial reproduction of narratives. *Personality and Social Psychology Bulletin, 26,* 594–604.

Kasser, T., & Ryan, R. M. (1996). Further examining the American dream: Differential correlates of intrinsic and extrinsic goals. *Personality and Social Psychology Bulletin, 22,* 280–287.

Kassin, S. M., & Kiechel, K. L. (1996). The social psychology of false confessions: Compliance, internalization, and confabulation. *Psychological Science, 7,* 125–128.

Kassin, S. M., & McNall, K. (1991). Police interrogations and confessions: Communicating promises and threats by pragmatic implication. *Law and Human Behavior, 15,* 233–251.

Kassin, S. M., & Neumann, K. (1997). On the power of confession evidence: An experimental test of the fundamental difference hypothesis. *Law and Human Behavior, 21,* 469–484.

Kassin, S. M., & Sommers, S. R. (1997). Inadmissible testimony, instructions to disregard, and the jury: Substantive and procedural considerations. *Law and Human Behavior, 23,* 1046–1054.

Kassin, S. M., & Wrightsman, L. S. (1985). Confession evidence. In S. M. Kassin & L. S. Wrightsman (Eds.), *The psychology of evidence and trial procedure* (pp. 67–94). Newbury Park, CA: Sage.

Katchadourian, L. K., Fincham, F., & Davila, J. (2004). The tendency to forgive in dating and married couples: The role of attachment and relationship satisfaction. *Personal Relationships, 11,* 373–393.

Katz, J., & Beach, S. R. H. (2000). Looking for love? Self-verification and self-enhancement effects on initial romantic attraction. *Personality and Social Psychology Bulletin, 26,* 1526–1539.

Kaufert, J. M., Rabkin, S. W., Syrotuik, J., Boyko, E., & Shane, F. (1986). Health beliefs as predictors of success of alternate modalities of smoking cessation: Results of a controlled trial. *Journal of Behavioral Medicine, 9,* 475–489.

Kaufman, M. R. (1970). Practicing good manners and compassion. *Medical Insight, 2,* 56–61.

Kawakami, K., & Dovidio, J. F. (2001). The reliability of implicit stereotyping. *Personality and Social Psychology Bulletin, 27,* 212–225.

Kawakami, K., Dovidio, J. F., Moll, J., Hermsen, S., & Russin, A. (2000). Just say no (to stereotyping): Effects of training in the negation of stereotypic associations on stereotype activation. *Journal of Personality and Social Psychology, 78,* 871–888.

Keating, C. F., Mazur, A., Segall, M. H., Cysneiros, P. G., DiVale, W. T., Kilbride, J. E., et al. (1981). Culture and the perception of social dominance from facial expression. *Journal of Personality and Social Psychology, 40,* 601–614.

Kelley, H. H. (1950). The warm-cold variable in first impressions of persons. *Journal of Personality,* 18, 431–439.

Kelley, H. H. (1967). Attribution theory in social psychology. In D. Levine (Ed.), *Nebraska symposium on motivation* (pp. 192–238). Lincoln: University of Nebraska Press.

Kelley, H. H. (1972). Attribution in social interaction. In E. E. Jones, D. E. Kanouse, H. H. Kelley, R. E. Nisbett, S. Valins, & B. Weiner (Eds.), *Attribution: Perceiving the causes of behavior* (pp. 1–26). Morristown, NJ: General Learning Press.

Kelley, H. H., Berscheid, E., Christensen, A., Harvey, J. H., Huston, T. L., Levinger, G., et al. (2002). *Close relationships.* Clinton Corners, NY: Percheron.

Kelley, H. H., & Thibaut, J. W. (1978). *Interpersonal relations: A theory of interdependence.* New York: Wiley-Interscience.

Kelly, J. R., & Karau, S. J. (1999). Group decision making: The effects of initial preferences and time pressure. *Personality and Social Psychology Bulletin, 25,* 1342–1354.

Kelman, H. C., & Hamilton, V. L. (1989). *Crimes of obedience: Toward a social psychology of authority and responsibility.* New Haven, CT: Yale University Press.

Kelman, H. C., & Hovland, C. I. (1953). "Reinstatement" of the communicator in delayed measurement of opinion change. *Journal of Abnormal and Social Psychology, 48,* 327–335.

Kendzierski, D., & Whitaker, D. J. (1997). The role of self-schema in linking intentions with behavior. *Personality and Social Psychology Bulletin, 23,* 139–147.

Kenny, D. A., & Acitelli, L. K. (2001). Accuracy and bias in perceptions of the partner in close relationships. *Journal of Personality and Social Psychology, 80,* 439–448.

Kenrick, D. T., Trost, M. R., & Sundie, J. M. (2004). Sex roles as adaptation: An evolutionary perspective on gender differences and similarities. In A. H. Eagly, A. E. Beall, & R. J. Sternberg (Eds.), *Psychology of gender* (2nd ed., pp. 65–91). New York: Guilford.

Kephart, W. (1967). Some correlates of romantic love. *Journal of Marriage and Family, 29,* 470–479.

Kernis, M. H., & Grannemann, B. D. (1990). Excuses in the making: A test and extension of Darley and Goethals' attributional model. *Journal of Experimental Social Psychology, 26,* 337–349.

Kernis, M. H., Paradise, A. W., Whitaker, D. J., Wheatman, S. R., & Goldman, B. N. (2000). Master of one's psychological domain? Not likely if one's self-esteem is unstable. *Personality and Social Psychology Bulletin, 26,* 1297–1305.

Kernis, M. H., & Wheeler, L. (1981). Beautiful friends and ugly strangers: Radiation and contrast effects in perception of same-sex pairs. *Personality and Social Psychology Bulletin, 7,* 617–620.

Kerr, N. L., & Park, E. S. (2001). Group performance in collaborative and social dilemma tasks. In M. A. Hogg & R. S. Tindale (Eds.), *Blackwell handbook of social psychology: Group processes* (pp. 107–138). Malden, MA: Blackwell.

Kerr, N. L., & Stanfel, J. A. (1993). Role schemata and member motivation in task groups. *Personality and Social Psychology Bulletin, 19,* 432–442.

Kertscher, T. (2003, September 12). Wrongly convicted man freed: Steven Avery tastes his first freedom in more than 17 years. *Milwaukee Journal Sentinel.* Retrieved August 16, 2004, from http://www.jsonline.com/news/state/sep03/169169.asp

Kertscher, T., & Garza, J. (2003, September 11). DNA clears prisoner 17 years into his term: Man was convicted of 1985 sex assault; now another inmate is implicated. *Milwaukee Journal Sentinel.* Retrieved August 16, 2004, from http://www.jsonline.com/news/racine/sep03/168842.asp

Keyes, C. L. M., Shmotkin, D., & Ryff, C. D. (2002). Optimizing well-being: The empirical encounter of two traditions. *Journal of Personality and Social Psychology, 82,* 1007–1022.

Kiecolt-Glaser, J. K., & Glaser, R. (1995). Psychoneuro immunology and health consequences: Data and shared mechanisms. *Psychosomatic Medicine, 57,* 269–274.

Kiecolt-Glaser, J. K., & Newton, T. L. (2001). Marriage and health: His and hers. *Psychological Bulletin, 127,* 472–503.

Kihlstrom, J. F. (2004). An unbalanced balancing act: Blocked, recovered, and false memories in the laboratory and clinic. *Clinical Psychology: Science and Practice, 11,* 34–41.

Killeya, L. A., & Johnson, B. T. (1998). Experimental induction of biased systematic processing: The directed thought technique. *Personality and Social Psychology Bulletin, 24,* 17–33.

Kilpatrick, D. G., Resick, P. A., & Veronen, L. J. (1981). Effects of a rape experience: A longitudinal study. *Journal of Social Issues, 37,* 105–122.

Kim, H., & Markus, H. R. (1999). Deviance or uniqueness, harmony or conformity? A cultural analysis. *Journal of Personality and Social Psychology, 77,* 785–800.

Kim, M. P., & Rosenberg, S. (1980). Comparison of two structural models of implicit personality theory. *Journal of Personality and Social Psychology, 38,* 375–389.

Kimball, M. M. (1986). Television and sex-role attitudes. In T. M. Williams (Ed.), *The impact of television: A natural experiment in three communities* (pp. 265–301). Orlando, FL: Academic Press.

Kinder, D. R., & Sanders, L. M. (1996). *Divided by color: Racial politics and democratic ideals.* Chicago: University of Chicago Press.

Kinder, D. R., & Sears, D. O. (1981). Prejudice and politics: Symbolic racism versus racial threats to the good life. *Journal of Personality and Social Psychology, 40,* 414–431.

King, C. E., & Christensen, A. (1983). The relationship events scale: A Guttman scale of progress in courtship. *Journal of Marriage and the Family, 45,* 671–678.

King, L. A., & Miner, K. N. (2000). Writing about the perceived benefits of traumatic events: Implications for physical health. *Personality and Social Psychology Bulletin, 26,* 220–230.

Kipnis, D. (1984). The use of power in organizations and in interpersonal settings. In S. Oskamp (Ed.), *Applied social psychology annual 5* (pp. 179–210). Beverly Hills, CA: Sage.

Kirscht, J. P., & Rosenstock, I. M. (1979). Patient's problems in following recommendations of health experts. In G. C. Stone, F. Cohen, & N. E. Adler (Eds.) *Health psychology: A handbook* (pp. 189–216). San Francisco: Jossey-Bass.

Kitayama, S. (1992). Some thoughts on the cognitive-psychodynamic self from a cultural perspective. *Psychological Inquiry, 3,* 41–44.

Kitayama, S., & Karasawa, M. (1997). Implicit self-esteem in Japan: Name letters and birthday numbers. *Personality and Social Psychology Bulletin, 23,* 736–742.

Kitayama, S., Markus, H. R., Matsumoto, H., & Norasakkunkit, V. (1997). Individual and collective processes in the construction of the self: Self-enhancement in the United States and self-criticism in Japan. *Journal of Personality and Social Psychology, 72,* 1245–1267.

Klar, Y., & Giladi, E. E. (1999). Are most people happier than their peers, or are they just happy? *Personality and Social Psychology Bulletin, 25,* 585–594.

Klauer, K. C., & Meiser, T. (2000). A source-monitoring analysis of illusory correlations. *Personality and Social Psychology Bulletin, 26,* 1074–1093.

Klein, K. J., & Hodges, S. D. (2001). Gender differences, motivation, and empathic accuracy: When it pays to understand. *Personality and Social Psychology Bulletin, 27,* 720–730.

Klonoff, E. A., & Landrine, H. (1992). Sex roles, occupational roles, and symptom-reporting: A test of competing hypotheses on sex differences. *Journal of Behavioral Medicine, 15,* 355–364.

Kluegel, J. R. (1990). Trends in whites' explanations of the black-white gap in socioeconomic status, 1977–1989. *American Sociological Review, 55,* 512–525.

Knight, G. P., Fabes, R. A., & Higgins, D. A. (1996). Concerns about drawing causal inferences from meta-analyses: An example in the study of gender differences in aggression. *Psychological Bulletin, 119,* 410–421.

Knight, G. P., Johnson, L. G., Carlo, G., & Eisenberg, N. (1994). A multiplicative model of the dispositional antecedents of a prosocial behavior. Predicting more of the people more of the time. *Journal of Personality and Social Psychology, 66,* 178–183.

Knight, G. P., & Chao, C. (1991). Cooperative, competitive, and individualistic social values among 8–12-year-old siblings, friends, and acquaintances. *Personality and Social Psychology Bulletin, 17,* 201–211.

Knight, G. P., & Kagan, S. (1977). Acculturation of prosocial and competitive behaviors among second- and third-generation Mexican-American children. *Journal of Cross-Cultural Psychology, 8,* 273–284.

Knowles, E. D., Morris, M. W., Chiu, C.-y., & Hong, Y.-y. (2001). Culture and the process of person perception: Evidence for automaticity among East Asians in correcting for situational influences on behavior. *Personality and Social Psychology Bulletin, 27,* 1344–1356.

Kobasa, S. C. (1979). Stressful life events, personality, and health: An inquiry into hardiness. *Journal of Personality and Social Psychology, 37,* 1–11.

Kohlberg, L. (1966). A cognitive-developmental analysis of children's sex-role concepts and attitudes. In E. E. Maccoby (Ed.), *The development of sex differences.* Stanford, CA: Stanford University Press.

Kohn, P. M., Lafreniere, K., & Gurevich, M. (1991). Hassles, health, and personality. *Journal of Personality and Social Psychology, 61,* 478–482.

Končni, V. J., & Ebbesen, E. B. (1976). Disinhibition versus the cathartic effect: Artifact and substance. *Journal of Personality and Social Psychology, 34,* 352–365.

Koole, S. L., Dijksterhuis, A., & van Knippenberg, A. (2001). What's in a name: Implicit self-esteem and the automatic self. *Journal of Personality and Social Psychology, 80,* 669–685.

Koole, S. L., Smeets, K., van Knippenberg, A., & Dijksterhuis, A. (1999). The cessation of rumination through self-affirmation. *Journal of Personality and Social Psychology, 77,* 111–125.

Koss, M. P. (1993). Rape: Scope, impact, interventions, and public policy responses. *American Psychologist, 48,* 1062–1069.

Koss, M. P. (2000). Blame, shame, and community: Justice responses to violence against women. *American Psychologist, 55,* 1332–1343.

Koss, M. P., Heise, L., & Russo, N. F. (1994). The global health burden of rape. *Psychology of Women Quarterly, 18,* 509–537.

Koss, M. P., & Oros, C. J. (1982). Sexual Experiences Survey: A research instrument investigating sexual aggression and victimization. *Journal of Consulting and Clinical Psychology, 50,* 455–457.

Kottler, J. A. (2000). *Doing good: Passion and commitment for helping others.* Philadelphia: Brunner-Routledge.

Kovera, M. B. (2002). The effects of general pretrial publicity on juror decisions: An examination of moderators and mediating mechanisms. *Law and Human Behavior, 26,* 43–72.

Kovera, M. B., & Borgida, E. (1997). Expert testimony in child sexual abuse trials: The admissibility of psychological science. *Applied Cognitive Psychology, 11,* 105–129.

Kovera, M. B., Gresham, A. W., Borgida, E., Gray, E., & Regan, P. C. (1997). Does expert testimony inform or influence jury decision making? A social-cognitive analysis. *Journal of Applied Psychology, 82,* 178–191.

Kovera, M. B., Levy, R. J., Borgida, E., & Penrod, S. D. (1994). Expert testimony in child sexual abuse cases: Effects of expert evidence type and cross-examination. *Law and Human Behavior, 18,* 653–674.

Kovera, M. B., & McAuliff, B. D. (2000). The effects of peer review and evidence quality on judge evaluations of psychological evidence: Are judges effective gatekeepers? *Journal of Applied Psychology, 85,* 574–586.

Kowalski, R. M., & Leary, M. R. (1990). Strategic self-presentation and the avoidance of aversive events: Antecedents and consequences of self-enhancement and self-depreciation. *Journal of Experimental Social Psychology, 26,* 322–336.

Krahe, B. (1991). Police officers' definitions of rape: A prototype study. *Journal of Community and Applied Social Psychology, 1,* 223–244.

Kramer, B. J., & Thompson, E. H. (Eds.) (2002). *Men as caregivers.* New York: Springer Publishing.

Kramer, T. H., Buckhout, R., & Eugenio, P. (1990). Weapon focus, arousal, and eyewitness memory: Attention must be paid. *Law and Human Behavior, 14,* 167–184.

Krantz, D. S., & Deckel, A. W. (1983). Coping with coronary heart disease and stroke. In T. G. Burish & L. A. Bradley (Eds.), *Coping with chronic disease: Research and applications.* New York: Academic Press.

Kraus, S. J. (1995). Attitudes and the prediction of behavior: A meta-analysis of the empirical literature. *Personality and Social Psychology Bulletin, 21,* 58–75.

Krauss, R. M., Geller, V., & Olson, C. (1976, September). *Modalities and cues in the detection of deception.* Paper presented at the annual meeting of the American Psychological Association, Washington, DC.

Kraut, R., & Kiesler, S. (2003). The social impact of Internet use. *Psychological Science Agenda,* American Psychological Association.

Kraut, R., Kiesler, S., Boneva, B., Cummings, J., Helgeson, V., & Crawford, A. (2002). Internet paradox revisited. *Journal of Social Issues, 58*(1), 49–74.

Kraut, R., Olson, J., Banaji, M., Bruckman, A., Cohen, J., & Couper, M. (2004). Psychological research online. *American Psychologist, 59,* 105–117.

Kraut, R. E. (1978). Verbal and nonverbal cues in the perception of lying. *Journal of Personality and Social Psychology, 36,* 380–391.

Kravitz, D. A., & Martin, B. (1986). Ringlemann rediscovered: The original article. *Journal of Personality and Social Psychology, 50,* 936–941.

Krosnick, J. A., Jussim, L. J., & Lynn, A. R. (1992). Subliminal conditioning of attitudes. *Personality and Social Psychology Bulletin, 18,* 152–162.

Kruegar, J. (1998). Enhancement bias in descriptions of self and others. *Personality and Social Psychology Bulletin, 24,* 505–516.

Krueger, J., & Dunning, D. (1999). Unskilled and unaware of it: How difficulties in recognizing one's own incompetence lead to inflated self-assessments. *Journal of Personality and Social Psychology, 77,* 1121–1134.

Krueger, J., & Rothbart, M. (1988). Use of categorical and individuating information in making inferences about personality. *Journal of Personality and Social Psychology, 55,* 187–195.

Krueger, J., & Zeiger, J. S. (1993). Social categorization and the truly false consensus effect. *Journal of Personality and Social Psychology, 65,* 670–680.

Kruglanski, A. W., Atash, M. N., DeGrada, E., Mannetti, L., Pierro, A., & Webster, D. M. (1997). Psychological theory versus psychometric nay-saying: Comment on Neuberg et al.'s (1997) critique of the Need for Closure Scale. *Journal of Personality and Social Psychology, 73,* 1005–1016.

Kruglanski, A. W., & Mackie, D. M. (1990). Majority and minority influence: A judgmental process integration. In W. Stroebe & M. Hewstone (Eds.), *European review of social psychology* (Vol. 1, pp. 229–262). Chichester, England: Wiley.

Kruglanski, A. W., Webster, D. M., & Klem, A. (1993). Motivated resistance and openness to persuasion in the presence or absence of prior information. *Journal of Personality and Social Psychology, 65,* 861–876.

Krysan, M. (1998). Privacy and the expression of white racial attitudes: A comparison across three contexts. *Public Opinion Quarterly, 62,* 506–544.

Kuhnen, U., Hannover, B., & Schubert, B. (2001). The semantic-procedural interface model of the self: The role of self-knowledge for context-dependent versus context-independent modes of thinking. *Journal of Personality and Social Psychology, 80,* 397–409.

Kulig, J. W. (2000). Effects of forced exposure to a hypothetical population on false consensus. *Personality and Social Psychology Bulletin, 26,* 629–636.

Kunda, Z. (1987). Motivated inference: Self-serving generation and evaluation of causal theories. *Journal of Personality and Social Psychology, 53,* 636–647.

Kunda, Z., & Sherman-Williams, B. (1993). Stereotypes and the construal of individuating information. *Personality and Social Psychology Bulletin, 19,* 90–99.

Kupersmidt, J. B., DeRosier, M. E., & Patterson, C. P. (1995). Similarity as the basis for children's friendships. *Journal of Social and Personal Relationships, 12,* 439–452.

Kurdek, L. A. (1993). The allocation of household labor in gay, lesbian, and heterosexually married couples. *Journal of Social Issues, 49,* 127–139.

Kurdek, L. A. (1998). Relationship outcomes and their predictors: Longitudinal evidence from heterosexual married, gay cohabiting, and lesbian cohabiting couples. *Journal of Marriage and Family, 60,* 553–568.

Kurdek, L. A. (2000). Attractions and constraints as determinants of relationship commitment: Longitudinal evidence from gay, lesbian, and heterosexual couples. *Personal Relationships, 7,* 245–262.

Kurdek, L. A. (in press). Are gay and lesbian cohabiting couples really different from heterosexual married couples? *Journal of Marriage and Family.*

Kurman, J. (2001). Self-enhancement: Is it restricted to individualistic cultures? *Personality and Social Psychology Bulletin, 27,* 1705–1716.

Kurman, J. (2003). The role of perceived specificity level of failure events in self-enhancement and in constructive self-criticism. *Personality and Social Psychology Bulletin, 29,* 285–294.

La Piere, R. T. (1934). Attitudes vs. actions. *Social Forces, 13,* 230–237.

Lacroix, J. M., Martin, B., Avendano, M., & Goldstein, R. (1991). Symptom schemata in chronic respiratory patients. *Health Psychology, 10,* 268–273.

LaFromboise, T., Coleman, H. L., & Gerton, J. (1993). Psychological impact of biculturalism: Evidence and theory. *Psychological Bulletin, 114,* 395–412.

Lagorce, A. (2004, April 7). The gay-marriage windfall. *Forbes Magazine.* Retrieved August 3, 2004 from Forbes.com

Lambert, A. J., & Raichle, K. (2000). The role of political ideology in mediating judgments of blame in rape victims and their assailants: A test of the just world, personal responsibility, and legitimization hypotheses. *Personality and Social Psychology Bulletin, 26,* 853–863.

Lambert, W. E., & Klineberg, O. (1967). *Children's views of foreign peoples.* New York: Appleton-Century-Crofts.

Landrine, H., & Klonoff, E. A. (1994). Cultural diversity in causal attributions for illness: The role of the supernatural. *Journal of Behavioral Medicine, 17,* 181–193.

Laner, M. R., & Ventrone, N. A. (1998). Egalitarian dates/traditionalist dates. *Journal of Family Issues, 19,* 468–477.

Langer, E. J., Blank, A., & Chanowitz, B. (1978). The mindlessness of ostensibly thoughtful action. *Journal of Personality and Social Psychology, 36,* 635–642.

Langlois, J. H., Kalakanis, L., Rubenstein, A. J., Larson, A., Hallam, M., & Smoot, M. (2000). Maxims or myths of beauty? A meta-analytic and theoretical review. *Psychological Bulletin, 126,* 390–423.

Laplace, A. C., Chermack, S. T., & Taylor, S. P. (1994). Effects of alcohol and drinking experience on human physical aggression. *Personality and Social Psychology Bulletin, 20,* 439–444.

Larson, J. R., Christensen, C., Franz, T. M., & Abbott, A. S. (1998). Diagnosing groups: The pooling, management, and impact of shared and unshared case information in team-based medical decision making. *Journal of Personality and Social Psychology, 75,* 93–108.

Larson, R., Csikszentmihalyi, M., & Graef, R. (1982). Time alone in daily experience: Loneliness or renewal? In L. A. Peplau & D. Perlman (Eds.), *Loneliness: A sourcebook of current theory, research and therapy,* (pp. 40–53). New York: Wiley-Interscience.

Lassiter, G. D., Geers, A. L., & Apple, K. J. (2002). Communication set and the perception of ongoing behavior. *Personality and Social Psychology Bulletin, 28,* 158–171.

Latane, B., (1981). The psychology of social impact. *American Psychologist, 36,* 343–356.

Latané, B., & Darley, J. M. (1970). *The unresponsive bystander: Why doesn't he help?* New York: Appleton-Century-Crofts.

Latané, B., Liu, J. H., Nowak, A., Bonevento, M., & Zheng, L. (1995). Distance matters: Physical space and social impact. *Personality and Social Psychology Bulletin, 21,* 795–805.

Latané, B., Williams, K., & Harkins, S. (1979). Many hands make light the work: The causes and consequences of social loafing. Journal of Personality and Social Psychology, 37, 822–832.

Lau, R. R., Kane, R., Berry, S., Ware, J. E., & Roy, R. (1980). Channeling Health: A review of the evaluation of televised health campaigns. *Health Education Quarterly, 7,* 59–89.

Laughlin, P. R., & Adamopoulos, J. (1980). Social combination processes and individual learning for six-person cooperative groups on an intellective task. *Journal of Personality and Social Psychology, 38,* 941–947.

Laurenceau, J-P., Barrett, L. F., & Pietromonaco, P. R. (1998). Intimacy as an interpersonal process: The importance of self-disclosure, partner disclosure, and perceived partner responsiveness in interpersonal exchanges. *Journal of Personality and Social Psychology, 74,* 1238–1251.

Lavine, H., Huff, J. W., Wagner, S. H., & Sweeney, D. (1998). The moderating influence of attitude strength on the susceptibility to context effects in attitude surveys. *Journal of Personality and Social Psychology 75,* 359–373.

Lazarus, R. S., & Folkman, S. (1984). *Stress, appraisal and coping.* New York: Springer.

Lazarus, R. S., & Launier, R. (1978). Stress related transactions between persons and environment. In L. A. Pervin & M. Lewis (Eds.), *Perspective in interactional psychology.* New York: Wiley.

Le, B., & Agnew, C. R. (2003). Commitment and its theorized determinants: A meta-analysis of the investment model. *Personal Relationships, 10,* 37–57.

Le Bon, G. (1896). *The crowd: A study of the popular mind.* London: Ernest Benn.

Leary, M. R., Cottrell, C. A., & Phillips, M. (2001). Deconfounding the effects of dominance and social acceptance on self-esteem. *Journal of Personality and Social Psychology, 81,* 898–909.

Leary, M. R., Gallagher, B., Fors, E., Buttermore, N., Baldwin, E., & Kennedy, K., et al. (2003). The invalidity of disclaimers about the effects of social feedback on self-esteem. *Personality and Social Psychology Bulletin, 29,* 623–636.

Leary, M. R., Haupt, A. L., Strausser, K. S., & Chokel, J. T. (1998). Calibrating the sociometer: The relationship between interpersonal appraisals and the state self-esteem. *Journal of Personality and Social Psychology, 74,* 1290–1299.

Leary, M. R., & Jones, J. L. (1993). The social psychology of tanning and sunscreen use: Self-presentational motives as a predictor of health risk. *Journal of Applied Social Psychology, 23,* 1390–1406.

Leary, M. R., Rogers, P. A., Canfield, R. W., & Coe, C. (1986). Boredom in interpersonal encounters: Antecedents and social implications. *Journal of Personality and Social Psychology, 51,* 968–975.

Leary, M. R., & Shepperd, J. A. (1986). Behavioral self-handicaps versus self-reported handicaps: A conceptual note. *Journal of Personality and Social Psychology, 51,* 1265–1268.

Leary, M. R., Tambor, E. S., Terdal, S. K., & Downs, D. L. (1995). Self-esteem as an interpersonal monitor: The sociometer hypothesis. *Journal of Personality and Social Psychology, 68,* 518–530.

LeBlanc, M. M., & Barling, J. (2004). Workplace aggression. *Current Directions in Psychological Science, 13,* 9–12.

Lee, A. Y., Aaker, J. L., & Gardner, W. L. (2000). The pleasures and pains of distinct self-construals: The role of interdependence in regulatory focus. *Journal of Personality and Social Psychology, 78,* 1122–1134.

Lee, H.-C.-B. (1991). The attitudes toward rape victims scale: Reliability and validity in a Chinese context. *Sex Roles, 24,* 599–603.

Lee, J. (2004, February 3). Hey Friendster, got a Match? *CNN/Money.* Retrieved August 20, 2004, from http://money.cnn.com/2004/02/02/technology/valentines_friendster.

Lee, J. A. (1988). Love-styles. In R. J. Sternberg & M. L. Barnes (Eds.), *The psychology of love* (pp. 38–67). New Haven, CT: Yale University Press.

Lee, J. (1973). *The colors of love: An exploration of the ways of loving.* Ontario, Canada: New Press.

Leippe, M. R., & Eisenstadt, D. (1994). Generalization of dissonance reduction: Decreasing prejudice through induced compliance. *Journal of Personality and Social Psychology, 67,* 395–413.

Leippe, M. R., & Elkin, R. A. (1987). When motives clash: Issue involvement and response involvement in determinants of persuasion. *Journal of Personality and Social Psychology, 52,* 269–278.

Lenton, A. P., Blair, I. V., & Hastie, R. (2001). Illusions of gender: Stereotypes evoke false memories. *Journal of Experimental Social Psychology, 37,* 3–14.

Leonard, K. E. (1989). The impact of explicit aggressive and implicit nonaggressive cues on aggression in intoxicated and sober males. *Personality and Social Psychology Bulletin, 15,* 390–400.

Lepore, S. J. (1995). Cynicism, social support, and cardiovascular reactivity. *Health Psychology, 14,* 210–216.

Lepore, S. J. (1997). Expressive writing moderates the relation between intrusive thoughts and depressive symptoms. *Journal of Personality and Social Psychology, 73,* 1030–1037.

Lepore, S. J., Ragan, J. D., & Jones, S. (2000). Talking facilitates cognitive-emotional processes of adaptation to an acute stressor. *Journal of Personality and Social Psychology, 78,* 499–508.

Lepowsky, M. (1994). Women, men, and aggression in an egalitarian society. *Sex Roles, 30,* 199–212.

Lerner, J. S., Goldberg, J. H., & Tetlock, P. E. (1998). Sober second thought: The effects of accountability, anger, and authoritarianism on attribution of responsibility. *Personality and Social Psychology Bulletin, 24,* 563–574.

Lerner, J. S., & Keltner, D. (2001). Fear, anger, and risk. *Journal of Personality and Social Psychology, 81,* 146–159.

Lerner, J. S., & Tetlock, P. E. (1999). Accounting for the effects of accountability. *Psychological Bulletin, 125,* 255–256.

Leventhal, H. (1970). Findings and theory in the study of fear communications. In L. Berkowitz (Ed.), *Advances in experimental social psychology,* (Vol. 5, pp. 120–186). New York: Academic Press.

Leventhal, H., & Nerenz, D. R. (1983). A model for stress research and some implications for the control of stress disorders. In D. Meichenbaum, & M. Jaremko (Eds.), *Stress reduction and management: A cognitive behavioral approach* (pp. 5–38). New York: Plenum Press.

Leventhal, H., Nerenz, D., & Strauss, A. (1980). Self-regulation and the mechanisms for symptom appraisal. In D. Mechanic (Ed.), *Psychological epidemiology* (pp. 76–82). New York: Watson.

Levesque, C., & Pelletier, L. G. (2003). On the investigation of primed and chronic autonomous and heteronomous motivational orientations. *Personality and Social Psychology Bulletin, 29,* 1570–1584.

Levesque, M. J., & Kenny, D. A. (1993). Accuracy of behavioral predictions at zero acquaintance: A social relations analysis. *Journal of Personality and Social Psychology, 65,* 1178–1187.

Levett, A., & Kuhn, L. (1991). Attitudes towards rape and rapists: A White, English-speaking South African student sample. *South African Journal of Psychology, 21,* 32–37.

Levine, J. M., & Moreland, R. L. (1998). Small groups. In D. T. Gilbert, S. T. Fiske, & G. Lindzey (Eds.), *Handbook of social psychology* (Vol. 2, pp. 415–469). Boston: McGraw-Hill.

Levine, R., Sato, S., Hashimoto, T., & Verma, J. (1995). Love and marriage in eleven cultures. *Journal of Cross-Cultural Psychology, 26,* 554–571.

LeVine, R. A., & Campbell, D. T. (1972). *Ethnocentrism: Theories of Conflict, ethnic attitudes, and group behavior.* New York: Wiley.

Levine, R. V. (1988). The pace of life across cultures. In J. E. McGrath (Ed.), *The social psychology of time: New perspectives* (pp. 39–60). Newbury Park, CA: Sage.

Levine, R. V. (2003). The kindness of strangers. *American Scientist, 91,* 226–233.

Levine, R. V., Martinez, T. S., Brase, G., & Sorenson, K. (1994). Helping in 36 U.S. cities. *Journal of Personality and Social Psychology, 67,* 69–82.

Levinson, R. M. (1975). Sex discrimination and employment practices: An experiment with unconventional job inquiries. *Social Problems, 22,* 533–543.

Levy, B., & Langer, E. (1994). Aging free from negative stereotypes: Successful memory in China and among the American deaf. *Journal of Personality and Social Psychology, 66,* 989–997.

Lewin-Epstein, N. (1991). Determinants of regular source of health care in black, Mexican, Puerto Rican, and non-Hispanic white populations. *Medical Care, 29,* 543–557.

Li, N. P., Bailey, J. M., Kenrick, D. T., & Linsenmeier, J. A. W. (2002). The necessities and luxuries of mate preferences: Testing the tradeoffs. *Journal of Personality and Social Psychology, 82,* 947–955.

Libby, L. K., & Eibach, R. P. (2002). Looking back in time: Self-concept change affects visual perspective in autobiographical memory. *Journal of Personality and Social Psychology, 82,* 167–179.

Liberman, A., & Chaiken, S. (1991). Value conflict and thought-induced attitude change. *Journal of Personality and Social Psychology, 32,* 346–360.

Liberman, N., & Förster, J. (2000). Expression after suppression: A motivational explanation of post-suppressional rebound. *Journal of Personality and Social Psychology, 79,* 190–203.

Lieberman, J. D., & Arndt, J. (2000). Understanding the limits of limiting instructions: Social psychological explanations for the failures of instructions to disregard pretrial publicity and other inadmissible evidence. *Psychology, Public Policy, and Law, 6,* 677–711.

Lieberman, J. D., & Sales, B. D. (1997). What social science teaches us about the jury instruction process. *Psychology, Public Policy, and Law, 3,* 589–644.

Lieberson, S. (2000). *A matter of taste: How names, fashions and culture change.* New Haven, CT: Yale University Press.

Lierman, L. M., Young, H. M., Kasprzyk, D., & Benoliel, J. Q. (1990). Predicting breast self-examination using the theory of reasoned action. *Nursing Research, 39,* 97–101.

Lindsay, D. S., & Johnson, M. K. (1989). The eyewitness suggestibility effect and memory for source. *Memory and Cognition, 17,* 349–358.

Lindsay, R. C. L., Wells, G. L., & Rumpel, C. M. (1981). Can people detect eyewitness identification accuracy within and between situations? *Journal of Applied Psychology, 66,* 79–89.

Linville, P. W. (1982). The complexity-extremity effect and age-based stereotyping. *Journal of Personality and Social Psychology, 42,* 193–211.

Linville, P. W. (1985). Self-complexity and affective extremity: Don't put all of your eggs in one cognitive basket. Depression [Special issue]. *Social Cognition, 3,* 94–120.

Linville, P. W., Fisher, G. W., & Salovey, P. (1989). Perceived distributions of the characteristics of in-groups and out-group members: Empirical evidence and a computer simulation. *Journal of Personality and Social Psychology, 52,* 166–188.

Linville, P. W., & Jones, E. E. (1980). Polarized appraisals of outgroup members. *Journal of Personality and Social Psychology, 38,* 689–703.

Linville, P. W., Salovey, P., & Fisher, G. W. (1986). Stereotyping and perceived distributions of social characteristics: An application to ingroup-outgroup perception. In J. F. Dovidio & S. L. Gaertner (Eds.), *Prejudice, discrimination, and racism* (pp. 165–208). New York: Academic Press.

Linz, D. G., Donnerstein, E., & Penrod, S. (1984). The effects of multiple exposures to filmed violence against women. *Journal of Communication, 34,* 130–147.

Linz, D. G., Donnerstein, E., & Penrod, S. (1988). Effects of long-term exposure to violent and sexually degrading depictions of women. *Journal of Personality and Social Psychology, 55,* 758–768.

Linz, D., Wilson, B. J., & Donnerstein, E. (1992). Sexual violence in the mass media: Legal solutions, warnings, and mitigation through education. *Journal of Social Issues, 48,* 145–171.

Lippa, R. A. (2002). *Gender, nature, and nurture.* Mahwah, NJ: Erlbaum.

Lips, H. M. (2003). The gender pay gap. *Analyses of Social Issues and Public Policy, 3,* 87–109.

Lisak, D., & Roth, S. (1988). Motivational factors in nonincarcerated sexually aggressive men. *Journal of Personality and Social Psychology, 55,* 795–802.

Livingston, R. W. (2001). What you see is what you get: Systematic variability in perceptual-based social judgment. *Personality and Social Psychology Bulletin, 27,* 1086–1096.

Livingston R. W., & Brewer, M. B. (2003). What are we really priming? Cue-based versus category-based processing of facial stimuli. *Journal of Personality and Social Psychology, 82,* 5–18.

Locke, K. D. (2003). Status and solidarity in social comparison: Agentic and communal values and vertical and horizontal directions. *Journal of Personality and Social Psychology, 84,* 619–631.

Locke, K. D., & Nekich, J. C. (2000). Agency and communion in naturalistic social comparison. *Personality and Social Psychology Bulletin, 26,* 864–874.

Lockwood, P. (2002). Could it happen to you? Predicting the impact of downward comparisons on the self. *Journal of Personality and Social Psychology, 82,* 343–358.

Lockwood, P., & Kunda, Z. (1997). Superstars and me: Predicting the impact of role models on the self. *Journal of Personality and Social Psychology, 73,* 91–103.

Lockwood, P., & Kunda, Z. (1999). Increasing the salience of one's best selves can undermine inspiration by outstanding role models. *Journal of Personality and Social Psychology, 76,* 214–228.

Loftus, E. F. (1975). Leading questions and the eyewitness report. *Cognitive Psychology, 7,* 560–572.

Loftus, E. F. (1979). *Eyewitness testimony.* Cambridge MA: Harvard University Press.

Loftus, E. F. (1994). The reality of repressed memories. *American Psychologist, 48,* 518–537.

Loftus, E. F., & Palmer, J. C. (1974). Reconstruction of automobile destruction: An example of the interaction between language and memory. *Journal of Verbal Learning and Verbal Behavior, 13,* 585–589.

London, K., & Nunez, N. (2000). The effect of jury deliberations on jurors' propensity to disregard inadmissible evidence. *Journal of Applied Psychology, 85,* 932–939.

Lonsway, K. A., & Fitzgerald, L. F. (1995). Attitudinal antecedents of rape myth acceptance: A theoretical and empirical reexamination. *Journal of Personality and Social Psychology, 68,* 704–711.

Lord, C. G., Lepper, M. R., & Mackie, D. (1984). Attitude prototypes as determinants of attitude-behavior consistency. *Journal of Personality and Social Psychology, 46,* 1254–1266.

Los Angeles Times, (2004, July 10). Highlights of report by Senate panel.

Lowery, B. S., Hardin, C. D., & Sinclair, S. (2001). Social influence effects on automatic racial prejudice. *Journal of Personality and Social Psychology, 81,* 842–855.

Luhtanen, R., & Crocker, J. (1992). A collective self-esteem scale: Self-evaluation of one's social identity. *Personality and Social Psychology Bulletin, 18,* 302–318.

Lundgren, S. R., & Prislin, R. (1998). Motivated cognitive processing and attitude change. *Personality and Social Psychology Bulletin, 24,* 715–726.

Lydon, J. E., Fitzsimons, G. M., & Naidoo, L. (2003). Devaluation versus enhancement of attractive alternatives. *Personality and Social Psychology Bulletin, 29,* 349–359.

Lydon, J. E., Jamieson, D. W., & Zanna, M. P. (1988). Interpersonal similarity and the social and intellectual dimensions of first impressions. *Social Cognition, 6,* 269–286.

Lyons, A., & Kasima, Y. (2003). How are stereotypes maintained through communication? The influence of stereotype sharedness. *Journal of Personality and Social Psychology, 85,* 989–1005.

Lyubomirsky, S., Caldwell, N. D., & Nolen-Hoeksema, S. (1998). Effects of ruminative and distracting responses to depressed mood on retrieval of autobiographical memories. *Journal of Personality and Social Psychology, 75,* 166–177.

Maass, A., & Clark, R. D. (1984). Hidden impact of minorities: Fifteen years of minority influence research. *Psychological Bulletin, 95,* 428–450.

Maass, A., Clark, R. K., & Haberkorn, G. (1982). The effects of differential ascribed category membership and norms on minority influence. *European Journal of Social Psychology, 12,* 89–104.

Maccoby, E. E. (1990a). Gender and relationships: A developmental account. *American Psychologist, 45,* 513–520.

Maccoby, E. E. (1990b, July). An interview with Eleanor Maccoby. *American Psychological Society Observer,* pp. 4–6.

Maccoby, E. E. (2002). Gender and group process: A developmental perspective. *Current Directions in Psychological Science, 11,* 54–58.

MacCoun, R. J., & Kerr, N. L. (1988). Asymmetric influences in mock deliberation: Jurors' bias for leniency. *Journal of Personality and Social Psychology, 54,* 21–33.

MacDonald, T. K., & Ross, M. (1999). Assessing the accuracy of predictions about dating relationships: How and why do lovers' predictions differ from those made by observers? *Personality and Social Psychology Bulletin, 11,* 1417–1429.

MacDonald, T. K., Zanna, M. P., & Fong, G. T. (1996). Why common sense goes out the window: Effects of alcohol on intentions to use condoms. *Personality and Social Psychology Bulletin, 22,* 763–775.

Mace, D., & Mace, V. (1960). *Marriage east and west.* New York: Doubleday.

Mack, D. E. (1971). Where the black matriarchy theorists went wrong. *Psychology Today, 4,* 86–87.

Mackey, R. A., Diemer, M. A., & O'Brien, B. A. (2000). Psychological intimacy in the lasting relationships of heterosexual and same-gender couples. *Sex Roles, 43,* 201–227.

Mackie, D. M. (1986). Social identification effects in group polarization. *Journal of Personality and Social Psychology, 50,* 720–728.

Mackie, D. M. (1987). Systematic and nonsystematic processing of majority and minority persuasive communications. *Journal of Personality and Social Psychology, 53,* 41–52.

Mackie, D. M., & Hunter, S. B. (1999). Majority and minority influence: The interactions of social identity and social cognition mediators. In D. Abrams & M. A. Hogg (Eds.), *Social identity and social cognition,* (pp. 332–353). Oxford, England: Blackwell Publishers.

Mackie, D. M., Worth, L. I., & Asuncion, A. G. (1990). Processing of persuasive in-group messages. *Journal of Personality and Social Psychology, 58,* 812–822.

MacLeod, C., & Campbell, L. (1992). Memory accessibility and probability judgment: An experimental evaluation of the availability heuristic. *Journal of Personality and Social Psychology, 63,* 890–902.

Macrae, C. N., Bodenhausen, G. V., & Milne, A. B. (1998). Saying no to unwanted thoughts: Self-focus and the regulation of mental life. *Journal of Personality and Social Psychology, 74,* 578–589.

Macrae, C. N., Bodenhausen, G. V., Milne, A. B., & Calvini, G. (1999). Seeing more than we can know: Visual attention and category activation. *Journal of Experimental Social Psychology, 35,* 590–602.

Macrae, C. N., Bodenhausen, G. V., Schloerscheidt, A. M., & Milne, A. B. (1999). Tales of the unexpected: Executive function and person perception. *Journal of Personality & Social Psychology, 76,* 200–213.

Macrae, C. N., Milne, A. B., & Bodenhausen, G. V. (1994). Stereotypes as energy-saving devices: A peek inside the cognitive toolbox. *Journal of Personality and Social Psychology, 66,* 37–47.

Macrae, C. N., Stangor, C., & Milne, A. B. (1994). Activating social stereotypes: A functional analysis. *Journal of Experimental Social Psychology, 30,* 370–389.

Madon, S., Smith, A., Jussim, L., Russell, D. W., Eccles, J., Palumbo, P., et al. (2001). Am I as you see me or do you see me as I am? Self-fulfilling prophecies and self-verification. *Personality and Social Psychology Bulletin, 27,* 1214–1224.

Madsen, M. C. (1971). Developmental and cross-cultural differences in the cooperative and competitive behavior of young children. *Journal of Cross-Cultural Psychology, 2,* 365–371.

Maheswaran, D., & Chaiken, S. (1991). Promoting systematic processing in low-motivation settings: Effect of incongruent information on processing and judgment. *Journal of Personality and Social Psychology, 61,* 13–25.

Mahler, H. I. M., & Kulik, J. A. (1998). Effects of preparatory videotapes on self-efficacy beliefs and recovery from coronary bypass surgery. *Annals of Behavioral Medicine, 20,* 39–46.

Maio, G. R., & Olson, J. M. (1998). Values as truisms: Evidence and implications. *Journal of Personality and Social Psychology, 74,* 294–311.

Major, B. (1989). Gender differences in comparisons and entitlement: Implications for comparable worth. *Journal of Social Issues, 45,* 99–115.

Major, B. (1993). Gender, entitlement, and the distribution of family labor. *Journal of Social Issues, 49*(3), 141–160.

Major, B., McFarlin, D. B., & Gagnon, D. (1984). Overworked and underpaid: On the nature of gender differences in personal entitlement. *Journal of Personality and Social Psychology, 47,* 1399–1412.

Major, B., Richards, C., Cooper, M. L., Cozzarelli, C., & Zubeck, J. (1998). Personal resilience, cognitive appraisals, and coping: An integrative model of adjustment to abortion. *Journal of Personality and Social Psychology, 74,* 735–752.

Major, B., Spencer, S., Schmader, T., Wolfe, C., & Crocker, J. (1998). Coping with negative stereotypes about intellectual performance: The role of psychological disengagement. *Personality and Social Psychology Bulletin, 24,* 34–50.

Major, B., Zubek, J., Cooper, M. L., Cozzarelli, C., & Richards, C. (1997). Mixed messages: Implications of social conflict and social support within close relationships for adjustment to a stressful life event. *Journal of Personality and Social Psychology, 72,* 1349–1363.

Malamuth, N. M. (1981). Rape proclivity among males. *Journal of Social Issues, 37,* 138–156.

Malamuth, N. M. (1993). Pornography's impact on male adolescents. *Adolescent Medicine: State of the Art Reviews, 4,* 563–576.

Malamuth, N. M., & Briere, J. (1986). Sexual violence in the media: Indirect effects on aggression against women. *Journal of Social Issues, 42,* 75–92.

Malamuth, N. M., & Ceniti, J. (1986). Repeated exposure to violent and nonviolent pornography: Likelihood of raping ratings and laboratory aggression against women. *Aggressive Behavior, 12,* 129–137.

Malamuth, N. M., Check, J. V., & Briere, J. (1986). Sexual arousal in response to aggression: Ideological, aggressive, and sexual correlates. *Journal of Personality and Social Psychology, 50,* 330–340.

Malamuth, N. M., Linz, D., Heavey, C. L., Barnes, G., & Acker, M. (1995). Using the confluence model of sexual aggression to predict men's conflict with women: A 10-year follow-up study. *Journal of Personality and Social Psychology, 69,* 353–369.

Malamuth, N. M., Sockloskie, R. J., Koss, M. P., & Tanaka, J. S. (1991). Characteristics of aggressors against women: Testing a model using a national sample of college students. *Journal of Consulting and Clinical Psychology, 59,* 670–681.

Malatesta, C. Z., & Haviland, J. M. (1982). Learning display rules: The socialization of emotion expression in infancy. *Child Development, 53,* 991–1003.

Malle, B. F., & Horowitz, L. M. (1995). The puzzle of negative self-views: An exploration using the schema concept. *Journal of Personality and Social Psychology, 68,* 470–484.

Malle, B. F., Knobe, J., O'Laughlin, M., Pearce, G. E., & Nelson, S. E. (2000). Conceptual structure and social functions of behavior explanations: Beyond person–situation attributions. *Journal of Personality and Social Psychology, 79,* 309–326.

Malle, B. F., & Pearce, G. E. (2001). Attention to behavioral events during interaction: Two actor-observer gaps and three attempts to close them. *Journal of Personality and Social Psychology, 81,* 278–294.

Malloy, T. E., Agatstein, F., Yarlas, A., & Albright, L. (1997). Effects of communication, information overlap, and behavioral consistency on consensus in social perception. *Journal of Personality and Social Psychology, 73,* 270–280.

Malloy, T. E., & Albright, L. (1990). Interpersonal perception in a social contest. *Journal of Personality and Social Psychology, 58,* 419–428.

Malloy, T. E., Albright, L., Diaz-Loving, R., Dong Q., & Le, Y. T. (2004). Agreement in personality judgments within and between nonoverlapping social groups in collectivist cultures. *Personality and Social Psychology Bulletin, 30,* 106–117.

Mandel, D. R., & Lehman, D. R. (1996). Counterfactual thinking and ascriptions of cause and preventability. *Journal of Personality and Social Psychology, 71,* 450–463.

Maner, J. K., Kenrick, D. T., Becker, D. V., Delton, A. W., Hofer, B., Wilbur, C. J., et al. (2003). Sexually selective cognition: Beauty captures the mind of the beholder. *Journal of Personality and Social Psychology, 85,* 1107–1120.

Maner, J. K., Luce, C. L., Neuberg, S. L., Cialdini, R. B., Brown, S., & Sagarin, B. J. (2002). The effects of perspective taking on motivations for helping: Still no evidence for altruism. *Personality and Social Psychology Bulletin, 28,* 1601–1610.

Manian, N., Strauman, T. J., & Denney, N. (1998). Temperament, recalled parenting styles, and self-regulation: Retrospective tests of the developmental postulates of self-discrepancy theory. *Journal of Personality and Social Psychology, 75,* 1321–1332.

Manis, M., Shedler, J., Jonides, J., & Nelson, T. E. (1993). Availability heuristic in judgments of set size and frequency of occurrence. *Journal of Personality and Social Psychology, 65,* 448–457.

Mann, S., Vrij, A., & Bull, R. (2004). Detecting true lies: Police officers' ability to detect suspects' lies. *Journal of Applied Psychology, 89,* 137–149.

Mann, T., Sherman, D., & Undegraff, J. (2004). Dispositional motivations and message framing: A test of the congruency hypothesis in college students. *Health Psychology, 23,* 330–334.

Manstead, A. S. R., Proffitt, C., & Smart, J. L. (1983). Predicting and understanding mothers' infant-feeding intentions and behavior: Testing the theory of reasoned action. *Journal of Personality and Social Psychology, 44,* 657–671.

Marcus, D. K., & Miller, R. S. (2003). Sex differences in judgments of physical attractiveness. *Personality and Social Psychology Bulletin, 29,* 325–335.

Marcus-Newhall, A., Pedersen, W. C., Carlson, M., & Miller, N. (2000). Displaced aggression is alive and well: A meta-analytic review. *Journal of Personality and Social Psychology, 78,* 670–689.

Marín, B. V., & Marín, G. (1990). Effects of acculturation on knowledge of AIDS and HIV among Hispanics. *Hispanics Journal of Behavioral Sciences, 12,* 110–121.

Marín, B. V., Marín, G., Otero-Sabogal, R., Sabogal, F., & Perez-Stable, E. J. (1990). Cultural differences in attitudes toward smoking: Developing messages using the Theory of Reasoned Action. *Journal of Applied Social Psychology, 20,* 478–493.

Marín, G., Marín, B., Otero-Sabogal, R., Sabogal, F., & Perez-Stable, E. J. (1989). The role of acculturation on the attitudes, norms, and expectancies of Hispanic smokers. *Journal of Cross-Cultural Psychology, 20,* 399–415.

Marín, G., & Triandis, H. C. (1985). Allocentrism as an important characteristic of the behavior of Latin Americans and Hispanics. In R. Diaz-Guerrero (Ed.), *Cross-cultural and national studies in social psychology* (pp. 69–80). Amsterdam: North-Holland.

Markman, K. D., & Tetlock, P. E. (2000). Accountability and close-call counterfactuals: The loser who nearly won and the winner who nearly lost. *Personality and Social Psychology Bulletin, 26,* 1213–1224.

Marks, G. (1984). Thinking one's abilities are unique and one's opinions are common. *Personality and Social Psychology Bulletin, 10,* 203–208.

Marks, G., & Miller, N. (1987). Ten years of research on the false-consensus effect: An empirical and theoretical review. *Psychological Bulletin, 102,* 72–90.

Markus, H., & Kitayama, S. (1991). Culture and the self: Implications for cognition, emotion, and motivation. *Psychological Review, 98,* 224–253.

Markus, H., & Nurius, P. (1986). Possible selves. *American Psychologist, 41,* 954–969.

Markus, H., & Ruvolo, A. (1989). Possible selves: Personalized representations of goals. In L. A. Pervin (Ed.), *Goal concepts in personality and social psychology* (pp. 211–241). Hillsdale, NJ: Erlbaum.

Markus, H., Smith, J., & Moreland, R. L. (1985). Role of the self-concept in the perception of others. *Journal of Personality and Social Psychology, 49,* 1494–1512.

Markus, H. R. (2004). A social psychological model of behavior. *Dialogue, 19*(Suppl. 1), 1–4.

Markus, H. R., & Kitayama, S. (1991). A collective fear of the collective: Implications for selves and theories of selves. Cognitive science and psychotherapy [Special Issue]. *Journal of Psychotherapy Integration, 4,* 317–353.

Markus, H. R., & Kitayama, S. (1994). A collective fear of the collective: Implications for selves and theories of selves. The self and the collective [Special Issue]. *Personality and Social Psychology Bulletin. 20,* 568–579.

Marsh, H. W., Kong, C. K., & Hau, K. T. (2000). Longitudinal multilevel modeling of the Big Fish Little Pond Effect on academic self-concept: Counterbalancing social comparison and reflected glory effects in Hong Kong high schools. *Journal of Personality and Social Psychology, 78,* 337–349.

Martin, B. A. (1989). Gender differences in salary expectations when current salary information is provided. *Psychology of Women Quarterly, 13,* 87–96.

Martin, C. L., & Fabes, R. A. (2001). The stability and consequences of young children's same-sex peer interactions. *Developmental Psychology, 37,* 431–446.

Martin, C. L., & Parker, S. (1995). Folk theories about sex and race differences. *Personality and Social Psychology Bulletin, 21*(1), 45–57.

Martin, C. L., & Ruble, D. (2004). Children's search for gender cues: Cognitive perspectives on gender development. *Current Directions in Psychological Science, 13,* 67–70.

Martin, C. L., Ruble, D. N., & Szkrybalo, J. (2002). Cognitive theories of early gender development. *Psychological Bulletin, 128,* 903–933.

Martin, R., & Hewstone, M. (2003) Social-influence processes of control and change: Conformity, obedience to authority and innovation. In M. A. Hogg & J. Cooper (Eds.), *The Sage handbook of social psychology* (pp. 347–366). Thousand Oaks, CA: Sage.

Martin, R., Suls, J., & Wheeler, L. (2002). Ability evaluation by proxy: Role of maximal performance and related attributes in social comparison. *Journal of Personality and Social Psychology, 82,* 781–791.

Maruyama, G., Fraser, S. C., & Miller, N. (1982). Personal responsibility and altruism in children. *Journal of Personality and Social Psychology, 42,* 658–664.

Maslach, C., Stapp, J., & Santee, R. T. (1985). Individuation: Conceptual analysis and assessment. *Journal of Personality and Social Psychology, 49,* 729–738.

Mason, H. R. C., Marks, G., Simoni, J. M., Ruiz, M. S., & Richardson, J. L. (1995). Culturally sanctioned secrets? Latino men's nondisclosure of HIV infection to family, friends, and lovers. *Health Psychology, 14,* 6–12.

Masuda, T., & Nisbett, R. E. (2001). Attending holistically versus analytically: Comparing the context sensitivity of Japanese and Americans. *Journal of Personality and Social Psychology, 81,* 922–934.

Matarazzo, J. D. (1980). Behavioral health and behavioral medicine: Frontiers for new health psychology. *American Psychologists, 35,* 807–817.

Matarazzo, J. D. (1983). Behavioral health: A 1990 challenge for the health science professions: In J. D. Matarazzo, N. E. Miller, S. M. Weiss, J. A. Herd, & S. M. Weiss (Eds.), *Behavioral health: A handbook of health enhancement and disease prevention* (pp. 3–40). New York: Wiley.

Matheson, K., Holmes, J. G., & Kristiansen, C. M. (1991).Observational goals and the integration of trait perceptions and behavior: Behavioral prediction versus impression formation. *Journal of Experimental Social Psychology, 27,* 138–160.

Matlin, M. (2004). *The psychology of women* (5th ed.). Belmont, CA: Wadsworth/Thomson Learning.

Mayer, J. D., Rapp, H. C., & Williams, L. (1993). Individual differences in behavioral prediction: The acquisition of personal-action schemata. *Personality and Social Psychology Bulletin, 19,* 443–451.

Mays, V. M., & Cochran, S. D. (1993). Ethnic and gender differences in beliefs about sex partner questioning to reduce HIV risk. *Journal of Adolescent Research, 8,* 77–88.

Mazzella, R., & Feingold, A. (1994). The effects of physical attractiveness, race, socioeconomic status, and gender of defendants and victims on judgments of mock jurors: A meta-analysis. *Journal of Applied Social Psychology, 24,* 1315–1344.

McAndrew, F. T. (1993). *Environmental psychology.* Pacific Grove, CA: Brooks/Cole.

McAndrew, F. T. (2002). New evolutionary perspectives on altruism: Multilevel-selection and costly-signaling theories. *Current Directions in Psychology, 11,* 79–82.

McArthur, L. Z., & Post, D. L. (1977). Figural emphasis and person perception. *Journal of Personality and Social Psychology, 13,* 520–535.

McArthur, L. Z., & Resko, B. G. (1975). The portrayal of men and women in American TV commercials. *Journal of Social Psychology, 97,* 209–220.

McAuley, E. (1993). Self-efficacy and the maintenance of exercise participation in older adults. *Journal of Behavioral Medicine, 16,* 103–113.

McCann, J. T. (2001). *Staking in children and adults.* Washington, DC: American Psychological Association.

McCarthy, M. (2004). Consumers decide ads not a match. *USA Today.* Retrieved August 20, 2004 from http://www.usatoday.com/money/advertising/adtrack/2003–04–28-match com_x.htm

McCaul, K. D., Veltum, L. G., Boyechko, V., & Crawford, J. J. (1990). Understanding attributions of victim blame for rape: Sex, violence, and foreseeability. *Journal of Applied Social Psychology, 20,* 1–26.

McCleod, J. D., & Kessler, R. C. (1990). Socioeconomic status differences in vulnerability to undesirable life events. *Journal of Health and Social Behavior, 31,* 162–172.

McClintock, C. G., & Liebrand, W. B. G. (1988). Role of interdependence structure, individual value orientation, and another's strategy in social decision making: A transformational analysis. *Journal of Personality and Social Psychology, 55,* 396–409.

McCloskey, M., & Zaragosa, M. S. (1985). Misleading postevent information and memory for events: Arguments and evidence against the memory impairment hypothesis. *Journal of Experimental Psychology: General, 114,* 1–16.

McClure, E. B. (2000). A meta-analytic review of sex differences in facial expression processing and their development in infants, children, and adolescents. *Psychological Bulletin, 126,* 424–453.

McConahay, J. B. (1986). Modern racism, ambivalence, and the modern racism scale. In J. F. Dovidio & S. L. Gaertner (Eds.), *Prejudice, discrimination, and racism* (pp. 91–126). New York: Academic Press.

McConahay, J. B., Hardee, B. B., & Batts, V. (1981). Has racism declined in America? It depends upon who is asking and what is asked. *Journal of Conflict Resolution, 25,* 563–579.

McConnell, A. R., Leibold, J. M., & Sherman, S. J. (1997). Within-target illusory correlations and the formation of context-dependent attitudes. *Journal of Personality and Social Psychology, 73,* 675–686.

McConnell, A. R., Sherman, S. J., & Hamilton, D. L. (1994). On-line and memory-based aspects of individual and group target judgments. *Journal of Personality and Social Psychology, 67,* 173–185.

McCrea, S. M., & Hirt, E. R. (2001). The role of ability judgments in self-handicapping. *Personality and Social Psychology Bulletin, 27,* 1378–1389.

McCullough, M. E. (2001). Forgiveness: Who does it and how do they do it? *Current Directions in Psychological Science, 10,* 194–197.

McDonald, H. E., & Hirt, E. R. (1997). When expectancy meets desire: Motivational effects in reconstructive memory. *Journal of Personality and Social Psychology, 72,* 5–23.

McDonald, J. (1990). Some situational determinants of hypothesis-testing strategies. *Journal of Experimental Social Psychology, 26,* 255–274.

McFarland, C., & Alvaro, C. (2000). The impact of motivation on temporal comparisons: Coping with traumatic events by perceiving personal growth. *Journal of Personality and Social Psychology, 79,* 327–343.

McFarland, C., & Buehler, R. (1995). Collective self-esteem as a moderator of the frog-pond effect in reactions to performance feedback. *Journal of Personality and Social Psychology, 68,* 1055–1070.

McFarland, C., Ross, M., & DeCourville, N. (1989). Women's theories of menstruation and biases in recall of menstrual symptoms. *Journal of Personality and Social Psychology, 57,* 522–531.

McFarlane, A. H., Norman, G. R., Streiner, D. L., Roy, R., & Scott, D. J. (1980). A longitudinal study of the influence of the psychosocial environment on health status: A preliminary report. *Journal of Health and Social Behavior, 21,* 124–133.

McGonagle, K. A., Kessler, R. C., & Schilling, E. A. (1992). The frequency and determinants of marital disagreements in a community sample. *Journal of Personal and Social Relationships, 9,* 507–524.

McGrath, J. E. (1984). *Groups: Interaction and performance.* Upper Saddle River, NJ: Prentice Hall.

McGregor, H., Lieberman, J. D., Solomon, S., Greenberg, T., Arndt, J., Simon, L., et al. (1998). Terror management and aggression: Evidence that mortality salience motivates aggression against worldview threatening others. *Journal of Personality and Social Psychology, 74,* 590–605.

McGuire, A. M. (1994). Helping behaviors in the natural environment: Dimensions and correlates of helping. *Personality and Social Psychology Bulletin, 20,* 45–56.

McGuire, W. J. (1964). Inducing resistance to persuasion: Some contemporary approaches. In L. Berkowitz (Ed.), *Advances in experimental social psychology* (Vol. 1, pp. 192–229). New York: Academic Press.

McGuire, W. J. (1985). Attitudes and attitude change. In G. Lindzey, & E. Aronson (Eds.), *Handbook of social psychology* (3rd ed., Vol. 2, pp. 223–346). New York: Random House.

McGuire, W. J., & McGuire, C. V. (1982). Significant others in self-space. In J. Suls (Ed.), *Psychological perspectives on the self* (Vol. 1, pp. 71–96). Hillsdale, NJ: Erlbaum.

McGuire, W. J., & Padawer-Singer, A. (1976). Trait salience in the spontaneous self-concept. *Journal of Personality and Social Psychology, 33,* 743–754.

McGuire, W. J., & Papageorgis, D. (1961). The relative efficacy of various types of prior belief defense in producing immunity against persuasion. *Journal of Abnormal and Social Psychology, 62,* 327–337.

McIntosh, D. N., Silver, R. C., & Wortman, C. B. (1993). Religion's role in adjustment to a negative life event: Coping with the loss of a child. *Journal of Personality and Social Psychology, 65,* 812–821.

McKenna, K Y. A., & Bargh, J. A. (2000). Plan 9 from cyberspace: The implications of the Internet for personality and social psychology. *Personality and Social Psychology Review, 4,* 57–75.

McKenna, K. Y. A., Green, A. S., & Gleason, M. E. J. (2002). Relationship formation on the Internet. *Journal of Social Issues, 58*(1), 9–32.

McKinney, K., & Maroules, N. (1991). Sexual harassment. In E. Grauerholz & M. A. Koralewski (Eds.), *Sexual coercion: A sourcebook on its nature, causes, and prevention* (pp. 29–44). Lexington, MA: Lexington Books.

McMullen, M. N., & Markman, K. D. (2000). Downward counterfactuals and motivation: The "wake-up call" and the "Pangloss" effect. *Personality and Social Psychology Bulletin, 26,* 575–584.

McNulty, S. E., & Swann, W. B., Jr. (1994). Identity negotiation in roommate relationships: The self as architect and consequence of social reality. *Journal of Personality and Social Psychology, 67,* 1012–1023.

Mealey, L., Bridgstock, R., & Townsend, G. C. (1999). Symmetry and perceived facial attractiveness: A monozygotic co-twin comparison. *Journal of Personality and Social Psychology, 76,* 151–158.

Medvene, L. (1992). Self-help groups, peer helping, and social comparison. In S. Spacapan & S. Oskamp (Eds.), *Helping and being helped: Naturalistic studies* (pp. 49–81). Newbury Park, CA: Sage.

Mehlman, R. C., & Snyder, C. R. (1985). Excuse theory: A test of the self-protective role of attributions. *Journal of Personality and Social Psychology, 49,* 994–1001.

Meissner, C. A., & Brigham, J. C. (2001). Thirty years of investigating the own-race bias in memory for faces: A meta-analytic review. *Psychology, Public Policy, and Law, 7,* 3–35.

Meissner, C. A., & Kassin, S. M. (2002). "He's guilty!": Investigator bias in judgments of truth and deception. *Law and Human Behavior, 26,* 469–480.

Mellor, D. (2003). Contemporary racism in Australia: The experience of aborigines. *Personality and Social Psychology Bulletin, 29,* 474–486.

Mendes, W. B., Blaskovich, J., Lickel, B., & Hunter, S. (2002). Challenge and threat during social interactions with white and black men. *Personality and Social Psychology Bulletin, 28,* 939–952.

Menon, T., Morris, M. W., Chiu, C.-y, & Hong Y.-y. (1999). Culture and the construal of agency: Attribution to individuals versus group dispositions. *Journal of Personality and Social Psychology, 76,* 701–717.

Merei, F. (1949). Group leadership and institutionalization. *Human Relations, 2,* 23–29.

Mesquita, B. (2001). Emotions in collectivist and individualist contexts. *Journal of Personality and Social Psychology, 80,* 68–74.

Messick, D., & Brewer, M. B. (1983). Solving social dilemmas: A review. In L. Wheeler & P. Shaver (Eds.), *Review of personality and social psychology* (Vol. 4, pp. 11–44). Beverly Hills: Sage.

Mestel, R. (2004, March 10). Obesity gaining on tobacco as top killer. *Los Angeles Times,* pp. A1 & A26.

Meyer, C. B., & Taylor, S. E. (1986). Adjustment to rape. *Journal of Personality and Social Psychology, 50, 1226–1234.*

Meyer, D., Leventhal, H., & Gutmann, M. (1985). Common-sense models of illness: The example of hypertension. *Health Psychology, 4,* 115–135.

Meyer, J. P., & Mulherin, A. (1980). From attribution to helping: An analysis of the mediating effects of affect and expectancy. *Journal of Personality and Social Psychology, 39,* 201–210.

Michaels, J. W., Bloommel, J. M., Brocato, R. M., Linkous, R. A., & Rowe, J. S. (1982). Social facilitation and inhibition in a natural setting. *Replications in Social Psychology, 2,* 21–24.

Mickelson, K. D., Kessler, R. C., & Shaver, P. R. (1997). Adult attachment in a nationally representative sample. *Journal of Personality and Social Psychology, 73,* 1092–1106.

Milavsky, J. R., Kessler, R., Stipp, H., Rubens, W. S., Pearl, D., Bouthilet, L., et al. (Eds.). (1982). *Television and behavior: Ten years of scientific progress and implications for the eighties. Vol. 2: Technical reviews* (DHHS Publication No. ADM 82–1196). Washington, DC: U.S. Government Printing Office.

Miles, D. R., & Carey, G. (1997). Genetic and environmental architecture on human aggression. *Journal of Personality and Social Psychology, 72,* 207–217.

Milgram, S. (1963). Behavioral study of obedience. *Journal of Abnormal and Social Psychology, 67,* 371–378.

Milgram, S. (1964). Issues in the study of obedience: A reply to Baumrind. *American Psychologist, 19,* 848–852.

Milgram, S. (1965). Some conditions of obedience and disobedience to authority. *Human Relations, 18,* 57–75.

Milgram, S. (1970). The experience of living in cities. *Science, 167,* 1461–1468.

Milgram, S. (1974). *Obedience to authority: An experimental view.* New York: Harper & Row.

Millar, M. G., & Tesser, A. (1989). The effects of affective-cognitive consistency and thought on the attitude-behavior relation. *Journal of Experimental Social Psychology, 25,* 189–202.

Millar, M. G., & Tesser, A. (1986). Thought-induced attitude change: The effects of schema structure and commitment. *Journal of Personality and Social Psychology, 51,* 259–269.

Miller, A. G. (1986). *The obedience experiments: A case study of controversy in social science.* New York: Praeger.

Miller, C. E. (1989). The social psychological effects of group decision rules. In P. B. Paulus (Ed.), *Psychology of group influence* (2nd ed., pp. 327–356). Hillsdale, NJ: Erlbaum.

Miller, D. T., & McFarland, C. (1986). Counterfactual thinking and victim compensation: A test of norm theory. *Personality and Social Psychology Bulletin, 12,* 513–519.

Miller, D. T., & Ross, M. (1975). Self-serving biases in the attribution of causality: Fact or fiction? *Psychological Bulletin, 82,* 213–225.

Miller, J. G. (1994). Cultural diversity in the morality of caring: Individually oriented versus duty-based interpersonal moral codes. *Cross-Cultural Research, 28,* 3–39.

Miller, J. G., Bersoff, D. G., & Harwood, R. L. (1990). Perceptions of social responsibilities in India and in the United States: Moral imperatives or personal decisions? *Journal of Personality and Social Psychology, 58,* 33–47.

Miller, L. C. (1990). Intimacy and liking: Mutual influence and the role of unique relationships. *Journal of Personality and Social Psychology, 59,* 50–60.

Miller, N., & Cooper, H. M. (Eds.). (1991). Meta-analysis in personality and social psychology [Special Issue]. *Personality and Social Psychology Bulletin, 17.*

Miller, P. A., Kozu, J., & Davis, A. C. (2001). Social influence, empathy, and prosocial behavior in cross-cultural perspective. In W. Wosinska, R. B. Cialdini, D. W. Barrett, & J. Reykowski (Eds.), *The practice of social influence in multiple cultures* (pp. 63–77). Mahwah, NJ: Erlbaum.

Miller, R. S. (1997). Inattentive and contented: Relationship commitment and attention to alternatives. *Journal of Personality and Social Psychology, 73,* 758–766.

Miller, S., & Sears, D. O. (1986). Stability and change in social tolerance: A test of the persistence hypothesis. *American Journal of Political Science, 30,* 214–236.

Miller, S. M., & Mangan, C. E. (1983). Interacting effects of information and copying style in adapting to gynecologic stress: Should the doctor tell all? *Journal of Personality and Social Psychology, 45,* 223–236.

Mills, J., & Clark, M. S. (1994). Communal and exchange relationships: Controversies and research. In R. Erber & R. Gilmour (Eds.), *Theoretical frameworks for personal relationships* (pp. 29–42). Hillsdale, NJ: Erlbaum.

Mills, J., & Clark, M. S. (2001). Viewing close, romantic relationships as communal relationships: Implications for maintenance and enhancement. In J. H. Harvey & A. Wenzel (Eds.), *Close romantic relationships: Maintenance and enhancement* (pp. 13–25). Mahwah, NJ: Erlbaum.

Mills, R. S. L., & Grusec, J. E. (1989). Cognitive, affective, and behavioral consequences of praising altruism. *Merrill-Palmer Quarterly, 35,* 299–326.

Minard, R. D. (1952). Race relations in the Pocahontas Coal Field. *Journal of Social Issues, 8,* 29–44.

Misumi, J. (1995). The development in Japan of the Performance-Maintenance (PM) theory of leadership. *Journal of Social Issues, 51,* 213–228.

Mita, T. H., Dermer, M., & Knight, J. (1977). Reversed facial images and the mere-exposure hypothesis. *Journal of Personality and Social Psychology, 35,* 597–601.

Miyamoto, Y., & Kitayama, S. (2002). Cultural variation in correspondence bias: The critical role of attitude diagnosticity of socially constrained behavior. *Journal of Personality and Social Psychology, 83,* 1239–1248.

Monahan, J., & Walker, L. (1998). *Social science in law: Cases and materials.* (4th Ed.). Westbury, NY: The Foundation Press.

Monin, B., & Miller, D. T. (2001). Moral credentials and the expression of prejudice. *Journal of Personality and Social Psychology, 81,* 33–43.

Monteith, M. J. (1993). Self-regulation of prejudiced responses: Implications for progress in prejudice-reduction efforts. *Journal of Personality and Social Psychology, 65,* 469–485.

Montgomery, B. M. (1988). Quality communication in personal relationships. In S. W. Duck (Ed.), *Handbook of personal relationships* (pp. 343–359). Chichester, England: Wiley.

Moorhead, G., Ference, R., & Neck, C. P. (1991). Group decision fiascoes continue: Space shuttle Challenger and a revised groupthink framework. *Human Relations, 44,* 539–550.

Moreland, R. L., & Beach, S. R. (1992). Exposure effects in the classroom: The development of affinity among students. *Journal of Experimental Social Psychology, 28,* 255–276.

Moreland, R. L., & Levine, J. M. (2003). Group composition. In M. A. Hogg & J. Cooper (Eds.), *The Sage handbook of social psychology* (pp. 367–380). Thousand Oaks, CA: Sage.

Moretti, M., & Higgins, E. T. (1990). Relating self-discrepancy to self-esteem: The contribution of discrepancy beyond actual self-ratings. *Journal of Experimental Social Psychology, 26,* 108–123.

Morf, C. C., & Rhodewalt, F. (1993). Narcissism and self-evaluation maintenance: Explorations in object relations. *Personality and Social Psychology Bulletin, 19,* 668–676.

Moriarty, T. (1975). Crime, commitment, and the responsive bystander. Two field experiments. *Journal of Personality and Social Psychology, 31,* 370–376.

Morier, D., & Seroy, C. (1994). The effect of interpersonal expectancies on men's self-presentation of gender role attitudes to women. *Sex Roles, 31,* 493–504.

Morling, B., Kitayama, S., & Miyamoto, Y. (2002). Cultural practices emphasize influence in the United States and adjustment in Japan. *Personality and Social Psychology Bulletin, 28,* 311–323.

Morling, B., Kitayama, S., & Miyamoto, Y. (2003). American and Japanese women use different coping strategies during normal pregnancy. *Personality and Social Psychology Bulletin, 29,* 1533–1546.

Morris, M. W., & Larrick, R. P. (1995). When one cause casts doubt on another. A normative analysis of discounting in causal attribution. *Psychological Review, 102,* 331–355.

Morris, M. W., & Peng, K. (1994). Culture and cause: American and Chinese attributions for social and physical events. *Journal of Personality and Social Psychology, 67,* 949–971.

Morris, W. N., & Miller, R. S. (1975). The effects of consensus-breaking and consensus-preempting partners on reduction in conformity. *Journal of Experimental Social Psychology, 11,* 215–223.

Morse, S. J., & Gergen, K. J. (1970). Social comparison, self-consistency and the presentation of self. *Journal of Personality and Social Psychology, 16,* 148–156.

Moscovici, S. (1985). Social influence and conformity. In G. Lindzey & E. Aronson (Eds.), *Handbook of social psychology* (Vol. 2, 3rd ed., pp. 347–412). New York: Random House.

Moscovici, S., Lage, E., & Naffrechoux, M. (1969). Influence of a consistent minority on the responses of a majority in a color perception task. *Sociometry, 32,* 365–379.

Moser, D. V. (1992). Does memory affect judgment? Self-generated versus recall memory measures. *Journal of Personality and Social Psychology, 62,* 555–563.

Moskalenko, S., & Heine, S. J. (2003). Watching your troubles away: Television viewing as a stimulus for subjective self-awareness. *Personality and Social Psychology Bulletin, 29,* 76–85.

Moskowitz, G. B., & Skurnik, I. (1999). Contrast effects as determined by the type of prime: Trait versus exemplar primes initiate processing strategies that differ in how accessible constructs are used. *Journal of Personality and Social Psychology, 76,* 911–927.

Muehlenhard, C. L. (1988). Misinterpreted dating behaviors and the risk of date rape. *Journal of Social and Clinical Psychology, 6,* 20–37.

Mueller, C. W., &Wallace, J. E. (1996). Justice and the paradox of the contented female worker. *Social Psychology Quarterly, 58,* 338–349.

Mullen, B. (1986). Atrocity as a function of lynch mob composition. *Personality and Social Psychology Bulletin, 12,* 187–198.

Mullen, B. (1991). Group composition, salience, and cognitive representations: The phenomenology of being in a group. *Journal of Experimental Social Psychology, 27,* 297–323.

Mullen, B. (2004). Sticks and stones can break my bones, but ethnopaulisms can alter the portrayal of immigrants to children. *Personality and Social Psychology Bulletin, 30,* 250–260.

Mullen, B., & Cooper, C. (1994). The relation between group cohesion and performance: An integration. *Psychological Bulletin, 115,* 210–227.

Mullen, B., & Johnson, C. (1995). Cognitive representation in ethnophaulisms and illusory correlation in Stereotyping *Personality and Social Psychology Bulletin, 21,* 420–433.

Mullin, C. R., & Linz, D. (1995). Desensitization and resensitization to violence against women: Effects of exposure to sexually violent films on judgments of domestic violence victims. *Journal of Personality and Social Psychology, 69,* 449–459.

Munro, G. D., & Ditto, P. H. (1997). Biased assimilation, attitude polarization, and affect in reactions to stereotype-relevant scientific information. *Personality and Social Psychology Bulletin, 23,* 636–653.

Murphy, S. T., & Zajonc, R. B. (1993). Affect, cognition, and awareness: Affective priming with optimal and suboptimal stimulus exposures. *Journal of Personality and Social Psychology, 64,* 723–739.

Murray, S. L. (1999). The quest for conviction: Motivated cognition in romantic relationships. *Psychological Inquiry, 10,* 23–34.

Murray, S. L., & Holmes, J. G. (1997). A leap of faith? Positive illusions in romantic relationships. *Personality and Social Psychology Bulletin, 23,* 586–604.

Mussweiler, T. (2001). Focus of comparison as a determinant of assimilation versus contrast in social comparison. *Personality and Social Psychology Bulletin, 27,* 38–47.

Mussweiler, T., & Förster, J. (2000). The sex → aggression link: A perception-behavior dissociation. *Journal of Personality and Social Psychology, 79,* 507–520.

Mussweiler, T., Gabriel, S., & Bodenhausen, G. V. (2000). Shifting social identities as a strategy for deflecting threatening social comparisons. *Journal of Personality and Social Psychology, 79,* 398–409.

Mussweiler, T., & Ruter, K. (2003). What friends are for! The use of romantic standards in social comparison. *Journal of Personality and Social Psychology, 85,* 467–481.

Mussweiler, T., Strack, F., & Pfeiffer, T. (2000). Overcoming the inevitable anchoring effect: Considering the opposite compensates for selective accessibility. *Personality and Social Psychology Bulletin, 26,* 1142–1150.

Mutchler, J. E., & Burr, J. A. (1991). Racial differences in health and health care service utilization in later life: The effect of socioeconomic status. *Journal of Health and Social, Behavior, 32,* 342–356.

Myers, A. M., & Gonda, G. (1982). Utility of the masculinity-femininity construct: Comparison of traditional and androgyny approaches. *Journal of Personality and Social Psychology, 43,* 514–523.

Nadler, A. (1991). Help-seeking behavior:Psychological costs and instrumental benefits. In M. S. Clark (Ed.), *Prosocial behavior* (pp. 290–311). Newbury Park, CA: Sage.

Narby, D. J., Cutler, B. L., & Moran, G. (1993). A meta-analysis of the association between authoritarianism and jurors' perceptions of defendant culpability. *Journal of Applied Psychology, 78,* 34–42.

National Center for Education Statistics. (2002). Indicators of school crime and safety: Nonfatal teacher victimization at school-teacher reports. http://nces.ed.gov/pubs2003/schoolcrime/10.asp?nav=3

National Center for Injury Prevention and Control. (2003). Intimate partner violence: Fact sheet. Retrieved November 22, 2004, from the Centers for Disease Control Web site: http://www.cdc.gov/ncipc/factsheets/ipvfacts.htm

National Institute of Mental Health. (1982). *Television and behavior: Ten years of scientific progress and implications for the eighties. Vol. I: Summary report.* Rockville, MD: National Institute of Mental Health.

Neff, L. A., & Karney, A. B. R. (2004). How does context affect intimate relationships? Linking external stress and cognitive processes within marriage. *Personality and Social Psychology Bulletin, 30,* 134–148.

Neff, L. A., & Karney, B. R. (2002). Judgments of a relationship partner: Specific accuracy but global enhancement. *Journal of Personality, 70,* 1079–1112.

Neil v. Biggers, 409 U.S. 188 (1972).

Nelson, A. (2000). The pink dragon is female: Halloween costumes and gender markers. *Psychology of Women Quarterly, 24,* 137–144.

Nelson, L. J., & Klutas, K. (2000). The distinctiveness effect in social interaction: Creation of a self-fulfilling prophecy. *Personality and Social Psychology Bulletin, 26,* 126–135.

Nemeth, C., & Kwan, J. (1987). Minority influence, divergent thinking, and detection of correct solutions. *Journal of Applied Social Psychology, 17,* 788–799.

Nemeth, C., Mosier, K., & Chiles, C. (1992). When convergent thought improves performance: Majority versus minority influence. *Personality and Social Psychology Bulletin, 18,* 139–144.

Nerenz, D. R., & Leventhal, H. (1983). Self-regulation theory in chronic illness. In T. G. Burish & L. A. Bradley (Eds.), *Coping with chronic disease: Research and applications* (pp. 13–35). New York: Academic Press.

Neuberg, S. L. (1989). The goal of forming accurate impressions during social interactions: Attenuating the impact of negative expectancies. *Journal of Personality and Social Psychology, 56,* 374–386.

Neuberg, S. L., Judice, T. N., & West, S. G. (1997). What the Need for Closure Scale measures and what it does not: Toward differentiating among related epistemic motives. *Personality and Social Psychology Bulletin, 72,* 1396–1412.

Neumann, R., & Strack, F. (2000). Approach and avoidance: The influence of proprioceptive and exteroceptive cues on encoding of affective information. *Journal of Personality and Social Psychology, 79,* 39–48.

Newcomb, T. M. (1961). *The acquaintance process.* New York: Holt.

Newman, K. S. (2004, April 17). Too close for comfort. *The New York Times,* late ed., p. A15.

Newman, L. S. (1996). Trait impressions as heuristics for predicting future behavior. *Personality and Social Psychology Bulletin, 22,* 395–411.

Newman, M. A., Jackson, R. A., & Baker, D. D. (2003). Sexual harassment in the federal workplace. *Public Administration Review, 63,* 472–483.

Newman, M. L., Pennebaker, J. W., Berry, D. S., & Richards, J. M. (2003). Lying words: Predicting deception from linguistic styles. *Personality and Social Psychology Bulletin, 29, 665–675.*

Newsom, J. T. (1999). Another side to caregiving: Negative reactions to being helped. *Current Directions in Psychological Science, 8,* 183–187.

Newsom, J. T., Adams, N. L., Rahim, A., Mowry, H., & Rogers, J. (1998, November). *Approaches to measuring care recipient's negative reactions to assistance.* Poster presented at the annual meeting of the Gerontological Society of America, Philadelphia.

Newtson, D. (1976). Foundations of attribution: The perception of ongoing behavior. In J. H. Harvey, W. J. Ickes, & R. F. Kidd (Eds.), *New directions in attribution research* (Vol. 1, pp. 223–248). Hillsdale, NJ: Erlbaum.

Nezlek, J. B., & Leary, M. R. (2002). Individual differences in self-presentational motives in daily social interaction. *Personality and Social Psychology Bulletin, 28,* 211–223.

Nezlek, J. B., & Plesko, R. M. (2001). Day-to-day relationships among self-concept clarity, self-esteem, daily events, and mood. *Personality and Social Psychology Bulletin, 27,* 201–211.

Niemann, Y. F., Jennings, L., Rozelle, R. M., Baxter, J. C., & Sullivan, E. (1994). Use of free responses and cluster analysis to determine stereotypes of eight groups. *Personality and Social Psychology Bulletin, 20,* 379–390.

Nienhuis, A. E., Manstead, A. S., & Spears, R. (2001). Multiple motives and persuasive communication: Creative elaboration as a result of impression motivation and accuracy motivation. *Personality and Social Psychology Bulletin, 27,* 118–132.

Nietzel, M. T., McCarthy, D. M., & Kern, M. J. (1999). Juries: The current state of the empirical literature. In R. Roesch, S. D. Hart, & J. R. P. Ogloff (Eds.), *Psychology and law: The state of the discipline* (pp. 23–52). New York: Kluwer Academic/Plenum Publishers.

Nisbett, R. E. (1993). Violence and U.S. regional culture. *American Psychologist, 48,* 441–449.

Nisbett, R. E., Caputo, C., Legant, P., & Maracek, J. (1973). Behavior as seen by the actor and as seen by the observer. *Journal of Personality and Social Psychology, 27,* 154–164.

Nisbett, R. E., & Kunda, Z. (1985). Perception of social distribution. *Journal of Personality and Social Psychology, 48,* 297–311.

Nisbett, R. E., & Ross, L. (1980). *Human inference: Strategies and shortcomings of social judgment.* Upper Saddle River, NJ: Prentice Hall.

Norenzayan, A., Choi, I., & Nisbett, R. E. (2002). Cultural similarities and differences in social inference: Evidence from behavioral predictions and lay theories of behavior. *Personality and Social Psychology Bulletin, 28,* 109–120.

Novak, D. W., & Lerner, M. J. (1968). Rejection as a consequence of perceived similarity. *Journal of Personality and Social Psychology, 9,* 147–152.

Nowak, A., Szamrej, J., & Latané, B. (1990). From private attitude to public opinion: A dynamic theory of social comparison. *Psychological Review, 97,* 362–376.

Nussbaum, S., Trope, Y., & Liberman, N. (2003). Creeping dispositionism: The temporal dynamics of behavior prediction. *Journal of Personality and Social Psychology, 84,* 485–497.

Oettingen, G., & Mayer, D. (2002). The motivating function of thinking about the future: Expectations versus fantasies. *Journal of Personality and Social Psychology, 83,* 1198–1212.

Oettingen, G., Pak, H.-j., Schnetter, K. (2001). Self-regulation of goal setting: Turning free fantasies about the future into binding goals. *Journal of Personality and Social Psychology, 80,* 736–753.

Ofshe, R., & Watters, E. (1994). *Making monsters: False memories, psychotherapy, and sexual hysteria.* New York: Scribners.

Ohbuchi, K., Kameda, M., & Agarie, N. (1989). Apology as aggression control: Its role in mediating appraisal of and response to harm. *Journal of Personality and Social Psychology, 56,* 219–227.

Öhman, A., Lundqvist, D., & Esteves, F. (2001). The face in the crowd revisited: A threat advantage with schematic stimuli. *Journal of Personality and Social Psychology, 80,* 381–396.

Oishi, S., & Diener, E. (2001). Goals, culture, and subjective well-being. *Personality and Social Psychology Bulletin, 27,* 1674–1682.

Oishi, S., & Diener, E. (2003). Culture and well-being: The cycle of action, evaluation, and decision. *Personality and Social Psychology Bulletin, 29,* 939–949.

Oishi, S., Wyer, R. S., & Colcombe, S. (2000). Cultural variation in the use of current life satisfaction to predict the future. *Journal of Personality and Social Psychology, 78,* 434–445.

Olczak, P. V., Kaplan, M. F., & Penrod, S. (1991). Attorneys' lay psychology and its effectiveness in selecting jurors: Three empirical studies. *Journal of Social Behavior and Personality, 6,* 431–452.

Oliner, S. P., & Oliner, P. M. (1988). *The altruistic personality: Rescuers of Jews in Nazi Europe.* New York: Free Press.

Oliver, M. B., & Hyde, J. S. (1993). Gender differences in sexuality: A meta-analysis. *Psychological Bulletin, 114,* 29–51.

Olsen, L. (1988). *Crossing the schoolhouse border: Immigrant students and the California Public Schools.* San Francisco: California Tomorrow.

Olson, J. M., & Janes, L. M. (2002). Vigilance for differences: Heightened impact of differences on surprise. *Personality and Social Psychology Bulletin, 28,* 1084–1093.

Olweus, D. (1979). Stability of aggressive reaction patterns in males: A review. *Psychological Bulletin, 86,* 852–875.

Omarzu, J. (2000). A disclosure decision model: Determining how and when individuals will self-disclose. *Personality and Social Psychology Review, 4,* 174–185.

Omoto, A. M., & Snyder, M. (1995). Sustained helping without obligation: Motivation, longevity of service, and perceived attitude change among AIDS volunteers. *Journal of Personality and Social Psychology, 68,* 671–686.

Omoto, A. M., & Snyder, M. (2002). Considerations of community: The context and process of volunteerism. *American Behavioral Scientist, 45,* 846–867.

Omoto, A. M., Snyder, M., & Martino, S. C. (2000). Volunteerism and the life course: Investigating age-related agendas for action. *Basic and Applied Social Psychology, 22,* 181–197.

Orbell, J. M., van de Kragt, A. J. C., & Dawes, R. M. (1988). Explaining discussion-induced cooperation. *Journal of Personality and Social Psychology, 54,* 811–819.

Orenstein, P. (2003, July 6). Where have all the Lisas gone? *The New York Times,* Section 6, p. 28.

Orina, M. M., Wood, W., & Simpson, J. A. (2002). Strategies of influence in close relationships. *Journal of Experimental Social Psychology, 38,* 459–472.

Ornstein, P. A., Ceci, S. J., & Loftus, E. F. (1998). Adult recollections of childhood abuse: Cognitive and developmental perspectives. *Psychology, Public Policy, and Law, 4,* 1025–1051.

Osborn, A. F. (1957). *Applied imagination.* New York: Scribners.

Osbourne, R. E., & Gilbert, D. T. (1992). The preoccupational hazards of social life. *Journal of Personality and Social Psychology, 62,* 219–228.

Osgood, C. E., Suci, G. J., & Tannenbaum, P. H. (1957). *The measurement of meaning.* Urbana: University of Illinois Press.

O'Sullivan, M. (2003). The fundamental attribution error in detecting deception: The boy-who-cried-wolf effect. *Personality and Social Psychology Bulletin, 29,* 1316–1327.

Ottati, V., Terkildsen, N., & Hubbard, C. (1997). Happy faces elicit heuristic processing in a televised impression formation task: A cognitive tuning account. *Personality and Social Psychology Bulletin, 23,* 1144–1156.

Otto, A. L., Penrod, S. D., & Dexter, H. R. (1994). The biasing impact of pretrial publicity on juror judgments. *Law and Human Behavior, 18,* 453–470.

Pachon, H., & Valencia, M. (1999, June 7). It's a white, white TV world out there. *Los Angeles Times.*

Pancer, S. M., & Pratt, M. W. (1999). Social and family determinanants of community service involvement in Canadian Youth. *Roots of Civic Identity* (pp. 32–55). New York: Cambridge University Press.

Park, B. (1986). A method for studying the development of impressions of real people. *Journal of Personality and Social Psychology, 51,* 907–917.

Park, B., & Krauss, S. (1992). Consensus in initial impression as a function of verbal information. *Personality and Social Psychology Bulletin, 8,* 439–446.

Park, B., & Rothbart, M. (1982). Perception of out-group homogeneity and levels of social categorization: Memory for the subordinate attributes of in-group and out-group members. *Journal of Personality and Social Psychology, 42,* 1051–1068.

Park, B., Ryan, C. S., & Judd, C. M. (1992). Role of meaningful subgroups in explaining differences in perceived variability for in-groups and out-groups. *Journal of Personality and Social Psychology, 63,* 553–567.

Park, B., Wolsko, C., & Judd, C. M. (2001). Measurement of subtyping in stereotype change. *Journal of Experimental Social Psychology, 37,* 325–332.

Park, C. L., Armeli, S., & Tennen, H. (2004). Appraisal-coping goodness of fit: A daily internet study. *Personality and Social Psychology Bulletin, 30,* 558–569.

Park, J., & Banaji, M. R. (2000). Mood and heuristics: The influence of happy and sad states on sensitivity and bias in stereotyping. *Journal of Personality and Social Psychology, 78,* 1005–1023.

Parker, S. D., Brewer, M. B., & Spencer, J. R. (1980). Natural disaster, perceived control, and attributions to fate. *Personality and Social Psychology Bulletin, 6,* 454–459.

Parks, C. D., & Sanna, L. J. (1999). *Group performance and interaction.* Boulder, CO: Westview Press.

Parlee, M. B. (1979, October). The friendship bond. *Psychology Today,* pp. 43–54.

Parmelee, L. F. (2001). A Roper Center data review: Mending the fabric: Race relations in black and white. *Public Perspective, 12,* 22–31.

Parrott, W. G., Sabini, J., & Silver, M. (1988). The roles of self-esteem and social interaction in embarrassment. *Personality and Social Psychology Bulletin, 14,* 191–202.

Partlett, D., & Nurcombe, B. (1998). Recovered memories of child sexual abuse and liability: Society, science and law in a comparative setting. *Psychology, Public Policy, and Law, 4,* 1253–1306.

Patrick, H., Neighbors, C., & Knee, C. R. (2004). Appearance-related social comparisons: The role of contingent self-esteem and self perceptions of attractiveness. *Personality and Social Psychology Bulletin, 30,* 501–514.

Paulus, D. L. (1998). Interpersonal and intrapsychic adaptiveness of trait self-enhancement: A mixed blessing? *Journal of Personality and Social Psychology, 74,* 1197–1208.

Paulus, D. L., & Bruce, M. N. (1992). The effect of acquaintanceship on the validity of personality impressions: A longitudinal study. *Journal of Personality and Social Psychology, 63,* 816–824.

Paulus, P. B., & Dzindolet, M. T. (1993). Social influence processes in group brainstorming. *Journal of Personality and Social Psychology, 64,* 575–586.

Paulus, P. B., Larey, T. S., & Dzindolet, M. T. (2001). Creativity in groups and teams. In M. E. Turner (Ed.), *Groups at work: Theory and research* (pp. 319–338). Mahwah, NJ: Erlbaum.

Paxton, P., & Moody, J. (2003). Structure and sentiment: Explaining emotional attachment to groups. *Social Psychology Quarterly, 66,* 34–47.

Payne, B. K. (2001). Prejudice and perception: The role of automatic and controlled processes in misperceiving a weapon. *Journal of Personality and Social Psychology, 81,* 181–192.

Pearlin, L. I., & Schooler, C. (1978). The structure of coping. *Journal of Health and Social Behavior, 19,* 2–21.

Pedersen, W. C., Gonzales, C., & Miller, N. (2000). The moderating effect of trivial triggering provocation on displaced aggression. *Journal of Personality and Social Psychology, 78,* 913–927.

Peffley, M., & Hurwitz, J. (1998). Whites' stereotypes of blacks: Sources and political consequences. In J. Hurwitz & M. Peffley (Eds.), *Perception and prejudice: Race and politics in the United States* (pp. 58–99). New Haven, CT: Yale University Press.

Pelham, B. W., & Hetts, J. J. (2001). Underworked and overpaid: Elevated entitlement in men's self-pay. *Journal of Experimental Social Psychology, 37,* 93–103.

Pelham, B. W., & Neter, E. (1995). The effect of motivation of judgment depends on the difficulty of the judgment. *Journal of Personality and Social Psychology, 68,* 581–594.

Pelham, B. W., & Swann, W. B., Jr. (1994). The juncture of intrapersonal and interpersonal knowledge: Self-certainty and interpersonal congruence. *Personality and Social Psychology Bulletin, 20,* 349–357.

Pendry, L. F., & Macrae, C. N. (1994). Stereotypes and mental life: The case of the motivated but thwarted tactician. *Journal of Experimental Social Psychology, 30,* 303–325.

Pennebaker, J. W. (1983). Accuracy of symptom perception. In A. Baum, S. E. Taylor, & J. Singer (Eds.), *Handbook of psychology and health* (Vol. 4, pp. 189–217). Hillsdale, NJ: Erlbaum.

Pennebaker, J. W., & Beall, S. (1986). Confronting a traumatic event: Toward an understanding of inhibition and disease. *Journal of Abnormal Psychology, 95,* 274–281.

Pennebaker, J. W., Colder, M., & Sharp, L. K. (1990). Accelerating the coping process. *Journal of Personality and Social Psychology, 58,* 528–537.

Pennebaker, J. W., & Lightner, J. M. (1980). Competition of internal and external information in an exercise setting. *Journal of Personality and Social Psychology, 39,* 165–174.

Pennington, J., & Schlenker, P. R. (1999). Accountability for consequential decisions: Justifying ethical judgments to audiences. *Personality and Social Psychology Bulletin, 9,* 1067–1081.

Pennington, N., & Hastie, R. (1988). Explanation-based decision making: Effects of memory structure on judgment. *Journal of Experimental Psychology: Learning, Memory, and Cognition, 14,* 521–533.

Pennington, N., & Hastie, R. (1992). Explaining the evidence: Tests of the story model for juror decision making. *Journal of Personality and Social Psychology, 62,* 189–206.

Peplau, L. A. (1984). Power in dating relationships. In J. Freeman (Ed.), *Women: A feminist perspective* (3rd ed., pp. 121–135). Palo Alto, CA: Mayfield.

Peplau, L. A. (2003). Human sexuality: How do men and women differ? *Current Directions in Psychological Science, 12,* 37–40.

Peplau, L. A., & Beals, K. P. (2004). The family lives of lesbians and gay men. In A. Vangelisti (Ed.), *Handbook of family communication* (pp.233–248). Mahwah, NJ: Erlbaum.

Peplau, L. A., & Campbell, S. M. (1989). The balance of power in dating and marriage. In J. Freeman (Ed.), *Women: A feminist perspective* (4th ed., pp. 121–137). Mountain View, CA: Mayfield.

Peplau, L. A., DeBro, S. C., Veniegas, R. C., & Taylor, P. L. (Eds.). (1999). *Gender, culture and ethnicity: Current research about women and men.* Mountain View, CA: Mayfield.

Peplau, L. A., Fingerhut, A., & Beals, K. P. (2004). Sexuality in the relationships of lesbians and gay men. In J. Harvey, A. Wenzel, & S. Sprecher (Eds.), *Handbook of sexuality in close relationships* (pp. 350–369). Mahwah, NJ: Erlbaum.

Perkins, H. W. (Ed.). (2003). *The social norms approach to preventing school and college age substance abuse: A handbook for educators, counselors, and clinicians.* San Francisco: Jossey-Bass.

Perlman, D. (1990, August). *Age differences in loneliness: A meta-analysis.* Paper presented at the annual meeting of the American Psychological Association. Boston.

Perlman, D., & Oskamp, S. (1971). The effects of picture content and exposure frequency on evaluations of Negroes and whites. *Journal of Experimental Social Psychology, 7,* 503–514.

Perlman, D., & Peplau, L. A. (1998). Loneliness. *Encyclopedia of Mental Health* (Vol. 2, pp. 571–581). New York: Academic Press.

Perry, D. G., Perry, L. C., & Weiss, R. J. (1989). Sex differences in the consequences that children anticipate for aggression. *Developmental Psychology, 25,* 312–319.

Pessin, J. (1933). The comparative effects of social and mechanical stimulation on memorizing. *American Journal of Psychology, 45,* 263–270.

Peterson, B. E., Doty, R. M., & Winter, D. G. (1993). Authoritarianism and attitudes toward contemporary social issues. *Personality and Social Psychology Bulletin, 19,* 174–184.

Peterson, B. E., & Lane, M. D. (2001). Implications of authoritarianism for young adulthood: Longitudinal analysis of college experiences and future goals. *Personality and Social Psychology Bulletin, 27,* 678–690.

Petrie, K. J., Booth, R. J., & Pennebaker, J. W. (1998). The immunological effects of thought suppression. *Journal of Personality and Social Psychology, 75,* 1264–1272.

Petrie, K. J., & Weinman, J. A. (Eds.). (1997). *Perceptions of health and illness: Current research and applications.* Reading, England: Harwood Academic.

Pettigrew, T. F. (1985). New black-white patterns: How best to conceptualize them? *Annual Review of Sociology, 11,* 329–346.

Pettigrew, T. F. (1997). Generalized intergroup contact effects on prejudice. *Personality and Social Psychology Bulletin, 23,* 173–185.

Pettigrew, T. F., & Meertens, R. W. (1995). Subtle and blatant prejudice in Western Europe. *European Journal of Social Psychology, 25,* 57–75.

Pettigrew, T. F., & Tropp, L. R. (2000). Does intergroup contact reduce prejudice? Recent meta-analytic findings. In S. Oskamp (Ed.), *Reducing prejudice and discrimination* (pp. 93–114). Mahwah, NJ: Erlbaum.

Petty, R. E., & Brock, T. C. (1981). Thought disruption and persuasion: Assessing the validity of attitude change experiments. In R. E. Petty, T. M. Ostrom, & T. C. Brock (Eds.), *Cognitive response in persuasion* (pp. 55–79). Hillsdale, NJ: Erlbaum.

Petty, R. E., & Cacioppo, J. T. (1977). Forewarning, cognitive responding, and resistance to persuasion. *Journal of Personality and Social Psychology, 35,* 645–656.

Petty, R. E., & Cacioppo, J. T. (1986). *Communication and persuasion: Central and peripheral routes to attitude change.* New York: Springer-Verlag.

Petty, R. E., & Cacioppo, J. T. (1990). Involvement and persuasion: Tradition versus integration. *Psychological Bulletin, 107,* 367–374.

Petty, R. E., Fleming, M. A., & White, P. H. (1999). Stigmatized sources and persuasion: Prejudice as a determinant of argument scrutiny. *Journal of Personality and Social Psychology, 76,* 19–34.

Petty, R. E., & Wegener, D. T. (1998). Attitude change: Multiple roles for persuasion variables. In D. Gilbert, S. Fiske, & G. Lindzey (Eds.), *Handbook of social psychology,* (4th ed., pp. 323–390). New York: McGraw-Hill.

Pfeifer, J. E., & Ogloff, J. R. P. (1991). Ambiguity and guilt determinations: A modern racism perspective. *Journal of Applied Social Psychology, 21,* 1713–1725.

Pham, A. (2001, May 17). Boy, you fight like a girl. *Los Angeles Times,* pp. A1, A18.

Pham, L. B., & Taylor, S. E. (1999). From thought to action: Effects of process versus outcome-based mental simulations on performance. *Personality and Social Psychology Bulletin, 25,* 250–260.

Pham, L. B., Taylor, S. E., & Seeman, T. E. (2001). Effects of environmental predictability and personal mastery on self-regulatory and physiological processes. *Personality and Social Psychology Bulletin, 27,* 611–620.

Phillips, M. R., McAuliff, B. D., Kovera, M. B., & Cutler, B. L. (1999). Double-blind photoarray administration as a safeguard against investigator bias. *Journal of Applied Psychology, 84,* 940–951.

Phinney, J. S. (1990). Ethnic identity in adolescents and adults: Review of research. *Psychological Bulletin, 108,* 499–514.

Phinney, J. S. (1991). Ethnic identity and self-esteem: A review and integration. *Hispanic Journal of Behavioral Sciences, 13,* 193–208.

Pickel, K. L. (1995). Inducing jurors to disregard inadmissible evidence: A legal explanation does not help. *Law and Human Behavior, 19,* 407–424.

Pickel, K. L. (1999). The influence of context on the "weapon focus" effect. *Law and Human Behavior, 23,* 299–312.

Piliavin, I. M., Rodin, J., & Piliavin, J. A. (1969). Good Samaritanism: An underground phenomenon? *Journal of Personality and Social Psychology, 13,* 289–299.

Piliavin, J. A., & Callero, P. L. (1991). *Giving blood: The development of an altruistic identity.* Baltimore, MD: Johns Hopkins University Press.

Pillai, R. (1996). Crisis and the emergence of charismatic leadership in groups. *Journal of Applied Social Psychology, 26,* 543–562.

Pinquart, M. (2003). Loneliness in married, widowed, divorced, and never-married older adults. *Journal of Social and Personal Relationships, 20,* 31–53.

Plaks, J. E., & Higgins, E. T. (2000). Pragmatic use of stereotyping in teamwork: Social loafing and compensation as a function of inferred partner-situation fit. *Journal of Personality and Social Psychology, 79,* 962–974.

Plaks, J. E., Stroessner, S. J., Dweck, C. S., & Sherman, J. W. (2001). Person theories and attention allocation: Preferences for stereotypic versus counterstereotypic information. *Journal of Personality and Social Psychology, 80,* 876–893.

Plant, E. A., & Devine, P. G. (2003). The antecedents and implications of interracial anxiety. *Personality and Social Psychology Bulletin, 29,* 790–801.

Plous, S., & Neptune, D. (1997). Racial and gender biases in magazine advertising. *Psychology of Women Quarterly, 21,* 627–644.

Podell, S., & Archer, D. (1994). Do legal changes matter? The case of gun control laws. In M. Costanzo & S. Oskamp (Eds.).

Violence and the law. Claremont symposium on applied social psychology (pp. 37–62). Thousand Oaks, CA: Sage.

Porter, S., Yuille, J. C., & Lehman, D. R. (1999). The nature of real, implanted, and fabricated memories for emotional childhood events: Implications for the recovered memory debate. *Law and Human Behavior, 23,* 517–537.

Posavac, S. S., Sanbonmatsu, D. M., & Fazio, R. H. (1997). Considering the best choice: Effects of the salience and accessibility of alternatives on attitude-decision consistency. *Journal of Personality and Social Psychology, 72,* 253–261.

Postmes, T., & Spears, R. (1998). Deindividuation and antinormative behavior: A meta-analysis. *Psychological Bulletin, 123,* 238–259.

Postmes, T., Spears, R., Sakhel, K., & de Groot, D. (2001). Social influence in computer-mediated communication: The effects of anonymity on group behavior. *Personality and Social Psychology Bulletin, 27,* 1243–1254.

Potegal, M., & Knutson, J. F. (1994). *The dynamics of aggression: Biological and social processes in dyads and groups.* Hillsdale, NJ, England: Erlbaum.

Potter, R., & Brewer, N. (1999). Perceptions of witness behaviour-accuracy relationships held by police, lawyers, and jurors. *Psychiatry, Psychology, and Law, 6,* 97–103.

Powlishta, K. K., Sen, M. G., Serbin, L. A., Poulin-Dubois, D., & Eichstedt, J. A. (2001). From infancy through middle childhood: The role of cognitive and social factors in becoming gendered. In R. K. Unger (Ed.), *Handbook of the psychology of women and gender* (pp. 116–132). New York: Wiley.

Pratkanis, A. R., Greenwald, A. G., Leippe, M. R., & Baumgardner, M. H. (1988). In search of reliable persuasion effects. III: The sleeper effect is dead. Long live the sleeper effect. *Journal of Personality and Social Psychology, 54,* 203–218.

Pratto, F., & John, O. P. (1991). Automatic vigilance: The attention-grabbing power of negative social information. *Journal of Personality and Social Psychology, 61,* 380–391.

Prentky, R. A., & Knight, R. A. (1991). Identifying critical dimensions for discriminating among rapists. *Journal of Consulting and Clinical Psychology, 59,* 643–661.

Presser, H. B. (1994). Employment schedules among dual-earner spouses and the division of household labor by gender. *American Sociological Review, 59,* 348–364.

Previti, D., & Amato, P. R. (2003). Why stay married? Rewards, barriers, and marital stability. *Journal of Marriage and Family, 65,* 561–573.

Previti, D., & Amato, P. R. (2004). Is infidelity a cause or a consequence of poor marital quality? *Journal of Social and Personal Relationships, 21,* 217–230.

Price, V., & Hsu, M. (1992). Public opinion about AIDS policies: The role of misinformation and attitudes toward homosexuals. *Public Opinion Quarterly, 56,* 29–52.

Price Waterhouse v. Hopkins, 490 U.S. 228, 104 L.Ed.2d 268, 109 S.Ct. 1775 (1989).

Priester, J. R., & Petty, R. E. (2001). Extending the bases of subjective attitudinal ambivalence: Interpersonal and intrapersonal antecedents of evaluative tension. *Journal of Personality and Social Psychology, 80,* 19–34.

Prislin, R., & Ouellette, J. (1996). When it is embedded, it is potent: Effects of general attitude embeddedness on formation of specific attitudes and behavioral intentions. *Personality and Social Psychology Bulletin,* Vol. 22, 845–861.

Pronin, E., Lin, D. Y., & Ross, L. (2002). The bias blind spot: Perceptions of bias in self versus others. *Personality and Social Psychology Bulletin, 28,* 369–381.

Pryke, S., Lindsay, R. C. L., Dysart, J. E., & Dupuis, P. (2004). Multiple independent identification decisions: A method of calibrating eyewitness identifications. *Journal of Applied Psychology, 89,* 73–84.

Pryor, J. B., Giedd, J. L., & Williams, K. B. (1995). A social psychological model for predicting sexual harassment. Gender stereotyping, sexual harassment, and the law. *Journal of Social Issues, 51,* 69–84.

Pryor, J. B., Reeder, G. D., & McManus, J. A. (1991). Fear and loathing in the workplace: Reactions to AIDS-infected co-workers. *Personality and Social Psychology Bulletin, 17,* 133–139.

Puente, S., & Cohen, D. (2003). Jealousy and the meaning (or non-meaning) of violence. *Personality and Social Psychology Bulletin, 29,* 449–460.

Putnam, R. (2000). *Bowling alone.* New York: Simon & Schuster.

Quinley, H. E., & Glock, C. Y. (1979). *Anti-Semitism in America.* New York: Free Press.

Radecki, C. M., & Jaccard, J. (1995). Perceptions of knowledge, actual knowledge, and information search behavior. *Journal of Experimental Social Psychology, 31,* 107–138.

Raghunathan, R., & Trope, Y. (2002). Walking the tightrope between feeling good and being accurate: Mood as a resource in processing persuasive messages. *Journal of Personality and Social Psychology, 83,* 510–525.

Räikkönen, K., Matthews, K. A., Flory, J. D., Owens, J. F., & Gump, B. B. (1999). Effects of optimism, pessimism, and trait anxiety on ambulatory blood pressure and mood during everyday life. *Journal of Personality and Social Psychology, 76,* 104–113.

RAND Corporation. (2004). Obesity and disability: The shape of things to come. http://www.rand.org/publications/RB/RB9043/Retrieved 7/1/2004.

Rands, M., & Levinger, G. (1979). Implicit theories of relationship: An intergenerational study. *Journal of Personality and Social Psychology, 37,* 649–661.

Raty, H., Vanska, J., Kasanen, K., & Karkkainen, R. (2002). Parents' explanations of their child's performance in mathematics and reading: A replication and extension of Yee and Eccles. *Sex Roles, 46,* 121–128.

Raven, B. H. (1992). A power/interaction model of interpersonal influence: French and Raven thirty years later. *Journal of Social Behavior and Personality, 7,* 217–244.

Raven, B. H., Schwarzwald, J., & Koslowsky, M. (1998). Conceptualizing and measuring a power/interaction model of interpersonal influence. *Journal of Applied Social Psychology, 28,* 307–332.

Read, S. J., & Cesa, I. L. (1991). This reminds me of times when...: Expectation failures in reminding and explanation. *Journal of Experimental Social Psychology, 27,* 1–25.

Redding, R. E. (2001). Sociopolitical diversity in psychology. *American Psychologist, 56,* 205–215.

Redlich, A. D., & Goodman, G. S. (2003). Taking responsibility for an act not committed: The influence of age and suggestibility. *Law and Human Behavior, 27,* 141–156.

Reeder, G. D., Kumar, S., Hesson-McInnis, M. S., & Trafimow, D. (2002). Inferences about the morality of an aggressor: The role of perceived motive. *Journal of Personality and Social Psychology, 83,* 789–803.

Reeder, G. D., Vonk, R., Ronk, M. J., Ham, J., & Lawrence, M. (2004). Dispositional attribution: Multiple inferences about motive-related traits. *Journal of Personality and Social Psychology, 86,* 530–544.

Regan, D. T. (1968). *The effects of a favor and liking on compliance.* Unpublished doctoral dissertation, Stanford University.

Regan, D. T., & Fazio, R. (1977). On the consistency between attitudes and behavior: Look to the method of attitude formation. *Journal of Experimental Social Psychology, 13,* 28–45.

Regan, D. T., & Totten, J. (1975). Empathy and attribution: Turning observers into actors. *Journal of Personality and Social Psychology, 32,* 850–856.

Regan, P. C. (2000). Love relationships. In L. T. Szuchman & F. Muscarella (Eds.), *Psychological perspectives on human sexuality* (pp. 232–282). New York: Wiley.

Regan, P. C., & Berscheid, E. (1996). Beliefs about the state, goals and objects of sexual desire. *Journal of Sex and Marital Therapy, 22,* 110–120.

Regan, P. C., & Dreyer, C. S. (1999). Lust? love? status? Young adults' motives for engaging in casual sex. *Journal of Psychology and Human Sexuality, 11,* 1–23.

Regan, P. C., Snyder, M., & Kassin, S. M. (1995). Unrealistic optimism: Self-enhancement or person positivity? *Personality and Social Psychology Bulletin, 21,* 1073–1082.

Reicher, S. (2003). The psychology of crowd dynamics. In M. A. Hogg & J. Cooper (Eds.), *The Sage handbook of social psychology* (pp.182–208). Thousand Oaks, CA: Sage.

Reifman, A., Gusick, S. M., & Ellsworth, P. C. (1992). Real jurors' understanding of the law in real cases. *Law and Human Behavior, 16,* 539–554.

Reis, H. T. (1998). Gender differences in intimacy and related behaviors: Context and process. In D. J. Canary & K. Dindia (Eds.), *Sex differences and similarities in communication* (pp. 203–231). Mahwah, NJ: Erlbaum.

Reis, H. T., Clark, M. S., & Holmes, J. G. (2004). Perceived partner responsiveness as an organizing construct in the study of intimacy and closeness. In D. J. Mashek & A. Aron (Eds.), *Handbook of closeness and intimacy* (pp. 201–225). Mahwah, NJ: Erlbaum.

Reis, H. T., Collins, W. A., & Berscheid, E. (2000). The relationship context of human behavior and development. *Psychological Bulletin, 126,* 844–872.

Reis, H. T., Senchak, M., & Solomon, B., (1985). Sex differences in the intimacy of social interactions: Further examination of potential explanations. *Journal of Personality and Social Psychology, 48,* 1204–1217.

Reis, H. T., & Shaver, P. (1988). Intimacy as an interpersonal process. In S. W. Duck (Ed.), *Handbook of personal relationships* (pp. 367–389). New York: Wiley.

Reis, H. T., Sheldon, K. M., Gable, S. L., Roscoe, J., & Ryan, R. M. (2000). Daily well-being: The role of autonomy, competence, and relatedness. *Personality and Social Psychology Bulletin, 26,* 419–435.

Reis, H. T., & Wheeler, L. (1991). Studying social interaction with the Rochester Interaction Record. In M. P. Zanna (Ed.), *Advances in experimental social psychology* (pp. 269–318). New York: Academic Press.

Reno, R., Cialdini, R., & Kallgren, C. A. (1993). The transsituational influence of social norms. *Journal of Personality and Social Psychology, 64,* 104–112.

Reynolds, D. J., Jr., & Gifford, R. (2001). The sounds and sights of intelligences: A lens model channel analysis. *Personality and Social Psychology Bulletin, 27,* 187–200.

Rhee, E., Uleman, J. S., Lee, H. K., & Roman, R. J. (1995). Spontaneous self-descriptions and ethnic identities in individualistic and collectivist cultures. *Journal of Personality and Social Psychology, 69,* 142–152.

Rhine, R. J., & Severance, L. J. (1970). Ego-involvement, discrepancy, source credibility, and attitude change. *Journal of Personality and Social Psychology, 16,* 175–190.

Rhodewalt, F., Sanbonmatsu, D. M., Tschanz, B., Feick, D. L., & Waller, A. (1995). Self-handicapping and interpersonal trade-offs: The effects of claimed self-handicaps on observers' performance evaluations and feedback. *Personality and Social Psychology Bulletin, 21,* 1042–1050.

Richards, J. M., & Gross, J. J. (2000). Emotion regulation and memory: The cognitive costs of keeping one's cool. *Journal of Personality and Social Psychology, 79,* 410–424.

Richmond, V. P., & McCroskey, J. C. (Eds.) (1992). *Power in the classroom: Communication, control, and concern.* Hillsdale, NJ: Erlbaum.

Riggio, R., Murphy, S. E., & Pirozzolo, F. J. (Eds.) (2001). *Multiple intelligences and leadership.* Mahwah, NJ: Erlbaum.

Risman, B. J. (1987). Intimate relationships from a microstructural perspective: Men who mother. *Gender and Society, 1,* 6–32.

Road and Travel Magazine (2004). Goodyear names Virginia trucker highway hero. Retrieved July 3, 2004, from http://www.roadandtravel.com/newsworthy/newsandviews04/goodyearhighwayhero.htm

Robins, R. W., & Beer, J. S. (2001). Positive illusions about the self: Short-term benefits and long-term costs. *Journal of Personality and Social Psychology, 80,* 340–352.

Robins, R. W., Mendelsohn, G. A., Connell, J. B., & Kwan, V. S. Y. (2004). Do people agree about the causes of behavior? A social relations analysis of behavior ratings and causal attributions. *Journal of Personality and Social Psychology, 86,* 334–344.

Robinson, M. D., & Ryff, C. D. (1999). The role of self-deception in perceptions of past, present, and future happiness. *Personality and Social Psychology Bulletin, 25,* 595–606.

Rodin, J., & Janis, I. L. (1979). The social power of health-care practitioners as agents of change. *Journal of Social Issues, 35,* 60–81.

Roebers, C. M., & Schneider, W. (2000). The impact of misleading questions on eyewitness memory in children and adults. *Applied Cognitive Psychology, 14,* 509–526.

Roese, N. J., & Olson, J. M. (1994). Attitude importance as a function of repeated attitude expression. *Journal of Experimental Social Psychology, 30,* 39–51.

Roger, M., & Gazzaniga, M. S. (2004). Automatic brains—interpretive minds. *Current Directions in Psychological Science, 13,* 56–59.

Rogers, R. W. (1984). Changing health-related attitudes and behavior: The role of preventative health psychology. In J. H. Harvey, J. E. Maddux, R. P. McGlynn, & C. D. Stoltenberg (Eds.), *Social perception in clinical and counseling psychology* (Vol. 2, pp. 91–112). Lubbock: Texas Tech University Press.

Rohlinger, D. A. (2002). Eroticizing men: Cultural influences on advertising and male objectification. *Sex Roles, 46,* 61–74.

Romero, A. A., Agnew, C. R., & Insko, C. A. (1996). The cognitive mediation hypothesis revisited: An empirical response to methodological and theoretical criticism. *Personality and Social Psychology Bulletin, 22,* 651–665.

Roney, C. J. R., Higgins, E. T., & Shah, J. (1995). Goals and framing: How outcome focus influences motivation and emotion. *Personality and Social Psychology Bulletin, 21,* 1151–1160.

Rose, S., & Frieze, I. H. (1989). Young singles' scripts for a first date. *Gender and Society, 3,* 258–268.

Rose, S., & Frieze, I. H. (1993). Young singles' contemporary dating scripts. *Sex Roles, 28,* 499–509.

Rosen, B., & Jerdee, T. H. (1978). Perceived sex differences in managerially relevant characteristics. *Sex Roles, 4,* 837–843.

Rosenberg, M. (1965). *Society and the adolescent self-image.* Princeton, NJ: Princeton University Press.

Rosenfield, S., Vertefuille, J., & McAlpine, D. D. (2000). Gender stratification and mental health. *Social Psychology Quarterly, 63,* 208–223.

Rosenstock, I. M. (1966). Why people use health services. *Millbank Memorial Fund Quarterly, 44,* 94ff.

Rosenthal, R. (1986). Media violence, antisocial behavior, and the social consequences of small effects. *Journal of Social Issues, 42,* 141–154.

Rosenthal, R. (1991). *Meta-analytic procedures for social research* (Rev. ed.). Newbury Park, CA: Sage.

Roskos-Ewoldsen, D. R., & Fazio, R. H. (1992). The accessibility of source likeability as a determinant of persuasion. *Personality and Social Psychology Bulletin, 18,* 19–25.

Ross, A. S. (1971). Effect of increased responsibility on bystander intervention: The presence of children. *Journal of Personality and Social Psychology, 19,* 306–310.

Ross, L. (1977). The intuitive psychologist and his shortcoming: Distortions in the attribution process. In L. Berkowitz (Ed.), *Advances in experimental social psychology* (Vol. 10, pp. 174–221). New York: Academic Press.

Ross, L., Greene, D., & House, P. (1977). The "false consensus effect": An egocentric bias in social perception and attribution processes. *Journal of Experimental Social Psychology, 19,* 306–310.

Ross, L. D. (2001). Getting down to fundamentals: Lay dispositionism and the attributions of psychologists. *Psychological Inquiry, 12,* 37–40.

Ross, L. T., Lutz, C. J., & Lakey, B. (1999). Perceived social support and attributions for failed support. *Personality and Social Psychology Bulletin, 25,* 896–909.

Ross, M., & Wilson, A. E. (2002). It feels like yesterday: Self-esteem, valence of personal past experiences, and judgments of subjective distance. *Journal of Personality and Social Psychology, 82,* 792–803.

Ross, M., Xun, W. Q. E., & Wilson, A. E. (2002). Language and the bicultural self. *Personality and Social Psychology Bulletin, 28,* 1040–1050.

Rothman, A. J., & Hardin, C. D. (1997). Differential use of the availability heuristic in social judgment. *Personality and Social Psychology Bulletin, 23,* 123–128.

Rothman, A. J., & Salovey, P. (1997). Shaping perceptions to motivate healthy behavior: The role of message framing. *Psychological Bulletin, 121,* 3–19.

Rothman, A. J., & Schwarz, N. (1998). Constructing perceptions of vulnerability: Personal relevance and the use of experiential information in health judgments. *Personality and Social Psychology Bulletin, 24,* 1053–1064.

Rotton, J., & Cohn, E. G. (2000). Weather, disorderly conduct, and assaults: From social contact to social avoidance. *Environment & Behavior, 32,* 651–673.

Rowley, S. J., Sellers, R. M., Chavous, T. M., & Smith, M. A. (1998). The relationship between racial identity and self-esteem in African American college and high school students. *Journal of Personality and Social Psychology, 74,* 715–724.

Rozin, P., Kabnick, K., Pete, E., Fischler, C., & Shields, C. (2003). The ecology of eating. *Psychological Science, 14,* 450–454.

Rozin, P., Lowery, L., & Ebert, R. (1994). Varieties of disgust faces and the structure of disgust. *Journal of Personality and Social Psychology, 66,* 870–881.

Rubin, L. (1976). *Worlds of pain.* New York: Basic Books.

Rubin, M., & Hewstone, M. (1998). Social identity theory's self-esteem hypothesis: A review and some suggestions for clarification. *Personality and Social Psychology Review, 2,* 40–62.

Rubin, Z. (1970). Measurement of romantic love. *Journal of Personality and Social Psychology, 16,* 265–273.

Rubin, Z. (1973). *Liking and loving.* New York: Holt, Rinehart and Winston.

Rubin, Z. (1980). *Children's friendships.* Cambridge, MA: Harvard University Press.

Rubin, Z., Hill, C. T., Peplau, L. A., & Dunkel-Schetter, C. (1980). Self-disclosure in dating couples: Sex roles and the ethic of openness. *Journal of Marriage and the Family, 42,* 305–317.

Ruble, D. N., & Stangor, C. (1986). Stalking the elusive schema: Insights from developmental and social-psychological analyses of gender schemas. *Social Cognition, 4,* 227–261.

Ruder, M., & Bless, H. (2003). Mood and the reliance on the ease of retrieval heuristic. *Journal of Personality and Social Psychology, 85,* 20–32.

Rudman, L. A., Ashmore, R. D., & Gary, M. L. (2001). "Unlearning" automatic biases: The malleability of implicit prejudice and stereotypes. *Journal of Personality and Social Psychology, 81,* 856–868.

Rudman, L. A., & Glick, P. (1999). Feminized management and backlash toward agentic women. *Journal of Personality and Social Psychology, 77,* 1004–1010.

Rudman, L. A., & Kilianski, S. E. (2000). Implicit and explicit attitudes toward female authority. *Personality and Social Psychology Bulletin, 26,* 1315–1328.

Rusbult, C. E. (1980). Commitment and satisfaction in romantic associations: A test of the investment model. *Journal of Experimental Social Psychology, 16,* 172–186.

Rusbult, C. E. (1983). A longitudinal test of the investment model: The development (and deterioration) of satisfaction and commitment in heterosexual involvements. *Journal of Personality and Social Psychology, 45,* 101–117.

Rusbult, C. E. (1987). Responses to dissatisfaction in close relationships. In D. Perlman & S. Duck (Eds.), *Intimate relationships: Development, dynamics, and deterioration* (pp. 209–237). Beverly Hills, CA: Sage.

Rusbult, C. E., & Martz, J. M. (1995). Remaining in an abusive relationship: An investment model analysis of nonvoluntary dependence. *Personality and Social Psychology Bulletin, 21,* 558–571.

Rusbult, C. E., & Van Lange, P. A. M. (1996). Interdependence processes. In E. T. Higgins & A. W. Kruglanski (Eds.), *Social psychology: Handbook of basic principles* (pp. 564–596). New York: Guilford.

Rusbult, C. E., Van Lange, P. A. M., Wildschut, T., Yovetich, N. A., & Verette, J. (2000). Perceived superiority in close relationships: Why it exists and persists. *Journal of Personality and Social Psychology, 79,* 521–545.

Rusbult, C. E., Wieselquist, J., Foster, C. A., & Witcher, B. S. (1999). Commitment and trust in close relationships: An interdependence analysis. In J. M. Adams & W. H. Jones (Eds), *Handbook of interpersonal commitment and relationship stability* (pp. 427–449). New York: Kluwer Academic/Plenum.

Rusbult, C. E., Zembrodt, I. M., & Gunn, L. K. (1982). Exit, voice, loyalty, and neglect: Responses to dissatisfaction in romantic involvements. *Journal of Personality and Social Psychology, 43,* 1230–1242.

Ruscher, J. B., Hammer, E. Y., & Hammer, E. D. (1996)., Forming shared impression through conversation: An adaptation of the continuum model. *Personality and Social Psychology Bulletin, 22,* 705–720.

Rush, M. C., & Russell, J. E. A. (1988). Leader prototypes and prototype-contingent consensus in leader behavior descriptions. *Journal of Experimental Social Psychology, 24,* 88–104.

Rushton, J. P., & Campbell, A. C. (1977). Modeling, vicarious reinforcement and extraversion on blood donating in adults: Immediate and long-term effects. *European Journal of Social Psychology, 7,* 297–306.

Rushton, J. P., & Teachman, G. (1978). The effects of positive reinforcement, attributions, and punishment on model-induced altruism in children. *Personality and Social Psychology Bulletin, 4,* 322–325.

Russano, M. B., Meissner, C. A., Narchet, F. M., & Kassin, S. M. (in press). Investigating true and false confessions within a novel experimental paradigm. *Psychological Science.*

Russell, D., Peplau, L. A., & Cutrona, C. E. (1980). The revised UCLA loneliness scale: Concurrent and discriminant validity evidence. *Journal of Personality and Social Psychology, 39,* 472–480.

Russell, J. A., & Bullock, M. (1985). Multidimensional scaling of emotional facial expressions: Similarity from preschoolers to adults. *Journal of Personality and Social Psychology, 48,* 1290–1298.

Rusting, C. L., & DeHart, T. (2000). Retrieving positive memories to regulate negative mood: Consequences for mood-congruent memory. *Journal of Personality and Social Psychology, 78,* 737–752.

Rusting, C. L., & Nolen-Hoeksema, S. (1998). Regulating responses to anger: Effects of rumination and distraction on angry mood. *Journal of Personality and Social Psychology, 74,* 790–803.

Ruvolo, A. P., & Markus, H. R. (1992). Possible selves and performance: The power of self-relevant imagery. *Social Cognition, 10,* 95–124.

Ryder, A. G., Alden, L. E., & Paulhus, D. L. (2000). Is acculturation unidimensional or bidimensional? A head-to-head comparison in the prediction of personality, self-identity, and adjustment. *Journal of Personality and Social Psychology, 79,* 49–65.

Sabini, J., Siepmann, M., & Stein, J. (2001). The really fundamental attribution error in social psychological research. *Psychological Inquiry, 12,* 1–15.

Saks, M. J., & Marti, M. W. (1997). A meta-analysis of the effects of jury size. *Law and Human Behavior, 21,* 451–467.

Salovey, P., & Birnbaum, D. (1989). Influence of mood on health-relevant cognitions. *Journal of Personality and Social Psychology, 57,* 539–551.

Saluter, A. F. (1996, February). Marital status and living arrangements: March, 1994. *Current population reports: Population characteristics (P20–484).* Washington, DC: U.S. Bureau of the Census.

Sanbonmatsu, D. M., & Fazio, R. H. (1990). The role of attitudes in memory-based decision making. *Journal of Personality and Social Psychology, 59,* 614–622.

Sanbonmatsu, D. M., Shavitt, S., & Gibson, B. D. (1994). Salience, set size, and illusory correlation: Making moderate assumptions about extreme targets. *Journal of Personality and Social Psychology, 66,* 1020–1033.

Sanchez, J. I., & Fernandez, D. M. (1993). Acculturative stress among Hispanics: A bidimensional model of ethnic identification. *Journal of Applied Social Psychology, 23,* 654–668.

Sandys, M., & Dillehay, R. C. (1995). First-ballot votes, predeliberation dispositions, and final verdicts in jury trials. *Law and Human Behavior, 19,* 175–195.

Sanna, L. J., Chang, E. C., & Meier, S. (2001). Counterfactual thinking and self-motives. *Personality and Social Psychology Bulletin, 27,* 1023–1034.

Sanna, L. J., & Shotland, R. L. (1990). Valence of anticipated evaluation and social facilitation. *Journal of Experimental Social Psychology, 57,* 819–829.

Sanna, L. J., Turley-Ames, K. J., & Meier, S. (1999). Mood, self-esteem, and simulated alternatives: Thought-provoking affective influences on counterfactual direction. *Journal of Personality and Social Psychology, 76,* 543–558.

Santos, M. D., Leve, C., & Pratkanis, A. R. (1994). Hey buddy, can you spare seventeen cents? Mindful persuasion and the pique technique. *Journal of Applied Social Psychology, 24,* 755–764.

Sarason, B. R., Sarason, I. G., & Gurung, R. A. R. (1997). Close personal relationships and health outcomes: A key to the role of social support. In S. Duck (Ed.), *Handbook of personal relationships* (pp. 547–573). New York: Wiley.

Sarason, I. G., Johnson, J. H., & Siegel, J. M. (1978). Assessing the impact of life changes: Development of the Life Experience Survey. *Journal of Consulting and Clinical Psychology, 46,* 932–946.

Satow, K. L. (1975). Social approval and helping. *Journal of Experimental Social Psychology, 11,* 501–509.

Satran, P. R., & Rosenkrantz, L. (2003). *Cool names for babies.* New York: St. Martin's Press.

Savage, D. G. (1992, June 25). Prayers banned at school ceremonies. *Los Angeles Times,* pp A1, A12.

Scanzoni, L. D., & Scanzoni, J. (1981). *Men, women, and change.* New York: McGraw-Hill.

Scarborough, R. (2004, July 1). Zarqawi targets female soldiers. *The Washington Times.* Retrieved August 20, 2004, from www.washtimes.com/national/20040701-122456-6466r.htm

Scarpaci, J. L. (1988). Help-seeking behavior, use, and satisfaction among frequent primary care users in Santiago de Chile. *Journal of Health and Social Behavior, 29,* 199–213.

Schachter, S. (1964). The interaction of cognitive and physiological determinants of emotional state. In L. Berkowitz (Ed.), *Advances in experimental social psychology* (pp. 49–80). New York: Academic Press.

Schaller, M. (1992). Sample size, aggregation, and statistical reasoning in social inference. *Journal of Experimental Social Psychology, 28,* 65–85.

Schaller, M., & Cialdini, R. B. (1988). The economics of empathic helping: Support for a mood management motive. *Journal of Experimental Social Psychology, 24,* 163–181.

Schaufeli, W. B. (1988). Perceiving the causes of employment: An evaluation of the causal dimensions in a real-life situation. *Journal of Personality and Social Psychology, 54,* 347–356.

Scheck, B., Neufeld, P., & Dwyer, J. (2000). *Actual innocence.* New York: Random House.

Scheier, M. F., Carver, C. S., & Bridges, M. W. (1994). Distinguishing optimism from neuroticism (and trait anxiety, self-mastery, and self-esteem): A reevaluation of the Life Orientation Test. *Journal of Personality and Social Psychology, 67,* 1063–1078.

Scher, S. J., & Cooper, J. (1989). Motivational basis of dissonance. The singular role of behavioral consequences. *Journal of Personality and Social Psychology, 56,* 899–906.

Scheufele, P. M. (2000). Effects of progressive relaxation and classical music on measurements of attention, relaxation, and stress responses. *Journal of Behavioral Medicine, 23,* 207–228.

Schifter, D. E., & Ajzen, I. (1985). Intention, perceived control, and weight loss: An application of the theory of planned behavior. *Journal of Personality and Social Psychology, 49,* 843–851.

Schimel, J., Arndt, J., Pyszczynski, T., & Greenberg, J. (2001). Being accepted for who we are: Evidence that social validation of the intrinsic self reduces general defensiveness. *Journal of Personality and Social Psychology, 80,* 35–52.

Schimel, J., Pyszczynski, T., Greenberg, J., O'Mahen, H., & Arndt, J. (2000). Running from the shadow: Psychological distancing from others to deny characteristics people fear in themselves. *Journal of Personality and Social Psychology, 78,* 446–462.

Schimmack, U., Radhakrishnan, P., Oishi, S., Dzokoto, V., & Ahadi, S. (2002). Culture, personality, and subjective well-being: Integrating process models of life satisfaction. *Journal of Personality and Social Psychology, 82,* 582–593.

Schlenker, B. R. (1980). *Impression management: The self-concept, social identity, and interpersonal relations.* Monterey, CA: Brooks/Cole.

Schlenker, B. R., Phillips. S. T., Boniecki, K. A., & Schlenker, D. R. (1995). Championship pressures: Choking or triumphing in one's territory? *Journal of Personality and Social Psychology, 68,* 632–643.

Schlenker, B. R., & Weigold, M. F. (1990). Self-consciousness and Self-presentation: Being autonomous versus appearing autonomous. *Journal of Personality and Social Psychology, 59,* 820–828.

Schmeichel, B. J., Vohs, K. D., & Baumeister, R. F. (2003). Intellectual performance and ego depletion: Role of the self in logical reasoning and other information processing. *Journal of Personality and Social Psychology, 85,* 33–46.

Schmidt, G., & Weiner, B. (1988). An attribution-affect-action theory of behavior: Replications of judgments of help-giving. *Personality and Social Psychology Bulletin, 14,* 610–621.

Schmitt, D. R., & Marwell, G. (1972). Withdrawal and reward reallocation as responses to inequity. *Journal of Experimental Social Psychology, 8,* 207–221.

Schneider, D. J. (2004). *The psychology of stereotyping.* New York: Guilford.

Schopler, J., Insko, C. A., Wieselquist, J., Pemberton, M., Witcher, B., & Kozar, R., et al. (2001). When groups are more competitive than individuals: The domain of the discontinuity effect. *Journal of Personality and Social Psycholgy, 80,* 632–644.

Schroeder, D. A., Penner, L. A., Dovidio, J. F., & Pieiavin, J. A. (1995). *The psychology of helping and altruism: Problems and puzzles.* New York: McGraw-Hill.

Schuller, R. A., Wells, E., Rzepa, S., & Klippenstine, M. A. (2004). Rethinking battered woman syndrome evidence: The impact of alternative forms of expert testimony on mock jurors' decisions. *Canadian Journal of Behavioural Science, 36,* 127–136.

Schult D. G., & Schneider, L. J. (1991). The role of sexual provocativeness, rape history, and observer gender in perceptions of blame in sexual assault. *Journal of Interpersonal Violence, 6,* 94–101.

Schulz, R., O'Brien, A. T., Bookwala, J., & Fleissner, K. (1995). Psychiatric and physical morbidity effects of dementia caregiving: Prevalence, correlates, and causes. *The Gerontologist, 35,* 771–791.

Schulz-Hardt, S., Frey, D., Luthgens, C., & Moscovici, S. (2000). Biased information search in group decision making. *Journal of Personality and Social Psychology, 78,* 655–669.

Schuman, H., Steeh, C., Bobo, L., & Krysan, M. (1997). *Racial attitudes in America: Trends and interpretations.* Cambridge, MA: Harvard University Press.

Schwartz, S. H., & Gottlieb, A. (1980). Bystander anonymity and reactions to emergencies. *Journal of Personality and Social Psychology, 39,* 418–430.

Schwartz, S. H., & Struch, N. (1989). Intergroup aggression: Its predictors and distinctness from in-group bias. *Journal of Personality and Social Psychology, 56,* 364–373.

Schwarzer, R., & Renner, B. (2000). Social-cognitive predictors of health behavior: Action self-efficacy and coping self-efficacy. *Health Psychology, 19,* 487–495.

Scott, B. (1994). Pornography and sexual aggression: Associations of violent and nonviolent depictions with rape and rape proclivity. *Deviant Behavior, 15,* 289–304.

Scully, D., & Marolla, J. (1984). Convicted rapists' vocabulary of motive: Excuses and justifications. *Social Problems, 31,* 530–544.

Sears, D. O. (1983). The person-positivity bias. *Journal of Personality and Social Psychology, 44,* 233–250.

Sears, D. O. (1986). College sophomores in the laboratory: Influences of a narrow database on social psychology's view of human nature. *Journal of Personality and Social Psychology, 51,* 515–530.

Sears, D. O., Citrin, J., Cheleden, S. V. & van Laar, C. (1999). Cultural diversity and multicultural politics: Is ethnic balkanization psychologically inevitable? In D. A. Prentice & D. T. Miller (Eds.), *Cultural divides: Understanding and overcoming group conflict.* New York: Russell Sage Foundation.

Sears, D. O., & Funk, C. L. (1991). The role of self-interest in social and political attitudes. In M. P. Zanna (Ed.), *Advances in experimental social psychology* (Vol. 24, pp. 1–91). New York: Academic Press.

Sears, D. O., & Henry, P. J. (2003). The origins of symbolic racism. *Journal of Personality and Social Psychology, 85,* 259–275.

Sears, D. O., & Levy, S. R. (2003). Childhood and adult political development. In D. O. Sears, L. Huddy, & R. Jervis (Eds.), *The Oxford Handbook of Political Psychology* (pp. 60–109). New York: Oxford University Press.

Sears, D. O., & McConahay, J. B. (1973). *The politics of violence: The new urban blacks and the Watts riot.* Boston: Houghton Mifflin.

Sears, D. O., Sidanius, J., & Bobo, L. (Eds.) (2000). *Racialized politics: The debate about racism in America.* Chicago: University of Chicago Press.

Sears, D. O., van Laar, C., Carrillo, M., & Kosterman, R. (1997). Is it really racism? The origins of white Americans' opposition to race-targeted policies. *Public Opinion Quarterly, 61,* 16–53.

Sears, R. R., Maccoby, E., & Levin, H. (1957). *Patterns of child rearing.* Evanston, IL: Row, Peterson.

Sears, R. R., Whiting, J. W., Nowlis, V., & Sears, P. S. (1953). Some child-rearing antecedents of aggression and dependency in young children. *Genetic Psychology Monographs, 47,* 135–263.

Sedikides, C. (1990). Effects of fortuitously activated constructs versus activated communication goals on person impressions. *Journal of Personality and Social Psychology, 58,* 397–408.

Sedikides, C. (1992). Attentional effects on mood are moderated by chronic self-conception valence. *Personality and Social Psychology Bulletin, 18,* 580–584.

Sedikides, C. (1993). Assessment, enhancement, and verification determinants of the self-evaluation process. *Journal of Personality and Social Psychology, 65,* 317–338.

Sedikides, C., & Anderson, C. A. (1994). Causal perceptions of intertrait relations: The glue that holds person types together. *Personality and Social Psychology Bulletin, 20,* 294–302.

Sedikides, C., Gaertner, L., & Toguchi, Y. (2003). Pancultural self-enhancement. *Journal of Personality and Social Psychology, 84,* 60–79.

Sedikides, C., & Green, J. D. (2000). On the self-protective nature of inconsistency-negativity management: Using the person memory paradigm to examine self-referent memory. *Journal of Personality and Social Psychology, 79,* 906–922.

Sedikides, C., Herbst, K. C., Hardin, D. P., & Dardis, G. J. (2002). Accountability as a deterrent to self-enhancement: The search for mechanisms. *Journal of Personality and Social Psychology, 83,* 592–605.

Sedikides, C., & Jackson, J. M. (1990). Social impact theory: A field test of source strength, source immediacy, and number of targets. *Basic and Applied Social Psychology, 11,* 273–281.

Sedikides, C., Oliver, M. B., & Campbell, W. K. (1994). Perceived benefits and costs of romantic relationships for women and men: Implications for exchange theory. *Personal Relationships, 1,* 5–21.

Sedikides, C., & Skowronski, J. J. (1993). The self in impression formation: Trait centrality and social perception. *Journal of Experimental Social Psychology, 29,* 347–357.

Segerstrom, S. C. (2001). Optimism and attentional bias for negative and positive stimuli. *Personality and Social Psychology Bulletin, 27,* 1334–1343.

Segerstrom, S. C., Taylor, S. E., Kemeny, M. E., & Fahey, J. L. (1998). Optimism is associated with mood, coping, and immune changes in response to stress. *Journal of Personality and Social Psychology, 74,* 1646–1655.

Sellers, R. M., Rowley, S. A., Chavous, N. M., Shelton, N. J., & Smith, M. A. (1997). Multidimensional Inventory of Black Identity: A preliminary investigation of reliability and construct validity. *Journal of Personality and Social Psychology, 73,* 805–815.

Selye, H. (1956). *The stress of life.* New York: McGraw-Hill.

Selye, H. (1976). *Stress in health and disease.* Woburn, MA: Butterworth.

Sengupta, J., & Johar, G. V. (2001). Contingent effects of anxiety on message elaboration and persuasion. *Personality and Social Psychology Bulletin, 27,* 139–150.

Seta, J. J., McElroy, T., & Seta, C. E. (2001). To do or not to do: Desirability and consistency mediate judgments of regret. *Journal of Personality and Social Psychology, 80,* 861–870.

Setterlund, B. M., & Niedenthal, P. M. (1993). "Who am I? Why am I here?" Self-esteem, self-clarity, and prototype matching. *Journal of Personality and Social Psychology, 65,* 769–780.

Shah, J., & Higgins, E. T. (2001). Regulatory concerns and appraisal efficiency: The general impact of promotion and prevention. *Journal of Personality and Social Psychology, 80,* 693–705.

Shakin, M., Shakin, D., & Sternglanz, S. H. (1985). Infant clothing: Sex labeling for strangers. *Sex Roles, 12,* 955–964.

Shapiro, P. N., & Penrod, S. (1986). Meta-analysis of facial identification studies. *Psychological Bulletin, 100,* 139–156.

Sharp, M. J., & Getz, G. J. (1996). Substance use as impression management. *Personality and Social Psychology Bulletin, 22,* 60–67.

Shaw, J. I., & Skolnick, P. (1999). Weapon focus and gender difference in eyewitness accuracy: Arousal versus salience. *Journal of Applied Social Psychology, 29,* 2328–2341.

Shaw J. S., III, Garven, S., & Wood, J. M. (1997). Co-witness information can have immediate effects on eyewitness memory reports. *Law and Human Behavior, 21,* 503–523.

Sheeran, P., Conner, M., & Norman, P. (2001). Can the theory of planned behavior explain patterns of health behavior change? *Health Psychology, 20,* 12–19.

Sheeran, P., & Orbell, S. (1999). Implementation intentions and repeated behaviours: Enhancing the predictive validity of the theory of planned behaviour. *European Journal of Social Psychology, 29,* 349–369.

Sheeran, P., Orbell, S., & Trafimow, D. (1999). Does the temporal stability of behavioral intentions moderate intention-behavior and past behavior-future behavior relations? *Personality and Social Psychology Bulletin, 25,* 721–730.

Sheets, V. L., & Braver, S. L. (1999). Organizational status and perceived sexual harassment: Detecting the mediators of a null effect. *Personality and Social Psychology Bulletin, 25,* 1159–1171.

Shepperd, J. A., & Arkin, R. M. (1989). Self-handicapping: The moderating roles of public self-consciousness and task importance. *Personality and Social Psychology Bulletin, 15,* 252–265.

Shepperd, J. A., Ouellette, J. A., & Fernandez, J. K. (1996). Abandoning unrealistic optimism: Performance estimates and the temporal proximity of self-relevant feedback. *Journal of Personality and Social Psychology, 70,* 844–855.

Shepperd, J. A., & Wright, R. A. (1989). Individual contributions to a collective effort: An incentive analysis. *Personality and Social Psychology Bulletin, 15,* 141–149.

Sherif, M. (1936). *The psychology of social norms.* New York: Harper.

Sherif, M., & Cantril, H. (1947). *The psychology of ego-involvements.* New York: Wiley.

Sherif, M., Harvey, O. J., White, B. J., Hood, W. R., & Sherif, C. W. (1961). *Intergroup conflict and cooperation: The robber's cave experiment.* Norman: University of Oklahoma Press.

Sherman, D. A. K., Nelson, L. D., & Steele, C. M. (2000). Do messages about health risks threaten the self? Increasing the acceptance of threatening health messages via self-affirmation. *Personality and Social Psychology Bulletin, 26,* 1046–1058.

Sherman, D. K., & Kim, H. S. (2002). Affective perseverance: The resistance of affect to cognitive invalidation. *Personality and Social Psychology Bulletin, 28,* 224–237.

Sherman, J. W., & Klein, S. B. (1994). Development and representation of personality impressions. *Journal of Personality and Social Psychology, 67,* 972–983.

Sherman, J. W., Lee, A. Y., Bessenoff, G. R., & Frost, L. A. (1998). Stereotype efficiency reconsidered: Encoding flexibility under cognitive load. *Journal of Personality and Social Psychology, 75,* 589–606.

Sherman, R. C., Buddie, A. M., Dragan, K. L., End, C. M., & Finney, L. J. (1999). Twenty years of PSPB: Trends in content, design, and analysis. *Personality and Social Psychology Bulletin, 25,* 177–187.

Sherrill, K., & Yang, A. (2000). From outlaws to in-laws: Anti-gay attitudes thaw. *Public Perspective, 11,* 20–23.

Shih, M., Pittinsky, T. L., & Ambady, N. (1999). Stereotype susceptibility: Identity salience and shifts in quantitative performance. *Psychological Science, 10,* 81–84.

Shotland, R. L., & Huston, T. L. (1979). Emergencies: What are they and do they influence bystanders to intervene? *Journal of Personality and Social Psychology, 37,* 1822–1834.

Shotland, R. L., & Straw, M. K. (1976). Bystander response to an assault: When a man attacks a woman. *Journal of Personality and Social Psychology, 34,* 990–999.

Showers, C. (1992). Compartmentalization of positive and negative self-knowledge: Keeping bad apples out of the bunch. *Journal of Personality and Social Psychology, 62,* 1036–1049.

Showers, C. J., & Ryff, C. D. (1996). Self-differentiation and well-being in a life transition. *Personality and Social Psychology Bulletin, 22,* 448–460.

Shrauger, S. J., Mariano, E., & Walter, T. J. (1998). Depressive symptoms and accuracy in the prediction of future events. *Personality and Social Psychology Bulletin, 24,* 880–892.

Shrum, L. J., & McCarty, J. A. (1992). Individual differences in differentiation in the rating of personal values: The role of private self-consciousness. *Personality and Social Psychology Bulletin, 18,* 223–230.

Shumaker, S. A., & Hill, D. R. (1991). Gender differences in social support and physical health. *Health Psychology, 10,* 102–111.

Sia, T. L., Lord, C. G., Blessum, K. A., Thomas, J. C., & Lepper, M. R. (1999). Activation of exemplars in the process of assessing social category attitudes. *Journal of Personality and Social Psychology, 76,* 517–532.

Sidanius, J., & Pratto, F. (1999). *Social dominance: An intergroup theory of social hierarchy and oppression.* New York: Cambridge University Press.

Siebenaler, J. B., & Caldwell, D. K. (1956). Cooperation among adult dolphins. *Journal of Mammology, 37,* 126–128.

Siegel, D., Grady, D., Browner, W. S., & Hulley, S. B. (1988). Risk factor modifications after myocardial infarction. *Annals of Internal Medicine, 109,* 213–218.

Signorielli, N., & Lears, M. (1992). Children, television, and conceptions about chores: Attitudes and behaviors. *Sex Roles, 27,* 157–170.

Silverman, F. H., & Klees, J. (1989). Adolescents' attitudes toward peers who wear visible hearing aids. *Journal of Communication Disorders, 22,* 147–150.

Simon, B., Pantaleo, G., & Mummedy, A. (1995). Unique individual or interchangeable group member? The accentuation of intragroup differences versus similarities as an indicator of the individual versus self versus the collective self. *Journal of Personality and Social Psychology, 69,* 106–119.

Simon, L., Greenberg, J., & Brehm, J. (1995). Trivialization: The forgotten mode of dissonance reduction. *Journal of Personality and Social Psychology, 68,* 247–260.

Simon, R. W., Eder, D., & Evans, C. (1992). The development of feeling norms underlying romantic love among adolescent females. *Social Psychology Quarterly, 55,* 29–46.

Simpson, J. A., Campbell, B., & Berscheid, E. (1986). The association between romantic love and marriage: Kephart (1967) twice revisited. *Personality and Social Psychology Bulletin, 12,* 363–372.

Simpson, J. A., Rholes, W. S., & Nelligan, J. S. (1992). Support seeking and support giving within couples in an anxiety-provoking situation: The role of attachment styles. *Journal of Personality and Social Psychology, 62,* 434–446.

Singelis, T. M. (1994). The measurement of independent and interdependent self-construals. *Personality and Social Psychology Bulletin, 20,* 580–591.

Sistrunk, F., & McDavid, J. W. (1971). Sex variable in conformity behavior. *Journal of Personality and Social Psychology, 17,* 200–207.

Sivacek, J., & Crano, W. D. (1982). Vested interest as a moderator of attitude-behavior. *Journal of Personality and Social Psychology, 43,* 210–221.

Skinner, N., & Brewer, N. (2002). The dynamics of threat and challenge appraisals prior to stressful achievement events. *Journal of Personality and Social Psychology, 83,* 678–692.

Skitka, L. J. (1999). Ideological and attributional boundaries on public compassion: Reactions to individuals and communities affected by a natural disaster. *Personality and Social Psychology Bulletin, 25,* 793–808.

Skolnick, A. S. (1987). *The intimate environment: Exploring marriage and the family.* Boston: Little, Brown.

Skolnick, P. (1977). Helping as a function of time of day, location, and sex of victim. *Journal of Social Psychology, 102,* 61–62.

Skowronski, J. J., Carlston, D. E., Mae, L., & Crawford, M. T. (1998). Spontaneous trait transference: Communicators take on the qualities they describe in others. *Journal of Personality and Social Psychology, 74,* 837–848.

Skrypnek, B. J., & Snyder, M. (1982). On the self-perpetuating nature of stereotypes about women and men. *Journal of Experimental Social Psychology, 18,* 277–291.

Sleek, S. (1994, January). APA works to reduce violence in the media. *APA Monitor, 25,* 6–7.

Sleek, S. (1998, September). Isolation increases with Internet use. *APA Monitor, 29,* 30–31.

Slovic, P., Fischhoff, B., & Lichtenstein, S. (1977). Behavioral decision theory. In M. R. Rosenzweig & L. W. Porter (Eds.), *Annual review of psychology* (Vol. 28, pp. 1–39). Palo Alto, CA: Annual Reviews.

Slusher, M. P., & Anderson, C. A. (1987). When reality monitoring fails: The role of imagination in stereotype maintenance. *Journal of Personality and Social Psychology, 52,* 653–662.

Smith, D. M., & Hand, C. (1987). The pornography/aggression linkage: Results from a field study. *Deviant Behavior, 8,* 389–399.

Smith, D. M., Neuberg, S. L., Judice, T. N., & Biesanz, J. C. (1997). Target complicity in the confirmation and disconfirmation of erroneous perceiver expectations: Immediate and longer term implications. *Journal of Personality and Social Psychology, 73,* 974–991.

Smith, E. E., & Medin, D. L. (1981). *Categories and concepts.* Cambridge, MA: Harvard University Press.

Smith, E. R., Fazio, R. H., & Cejka, M. A. (1996). Accessible attitudes influence categorization of multiply categorizable objects. *Journal of Personality and Social Psychology, 70,* 893–912.

Smith, S. M., Lindsay, R. C. L., & Pryke, S. (2000). Postdictors of eyewitness errors: Can false identifications be diagnosed? *Journal of Applied Psychology, 85,* 542–550.

Smith, S. S., & Richardson, D. (1983). Amelioration of deception and harm in psychological research: The important role of debriefing. *Journal of Personality and Social Psychology, 44,* 1075–1082.

Smith, T. M., Limon, J. P., Gallo, L. C., & Ngu, L. Q. (1996). Interpersonal control and cardiovascular reactivity: Goals, behavioral expression, and the moderating effects of sex. *Journal of Personality and Social Psychology, 70,* 1012–1024.

Smith, T. W., & Frohm, K. D. (1985). What's so unhealthy about hostility? Construct validity and psychosocial correlates of the Cook and Medley HO scale. *Health Psychology, 4,* 503–520.

Smith, T. W., Ruiz, J. M., & Uchino, B. N. (2000). Vigilance, active coping, and cardiovascular reactivity during social interaction in young men. *Health Psychology, 19,* 382–392.

Snider, R. (2004, January 29). Terp turns to state to muzzle vulgar fans. *The Washington Times.* Retrieved July 8, 2004, from http://www.washingtontimes.com/functions/print.php?storyID=200

Sniderman, P. M., Crosby, G. C. & Howell, W. G. (2000). The politics of race. In D. O. Sears, J. Sidanius, & L. Bobo (Eds.), *Racialized politics: The debate about racism in America* (pp. 236–279). Chicago, IL: University of Chicago Press.

Snodgrass, S. E. (1992). Further effects of role versus gender on interpersonal sensitivity. *Journal of Personality and Social Psychology, 62,* 154–158.

Snodgrass, S. E., Hecht, M. A., & Ploutz-Snyder, R. (1998). Interpersonal sensitivity: Expressivity or perceptivity. *Journal of Personality and Social Psychology, 74,* 238–249.

Snyder, C. R., & Fromkin, H. L. (1980). *Uniqueness: The human pursuit of difference.* New York: Plenum Press.

Snyder, C. R., & Higgins, R. L. (1988). Excuses: Their effective role in the negotiation of reality. *Psychological Bulletin, 104,* 23–25.

Snyder, M., Clary, E. G., & Stukas, A. A. (2000). The functional approach to volunteerism. In G. R. Maio & J. M. Olson (Eds.), *Why we evaluate: The function of attitudes* (pp. 365–393). Mahwah, NJ: Erlbaum.

Snyder, M., & Gangestad, S. (1981). Hypothesis-testing processes. In J. H. Harvey, W. Ickes, & R. F. Kidd (Eds.), New *directions in attribution research* (Vol. 3, pp. 171–198). Hillsdale, NJ: Erlbaum.

Snyder, M., & Haugen, J. A. (1995). Why does behavioral confirmation occur? A functional perspective on the role of the target. *Personality and Social Psychology Bulletin, 21,* 963–974.

Snyder, M., & Omoto, A. M. (1992). Volunteerism and society's response to the HIV epidemic. *Current Directions in Psychological Science, 1,* 113–116.

Snyder, M., & Omoto, A. M. (2001). Basic research and practical problems: Volunteerism and the psychology of individual and collective action. In W. Wosinska, R. B. Cialdini, D. W. Barrett, & J. Reykowski (Eds.), *The practice of social influence in multiple cultures* (pp. 287–307). Mahwah, NJ: Erlbaum.

Snyder, M., & Swann, W. B., Jr. (1978). Hypothesis-testing processes in social interaction. *Journal of Personality and Social Psychology, 36,* 1202–1212.

Snyder, M., Tanke, E. D., & Berscheid, E. (1977). Social perception and interpersonal behavior: On the self-fulfilling nature of social stereotypes. *Journal of Personality and Social Psychology, 35,* 656–666.

Soderstrom, M., Dolbier, C., Leiferman, J., & Steinhardt, M. (2000). The relationship of hardiness, coping strategies, and perceived stress to symptoms of illness. *Journal of Behavioral Medicine, 23,* 311–328.

Sohlberg, S., & Birgegard, A. (2003). Persistent complex subliminal activation effects: First experimental observations. *Journal of Personality and Social Psychology, 85,* 302–316.

Solomon, S. E., Rothblum, E. D., & Balsam, K. F. (2004). [Money, housework, sex, and conflict: Same-sex couples in civil unions, those not in civil unions, and heterosexual married siblings]. Unpublished raw data.

Sommer, K. L., & Baumeister, R. F. (2002). Self-evaluation, persistence, and performance following implicit rejection: The role of trait self-esteem. *Personality and Social Psychology Bulletin, 28,* 926–938.

Sommers, S. R., & Ellsworth, P. C. (2000). Race in the courtroom: Perceptions of guilt and dispositional attributions. *Personality and Social Psychology Bulletin, 26,* 1367–1379.

Sommers, S. R., & Ellsworth, P. C. (2001). White juror bias: An investigation of prejudice against Black defendants in the American courtroom. *Psychology, Public Policy, and Law, 7,* 201–229.

Sorensen, J. W., & White, S. B. (1992). A sociocultural view of sexual assault: From discrepancy to diversity. *Journal of Social Issues, 48,* 187–195.

Sorrentino, R. M., & Roney, C. J. R. (1986). Uncertainty orientation, achievement-related motivation, and task diagnosticity as determinants of task performance. *Social Cognition, 4,* 420–436.

Speca, M., Carlson, L. E., Goodey, E., & Angen, M. (2000). A randomized, wait-list controlled clinical trial: The effect of a mindfulness meditation-based stress reduction program on mood and symptoms of stress in cancer outpatients. *Psychosomatic Medicine, 62,* 613–622.

Spence, J. T. (1991). Do the BSRI and PAQ measure the same or different concepts? *Psychology of Women Quarterly, 15,* 141–165.

Spence, J. T., & Buckner, C. E. (2000). Instrumental and expressive traits, trait stereotypes, and sexist attitudes. *Psychology of Women Quarterly, 24,* 44–62.

Spence, J. T., & Helmreich, R. L. (1972). The Attitudes Toward Women Scale: An objective instrument to measure attitudes toward the rights and roles of women in contemporary society. *JSAS Catalog of Selected Documents in Psychology, 2,* 667–668.

Spencer, S. J., Steele, C. M., & Quinn, D. M. (1999). Stereotype threat and women's math performance. *Journal of Experimental Social Psychology, 35,* 4–28.

Spencer, M. B., & Markstrom-Adams, C. (1990). Identity processes among racial and ethnic minority children in America. *Child Development, 61,* 290–310.

Sporer, S. L., Penrod, S. D., Read, J. D., & Cutler, B. L. (1995). Choosing, confidence, and accuracy: A meta-analysis of the confidence-accuracy relation in eyewitness identification studies. *Psychological Bulletin, 118,* 315–327.

Spradley, J. P., & Phillips, M. (1972). Culture and stress: A quantitative analysis. *American Anthropologist, 74,* 518–529.

Sprafkin, J. N., Liebert, R. M., & Poulos, R. W. (1975). Effects of prosocial televised example on children's helping. *Journal of Experimental Child Psychology, 20,* 119–126.

Spragins, E. (1996, June 24). Does your HMO stack up? *Newsweek,* pp. 56–61, 63.

Sprecher, S. (1992). How men and women expect to feel and behave in response to inequity in close relationships. *Social Psychology Quarterly, 55,* 57–69.

Sprecher, S. (1999). "I love you more today than yesterday": Romantic partners' perceptions of changes in love and related affect over time. *Journal of Personality and Social Psychology, 76,* 46–53.

Sprecher, S. (2001). Equity and social exchange in dating couples: Associations with satisfaction, commitment and stability. *Journal of Marriage and the Family, 63,* 599–613.

Sprecher, S., & Regan, P. C. (2002). Liking some things (in some people) more than others: Partner preferences in romantic relationships and friendships. *Journal of Social and Personal Relationships, 19,* 463–481.

Sprecher, S., Sullivan, Q., & Hatfield, E. (1994). Mate selection preferences: Gender differences examined in a national sample. *Journal of Personality and Social Psychology, 66,* 1074–1080.

Stalder, D. R., & Baron, R. S. (1998). Attributional complexity as a moderator of dissonance-produced attitude change. *Journal of Personality and Social Psychology, 75,* 449–455.

Stangor, C. (1990). Arousal, accessibility of trait constructs, and person perception. *Journal of Experimental Social Psychology, 26,* 305–321.

Stangor, C., Sechrist, G. B., & Jost, J. T. (2001). Changing racial beliefs by providing consensus information. *Personality and Social Psychology Bulletin, 27,* 486–496.

Stangor, C., Sullivan, L. A., & Ford, T. E. (1991). Affective and cognitive determinants of prejudice. *Social Cognition, 9,* 359–380.

Stanton, A. L., Kirk, S. B., Cameron, C. L., & Danoff-Burg, S. (2000). Coping through emotional approach: Scale construction and validation. *Journal of Personality and Social Psychology, 78,* 1150–1169.

Stapel, D. A., & Koomen, W. (2000). Distinctness of others, mutability of selves: Their impact on self-evaluations. *Journal of Personality and Social Psychology, 79,* 1068–1087.

Stapel, D. A., & Koomen, W. (2001). When we wonder what it all means: Interpretation goals facilitate accessibility and stereotyping effects. *Personality and Social Psychology Bulletin, 27,* 915–929.

Stapel, D. A., Koomen, W., & Ruys, K. I. (2002). The effects of diffuse and distinct affect. *Journal of Personality and Social Psychology, 83,* 60–74.

Stapel, D. A., Koomen, W., & Zeelenberg, M. (1998). The impact of accuracy motivation on interpretation, comparison and correction processes: Accuracy X knowledge accessibility effects. *Journal of Personality and Social Psychology, 74,* 878–893.

Stapel, D. A., Martin, L. L., & Schwarz, N. (1998). The smell of bias: What instigates correction processes in social judgments? *Personality and Social Psychology Bulletin, 24,* 797–806.

Stapel, D. A., & Tesser, A. (2001). Self-activation increases social comparison. *Journal of Personality and Social Psychology, 81,* 742–750.

Staples, R., & Mirande, A. (1980). Racial and cultural variation among American families: A decennial review of the literature on minority families. *Journal of Marriage and the Family, 42,* 887–903.

Statistics Canada. (2004). Ethnocultural portrait of Canada. Retrieved July 22, 2004, from http://www12.statcan.ca/english/census01/products/standard/themes

Steblay, N., Dysart, J., Fulero, S., & Lindsay, R. C. L. (2001). Eyewitness accuracy rates in sequential and simultaneous lineup presentations: A meta-analytic comparison. *Law and Human Behavior, 25,* 459–474.

Steblay, N., Dysart, J., Fulero, S., & Lindsay, R. C. L. (2003). Eyewitness accuracy rates in police showup and lineup presentations: A meta-analytic comparison. *Law and Human Behavior, 27,* 523–540.

Steblay, N. M. (1992). A meta-analytic review of the weapon focus effect. *Law and Human Behavior, 16,* 413–424.

Steblay, N. M. (1997). Social influence in eyewitness recall: A meta-analytic review of lineup instruction effects. *Law and Human Behavior, 21,* 283–297.

Steblay, N. M., Besirevic, J., Fulero, S. M., & Jimenez-Lorente, B. (1999). The effects of pretrial publicity on juror verdicts: A meta-analytic review. *Law and Human Behavior, 23,* 219–236.

Steele, C. M. (1988). The psychology of self-affirmation: Sustaining the integrity of the self. In L. Berkowitz (Ed.), *Advances in Experimental Social Psychology* (Vol. 21, pp. 261–302). New York: Academic Press.

Steele, C. M., & Aronson, J. (1995). Stereotype threat and the intellectual test performance of African Americans. *Journal of Personality and Social Psychology, 69,* 797–811.

Steele, C. M., & Southwick, L. (1985). Alcohol and social behavior: I. The psychology of drunken excess. *Journal of Personality and Social Psychology, 48,* 18–34.

Stein, J. A., Fox, S. A., & Murata, P. J. (1991). The influence of ethnicity, socioeconomic status, and psychological barriers on use of mammography. *Journal of Health and Social Behavior, 32,* 101–113.

Stein, J. A., Newcomb, M. D., & Bentler, P. M. (1992). The effect of agency and communality on self-esteem: Gender differences in longitudinal data. *Sex Roles, 26,* 465–483.

Steinpreis, R. E., Anders, K. A., & Ritzke, D. (1999). The impact of gender on the review of the curricula vitae of job applicants and tenure candidates: A national empirical study. *Sex Roles, 41,* 509–528.

Stephens, M. A. P., & Franks, M. M. (1999). Parent care in the context of women's multiple roles. *Current Directions in Psychological Science, 8,* 149–152.

Sternberg, R. J. (1986). A triangular theory of love. *Psychological Review, 93,* 119–135.

Stolberg, S. (1993, October 22). Researchers link gene to aggression. *Los Angeles Times,* pp. A36–A37.

Stolberg, S. G. (2002, October 3). War, murder and suicide: A year's toll is 1.6 million. *The New York Times,* p. A11.

Stone, J. (2002). Battling doubt by avoiding practice: The effects of stereotype threat on self-handicapping in white athletes. *Personality and Social Psychology Bulletin, 28,* 1667–1678.

Stone, J. (2003). Self-consistency for low self-esteem in dissonance processes: The role of self- standards. *Personality and Social Psychology Bulletin, 29,* 846–858.

Stone, J., & Cooper, J. (2001). A self-standards model of cognitive dissonance. *Journal of Experimental Social Psychology, 37,* 228–243.

Stone, R. (1993, June 11). Panel finds gap in violent studies. *Science, 260,* 1582–1585.

Stoner, J. (1968). Risky and cautious shifts in group decisions. *Journal of Experimental Social Psychology, 4,* 442–459.

Story, A. L. (1998). Self-esteem and memory for favorable and unfavorable personality feedback. *Personality and Social Psychology Bulletin, 24,* 51–64.

Stouffer, S. A., Suchman, E. A., DeVinney, L. C., Star, S. A., & Williams, R. M., Jr. (1949). *The American soldier: Adjustment during army life.* New York: Wiley.

Strack, F., & Neumann, R. (2000). Furrowing the brow may undermine perceived fame: The role of facial feedback in judgments of celebrity. *Personality and Social Psychology Bulletin,* 26, 762–768.

Strahan, E. J., Spencer, S. J., & Zanna, M. P. (2002). Subliminal priming and persuasion: Striking while the iron is hot. *Journal of Experimental Social Psychology, 38,* 556–568.

Strauman, T. J. (1996). Stability within the self: A longitudinal study of the structural implications of self-discrepancy theory. *Journal of Personality and Social Psychology, 71,* 1142–1153.

Straus, M. A., Gelles, R. J., & Steinmetz, S. K. (1980). *Behind closed doors: Violence in American Families.* New York: Doubleday.

Strayer, F. F., Wareing, S., & Rushton, J. P. (1979). Social constraints on naturally occurring preschool altruism. *Ethology and Sociobiology, 1,* 3–11.

Strier, F. (1999). Whither trial consulting? Issues and projections. *Law and Human Behavior, 23,* 93–116.

Strömwall, L. A., & Granhag, P. A. (2003). How to detect deception? Arresting the beliefs of police officers, prosecutors, and judges. *Psychology, Crime, and Law, 9,* 19–36.

Studebaker, C. A., Robbenolt, J. K., Penrod, S. D., Pathak-Sharma, M. K., Groscup, J. L., & Devenport, J. L. (2002). Studying pretrial publicity effects: New methods for improving ecological validity and testing external validity. *Law and Human Behavior, 26,* 19–42.

Suh, E. (2002). Culture, identity consistency, and subjective well-being. *Journal of Personality and Social Psychology, 83,* 1378–1391.

Suh, E., Diener, E., Oishi, S., & Triandis, H. C. (1998). The shifting basis of life satisfaction judgments across cultures: Emotion versus norms. *Journal of Personality and Social Psychology, 74,* 482–493.

Suls, J., & Fletcher, B. (1985). The relative efficacy of avoidant and nonavoidant coping strategies: A meta-analysis. *Health Psychology, 4,* 249–288.

Suls, J., Green, P., & Hillis, S. (1998). Emotional reactivity to everyday problems, affective inertia, and neuroticism. *Personality and Social Psychology Bulletin, 24,* 127–136.

Suls, J., Lemos, K., & Stewart, H. L. (2002). Self-esteem, construal, and comparisons with the self, friends, and peers. *Journal of Personality and Social Psychology, 82,* 252–261.

Suls, J., & Mullen, B. (1981). Life change in psychological distress: The role of perceived control and desirability. *Journal of Applied Social Psychology, 11,* 379–389.

Surgeon General's Scientific Advisory Committee. (1972). *Television and growing up: The impact of televised violence: Report to the Surgeon General.* U.S. Public Health Service, Department of Health, Education, and Welfare Publication N. HSM 72-9086. Rockville, MD: National Institute of Health.

Surra, C. A. (1990). Research and theory on mate selection and premarital relationships in the 1980s. *Journal of Marriage and the Family, 52,* 844–865.

Surra, C. A., & Gray, C. R. (2000). A typology of processes of commitment to marriage. In L. J. Waite, C. Backrach, M. Hindin, E. Thomson, & A. Thornton (Eds.), *The ties that bind: Perspectives on marriage and cohabitation* (pp. 253–280). New York: Aldine de Gryter.

Surra, C. A., & Longstreth, M. (1990). Similarity of outcomes, interdependence, and conflict in dating relationships. *Journal of Personality and Social Psychology, 59,* 501–516.

Swann, W. B., Jr. (1983). Self-verification: Bringing social reality into harmony with the self. In J. Suls & A. G. Greenwald (Eds.), *Social psychology perspectives* (Vol. 2, pp. 33–66). Hillsdale, NJ: Erlbaum.

Swann, W. B., Jr., & Ely, R. J. (1984). A battle of wills: Self-verification versus behavioral confirmation. *Journal of Personality and Social Psychology, 46,* 1287–1302.

Swann, W. B., Jr., Giulano, T., & Wegner, D. M. (1982). Where leading questions can lead: The power of conjecture in social interaction. *Journal of Personality and Social Psychology, 42,* 1025–1035.

Swann, W. B., Jr., & Pelham, B. W. (1990). [Embracing the bitter truth: Positivity and authenticity in social relationships.] Unpublished raw data.

Swann, W. B., Jr., & Read, S. J. (1981). Self-verification processes: How we sustain our self-conceptions. *Journal of Experimental Social Psychology, 17,* 351–370.

Swann, W. B., Jr., & Schroeder, D. G. (1995). The search for beauty and truth: A framework for understanding reactions to evaluations. *Personality and Social Psychology Bulletin, 21,* 1307–1318.

Swann, W. B., Jr., Stein-Seroussi, A., & Giesler, R. B. (1992). Why people self-verify. *Journal of Personality and Social Psychology, 62,* 392–401.

Swensen, C. H. (1972). The behavior of love. In H. A. Otto (Ed.), *Love today* (pp. 86–101). New York: Dell.

Swim, J., Borgida, E., Maruyama, G., & Myers, D. G. (1989). Joan McKay versus John McKay: Do gender stereotypes bias evaluations? *Psychological Bulletin, 105,* 409–429.

Swim, J. K., Aikin, K., Hall, W. S., & Hunter, B. A. (1995). Sexism and racism: Old-fashioned and modern prejudices. *Journal of Personality and Social Psychology, 68,* 199–214.

Swim, J. K., & Sanna, L. J. (1996). He's skilled, she's lucky: A meta-analysis of observers' attributions for women's and men's successes and failures. *Personality and Social Psychology Bulletin, 22,* 507–519.

Swim, J. K., & Stangor, C. (Eds.). (1998). *Prejudice: The target's perspective.* New York: Academic Press.

Swim, J. K., Scott, E. D., Sechrist, G. B., Campbell, B., & Stangor, C. (2003). The role of intent and harm in judgments of prejudice and discrimination. *Journal of Personality and Social Psychology, 84,* 944–959.

Szapocznik, J. (1995). Research on disclosure of HIV status: Cultural evolution finds an ally in science. *Health Psychology, 14,* 4–5.

Tafarodi, R. W., Marshall, T. C., & Milne, A. B. (2003). Self-esteem and memory. *Journal of Personality and Social Psychology, 84,* 29–45.

Tajfel, H. (1969). Cognitive aspects of prejudice. *Journal of Social Issues, 25,* 79–97.

Tajfel, H. (1981). *Human groups and social categories.* Cambridge, England: Cambridge University Press.

Tajfel, H. (Ed.). (1982). *Social identity and intergroup relations.* Cambridge, England: Cambridge University Press.

Tajfel, H., Billig, M. G., Bundy, R. P., & Flament, C. (1971). Social categorization and intergroup behavior. *European Journal of Social Psychology, 1,* 149–178.

Tajfel, H., & Turner, J. C. (1986). The social identity theory of intergroup behavior. In S. Worchel & W. G. Austin (Eds.), *Psychology of intergroup relations* (2nd ed., pp. 7–24). Chicago: Nelson-Hall.

Takata, T. (1987). Self-deprecative tendencies in self-evaluation through social comparison. *Japanese Journal of Experimental Social Psychology, 27,* 27–36.

Tamir, M., Robinson, M. D., & Clore, G. L. (2002). The epistemic benefits of trait-consistent mood states: An analysis of extraversion and mood. *Journal of Personality and Social Psychology, 83,* 663–677.

Tamir, M., Robinson, M. D., Clore, G. L., Martin, L. L., & Whitaker, D. J. (2004). Are we puppets on a string? The contextual meaning of unconscious expressive cues. *Personality and Social Psychology Bulletin, 30,* 237–249.

Tarde, B. (1903). *The laws of imitation.* New York: Holt, Rinehart and Winston.

Tarman, C., & Sears, D. O. (2005). The conceptualization and measurement of symbolic racism. *Journal of Politics.*

Taylor, D. W., Berry, P. C., & Block, C. H. (1958). Does group participation when using brainstorming facilitate or inhibit creative thinking? *Administrative Science Quarterly, 2,* 23–47.

Taylor, K. M., & Shepperd, J. A. (1998). Bracing for the worst: Severity, testing, and feedback timing as moderators of the optimistic bias. *Personality and Social Psychology Bulletin, 24,* 915–926.

Taylor, L. (1992). Relationship between affect and memory: Motivation-based selective generation. *Journal of Personality and Social Psychology, 62,* 876–882.

Taylor, S. E. (1981). A categorization approach to stereotyping. In D. L. Hamilton (Ed.), *Cognitive processes in stereotyping and intergroup behavior* (pp. 83–114). Hillsdale, NJ: Erlbaum.

Taylor, S. E. (1983). Adjustment to threatening events: A theory of cognitive adaptation. *American Psychologist, 38,* 1161–1173.

Taylor, S. E. (1991). Asymmetrical effects of positive and negative events: The mobilization-minimization hypothesis. *Psychological Bulletin, 110,* 67–85.

Taylor, S. E. (2002). *The tending instinct.* New York: Holt.

Taylor, S. E. (2003). *Health psychology* (5th ed.). New York: McGraw-Hill.

Taylor, S. E., & Aspinwall, L. G. (1990). Psychological aspects of chronic illness. In G. R. VadenBos & P. T. Costa, Jr. (Eds.), *Psychological aspects of serious illness* (pp. 3–60). Washington, DC: American Psychological Association.

Taylor, S. E., & Brown, J. (1988). Illusion and well-being: A social psychological perspective on mental health. *Psychological Bulletin, 103,* 193–210.

Taylor, S. E., & Clark, L. F. (1986). Does information improve adjustment to noxious events? In M. J. Saks & L. Saxe (Eds.), *Advances in applied social psychology* (Vol. 3, pp. 1–28). Hillsdale, NJ: Erlbaum.

Taylor, S. E., & Crocker, J. (1981). Schematic bases of social information processing. In E. T. Higgins, C. P. Herman, & M. P. Zanna (Eds.), *Social Cognition: The Ontario Symposium* (Vol. 1, pp. 89–134). Hillsdale, NJ: Erlbaum.

Taylor, S. E., & Fiske, S. T. (1975). Point of view and perceptions of causality. *Journal of Personality and Social Psychology, 32,* 439–445.

Taylor, S. E., & Fiske, S. T. (1978). Salience, attention, and attribution: Top of the head phenomena. In L. Berkowitz (Ed.), *Advances in experimental social psychology,* (Vol. 11, pp. 249–288). New York: Academic Press.

Taylor, S. E., Fiske, S. T., Close, M., Anderson, C., & Ruderman, A. (1977). *Solo status as a psychological variable: The power of being distinctive.* Unpublished manuscript, Harvard University, Cambridge, MA.

Taylor, S. E., Fiske, S. T., Eticoff, N. C., & Ruderman, A. J. (1978). Categorical and contextual bases of person memory. *Journal of Personality and Social Psychology, 36,* 778–793.

Taylor, S. E., & Gollwitzer, P. M. (1995). The effects of mindset on positive illusions. *Journal of Personality and Social Psychology, 69,* 213–226.

Taylor, S. E., Helgeson, V. S., Reed, G. M., & Skokan, L. A. (1991). Self-generated feelings of control and adjustment to physical illness. *Journal of Social Issues, 47,* 91–109.

Taylor, S. E., Kemeny, M. E., Reed, G. M., Bower, J. E., & Gruenewald, T. L. (2000). Psychological resources, positive illusions, and health. *American Psychologist, 55,* 99–109.

Taylor, S. E., & Koivumaki, J. H. (1976). The perception of self and others: Acquaintanceship, affect, and actor-observer differences. *Journal of Personality and Social Psychology, 33,* 403–408.

Taylor, S. E., Lerner, J. S., Sherman, D. K., Sage, R. M., & McDowell, N. K. (2003). Portrait of the self-enhancer: Well-Adjusted and Well-Liked or Maladjusted and Friendless? *Journal of Personality and Social Psychology, 84,* 165–176.

Taylor, S. E., Lichtman, R. R., & Wood, J. V. (1984). Attributions, beliefs about control, and adjustment to breast cancer. *Journal of Personality and Social Psychology, 46,* 489–502.

Taylor, S. E., & Lobel, M. (1989). Social comparison activity under threat: Downward evaluation and upward contacts. *Psychological Review, 96,* 569–575.

Taylor, S. E., Pham, L. B., Rivkin, I. D., & Armor, D. A. (1998). Harnessing the imagination: Mental simulation, self-regulation, and coping. *American Psychologist, 53,* 429–439.

Taylor, S. E., Repetti, R. L., & Seeman, T. E. (1997). Health psychology: What is an unhealthy environment and how does it get under the skin? *Annual Review of Psychology, 48,* 411–447.

Taylor, S. E., & Thompson, S. C. (1982). Stalking the elusive "vividness" effect. *Psychological Review, 89,* 155–181.

Taylor, S. E., Wood, J. V., & Lichtman, R. R. (1983). It could be worse: Selective evaluation as a response to victimization. *Journal of Social Issues, 39,* 19–40.

Taylor, S. P., & Gammon, C. B. (1975). Effects of type and dose of alcohol on human physical aggression. *Journal of Personality and Social Psychology, 32,* 169–175.

Taylor, S. P., Gammon, C. B., & Capasso, D. R. (1976). Aggression as a function of the interaction of alcohol and frustration. *Journal of Personality and Social Psychology, 34,* 938–941.

Taylor, S. P., Schmutte, G. T., Leonard, K. E., & Cranston, J. W. (1979). The effects of alcohol and extreme provocation on the use of a highly noxious electric shock. *Motivation and Emotion, 3,* 73–81.

Taylor, S. P., & Sears, J. D. (1988). The effects of alcohol and persuasive social pressure on human physical aggression. *Aggressive Behavior, 14,* 237–243.

Tedesco, L. A., Keffer, M. A., & Fleck-Kandath, C. (1991). Self-efficacy, reasoned action, and oral health behavior reports: A social cognitive approach to compliance. *Journal of Behavioral Medicine, 14,* 341–355.

Terry, D. J., & Hogg, M. A. (1996). Group norms and the attitude-behavior relationship: A role for group identification. *Personality and Social Psychology Bulletin, 22,* 776–793.

Terry, D. J., & Hynes, G. J. (1998). Adjustment to a low-control situation: Reexamining the role of coping responses. *Journal of Personality and Social Psychology, 74,* 1078–1092.

Tesser, A. (1978). Self-generated attitude change. In L. Berkowitz (Ed.), *Advances in experimental social psychology* (Vol. 11, pp. 290–338). New York: Academic Press.

Tesser, A. (1988). Toward a self-evaluation maintenance model of social behavior. In L. Berkowitz (Ed.), *Advances in experimental social psychology* (Vol. 21, pp. 181–227). New York: Academic Press.

Tesser, A., & Collins, J. E. (1988). Emotion in social reflection and comparison situations: Intuitive, systematic, and exploratory approaches. *Journal of Personality and Social Psychology, 55,* 695–709.

Tesser, A., & Conlee, M. C. (1975). Some effects of time and thought on attitude polarization. *Journal of Personality and Social Psychology, 31,* 262–270.

Tesser, A., Crepaz, N., Collins, S. R., Cornell, D., & Beach, J. C. (2000). Confluence of self-esteem regulation mechanisms: On integrating the self-zoo. *Personality and Social Psychology Bulletin, 26,* 1476–1489.

Tesser, A., Pilkington, C. J., & McIntosh, W. D. (1989). Self-evaluation maintenance and the mediational role of emotion: The perception of friends and strangers. *Journal of Personality and Social Psychology, 57,* 442–456.

Testa, R. J., Kinder, B. N., & Ironson, G. (1987). Heterosexual bias in the perception of loving relationships of gay males and lesbians. *Journal of Sex Research, 23,* 163–172.

Tetlock, P. E. (1999). Accountability theory: Mixing properties of human agents with properties of social systems. In J. Levine, L. Thompson, & D. Messick (Eds.), *Shared cognition in organizations: The management of knowledge* (pp. 111–137). Hillsdale, NJ: Erlbaum.

Tetlock, P. E., & Boettger, R. (1989). Accountability: A social magnifier of the dilution effect. *Journal of Personality and Social Psychology, 57,* 388–398.

Tetlock, P. E., Peterson, R. S., McGuire, C., & Chang, S., et al. (1992). Assessing political group dynamics: A test of the groupthink model. *Journal of Personality and Social Psychology, 63,* 403–425.

Thibaut, J. W., & Kelley, H. H. (1959). *The social psychology of groups.* New York: Wiley.

Thibodeau, R. (1989). From racism to tokenism: The changing face of blacks in New Yorker cartoons. *Public Opinion Quarterly, 53,* 482–494.

Thoits, P. A. (1994). Stressors and problem-solving: The individual as psychological activist. *Journal of Health and Social Behavior, 35,* 143–159.

Thompson, E. P., Roman, R. J., Moskowitz, G. B., Chaiken, S., & Bargh, J. A. (1994). Accuracy motivation attenuates covert priming: The systematic reprocessing of social information. *Journal of Personality and Social Psychology, 66,* 474–489.

Thompson, S. C., Nanni, C., & Levine, A. (1994). Primary versus secondary and central versus consequence-related control in HIV-positive men. *Journal of Personality and Social Psychology, 67,* 540–547.

Thompson, S. C., & Spacapan, S. (1991). Perceptions of control in vulnerable populations. *Journal of Social Issues, 47,* 1–21.

Thompson, T. L., & Zerbinos, E. (1995). Gender roles in animated cartoons: Has the picture changed in 20 years? *Sex Roles, 32,* 651–673.

Thompson, V. L. S. (1990). Factors affecting the level of African American identification. *The Journal of Black Psychology, 17,* 19–35.

Thompson, V. L. S. (1991). Perceptions of race and race relations which affect African American identification. *Journal of Applied Social Psychology, 21,* 1502–1516.

Thornton, B., Ryckman, R. M., Kirschner, G., Jacobs, J., Kaczor, L., & Kuehnel, R. H. (1988). Reaction to self-attributed victim responsibility: A comparative analysis of rape crisis counselors and lay observers. *Journal of Applied Social Psychology, 18,* 409–422.

Tice, D. M. (1992). Self-concept change and self-presentation: The looking glass self is also a magnifying glass. *Journal of Personality and Social Psychology, 63,* 435–451.

Tichenor, V. J. (1999). Status and income as gendered resources: The case of marital power. *Journal of Marriage and the Family, 61,* 638–650.

Tidwell, M. O., Reis, H. T., & Shaver, P. R. (1996). Attachment, attractiveness, and social interaction: A diary study. *Journal of Personality and Social Psychology, 71,* 729–745.

Tiedens, L. Z., & Fragale, A. R. (2003). Power moves: Complementarity in dominant and submissive nonverbal behavior. *Journal of Personality and Social Psychology, 84,* 558–568.

Tiedens, L. Z., & Linton, S. (2001). Judgment under emotional certainty and uncertainty: The effects of specific emotions on information processing. *Journal of Personality and Social Psychology, 81,* 973–988.

Tilker, H. A. (1970). Socially responsible behavior as a function of observer responsibility and victim feedback. *Journal of Personality and Social Psychology, 14,* 95–100.

Toi, M., & Batson, C. D. (1982). More evidence that empathy is a source of altruistic motivation. *Journal of Personality and Social Psychology, 43,* 281–292.

Tomaka, J., Blascovich, J., Kibler, J., & Ernst, J. M. (1997). Cognitive and physiological antecedents of threat and challenge appraisal. *Journal of Personality and Social Psychology, 73,* 63–72.

Tong, Y.-y., & Chiu, C.-y. (2002). Lay theories and evaluation-based organization of impressions: An application of the memory search paradigm. *Personality and Social Psychology Bulletin, 28,* 1518–1527.

Tordesillas, R. S., & Chaiken, S. (1999). Thinking too much or too little? The effects of introspection on the decision-making process. *Personality Bulletin, 25,* 623–629.

Toris, C., & DePaulo, B. M. (1984). Effects of actual deception and suspiciousness of deception on interpersonal perceptions. *Journal of Personality and Social Psychology, 47,* 1063–1073.

Tormala, Z. L., & Petty, R. E. (2001). On-line versus memory-based processing: The role of "need to evaluate" in person perception. *Personality and Social Psychology Bulletin, 27,* 1599–1612.

Tormala, Z. L., Petty, R. E., & Briñol, P. (2002). Ease of retrieval effects in persuasion: A self-validation analysis. *Personality and Social Psychology Bulletin, 28,* 1700–1712.

Tougas, F., Brown, R., Beaton, A. M., & Joly, S. (1995). Neosexism: Plus ca change, plus c'est pareil. *Personality and Social Psychology Bulletin, 21,* 842–849.

Trafimow, D. (1998). Situation-specific effects in person memory. *Journal of Personality and Social Psychology, 46,* 314–321.

Trafimow, D., & Finlay, K. A. (2001). Evidence for improved sensitivity of within-participants analyses in tests of the theory of reasoned action. *The Social Science Journal, 38,* 629–635.

Trafimow, D., Triandis, H. C., & Goto, S. G. (1991). Some tests of the distinction between the private self and the collective self. *Journal of Personality and Social Psychology, 60,* 649–655.

Triandis, H. C. (1990). Cross-cultural studies of individualism and collectivism. In J. Berman (Ed.), *Nebraska Symposium on Motivation, 1989* (pp. 41–122). Lincoln: University of Nebraska Press.

Triandis, H. C. (1995). *Individualism and collectivism.* Boulder, CO: Westview Press.

Triandis, H. C., Bontempo, R., Villareal, M. J., Asai, M., & Lucca, N. (1988). Individualism and collectivism: Cross-cultural perspectives on self-ingroup relationships. *Journal of Personality and Social Psychology, 54,* 323–338.

Triandis, H. C., McCusker, C., & Hui, C. (1990). Multimethod probes of individualism and collectivism. *Journal of Personality and Social Psychology, 59,* 1006–1020.

Trickett, P. K., & Putnam, F. W. (1993). Impact of child sexual abuse on females: Toward a developmental, psychobiological integration. *Psychological Science, 4,* 81–87.

Trimble, J. E. (1988). Stereotypical images, American Indians, and prejudice. In P. A. Katz & D. A. Taylor (Eds.), *Eliminating racism: Profiles in controversy,* (pp. 181–202). New York: Plenum.

Trivers, R. L. (1971). The evolution of reciprocal altruism. *Quarterly Review of Biology, 46,* 35–57.

Trope, Y. (1975). Seeking information about one's own ability as a determinant of choice among tasks. *Journal of Personality and Social Psychology, 32,* 1004–1013.

Trope, Y. (1983). Self-assessment in achievement behavior. In J. M. Suls & A. G. Carver (Eds.), *Psychological perspectives on the self* (Vol. 2, pp. 93–122). Hillsdale, NJ: Erlbaum.

Trope, Y., & Bassok, M. (1982). Confirmatory and diagnosing strategies in social information gathering. *Journal of Personality and Social Psychology, 43,* 22–34.

Trope, Y., & Gaunt, R. (1999). A dual-process model of overconfident attributions. In S. Chaiken & Y. Trope (Eds.), *Dual-process theories in social psychology.* New York: Guilford Press.

Trope, Y., & Gaunt, R. (2000). Processing alternative explanations of behavior: Correction or integration. *Journal of Personality and Social Psychology, 79,* 344–354.

Trope, Y., & Liberman, A. (1993). The use of trait conceptions to identify other people's behavior and to draw inferences about their personalities. *Personality and Social Psychology Bulletin, 19,* 553–562.

Trost, M. R., Maass, A., & Kenrick, D. T. (1992). Minority influence: Personal relevance biases cognitive processes and reverses private acceptance. *Journal of Experimental Social Psychology, 28,* 234–254.

Trzebinski, J., & Richards, K. (1986). The role of goal categories in person impression. *Journal of Experimental Social Psychology, 22,* 216–227.

Tucker, J. S., & Mueller, J. S. (2000). Spouses' social control of health behaviors: Use and effectiveness of specific strategies. *Personality & Social Psychology Bulletin, 26,* 1120–1130.

Turk, D. C., & Meichenbaum, D. (1991). Adherence to self-care regimens: The patient's perspective. In R. H. Rozensky, J. J. Sweet, & S. M. Tovian (Eds.), *Handbook of clinical psychology in medical settings* (pp. 249–266). New York: Plenum Press.

Turner, J. C., Hogg, M. A., Oakes, P. J., Reicher, S. D., & Wetherell, M. (1987). *Rediscovering the social group: A self-categorization theory.* Oxford, England: Basil Blackwell.

Turner, J. C., Oakes, P. J., Haslam, S. A., & McGarty, C. (1994). Self and the collective: Cognition and social context. *Personality and Social Psychology Bulletin, 20,* 454–463.

Turner, R. H. (1962). Role-taking: Process versus conformity. In A. H. Rose (Ed.), *Human behavior and social processes* (pp. 20–40). Boston: Houghton Mifflin.

Turner-Cobb, J. M., Sephton, S. E., Koopman, C., Blake-Mortimer, J., & Spiegel, D. (2000). Social support and salivary cortisol in women with metastatic breast cancer. *Psychosomatic Medicine, 62,* 337–345.

Tversky, A., & Kahneman, D. (1974). Judgment under uncertainty: Heuristics and biases. *Science, 185,* 1124–1131.

Tversky, A., & Kahneman, D. (1982). Evidential impact of base rates. In D. Kahneman, P. Slovic, & A. Tversky (Eds.), *Judgment under uncertainty: Heuristics and biases.* New York: Cambridge University Press.

Twenge, J. M. (1997). Attitudes toward women, 1970–1995. *Psychology of Women Quarterly, 21,* 35–51.

Twenge, J. M., Baumeister, R. F., Tice, D. M., & Stucke, T. S. (2001). If you can't join them, beat them: Effects of social exclusion on aggressive behavior. *Journal of Personality and Social Psychology, 81,* 1058–1069.

Twenge, J. M., Catanese, K. R., & Baumeister, R. F. (2003). Social exclusion and the deconstructed state: Time perception, meaninglessness, lethargy, lack of emotion, and self-awareness. *Journal of Personality and Social Psychology, 85,* 409–423.

Tykocinski, O. E. (2001). I never had a chance: Using hindsight tactics to mitigate disappointments. *Personality and Social Psychology Bulletin, 27,* 376–382.

Tyler, T. R. (1997). The psychology of legitimacy: A relational perspective on voluntary deference to authorities. *Personality and Social Psychology Review, 1,* 323–345.

Tyler, T. R., & Degoey, P. (1995). Collective restraint in social dilemmas: Procedural justice and social identification effects on support for authorities. *Journal of Personality and Social Psychology, 69,* 482–497.

U.S. Census Bureau. (2001). Retrieved August 5, 2001, from http://www.census.gov/population

U.S. Census Bureau. (2004). Projected population of the United States, by race and Hispanic origin: 2000 to 2050. Retrieved July 22, 2004, from http://www.census.gov/vlipc/www/usinterimproj/

U.S. Department of Health. (2002). National crime victimization survey. Retrieved on 7/1/04, from http://www.rainn.org/ncvs_2002.pdf

U.S. Department of Justice. (2000). Criminal victimization 2000: Changes 1999–2000 with trends 1993–2000. *National Crime Survey.* Retrieved on 7/1/04, from http://www.rainn.org/Linked%20files/NCVS%202000.pdf

U.S. Department of Justice. (2002). Bureau of justice statistics: Crime characteristics. Retrieved on 7/1/04, from http://www.ojp.usdoj.gov/bjs/cvict_c.htm

U.S Department of Transportation. (2003). Traffic safety facts 2002: Alcohol. *National Highway Traffic Safety Administration.* Retrieved on 7/1/04, from http://www-nrd.nhtsa.dot.gov/pdf/nrd-30/NCSA/ TSF2002/2002alcfacts.pdf

Uleman, J. S., Hon, A., Roman, R. J., & Moskowitz, G. B. (1996). Online evidence for spontaneous trait inferences at encoding. *Personality and Social Psychology Bulletin, 22,* 377–394.

Uleman, J. S., & Moskowitz, G. B. (1994). Unintended effects of goals on unintended inferences. *Journal of Personality and Social Psychology, 66,* 490–501.

Updegraff, J. A., Gable, S. L, & Taylor, S. E. (2004). What makes experiences satisfying? The interaction of dispositional motivations and emotion in cognitive well-being. *Journal of Personality and Social Psychology, 86,* 496–504.

Uzark, K. C., Becker, M. H., Dielman, T. E., & Rocchini, A. P. (1987). Psychosocial predictors of compliance with a weight control intervention for obese children and adolescents. *Journal of Compliance in Health Care, 2,* 167–178.

Vallone, R. P., Griffin, D. W., Lin, S., & Ross, L. (1990). Overconfident prediction of future actions and outcomes by self and others. *Journal of Personality and Social Psychology, 58,* 582–592.

van Baaren, R. B., Horgan, T. G., Chartrand, T. L., & Dijkmans, M. (2004). The forest, the trees, and the chameleon: Context dependence and mimicry. *Journal of Personality and Social Psychology, 86,* 453–459.

van Boven, L., & Gilovich, T. (2003). To do or to have? That is the question. *Journal of Personality and Social Psychology, 85,* 1193–1202.

Van Lange, P. A. M. (1999). The pursuit of joint outcomes and equality of outcomes: An integrative model of social value orientation. *Journal of Personality and Social Psychology, 77,* 337–349.

Van Lange, P. A. M., Rusbult, C. E., Drigotas, S. M., Arriaga, X. B., Witcher, B. S., & Cox, C. L. (1997). Willingness to sacrifice in close relationships. *Journal of Personality and Social Psychology, 72,* 1373–1395.

Van Overwalle, F., & Van Rooy, D. (2001). How one cause discounts or augments another: A connectionist account of causal competition. *Personality and Social Psychology Bulletin, 27,* 1613–1626.

Van Rijswijk, W., & Ellemers, N. (2002). Context effects on the application of stereotype content to multiple categorizable targets. *Personality and Social Psychology Bulletin, 28,* 90–101.

Van Vugt, M., & Hart, C. M. (2004). Social identity as social glue: The origins of group loyalty. *Journal of Personality and Social Psychology, 86,* 585–598.

Van Yperen, N. W., & Buunk, B. P. (1990). A longitudinal study of equity and satisfaction in intimate relationships. *European Journal of Social Psychology, 20,* 287–309.

Van Yperen, N. W., & Buunk, B. P. (1991). Sex-role attitudes, social comparison, and satisfaction with relationships. *Social Psychology Quarterly, 54,* 169–180.

Vandello, J. A., & Cohen, D. (1999). Patterns of individualism and collectivism across the United States. *Journal of Personality and Social Psychology, 77,* 279–292.

Verplanken, B., & Holland, R. W. (2002). Motivated decision making: Effects of activation and self-centrality of values on choices and behavior. *Journal of Personality and Social Psychology, 82,* 434–447.

Verplanken, B., Jetten, J., & van Knippenberg, A. (1996). Effects of stereotypicality and perceived group variability on the use of attitudinal information in impression formation. *Personality and Social Psychology Bulletin, 22,* 960–971.

Viemero, V., & Paajanen, S. (1992). The role of fantasies and dreams in the TV viewing-aggression relationship. *Aggressive Behavior, 18,* 109–116.

Vitaliano, P. P., DeWolfe, D. J., Maiuro, R. D., Russo, J., & Katon, W. (1990). Appraised changeability of a stress as a modifier of the relationship between coping and depression: A test of the hypothesis of fit. *Journal of Personality and Social Psychology, 59,* 582–592.

Vogel, D. A., Lake, M. A., Evans, S., & Karraker, K. H. (1991). Children's and adults' sex-stereotyped perceptions of infants. *Sex Roles, 24,* 605–616.

Vogel, D. L., & Wester, S. R. (2003). To seek help or not to seek help: The risks of self-disclosure. *Journal of Counseling Psychology, 50,* 351–361.

Volpato, C., Maass, A., Mucchi-Faina, A., & Vitti, E. (1990). Minority influence and social categorization. *European Journal of Social Psychology, 20,* 119–132.

von Baeyer, C. L., Sherk, D. L., & Zanna, M. P. (1981). Impression management in the job interview: When the female applicant meets the male (chauvinist) interviewer. *Personality and Social Psychology Bulletin, 7,* 45–52.

von Hecker, U. (1993). On memory effects of Heiderian balance: A code hypothesis and an inconsistency hypothesis. *Journal of Personality and Social Psychology, 29,* 45–52.

von Hippel, W., Hawkins, C., & Schooler, J. W. (2001). Stereotype distinctiveness: How counterstereotypic behavior shapes the self-concept. *Journal of Personality and Social Psychology, 81,* 193–205.

Vondello, J. A., & Cohen, D. (2003). Male honor and female fidelity: Implicit cultural scripts that perpetuate domestic violence. *Journal of Personality and Social Psychology, 84,* 997–1010.

Vonk, R. (1993). The negativity effect in trait ratings and in open-ended descriptions of persons. *Personality and Social Psychology Bulletin, 19,* 269–278.

Vonk, R. (1999). Impression formation and impression management: Motives, traits, and likeability inferred from self-promoting and self-deprecating behavior. *Social Cognition, 17,* 390–412.

Vrij, A. (2000). *Detecting lies and deceit.* Chichester, U.K.: Wiley.

Vrij, A., Edward, K., & Bull, R. (2001). Stereotypical verbal and nonverbal responses while deceiving others. *Personality and Social Psychology Bulletin, 27,* 899–909.

Walker, L., & Monahan, J. (1996). Daubert and the Reference manual: An essay on the future of science and law. *Virginia Law Review, 82,* 837–857.

Walker, W. D., Rowe, R. C., & Quinsey, V. L. (1993). Authoritarianism and sexual aggression. *Journal of Personality and Social Psychology, 65,* 1036–1045.

Waller, W. (1938). *The family: A dynamic interpretation.* New York: Dryden Press.

Wallston, B. S., Alagna, S. W., DeVellis, B. M., & DeVellis, R. F., (1983). Social support and physical health. *Health Psychology, 2,* 367–391.

Walster, E., Aronson, E., Abrahams, D., & Rottman, L. (1966). Importance of physical attractiveness in dating behavior. *Journal of Personality and Social Psychology, 4,* 508–516.

Walster, E., Walster, G. W., & Berscheid, E. (1978). *Equity: Theory and research.* Boston: Allyn & Bacon.

Wänke, M., Bless, H., & Biller, B. (1996). Subjective experience versus content of information in the construction of attitude judgments. *Personality and Social Psychology Bulletin, 22,* 1105–1113.

Wänke, M., Bless, H., & Igou, E. R. (2001). Next to a star: Paling, shining, or both? Turning inter-exemplar contrast into inter-exemplar assimilation. *Personality and Social Psychology, 27,* 14–29.

Ware, J. E., Jr., Davies-Avery, A., & Stewart, A. L. (1978). The measurement and meaning of patient satisfaction: A review of the literature. *The Health and Medical Care Services Review, 1,* 1–15.

Waring, E. M., Tillman, M. P., Frelick, L., Russell, L., & Weisz, G. (1980). Concepts of intimacy in the general population. *Journal of Nervous and Mental Disease, 168,* 471–474.

Warner, M. G., & Fineman, H. (1988, September 26). Bush's media wizard: A down-and-dirty street fighter reshapes the veep. *Newsweek,* pp. 19–20.

Watanabe, T. (1992, October 27). "Doll wars" challenge female. *Los Angeles Times,* p. H2.

Waters, E., Merrick, S. K., Albersheim, L. J., & Treboux, D. (1995, April). *Attachment security from infancy to early adulthood: A 20-year longitudinal study.* Poster presented at the Biennial Meeting of the Society for Research in Child Development, Indianapolis, IN.

Watson, R. I., Jr. (1973). Investigation into deindividuation using a cross-cultural survey technique. *Journal of Personality and Social Psychology, 25,* 342–345.

Watts, W. A., & Holt, L. E. (1979). Persistence of opinion change induced under conditions of forewarning and distraction. *Journal of Personality and Social Psychology, 37,* 778–789.

Weary, G., Reich, D. A., & Tobin, S. J. (2001). The role of contextual constraints and chronic expectancies on behavior categorizations and dispositional inferences. *Personality and Social Psychology Bulletin, 27,* 62–75.

Webb, B., Worchel, S., Riechers, L., & Wayne, W. (1986). The influence of categorization on perceptions of crowding. *Personality and Social Psychology Bulletin, 12,* 539–546.

Weber, S. J., & Cook, T. D. (1972). Subject effects in laboratory research: An examination of subject roles, demand characteristics, and valid inferences. *Psychological Bulletin, 77,* 273–295.

Webster, G. D. (2003). Prosocial behavior in families: Moderators of resource sharing. *Journal of Experimental Social Psychology, 39,* 644–652.

Wegner, D. M. (1994). Ironic processes of mental control. *Psychological Review, 101,* 34–52.

Wehrle, T., Kaiser, S., Schmidt, S., & Schere, K. R. (2000). Studying the dynamics of emotional expression using synthesized facial muscle movements. *Journal of Personality and Social Psychology, 78,* 105–119.

Weiner, B. (1980). A cognitive (attribution)-emotion-action model of motivated behavior: An analysis of judgments of help-giving. *Journal of Personality and Social Psychology, 39,* 186–200.

Weiner, B. (1982). The emotional consequences of causal attributions. In M. S. Clark & S. T. Fiske (Eds.), *Affect and cognition: The 17th annual Carnegie Symposium on Cognition* (pp. 185–210). Hillsdale, NJ: Erlbaum.

Weiner, B., Amirkhan, J., Folkes, V. S., & Verette, J. A. (1987). An attributional analysis of excuse giving: Studies of a naïve theory of emotion. *Journal of Personality and Social Psychology, 52,* 316–324.

Weinman, J., Petrie, K. J., Moss-Morris, R., & Horne, R. (1996). The illness perception questionnaire: A new method for assessing the cognitive representation of illness. *Psychology and Health, 11,* 431–445.

Weinstein, N. D. (1993). Testing four competing theories of health-protective behavior. *Health Psychology, 12,* 324–333.

Weisbuch, M., Mackie, D. M., & Garcia-Marques, T. (2003). Prior source exposure and persuasion: Further evidence for misattributional processes. *Personality and Social Psychology Bulletin, 29,* 691–700.

Weiss, R. S. (1973). *Loneliness: The experience of emotional and social isolation.* Cambridge, MA: MIT Press.

Weiss, W., & Fine, B. J. (1956). The effect of induced aggressiveness on opinion change. *Journal of Abnormal and Social Psychology, 52,* 109–114.

Weisz, M. G., & Earls, C. M. (1995). The effects of exposure to filmed sexual violence on attitudes toward rape. *Journal of Interpersonal Violence, 10,* 71–84.

Welbourne, J. L. (2001). Changes in impression complexity over time and across situations. *Personality and Social Psychology Bulletin, 27,* 1071–1085.

Wells, G. L. (1978). Applied eyewitness testimony research: System variables and estimator variables. *Journal of Personality and Social Psychology, 36,* 1546–1557.

Wells, G. L. (1984). The psychology of lineup identifications. *Journal of Applied Social Psychology, 66,* 688–696.

Wells, G. L. (2002). Eyewitness identifications: Scientific status. In D. L. Faigman, D. H. Kaye, M. J. Saks, & J. Sanders (Eds.), *Modern scientific evidence: The law and science of expert testimony,* (Vol. 2, 2nd ed., pp. 230–262). St. Paul, MN: West Publishing Co.

Wells, G. L., & Luus, C. A. E. (1990). Police lineups as experiments: Social methodology as a framework for properly conducted lineups. *Personality and Social Psychology Bulletin, 16,* 106–117.

Wells, G. L., Malpass, R. S., Lindsay, R. C. L., Fisher, R. P., Turtle, J. W., & Fulero, S. M. (2000). From the lab to the police station: A successful application of eyewitness research. *American Psychologist, 55,* 581–598.

Wells, G. L., & Olson, E. A. (2003). Eyewitness testimony. *Annual Review of Psychology, 54,* 277–295.

Wentura, D., Rothermund, K., & Bak, P. (2000). Automatic vigilance: The attention-grabbing power of approach- and avoidance-related social information. *Journal of Personality and Social Psychology, 78,* 1024–1037.

Whitborne, S. K., Zuschlag, M. K., Elliot, L. B., & Waterman, A. S. (1992). Psychosocial development in adulthood: A 22-year sequential study. *Journal of Personality and Social Psychology, 63,* 260–271.

White, G. L., & Mullen, P. E. (1989). *Jealousy: Theory, research, and clinical strategies.* New York: Guilford Press.

White, J. W., & Sorensen, S. B. (1992). A sociocultural view of sexual assault: From discrepancy to diversity. *Journal of Social Issues, 48,* 187–195.

Whitley, B. E. (1983). Sex role orientation and self-esteem: A critical meta-analytic review. *Journal of Personality and Social Psychology, 44,* 765–778.

Whitley, B. E. (1988). Masculinity, femininity, and self-esteem: A multitrait-multimethod analysis. *Sex Roles, 18,* 419–431.

Whitley, B. E., Jr. (1990). The relationship of heterosexuals' attributions for the causes of homosexuality to attitudes toward lesbians and gay men. *Personality and Social Psychology Bulletin, 16,* 369–377.

Whitney, K., Sagrestano, L. M., & Maslach, C. (1992). [The behavioral expression of individuation through creativity, leadership, and non-verbal expressiveness]. Unpublished raw data.

Whitney, K., Sagrestano, L. M., & Maslach, C. (1994). Establishing the social impact of individuation. *Journal of Personality and Social Psychology, 66,* 1140–1153.

Whitton, S., Stanley, S., & Markman, H. (2002). Sacrifice in romantic relationships. In A. Vangelisti & H. Reis (Eds.), *Stability and change in relationships* (pp. 156–181). New York: Cambridge University Press.

Wichman, H. (1970). Effects of isolation and communication on cooperation in a two-person game. *Journal of Personality and Social Psychology, 6,* 114–120.

Wicker, A. W. (1969). Attitudes versus action: The relationship of verbal and overt behavior responses to attitude objects. *Journal of Social Issues, 25,* 41–78.

Wicklund, R. A., Cooper, J., & Linder, D. (1967). Effects of expected effort on attitude change prior to exposure. *Journal of Experimental Social Psychology, 3,* 416–428.

Wicklund, R. A., & Frey, D. (1980). Self-awareness theory: When the self makes a difference. In D. M. Wegner & R. R. Vallacher (Eds.), *The self in social psychology* (pp. 31–54). New York: Oxford University Press.

Wicklund, R. A., & Gollwitzer, P. M. (1982). *Symbolic self-completion.* Hillsdale, NJ: Erlbaum.

Wickrama, K., Conger, R. D., & Lorenz, F. O. (1995). Work, marriage, lifestyle, and changes in men's physical health. *Journal of Behavioral Medicine, 18,* 97–112.

Widmer, E. D., Treas, J., & Newcomb, R. (1998). Attitudes toward nomarital sex in 24 countries. *Journal of Sex Research, 35,* 349–358.

Wiener, R. L., Hurt, L. E., Thomas, S. L., Sadler, M. S., Bauer, C. A., & Sargent, T. M. (1998). The role of declarative and procedural knowledge in capital murder sentencing. *Journal of Applied Social Psychology, 28,* 124–144.

Wieselquist, J., Rusbult, C. E., Foster, C. A., & Agnew, C. R. (1999). Commitment, pro-relationship behavior, and trust in close relationships. *Journal of Personality and Social Psychology, 77,* 942–966.

Williams, D. R., & Collins, C. (1995). U.S. socioeconomic and racial differences in health: Patterns and explanations. *Annual Review of Sociology, 21,* 349–386.

Williams, J. E., & Best, D. L. (1990). *Sex and psyche: Gender and self viewed cross-culturally.* Newbury Park, CA: Sage.

Williams, K. D. (2001). *Ostracism: The power of silence.* New York: Guilford.

Williams, K. D., Cheung, C. K. T., & Choi, W. (2000). Cyberostracism: Effects of being ignored over the Internet. *Journal of Personality and Social Psychology, 79,* 748–762.

Williams, K. D., Harkins, S. G., & Karau, S. J. (2003). Social performance. In M. A. Hogg & J. Cooper (Eds.), *The Sage handbook of social psychology* (pp. 327–346). Thousand Oaks, CA: Sage.

Williams, K. D., & Karau, S. J. (1991). Social loafing and social compensation: The effects of expectations of co-worker performance. *Journal of Personality and Social Psychology, 61,* 570–581.

Williams, R. D., Jr., & Barefoot, J. C. (1988). Coronary-prone behavior: The emerging role of the hostility complex. In B. K. Houston & C. R. Snyder (Eds.), *Type A behavior pattern: Current trends and future directions* (pp. 189–221). New York: Wiley.

Williamson, G. M., & Clark, M. S. (1989). Providing help and desired relationship type as determinants of changes in moods and self-evaluations. *Journal of Personality and Social Psychology, 56,* 722–734.

Williamson, G. M., & Clark, M. S. (1992). Impact of desired relationship type on affective reactions to choosing and being required to help. *Personality and Social Psychology Bulletin, 18,* 10–18.

Wills, T. A. (1981). Downward comparison principles in social psychology. *Psychological Bulletin, 90,* 245–271.

Wills, T. A. (1992). The helping process in the context of personal relationships. In S. Spacapan & S. Oskamp (Eds.), *Helping and being helped in the real world* (pp. 17–48). Newbury Park, CA: Sage.

Wilson, A. E., & Ross, M. (2000). The frequency of temporal-self and social comparisons in people's personal appraisals. *Journal of Personality and Social Psychology, 78,* 928–942.

Wilson, A. E., & Ross, M. (2001). From chump to champ: People's appraisals of their earlier and present selves. *Journal of Personality and Social Psychology 80,* 572–584.

Wilson, T. D., & Hodges, S. D. (1992). Attitudes as temporary constructions. In L. L. Martin & A. Tesser (Eds.), *The construction of social judgments* (pp. 37–65). Hillsdale, NJ: Erlbaum.

Wilson, T. D., Hodges, S. D., & LaFleur, S .J. (1995). Effects of introspecting about reasons: Inferring attitudes from accessible thoughts. *Journal of Personality and Social Psychology, 69,* 16–28.

Wilson, T. D., & LaFleur, S. J. (1995). Knowing what you'll do: Effects of analyzing reasons on self-prediction. *Journal of Personality and Social Psychology, 68,* 21–35.

Wilson, T. D., Lisle, D. J., Kraft, D., & Wetzel, C. G. (1989). Preference as expectation-driven inferences: Effects of affective expectations on affect experience. *Journal of Personality and Social Psychology, 56,* 519–530.

Wilson, T. D., Meyers, J., & Gilbert, D. T. (2001). Lessons from the past: Do people learn from experience that emotional reactions are short-lived? *Personality and Social Psychology Bulletin, 27,* 1648–1661.

Wilson, T. D., Wheatley, T. P., Meyers, J. M., Gilbert, D. T., & Axsom, D. (2000). Focalism: A source of durability bias in affective forecasting. *Journal of Personality and Social Psychology, 78,* 821–836.

Winquist, J. R., & Larson, J. R. (1998). Information pooling: When it impacts group decision making. *Journal of Personality and Social Psychology, 74,* 371–377.

Winter, D. G. (1988). The power motive in women—and men. *Journal of Personality and, Social Psychology, 54,* 510–519.

Wisconsin Innocence Project. (2003). *Steven Avery exonerated after 18 years in prison.* Retrieved August 16, 2004, from University of Wisconsin Law School Web site: http://www.law.wisc.edu/FJR/innocence/AverySummaryPage.htm.

Wise, R. A., & Safer, M. A. (2004). What U.S. judges know and believe about eyewitness testimony. *Applied Cognitive Psychology, 18,* 427–443.

Wisman, A., & Koole, S. L. (2003). Hiding in the crowd: Can mortality salience promote affiliation with others who oppose one's worldviews? *Journal of Personality and Social Psychology, 84,* 511–526.

Wittenbaum, G. M., & Park, E. S. (2001). The collective preference for shared information. *Current Directions in Psychological Science, 10,* 70–73.

Wittenbaum, G. M., Vaughan, D. I., & Stasser, G. (1998). Coordination in task-performing groups. In R. S. Tindale, L. Heath, J. Edwards, E. J. Posavac, F. B. Bryant, Y. Suarez-Balcazay et al. (Eds.), *Theory and research on small groups* (pp. 117–204). New York: Plenum.

Wittenbrink, B., Judd, C. M., & Park, B. (2001a). Evaluative versus conceptual judgments in automatic stereotyping and prejudice. *Journal of Experimental Social Psychology, 37,* 244–252.

Wittenbrink, B., Judd, C. M., & Park, B. (2001b). Spontaneous prejudice in context: Variability in automatically activated attitudes. *Journal of Personality and Social Psychology, 81,* 815–827.

Witvliet, C. v., Ludwig, T. E., & Vander Laan, K. L. (2001). Granting forgiveness or harboring grudges: Implications for emotion, physiology and health. *Psychological Science, 12,* 117–123.

Wogalter, M. S., Malpass, R. S., & McQuiston, D. E. (2004). A national survey of U.S. police on preparation and conduct of identification lineups. *Psychology, Crime, and Law, 10,* 69–82.

Woike, B., Gershkovich, I., Piorkowski, R., & Polo, M. (1999). The role of motives in the content and structure of autobiographical memory. *Journal of Personality and Social Psychology, 76,* 600–612.

Woike, B., Mcleod, S., & Goggin, M. (2003). Implicit and explicit motives influence accessibility to different autobiographical knowledge. *Personality and Social Psychology Bulletin, 29,* 1046–1055.

Wolsko, C., Park, B., Judd, C. M., & Wittenbrink, B. (2000). Framing interethnic ideology: Effects of multicultural and color-blind perspectives on judgments of groups and individuals. *Journal of Personality and Social Psychology, 78,* 635–654.

Wong, P. T. P., & Weiner, B. (1981). When people ask "why" questions, and the heuristics of attributional search. *Journal of Personality and Social Psychology, 40,* 650–663.

Wood, J. V. (1989). Theory and research concerning social comparisons of personal attributes. *Psychological Bulletin, 106,* 231–248.

Wood, J. V., Heimpel, S. A., & Michela, J. L. (2003). Savoring versus dampening: Self-esteem differences in regulating positive affect. *Journal of Personality and Social Psychology, 85,* 566–580.

Wood, W., & Eagly, A. H. (2002). A cross-cultural analysis of the behavior of women and men: Implications for the origins of sex differences. *Psychological Bulletin, 128,* 699–727.

Wood, W., & Kallgren, C. A. (1988). Communicator attributes and persuasion: Recipients' access to attitude-relevant information in memory. *Personality and Social Psychology Bulletin, 14,* 172–182.

Wood, W., Kallgren, C. A., & Priesler, R. (1985). Access to attitude relevant information in memory as a determinant of persuasion. *Journal of Experimental Social Psychology, 21,* 73–85.

Wood, W., Lundgren, S., Ouellette, J. A., Busceme, S., & Blackstone, T. (1994). Minority influence: A meta-analytic review of social influence processes. *Psychological Bulletin, 115,* 323–345.

Wood, W., Quinn, J., & Kashy, D. (2002). Habits in everyday life: Thought, emotion, and action. *Journal of Personality and Social Psychology, 83,* 1281–1297.

Woodall, K. L., & Matthews, K. A. (1993). Changes in and stability of hostile characteristics: Results from a four-year longitudinal study of children. *Journal of Personality and Social Psychology, 64,* 491–499.

Woodworth, R. D. (1938). *Experimental psychology.* New York: Holt.

Woolfolk, R. L., Novalany, J., Gara, M. A., Allen, L. A., & Polino, M. (1995). Self-complexity, self-evaluation, and depression: An examination of form and content within the self-schema. *Journal of Personality and Social Psychology, 68,* 1108–1120.

Worchel, S., & Teddie, C. (1976). The experience of crowding: A two-factor theory. *Journal of Personality and Social Psychology, 34,* 30–40.

WREI (Women's Research and Education Institute). (2004). Women in the military. Retrieved August 16, 2004, from http://www.wrei_org/projects/wiu/wim/didyouknow.htm#aa

Wright, J. C., & Dawson, V. L. (1988). Person perception and the bounded rationality of social judgment. *Journal of Personality and Social Psychology, 55,* 780–794.

Wrightsman, L. S., Greene, E., Nietzel, M. T., & Fortune, W. H. (2002). *Psychology and the legal system* (5th ed.). Belmont, CA: Wadsworth.

Wrosch, C., Scheier, M. F., Miller, G. E., Schulz, R., & Carver, C. S. (2003). Adaptive self-regulation of unattainable goals: Goal disengagement, goal reengagement, and subjective well-being. *Personality and Social Psychology Bulletin, 29,* 1494–1508.

Wulfert, E., & Wan, C. K. (1993). Condom use: A self-efficacy model. *Health Psychology, 12,* 346–353.

Wurtele, S. K., & Maddux, J. E. (1987). Relative contributions of protection motivation theory components in predicting exercise intentions and behavior. *Health Psychology, 6,* 453–466.

Wyer, R. S., Jr., Budesheim, T. L., Lambert, A. J., & Swan, S. (1994). Person memory and judgment: Pragmatic influences on impressions formed in a social context. *Journal of Personality and Social Psychology, 66,* 254–267.

Wyer, R. S., Jr., & Srull, T. K. (1981). Category accessibility: Some theoretical and empirical issues concerning the processing of social stimulus information. In E. T. Higgins, C. P. Herman, & M. P. Zanna (Eds.), *The Ontario Symposium on Personality and Social Psychology: Social Cognition* (pp 161–198). Hillsdale, NJ: Erlbaum.

Wyer, R. S., Jr., & Srull, T. K. (1986). Human cognition in its social context. *Psychological Review, 93,* 322–359.

Yammarino, F. J., & Bass, B. M. (1990). Transformational leadership and multiple levels of analysis. *Human Relations, 43,* 975–995.

Ybarra, O. (1999). Misanthropic person memory when the need to self-enhance is absent. *Personality and Social Psychology Bulletin, 99,* 261–269.

Ybarra, O., Schaberg, L. A., & Keiper, S. N. (1999). Favorable and unfavorable target expectancies and social information processing. *Journal of Personality and Social Psychology, 77,* 698–709.

Ybarra, O., & Stephan, W. G. (1999). Attributional orientations and the prediction of behavior: The attribution-prediction bias. *Journal of Personality and Social Psychology, 76,* 718–727.

Ybarra, O., & Trafimow, D. (1998). How priming the private self or collective self affects the relative weights of attitudes and subjective norms. *Personality and Social Psychology Bulletin, 24,* 362–370.

Yee, D. K., & Eccles, J. S. (1988). Parent perceptions and attributions for children's math achievement. *Sex Roles, 19,* 317–333.

Yelsma, P., & Athappilly, K. (1988). Marital satisfaction and communication practices: Comparisons among Indian and American couples. *Journal of Comparative Family Studies, 19,* 37–54.

Yik, M. S. M., Bond, M. H., & Paulhus, D. L. (1998). Do Chinese self-enhance or self-efface? It's a matter of domain. *Personality and Social Psychology Bulletin, 24,* 399–406.

Yoder, J. D., & Kahn, A. S. (2003). Making gender comparisons more meaningful: A call for more attention to social context. *Psychology of Women Quarterly, 27,* 281–290.

Young, R. L. (2004). Guilty until proven innocent: Conviction orientation, racial attitudes, and support for capital punishment. *Deviant Behavior, 25,* 151–167.

Yzerbyt, V. Y., Corneille, O., Dumont, M., & Hahn, K. (2001). The dispositional inference strikes back: Situational focus and dispositional suppression in causal attribution. *Journal of Personality and Social Psychology, 81,* 365–376.

Yzerbyt, V. Y., & Leyens, J.-P. (1991). Requesting information to form an impression: The influence of valence and confirmatory status. *Journal of Experimental Social Psychology, 30,* 138–164.

Yzerbyt, V. Y., Schadrom, G., Leyens, J.-P., & Rocher, S. (1994). Social judgeability: The impact of meta-informational cues on the use of stereotypes. *Journal of Personality and Social Psychology, 66,* 48–55.

Zaccaro, S. J. (2001). *The nature of executive leadership.* Washington, DC: American Psychological Association.

Zajonc, R. B. (1965). Social facilitation. *Science, 149,* 269–274.

Zajonc, R. B. (1968). Attitudinal effects of mere exposure [Monograph]. *Journal of Personality and Social Psychology, 9,* 1–27.

Zajonc, R. B. (2001). Mere exposure: A gateway to the subliminal. *Current Directions in Psychological Science, 10,* 224–228.

Zanna, M. P., & Hamilton, D. L. (1977). Further evidence for meaning change in impression formation. *Journal of Experimental Social Psychology, 13,* 224–238.

Zebrowitz, L. A., Hall, J. A., Murphy, N. A., & Rhodes, G. (2002). Looking smart and looking good: Facial cues to intelligence and their origins. *Personality and Social Psychology Bulletin, 28,* 238–249.

Zeichner, A., & Pihl, R. (1979). Effects of alcohol and behavior contingencies on human aggression. *Journal of Abnormal Psychology, 88,* 153–160.

Zelenski, J. M., & Larsen, R. J. (2002). Predicting the future: How affect-related personality traits influence likelihood judgments of future events. *Personality and Social Psychology Bulletin, 28,* 1000–1010.

Zelli, A., Dodge, K. A., Lochman, J. E., Laird, R. D., & Conduct Problems Prevention Research Group (1999). The distinction between beliefs legitimizing aggression and deviant processing of social cues: Testing measurement validity and the hypothesis that biased processing mediates the effects of beliefs on aggression. *Journal of Personality and Social Psychology, 77,* 150–166.

Zeprun, J. G. (1990, January 22). Sexual assault victims faced with legal bias. *Boston Globe,* p.10.

Ziegler, R., Diehl, M., & Ruther, A. (2002). Multiple source characteristics and persuasion: Source inconsistency as a determinant of message scrutiny. *Personality and Social Psychology Bulletin, 28,* 496–508.

Zillmann, D. (1988). Cognition-excitation interdependencies in aggressive behavior. [Aggressive Behavior. Special Issue] *Current theoretical perspectives on aggressive and antisocial behavior, 14,* 51–64.

Zillmann, D., & Bryant, J. (1994). Entertainment as media effect. In J. Bryant & D. Zillmann (Eds.), *Media effects: Advances in theory and research.* Hillsdale, NJ: Erlbaum.

Zimbardo, P. G. (1960). Verbal ambiguity and judgmental distortion. *Psychological Reports, 60,* 57–58.

Zimbardo, P. G. (1970). The human choice: Individuation, reason and order versus deindividuation, impulse and chaos. In N. J. Arnold & D. Levine (Eds.), *Nebraska Symposium on Motivation, 1969,* (p. 298). Lincoln: University of Nebraska Press.

Zuckerman, M., DePaulo, B. M., & Rosenthal, R. (1981). Verbal and nonverbal communication in deception. In L. Berkowitz (Ed.), *Advances in experimental social psychology* (Vol. 14, pp. 2–60). New York: Academic Press.

Zuckerman, M., Kieffer, S. C., & Knee, C. R. (1998). Consequences of self-handicapping: Effects on coping, academic performance, and adjustment. *Journal of Personality and Social Psychology, 74,* 1619–1628.

Zuckerman, M. Larrance, D. T. Spiegel, N. H. & Klorman, R. (1981). Controlling nonverbal displays: Facial expressions and tone of voice. *Journal of Experimental Social Psychology, 17,* 506–524.

Zurbriggen, E. L. (2000). Social motives and cognitive power-sex associations: Predictors of aggressive sexual behavior. *Journal of Personality and Social Psychology, 78,* 559–581.

Zuwerink, J. R., & Devine, P. G. (1996). Attitude importance and resistance to persuasion: It's not just the thought that counts. *Journal of Personality and Social Psychology, 70,* 931–944.

Photo Credits

CHAPTER 1 1-1 AP/Wide World Photos; 1-2 Bob Daemmrich/The Image Works; 1-3 David R. Frazier/Photo Researchers, Inc.; 1-4 George Holon/Photo Researchers, Inc.; 1-5 Getty Images, Inc.; 1-6 A. Ramey/PhotoEdit; 1-7 The Image Works; 1-8 David Young-Wolff/PhotoEdit.

CHAPTER 2 2-1 Getty Images; 2-2 PhotoEdit; 2-3 Photolibrary.com; 2-4 Margaret Miller/Photo Researchers, Inc.; 2-5 Pat Graham; 2-6 Folio Inc.; 2-7 Los Angeles Times Syndicate; 2-8 Arlene Collins; 2-9a Paul Ekman, Ph.D, Professor of Psychology; 2-9b Paul Ekman, Ph.D. Professor of Psychology; 2-9c Paul Ekman, Ph.D. Professor of Psychology; 2-9d Paul Ekman, Ph.D. Professor of Psychology; 2-9e Paul Ekman, Ph.D. Professor of Psychology; 2-9f Paul Ekman, Ph.D. Professor of Psychology; 2-10 Michael J. Okoniewski/The Image Works; 2-11a Bernard Pierre Wolff/Photo Researchers, Inc.; 2-11b Phyllis Picardi/Stock Boston.

CHAPTER 3 3-1 AP/Wide World Photos; 3-2 Eric Neurath/Stock Boston; 3-3 Grant LeDuc; 3-4 Getty Images, Inc.-Taxi; 3-5 Steve Mason/Getty Images, Inc.; 3-6 Stuart Cohen/Comstock Images; 3-7 William Sallaz/Duomo Photography Incorporated; 3-8 Mark D. Phillips/Photo Researchers, Inc.

CHAPTER 4 4-1 Getty Images; 4-2 Stephen McBrady/PhotoEdit; 4-3 Gary Connor/PhotoEdit; 4-4 PhotoEdit; 4-5 Jose Luis Pelaez, Inc., Corbis/Bettman; 4-6 Bob Daemmrich/The Image Works; 4-7 Paul S. Conklin/PhotoEdit; 4-8 Grant LeDuc.

CHAPTER 5 5-1 AP/Wide World Photos; 5-2 Bob Daemmrich/Stock Boston; 5-3 AP/Wide World Photos; 5-4 Dana White/PhotoEdit; 5-5 AP/Wide World Photos; 5-6 Steve Skjoid/PhotoEdit; 5-7 Elena Rooraid/PhotoEdit; 5-8 Ellen B. Neipris/Impact Visuals Photo & Graphics, Inc.

CHAPTER 6 6-1 Corbis/Bettmann; 6-2 Library of Congress; 6-3 UPI/Corbis/Bettmann; 6-4 The Image Works; 6-5 Smiley N. Pool/Corbis/Bettman; 6-6 Corbis/Bettman; 6-7 AP/Wide World Photos; 6-8 Tony Freeman/PhotoEdit; 6-9 PhotoEdit.

CHAPTER 7 7-1 PhotoEdit; 7-2 Michael A. Dwyer/Stock Boston; 7-3 James Madison University, Office of Health Promotion, Harrisonburg, VA. Bruce Campbell, Simmons. 1999-2000. Most of Us Social Marketing Campaign; 7-4 Brown Brothers; 7-5 Barbara Rios/Photo Researchers, Inc.; 7-6 Paolo Koch/Photo Researchers, Inc.; 7-7 Michael Newman/PhotoEdit; 7-8abc, Copyright 1965 by Stanley Milgram. From the film OBEDIENCE, distributed by Penn State Media Sales.

CHAPTER 8 8-1 Corbis/Bettman; 8-2 Photo Researchers, Inc.; 8-3 Michael Newman/PhotoEdit; 8-4 Myrleen Ferguson/PhotoEdit; 8-5 PhotoEdit; 8-6 Jonathan Nourok/PhotoEdit; 8-7 Getty Images, Inc.-Image Bank; 8-8 Getty Images, Inc.-Taxi; 8-9 Getty Images-Photodisc.

CHAPTER 9 9-1 AP/Wide World Photos; 9-2 Bruno Herdt/Getty Images, Inc.; 9-3 Barbara Rios/Photo Researchers, Inc.; 9-4 George E. Jones, III/Photo Researchers, Inc.; 9-5 Jean-Claude Lejeune/Stock Boston; 9-6 Dorothy Littell Greco/The Image Works; 9-7 PhotoEdit; 9-8 Myrleen Ferguson/PhotoEdit; 9-9 Alamy Images.

CHAPTER 10 10-1 AP/Wide World Photos; 10-2 Jonathan Fickies/AP/Wide World Photos; 10-3 Amy C. Etra/PhotoEdit; 10-4 Adam Woolfitt/Corbis/Bettmann; 10-5 Black Star; 10-6 Alamy Images; 10-7 Spencer Grant III/Stock Boston; 10-8 AP/Wide World Photos; 10-9 AP/Wide World Photos.

CHAPTER 11 11-1 Corbis/Bettmann; 11-2 PhotoEdit; 11-3 Rick Maiman/Corbis/Sygma; 11-4 PhotoEdit; 11-5a David Burges/FSP/Gamma Liaison/Getty Images, Inc.; 11-5b David Burges/FSP/Gamma Liaison/Getty Images, Inc.; 11-6 Getty Images, Inc.-Stone Allstock; 11-7 Getty Images, Inc.-Taxi; 11-8 Getty Images-Photodisc; 11-9 Tony Freeman/PhotoEdit.

CHAPTER 12 12-1 The Goodyear Tire & Rubber Company; 12-2 Rhoda Sidney; 12-3 Alan S. Weiner/New York Times Pictures; 12-4 Ariel Skelley/Corbis/Bettmann; 12-5 Michael Newman/PhotoEdit; 12-6 Peter Hvizdak/The Image Works; 12-7 Tony Freeman/PhotoEdit; 12-8 Kathy McLaughlin/The Image Works; 12-9 Getty Images, Inc.-Stone Allstock.

CHAPTER 13 13-1 AP/Wide World Photos; 13-2 AP/Wide World Photos; 13-3 UNICEF/ICEF 8181/Lazopina; 13-4a Reuters/Charles Platiau/Corbis; 13-4b Craig Filipacchi/Getty Images, Inc.; 13-5 Robert Brenner/PhotoEdit; 13-6 Davis S. Strickler/The Image Works; 13-7 Bill Aron/PhotoEdit; 13-8 Michael Newman/PhotoEdit; 13-9 AP/Wide World Photos.

CHAPTER 14 14-1 Corbis/Bettmann; 14-2 Randy Matusow; 14-3 The Image Works; 14-4 Myrleen Ferguson/PhotoEdit; 14-5 Susan Lapides/Design Conceptions; 14-6 Michael Newman/PhotoEdit; 14-7 Janice Fullman/Index Stock Imagery, Inc.

CHAPTER 15 15-1 AP/Wide World Photos; 15-2 VCL/Chris Ryan/Getty Images, Inc.; 15-3 Bryan Singer/Picture Desk, Inc./Kobal Collection; 15-4 Getty Images, Inc.-Stone Allstock; 15-5 David Longstreath/AP/Wide World Photos; 15-6 Corbis-NY; 15-7 AP/Wide World Photos; 15-8 Getty Images, Inc.-Stone Allstock; 15-9 Jeff Siner/Corbis/Sygma.

Name Index

Name Index

Subject Index